DEBATES ON
U.S. IMMIGRATION

DEBATES ON U.S. IMMIGRATION

EDITORS

JUDITH GANS
University of Arizona

ELAINE M. REPLOGLE | DANIEL J. TICHENOR
University of Oregon

⑤SAGE reference

Los Angeles | London | New Delhi
Singapore | Washington DC

Los Angeles | London | New Delhi
Singapore | Washington DC

FOR INFORMATION:

SAGE Publications, Inc.
2455 Teller Road
Thousand Oaks, California 91320
E-mail: order@sagepub.com

SAGE Publications Ltd.
1 Oliver's Yard
55 City Road
London, EC1Y 1SP
United Kingdom

SAGE Publications India Pvt. Ltd.
B 1/I 1 Mohan Cooperative Industrial Area
Mathura Road, New Delhi 110 044
India

SAGE Publications Asia-Pacific Pte. Ltd.
3 Church Street
#10-04 Samsung Hub
Singapore 049483

SAGE REFERENCE

Publisher: Rolf A. Janke
Acquisitions Editor: Jim Brace-Thompson
Assistant to the Publisher: Michele Thompson
Production Editor: Tracy Buyan
Reference Systems Team: Leticia Gutierrez,
　　　　　　Laura Notton, Anna Villasenor
Typesetter: Hurix Systems Pvt Ltd.
Proofreader: Jennifer Thompson
Indexer: Scott Smiley
Cover Designer: Gail Buschman
Marketing Manager: Carmel Schrire

MTM PUBLISHING, INC.

Editorial and Book Development Services,
New York City; www.mtmpublishing.com
Publisher/President: Valerie A. Tomaselli
Vice President, Book Development: Hilary Poole
Additional Research and Writing: Tim Anderson
Copy Editor: Peter Jaskowiak
Editorial Assistants: Anna Luciano, Meghan McHugh

Printed in the United States of America.

Library of Congress Cataloging-in-Publication Data

Debates on U.S. immigration / editors, Judith Gans, Elaine M. Replogle, Daniel J. Tichenor.

p. cm.

Includes bibliographical references and index.

ISBN 978-1-4129-9601-3 (cloth)

1. United States—Emigration and immigration—Government policy. 2. United States—Emigration and immigration—Public opinion. 3. Public opinion—United States. I. Gans, Judith. II. Replogle, Elaine M. III. Tichenor, Daniel J., 1966- IV. Title: Debates on United States immigration.

JV6483.D422 2012

325.73—dc23　　　　　　　　　　　2012016287

12 13 14 15 16 10 9 8 7 6 5 4 3 2 1

CONTENTS

ECONOMIC, LABOR, AND DEMOGRAPHIC DEBATES

ABOUT THE EDITORS

Judith Gans manages the immigration policy program at the Udall Center for Studies in Public Policy at the University of Arizona. Her areas of expertise include immigration and globalization, U.S. immigration policy, economics, and trade. The focus of her work is to provide conceptual frameworks for understanding the complexities of U.S. immigration policy rather than to advocate a particular policy position. She has written extensively on immigration including *Immigrants in Arizona: Fiscal and Economic Impacts* and a *Primer on U.S. Immigration in a Global Economy*. She has a BA degree in economics from Stanford University, an MBA from UCLA's Graduate School of Management, and a master's in public administration from Harvard University. She has two grown children, was raised in Mexico and Brazil, and is fluent in Portuguese.

Elaine M. Replogle teaches in the Sociology Department at the University of Oregon. Her research and publications have focused on the sociology of health and medicine, social inequality, and immigrant and second-generation social adjustment. She is author of *Head Start as a Family Support Program: Renewing a Community Ethic* (Harvard Family Research Project). She is currently working on a book on the intersection of mental health and intergenerational conflict among second-generation South Asian Americans (her dissertation research). Her work on mob violence toward women, adolescent health, patterns in smoking trajectories among black and white youth, and Head Start, has appeared in publications such as *Sociological Forum, Evaluation Review, Children Today, Drug and Alcohol Dependence,* and the *Macmillan Encyclopedia of Aging.*

Daniel J. Tichenor is the Philip H. Knight Professor of Political Science and director of the Politics and Policy Program at the Wayne Morse Center for Law and Politics at the University of Oregon. He has published extensively on immigration politics and policy, the American presidency, civil liberties, interest groups, social movements, political parties, and U.S. political history. He is the author of *Dividing Lines: The Politics of Immigration Control in America*, which won the American Political Science Association's Gladys M. Kammerer Award for the best book in American national policy. Other works include *The Politics of International Migration* and *A History of the U.S. Political System*, a three-volume set examining the development of American political thought, institutions, behavior, and public policy. He has been a Faculty Scholar at the Center for the Study of Democratic Politics at Princeton University, Research Fellow in Governmental Studies at the Brookings Institution, Abba P. Schwartz Fellow in Immigration and Refugee Policy at the John F. Kennedy Presidential Library, Research Scholar at the Eagleton Institute of Politics, a visiting scholar at Leipzig University, and a faculty associate at Princeton's Center for Migration and Development and the Center for Comparative Immigration Studies at the University of California, San Diego.

ABOUT THE CONTRIBUTORS

Francisco J. Alatorre is an assistant professor in the Department of Criminal Justice at New Mexico State University in Las Cruces. A graduate from Arizona State University, he also received a law degree in Mexico. He is currently researching immigration issues, specifically how immigration affects women and youth.

Catalina Amuedo-Dorantes is an economics professor at San Diego State University, a research fellow at CReAM, FEDEA, and IZA, and an advisory committee member of the Americas Center Advisory Council at the Federal Reserve Bank of Atlanta. Her areas of interest include labor economics, international migration, and international finance, and she has published on contingent work contracts, the informal work sector, immigrant saving, international remittances, and immigrant health care. Her work has been funded by the Robert Wood Johnson Foundation, the Hewlett Foundation, and the National Institutes of Health, among other agencies.

Cynthia Bansak is an associate professor of economics at St. Lawrence University, and she was an assistant professor at San Diego State University and an economist at the Board of Governors of the Federal Reserve System, prior to her current position. Her research interests are in labor economics and monetary policy, and she has published research on immigration policy, including the impact of employer sanctions, amnesty, border enforcement, and E-Verify on labor market outcomes. Her research has been funded by the National Poverty Center, the W.E. Upjohn Institute for Employment Research, and the Robert Wood Johnson Foundation.

Frank D. Bean is Chancellor's Professor of Sociology and director of the Center for Research on Immigration, Population, and Public Policy at the University of California, Irvine. His latest book, *The Diversity Paradox: Immigration and the Color Line in 21st Century America,* won the 2011 American Sociological Association's Population Section Otis Dudley Duncan Award for Distinguished Scholarship in Social Demography.

Sarah E. Bohn is an economist and fellow at the Public Policy Institute of California. Her work focuses on issues at the intersection of public policy and labor markets, with particular attention to low-income and vulnerable populations. She has published research on the role of employment opportunities in the location choice of immigrants, the labor market impact of immigration and immigration enforcement, underground labor, income inequality, and poverty.

Susan K. Brown is associate professor of sociology and an affiliate of the Center for Research on Immigration, Population, and Public Policy at the University of California, Irvine. She is the author of *Beyond the Immigrant Enclave: Network Change and Assimilation* (2004). Her research focuses on the incorporation of immigrants into the United States, residential segregation, and inequality of access to higher education.

Philip Cafaro is a professor of philosophy at Colorado State University in Fort Collins, Colorado, and an affiliated faculty member of CSU's School of Global Ecological Sustainability. A former ranger with the U.S. National Park Service, his main research interests are in environmental ethics, consumption and population issues, and wildlands preservation. He is the author of *Thoreau's Living Ethics* and coeditor of the forthcoming anthology *Life on the Brink: Environmentalists Confront Overpopulation,* both from the University of Georgia Press.

Trista R. Chaney is currently state and local counsel at the Federation for American Immigration Reform (FAIR) in Washington, D.C. For 2 years prior to joining FAIR, she was employed as an attorney at the Immigration Reform Law Institute (IRLI). She has worked extensively in matters involving illegal immigration and its effects on United States citizens and legal residents. Trista has written on immigration topics for the *IRLI Monthly Bulletin* and *IRLI Legal Manual.* She was also an editor of the *FAIR State and Local Guide to Action.* Trista graduated from the University of Guelph in 2006 and earned her JD in 2008 from Cleveland-Marshall College of Law. She has been a member of the Ohio Bar since 2009.

Shinwoo Choi is with the University of Illinois at Urbana-Champaign.

Carol L. Cleaveland is an assistant professor in the Department of Social Work at George Mason University. She has been engaged in qualitative research with Latino immigrants since 2004.

Lillie Coney is associate director of the Electronic Privacy Information Center (EPIC), a nonprofit civil society organization based in Washington, D.C. Ms. Coney's work includes civic participation with a focus on voting rights. She conducts privacy analyses of emerging technology, new business practices, and changes in government policy. Government issued ID requirements; civil rights privacy policy; body scanners; fusion centers; smart grid, civil society, and cyber-security policy; E-Verify; and Secure Communities are her contributions to EPIC's policy work. She leads EPIC's coalition efforts: Privacy Coalition (domestic) and the Public Voice Annual Meeting (international).

Carolyn J. Craig specializes in comparative politics and women and politics. She holds a PhD, and her research has examined the politics of immigration reform in the United States, free trade in Central America, and gender and development throughout the Americas. She is collaborating with scholars based in the United States and Japan to establish an institute dedicated to the development and dissemination of research on citizen-based peace initiatives across the globe.

Karen Manges Douglas is with Sam Houston State University.

James R. Edwards Jr. is a Washington consultant with experience on Capitol Hill, where he served as U.S. Rep. Ed Bryant's legislative director and worked for other lawmakers. He coauthored *The Congressional Politics of Immigration Reform* and is a fellow with the Center for Immigration Studies.

Edward J. Erler is professor of political science at California State University, San Bernardino and a senior fellow at the Claremont Institute. He is the coauthor of *The Founders on Citizenship and Immigration* (2007).

Walter A. Ewing is senior researcher at the Immigration Policy Center (IPC) of the American Immigration Council in Washington, D.C. He writes about the economics of immigration, the relationship between immigration and crime, and the quest for "security" along the U.S.-Mexico border. He received his PhD in anthropology from the City University of New York (CUNY) Graduate School in 1997.

Alexandra Filindra is an assistant professor of political science at the University of Illinois at Chicago and a research associate with the Center for the Study of Human Development at Brown University. She received her PhD in political science from Rutgers University. Dr. Filindra's research focuses on immigration policy, race, federalism, and state-level policymaking. Her work has been published in several academic journals such as the *Harvard Educational Review, Urban Affairs Review,* and *State Politics and Policy Quarterly.*

Marshall Fitz is director of immigration policy at the Center for American Progress. He holds a JD and BA from the University of Virginia, and prior to joining American Progress served as the director of advocacy for the American Immigration Lawyers Association.

Rodolfo O. de la Garza, Eaton Professor of Administrative Law and Municipal Science at Columbia University, is a specialist in Latino political participation, migration, and immigrant incorporation whose publications include 18 books of which he is coauthor or editor and articles in leading political science and policy analysis journals. He is also the author of *Migration and Development: The Children Left Behind,* a UNICEF report published in 2007–2008. He has published extensively on voting rights and has served as an expert witness in voting rights cases for over 30 years. He served as the vice president of the American Political Science Association and received the APSA's Lifetime Achievement Award for his contributions to the study of Latino politics.

Jack Glaser is an associate professor in the Goldman School of Public Policy at the University of California, Berkeley. He received his PhD in psychology from Yale University in 1999. Professor Glaser's primary research interest is intergroup bias, particularly implicit biases, as well as racial biases in criminal justice.

Jeffrey L. Gower has a BS from Butler University; a JD from University of Akron; and a certificate from Ray C. Bliss Institute of Applied Politics, University of Akron. He is a National Science Foundation IGERT Fellow and a PhD candidate in geography, University at Buffalo–SUNY. He is the author of the article "As Dumb as We Wanna Be: U.S. H-1B Visa Policy and the 'Brain Blocking' of Asian Technology Professionals," which appeared in *Rutgers Race and the Law Review.*

David W. Haines is professor of anthropology at George Mason University and author of *Cultural Anthropology: Adaptations, Structures, Meanings* (2005), *The Limits of Kinship: Vietnamese Households* (2006), and *Safe Haven? A History of Refugees in America* (2010). He is also the editor or coeditor of several collected volumes on refugees and immigrants, including the forthcoming *Wind Over Water: East Asian Migration* (with Keiko Yamanaka and Shinji Yamashita).

Ron Hayduk is a professor of political science at Queens College, CUNY. Hayduk has written about elections, social movements, immigration, and race, including *Democracy for All: Restoring Immigrant Voting Rights in the United States*. Hayduk is cofounder of the Coalition to Expand Voting Rights (www.ivotenyc.org).

Marielena Hincapié is the executive director of the National Immigration Law Center (NILC). She also is a frequent lecturer at national and international conferences addressing issues of migration and works closely with emerging leaders in the social justice movement. Hincapié began at NILC in 2000 as a staff attorney, then served as NILC's director of programs from 2004 and 2008. Before joining NILC, Hincapié worked for the Legal Aid Society of San Francisco's Employment Law Center, where she founded the Center's Immigrant Workers' Rights Project. She holds a JD degree from Northeastern University School of Law, served on the American Bar Association's Commission on Immigration, and is a member of the Jobs with Justice Board of Directors.

Elizabeth Hull is professor of political science at Rutgers University in Newark, New Jersey. She has written extensively on issues relating to immigration, including *Without Justice for All: The Constitutional Rights of Aliens*.

Kristin Johnson is an assistant professor of political science at the University of Rhode Island. Her recent published work focuses on state capacity, political violence, prospects for state building, and poverty and human development with a concentration on the developing world.

Donald M. Kerwin Jr. directs the Center for Migration Studies (CMS), a New York–based educational institute devoted to the study of migration, to the promotion of understanding between immigrants and receiving communities, and to public policies that safeguard the dignity and rights of migrants, refugees, and newcomers. Prior to joining CMS, he served as vice president for programs at the Migration Policy Institute and as Executive Director at the Catholic Legal Immigration Network, Inc. He also serves as a non resident senior fellow at MPI, an associate fellow at the Woodstock Theological Center, a member of the American Bar Association's Commission on Immigration, and a board member of the Border Network for Human Rights.

David C. Koelsch is an associate professor and director of the Immigration Law Clinic at the University of Detroit Mercy School of Law. The Immigration Law Clinic represents immigrants on a variety of legal issues, including abandoned immigrant children and abused immigrant women. Professor Koelsch also teaches U.S. and Canadian immigration law. He was named Outstanding Immigration Law Professor in 2009 by the American Immigration Lawyers Association.

Mark Krikorian has headed the Center for Immigration Studies since 1995. He holds a master's degree from the Fletcher School of Law and Diplomacy, a bachelor's degree from Georgetown University, and spent 2 years at Yerevan State University in then-Soviet Armenia. Before joining the Center he held a variety of editorial and writing positions. He is one of the most frequently cited experts on immigration, and the author of *The New Case Against Immigration, Both Legal and Illegal*. His writing appears in major news and opinion outlets nationwide.

Alida Y. Lasker is an associate at the law firm of Cleary Gottlieb Steen & Hamilton LLP in New York and co-coordinator of the firm's pro bono immigration practice. Ms. Lasker received a JD, magna cum laude, from Brooklyn Law School, where she was the Executive Notes & Comments Editor of the *Brooklyn Journal of International Law*, and received a bachelor's degree, magna cum laude, from Columbia University. From 2008 to 2009, she served as law clerk to the Honorable Dolores K. Sloviter of the U.S. Court of Appeals for the Third Circuit. Ms. Lasker also serves as the law firm coordinator of the Asylum Representation Project, a 2011 initiative of the Leon Levy Foundation, Human Rights First, the Public Service Committee of the Federal Bar Council, and the Study Group on Immigrant Representation launched by the Honorable Robert A. Katzmann of the U.S. Court of Appeals for the Second Circuit.

Anna O. Law is an associate professor of political science at DePaul University. She is also the author of *The Immigration Battle in American Courts,* published by Cambridge University Press in 2010. She teaches and conducts research in immigration law and policy and law and courts more broadly.

Karey Leung is an instructor in the political science department at Rutgers University. Her research interests include race, gender, class, and religion in American politics and political philosophy.

Calvin L. Lewis is associate dean for student affairs and diversity at Texas Tech University School of Law. Lewis joined the faculty at Tech Law in 2003 after 25 years of distinguished service in the U.S. Army Judge Advocate General's Corps. In addition to performing his many administrative duties, he has taught immigration law, criminal law, and trial advocacy, and he has published in the areas of immigration law, criminal law, and military law.

Andrew Light is director of the Center for Global Ethics and associate director of the Institute for Philosophy and Public Policy at George Mason University. He is also a senior fellow and director of international climate policy at the Center for American Progress (CAP) in Washington, D.C. He has written over 80 scholarly articles and authored, coauthored, and edited 17 books including *Environmental Pragmatism* (1996), *Technology and the Good Life?* (2000), and *Environmental Values* (2008). In his policy career he is chief adviser on international environmental affairs to CAP's chairman, John Podesta, and leads CAP's work on bilateral and multilateral climate and energy agreements, most recently with a focus on climate finance.

Nelson Lim is a senior social scientist at the RAND Corporation and a professor at the Pardee RAND Graduate School. Lim serves as research director for the Military Leadership Diversity Commission, which is conducting a comprehensive evaluation and assessment of policies that provide opportunities for the promotion and advancement of minority members of the Armed Forces, including minority members who are senior officers. Lim received his PhD in sociology from the University of California, Los Angeles.

Andrew D. Linenberg is an associate attorney at Hinkle, Fingles & Prior, P.C., in Lawrenceville, New Jersey, where he focuses his practice on special education litigation, guardianships, and other legal issues for individuals with disabilities and their families. Prior to joining the firm, Mr. Linenberg was a private immigration practitioner who represented clients before various immigration courts in Pennsylvania and New Jersey. Mr. Linenberg received his JD from Rutgers University School of Law–Camden and served in a prestigious clerkship with the Honorable Linda R. Feinberg, Assignment Judge for Mercer County Superior Court. Mr. Linenberg is licensed to practice in Pennsylvania and New Jersey and is fluent in Spanish.

Magnus Lofstrom is a research fellow at the Public Policy Institute of California, a nonprofit, nonpartisan think tank located in San Francisco. He has a PhD in economics from the University of California, San Diego and his research interests include immigration, entrepreneurship, and education.

John "Jack" L. Martin, a graduate of Lewis and Clark College (1961) in Portland, Oregon is a retired foreign service officer (1961–1989). He is also a graduate of the Armed Services Staff College in Norfolk, Virginia (1971–72). He has worked on immigration issues since 1992, first as research director at the Center for Immigration Studies in Washington, D.C., and since 1996 as special projects director at the Federation for American Immigration Reform (FAIR), also in Washington, D.C. His publications are numerous dating back to 1974 with a study on a Real Industrial Wage Index for Latin America in the *Statistical Abstract for Latin America* published by the UCLA University Press. FAIR recently published his study "The Fiscal Burden of Illegal Immigration on United States Taxpayers."

Karin D. Martin is a PhD candidate in public policy at the University of California, Berkeley. She received her MPP and MA in political science at UC Berkeley and an AB degree in psychology from Stanford University. Her research interests include attitudes about racial profiling, popular support for punitive crime policy, race in criminal sentencing, monetary sanctions, and multimethod research design. She is a fellow in the Center for Research on Social Change and was previously a Berkeley Empirical Legal Studies Fellow and a National Science Foundation–funded fellow in the Integrated Graduate Education Research and Training (IGERT) program in politics, economics, psychology, and public policy.

Clarissa Martínez-De-Castro, director of immigration and civic engagement at the National Council of La Raza (NCLR), oversees the organization's work on immigration and efforts to expand Latino electoral participation and advocacy in public policy debates. She received her undergraduate degree from Occidental College and her master's degree from Harvard University and is a frequent commentator on the Latino electorate and immigration issues on CNN, MSNBC, FOX, Univision, Telemundo, *The Washington Post, The New York Times*, and other news outlets.

Norman Matloff is a professor of computer science at the University of California, Davis. He was formerly a professor of statistics at that institution, before which he was a software developer in Silicon Valley. He is the author of numerous publications on computer science, statistics, and the H-1B issue, and is frequently quoted in the press on the latter.

Carl Matthies is with the Vera Institute of Justice and earned a PhD in policy analysis from the Pardee RAND Graduate School in 2011. He was the 2010 recipient of the PRGS Paul Volcker Award, given to fund research aimed at improving the effectiveness of civil service employees. His RAND research spans a variety of public safety topics including police recruitment, organized crime, and forensic DNA database policies.

K.C. McAlpin graduated from the University of Texas at Austin and has a master's degree in international management from the Thunderbird School of Global Management in Glendale, Arizona. His early career spent working overseas and speaking foreign languages helped him appreciate the vital role that language fills in promoting empathy and understanding between peoples from different backgrounds. For 10 years he served as executive director of ProEnglish—a national organization that advocates for making English the official language of U.S. government operations—and today serves on its national board of directors.

Kathryn Miller is a doctoral student of political science at the University of Oregon. She has a master's degree in political science from the University of Colorado, Denver. Miller studies language politics in the U.S. context and immigration, with an emphasis on gender issues and forced migration.

Ali Noorani is the executive director of the National Immigration Forum, one of the nation's leading pro-immigrant advocacy organizations. Born in California, Noorani is the son of Pakistani immigrants and one of the few national leaders of Muslim heritage. Under Noorani's leadership since May 2008, the Forum is a powerful and key advocate on a range of immigration issues, working closely with business, law enforcement, and faith and civic leadership across the country to advance much needed reforms to our nation's immigration system.

Morris I. Onyewuchi practices immigration law with a federal agency. He holds a master of studies in international human rights law from the University of Oxford, U.K.; a JD from Thurgood Marshall School of Law at Texas Southern University; a mediation certificate from Harvard Law School, and a BA from Georgia State University. Onyewuchi has also taught immigration law as an adjunct law professor. In addition, he has trained local, state, and federal law enforcement officers in Georgia, North Carolina, and South Carolina in immigration, customs, civil rights, and constitutional laws.

Maura Ooi is a law student at Georgetown University Law Center.

Hye Joon Park is with the University of Illinois at Urbana-Champaign.

Andrew J. Parr earned his PhD in educational leadership (K–12 school administration) from the University of Nevada, Reno. Parr currently works as an education programs professional for the Nevada Department of Education, Office of Assessments, Program Accountability, and Curriculum.

Lissette M. Piedra is with the University of Illinois at Urbana-Champaign.

Rosalie Pedalino Porter is best known for her influential *Forked Tongue: The Politics of Bilingual Education* (1990 and 1996). Her newest book is *American Immigrant: My Life in Three Languages* (2011). Her professional career as teacher, administrator, researcher, advocate, and expert witness in court cases on education policy for non-English-speaking children spans 3 decades. She holds an EdD degree and is chairman of the board of ProEnglish in Washington, D.C.

Ann Robertson is a freelance writer in Washington, D.C. She has a doctorate in political science and master's in Russian and East European studies from George Washington University.

Eric A. Ruark is the director of research for the Federation for American Immigration Reform (FAIR). He has a background in intellectual history and legal theory, and the history of technology and society. He has published extensively on the impact of immigration on the American economy and environment, and he has provided testimony to the U.S. Senate.

Jessica Saunders is a criminologist at the RAND Corporation. Her research projects include innovations in policing, immigration and crime, developmental criminology, criminal justice program evaluation, correctional education, and quantitative methods. Saunders received her PhD from John Jay College of Criminal Justice.

Peter H. Schuck is the Simeon E. Baldwin Professor Emeritus at Yale University, where he has taught since 1979. His many books and hundreds of articles include *Meditations of a Militant Moderate: Cool Views on Hot Topics* (2006) and *Understanding America: The Anatomy of an Exceptional Nation* (2008), coedited with James Q. Wilson.

Melysa Sperber is an adjunct professor at George Washington University Law School, where she teaches refugee and asylum law and public interest lawyering. She is a director of human rights at Vital Voices Global Partnership, an international women's organization based in Washington, D.C. In addition to managing a portfolio of overseas programming, she lobbies the federal government to strengthen policies and programs on violence against women. Prior to joining Vital Voices, she was a staff attorney at the Tahirih Justice Center, a nonprofit legal services agency that provides services to women fleeing gender-based persecution. Sperber handled a caseload of over 80 immigration matters involving domestic violence survivors, human trafficking victims, asylum seekers, and victims of violent crime.

Winthrop R. Staples III is an endangered species biologist and environmental philosopher. He has conducted research and recovery efforts on lynx, coyote, the Amur leopard, and the American chestnut. Staples's work in environmental philosophy, "For a Species Right to Exist," will be published in the anthology *Life on the Brink: Environmentalists Confront Overpopulation.*

Madeleine Sumption is a policy analyst at the Migration Policy Institute, an independent, nonpartisan, nonprofit think tank in Washington, D.C., dedicated to the analysis of the movement of people worldwide. Her recent publications include *Policies to Curb Unauthorized Employment, Aligning Temporary Immigration Visas With US Labor Market Needs* (coauthor), *Migration and Immigrants Two Years After the Financial Collapse* (BBC World Service and Migration Policy Institute, coeditor and author), *Immigration and the Labor Market: Theory, Evidence and Policy* (Equality and Human Rights Commission, coauthor), *Migration and the Economic Downturn: What to Expect in the European Union* (coauthor), and *Social Networks and Polish Immigration to the UK* (Institute for Public Policy Research).

Roberto Suro is a professor of journalism and public policy at the University of Southern California and is director of the Tomás Rivera Policy Institute. He is coeditor of *Writing Immigration: Scholars and Journalists in Dialogue* (2011) and author of *Strangers Among Us: Latino Lives in a Changing America* (1999), among many other publications on immigration.

Matthew K. Tabor is the editor of EducationNews.org, which provides daily coverage of K–12 and higher education worldwide, and *Education Debate at OnlineSchools.* His background includes work in higher education, executive recruiting and government, and he currently serves as CEO/president of Koala Fight Media, Inc. Tabor comments on education and politics at *Education for the Aughts* at www.matthewktabor.com. He writes out of Cooperstown, New York.

Nik Theodore is an associate professor in the Department of Urban Planning and Policy of the University of Illinois at Chicago. Prior to joining UIC he was a 1997–98 Atlantic Fellow in Public Policy at the University of Manchester and a researcher for the Chicago Urban League (1988–1997).

Jessica M. Vaughan is director of policy studies at the Center for Immigration Studies. She has been with the center since 1992, and her area of expertise is the administration and implementation of immigration policy, covering topics such as visa programs, immigration benefits, and immigration law enforcement. She is frequently cited as an expert and is often invited to testify before Congress and state legislatures. Her writings have appeared in publications such as *The Washington*

Post and *Boston Globe.* Prior to joining the center, she was a foreign service officer with the U.S. State Department. She has a master's degree from Georgetown University and a bachelor's degree from Washington College in Maryland.

Laura Vazquez is the immigration legislative analyst for the National Council of La Raza (NCLR), the largest national Latino civil rights and advocacy organization in the United States. She monitors immigration policy and conducts legislative and administrative advocacy in order to advance just and humane reforms to the current immigration system. Vazquez holds an MA in Latin American studies from the University of California, San Diego and a BA in political science and Spanish from Kenyon College.

Shoba Sivaprasad Wadhia is a professor at Penn State Law and the founder/director of Penn State's Center for Immigrants' Rights. She researches the role of prosecutorial discretion in immigration law; the association between detention, removal, and due process; and the intersection between immigration, national security, and race. Prior to joining Penn State Law, she was deputy director for legal affairs at the National Immigration Forum in Washington, D.C., where she worked on issues surrounding the creation of the U.S. Department of Homeland Security and post-9/11 executive branch policies impacting immigrant communities. She serves on the ABA Commission on Immigration and is a member of the American Immigration Lawyers Association and National Immigration Project of the National Lawyers Guild.

Michele Waslin is senior policy analyst at the Immigration Policy Center, a division of the American Immigration Council located in Washington, D.C. In her capacity, Waslin tracks and analyzes immigration policy and the immigration debate, writes articles on a multitude of immigration-related topics, coordinates the IPC research agenda and builds relationships with academics and other authors, provides technical assistance to organizations, conducts public education events, and maintains relationships with a wide array of national, state, and local advocacy organizations as well as federal agencies. She has authored several publications on immigration policy and post-9/11 immigration issues and appears regularly in English- and Spanish-language media. She received her PhD in 2002 in government and international studies from the University of Notre Dame.

Philip E. Wolgin is immigration policy analyst at the Center for American Progress. He holds an MA and a PhD in American history from the University of California, Berkeley and a BA from New York University.

Julie Myers Wood is a former federal prosecutor and former assistant secretary/director of immigration and customs enforcement. After leaving government, she founded ICS Consulting, LLC, a company that develops software and assists businesses in developing compliance solutions.

Priscilla Yamin is an assistant professor of political science at the University of Oregon. Her areas of study include gender, race, and sexuality in American politics.

PREFACE

Ours is a nation of immigrants. Yet while the lofty words enshrined with the Statue of Liberty stand as a source of national pride, the rhetoric and politics surrounding immigration policy have often proven far less lofty. In reality, the apparently open invitation of Lady Liberty seldom has been entirely without restriction, and each wave of newcomers has provoked anxiety among the general population. Throughout our history, impassioned debates—about who constitutes a "desirable" American, about whether to limit immigration and, if so, how to go about it—have emerged and mushroomed among politicians, scholars of public policy, and the public. The chapters in this volume aim to keep students, researchers, and other interested readers informed and up-to-date on the most contentious aspects of U.S. immigration policy. Introductory essays followed by Point–Counterpoint essays provide readers with views on multiple sides of this complex issue.

This book is divided into three sections. The first section, on Political Debates, looks at public policy issues regarding who should become an American and who should not, as well as what to do about people who enter the country illegally. The next section, on Economic, Labor, and Demographic Debates, considers both positive and negative aspects of immigration on American finances, work lives, and environment. The final section, on Social and Cultural Debates, explores the impact that newcomers have had and continue to have on the proverbial American melting pot.

In each of these sections, critical issues are considered in a Point–Counterpoint format. The editors of each section selected the debate topics with two main things in mind: to ensure that the general issues surrounding immigration are comprehensively discussed and to analyze the most contentious aspects of both legal and illegal immigration, in an effort to lay out the pros and cons in an analytical and objective manner.

While the authors strongly make the case for each side, the Point and Counterpoint sections taken together will give the reader a well-rounded sense of the entire issue, allowing for an appreciation of both sides. It is possible that a reader might see the merits of the argument made on the Point side of the debate and then feel the same way about the Counterpoint. Often the validity of the conclusions of one side will not preclude the validity of those on the other—this represents just how complex and difficult these issues are to confront and solve. The goal is careful consideration of all aspects of immigration—from all perspectives.

That said, it is worth pointing out that the authors do, indeed, have strong points of view. Nonetheless, some authors contributed both Point and Counterpoint sides of particular debates; they were willing and able to set those views aside momentarily to explore aspects of the debate with which they may not personally agree.

The introductions to each chapter aim to introduce these conflicting points of view. Written in an effort to contextualize each debate, they help summarize the positions taken by the authors and indeed will offer readers a road map into the Point and Counterpoint essays. The introductions invoke considerations for readers to be alert to as they reason through the arguments presented in each chapter.

The chapters are followed and supported by a documents Appendix, which presents key speeches, court findings, and testimonies that highlight critical ideas from the last century of immigration policy. It is meant to offer a mini-history of the milestones concerning immigration since the signing of the Immigration Act of 1924, which set the stage for immigration policy in the twentieth century.

Political Debates

Introduction

The Politics section of this volume covers 13 of the key debates on immigration: amnesty, Arizona's S.B. 1070, birthright citizenship, immigration and crime, the provision of driver's licenses to undocumented immigrants, federal policy, voting, the selection system, nativism, the naturalization process, border control, gender and refugee status, and detention and deportation. These issues underscore the reality that the United States is a nation built upon immigration, and yet immigration has long been one of the most contentious issues in American law and politics. Indeed, Americans have been arguing over immigrant admissions and rights since the earliest days of the republic. Over time, each generation has disagreed about the impact of newcomers on jobs and economic growth, law and order, social relations, the welfare state, and the distribution of political power. Traditionally, leaders and ordinary citizens have celebrated the nation's immigrant history while expressing anxieties about recent arrivals. Here, in this introduction, we review some of the key legislative decisions of the past 25 years regarding immigration reform. They are the backdrop to the controversies covered in the following chapters.

In 2012, Americans were as at odds as they were at the country's founding over who is "fit for our society," how many immigrants to accept, and what rights should be extended to noncitizens already residing in U.S. territory. But the contemporary national debate over immigration is particularly focused on the challenges posed by unauthorized immigration and by millions living in the country unlawfully. These issues come up in all chapters in this volume, but are particularly noted in Andrew Linenberg's chapter on amnesty, Calvin Lewis and Roberto Suro's debate on Arizona's S.B. 1070, David Haines and Madeline Sumption's piece on the legal immigration system, Karey Leung's contribution on the naturalization process, Michele Waslin and Julie Myers Wood's chapter on driver's licenses, and the chapter on border control by Catalina Amuedo-Dorantes, Cynthia Bansak, and Melysa Sperber. The politics of illegal immigration—and the Washington deadlock over comprehensive immigration reform—drive these conflicts. The reverberations of this impasse are profound for nearly every other facet of U.S. immigration policy, from legal immigration and refugee admissions to naturalization. Understanding the dynamics and implications of elusive immigration reform is crucial for explaining the current state of American immigration law and politics.

For at least two decades, successive U.S. presidents and Congresses have characterized the immigration system as "broken." In particular, elected officials have viewed porous national borders and the presence of 10 to 12 million undocumented immigrants in the country as a pressing problem. A majority of Americans have shared the perspective that significant reform is urgently needed, and new grassroots movements have emerged favoring immigrant rights, on the one side, and tougher enforcement and border control, on the other. Against this backdrop, the White House and Congress have worked together several times to advance a comprehensive immigration reform package comprising four core elements: (1) new measures to strengthen enforcement of immigration laws and border control, (2) improved employer sanctions to penalize those who knowingly hire undocumented immigrants, (3) an earned legalization program that would allow most undocumented immigrants living in the country to gain legal status, and (4) revision of the legal immigration preference system to allow U.S. businesses to have easier access to immigrant workers or foreign guest workers. In this volume, the chapters on federal policy (Ali Noorani, and Anna Law), naturalization (Karey Leung), and the legal immigration system (David Haines and Madeline Sumption) all discuss these elements.

While national policymakers largely agree on the essential building blocks of comprehensive immigration reform, each legislative effort has been derailed by disputes over which of these elements should take precedence over the others. On record promising to secure sweeping immigration reform that would enhance border control while ensuring a path to citizenship for undocumented immigrants, President Barack Obama has languished nearly as much as his predecessor, George W. Bush, in efforts to find an opening for major policy change. How can this be? What are the chief obstacles confronting comprehensive immigration reform? More generally, why has major immigration reform proven so elusive in recent decades?

To understand why U.S. policymakers have struggled to address the nation's most significant immigration problems, it is useful to identify four daunting barriers to reform. First, the rival ideas and interests inspired by this issue make problem definition and legislative majorities elusive. A second formidable challenge is that policymakers are well aware that major reform in this area entails difficult negotiations that produce painful compromise packages. Third, past implementation failures and policy inertia generally have expanded illegal immigration, compounding over time the problems associated with porous borders. Equally important, the federal government's failure to control the borders in either the distant or recent past has bred widespread cynicism and mistrust about the capacity and will of the national state to enforce its immigration laws. Finally, the most prominent policy prescriptions on the table today appear inadequate to meet the problem and draw fire from all sides. Each of these dynamics will be considered in turn.

Political Cacophony: Elusive Problem Definition and Congressional Majorities

Immigration is a potent cross-cutting issue in American national politics, one that defies the standard liberal-conservative divide and often polarizes major party coalitions. One can point to four rather durable ideological traditions that have found expression in national debates and political struggles over immigration (Tichenor, 2002). Consider two dimensions. The first focuses on immigration numbers and divides those who support expansive immigration opportunities and robust numbers from those who favor substantial restrictions on alien admissions. The second concentrates on the rights of noncitizens residing in the United States and distinguishes those who endorse the provision of a broad set of civil, political, and social rights (as defined by T. H. Marshall in *Citizenship and Social Class and Other Essays* [1950]) to newcomers from those who advocate strict limitations on the rights accorded to noncitizens. These two dimensions of immigration policy reveal tensions between cosmopolitans versus economic protectionists on the Left, and between pro-business expansionists versus cultural protectionists and border hawks on the Right. Tellingly, these conflicts are especially pronounced when the agenda focuses on unauthorized immigration and those residing in the country illegally (in this volume, see Lewis and Suro's chapter on S.B. 1070, Waslin and Myers Wood's on driver's licenses, Chaney and Ewing's on crime, and Hayduk and de la Garza's on voting).

The rival commitments of ideology and interest unleashed by illegal immigration make basic problem definition a tall order for policymakers. Indeed, recent immigration reform efforts captured profoundly different assumptions and conceptions of what the problem is, or, for some, whether a problem even exists. Carolyn Craig's chapter on nativism, in this volume, reviews the history of that sentiment in this country and the accompanying incompatible assumptions of those for and against restrictionist policies, both in the past and in the present. It is clear that powerful organized interests and competing constituencies—from agribusinesses, service industries, and Microsoft to labor unions, ethnic and civil rights advocates, and church groups, to anti-immigrant activists of the Minuteman Project and Tea Party movement—regularly mobilize and clash over immigration reform. The resulting battles not only pit interest groups and constituencies allied with the Republican Party against those allied with the Democratic Party, they also divide organized interests within these partisan coalitions, and sometimes even among those associated with the same interest or constituency—such as internal fights on this issue within the labor movement or among environmental and population control groups.

For cosmopolitans, or pro-immigration liberals, the problem is not *the presence* of millions of undocumented aliens in the United States but rather *their status* as vulnerable, second-class persons. This reality comes out particularly strongly in Andrew Linenberg's chapter on amnesty, Alexandra Filindra and Edward Erler's debate on birthright citizenship, Michele Waslin and Julie Myers Wood's debate on driver's licenses, and Priscilla Yamin's chapter on the arguable need for the United States to expand refugee relief to those fleeing both gender-based violence and persecution on the basis of sexual orientation. The chief imperative for pro-immigration activists is to make the estimated 12 million unauthorized migrants living in the country eligible for legal membership. Representative Luis Gutierrez (D-IL) explained in a 2006 interview, "What we want . . . is a pathway to their legalization so that they can come out of the shadows of darkness, of discrimination, of bigotry, of exploitation, and join us fully." Latino immigrants such as the journalist and scholar Edward Schumacher-Matos add that Hispanics have proven their loyalty to the nation in countless ways, including joining the military at higher rates than most groups. In a 2009 editorial, Schumacher-Matos argued, "we have earned our say over the direction of the country . . . and what we do on immigration." Since powerful democracies such as the United States profit from the economic exploitation of unauthorized immigrants, in an online debate in 2007, Marc Rosenblum of the Migration Policy Institute argued that "all American employers, consumers, and lawmakers—all of us—share the 'blame' for undocumented migration." Legalization or "earned citizenship" initiatives, discussed in the Linenberg chapter on amnesty, draw strong support from immigrant advocate and civil rights groups; Latino, Asian, and other organizations; religious associations; and the leading federations of organized labor.

Predictably, Obama's announcement in June 2012 that his administration would no longer deport eligible, young, illegal immigrants was met with applause from liberals, who argue that the policy is a question of fairness to young people who would otherwise be punished for choices that others made for them, and scorn from conservatives, who tend to be hostile toward any kinds of accommodation to those in our country illegally. Though Obama's new policy did *not* essentially change existing immigrant prioritization schemes—as explained in Kathryn Miller's chapter on deportation—it does allow those who meet certain criteria to apply for temporary 2-year work visas and thus theoretically encourages the "best" (most productive) immigrants to stay. The new rules do *not* allow them to become citizens or to apply for permanent resident status.

Economic protectionists have been particularly hostile toward illegal immigration, which they view as enhancing the wealth of corporate and professional America with little concern about the consequences for blue-collar workers or the unemployed. As much as Cesar Chavez complained in the late 1960s that undocumented Mexicans were being recruited to undermine his efforts to organize legal farm workers, in the introduction to *Debating Immigration* (2007), Carol Swain pointed to the deleterious "impact that high levels of illegal immigration [are] having in the communities when it comes to jobs, when it comes to education, when it comes to health care." Former CNN newsman Lou Dobbs regularly sounds similar themes—claiming in 2007, for example, that illegal immigration has "a calamitous effect on working citizens and their families" and "that the industries in which illegal aliens are employed in the greatest percentages also are suffering the largest wage declines." Economic protectionists endorse employer sanctions against unscrupulous employers who knowingly hire undocumented aliens, and they vehemently oppose guest worker programs that they associate with a captive workforce subject to exploitation, abuse, and permanent marginalization. These views resonate among many rank-and-file members of labor unions and the constituencies of moderate Democrats in Congress.

For pro-business conservatives, the chief problem is that existing federal policies fail to address, in the words of former president George W. Bush, "the reality that there are many people on the other side of our border who will do anything to come to America to work." In short, the argument is that the U.S. economy has grown dependent on this supply of cheap, unskilled labor. The solution for this camp lies in regularizing employers' access to this vital foreign labor; if the back door is to be closed, then this labor supply must be secured through temporary worker programs and an expansion of employment-based legal immigration. Powerful business groups in this camp also oppose employer sanctions as an unwelcome and unfair regulatory burden placed on American businesses large and small.

Border hawks today see the illegal immigration problem as nothing short of an unprecedented breakdown of American sovereignty, one that compromises national security, the rule of law, job opportunities for citizens, public education, and social services. (See, for example, *In Mortal Danger*, published by the former legislator Tom Tancredo in 2006.) Mobilized by conservative talk radio, columnists, and television commentators, many grassroots Republicans are outraged that the nation's fundamental interest in border control and law enforcement has been trumped by the power of immigrant labor, rights, and votes. Amnesty or legalization proposals inspire hostile resistance from this camp as unethical rewards to those who break the rules and as stimulants to new waves of undocumented immigrants anticipating similar treatment. Likewise, temporary worker programs are scorned by these activists because many guest workers historically have remained in the country illegally, and because they contest the notion that only foreign workers will do certain menial jobs. Border hawks believe enforcement must come first. They favor a strengthened Border Patrol and tougher security measures along the nation's borders, as well as crackdowns on unauthorized immigrants and their employers within U.S. territory. They endorse a strategy of attrition in which targeted deportation efforts, workplace enforcement, and denial of social services and other public benefits would persuade many unauthorized migrants to return home.

It is hard to imagine more widely divergent definitions of a public policy problem or, concomitantly, more disparate blueprints for reform. Building majority support for legislation involving tough choices is always challenging, but it is especially so amid ideological disorientation and intraparty warfare. Clashing interests and ideals have meant that when policy initiatives are designed to meet the demands of one important constituency, they invariably incur the wrath of others. The diverse responses of states and localities to immigration enforcement and immigrant policy, as subnational governments enter the void when Washington fails to act, further cloud the picture.

The Long Way Home: Prolonged Negotiation and Unpalatable Compromise

National policymakers are well aware of the tortured path that earlier reformers traversed to secure comprehensive legislation on illegal immigration. False starts, grueling negotiations, and unappealing compromises have been par for the course over the past quarter-century. For much of the 1970s, liberal House Democrat Peter Rodino of New Jersey waged a quixotic campaign for employer sanctions legislation to discourage unauthorized entries. This effort to punish employers who knowingly hired undocumented aliens was strongly advocated by the AFL-CIO and labor unions. But organized agricultural interests initially succeeded in stalling Rodino's legislation in the Senate, where conservative Democrat James Eastland of Mississippi refused to allow the Judiciary Committee he chaired to take action. When Rodino again pressed the initiative later in the decade, new resistance emerged in both the House and Senate from liberal Democrats who warned that the measure would lead to job discrimination against Latinos, Asians, and anyone who looked or sounded foreign. Archival documents from the National Council of La Raza (NCLR) from this period indicate that Latino organizations and civil rights groups were now lined up in opposition to employer sanctions.

During the next decade, the bipartisan team of Senator Alan Simpson (R-WY) and Congressman Romano Mazzoli (D-KY) took the lead in pressing for immigration reform. Early in 1982, the pair introduced omnibus legislation on illegal and legal immigration. The measure met fierce resistance from a broad coalition of business interests (the U.S. Chamber of Commerce, National Association of Manufacturers, agribusinesses, the Business Roundtable), ethnic and civil rights groups such as NCLR and the Mexican American Legal Defense and Educational Fund (MALDEF), the American Civil Liberties Union (ACLU), religious lobbies, and a new immigrant rights organization, the National Immigration Forum. Left-Right opposition to the Simpson-Mazzoli initiative was reflected in the resistance of key figures in the Reagan administration, who saw employer sanctions and national identification cards working at cross-purposes with its regulatory relief agenda, and House Democrats led by the Hispanic and Black Caucuses, who raised familiar concerns about discriminatory impacts of sanctions and other provisions. Simpson and Mazzoli got nowhere for 5 years before 11th-hour deal making produced the compromise Immigration Reform and Control Act of 1986 (IRCA). Gridlock was overcome by a compromise package of watered-down employer sanctions provisions, legalization for undocumented aliens living in the country since 1982, and a new Seasonal Agricultural Worker program to appease grower interests. Final vote tallies were tight, and major components of the "grand bargain" were almost undone during bruising amendment battles on the floor. This history of painful negotiations and compromises has only intensified national policymakers' dread of the illegal immigration problem.

Implementation Failures and Inertia: Fostering Cynicism and Illegal Expansion

The capacity and will of the national state to enforce its immigration laws has long been beleaguered by a tradition of inadequate resources, erratic enforcement, and poor oversight. Nearly all advanced industrial democracies have struggled to control their borders, and scholars like Mae Ngai remind us that the presence of undocumented immigrants is inevitable. (See, for example, Ngai's 2005 work, *Impossible Subjects*.) Yet the recognition that governments cannot eliminate illegal immigration does not mean that they are incapable of exercising a measure of control over their borders. Moreover, early policy choices (and silences) by wealthy democracies are significant because they can nurture and entrench the forces that spur large-scale illegal immigration. Indeed, policy inertia often has had the effect of expanding unauthorized flows. Equally important, past implementation failures have bred deep mistrust or cynicism among ordinary citizens and enforcement-minded lawmakers that the federal government will control its borders. This skepticism is a major impediment to immigration reform today.

A contemporary illustration of lax enforcement can be seen in the implementation of the IRCA's employer sanctions provisions. As stated above, the absence of a reliable identification system for verifying employee eligibility made it relatively easy for undocumented aliens to evade detection at the workplace. Soon after passage of the IRCA, an underground industry of fraudulent documents flourished in both Mexico and the United States, enabling unauthorized migrants to obtain work with ease. But if the legislative design of employer sanctions discouraged their efficacy, the Reagan administration was less than zealous in their enforcement. The Immigration and Naturalization Service (INS) tended to enforce employer sanctions with considerable forbearance toward offenders. According to Tichenor's interviews with Reagan administration officials, Alan Nelson, the INS Commissioner under Reagan, was urged to pursue a policy of "least employer resistance" by stressing business education over penalties. The IRCA authorized a 70 percent increase in the INS budget, with an annual $100 million targeted for employer sanctions enforcement. Tellingly, $34 million was spent on enforcing sanctions in fiscal year 1987, $59 million in 1988, and below $30 million annually in ensuing years.

From his perch on the Senate Immigration Subcommittee, Senator Simpson pressed the Reagan and Bush administrations to take a harder line on employer sanctions. Yet, despite his clout as Republican minority whip, Simpson made little headway during either Republican presidency. Few of Simpson's congressional colleagues shared his alarm over the inefficacy or uneven enforcement of employer sanctions. In fact, the most vigorous oversight of sanctions focused on whether they should be repealed because they unfavorably burdened small businesses (led by Orrin Hatch) or because they engendered increased job discrimination against legal aliens or citizens who look or sound foreign (led by Edward Kennedy). Few conservative politicians of the 1980s, most of whom embraced "regulatory relief" and free markets, or their liberal counterparts, dedicated to universal rights and inclusion, worried about the efficacy of employer sanctions.

IRCA's implementation failures helped fuel the dramatic expansion of illegal immigration in recent decades, yielding an undocumented population in the United States that estimates suggest is three to four times larger than it was in the early 1980s. They also have raised profound doubts among activists, policymakers, and citizens that the federal government either can or will adequately control its borders. The resulting cynicism poses substantial hurdles to reform. It is not simply an educational exercise that every chapter in this volume contains a "Point" half and "Counterpoint" half; it is an accurate portrayal of the sometimes irreconcilable differences found in every immigration-related policy battle.

Bad Options: Inadequate or Unappealing Policy Solutions

A final major constraint for political leaders tackling illegal immigration is that many of the most prominent policy prescriptions on the table today appear inadequate, too costly, unpopular, or likely to have unintended consequences. A few examples from recent immigration reform are illustrative. Amnesty or legalization programs (see, in particular, the chapters by Linenberg, Haines and Sumption, and Leung) are designed to adjust the status of undocumented immigrants living and working in the country for a given duration of time, but they may serve as a magnet for new unauthorized entries by migrants hoping for similar treatment in the future. Efforts to make past "amnesty" programs into "earned citizenship" (through payment of fines, back taxes, and "touch back" provisions requiring immigrants to return to their home countries) face potentially large numbers of undocumented immigrants refusing to participate. As a result, many of these unauthorized residents, perhaps millions, would remain "illegal." Likewise, the adoption of new guest worker programs to meet business demands and to regularize the flow of foreign workers overlooks the fact that similar programs in the past were accompanied by unauthorized flows, and that many temporary workers chose to remain illegally. (See, for example, Kitty Calavita's 1992 book, *Inside the State*.)

Enforcement proposals feature their own share of potential woes. Creating strict, militarized control over the 2,000-mile U.S.-Mexico border will not come cheap in terms of constructing border fences, surveillance technology, or personnel. This is true despite the compelling evidence that Amuedo-Dorantes and Bansak present in their chapter, showing that border enforcement patrols *have* contributed to a decrease in successful border crossings. Yet, according to Jorge Durand and Douglas Massey (2004), adequate enforcement will slow the movement of tourists and commercial goods, and it will reinforce the incentives for those who entered without inspection (EWIs) to avoid returning home and thereby risk not getting back in. The notion of mass deportation campaigns or systematic internal enforcement draw little support in opinion polls, would require major new budget commitments, and could involve significant incursions upon the civil liberties of legal immigrants and citizens. Along similar lines, effective employer sanctions would entail new mechanisms for verifying employee eligibility that will produce sacrifices in privacy as well as higher costs for businesses and consumers alike. Whereas legal immigration reform has recently included something to please almost everyone mobilized on the issue, comprehensive initiatives on illegal immigration promise plenty of bitter pills for all.

Mission Impossible: Bush and Immigration Reform

Between 1990 and 2000 in sheer numbers, more immigrants arrived in the United States than during any previous period in American history. In that decade alone, the immigrant population in the United States grew by roughly 1 million persons per year, rising from 19.8 million to 31.1 million. By the 2000 election, Republican national and state organizations drew up plans to attract new Asian and Latino voters. Bush dramatically outspent Democrats in his appeal to Latino voters in 2000, devoting millions of campaign dollars to Spanish-language advertising and direct-mail appeals. Bush's "compassionate conservatism" on immigration policy and his direct campaigning had clear electoral ramifications. An estimated 7.8 million Latino voters, or 6 percent of all voters (up from 4 percent in 1996), cast ballots in the 2000 election. Al Gore maintained the Democrats' traditional edge in Latino voting, but Bush gained an estimated 34 percent among Latinos. In a 2005 report, *Hispanics and the 2004 Election,* Jeffrey Passel, Richard Fry, and Roberto Suro reported that Bush's portion of the Latino vote was 13 points higher than Dole's 1996 total and only 3 points off the previous GOP record of 37 percent attained by Ronald Reagan in the

1984 election. The Bush team clearly was focused on adding more Latinos, the fastest-growing sector of the electorate and a crucial swing constituency in battleground states, to the GOP base.

Expanding its electoral coalition was certainly not the only factor that informed the Bush administration's decision to take the initiative on controversial immigration reform soon after taking office. Bush personally believed that his plan was a sound policy solution to a bedeviling problem. Indeed, the president regularly explained that as a Texan he particularly understood the need to streamline and expand the inflow of workers from abroad; in a December 24, 2003, article in *The Washington Post,* Bush was quoted as saying that undocumented immigrants in the country should be allowed to stay since "compassion" and "family values don't stop at the Rio Grande" (Allen, 2003). Moreover, Bush's immigration initiatives clearly benefited and appealed to the business community that was squarely rooted in his coalition. Various employers of low-wage, low-skill workers readily supported the president's proposals, from Fortune 500 companies to smaller agribusinesses, builders, restaurant owners, and other service companies. Finally, Bush's decision to pursue a contentious immigration initiative also reflected steady political demands for border control, while public opinion was uneven on specific proposals (such as the legalization of undocumented immigrants) and seemingly open to presidential influence.

Initially, Bush and President Vicente Fox of Mexico worked together on blueprints for both a large new temporary worker program and the legalization of undocumented Mexican immigrants who worked and paid taxes in the United States. In August 2001, new polling found that 59 percent of Americans favored reductions in legal immigration, but 62 percent also endorsed legalizing a significant number of taxpaying undocumented aliens. After the 9/11 attacks, however, the Bush administration determined that it had little choice but to shelve comprehensive reform. Border hawks like Representative Tom Tancredo (R-CO) made headlines in December 2001 by underscoring how porous borders presented an appalling national security problem. Organized interests favoring immigration restriction and strict border control ran ads around the country blaming lax immigration policies for the September 11 terrorist attacks. Plans for a guest worker program and legalization fell off the agenda. Instead, large bipartisan majorities in Congress agreed in 2002 to abolish the INS in favor of a new agency, Immigration and Customs Enforcement (ICE), housed in the freshly created Department of Homeland Security. Comprehensive immigration reform was off the agenda.

Soon after the 2004 election, Bush met privately with a handful of pro-immigration Republicans in Congress to discuss reviving the derailed White House plan for a new guest worker program that would regularize flows and grant legal status to millions of undocumented immigrants. *The Washington Times* reported on November 10, 2004, that Press Secretary Scott McClellan underscored that immigration reform was "a high priority" and that the president "intends to work with members to get moving again in the second term. It's something he believes very strongly in" (Sammon, 2004). Restrictionists were aghast. Federation for American Immigration Reform (FAIR) president Dan Stein told the *Times* that he doubted Republican lawmakers would follow the administration "over a cliff" on the issue. He was right. In late November, House Republicans blocked an intelligence overhaul bill to signal Bush that his immigration initiative would split the party and stall action in his second term.

Polls indeed found that most conservative Republicans disapproved of plans for granting legal status to undocumented immigrants. In truth, however, the business base of the Republican Party was a zealous and unwavering supporter of the president's guest worker plans throughout his two terms in office. The most active business lobbyists favoring the Bush initiatives formed the Essential Worker Immigration Coalition (EWIC), an alliance of immigrant-dependent industry associations headed by the U.S. Chamber of Commerce. The coalition would bring together powerful associations such as the American Health Care Association, American Hotel and Lodging Association, National Council of Chain Restaurants, National Retail Federation, and Associated Builders and Contractors.

Illegal immigration and insecure borders were hot-button issues for many Republicans, and their disquietude was fueled by local and national talk radio, television commentators like Lou Dobbs and Pat Buchanan, and restrictive politicians such as Tancredo and his House Immigration Reform Caucus. New citizen patrols also popped up along the U.S.-Mexico border. In 2004 an accountant and decorated former Marine, James Gilchrist, founded the all-volunteer Minuteman Project to patrol the Arizona border armed with binoculars and cell phones. A former California schoolteacher, Chris Simcox, established the separate Minuteman Civil Defense Corps as an extension of this citizen patrol movement. Described as "vigilantes" by Bush, surveys showed that most ordinary citizens approved of the Minuteman movement. (The Minuteman movement is discussed in Craig's chapter on nativism.)

In the winter of 2005, H.B. 4437, a punitive bill focused on border enforcement narrowly passed the Republican-controlled House. It proposed for the first time to make illegal presence in the United States a felony, and it made it a crime for any persons or organizations to lend support to undocumented immigrants. The bill was also a direct attack on day laborer centers. From March through May 2006, demonstrations against the bill by largely Latino immigrants and their supporters, unprecedented in number and size, took place in a wide array of cities and towns across the United States. These nationwide rallies, protests, and boycotts drew negative reactions from most Americans: just 24 percent offered a favorable view of people who marched and protested for immigrant rights in major cities, while 52 percent were unfavorable. Overall, however, public opinion remained open to varied policy solutions: majorities favored legal status and earned citizenship for undocumented immigrants, stricter employer penalties, and tougher enforcement. Opinion was far from locked in either a restrictive or expansive position.

In the spring of 2006, a Senate plan emerged that was designed to satisfy disparate camps by including tough new language on border and interior enforcement, employment verification, and an expanded guest worker program, along with earned legalization for millions of undocumented people, a reduction of the family immigration backlog, and a provision extending legal status for many undocumented agricultural workers. The bill passed the full Senate that spring, but died in the more polarized House. With a majority of the House supporting a law-and-order approach to the issue and the Senate favoring a more liberal bill, immigration reform was tabled until after the election. In November, Democrats gained control of the House and Senate. Bush now spoke hopefully about a fresh "bipartisan effort" on immigration reform in the new term.

During the spring of 2007, a bipartisan Senate coalition led by Edward Kennedy negotiated behind the scenes with administration officials and eventually put forward the Border Security and Immigration Reform Act of 2007, a "grand bargain" that had the support of President Bush and became the focus of all meaningful subsequent discussion (Pear & Rutenberg, 2007). Emerging in June 2007, the grand bargain included significant new funding for border security and other interior enforcement measures. It imposed criminal penalties for illegal entry and replaced the current family- and employment-based admissions system with a new visa system. The bill provided a Z visa for undocumented immigrants covering those who were employed and their families, provided that they pay fees and penalties. It also contained a temporary Y worker program for 200,000 workers to be admitted on a 2-year basis, and that could be renewed twice as long as the worker spent a period of 1 year outside of the country between each admission.

Subject to intense media scrutiny and commentary, the public response to the compromise Senate immigration plan ranged from hostile to tepid. Many members of Congress were deluged with angry phone calls, e-mails, and letters from constituents and other activists. Surveys indicated that most Republicans, Democrats, and Independents opposed the measure, with only 23 percent in favor. Significantly, most Americans opposed the initiative not because they opposed "amnesty" or other proposals for legalizing millions of undocumented immigrants in the country (roughly two-thirds supported earned citizenship options over deportation), but because they had little faith that it would provide genuine border security. Ultimately, the "grand bargain" developed by Bush, Kennedy, and McCain fell 14 votes short of the 60 needed to force a final vote, and 15 Democrats were among those who helped kill the bill.

Bush had pursued comprehensive immigration reform out of a strong conviction that the best solution to the bedeviling problems associated with unauthorized flows was an expansive guest worker program that matched willing employers and laborers. He also believed that stricter enforcement of employer sanctions, improved efforts at the border, and earned citizenship for undocumented immigrants were necessary features of an effective compromise package. He and his advisers were also convinced that public opinion could be swayed on the issue, that his conservative base would hold and not rebel, and that his compassionate pragmatism on immigration reform would draw unprecedented numbers of Latino voters into the Republican fold. Yet whatever GOP inroads were made in 2000 and 2004 with Latinos and other new immigrant voters were forgotten by 2008. Consistent with trends that began in 2005 when Latinos soured on Bush's immigration plan and on House Republicans viewed as anti-immigrant, Barack Obama and the Democrats dominated the Latino vote in 2008, with more than two-thirds support in crucial battleground states from Florida to the Southwest. Equally striking was the fact that Latino turnout increased to 11 million voters (9 percent of the total) in 2008, double the turnout in 2000. Bush's gamble on immigration reform also sealed the fate of his second-term domestic agenda; he had no political capital left to expend on Capitol Hill.

Obama and the Immigration Minefield

Barack Obama ran for president promising in his first year to secure sweeping immigration reform that would enhance border control while extending legal status to roughly 12 million undocumented immigrants. When the dust settled, Obama's pro-immigration appeals helped him garner 67 percent of the Latino and 64 percent of the Asian vote in 2008. Yet neither this support nor his broader popularity upon entering office, the new president believed, was sufficient to propel major policy innovation. Even in an era of partisan polarization, few issues rivaled illegal immigration for how great the divide was between the Democratic and Republican base—ideological distance replicated in Congress.

Moreover, conflicts *within* each party on how to govern immigration remained profound. Against this backdrop, Obama officials explained soon after entering office that an immigration initiative would have to come after more looming priorities such as health care, energy, and financial regulatory reform. Considered too politically hot to handle, the Obama White House resolved to keep the immigration issue off its initial agenda.

During the heat of the 2010 election, illegal immigration was again center stage. In races across the country, Republican candidates railed against "illegal aliens who take our jobs" and increase taxes by placing strains on the U.S. health-care, justice, and education systems. During the hotly contested Nevada Senate campaign, the Republican challenger Sharron Angle ran negative ads blaming incumbent Senator Harry Reid for "millions of illegal aliens, swarming across our border, joining violent gangs, forcing families to live in fear." By contrast, President Obama sought to rally Latino voter support during the waning stages of the election by renewing his pledge to secure comprehensive immigration reform. In an interview with a popular Univision radio show in October 2010, Obama told the audience that his hopes for significant policy change were frustrated early in his term by "anti-immigrant" Republicans in Congress. Nevertheless, he promised listeners that he was "committed" to winning major reform that would include a "path to citizenship" for millions of undocumented immigrants.

In May 2011, President Obama went to El Paso, Texas, to deliver a speech that outlined his blueprint for comprehensive immigration reform. His plan centered on four key elements of a compromise package: a "threshold responsibility" of the government to "secure our borders and enforce our laws," stronger sanctions against employers who knowingly hire undocumented immigrants, "earned" legalization for undocumented immigrants (requiring applicants to pay a fine, learn English, and pass a background check), and revision of the legal immigration system to provide U.S. businesses which rely on immigrant labor "a legal way to hire workers . . . and a path for those workers to earn legal status." The proposal was largely centrist and designed to provide a "grand bargain" that would attract the kind of bipartisan coalition that propelled reform in the past. Indeed, while reading through the chapters here, one will notice that the "Point" and "Counterpoint" halves are often more polarized than was Obama's (probably destined to fail) attempt at a centrist immigration reform bill.

Gridlock in Washington over immigration reform has made state and local governments restive, with many protesting that inaction has significant implications for their budgets, public safety, the utilization and quality of their services, and the character of their communities. Amid intense media scrutiny, bruising debates, and legal uncertainty, a number of state and local leaders have seized the initiative by adopting their own policy responses. Arizona gained notoriety in 2010 when it enacted legislation—S.B. 1070—requiring state and local law enforcement officers to determine the immigration status of anyone involved in a lawful stop, detention, or arrest where "reasonable suspicion exists" that the person is unlawfully present. As Lewis and Suro, in this volume, show, critics charged that the measure would spur racial profiling by targeting people who look or sound foreign, especially anyone of Latino descent, while defenders retorted that strong action was required now, and law enforcement would be sensible and respectful in enforcing the law. Immigrant rights advocates vowed to boycott Arizona tourism and products, while their rivals promised to promote them. In polls, most Americans expressed support for Arizona lawmakers and their efforts to address illegal immigration while the federal government remained stuck in neutral.

Within days of its signing, S.B. 1070 was challenged in federal court as an unconstitutional violation of equal protection, due process, and the supremacy of the national government over immigration matters. President Obama also wasted no time in denouncing the law and its potential for discrimination, declaring that no one "should be subject to suspicion simply because of what they look like." U.S. Justice Department lawyers were prominent among those aligned against the law in federal court, but the core of their argument was that Arizona had infringed on exclusive federal powers and thereby violated the Constitution's supremacy clause. Before S.B. 1070 went into effect, federal judge Susan Bolton ruled that key provisions were indeed unconstitutional, including the mandate that Arizona police determine immigration status during any lawful stop. Governor Jan Brewer appealed the court's decision, and in December 2011 the U.S. Supreme Court agreed to hear the case.

Undaunted by the controversy that swirled around S.B. 1070, other states followed suit with legislation requiring police to check the immigration status of criminal suspects, compelling businesses to check the legal status of workers using a federal system called E-Verify, and forcing applicants for public benefits to verify eligibility with new documentation of lawful presence. In Alabama, for instance, a state where the undocumented immigrant population grew fivefold to roughly 120,000 in 10 years, Republican Governor Robert Bentley hailed new legislation in 2011 as the "strongest" and "toughest" in the nation. Along with familiar law enforcement, employment, and public benefits provisions, the Alabama law went further than most in mandating schools to determine the legal status of students and making it a crime to knowingly rent or give a ride to an undocumented immigrant. In August 2011, Mary Bauer, director for the Southern Poverty Law Center, told the PBS Newshour that S.B. 1070 is "clearly unconstitutional. It's mean-spirited, racist, and we think a court will enjoin it."

On June 25, 2012, the Supreme Court showed that it largely agreed with Bauer, striking down three of the four major provisions of S.B. 1070. Though the Court allowed for the right of police officers to check immigration status if they suspect the person they are dealing with is here illegally, their decision arguably reinforces a longstanding doctrine that states may not supersede or ignore federal policies in the field of immigration. The so-called plenary power doctrine, or the idea that the federal government exercises unchallenged power and control, remained as strong as ever. See Calvin Lewis and Roberto Suro's chapter in this volume on S.B. 1070 to learn about the debate over, and the realities of, collaborative and sometimes conflicting implementations of policy in practice.

While restrictive laws in states like Arizona and Alabama continue to steal most of the headlines, numerous other states have adopted very different approaches. A dozen states offer tuition breaks to undocumented immigrants to attend public colleges and universities, including a California law providing reduced university tuition to graduates of the state's high schools that withstood a challenge that found its way to the U.S. Supreme Court. From New York to California, state lawmakers have passed bills aimed at helping legal and undocumented immigrants in housing, health, employment, education, and other areas of integration. In Utah, a bipartisan coalition of government, business, religious, and civic leaders drafted a "Compact" on immigration reform endorsing a balance of federal solutions, effective law enforcement, protection of families, recognition of immigrants as valuable workers and taxpayers, and "humane" treatment of immigrants. In the winter of 2011, Utah legislators passed a package of bills for a temporary worker program, law enforcement, public benefits, and immigrant services. Meanwhile, cities and towns across the country have joined a "new sanctuary movement" that refuses to cooperate with federal efforts to identify and remove undocumented immigrants. In response, restriction-minded members of Congress, such as Representative Steve King (R-IA), have demanded that all federal funds be cut to sanctuary cities.

The Constitution is often vague in its division of powers between the national government and states. Immigration policy is not one of them. According to the Constitution, as the federal courts clarified in the nineteenth century, the federal government is granted exclusive authority to control immigration. It is telling, then, that contemporary battle lines over immigration policy cut across federal and state politics, and that even in this volume there is disagreement over what the Constitution says about immigration (see the chapter on birthright citizenship by Alexandra Filindra and Edward Erler).

Today's Immigration reform struggles powerfully capture the clashes and interdependence of national and state governments over policy, as well as the striking diversity of states and localities in how they respond to new challenges. It also captures a familiar conflict between Jeffersonian and Hamiltonian conceptions of federal-state relations. Like the Anti-Federalists before them, immigration restrictionists advancing tough enforcement measures from Arizona to Georgia view the federal government as too remote and insulated to understand the problems associated with porous borders. Their opponents, however, view national reform as essential for restoring coherence and respect for human rights in how the United States governs immigration.

In the end, the votes of immigrants and kindred ethnics, especially Latinos, were pivotal for Obama's presidential victory in 2008, and they will be critical to his reelection. During his first term in office, Obama promised a sensible overhaul of national immigration policy that would provide legal status to undocumented immigrants, clear backlogs in the current admissions system, target employers who knowingly hire unauthorized laborers, and regain control of the nation's borders. As Bush and reform-minded lawmakers of the 110th Congress learned, however, the impediments to major immigration reform have grown decidedly more daunting over time. American political leaders and ordinary citizens alike advance such deeply conflicting ideas and interests on illegal immigration that fierce battles rage both within and across the major parties and defy the usual ideological alliances. Basic problem definition and coalition building are consequently as elusive as ever. Moreover, the failure of past reforms like the Immigration Reform and Control Act of 1986 have inspired widespread cynicism about the federal government's will or capacity to curtail illegal immigration, and in turn have intensified opposition to familiar compromise packages. To make matters worse, the leading policy proposals of warring camps contain fatal flaws that do little to dampen public cynicism and frustration. At the end of the day, the bruising politics of health-care reform may seem like a welcome respite from the pitched battles ahead over immigration.

Illegal immigration has emerged as one of the nation's most formidable modern policy dilemmas and a cornerstone of contemporary political debate. How policymakers ultimately address comprehensive immigration reform after the 2012 election will not only have profound implications for age-old conflicts over the size, composition, legal rights, and status of the nation's foreign-born population, but will also shape the very character of American politics and society.

REFERENCES AND FURTHER READING

Allen, M. (2003, December 24). Immigration reform on Bush agenda. *The Washington Post,* p. 1.

Biemiller, Andrew to Peter Rodino, September 8, 1972; Biemiller to Rodino, March 23, 1973; Rodino to Biemiller, May 15, 1973, Papers of the Legislation Department of the AFL-CIO, Box 71, Folder #28, George Meany Archives.

Briscoe, D. (2004, November 22). Immigration—a hot topic. *Newsweek,* p.10.

Bush, G. W. (2006, May 15). Address to the nation on immigration reform, Washington, D.C., May 15, 2006. Retrieved from http://www.nytimes.com/2006/05/15/washington/15text-bush.html?pagewanted=all

Calavita, K. (1992). *Inside the state: The Bracero program, immigration, and the I.N.S.* New York, NY: Routledge.

Congressional Record. (1972, September 12). pp. 30164, 30182–30183.

Dobbs, L. (2007, April 25). *Big media hide truth about immigration.* Retrieved from http://articles.cnn.com/2007-04-24/us/Dobbs.April25_1_illegal-immigration-illegal-aliens-texas-and-florida?_s=PM:US

Durand, J., & Massey, D. (Eds.). (2004). *Crossing the border.* New York, NY: Russell Sage Foundation.

Gilchrist, J., & Corsi, J. (2006). *Minutemen: The battle to secure America's borders.* Los Angeles, CA: World Ahead.

Gutierrez, L. (2006, May 2). Interview with Representative Luis Gutierrez, Democracy Now Radio and Television. Transcript available at http://www.democracynow.org/2006/5/2/over_1_5_million_march_for

Marshall, T. H. (1950). *Citizenship and social class and other essays.* Cambridge, UK: Cambridge University Press.

McCarty, N., Poole, K., & Rosenthal, H. (2006). *Polarized America: The dance of ideology and unequal riches.* Cambridge, MA: MIT Press.

Narro, V., Wong, K. & Sahdduck-Hernandez, J. (2007). The 2006 immigrant uprising: Origins and future. *New Labor Forum, 16*(1), 49–56.

Ngai, M. M. (2005). *Impossible subjects: Illegal aliens and the making of modern America.* Princeton, NJ: Princeton University Press.

Obama, B. (2011). Remarks by the President on comprehensive immigration reform, El Paso, Texas, May 10, 2011. Retrieved from http://www.whitehouse.gov/the-press-office/2011/05/10/remarks-president-comprehensive-immigration-reform-el-paso-texas

Ong Hing, B., & Johnson, K. R. (2007). The Immigrant rights marches of 2006 and the prospects of a new civil rights movement. *Harvard Civil Rights-Civil Liberties Law Review, 42,* 99–138.

Passel, J., Fry, R., & Suro, R., (2005). *Hispanics and the 2004 election: Population, electorate, and votes.* Pew Hispanic Center Report. Retrieved from http://www.pewhispanic.org/2005/06/27/hispanics-and-the-2004-election

Pear, R., & Rutenberg, J. (2007, May 18). Senators in bipartisan deal on immigration bill. *The New York Times,* p. A-1.

Rosenblum, M. (2007). A "path to citizenship" or current illegal immigrants? Online Debate, Council of Foreign Relations website, April 1, 2007. Retrieved from http://www.cfr.org/immigration/path-citizenship-current-illegal-immigrants/p12971

Sammon, B. (2004, November 10). Bush revives bid to legalize illegal aliens. *The Washington Times,* p. 1.

Schumacher-Matos, E. (2009, August 28). Immigration reform must wait. *North County Times.* Retrieved from http://www.nctimes.com/news/opinion/columnists/schumacher-matos/article_6eef2ae8-c637-5ed9-90e6-c92416595736.html

Swain, C. (2007). Introduction. In C. Swain (Ed.), *Debating immigration* (pp. 1–16). New York, NY: Cambridge University Press.

Tancredo, T. (2006). *In mortal danger.* Nashville, TN: WND Books.

Tichenor, D. J. (2002). *Dividing lines: The politics of immigration control in America.* Princeton, NJ: Princeton University Press.

Tichenor, D., & Filindra, A. (2009). *Beyond myths of federal exclusivity: Governing immigration in the states and localities.* American Political Science Association paper.

Elaine M. Replogle and Daniel J. Tichenor
University of Oregon

Legal Immigration Selection System

POINT: The current U.S. legal immigration selection system reflects a sensible and appropriate balance between family-based and economic-based visa preferences. While far from perfect, the current system essentially works well.

David W. Haines, George Mason University

COUNTERPOINT: The current U.S. legal immigration selection system is deeply flawed and in need of serious reform. Backlogs, illegal immigration, too few skilled workers, and inflexible categories are some of the indicators of a broken system.

Madeleine Sumption, Migration Policy Institute

Introduction

The expression "America is a nation of immigrants" has reached the level of cliché, but the statement is no less true for being so. But while the practice of immigration is as old as the country itself, the laws and policies that regulate it are comparatively young. Like all laws, immigration laws have evolved over time as the national agenda has evolved. In this chapter, David Haines and Madeleine Sumption debate whether the current selection system for legal immigrants is appropriate, effective, and just.

The first laws relating to immigration were written in the late eighteenth century and simply involved the definition of citizenship, which in 1790 was limited to "free white persons" possessing "good moral character." Immigrants could petition a U.S. court for citizenship after several years of residency. From the beginning, therefore, two fundamental principles of immigration law can be observed. The first is that legislators have long attempted to select new citizens by sorting out desirable citizens from, in their view, less desirable ones. And the second principle of note is that proximity to the United States has always been an important consideration. In other words, the vast majority of immigrants who become citizens are people who are already in the United States and have been for some time. Location and connection matter.

A proverbial great leap forward in citizenship rights was one outcome of the Civil War. In 1868, the Fourteenth Amendment was added to the Constitution, including the Citizenship Clause, which states: "All persons born or naturalized in the United States, and subject to the jurisdiction thereof, are citizens of the United States and of the State wherein they reside." On paper at least, the Fourteenth Amendment removed the racial component from the equation.

But while racial background may have been removed from the formal definition of citizenship, race has had a major role to play in the question of naturalization. For example, the Chinese Exclusion Act, which followed the Fourteenth Amendment by 20 years, barred Chinese people, whether skilled or unskilled from entering the United States. The Chinese Exclusion Act was followed by a number of other laws that sought to tilt the balance of immigration toward the "desirable"—defined, generally speaking, as Northern Europeans—and away from the "undesirable,"—most everyone else. Quotas were set in place such that, for example, it was far easier for a person of British or German extraction to immigrate, but more difficult for an Italian or Greek, and impossible for a Malaysian.

The quota system would be adjusted in a variety of ways throughout the first half of the twentieth century and finally abolished by the Immigration and Nationality Act of 1965, also known as the Hart-Cellar Act. Hart-Cellar replaced the national origin focus of earlier immigration law with a new, bifurcated focus: the skill sets of the immigrants themselves, on the one hand, and their family relationships with U.S. citizens on the other. To these concepts a third would be added in 1980: the Refugee Act adopted the definition of *refugee* as accepted by the United Nations, and provided for 50,000 refugee admissions annually.

These three priorities—skills, family relationships, and refugee status—continue to govern the legal immigration system as it currently exists in the twenty-first century. But the three "legs" of the naturalization stool are not given equal weight. Family reunification far outweighs economic considerations when it comes to choosing new Americans—about 70 percent of legal immigration falls into various family-related categories. Indeed, relative to other countries' policies on immigration, the United States relies more on family reasons for immigration than it does on economic reasons.

Some see our system as one that works relatively well. In the Point section below, David Haines argues that the focus on family reunification helps guarantee that immigrants will adapt fairly smoothly to their new country because they already have ties here. He further points out that a visa lottery system, instituted in 1990, does provide openings for limited numbers of newcomers who do not have family here already, thus keeping the door somewhat open and allowing for an "eclectic" mix that Haines views as "quite appropriately American."

Madeleine Sumption, on the other hand, casts an economist's eye on the legal selection system and finds it wanting on a number of fronts. She argues that the system "fails dramatically" in several ways, imposing "awesome complexity on employers and [failing] systematically to adjust to changing economic needs and circumstances."

As you read this debate, consider what you believe to be the most important goals for U.S. immigration policy. Economic benefit? Family stability? Humanitarian? What mix of these priorities would be the most effective? What role does unauthorized immigration have to play in changing the mix? Are some problems better dealt with through, for example, labor policy, rather than legal immigration reform? Does the legal selection system require a complete overhaul, or merely some structural tweaks in order to work more effectively?

POINT

Complaints about immigration seem endless, and they are usually linked to resounding calls for "comprehensive immigration reform." But what exactly is this immigration system that is supposedly so flawed? The discussion that follows addresses this question by looking at the actual numbers, types, and origins of recently arriving legal immigrants, and by considering whether those numbers, types, and origins make sense in terms of America's immigration history and its current and future needs.

The discussion is in three parts. The first part involves the overall scale of legal immigration to the United States. A review of the historical data suggests the central point that, with about a million new legal immigrants a year, the percentage of the foreign-born in the United States has now reached about 13 percent, which is almost exactly what it was up until the beginning of the Great Depression in 1929. So, in terms of overall scale, American is now "back to normal," and there seems no reason to believe that the country cannot absorb that number of immigrants. There is thus no need for concern or change, although some might argue for somewhat higher numbers.

The second part of the discussion concerns the overall emphasis in legal immigration on people who already have ties to the United States. Slightly over half of the immigrants to the United States, for example, are admitted as relatives of U.S. citizens. Indeed, the majority of legal new immigrants are actually already living in the United States. In the main, then, America accepts people as immigrants who are already connected to it. Such an approach recognizes the desire of Americans to unite or reunite with foreign kin. The approach also helps ensure that newcomers are able to adapt relatively smoothly to their new country, since they already have anchor relatives who can help orient them to a new life. Here again, there is no great need for concern or change—although some might argue, quite reasonably, for modest changes in particular categories of admission.

The third part of the discussion concerns the many other components of legal U.S. immigration. These components represent a very comprehensive attempt to deal with all the other possible reasons that newcomers might wish to come to the United States. Such persons include high-tech entrepreneurs, badly needed professionals (nurses, for example), and refugees fleeing for their lives and their futures. There is also a visa lottery for people who do not have previous connections to the United States but wish to come here. There is a kind of eclectic inclusion in all these varied entry tracks that seems quite appropriately American, both in historical terms and in the current American emphasis on full engagement in a rapidly globalizing world.

THE SCALE OF IMMIGRATION

The United States is, as everyone knows, an "immigration country" (Cornelius et al., 2004). At nearly every stage of U.S. history, immigrants have made the difference between America as one of many countries in the world and America as an expansive and ultimately dominant world power in economic, political, cultural, and military dimensions. The majority of Americans have thus always been either immigrants, the children of immigrants, or relatively recent descendants of immigrants.

Perhaps the best indicator of the importance of immigration is the percentage of the foreign-born compared to the overall U.S. population. Consider the percentage of foreign-born residents at different periods in U.S. history. Data for the colonial period are sketchy, but by 1850 the U.S. Census was including a question on nativity. The first comprehensive data from that year indicate that roughly 10 percent of the population was foreign-born. That number jumped to 13 percent by 1860, due to the massive influx during that decade from Europe, and it stayed at roughly the same percentage for the rest of the nineteenth century (and through the first two decades of the twentieth century as well). All that massive immigration from western, then, central and southern Europe—that foundation of all the great paeans to America as beacon of hope and opportunity—only resulted, then, in a relatively constant proportion of the population being foreign-born.

Something did change very drastically in the 1920s, however, as alarmist fears of immigration led to serious restrictions in entry. As the doors slammed shut, the percentage of the foreign-born began to gradually drop. By 1970 the number of the foreign-born had dropped below 10 million, and their percentage of the total population dropped below 5 percent. But by then, the 1965 amendments to the Immigration and Nationality Act were beginning to take hold, and the gates that had been slammed shut were opened again. The result? By 2010 the percentage of the population that was foreign-born was

Table 1.1   Percentage foreign-born (1850–2010)

Year	Number	Percent
2010	36,700,000 (est.)	12.9
2000	31,107,889	11.1
1990	19,767,316	7.9
1980	14,079,906	6.2
1970	9,619,302	4.7
1960	9,738,091	5.4
1950	10,347,395	6.9
1940	11,594,896	8.8
1930	14,204,149	11.6
1920	13,920,692	13.2
1910	13,515,886	14.7
1900	10,341,276	13.6
1890	9,249,547	14.8
1880	6,679,943	13.3
1870	5,567,229	14.4
1860	4,138,697	13.2
1850	2,244,602	9.7

Sources: Gibson & Lennon (1999) for data through 1990; Malone et al. (2003) for 2000; U.S. Census Bureau (2010) for 2010.
Note: See the originals for sources of individual year calculations. Data are from decennial census, except for 2010 estimates.

nearing 13 percent again. America was back to "normal," at least to the extent that any norm can be established for such a young country. America has become again, as Randolph Bourne put it so evocatively a century earlier in 1916, a country that is truly international, truly cosmopolitan, truly what is now called "global." "Only America," Bourne suggested, "can lead in this cosmopolitan enterprise. . . . Only the American . . . has the chance to become that citizen of the world. America is coming to be, not a nationality but a transnationality, a weaving back and forth, with the other lands, of many threads of all sizes and colors" (Sheffer, 2002, p. 66). Bourne conveyed eloquently the glory of American immigration and the way it consistently reenergizes and reglobalizes America. The 13 percent solution seems to have worked very well: traditional and moderate, but effective and energizing.

BUT WHICH IMMIGRANTS?

These overall immigration numbers, and the quite traditional figure of 13 percent foreign-born, lead to the question of what kind of immigrants have come to the United States. In terms of national origins, the answer has shifted greatly over time, from an early preponderance of the English, and then western Europeans, then eastern and southern Europeans, and now to a very wide range of origin countries. The numbers by region, for example, now indicate roughly one-third each from Asia and North America, a bit above a tenth from Europe, and a bit below a tenth from Africa (see Table 1.2), greatly favoring North America and Asia as source countries. But the differences are hardly surprising and, at the least, are greatly reduced from the very lopsided European origins of American immigrants a century ago.

In terms of specific source countries, there are also great variations. A few countries stand out as major sources of immigrants, particularly Mexico (16 percent of the total), and China, India, and the Philippines (about 6 percent each). All these cases make sense: Mexico as our most populous neighbor, China and India as the world's most populous countries, and the Philippines as a former colony and close political ally. The more impressive fact, however, may be the sheer number of countries from which immigrants now come. Twenty-six countries have averaged at least 10,000 admissions per year over the last decade, and many, many more have contributed at least some immigrants. These numbers underscore the great national, linguistic, and cultural breadth of those coming to the United States.

A related question involves the immigration categories under which all of these people from all of these countries are admitted legally to the United States, and whether it is a reasonable system. What are the legal categories that produce the 13 percent solution, and is it the right 13 percent? Table 1.3 presents the major categories of admission to the United States over the last decade. The numbers break out into three major categories. The most overwhelming one, and accounting for fully two-thirds of all legal immigration, involves family.

There are two major parts to the family component of immigration. The larger family-related component of immigration—at about 45 percent of total admissions each year—involves immediate relatives of U.S. citizens. These are mostly spouses, but also some unmarried children under the age of 21, and some parents. This category is not subject to any numerical limitation, and it is hard to imagine how it ever could be. But it is also not surprising that there are often complaints about marriage fraud. Anybody at all interested in coming to the United States would immediately recognize that this is the biggest category of admission, and that it is not subject to any limitation other than proof of relationship and occasional procedural delays. This, the biggest single category of legal immigration, is thus also the least controlled. It is a useful reminder that much of immigration is not subject to direct policy control. Because of these immediate relatives,

Table 1.2 Immigrant origins (annual average, 2001–2010)

	Number	Percent
TOTAL	1,050,105	100.0
By region		
Africa	86,045	8.2
Asia	378,455	36.0
Europe	126,394	12.0
North America	360,511	34.3
Oceania	5,814	0.6
South America	90,599	8.6
Unknown	2,288	0.2
By country (With over 10,000 annually only)		
Bangladesh	10,674	1.0
Brazil	12,379	1.2
Canada	16,818	1.6
China, People's Republic	66,268	6.3
Colombia	25,132	2.4
Cuba	31,839	3.0
Dominican Republic	32,913	3.1
Ecuador	11,255	1.1
El Salvador	25,283	2.4
Ethiopia	10,973	1.0
Guatemala	16,068	1.5
Haiti	21,375	2.0
India	66,245	6.3
Iran	12,593	1.2
Jamaica	18,072	1.7
Korea, South	22,151	2.1
Mexico	169,324	16.1
Nigeria	11,121	1.1
Pakistan	15,696	1.5
Peru	14,566	1.4
Philippines	58,724	5.6
Poland	11,682	1.1
Russia	13,972	1.3
Ukraine	14,929	1.4
United Kingdom	15,346	1.5
Vietnam	30,612	2.9

Sources: U.S. Department of Homeland Security (2011).

the remaining more planned, controlled, and controllable parts of immigration account for only the bare majority of all admissions.

The other part of family-based immigration—and the smaller one, at 20 percent of the total—involves a series of preference categories that are subject to numerical restrictions. The priorities stem in part from the legal status of the U.S.-based relative. For example, the spouse of a citizen is (as noted above) not subject to any numerical restriction, while the spouse of a noncitizen permanent legal resident (a "green card" holder) is subject to numerical restriction. Such a spouse must wait in a queue after being approved until a "slot" is available. These relatives are also prioritized by the closeness of their relationship to the U.S.-based relative. Unmarried children, for example, have a higher priority than married children; both have higher priority than siblings. Overall, about 200,000 people a year, roughly one-fifth of all immigrants, are such sponsored relatives. There is a large backlog of applicants for these slots, and the result can be a long wait. Only in 2011, for example, were most Filipinos who had applied in the 1990s to join family in the United States being processed. The waiting time has been similar for Mexicans. These delays reflect the nearly three million people who queue up each year for the roughly 200,000 slots available for this admissions category.

The two other major segments of the immigration picture are economic-based immigrants (about 15 percent of the total) and a set of categories that, for the sake of convenience, will be designated here as "humanitarian admissions" (also about 15 percent of the total). Both represent more formal government decisions and control about the kind of new people (not just relatives) who ought to be admitted to the United States. On the economic side, many other countries place more emphasis on economic factors in admission (Cornelius et al., 2004). They often use some kind of point system that is based directly on potential immigrant economic contributions, or that attempts to balance economic factors with family ties and cultural compatibility (e.g., English language skills). The United States, however, has largely been content with this smaller explicitly economic stream for admissions, despite the frequent exhortations of critics that America is losing out to other countries in the quest for the best international migrants (Papademetriou & Sumption, 2011).

On the humanitarian side, the United States has always prided itself on being a haven for the oppressed and the persecuted. The percentage of all immigrants who are refugees or other kinds of humanitarian cases has varied greatly—from the years after World War II (when they were a very major part of American immigration) to the virtual shutdown of the refugee program in the months after 9/11.

Table 1.3 Annual admissions by category (annual average, 2001–2010)

Type of admission	Number	Percent
TOTAL	1,050,105	100.0
Total of immediate relatives of U.S. citizens	468,458	44.6
Spouses	272,556	26.0
Children (unmarried under the age of 21)	96,091	9.2
Parents (if U.S. relative is over 21)	99,812	9.5
Total of family-sponsored preferences	207,604	19.8
1: Unmarried sons/daughters of U.S. citizens and their children	24,853	2.4
2: Spouses, children, and unmarried sons/daughters of alien residents	93,606	8.9
3: Married sons/daughters of U.S. citizens and their spouses and children	25,493	2.4
4: Siblings of U.S. citizens (at least 21 years of age) and their spouses and children	63,653	6.1
Total of employment-based preferences	161,112	15.3
1: Priority workers	36,863	3.5
2: Professionals with advanced degrees or aliens of exceptional ability	41,302	3.9
3: Skilled workers, professionals, and unskilled workers	73,932	7.0
4: Certain special immigrants	8,020	0.8
5: Employment creation (investors)	996	0.1
Total of humanitarian admissions	164,074	15.6
Refugees	87,668	8.3
Asylees	44,869	4.3
Parolees (a mechanism to "parole" people into the country quickly)	4,212	0.4
Children born abroad to alien residents	686	0.1
Nicaraguan Adjustment and Central American Relief Act (NACARA)	3,576	0.3
Cancellation of removal	20,021	1.9
Haitian Refugee Immigration Fairness Act (HRIFA)	3,043	0.3
Diversity	45,346	4.3
Other	3,511	0.3

Source: U.S. Department of Homeland Security (2011).
Note: The overall "humanitarian" category is created here for simplicity. It is not used in the original DHS tables.

The overall figures for the 2010s suggest something more moderate and not too greatly different from the equivalent figure for economic-based migrants. The two farthest wings of American immigration—those based on economic benefit and humanitarian need—provide roughly 15 percent each of total immigration, surrounding the overwhelming core of American immigration, the roughly two-thirds who are family-based immigrants.

WHAT DO THOSE ADMISSIONS NUMBERS MEAN?

These basic numbers suggest that U.S. immigration is based on three main principles: family reunion, economic development, and humanitarian relief. These are all important goals, as they reflect fundamental features of American history, and they all remain highly appropriate in the contemporary world. But what is the proper mix? If the 13 percent solution is indeed a good one—not too few but not too many—then expanding the people admitted under any of these three goals would be at the expense of the other. Furthermore, with the exception of immediate relatives of citizens, there are long waiting lists for all these categories of immigration: long pending applications for family sponsorship, long lists of people who want to work in America, and long lists of people who need refuge in America. So to change the mix will require a decision to have one category of immigrant bear the cost of increased numbers in other categories. It would pit Americans who want to reunite with their relatives against business interests looking for fresh labor, and against humanitarian activists.

HUMANITARIAN ADMISSIONS

Another important characteristic of the U.S. legal immigration system is that about 60 percent of new admissions each year are people who are already in the United States. Thus, over half of new admissions are not new arrivals. They are already here, living under a variety of legal statuses, including being undocumented. Not surprisingly, the characteristics of the immigrants coming from abroad and those already in the country differ somewhat in terms of country of origin and legal admission category. The result is that there are two somewhat different U.S. immigration systems, depending on whether legal permanent resident status involves a new arrival or a change of status for someone already in the United States.

Humanitarian admissions provide a particularly good example of the differing effects of these two systems: legal admission *before* physical arrival versus legal admission *after* physical arrival. In the humanitarian case, there are many admissions categories: some are temporary—as in temporary protected status (TPS)—while others yield permanent legal status, or at least a path to it. Some are potentially available to all groups, while some are limited to a specific group (such as Cubans under the Cuban Adjustment Act), some are for groups as a whole, and some are for particular individuals (such as cancellation of removal). The two main legal statuses, however, stem from the U.S. Refugee Act of 1980, which created two separate tracks, one for people whose status is determined before arrival in the United States (legal admission before physical arrival) and the other for people whose status is determined after arrival in the United States (legal admission after physical arrival). The standard is the same, but the processes are quite different, providing a good example of this question of whether the newly admitted are already here or not.

Some general background on the relationship between America and refugees may be helpful. America has a long history of providing refuge to the oppressed. Indeed much of America's early history can be seen as the interplay of northern colonies based on America as a "land of refuge" (especially for freedom of religion) versus southern colonies based more on America as "land of economic opportunity." The subsequent history of America as a land of refuge is a long and contorted one, with periods of acceptance of refugees alternating with periods of exclusion—often depending on the specific economic, racial, religious, and social characteristics of particular refugee groups. The Refugee Act of 1980, spurred by the late Senator Edward Kennedy, aimed to reconcile that long American history as land of refuge with the more international and legalistic definitions of refugee embodied in international law and practice, particularly the definition in the United Nations Refugee Convention of 1951. That definition specifies that a refugee is someone who has fled across a national border because of a well-founded fear of persecution, not simply because of generalized violence or disorder. Among other issues, the Refugee Act of 1980 provides a reminder that U.S. immigration law is often interwoven with America's stance in the wider world, and with a commitment to shoulder a fair share of the world's migration problems.

There is, then, a legal definition of *refugee* in U.S. law, and that definition largely matches international standards. But where does the application of the definition to particular people take place? How do people who have fled—who are refugees in the general sense—become refugees in the more specific "legal immigration" sense? Here is where the two tracks arise. The first track is one where refugees are identified overseas, often in refugee camps that are just across the border from the countries from which they have fled, such as the Southeast Asian refugee camps that became so large in the late 1970s and early 1980s in Thailand, Malaysia, the Philippines, Indonesia, and Hong Kong, or the massive refugee camps today in Kenya, swollen further in late 2011 by famine in Somalia. This has been by far the major track, bringing in nearly 100,000 people per year from 1975 to 2000, although a much smaller number—a little over 50,000 per year—in the first decade of this century (Haines, 2010, pp. 4, 175).

This track has some procedural advantages. The refugees are together as a group, so there can be efficiency in processing and a better chance to be sure that the people really are bona fide refugees. A claim to have fled across a border, for example, is quite easily verified, and the conditions at the time of flight are readily knowable. Furthermore, the issue of legal status is determined before arrival in the United States, so the inevitable problems of adjustment are not further complicated by legal questions. The many organizations that reach out to these newcomers to offer assistance have some assurance that these people really are refugees.

In the second track, refugee status is sought by people who themselves make the journey to America, either claiming to be refugees at the border, or—and this is the wiser practical strategy—entering the country illegally and then finding the community and legal resources to make a claim to refugee status. In the past, this has been by far the minor track, but has expanded greatly in recent decades with the number of asylees exceeding 20,000 in 2008, 2009, and 2010 (Martin, 2011). This track involves a more individualized process taking place far away from the country from which the refugees have fled, making it far more difficult for those adjudicating the case to know of the severity of conditions in that country and whether those conditions may have changed. These people are thus not yet legally refugees, whatever their personal experiences may have been. Rather, they are "asylum-seekers" about whom the public reaction is often confused, precisely because their legal status remains uncertain. And the legal terminology becomes even more confusing because asylum seekers who meet the refugee standard are, in legal terms, not refugees even then; instead, they are "asylees." There are still many organizations that aim to aid these newcomers, including making sure they gain access to legal representation, without which their claim is in far greater jeopardy. Yet, still, the process is shrouded in uncertainty: for the asylum seekers, for those who seek to aid them, for the government as it attempts to impose consistent migration controls, and for the general public, who are likely to be, at the least, a little confused.

These dual tracks for refugees are a particularly strong reminder of the extent to which American immigration policy is both about accepting people from somewhere else and about accepting people who are already here. Clearly, people who arrive in the United States claiming refuge cannot be sent back to some camp in another country to await proper processing there; clearly, people who are waiting in camps cannot be told they must make a clandestine trip to the United States in order to gain direct access to the U.S. legal system. While people may well be confused about these twin statuses of "refugee" and "asylee"—including refugees themselves—the need for both tracks is still manifest. Here, then, policy and operational complexity may seem to burden the system and confuse the citizenry; yet the complexities are necessary to meet the goals of humanitarian relief both overseas and in the United States.

ADD A LITTLE COMPLEXITY, THEN STIR

The refugee case suggests that the broad goals of family reunion, economic development, and humanitarian relief mask an immigration system that is complex in its categories, policies, and procedures. Just as there are many different kinds of humanitarian migration statuses, so too are there many different kinds of family-sponsored immigrants (married children, unmarried children, siblings, parents, etc.) and economic-based immigrants (and temporary migrant workers of all kinds). Many of these operate as virtually independent immigration programs, each with its own particular logic. A few examples may help to indicate how specialized immigration law and policy can be.

Consider, for example, nurses and preachers. One set of people ministers to the body and another to the spirit. Both are important and, of course, both tend to be rather underpaid considering their skills and education. So there is likely to be a shortage of them in at least some areas, and thus they become candidates for special consideration as immigrants. In the case of nurses, processing is under the third preference for employment-based immigration, and there are fairly extensive requirements in terms of educations and certification in the country of origin. In this case, the net numbers are not large, since the nurses must compete among each other and other third-preference employment-based immigrants, but the result remains something of a special channel for nurses. In the case of preachers, there is a special category under the fourth preference for employment-based immigration for religious ministers that, among other things, requires proof of already belonging to an established religious denomination in the United States. In 2010, there were 2,074 people admitted in this category, most of whom were already in the United States.

Both of these cases represent an attempt in immigration policy to address quite specific employment needs. This is not a grand policy of skills-based migration, but rather a more focused kind of mini-program to address particular needs. While such programs have the disadvantage of complexity (i.e., separate programs for separate groups), they have the decided advantage of addressing particular needs that have become apparent enough to attract some governmental support. It may seem a disorganized approach to immigration policy, with a little piece here and a little piece there, linked together in a seemingly uncoordinated fashion, but it addresses the component issues and, after all, seems to work—and it does so with a certain American inventiveness.

As another example, consider the diversity program. The logic is fairly simple. Because existing streams of immigrants to America create future immigration by relatives, yesterday's immigrants bring today's immigrants, and today's immigrants tend to bring in tomorrow's immigrants. The result is large numbers of immigrants from particular countries, and often from particular places within those countries. But should America not be open to everybody on an equal opportunity basis? Here again is a kind of special need, and the answer again has not been to change the entire immigration system, but simply to add a separate program for people from countries underrepresented as sources of immigration to the United States. People in such countries now have the opportunity to apply for a special kind of immigration slot, with the results chosen by random lot. This is the diversity visa program—the diversity lottery—with roughly 50,000 people selected each year by random number from a web-based application system operated by the U.S. Department of State. It is another kind of Rube Goldberg invention: don't redo the whole system, just add another component to clank along to its own rhythm in the overall cacophony of American immigration. No smooth, well-polished and integrated immigration system here. Instead, it is a complex and at times internally inconsistent system. Yet it is a system that, by aiming at the component issues in immigration, may actually achieve its goals more effectively than a more formalized and integrated policy. It may be hard to explain this big clanking machine to the public, but that does not mean there is a need for comprehensive immigration reform, just that there is a need for a more comprehensive explanation of this great big wondrous American immigration process.

CONCLUSION

To reiterate all three parts of the discussion, contemporary legal immigration to the United States demonstrates an overall scale of immigration that is quite consistent with historical trends, a preponderant but not exclusive emphasis on existing ties, yet also a recognition of the many other reasons for immigration. Contemporary legal immigration to the United States can thus quite easily be argued to be nicely comprehensive, responsive, flexible, and practical, as well as eminently sensible in terms of America's history, society, and role in the world.

That does not mean that contemporary U.S. immigration is without problems. There are serious migration-related problems in America today, perhaps especially with a high level of undocumented migration. That undocumented migration, in turn, reflects an enduring ambivalence about the extent to which American labor needs should be met with the use of temporary and low-wage imported labor (whether as legal immigrants, legal but temporary workers, or a tacit system of using undocumented labor). But these problems would be better addressed by focusing on them directly, rather than calling for "comprehensive immigration reform" when the current legal immigration system itself seems in quite good shape. In other words, the legal immigration system should not be asked to resolve problems that lie elsewhere. Much of the concern with Mexican undocumented migration, for example, might be better addressed by thinking about U.S. labor policy, the global rush to the bottom in terms of wages, and the desperate need for a better good neighbor policy toward our most populous neighbor. A legal immigration system that is working pretty well should be kept, and the focus should instead be on the real problems, such as a better neighbor policy and a better labor policy.

REFERENCES AND FURTHER READING

Barkan, E. R., Diner, H., & Kraut, A. M. (Eds.). (2008). *From arrival to incorporation: Migrants to the U.S. in a global era*. New York, NY: New York University Press.

Bon Tempo, C. (2008). *Americans at the gate: The United States and refugees during the Cold War*. Princeton, NJ: Princeton University Press.

Cornelius, W., Tsuda, T., Martin, P. L., & Hollifield, J. F. (2004). *Controlling immigration: A global perspective* (2nd ed.). Stanford, CA: Stanford University Press.

Daniels, R. (2004). *Guarding the golden door: American immigration policy and immigrants since 1882*. New York, NY: Hill & Wang.

Divine, R. A. (1972). *American immigration policy, 1924–1952*. New Haven, CT: Yale University Press. (Original work published 1957)

Gibson, C. J., & Lennon, E. (1999). *Historical census statistics on the foreign-born population of the United States: 1850–1990* (Working Paper No. 29). Washington, DC: U.S. Census Bureau, Population Division.

Haines, D. (2010). *Safe haven? A history of refugees in America*. Sterling, VA: Kumarian Press.

Haines, D., & Rosenblum, K. (Eds.). (1999). *Illegal immigration in America: A reference handbook*. Westport, CT: Greenwood.

Malone, N., Baluja, K. F., Costanzo, J. M., & Davis, C. J. (2003). *The foreign-born population 2003*. Washington, DC: U.S. Census Bureau.

Martin, D. C. (2011). *Refugees and asylees: 2010.* Washington, DC: Department of Homeland Security, Office of Immigration Statistics.

Ngai, M. (2005). *Impossible subjects: Illegal aliens and the making of modern America.* Princeton, NJ: Princeton University Press.

Papademetriou, D. G., & Sumption, M. (2011). *The role of immigration in fostering competitiveness in the United States.* Washington, DC: Migration Policy Institute.

Pew Research Center. (2011). *Illegal immigration: Gaps between and within parties.* Retrieved from http://www.people-press.org/2011/12/06/illegal-immigration-gaps-between-and-within-parties/?src=prc-headline

Portes, A., & Rumbaut, R. G. (2006). *Immigrant America: A portrait* (3rd ed.). Berkeley, CA: University of California Press.

Sheffer, M. S. (Ed.). (2002). *In search of a democratic America: The writings of Randolph S. Bourne.* Lanham, MD: Lexington Books.

U.S. Census Bureau. (2010, October 19). Nation's foreign-born population nears 37 million [News release]. Retrieved from http://www.census.gov/newsroom/releases/archives/foreignborn_population/cb10-159.html

U.S. Department of Homeland Security. (2011). *Yearbook of immigration statistics.* Washington, DC: Author.

Waters, M., & Ueda, R. (Eds.). (2007). *The new Americans: A guide to immigration since 1965.* Cambridge, MA: Harvard University Press.

David W. Haines

COUNTERPOINT

Selection is perhaps the most fundamental component of a nation's immigration policy. The selection system determines who gets in and who doesn't, and this gives it a central role in shaping the role of immigration in the receiving country's economy and society.

The definition of "good" selection policies depends on their goals, and most immigration systems balance several, including enabling family unification, contributing to economic growth, and meeting humanitarian obligations. These goals are translated into specific eligibility criteria that determine which immigrants can be admitted. For example, humanitarian migrants are generally admitted on the basis of their ability to establish a well-founded fear of persecution, and family migrants are admitted on the basis of specified family relationships with U.S. citizens or permanent residents.

This chapter takes an economic perspective on selection policies, focusing on the economic goals of immigrant selection and, more specifically, on the system for allocating work visas. This system is also known as "economic-stream" or "employment-based" selection. Immigrants admitted through this part of the immigration system are expected to contribute directly to the national economic interest. Arguably, the work visa system represents selection at its most deliberate; it is also the area in which policymakers have most discretion over whether workers are eligible to immigrate or not, and over which criteria should govern their admission.

From an economic perspective, good selection policies should ideally achieve various goals. First, they should provide a screening mechanism to determine whether a prospective immigrant brings economic value, or (another way of approaching the same problem) which people from the pool of those who would like to come to the United States would bring the most economic value. Defining economic value in this context is not straightforward, but immigration policy tends to focus on a few intermediate goals designed to support national economic interests. These may include ensuring that the door is open to the most exceptional individuals who could make disproportionate contributions to economic growth and productivity, thus ensuring that immigrants who are admitted have skills and attributes that U.S. employers value and that they are able to put these skills to good use; enhancing the country's "human capital pool" (for example, by bringing in scientists and researchers who contribute to the excellence of research centers and to knowledge and technological progress); and, more generally, facilitating immigration where employers find it difficult to meet labor demand from the domestic labor market.

A second goal of good selection policies is to be "user-friendly" for immigrants and their employers, while also discouraging abuses of the letter or spirit of the law. On the one hand, this means implementing policies that lead to predictable outcomes, so that immigrants and employers can plan ahead, make investments, and avoid the expense and disruption of unpredictable events. At the same time, the system must be capable of deterring abuse through regulations that are well designed and enforceable. This often leads to a tradeoff between the desire to fine-tune policies to meet a complex set of objectives, and the need to avoid excessive administrative complexity.

Finally, a good selection system has sufficient flexibility to adjust over time to changing circumstances. This includes the ability to generate evidence about the impacts of policy choices and respond to it by adjusting policy accordingly.

As this chapter explains, the U.S. immigrant selection system is partially successful on the first count—screening for immigrants with valuable skills. This is in large part because of the central role it gives to employers to select immigrants. However, a heavy reliance on numerical limits on the number of visas that can be issued undermines some of the benefits of the employer-led system. Meanwhile, U.S. policy fails dramatically on the second two counts (effective regulation and adjusting to evidence); instead, it imposes awesome complexity on employers and fails systematically to adjust to changing economic needs and circumstances.

Of course, while selection is central to determining the impact of immigration, it is not the whole story. In particular, policies that facilitate the economic and social integration of immigrants once they arrive can have a significant impact on immigration's economic role, not to mention the public's acceptance of its value.

CONTEXT: THE U.S. SELECTION SYSTEM

The U.S. immigration selection system has a few attributes that are worth emphasizing by way of context: a small share of employment-based visas relative to visas issued for other purposes, such as family unification; a bias toward admitting highly skilled workers, at least within employment-based routes, coupled with high levels of illegal immigration at the less-skilled level; heavy use of temporary visas as an initial entry route within the economic stream; and a central role for employers in determining which foreign workers gain admission.

The U.S. immigration system as a whole is, for the most part, not designed with economic goals in mind. Two-thirds of permanent visas—known as green cards—go to family members of U.S. citizens or existing green card holders (of these, two-fifths are issued to the spouses of U.S. citizens, and the rest to the children, siblings, or parents of U.S. citizens, or to the spouses of permanent residents). A further 15 percent of green card recipients enter as refugees or asylum seekers, making the United States the largest global recipient of humanitarian migrants. Only about 15 percent of green cards are issued to economic-stream immigrants in the United States, of which about half go to family members of employer-sponsored immigrant workers themselves (the principal applicants). Finally, about 5 percent of permanent visas are issued in a lottery available to nationals of countries that do not send large numbers of immigrants to the United States, primarily countries in Africa and Europe. (The green card lottery has been slated for abolition in various pieces of legislation in recent years, and its demise may well be the outcome of future efforts to increase the allocation of visas elsewhere in the system.) In addition to these flows, about 3 in 10 immigrants in the United States were not selected at all, but arrived illegally or overstayed their visas. (According to government estimates, approximately 10.8 million unauthorized immigrants lived in the United States in 2010.)

The employment-based immigration system is divided into two components: temporary and permanent. (Some temporary visas exist in other streams, such as the family route, but by far the most significant use of temporary visas occurs in the economic stream of the immigration system.) Temporary work visas, typically lasting up to about 6 years, provide the initial entry route into the labor market for the overwhelming majority of immigrants, and many of these visas allow their holders eventually to apply for a more limited number of green cards.

Although most immigration to the United States is not selected on the basis of skills, legal *employment-based* immigration is heavily skewed towards skilled and highly skilled workers. Most immigrants coming on work visas must have a bachelor's degree or higher, and the higher the skill level, the easier it is for them to gain permanent residence rights. At lower skill levels, visas are fewer, of shorter duration and more tightly controlled, and adjusting to permanent residence is extremely difficult. Instead, family and illegal immigration represent the main entry routes for less-skilled immigrants.

Finally, work-based immigration in the United States relies heavily on employers, who select prospective foreign employees and apply for visas on their behalf. These workers may apply directly from abroad, they might be recruited as an international student from within the country, or they might be transferred from an overseas office of a multinational corporation. Once an employer has selected a candidate, several conditions must be in place in order for the worker to be eligible for admission, including the following:

- The worker must meet the criteria for the visa in question, such as educational requirements or a clean criminal record.
- The employer must agree to pay a wage comparable to what U.S. workers (that is, U.S. citizens and green card holders) would receive in the same job.

- The employer may be required to demonstrate that it has advertised the vacancy to U.S. workers and failed to find suitable candidates.

- There must be a sufficient number of visas remaining under the system of annual numerical limits on visa issuances.

By way of comparison, employers are less dominant in some other immigration systems. In Canada and Australia, for example, work-motivated immigrants can apply for a visa without an employer sponsor. Under this policy, the government awards prospective immigrants points for individual characteristics considered desirable (these include education, language ability, or work experience), and applicants who gain sufficient points can enter the country to find a job. However, immigrants arriving in both Canada and Australia without a job offer fare worse in the labor market than employer-selected workers in the same country. As a result, both countries have moved away from "pure" government selection of this kind, and are placing ever greater emphasis on admitting immigrants with prearranged employment, bringing their policies somewhat closer to the U.S. model. (By contrast, a 2007 legislative proposal for comprehensive immigration reform would have moved in the opposite direction, introducing a points system to replace employer-led selection, but the bill was unsuccessful.)

PROBLEMS WITH THE SELECTION SYSTEM

Perhaps the greatest asset of the U.S. immigration system is employer-driven selection, and there is no need to change this basic principle. Because employers individually screen candidates and assess the relevance of their skills before offering them a job, employer selection guarantees immigrants' employability and ensures that they have a job waiting for them on arrival; compelling evidence from around the world demonstrates that this improves their long-term integration. However, a wide range of flaws undermine the system's ability to meet the goals described earlier.

Heavy reliance on numerical limits instead of more effective selection criteria. U.S. work visa policy has proved extremely inflexible in the face of changing circumstances. One reason for this is a heavy reliance on numerical limits and Congress's unwillingness to adjust them regularly or systematically. Numerical limits or "caps" on immigration regulate the number of visas that U.S. Citizenship and Immigration Services (USCIS), the agency responsible for adjudicating visa applications, can issue to certain categories of worker. Current law allocates 140,000 green cards per year for permanent employment-based immigration, for example, and 226,000 for family immigrants other than "immediate relatives" (that is, the spouses, unmarried minor children, and parents of U.S. citizens), for whom no limits are imposed. Temporary H-1B visas—the most commonly used work visa for skilled professionals—are limited to 85,000 per year, although certain types of employers, such as universities and other nonprofit or public sector research organizations, receive H-1B visas exempt from the cap.

Caps are a blunt instrument for managing visa policy, but over the years they have become one of the most influential features of the U.S. employment-based immigration system. Caps have a significant political function, since they allow the government to demonstrate to the public that immigration is under control and that the system does not allow excessive immigration.

However, numerical limits regulate the quantity of immigrants but do nothing to improve their "quality." Indeed, while the number of skilled and highly skilled workers who would like to work in the United States vastly exceeds the number of visas available for them, the selection system does relatively little to prioritize applications that are potentially the most beneficial economically. The United States allocates H-1B visas, for example, on a first-come, first-served basis to workers whose applications meet the basic eligibility criteria (in particular, possessing a bachelor's degree or equivalent). Entry-level IT workers essentially compete with seasoned business managers or specialized health workers, depending on their employers' ability to submit their application early (several months in advance of their employment start date). In some years, H-1B visas for skilled professionals have sold out after a matter of days, leaving none available for the rest of the year (see Figure 1.1). Even extremely high-caliber candidates may fail to get a visa if the vacancy for which they are selected does not happen to open up at the right time of year. Meanwhile, employers are forced to guess their need for workers 6 to 18 months in advance in order to apply for a visa at the specified time (April for H-1B visas). This makes

Figure 1.1   Time taken to fill H-1B cap, 2003–2010

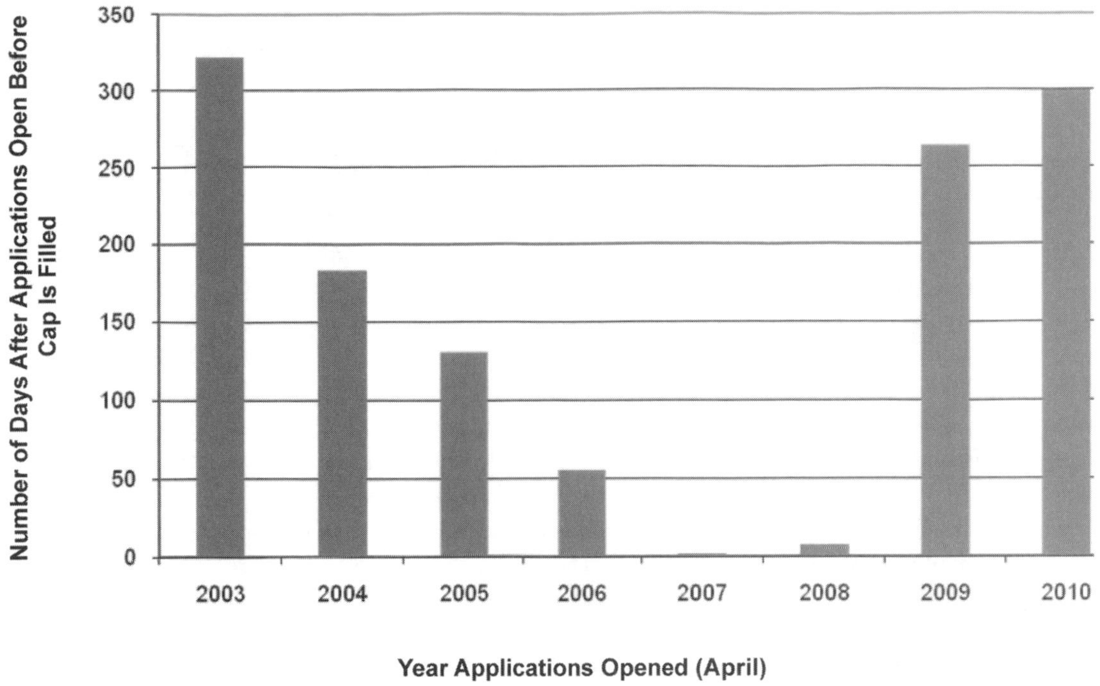

Source: USCIS Press Releases, 2003–2010.

Note: Employers can apply for H-1B visas in April for employment start dates during the next fiscal year, beginning in October. This chart tracks the baseline congressionally mandated H-1B cap of 65,000 as of 2004, and does not include the 20,000 additional visas set aside for graduates of master's degree programs in U.S. universities.

strategic staffing decisions difficult, undermining the predictability of the U.S. business environment and encouraging a stampede for visas each time applications are reopened.

For permanent visas, demand also exceeds the number of visas available, and applications roll over from one year to the next, creating long backlogs and a waiting time of several years in the more oversubscribed visa categories. Since most workers require their employer's support to make the transition from temporary to permanent residence, it is often difficult to move between employers while a green card application is pending.

Backlogs in the permanent system and long blackout periods in the temporary system result from a simple disequilibrium between the supply and demand for a scarce good: visas. To remedy the problem, one or both of two things must happen. Policymakers must either make more visas available, or they must raise the bar for eligibility so that fewer applications are made. From an economic perspective, no "optimal" number of visas exists, and choosing how wide to open the door to immigrant workers is in large part a political decision. But regardless of the number of visas ultimately issued, more effective mechanisms are needed to ensure that the visas available go to the most compelling applicants and that employers seeking to bring in the highest caliber workers are able to do so according to a predictable timeline. Efforts to bring supply and demand closer into balance without simply removing the immigration cap could involve providing cap exemptions for high-earning or otherwise desirable immigrants, raising eligibility requirements for some or all of the visas available, or charging higher fees to employers (fees could be charged either across the board or in order to gain exemption from numerical limits; either way, this policy might require employers to demonstrate that they face a genuine "need" for the worker in question).

In other words, immigration caps may be useful as a political safety valve, but they do not in themselves make good selection policies. Instead, other policies, such as eligibility requirements or fees, are better able to bear the burden of deciding which immigrants are eligible and which are not. But with visas vastly oversubscribed—even if current economic weakness has provided some temporary respite—simply allowing visas to run out within days is not an effective allocation mechanism.

Lack of flexibility, especially on numerical limits. The impact of reliance on numerical limits could be mitigated if the limits themselves were more flexible. As Figure 1.1 shows, the demand for visas varies year by year, but caps typically do not. Other countries with numerical targets for immigration review the size of the limit on at least an annual basis, in recognition of the fact that the need for immigrant workers varies over time, not least with changing economic conditions. By contrast, cap adjustments in the United States are generally ad hoc and occur only when political coalitions are able to bring them about—something that does not happen particularly often. Proposed legislation debated in 2006, for example, would have increased both temporary and permanent employment-based visa numbers and allowed the H-1B cap to increase automatically over time, but the bill did not gather enough support to become law. As a result, the current employment-based green card cap has not changed since 1990. The cap on H-1B visas has changed more often, but not in response to any systematic evaluation of need. Other countries that use numerical limits typically adjust them at least on an annual basis.

Inflexibility in the United States is, in part, a natural consequence of the country's political system, which makes it more difficult to legislate on controversial topics such as immigration. But the problem is sufficiently important to warrant efforts to push against this tendency. One way of doing this would be to build greater institutional flexibility into the system, creating an independent government agency that would provide systematic evaluation of numerical limits and other employment-based immigration policies, as well as analytical support and regular recommendations to Congress. Legislation could even require Congress to respond to the recommendations or, more controversially, provide for recommendations that would automatically come into effect if Congress failed to act.

Analytical capacity of this kind could also help to inform more flexible policies in other areas of the selection system. Other major immigrant-receiving countries tend to adjust their selection criteria and employer regulations much more often than the United States. Some—such as Australia, Canada, and New Zealand—also collect detailed data on how immigrants fare when they arrive in the country and on their journey through the migration system (from one visa category to another and eventually to permanent residence). This enables them to adjust selection policies on the basis of evidence, selecting more explicitly for individuals with better prospects in the labor market. Since no immigration policy is perfect, this ongoing monitoring and adjustment is essential in dealing with unintended consequences or changing economic circumstances—a capacity that is sorely lacking in the current U.S. system.

Bureaucratic procedures that create costs with no clear benefit. The U.S. employment-based immigration system is an administrative obstacle course. Administrative checks and balances are necessary and inevitable in order to reduce the risk that employers or workers will use the system in ways for which it was not intended. For example, many of the rules in place seek to meet the apparently reasonable goal of ensuring that employers do not use foreign workers simply to undercut potential local hires, pay workers less than they are worth, or discriminate against local candidates. However, administrative requirements impose costs on everyone, including employers who play by the rules. This makes it important both to avoid requirements that fail to create palpable benefits, and to find ways of targeting administrative checks towards employers who pose the greatest risks. The U.S. system fails to do this in several ways.

Perhaps the clearest example is the process for adjusting from temporary to permanent residence. The permanent employment-based visa system is essentially no longer used, as it once was, to bring workers to the United States for the first time, but rather to allow them to stay permanently after spending some time on a temporary work visa. However, the application process for the main categories of permanent work visa includes features that are much more appropriate for initial recruitment than for workers who have already been in the country for several years.

One of these features is the requirement that employers sponsor their workers twice—once when the workers enter the country, and again when they apply for permanent residence. The fact that the worker received employer sponsorship the first time and has been able to hold down a job for several years already provides a screening mechanism to demonstrate that demand for his or her skills exists. While the second round of employer sponsorship may provide an additional guarantee that the worker is still needed, this benefit is probably small compared to the additional cost it creates for employers and the uncertainty it imposes on workers reliant on their employer's willingness and ability to support their future green card application. Since temporary visas are valid for several years and employers have no incentive to sponsor green card applications until the temporary visa is close to expiration, these rules also reduce immigrant workers' ability to switch between employers.

A second example of a regulatory failure is the labor certification process for permanent employment-based immigration. In most cases, employers who petition for a green card to allow existing employees on temporary work visas to stay permanently must advertise the worker's job despite the fact that no real vacancy exists, in order to "prove" that U.S. workers are not available. This makes little sense, given that many of these workers enter on H-1B visas, which do not require employers to advertise vacancies. At the very minimum, bringing forward the advertising process to the point at which the worker is actually recruited, rather than requiring it up to 6 years later, would bring a clear improvement.

Advertising requirements such as these do not have to be burdensome, since many employers advertise their vacancies anyway. However, several aspects of the design of these requirements are out of step with the natural process that reasonable, law-abiding employers tend to follow. Employers may be required to advertise in outdated print media or Sunday newspapers, for example. More significantly, current law requires employers to offer jobs to any U.S. worker who meets the advertised job's minimum qualifications (who is "minimally qualified"), before they can hire a better-qualified foreign worker. Employers, of course, prefer to hire the best candidates, even if other candidates are available who would perform the work to an acceptable but lesser standard, creating a clear incentive to bend the rules. Moreover, enforcing these distinctions on a case-by-case basis is highly subjective and not something for which government agencies are naturally suited. As a result, many of these rules simply encourage reasonable employers to game the system.

Finally, the U.S. immigration system makes little effort to distinguish between employers that pose higher and lower levels of risk. While some employers who are considered "dependent" on skilled foreign workers face somewhat stricter eligibility requirements and higher visa fees, the vast majority of employers sponsoring workers are treated the same. In other words, they face the same level of paperwork regardless of whether they are applying for the first time and still need to prove their credentials to the immigration authorities, or whether they have become a known quantity to the immigration agency. Creating a registered employer system in which employers who demonstrate a high level of compliance with the rules face lower paperwork—or even greater access to visas or an exemption from numerical limits—would help to alleviate this problem.

The balance of family and employment-based immigration. Employment-based immigrants make up a much smaller proportion of overall inflows in the United States than in other English-speaking countries of immigration. Most immigration is based on family ties, and the United States allows much more generous family unification policies than other countries. (Americans can apply for green cards on behalf of their adult siblings, for example.) This is a central reason for the relatively low skill profile of immigrants in the United States compared to comparable English-speaking countries of immigration. Employment-based immigrants tend to have higher skill levels and fare significantly better in the labor market than other groups of immigrants, with higher employment rates and a higher incidence of skilled employment, according to the available evidence. This advantage persists over time, and even later in their careers immigrants who initially entered the labor market on a work visa fare measurably better than others.

The balance between family and economic-stream immigration is a philosophical and political question, as much as it is an economic one. However, shifting the balance toward more highly skilled economic-stream flows would almost certainly make the economic impact of immigration more beneficial.

CONCLUSION

Nobody starting from scratch to design an immigration selection system would propose the status quo as a sensible policy option, regardless of their political convictions. As this chapter has argued, the U.S. system is riddled with conflicting rules and requirements that have become outdated or fail to achieve their intended goals.

Many of the problems are not ideological, but rather the product of a system that has evolved over time through ad hoc adjustments, fixes, and compromises. While some of them can be addressed with more ad hoc fixes, others require more ambitious, systemic changes to the employment-based visa regime. Above all, bringing the supply and demand for employment-based visas into balance is essential if the U.S. immigration system is to be a functional system. This will require either increases in the number of visas available or policies to tighten eligibility criteria or increase visa fees—or (most likely) some of both. Greater flexibility will be needed in order to prevent the rapid exhaustion of visa limits in years of high demand, alongside more effective differentiation between applications to ensure that the highest-value ones are systematically satisfied. A faster, less bureaucratic path from temporary to permanent residence is needed to reduce unnecessary costs in the immigration system and reduce uncertainty facing immigrants and their employers. And finally, U.S. immigration policymaking requires a more evidence-based approach, relying on systematically collected and regularly reported data on the outcomes it produces for employers, immigrants, and the U.S. economy.

References and Further Reading

Bodvarsson, O., & Van den Berg, H. (2009). *The economics of immigration: Theory and policy.* New York, NY: Springer.

Ehrenberg, R., & Smith, R. (2012). *Modern labor economics: Theory and public policy* (see chapter 10). Upper Saddle River, NJ: Prentice Hall.

Holzer, H. J. (2010). *Immigration policy and less-skilled workers in the United States: Reflections on future directions for reform.* Retrieved from Migration Policy Institute website: http://www.migrationpolicy.org/pubs/Holzer-January2011.pdf

Orrenius, P. M., & Zavodny, M. (2010). *Beside the golden door: U.S. immigration reform in a new era of globalization.* Washington, DC: American Enterprise Institute.

Papademetriou, D. G., Fix, M., & Sumption, M. (2012). *Immigrants in a changing labor market: Responding to economic needs* Washington, DC: Migration Policy Institute.

Papademetriou, D. G., Meissner, D., Rosenblum, M., & Sumption, M. (2009, May). *Harnessing the advantages of immigration for a 21st-century economy: A Standing Commission on Labor Markets, Economic Competitiveness, and Immigration.* Retrieved from Migration Policy Institute website: http://www.migrationpolicy.org/pubs/StandingCommission_May09.pdf

Papademetriou, D. G., Meissner, D., Rosenblum, M., & Sumption, M. (2009, July). *Aligning temporary immigration visas with U.S. labor market needs: The case for provisional visas.* Retrieved from Migration Policy Institute website: http://www.migrationpolicy.org/pubs/Provisional_visas.pdf

von Weizsacker, J. (2008). *Divisions of labour: Rethinking Europe's migration policy.* Retrieved from Bruegel website: http://www.bruegel.org/publications/publication-detail/publication/10-divisions-of-labour-rethinking-europes-migration-policy

Madeleine Sumption

Gender and Refugee Status

POINT: The United States has long been committed to providing refugee status to people escaping persecution. Therefore, we should expand refugee relief to those fleeing gender-based violence and persecution on the basis of sexual orientation.

Priscilla Yamin, University of Oregon

COUNTERPOINT: The concept of a "refugee" has now been stretched much too far. Granting refugee status on the basis of gender-based violence or sexual orientation discrimination opens the gates to a potentially limitless number of victims from around the world.

Priscilla Yamin, University of Oregon

Introduction

The United States prides itself on being a "nation of immigrants" and a place of refuge for people fleeing religious and political persecution. The famous Emma Lazarus poem, engraved on the base of the Statue of Liberty, implores, "Give me your tired, your poor / Your huddled masses yearning to breathe free." This image of the United States as a place of safety, however, has been superseded in recent years by an emphasis on illegal immigration rather than one on immigrants as refugees. Indeed, most immigration policy since the 1980s has focused on immigration reform—ways to control (and limit) the numbers seeking homes within U.S. borders—rather than on how to expand the definition of "refugee" in order to take in more people who, from a human rights perspective, are the most necessitous strangers.

This chapter explores a controversial debate: should the traditional definition of "refugee" be reasonably expanded to include those who face gender-based sexual violence or persecution on the basis on sexual orientation? If it can, what challenges does this pose to U.S. immigration policies?

The United States adopted the international definition of "refugee" in the Refugee Act of 1980, reflecting the universalism of human rights. This definition, which states that refugees are "persons outside their own countries who [have] a well-founded fear of persecution on the basis of race, religion, nationality, membership in a particular group, or political opinion," brought U.S. refugee policy up to date with contemporary international human rights principles. Some argue that claims for refugee status and asylum on the basis of gender-based violence or persecution due to sexual orientation are covered under the part of the definition that refers to "membership in a particular group." But this assignment has generated debate about what constitutes a "social group" and what defines membership in one.

Accepting individuals for asylum based on violence such as systematic rape, female genital cutting, or persecution for transsexual, lesbian, or gay identity can be rather easily argued to acknowledge the *political* role that gender and sexuality have in social and political life. But, as argued in the Counterpoint section, this potentially makes a tremendous number of people eligible for refugee status in the United States.

Disturbing levels of sexual violence in war zones alone confirm the reality that many women (and men) the world over are potentially eligible for refugee status based on their victimization. For example, consider the alleged systematic rape by Qaddafi forces in Libya, best symbolized perhaps by Eman al-Obedi, a young law student who in March 2011 burst into a hotel filled with foreign journalists, claiming that she'd been gang-raped by government forces; al-Obedi has successfully sought asylum in the United States. There is also the widely publicized problem of extensive rape in the Democratic Republic of the Congo. In Egypt, the "Arab Spring" has been seriously marred by news of forced "virginity tests" and gang assaults, widespread sexual harassment, and gang-rapes on both protesters and journalists. These are, of course, just a few of the dozens of examples one could cite to show the prevalence of gender-based violence. (For more information, consult the variety of sources in the Point reading list, particularly works by Susan Bartels and colleagues, Nicholas Kristof and Sheryl WuDunn, and the Women Under Siege project.)

If one further considers the prevalence of female genital cutting (the World Health Organization estimates 140 million girls and women worldwide have undergone the procedure) and the persecution of individuals based on their sexual identity (75 countries in the world criminalize same-sex relationships, and 7 countries consider it a crime punishable by death, according to the United Nations), one begins to see that adapting such a broad definition of "refugee" risks opening the door to an unmanageable flow of potential new citizens.

But the example of female genital cutting raises yet another conundrum: many forms of what people in the United States might call gender-based violence and persecution are culturally normative in the places they are practiced. Can the United States afford, not merely economically but also politically, to accept refugees by inadvertently declaring a "war" of sorts on the cultures they come from?

In reading this chapter, think of the tension between the traditional definition of refugee—a person fleeing political persecution by the state—and the more radical one that would acknowledge gender-based violence and sexual orientation persecution as a valid basis for refugee status. How can U.S. refugee policy adequately address the needs of women and men who so urgently seek safety from violence due to their gender or their sexual identity, violence often seen as normative in their own cultures?

POINT

At the 1980 Republican Convention, President Reagan quoted a line from Emma Lazarus's 1883 poem, "The New Colossus," engraved on a plaque at the base of the Statue of Liberty. The promise of the United States to open its arms to the masses "who yearn to breathe free" is as powerful now as it was then. To honor that promise, the United States should expand its refugee relief to those fleeing gender-based violence and persecution on the basis of sexual orientation. While gender identity and sexual activity are usually thought of as private matters, they become public when people whose identities or behaviors seem nonnormative face persecution (often public). Moreover, it involves an understanding that discrimination and violence against women or gays and lesbians are political acts, and that the United States must provide protection and freedom for those affected by this kind of violence. Many international institutions, such as the United Nations, already recognize that women and gays and lesbians can and should be provided protection and asylum, and at the very least it is in the interest of the United States to keep up with broadly accepted principles of human rights.

In order to make the claim that the U.S. definition of "refugee" should include gender-based violence and persecution based on sexual orientation, it is important to understand that the concept of refugee in U.S. policy has developed over time, and that it must continue to evolve and change with demands of a changing world. The United States adopted the internationally accepted definition of a refugee as part of the Refugee Act of 1980, which amended earlier immigration laws to create a systematic process for accepting refugees from other nations. This new definition involved "persons outside their own countries who had a well-founded fear of persecution on the basis of race, religion, nationality, membership in a particular social group, or political opinion." Prior to this point, the U.S. definition of refugee had been Cold War–focused, designed to protect those fleeing Communism and Communist-dominated countries. The implementation and processing of refugee applications seemed to run on a case-by-case basis, implementing policy in an ad hoc basis.

The Refugee Act of 1980 removed the ideological focus on Communist countries. It also adopted the process through which annual decisions would be made on the number and composition of the refugee population to be admitted for resettlement. This law also established an asylum program for the protection of refugees who arrived on their own, and a domestic assistance program to help refugees adapt to life in the United States. According to immigration scholar Susan Martin (2011), the impetus for the law was to bring U.S. refugee policy into line with international human rights principles. This view was shared by congressional reformers, who wanted more control over refugee admissions, and the Carter administration, which had also established a new State Department bureau on human rights. The law was signed on March 17 and went into effect on April 1, 1980.

The Refugee Act accomplished a number of notable reforms. The approach prior to this law was to basically respond to each refugee crisis as it arose. In contrast, the new act provided a permanent authority for admission of refugees, recognizing the recurrence of these crises. It allowed the president to have a flexible mechanism through which to make decisions on refugees that involve foreign policy issues, while at the same time allowed Congress to play a deciding role (Martin, 2011).

The 1980s was an important decade in the development of refugee policy and for the question of where gender and sexual orientation fits within that policy. For most of the decade, the United States struggled with having a universalistic commitment to refugee protection while also keeping in line with domestic interests and foreign policy issues that circumscribed who would be admitted. Refugees accepted into the United States mostly hailed from Communist states or those that had been previously allied with the United States in Cold War–related conflicts, including Cuba and countries in Southeast Asia. Meanwhile, Haitians, Salvadorans, and Guatemalans were rejected. The U.S. government rejected Haitian immigrants because the Haitian government was seen as anti-Communist, even though it was itself authoritarian. Thus, Haitians seeking refuge in the United States did not fit the definition of individuals fleeing Communist-led countries (Martin, 2011).

Claims for refugee and asylum due to gender-based violence and persecution on the basis of sexual orientation have fallen under the category of "membership in a particular social group." However, of the five protected grounds for refugee status and asylum, "membership in a particular social group" has always generated the most debate. It does so because it raises many questions about what constitutes a social group and what defines membership in such a group. The seminal 1985 decision of the U.S. Board of Immigration Appeals (BIA) in deportation proceedings referred to as *Matter of Acosta* defines "particular social group" as a group of persons all of whom share a common, "immutable" characteristic. Often referred to as the Acosta standard, this means a characteristic that an individual either cannot change or should not be required to change because it is fundamental to that person's identity (Kerwin, 2011; *Matter of Acosta*). As was explained in the case, that characteristic might be an "innate one such as sex, color, kinship ties" or "a shared past experience such as a former military leadership or landownership."

The United States (along with Canada, New Zealand, and the United Kingdom) follows this protected characteristic approach in cases regarding gender and sexual orientation. Arguing that the United States should accept individuals based on gender or sexual orientation violence claims is more than merely an issue of semantics or legalities. Rather, it amounts to acknowledging the important political role gender and sexuality plays in the political field, and that the policing and regulating of these categories sometimes occurs through violence and persecution. Individuals who do not conform to regulated roles can pay a price. Refugee definitions traditionally privilege more male-dominated public activities over the activities or roles of women or the expressions of sexuality, all of which are generally designated as private and domestic (Randall, 2002).

GENDER-BASED CLAIMS

In the United States, the notions of gender asylum and the granting of refugee status to women based on gender-based violence are some of the most debated refugee issues in recent times. Granting either asylum or refugee status based on gender comes from two kinds of claims. One is when the form of persecution is unique to women, such as female genital cutting (FGC, also called female genital mutilation, or FGM), domestic violence, rape, or forced marriage. The other is when a woman or a man has suffered a gendered form of harm such as rape or sexual assault that occurred because of nongendered reasons, such as political opinion or war (Musalo, 2010). The use of rape as a political tactic of control can happen to both men and women. Domestic violence, in contrast, is a form of gender-based violence almost exclusively unique to women. Yet the claims to domestic violence, in particular, have not been widely accepted as terms of persecution (Musalo, 2010).

There are three reasons why gender- and sexuality-based claims have not been widely accepted as terms of persecution and, therefore, as legitimate bases for refugee status. First, women were not, according to the 1951 United Nations Convention Relating to the Status of Refugees, named as a protected social group. However, according to Deborah Anker, the director of Harvard Law School's Immigration and Refugee Clinic, "the experiences of women are beginning to be incorporated into the interpretation of 'refugee.'" As discussed above, forms of violence against women such a rape and other sexual assaults are often considered "private" (Anker, 2001), whereas most claims for asylum or refugee relief occur because of public persecution and state actions. In gender cases, harm and persecution occurs in private homes and spaces and are therefore difficult to document. That said, just because contemporary violence and persecution may look different from older conceptions of refugee, this does not mean the United States should not adopt and update its definition.

The second reason, related to the first, is that often nonstate actors, such as husbands, fathers, or members of the applicant's extended community, are the perpetrators of gender violence. This contradicts, or does not fit within, the overarching refugee relief paradigm where the state is the persecuting agent. Thus, there is resistance to accepting such claims, since they do not immediately conform to the other categories within the refugee definition.

The third reason that gender-based violence as a basis for refugee status is debated is that harms suffered by women, such as FGC or forced marriage, are often also cultural practices accepted as social norms. The characterization of these practices as social and cultural norms rather than political acts usually results in a resistance to define them as forms of persecution. The Acosta standard was used in a 1995 case, *Matter of Kasinga,* which involved Fauziya Kassindja, a young woman fleeing female genital mutilation (FGM) and forced marriage in Togo. In her tribe, social customs required FGM and forced polygamous marriage. Women were not expected to get an education, wife beating was widespread, and the authorities did little to protect women. Her initial claim for gender asylum was rejected. On her appeal, the Board of Immigration Appeals (BIA) found that FGM could be understood as persecution and that she could be considered a member of a particular social group defined by gender with immutable characteristics (Musalo, 2010).

As the Immigration and Naturalization Service argued in 1996, during the appeal of the *Matter of Kasinga* case, it is difficult to consider FGM persecution, because "most of its practitioners believe that they are simply performing an important cultural rite that bonds the individual to society." Women's claims based on gender persecution are commonly framed as social group claims rather than political ones. This is true despite the fact that much of the experience of gender persecution arose from a perception of gender nonconformity as a threat to the state's notion of the natural order (Millbank, 2003).

These three reasons explain why gender-based violence has not been widely accepted as a cause for refugee status. At the same time, they also show how the qualifications of the status of "refugee" could be expanded to include "women who seek safety from gendered violence," because they show how women do constitute a social group, and that there are clear and consistent social patterns of women's persecution. Thus, the notion of "refugee" needs to be expanded to include gender and sexual orientation. Likewise, nation-states and international organizations must acknowledge and accept that some forms of oppression and persecution do not fall along established understandings of what constitute legitimate persecution.

There is clear precedent for this expansion from international bodies. Beginning in 1985, The United Nations High Commissioner for Refugees (UNHCR) and its Executive Committee (EXCOM) issued guidance that directly addressed the issue of refugee women and the interpretive barriers that curtailed protection. In 1985, EXCOM made its first pronouncement on gender-related asylum, saying states could acknowledge that women asylum-seekers who face harsh or inhuman treatment due to their having transgressed the social mores of the society in which they live may be considered a "particular social group" within the meaning of Article 1 A(2) of the 1951 United Nations Refugee Convention (Musalo, 2010). This laid the ground to claim that violence toward women who transgress social norms (such as seeking education in countries where women are not allowed to do so) could constitute persecution, and that women in these circumstances could be considered members of a "particular group."

Even with this precedent, a concern raised by opponents of expanding the status of "refugee" to include women suffering gender-based violence and allowing for protection based on gender is that this will result in a rapid increase of such claims. According to Karen Musalo, a law professor at the University of California and director of the Center for Gender and Refugee Studies, these claims are unsubstantiated. On the one hand, the United Nations High Commissioner for Refugees (UNHCR) has already recognized that gender claims come within the 1951 Refugee Convention's intended scope of protection. On the other hand, the acceptance of gender asylum has not created a surge in the number of claims (Musalo, 2010, p. 48). Canada began granting gender asylum in 1993, and the United States did so after the 1996 decision in *Matter of Kasinga.*

Another case that took over 10 years to be resolved favorably began 3 years after the *Matter of Kasinga,* in 1999. In this case, *Matter of Rody Alvarado,* the BIA denied asylum to Rody Alvarado, a 16-year-old Guatemalan who sought asylum in the United States from her husband's abuse and violent threats because her native country did not offer her protection. In denying asylum, the BIA did not contest that Alvarado suffered abuse, nor that this abuse constituted persecution, but it stated that she failed to establish that the harm she suffered was because she was a member of a particular social group, as defined by the Acosta standard. This decision generated a lot of criticism from many corners, and it was not until Barack Obama took office as president that Alvarado was granted asylum (Musalo, 2010).

According to Human Rights Watch, violence by domestic partners is a leading factor in murder rates against women; studies by the World Health Organization and the United Nations have shown domestic violence to be widespread around the world. Insufficient government regulation and enforcement in many countries offer women inadequate protection against domestic abuse, including marital rape; physical, psychological, and sexual abuse; and even murder. This suggests that gender is not a special category of refugee law. Rather, gender-based violence should be considered a form of persecution, even though it is not currently considered one of the five Refugee Convention grounds. The United States is headed in this direction: regulations proposed by the U.S. Department of Justice in December 2000 provide principles for deciding asylum cases that are based on domestic violence, and these principles clarify that gender can form the basis of a "particular social group."

SEXUAL ORIENTATION

The obstacles to accepting sexual orientation as a legitimate cause for refugee relief are both similar to and different from those related to gender-based violence. Similar to gender-based violence, many states do not recognize the risks faced by lesbian, gay, bisexual, transgender, and intersex (LGBTI) people, and therefore do not grant refugee status or asylum based on that status. Instead, people seeking refugee status based on LGBTI persecution are often sent back to their country of origin. Sexuality claims, like gender claims, are rarely articulated and almost never received as political claims (Millbank,

2003). That nonnormative practices of sexuality and gender are not obvious forms of persecution should not be the reason they are not accepted as legitimate, when in fact there is plenty of evidence that people are often brutally persecuted for so-called nonnormative behaviors.

Yet there are ways that LGBTI claims are different from gender claims. LGBTI people are often forced to lead closeted lives, as their LGBTI identity and nonconformist sexual activity is considered punishable by torture or death in many countries. With continuing recognition of sexual orientation, an increasing number of LGBTI-identified people try to escape their persecution and oppression by seeking refugee relief in foreign states. Interestingly, while gender-based claims to violence are generally not considered a public matter, institutional sanctions such as criminal provisions for gay sex are explicit official positions in nations that condemn homosexuality—they are, in other words, openly political positions. Many of these criminal provisions make express reference to the "natural order" or "offenses against nature," clearly articulating homosexuality as a threat to the heterosexual order that is posited as the stable and natural basis of the nation. The passage and enforcement of such laws are clearly public and political and should be accepted as such (Millbank, 2003).

At the same time, in some of the applicants' countries of origin, homosexuality is believed to not exist at all (as is the case with Tanzania and Pakistan). In other countries, such as Zimbabwe and Iran, the more common official view is that homosexuality is an expression of Western decadence. In China the government tolerates homosexuality only as private sexual behavior that is invisible and not an expression of political status (Millbank, 2003).

With sexual orientation, there are public laws against nonconformist sex and relationships as well as forms of private persecution caused from either living a closeted life or public denial of one's self-identity. There are similarities among applicants in the way their actual or alleged same-sex attractions and relationships subject them to, or threaten them with, violence. Thus, just as with gender-based violence claims, the experience of being or being named as LGBTI has material consequences and does raise issues of safety and well-being.

For these reasons, LGBTI identity and nonconformist sexual activity should constitute membership in a particular social group, because the essential and unifying element in each claimant's case is that they did not, or could not, conform to the heterosexual norms that their own culture imposed. Some seeking refuge based on sexual orientation may have been politically active around sexuality issues in their home country, or they may not have been politically active at all. In either case, their sexuality was received as a sufficient threat to the state, family, or the natural order that they were put in jeopardy. Because this is the case, sexuality should be considered as a political experience, not only a private or social one, lending support to the argument that gendered-based forms of violence are grounds for asylum and refugee relief.

There should be a right to be publicly identified as gay or lesbian, which would be grounded in concepts such as self-identity, self-respect, and self-expression. To bring a claim of asylum, LGBTI applicants must first prove that they were themselves victims of persecution based on their sexual identity or related political opinions. One of the biggest obstacles to proving persecution and winning LGBTI asylum claims is the argument that one's identity as lesbian, gay, bisexual, transgender, transsexual, or intersex can be held private, which might enable people to protect themselves from the threat of persecution to a large extent. This argument presumes that leading a double life is possible, and that applicants are sufficiently shielded from persecution if they merely mute their sexuality. Heterosexuals are not asked to keep their sexuality private, because in many cases the heterosexual family is understood as the basis of the nation, because it theoretically provides stability. However, in practice, publicly proclaiming heterosexuality or gender conformity does not prevent harassment on the basis of *rumored* homosexuality or the eventual discovery of an immaculately hidden private life (Fahamu Refugee Legal Aid).

There is also precedent for acknowledging claims based on sexual orientation. In 1995 the United Nations High Commissioner for Refugees (UNHCR) accepted that lesbians and gay men can constitute members of a "particular social group" and are eligible for protection under the terms of the Refugee Convention (Millbank, 2003). For both gender-based violence and sexual orientation, accepting these as legitimate claims for refuge relief is part of an ongoing process of addressing and transforming oppressive discriminatory attitudes that pose significant threat and harm to the well-being of many individuals across the globe.

CONCLUSION

Karen Musalo explains that one reason why there is resistance to protecting victims of gender-related violence and sexual orientation is what she calls an "interpretative barrier" (Musalo, 2010, p. 48). Harm or violence against women, in particular, is often misunderstood as an act condoned or required by social or cultural norms such as FGC and forced marriage. There is more involved in accepting individuals affected by gender or sexual orientation persecution under the banner of refugee; it also represents a crucial sea change in how we understand politics and power, borders, and human security. This interpretative barrier is precisely why it is necessary to acknowledge that gender and sexual orientation are part of a "particular social group."

There are two factors in particular that should be acknowledged in accepting these kinds of claims. The first is that what happens in the private spheres of families, or what is also considered cultural tradition, can in some instances be considered a kind of violence or persecution that is eligible for refugee status. The second is that the perpetrators of violence based on gender and sexual orientation are usually nonstate actors such as fathers, husbands, or members of the applicant's extended community. Usually, refugee claims target the state as the persecuting agent. Although the perpetrators in these cases are rarely "the state," the claims can still be understood as legitimate, due in part to the expansion of the definition of "refugee."

References and Further Reading

Anker, D. (2001). Refugee status and violence against women in the "domestic" sphere: The non-state actor question. *Georgetown Immigration Law Journal, 15*(3), 391–402.

Bartels, S., VanRooyen, M., Leaning, J., Scott, J., & Kelly, J. (2010). *Now, the world is without me: An investigation of sexual violence in eastern Democratic Republic of the Congo.* Cambridge, MA: Harvard Humanitarian Initiative.

Fahamu Refugee Legal Aid. (n.d.). *Sexual orientation and gender identity: LGBTI resources listed by country.* Retrieved from http://www.srlan.org/content/sexual-orientation-and-gender-identity

Kerwin, D. M. (2011). *The faltering U.S. refugee protection system: Legal & policy responses to refugees, asylum seekers, and others in need of protection.* Washington, DC: Migration Policy Institute. Retrieved from http://www.migrationpolicy.org/pubs/refugeeprotection-2011.pdf

Kristof, N., & WuDunn, S. (2010). *Half the sky: Turning oppression into opportunity for women worldwide.* New York, NY: Vintage.

Martin, S. F. (2011). *A nation of immigrants.* New York, NY: Cambridge University Press.

Matter of Acosta in Deportation Proceedings [A-24159781], United States Board of Immigration Appeals, 1 March 1985. Retrieved from http://www.justice.gov/eoir/vll/intdec/vol19/2986.pdf

Millbank, J. (2003). Gender, sex and visibility in refugee claims on the basis of sexual orientation. *Georgetown Immigration Law Journal, 18,* 71–110.

Musalo, K. (2010). A short history of gender asylum in the United States: Resistance and ambivalence may very slowly be inching towards recognition of women's claims. UNHCR's *Refugee Survey Quarterly, 29*(2), 46–63.

Randall, M. (2002). Refugee law and state accountability for violence against women: A comparative analysis of legal approaches to recognizing asylum claims based on gender persecution. *Harvard Women's Law Review Journal, 25,* 281–315.

United Nations Convention Relating to the Status of Refugees. Retrieved from http://www.unhcr.org/3b66c2aa10.html

United Nations High Commissioner for Refugees. (2011, June 29). *Q&A: Reaching out to refugees persecuted for sexual orientation, gender identity.* Retrieved from http://www.unhcr.org/4e0adced9.html.

Women's Media Center, Women Under Siege Project: http://www.womenundersiegeproject.org

World Health Organziation. (2012). Female genital mutilation: Fact sheet no. 241, February 2012. Retrieved from http://www.who.int/mediacentre/factsheets/fs241/en

Priscilla Yamin

COUNTERPOINT

There are many reasons to be cautious about changing refugee policy to meet the needs of individuals who are victims of gender-based violence or sexual orientation discrimination. The argument against expanding the definition of refugee or sexual orientation can only be made and analyzed outside the emotional and volatile context of the topic. Violence of any kind must be quelled and prevented if possible. However, the issue of political refugees or political asylum raises questions about the role of the refugee and asylum process in U.S. politics and foreign policy. One question is whether the granting of asylum is meant to create the conditions for a permanent resettlement for a large number of individuals who have endured oppressive cultural and civil norms and traditions, or whether it is meant to provide temporary protection for individuals who have been persecuted or discriminated against but who seek positive change in their originating country (Stein, 1996). These are hard questions. Another one is, whatever the intent of the policy, how can we ensure it? In other words, how can we make sure that those who arrive under temporary protection do in fact return to their home countries when the time comes? These questions are directly related to the concern of opening the gate to a potentially limitless number of victims in the world. It is unclear whether the United States can control the numbers, and therefore it is reasonable for the United States to limit refugee access and not expand the definition of "refugee."

The current statutory definition of refugee and asylum in the United States protects those who can demonstrate a fear of political persecution on account of race, religion, nationality, or membership in a particular group or political opinion. This definition is very open and could qualify millions for asylum in the United States. Yet allowing and providing for the resettlement of this many individuals from regions and cultures across the globe is more than the American system can handle in terms of resources, jobs, and services. There is a common misconception that asylum means providing temporary protection for those who challenge their governments and cultures, and who work for positive change in their home countries. In fact, most asylees do not return to their home country. In addition, the number of recent asylum cases has skyrocketed from a few thousand a year to over 100,000 a year. The rapid increase has put more pressure on the system and resulted in backlogs and administrative delays. Further pressure would come if human rights activists succeed in expanding the definitions of political asylum to include cultural asylum, sexual preference, and gender-based asylum (Stein, 1996).

Thus, a primary reason not to stretch the definition of refugee and political asylum to include gender and sexual orientation is that the United States is already overburdened with refugees and immigrants. In fact, there are other ideas about revising, expanding, or limiting U.S. asylum law and refugee policy that are equally valid. One example, is a 2007 statement from the Federation for American Immigration Reform (FAIR) written by Jack Martin, special projects director at FAIR, that raises the possibility of a range of changes, including scaling back the refugee resettlement program and focusing refugee policy to track Islamic refugees who fit the profile of a population among whom jihadists have shown an ability to recruit. To some, this plan might serve a more direct and obvious benefit to this country than providing asylum to abused women or homosexuals. So why would the United States agree to open the gates for some and not others?

In arguing against the expansion of the definition of refugee to explicitly include gender and sexual orientation–related violence, it is important first to keep in mind the question of whether a policy that was forged under the Cold War, as U.S. refugee policy was, can adapt to a changing world. Most people who have been granted refugee status have fled from a Communist or Socialist country. From 1946 through 2000, the United States granted permanent resident status to 3.5 million refugees. Over half (53%) were from three countries: Vietnam (19%), Cuba (18%), and the former Soviet Union (16%) (Wasem, 2005). Even with a clearly defined policy, the history of refugee policy in the United States shows how quickly the need overtakes the process.

HISTORICAL EXAMPLES

At every historical moment since the United States began letting in refugees, the process and number of those wanting and gaining access to the United States has ballooned beyond what administrators, officials, and politicians would have imagined. In other words, one cannot always know what will happen once the gates are opened. Thus, the utmost caution should be used in opening up refugee policy and allowing more people into the United States under new and different categories.

In the decades before the passage of the Refugee Act of 1980, U.S. refugee policy was circumscribed by the Cold War politics of the 1950s and 1960s. There was an Eastern Hemisphere quota for refugees fleeing Communism and Communist-dominated countries. This meant that United States gave priority to those who desired to live in a democratic, market-based economy but whose country actively suppressed those political and economic ideas. Yet the cap on annual immigration was inadequate to meet demand. Between the years of 1965 and 1980, the United States admitted refugees from Communist countries, in particular, above the limited allowable number.

From the years prior to 1980, there are three examples of when the practice of accepting fleeing refugees from authoritarian countries swelled larger than the United States had anticipated and put stress on agencies and government resources that were already overtaxed. These examples (detailed below) illustrate what can happen when the United States opens its doors to all forms of persecution, and therefore why it is necessary to limit the definition of refugee to a purely political question of the state.

The first example is Cuba. Cubans began to seek refugee status in the United States after the Cuban Revolution, and particularly after Fidel Castro established Cuba as a Communist country. President Lyndon Johnson supported granting asylum to fleeing Cubans and, along with the Red Cross, the United States organized two chartered flights each day, called Freedom Flights, that carried fleeing Cubans to U.S. shores. The flights continued consistently between 1965 and 1971, and less frequently for two more years. Cubans who had family in the United States were given priority. Almost 300,000 Cubans were a part of the airlift. Funding to assist the new Cuban arrivals came from all levels of the nation. President Johnson designated supplemental federal funds, he enlisted voluntary organizations and agencies to assist, and, realizing that Florida would absorb the most impact, other states were asked to receive Cubans as well.

The Cuban program had been established by the Migration and Refugee Assistance Act of 1962. The federal government provided grants to voluntary agencies for aiding in the resettlement program. States received funds to help with additional costs in education, health care, and other social services. Even though many of the Cubans who came during this period were middle-class trained professionals who brought financial and business capital with them, they nonetheless required assistance in the form of federally financed business loans. Special programs were implemented to help professionals, particularly doctors, receive the training needed to pass qualifying exams. In addition, many who came were in need of cash and medical assistance programs. By 1980 the total amount spent to assist the resettlement of Cubans came to $1.4 billion (Martin, 2011).

The next major challenge to the U.S. refugee policy came from Vietnam in 1975. From 1975 to 1985, more than 1 million Indochinese refugees from Vietnam, Cambodia, and Laos came to the United States after the fall of the South Vietnamese government. The United States accepted responsibility for assisting these refugees, and it mounted a resettlement program that brought about 600,000 Southeast Asian refugees to the United States. Indochinese refugees came to the United States in three ever-increasing waves, beginning with the evacuation of Saigon in 1975. Due to the large number of fleeing refugees and the fast pace at which they arrived, the federal government engaged in an unprecedented role in resettlement. Between April and December of 1975, more than 130,000 refugees came under the attorney general's parole authority. Once in the country, the refugees were sent to either Camp Pendleton in California, Fort Chaffee in Arkansas, Fort Indiantown Gap in Pennsylvania, or Eglin Air Force Base in Florida (Martin, 2011).

The program set up to manage and handle Indochinese refugees resided in the Interagency Task Force for Indochina Refugees, which was housed in the State Department and made up of twelve agencies. It was responsible for allocating funds and coordinating activities, for processing and resettling, and for consulting public and private agencies involved in the program. For example, at the camps, the military was in charge of food, clothes, and housing. The INS processed applications for admission and security checks. The Department of Health, Education, and Welfare conducted medical screenings, assigned social security numbers, and provided some educational services. Although the war in Vietnam had been extremely controversial in the United States, the admission of refugees was easily justified on both foreign policy and humanitarian interests. From 1977 to 1980, the number of those fleeing the Communist takeover of Laos, Cambodia, and Vietnam continued to increase.

The refugees who came later than 1975 had fewer personal and financial resources than those who came in the first waves. The Cambodians in particular had suffered through 4 years of living under harsh and psychologically damaging conditions of killings, dislocations, and famine. Many of them came with little to no education. A disproportionately large number of households headed by women were resettled. Those coming from Laos had no skills that were readily transferable to rural or urban America. Although the Vietnamese came with more education, they had less human capital than those who preceded them. Most Southeast Asian refugees settled in California, but also in parts of Virginia, as well as big cities like Chicago, Houston, and Seattle. The issue of refugee policy goes beyond letting in individuals and making humanitarian statements; it includes a range of economic, social, and political issues on the ground. How equipped are refugees to be economically independent, socially secure, and generally able to add to American society and not just take from it?

The last example of a strained U.S. refugee system came in the form of the refugees from the Soviet Union who arrived in the 1970s. During this decade, there was a resurgence of immigration to the United States from the Soviet Union as an increasing number of Jews, ethnic Germans, and Christian Pentecostals sought to leave their country. The lifting of the Iron Curtain was a central tenet of U.S. foreign policy. The plight of the Soviet Jews was a particular focus due to rising anti-Semitism in the USSR. Those who applied for exit permission from the Soviet Union were often denied. In response, Congress threatened to pass legislation that barred a trade agreement, forcing the Soviet Union to grant permission. This allowed roughly 35,000 Soviet Jews to flee the USSR in 1973 alone. Soviet Jewish emigration changed over time, but during the course of the 1970s, 250,000 entered the United States (Martin, 2011).

Movement to change refugee policy came in the late 1970s, when critiques arose over the ad hoc fashion in which the United States reacted to refugee crises. There was a political call to develop more realistic projections of a U.S. refugee program and to establish and define realistic financial needs. Senior officials saw refugee admission as part of foreign policy. Members of Congress felt squeezed as they were asked to provide funding after refugees were already in the country, and yet did not have input into the actual decisions to admit refugees. In addition, states and voluntary agencies incurred costs not knowing if Congress would reimburse them (Martin, 2011). With the Refugee Act of 1980, a universal definition of refugee was established, which then led the way for a shift from the ideological policy that focused on repressive (from America's perspective) governments. The issue at hand is that refugee policy is not only about the individuals fleeing. It also crosses over into foreign policy, partisan politics, and domestic resources that are equally important in deciding on refugee policy.

Even with the changes implemented with the Refugee Act of 1980, the examples above suggest the reasonable likelihood that it will be difficult to predict or even control before a policy is implemented how many refugees will come and whether the United States can handle the influx. Even with changes to the law, as explained below, it is likely that expanding the definition of refugee and asylum to include gender-based violence or sexual orientation discrimination would result in a deluge of claims.

THE REFUGEE ACT

The Refugee Act of 1980 was passed to give the United States a standing in international human rights issues, but also to assure greater equity in the treatment of refugees and more effective procedures in dealing with them. The solution was devised legislatively with the creation of a "normal flow" refugee program of 50,000 admissions per year and a special mechanism by which the president could exceed that number after holding consultations with Congress. As discussed above, the Refugee Act gave the UN definition of "refugee" meaning in the United States legal code.

The intention of the Refugee Act was to limit expanding refugee and asylum claims and to institutionalize the processing and clarify the decision-making process. Allowing individuals refugee or asylum status based on gender or sexual orientation may circumvent the aims of the Refugee Act to manage refugee flow. The definition of refugee in the 1980 act was not intended to expand protection in these situations, but rather to limit the already expanding number of refugee claims and costs.

In particular, "gender," or "sexual orientation" are not explicitly among the stated five grounds, and so therefore cannot be considered automatically valid without much deliberation. It is difficult to adopt a policy for these two specific groups because gender-related violence or persecutions based on sexual orientation are difficult to separate from cultural norms and practices. What is a harmful cultural practice and what is not? Is it appropriate for the United States to, in effect, accuse another country of discriminatory cultural practices? Harm or violence against women, in particular, can be understood or perceived as acts condoned or required by social or cultural norms, such as female genital cutting (FGC, also called female genital mutilation, or FGM) and forced marriage. In addition, the perpetrators of violence based on gender and sexual orientation are usually nonstate actors such as fathers, husbands, or members of the applicant's extended community. Refugee status is based on the paradigm that the state is the persecuting agent, and nonstate actors as agents of violence or persecution do not fall within the definition of refugee. It is also difficult to prove or establish gender-based violence or persecution based on sexual orientation. The line must be drawn somewhere, and U.S. refugee policy has been historically maintained as politically circumscribed.

Moreover, even if "gender" were added into the formal definition of "refugee," its range would still be unclear. In other words, how would the government determine or define "persecution" on the basis of gender or sexual orientation that exists across all countries and cultures? What would it cover, exactly? There are many actions that fall under the definition of gender-based violence, including domestic violence, forced marriage, and FGM. So, too, with sexual orientation, which is even harder to quantify or define. Because gender-related violence and sexual orientation discrimination are hard to define and prove, they should not be included in refugee policy.

Another argument against expanding the notion of refugee is that individuals and organizations with anti-immigrant views will be against expansion no matter how rational or right the argument is. They think that allowing more immigrants into the country will harm the public, create social ills, cause crime and disease, and create job displacement. In addition, they argue that gender and sexual orientation persecution is so prevalent and systematic in other societies that asylum should not be used to battle the worlds' cultural and political inequalities. They also say the United States should focus on spreading its democratic values rather than setting up policies designed to "save" the world and let in more immigrants, which will result in unintended consequences (Twibell, 2010).

Another issue to consider is the connection between foreign policy and refugee policy. National refugee policy exemplifies the level of commitment a state has to act on its international human rights promises. Refugee status is based on a notion of rights that are considered fundamental to individual persons and, if violated, worthy of granting asylum to a foreign national. In terms of foreign policy, the granting of refugee status to a foreign national risks implicitly or explicitly criticizing another state's domestic laws and traditions. Thus, the policy to allow in individuals persecuted by a Communist state worked with already established American Cold War foreign policy, rather than against it. Accepting nationals or refugees from Cuba and the Soviet Union was not threatening to relations between the two countries beyond already antagonistic relations. By contrast, expanding the notion of refugee to include gender does not coincide with existing foreign policy. At the moment we do not sanction countries that make women wear veils, for example.

Letting in individuals based on gender or sexual orientation violence poses another challenge: Gender and sexual-orientation persecution are cultural issues, not political ones. A large part of U.S. refugee policy is the resettlement program, which is designed to aid displaced members of a community to come together around common cultural traditions that exist outside of political differences in order to assist in acclimation to the United States. If cultural traditions or norms ostracize a woman so much that she needs to flee her home country, how will she "resettle" in the United States with others from her community? How can the United States design policies to help her? Are there enough resources?

There are many obstacles to implementing a definition of refugee that encompasses persecution based on gender or sexual orientation. The most notable is the current political and social trend of the United States that seeks to restrict the ability to obtain asylum and immigration generally, rather than open it up and stretch it to include controversial refugee and asylum claims. Immigration restrictionists argue that it is necessary to protect the United States against immigrants who take jobs from native-born Americans, or that doing so will create all kinds of societal ills, from crime to disease. Any policy on refugees and asylum must have public support. It must also be practical and administratively allowable.

As the above examples illustrate, the burden of providing asylum to refugees who are victims of gender-based violence or sexual orientation discrimination can be heavy. It suggests that rather than pushing for the United States to expand their policies, the United States might do better to coordinate with international institutions to create an international standard and coordination of efforts to provide refugees with asylum.

Yet advocates of adding gender and sexual orientation to asylum cases argue there are special considerations for women and gays and lesbians that make them legitimate categories for protection. Rapes, beatings, assaults, and other related violence, they argue, have a political dimension that makes them appropriate and necessary to consider the decision to flee as a flight from officially sanctioned persecution. Other forms of gender-based violence and sexual orientation persecution include coercive marriage, the loss of marriage-based property rights, and female genital mutilation. These can be considered broad-based civil crimes and cultural norms that affect particular members of a society, such as women or gays and lesbians, especially where society fails to intervene and protect members in abusive situations. At the same time, making these kinds of claims and the acceptance of such claims by receiving countries such as the United States has been and continues to be controversial. In other words, not all claims to gender-based violence or persecution based on sexual orientation are accepted as forms of human rights violations or included within the concept of persecution.

Moreover, there are economic and political issues to consider. Returning to the questions that were raised at the beginning of this essay, it is not known if asylees will stay or return, even if only granted a temporary stay. Once individuals are let in, the country has to be prepared to support and aid them. This is not possible in all cases. Thus, as much as one would like to see these practices stopped, asylum and refugee policy is not the place to fight this battle over cultural and civil norms in other countries. Asylum was designed to protect people from governments, not from cultural traditions and norms, no matter how much one might disagree with them.

REFERENCES AND FURTHER READING

Martin, J. (2007). Reforming refugee admissions, Comment from the Federation for American Immigration Reform (FAIR) to the FY-2008 Refugee Admissions Program stakeholders' meeting, Chaired by Asst. Secretary of State Ellen Sauerbrey. Retrieved from http://www.fairus.org/site/PageNavigator/issues/reforming_refugee_admissions

Martin, S. F. (2011). *A nation of immigrants.* New York, NY: Cambridge University Press.

Stein, D. (1996). Gender asylum reflects mistaken priorities. *Human Rights Brief, 3*(3). Retrieved from http://www.wcl.american.edu/hrbrief/v3i3/stein33.htm

Twibell, T. S. (2010). The development of gender as a basis for asylum in United States immigration law and under the United Nations Refugee Convention: Case studies of female asylum seekers from Cameroon, Eritrea, Iraq and Somalia. *Georgetown Immigration Law Journal, 24*(2), 189.

Wasem, R. E. (2005). *U.S. immigration policy on asylum seekers* (CRS Report for Congress, updated May 5, 2005). Washington, DC: Congressional Research Service, Library of Congress.

Priscilla Yamin

Naturalization Process

POINT: Significant backlogs in processing naturalization applications, increased fees, and the current citizenship test all point to a flawed naturalization process in need of reform.

Karey Leung, Rutgers University

COUNTERPOINT: The naturalization process in the United States works effectively, especially compared to that of other advanced industrial democracies. If anything, the process may be too streamlined.

Karey Leung, Rutgers University

Introduction

The question of who should be allowed to become an American has long vexed citizens and lawmakers alike. Prior to 1882, the United States had no real immigration policy per se, although only whites were allowed to fully naturalize as citizens. Since then, naturalization policy has swung on a pendulum, from extremely restrictive—during the Great Depression, for example, no new citizens were welcomed at all—to much more liberal—perhaps most notably during the 1980s period of amnesty. Through it all, the fundamental question has remained the same: What *kind* of new citizens does America want? In this chapter, Karey Leung explores the debate surrounding the priorities of the current naturalization system, particularly the citizenship test. (A related debate, about the ideological priorities of the legal immigration selection system as a whole, is covered in Chapter 1.)

Oversight of the naturalization process falls to an agency called U.S. Citizenship and Immigration Services (USCIS), which is a part of the Department of Homeland Security (DHS). The USCIS was created in 2002, taking over a role that had been formerly handled by the Immigration and Naturalization Service, under the Department of Justice. Significantly, funding for the USCIS comes almost entirely from the fees charged to prospective new citizens. (The federal government does occasionally step in with additional funding, as happened in 2010, when Congress appropriated $50 million to help pay the naturalization fees of asylum seekers and military personnel.) In general, however, the USCIS depends on collecting fees in order to operate.

The fee question is significant because in 2008, as part of a general overhaul of the naturalization process, the USCIS raised the fee for individual applications 69 percent, from $405 to $675 (as of 2012 the fee had gone to $680). Prospective citizens whose income is 150 percent of the poverty level are eligible for a fee waiver; however, since the fee has gone up, requests for waivers have outstripped the funds to cover them. Defenders of the fees point out that, absent even more funding from the federal government, the money to cover the naturalization process has to come from somewhere. But the significant fee increases, combined with the shortage of fee waivers, has led some critics of USCIS policies to suggest a deliberate attempt to weed out low-income immigrants.

Indeed, the fee question is one part of the larger debate: What are the appropriate standards and requirements to ask of prospective citizens? Is basic fluency in English, for example, a fair and appropriate expectation? Perhaps it may seem obvious at first that English should be required, but, on the other hand, the government does not require English proficiency for obtaining driver's licenses or, perhaps more significantly, passports. As Leung notes in the Point section of this chapter, this raises a fundamental question: What defines a citizen?

Nowhere is this issue more hotly contested than with regard to the citizenship test itself, which is why Leung devotes considerable time in this chapter to analyzing it. In 2008, the USCIS revised its citizenship test to include questions on "American history, democratic principles and civic duties"—types of questions that were designed to be more abstract than those on previous tests that, in the eyes of critics, were more focused on "trivia." Prospective citizens might be asked to explain the meaning of the phrase, "the rule of law," or to know who Susan B. Anthony was, or who wrote the Federalist Papers. The idea behind the test is to transmit a basic level of civics knowledge, thus helping to bind new citizens to the foundational ideas of their new country. The question is, when polls show that a majority of natural-born Americans cannot name the Chief Justice of the Supreme Court, is it fair to ask new citizens to acquire this knowledge? Perhaps it is, in the sense that a basic knowledge of the politics of the United States might be considered a small thing to ask when weighed against the many opportunities that citizenship offers. On the other hand, can loyalty to a country be memorized for a test?

Critics of both the higher fee and the newer test argue that lower-income, less-educated immigrants may be discouraged from applying. Some further argue that the new citizenship test may be linked to a conservative agenda, and that data already show it to be a considerable barrier to naturalization among those with limited English skills and little education. Readers should ask themselves: Is the new citizenship test simply a new way to limit "undesirable" immigrants? What is the "right" kind of test for naturalization? Or should there even be a test? Some immigrant advocates argue that a required civics class, rather than a test based on rote memorization, would be a more appropriate way to transition new citizens into their civic duties as Americans. Are the barriers to naturalization set too high? Or not high enough?

POINT

Supporters of the American naturalization process argue that the requirements for citizenship prepare potential new citizens with the knowledge of the rights and responsibilities of citizenship. In 2008, the U.S. Citizenship and Immigration Services (USCIS) revised the existing citizenship test to include more abstract questions regarding American history, democratic principles, and the civic duties of citizens. While supporters of this revised version of the test claim that the queries would make citizenship preparation more meaningful to the applicant, critics of the revisions argue that to raise standards without public assistance is to vet out the most vulnerable groups of legal permanent residents (LPRs) eligible for citizenship. Critics raise several concerns: (1) the American naturalization process does not prepare applicants for citizenship if there is a lack of sufficient public assistance in the form of subsidies to help applicants pay for increased fees; (2) civics and English language classes are unavailable or under-resourced, and thus do not adequately help applicants pass a more difficult citizenship test; and (3) fluctuating backlogs in application processing are dealt with inefficiently. Rather than being a more meaningful process to prepare applicants for citizenship, the naturalization process ends up limiting access to citizenship, particularly for low-income applicants and those without English language proficiency.

BACKLOGS IN APPLICATION PROCESSING

The current structure of the USCIS is unprepared to handle massive backlogs in application processing. In 2007 there was a surge in applications attributed to an attempt to get applications in before a pending 69 percent fee increase. Citizenship drives by immigrant advocacy groups and hostile immigration debates in Congress and state legislatures also contributed to an increased backlog of over 1.47 million applications (Migration Policy Institute, 2008; U.S. Government Accountability Office, 2009). Besides advocating for federal funding to prevent the cycle of backlogs and temporary backlog reduction plans, immigrant advocates urged the USCIS to fully digitize and streamline the application process and to avoid redundant background checks through the FBI (National Immigration Forum, 2008).

Backlogs in processing naturalization applications fluctuate depending on external and internal circumstances. After receiving federal appropriations to alleviate an all-time high of 6 million pending applications in 2003 (Bustos, 2005), the USCIS relied on certain employers to apply for work visas to pay Premium Processing Service fees of an extra $1,000 to reduce processing time to within 15 calendar days to further reduce the processing backlogs. Immigrant rights advocates caution that relying on Premium Processing fees to reduce backlogs creates a reverse incentive for the USCIS to work less efficiently to process applications, since employers will be less likely to pay for Premium Processing if application processing times are reduced. Moreover the USCIS will be unprepared for application surges that arise due to fee increases and changes in the political climate toward immigrants (Migration Policy Institute, 2008).

A study by the U.S. Government Accountability Office (GAO) evaluated the USCIS based on the GAO's principles of "equity, efficiency, revenue adequacy, and administrative burden." The GAO found that the Premium Processing Service had unforeseen costs that the $1,000 fee did not cover. Therefore, costs for Premium Processing had to come out of regular user fees that did not satisfy the equity dimension of the evaluation. Because the Premium Processing costs and fees were "misaligned," this backlog reduction plan not only became an unreliable temporary fix, it also resulted in extra costs to the agency. The GAO also found that the USCIS has insufficient methods to make accurate projections in future application surges by not always recording "application volume drivers such as policy decisions and known demographic trends" (U.S. Government Accountability Office, 2009, pp. 3–6).

INCREASED APPLICATION FEES

Without federal funding, the USCIS is 90 percent funded by immigration application fees. In 2007, the fee increase for naturalization applications increased 69 percent, from $400 to $675. This was the sixth time that immigration application fees had risen since 1988, when amendments to the Immigration and Nationality Act defunded the Immigration and Naturalization Service (INS) to base revenue on application fees alone. At $675, the application fee for naturalization costs more in the United States than in other advanced industrialized nations with comparable migration populations.

According to the Migration Policy Institute, in 2007 the U.S. naturalization application fee for adults was comparable to the United Kingdom ($525), but above that of Germany ($330), New Zealand ($321), Australia ($93), and Canada ($85).

Critics of the USCIS fee-funded structure claim the higher fees may discourage lower-income immigrants from applying. Immigrant advocates argue this places an unfair burden on legal permanent residents (LPRs) who are from less advantaged economic backgrounds and have less English language skills (Fix, Passel, & Sucher, 2003). While the USCIS aims to provide a fee waiver for those who meet the eligibility criteria based on a combination of income level (150% below the poverty line), age, and disability, funding is not enough to meet the demand, which has reached record highs. When the application fee increase came into effect on January 2007, applications for fee waivers soared to 300 percent from the previous year and a half (GAO, 2010, p. 27). As the fee waiver pool is taken out of 15 percent of user fees, USCIS could not satisfy the demand for fee waivers. While Congress provided appropriations for fee waiver and fee-exempt applications in fiscal year 2010, these funds ($50 million) are restricted for naturalization applications for asylum and refugee seekers, military personnel, and other "humanitarian parole" cases (GAO, 2010, p. 13). The USCIS's revenue inadequacies fall short of promised goals to waive fees for those who are unable to pay.

A MORE MEANINGFUL CITIZENSHIP TEST?

In 2006, advocates of comprehensive immigration reform urged USCIS to revise the citizenship test to introduce more meaningful queries related to knowledge of democratic principles and the civic responsibilities of citizens (Senate Hearings, 2005). The 2008 overhaul of the citizenship test incorporated more abstract conceptual questions considered too demanding for legal permanent residents with lower literacy and English-speaking levels, such as "What is the rule of law?" Moreover, critics point out that the new civics test has been politicized to link American historical queries with a conservative agenda that has little direct relevance for new citizens. Critics have called this the "second wall," a reference to the physical wall between the United States and Mexico, and claim such changes are designed to keep legal immigrants from attaining full citizenship rights (Mehta, 2006).

For critics, a call to make the citizenship test more meaningful and, in essence, harder without providing public funding to support applicants is a means to vet applicants who have limited English proficiency and lack the means to pay for civics or English language instruction. While naturalization rates would be even lower without the help of nonprofit ethnic, religious, and immigrant organizations that volunteer to help eligible LPRs meet the civics and language requirements for citizenship, it is questionable for the USCIS to push the entire responsibility for meeting eligibility requirements onto potential new citizens themselves.

Immigrant advocates claim that the current citizenship test creates a considerable barrier for eligible applicants with lower education and limited English proficiency—a group more concentrated among Latino applicants, especially those born in Mexico (Fix et al., 2003). Immigrant advocate Michele Waslin reports that the Department of Homeland Security (DHS) and USCIS "discourage Latino naturalization" (pp. 2–3; cited in Félix et al., 2008, p. 620). According to the Urban Institute, statistically significant differences between naturalized citizens and eligible LPRs along the lines of class, educational attainment, and English language ability warrant a careful consideration of how the American naturalization process presents formidable barriers against eligible LPRs who are concentrated on the lower end of the economic and educational spectrum. Researchers urge that intensive language and civics training should replace the citizenship test (Fix et al., 2003, p. 8). While supporters of the 2008 citizenship test claim that memorizing civics facts or trivia do little to inspire civic consciousness among potential new citizens, critics claim that the revised test requires similar memorization techniques, but for more abstract and difficult concepts. Learning by rote memorization for a citizenship test, whether of civics trivia or more abstract terminologies, is less relevant in promoting good citizenship than are civic values, which can be taught in civics classes (Etzioni, 2007; Fix et al., 2003).

Immigrant rights advocates argue that the current citizenship test sets up a barrier against those who are less educated. The old questions allowed for multiple answers, but answers to the new questions need to be known exactly as printed in study booklets. A member of the committee to revise the new citizenship test, Karen K. Narasaki, the director of the Asian American Justice Center, admits that the test has been made too difficult for potential new citizens. Narasaki also claims that there is a hidden agenda to use the test as a means to promote a conservative agenda. Narasaki notes Senator James M. Inhofe of Oklahoma, a Republican, added an amendment during debates in 2006 on the proposed Comprehensive Immigration Reform Act to require applicants to answer a question about the Federalist Papers. While Inhofe's rationale was to require LPRs to know more about America's Founding Fathers, Narasaki questions whether these questions are necessarily relevant to assist LPRs to prepare for citizenship (Gaouette, 2007, p. A1). An immigrant advocate from the Illinois Coalition for Immigrant and Refugee Rights, Flavia Jimenez, warns that the revised test strains the capacities of ethnic and immigrant groups to provide English and civics classes to help applicants pass the revised test (Hanna, 2008).

The sociologist Amitai Etzioni (2007) argues that citizenship tests are introduced and revised based not on the need to initiate citizens into the American democratic process, but on the desire to limit certain groups of "undesirable" immigrants. Etzioni calls citizenship tests a "modern form of nativist sentiment" (p. 354). Throughout U.S. history, literacy and civics tests have served a vetting role to control naturalization rates for Irish Catholics, non-western Europeans, Chinese, and other groups from Asia and Africa. Besides ethnic and religious groups, the United States also restricted immigration and naturalization based on political ideologies. For example, the Immigration and Nationality Act of 1952 created a citizenship and language test that sought to limit the naturalization of not only Asians but also those suspected of having communist alliances (p. 354).

In a more radical critique of the American naturalization requirements, scholar Joseph Carens (1998) argues that while the hope that the naturalization process can build a stronger civil society and integrate new citizens into the political process is well intentioned, this desire to instill patriotism and civic engagement cannot be encapsulated in a citizenship test. Since LPRs are in this country legally and can stay and work in the United States indefinitely, they have already been admitted as part of the American economic and political community. If a test is necessary, then it should be made as easy as possible and not more difficult. Otherwise, those who are most in need of help will find the obstacles harder to overcome. As Carens notes, "People who do not have a good education or who are just not good at taking tests have the right to be citizens too." He adds, "What about the few who fail? Are we confident that they are not competent?" (p. 141). While 92 percent of applicants pass the citizenship on the first try (USCIS, 2011), Carens suggests that the few who fail the test are not necessarily inadequate for citizenship, as literacy and knowledge of civics and American history are not necessarily related to a commitment towards the general good.

Carens's significant contribution to the debate on U.S. naturalization requirements is in distinguishing between legal requirements and the "norms and aspirations" that a nation hopes its new citizens acquire in order to participate meaningfully in the American democratic process. For Carens, those who claim that the citizenship test should instill American values of civic participation are misguided in their faith on an inappropriate mechanism to achieve such hopes of civic-mindedness. Such democratic and participatory values for citizenship cannot be drilled into the mind of the potential citizen through test preparation but should arise organically through the associations one makes after the applicant has been fully admitted as a citizen. Carens argues that the only legitimate requirement for citizenship should be length of residence. As with acquiring basic language proficiency, knowledge of American history and laws and civic engagement are expectations that some may hope for citizens to attain, but they cannot be legally enforceable. USCIS should not confuse legal requirements with normative goals of achieving a more vibrant civic society. To detach English proficiency from political engagement, Carens further contends that knowledge of English is a poor indicator of competency in the political realm, as information and knowledge of politics can be attained through one's social and non-English media networks (pp. 144–145). Moreover, feelings of patriotism and loyalty are not created by force in a liberal democratic society.

Language testing scholar Antony John Kunnan (2009) argues that the English-proficiency requirement of the naturalization test is akin to the literacy tests for voting that were struck down by the U.S. Supreme Court as unconstitutional. According to Kunnan, since U.S.-born citizens are not required to pass English language or civics the tests to receive passports or driver's licenses, LPRs should not be required to demonstrate such skills and knowledge when applying for citizenship (p. 95). Since the level of English proficiency required to pass the English portion of the test does not meet the standards of the language assessment community, Kunnan argues that the naturalization test does little to socially integrate citizens. Kunnan advocates adult language schools in partnership with local community colleges and high schools to provide English language and civics instruction that would satisfy an ideologically "middle-of-the-road position in terms of language rights and civic nationalism: a nation where there would be neither a policy of national monolingualism nor an overt policy of individual language rights" (p. 96).

Looking beyond the utilitarian aspects of naturalization testing as a means to prepare citizens with the skills required to participate in society, the political scientists Oded Löwenheim and Orit Gazit (2009) illustrate that the testing procedure itself constructs a power relationship between the new citizen and the state. While states have a right to set criteria for citizenship for the sake of the integration, Löwenheim and Gazit argue that citizenship testing serves other ideological functions that objectify national histories, institutionalize state authority, and reward citizens' complacency with the status quo. Using the social theorist Michel Foucault's notion that state power is often reproduced and legitimized through mundane practices, Löwenheim and Gazit apply this theory to the citizenship testing process, which leads to the "subjectification of individuals and the construction of their identity as governable 'citizens'" (p. 147).

As a ritual that may induce applicants' anxiety and fears of not passing, the naturalization testing procedure itself becomes a disciplining technology that emphasizes compliance with state authority. Not only does the lack of open-ended questions on the citizenship exam objectify "correct" answers as uncontested, the requirement for applicants to confess their loyalty to the state serves to further discipline the potential new citizen through a "bureaucratic confession of faith" (Marx, 1970, p. 51; quoted in Löwenheim & Gazit, 2009, p. 156). Rather than encourage citizens to achieve a critical distance from state power, the naturalization process produces subjects who may view dissent as unpatriotic. Moreover, as the naturalization process confers the responsibility to linguistically and socially integrate into civil society, the state may eschew responsibility for assisting immigrants after the naturalization process is over. The flip side of this "responsibilization" is that the government can blame new citizens for their own social and economic ostracism as a function of the new citizen's inability to use those tools of integration (Löwenheim & Gazit, 2009, p.159).

Making the naturalization test more substantive does not necessarily mean applicants would have a more meaningful relationship with the process of becoming a citizen. While the desire to foster civic engagement among potential new citizens is understandable, testing is not the way to inculcate these democratic principles. Testing rarely ensures civic-mindedness and civic engagement, since these sensibilities are not based on factual information absorbed through study and memorization in preparation for a civics text, but are instead derived from an internal drive to make connections beyond one's close circle of family and friends. This internal drive to give one's time and energy to participating in the public sphere can be encouraged through a more generous attitude towards immigrants in assisting their efforts in becoming full members of the American polity. The availability of publicly funded civics classes may have the effect of generating gratitude and may do more to encourage new citizens to dedicate their time and attention to civic associations and to engage in local politics. New citizens would feel a part of the local and national polity from the start. Rather than leave LPRs to fend for themselves in passing a difficult test and leaping bureaucratic hurdles, new citizens may gain a sense of loyalty, and thus value their role as citizens.

COMPARISONS TO OTHER ADVANCED INDUSTRIAL NATIONS

Supporters of the American naturalization process claim that advanced industrialized countries in Europe have more restrictive immigration policies than the United States. While this may be true, the political theorist Seyla Benhabib (2002) notes that certain European countries also grant foreign nationals from European Union (EU) countries voting rights in local elections. For Benhabib, the status of non-EU foreign nationals may be treated with more restrictive immigration policies than immigrants in the United States, and U.S. policy may therefore be considered more equitable than that of some EU countries. However, rather than focusing on naturalization policy as the only means of inclusion, which necessarily assumes only citizens have voting rights and can run for political office, Benhabib proposes a "politics of inclusion" that seeks to expand the boundaries of citizenship rights to LPRs.

According to the political sociologist Thomas Janoski (2010), comparing the United States to western European countries does not adequately take into account the fact that the United States has a different historical relationship to immigration than do countries in western Europe. He instead compares U.S. naturalization rates to those of Canada, Australia, and New Zealand, due to their shared characteristic as "settler" nations. Janoski categorizes the United States, Canada, Australia, and New Zealand as "settler" countries that have depended on mass immigration to work land that was acquired through the persecution of indigenous peoples (p. 12). While these countries depended on immigration for labor to occupy indigenous land, this does not mean that such countries promoted citizenship among its immigrant populations. On the contrary, since it was expensive to provide the full rights and privileges to migrants, these countries sought to slow down the acquisition of citizenship for particular groups of migrants (p. 13). In fact, all four countries have had naturalization policies that "were hostile to Asians and Africans" in their past (p. 100). Janoski places the introduction of English tests in the context of the history of the Chinese Exclusion Act (p. 103).

According to Janoski, there should be a more focused comparison among countries within their regime-type categories: colonizing; occupying; noncolonizing but occupying; settler; and noncolonizing Nordic countries. It is important to distinguish countries with different migrant needs, because comparing countries based solely on their advanced industrialized status or demographic similarities does not take into account the countries' institutional or regime-type factors. When compared to colonizing (France, United Kingdom, the Netherlands, Austria, Portugal), occupying (Japan, Belgium, Germany, Italy), and noncolonizing but occupying (Ireland, Finland, Switzerland) nations, the United States may seem to have less restrictive naturalization requirements. Yet within settler countries, the United States has one of the lowest rates of naturalization. Moreover, noncolonizing Nordic countries (Sweden and Denmark) have at times had a higher rate of naturalization than most settler countries, partly due to the efforts of social democrats to open naturalization policies. Putting the U.S. naturalization process into a more nuanced perspective, Janoski (2010) points out that while the United States is "seen as the premier naturalizer, perhaps because of the size of absolute numbers of naturalizations . . . relative to its population of foreign persons, Canada is the clear leader, with rates twice as high as the US. Only from 1995 to 2003 was the naturalization rate very high in the US" (p. 90). Only 7.9 percent of the U.S. population was born in foreign countries, whereas Australia is the highest in this regard, with 21.1 percent, followed by Canada, with 17.4 percent, and New Zealand, with 16.3 percent of its population born elsewhere (p. 90). Janoski concludes, "For overall population size, the United States has the lowest naturalization rates, lowest percentages of foreign population, and lowest acceptance rates of refugees. It clings to an assimilationist view of integration like France instead of a pluralist or multicultural view as in other settler countries" (p. 122).

In a more focused study comparing the naturalization rates of Canada and the United States, the sociologist Irene Bloemraad (2002) reveals why the United States lags behind Canada in naturalization rates. Bloemraad shows that how a nation institutionally welcomes potential new citizens has a large impact on the rate of naturalization. Rather than link naturalization rates to the characteristics of applicants, Bloemraad shows how Canada's federal policy directly encourages citizenship through the appropriation of public funds given to local ethnic communities to help applicants pass the citizenship test. The availability of institutional resources accounts for the gap in naturalization rates between Canada and the United States. While ethnic groups in the Toronto area receive federal funding to encourage naturalization, those in Boston have to rely on grassroots fundraising efforts to help immigrant groups provide free civics and English language classes to applicants for citizenship. This study shows that while the efforts by U.S. ethnic and immigrant advocacy groups are admirable, such efforts in helping LPRs attain citizenship would be greatly enhanced with public financial support. The sole reliance on grassroots community organizations to provide language and civics classes does not adequately meet the needs of LPRs who have low incomes and poor English skills.

CONCLUSION

Based on absolute numbers, the United States may be a nation of immigrants; however, this does not necessarily mean that the United States is a nation that encourages immigrants to become citizens. Scholars and immigrant advocates point out that a set of legal and informal barriers restrict particular groups of LPRs from gaining full entry into American civil society as citizens. To match the rhetoric of inclusivity made by the U.S. Citizenship and Immigration Services (USCIS), the naturalization process needs to be reformed to ensure all LPRs, regardless of income, educational level, or English skills, are provided with the means to meet the requirements for citizenship. If funds are unavailable to help potential new citizens take civics or language classes, the requirements for citizenship should be made less difficult in order to include the most vulnerable groups of LPRs. Because LPRs who are permitted to reside in the country on a permanent basis are expected to pay taxes to the government at all levels, and as such are already included as part of the American polity, it is appropriate to provide resources to help these applicants meet the costs associated with citizenship preparation. Otherwise, the increased application fee and difficulty of the citizenship test essentially vet out those applicants with low English proficiency and income levels.

The ethical imperative to care for oneself and others cannot be imposed from without. No country can legislate that fellow citizens love one another, but naturalization policies can help construct a relationship between immigrant and nonimmigrant that is not solely an example of a more powerful group using the other for material gain. If the United States treats LPRs in purely instrumentalist terms of gaining more taxpayers or workers, then potential new citizens have no incentive to think of their citizenship beyond what is materially beneficial. Instead, a feeling of distrust will result, and going beyond self-interest will be seen as providing no positive gains. To instill the sense of the general good, the United States should foster a sense of inclusion among LPRs when they are preparing for citizenship.

If the American naturalization process is to be made more meaningful, then it should promote the feeling of the general good, not through testing, but through encouraging a genuine commitment to the polity on the part of potential new citizens. Printing free manuals or booklets to help LPRs study for a test does not accomplish this. More available and affordable civics classes and English instruction for adults is needed. If public funds for these are unavailable, then the requirements for citizenship must be made more attainable for all eligible LPRs regardless of income, education, or English proficiency. In an economic crisis, it will be hard to convince public officials to spend money on those who are not citizens. Yet it is also important not to treat LPRs simply as foreigners. Those who are eligible have met the criteria of residency and have already been admitted as permanent members of American society. If the government is not willing to meet potential citizens part of the way in providing services to help them pass the more difficult civics test, then the most vulnerable members will not be able to pass. The call for a genuine commitment to civic participation on the part of citizens should be matched by a reciprocal commitment on the part of the government to provide adequate resources for eligible applicants for citizenship.

References and Further Reading

Benhabib, S. (2002). Political theory and political membership in a changing world. In I. Katznelson & H. Milner (Eds.), *Political science: State of the discipline* (pp. 404–432). New York, NY: W.W. Norton.

Bloemraad, I. (2002). The North American naturalization gap: An institutional approach to citizenship acquisition in the United States and Canada. *International Migration Review, 36*(1), 193–228.

Bustos, S. (2005, January 26). Backlog keeps immigrants waiting years for green cards. *USA Today.* Retrieved from http://www.usatoday.com/news/washington/2005–01–26-immigration-wait_x.htm

Carens, J. H. (1998). Why naturalization should be easy: A response to Noah Pickus. In N. Pickus (Ed.), *Immigration and citizenship in the 21st century* (pp. 141–146). Lanham, MD: Rowman & Littlefield.

Etzioni, A. (2007). Citizenship tests: A comparative, communitarian perspective. *Political Quarterly, 78*(3), 353–363.

Fix, M., Passel, J., & Sucher, K. (2003, September). *Trends in naturalization* (Immigrant Families and Workers, Facts and Perspectives Brief No. 3). Retrieved from Urban Institute website: http://www.urban.org/UploadedPDF/310847_trends_in_naturalization.pdf

Gaouette, N. (2007, September 28). Government unveils new citizenship test. *Los Angeles Times.* Retrieved from http://articles.latimes.com/2007/sep/28/nation/na-citizenship28

Hanna, J. (2008, October 1). Could you pass the new citizenship test? Retrieved from CNN website: http://articles.cnn.com/2008-10-01/us/citizenship.test_1_civics-questions-prospective-citizens?_s=PM:US

Janoski, T. (2010). *The ironies of citizenship: Naturalization and integration in industrialized countries.* Cambridge, UK: Cambridge University Press.

Kunnan, A. J. (2009). Testing for citizenship: The U.S. Naturalization Test. *Language Assessment Quarterly, 6,* 89–97.

Löwenheim, O., & Gazit, O. (2009, April). Power and examination: A critique of citizenship tests. *Security Dialogue, 40*(2), 145–167.

Marx, K. (1970). *A critique of Hegel's philosophy of right.* Cambridge, UK: Cambridge University Press. (Original work published 1843)

Mehta, S. (2006, November 15). Barriers inhibit legal road to U.S. citizenship. *The New Standard.* Retrieved from http://newstandardnews.net/content/index.cfm/items/3891

Migration Policy Institute. (2007, February). *Immigration fee increases in context* (Immigration Fact Sheet No. 15). Retrieved from http://www.migrationpolicy.org/pubs/FS15_CitizenshipFees2007.pdf

Migration Policy Institute. (2008, February). *Behind the naturalization backlog: Causes, context, and concerns* (Immigration Fact Sheet No. 21). Retrieved from http://www.migrationpolicy.org/pubs/FS21_NaturalizationBacklog_022608.pdf

National Immigration Forum. (2008, August). *Out of focus: The hidden crisis of the latest backlogs in naturalization processing.* Retrieved from http://www.immigrationforum.org/images/uploads/OutofFocus_BacklogReport.pdf

Senate Hearings before the Committee on Appropriations: Department of Homeland Security, fiscal year 2006. (2005, March 2). S. HRG. 109–195. H.R. 2360. Washington, DC. Retrieved from http://www.gpo.gov/fdsys/pkg/CHRG-109shrg99863/pdf/CHRG-109shrg99863.pdf

U.S. Citizenship and Immigration Services. (2011, August 23). *Applicant performance on the naturalization test.* Retrieved from http://www.uscis.gov/portal/site/uscis/menuitem.eb1d4c2a3e5b9ac89243c6a7543f6d1a/?vgnextoid=6c40ec90d8668210VgnVCM100000082ca60aRCRD&vgnextchannel=6c40ec90d8668210VgnVCM100000082ca60aRCRD

U.S. Government Accountability Office (GAO). (2009, January). *Federal user fees: Additional analyses and timely reviews could improve immigration and naturalization user fee design and USCIS operations* (Report to Congressional Requesters). Retrieved from http://www.gao.gov/new.items/d09180.pdf

U.S. Government Accountability Office (GAO). (2010, March 23). *Federal user fees: Fee design characteristics and trade-offs illustrated by USCIS's immigration and naturalization fees.* Statement of Susan J. Irving, Director, Federal Budget Analysis, Strategic Issues. Testimony before the Subcommittee on Immigration, Citizenship, Refugees, Border Security, and International Law, Committee on the Judiciary, U.S. House of Representatives. Retrieved from http://www.gao.gov/new.items/d10560t.pdf

Waslin, M. (2008). *Latino naturalization and the federal government's response* (Unpublished manuscript). Cited in A. Félix, C. González, & R. Ramírez (Eds.), Political protest, ethnic media, and Latino naturalization. *American Behavioral Scientist, 52*(4), 618–634.

Karey Leung

COUNTERPOINT

The American naturalization process does not need to be reformed. The U.S. Citizenship and Immigration Services (USCIS) has effectively reduced the number of pending applications to a manageable level since the 2007 surge in applications (which was partly due to factors beyond the control of the agency). Since Congress voted to turn the Immigration and Naturalization Service (INS) into a user-funded institution in 1988, USCIS has had to raise fees periodically to keep up with processing, administration, and overhead costs. Fee waivers aim to spread the fee burden across the applicant pool according to need. For those who cannot afford to pay the application fee, USCIS grants fee waivers for applicants who fall under 150 percent of the poverty line. While the fee waiver pool covers an average of 83 percent of all fee waiver applicants, USCIS prioritizes those individuals who are considered most in need of waivers based on a combination of factors including income, disability, and age (USCIS, 2011, p. 1).

In order to pay for fee waivers, USCIS designates 15 percent of the application fee, which is partly responsible for the high cost of naturalization. The U.S. Government Accountability Office (GAO) reviews the fee structure of USCIS every 2 years to ensure the agency satisfies the criteria set forth by the agency. Fee increases are not approved until an oversight committee evaluates the need based on the following criteria: equity, efficiency, revenue adequacy, and administrative burden (GAO, 2010). While fee increases are an unfortunate necessity to keep up with operational, overhead, administrative, and fee waiver costs, USCIS makes every effort to maintain transparency. Ideally, USCIS would be able to grant waivers to all who are eligible, but the unavailability of federal funding means that tough decisions have to be made on an individual case-by-case basis.

THE 2008 REVISED CITIZENSHIP TEST

Acquiring citizenship should be a momentous experience that challenges the individual to be a part of the democratic polity in active and engaging ways. Otherwise, the process is merely procedural, and therefore meaningless. The improved citizenship test is geared to promote not only knowledge of U.S. history and government, but also civic-mindedness and civic participation. Moving away from questions on civics trivia to more significant inquiries regarding the principles of American democracy, the new citizenship test promotes civic integration into the American polity on both the local and national level. Moreover, the test includes more questions regarding historically marginalized groups such as Native Americans and African Americans, and thus represent the heterogeneity of the U.S. population in the past and present.

USCIS consulted groups from the full range of the political and ideological spectrum to make recommendations to the pilot committee. After the pilot test, another review process revised ambiguous or vague questions. After 10 years of consultations with both liberal and conservative research institutes and scholars, USCIS released a new version of the citizenship test in 2008. A number of academics and policy advisors in education and testing were contracted to administer the restructuring of the citizenship test. These academics included individuals from the fields of political science, history, English, testing, psychometrics, and Teachers of English to Speakers of Other Languages (TESOL). In consultation with experts in the above fields of education, testing, and civics, the English and civics portion of the test went through a series of in-depth evaluations that sought to transform the test into a more meaningful process without unduly raising the difficulty of the test (Chenoweth & Burdick, 2007, cited in Laglagaron & Devani, 2008, pp. 15–16; Committee on the U.S. Naturalization Test Redesign, 2004). In fact, the test has had a higher passing rate than the previous test, up from 85 percent to 92 percent of the applicant pool (Semple, 2008). This rate is much higher than the passing rate for the equivalent citizenship test in the United Kingdom, *Life in the UK,* which is around 75 percent (White, 2008, p.222).

While critics claim that the current test exceeds the language level of those with the lowest education and English proficiency, this does not mean that changes to the citizenship test are not useful for the applicant. On the query of voting rights, the current test inverted the question from "What's one of the constitutional amendments that focuses on voting rights?" to "There are four amendments to the Constitution about who can vote? Describe one of them." The answer to the previous question could be Amendment 15, 19, 24, or 26, while that of the revised query can be one of the following: "citizens eighteen (18) and older (can vote); you don't have to pay (a poll tax) to vote; any citizen can vote (women and men can vote); and a male citizen of any race (can vote)" (Ratliff, 2004). The earlier question required applicants to memorize the number of one of these four amendments to answer the question correctly. To avoid applicants' needing to memorize a number, the test question was revised to stress the content of the amendments, and thus requires a more substantive answer than the number itself. In this way, the applicant may be able to come away from the process with the knowledge that voting rights are protected by the Constitution. This change does require the applicant to learn a more substantive answer, but the answer is one that may potentially aid in combating possible infringements of a citizen's voting rights in the future.

Critics have pointed out that the citizenship test requires a substantial commitment of time and resources on the part of the applicant. However, the public policy scholar Noah Pickus (1998) argues that civic associations can help applicants prepare for the civics and English portion of the citizenship test. Studying for a civics exam may not be the ideal way to inculcate democratic engagement, but immigrant advocacy, grassroots, and religious organizations may form connections with applicants, whose sense of civic community will be strengthened from the very start of their journey through the naturalization process (pp. 130–131). By forging this bond with such community organizations, new citizens may be more likely to contribute time and resources to help these organizations continue the work of helping future applicants, or they may work on other similar issues for the public good. For those who argue that citizenship should be made available for all who meet the residency requirement, Pickus quotes Chief Justice William Rehnquist, who stated in *Sugarman v. Dougall* that naturalization is "a status in and relationship with a society which is continuing and more basic than mere presence or residence" (*Sugarman v. Dougall,* 1973; quoted in Pickus, 1998, p. 125). Preparing for citizenship instills a sense of allegiance to the country. Moreover, applicants need a basic knowledge of U.S. history and democratic institutions to become a part of an informed citizenry. While critics may claim that many native-born citizens could not pass the citizenship test, and therefore that legal permanent residents (LPRs) seeking citizenship should not be expected to meet such higher standards, lowering the bar for citizenship based on the lowest common denominator would not be in the country's best interest. Instead, USCIS should maintain a higher standard of excellence and expect more from those who are actively choosing to be a part of the American citizenry. In this way, those who are newly admitted may help raise the standards of civic engagement of the entire polity.

Since many native-born or previously naturalized citizens may have attended civics and government classes, those who have not had such educational opportunities may need to be exposed to the workings of American political institutions before becoming citizens. While some critics argue for the alternative of providing civics and English classes to eligible LPRs, rather than testing, requiring applicants to take classes presents a much greater burden in terms of time commitment and resources for the applicant. Moreover, coordinating classes on a national scale requires substantial resources. Testing is a more flexible alternative to enforced, mandatory classes, since applicants may study for the test in the convenience of their homes or local community centers.

While the fee-funded nature of USCIS prevents free civics or language instruction, test booklets and manuals that lay out all aspects of the testing procedure are available for all. Whereas the naturalization process was once contingent on locale or interviewer temperament, the process is now routinely standardized to ensure fairness for LPRs who decide to take the test. Moreover, those who fail to answer 6 out of 10 questions may retake the test without paying the application fee. USCIS understands that unforeseen contingencies may affect one's ability to pass the test, and will therefore give applicants another chance to pass in case the conditions during the first test are not optimal. Because USCIS is a fee-funded institution, however, funds are limited to two attempts. Also, the finite number of times an applicant can take the test without repaying the fee may encourage applicants to take the citizenship test more seriously.

Some critics argue that multimedia materials ought to replace the citizenship exam. However, the viewing of DVDs, museum installations, books, and pamphlets eliminates a certain level of human interaction with USCIS representatives during the interview process. Moreover, USCIS is less able to determine the level of engagement with installations or books. Testing encourages the applicant to at least absorb the information well enough to recall the answers on test day. Memorized material can be easily forgotten, but at least the individual would have gone through the mental steps to incorporate the material at least once or twice. This does not guarantee applicants will retain the information, but at least at one point in the process their knowledge of civics and American history would be most acute.

Historically, literacy tests have been used to weed out "undesirable" immigrants, but the current tests aim to prepare applicants to have the basic knowledge required to participate in the complex historical institutions that make American democracy unique and one of the most progressive nations in the world. Without a basic knowledge of the workings of American political institutions, a new citizen would be ill-prepared for civic participation and unaware of the full rights and responsibilities of citizenship that some citizens may have learned through years of schooling in civics classes. Although the naturalization process requires an initial time commitment and substantial resources, the process is designed to make sure new and older citizens are equivalent in their level of civics knowledge. Of course, not all citizens have gone through an adequate civics education, but this does not mean one should expect less from new citizens. Indeed, new citizens may need such information the most, as they may be more vulnerable to anti-immigrant sentiments, particularly in times of economic crisis.

John Fonte, the director of the Hudson Institute's Center for American Common Culture, describes the American naturalization process as a rite of passage, much like a marriage marks the beginning of a commitment to one's beloved. The experience encompasses more than taking a test; it starts with the application process, studying, passing the citizenship and English language tests, and finally attending the swearing-in ceremony, all of which should encapsulate the spirit of being a patriotic citizen of the United States. The citizenship test is not simply another test one takes in school, but a test that should carry enormous normative weight to instill patriotism through elaborate final ceremonies and testing procedures. Because the citizenship test is a way to "attach" potential citizens to the well-being of the state, it is important to focus on the "more celebratory version" of the test, which may differ from a history test in high school or grade school. The purposes of the citizenship test should not simply be to learn content, but also to bring out loyalty toward the government. Fonte believes this is consistent with the purposes of the Immigration and Nationality Act of 1952. In the post-9/11 world, knowledge of U.S. government is not enough; the naturalization process must work toward changing the hearts of new citizens to be loyal to the country. While taking part in a 2004 panel discussion, Fonte cited James Madison, who wrote in *Federalist* No. 49 that "both enlightened reason and a certain degree of veneration" is needed for the full functioning health of the republic. Hence, the citizenship process should not be simply a procedural formality, it should require dedicated preparation on the part of the potential citizen.

Critics of the naturalization process charge that it has reintroduced assimilationist ideology in order to reduce the cultural, ethnic, religious, and racial diversity of new immigrants. In contrast, the American sociologist Rogers Brubaker (2001) has resuscitated the word "assimilation" from its negative historical connotations. Brubaker detaches the word from its darker historical meaning as "cultural assimilation" and applies the notion of "civic assimilation" into the nation's democratic polity. Understanding the elaborate political mechanisms that keeps American democracy stable through a system of checks and balances requires a more in-depth appreciation of the ways in which the Founding Fathers designed the Constitution. Brubaker also contends that English language skills may be necessary for a new citizen to fully take part in civil society. He notes that assimilation in the new sense does not automatically mean a form of acculturation in which whole cultures are seen as inferior to the dominant one. Brubaker maps out the two meanings of "assimilation" in both its earlier negative and later positive forms in order to maintain the necessary and desirable aspects of "civic commonality" needed in a thriving democratic society (pp. 533–535). To become a citizen is to become similar to other citizens regarding certain aspects of public identity, and this requires the acquisition of knowledge and sentiments correlated with citizenship. This process does not dissolve the applicant's individuality in terms of cultural and linguistic traditions. Rather, the process insures that a

Assimilation (OLD): cultural, ethnic, religious, and racial homogenization
Assimilation (NEW): civic commonality, shared civic vocabulary, and knowledge of political institutions

set of codes is properly instilled in the mindset of the potential new citizen so as to facilitate a more substantive participatory society. The pre-1965 notion of assimilation as adopting white Anglo-Saxon Protestant cultural traditions is not the only way of thinking about assimilation.

This newer notion of assimilation applies to the American naturalization process. Alfonso Aguilar, the head of the citizenship office at USCIS, notes, "the [citizenship test] redesign is part of the Bush administration's efforts to improve immigrant assimilation," but this statement does not automatically signal that the naturalization process aims to reduce the diversity of immigrants' cultural and linguistic backgrounds (Semple, 2008). Rather, immigrants are gaining competency in a civics language that does not take away one's cultural or ethnic distinctiveness. Given Brubaker's framework of rethinking assimilation to connote civic similarity, not cultural absorption, the American naturalization process can be similarly understood as geared toward making citizens alike in their knowledge of democratic procedure and their adoption of core liberal values of tolerance and participation. The adoption of such democratic discourses may in turn foster a greater diversity of views by activating citizens' voices in the public realm. In fact, test questions regarding the diversity of groups among Native American tribes and African Americans celebrate America's cultural diversity. The desire to give potential new citizens the proper tools to fully engage in democratic life does not mean that applicants have to lose what makes them unique. While acquiring basic English proficiency may be necessary for citizens to act as full members of the economic, political, and social life of the nation, one should think of such language acquisition in an additive fashion. To meaningfully connect with one's fellow citizens, a minimum level of civics and English proficiency is necessary.

COMPARISON TO ADVANCED INDUSTRIALIZED DEMOCRACIES

The U.S. naturalization process is inclusive compared to the most prohibitive European countries, such as Germany, Denmark, and Austria, as well as exclusive states such as Greece, Spain, Italy, and Luxembourg, which has the lowest naturalization rate in Europe. Other advanced industrial democracies require higher application fees, longer periods of legal residence, and pre-arrival or soon-after-arrival language and civics tests that may or may not come with study guides. In addition, some countries unfairly target certain groups of immigrants for civics and language testing based on country of origin and religion. The Netherlands and Germany exempt most immigrants from pre-entry testing, except for Muslims from Turkey and Morocco (Goodman, 2010; Joppke, 2008).

Discussion of EU-style politics has sparked scholars to insist on a North American union made up of Canada, the United States, and Mexico. Although this inclusive proposal to eliminate barriers among neighboring countries may sound cosmopolitan, scholars warn that modeling citizenship on EU immigration policy ignores the ways in which the EU has encountered problems in terms of engagement and cohesion. The political scientist Richard Bellamy (2011) notes that language and cultural barriers among European countries may prohibit a truly meaningful notion of cosmopolitanism, as well as dilute civic connection to the polity, because an individual's vote has less weight as the EU grows (p. 596).

While the Comprehensive Immigration Reform Act of 2006, which was not passed, sought to standardize naturalization procedure so that all applicants would be tested for the same aptitude in English and civics knowledge, certain advanced western European countries have not undergone such standardization. German naturalization procedure can differ dramatically from one state to the next (Goodman, 2011, p. 238). The Dutch philosopher René Boomken (2010) notes that a series of post-9/11 events in the Netherlands redirected the public discourse on immigration toward a promotion of "cultural citizenship" that targeted immigrants from Muslim countries as backward and prone to terrorism (p. 313). According to the sociologist Willem Schinkel (2010), Dutch naturalization policy, in the guise of aiming to assimilate potential new citizens into the liberal democratic framework, took a cultural assimilationist turn that isolated certain cultural traits as undesirable, particularly those of Islam (p. 269). Schinkel notes that the Dutch citizenship debates linked undesirable cultural traits to "Islamic fundamentalism," and particularly to Muslim immigrant populations of Antillians and Moroccans (p. 273). He claims that a "neo-nationalism" is taking hold in western European countries that seeks to promote a culture-based politics of citizenship that unfairly isolates those deemed disloyal or impossible to integrate (p. 279).

Coupled with the fear of Muslims, this culturalist turn in citizenship policy signals a return of racist politics. In May 2008, Human Rights Watch (HRW) published *The Netherlands: Discrimination in the Name of Integration*, which condemns the specific targeting of migrants from Morocco and Turkey to take an "overseas integration test" before entry into the country (p. 1). This blatant case of discrimination violates international human rights law. The political scientist Sara Wallace Goodman (2011) illustrates that the trend in requiring civic integration before an immigrant is allowed permanent residency status posits an extreme form of immigration control in the guise of inclusive integration. Because the Netherlands has a reputation as one of the most liberal and tolerant societies in western Europe, the pre-entry integration test has become a model for other European countries to enact similar legislation (p. 252). This trend of pre-entry civics and language testing has inspired similar proposals in Germany, Denmark, France, and the United Kingdom. In August 2007, a new German law was passed stating that foreign spouses of German citizens must take a pre-entry German language test to gain entry. Denmark and France have approved new laws to require language and civics testing (Denmark) and courses (France) in the applicant's home country before applying for a visa (Human Rights Watch, 2008, p. 11). The pre-entry exam puts the entire responsibility of preparation on the part of the applicant prior to residence. As these policies of exclusion are aimed at preventing family reunification of mostly Muslim families, this violates basic notions of fairness in human rights law. Unlike countries in the European Union, the United States has one of the highest rates of migration via family reunification (close to 70% of total migration) in the world (Goodman, 2011, p. 252).

Critics of the American naturalization process argue that the United States should have more porous boundaries with neighboring countries, similar to that among countries within the European Union. The Dutch public administration scholar Berry Tholen (2009) notes, however, that EU states may form cultural boundaries that exclude those considered "undesirable" by the supranational community. The development of open borders for EU countries leads to an exclusion of cultures seen as impossible to civically integrate. Tholen also notes that EU immigration policies discriminate against those from countries and religions considered "non-Western" in the name of integration. To maintain porous national borders, EU states rely on de facto cultural boundaries that are subject to age-old xenophobic sentiments. Rather than providing clear-cut criteria for naturalization, Tholen argues, EU citizenship policy becomes tangled with growing anti-Muslim hysteria that unjustly equates Islam with violent fundamentalism (p. 48). Through external and internal review processes, USCIS aims to prevent such cultural assimilationist ideologies from affecting the American naturalization process.

CONCLUSION

Although nativist sentiments have also historically plagued U.S. naturalization policies, this does not mean that the process cannot be redeemed. While some critics argue that the requirements for citizenship should be made as easy as possible, this would lower the standards that might help initiate a potential new citizen to be an active member of the civic community. Rather than assume the lowest common denominator of language and civics knowledge, U.S. Citizenship and Immigration Services (USCIS) should maintain a more meaningful naturalization process. If citizenship requirements are made meaningless through mere civics trivia questions, there might be less pride in attaining citizenship, as the rite of passage in the final ceremony would be reduced to a procedural chore. While making the test more meaningful may pose more difficulties for applicants with limited English ability or low education levels, grassroots organizations can work with legal permanent residents (LPRs) to fill the gap to provide assistance as well as strengthen the bonds of civil society. This collaboration fosters a sense of civic community between immigrant advocacy organizations and the applicant, who in turn may be encouraged to help future applicants. By forging a link between new and old citizens, the naturalization process becomes a way in which civil society grows through mutual assistance. Given the high passing rate of those taking the citizenship exam, the citizenship test does not pose a serious barrier to most who take the exam. After almost a decade of review, the new citizenship test has met the criteria of fairness, according to the policy experts and academics who have been consulted.

The requirement that all new citizens acquire basic language and civics knowledge is not asking too much. Rather than leave applicants on their own to study, USCIS has made efforts with the limited funds available to provide resources in the form of booklets, online brochures, and study guides available at public libraries throughout the United States. If LPRs have successfully made it far enough in the naturalization process to attain a visa and stay the requisite number of years as permanent residents, then it is not too much to ask them to fulfill these last steps toward becoming full citizens. While it is true that loyalty and patriotism cannot be learned by rote, the hope of fostering allegiance to the United States requires basic civics knowledge. These steps serve to prepare applicants for entry into American society, not merely as consumers, but as active citizens who have at their disposal the right tools for civic engagement at all levels.

Given that most advanced industrialized western European countries have or are in the process of designing stricter rules of naturalization in terms of civics and language testing before entry, it is important to view the United States in this comparative perspective. While the United States has had a dark history of anti-immigrant naturalization policies, the current naturalization process is devoid of such discriminatory effects. Thorough consultation with advisors from all sides of the political spectrum has made the citizenship test more substantive, but without raising the difficulty level to a statistically significant level. The call to lift all requirements except a minimum number of years of residency does not respect the ways in which this process has been a source of pride for many applicants who have met the requirements. Taking this process away from the applicant would be a disservice to those who have come to value their citizenship. Since LPRs must meet the 5-year eligibility requirement, there is ample time to most applicants to acquire the skills or seek help in studying for the civics and English language exams. If the tests were eliminated or made easier, then the oath of allegiance might be perceived as less meaningful to the applicant. Citizenship status is one of the most significant identities of a person residing in a country, and citizenship must not be reduced to a simple procedural formality automatically conferred after residing in the country.

References and Further Reading

Bellamy, R. (2011). Citizenship. In G. Klosko (Ed.), *The Oxford handbook of the history of political philosophy* (pp. 586–598). Oxford, UK: Oxford University Press.

Boomken, R. (2010). Cultural citizenship and real politics: The Dutch case. *Citizenship Studies, 14*(3), 307–316.

Brubaker, R. (2001). The return of assimilation? Changing perspectives on immigration and its sequels in France, Germany, and the United States. *Ethnic and Racial Studies, 24*(4), 531–548.

Chenoweth, J., & Burdick, L. (2007, January). *A more perfect union.* Washington, DC: Catholic Legal Immigration Network.

Committee on the U.S. Naturalization Test Redesign. (2004). *Redesigning the U.S. naturalization tests: Interim report.* Washington, DC: The National Academies Press.

Fonte, J. (2004, July 13). *Testing for citizenship: Update on the redesign of the naturalization exam* (Panel discussion transcript). Retrieved from Center for Immigration Studies website: http://www.cis.org/articles/2004/exampanel071304.html

Goodman, S. W. (2010, May). Integration requirement for integration's sake? Identifying , categorising and comparing civic integration policies. *Journal of Ethnic and Migration Studies, 36*(5), 753–772.

Goodman, S. W. (2011). Controlling immigration through language and country knowledge requirements. *West European Politics, 34*(2), 235–255.

Human Rights Watch. (2008, May). *The Netherlands: Discrimination in the name of integration.* Retrieved from http://www.hrw.org/en/reports/2009/04/13/netherlands-discrimination-name-integration

Joppke, C. (2008) Comparative citizenship: A restrictive turn in Europe? *Journal of Law and Ethics of Human Rights, 2*(1), 1–41.

Laglagaron, L., & Devani, B. (2008, September). High stakes, more meaning: An overview of the process of redesigning the US citizenship test. Retrieved from Migration Policy Institute website: http://www.migrationpolicy.org/pubs/BR6_NatzTest_092908.pdf

Pickus, N. (1998). Creating citizens for the 21st century. In N. Pickus (Ed.), *Immigration and citizenship in the 21st century* (107–139). Lanham, MD: Rowman & Littlefield.

Ratliff, G. (2004, July 13). *Testing for citizenship: Update on the redesign of the naturalization exam* (Panel discussion transcript). Retrieved from Center for Immigration Studies website: http://www.cis.org/articles/2004/exampanel071304.html

Schinkel, W. (2010). The virtualization of citizenship. *Critical Sociology, 36*(2), 265–283.

Schneider, D. (2001, Fall). Naturalization and United States citizenship in two periods of mass migration: 1894–1930, 1965–2000. *Journal of American Ethnic History, 21*(1), 50–82.

Semple, K. (2008, September 23). Citizenship seekers told not to fear a new test. *The New York Times.* Retrieved from http://www.nytimes.com/2008/09/24/us/24test.html

Sugarman v. Dougall, 413 U.S. 634 (1973).

Tholen, B. (2009). Privileging the near and dear? Evaluating special ties considerations in European Union Migration Policy. *Ethnicities, 9*(1), 32–52.

U.S. Citizenship and Immigration Services (USCIS). (2011, February 24). *Questions & answers: USCIS Quarterly National Stakeholder Engagement.* Retrieved from http://www.uscis.gov/USCIS/Outreach/Public%20Engagement/National%20Engagement%20Pages/2011%20Events/February%202011/QA%20-%20Quarterly%20National%20Stakeholder%20Meeting.pdf

U.S. Government Accountability Office (GAO). (2010, March 23). *Federal user fees: Fee design characteristics and trade-offs illustrated by USCIS's immigration and naturalization fees.* Statement of Susan J. Irving, Director, Federal Budget Analysis, Strategic Issues. Testimony before the Subcommittee on Immigration, Citizenship, Refugees, Border Security, and International Law, Committee on the Judiciary, U.S. House of Representatives. Retrieved from http://www.gao.gov/new.items/d10560t.pdf

White, P. (2008, April–June). Immigrants into citizens. *Political Quarterly, 79*(2), 221–231.

Karey Leung

4

Legalization (Amnesty) for Unauthorized Immigrants

POINT: What to do about the 11 million or more unauthorized immigrants living in the United States is one of the most contentious issues in American politics today. Providing a path to (earned) legal status for most of this unauthorized population is practical, necessary, and in the national interest. It is required out of fairness to millions of unauthorized immigrants who have established their lives here and have no way to exercise their civil rights, nor any pathway to social mobility or integration with the rest of society.

Andrew D. Linenberg, Hinkle, Fingles & Prior, P.C.

COUNTERPOINT: Amnesty or legalization for unauthorized immigrants is unfair, illogical, and imperils the national interest. It is unfair to the millions of would-be immigrants who play by the rules and wait their turn under the legal visa system. It is illogical because it rewards those who do not play by the rules, and it imperils national security by encouraging more illegal immigration in the future. Legalization is wrong on a moral level, and on a practical level, would hurt the U.S. economy and increase competition in an already difficult job market.

Andrew D. Linenberg, Hinkle, Fingles & Prior, P.C.

Introduction

Of the 38.2 million immigrants estimated to be living in the United States as of March 2010, approximately 10 million were not in this country legally. Experts agree that the current U.S. immigration system is dysfunctional at best, with inconsistent and ineffective enforcement that fails to stop unauthorized immigrants from entering the country while deterring them from returning to their home countries. These inconsistencies render the system unfair and unpredictable for many of the hard-working, long-time resident unauthorized immigrants who have been contributing to this nation's economy and strengthening its communities for years. Experts also agree unauthorized immigrants will continue to arrive and stay in the country as a result of multiple national and international conditions. However, unauthorized immigrants are rarely able to legitimize their status, because no official path to do so currently exists for that population. Meanwhile, removal of all unauthorized immigrants via enforcement is an impossibility.

The current immigration system amounts to an untenable regime in which a large population of foreign-born people is here to stay, but whose members are relegated to a caste-like subclass in many settings, with few, if any, ways to access and protect their rights. The question, therefore, is how to improve this situation in a way that is fair to unauthorized immigrants, while helping to resolve some of the alleged problems resulting from the current immigration system. The following debate examines whether an earned legalization program (sometimes referred to as "amnesty") is the answer.

An earned legalization program is *not* a magic wand by which all unauthorized immigrants in the country are instantly granted legal immigration status. Nor does earned legalization represent a governmental condoning of illegal activity.

Even legalization proponents do not entirely agree about what form such a program should take and whom it should include. But in essence, any earned legalization program would provide legal immigration status, or at least a pathway to legalized status, for those who have earned it by meeting specific criteria. Any design for an earned legalization program strives to balance the following competing goals: (1) reducing the unauthorized immigrant population; (2) imposing requirements on unauthorized immigrants to "earn" legalized status, so as to avoid rewarding rule-breaking and deter opening the floodgates to further unauthorized immigration; and (3) increasing the economic benefits and decreasing security concerns to the nation as a whole.

The Counterpoint essay takes the position that a legalization program would exacerbate, rather than resolve, the issues with the current immigration regime and large unauthorized immigrant population. This is true for multiple reasons. First, any legalization program is set up to fail. History demonstrates that the requirements for obtaining permanent status, along with unauthorized immigrants' inherent distrust of the government, will leave a substantial portion of the target population with unauthorized status. Second, such a program is immoral, in the sense that it rewards those who have violated the nation's immigration laws. It is also unfair to those who have spent sometimes substantial amounts of time and money to obtain permanent resident status through proper, albeit backlogged, legal channels. Third, legalization is impractical and counterproductive, as it would encourage increased unauthorized immigration. Migrants would descend upon the United States believing they too could skirt the country's immigration laws, and still eventually earn permanent status by coming and staying in the country for the requisite period of time. Finally, a legalization policy would be financially and administratively costly, would increase job competition for unskilled and low-skilled laborers legally in the United States, and would otherwise hurt the U.S. economy while endangering national security.

Terminology

Before delving into the debate, it is important to clarify key terminology. With respect to the subject population, this article uses the terms "authorized" and "unauthorized" immigrant, rather than "legal immigrant" and "illegal alien" or "illegal immigrant," on grounds that this choice will lead to more meaningful, less inflammatory debate about the tough substantive issues at stake.

As Kevin Johnson, dean of the Law School of the University of California at Davis, has stated, using the term "illegal" inflames emotion, because many feel it is a loaded term that ends up blocking meaningful debate about the substance of immigration policy issues. Johnson notes that violations of immigration law are administrative offenses more akin to violating traffic or child labor laws than criminal law. Just as it would be illogical to label those who violate such laws as "illegal drivers" or "illegal children," it is irrational to label immigration law violators "illegal immigrants." As George Lakoff and Sam Ferguson argue in "The Framing of Immigration" (2006), using the term "illegal immigrant" connotes criminality and "otherness." This results in framing the entire immigration debate in a self-confining, less meaningful way, which constricts consideration of possible solutions to the "illegal immigrant problem." At the same time, the term "undocumented" is not a wholly satisfactory alternative. While less inflammatory, characterizing these individuals as "undocumented" is often inaccurate, because many have entered the country legally with official documentation but have overstayed the scope or duration of their permitted stay. Thus, the reference to "unauthorized" and "authorized" immigrants in the discussion here.

Authorized immigrants (or "aliens," in the language of the immigration statute) are persons present in the United States with valid legal immigration status. They have been inspected and admitted, and have complied with all conditions on their presence in this country. Jeffrey S. Passel, a senior demographer at the Pew Hispanic Center, has defined "authorized immigrant" as an individual who has been granted any of the following forms of immigration status: (1) legal permanent residence (LPR) status; (2) asylum; (3) admission as a refugee; (4) admitted for specified, but temporary statuses for longer-term residence and work; (5) naturalized citizen; and (6) legal temporary migrant, who has received permission to live, and sometimes even work, in the United States for defined periods of time (usually over 1 year). Unauthorized immigrants are persons who entered the country without permission—either by surreptitiously crossing the border or by presenting false documents to officials—as well as those who initially entered legally but then fell "out of status" by overstaying the duration of their permitted stay or surpassing the scope of their permitted conduct while here. This latter group, so-called overstays or out-of-status immigrants, includes students, temporary workers, tourists, and those whose asylum cases were denied. According to the Pew Hispanic Center, this category accounted for as much as 45 percent of the entire unauthorized immigrant population in 2006.

One additional terminological point: although "amnesty" is an oft-heard term with regard to these types of programs, this chapter prefers the terms "legalization" or "regularization." As Andrew Wroe, a lecturer in American politics at Kent University, has stated, the term "amnesty" implies that unauthorized immigrants have committed a moral wrong or violated a criminal law for which they must be punished, but for which they may now, beneficently, be shown mercy by the government. In contrast, this chapter employs the term "legalization," particularly "earned legalization," on grounds that these do not carry the same negative baggage and more neutrally describe policies designed to provide a definite path to some form of permanent legal status for unauthorized immigrants.

In reading the debate, consider the following. First, much of the legalization debate focuses on fairness, but to whom are such programs fair and unfair? Second, what are the long-term implications of implementing an earned legalization program? Third, an earned legalization program or increasing enforcement efforts are each only one piece of improving the current immigration system. Because neither approach, by itself, is meant to completely solve all the problems with the current system, it is important to think of what other initiatives may help to improve the existing immigration regime.

POINT

The Department of Homeland Security (DHS), which is responsible for controlling the country's immigration system, estimates that as of January 2010 there were approximately 10.8 million unauthorized immigrants in the country. Unauthorized immigration increased by 27 percent between 2000 and March 2010, despite two recessions and a net loss of one million jobs during that decade. According to the Pew Hispanic Center, this represents the highest level of unauthorized immigration in the nation's history. In 2010, unauthorized immigrants were estimated to comprise 5 percent of the nation's workforce and 4 percent of the overall U.S. population.

This may not seem alarming at first. After all, surely a substantial portion of this unauthorized immigrant population can satisfy whatever is necessary under the immigration laws to obtain legal status. The reality is, however, that this is largely impossible. Immigration laws provide virtually no pathway for unauthorized immigrants to obtain legal status to work and live in the United States. Whether by choice or because they are unable to return home for various reasons, the vast majority of unauthorized immigrants are here to stay. The result of all this is a caste-like underclass with little or no route to legal status, social integration, or social mobility.

Given the high numbers of long-term unauthorized immigrants, what has the United States done to attempt to address the situation? The government's response to the high numbers of unauthorized immigration has exclusively focused on enforcement. Enforcement efforts have included erecting miles of fencing along the U.S.-Mexico border and adding agents to patrol the physical borders and points of entry. Immigration laws have been amended to increase the grounds for deporting immigrants. Immigration authorities have stepped up internal deportation initiatives, such as increasing workplace raids, and in some circumstances providing for expedited removal procedures.

In "Five Myths About Immigration" (2005), the sociologist Douglas S. Massey argues that, for the most part, these enforcement policies have failed to deter ingress of new immigrants, but meanwhile have served to prevent those already present from returning home. Border enforcement in particular has also increased the costs of unauthorized immigration, causing markets for human trafficking to soar and forcing unauthorized immigrants to cross the border in more dangerous places. This has significantly increased the number of deaths of potential unauthorized immigrants.

It is true that from 2007 to 2009, the number of unauthorized immigrants fell by one million. However, the Migration Policy Institute (MPI) and many other experts attribute this decline to the recent economic recession, rather than to increased effectiveness of enforcement efforts (Chishti & Bergeron, 2010). They point to the fact that with the exception of enforcement efforts, everything else regarding the immigration system has remained largely unchanged, demonstrating that an enforcement-only approach has caused the number of unauthorized immigrants to increase by trapping those in the United States who otherwise would have returned to their countries (see, e.g., Papademetriou, 2005).

Opponents of a legalization program claim enforcement has been effective in reducing the number of unauthorized immigrants in the United States, particularly with respect to unauthorized immigrants who have also violated criminal laws. (Strictly speaking, a violation of an immigration law is not automatically a criminal law violation.) Yet, even after Immigration and Customs Enforcement (ICE) made removing criminal immigrants a high priority, it was only able to remove 89,406 criminal immigrants in 2005—only a small percentage of removable immigrants in custody or probation/criminal parole in the country at any given time.

The inadequacies of the current immigration system can be felt most on the state and local level. The large number of unauthorized immigrants in local communities has caused tensions among U.S. citizens and authorized immigrants on the one hand, and unauthorized immigrants on the other. For instance, because unauthorized immigrants cannot obtain health insurance, they do not go to primary care physicians for medical care, relying instead on hospital emergency rooms for treatment. This increases emergency room wait times and the cost of hospital medical care for all. The impact of the large number of unauthorized immigrants can also be felt in financially strapped public school systems, which the children of unauthorized immigrants are permitted to attend. U.S. citizens and authorized immigrants claim to be competing with unauthorized immigrants for jobs and housing, amid stereotypes about and xenophobic fears of unauthorized immigrants. These concerns and financial constraints, along with the high number of unauthorized immigrants currently present in the United States, illustrate the inadequacies of the current immigration system and the ineffective nature of enforcement efforts.

Given these inadequacies, and in an effort to "save" local communities from what is viewed as the "unauthorized immigrant problem," states and localities have undertaken to write their own laws to deal with unauthorized immigrants. It is important to note the distinction between laws governing the immigration status of an individual—which concern who may enter and stay, and who must leave the United States—and laws governing the behavior of immigrants (authorized and unauthorized) in the United States. The former can be termed "immigration laws"; the latter, "immigrant laws." For instance, immigrant laws seek to regulate the housing, jobs, and public benefits of people based on whether they are unauthorized or authorized immigrants.

The result of these state and local initiatives is an uneven patchwork of state and local laws attempting to deal with unauthorized immigrants; some of these laws have led to the violation of the constitutional right to privacy of valid visa holders, legal permanent residents (LPRs), and even naturalized and birthright citizens who "look unauthorized." For example, the controversial ordinance enacted in Hazelton, Pennsylvania, revoked permits and licenses for businesses that employed unauthorized workers, fined landlords who rented to unauthorized immigrants, and made English the city's official language. The effect was displacement of unauthorized immigrants, an increase in discrimination and xenophobia, and a backlash against a large number of authorized immigrants and U.S. citizens, particularly Hispanics.

Many believe that the net result of such laws has been increased racial profiling, decreased immigrant societal integration, and the increased security concerns that go with pushing huge numbers of people even further underground. For example, in the face of Arizona's anti-immigrant law S.B. 1070, unauthorized immigrants are reluctant to send their children to public school, if not utterly opposed to doing so (Waslin, 2012). Their children are thus deprived an opportunity for social mobility, magnifying the caste-like effects of the federal immigration laws. Unauthorized immigrants in communities with such anti-immigrant laws are even less likely to seek health care, even when there is true medical need (Waslin, 2012). Advocates argue this increases the risk of public health epidemics for all. Similarly, many legalization advocates contend such anti-immigrant laws have made unauthorized immigrants even less likely to trust the police or report crimes—further jeopardizing public safety for all. In the long run, this would decrease the potential for the social integration of unauthorized immigrants (as well as those perceived to be unauthorized immigrants, regardless of their true immigration or citizenship status).

The ineffective immigration regime has also sparked state and local law enforcement officers to enter agreements with the federal government to enforce the federal immigration laws, pursuant to Section 287(g) of the Immigration and Nationality Act (INA). The result is inconsistent enforcement of the country's immigration laws and movement of unauthorized immigrants to less anti-immigrant states—movement that is contrary to natural migration patterns.

An earned legalization program is absolutely essential for dealing with the unauthorized population in a fair and logical way, while providing solutions for many of the aforementioned problems with the current immigration system.

DEFINING A LEGALIZATION PROGRAM

A legalization program is one component of a multipronged approach to improving the nation's immigration system to more effectively and efficiently address the reality of current immigration trends and the forces behind them. The existing immigration system is based on fundamental misunderstandings of natural migration patterns and the forces that cause immigration. It amounts to a "Band-Aid approach"—attempting to temporarily treat only the symptoms (e.g., large numbers of unauthorized immigrants in the United States), rather than the underlying causes of those symptoms (e.g., what motivates unauthorized immigrants to come to and stay in the United States)—and inevitably fails to accomplish even that.

It is important to note from the outset that there is no singular "legalization" program. Even among legalization proponents, there is great debate regarding the form such a program should take. This essay aims to provide an overview of the basic considerations and contours such proposed legalization programs could take.

Any legalization program is designed to accomplish multiple goals. It seeks to substantially shrink the large unauthorized immigrant population. As discussed further below, this is done to be fair to unauthorized immigrants who are stuck in limbo: physically present in the United States for more than a temporary stay, but mired in the tangled web of immigration laws and policies that offer no path to legal status. Legalization is also designed to help the government more efficiently and effectively use its limited resources to identify and track unauthorized immigrants. This enables the government to focus its deportation efforts on individuals who represent true threats to the nation's security, such as those with serious criminal histories. To garner bipartisan support and to appease those who wish to avoid rewarding rule-breaking, all earned legalization programs impose prospective requirements on participants to make them "earn" permanent status. Finally, all legalization programs seek to deter further unauthorized immigration, prevent the regeneration of the unauthorized population, and ensure maximum societal integration for participants.

The following is a description of the major considerations evaluated when designing a legalization program.

Consideration 1: Partial versus complete legalization. One initial point of debate by legalization proponents is whether such a program should be complete or partial. Complete legalization programs aim to include as many unauthorized immigrants as possible. Partial legalization programs target a specific segment of the unauthorized population. While partial legalization programs are cheaper and more easily garner political support, they also fail to provide more long-term, far-reaching solutions.

To illustrate this point, it is helpful to describe the best-known proposed partial legalization program, the Development, Relief, and Education for Alien Minors (DREAM) Act. The DREAM Act evolved from legislation first introduced by Senators Orrin Hatch (R-UT) and Richard Durbin (D-IL) in 2001. The DREAM Act is meant to serve as an acknowledgement that the children of unauthorized immigrants were brought here when they were very young, through no fault of their own, have spent essentially their entire lives in the United States, and have become "Americans" for all practical purposes. The DREAM Act does not provide outright permanent legal status to potential beneficiaries. Instead, candidates who meet the eligibility criteria can apply for a 6-year conditional residency status. They can then apply for legal permanent resident status if they meet additional requirements, including postsecondary education or military service. To be eligible for the DREAM Act, upon the law's enactment, an individual must be under age 35, have entered the United States prior to turning 16 years old, have at least 5 years of continuous physical presence in the United States, and have obtained a U.S. high school diploma or GED. After satisfying these criteria, participants can apply for conditional resident status. After 6 years of conditional status, they can then apply for full legal permanent resident status, as long as they can demonstrate they completed 2 years of college, vocational training, or military service, and have had "good moral character" during conditional status (e.g., no serious crimes, no lies to immigration applications, and paid-up on taxes).

This is a partial legalization program, because, as estimated by the Migration Policy Institute (MPI), only 2.1 million unauthorized youth and young adults would be eligible to apply for legal status under the DREAM Act. Further, historical trends dictate postsecondary education requirements would block eligible conditional residents from gaining permanent status (Batalova & McHugh, 2010). In the end, MPI estimates only 38 percent of potential beneficiaries—or 825,000 people of the nearly 11 million unauthorized immigrants in the United States—would obtain permanent legal status through the DREAM Act.

In weighing complete versus partial incorporation, many legalization proponents desire partial legalization programs, because at least it helps a portion of the unauthorized immigrant population and thus represents a step in the right direction. Yet a partial legalization program would be insufficient to others, on grounds that it does not systematically address the huge number of unauthorized immigrants, by failing to incorporate the vast majority of unauthorized immigrants.

Consideration 2: "One-shot" versus "rolling" legalizations. There is also debate as to whether any legalization should be a one-time occurrence ("one-shot" legalization), or should occur repeatedly on a rolling basis. Although subject to debate, the consensus among legalization advocates seems to be that an earned legalization program should be a one-shot program. Like the 1986 Immigration Reform and Control Act (IRCA), an earned legalization program would likely be designed to cover a larger potential group of unauthorized immigrants, and it could impose requirements and spread costs to participants over a period of time to make it more affordable for unauthorized immigrants and truly reduce the unauthorized immigrant population. Although a rolling program would be cheaper and would not require nearly as much administrative costs and resources, in the long run, having repeated, rolling-basis legalizations could become very expensive, and it runs the risk of encouraging increased unauthorized immigration. As a practical matter, a one-shot program is more likely to muster the requisite political support for enactment than would repeated, rolling legalizations.

Consideration 3: What benefits will a legalization program confer? Closely linked with the debate about whether a legalization program should occur repeatedly or only once, is the ongoing controversy about whether benefits of a legalization program should be provided at once or in phases. In *Immigration Legalization in the United States and the European Union* (2010), Marc R. Rosenblum of the MPI outlines a number of important policy concepts. Under a one-stage benefits system, as soon as the individual fills out the application and demonstrates that he or she meets the requirements for legalization (what those requirements should be is discussed below), some form of temporary legalized status will be conferred. As to what the temporary status should be, suggestions include the following: (1) strictly temporary status with no possibility of renewal or adjustment to permanent status, (2) a temporary visa with multiple opportunities for renewal, (3) a temporary visa with the possibility to adjust to LPR status after meeting prospective requirements, and (4) granting permanent resident status outright to qualifying unauthorized immigrants. Disputes also ensue regarding the proposed duration of any such temporary visa status, with suggestions spanning from 2 to 5 years. Option 3 from the list above is the most commonly discussed, though advocates vary widely regarding the exact prospective requirements for adjustment to permanent status.

An "earned legalization" program is a phased system. Stage one is an initial registration period during which unauthorized immigrants demonstrate they meet the qualifications to receive temporary status. Stage two takes place during the immigrants' time as temporary residents. It involves meeting a set of prospective requirements in order to qualify for adjustment to LPR status. Under many potential phased programs, if the temporary status expires before the immigrants have met the requirements for adjusting to permanent status, the temporary visa can be renewed for another short term of years.

The MPI and many other scholars (though not all) argue a phased system is preferable to bestowing all benefits at once. An initial registration period would allow qualified unauthorized immigrants to receive temporary legal status to protect them from deportation and provide them with authorization to work and travel. With temporary status, they could then work toward the requirements needed for adjustment to LPR status.

This approach would arguably benefit everyone. The government could impose fines or fees upon unauthorized immigrants who seek to participate in the legalization program. This would allow the government to offset the administrative costs involved while spreading costs to participants over a longer period of time, which would ensure as many unauthorized immigrants as possible are not precluded from participation due to fines and fees.

An earned legalization program with easy-to-satisfy eligibility requirements for the first phase and stricter requirements for permanent legal status would reach the maximum number of unauthorized immigrants and ensure the greatest chance of their societal integration upon completion of the program. Because unauthorized immigrants would voluntarily opt into a system with less stringent initial requirements to gain some form of status, such an earned legalization program would be less expensive to administer. Once they begin participating, unauthorized immigrants would have a strong incentive to satisfy the prospective requirements for permanent status and to not allow their temporary status to lapse, because the government would have their information and could more easily deport them. Thus, an earned legalization regime is self-enforcing.

Such earned legalization programs are more expensive and much more burdensome administratively than programs that grant only temporary status. However, temporary visas are economically inefficient, because they lack the stability and security immigrants need to make long-term investments in business opportunities, homeownership, community ties, education, and other social and economic investments that would further strengthen the country and encourage immigrant societal integration. Moreover, without the possibility of more long-term status, employers are also less likely to invest in immigrant workers.

For these reasons, in the long run, temporary visas alone are not as cost-effective as a phased system that provides a path to earning permanent status.

Consideration 4: Retrospective qualifications versus prospective ("earned") requirements. Advocates also debate the related issue of whether a legalization program should consist of retrospective qualifications in order to participate, prospective requirements, or a combination of both. Retrospective requirements might include demonstrating entry into the United States before a certain date and a certain period of continuous physical presence since entering, proof of a certain period of work history in the United States, and proof of having paid taxes for each year in the country. There is debate among advocates about what those prospective requirements would look like, but they would likely include demonstrating a certain period of continuous physical presence in the country and a specified period of work history, contributions to the United States, English language facility and knowledge of U.S. civics, and payment of fines and application fees (Rosenblum, 2010).

Any legalization program that requires participants to meet prospective requirements is essentially an earned legalization program. Satisfying those prospective requirements enhances the chances for immigrant integration into society while at the same time imposing a kind of penalty on previously unauthorized immigrants, such that granting them permanent status seems fair in spite of their unauthorized entry or overstay.

A legalization program that focuses on prospective requirements is preferable to a totally retrospective qualification-based system. For one thing, prospective requirements make it possible to track participants who were previously living "off the radar." During the initial registration phase of a phased system, unauthorized immigrants would have to submit to biometric testing such as fingerprinting to verify their identity. Second, retrospective requirements are less reliable, because they rely on historical documents, affidavits from landlords and employers, and sworn statements from unauthorized immigrants. This precludes many unauthorized immigrants from participating because they have gone out of their way to avoid creating a paper trail of their residence and work histories, which could lead to detection; in fact, aggressive enforcement efforts in the last 6 years have driven many unauthorized immigrants even further underground (Rosenblum, Capps, & Yi-Ying Lin, 2011). Because of reliance on such documents to prove past facts, retrospective-based programs breed fraud. For instance, MPI estimates indicate that as much as 73 percent of all applications submitted under IRCA were fraudulent (Papademetriou, 2005).

In addition, a prospective system is more beneficial than a retrospective system, because prospective requirements are generally easier for officials to check (Rosenblum, 2010). It would be much easier and cheaper, therefore, to enforce a prospective-based system. For instance, if the prospective requirements are that participating immigrants pass an English language exam and pay required fines and fees, immigrants have either done these things or have not. The official's job in evaluating the eligibility for adjustment to permanent status is easy in that regard.

Finally, a system with prospective requirements presents an opportunity to impose fines for any immigration law violations in the first place, as well as fees for the various stages of the earned legalization process. Essentially, a prospective-based earned legalization program provides the government with an opportunity to generate revenue that could be used to help support the administrative functions necessary to operate the legalization program.

There is no consensus as to the requirements an earned legalization program should contain. As a composite, earned legalization programs that emphasize prospective requirements, but that also contain *prerequisite qualifications* for participation in the initial phase, tend to include the following qualifications. The immigrant must (1) have entered the United States by a certain cut-off date (though the actual cut-off date is hotly debated); (2) have remained continuously physically present in the United States for the requisite length of time (though what that time period is varies greatly); (3) have demonstrated a certain number of years of employment history (again, that number varies widely); and (4) not have committed any serious crimes (though what crimes will preclude participation also differs, depending on the source).

After that initial phase of an earned legalization, participants would have to demonstrate an array of prospective requirements to qualify for permanent legal immigration status, including the following:

- *Good moral character.* First, immigrants must demonstrate good moral character. However, there is debate as to whether the period of good moral character would be only the period of the conditional status or longer. Good moral character refers to two essential requirements: lack of a serious criminal record (commission of a serious crime, or even multiple lesser crimes could preclude adjusting to permanent status, and perhaps even deportation); and having paid taxes for the requisite period of good moral character, along with any back taxes owed.

- *English.* Many proposed legalization programs require that immigrants demonstrate basic English language proficiency by passing an English exam.

- *Employment.* Many call for an employment requirement, that participants prove a certain number of years of prior employment, say the past 2 to 3 years prior to applying for legalization, and that they remain employed during the conditional status period, say 6 years (or however long that period ends up being depending on the proposal considered).

- *Civics test.* Still others would also require that immigrants pass a basic American history and civics exam (to mimic the requirements needed to become a U.S. citizen).

- *Valid temporary status.* Every program would require that immigrants stay in valid conditional or temporary status for a certain number of years before being eligible to apply for adjustment to permanent status. However, the number of years of such a program varies greatly among proposals.

- *Fine and fees.* Many proposed earned legalization programs would also impose both fines and fees on participants, with the fines to penalize them for violating the immigration laws and the fees to cover the costs of administering the program.

- Though not a qualification or requirement, it is important to note that many of the proposed bills would increase enforcement efforts to balance out the legislation in an attempt to garner bipartisan support to raise the probability of the legislation actually being enacted. However, that is a function of politics, rather than a necessary component to any immigration reform effort generally, or to an earned legalization program specifically.

MORAL JUSTIFICATIONS FOR A LEGALIZATION PROGRAM FOR UNAUTHORIZED IMMIGRANTS

Aside from the debates over the specific features any regularization program might have, there is debate about whether unauthorized immigrants have a moral right to legal immigration status in this country. Many scholars, such as Linda Bosniak, argue that unauthorized immigrants have such a moral right. At one end of the spectrum are those who contend the United States must provide open borders once someone is present within the jurisdiction of the United States. That is, some maintain the position that controlling borders at the edges of the country is legitimate, but once someone is present inside those borders, and thus subject to the jurisdiction of the United States, internal borders are illegitimate. This is because, as a liberal democracy, the United States owes basic civil and human rights to everyone within its borders regardless of immigration status. For example, immigration status aside, the United States has a moral duty to provide every person within its jurisdiction personal safety and safety of their property, as well as protection from acts of violence and oppressive working conditions (Bosniak, 2010).

Such scholars argue it is morally abhorrent to create a system in which unauthorized immigrants come to the United States and are here to stay due to a variety of factors, yet not offer such individuals even a pathway to legalize their immigration status. They contend this is morally wrong because it creates a large caste-like underclass of people with no way of exercising their civil rights due to constant fear of deportation, while the United States profits from the labor of such individuals. On this basis, such scholars further argue "open borders" is the only way to truly ensure the unauthorized immigrants are able to access their civil and human rights, because it is the only way to remove the constantly looming threat of deportation that impedes the exercise of those rights. They argue that unauthorized immigrants have a moral right to a pathway to legalized status, and that the U.S. government has a corresponding moral obligation to offer such an opportunity to them (Bosniak, 2010).

Other scholars, such as Joseph Carens (though best known for his position that borders of liberal states themselves need critique), have recently contended that even if it is assumed for the sake of argument—in order to garner support for legalization in the practical political climate in which the United States currently finds itself—that the government has a moral right to control its borders and decide who can stay and who must leave, unauthorized immigrants still have a moral justification for a legalization program (Carens, 2010). They derive this moral right by living in the United States continuously for a long enough period of time, where the length of their presence serves as a proxy for their social membership and ties to the community. Relying on physical presence as a proxy for social ties, as opposed to evaluating social membership itself, is preferable, because allowing officials the discretion to determine actual ties leaves too much room for discrimination (Ngai, 2010). Once unauthorized immigrants develop such ties, it would be immoral to uproot them from the lives they have established here. At that point, as Carens argues, their *de facto* social membership should be officially recognized by *de jure* legal immigration status.

All proponents of unauthorized immigrants' moral claim to regularize their status agree that unauthorized immigrants are entitled to certain human and civil rights while in the United States. Here's the rub: If the government has a moral and legal right to deport unauthorized immigrants (at least until they meet the requisite criteria to trigger their claim to regularize their immigration status), unauthorized immigrants will never be able exercise those human and civil rights, less they risk deportation (Bosniak, 2010). Theoretically, a legal firewall could be developed such that unauthorized immigrants could exercise their rights without fear that they would be indirectly telegraphing their information to the deportation authorities. Such firewalls are practically in place in a number of contexts, such as when police departments specifically state they will not share information to the immigration authorities about individuals who report crimes. Yet even with such firewalls in place, immigrants are still highly reluctant to exercise their rights. With little more than a promise from one part of the government not to report them to another part of the government, many unauthorized immigrants may still feel the risk of exposure and deportation is still too great to exercise their rights.

Another moral justification for earned legalization of unauthorized immigrants is premised upon their contributions to the country instead of the length of time they have been present in the country. Advocates of this school of thought argue individuals may have been present for ages without contributing anything to the country and without forming any community ties, whereas others dig in and try to improve their communities right away.

Ultimately, whatever their differences, most scholars agree on the same point: many, if not all, unauthorized immigrants have a moral right to a pathway to legal status that should be recognized by implementing an earned legalization program.

PRAGMATIC JUSTIFICATIONS FOR A LEGALIZATION PROGRAM FOR UNAUTHORIZED IMMIGRANTS

In addition to the moral justifications for a legalization program for unauthorized immigrants, there are also several pragmatic reasons to support such a program. First and foremost, a legalization program will help substantially reduce the unauthorized immigrant population in a way that is fair to unauthorized immigrants, while also making the entire immigration system more manageable.

Economic benefits. A legalization program is a more cost-effective way to reduce the unauthorized population in the United States when compared to the cost of identifying, detaining, and removing people on an individual basis, which often has a limited impact on the overall system. As Bill Ong Hing and Douglas Massey have argued on numerous occasions, the current immigration system fails to account for the natural movement of labor between the United States and Mexico. For instance, between 1965 and 1976, Congress ended a 22-year-old temporary worker agreement with Mexico, enacted new caps on immigrants from the Western Hemisphere, and imposed country-specific quotas on legal immigration. This pulled out the carpet from the 450,000 annual guest worker visas and unlimited residence visas available to Mexico. These policies replaced decades of 2- to 3-year cycles of Mexican laborers coming to the United States and returning to Mexico, leaving merely 20,000 visas for permanent residence available to Mexico and eliminating Mexican guest worker availability. Nothing since that time, including IRCA, has done anything to recognize the reality that the same demand for labor and movement of labor from Mexico continued. The only thing that changed was the legal status of such workers. Given these realities of supply and demand for Mexican laborers in this country, enforcement alone is insufficient to staunch the constant flow of unauthorized immigrants. In the 2010 article, *Babies R' Us: Challenges to Birthright Citizenship Are Just a Distraction,* Hing further argues the "enforcement-only" approach has been the sole focus of policymakers since 1986. It has cost billions of dollars and resulted in increased deaths as people try to surreptitiously cross the border in even more dangerous ways and locations. It has also increased human smuggling and document fraud, separated families, and filled detention facilities to capacity. The result? Nearly 11 million unauthorized immigrants are still in the United States.

In terms of the labor market, whereas intensified enforcement efforts also push unauthorized immigrants further underground, MPI argues an earned legalization program would encourage unauthorized immigrants to switch from the informal to formal economic markets in order to satisfy any employment-based requirements for an earned legalization program (Rosenblum, 2010). This switch would increase tax revenues and wages, which in turn would stimulate the economy—thereby benefiting unauthorized and authorized immigrants, as well as U.S. citizens. By reducing the informal economy, legalization would also help to eliminate unsafe and unfair working conditions. Legalization, in short, would level the playing field for all workers. It would also allow the government to more easily identify and punish employers who violate the nation's labor laws.

An earned legalization program would also improve the tax and public benefits systems. Approximately 5 percent of the U.S. workforce in 2010 comprised unauthorized immigrants. The Brookings Institute reported in 2010 that although most unauthorized immigrants cannot benefit from the Social Security system, a comparatively high number of unauthorized immigrants (1) apply for Individual Taxpayer Identification Numbers (ITINs) and (2) pay taxes and contribute to the Social Security system through wage withholdings. Brookings explains that even unauthorized immigrants would contribute to such official systems if the threat of deportation were removed. This suggests that legalization would boost the U.S. economy by encouraging increased tax, social security, and other monetary contributions from an even greater number of unauthorized immigrants. Douglas Massey's (2005) research has returned similar findings:

> While 66 percent of Mexican immigrants report the withholding of Social Security taxes from their paychecks and 62 percent say that employers withhold income taxes, only 10 percent say they have ever sent a child to U.S. public schools, 7 percent indicate they have received Supplemental Security Income, and 5 percent or less report ever using food stamps, welfare, or unemployment compensation.

Not only do unauthorized immigrants contribute to the nation's public benefits systems, they are strictly prohibited from benefiting from many of those systems. In a series of 1996 laws, the government barred unauthorized immigrants from receiving Social Security, limited their eligibility for educational benefits, and made public assistance available only to U.S. citizens. Those laws even precluded legal immigrants from receiving food stamps or Supplemental Security Income (SSI), and they restricted legal immigrants from receiving certain federal public benefits for at least 5 years after admission to the country. Studies indicate that unauthorized immigrants use public services at far lower rates than authorized immigrants.

Legalization would also help produce safer working conditions and fairer wages for U.S. citizens, authorized immigrants, and for the benefited immigrants themselves. Presently, employers take advantage of unauthorized immigrants for low-skilled and unskilled labor jobs. Granting immigration status to those who have earned legalization would mean more people could join authorized immigrants and U.S. citizens in unions to fight for fairer wages and better working conditions for all (Massey, 2005).

Safety and national security. A legalization program would also significantly enhance national security and reduce crime. As mentioned above, with nearly 11 million unauthorized immigrants in the United States without a pathway to legal status, the present regime has created a large caste-like population, marginalized in many respects from the rest of society. Such marginalization is detrimental not only for unauthorized immigrants themselves but also for the rest of the nation.

According to Massey (2005), unauthorized immigrants live in a daily stalemate of economic strife and political disenfranchisement. They avoid any official institutions, such as health-care providers and schools, out of fear of detection, detention, and, ultimately, deportation. At any moment, their families could be ripped apart by deportation. They have no access to health care, and thus often avoid medical attention even when they are in dire need of it. When they do seek medical care, they usually rely on hospital emergency rooms rather than on primary care physicians. This increases the wait times and costs of emergency medical attention for all, and it poses public health risks. The constant threat of deportation paralyzes many unauthorized immigrants with such fear that they refuse to send their children to public schools, despite the rights of such children to receive a public education—as the Supreme Court decided in *Plyler v. Doe* (1982). This has a ripple effect of hindering the social mobility of such children, further contributing to the caste-like system brought about by the immigration regime, which takes its toll on everyone in the United States, as discussed above.

Further, unauthorized children who grow up in the United States and attend school here will eventually hit a ceiling on their social mobility. They are unable to receive federal tuition assistance or work authorization due to their lack of immigration status.

For these reasons, Massey notes, "if U.S. officials had set out to intentionally create a new underclass, they could hardly have done a better job" (Massey, 2005). Such an underclass is deterred from investing in, participating in, and integrating into the rest of society. This poses safety issues for everyone, because it prevents unauthorized immigrants from reporting information about crime to the police out of fear they will be reported.

A legalization program could help resolve many of these problems and would increase the safety of unauthorized immigrants and the rest of the nation. First, in an earned legalization program with an initial registration period, most of the unauthorized population would voluntarily report to immigration authorities. They would be properly tracked by biometrics to confirm their identities. This would reduce the chance of fraud and would help the government identify and monitor large numbers of unauthorized immigrants presently living off the radar. The government could then concentrate on true threats to the nation's safety, including unauthorized immigrants who have committed serious crimes (Kerwin & Laglagaron, 2010).

Legalization would also reduce crime, by providing the guarantee of secure legal status unauthorized immigrants need to feel comfortable reporting crimes. An earned legalization program would also bolster national security by permitting more talented young immigrant men and women who are currently unauthorized to join the military. Finally, an earned legalization program would enable the government to impose fines and fees on the unauthorized population. This would help defray the costs of administering a legalization program, while making immigrants so invested that they are less likely to abandon the program and go back into hiding.

CONCLUSION

This essay demonstrates that legalization programs are extremely controversial. There are many who oppose any form of legalization, because it purportedly would reward rule-breaking and encourage future unauthorized immigration. Others advocate for a legalization program, because it is the morally right thing to do to be fair to unauthorized immigrants currently stuck in a stalemate with no route to legal status. There are others who support legalization for unauthorized immigrants because (apart from what is best for unauthorized immigrants), pragmatically speaking, a legalization program will strengthen the U.S. economy and increase the nation's safety.

Even among those who support a legalization program for unauthorized immigrants, there is wide debate about the qualifications and requirements, and about the form such a program should take. These include relevant entry dates, length of continuous physical presence and employment history, and whether immigrants would have to demonstrate English language proficiency and pay some amount of fines to ultimately adjust to permanent status.

Despite the debates, most experts agree on one thing: the current immigration system is not operating in the most logical, efficient, or fair manner. Many of its aspects are nearly impossible to enforce. This has contributed to the number of unauthorized immigrants living in the United States. Therefore, legalization is necessary, and it should be viewed as one of many tools in a multipronged approach for comprehensive immigration reform.

References and Further Reading

Akers Chacon, J., & Davis, M. (2006). *No one is illegal: Fighting racism and state violence on the U.S.-Mexico border.* Chicago, IL: Haymarket Books.

Batalova, J., & McHugh, M. (July 2010). *Dream vs. reality: An analysis of potential DREAM Act beneficiaries.* Migration Policy Institute. Retrieved from http://www.migrationpolicy.org/pubs/DREAM-Insight-July2010.pdf

Bosniak, L. (2010). Forum response to Joseph Carens' *Immigrants and the right to stay.* Cambridge, MA: MIT Press.

Bosniak, L. S. (2007). The Undocumented immigrant: Contending policy approaches. In C. M. Swain (Ed.), *Debating immigration* (pp. 93–94). New York, NY: Cambridge University Press.

Camarota, S. A. (2007). Immigrant employment gains and native losses. In C. M. Swain (Ed.), *Debating immigration* (pp. 39–40). New York, NY: Cambridge University Press.

Camarota, S. A. (2010). *Immigration and economic stagnation: An examination of trends 2000 to 2010.* Center for Immigration Studies. Retrieved August 1, 2011 from http://www.cis.org/highest-decade

Camarota, S. A., & Jensenius, K. (2009). *A shifting tide: Recent trends in the illegal immigrant population.* Retrieved from http://cis.org/IllegalImmigration-ShiftingTide

Carens, J. (2005). On belonging: What we owe people who stay. *Boston Review,* Summer 2005. Retrieved from http://bostonreview.net/BR30.3/carens.php

Carens, J. (2010). *Immigrants and the right to stay.* Cambridge, MA: MIT Press.

Chishti, M., & Bergeron, C. (2010). *Increasing evidence that recession has caused number of unauthorized immigrants in U.S. to drop.* Migration Policy Institute. Retrieved from http://www.migrationinformation.org/USFocus/display.cfm?ID=774

Hing, B. O. (2010, August 4). *Babies r' us: Challenges to birthright citizenship are just a distraction.* Retrieved from http://www.slate.com/articles/news_and_politics/politics/2010/08/babies_r_us.html

Hing, B. O. (2011, July 12). Control the border: Invest in Mexico. *Huffington Post* blog post. Retrieved from http://www.huffingtonpost.com/bill-ong-hing/invest-in-mexico-b_896473.html

Hoefer, M., Rytina, N., & Baker, B. C. (2010). *Estimates of the unauthorized immigrant population residing in the United States: January 2010* (Population Estimate Report dated Feb. 2011). Department of Homeland Security, Office of Immigration Statistics. Retrieved from http://www.dhs.gov/xlibrary/assets/statistics/publications/lpr_fr_2010.pdf

Kerwin, D. M., & Laglagaron, L. (2010). *Structuring and implementing an immigrant legalization program: Registration as the first step.* Migration Policy Institute policy brief. Retrieved from http://www.migrationpolicy.org/pubs/legalization-registration.pdf

Lakoff, G., & Ferguson, S. (2006, May 22). *The framing of immigration.* Retrieved from http://buzzflash.com/contributors/06/05/con06208.html

Levinson, A. (2005). *Migration fundamentals: Why countries continue to consider regularization.* Retrieved from http://www.migrationinformation.org/Feature/display.cfm?ID=330

Massey, D. S. (2005). Five myths about immigration: Common misconceptions underlying U.S. border-enforcement policy. *Immigration Daily.* Retrieved from http://www.ilw.com/articles/2005,1207-massey.shtm

Massey, D. S. (2007). Borderline madness: America's counterproductive immigration policy. In C. M. Swain (Ed.), *Debating immigration* (pp. 136–138). New York, NY: Cambridge University Press.

Massey, D. S. (2010). Forum response to Joseph Carens' *Immigrants and the right to stay.* Cambridge, MA: MIT Press.

Ngai, M. M. (2010). Forum response to Joseph Carens' *Immigrants and the right to stay.* Cambridge, MA: MIT Press.

Papademetriou, D. G. (2005). *The regularization option in managing illegal migration more effectively: A comparative perspective.* Migration Policy Institute. Retrieved from http://www.migrationpolicy.org/pubs/PolicyBrief_No4_Sept05.pdf

Papademetriou, D. G. (2005, September). *National earned regularization program: The credit system.* Migration Policy Institute. Retrieved from http://www.migrationpolicy.org/pubs/PolicyBrief_No4_Sept05.pdf

Passel, J., & Cohn, D. (2011). *Unauthorized immigrant population: National and state trends, 2010.* Pew Hispanic Center. Retrieved from http://www.pewhispanic.org/2011/02/01/unauthorized-immigrant-population-brnational-and-state-trends-2010

Rosenblum, M. R. (2010). *Immigration legalization in the United States and the European Union: Policy goals and program design.* Migration Policy Institute. Retrieved from http://www.migrationpolicy.org/pubs/legalization-policydesign.pdf

Rosenblum, M. R., Capps, R., & Yi-Ying Lin, S. (2011). *Earned legalization: Effects of proposed requirements on unauthorized men, women, and children.* Migration Policy Institute. Retrieved from http://www.migrationpolicy.org/pubs/legalization-requirements.pdf

Waslin, M. (2012, February 6). *New report examines dire consequences of "attrition through enforcement" immigration strategy.* Retrieved from http://immigrationimpact.com/2012/02/06/new-report-examines-dire-consequences-of-attrition-through-enforcement-immigration-strategy

Weissbrodt, D., & Danielson, L. (2005). *Immigration law and procedure in a nutshell* (5th ed.). St. Paul, MN: Thomson/West.

Which is acceptable: "Undocumented" vs. "illegal" immigrant? Radio show broadcast, on *Tell Me More.* (2010, January 7). National Public Radio. Retrieved from http://www.npr.org/templates/story/story.php?storyId=122314131

Wong, C. (2006). *Lobbying for inclusion: Rights politics and the making of immigration policy.* Palo Alto, CA: Stanford University Press.

Wroe, A. (2008). *The Republican Party and immigration politics: From Proposition 187 to George W. Bush.* New York, NY: Palgrave Macmillan.

Yen, H. (Associated Press). (2011, February 1). *Number of illegal immigrants in U.S. steady at 11.2m.* Retrieved from http://www.cnsnews.com/news/article/number-illegal-immigrants-us-steady-112m

Andrew D. Linenberg

COUNTERPOINT

As noted previously, it has been estimated that there are at least 10.8 million unauthorized immigrants presently in the United States. Increased efforts to enforce the nation's immigration laws have proven successful in helping to reduce the number of unauthorized immigrants. However, experts agree such enforcement efforts alone are insufficient to deal with the unauthorized population. The question, therefore, becomes: How can the United States improve the current immigration system, while reducing the unauthorized population in a way that is fair to everyone and ensures national security? Many scholars and politicians believe implementing a legalization program is the answer. Any legalization program (sometimes also referred to as an "amnesty" or "regularization" program) would provide temporary legal immigration status, and a pathway to permanent legalized status, to those who meet specific requirements.

Despite the clamoring by many for some form of regularization, such a program will do more harm than good. This Counterpoint essay first discusses how current enforcement practices have helped to reduce the unauthorized immigrant population, and it then sketches a composite earned legalization program, highlighting the deficiencies and structural objections to any such program. The essay goes on to explain the moral objections and pragmatic consequences of an earned legalization program, and to offer alternatives to earned legalization to deal with the current unauthorized immigration population.

ENFORCEMENT INITIATIVES

The number of unauthorized immigrants in the United States has recently begun to decline. In March 2010, the U.S. Department of Homeland Security (DHS) estimated there were approximately 10.8 million unauthorized immigrants in the United States. DHS noted in March 2010 that this number was down from the all-time high of 11.8 million unauthorized immigrants in the country in January 2007. However, the unauthorized population rose overall by 27 percent from 2000 through 2010 (Hoefer, Rytina, & Baker, 2010). These figures demonstrate there is still a huge unauthorized immigrant population in the United States, which, by and large, is here to stay.

According to a July 2009 report by the Center for Immigration Studies (CIS), although the recession and unemployment rate marginally helped reduce the unauthorized immigrant population, increased immigration enforcement efforts had a substantial impact on that population. One reason for this conclusion is that as the number of Border Patrol agents doubled between 2007 and 2009 and a substantial portion of fencing was added along the U.S.-Mexico border, the number of unauthorized immigrants decreased by about one-third. During the same time frame, the number of unauthorized immigrants returning home more than doubled (compared to return migration between 2000 and 2009). In fact, enforcement efforts contributed to a decline in the number of unauthorized immigrants even before the rise in the rate of unemployment in this population (Camarota & Jensenius, 2009).

Immigration enforcement initiatives are not limited to increased border agents and fencing. Rather, enforcement occurs in the nation's interior as well. For example, in recent years, efforts have focused on enhancing the effectiveness of the nation's employer sanctions provisions. E-Verify—a voluntary program that allows employers to check if their employees are authorized to work in the United States—now covers over 1 in every 10 newly hired employees in the United States. CIS noted in 2009 that the program doubled in size between 2007 and 2008. Further, Immigration and Customs Enforcement (ICE), the agency responsible for enforcing the immigration laws and capturing violators, has increased worksite raids. Since 2005, those efforts resulted in a fivefold increase in the number of criminal and administrative (e.g., immigration law violation) arrests (Camarota & Jensenius, 2009).

In addition to the growing effectiveness of workplace enforcement efforts, legislatures have attempted to respond to the number of unauthorized immigrants still in the United States. The federal government has considered a vast number of legislative proposals related to immigration in the past decade. These proposals have included the Comprehensive Immigration Reform for America's Security and Prosperity Act of 2009, Secure America and Orderly Immigration Act of 2005, Comprehensive Enforcement and Immigration Reform Act of 2005, and the REAL GUEST Act of 2005—all of which sought, among other things, to increase immigration enforcement efforts.

Additionally, public frustration with unauthorized immigration resulted in over 1,592 proposed bills in state capitals, a 13.7 percent increase, in 2005, according to an August 2011 report by the National Conference of State Legislatures (NCSL). Although that figure includes pro-immigrant and anti-immigrant bills alike, and the number of such proposed bills actually enacted dropped by one-fourth since 2005, the decline is most likely due to the expense and backlash Arizona has faced in its battle in favor of its famed S.B. 1070 anti-immigration legislation.

The majority of such proposed state and local anti-immigrant bills and resolutions aim for "self-deportation," also referred to as "attrition through enforcement" (Waslin, 2012). In other words, anti-immigrant bills—like those enacted in Arizona, Alabama, Georgia, Indiana, South Carolina, and Utah, just to name a few—seek to make the daily lives of unauthorized immigrants so unbearable that they will leave the United States voluntarily. Although they vary in their requirements and level of severity, according to an article in August 2011 by Southern California Public Radio, many of these state laws and their local government counterparts require (1) the police to make warrantless arrests of individuals assumed to be out of immigration status; (2) the police to attempt to determine the immigration status of a person involved in a lawful stop; (3) that state residents be permitted to bring suit against federal immigration authorities for failure to enforce the immigration laws; (4) the mandatory implementation of E-Verify to check whether an employee is authorized to work in the United States; and (5) criminalization of an individual's failure to carry an alien registration document.

All of these efforts have proven effective in helping reduce the unauthorized immigrant population, obviating any need for a legalization program.

STRUCTURAL OBJECTIONS TO AN EARNED LEGALIZATION PROGRAM

No matter how it is designed, any legalization program for illegal immigrants will contain multiple deficiencies that render its success impossible.

On a fundamental level, an earned legalization program consists of two phases. In most such programs, phase one consists of retrospective eligibility qualifications for some form of temporary status. In phase two, participants must satisfy various prospective requirements while in temporary immigration status to obtain permanent legal immigration status. Even earned legalization advocates, however, disagree about what those requirements should be.

As a composite, for the initial phase, unauthorized immigrants would need to prove they (1) entered the United States by a certain cut-off date (though the actual cut-off date is hotly debated), (2) remained continuously physically present in the United States for the requisite length of time (again, the requisite period varies greatly), (3) can demonstrate a certain number of years of employment history (the number varies widely), and (4) have not committed any serious crimes (though what crimes will preclude participation is also debated). A composite of potential prospective requirements to satisfy the second phase would include (1) demonstrating they have still not committed any serious crimes and are paid up on all their taxes for a certain period of time (which is currently in contention, but with the minimum period, the time in temporary status from phase one of the legalization program), (2) a certain number of years of continued employment during temporary status, (3) passing an English language proficiency exam, (4) passing a basic U.S. history and civics exam, (5) staying in valid temporary or conditional status for the requisite period of years (again, that number is contested), and (6) paying penalty fines for their immigration violations, along with application fees for participating in the program.

Many unauthorized immigrants will not participate in a legalization program because they fear interacting with the government. A substantial portion of the nearly 11 million unauthorized immigrants will refuse to even participate in the legalization program out of distrust of the government and the ever-present threat of deportation. As Demetrios G. Papademetriou (2005) of the Migration Policy Institute (MPI) has noted, this is exactly what happened in the aftermath of the Immigration Reform and Control Act (IRCA) of 1986—the last general legalization program passed in the United States. As much as 12 percent of temporary status applicants in IRCA dropped out before attaining permanent status, causing a huge number of people to revert to unauthorized status (Cooper & O'Neil, 2005). That experience has shown that an earned legalization program would fail to substantially reduce the unauthorized population, let alone achieve other stated goals of legalization, such as decreasing informal sector employment and increasing national security (Papademetriou, 2005).

Prospective requirements will fail to encompass a large portion of the unauthorized population. The prospective requirements of any earned legalization program would inherently exclude huge numbers of unauthorized immigrants. To begin, according to MPI, such requirements have not received in-depth evaluation in research, nor have they been implemented in practical experimentation. For instance, there is no empirical evidence that requiring formal sector employment would prompt unauthorized immigrants to withdraw from thriving informal labor markets to enter formal markets (Papademetriou, 2005).

According to Mark Rosenblum, Randy Capps, and Serena Yi-Ying Lin (2011), each prospective requirement would have a different exclusionary effect on the number of unauthorized immigrants that an earned legalization program could legalize. An English language requirement would exclude between 3.3 and 3.8 million of the unauthorized immigrants in the United States and could cost between $6 million and $12 million in language instruction programs (given current per student costs). Employment requirements would exclude a huge number of unauthorized immigrants, disproportionately precluding unauthorized women, because they are less likely than men to be in the workforce. Continuous physical presence requirements would disproportionately exclude unauthorized children, because they are less likely to have accrued the requisite time present. Of course, this would depend on what the requisite number of years is, with most estimates calling for 5 years. Moreover, although the amount of any penalty fines is debated, requiring legalization program participants to pay penalty fines could preclude as many as 25 percent, or 2.5 million unauthorized immigrants, from participating.

A legalization program would actually increase unauthorized immigration. Implementing an earned legalization program would increase unauthorized immigration. IRCA was only able to garner sufficient bipartisan political support for passage on grounds that it would be a one-time effort to eliminate the unauthorized population. Having another legalization program would signal to unauthorized immigrants that they should illegally migrate to the United States immediately and stay undetected as long as possible, in the hopes they will then be able to meet the entry date and continuous physical presence prospective requirements to participate in the next legalization program (Papademetriou, 2005). This conclusion is based partially on surveys of immigrants apprehended at the border who state future regularization programs as one reason for their illegal entry.

In fact, MPI notes most studies demonstrate a large-scale amnesty will increase unauthorized immigration, rather than decrease it. For instance, after IRCA the unauthorized immigration population soared through the 1990s and most of the 2000s, reaching 12 million in 2007—the highest level in the nation's history. A similar result occurred when Congress merely considered passing a legalization program in the summer of 1997: the number of Hispanic unauthorized immigrants skyrocketed to an all-time high and quickly fell once the bill failed to pass for a second time. The sociologist Douglas Massey (2010) has reached similar conclusions, stating that history demonstrates unauthorized immigrants will come again if the United States legalizes those who are here now and have been here for long enough to qualify for a legalization program. For example, he notes that although the United States engaged in stricter border enforcement in 1993, increased numbers of unauthorized immigrants entered the country during that time and thereafter.

Any earned legalization program is administratively inefficient. An earned legalization program would be administratively illogical. It will be very expensive, require myriad government resources at a time when government is already severely strapped, and aggravate existing administrative inefficiencies. MPI notes that "large numbers of applicants, combined with staffing shortages, led to backlogs, slow application processing, and, ultimately, weak or ineffective [legalization] programs in the UK, Greece, Italy, Spain, and Belgium" (Levinson, 2005).

Any proposed legalization in the United States would require large numbers of staff to evaluate whether participants have satisfied the eligibility criteria for permanent immigration status. Legalizing millions of individuals would create an enormous backlog for *legal* immigration categories. Such a backlog occurred in the aftermath of IRCA, with participants forced to wait years to obtain permanent status before they could even apply for status for their qualifying family members. The resulting bottlenecks, in turn, forced millions of people with approved petitions based on relationships with qualifying United States citizens or legal permanent residents to wait additional years in unauthorized status until their visa numbers became current. In other words, earned legalization disadvantaged those who played by the rules. In fact, as was the case with IRCA, implementing an earned legalization program today would create a ripple effect for years, with MPI estimating such a program would triple the workload of U.S. Citizenship and Immigration Services (USCIS)—the agency charged with determining immigration benefits (Kerwin & Laglagaron, 2010).

A related administrative concern is that an earned legalization program would encourage fraud. For instance, MPI estimates that as much as 73 percent of all IRCA applications were fraudulent. IRCA was arguably more prone to fraud than earned legalization programs proposed today, because IRCA necessitated presenting affidavits from friends, family, and employers to demonstrate retrospective physical presence and employment history requirements. The danger of fraud with current proposed earned legalization programs nonetheless remains, especially because the initial phase of earned legalization would be based on satisfying retrospective requirements. In fact, the motivation for fraud is arguably even greater today, because whereas IRCA only required participants to demonstrate 4 years of physical presence (entry before 1982), many current proposals call for demonstrating at least 5 years of continuous physical presence and employment history.

Given the structural weaknesses of an earned legalization program, the administrative and financial costs, and the risk of increasing unauthorized immigration, critics argue the country is better served by continuing to crack down on immigration and labor law violators by ramping up enforcement.

MORAL OBJECTIONS TO A LEGALIZATION PROGRAM FOR UNAUTHORIZED IMMIGRANTS

Critics contend a legalization program is immoral for various reasons. First, those who oppose legalization argue the U.S. government has its own moral and legal right to control its borders. While legalization proponents argue that, as a liberal democracy, the United States owes a moral duty to provide basic human and civil rights to anyone within its jurisdiction, critics counter that states are entitled to, and indeed required to, enforce laws for the protection of their citizens. A self-governing democracy has the inherent right to define who is entitled to become part of the democracy and who cannot, and to ensure that foreign-born persons do not unilaterally bestow membership upon themselves without the official permission of the country's population (Aleinkoff, 2010). The U.S. government, in short, must have the right to deter their entry and remove them once present.

Second, some legalization proponents argue that unauthorized immigrants have a moral right to legalization because, despite their economic contribution, U.S. immigration laws relegate them to a caste-like subclass without any pathway to legitimized status. In response, critics insist that argument is merely illusory. To the extent any caste-like subclass exists involving unauthorized immigrants, it is created by the unauthorized entry and presence of such unauthorized migrants themselves, rather than by any legal construct of the U.S. government. To be clear, those who oppose legalization do not argue unauthorized immigrants are not entitled to exercise their civil rights. Rather, critics maintain that if unauthorized immigrants do not exercise their rights due to fear that doing so will alert their presence and immigration violations to the authorities, that is a function of their immigration rule-breaking in the first place. Such violations and the resulting fear of deportation do not somehow transform into a governmental duty to provide totally open borders or legal status for all.

Third, the length of unauthorized immigrants' physical presence in the United States does not trigger a moral claim to legalized status. Some legalization proponents, such as Joseph Carens (2010), argue there comes a point at which unauthorized immigrants have accrued enough physical presence in the United States that it is immoral to uproot them through deportation, because they have created social ties here (as measured by time as a proxy for such ties). This argument is unpersuasive. As Carens himself acknowledges, selecting a threshold time period for physical presence involves a certain amount of arbitrariness. Normatively speaking then, it is not clear why a moral imperative to legalize unauthorized immigrants would arise after that arbitrary threshold is met, but not before it. Additionally, the "time matters" argument cuts both ways. While legalization proponents may argue that the longer the unauthorized stay, the stronger the moral claim to legalized status, critics contend the longer the unauthorized presence, the greater the immorality of unauthorized immigrants' initial law-breaking act. If anything, the longer the unauthorized immigrants' unauthorized stay, the stronger the government's moral right to deport them.

To the extent Carens and other proponents argue that accruing the requisite length of physical presence as a proxy for social ties is what triggers unauthorized immigrants' moral claim to legalized status, this argument lacks merit. Although individually evaluating such ties is fraught with its own problems (e.g., limited resources and the possibility of abuse of discretion by officials), the social ties themselves, and not time as a proxy for those ties, are what really matter; therefore, the ties themselves are what should be evaluated. Why? Many immigrants stay in the United States for virtually their entire lives without developing social ties outside of their own particular immigrant community, whereas others form ties with the rest of society almost immediately (Bosniak, 2010).

The time-matters argument also excludes a substantial portion of the unauthorized population from participating in the legalization program. By having a minimum period of physical presence needed to accrue a moral claim to legalized status, there is by definition a substantial group of people who lack the requisite physical presence. What becomes of those people? Do they stay in limbo hoping to avoid detection for long enough to meet the arbitrary threshold for a moral claim to any future legalization program? Or perhaps they obtain temporary legal status, only to revert to unauthorized status upon expiration of the temporary visa. Either way, the United States is left with an ongoing large resident unauthorized population.

Fourth, any moral claim for earned legalization overlooks the inherent immorality of the injustice to applicants of the *legal* immigration system. Legal immigration applicants have waited very long periods of time by going through the proper channels, and they have expended significant resources to play by the rules. It would be unfair to such people to legalize unauthorized immigrants. This is especially true when considering that unauthorized immigrants entering the legal immigration system through a legalization program will cause even further backlogs and waits for those attempting to play by the rules. Indeed, in weighing decisions about to whom the U.S. government owes a moral duty, Carol Swain

(2010) argues that the United States has a greater moral obligation to help its own citizens—especially African Americans and other minorities "who continue to suffer racial discrimination, wanton neglect, and outright rejection"—than to help unauthorized immigrants. Opponents claim the moral arguments in favor of legalization fail to account for the "impact of illegal immigration on the most vulnerable members of American society: native-born Americans and legal immigrants with low skills and low levels of education" (Swain, 2010).

Given all these reasons, earned legalization is immoral. It is unfair to those who follow U.S. immigration laws. Accordingly, the United States should not implement an earned legalization program.

PRAGMATIC OBJECTIONS TO A LEGALIZATION PROGRAM FOR UNAUTHORIZED IMMIGRANTS

One pragmatic objection to earned legalization is that implementing such a program would increase national security threats. National security would be implicated by taking in such a large number of people—whom the United States knows little to nothing about—and granting them legal status through a rushed, overburdened process. Such concerns led to the increased enforcement efforts that attempted to prevent such unauthorized immigration in the wake of the September 11, 2001, attacks. Legalization would further endanger communities in respect to crime. Most research indicates the unauthorized population consists primarily of young, low-educated males—a demographic most prone to resort to crime, especially during periods of recession. In 2007 it was estimated that over 600,000 immigrants were criminally incarcerated (as opposed to placed in immigration detention facilities) each year (Pickus & Skerry, 2007). While recent enforcement efforts have proven successful in reducing the unauthorized population overall, Immigration and Customs Enforcement (ICE) has had less success removing criminal immigrants. For example, in 2005, ICE was only able to remove 89,406 criminal immigrants—a small percentage of removable immigrants in custody or probation/criminal parole in the United States at that time. Thus, legalizing unauthorized immigrants would open the nation's doors to a large number of criminals, thereby further jeopardizing public safety (Pickus & Skerry, 2007).

Likewise, earned legalization would be detrimental to a range of public institutions, including educational institutions, hospitals and clinics, jails and prisons, and low-income housing (Swain, 2007). Noted scholar, Carol M. Swain (2007), has stated the problem is "dire" because of the sheer number of unauthorized immigrants saturating these public systems. The Federation for American Immigration Reform (FAIR) has discussed how unauthorized immigration has negatively impacted educational institutions. Public schools across the states are already laying off teachers, increasing class sizes, and decreasing special programs, sports, and language learning, all because of budget cuts. States spend almost $12 billion per year on K–12 education of unauthorized immigrant children, while spending an additional $16.6 billion in K–12 education of U.S.-born children of unauthorized immigrant parents. Schools have additional expenses in the form of between $290 and $879 per-pupil costs associated with dual-language programs, along with more expenditures for supplemental feed programs for impoverished children—many of whom are the children of unauthorized immigrants. Scholars argue these expenditures unfairly disadvantage children of U.S. citizens and authorized immigrants, who are already suffering the consequences of overburdened, and increasingly over-enrolled, public schools.

Similarly, in terms of health care, the Pew Hispanic Center notes that in 2007, 60 percent (or 6 in every 10) Latino unauthorized immigrants in the United States lacked health insurance, and unauthorized immigrants and their children comprised 70 percent of the 46 million Americans without health care in 2009 (Livingston, 2009). According to Pew, 37 percent of noncitizen/non-LPR Latino adults (98% of whom are unauthorized immigrants) have no usual health-care provider; 41 percent use community clinics or health centers for medical care (regardless that such centers are designed as a safety net for vulnerable populations and are partially funded by federal and state governments), and 6 percent use emergency rooms. However, Pew and other sources note that many unauthorized immigrants do not seek medical care unless they are severely ill. Given these statistics, unauthorized immigrants endanger public health by not seeking treatment for illnesses; they increase wait times and decrease level of care for all; and they increase the costs of such medical care by millions of dollars—though Pew and other researchers indicate it is impossible to accurately estimate how much the unauthorized immigrant population drives up health-care costs.

A third pragmatic objection to earned legalization is that it would be detrimental to U.S. workers. Over 8 million unauthorized immigrants were part of the workforce at the beginning of 2010. This represents approximately 5 percent of the nation's entire workforce. Many commentators argue unauthorized immigrants take jobs from low-skilled and unskilled native workers (used in this article to mean authorized immigrants or U.S. citizens). They argue earned legalization would have a disparate impact on poorly educated African American and Hispanic U.S. citizens, legal permanent residents (LPRs), and authorized immigrants. While less-skilled unauthorized immigrants create an economic boon for U.S. consumers by producing and selling products at cheaper rates (because unauthorized immigrants receive subpar wages), legalizing more unauthorized immigrants would negatively impact U.S. workers competing for similar low-skilled and unskilled jobs (Holzer, 2011).

In 2010, an estimated 6 to 7 million unauthorized immigrants were working in low-wage, low-skill positions that low-educated native workers in the United States could fill (Swain, 2010). The unemployment rates for U.S.-born blacks and Hispanics without a high school education (24.7 percent and 16.2 percent, respectively) support this argument (Swain, 2010). In contrast, the unemployment rate for immigrants with less than a high school education—both authorized and unauthorized—is much lower, at 10.6 percent (Swain, 2010). Vernon Briggs Jr. (2010) of the Center for Immigration Studies (CIS), has reached similar conclusions in his research.

Critics of legalization urge the government to make E-Verify mandatory and expand it. They argue that using that system to check Social Security numbers for each employee against a national database ("with a 99.6 % accuracy rate" that yields results in seconds) would enable employers and the government to identify authorized and unauthorized immigrant workers. The employer would then have to terminate any unauthorized immigrant workers.

The problem up to this point has been that participation in E-Verify has been voluntary. Making E-Verify mandatory would prevent employers from employing unauthorized immigrants for subpar wages, and it would prevent unauthorized immigrant workers from avoiding detection by moving to states or employers who previously had opted not to participate in E-Verify (Rosenblum & Hoyt, 2011). E-Verify has three huge benefits: (1) it helps identify unauthorized workers; (2) it is more secure than traditional measures to identify fraudulent employment/immigration documents; and (3) it provides assurances to employers that their employees are authorized to work in the United States, thereby decreasing apprehension to hire those who "look" unauthorized but are authorized to work in the United States (e.g., Hispanic immigrants and Hispanic U.S. citizens) (Rosenblum & Hoyt, 2011).

If instead of requiring E-Verify, the government implements a legalization program, the consequences of unauthorized immigration on the country would be magnified. Legalization would encourage increased unauthorized immigration, further disadvantaging native workers in terms of working conditions and minimum wages. It would also mean a sudden, huge population of people who would become authorized for employment in the United States, thereby overwhelming already dry job markets with competition for low-skilled and unskilled labor. Further, the timing for legalization could not be worse. Unemployment rates are hovering between 8.5 and 9 percent.

Critics agree the United States is best served by deporting surplus workers who are unauthorized immigrants, rather than providing them with a legalized status. This would force U.S. employers to raise wages in various industries and improve working conditions for native employees.

UNITED STATES SHOULD INCREASE SPECIFIC ENFORCEMENT INITIATIVES

The United States should channel its resources into increasing specific enforcement initiatives to decrease the unauthorized immigrant population, instead of implementing an earned legalization program. Such enforcement initiatives include increasing border patrol and other enforcement technologies to expand the country's virtual borders, and collaboration between the federal immigration enforcement authorities and state and local law governments.

Many legalization proponents question why the government should invest in increased enforcement efforts when the sheer number of unauthorized immigrants seems to suggest enforcement is not effective. Yet statistics indicate enforcement mechanisms have played a role in decreasing the unauthorized immigrant population over the past few years. For instance, over the past 15 years, U.S. immigration enforcement has focused on securing the Southwest border with Mexico (McCabe & Meissner, 2010). Such efforts have included increasing the number of Border Patrol agents to over 20,000, and implementing new technology, such as drone aircraft, sensors, and cameras. Significant fencing was also erected along the U.S.-Mexico border. These initiatives closed off the most commonly used physical entry points for unauthorized immigration, forcing immigrants to cross in more dangerous locations over more unforgiving terrain. This has made unauthorized immigration both more dangerous and more costly for migrants, which the United States hopes will deter future potential unauthorized immigrants. Critics call for the expansion of such efforts to further reduce unauthorized immigration.

In addition to increasing Border Patrol agents and border enforcement technologies, legalization opponents maintain the federal government must expand collaboration efforts with state and local governments. One way to do this would be to increase memoranda of understanding (MOUs) between federal authorities and state and local law enforcement personnel. The purpose of such MOUs is to enable state and local law enforcement agents to help enforce the federal immigration laws, pursuant to Section 287(g) of the Immigration and Nationality Act. Despite claims by legalization advocates that MOUs lead to racial profiling of foreign-looking people regardless of their immigration status, critics argue the federal government's limited resources make increasing MOUs necessary to more effectively detect, capture, and ultimately deport immigration law violators.

A second way to increase federal and local collaboration to enforce the federal immigration laws would be to expand the Secure Communities program. First introduced in May 2008, this program essentially enables local law enforcement agents "to check the immigration status of any individuals booked in participating state prisons and local jails . . . [in order to] prioritize the removal of the most dangerous criminal aliens" (McCabe & Meissner, 2010).

While earned legalization opponents generally agree that increased enforcement is essential to reducing the unauthorized population, there is great debate as to how to best ratchet-up enforcement efforts. To illustrate this point, the following is a sampling of some of the legislative proposals calling for various enforcement initiatives. The Comprehensive Immigration Reform for America's Security and Prosperity Act of 2009 (CIR-ASAP) and the Secure America and Orderly Immigration Act of 2005 would raise the number of border patrol officers, provide for more Customs and Border Protection agriculture specialists, and add to the support personnel of all ports of entry. The latter bill would also make E-Verify mandatory and would double the existing INA minimum and maximum employer penalties. The Comprehensive Enforcement and Immigration Reform Act would make any worker who fails to comply with mandatory departure ineligible for legal reentry to the United States for 10 years, and it would raise the number of beds in ICE detention facilities by 10,000, while expanding expedited removal to the entire U.S. border. The REAL GUEST Act of 2005 goes even further. It would make unauthorized entry and unauthorized presence in the United States a criminal felony, while preventing children born in the United States to unauthorized parents from entitlement to citizenship, and allowing the military to assist in border enforcement.

These are just a sampling of proposals by legalization opponents. In general, opponents to legalization contend more enforcement is the only way to reduce the unauthorized population and deter future unauthorized immigration.

CONCLUSION

This Counterpoint essay demonstrates that any legalization program for unauthorized immigrants presents too many risks and consequences to make it a worthwhile endeavor. First, it would be very expensive and time-consuming. The current immigration system is simply not administratively equipped to handle a regime in which, in a very short time frame, millions of people are evaluated for and granted legal status. Second, any earned legalization program would encourage increased unauthorized immigration. Yet such legalization program proposals inherently fail to include a large number of the current unauthorized population—whether because such people would revert to unauthorized status because they lack the ability to satisfy any prospective requirements needed to gain permanent status, or because they would not even participate from the outset for fear of deportation as was the case with IRCA.

Legalization is also morally unfair to those who have played by the rules by trying to immigrate through the proper channels. At the same time, it would be immoral and unjust to reward those who broke the law—whether by crossing the border without authorization or overstaying their permitted status—with legal status.

In addition to such structural and moral objections, a legalization program would have multiple pragmatic consequences. It would hurt the U.S. economy and negatively impact job prospects for U.S. citizens and authorized workers already struggling to find jobs, given the high unemployment rate. It would have a disproportionately harmful impact on job prospects for low-educated black and Hispanic U.S. citizens and authorized workers. It could also further endanger national security and increase the crime rate.

For all these reasons, an earned legalization program is not in the country's best interest. Rather, the United States should continue to invest in increased enforcement initiatives to reduce the current unauthorized population and effectively deter future unauthorized immigration.

References and Further Reading

Aleinkoff, A. (2010). Forum response to Joseph Carens' *Immigrants and the right to stay.* Cambridge, MA: MIT Press.

Bosniak, L. (2010). Forum response to Joseph Carens' *Immigrants and the right to stay.* Cambridge, MA: MIT Press.

Briggs, V. A., Jr. (2010). *Illegal immigration and immigration reform: Protecting the employment rights of the American labor force (native-born and foreign-born) who are eligible to be employed.* Center for Immigration Studies. Retrieved from http://www.cis.org/employment-rights

Camarota, S. A. (2007). Immigrant employment gains and native losses. In C. M. Swain (Ed.), *Debating immigration* (pp. 39–40). New York, NY: Cambridge University Press.

Camarota, S. A. (2010). *Immigration and economic stagnation: An examination of trends 2000 to 2010.* Center for Immigration Studies. Retrieved from http://www.cis.org/highest-decade

Camarota, S. A., & Jensenius, K. (2009). *A shifting tide: Recent trends in the illegal immigrant population.* Center for Immigration Studies. Retrieved from http://www.cis.org/IllegalImmigration-ShiftingTide

Carens, J. (2005). On belonging: What we owe people who stay. *Boston Review,* Summer 2005. Retrieved from http://bostonreview.net/BR30.3/carens.php

Carens, J. (2010). *Immigrants and the right to stay.* Cambridge, MA: MIT Press.

Chishti, M., & Bergeron, C. (2010). *Increasing evidence that the recession has caused number of unauthorized immigrations in U.S. to drop.* Migration Policy Institute. Retrieved from http://www.migrationinformation.org/USFocus/display.cfm?ID=774

Chishti, M., & Bergeron, C. (2010). *New immigration bill edges comprehensive immigration reform back on the legislative agenda.* Migration Policy Institute. Retrieved from http://www.migrationinformation.org/Profiles/display.cfm?ID=769

Cooper, B., & O'Neil, K. (2005). *Lessons from the Immigration Reform and Control Act of 1986.* Migration Policy Institute. Retrieved from http://www.migrationpolicy.org/pubs/PolicyBrief_No3_Aug05.pdf

Federation for American Immigration Reform. (2005). *Breaking the piggy bank: How illegal immigration is sending schools into the red.* Retrieved from http://www.fairus.org/site/News2?page=NewsArticle&id=17193&security=1601&news_iv_ctrl=1901

Hing, B. O. (2010, August 4). *Babies r' us: Challenges to birthright citizenship are just a distraction.* Retrieved from http://www.slate.com/articles/news_and_politics/politics/2010/08/babies_r_us.html

Hing, B. O. (2011, July 12). Control the border: Invest in Mexico. *Huffington Post* blog post. Retrieved from http://www.huffingtonpost.com/bill-ong-hing/invest-in-mexico_b_896473.html

Hoefer, M., Rytina, N., & Baker, B. C. (2010). *Estimates of the unauthorized immigrant population residing in the United States: January 2010* (Population Estimate Report dated Feb. 2011). Department of Homeland Security, Office of Immigration Statistics. Retrieved from http://www.dhs.gov/xlibrary/assets/statistics/publications/lpr_fr_2010.pdf

Holzer, Harry J. (2011). *Immigration policy and less-skilled workers in the United States: Reflections on future directions for reform.* Urban Institute. Retrieved from http://www.urban.org/publications/1001488.html

Kerwin, D. M. (2010). *More than IRCA: U.S. legalization programs and the current policy debate.* Migration Policy Institute. Retrieved from http://www.migrationpolicy.org/pubs/legalization-historical.pdf

Kerwin, D. M., & Laglagaron, L. (2010). *Structuring and implementing an immigrant legalization program: Registration as the first step.* Migration Policy Institute. Retrieved from http://www.migrationpolicy.org/pubs/legalization-registration.pdf

Levinson, A. (2005). *Migration fundamentals: Why countries continue to consider regularization.* Migration Policy Institute. Retrieved from http://www.migrationinformation.org/Feature/display.cfm?ID=330

Livingston, G. (2009). *Hispanics, health insurance and health care access.* Pew Hispanic Center. Retrieved from http://www.pewhispanic.org/2009/09/25/hispanics-health-insurance-and-health-care-access

Massey, D. S. (2005). Five myths about immigration: Common misconceptions underlying U.S. border-enforcement policy. *Immigration Daily.* Retrieved from http://www.ilw.com/articles/2005,1207-massey.shtm

Massey, D. S. (2007). Borderline madness: America's counterproductive immigration policy. In C. M. Swain (Ed.), *Debating immigration* (pp. 136–138). New York, NY: Cambridge University Press.

Massey, D. S. (2010). Forum response to Joseph Carens' *Immigrants and the right to stay.* Cambridge, MA: MIT Press.

McCabe, K., & Meissner, D. (2010). *Immigration and the United States: Recession affects flows, prospects for reform.* Migration Policy Institute. Retrieved from http://www.migrationinformation.org/Profiles/display.cfm?ID=766#top

Papademetriou, D. G. (2005). *The "regularization" option in managing illegal migration more effectively: A comparative perspective.* Migration Policy Institute. Retrieved from http://www.migrationpolicy.org/pubs/PolicyBrief_No4_Sept05.pdf

Pickus, N., & Skerry, P. (2007). Good neighbors and good citizens In C. M. Swain (Ed.), *Debating immigration* (pp. 95–113). New York, NY: Cambridge University Press.

Rosenblum, M. R. (2010, December). *Immigration legalization in the United States and the European Union: Policy goals and program design,* Migration Policy Institute. Retrieved from http://www.migrationpolicy.org/pubs/legalization-policydesign.pdf

Rosenblum, M., & Hoyt, L. (2011). *The basics of E-Verify, the U.S. employer verification system.* Migration Policy Institute. Retrieved from http://www.migrationinformation.org/Feature/display.cfm?ID=846

Rosenblum, M. R., Capps, R., & Yi-Ying Lin, S. (2011). *Earned legalization: Effects of proposed requirements on unauthorized men, women, and children.* Migration Policy Institute. Retrieved from http://www.migrationpolicy.org/pubs/legalization-requirements.pdf

Shuck, P. H. (2007). The disconnect between public attitudes and policy outcomes in immigration. In C. M. Swain (Ed.), *Debating immigration* (pp. 17–31). New York, NY: Cambridge University Press.

Swain, C. (2010). Forum response to Joseph Carens' *Immigrants and the right to stay.* Cambridge, MA: MIT Press.

Swain, C. M. (2007). Introduction. In C. M. Swain (Ed.), *Debating immigration* (pp. 1–16). New York, NY: Cambridge University Press.

Waslin, M. (2012). *New report examines dire consequences of "attrition through enforcement" immigration strategy.* Retrieved from http://immigrationimpact.com/2012/02/06/new-report-examines-dire-consequences-of-attrition-through-enforcement-immigration-strategy

Andrew D. Linenberg

Note: The author is extremely grateful for the mentorship and guidance in developing this article from Linda S. Bosniak, a noted scholar on immigration law, citizenship, and constitutional law and theory at Rutgers University School of Law–Camden.

Birthright Citizenship

POINT: The Fourteenth Amendment to the U.S. Constitution is unambiguous in extending citizenship to anyone born on U.S. soil, including, as the Supreme Court concluded in *United States v. Wong Kim Ark* (1898), "all children here born of resident aliens." The Court reiterated this view in *Plyler v. Doe* (1982), holding that the Fourteenth Amendment extends to everyone "who is subject to the laws of a state," including the U.S.-born children of unauthorized aliens.

Alexandra Filindra, University of Illinois at Chicago

COUNTERPOINT: The authors of the Fourteenth Amendment did not intend to grant birthright citizenship to the children of unauthorized aliens. Today, pregnant women can enter the United States illegally and have their newborns gain citizenship, and these children can later sponsor their parents for citizenship. This practice is clearly at odds with the original purposes of the Fourteenth Amendment.

Edward J. Erler, California State University, San Bernardino

Introduction

The phrase *birthright citizenship* alludes to an ongoing debate over whether or not to grant automatic U.S. citizenship to children born to mothers who are present in the United States illegally. People on both sides of the debate agree that jurisdiction over this question is covered by Section 1 of the Fourteenth Amendment to the Constitution, which states:

> All persons born or naturalized in the United States, and subject to the jurisdiction thereof, are citizens of the United States and of the state wherein they reside. No state shall make or enforce any law which shall abridge the privileges or immunities of citizens of the United States; nor shall any state deprive any person of life, liberty, or property, without due process of law; nor deny to any person within its jurisdiction the equal protection of the laws.

However, defenders and critics of birthright citizenship do not agree on the intention of that amendment or to whom it should apply.

The true intent of the Fourteenth Amendment became a hot political issue in the 1990s, when it was raised in the halls of Congress, as well as in some state houses. But the amendment itself, of course, is far older—passed in 1868, the amendment is a child of the Civil War and the Reconstruction period that followed. The amendment was necessary in order to undo the *Dred Scott v. Sandford* decision of 1857, in which the U. S. Supreme Court declared that black people were not American citizens.

Some who argue against the Fourteenth Amendment being applicable to undocumented immigrants point out that there was no concept of "undocumented immigrant" in the mid-nineteenth century. Indeed, although there was some attempt made to discourage so-called undesirable immigrants, as Alexandra Filindra points out in the Point section of this debate, there was no real border enforcement at all. Thus, according to critics, it is impossible that the authors of the Fourteenth Amendment could have intended the language to cover this new circumstance. Filindra argues, however, that state and local ordinances did exist that attempted to restrict immigration, and that the authors of the Fourteenth Amendment were, indeed, well aware that their language might be used to allow children of these "undesirables" to become citizens. Defenders of the Fourteenth Amendment as it applies to immigrants also point to the 1982 decision, *Plyer v. Doe,* which specifically states that there should be no difference in the applicability of the Fourteenth Amendment to lawfully or unlawfully entered immigrants.

But Edward Erler, arguing in the Counterpoint essay, locates his objections to the Fourteenth Amendment's application to immigrants in another place: automatically bestowed citizenship, he argues, is a form of "perpetual allegiance"—a relic of the feudal era that was expressly rejected by the Declaration of Independence, which is based on the "consent of the governed." This question of allegiance—what is it, who can be said to have it or not—is central to the birthright citizenship debate because the Fourteenth Amendment only applies to those "subject to the jurisdiction of the United States." Does *jurisdiction,* as Filindra would argue, refer simply to anyone within the physical borders of the country? Or, as Erler states, does it mean something more?

Another important question to consider when thinking about the true meaning of the Fourteenth Amendment is the language that states, "no state shall make or enforce any law. . . ." This language was designed to lift the question of citizenship above the states and make it a federal concern. Prior to the amendment, citizenship was a state-level matter. Again, this was in direct response to the events of the Civil War, and to concerns that some states would attempt to write their own citizenship rules if allowed to do so, to the detriment of freed slaves. As you read this chapter, consider whether you believe citizenship ought to be a state or federal matter. In 2012, lawmakers in at least 40 states were considering bills that would deny citizenship to American-born children of undocumented immigrants, which would suggest that the state argument does have some appeal to at least part of the U.S. body politic.

Meanwhile, at the federal level, the Birthright Citizenship Act of 2011 was proposed both in the House (by Rep. Steve King [R-IA]) and in the Senate (by Sen. David Vitter [R-LA]). While the bills did not make it out of committee in that legislative year, it is worth noting that both bills attracted considerably more support than similar attempts had in the past. Immigrant rights activists voice concerns that the denial of birthright citizenship would create a two-tiered social structure in the United States, leading to an entire generation of people born within U.S. borders and yet without citizenship rights. Would this situation unfairly punish children for the "sins" of their parents? Finally, how might a reinterpretation of the Fourteenth Amendment serve or not serve the ultimate goal of reducing illegal immigration?

POINT

The right to citizenship for the American-born children of undocumented immigrants came under increased scrutiny in 2010–2011. Not only does a portion of the American public favor an explicit bar of these children from "automatic" American citizenship, but legislators in as many as 40 states are considering bills that would deny birthright citizenship to the American-born children of undocumented immigrants (Preston, 2011; Reuters, 2011). Similarly, Republicans in Congress recently introduced legislation and proposals for a constitutional amendment aimed at changing the citizenship clause of the Fourteenth Amendment and precluding these children from access to birthright citizenship (Rubin, 2011). Similar proposals have been around since the mid-1990s when a new generation of conservative Republicans dominated Congress. Specifically, in 1993, Representative Elton Gallegly proposed both a constitutional amendment and legislation that would limit birthright citizenship to children whose mothers are U.S. citizens or permanent residents (See 139 Cong. Rec. H1005, daily ed., Mar. 3, 1993). Some politicians, conservative journalists, and a small number of legal scholars have argued that the Fourteenth Amendment, which defines the idea of birthright citizenship, can be understood to exclude the children of undocumented immigrants (Coulter, 2010; Graglia, 2009; Lacey, 2011; Schuck & Smith, 1985; Will, 2010). Proponents of this revisionist view argue that "the simple" solution to unauthorized immigration is a reinterpretation of the Fourteenth Amendment's citizenship clause to end birthright citizenship for children of unauthorized immigrants.

This essay argues that the United States should continue to recognize the birthright citizenship of the U.S.-born children of undocumented citizens because it is consistent with the U.S. Constitution; the country's principles of justice; its economic and political interests, which include assisting in the social integration of immigrants; and the obligation to prevent the establishment of a permanent and hereditary caste system. There is a strong constitutional tradition going back to the late nineteenth century that recognizes the citizenship rights of the American-born children of undocumented immigrants. Mainstream interpretations of the Constitution, which are accepted by the majority of jurists, legal scholars, and legal historians, argue for inclusion of these children in the category of "American citizen." In addition to a strong constitutional foundation, the principle of extending birthright citizenship to all children born on American soil makes good sense for social, political, and moral reasons. History—both in the United States and in other countries—has shown that justice cannot be served by having second-class citizens who do not enjoy equal rights within a state's territory. Furthermore, Americans themselves do not favor a change to this long-standing principle (Kettner, 1978). Not all countries, however, have a birthright citizenship principle in their laws. Among the countries that do are Canada, Australia (with some restrictions), Mexico, Brazil, Argentina, Colombia, Peru, Uruguay, and Romania. The United Kingdom recently revised its birthright citizenship laws making them more exclusionary, while Germany introduced the concept of birthright citizenship in 2000.

This essay starts with explaining what "birthright citizenship" means in the American context. Then the various constitutional and political arguments that are brought up in conjunction with revising the citizenship clause will be discussed. The third section examines the social and economic consequences, as well as the moral implications, of creating a caste of American-born perpetual foreigners.

WHAT IS BIRTHRIGHT CITIZENSHIP?

Birthright citizenship refers to the principle that individuals born within the territory of a given country should be recognized by the country's authorities as full members of the country's political society—that is, as "citizens." Birthright citizenship obliges countries that have included the principle in their law to confer citizenship to all children born within their borders regardless of the citizenship status of their parents. The only commonly held exception in U.S. law is children of foreign diplomats and dignitaries. The practice of birthright citizenship in the United States is derived from the first section of the Fourteenth Amendment to the federal Constitution, commonly known as "the citizenship clause," which states, "All persons born or naturalized in the United States, and subject to the jurisdiction thereof, are citizens of the United States."

The Fourteenth Amendment, one of the Reconstruction Amendments, was passed in 1868 in the aftermath of the American Civil War. One of the key motivations for the birthright citizenship provision was the reversal of the 1857 Supreme Court decision in *Dred Scott v. Sandford*, which had determined that blacks born in the United States could not be recognized as American citizens and members of the national political community under the federal Constitution. The *Dred Scott* decision put the official seal of the Supreme Court on the belief that black people were racially inferior to whites, and therefore not deserving of any political, economic, and social rights associated with U.S. citizenship. According to Chief Justice Roger B. Taney's decision in *Dred Scott*, blacks could not be recognized as U.S. citizens because they were "beings of an inferior order, and altogether unfit to associate with the white race, either in social or political relations, and so far inferior that they had no rights which the white man was bound to respect." The Fourteenth Amendment sought to reverse this decision and establish political membership rights for blacks, the era's "undesirable" population, and to reaffirm the Constitution's foundational principle of equality under the law for all people, regardless of their race, nativity, or parentage (Notes, 1994).

The applicability of the Fourteenth Amendment's citizenship clause to the American-born children of undocumented immigrants has come under scrutiny since the 1980s, first in academia (Schuck & Smith, 1985) and soon after in the political arena (Nelan, 1993; Wilson, 1993). Representative Gallegly (R-CA) introduced a constitutional amendment seeking to revise the citizenship clause in 1993, and has done so every year since. In 1996 the Republican Party endorsed the idea of excluding the American-born children of undocumented immigrants from birthright citizenship (Smith, 2009). Opponents of the Gallegly Amendment have put forth several legal, moral, and social arguments explaining why changing the citizenship clause is bad policy and inconsistent with America's foundational principles.

"UNDESIRABLE" ALIENS AND THE CONSTITUTION

Proponents of the Gallegly Amendment and other similar proposals argue that the Fourteenth Amendment does not apply to the children of undocumented immigrants because undocumented immigration was not an issue in the 1860s, and thus the framers of the Amendment could not have possibly meant to include them in its provisions. In this view, in the 1860s, the U.S. government had not yet instituted laws that regulated the entry and admission of immigrants. At the time, the United States did not have any type of immigration enforcement authorities and no border patrol. Because of this lack of legal and administrative frameworks, the concept of "illegal" or "undocumented" immigrant did not exist (Ngai, 2005). If a country does not have laws that define who can be admitted and who cannot, and if there is no process of formal admission, then there is no way to classify people as "legal" entrants or "illegal" entrants. Proponents of the redefinition of the Fourteenth Amendment argue that birthright citizenship could not possibly apply to undocumented immigrants because the category of "undocumented" did not exist in 1868. Therefore, the Congress of the time could not have contemplated what to do with the children of this particular class of undesirable aliens.

Congress may not have had a conception of "undocumented" or "illegal" immigrants in the 1860s, but there were other groups of noncitizens who were considered "undesirable" aliens at the time, and Congress was well informed and had positions on them. Federal regulation of immigrants did not start until later in the nineteenth century, but as early as 1808, Congress had implemented laws barring the entry of another group of aliens: slaves, imported from Africa. Because traders ignored the prohibition, this relegated imported slaves to the category of "illegal commodity" if not "illegal alien."

Even if the federal government came late to the game of immigration control, that does not mean that there were no immigration controls or laws that applied to noncitizens. States and localities had been enacting restrictions on immigration since colonial times. States (and colonies) had "pauper laws" targeted at immigrants from Europe, and many later introduced head taxes to discourage the entry of poor Europeans. A number of southern states also had laws targeting foreign black sailors: for example, blacks who worked on British ships were not allowed to disembark their vessel in Southern Carolina because white elites in the state feared that the presence of free blacks could incite slave rebellions (Neuman, 1996).

The framers of the Fourteenth Amendment were well aware that the language used in the citizenship clause would enable a number of "undesirable" groups to get access to citizenship. For example, a key concern in the late 1860s was that the children of Chinese immigrants would become citizens. The Chinese were the "undesirables" of the late nineteenth century, and western states resisted the idea of granting citizenship to the offspring of Chinese immigrants, fearing that it would encourage the settlement and growth of Chinese communities. This was a scary prospect for white Americans who held numerous negative racial views of the Chinese, and perceived them as both an economic and a racial threat (Takaki, 1989). Congress knew that, as a result of the Fourteenth Amendment, the children of Chinese immigrants would receive citizenship. Senator Edgar Cowen (R-PA), fearful of precisely this outcome, insisted that the amendment should be formulated so that "if [a state] were overrun by another and a different race, it would have the right to absolutely expel them." Acknowledging that this was precisely the outcome Congress sought to avoid, Senator John Conness (R-CA) responded,

> the proposition before us . . . relates simply in that respect to the children begotten to Chinese parents in California, and it is proposed to declare that they shall be citizens. . . . I am in favor of doing so. . . . We are entirely ready to accept the provision proposed in this constitutional amendment, that the children born here of Mongolian parents shall be declared by the Constitution of the United States to be entitled to civil rights and to equal protection before the law with others. (*Cong. Globe*, 39th Cong., 1st Sess. 2891 [1866])

In spite of any political and popular objections, the Supreme Court, in *U.S. v. Wong Kim Ark* (1898), formally recognized that the American-born children of Chinese immigrants have a right to birthright citizenship on the basis of the Fourteenth Amendment. Almost a century later, in 1982, the Supreme Court again affirmed this inclusive interpretation of the Citizenship Clause. In his majority decision in *Plyler v. Doe*, Justice William J. Brennan wrote, "no plausible distinction with respect to Fourteenth Amendment 'jurisdiction' can be drawn between resident aliens whose entry into the United States was lawful, and resident aliens whose entry was unlawful." These Supreme Court decisions indicate that the principle of birthright citizenship applies to all U.S.-born children, regardless of parentage.

THE PROBLEM OF "THE JURISDICTION THEREOF"

The birthright citizenship clause of the Fourteenth Amendment specifies that the United States is obligated to confer birthright citizenship to individuals born in the United States and under "the jurisdiction thereof." This issue of "jurisdiction" is alluded in the *Plyler v. Doe* decision written by Justice Brennan. These three words are where the legal debate has focused for the past 30 years. What does this phrase mean, and to whom does it apply?

Some scholars have argued that for a foreigner to be "in the jurisdiction of" the United States, this person must "owe allegiance" to the United States (Eastman, 2008; Graglia, 2009; Schuck & Smith, 1985). The meaning of "allegiance" is complex and technical, but it implies that mere territorial presence is not sufficient for a foreigner to be in the jurisdiction of the United States. Some form of "loyalty" to the political community of the country is also required before a foreigner can be considered to be in "the jurisdiction thereof," and thus eligible for citizenship. This loyalty, in turn, rests on legal territorial presence.

However, many legal scholars disagree with this interpretation of the phrase. According to Neuman (1996), being "subject to the jurisdiction" of the United States has nothing to do with loyalty. It means no more than being subject to the laws and rules of the U.S. government. The Supreme Court has also used this understanding of jurisdiction in its decisions. According to Justice Antonin Scalia, in his dissent in *Spector v. Norwegian Cruise Line Ltd.* (2005), when Congress says that a group of people are subject to the jurisdiction of the United States, this means that Congress "has made clear its intent to extend its laws [to this group]." Undocumented immigrants are not exempt from U.S. laws just because they do not have proper immigration paperwork, nor are they exempt because they may not have feelings of loyalty to the American government. The country's civil and criminal laws apply to them the same way that they apply to all others. Therefore, the jurisdictional argument is very problematic.

In addition, the United States has always promoted equality under the law, and the idea of punishing children for the acts of their parents violates the country's principles of justice. Discrimination based on status at birth is not permitted under the U.S. Constitution (*Weber v. Aetna Casualty & Surety Co.*, 1972). For example, the Supreme Court has struck down laws that penalize children born out of wedlock and found that not only did children have no responsibility for the actions of their parents but also that these policies made little sense and were ineffectual as a deterrent for parents. As the Court stated in *Trimble v. Gordon* (1977), the government should not "attempt to influence the actions of men and women by imposing sanctions on the children." Furthermore, the Court determined in *Weber v. Aetna Casualty & Surety Co.* (1972) that "[discriminating against] an illegitimate child is an ineffectual—as well as an unjust—way of deterring the parent."

Finally, even if one were to assume that there was a time when the American people had not given "consent" to birthright citizenship privileges for the U.S.-born children of the undocumented, surely that is no longer the case. The

Table 5.1   Poll results on birthright citizenship for the American-born children of undocumented immigrants (2010–2011)

	Wording indicating support for revision of automatic citizenship	(%)	Wording indicating opposition to elimination of automatic citizenship	(%)
Time Poll (June 2011)	Revise the 14th Amendment	35	Do not revise the 14th Amendment	62
USA Today/Gallup (January 2011)	Deny automatic citizenship (strongly favor/favor)	44	Deny automatic citizenship (oppose/strongly oppose)	54
Pew Center (September 2010)	Change the 14th Amendment	46	Leave the 14th Amendment as is	49
CNN/Opinion Research Corporation (August 2010)	Favor constitutional amendment to prevent automatic citizenship	49	Oppose constitutional amendment to prevent automatic citizenship	51
CBS News/*New York Times* (August 2010)	Change law to deny automatic citizenship	47	Keep the law as is and allow automatic citizenship	49
Associated Press/National Constitution Center (August 2010)	Favor constitutional amendment to prevent automatic citizenship	49	Oppose constitutional amendment to prevent automatic citizenship	51
Time/CNN Trends (September 1993)	Favor constitutional amendment to prevent automatic citizenship	49	Oppose constitutional amendment to prevent automatic citizenship	47

Sources: The PollingReport.com; CNN.com.

Supreme Court has accepted the precedent set by *U.S. v. Wong Kim Ark* in 1898 when it determined that the U.S-born children of Chinese immigrants are American citizens, and it conferred rights to the children of undocumented immigrants in *Plyler v. Doe* (1982). The issue of revising the citizenship clause has been on the public agenda since the early 1990s. Most legal scholars and jurists continue to be resistant to a reinterpretation of the Fourteenth Amendment that would exclude the U.S.-born children of undocumented immigrants from American citizenship. Congress has held hearings on the matter and political leaders and pundits have expressed their views but this has not helped to sway the public. American citizens remain divided on the issue, but recent polls indicate that they continue to lean towards preserving the Fourteenth Amendment intact. The year 2011 was marked by renewed debate on the merits of changing state and federal laws to exclude these children from citizenship (see Lacey, 2011; Preston, 2011; Reuters, 2011). The public, however, remains reluctant to endorse such a fundamental reform of the country's Constitution.

A number of public opinion polls conducted in 2010 and in 2011 showed a division among Americans on this issue. In fact, these polls mirror public opinion divides that have existed since the 1990s (see Table 5.1). Overall, a majority of Americans oppose any change or reinterpretation of the Fourteenth Amendment that would lead to an exclusion of these children from birthright citizenship. Polls conducted between August 2010 and June 2011 showed that between 49 and 62 percent of Americans do not want to see revisions of the Fourteenth Amendment.

According to a CBS News/*New York Times* poll conducted in August 2010, views on birthright citizenship for the children of undocumented immigrants are split along partisan lines. Opposition to any changes to birthright citizenship is strongest among Democrats (59%) and independents (47%) and weakest among Republicans (39%). But most polls show that only a minority of Americans (sizeable as it may be) supports a change in the rules that govern birthright citizenship, and this support seems to have become weaker over time. This indicates that the American people have consented to the established practice of conferring birthright citizenship to all U.S.-born children, including those of undocumented parentage.

THE SOCIAL COSTS OF DENYING BIRTHRIGHT CITIZENSHIP TO AMERICAN-BORN CHILDREN OF UNDOCUMENTED PARENTAGE

It is not sufficient to discuss the legal issues involved in excluding the American-born children of undocumented immigrants from birthright citizenship. Normative legal principles have implications for day-to-day life. One thus needs to ask what would be the social, economic, and moral implications of a policy that excludes the U.S.-born children of undocumented immigrants from birthright citizenship. As the Supreme Court has noted, policies that target children are not likely to be a deterrent for the actions of their parents. This means that, more likely than not, undocumented immigration will continue as long as the economic, social, and political conditions that feed it persist. If undocumented immigrants continue to arrive, and their children continue living in the United States and seeking to make a life here, what does that mean for these children and for American society?

It is important to understand that a policy that would deny birthright citizenship to the American-born children of undocumented immigrants has the potential to affect the lives of millions of children. In a recent study, the Pew Hispanic Center estimated that annually about 340,000 children born in the United States (or 8 percent of the total) have undocumented immigrant parents. In all, about 4 million U.S.-born children of undocumented immigrant parentage live in the United States, along with about 1.1 million foreign-born (and thus undocumented) siblings (Passel & Taylor, 2010). These American-born children (and their undocumented siblings) speak the English language; go to local schools; participate in community service, athletics, and arts; and contribute actively to their families, schools, and towns (Gonzales, 2009). Having been born in the United States, these children enjoy all the rights and privileges that are conferred by American citizenship, including the right to work for pay, vote and run for political office (when they turn 18 years of age), join the U.S. military, and receive services and social benefits.

A change to the current interpretation of the Fourteenth Amendment would relegate these individuals who are born in the United States—and who have developed economic, social, and emotional bonds with this country—to second-class citizenship status. Research shows that most of the children of immigrants who grow up in the United States speak English as their primary language (Alba, 2004; Portes & Hao, 2002; Portes & Rivas, 2011; Portes & Rumbaut, 2001). These children (and even their undocumented brothers and sisters) also tend to identify culturally and politically with the United States and not with the country of origin of their parents. In short, because they have grown up in the United States and been exposed to American education and culture, they have an American identity and an American way of life. Growing up in the United States also means that these children have families, friends, and a variety of groups to which they belong here in the United States. Socially, they belong in this country. Taking away their American citizenship would not make these children any less American in identity or any more likely to leave the United States. What a change in birthright citizenship would do is to create a generation of children who would be forced to live in the shadows as second-class citizens. Denial of birthright citizenship could also foster resentment among these U.S.-raised and educated children, limiting their commitment to the United States and opening the possibility of anti-American radicalization within the U.S. territory.

In the 1860s, according to the U.S. Census, there were about 4 million black slaves in the United States, most of whom were born in the country. Changing the Fourteenth Amendment would have the potential to create a similarly large number of American-born, undocumented children—many of them Latino and Asian—with no access to jobs, higher education, political rights, or formal permanent residence. Much like slaves, these children would be vulnerable to exploitation, cruelty, and other injustices. Government authorities could arbitrarily use the power of the state against these individuals. Not only is this incompatible with American principles of justice, it would lead to a host of social and economic problems, and these children and their descendants would be forced into a life of extreme poverty, an existence in the shadows, and fear of government and law enforcement. In effect, this policy would be creating a caste of perpetual undesirables, of people who generation after generation could be nothing but aliens, never able to become part of U.S. political society.

CONCLUSION

The repeal of birthright citizenship for the children of undocumented immigrants is neither a "simple" nor a fair solution to the challenges of immigration, as suggested by proponents of the Gallegly Amendment. This type of legislation is inconsistent with the principles and values embedded in the Constitution. The United States has embraced the principle of equality under the law, which implies that children cannot be held responsible for the sins of their parents, especially when this would translate into perpetual exclusion from American society. America has long sought to build social unity through integration of the children of immigrants.

Dr. Martin Luther King (1963) described the life of an African American under Jim Crow laws as "crippled by the manacles of segregation and the chains of discrimination," living "in a lonely island of poverty in the midst of a vast ocean of material prosperity," and "languished in the corners of American Society . . . an exile in his own land." The civil rights legislation of the 1950s and 1960s addressed many of these injustices and restored the political rights of America's blacks. Eliminating birthright citizenship for the American-born children of undocumented immigrants threatens to reinstate a system that America rejected 50 years ago because of its cruelty and injustice. As Professor Neuman (1996) put it, the authors of the Fourteenth Amendment and civil rights legislation "refused the invitation to create a hereditary caste of voteless denizens, vulnerable to expulsion and exploitation." Contemporary scholars, politicians, and pundits, as well as everyday citizens and students, would do well to follow the same course.

REFERENCES AND FURTHER READING

Alba, R. (2004). *Language assimilation today: Bilingualism persists more than in the past, but english still dominates.* Retrieved from Lewis Mumford Center for Comparative Urban and Regional Research website: http://mumford.albany.edu/children/reports/language_assimilation/language_assimilation_brief.pdf

Coulter, A. (2010, August 4). Justice Brennan's footnote gave us anchor babies. *Townhall.* Retrieved from http://townhall.com/columnists/anncoulter/2010/08/04/justice_brennans_footnote_gave_us_anchor_babies

Eastman, J. C. (2008). Born in the U.S.A: Rethinking birthright citizenship in the wake of 9/11. *Texas Review of Law and Politics, 12,* 168–179.

Gonzales, R. (2009). *Young lives on hold: The college dreams of undocumented students.* Retrieved from College Board Advocacy website: http://professionals.collegeboard.com/profdownload/young-lives-on-hold-college-board.pdf

Graglia, L. A. (2009). Birthright citizenship for children of illegal aliens: An irrational public policy. *Texas Review of Law and Politics, 14*(1), 1–14.

Kettner, J. H. (1978). *The development of American citizenship, 1608–1870.* Chapel Hill, NC: University of North Carolina Press.

King, M. L., Jr. (1963). I Have a Dream. Retrieved from American Rhetoric: Top 100 Speeches website: http://www.americanrhetoric.com/speeches/mlkihaveadream.htm

Lacey, M. (2011, January 5). Birthright citizenship looms as next immigration battle. *The New York Times.* Retrieved from http://www.nytimes.com/2011/01/05/us/politics/05babies.html

Nelan, B. W. (1993, December 2). Not quite so welcome anymore. *Time.* Retrieved from http://www.time.com/time/magazine/article/0,9171,979734,00.html

Neuman, G. (1996). *Strangers to the Constitution: Immigrants, borders and fundamental law.* Princeton, NJ: Princeton University Press.

Ngai, M. M. (2005). *Impossible subjects: Illegal aliens and the making of America.* Princeton, NJ: Princeton University Press.

Notes: The birthright citizenship amendment: A threat to equality. (1994, March). *Harvard Law Review, 107*(5), 1026–1043.

Passel, J. S., & Taylor, P. (2010). *Unauthorized immigrants and their U.S.-born children.* Washington, DC: Pew Hispanic Center.

Pear, R. (1996, August 7). Citizenship proposal faces obstacle in the Constitution. *The New York Times.* Retrieved from http://www.nytimes.com/1996/08/07/us/citizenship-proposal-faces-obstacle-in-the-constitution.html?scp=1&sq=illegal%20immigration%20birthright%20citizenship%201995&st=cse (Last accessed July 8, 2011).

Perez, W. (2009). *We are Americans: Undocumented students pursuing the American dream.* Sterling, VA: Stylus.

Portes, A., & Hao, L. (2002). The price of uniformity: Language, family and personal adjustment in the immigrant second generation. *Ethnic and Racial Studies, 25,* 889–912.

Portes, A., & Rivas, A. (2011). The adaptation of migrant children. *The Future of Children, 21*(1), 219–246.

Portes, A., & Rumbaut. R. (2001). *Legacies: The story of the immigrant second generation.* Berkeley, CA: University of California Press.

Preston, J. (2011, January 6). State lawmakers outline plans to end birthright citizenship, drawing outcry. *The New York Times,* p. 16.

Reuters. (2011, January 6). *State lawmakers target children of illegal immigrants.* Retrieved from http://www.reuters.com/article/2011/01/06/us-states-immigration-idUSTRE7045VO20110106

Rubin, J. (2011, January 30). Birthright citizenship. *The Washington Post.* Retrieved from http://voices.washingtonpost.com/right-turn/2011/01/birthright_citizenship.html

Schuck, P. H., & Smith, R. M. (1985). *Citizenship without consent: Illegal aliens in the American polity.* New Haven, CT: Yale University Press.

Smith, R. M. (2009). Birthright citizenship and the 14th Amendment in 1868 and 2008. *University of Pennsylvania Journal of Constitutional Law, 11,* 1329–1335.

Takaki, R. (1989). *Strangers from a different shore: A history of Asian Americans.* New York, NY: Little, Brown.

Will, G. F. (2010, March 28). An argument to be made about immigrant babies and citizenship. *The Washington Post.* Retrieved from http://www.washingtonpost.com/wp-dyn/content/article/2010/03/26/AR2010032603077.html

Wilson, P. (1993, August 20). Crack down on illegals. *USA Today,* p. 12A.

Alexandra Filindra

Note: Parts of this essay were originally intended as a response to an opinion editorial written by George F. Will in *The Washington Post* (2010). That version of the discussion benefitted from the active input of Jim Oberly, Donna R. Gabaccia, Katherine Fennelly, and Gerald Neuman. I would like to thank them for their suggestions, contributions, and edits.

COUNTERPOINT

A serious debate about the meaning of the Fourteenth Amendment's citizenship clause ("All persons born or naturalized in the United States, and subject to the jurisdiction thereof, are citizens of the United States and of the State wherein they reside") has arisen in recent years, provoked by issues surrounding illegal immigration. It has been assumed as a matter of course that the citizenship clause means that all persons born within the geographical limits of the United States are automatically citizens of the United States. But there are several flaws in this assumption that are easily demonstrated.

CITIZENSHIP AND THE DECLARATION OF DEPENDENCE

The Constitution mentions "citizens," but nowhere does it define "citizenship." Before they can be elected, members of the House of Representatives must be citizens for 7 years, while members of the Senate must be citizens for 9 years. The president, however, must be a "natural born Citizen, or a Citizen of the United States, at the time of the Adoption of the Constitution" and "been fourteen years a Resident within the United States." Thus, citizenship clearly precedes the Constitution. What, then, is the origin of American citizenship?

The Preamble to the Constitution states that "We the people of the United States . . . do ordain and establish this Constitution for the United States of America." Thus, the people created the Constitution, the Constitution did not create the people. When, then, did Americans become a "people"? Article VII specifies that the Constitution was "Done in Convention by the Unanimous Consent of the States present the Seventeenth Day of September in the Year of our Lord one thousand seven hundred and Eighty seven and of the Independence of the United States of America the Twelfth." Thus the "independence of the United States" is fixed on the date of the Declaration of Independence. The Declaration, of course, refers to Americans as "one people" and as "the good People," and it denominates "the people" as the ultimate authority for independence. Thus, one can conclude that the people who established and ordained the Constitution were the same people who dissolved "all Allegiance to the British Crown." The Declaration specifies that the only legitimate basis for citizenship is "the consent of the governed." The doctrine of social compact is thus intrinsic to the principles of the Declaration.

James Madison famously remarked that "compact, express or implied is the vital principle of free Governments." If it is true that "all men are created equal," then no one is by nature the ruler of another; legitimate rule must therefore be based on the consent of each and every person. John Adams gave a fuller explication of social compact in the Massachusetts Bill of Rights (1780):

> The end of the institution, maintenance and administration of government, is to secure the existence of the body politic, to protect it, and to furnish the individuals who compose it with the power of enjoying in safety and tranquility their natural rights . . . and whenever these great objects are not obtained, the people have a right to alter the government. . . . The body politic is formed by a voluntary association of individuals; it is a social compact by which the whole people covenants with each citizen and each citizen with the whole people that all shall be governed by certain laws for the common good. (Commager, 1973, p. 107)

The establishment of civil society thus requires reciprocal consent. Once civil society is established by the voluntary and unanimous consent of its members, new members can be added only with the consent of those who already constitute civil society. Just as no individual can be ruled without his consent, no one can join an already established civil society without the consent of the community. Naturalization is thus the result of a contract—an offer on one side and an acceptance of its conditions on the other. No community, of course, is obliged to accept new members; the determination to add new members is a matter of prudence and will be dictated by the "safety and happiness of the body politic."

Congress has the exclusive power under Article I of the Constitution "To establish an uniform Rule of Naturalization." A necessary inference from this power is that Congress also has exclusive power to regulate immigration as well as define the qualifications for citizenship. As a practical matter, however, until the adoption of the Fourteenth Amendment, state citizenship determined federal citizenship—those who were citizens of states were automatically deemed citizens of the United States.

THE FOURTEENTH AMENDMENT AND CITIZENSHIP

The Fourteenth Amendment reversed the relationship between state citizenship and federal citizenship, as federal citizenship became primary and state citizenship derivative. This change was necessary to prevent southern states from withholding federal citizenship—along with the whole panoply of privileges and immunities that attach to federal citizenship—from the newly freed slaves by withholding state citizenship. Everyone seems to agree that the principal purpose of the amendment was to overturn the *Dred Scott* decision and give constitutional status to the citizenship of African Americans. In doing so, the framers of the Fourteenth Amendment sought to fulfill the promise of the Declaration of Independence by completing the regime of the founding. Representative Thaddeus Stevens, a prominent member of the Joint Committee on Reconstruction, made the following remark during floor debate on May 8, 1866:

> Consider the magnitude of the task which was imposed upon the [members of the Joint Committee on Reconstruction]. They were expected to suggest a plan for rebuilding a shattered nation . . . It cannot be denied that this terrible struggle sprang from the vicious principles incorporated into the institutions of our country. Our fathers had been compelled to postpone the principles of their great Declaration, and wait for their full establishment till a more propitious time. That time ought to be now. (*Cong. Globe,* 39th Cong., 1st Sess. 2459 [1866])

Thus, for Stevens, the Fourteenth Amendment was intended to be a completion of the founding. The founding was incomplete because of the compromises with slavery. Insofar as the Constitution of 1789 tolerated the continued existence of slavery, it remained an incomplete expression of the principles of the Declaration of Independence. The protections for slavery were necessary to purchase the support of the slaveholding states for a strong national government. And, as the most perceptive Federalists understood, without a strong national government, the prospects of ever ending slavery were remote. Madison defended the compromises in the Virginia Ratifying Convention on June 17, 1788. "Great as the evil is," Madison remarked, "a dismemberment of the union would be worse." Without protections for slavery, "the southern states would not have entered into the union of America . . . [a]nd if they were excluded from the union, the consequences might be dreadful to them and to us." These compromises were justified, of course, only to the extent that they provided a foundation for eventual emancipation. The Constitution's grounding in the principles of the Declaration made the eventual abolition of slavery a moral imperative.

On February 15, 1866 Representative William Newell commented on the relation of the Declaration and the Constitution, noting, "the framers of the Constitution did what they considered best under the circumstances. They made freedom the rule and slavery the exception in the organization of the Government. They declared in favor of the former in language most emphatic and sublime in history, while they placed the latter, as they fondly hoped, in a position favorable for ultimate extinction" (*Cong. Globe,* 39th Cong., 1st Sess. 866 [1866]). Newell here was echoing the words of Abraham Lincoln, whose omnipresent spirit surely animated the deliberations of the 39th Congress. Lincoln always maintained that the Constitution, understood properly in the light of the principles of the Declaration, had put slavery "in course of ultimate extinction." References to the Declaration as "organic law" were so frequent throughout the debates that one can hardly doubt that the Reconstruction Congress conceived its principal task as completing the regime of the founding, a founding that had been rendered incomplete because of its compromises with slavery.

THE CITIZENSHIP CLAUSE

The Fourteenth Amendment specifies two requirements to become a citizen: one must be born or naturalized in the United States, and one must be "subject to the jurisdiction" of the United States. If it is argued that everyone born within the territorial limits of the United States is automatically subject to the jurisdiction of the United States, then the requirement of "jurisdiction" is rendered superfluous. But a principle of construction that is intrinsic to a written constitution dictates that no interpretation can render any provision without force or effect. This would be tantamount to an amendment of the Constitution by interpretation. If the framers of the Fourteenth Amendment had intended that everyone born within the geographical limits of the United States were automatically subject to its jurisdiction, they would simply have omitted this phrase—precisely what liberal constitutionalists have done in their insistence on automatic birthright citizenship.

Senator Jacob Howard of Michigan was a member of the Joint Committee on Reconstruction (1865–1867) and one of the architects of the citizenship clause. During Senate debate, he defended his handiwork against the charge that it would make Native Americans citizens of the United States. "Indians born within the limits of the United States, and who maintain their tribal relations," he assured a skeptical Senate on May 30, 1866, "are not, in the sense of this amendment, born subject to the jurisdiction of the United States." Senator Lyman Trumbull of Illinois, chairman of the Senate Judiciary Committee, supported Howard, contending that "subject to the jurisdiction thereof" meant "not owing allegiance to anybody else . . . subject to the complete jurisdiction of the United States." Indians, he maintained, were not "subject to the jurisdiction" of the United States because they owed allegiance—even if only partial allegiance—to their tribes. Native Americans were, of course, born within the geographical limits of the United States, but from the point of view of the principal framers of the Fourteenth Amendment, this did not make them automatically "subject to the jurisdiction" of the United States.

Jurisdiction did not mean, as liberal constitutionalists casually argue, simply subject to the laws of the United States or subject to the jurisdiction of its courts. Rather, "jurisdiction" meant exclusive "allegiance" to the United States. Not all who are subject to the laws of the United States owe allegiance to the United States. As Senator Howard remarked, the requirement of "jurisdiction," understood in the sense of "allegiance," "will not, of course, include persons born in the United States who are foreigners, aliens, who belong to the families of ambassadors or foreign ministers accredited to the Government of the United States." Speaking in support of the citizenship clause, Senator John Bingham of Ohio, another member of the Joint Committee on Reconstruction, remarked on March 9, 1866, that the citizenship clause "is simply declaratory of what is written in the Constitution, that every human being born within the jurisdiction of the United States of parents not owing allegiance to any foreign sovereignty is, in the language of our Constitution itself, a natural-born citizen." Thus, Bingham also understood jurisdiction in terms of allegiance. For the framers of the Fourteenth Amendment, jurisdiction did not mean merely subject to the laws or the courts.

It is impossible to believe that the framers of the Fourteenth Amendment intended to confer the boon of citizenship on the children of illegal aliens when they explicitly denied that boon to Native Americans. It is also common for liberal interpreters to say that denying birthright citizenship to the children of illegal aliens unjustly visits the sins of the parents upon the children. But, of course, these children are not denied any rights that they would otherwise be entitled to.

COMMON LAW AND CITIZENSHIP

In 1898, the Supreme Court, in *U.S. v. Wong Kim Ark,* proclaimed that the Fourteenth Amendment adopted the common law definition of citizenship and therefore must be interpreted in terms of common law principles. The problem with this assertion is manifest: the idea of citizenship is utterly unknown to the common law.

The common law recognizes "subjectship" but not citizenship. William Blackstone's *Commentaries on the Laws of England* (1765–1769), the authoritative source for interpreting the common law, details the common law of "subjectship." At the core of "subjectship," Blackstone argued, is the idea of "perpetual allegiance" or "natural allegiance." "Natural allegiance," according to Blackstone,

> is such as is due from all men born within the king's dominions immediately upon their birth. For immediately upon their birth, they are under the king's protection. . . . Natural allegiance is therefore a debt of gratitude which cannot be forfeited, cancelled, or altered, by any change of time, place, or circumstance. . . . For it is a principle of universal law, that the natural-born subject of one prince cannot by any act of his own, no, not by swearing allegiance to another, put off or discharge his natural allegiance of the former: for this natural allegiance was intrinsic, and primitive, and antecedent to the other. (pp. 350–351)

Blackstone admitted that the common law doctrine of birthright subjectship, originally propounded by Lord Edward Coke in *Calvin's Case* (1608), was an inheritance from the "feudal system," deriving from the "mutual trust or confidence subsisting between the lord and vassal," and "by an easy analogy the term allegiance was soon brought to signify all other engagements, which are due from subjects to their prince" (pp. 354–355).

The idea of citizenship, of course, was impossible in the feudal regime. Neither Coke nor Blackstone ever refers to birthright citizenship, and both describe the allegiance due to a king as involuntary and perpetual. This is the relation of master and subject, in which subjects can never gain the elevated status of citizens who not only freely accept obligations but also have the obligation to assert rights. James Wilson almost certainly had Blackstone in mind when, in 1793, he noted, "under the Constitution of the United States there are citizens, but no subjects." Wilson, a member of the Constitutional Convention, and later a justice of the Supreme Court, thus rendered his judgment that American citizenship did not derive from the common law.

The Declaration of Independence was an unambiguous repudiation of the "feudal" doctrine of perpetual allegiance that was at the heart of "birthright subjectship." The Declaration emphatically announced that "these United Colonies are . . . Absolved from all Allegiance to the British Crown, and that all political connection between them and the State of Great Britain, is and ought to be totally dissolved." The dissolution of perpetual allegiance, of course, is impossible under the common law. It is therefore improbable that the founders of the American regime adopted the principle of birthright allegiance as the basis for American citizenship at the same time that they were dissolving their perpetual allegiance to the King of England. The principles of the Declaration transform subjects into citizens by making consent of the governed—not accident of birth—the ground of citizenship. Chief Justice Melville Fuller, in his dissenting opinion in *Wong Kim Ark,* rightly noted that "from the Declaration of Independence to this day the United States have rejected the doctrine of indissoluble allegiance." It is difficult to avoid the conclusion that birthright allegiance and birthright subjectship were rejected by the Declaration no less than by the framers of the Fourteenth Amendment. To say nothing of other considerations no less important, "subjectship" and "citizenship" are not convertible terms.

THE EXPATRIATION ACT OF 1868

This conclusion is amply supported by the debate surrounding the passage of the Expatriation Act of 1868—indeed, this act should be properly considered as a necessary companion piece to the citizenship clause of the Fourteenth Amendment. The act provided, in relevant part, that "the right of expatriation is a natural and inherent right of all people, indispensable to the enjoyment of the rights of life, liberty, and the pursuit of happiness."

Senator Howard, whom we have already seen as one of the architects of the Fourteenth Amendment's citizenship clause, was a prominent figure in support of the legislation. He noted that the principles of the Declaration of Independence—reflected in the language of the act itself—meant that "the right of expatriation . . . is inherent and natural in man as man." The notion of birthright citizenship was frequently described in the debate as an "indefensible feudal doctrine of indefeasible allegiance." One member of the House of Representatives expressed the general sense of the Congress when he concluded that "it is high time that feudalism were driven from our shores and eliminated from our law, and now is the time to declare it."

Representative Frederick Woodbridge of Vermont, one of the principal proponents of the legislation, argued before the House on January 30, 1868, that the doctrine of perpetual allegiance "is based upon the feudal systems under which there were no free citizens . . . and the individual man [had] no personal rights; and it was from this source and system that Blackstone derived his idea of indefeasible and perpetual allegiance to the English Crown." But, Woodbridge continued,

> the old feudal doctrine stated by Blackstone and adopted as part of the common law of England, that once a citizen by the accident of birth expatriation under any circumstances less than the consent of the sovereign is an impossibility. The doctrine . . . is not only at war with our institutions, but is equally at war with every principle of justice and of sound public law. (*Cong. Globe,* 40th Cong., 2nd Sess. 868 [1868])

This unequivocal repudiation of Blackstone makes it impossible to maintain that the common law was the basis of American citizenship. Perpetual allegiance and birthright subjectship are utterly alien to the principles of the Declaration, which grounds citizenship on the consent of the governed.

THE *WONG KIM ARK* CASE

Wong Kim Ark involved the question of whether someone born in the United States of legal immigrants was a natural born citizen in terms of the Fourteenth Amendment. Wong Kim Ark's parents were, by treaty and statute, ineligible for American citizenship, and they freely acknowledged that they retained their allegiance to the emperor of China. It is clear that the framers of the Fourteenth Amendment would not have considered the children of these parents, though born in the United States, to be subject to the jurisdiction of the United States. Since the parents owed no allegiance to the United States, their children would follow the allegiance of the parents who, while subject to the laws of the United States, were not subject to its jurisdiction as understood by the framers of the citizenship provisions of the Fourteenth Amendment.

Ever since *Wong Kim Ark*'s mistaken holding that the Fourteenth Amendment adopted the common law of "birthright citizenship," it has been assumed that all persons born within the geographical limits of the United States are automatically citizens of the nation, regardless of whether the parents are within the jurisdiction of the United States or have legal residence in the country. Although some of the language of the majority opinion in *Wong Kim Ark* seems capacious enough to include the children of illegal aliens, there has been no Supreme Court decision explicitly holding that the children of illegal aliens are automatically accorded birthright citizenship.

SECTION 5 OF THE FOURTEENTH AMENDMENT

After the passage of the Fourteenth Amendment (which all sides agreed did not extend citizenship to Native Americans), Congress began to pass legislation inviting members of various Indian tribes to become citizens of the United States. Any tribal member who consented to become a citizen would thus become "subject to the jurisdiction" of the United States by legislative enactment. Under Section 5 of the Fourteenth Amendment, Congress has the power to implement the provisions of the amendment. In the offer of citizenship to Native persons, Congress extended "jurisdiction" to those who had been admittedly excluded at the time of the adoption of the Fourteenth Amendment, and in 1924 this offer was extended to all Native persons. Here was an offer of citizenship that could be accepted by anyone consenting to the terms of the proffer. This was a perfect example of the social contract basis of citizenship derived from reciprocal consent that was described by John Adams in the Massachusetts Bill of Rights of 1780 (and quoted *in extenso* earlier in this essay).

Presumably, Congress could exercise the same legislative power under Section 5 to exclude as well as include people who are "subject to the jurisdiction" of the United States. It would not require a constitutional amendment, as some claim, to exclude from "jurisdiction" the children of illegal alien parents who are born within the geographical limits of the U.S. Congress can simply exercise its Section 5 powers—as it has done many times in the case of Native Americans—to define by legislation those who are properly within the jurisdiction of the United States.

Such legislation, of course, would not affect anyone who is currently a citizen of the United States. It has been well established by the Supreme Court that involuntary expatriation is virtually impossible without the knowing consent of the parties involved. The Court has held involuntary expatriation to be a violation of the Eighth Amendment's prohibition on cruel and unusual punishment. American citizenship, once vested, cannot be divested. Nor, would Section 5 legislation create second-class citizens or lead to a legal caste system. These arguments against reforming automatic birthright citizenship are at best misdirected. All citizens have constitutional protections, most importantly the Fifth and Fourteenth Amendment guarantees of equal protection of the laws. Equal protection of the laws is at the very core of the social compact understanding of the origin of civil society: members of civil society consent to be governed in exchange for the equal protection of equal rights. It is this understanding of civil society and citizenship that animated the framers of the Fourteenth Amendment.

A prospective law that would apply to any future children born in the United States of illegal alien parents would be unobjectionable under the core theory of the Fourteenth Amendment. Opponents of such legislation apparently believe that illegal aliens can unilaterally put themselves within the jurisdiction of the United States—not only without its consent but in express violation of its laws—and thus confer citizenship upon their children without the consent of the United States. It should seem obvious that the citizenship clause cannot be read in a manner to dissolve the sovereignty of the United States. After all, a country that cannot determine who becomes citizens—or distinguish between citizens and aliens—is no longer sovereign.

POSTMODERN CITIZENSHIP

President George W. Bush famously announced that "family values don't stop at the border." Here the president, a supporter of amnesty and a path to citizenship for illegal aliens, clearly indicated that certain "universal values" transcend a nation's sovereignty. If the United States is more interested in promoting "family values" for citizens of other countries, then the nation's sovereignty—and the privileges and immunities that attach particularly to American citizenship—will be in grave danger.

One of the principal causes of the decline in citizenship based on the nation-state, according to David A. Jacobson, in his *Rights Across Borders: Immigration and the Decline of Citizenship* (1997), is "that the state has lost control of international migration. The transnational lines that have developed, as a consequence, between the aliens and their associations and groups in the host society have had the effect of loosening state-society ties . . . Most important," Jacobson concludes, "the fundamental relationship between state and citizen is broken" (p. 70).

The same kind of confusion that has led to an acceptance of birthright citizenship for the children of illegal aliens has led to the toleration of dual citizenship. The framers of the Fourteenth Amendment specified that those who are naturalized must owe exclusive allegiance to the United States to be included within its jurisdiction. The citizenship oath still requires a pledge of exclusive allegiance to the United States. In practice, however, dual citizenship—and dual allegiance—is allowed. To some, including this author, this casual acceptance of dual citizenship is a sign of the decline of American citizenship and America's decline as a nation-state. Dual citizenship, of course, involves multiple allegiances. It is remarkable that 85 percent of all immigrants arriving in the United States come from countries that allow—and encourage—dual citizenship. Dual citizens, of course, give the sending countries a unique political presence in the United States, and many countries use their dual citizens to promote their own interests by exerting pressure on American politicians and policymakers. Such foreign meddling in the internal political affairs of the United States has become quite routine, creating the impossible situation whereby a newly naturalized citizen can swear exclusive allegiance to the United States but retain allegiance to a vicious despotism or a theocratic tyranny.

DO ILLEGAL ALIENS WANT AMERICAN CITIZENSHIP?

It is often said that illegal aliens come to the United States not to seek citizenship for themselves or for their children, but for economic advantages, to improve the lives of themselves and their families. The government of Mexico, of course, actively abets and aids the illegal crossing of the U.S.-Mexico border. Mexico has a strong interest in increasing the number of illegal immigrants in the United States, and it is only too willing to exploit its own citizens. Illegal immigration provides a convenient outlet for Mexico's desperately poor and malcontent. The remittances sent home to Mexico by illegal aliens in the United States form a significant component of the Mexican economy. Another spur to illegal immigration in recent years has been the rise of violence in Mexico due to the illegal drug trade. Mexico is on the verge of becoming a failed state, and many Mexicans are desperate to find refuge in the United States.

Despite assurances that illegal immigrants are not interested in American citizenship, there has been a steady drum beat of demands emanating from immigrant advocacy groups, not only for amnesty for lawbreakers, but for a path to citizenship as well. These advocacy groups know the value that illegal aliens attach to American citizenship. As conditions in Mexico deteriorate, demands for a path to citizenship increase. Desperate Mexicans, along with other desperate people in the world, recognize the benefits of American citizenship. To such individuals, the United States is not only a place for political refuge, but also one with enormous economic benefits. Children of illegal immigrants born in the United States are immediately eligible for welfare benefits, and these benefits can extend to their parents as well. As anyone who has traveled extensively in the less developed regions of the world knows, the desperate and unfortunate of the world recognize the value of American citizenship.

BIRTH TOURISM

Birth tourism to the United States has increased in recent years. Wealthy and middle-class women travel to the United States from all parts of the globe to give birth to their children. This, of course, confers valuable birthright citizenship on the children. Dual citizenship, in these cases, provides advantages in the country of origin as well as in the United States. By all accounts, the number of women who travel to the United States for this purpose, both legally and illegally, is not large, but it is increasing. This phenomenon seems to be proof—as if proof were necessary—that many parts of the world consider American citizenship to be of almost inestimable value. It is difficult, if not impossible, however, to believe that the framers of the Fourteenth Amendment, who believed that allegiance was a crucial element in American citizenship, could have anticipated that such casual sojourners in the United States would fall within the jurisdiction requirements of the citizenship clause. It may well be argued—as President Bush did argue—that we should be more than willing to extend compassion to our less fortunate neighbors. Compassion, however, is not a solid basis either for foreign policy or immigration policy. Compassion is more likely to lead to contempt than gratitude in both policy areas, as recent history has amply demonstrated.

President Barack Obama's policy of "engagement" with such nations as Iran, Egypt, North Korea, and Syria (and even such Cold War adversaries as the former Soviet Union and China) has been contemptuously rebuffed by those countries. These failures serve as reminders of the useful Machiavellian adage that in the *real politik* world of foreign affairs it is better to be feared than loved. Fear is more likely to engender respect, whereas love or compassion is more likely to be regarded as a contemptible sign of weakness.

Similarly, the 1986 Immigration Reform and Control Act, which provided amnesty for illegal aliens, was widely touted as an act of compassion or humanity. Three million illegal aliens were granted amnesty in what President Ronald Reagan said was a way of "humanely" dealing with the issue of illegal immigration. The act, Reagan claimed in his signing statement, "is both generous to the alien and fair to the countless thousands of people throughout the world who seek legally to come to America." This act, of course, fueled expectations—and even demands—from those "countless thousands" for additional amnesties, even that amnesties become a regular feature of American immigration policy. Amnesty and a path to citizenship was, of course, an integral part of President George W. Bush's "compassionate conservatism." Delays in implementing new amnesties have been treated with contempt by immigration activists and proffered as evidence that the American people are "heartless" (to use the characterization of a candidate for the 2012 Republican nomination for president). In some activist quarters, amnesty—and even citizenship—is considered to be a right that attaches to "universal personhood."

In any case, since the Constitution authorizes Congress only to pass a "uniform Rule of Naturalization," there is a serious question about whether a law that targets a discrete group for amnesty or naturalization can pass constitutional muster, since the law would obviously not be "uniform." However noble and inspiring the sentiments on the Statue of Liberty may be, they are not part of the Constitution. The Constitution, of course, commands that the interests of American citizens take precedence over any demands emanating from the "world community."

SOVEREIGNTY AND CONSTITUTIONAL DEMOCRACY

Historically, constitutional democracy has existed only in the nation-state. When citizenship is debased and diluted—when a nation no longer controls who becomes citizens—a nation's sovereignty is undermined. As Jeremy A. Rabkin, in *Law Without Nations? Why Constitutional Government Requires Sovereign States* (2005), observes:

> In the modern world, sovereignty has been closely associated with constitutional government, at least in the sense that constitutional government has only been achieved in sovereign states. And it is only in the modern practice of constitutional government that guarantees of personal liberty have been combined with political structures capable of sustaining stable democracy. (p. 16)

The demise of the nation-state will almost certainly be the demise of constitutional democracy. No one believes that the European Union or similar organizations will ever produce constitutional government. The EU is well on the road to becoming an administrative tyranny (if it survives its current economic crisis). The homogeneous world state—the EU on a global scale—will not be a constitutional democracy; it will be the administration of "universal personhood" without the inconvenience of having to rely on the consent of the governed. Thus, after many centuries we seem to be on the verge of reinstituting feudalism, this time on a world scale, where citizenship will be replaced by the master-servant relationship—or to use slightly different language, where all people will become clients of the world administrative state. The continued vitality of the nation-state, and the continued vitality of constitutional government, depends on the continuing vitality of a citizenship that carries with it exclusive allegiance to a "separate and equal" nation. This author thinks everyone realizes that in the world homogeneous state of the future, there will be subjects but no citizens.

REFERENCES AND FURTHER READING

Blackstone, W. (1979). Of the people, whether aliens, denizens, or natives. In *Commentaries on the Laws of England* (Vol. 1). Chicago, IL: University of Chicago Press. (Original work published 1765–1769)

Commanger, H. S. (Ed.). (1973). *Documents of American history* (Vol. 1). Englewood Cliffs, NJ: Prentice Hall.

Congressional Globe, 39th Cong. 1st Sess. (1866).

Congressional Globe, 40th Cong. 2nd Sess. (1868).

Erler, E. J. (2003). From subjects to citizens: The social compact origins of American citizenship. In R. J. Pestritto & T. G. West (Eds.), *The American founding and the social compact* (pp. 163–197). Lanham, MD: Lexington Books.

Erler, E. J., West, T. G., & Marini, J. (2007). *The Founders on citizenship and immigration.* Lanham, MD: Rowman & Littlefield.

Graham, H. D. (2002). *Collision course: The strange convergence of affirmative action and immigration policy in America.* New York, NY: Oxford University Press.

Huntington, S. P. (2004). *Who are we: Challenges to America's national identity.* New York, NY: Simon & Schuster.

Jacobson, D. A. (1997). *Rights across borders: Immigration and the decline of citizenship.* Baltimore, MD: Johns Hopkins University Press.

Kettner, J. H. (1978). *The development of American citizenship, 1608–1870.* Chapel Hill, NC: University of North Carolina Press.

Pickus, N. (2005). *True faith and allegiance: Immigration and American civic nationalism.* Princeton, NJ: Princeton University Press.

Rabkin, J. A. (2005). *Law without nations? Why constitutional government requires sovereign states.* Princeton, NJ: Princeton University Press.

Schuck, P. H. (1998). *Citizens, strangers, and in-betweens: Essays on immigration and citizenship.* Boulder, CO: Westview.

Edward J. Erler

Immigrant Voting

POINT: For most of America's history, voting by noncitizens was the norm rather than the exception in the vast majority of the country. Although it is not widely known, noncitizens can currently vote in local elections in Chicago and Maryland, while campaigns to expand the franchise to noncitizens have been launched in at least a dozen other jurisdictions since 1990.

Ron Hayduk, Queens College, City University of New York

COUNTERPOINT: Immigrant voting does not enhance American democracy or democratic polities in general. Indeed, it may not be in the interest of immigrants either, because noncitizen voting could contribute to making the polity to which they have migrated a less attractive and more undemocratic place to live.

Rodolfo O. de la Garza, Columbia University

Introduction

When the American media focuses its attention on immigration, it tends to dwell on the more sensationalistic aspects, such as "illegal aliens" or immigrants who commit crimes. But those stories overlook an important, albeit less dramatic, fact: 30 million people in the United States, or roughly 1 in 10, are noncitizen immigrants. They pay taxes, they are subject to U.S. laws, some even serve in the military—but as noncitizens they are ineligible to vote. In this chapter, Ron Hayduk and Rodolfo O. de la Garza debate whether suffrage should be extended to legal immigrants who are not citizens.

In the Point essay, Hayduk points out that noncitizen voting has a long history in the United States. Many people might be surprised to hear that noncitizens have frequently been allowed to vote in the past: there is nothing in the U.S. constitution that forbids the practice, and between 1776 and 1926, 40 states allowed noncitizens to vote and to hold office. Even today, many cities across the country do allow some voting among noncitizens, especially in school board and local elections. Nearly 60 countries around the world today allow resident noncitizens to vote in at least some circumstances.

Hayduk argues that late-twentieth-century globalization has made the suffrage issue more pertinent than ever. Some cities, such as Los Angeles and New York, have immigrants as a sizeable portion of the voting-age population. But despite their numbers, noncitizens are excluded from the decision-making process that touches their daily lives in many ways. On the most basic level, legal immigrants pay taxes that go toward the salaries of elected representatives, and yet they have no say in who those representatives are. The concept of "no taxation without representation" was central to the foundation of the United States, and yet it plays virtually no role for about one-tenth of America's adult population. Groups that had historically been excluded from the political process, such as African Americans and women, have seen their fortunes rise after suffrage was obtained. As Hayduk points out, "without the vote, noncitizens are at risk of discrimination and bias because policymakers can, and often do, ignore their interests."

In the Counterpoint essay, however, de la Garza makes the case that areas with large immigrant populations already have representatives who concern themselves with ethnic voters who live in their districts, if not the noncitizen voting bloc as a whole. "The congressmen and women who are elected from these districts," de la Garza notes, "are such strong immigrant advocates that it is difficult to imagine how immigrant voting could further influence them."

More importantly, de la Garza worries that to extend suffrage too far is to cheapen it—the preservation of democracy depends on citizens who understand and appreciate what is at stake in any given election. He argues that extending that privilege to people who have one foot in one land and one in another would prove a grave mistake. "Throughout their stay," de la Garza writes, "the right to vote will have enabled [immigrants] to influence policy to benefit themselves and their homeland while de-emphasizing their concern for the well-being of the receiving state."

While reading this chapter, consider whether immigrants have legitimate claims on the American polity, and by what measure is a claim by an immigrant judged to be "legitimate"? Does giving voting rights to noncitizens cheapen the value of U.S. citizenship? Or would granting the vote to immigrants make the U.S. government more responsive to their needs and, in turn, make immigrants more faithful to the United States? Would opening suffrage to noncitizens imperil our democracy? Why or why not?

POINT

Immigrants, or noncitizens, are as varied as the hundreds of countries they come from, but they all have one thing in common: they are without a formal political voice. Today, more than 30 million people in every walk of life, or 1 in 10 U.S. residents, are immigrants who are not U.S. citizens. They include teachers, students, firefighters, police officers, shopkeepers, nurses, doctors, athletes, movie stars, musicians, construction workers, gardeners, nannies, scientists, and workers of every kind, and they live in every state, city, suburb, and nearly every town in America. Like citizens, noncitizen immigrants work in every sector of the economy, own businesses, pay taxes, raise families, make countless social and cultural contributions, are subject to all U.S. laws, and participate in every aspect of daily social life. Although noncitizens behave in much the same ways as citizens, they possess fewer rights and benefits. For one, they cannot vote for the representatives who make the policies that affect their daily lives.

According to projections by the U.S. Census Bureau, immigrants are here to stay, and their numbers will only increase. However, immigrants who want to become U.S. citizens are often stymied, largely due to bureaucratic red tape. The average time it takes many immigrants to become a U.S. citizen—or to "naturalize"—is 10 years or longer after they arrive in America, up from 8 years in 1960, according to the U.S. Census Bureau. In addition, unlike in earlier times, when almost everyone who came to the United States was able to naturalize, not all immigrants are eligible to become U.S. citizens today, for it is a much harder and lengthier process today than it was in the past. In many jurisdictions in the early twenty-first century, anywhere from 10 to 50 percent of the adult population are barred from voting because they are noncitizens. The political exclusion of noncitizens raises troubling questions about the nature of U.S. democracy. Why shouldn't immigrants be able to vote?

The idea of allowing noncitizens to vote may sound odd or outlandish. For most Americans, voting is the essence of citizenship. But it was not always so, nor need it be. In considering the case for immigrant voting rights, there are three things to keep in mind:

1. *It's legal.* The U.S. Constitution does not preclude it and the courts, including the Supreme Court, have upheld voting by noncitizens. Noncitizens have enjoyed voting rights for most of U.S. history, and they continue to do so today.

2. *It's rational.* There are moral and practical reasons to restore immigrant voting—including notions of equal rights and treatment—as well as mutual benefits that accrue to all community members, citizen and noncitizen alike.

3. *It's feasible.* Noncitizen voting is making a comeback in the United States and is expanding globally.

Americans are usually surprised to learn that immigrants enjoyed voting rights for most of American history and throughout the vast majority of the country. In fact, from 1776 to 1926, 40 states and federal territories permitted noncitizens to vote in local, state, and even federal elections. Noncitizens also held public office, such as alderman, coroner, and school board member. In practice, immigrant voting promoted civic education and citizenship. Immigrants learned civics by practice, and immigrant voting was an effective method for facilitating the incorporation of immigrants. The notion that noncitizens should have the vote is older, was practiced longer, and is more consistent with democratic ideals than the idea that they should not. Curiously, this 150-year history has been eviscerated from American national memory.

Nor is immigrant voting merely a relic of the distant past. Noncitizens currently vote in local elections in over a half dozen cities and towns in the United States, most notably in Chicago's school elections and in all local elections in six towns in Maryland. In addition, campaigns to expand the franchise to noncitizens, primarily in local elections, have been launched in more than a dozen other jurisdictions since 2000, including in New York, Massachusetts, Washington, D.C., California, Maine, Colorado, Minnesota, Wisconsin, Connecticut, Vermont, New Jersey, and Texas. These campaigns propose to restore voting rights for immigrants in local elections, though only a few have contemplated state-level elections, and none would grant voting to immigrants in any national election. There are slight variations in which categories of noncitizens can vote. Some cities and towns allow all immigrants to vote, including undocumented or "illegal" immigrants (in Chicago and Maryland), while other places grant suffrage only to documented or "legal" immigrants (Massachusetts). Differences also exist regarding which elections noncitizens can vote in, such as in school board elections, municipal elections, or state races. Although different terms are used to describe immigrant voting, including "noncitizen voting," "resident voting," "local citizenship," and "alien suffrage," they all mean essentially the same thing: enfranchising or restoring voting rights to those who are excluded from the electorate, namely immigrants who are not U.S. citizens.

The effort to expand the franchise to immigrants is not particular to the United States; it is a global phenomenon. (See Table 6.1 at the end of this essay for more details on noncitizen voting rights in other countries.) Nearly 60 countries on nearly every continent allow resident noncitizens to vote at the local, regional, or national level, and most adopted such legislation during the past three decades. Europe provides a compelling case for noncitizen voting rights. The 1993 Maastricht Treaty granted all Europeans the right to vote in European countries other than their own, expanding what has been practiced for years in Sweden (since 1975), Ireland (1975), the Netherlands (1975), Denmark (1977), and Norway (1978). In the 1980s, the Netherlands, Venezuela, Ireland, Spain, and Iceland enacted legislation enfranchising resident aliens; several Swiss cantons (e.g., Neuchâtel and Jura) have long permitted noncitizen voting; Finland and Iceland allow Nordic citizens voting rights; and Estonia allows noncitizen voting at the local level. In fact, noncitizen immigrants vote on nearly every continent, including in Latin America, New Zealand, and the Caribbean, and in countries as varied as Barbados, Belize, Canada, Chile, Iceland, Israel, New Zealand, Uruguay, and Venezuela.

These policy changes reveal much about the evolution of citizenship and the practice of democracy in the era of globalization. Just as goods and services (products and people) are highly mobile today, notions that rights should follow migrants and apply to immigrants have also become more common. In short, struggles for human rights are on the rise.

This essay examines the politics and practices of noncitizen voting in the United States, chronicling the rise and fall—and reemergence—of immigrant voting. In addition, this essay looks at the arguments for and against noncitizen voting, and its impact on policy and American political development.

THE RISE OF IMMIGRANT VOTING

Contrary to the dominant narrative about a consistent expansion of democracy and political participation in the United States, the history of immigrant suffrage provides a more accurate lens to expose a recurring pattern that runs throughout the history of American voting rights: one step forward and two steps back. At various points in American history, an influx of newer immigrants has sparked a wave of nationalism and nativism—often associated with war or political conflict—and a rollback of voting rights. Alternatively, and sometimes simultaneously, struggles to expand democratic participation and economic imperatives—such as westward expansion and the need for labor—have spurred further cycles of migration and conflict, which have led to additional changes in electoral arrangements.

Before the American Revolution, Benjamin Franklin framed the importance of voting rights pointedly: "They who have no voice nor vote in the electing of representatives do not enjoy liberty, but are absolutely enslaved to those who have votes." Many of the early colonies had already allowed noncitizen residents to vote, and the practice was continued when the new states formed their constitutions. The emerging republicanism and liberalism in early America made noncitizen voting a reasonable practice that was difficult to challenge. America's diversity was evident at the time of the Revolution, and alien suffrage was a logical extension of the Revolutionary cry, "No taxation without representation!" Democratic notions, such as the belief that governments derive their "just powers from the consent of the governed," became "common sense."

During the first decades of U.S. history, voting rights were determined not by citizenship but by whether or not one was a white, male property holder. Thus, women and post-emancipation blacks—who were citizens—could be denied voting rights on the basis of sex or race, not citizenship per se. "Alien suffrage" was compatible with the exclusion of other categories of residents (women, men without property, and blacks) and actually buttressed the privileging of propertied white, male Christians.

However, early Americans also viewed alien suffrage as an effective method to encourage newcomers to make America their home. Budding Americans learned civics by practice, and getting a taste for democracy furthered immigrants' understanding of the political system and nurtured attachments to their adopted communities. Congress promoted noncitizen voting in the Northwest Ordinance of 1789, which gave "freehold aliens" with 2 years of residency the vote for territorial legislative representatives. Furthermore, it granted "wealthier" resident aliens with 3 years of residency the right to serve in territorial legislatures. Subsequently, Congress granted voting rights for immigrants in the new territories of Washington, Kansas, Nebraska, Nevada, the Dakotas, Wyoming, and Oklahoma, and also authorized the right of aliens to vote for representatives to statewide constitutional conventions in Ohio, Indiana, Michigan, and Illinois.

Wisconsin developed a formula in 1848, which became a model for other states and Congress going forward, which allowed aliens who "declared" their intent to become citizens the right to vote. The declarant alien qualification helped weaken objections of nativists, recasting how alien suffrage was conceived and practiced. Alien suffrage was now seen more clearly to be a pathway to citizenship rather than a substitute for it—a kind of pre-citizen voting. Declarant aliens were now presumed to be on the citizenship track, a line of reasoning that proved effective to deflect opponents' objections that immigrant voting would deter newcomers from naturalizing.

Soldiers returning from the Civil War demanded the right to vote, providing another effective argument for alien suffrage. Immigrant soldiers argued for and obtained what many perceived as their just reward for service, particularly given they fought for the freedom and voting rights of blacks. Another Civil War–related reason was the need to attract cheap labor, particularly in the South and West after the abolition of slavery. Many new states and territories used voting rights as an incentive to attract new immigrant settlers and as a pathway to citizenship, though not as a substitute.

THE DECLINE OF IMMIGRANT VOTING

Voting rights have always been linked to questions about race, class, and who should wield political power. With the influx of different kinds and larger numbers of immigrants, noncitizen voting began to be disputed, especially for newcomers who held political views that challenged dominant groups. For example, the War of 1812 slowed and even reversed the spread of alien suffrage, in part by raising the specter of foreign "enemies." Leading up to the Civil War, the South opposed immigrant voting because many of the new immigrants opposed slavery. One of the first planks in the Confederate Constitution was to exclude voting to anyone who was not born in the United States (there would be no "naturalization"). Nevertheless, after the Civil War and during Reconstruction, alien suffrage spread in the South and West with the growing need for new labor. Immigrant voting was practiced most widely during the 1870s and 1880s.

But as the twentieth century approached, large numbers of southern and eastern European immigrants—who were not universally seen as "white" at the time, and who often held politically "suspect" views—came to the United States. Their voting rights were increasingly challenged. These newer immigrants, coupled with the rise of mass social movements and third political parties (e.g., Labor, Populist, Socialist), posed a potential threat to the dominant political and social order, and noncitizen voting was gradually eliminated state by state. Both the anti-immigrant backlash at the turn of the twentieth century and wartime hysteria during World War I led to the elimination of this long-standing practice.

The case of Minnesota provides insight into both the rise and fall of noncitizen voting, particularly that of other Midwestern and northwestern states. The federal Organic Act of 1849 created the territorial government of Minnesota, which allowed declarant aliens the right to vote. It stated the following:

> That every free white male inhabitant above the age of twenty-one years, who shall have been a resident of said Territory at the time of the passage of this act, shall be entitled to vote at the first election, and shall be eligible to any office within the said Territory; but the qualifications of voters and of holding office at all subsequent elections shall be such as shall be prescribed by the legislative assembly; provided, that the right of suffrage and of holding office shall be exercised only by citizens of the United States and those who shall have declared on oath their intention to become such, and shall have taken an oath to support the constitution of the United States and the provisions of this act.

When Congress was considering legislation that would enable the territory of Minnesota to be admitted to statehood in 1857, a contentious debate ensued. Senator Asa Biggs of North Carolina stated that "the right of suffrage ought to be confined to citizens of the United States," and he introduced an amendment that would have required voters on the statehood issue to be U.S. citizens. Other supporters of the Biggs amendment defended this position by pointing out the dangers of foreign influence in elections, even while they claimed no affiliation with the nativist Know-Nothing Party.

One supporter, Senator Albert G. Brown of Mississippi, proclaimed his disdain of immigrants and a fear that new immigrants would be susceptible to manipulation by political parties: "There may be in this Territory Norwegians, who do not read one word of English. . . . What a mockery, and what a trifling with sacred institutions it is to allow such people to go to the polls and vote! Who does not know that they are led up like cattle to the ballot-boxes, and vote as they are told to vote?" (*Cong. Globe,* 34th Cong., 3rd sess. 810 [1857]). Moreover, Senator Brown claimed it was important to set limits in order to prevent claims that suffrage should be extended to "both sexes, male and female . . . to black and red as well as white" (*Cong. Globe,* 34th Cong., 3rd sess. 814 [1857]).

Equally important and revealing, some representatives from slave states feared that abolitionist noncitizen voters might tilt the delicate balance that existed between North and South on slavery. For example, Senator Bell of Tennessee worried that

> looking to the general aspect of the party divisions by which the country is distracted, and more particularly to the point of the intensity and magnitude of the interests depending on our national elections, you will see that foreigners not naturalized constitute an element of strength, distributed as they are in several of the northern and northwestern States, destined often to control our national elections, if they shall be allowed the privilege of voting; and thus they may, in the end, exert a powerful influence in changing the policy and even the vital principles of our Government. (*Cong. Globe*, 34th Cong., 3rd Sess. 811 [1857])

Supporters of declarant alien voting, such as Senator William H. Seward of New York, countered that noncitizens were capable of exercising self-government just as were citizens, and that alien suffrage was desirable "precisely for the reason that these new States are to be made chiefly by aliens and foreigners" (*Cong. Globe*, 34th Cong., 3rd sess. 813 [1857]). Although the Senate did adopt Senator Biggs's amendment in the bill, the final act allowed any "legal voter," which included qualified aliens, to vote on statehood. Minnesota subsequently reaffirmed its commitment to declarant alien suffrage in its first state constitution, adopted in 1857.

But in 1896, after the influx of more and newer immigrants, Minnesota discontinued its practice of noncitizen voting by referendum. By a vote of 97,980 to 52,454, Minnesota voters approved a constitutional amendment that prohibited noncitizen voting. A 1902 editorial in *The Washington Post* captured the prevailing attitude of the times. It criticized the states that had not yet repealed alien suffrage, referring to the "marked and increasing deterioration in the quality of immigration," and stated, "Men who are no more fit to be trusted with the ballot than babies are to be furnished with friction matches for playthings are coming in by the hundred thousand."

Mass immigration sparked intense debate about the impacts of immigrants on nearly everything. As a result, a host of laws were enacted that constricted the franchise, and not merely for noncitizens. For example, 18 states adopted literacy requirements aimed at restricting the flow of immigrants and their political participation, as well as that of other working-class constituencies and African Americans. By 1900, only eleven states retained immigrant voting rights. In the years leading up to, and with the advent of, World War I, these remaining states moved to end alien suffrage, usually by constitutional amendment. The states that did so were Alabama (1901), Colorado (1902), Wisconsin (1908), Oregon (1914), Kansas (1918), Nebraska (1918), South Dakota (1918), Indiana (1921), Texas (1921), Missouri (1921), and Arkansas (1926).

In fact, noncitizen voting was abolished at the same time that other restrictive measures were also enacted by elites, including literacy tests, poll taxes, felony disenfranchisement laws, and restrictive residency and voter registration requirements—all of which combined to disenfranchise millions of voters. Such disenfranchising measures were promoted and enacted by powerful economic and political elites (in both the Democratic and Republican parties) just when the electoral potential for working-class constituencies, progressive social movements, and third party mobilization was growing. The impact of noncitizens in elections had increased with their numbers—making the difference in several state elections—which fed critics of "the weight of a foreign element" in politics. Elites viewed noncitizen voters as a threat because of the appeal that third-party challenges had to immigrants and the working class more generally.

Disenfranchising measures and the elimination of noncitizen voting rights contributed to the precipitous decline in voter participation during the Progressive Era. From 1840 to 1900, voter turnout in presidential elections ranged from 70 to 80 percent, but dropped to 49 percent by 1924. Voter turnout in state and local elections also fell dramatically.

In the same period, anti-immigrant federal legislation was enacted, sharply limiting the influx of immigrants. From 1882 until 1924, federal laws were enacted to exclude the entrance of persons on qualitative grounds—the Chinese, criminals, prostitutes, the physically and mentally ill, the illiterate, "anarchists," and paupers. The 1924 National Origins Act drastically reduced the flow of immigrants, limiting in particular the proportion of non–western European immigrants.

Taken together, these developments limited democratic politics and progressive possibilities in the United States for years to come. (See Table 6.2 at the end of this Point essay for more details on noncitizen voting in particular states.) The legacy of these changes on American political and social development throughout the twentieth century to this day has been significant, blunting more democratic forms of participation and policy outcomes. It is revealing—but not coincidental—that immigrant voting has been buried in the annals of American history.

THE REVIVAL OF IMMIGRANT VOTING

This silence is striking for a second reason: immigrant voting is being revived today. Since 1970, immigrant voting rights have been restored in several municipalities. Chicago permits noncitizens to vote in school board elections (as did New York City from 1969 until 2003, when school boards were eliminated for unrelated reasons), and noncitizens currently vote in six municipalities in Maryland. These jurisdictions make no distinction between documented and undocumented immigrants—all noncitizens are permitted to vote in these local elections (as was true in New York City). Cambridge, Amherst, Newton, and Brookline, Massachusetts, have extended the right for documented noncitizens in local elections (but state action is needed to implement these local laws).

In addition, over a dozen other jurisdictions from coast to coast have considered moving toward enfranchising noncitizens in local elections, including San Francisco and several other cities in California (e.g., San Bernardino and Los Angeles); Washington, D.C.; Boston; New York City; Denver; Madison, Wisconsin; and Portland, Maine; as well as several states, such as Connecticut, Minnesota, and Texas.

Globally, about 60 countries on nearly every continent permit voting by resident immigrants. The 1993 Maastricht Treaty granted all Europeans the right to vote in European Union countries other than their own, expanding what has been practiced for years in Ireland (1963 and 1975), Sweden (1975), the Netherlands (1975), Denmark (1977), and Norway (1978). In the 1980s, the Netherlands, Venezuela, Ireland, Spain, and Iceland enacted legislation enfranchising resident aliens; several Swiss cantons (e.g., Neuchâtel and Jura) have permitted noncitizen voting for over a century; Finland and Iceland allow Nordic citizens voting rights; and Estonia allows noncitizen voting at the local level. Belgium and Rome have more recently joined the fold. Noncitizens vote in countries in Latin America, the Caribbean, the Middle East, North Africa, and New Zealand. Thus, the trend to expand the franchise is hardly unique to the United States.

WHY IMMIGRANT VOTING TODAY?

The revival of immigrant voting is, in part, a civil-rights and human-rights response to economic and cultural globalization and its consequences. Globalization has propelled mass migration and has also led to more widespread acceptance of ideas about "citizens without borders" or "global citizens." The extension of free trade across the globe makes products and people from remote parts of the world highly mobile and readily exchangeable. These changes have prompted heated debate about newcomers and national immigration policy. Controversy swirls about the impact of immigrants on everything from labor markets and wages, crime and public morals, electoral outcomes and public spending to awareness about race, ethnic, and national identity, and basic questions about *what* is "America" and *who* is an "American." Nativistic responses have led to proposals to restrict immigration and limit eligibility to health care, education, and other public services. Immigrant advocates, on the other hand, see demographic changes as leading to the inevitable triumph of multiculturalism and progressive politics. Consequently, emerging patterns of immigration have changed the political arithmetic, compelling parties and politicians to adjust campaign strategies to reflect evolving electoral conditions.

Immigrants have reemerged as pivotal players in contemporary American politics, although their numbers exceed their political representation and clout. Witness the proliferation of immigrant organizations that engage in advocacy and have built alliances with other groups on a range of issues, including labor, housing, education, health, language access, social welfare, and foreign policy. In recent years, millions of immigrants have marched in the streets in hundreds of cities, walked picket lines, and lobbied legislatures with greater frequency and force. Immigrant groups have also mobilized to promote naturalization, voter registration, and get-out-the-vote efforts, which contributed to increased turnout and victories for Democrats in Congress in 2006 and to the election of President Obama in 2008. Immigrant voters showed up in the 2010 elections, having significant impacts in California and Nevada's elections, for example. Such activity reveals a growing awareness among immigrants that they possess legitimate claims on the American polity, and they are commanding greater attention. One form that immigrant mobilization has taken is in campaigns to gain the vote.

The rising number of noncitizens has significant political implications, especially in the states and metropolitan areas where immigrants are concentrated. Because noncitizens are counted for districting purposes, they affect the apportionment of seats in the House of Representatives and can have an impact on presidential elections, because electoral votes are allocated based on representation in Congress. At the state and local levels, where they make up a larger proportion of the potential electorate, immigrants can have an even greater impact. Although immigrants who have naturalized hold the capacity to influence winners and losers in close contests, noncitizen adults are denied a political voice. The numbers are staggering: noncitizens make up over 10 percent of the voting-age population in many states (over 20% in California), and they are even more highly concentrated at the local level. Adult noncitizens in Los Angeles make up more than a third of the voting-age population; in New York City, they are 22 percent of adults. In some cities and towns, a quarter to a half of the adult population is excluded from selecting representatives who make the policies that affect daily life. The level of political exclusion in these jurisdictions approximates the level of disenfranchisement associated with the exclusion of women and African Americans. It is no surprise that immigrants rank at the bottom of the social order.

What do these conditions mean for such basic democratic principles as "one person, one vote," "government rests on the consent of the governed," and "no taxation without representation"? Immigrant political exclusion challenges the ideals of a modern democracy, cutting to the heart of our political practice. Restoring immigrant voting rights would help address these inequities.

CONTEMPORARY CAMPAIGNS IN THE UNITED STATES: FOR AND AGAINST

Several characteristics stand out in nearly every campaign to restore immigrant voting in the contemporary period: demographic shifts have propelled immigrant mobilization; proponents of noncitizen voting (ethnic associations, civic groups, labor unions, faith-based organizations) have engaged in grassroots organizing, coalition building, and employing effective media strategies and lobbying; and sympathetic politicians, mostly liberal Democrats and some Green Party members, have enacted or supported legislation. Opponents of noncitizen voting have been conservative Democrats and Republicans, representatives who view noncitizen voters as a potential threat to their incumbency, and community residents and groups that express anti-immigrant sentiments or object to immigrant voting on other grounds. Campaigns have often appeared in clusters. For example several campaigns occurred in the early 1990s, including the successful campaigns in Maryland and Massachusetts. In 2004, three campaigns were launched—in New York City, Washington, D.C., and San Francisco (all three unsuccessfully). In 2010, campaigns were conducted in Portland, Maine; Brookline, Massachusetts; New York City; and San Francisco (one successfully).

In every case, campaigns were contentious and the outcomes quite close. In 2010, two cities held referendums on immigrant voting: voters in San Francisco narrowly defeated a ballot proposal, Proposition D (by a margin of 54.91% to 45.09%), that would have granted all parents and guardians of children in the public school system voting rights in school board elections, regardless of their immigrant status, and voters in Portland, Maine, narrowly defeated a ballot proposal (by a margin of 52.43% to 47.57%) that would have granted voting rights in all municipal elections to legal permanent residents. Brookline, Massachusetts, on the other hand, successfully passed legislation in 2010 allowing legal residents the right to vote in local elections. Similarly, momentum has been building to do the same in New York City, where a recent bill obtained significant support in the New York City Council.

Opponents to noncitizen voting raise several objections, including claiming it is illegal, it diminishes the value and meaning of citizenship, it blurs the lines between citizens and noncitizens, and it reduces incentives for immigrants to naturalize. Some object that immigrants already have a pathway to voting—by becoming a citizen. These opponents argue that individuals wishing to vote should take the steps to naturalize, "like everyone else," and that people should have loyalty to one country, not two. They also argue that granting immigrants voting rights would lead to less informed voters, increase vote fraud, make the difference in close elections, and affect contentious public policy issues.

Immigrant rights advocates have their own concerns. Some worry that immigrants would become further exposed and made more vulnerable if voting rights laws are not crafted carefully, protecting registrants' confidentiality. Some minority group members worry their voting power and number of representatives would be diluted at a time when they are reaching parity with whites in many areas and levels of governance.

Advocates contend that immigrant voting is legal and feasible. They note that the U.S. Constitution does not preclude voting by noncitizens, and both state and federal courts have upheld noncitizen voting. In *Minor v. Happersett* (1874), for example, the Supreme Court ruled that "citizenship has not in all cases been made a condition precedent to the enjoyment of the right of suffrage." (Ironically, *Minor v. Happersett* upheld Missouri voting legislation that limited suffrage to male citizens, and it was thus considered a defeat for the women's suffrage movement at the time.) Subsequent federal and state court rulings have upheld voting by noncitizens. The decision about who holds the franchise has—with very few exceptions—always rested with states and localities. Some campaigns to restore immigrant voting have been conducted through the use of local referendum (Takoma Park, Maryland, and San Francisco), though most have been enacted by local statute (Chicago, New York). In jurisdictions where a change to state law—or approval by the state of a local change—is required, campaigns have been less successful. State constitutional provisions prohibiting voting by noncitizens create the biggest obstacle to advocates, though some have developed savvy legal strategies to get around such barriers. San Francisco, for example, is a charter city and thus has substantial independent authority from the state regarding its governance.

In addition, advocates argue there are moral and practical reasons to restore immigrant voting rights. The acquisition of political rights—including voting rights—has been a vital tool for every disempowered group in America's history to achieve economic, social, and civil rights and equality. Because legislative bodies confer rights and make public policy, it is critical to possess the capacity to influence and select representatives. Legal barriers to political participation, however, have historically hampered the attainment of such rights by distinct classes of citizens, including African Americans, women, young people, and the poor. Previously excluded groups have gained access to the franchise principally through political struggle. They fought their way into the polity through political agitation, sometimes with the support of factions within political parties or via third parties, through social movements and independent organizations, or by using the courts as a tool. Ultimately, they needed the support of other sectors in society to win political rights. The agitation of the propertyless encouraged sectors of the propertied to extend the franchise; the abolitionist movement and civil rights movements led to the enfranchisement of African American men (14th and 15th Amendments); the women's suffrage movement (19th Amendment) compelled men to include women among the voting citizenry; and younger adults, after participation in the social movements of the 1960s and 1970s, were granted voting rights by older adults when the voting age was lowered from 21 to 18 in 1971 with the passage of the Twenty-sixth Amendment. The question therefore becomes: Why not for immigrants too?

Advocates argue that without the vote, noncitizens are at risk of discrimination and bias because policymakers can, and often do, ignore their interests. Immigrants score lowest in indicators of well-being, including in employment, housing, education, and health. A 2002 report published by the Urban Institute found that one in four low-income children is the child of an immigrant, while one in four low-wage workers is foreign-born. Even though immigrants work more hours than most other U.S. citizens, an alarmingly large number of immigrants and their families lack health insurance and are food insecure (that is, they often go hungry). Children of immigrants are more likely to have poor health, lack health insurance, and lack access to health care than natives. Discriminatory public policy and private practices—in employment, housing, education, health care, welfare, and criminal justice—are the inevitable by-products of immigrant political exclusion.

Restoring immigrant voting rights would extend the visibility and voices of immigrants, which in turn could make government more representative, responsive, and accountable. Winning immigrant voting rights could help reverse such inequities. Moreover, noncitizen voting might help advance other issues important to immigrants, from obtaining language assistance in public facilities to speeding up the naturalization process and eliminating racial profiling and hate crimes.

Creating universal suffrage would facilitate immigrant political incorporation and ultimately bring benefits to the larger society as a whole. All residents of U.S. cities and towns should be encouraged to participate in the life of their communities—regardless of whether they come from Iowa or Ireland—because all residents have the same interests in ensuring there are good schools, safe streets, living-wage jobs, and affordable health care and housing. Society is stronger when everyone participates, because everyone benefits if decisions are made democratically. And as Richard Wilkinson and Kate Pickett find in their 2009 book, *The Spirit Level*, societies that have a higher level of equality do better on most key levels.

Most immigrants want to become citizens, but they are often deterred for little reason other than bureaucratic roadblocks that have been erected. Technically, immigrants that obtain legal permanent residency (green cards) can apply for citizenship after 5 years. But the path to legal permanent residency can take 10 years or more for many immigrants. In addition, immigrants face daunting obstacles in the process, including application fees, lack of access to the English and civics classes needed to prepare for the naturalization examination, and application backlogs that can range from 6 months to nearly 2 years.

Moreover, millions of immigrants are not eligible to become U.S. citizens because the pathways to citizenship are restricted to certain categories of individuals, such as family members, asylum seekers, and military personnel. Thus, it is not only undocumented or "illegal" immigrants who are not eligible for citizenship, but also the millions of documented or "legal" immigrants who may possess any one of the nearly two dozen types of visas (including long-term worker and student visas) that also are precluded from becoming citizens.

In the meantime, these newest Americans are subject to U.S. laws, work in every sector of the economy, own businesses, send their children to school, have revitalized neighborhoods in every city in the country, contribute billions of dollars in taxes each year, serve in the military, and even die defending the country they live in. Yet they cannot vote on issues crucial to the quality of their daily lives. Excluding such a significant portion of the population from political participation closes off a proven pathway to promote civic education and citizenship. Worse, it undermines the health and legitimacy of U.S. laws and public policies. Rather than undermining democracy, as some argue, resident voting could lead to more robust democratic politics and policymaking. Instead of diluting the concept of citizenship, as its critics maintain, resident voting can enrich citizenship by encouraging immigrants to participate in the political life of their communities. Ultimately, advocates must make a compelling case that immigrant voting is the right thing to do and that benefits will accrue to all members of a community.

MUTUAL BENEFITS

To illustrate this latter point—that mutual benefits accrue to all community members—consider the following example from New York City. Noncitizen immigrants voted and ran for office in community school board elections from 1969 to 2002. Each of the 32 community school boards had significant powers, such as hiring superintendents and principals and allocating funding for certain programs. During the 1980s, many school districts were characterized by overcrowded schools, out-of-date textbooks, lack of language access or cultural competency, crumbling facilities, and no after school programs—all combining to produce poor education for the students, which contributed to and further perpetuated the low socioeconomic status of their families. In Washington Heights, a predominantly Dominican section of northern Manhattan, a vibrant voter registration drive in 1986 brought in 10,000 parent voters—most of them immigrants—who turned out in record numbers. This political mobilization led to the election on the local school board of a majority of advocates for immigrants, including the first Dominican ever elected in the United States, Guillermo Linares, who became the president of the school board. These developments, in turn, contributed to improvements in the schools and helped reshape community politics. (Linares later became a member of the City Council, and then head of Mayor Bloomberg's Office of Immigrant Affairs, and he is currently a member of the New York State Assembly.)

As a result of this mobilization—and similar efforts in other districts—the city devoted more funds to improve and build new schools in Washington Heights. In the end, it was not only Dominicans that benefited. All community residents—including older stock Irish, Italian, Jewish, Puerto Rican, and black families who still lived there—benefited from improved educational opportunities. Moreover, it was not just residents in Washington Heights who benefited: school budgets grew in other districts in New York City, producing improvements in student and family outcomes. Importantly, these examples were not isolated to districts in New York City; similar positive results are also evident in other cities where immigrants have voted (and still do), such as in Chicago and in Maryland. Even in cases where immigrant voting campaigns have thus far failed to win, immigrants and their neighbors have won improvements to public services and made policy gains due in part to their political mobilization and advocacy, including regarding schools, hospitals, transportation, housing, jobs, and so on.

EXPAND THE FRANCHISE

Campaigns for noncitizen voting rights provide immigrants with a crucial tool to defend themselves against nativist attacks. It also gives other minority groups greater means to forge winning voting blocs that can advance their mutual interests. Immigrant taxation without representation not only challenges the legitimacy of America's mantle of democratic governance, it also provides a rationale and opportunity for organizing a progressive political majority.

Just as the civil rights movement sought to extend the franchise to African Americans and others who had been barred from voting to attain equitable representation, renewed efforts to extend the franchise to new Americans would advance the cause of human rights. True universal suffrage could boost possibilities for working-class electoral majorities and strengthen chances for winning progressive policies. Of course, progressives run the risk—one they willingly accept for the sake of democratic principles—that enfranchised immigrants might vote for conservative candidates and issues.

Essentially, the issue is about fairness. It is only fair that persons who are part of a local community and contribute to its tax base and economy should have a say in the formulation of laws and policies that will have a direct bearing on their well-being. As the new century progresses, the political process must be made more accessible to everyone. This will help politically integrate individuals and groups who have a vested interest in their collective future. Everyone has common interests in good public services and in accessible and affordable public goods, from quality education and health care to jobs. Such outcomes are likely to be more widely available if all community members participate in decision-making processes.

As Jamin Raskin (1993), one of the most outspoken and prominent intellectual voices of the contemporary movement for noncitizen voting rights in the United States, has said, "immigrant rights are the civil rights" of the day, and "by that logic, noncitizen voting is the suffrage movement" of our time. The burgeoning movement to create a truly universal suffrage calls forth America's past and future as an immigrant nation. Restoring voting rights to all residents would update our democracy for these global times.

REFERENCES AND FURTHER READING

Aleinikoff, T. A., & Klusmeyer, D. (2002). *Citizenship policies for an age of migration*. Washington, DC: Carnegie Endowment for International Peace.

Bauböck, R. (2005). Expansive citizenship: Voting beyond territory and membership. *PS: Political Science and Politics, 38*(4), 683–687.

Bedolla, L. G. (2006). Rethinking citizenship: Noncitizen voting and immigrant political engagement in the United States. In T. Lee, S. K. Ramakrishnan, & R. Ramírez (Eds.), *Transforming politics, transforming America: The political and civic incorporation of immigrants in the United States*. Charlottesville, VA: University of Virginia Press.

Capps, R., Fix, M., Ost, J., Reardon-Anderson, J., & Passel, J. S. (2004). *The health and well-being of young children of immigrants*. Washington, DC: Urban Institute.

Capps, R., Fix, M., & Passel, J. S. (2002). *The dispersal of immigrants in the 1990s*. Washington, DC: Urban Institute.

Chishti, M., & Bergeron, C. (2008, February). *USCIS: Backlog in naturalization applications will take nearly three years to clear*. Retrieved from Migration Policy Institute website: http://www.migrationinformation.org/USfocus/display.cfm?id=673

Coll, K. (2010, March). *Remaking citizenship: Latina immigrants and new American politics*. Palo Alto, CA: Stanford University Press.

Earnest, D. (2008). *Old nations, new voters: Nationalism, transnationalism and democracy in the era of global migration*. Albany, NY: State University of New York Press.

Fix, M., Passel, J. S., & Sucher, K. (2003, September 17). *Trends in naturalization* (Immigrant Families and Workers: Facts and Perspectives Brief No. 3). Retrieved from Urban Institute website: http://www.urban.org/publications/310847.html

For intelligent suffrage. (1902, July 29). *The Washington Post*.

Gordon, J. (1999). Let them vote. In O. M. Fiss, J. Cohen, J. Rogers, & E. Danticat (Eds.), *A community of equals: The constitutional protection of new Americans*. Boston: Beacon Press.

Harper-Ho, V. (2000). Noncitizen voting rights: The history, the law and current prospects for change. *Law and Inequality Journal, 18*, 371–322.

Hayduk, R. (2006). *Democracy for all: Restoring immigrant voting in the United States*. New York, NY: Routledge.

Keyssar, A. (2000). *The right to vote: The contested history of democracy in the United States*. New York, NY: Basic Books.

Kini, T. (2005, January). Sharing the vote: Noncitizen voting rights in local school board elections. *California Law Review, 93*(1), 271–321.

Kleppner, P. (1992). Defining citizenship: Immigration and the struggle for voting rights in antebellum America. In D. W. Rogers & C. Scriabine (Eds.), *Voting and the spirit of American democracy: Essays on the history of voting and voting rights in America* (pp. 43–54). Urbana, IL: University of Illinois Press.

Minnesota Legislative Reference Library. (n.d.). *State constitutional amendments considered*. Retrieved from http://www.leg.state.mn.us/lrl/mngov/constitutionalamendments.aspx

Minnesota Territorial Government Act, Ch. 121, Sec. 5, 9 Stat. 403, 405 (1849).

Neuman, G. (1992). "We Are the People": Alien suffrage in German and American perspective. *Michigan Journal of International Law, 13*(2), 259–295.

New York Coalition to Expand Voting Rights. http://www.ivotenyc.org

Noel, I. (1995). *How the Irish became white*. New York, NY: Routledge.

Porter, K. H. (1971). *A history of suffrage in the United States*. New York, NY: AMS Press. (Originally published 1918)

Raskin, J. B. (1993). Legal aliens, local citizens: The historical, constitutional, and theoretical meanings of alien suffrage. *University of Pennsylvania Law Review, 141*(4), 1391–1470.

Rosberg, G. M. (1977, April–May). Aliens and equal protection: Why not the right to vote? *Michigan Law Review, 75*(5–6), 1092–1136.

Smith, R. (1997). *Civic ideals: Conflicting visions of citizenship in U.S. history*. New Haven, CT: Yale University Press.

Spiro, P. J. (1999). Questioning barriers to naturalization. *Georgetown Immigration Law Journal, 13*, 479–519.

Tienda, M. (2002). Demography and the social contract. *Demography, 39*(4), 587–616.

Ron Hayduk

Table 6.1 International voting rights in other countries

Country	Date measure passed or defeated	Type of voting rights	Geographic limitations	Nationality limitations	Residency requirements
Australia	Passed in 1947; retracted in 1984 w/a grandfather clause	(National)	(N/A)	(British only)	
Austria	Passed in 2002	Local	Vienna only	None	5 years of legal residency
Barbados	Passed in 1990	National	N/A	Commonwealth citizens only	3 years
Belgium	Proposed in Belgium's Parliament (Feb. 2004)	(Local)	(None)	(None)	(Legal residency for 5 years; sign declaration to respect Belgium's laws and Constitution)
Belize		Local		None	3 years
Bolivia	Constitution changed in 1994 to allow noncitizens to vote; has not been implemented	(Local)	(None)	(None)	
Brazil	Ended 1975	National	N/A	Portuguese only	
Canada	1975 to date	National	N/A	(Commonwealth citizens)	
		Provincial and local	Provinces of Saskatchewan and Nova Scotia	British only	
Chile	Passed in 1989	National and local	N/A	None	5 years
Colombia	Constitution changed in 1991 to allow noncitizens to vote; has not been implemented	(Local)	(None)	(None)	
Denmark	Originally in 1977; expanded to current level in 1981	Local	None	None	1 year
Estonia		Local		Russian-speaking minority only—they are not Estonian citizens	Must be "permanent residents"
Finland	Original law, 1919; expanded to current level in 1991	Local	None	None	4 years
France	Failed 1981 and 2000	Local	None		

Country		Elections	Where implemented	Citizenship restrictions	Residency requirement
Germany	Passed in 1989; struck down by Constitutional Court in 1990	(Local)	(State of Schleswig-Holstein)	(Danish, Irish, Dutch, Norse, Swedish & Swiss)	(5 years)
	Passed in 1989; struck down by Constitutional Court in 1990	(Local)	(State of Hamburg)	(None)	(8 years)
	Passed in 1989; struck down by Constitutional Court in 1990	(Local)	(West Berlin)		(5 years)
Hungary	1990	Local	None	None	"all permanent residents"
Iceland	Passed 1986; grandfathered from 1920 constitution	Local	None	None	
Ireland	Passed in 1963	Local	None	None	6 months
	Passed in 1984	National	N/A	British citizens	
Israel	Passed in 1950	Local only	None	Based on Law of Return—Jewish residents only	
Italy	Passed in 2004	Vote for 4 nonvoting members of City Council (one from Africa, Asia, Latin American & E. Europe) and 1 nonvoting seat at each of 19 district councils	Rome	None	
Japan	Supreme Court ruled in 1995 that noncitizens do not have the right to vote; legislation considered in 2000, but did not pass				
Latvia	Parliament considered legislation in 2000, but did not pass it				
Lithuania		Local		None	
Netherlands	1979	Local	Rotterdam	None	5 years
	1981	Local	Amsterdam	None	5 years
New Zealand	1975 (earlier for British residents)	All national and local elections	N/A	None	1 year
Norway	Original 1978; expanded in 1982	Local	None	None	3 years
Portugal	1976	National	N/A	"Subject to reciprocity"; in practice, Brazilian citizens only	

(*Continued*)

Table 6.1 (Continued)

Country	Date measure passed or defeated	Type of voting rights	Geographic limitations	Nationality limitations	Residency requirements
Spain	Passed 1985	Local	None	None	
Sweden	Passed in1976	Local only (and some national referenda)	None	None	3 years
Switzerland	Original 1849; restored late 19th century	Local only	Canton of Neuchâtel		
	1979	Local only	Canton of Jura (7 additional cantons)		
	Considered but rejected measures.				
United Kingdom	1948	National	N/A	Commonwealth and Irish citizens only	
Uruguay	1952	National	N/A	None	15 years
Venezuela	1983	State and local	None	None	10 years

Sources: Compiled by author from Aleinikoff and Klusmeyer (2002), Bauböck (2005), and Earnest (2008).

Note: Items in parentheses indicate noncitizen voting that is either proposed or no longer currently in practice.

Table 6.2 Noncitizen voting rights in the United States

State	Time period when noncitizens held voting rights	State	Time period when noncitizens held voting rights	State	Time period when noncitizens held voting rights
Alabama	1868–1901	Louisiana	1879–?	North Dakota	1861–1889/1909
Alaska	none	Maine	none	Ohio	1802–1851
Arizona	none	Maryland	1776–1851 for state and federal elections; six towns allow noncitizen voting in local elections.	Oklahoma	1850–1907
Arkansas	1874–1926			Oregon	1848–1914
California	none	Massachusetts	1780–1822	Pennsylvania	1790–1838
Colorado	1876–1902	Michigan	1835–1894	Rhode Island	1762–1842
Connecticut	1776–1819	Minnesota	1849–1896	South Carolina	1790–?
Delaware	1776–1831	Mississippi	none	South Dakota	1850–1918
District of Columbia	none	Missouri	1865–1921	Tennessee	1796–1834
Florida	1868–1894	Montana	1864–1889	Texas	1869–1921
Georgia	1868–1877	Nebraska	1854–1918	Utah	none
Hawaii	none	Nevada	1848–1864	Vermont	1767–1828
Idaho	1863–1890	New Hampshire	1792–1814	Virginia	1776–1818
Illinois	1818–1848	New Jersey	1776–1820	Washington	1850–?
Indiana	1851–1921	New Mexico	none	West Virginia	none
Iowa	none	New York	1776–1804	Wisconsin	1848–1908
Kansas	1854–1918	North Carolina	1704–1856	Wyoming	1850–1899
Kentucky	1789–1799				

Sources: Compiled by author from Harper-Ho (2000), Keyssar (2000), Kleppner (1992), Neuman (1992), Porter (1971), Raskin (1993), Rosberg (1977), and Tienda (2002).

COUNTERPOINT

This essay argues that noncitizens in the United States should not have the right to vote in U.S. elections. It focuses on two distinct but related issues: the elements that constitute the core of a democratic polis, and the individual rights enjoyed by citizens of a democracy. It should be noted that democratic theory engaged this debate after the Peace of Westphalia in 1648, which institutionalized the concept of nation-state sovereignty that reached its heyday in the late nineteenth century and converted the long-established movement of people into the phenomenon of international migration. Democratic theorists have thus confronted immigration-related issues for a relatively brief time.

DEFINING THE DEMOCRATIC POLITY

Democratic theorists agree that a democratic polis is more than the sum of the contribution of its citizens. Both David Miller (2008) and Theordora Kostakopoulou (2009), for example, point out that a democratic polis is a complex set of institutions that promote and defend a distinct set of values. Miller goes so far as to argue that if states did not protect and promote these values, they would have no reason to exist.

A democratic polis requires two distinct types of characteristics to be viable and successful: (1) an infrastructure comprising a variety of institutions that are necessary but not sufficient to maintain and enhance democracy and (2) an infrastructure with accountable governmental elites and transparent electoral procedures that enable citizens to express their preferences regarding officeholders and public policies. These policies must provide all citizens with equal opportunity to participate fully in all aspects of society, and must therefore be intolerant of all types of discrimination. Because no state ever satisfies these conditions completely, democratic polities must constantly attempt to improve their performance regarding these conditions. Additionally, state efforts dealing with these types of issues must be subject to the rule of law and open to continuous scrutiny by an autonomous legal process so that they earn the trust of all citizens.

Theorists also insist, with equal vigor, that for a democratic polis to be viable and thrive it must be constructed on a community that shares history, language, and culture. This is most powerfully articulated by Theodora Kostakopoulou, who argues that there can be no democracy absent either a community of fate (i.e., a community with deep historical roots) or a liberal contractual community. This perspective is shared by other theorists. With regard to language, this means that citizens may be multilingual so long as they share language to the extent that they are able to dialogue meaningfully. Such abilities are essential to the kinds of deliberations that make democracy possible.

These shared values are not immutable, however. Instead, they are subject to continuous scrutiny, following the procedures described above. As established values are challenged, they may be altered, but only if the proposed changes respect the rights of all citizens and adhere to the rule of law. Thus, enabling women's suffrage was a legitimate policy change because it enhanced democracy by terminating gender-based disenfranchisement. Current attempts to use race and ethnicity to target immigrants for harassment and arrest are illegitimate, however, since they diminish the civil and political rights of community members. These examples illustrate why changes in state policies must be evaluated to determine their impact on a community's democratic institutions. If they diminish democracy, society must resist them.

It is also essential to acknowledge that, democratic principles aside, nation-states have the authority and right to provide their native citizens distinctive privileges, whether citizenship is based on *jus sanguinis* (family lineage or blood), or on *jus soli* (place of birth). The former, as exemplified by Nazi-era Germany, assumes an immutable essence that easily leads to various types of anti-democratic policies, while the latter is geographically determined, more open to democratic practices, and rejects claims that some groups are characterized by an essentialist psychological or cultural characteristic. That Western democracies have been unable to eradicate antiblack racism illustrates the staying power of biases regarding the immutable essence of groups.

Nonetheless, all states provide benefits to their "natural" citizens—the native-born and those whose citizenship is based on familial lineage—that are denied to naturalized immigrants. For example, the United States and many other nation-states require that immigrants who seek citizenship pass tests demonstrating their knowledge of the receiving country's history and culture. Unlike immigrants, native-born citizens in the United States and elsewhere are not required to take such tests. Similarly, many nation-states prohibit naturalized citizens from holding key positions. Only native-born citizens may be elected president or vice president of the United States, for example. These laws are discriminatory but well within the historical rights of nation-states.

From the perspective of democratic theory, the question regarding the right of noncitizen immigrants to vote must first be evaluated within this context. Democratic polities cannot exist if immigrant rights take precedence over the need to sustain democracy. Once the democratic polity is protected, it is possible and necessary to turn to the political rights of immigrants so that, to the extent possible, the rules and procedures that govern their political incorporation are as respectful of democracy as possible.

The United States and most democratic polities subscribe to this approach. This is evident in how they restrict immigrant voting. Only a small number of the world's states seem to have no regulations governing the political and voting rights of immigrants. Indeed, most restrict voting by noncitizen immigrants to different degrees and in a variety of ways. The general pattern is to be more open to immigrants who are from states that are co-members of regional organizations or that have deep historical linkages to the state in which the immigrants have taken up residence.

States that are members of the European Union (EU) permit immigrants from EU states to vote in local and subnational elections. In numerous cases—such as Greece, Cyprus, and Finland—there appears to be no residency requirement restricting immigrant voting. In others, such as Belgium and Estonia, this right may be exercised only after meeting a residency requirement that ranges from 3 to 5 years. In some federal states, subnational jurisdictions establish their own residence requirements. In Germany this ranges up to 8 years. Immigrants from Denmark, Sweden, Norway, Finland, and Iceland do not have to meet any residency requirements to vote in any of these countries, because they are all members of the Nordic Passport Union.

The Latin American pattern is similarly varied. Argentina prohibits noncitizen voting in federal or national elections, and although states may determine if they or their municipalities will allow noncitizens to vote, noncitizen voting is prohibited overall. Brazil limits noncitizen voters to immigrants from Portugal who have resided in Brazil for at least 3 years. Noncitizen Chileans may vote if they have resided in Chile for more than 5 years, and Colombia has similar restrictions.

INCORPORATING IMMIGRANTS INTO A DEMOCRATIC POLITY

A clear pattern emerges from these regulations. The great majority of nation-states restrict noncitizen voting to immigrants from states with which they have special cultural and historical relations. Even in these cases, however, immigrants usually must meet a residency requirement of at least 3 years. This pattern illustrates the extent to which democratic polities see a need for voters to be knowledgeable about, and support the core values of, the polity in which they have chosen to reside, regardless of what they contribute to society and the economy at large.

Evidence that immigrant voting without such restrictions can undermine the polis is evident in several ways. First, immigrants do not immediately develop an understanding of how the polity functions. Junn et al. (2011) report that Asian and Latino immigrants are significantly less informed than non-Hispanic whites and the American public at large about the meaning of partisanship in U.S. politics (p. 527). Given the significance of partisanship in American elections, this finding suggests that immigrants are not necessarily sufficiently informed to participate meaningfully in elections. They also cannot be assumed to arrive with the linguistic capability to participate in the deliberations that are the bedrock of contemporary political life. While this is especially true in linguistically distinct states such as Norway and Finland, it is also true in the United States, where there are many Chinese, Korean, and Latin American immigrants. In the United States, the evidence overwhelmingly indicates that immigrants develop English competency, but despite a genuine interest in becoming fluent in English, the pace of this learning is especially slow for those who arrive as adults rather than as children.

Absent this skill, immigrants are much slower to develop an understanding of American political values. If they are from China, Mexico, or Central America, for example, they are likely to be diffident regarding participating in public affairs. Immigrants must be socialized out of this attitude if the democratic polity is to thrive.

If they have the right to vote upon arrival or soon thereafter, it would not be unreasonable for them to attempt to recreate the types of institutions with which they are familiar, or to introduce policies supportive of cultural practices that reinforce their identity and support the values with which they arrived. For example, if they were enfranchised, noncitizen Latino immigrants in the many areas where they constitute a substantial portion of the electorate could use their vote to pressure school districts to unfairly expand minority hiring and change curricula to emphasize Spanish and home-country history. Similarly, Muslims could institutionalize a major role for Sharia law in communities such as Southend, a section of Dearborn, Michigan, where they make up approximately 97 percent of the population (Durán & Pipes, 2002). Such initiatives indicate an unwillingness to abide by the nation's historically constructed core values and democratic institutions. Public protests notwithstanding, there is no evidence that they pose a greater threat than Navajo tribal law or Jewish law. The state must therefore act to defuse whatever public discontent such activities engender. This could be expensive in the short term, but that cost should be eliminated as immigrants are socialized into the polity.

The potential impact that immigrants who are unsocialized into the polity's norms can have on the polis is illustrated by two examples. First is the case of the Rajneeshi movement in Oregon in the 1980s. Movement members, who included native-born Americans as well as European and Indian immigrants, voted themselves into office and took over the town of Antelope, which they renamed Rajneesh. They then used violence and intimidation to expand their control. Although Oregon's attorney general successfully challenged the takeovers, the state supreme court upheld them in 1987, after the movement had dissipated.

A second example involves Islamberg, a private Muslim community in the Catskills, 150 miles northwest of New York City. A town with only 100 residents, which press reports indicate is accessed by a dirt road that passes through a gate on which "No Trespassing" signs are posted, Islamberg was founded by a radical Muslim cleric from Pakistan who was allegedly one of the founders of Jamaat al-Fuqra, an organization implicated in dozens of bombings and murders across the United States, and in the planning of the 1993 World Trade Center bombing.

It must be emphasized that there is no evidence that the overwhelming majority of Latino or Muslim immigrants support such activities. However, enfranchised immigrants who are unsocialized into the polity are more likely than naturalized immigrants and native-born citizens, who have more experience with U.S. society and the nation's democratic institutions, to fall prey to co-ethnic political entrepreneurs who support such anti-democratic activities.

It is also necessary to acknowledge that becoming socialized into the polity can produce antisystemic values, as the examples of the Black Panthers, the Black Muslims, the Brown Berets, and the American Indian Movement illustrate. Such groups constitute a small percentage of the population they claim to represent, and it is clear that the majorities of these populations are supportive of the polity's democratic norms.

UNFORESEEN POTENTIAL CONSEQUENCES OF NONCITIZEN VOTING RIGHTS

Offering noncitizen immigrants the right to vote may also constitute an incentive to emigrate. Relocating to democratic polities that offer substantial social services provides immigrants an opportunity to influence policy to their benefit, regardless of the cost to citizens. Immigrants who respond to such incentives do not necessarily have any commitment to the polities where they will reside. In time, they could develop such commitments, but they may be just as likely to migrate simply to improve their economic situation. Once they have accomplished that, there is no reason not to return to their homeland. Throughout their stay, however, the right to vote will have enabled them to influence policy to benefit themselves and their homeland while de-emphasizing their concern for the well-being of the receiving state.

To the extent that enfranchisement provides an incentive to migrate, it detracts from the well-being of the sending state. This is especially evident among high-skilled or well-educated emigrants. These are the individuals who benefited the most from the social policies of the homeland. Such highly skilled workers have developed their abilities under the tutelage of home country institutions. They might have apprenticed under a tradesman or been trained as office managers. Having mastered valuable skills, these emigrants are in a position to leave their home country and earn higher wages in a new state. In liberal regimes, the emigrant is free to do so without in any way repaying the homeland society for the training and knowledge received. This imbalance is even more evident in the case of university-educated professionals, who have benefited the most from their homeland's institutions.

Liberal nation-states such as the United States have historically enticed emigrants by promising improved economic and social conditions. Adding political influence to this bundle of benefits further enhances the appeal of emigration. However, the damage done by democratic polities such as the United States to sending states through such inducements is akin to encouraging foreign citizens to avoid paying taxes. That is, emigrants who leave after they profit from their home-state experiences without repaying the cost of their training and education weaken sending states at least as much as tax evaders do. How can a democratic state, which should have as a priority the promotion of democracy throughout the world, justify public policy that weakens the ability of other states to join the ranks of democratic polities?

From the perspective of democratic theory, the argument is clear. A democratic polity can only be sustained if its constituents have the knowledge to participate in democratic deliberations and are committed to the values of the polity. It is unreasonable to expect immigrants to meet these standards without having experienced life in the polity. While there is no guarantee that they will ever gain this knowledge or develop these commitments, they are more likely to do so if they develop an understanding of the demos they will join as permanent members.

AN EMPIRICALLY GROUNDED REFUTATION OF REINSTITUTING NONCITIZEN VOTING

The argument for allowing immigrant noncitizens to vote has several aspects. These include appeals to history, the debt owed to residents who function as good citizens and contribute positively to virtually all sectors of society, and an acceptance of limiting their voting rights to local issues.

The appeal to history is unpersuasive because it is not fully contextualized. First, not all immigrants were enfranchised prior to becoming citizens. The only groups who enjoyed this privilege were those defined as whites, and therefore as nascent members of the polity. Asians, African Americans (forced migrants), Mexicans, and all women were denied enfranchisement. Indeed, the political incorporation of Irish immigrants was delayed until it was clear they would identify with whites against African Americans (Ignatiey, 1995).

It is true that, for several decades, European male immigrants in many states could vote in local, state, and even federal elections if they signed a statement of intent to become a citizen. Arkansas ended this practice in 1926. The policy came to an end as the nation's mood changed with the rise of nativism in the 1830s, the public's anger toward immigrants following President McKinley's assassination by an immigrant, and the "Red Scare" that followed World War I.

Ironically, in the most anti-immigrant climate the polity has experienced in more than half a century, noncitizen voting is being pursued again in the early twenty-first century. Moreover, the conditions that influenced the end of this policy in 1926 are somewhat analogous to contemporary concerns such as post-9/11 terrorism, the violence engendered by cross-border narco-traffickers, and the fear regarding the cultural impact of today's large Latino and Asian influx.

Moreover, historical precedent does not legitimize resuscitating old policies. Slavery was once legal, and women were long denied the vote. As noted previously, historical precedent is less significant than how noncitizen voting would affect the polity today.

First, in the United States and other democratic polities, noncitizen voting would invite individuals unfamiliar with, and not obviously committed to, the values of the polity to influence public policy. Second, the current environment does not facilitate distinguishing between authorized and unauthorized immigrants. Consequently, either both types of immigrants would be invited to vote, or undocumented immigrants would somehow be identified and prevented from voting. Given that the unauthorized have essentially the same characteristics as legal immigrants and make the same types of contributions to society, however, advocates of immigrant voting have no obvious basis for denying them the vote. Furthermore, whatever the procedure that would be used to identify legal immigrants could also be used to identify the unauthorized. For example, legal immigrants would surely use voter registration cards to protect themselves from arrest and deportation. Immigrants without such cards would immediately be viewed as probable illegals. Authorized immigrants would thus probably rush to register, while the undocumented would be pushed further underground or risk easier arrest.

History aside, enfranchising immigrants could easily result in two negative outcomes. Giving all immigrants, regardless of status, the right to vote would either (1) force the state to effectively abandon all efforts to regulate immigration or (2) discriminate against the unauthorized and make them more vulnerable to labor exploitation, social discrimination, and deportation. Both of these outcomes undermine a democratic polity, and the latter threatens the well-being of millions of unauthorized immigrants who already live difficult lives in American society.

A second reason why the appeal to history is misleading is that the nation's original reasons for promoting immigration and immigrant voting are no longer viable. In the nineteenth and early twentieth centuries, the United States was in its nation-building phase. It needed immigrants to populate its land and meet the labor market needs for its expanding economy. Because it had not yet developed its welfare state component, workers came cost-free. Those conditions no longer exist. The national territory is well populated, and the needs of the labor market are much more specialized. The U.S. is unlikely to ever have enough highly skilled and educated immigrants, but it has particular needs for low-skilled workers. Recruiting them generates a large array of expensive social services, which are costly to satisfy in the short and medium term.

Immigrants who came during the nation-building phase migrated because their homelands offered few opportunities. While 30 percent of immigrants who came before 1920 returned (Bryant, 1999), the great majority arrived committed to becoming members of the American nation, in part because of the distance they had traveled and the cost of returning, and in part because the opportunities they found or expected stimulated their rapid attachment to the American state. Whatever cultural loyalties they maintained did not sustain political ties to the home country to the same extent that new communication technologies and the increased availability of dual citizenship enable today's sending states to encourage current immigrants to maintain political loyalties to the homeland.

The argument that noncitizen immigrants earn the right to vote because of their contributions to society and the polity is also inadequately developed. This view commodifies membership in the polity and grossly demeans the meaning of citizenship. Further, it implies that uneducated and unskilled immigrants are less deserving than their more fortunate brethren to be full members of the polity because they contribute less to the nation's economy and society's overall well-being. In addition, by implying that voting rights be extended to those who contribute to society, it suggests that some foreign residents should also be enfranchised. Foreign investors, for example, could claim the United States as a state of residence and make major contributions to national well-being through their contributions to the American economy without drawing down resources through their use of social services. The logic of commodifying membership in the polity could lead to arguing that they be enfranchised, a position no one would support.

A third claim regarding immigrant enfranchisement is that it could be limited to local elections that directly affect their most pressing interests. This proposal seems to overcome the almost universally shared concern regarding the fear that voting in national elections would allow noncitizens to vote on security issues in support of foreign states and against U.S. foreign policy concerns. In principle, this appears persuasive. In practice, however, it is difficult to determine the boundaries of policy decisions. Educational policy, for example is both local and national. School districts, perhaps the jurisdiction with the greatest local impact, determine curricula, but the state and national authorities invest substantial funds to educate teachers and finance education. Indeed, as the response to the Soviet Union's scientific advances in the Sputnik era and the "No Child Left Behind" policy of the George W. Bush Administration illustrate, the federal government sets national standards that impact the policies of local- and state-level educational authorities.

Conversely, local political jurisdictions can block the implementation of national policy through opposing proposals that are linked to national defense but are not clearly defined as national defense issues. The right to vote in local elections could enable noncitizens to swing electoral outcomes regarding the approval of issues such as a community's willingness to approve a nuclear plant or waste site established within its boundaries. Limiting the types of issues on which immigrants may vote, in short, cannot be determined *a priori* by geographical boundaries. Instead, it would require that the reach of all issues be determined on a case-by-case basis, which would be so cumbersome as to be impossible.

A liberal democratic polity must, however, recognize that all residents have political rights, including freedom of speech, freedom of assembly, the right to publish and access public information, the right of due process, and the right to attempt to influence decision makers and the policy process. Because of how its political institutions are constructed, noncitizen immigrants in the United States enjoy all of these.

It is especially noteworthy that the design of the electoral system guarantees that they are positioned to influence elections. Except for officials elected on a statewide basis (such as the president and vice president, senators, and governors), the overwhelming majority of officials are elected by district. Districts are designed based on total population. That is, noncitizen immigrants count as much as native-born and naturalized immigrants in determining the population that makes up a district. Because many immigrant groups, especially Latinos and Asians, live in geographically distinct ethnic communities, many districts that contain these communities include large numbers of noncitizen immigrants. The congressmen and women who are elected from these districts (such as California's Javier Becerra and Lucille Roybal-Allard, and Chicago's Luis Gutierrez) are such strong immigrant advocates that it is difficult to imagine how immigrant voting could further influence them. Similarly, city council members in cities with large numbers of immigrants—whether in New York, Rhode Island, Texas, or California—emulate this behavior. Ironically, the design of the polity is so open to the influence of immigrants in such locales that it could be argued that newcomers from Venezuela, most of Central America, and (at least until recently) Mexico were better represented in the United States than they had been in their home countries.

Such indirect representation would be meaningless if the polity never permitted immigrants to naturalize or required an excessively long time before they were allowed to do so, as was true from 1798 to 1800, when aliens were required to be residents for 14 years before being eligible to naturalize. Today, authorized immigrants are eligible for naturalization after 5 years of residency, unless they have committed a felony or have some other documented legal problems. The cost of naturalization is $680, which is less than the cost or applying for permanent legal resident status. Although costly given the income of many immigrants, this fee cannot be considered a major impediment to becoming a citizen.

Nonetheless, there is one group of immigrants who should be granted citizenship immediately: those who have willfully enlisted in the armed forces. The sacrifice they are willing to make exceeds what most native-born citizens are now willing to emulate. At a minimum, the polity should grant them citizenship when they have completed basic training.

CONCLUSION

Noncitizen voting impedes the creation and maintenance of a democratic polity. A democracy is built on a complex set of institutions held together by the shared commitment of its citizens to a core set of values, some of which are historically rooted and others adopted over time. Perhaps due to their institutional complexity, democratic polities are fragile and require the continuous attention and involvement of their citizens. Immigrants who are eligible to naturalize but choose not to have no reasonable basis for seeking noncitizen enfranchisement, because they would gain the vote if they naturalized. That they have not done so suggests they may not be committed to the polity's core values. Those who are relatively new to the polity are unlikely to have learned enough about its core values to be committed to them. In short, a democratic polity should not risk its well-being by allowing noncitizen voting.

Voting, even in local elections would provide immigrants rights without responsibilities in their communities of origin, as well as in the communities in which they settled. This is why the theorist Claudio López-Guerra (2005) argues that emigrants should not be allowed to vote in sending-state elections. Such individuals could attempt to influence policy to maximize their interests, regardless of how this would impact the polity where they reside or from which they migrated. If their efforts damage the receiving polity and make it a less desirable place to live, they have the right to return to their countries of origin. The citizens of the receiving polity have no such option. Noncitizen voting could thus contribute to making the polity to which they have migrated a less attractive and more undemocratic place to live.

In conclusion, immigrant voting does not enhance American democracy or democratic polities in general, and it may not serve the long-term interests of immigrants either.

REFERENCES AND FURTHER READING

Abizadeh, A. (2002). Does liberal democracy presuppose a cultural nation? Four arguments. *American Political Science Review, 96,* 495–509.

Bauböck, R. (2006). Free movement and the asymmetry between exit and entry. *Ethics and Economics, 4*(1). Retrieved from https://papyrus.bib.umontreal.ca/jspui/bitstream/1866/3369/1/2006v4n1_BAUBOCK.pdf

Brubaker, R. (1992). *Citizenship and nationhood in France and Germany.* Cambridge, MA: Harvard University Press.

Bryant, J. (1999). *Immigration and modern life: Volume III.* Retrieved from Yale-New Haven Teachers Institute website: http://www.yale.edu/ynhti/curriculum/units/1999/3

Carens, J. H. (1987). Aliens and citizens: the case for open borders. *Review of Politics, 49,* 251–273.

Carens, J. H. (2010). *Immigrants and the right to stay.* Cambridge, MA: MIT Press.

Durán, K., & Pipes, D. (2002, August). *Muslim immigrants in the United States.* Washington, DC: Center for Immigration Studies.

Goodin, R. (2007). Enfranchising all affected interests, and its alternatives. *Philosophy and Public Affairs, 35,* 40–68.

Hayduk, R. (2006). *Democracy for all: Restoring immigrant voting rights in the U.S.* New York, NY: Routledge.

Ignatiev, N. (1995). *How the Irish became white.* New York, NY: Routledge.

Junn, J., Wong, J., Ramakrishnan, S. K., & Lee, T. (2011). *Asian American political participation: Emerging constituents and their political identities*. New York, NY: Russell Sage Foundation.

Kostakopoulou, T. (2009). Citizenship goes public: The institutional design of national citizenship. *Journal of Political Philosophy, 17*(3), 227–306.

Kymlicka, W. (1995). *Multicultural citizenship*. Oxford, UK: Oxford University Press.

López-Guerra, C. (2005). Should expatriates vote? *Journal of Political Philosphy, 13*(2), 216–234.

Macedo, S. (2009). *Domestic and global justice: The problem of priorities and some problems concerning immigration*. Stanford, CA: Stanford Political Theory Workshop. Retrieved from http://iis-db.stanford.edu/evnts/5581/Macedo_on_Immigration_1-09.pdf

Miller, D. (2008). Immigrants, nations, and citizenship. *Journal of Political Philosophy, 16*(4), 374–390.

Rodriguez, C. M. (2010). Noncitizen voting and the extraconstitutional construction of the polity. *International Journal of Constitutional Law, 8*(1), 30–49.

Rosberg, G. (1977, April–May). Aliens and equal protection: Why not the right to vote? *Michigan Law Review, 75*(5–6), 1092–1136.

Shachar, A., & Hirschl, R. (2007). Citizenship as inherited property. *Political Theory, 35*, 253–287.

Shapiro R. Y., & Jacobs, L. R. (2011). *The Oxford handbook of American public opinion and the media*. New York, NY: Oxford University Press.

Walter, M. (1979). The alien's right to work and the political community's right to govern. *Wayne Law Review, 25*, 1181–1215.

Ypi, L. (2008). Justice in migration: A closed border utopia. *Journal of Political Philosophy, 16*(4), 391–418.

Rodolfo O. de la Garza

Nativism

POINT: The United States is a nation of immigrants, but it is also one that long has harbored strong anti-immigrant movements as well as deep fears and hostilities toward the latest newcomers. This is no less true today than in the past, as witnessed by contemporary rhetoric, political movements, and policy proposals.

Carolyn J. Craig, University of Oregon

COUNTERPOINT: The immigration restriction movement today is not driven by xenophobia or hostility toward new immigrants on the basis of national origin—the defining features of earlier nativist movements. Rather, it focuses on real costs and serious threats posed by current immigration.

Carolyn J. Craig, University of Oregon

Introduction

While America is widely known as a "nation of immigrants," the country has not always been a hospitable place for them. This chapter examines the nature of anti-immigrant or "restrictionist" movements in the United States in the late twentieth and early twenty-first centuries. It analyzes the contemporary debates over immigration in the context of previous periods of heightened anti-immigrant sentiment and political organization, highlighting similarities and differences between previous periods' immigration politics and those of the 1990s and early twenty-first century. This analysis will allow readers to consider the extent to which contemporary restrictionist movements and policies reflect older forms of nativism, or if they represent a new set of perspectives about immigrants and immigration in the United States.

The Point section of the chapter advances the argument that contemporary anti-immigrant rhetoric, political movements, and policy proposals exhibit the same kind of fear of, and hostility toward, immigrants that emerged in previous eras in the United States. This anti-immigrant sentiment and the associated support for public policies that would restrict immigration and immigrants' rights came to be known as "nativism" in the 1830s. In general terms, and to use a definition provided by John Higham in his seminal work on the topic, nativism may be defined as "an intense opposition to an internal minority on the grounds of its foreign (i.e. "un-American") connections" (Higham, 2002, p. 4). The first part of this chapter discusses the emergence of nativism and the development of nativist policies in America during the country's first few centuries, demonstrating how current anti-immigrant sentiment toward immigrants in general—and nonwhites such as Latinos, Arabs, and Southeast Asians (among others) in particular—echoes that of earlier eras. This historical perspective illuminates how both older and contemporary restrictionist movements and policies are fundamentally manifestations of their proponents' perceptions of foreigners as threats to the fabric of American society and prosperity.

The Counterpoint section of the chapter advances the argument that contemporary restrictionist rhetoric, political movements, and policy proposals are based on new and different concerns about immigration and its threat to the national interest. This section makes the case that restrictionist policy is necessary because America has undergone significant transformations since the end of World War II, the nature of immigration to the United States has changed significantly, and globalization has put pressures on modern states that make large-scale immigration untenable. Given these changes, the costs of mass immigration—in terms of jobs, social cohesion, public safety, and public well-being—far outweigh its benefits to the nation. In this view, current restrictionist sentiment is based on rational arguments and born of genuine concern about the country's and immigrants' well-being, not of racism or xenophobia.

Given that nativism has been associated with racism, these two sections will challenge readers to consider the extent to which, and how, race and ethnicity factor into contemporary immigration debates. While the label "nativist" was once claimed by explicitly racist restrictionists, it is no longer used in service to restrictionist goals, and, indeed, some restrictionists go to great lengths to declare or demonstrate that they are not racist, and that they want to restrict immigration so that Americans of all colors can live peacefully in a prosperous country. To the extent that the term "nativism" does circulate in immigration debates, it is used primarily by immigrants' rights proponents to delegitimize restrictionists as xenophobic (Bosniak, 1994; Jacobson, 2008). At the same time, the physical and cultural differences of most immigrants make it difficult to distinguish restrictionist sentiment from the xenophobia at the heart of nativism.

A provocative 2004 *Foreign Policy* article, "The Hispanic Challenge," exemplifies the imbrication of race, ethnicity, and restrictionist claims. In the article, the late Harvard professor of government Samuel P. Huntington argues that the unprecedented level of immigration from south of the U.S. border is on track to divide American society and thus perilously weaken the nation's political institutions and enervate its economy. As discussed in the pages that follow, arguments like Huntington's can be read in different ways, which in turn has implications for contemporary immigration debates and policy. This chapter will equip students and others with information and perspectives they need to better understand how and why restrictionist sentiments have and continue to circulate in "a nation of immigrants," and to advance their own position within the debates over immigration.

POINT

In the early hours of Friday, July 8, 2011, a female student at a state university in Oregon was attacked by a man who, before slapping her to the ground, yelled at her to "speak American." As the woman fled her attacker, she could hear him yelling obscenities at her based on his perceptions of her ethnic origin. The woman reported the assault to the local police department, and the incident was publicized on the university's website as an incident of "bias crime" (University of Oregon Department of Public Safety, 2011). While the attacker's actions constitute a crime today, such expressions of anti-immigrant sentiment have been, and continue to be, voiced by citizens and politicians who view immigrants as a threat to American society and democracy.

This sentiment is at the heart of nativism: a strong distrust and dislike—if not hatred—of foreigners. While American history acknowledges and often celebrates the fact that America was founded and built up by individuals who immigrated to the "New World" from Europe, and then from across the globe, the historical record also reveals a current of hostility toward foreigners since the nation's founding. Nativism has bedeviled the project of building America's political, social, and economic systems since the first European colonists arrived in what is now known as the Americas, and it is alive and well today among anti-immigrant individuals and groups who seek to restrict immigration to America and limit the rights of immigrants living on American soil.

The rest of this chapter on nativism is divided into five sections. The first section explains what nativism is and identifies four themes within American nativism. The next three sections discuss nativism in the United States over the course of American history, beginning with its origins in the colonists' antipathy toward American Indians, and highlighting subsequent moments when nativism became politically salient. In these moments, nativism has served as the organizing principle of political parties; as the foundation for federal legislation restricting the immigration of specific races and ethnicities; as a driving force behind efforts to make English the official language of states and the nation; and, very recently, as motivation for state and federal policies that encourage racial profiling and withholding public assistance to immigrants in the name of protecting the national interest. Together, these sections illuminate the four themes of nativism that continue to circulate in American society and politics. The final section reiterates the argument that while anti-immigrant sentiment in the United States today may seem different from earlier expressions of nativism, it is not fundamentally different from the nativism that emerged in previous eras.

WHAT IS "NATIVISM"?

Nativism, like other "isms," refers to a belief system that puts one group of people or way of doing things above all others. Nativism marks those who are considered from, or "native" to, a particular territory—either because they were born there, or because they are linked by blood to a people who made the territory their homeland—as distinct from those who trace their roots elsewhere. At the most basic level, nativism reflects a tendency for humans to organize themselves into social groupings whose members, or "insiders," are considered distinct in important ways from nonmembers, or "outsiders." But nativism does not simply differentiate those who are native from those who are foreign; nativism makes the distinction and expresses preferential treatment of natives. Nativists' distinctions between the native and "the Other" have generated and perpetuated distrust, disdain, and conflict between many groups across place and time.

Nativism is expressed in the form of rhetoric—from seemingly rational explanations for the need to exclude certain people from the polity, to explicitly xenophobic vitriol. In the United States, nativism can become institutionalized through discriminatory policies and laws that limit what certain groups of immigrants can do or the public benefits they can receive; through programs and policies that punish foreigners for failing to assimilate to "American" practices—such as religious conformity or conversion—and laws declaring English as the official language; and through restrictions, or quotas, on the numbers of immigrants from particular countries or regions who are permitted to enter the country and become citizens. Nativism can be manifested in subtle, "acceptable" forms of violence against foreign individuals or groups, such as the expression of racial epithets and racist jokes, the subjection of undocumented workers, and poor or dangerous working conditions. Perhaps the most obviously malicious expressions of nativism are blatant attacks on foreigners, like the one described at the beginning of this chapter, or the formation of Minutemen organizations—groups of civilians who have taken up arms and stationed themselves along the border between Mexico and the United States, claiming they are "doing for our country what our government won't."

Over the course of American history, nativism has inspired individuals to organize groups, movements, and political parties dedicated to keeping immigrants out of the country or limiting their rights while residing within it. These organizations have advanced arguments for the restriction of immigration that can be categorized into four themes (Feagin, 1997). One nativist theme is rooted in beliefs that certain "races" or groups of people are intellectually or culturally inferior. Nativists who subscribe to this view believe that certain immigrants should not be permitted to enter the country, or at least not in large numbers. A second form of nativism expresses anxiety about immigrants' willingness or capacity to assimilate to American culture. A third strain focuses on the argument that immigrants take jobs from native-born Americans. Finally, a fourth concern expressed by nativists is that immigrants cripple the capacity of governments at all levels to provide public services such as welfare, health care, and education. Each of these themes has been present in arguments for restricting immigration and immigrants' rights since the first self-proclaimed nativist political parties emerged in America in the 1830s. The following sections trace the emergence of and peaks in nativist organizations and legislation in the United States, highlighting nativism's manifestations in each of the four areas described above.

NATIVISM FROM COLONIZATION THROUGH WORLD WAR II

Nativism has its origins in the colonization of the land that is modern-day America. The first groups of Europeans who settled in the New World in the late sixteenth and seventeenth centuries were primarily Protestants from Great Britain. While there were class, linguistic, and religious differences among these early settlers, they generally had the English language in common, and they shared many beliefs and values that originated with the Protestant variant of Christianity. Both their cultural practices and their appearances set them apart from the indigenous Native American populations. Despite variations among the colonists' practices, their ideas about how society should be organized and their relationship toward their environment differed greatly from the indigenous peoples they encountered. Committed to capitalism and Christianity—both of which conflicted with Native American political, economic, social, and spiritual traditions—the colonists viewed American Indians as backward and savage. The colonists used their beliefs about their moral superiority to justify their wars with, and subjugation and extermination of, Native Indian populations for centuries to come. Moreover, the physical differences between the Europeans and the Native Americans, particularly in terms of facial features and skin tone, accentuated the colonists' perceptions of the Native Americans as the Other; this association of differences in appearance with inferior or dangerous peoples would establish a foundation for discrimination against non-Anglo immigrant populations that arrived on American shores.

But physical difference was not the sole basis of some of America's first laws passed for the purpose of protecting it from dangerous foreigners. One of the earliest expressions of fear of the Other was the Alien and Sedition Acts of 1789. These four laws were promoted by the Federalists on the grounds that they would strengthen the country as it was facing the threat of a war with France. These laws made citizenship more difficult to achieve and curtailed people's freedom of expression in the name of national security. The first of the laws, the Naturalization Act, required aliens to reside on American soil for 14 years (instead of 5) to be eligible for citizenship. The second law, the Alien Act, gave the president the authority to arrest, imprison, and deport aliens deemed to be a threat to peace and safety during wartime. While these laws proved widely unpopular with the public—to the extent that they are associated with the defeat of the Federalists in the next election and were eventually repealed or allowed to expire—they solidified the idea that foreigners provide a unique threat to the nation. This view reflects a "primordial view" of identity, which sees identities, including national identities, as fixed and unchanging. The legacy of the Alien and Sedition Acts is apparent in contemporary arguments for deporting undocumented immigrants, and in laws restricting immigration for the sake of keeping Americans safe.

America's fears of, and antipathy toward, non-Anglos during its first two centuries of development helped give rise to nativism as a coherent political ideology in the 1830s. It was during that decade that Anglo-Americans distrustful of immigrants who were not assimilating to their satisfaction organized "Native American" political parties—and later the American Party—around their shared disdain for and fear of the Other. The emergence of these parties was tied directly to the long-standing antipathy toward Catholics, and Irish Catholics in particular, of their mostly Protestant members. Prior to the American Revolution, American colonies had penal laws that forbade the practice of Catholicism, and states retained discriminatory laws against Catholics—such as preventing them from holding public office—well into the nineteenth century. Protestants were deeply suspicious of Catholicism, given the Catholic Church's hierarchical doctrine and its long-standing association with authoritarian rule in Europe. They were also directly hostile toward them; the Bible Riots in Philadelphia in 1844 killed 20 people and destroyed more than 100 Catholic churches, schools, and homes.

The popularity of the nativist parties grew in the 1840s and 1850s as immigration from Ireland increased, especially following that country's Great Famine, which left nearly a million people dead. Much like those who sound the alarm about immigrants in America today, and Mexicans in particular, the nativist parties mobilized support for their restrictionist cause by warning that the Irish immigrants were taking jobs and debasing the country. The relatively poorer Irish immigrants—many of whom performed hard labor in construction and agriculture for meager wages—lived in overcrowded conditions without adequate basic services. Protestants perceived and presented their poverty and their cultural practices as evidence that the Irish were filthy, lazy, morally corrupt, and un-American.

The central organizing principle of the American Party was the protection and promotion of Americanism through the reduction of immigration. Indeed, American party members took secret oaths pledging to fight immigration; their refusal to discuss the pledge outside of their party, and to reply "I know nothing" if asked about it, earned them the name of the "Know-Nothings." The disdain toward the Irish for their cultural differences would soon be directed with just as much vehemence toward immigrants from southern and eastern Europe, and toward Jews. In its earliest form, therefore, nativism established cultural difference as a grave threat to America. In the later half of the nineteenth century and the early part of the twentieth century, concerns about culture would merge with new "scientific evidence" that established the concept of different and unequal races, and of the superiority of Anglo-Saxons, or the "white race." This would lead to the adoption of legislation restricting the numbers of immigrants of particular races, especially southern and eastern Europeans, Jews, Asians, and Africans.

The idea that certain groups of people, or "races," were superior was advanced through the triumph of democracy in the late eighteenth century, along with a growing area of scientific inquiry into intelligence during the two centuries that followed. Following the American Revolution and the creation of what was proving to be a relatively stable democracy, prominent social thinkers produced texts advancing the idea that, as the founders of liberalism, Anglo-Saxons were uniquely disposed to political freedom, and were duty bound to promote it. The idea was used to justify America's westward expansion, and it fed a growing sense of a racial nationalism even before the concept of a superior "white race" was established (Higham, 2002). The idea that Anglo-Saxons were naturally superior was reinforced by studies performed by natural scientists and psychologists in Europe and America. The findings of European scientists engaged in eugenics—the study of human traits for the purpose of improving future generations, and based on the idea that some races are inherently superior to others—traveled to the United States. The findings of the biased research were advanced as proof of why foreigners should be prevented from coming to or staying in America. Though the eugenics research would later be discredited for its deficiencies as a scientific enterprise, it helped give rise to the notion of a superior white race and fueled concerns emerging at the time about the entry of people of "inferior" races—namely southern and eastern Europeans.

The growing hostility toward particular races ultimately became institutionalized in federal law. In 1882, Congress passed the Chinese Exclusion Act, the first major federal law banning a category of people from immigrating. While the primary target of the act was Chinese laborers, it reflected growing hostility toward Chinese and Asians in general. Over the next six decades, Congress would pass more laws explicitly barring certain categories of people from immigrating to the United States. That the laws sought to maintain the purity of the nation can be seen in the exclusion of certain races, along with criminals, people with disease or disabilities, and people who failed to meet certain moral standards (Daniels, 2008).

The Immigration Act of 1924—which established quotas to drastically reduce the number of immigrants from southern and eastern Europe, Asia, and Africa—marked the height of nativism in the early twentieth century. This law emerged from existing animosity toward eastern and southern Europeans combined with fears among Americans that the aftermath of World War I and the 1917 Bolshevik Revolution in Russia would cause a surge in immigration to the United States from those regions. Leading up to the law, the House of Representatives approved a bill in 1921 that, had it been approved by the Senate, would have suspended all immigration for 14 months. The 1924 Immigration Act set quotas for who could enter the United States based on the U.S. population; the quotas allotted to foreign countries were determined by the percentage of American citizens who had ties to the country, which meant significantly higher quotas were allotted to immigrants from Britain. The law also prevented the immigration of individuals from countries or members of races barred from citizenship. This intentionally resulted in the exclusion of Japanese altogether, even at the risk of harming U.S.-Japan relations at a crucial time. The nativist arguments for creating such a restrictive immigration policy was explicitly racist; for example, the chairman of the Immigration Committee of the House of Representatives claimed that restrictions on immigration from southern and eastern Europe were needed to prevent the United States from being overrun by "abnormally twisted" and "unassimilable" Jews, who were "filthy, un-American and often dangerous in their habits" (Daniels, 2008).

The 1924 Immigration Act remained the guiding policy on immigration until the 1960s. The law succeeded in keeping immigration levels low, and in creating a new type of immigrant, the "illegal" immigrant (Ngai, 2005). Its creation of quotas for immigrants from different parts of the globe, and the racial hierarchy this created, was matched with unprecedented levels of the American government's surveillance of immigrants and the country's borders. As a result, the legislation went beyond simply creating a mechanism for legal exclusion, as it led to the social construction of immigrants as undesirable criminals—particularly those from the non-European countries awarded the lowest or no quotas. From this point forward, Americans would use legal status as a justification for depriving immigrants rights afforded to American citizens; even those immigrants who had legal status but had the characteristics associated with illegal immigrants would become the targets of hostility by citizens.

NATIVISM IN THE SECOND HALF OF THE TWENTIETH CENTURY

In the middle of the twentieth century, the discourse surrounding immigrants began to change. Though fundamentally the same song, nativism has developed a new sound since the civil rights movement of the 1950s and 1960s revealed a widespread and growing intolerance for bigotry. This intolerance was ultimately institutionalized in laws at all levels of government, but most notably in federal laws like the Civil Rights Act of 1964, which made it illegal for employers and landlords to discriminate on the basis of race, color, religion, sex, or national origin. Of particular significance was passage of the Immigration and Nationality Services Act of 1965, which replaced discriminatory country quotas with a uniform cap of 20,000 people from any one nation annually, as well as two hemispheric caps: 170,000 for the Eastern Hemisphere and 120,000 for the Western Hemisphere. Moreover, the law contained other provisions for immigration not subjected to these limits, and it expanded the categories of family members of citizens and resident aliens who could immigrate to the United States (Daniels, 2008). This law embodied the prevailing spirit of atonement and acceptance at the time, opening the door for more immigrants than ever before from Asia, Latin America, and Africa to come to the United States.

However, the implementation of the 1965 immigration legislation and the increased immigration from Asia, Latin America, and Africa to the United States was met with a "new" kind of nativism (Jacobson, 2008; Perea, 1997). Despite their arrival during and following the expansion of civil rights in America for people of color, the large number of non-white immigrants, and of immigrants with non-Western customs, were increasingly received with distrust and hostility. Unlike the nativism of previous eras, however, the nativism that has accompanied post-1965 immigration is rarely explicitly racist. The laws that emerged from the civil rights era prohibit it, and American society at large shuns it. Like nativists of earlier eras who alleged immigrants were costly to society—the Irish and Italians, for example, were faulted for contributing to unemployment and crime—new nativists portray immigrants as a threat to the well-being of individual Americans, communities, and the nation as a whole. But rather than express the idea that the new immigrants are essentially inferior or undesirable, new nativists focus more on the immigration status of immigrants; their impact on government resources; and a perceived unwillingness—not inability—of recent immigrants to fully assimilate. Moreover, the new nativists take strides to eschew the image of their cause as being racially motivated; even the Minuteman Project, a group of armed civilians who have taken it upon themselves to police the U.S.-Mexican border proclaim to be "a multiethnic immigration law enforcement advocacy group."

Despite their overtures to nonwhites, new nativists share old nativists' underlying concern about foreign peoples' foreign ways. A prime example of this is the movement surrounding language that emerged in the 1980s. The movement sought to make English the official language of states and the nation as a whole; it achieved significant success at the state level in the 1980s and 1990s, and it remains a hallmark of nativism at the turn of the twentieth century. Prior to 1980, only three states had adopted legislation establishing English as the official language. Between 1981 and 1990, ten Southern and Midwestern states established English as their official language; by the mid-1990s, 22 states had passed official language laws; and as of December 2011, 31 states had laws that established English as the official language (Tatalovich, 1997; U.S. English, 2011). Some of the leading proponents of making English the official language at the state and even federal level expressed exasperation at not being able to communicate effectively with people who are not fluent in English or who have heavy accents. For example, Senator Robert Byrd of West Virginia made the following remarks on the Senate floor in 1992 while debating immigration: "I pick up the telephone and call the local garage . . . I can't understand the person on the other side of the line. I'm not sure he can understand me. They're all over the place, and they don't speak English. We want more of this?" (Tatalovich, 1997, p. 78).

The fact that the senator apologized shortly after making these remarks reveals that statements that smack of xenophobia are, in general, less acceptable following the civil rights era. Yet in March 2011, two federal lawmakers introduced the English Language Unity Act of 2011, indicating the contemporary currency of concern about language. The cosponsors of the bill asserted that the legislation was necessary to unite a nation of immigrants; the bill requires that all official government business be conducted in English, and it contains a naturalization stipulation that prospective citizens attain a certain level of English proficiency.

As a result of America's intolerance of intolerance, nativists justify making English the official language on the grounds that failing to do so creates a financial burden for local governments, or that making English the official language is necessary to promote and maintain national unity. Because most of the state laws that do declare English as the official language do not have significant policy implications, such laws function symbolically to propagate the idea that multiculturalism is a threat to the nation. Indeed, like the attacker in the scenario described at the opening of this chapter, those advocating for making English the official language really want everyone to speak "American." Laws that declare English as the official language reflect fears that immigrants won't adopt the dominant American culture—as envisioned by nativists—and must be forced to assimilate. Studies have shown, however, that most immigrants' children do assimilate. These studies show that the children of immigrants are more likely to do better economically than their parents, indicating their incorporation into and facility with American culture. Moreover, the grandchildren of immigrants usually do not speak the mother tongue of their ancestors (Waters and Jiménez, 2005).

By the 1990s, the openness to immigration embodied in the 1965 immigration law was overshadowed by the resurgence of restrictionist sentiment. As the twentieth century drew to a close, America's most populous state and the federal government adopted legislation that restricted immigrants' access to basic services, most notably health care and education. On November 8, 1994, voters in California overwhelmingly passed Proposition 187, also known as the Save Our State initiative, which denied undocumented immigrants access to non-emergency health care and public education. It also toughened penalties for immigrants with false residency papers, and required officials who provided public services to anyone they suspected of being in the country illegally to report those individuals to the Immigration and Naturalization Service (INS). While courts struck down its provisions and the proposition was not implemented, it generated copycat legislation and altered the national discourse on immigration, just as immigration reform was being pursued at the federal level. In 1996, Congress approved, and President Bill Clinton, a Democrat, signed, the Personal Responsibility and Work Opportunity Reconciliation Act (PRWORA), a sweeping piece of welfare reform legislation that, among many other provisions, denied most legal immigrants residing in the country public assistance for 5 years or until they attained citizenship.

Emerging from a state with mostly Latino and Asian immigrant populations, Proposition 187 and the debate that ensued redefined the political community along racial lines; peoples' support for legislation that denied basic public services to undocumented immigrants ultimately became support for the denial of basic services to people according to their race. Proponents of Proposition 187 advanced arguments that highlighted the cost of immigration and undocumented immigrants in particular, rather than the immorality or inferiority of particular immigrant populations. Moreover, many of the proponents of Proposition 187 and similar legislation articulate a "color-blind" form of conservatism that sees no role for the state in acknowledging racial difference (Jacobson, 2008). The denial of race, however, obfuscates the existence of inequalities created by both explicitly racist policies in the past, and current policies that have a disproportionate impact on nonwhites. In this way, the nativist spirit behind the proposition was given a voice very different from the explicitly racist nativism of the late 1800s and early 1900s. Nevertheless, Proposition 187 emerged from the same place as the Chinese Exclusion Act and the Immigration Act of 1924—a perception of the Other as inherently threatening to American society. And just like the nativism of old, the new nativist messages and accompanying policies deny the humanity of immigrants and negate all current and prospective benefits they provide local communities and the nation as a whole.

NATIVISM AFTER SEPTEMBER 11, 2001

The events of September 11, 2001, emboldened the new nativists. On that day, four commercial passenger jets were hijacked by self-proclaimed enemies of America of Arabic descent, and three of them were flown into symbols of America's economic and political power: the twin towers of the World Trade Center in New York City, and the Pentagon in Washington, D.C., the building that houses the Department of Defense. Passengers on the fourth plane managed to prevent the hijackers from reaching their target, but it is believed that plane was bound for the Capitol building in Washington, D.C. The loss of life and the implosion of the twin towers shook the country to its core, making real something most people could never imagine possible, at least not outside of a movie theater. As nationals of countries from the Middle East, the hijackers embodied the threat of foreignness; indeed, they succeeded in instilling fear in many Americans, and in inciting retribution upon the Other. Immediately following the 9/11 attacks, the United States saw a spike in the number of hate crimes toward people with dark skin and those with ties to the Middle East—a phenomenon so worrisome that the United States Department of Justice created the Initiative to Combat Post-9/11 Discriminatory Backlash within its Civil Rights Division. While the federal government and some localities took steps to prevent or mitigate the violence, the events of September 11 became a rallying call for political and legal action to interrogate those on American soil who resembled—in terms of religion, language, lineage, and skin color—the hijackers, along with others whose allegiance to the United States was deemed questionable due to their foreign origins or cultural practices. As a result, September 11 became a justification for "cracking down on illegal immigration" and "securing America's borders" (Council on American-Islamic Relations, 2005).

Riding the tide of concern over immigration, President George W. Bush and federal lawmakers attempted to pass immigration reform legislation in 2005. On December 16 of that year, the House of Representatives passed House Bill 4437, the Border Protection, Antiterrorism, and Illegal Immigration Control Act of 2005. The title of the legislation represents the fusion of terror and immigration that dominated public discourse on immigration following September 11. Even though immigration reform had been on federal lawmakers' agendas since passage of the Immigration Act and the establishment of the Commission on Immigration Reform in 1990, the events of September 11 gave the subject new urgency, and immigration reform became a salient public policy matter for citizens and lawmakers alike. H.B. 4437 followed President George W. Bush's call for a temporary "guest worker" program so that employers could "find needed workers in an honest and orderly system"—a system that he argued would "help protect our homeland, allowing Border Patrol and law enforcement to focus on true threats to our national security" (Bush, 2004).

Yet the "true threat" that emerged was more of a threat to the undocumented workforce and future immigrants from south of the U.S. border; H.B. 4437 legislation focused on criminalizing undocumented workers and beefing up security along the U.S.-Mexican border, and it failed to provide a path to citizenship for undocumented workers who had been working and living in the United States. Although it roused significant opposition by immigrants and immigrants' rights supporters, and was ultimately not passed, Congress and President Bush did enact a law that provided more funds for erecting a wall along portions of the U.S.-Mexican border.

The new nativism is apparent in the significant increase in local- and state-level laws aimed at identifying undocumented immigrants; restricting their access to public goods and services; promoting assimilation, especially through English-only education; and discouraging immigration or encouraging the emigration of nonnative residents through the intensification of identification requirements for everything from driving to attending school. Since 2007, the last year that Congress made a concerted effort to pass immigration reform, states have proposed or enacted record-breaking numbers of bills addressing immigration. In 2009, according to the National Conference of State Legislatures, 222 laws were enacted and 131 resolutions were passed regarding immigration in 48 states. In June 2010, the governor of Arizona approved a law that has become a national symbol of local efforts to control, criminalize, or reduce migration and migrants. The Arizona law, S.B. 1070, expanded the state's power to identify and penalize immigrants by making the failure to carry immigration documents a crime, and by authorizing local police to detain anyone suspected of being in the country illegally. S.B. 1070 was the first state law mandating that immigrants carry documents that legitimize their presence on American soil.

While proponents of the law argue that it is necessary in a border state that is home to high levels of immigration, much of which involves migrants without proper documentation, critics point out that the nature of the legislation legitimates racial profiling. Given that concerns about immigration are based upon the state's proximity to Mexico, the targets of the expanded police powers will inevitably be Latino. This law therefore reflects the nativism legislated in previous eras. While justification for the law is couched in terms of promoting order and the safety and well-being of the community at large, it clearly stands to penalize one particular ethnic or racial group. In summer 2011, Alabama followed Arizona's lead and passed legislation expanding local powers in the policing of immigration, and went even further in promoting the identification and punishment of immigrants. Among other provisions, the Alabama law requires that police officers try to verify the immigration status of individuals they stop for traffic violations.

These state laws have proved to be the latest expression of American nativism. While the laws are championed by their supporters as being good for local economies and communities, they are leaving small businesses and farmers short on much-needed labor. News of fruit and vegetables rotting on vines at a time of heightened food insecurity, and of small businesses on the brink of failure, reveals that the laws are not producing the economic and social benefits their proponents proclaimed they would. Moreover, the laws, even those passed in America's "Bible Belt," have been criticized by Christian organizations, which see them as in direct conflict with their mission to witness broadly and serve the needy, to be Good Samaritans (Robertson, 2011). The state laws thus show the extent to which some individuals and groups will go to keep foreigners out of their communities—they will do it even if it directly undermines their fellow Americans' well-being, and contradicts the tenets of their own faith.

CONCLUSION

Even though the foremost restrictionists no longer self-identify as "nativists" and may deny any dislike or distrust of foreigners, their concerns about immigrants and immigration are fundamentally the same as those that emerged with the "Know-Nothings," that culminated in quotas in the early twentieth century, that propelled Proposition 187 onto the ballot and turned it into law, and that drive "immigration reform" legislation that seeks to imprison or deport undocumented workers and build a wall between the United States and Mexico. Contemporary debates about immigration reveal the recurring reluctance or downright refusal among some groups of Americans to welcome newcomers.

Although race continues to play an important role in restrictionist agendas, contemporary arguments for restricting immigrants' rights and reducing immigration are generally not explicitly racist. As the preceding sections reveal, arguments for excluding certain categories of people, or races, had a much stronger public voice in the United States prior to the 1960s. Since then, and especially since the beginning of the twenty-first century, distrust of or distaste for the presence of foreigners has been expressed primarily in the form of rational arguments about immigrants' impact on employment opportunities for natives, government services, the unity of American society, and the safety of a country embroiled in several overseas wars. The ostensibly neutral language of the anti-immigrant activity masks concerns about the presence, and prospective increases in numbers, of nonwhites and non-Europeans in America.

While restrictionists deny allegations that their positions are racist, their overall goals are, by their very nature, exclusionary and privilege those born on American soil and who are white. Many of the demands from restrictionists—and state responses to them—target immigrants of color, especially those from the Middle East and Latin America. Legislation that requires police to check the immigration status of those "suspected" of being in the United States illegally, building a wall between the United States and Mexico, calls for making English the official language of the land, and federal raids on particular industries all single out groups of people with darker skin and from countries where English is not widely spoken. While these laws and associated actions are not justified by elected officials or restrictionist leaders with the baldly xenophobic language used by nativists of the past, their focus and impact on particular racial and ethnic groups is undeniable.

REFERENCES AND FURTHER READING

Bush, G. W. (2004, January 20). *Address before a Joint Session of Congress on the State of the Union.* Retrieved from the American Presidency Project website: http://www.presidency.ucsb.edu/ws/index.php?pid=29646

Council on American-Islamic Relations (CAIR). (2005). *The status of Muslim civil rights in the United States 2005.* Washington, DC: Author.

Daniels, R. (2008). *The Immigration Act of 1965: Intended and unintended consequences.* Retrieved from U.S. Department of State website: http://www.america.gov/st/educ-english/2008/April/20080423214226eaifas0.9637982.html

Feagin, J. R. (1997). Old poison in new bottles. In J. F. Perea (Ed.), *Immigrants out!: The new nativism and the anti-immigrant impulse in the United States* (pp. 13–43). New York, NY: New York University Press.

Higham, J. (2002). *Strangers in the land: Patterns of American nativism, 1860–1925.* New Brunswick, NJ: Rutgers University Press. (Original work published 1955)

Huntington, S. P. (2004, March). The Hispanic challenge. *Foreign Policy.* Retrieved from http://www.foreignpolicy.com/articles/2004/03/01/the_hispanic_challenge

Jacobson, R. D. (2008). *The new nativism: Proposition 187 and the debate over immigration.* Minneapolis, MN: University of Minnesota Press.

Ngai, M. M. (2005). *Impossible subjects: Illegal aliens and the making of modern America.* Princeton, NJ: Princeton University Press.

Perea, J. F. (Ed.). (1997). *Immigrants out!: The new nativism and the anti-immigrant impulse in the United States.* New York, NY: New York University Press.

Robertson, C. (2011, August 13). Bishops criticize tough Alabama immigration law. *The New York Times.* Retrieved from http://www .nytimes.com/2011/08/14/us/14immig.html?_r=2&nl=todaysheadlines&emc=tha23

Tatalovich, R. (1997). Official English as nativist backlash. In J. F. Perea (Ed.), *Immigrants out! The new nativism and the anti-immigrant impulse in the United States* (pp. 78–102). New York, NY: New York University Press.

University of Oregon Department of Public Safety. (2011). *Campus crime alert: Sexual assault.* Retrieved from http://safetyweb .uoregon.edu/node?page=1

U.S. English. (2011). *Facts and figures.* Retrieved from http://www.usenglish.org/view/3

Waters, M. C., & Jiménez, T. R. (2005). Assessing immigrant assimilation: New empirical and theoretical challenges. *Annual Review of Sociology, 31,* 105–125.

Carolyn J. Craig

COUNTERPOINT

When America's leaders and textbooks refer to America as "a nation of immigrants," they celebrate the contributions of immigrants to the country's development and prosperity. For the first few centuries of the nation's history, immigrants were necessary for settlement, growth, and expansion. They contributed and adapted to the emerging American way of life, making this country exceptionally successful, with high levels of immigration of peoples from an array of cultures. However, due to contemporary features of American society, politics, and the economy, as well as various features of globalization, America's relationship with immigration and immigrants has changed. Factors ranging from an overabundance of low-skilled labor to improved communications and transportation technologies and multiculturalism, make large-scale immigration problematic, and even dangerous, for those who currently reside on American soil. Those advocating for greater restrictions on immigration and cultural assimilation in the early twenty-first century are motivated by concerns about the threats immigration poses to America's economic growth, social cohesion, political institutions, environment, and national security—particularly in the wake of the terrorist attacks of September 11, 2001. Contemporary restrictionists do not oppose immigration because of fears of strangers or moral indignation, but because the real costs associated with high numbers of foreigners coming to and remaining in America far outweigh the benefits.

The rest of this chapter explains contemporary restrictionists' rational arguments that immigration threatens American society, economy, and political institutions. It begins with a brief review of America's history with immigration and immigrants prior to the 1960s. This section highlights the very different nature of immigration and the country's capacity to accommodate high levels of unskilled labor in earlier eras. It then examines the changes to American society and immigration policy, beginning in the1960s, that have made it more difficult for America to absorb immigrants, and less likely that immigrants will assimilate. The second section focuses on how these changes have made it less likely that immigrants will sever ties with their nations of origin and adopt American cultural practices. The third section highlights the ways in which immigration has become a financial burden on governments and a threat to employment opportunities for Americans. The fourth section highlights the threat of immigration to America's national sovereignty and security. The concluding section reiterates the rational nature of restrictionists' arguments and the distinction between these arguments and the racist and xenophobic agendas of the nativist movements that emerged earlier in American history.

THE ROLE OF IMMIGRANTS FROM AMERICA'S FOUNDING THROUGH THE 1960s

From the Europeans' discovery of the New World through the middle of the twentieth century, immigrants and immigration played a key role in America's prosperity. America was founded and built by immigrants, beginning with the Puritan settlers who arrived on the shores of modern-day New England. For over three centuries, immigrant labor and ingenuity proved invaluable to the country's economic development. While not everyone already residing on American soil approved of newcomers who looked different or practiced different customs, immigrants were crucial to the development of industry, infrastructure, and even American society. In order to understand why high levels of immigration will no longer benefit America or most immigrants now, one must recognize that several factors contributed to America's historic success with immigration from its founding through World War II—factors that no longer exist.

First, America had an abundance of jobs for low-skilled workers, both in burgeoning cities and rural areas, as the country was developed. Second, expectations for government assistance in general were much lower; government at all levels simply did not provide individuals and communities much in terms of education, health care, and security until the early twentieth century, so there were very little public cost associated with sustaining each newcomer. Third, assimilation was widely recognized by native-born Americans and immigrants alike as crucial for individual and familial advancement. As a result, mass migration to America prior to World War II provided the labor needed to develop the country, and the migrants who remained expanded the American nation by adopting an American identity and raising their offspring with that identity.

During America's earliest years, the American colonies relied upon a steady stream of immigrants from northern Europe to establish viable communities. These migrants settled in places that were largely undeveloped, and they worked together to create villages, commerce, and industry where none existed. Members of these communities shared cultural and religious institutions that helped produce the democratic system of government that exists today. The Industrial Revolution and the jobs that came with it created a demand for more labor, which in turn led to the recruitment of foreigners from near and far. French Canadians living in Quebec were recruited to work in the garment mills in New England and Chinese were brought over to help build America's railroads. Irish Catholics and southern Europeans came to work in the burgeoning cities. Westward expansion also required, and could accommodate, large numbers of immigrants from around the world. The abundance of natural resources—from seemingly endless tracts of land that could be used to grow corn and cotton, to lumber, precious metals, and oil—created demand for labor and offered opportunities for widespread prosperity into the twentieth century. The more the country developed, the more it needed labor and looked to foreign countries to provide it.

While some of the immigrants who came to America returned home, either by choice or by force, most remained on American soil. The extent to which first-generation immigrants spoke English or changed other cultural practices depended on many factors, but for many second- and third-generation immigrants, the English language and the practice of American customs became "natural." As the educational system expanded during the nineteenth century, local jurisdictions deliberately promoted Americanization through English-only instruction, citizenship programs, and rituals like the Pledge of Allegiance. Moreover, major industrialists like Henry Ford required workers to take English language classes, encouraged workers to play sports like baseball together to promote assimilation, and mandated workers' declaration of allegiance to the United States. Thus, even though many immigrants lived in neighborhoods populated mostly by others from their homeland, they and their progeny were the subject of deliberate efforts by America's elite, churches, neighborhood associations, and national nonprofit organizations to assimilate them—to have them become "Americans." Immigrants who were not directly affected by these programs were still aware of the benefits that came with assimilation. Recognizing these benefits, many second-generation immigrants raised their children in English-only homes, and as educational opportunities expanded, immigrants' children grew up more heavily influenced by national customs and at a time of expanding employment options. In general, immigrants who came to the United States prior to World War II ultimately embraced their new homeland, and those who did find a better life here often proudly came to identify as American (Fuchs, 1991; Huntington, 2004).

Immigration to the United States in the second half of the twentieth century differed from that which preceded it; the changes in the nature of those who came to the United States, combined with changes in American society and infrastructure, have altered the dynamics of immigration and the role of immigrants in the United States. In the most general terms, America became more welcoming of immigrants, while the opportunities for prosperity available in earlier eras to immigrants and native-born Americans were decreasing. At the same time, the mandates, expectations, and incentives for immigrant assimilation receded, so that immigrants to postwar America, and after 1965 in particular, have maintained attachments to their countries of origin or developed transnational identities. The resulting multiculturalism and the proliferation of transnational identities weaken the national collective identity necessary for making America strong (Reimers, 1992).

While the two world wars that occurred in the first half of the twentieth century took a toll on American society, the country emerged from World War II strong and a model for democratic development around the world. As such, it was taken to task by its own citizens for its own failures to promote democracy at home, and for its neglect of or promotion of inequalities rooted in race and gender. The civil rights movement demanded that the country ensure the enfranchisement of African Americans in particular, and raised a collective consciousness about violations of peoples' liberties based on an array of physical characteristics. Conceived during this heightened sensitivity toward "difference," the 1965 Immigration Act abolished country-specific quotas and encouraged the migration of people from the non-Western world—170,000 for the Eastern Hemisphere and 120,000 for the Western Hemisphere annually—and expanded the categories of family members permitted to immigrant. While not intended to do so, the 1965 Immigration Act precipitated the largest wave of immigration in the nation's history.

Prior to 1965, most of those who immigrated to the United States came from European countries. Even though there were some religious ethnic divisions among the Europeans, most were Christian and shared a broad range of other cultural practices. Most of those who have migrated to the United States since 1960 have been Asian and Latin American, and a majority of them are from Mexico. As Samuel Huntington argues in "The Hispanic Challenge" (2004), the migration of people from Mexico is "without precedent in U.S. history," and the "experience and lessons of past immigration have little relevance to understanding its dynamics and consequences" (p. 33).

The nature of the immigration from Mexico since 1965 is significant for a number of reasons. First, it represents the largest mass migration from a developing country to a developed country, meaning that the population of newcomers is significantly poorer than most of those already living in the United States. This has consequences for both society and the labor force, since these migrants are willing to work for much less in terms of wages and protections than most Americans. Second, given the proximity of the country, a great deal of the immigration can and does occur illegally. The presence of undocumented immigrants contributes to the development of an underclass of people who lack both the rights and responsibilities of citizens. These factors contribute to a third problem: the existence of a large group of people who have it in their interest to remain hidden in society and from the law, both of which undermine social cohesion. The proximity of their homeland, combined with improvements in transportation and communication technologies, means that many of these immigrants maintain ties and allegiances to their native land.

In sum, immigration to America in recent decades has occurred, and continues to occur, under circumstances that are very different from those that existed prior to the 1960s. Immigration has always brought foreigners to American soil, but in the past those foreigners usually did not arrive in numbers as high as they have in recent decades, and they wanted to, were encouraged, and were given opportunities to become successful Americans. Today, advanced communication technologies enable immigrants to maintain ties with their homeland, and the popularity of multiculturalism throughout the advanced industrialized world means that immigrants are much less likely to sever old ties and adopt the identity of their new homeland. Moreover, the lack of employment opportunities for the mostly undereducated immigrants coming to America means that many immigrants cannot contribute to the economic development of the country in the ways that newcomers once did, and that they will in fact be a drain on public services financed by working people. High levels of legal and illegal migration now pose an unprecedented threat to employment opportunities, to governments' capacities to provide services, and to the promotion of an American identity that inspires individual investment in and sacrifice for the nation (Borjas, 1999; Brimelow, 1995; Camarota, 2004; Rector, 2006).

IMMIGRATION AND SOCIETY

One of the greatest costs of mass immigration to America today is its toll on social cohesion. As a result of the changes in American society and communication technologies, as well as changes in the nature of immigration to the United States, the Americanization of immigrants is not taking place. As a result, American unity is threatened by the existence of people who do not identify first and foremost as Americans; this contributes to divisions within society and a decline in overall civic engagement, both of which undermine core democratic values and threaten the strength and stability of the national community (Putnam, 2007).

The civil rights movement gave rise to norms and policies that promoted cultural diversity and provided legal protection of the rights of people based on various aspects of their identity, including ethnicity, race, religion, and nationality. As a result, multiculturalism is now institutionalized in America; indeed, Americans tend to be quite tolerant of difference, at least compared to those in other countries around the world. The institutionalization of multiculturalism in America means that immigrants are not encouraged to assimilate to American culture and customs, as they were in the nineteenth century and through the middle of the twentieth century. Instead, immigrants are encouraged to maintain the cultural practices that they bring with them, which not only differ from but also sometimes directly conflict with deeply held democratic values, such as the rule of law and equality between the sexes. The fact that immigrants are now able and even encouraged to maintain attachments to foreign cultural practices and countries is new in the history of immigration in America, and poses a new threat to the strength of American society, its democratic system of government, and its national security (Fonte, 2005; Renshon, 2005).

The rise of multiculturalism has been accompanied by a rise in "transnationalism," or the proliferation of cross-border attachments and identities (Levitt, 2001; Portes, 1996). This phenomenon is found among business, governmental and nongovernmental organizations, and individuals to an unprecedented extent across the globe. Transnationalism has been facilitated by improvements in communication and transportation technologies, and by policies that encourage and permit the flow of goods and capital. While interconnection and interdependence is not likely to decrease in the future, and indeed has many benefits, transnationalism among individuals permits people to maintain their allegiances to their homeland and interferes with their assimilation and patriotic attachment to America. For immigrants, advances in communications technologies mean that they can maintain ties primarily with those of their native national community.

Transnationalism among immigrants undermines national unity and impedes democracy. As the scholar Robert Putnam argues in *Bowling Alone* (2000), Americans are spending less time engaging with members of their community in social activities like bowling leagues, which in turn has depleted the "social capital" that contributed to the success of American democracy. The atomization of American society has been exacerbated by the Internet, which permits people to shop, learn, and even socialize without leaving their homes or encountering many people who share different views or experiences. Immigrants who maintain ties and allegiances to other countries simply will not become as invested in the development and prosperity of America.

The high level of migration from Mexico and Latin America is especially problematic, not because of the nature of the cultural differences between Americans and Latinos per se, but because the mass migration of Latinos is introducing a very large, homogenous population of immigrants. In previous eras, the population of immigrants was more diverse, not only in terms of their countries of origin, but also their customs and, particularly, their language. The numbers of migrants from south of the U.S. border with Mexico is larger and more homogenous than any other immigrant group, and this migration is occurring at a time when there are far fewer incentives and capacities for immigrants to become American than there were before. As a result we are witnessing the emergence of a separate national community, a Hispanic Volk, that undermines national unity and ultimately national harmony and security (Krikorian, 2008).

IMMIGRATION, THE ECONOMY, AND JOBS

The impact of mass migration on jobs is another major threat to Americans. Much of the migration that has occurred over the course of the country's history was of unskilled workers, and over much of America's history that type of labor was needed. But the American economy underwent a major shift in the decades leading up to the turn of the twenty-first century, and the need for unskilled labor is now much lower. The need for skilled labor, meanwhile, for those who can contribute to economic growth in an information and service-based economy, is much higher.

The largest wave of immigration to the United States that followed the 1965 Immigration Act began when America's manufacturing-based economy was thriving and its position as one of the most prosperous advanced industrialized countries was secure. But this would not last for long; by the 1960s the United States was well on its way to being a postindustrial society, where the manufacturing sector is smaller than the service sector. This transformation requires a more highly educated workforce, but most immigrants coming to America over the past decades have arrived with low levels of education. This has increased the supply of low-skill workers to the point where it has exceeded demand. This has not only contributed to unemployment, it has also driven wages down, meaning that low-skill workers, among both the native and nonnative populations, are destined for a lower quality of life than was previously available to them in the "land of opportunity." While the prospects for employment do change with economic cycles, the days when poor workers could come to America and realistically expect to achieve a middle class standard of living are essentially gone.

Simply raising the bar for immigrants is not a solution, however, and in fact the immigration of skilled workers would also have a pernicious effect. First, the impetus for immigration for many immigrants is an expectation of an improved standard of living and opportunities down the road. This impetus exists primarily for the unskilled, since they are the ones who have fewer opportunities for advancement in their home countries. Second, an immigration policy that permits hundreds of thousands of skilled workers to come to America would make it more difficult for skilled Americans to find jobs. Moreover, it would decrease the incentives for Americans to get a college degree, which requires an investment with no guarantee of any return. At the same time, allowing the mass migration of skilled workers would create a disincentive for investment in the American educational system, since highly skilled workers could be "imported" from abroad, with the expenses of their education already paid for by their home countries (Krikorian, 2008).

IMMIGRATION AND THE COST TO SOCIETY AND GOVERNMENT

Another way that mass migration weakens the American state is through the toll immigrants take on public services. Spending on services such as health care, education, and law enforcement associated with mass migration has stressed local and state governments and is an added drain on federal coffers (Camarota, 2004; Rector, 2006). In previous eras of mass migration, local governments were not obligated to provide the services that they are today. Moreover, the wave of illegal immigration seen in the last several decades is a recent phenomenon. The fact that immigrants in the past had documentation meant that they could be easily identified, and they had few incentives to hide from the law or remain isolated from society.

In the wake of the federal government's failure to pass comprehensive immigration reform, state and even local governments have passed laws to address the drain of immigrants on public services and to make immigration control more efficient. One of the most significant pieces of state legislation in this regard was California's Proposition 187. This proposition was overwhelmingly approved by California voters in November of 1994 as a direct result of a financial crisis associated with the steady increase in legal and illegal migration to the state in previous decades. The primary goal of the legislation was to prevent illegal aliens from receiving public assistance paid for primarily by American citizens and legal residents. The federal government followed suit in 1996 when it passed comprehensive welfare reform legislation, the Personal Responsibility and Work Opportunity Reconciliation Act (PRWORA). PRWORA not only denied federal benefits to illegal immigrants, it also denied it to legal residents for 5 years or until they became citizens. Attaching citizenships status to the receipt of government assistance is important because it requires immigrants to pledge their allegiance to the country—an acknowledgement and affirmation of their identification with the American nation and duties as a member of it. Failing to require recipients of public assistance to make such an affirmation permits the fraying of the nation's social fabric. Such requirements are not born of fear of "the Other," but of an understanding that a country's prosperity requires a strong collective identity, and that its security requires its members' allegiance to it. No nation can survive for very long if it permits foreigners to use its resources without giving something in return, in both the short and long term.

Immigration has, and will continue to have, a considerable affect on America's quality of life—particularly if mass migration is permitted. Even setting aside the contemporary challenges to assimilation and the proliferation of multiculturalism and transnationalism, mass migration means more people on American soil. The presence of more people, and poor people in particular, interferes with some American quality-of-life values, including low-density living and a healthy environment that includes wide-open spaces and wilderness. Contrary to the belief that mass migration can counter the demographic shift toward an older population, mass migration will simply mean more and more people—including older people—living within America's borders. In the past, population growth was driven largely by those already living in America, and immigrants contributed only about 20 percent of the population growth. Recent projections indicate that immigration will account for 82 percent of population growth in the United States between 2005 and 2050 (Passel & Cohn, 2008).

Since the 1990s, the presence of more people in the United States due to mass migration has contributed to increases in carbon dioxide emissions, the production of billions of tons more waste, and the conversion of open space and farmland to housing developments. The demand for housing in urban areas—desirable in part due to the proximity to work for many people—has caused a significant increase in the property values, which in turn has forced more people to seek housing in the suburbs or more rural areas. This has contributed to the carbon dioxide emission increases and development mentioned above, as well as more time that Americans must spend commuting, and less time available for civic engagement in their home communities. In previous eras Americans and immigrants alike could live close to work, and recreate close to where they lived, but the development of America makes this more difficult as more people make the country their home. Mass migration is therefore a problem of numbers, one that will not be resolved even if the problems related to multiculturalism and transnationalism did not exist or were somehow resolved.

The presence of more people on American soil has become especially pronounced since the economic downturn of 2008. Unemployment has been maintained at levels not seen since the Great Depression, and governments at all levels are experiencing financial crises of unprecedented proportions. All services are being drastically reduced, even the most sacred: urban school districts with already overcrowded classrooms are closing and laying off teachers, and law enforcement agencies have imposed hiring freezes while crime rates rise and their services are increasingly in demand. State laws have been changed to permit, and courts have mandated, the early release of incarcerated criminals because prisons have become dangerously and inhumanely overcrowded. Passing legislation that restricts the entry of foreigners into the country, and that encourages or returns those here illegally, is not a consequence of ill-will toward immigrants, but rather a matter of wise and responsible policy—for both Americans and most immigrants.

IMMIGRATION AND THREATS TO SOVEREIGNTY AND NATIONAL SECURITY

Another unprecedented threat posed by mass migration is the erosion of national sovereignty. Modern states have entered into a record number of international treaties and trade agreements, and the proliferation of capitalism has contributed to interdependence, but democracy requires that states maintain the authority to govern those who reside within their borders. The mass migration of immigrants from Mexico has led to the development of the largest network of foreign consulates anywhere; Mexico has established more than 50 consulates and consular agencies in over 25 states, while the United States has only 9 consulates and 13 consular agencies in Mexico. In the past, when immigrants came to America they usually settled here for good, and their home countries took little interest and invested few resources in advancing their social or political relocation in America. This has changed, in part due to communication technologies, and in part due to the rise of identity politics and global norms that seek to protect group-based rights. While all foreign countries can now extend their reach into countries that house their emigrants, the capacity of foreign countries to weaken receiving states is made most evident by the growing influence of Mexico in the United States. The physical presence of the Mexican state within the United States—including its investment in protecting illegal immigrants, promoting Mexican culture, and seeking to expand the rights of Mexican immigrants in the United States—is an unprecedented display of foreign intrusion in politics and society, and is linked explicitly to mass migration.

The Mexican state has attempted to prevent the enforcement of U.S. immigration laws, first by declaring that it will not abide by them, and second by instructing Mexican immigrants on matters like successful illegal migration across the border and evading deportation. It has invested heavily in lobbying American officials at the state and local levels to promote the provision of public services to Mexican immigrants; it has supported political candidates or referenda positions that seek to protect Mexicans, including those in the United States illegally; it has advocated on behalf of Mexican immigrants tried in American courts; it has promoted pro-immigrants' rights marches and demonstrations that contest legislation meant to stop illegal immigration; and it has distributed textbooks that are not only in Spanish, but that celebrate Mexican history more so than American history. These actions obviously inhibit assimilation, and they work to weaken the American state by making it difficult to enforce its laws and govern with efficiency and legitimacy. The Mexican government's success in asserting itself in areas of immigration law and policy reveals the capacity of foreign countries to impose on America's national sovereignty when they have a large population residing within its borders.

CONCLUSION

Support for policies that seek to restrict immigration are, for the most part, born of genuine concern about the country's and immigrants' well-being, not racism or xenophobia. This restrictionist sentiment has emerged as a consequence of Americans' realization that America can no longer successfully adapt to mass migration. For centuries, immigration helped make America the great country that it is. Since World War II, however, America has undergone significant transformations, and forces associated with globalization have put pressures on modern states that make large-scale immigration untenable. In order to adequately meet the challenges of modern life at the turn of the twenty-first century, and to protect the opportunities for individual success and a high quality of life for all Americans, the country needs a more restrictive immigration policy and must actively promote assimilation.

The shift in the country's economic base means that it cannot absorb a large number of unskilled workers. Moreover, technological advances enable newcomers to maintain ties with their native lands, which undermines their attachment to this nation and their adoption of American values and customs. The lack of attachment to America contributes to social decay and makes the country vulnerable to outside attacks and weak on the international stage. These are the concerns that motivate elected officials and civic organizations that are calling for enhanced border security, a crackdown on undocumented immigrants, and assimilation to America's culture and mores. These are genuine concerns about the well-being of Americans and the nation at an unprecedented time of global competitiveness, vulnerability, and change.

REFERENCES AND FURTHER READING

Borjas, G. J. (1999). *Heaven's door: Immigration policy and the American economy.* Princeton, NJ: Princeton University Press.

Bosniak, L. (1994). Immigration crisis, nativism, and legitimacy. *Proceedings of the Annual Meeting of the American Society of International Law*: Vol. 88. The Transformation of Sovereignty (pp. 440–446).

Brimelow, P. (1995). *Alien nation.* New York, NY: Random House.

Camarota, S. A. (2004). *The high cost of cheap labor: Illegal immigration and the federal budget.* Retrieved from Center for Immigration Studies website: http://www.cis.org/node/54

Fonte, J. (2005). *Dual allegiance: A challenge to immigration reform and patriotic assimilation.* Retrieved from Center for Immigration Studies website: http://www.cis.org/node/648

Fuchs, L. H. (1991). *The American kaleidoscope: Race, ethnicity, and the civic culture.* Hanover, NH: Wesleyan University Press.

Huntington, S. P. (2004, March). The Hispanic challenge. *Foreign Policy.* Retrieved from http://www.foreignpolicy.com/articles/2004/03/01/the_hispanic_challenge

Krikorian, M. (2008). *The new case against immigration—Both legal and illegal.* New York, NY: Penguin.

Levitt, P. (2001). *The transnational villagers.* Berkeley, CA: University of California Press.

Passel, J., & Cohn, D. (2008, February 11). *Immigration to play lead role in future U.S. growth: U.S. population projections: 2005–2050.* Retrieved from Pew Research Center website: http://pewresearch.org/pubs/729/united-states-population-projections

Portes, A. (1996, March). Global villagers: The rise of transnational communities. *American Prospect, 7*(25). Retrieved from http://prospect.org/article/global-villagers-rise-transnational-communities

Putnam, R. (2000). *Bowling alone: The collapse and revival of American community.* New York: Simon & Schuster.

Putnam, R. (2007, June). *E Pluribus Unum:* Diversity and community in the twenty-first century: The 2006 Johan Skytte Prize Lecture. *Scandinavian Political Studies, 30*(2), 137–174.

Rector, R. (2006, May 12). *Backgrounder no. 1936: Amnesty and continued low skill immigration will substantially raise costs and poverty.* Retrieved from Heritage Foundation website: http://www.heritage.org/research/reports/2006/05/amnesty-and-continued-low-skill-immigration-will-substantially-raise-welfare-costs-and-poverty

Reimers, D. M. (1992). *Still the golden door: The Third World comes to America* (2nd ed.). New York, NY: Columbia University Press.

Renshon, S. A. (2005). *The 50% American: Immigration and national identity in an age of terror.* Washington, DC: Georgetown University Press.

Carolyn J. Craig

8

Federal Policy Versus Decentralized Policy

POINT: Despite the understandable frustration with Washington's seeming inability to deal with the immigration problem, states and localities should not enact their own immigration enforcement laws. State and local law enforcement officers, untrained in immigration law, will (and do) use race and ethnicity as a shortcut for suspecting someone is in the country illegally. A patchwork of policies will mean unequal treatment under the law, and documents required to prove lawful status or citizenship will differ from state to state.

Ali Noorani, National Immigration Forum

COUNTERPOINT: State and local governments confront the most immediate challenges of immigration, while the federal government has abdicated responsibility for enforcing laws designed to curb undocumented immigration. State and local governments should therefore be allowed to enact their own immigration policies that reflect their own interests.

Anna O. Law, DePaul University

Introduction

In 2010 there were an estimated 10.8 million undocumented immigrants in the United States. Though data on the cost of these immigrants is conflicting—some studies find that illegal immigrants contribute more to the economy than they take in services, while others find the opposite—many states, particularly since the late 2000s, have launched their own attempts to deal with illegal immigration. Arizona's S.B. 1070 and South Carolina's Illegal Immigration and Reform Act are two cases in point—and both have been the subject of lawsuits filed by the U.S. Department of Justice, which has argued in both cases that the laws are unconstitutional because they attempt to exert state authority over a federal matter. The specifics of Arizona's legislation are discussed in a separate debate. In this chapter, Ali Noorani and Anna O. Law debate the broader philosophical question of whether or not federal policy is the best arena in which to deal with immigration questions, or whether these issues should be left to the states.

Writing for the Point side of the debate, in favor of maintaining federal jurisdiction over immigration policy, Noorani acknowledges the importance of the illegal immigration problem, and he expresses sympathy with those who feel dismay at "the seeming inability of Congress" to solve it. Nevertheless, in his view, the Constitution is quite clear: according to Article I, Section 8, which reserves the right of the federal government to make a "uniform rule of naturalization," power over immigration policy rests in the hands of the federal government.

Beyond the legalistic argument, Noorani also outlines a number of reasons why federalized immigration policy is in the best interest of citizens. Allowing states to create their own laws results in a patchwork of policies, with inconsistent rules across state lines. And while it is true, as Anna Law points out in the Counterpoint essay, that "states and localities bristle at the thought of having to provide services for undocumented immigrants," Noorani argues that enforcement of state-level laws carries its own costs. Laws perceived as anti-immigrant tend to drive away not only immigrants but those sympathetic to them, and businesses suffer. The costs of fighting lawsuits filed in relation to these local laws can be tens of thousands of dollars, in the case of towns, and hundreds of thousands in the case of states.

Noorani also worries about the impact of these laws on the overall cohesion of communities. He points out that police officers often object to the laws. Because local policing depends in no small part on a cooperative populace, law enforcement often takes a dim view of anti-immigrant laws, which can make the job of policing more difficult. Immigrants' trust in police will erode, leaving their communities less protected than others and leaving police less able to solve crimes.

In the Counterpoint essay, Anna O. Law points to a different part of the Constitution—the all-important Tenth Amendment, which states that "powers not delegated to the United States by the Constitution, nor prohibited by it to the States, are reserved to the States respectively, or to the people." The notion of a "uniform rule of naturalization" is a far cry from the many complex issues that illegal immigrants pose to states and localities.

Fundamentally, the state argument is based on the total failure of the federal government—first to prevent the arrival of more than 10 million undocumented immigrants within U.S. borders, then a failure to find and deport the undocumented, and finally years of failure in both the legislative and executive branches of the federal government to develop a real solution to the problem. Supporters of states' right to enact their own immigration policy point out that the states must deal with the results of these federal failures: increased spending on education and other social services, increased policing expenses, and the risk of increased crime. In a December 2011 statement on behalf of South Carolina governor Nikki Haley, spokesman Rob Godfrey said, "If the feds were doing their job, we wouldn't have had to address illegal immigration reform at the state level. But, until they do, we're going to keep fighting in South Carolina to be able to enforce our laws."

In reading this debate, it is important to consider what kinds of national solutions exist for the "immigration problem." Are readers convinced that a one-size-fits-all approach would be best? Or should states be free to design their own approaches to dealing with undocumented immigrants? On the other hand, what might be the unintended consequences of the development of a patchwork of conflicting immigration laws across the 50 states?

POINT

During the 1990s, and continuing to a lesser extent through the mid-2000s, America's growing economy attracted millions of immigrants. Many of those immigrants came to the United States illegally, as the demand for labor generated by the growing economy outstripped the supply of immigrants who could come legally. In the early 2010s, there is a significant population of immigrants who are not authorized to be in the country—10.8 million in January 2010, according to official estimates (Hoefer, Rytina, & Baker, 2011).

There is broad consensus among both lawmakers and the general public that the immigration system is broken, yet there is no consensus on how to fix it. In particular, Congress has not been able to bridge different visions for handling the unauthorized immigrant population. Outside of Washington, congressional stalemate has generated much frustration with the federal government, and several states and a number of localities have decided not to wait, and have instead enacted their own immigration policies.

However, despite the seeming inability of Congress to fix the immigration system, states do not have the authority to enact their own immigration policies. The U.S. Constitution, in Article I, Section 8, leaves immigration policy in the realm of the federal government, stating Congress shall have the power "To establish an uniform rule of Naturalization." The patchwork of state and local policies that are developing are, for the most part, under legal challenge, and the country is a long way from a final determination on what is permissible for states—something that will ultimately be decided by the Supreme Court.

FROM CALIFORNIA TO HAZELTON

California pioneered in the effort of states to enact their own immigration policies. In the early 1990s, rising unemployment in California, coupled with a rapid increase in the Hispanic population, led to a rise in anti-immigrant sentiment. In 1994, California voters approved a ballot initiative known as Proposition 187. The initiative would have denied public benefits to unauthorized immigrants, and it would have required police and providers of various public services to verify the immigration status of individuals and to report those suspected of being in the country illegally to the U.S. Immigration and Naturalization Service. Despite its popularity, the law never went into effect, as District Court Judge Mariana Pfaelzer issued injunctions against it and ultimately declared much of the law unconstitutional on the grounds that the federal government has jurisdiction over immigration. After Gray Davis became governor in 1999, the state's appeal to the Court of Appeals for the Ninth Circuit was terminated.

Since the passage of Proposition 187, a number of states and localities have passed measures with elements similar to California's, while also taking different approaches. In 2006, for example, the town of Hazelton, Pennsylvania, adopted the Illegal Immigration Relief Act, aiming to regulate immigration by prohibiting businesses operating in the town from employing persons not authorized to work in the United States. It requires businesses to sign an affidavit affirming they do not employ unauthorized workers. Private citizens may bring complaints to the city, alleging an employer is employing unauthorized immigrants, triggering a city investigation. In addition, landlords in the town are prohibited from renting to unauthorized immigrants, and Hazelton requires anyone who wants to rent within the town to apply to the town for an occupancy permit, which they will receive only after proving legal residency. The law is still under court review.

ARIZONA'S S.B. 1070

The issue of state-enacted immigration rules exploded in the national press when, in 2010, the Arizona legislature passed, and Governor Jan Brewer signed, Senate Bill 1070, generally known as S.B. 1070. The law proved so controversial that organizations and even towns and cities across the United States pledged to boycott Arizona. The most controversial sections of the law have since been put on hold by a federal district judge in Arizona.

The law contains a number of sections that attempt to regulate immigration in different ways. It requires state and local police to attempt to determine a person's immigration status if, after a lawful stop, detention, or arrest, the officer has a reasonable suspicion that the person is in the country unlawfully, and it requires an immigration status determination for all persons arrested. The law prohibits Arizona state and local enforcement agencies from having policies that might restrict the enforcement of immigration law, and it gives citizens the right to sue such agencies. In addition, persons are prohibited from stopping and picking up day laborers, and criminal sanctions have been created for unauthorized persons who solicit work. The law makes it a crime to "harbor" or transport an unauthorized immigrant, and it contains sanctions for employers who hire unauthorized immigrants. There are several other provisions as well.

The law faced a number of challenges immediately after the governor signed it, including a lawsuit by the U.S. Department of Justice, and a federal district court issued an order halting the implementation of much of the law. The district court's order has been upheld by the Court of Appeals for the Ninth Circuit.

Despite court actions that have raised questions about whether the Arizona law will ever be fully implemented, a number of state legislatures introduced similar laws in 2011, some of which have been enacted and subsequently put on hold by courts. Given that a number of states are trying to emulate Arizona, this law will be used here as an example in making arguments against state and local immigration enforcement laws.

DISCRIMINATORY EFFECTS

The most controversial part of Arizona's law is that which requires state and local officers to make a "reasonable attempt" to determine the immigration status of a person when, in the course of enforcing any other state or local law or ordinance, there is "reasonable suspicion" that the individual in unlawfully present in the United States. The law also requires that for any person arrested, immigration status will be determined before release.

Immigration law is complicated, and state and local law enforcement officials are not trained in enforcing immigration law. The question then becomes, who gets stopped? The chief concern is that Hispanics will be disproportionately singled out, regardless of their citizenship status, and will be forced to repeatedly prove their authorization to be in the United States.

In 2009, the Warren Institute on Race, Ethnicity, and Diversity (now the Chief Justice Earl Warren Institute on Law and Social Policy) obtained arrest records of the Irving, Texas, Police Department. The records were analyzed for disparities in the ethnic makeup of arrestees. The town participated in an immigration enforcement program known as the Criminal Alien Program. In this program, local enforcement agents take the fingerprints of persons booked in local jails, and then submit them to U.S. Immigration and Customs Enforcement (ICE), the federal agency charged with enforcing immigration laws in the interior of the United States. ICE checks the fingerprints against databases maintained by the Department of Homeland Security. If the prints match those of an immigrant known to be here without authorization, ICE will ask the local enforcement agency to hold the immigrant until ICE can assume custody.

The Warren Institute found that, when Irving police gained easy, round-the-clock access to ICE fingerprint verification support, the number of Hispanics that were being stopped for minor issues went up compared to other ethnic groups. Indeed, the Warren Institute found that, when the CAP program expanded in Irving in April 2007, arrests of Hispanics for Class C misdemeanors more than doubled. Class C misdemeanors are offenses for which the maximum fine (in Texas) was $500, and for which an officer has considerable discretion not to arrest a person and bring the individual to a detention facility. Arrests for minor infractions went up for Hispanics far more than for other groups, and community members felt that officers were using minor violations as a pretext to arrest Hispanics to bring them into the detention facility, take their fingerprints, and check with ICE as to whether the person was unauthorized. For minor traffic infractions, the increase in arrests of Hispanics was even more dramatic (Gardner & Kohli, 2009). Not only were Hispanics being singled out for arrest, the majority of them were found to be in the country lawfully. These individuals—legal residents and citizens—were held unnecessarily pending word from ICE that they were lawfully present in the country.

The same fear of unnecessary apprehension and detention is applied to the Arizona law (and similar state laws). Decisions about who is stopped for a minor infraction, particularly in situations where the officer has discretion not to do so, are bound to be influenced by ethnicity. Once there is an arrest (according to the law), a determination will have to be made that the individual is in the country legally. In ordinary circumstances, an officer might not arrest someone for a minor infraction, but the infraction might provide an opportunity for a determination to be made regarding the individual's immigration status. Many of the people stopped will be authorized immigrants and even U.S. citizens, but they will have to prove their right to be in the United States. Many will be forced to do so repeatedly. Each time their status is challenged, they will be deprived of their liberty while the databases are checked. For U.S. citizens who may be suspected of being in the country illegally, a status resolution is more complicated—the Department of Homeland Security may not have any record in its databases of someone who was born here.

Indeed, in its argument for an injunction against the Arizona law, the Department of Justice highlighted its concern about the discriminatory effect of the law, citing the U.S. system of uniform rules governing the treatment of immigrants and visitors, a system that does not treat aliens as "a thing apart" (*U.S. v. Arizona,* Plaintiff's Motion, July 2010).

In Arizona, concerns about discriminatory treatment, or racial profiling, are not a theoretical matter. Arizona is home to Sheriff Joe Arpaio, whose department is notorious for its sweeps through Hispanic neighborhoods, picking up suspected "illegal aliens." The Maricopa County Sheriff's Office is under investigation by the Civil Rights Division of the U.S. Department of Justice over allegations of discrimination in its police practices and jail operations. Hundreds of private lawsuits have been filed against the office.

Related to the problem of discrimination, there is also a question about documentation with such laws. If states are allowed to set their own immigration rules, what documents will be needed to satisfy law enforcement officials in state X to prove that an individual is in the country legally? How about in state Y? In the United States today, citizens are not required to carry documents proving U.S. citizenship. If states set their own rules, a citizen will need a U.S. passport, or some other document proving citizenship, to avoid being challenged by local law enforcement officials who might suspect the citizen is an unauthorized immigrant.

UNEQUAL TREATMENT UNDER THE LAW

There are other issues related to discrimination. For example, the Arizona law makes it a state crime for an immigrant to fail to carry a federal alien registration card. A separate punishment is attached. This is already a federal offense, with a set punishment specified in federal law. In this case, immigrants in Arizona (and in states that adopted similar laws) would face greater punishment for the same violation of federal law as immigrants in other states.

Unauthorized immigrants may be out of status for different reasons. Some crossed the border illegally, which is a federal criminal offense. Some came legally but overstayed the term of their visitor or temporary immigrant visa. An individual who stays after the expiration of a visa has committed a civil offense; there are no criminal penalties attached. Unlawful presence is not a crime.

The Arizona law, and other state laws modeled after it, criminalizes unlawful presence, contradicting federal immigration law. This matters because immigration consequences can attach to crimes. If the state makes unlawful presence a crime, it may interfere with the federal government's ability to offer the individual some immigration benefit in the future. In making its own determination about how to sanction violations of federal immigration law, Arizona is, in effect, stepping into the realm of immigration admissions policy. A person who is found to be unlawfully present and is allowed to depart the United States voluntarily may be able to return legally in the future. If, however, the person had been convicted of a crime, return might not be possible.

CONFLICT WITH FEDERAL PRIORITIES

From the federal perspective, having states enact their own immigration enforcement policies makes it impossible for the federal government to set national priorities. Currently, the federal government has prioritized the removal of unauthorized immigrants who may pose a national security risk or who may be a threat to public safety (Morton, 2011). If, for example, Arizona's law goes into effect, resources of the federal government will be diverted due to a flood of inquiries from Arizona law enforcement officers who have "reasonable suspicions" that someone they have "lawfully stopped" is in the country illegally. The Arizona law sets no priorities for making the immigration inquiries to the federal government. It requires an immigration status check of all persons arrested, and officers are required to make a "reasonable attempt" to determine the immigration status of all persons stopped, detained, or arrested when the officer has "reasonable suspicion" that the person is in the country unlawfully. Indeed, the Justice Department, in its request for an injunction against the Arizona law, stated that the law would interfere with its priorities and thus is preempted by federal law. Even if the person is found to be in the United States unlawfully, a trained federal immigration enforcement agent may decide not to arrest that person for a variety of humanitarian reasons. For example, an immigrant might claim a fear of persecution if sent back to his or her home country, and might therefore be offered a chance to apply for asylum in the United States. State and local law enforcement agents do not have training to recognize that someone they encounter may be eligible for one of a number of humanitarian programs that exist in the 1952 Immigration and Nationality Act (the federal law governing immigration).

State laws that impose their own punishment schemes on foreigners may interfere with U.S. foreign policy objectives. The federal government must have control over the treatment of foreign nationals in the United States, not just in parts of the United States. States that enact their own laws governing the treatment of foreign nationals may taint the foreign policy interests of the nation as a whole.

In the Arizona case, much of the vitriol surrounding the debate was aimed at Mexican nationals, and Mexico reacted to the passage of the law in negative ways that affected not just Arizona, but the United States as well. For example, the Mexican Senate, angry over the passage of Arizona's S.B. 1070, postponed consideration of the ratification of an important agreement between the United States and Mexico having to do with response to natural disasters and accidents. The 2010 annual Border Governors Conference—attended by governors in the U.S. and Mexican states on the U.S.-Mexico border—was cancelled when all of the Mexican governors refused to travel to Arizona where the conference was to be held. Mexico issued a travel alert for its citizens planning a visit to or visiting or residing in Arizona.

SETTLED EXCEPTION

The above discussion has focused on the Arizona law as an example of efforts by states and localities to enact their own immigration laws. The Arizona law contains other provisions not addressed above, and other state and local ordinances attempt to control immigration in other ways. The ultimate legality of many of these strategies, as mentioned above, is yet to be decided by the U.S. Supreme Court.

One strategy used in several state and local ordinances is to punish businesses by tying behavior regarding the hiring of workers to locally regulated business licenses. Again, Arizona is the example. A law passed in 2007 (the Legal Arizona Workers Act) prohibits employers from knowingly employing unauthorized workers, and it requires employers to use the federal E-Verify electronic worker verification system to verify that their employees are authorized to work in the United States. The state will deny a license to operate to any business found to employ unauthorized workers or to businesses not using the E-Verify system. In May 2011, the Supreme Court upheld the Arizona law in *Chamber of Commerce of the United States v. Whiting*.

The basis of the Court's ruling was the 1986 Immigration Reform and Control Act (IRCA). In that law, Congress expressly exempted a state's licensing function from its preemption of state or local laws that would impose separate civil or criminal sanctions against employers. The Court ruled that because the Arizona law prohibits businesses from employing unauthorized workers as a condition of holding a license to operate within the state, and because the licensing function was expressly exempted by Congress' preemption language, the Arizona law was not preempted by federal law. This narrow ruling may or may not have an impact on other strategies that states and localities have used in their own efforts to regulate immigration.

ADDING UP THE COSTS

While there are many legal arguments to be made against states and localities enacting their own immigration enforcement laws—and these arguments are being made in the courts—it is also true that states and localities that have enacted their own immigration enforcement schemes have found there is an economic downside to such laws.

Although jurisdictions enacting their own immigration enforcement legislation often claim they are doing so to rid themselves of costs associated with providing services to unauthorized immigrants, jurisdictions often find that enacting these laws can prove costly. In addition to the legal costs necessary to defend the jurisdiction in a lawsuit, the laws, and the climate in which they are enacted, drive people away along with their associated economic activity. Even unauthorized immigrants create economic activity and tax revenues for jurisdictions.

For example, the Texas Office of the Comptroller attempted to estimate the impact on the state's economy if the entire unauthorized immigrant population left the state. In a 2006 report, the comptroller estimated that the absence of the estimated 1.4 million unauthorized immigrants living in Texas in 2005 would have depressed the gross state product by $17.7 billion. The comptroller also estimated that taxes received from unauthorized immigrants exceeded the cost of services provided to them. As a result, the absence of unauthorized immigrants would have depressed state revenues by an estimated $424.7 million in 2005 (Strayhorn, 2006).

In smaller jurisdictions, the economic consequences of immigration enforcement ordinances are magnified. For example, in the small town of Riverside, New Jersey, an estimated 3,000 immigrants arrived between 2000 and 2006. With the influx of immigrants, a long economic decline was reversed, as new businesses opened up in the boarded-up shops of downtown Riverside. Not everyone was happy about the arrival of Latin American immigrants, chiefly from Brazil. In 2006, the town passed its own Illegal Immigration Relief Act, which imposed fines and jail sentences on employers who hired unauthorized workers, and on landlords who rented to them. After the law was enacted, thousands of immigrants fled the town. Businesses suffered, and the downtown again became blighted with boarded-up store fronts. The town spent $82,000 defending itself in lawsuits related to the ordinance. A year later, the town rescinded the ordinance (Martinez, 2011).

Arizona's S.B. 1070 proved very controversial across the nation, and many organizations that planned conferences in that state cancelled those conferences. Organizations and other local jurisdictions announced boycotts of the state. The Center for American Progress estimated in a November 2010 study that losses resulting from conference cancellations amounted to $253 million in lost economic output for the state over a period of 2 to 3 years, while tax receipts would be $9.4 million lower as a result (Fitz & Kelley, 2010).

UNCIVIL ACTION

The debate surrounding local immigration enforcement initiatives is often toxic, tearing communities apart and ultimately damaging their reputation. Hispanics often view these initiatives as being aimed at them, and they become distrustful of others in the community and of the government.

In 2007, Prince William County in Virginia enacted an ordinance that would have required police to inquire about the immigration status of anyone they detained, provided there was "probable cause" that the individual was not in the country legally. For weeks leading up to the passage of the ordinance, and its following passage, the community was split between supporters of the relatively new Hispanic community and others who felt that their community had been "invaded." The police chief, who opposed the ordinance as it was first proposed, was accused of treason.

In the aftermath of the passage of the ordinance, according to an exhaustive report prepared for the Prince William County Police Department, there was a dramatic change in the way Hispanics viewed their life in the county. There was a sense of feeling unwelcome, and some—including legal immigrants—left the county. Distrust of county government increased, and police-community relations were disrupted. In 2008 the ordinance was modified so that police would determine immigration or citizenship status of persons only after a physical custodial arrest. Aggressive outreach by the police to the Hispanic community had rebuilt trust by the time the report was released (in 2010), but Hispanic population growth in the country lagged behind other areas in the region. The extensive coverage of the fight over the ordinance, especially in Spanish-language media, damaged the county's reputation as a welcoming place for Hispanics (Guterbock et al., 2010).

KEEPING COMMUNITIES SAFE

Another reason immigration enforcement is best left to federal officials is that, in areas where there are large immigrant communities, the enforcement of immigration laws by state and local police interferes with their ability to protect the public. Thus, when state and local ordinances are proposed, they are often opposed by police. As the Police Foundation noted in a 2007 national survey of law enforcement executives, the nature of law enforcement often causes police to see immigration enforcement from a different perspective than other members of the community, including the political leaders (Khashu, 2009).

Police must protect all members of the community, and to do that they rely on the community's trust in the police. Through community-oriented policing programs, police departments have worked hard to gain the trust of community members, including immigrant communities. As police become involved in immigration enforcement, immigrants begin to see them not at protectors but as agents of the immigration system. Contact with the police is avoided, because it might lead to deportation or the deportation of a family member. (Many immigrants live in "mixed-status" families, in which there may be unauthorized immigrants, legal residents, and even U.S. citizens. It is not only unauthorized immigrants who may fear police, but legal residents may fear getting a family member in trouble.)

If members of a community distrust the police, it becomes that much harder for the police to gain the cooperation of witnesses and victims of crimes. Thus, it becomes harder to prosecute criminals, and the entire community is less safe.

WHY THE HYSTERIA?

In the wake of the passage of Arizona's S.B. 1070, other states have vied to be the toughest on immigration, and the phenomenon of state and local immigration enforcement ordinances continues to spread. Stepping back from the hysteria, one might ask why these ordinances are necessary. When she signed S.B. 1070, Governor Jan Brewer said that she believed it was necessary because of "the crisis caused by illegal immigration and Arizona's porous border" (Brewer, 2010). In reality, in Arizona—and elsewhere where immigration enforcement laws are enacted ostensibly to deal with crime caused by "illegal immigrants"—it is hard to justify the hysteria when looking at trends and statistics.

In Arizona, despite the oft-repeated charge that violence along the border was out of control, police and FBI records indicated the opposite (Wagner, 2010). In Hazelton, the town's claim that "illegal immigrants" were causing much of the town's crime problems was not supported by the records of the Hazelton Police Department (Lozano v. Hazelton, 2008). In Prince William County, Virginia, enactment of the immigration enforcement ordinance did not affect most types of crimes in that community (Guterbock et al., 2010).

Scholars who have studied the issue of undocumented immigrants and crime have found that there is usually a negative correlation between the size of the undocumented population and the crime rate. Incarceration rates for young men (who are most prone to incarceration) are lowest for immigrant groups—including Mexicans, Salvadorans, and Guatemalans, who make up the bulk of the unauthorized immigrant population. Nationally, the unauthorized immigrant population increased sharply in the 1990s. At the same time, rates of violent and property crime decreased significantly. This pattern is more pronounced in some cities with large immigrant populations. Some scholars suggest that one of the reasons for the decrease in crime rates in the late 1990s and continuing into the 2000s is increased immigration (Rumbaut, 2009).

While local politicians have made claims about the burden being placed on their jurisdictions by unauthorized immigrants due to crime and other factors, they have also made claims that the federal government is doing little to nothing to enforce immigration laws. In fact, the federal government is currently spending a record amount on immigration enforcement, and this has manifested itself in a record number of removals of unauthorized immigrants—nearly 400,000 per year in 2010, or twice as many as 10 years earlier (Office of Immigration Statistics, 2011)—and the record amount of resources deployed to the border has yielded the lowest number of attempted illegal crossings of the border in many years (Fitz, 2011).

CONCLUSION

In conclusion, states and localities should stay out of the business of creating a patchwork of immigration policies across the nation. Laws such as Arizona's S.B. 1070 have a discriminatory effect on residents. They interfere with the federal government's ability to set immigration enforcement priorities, they interfere with the nation's foreign policy objectives, and they create inconsistent requirements for documentation and employment from state to state. States and localities that enact such laws suffer negative economic consequences as a result. These laws are extremely divisive and damage community reputations, and they interfere with the ability of police to keep a community safe. Finally, such laws are not necessary, for the claims made about the burdens unauthorized immigrants place on states and localities are exaggerated, and the federal government continues to step up its enforcement of immigration laws.

A more productive route for local politicians wanting to do something about unauthorized immigration would be to pressure their representatives in Congress to reform the immigration system and find a national solution to the problem of unauthorized immigrants and a visa allocation system that has not kept up with the changes in the U.S. economy.

REFERENCES AND FURTHER READING

Brewer, J. (2010, April 23). *Statement by Governor Jan Brewer.* Phoenix, AZ: State of Arizona, Office of the Governor. Retrieved from http://www.azgovernor.gov/dms/upload/PR_042310_StatementByGovernorOnSB1070.pdf

Chamber of Commerce of the United States v. Whiting, 131 S. Ct. 1968 (2011). Retrieved from Supreme Court website: http://www.supremecourt.gov/opinions/10pdf/09-115.pdf

Fitz, M. (2011, August). *Safer than ever: A view from the U.S.-Mexico border: Assessing the past, present, and future.* Retrieved from Center for American Progress website: http://www.americanprogress.org/issues/2011/08/pdf/safer_than_ever_report.pdf

Fitz, M., & Kelley, A. (2010, November). *Stop the conference: The economic and fiscal consequences of conference cancellations due to Arizona's S.B. 1070.* Retrieved from Center for American Progress website: http://www.americanprogress.org/issues/2010/11/pdf/az_tourism.pdf

Gardner, T., II, & Kohli, A. (2009, September). *The C.A.P. Effect: Racial profiling in the ICE Criminal Alien Program* (Policy Brief). Retrieved from Chief Justice Earl Warren Institute on Race, Ethnicity, and Diversity website: http://www.law.berkeley.edu/files/policybrief_irving_0909_v9.pdf

Guterbock, T. M., Vickerman, M., Walker, K. E., Koper, C. S., Taylor, B., & Carter, T. (2010, November). *Evaluation study of Prince William County's illegal immigration enforcement policy: Final Report 2010.* Prepared for the Prince William County Police Department by the Center for Survey Research, University of Virginia, and the Police Executive Research Forum. For discussion of the effects of the ordinance on the county's internal and external reputation for inclusiveness, see pp. 145–154. Retrieved from Center for Survey Research website: http://www.coopercenter.org/sites/default/files/csr/Final_Report_Consolidated_final.to%20printer.v2%2011.18.10s.pdf

Hoefer, M., Rytina, N., & Baker, B. C. (2011, February). Estimates of the unauthorized immigrant population residing in the United States: January 2010. *Population Estimates.* Retrieved from Department of Homeland Security, Office of Immigration Statistics website: http://www.dhs.gov/xlibrary/assets/statistics/publications/ois_ill_pe_2010.pdf

Inniss, L. K. B. (1996, Summer). California's Proposition 187: Does it mean what it says? Does it say what it means? A textual and constitutional analysis. *Georgetown Immigration Law Journal, 10,* 577–622.

Khashu, A. *The role of local police: Striking a balance between immigration enforcement and civil liberties.* (2009, April). For a discussion of the impact of immigration enforcement on community policing, see pp. 25–25, 48 (in a summary of police focus groups), and 169–178. Retrieved from Police Foundation website: http://www.policefoundation.org/pdf/strikingabalance/Role%20of%20Local%20Police.pdf

Lozano, et al. v. City of Hazelton. (2008, April 8). *Brief of appellees, on appeal from the United States District Court for the Middle District of Pennsylvania.* Retrieved from ACLU of Pennsylvania website: http://www.aclupa.org/downloads/Hzpsbrief3d.pdf

Martinez, G. (2011, January). *Unconstitutional and costly: The high price of local immigration enforcement.* Retrieved from Center for American Progress website: http://www.americanprogress.org/issues/2011/01/pdf/cost_of_enforcement.pdf

McKanders, K. M. (2007, Fall). Welcome to Hazleton! "Illegal" immigrants beware: Local immigration ordinances and what the federal government must do about it. *Loyola University Chicago Law Journal, 39,* 1–49.

Morton, J. (2011, March 2). Civil immigration enforcement: Priorities for the apprehension, detention, and removal of aliens [Memorandum]. Retrieved from U.S. Immigration and Customs Enforcement website: http://www.ice.gov/doclib/news/releases/2011/110302washingtondc.pdf

National Conference of State Legislatures. (2011, March 31). *2011 Immigration-related laws, bills and resolutions in the states: Jan. 1–March 31, 2011.* Retrieved from http://www.ncsl.org/default.aspx?tabid=13114 (Lists from previous years back to 2006 can be accessed at http://www.ncsl.org/default.aspx?TabID=756&tabs=951,119,860#860)

Office of Immigration Statistics. (2011, June). *Immigration Enforcement Actions: 2010* (Annual Report). Retrieved from http://www.dhs.gov/xlibrary/assets/statistics/publications/enforcement-ar-2010.pdf

Rumbaut, R. (2009, April). Undocumented immigrants and rates of crime and imprisonment: Popular myths and empirical realities. In A. Khashu (Ed.), *The role of local police: Striking a balance between immigration enforcement and civil liberties* (Appendix D, pp. 119–139). Retrieved from the Police Foundation website: http://www.policefoundation.org/pdf/strikingabalance/Role%20of%20Local%20Police.pdf

Senate Bill 1070, "Support Our Law Enforcement and Safe Neighborhoods Act," as amended by HB 2162, enacted as Laws 2010, Chapter 113. Retrieved from Arizona State Legislature website: http://www.azleg.gov/legtext/49leg/2r/summary/h.sb1070_asamendedbyhb2162.doc.htm

Silver, Mariko. (2010, June 24). Declaration of Mariko Silver, in *United States v. Arizona.* Retrieved from http://www.justice.gov/opa/documents/declaration-of-mariko-silver.pdf

Strayhorn, C. K. (2006, December). *Undocumented immigrants in Texas: A financial analysis of the impact to the state budget and economy* (Special Report). Retrieved from Texas Office of the Comptroller website: http://www.window.state.tx.us/specialrpt/undocumented/undocumented.pdf

United States v. Arizona. (2010, July 6). *Plaintiff's motion for preliminary injunction and memorandum of law in support thereof.* Retrieved from U.S. Department of Justice website: http://www.justice.gov/opa/documents/pi-brief.pdf

Wagner, D. (2010, May 2). Violence is not up on Arizona border despite Mexican drug war. *Arizona Republic.* Retrieved from http://www.azcentral.com/news/articles/2010/05/02/20100502arizona-border-violence-mexico.html

Ali Noorani

COUNTERPOINT

In 2010, Arizona's controversial immigration law garnered national attention for its aggressive targeting of undocumented immigrants, and especially for the provision that local law enforcement would be able to stop persons and ask for their immigration status. Arizona's S.B. 1070 not only sparked copycat legislation around the country, it also reignited a national debate about whether the national government or its subnational units (or some combination thereof) should create and implement immigration policy. Arizona's law and similar legislation in other states, such as Utah and Alabama (in 2011), were immediately challenged by the federal government in the federal courts on the grounds that states cannot make their own immigration policy, and that the federal government has exclusive control over this area. In fact, the United States is a federal system in which national and subnational units share power, and the authority of the national government does not automatically trump the authority of states and local governments (e.g., counties). In recognition of the fact that a one-size-fits-all approach in public policy is not always the best way to go, one of the strengths of the federal system is that it allows for variation and flexibility by creating 50 laboratories for democracy. But with a 50-laboratories system, one has to take the good along with the bad—some states and localities will come up with policies to one's liking, while others will not. Moreover, one should not assume that a centralized and unified policy carried out by the federal government would be to one's liking either.

CONSTITUTIONAL AUTHORITY FOR FEDERAL SYSTEM

One precondition of a federal system is that a written constitution clearly stipulates that power between the national government and its subnational units is shared in some areas and divided in others. The U.S. Constitution guarantees that the authority of the national government does not automatically override the subnational governments as it would in a unitary system, and that the subnational units maintain some level of integrity and autonomy. Regarding national power, the Constitution states, in Article I, Section 8, that Congress is authorized "To make all Laws which shall be necessary and proper for carrying into Execution the foregoing Powers [the foregoing enumerated powers], and all other Powers vested by this Constitution in the Government of the United States, or in any Department or Officer thereof." For the states, the Tenth Amendment guarantees "The powers not delegated to the United States by the Constitution, nor prohibited by it to the States, are reserved to the States respectively, or to the people." Therefore, in claiming authority to create and regulate any kind of policy, including immigration policy, both the national government and states and localities can point to the constitutional text for support.

Specific to the subject of immigration, the Constitution states, in Article I, Section 8, that Congress has the right to "establish an uniform rule of naturalization." This brief clause is the only source of textual support for the national government's ability to regulate immigration. That very narrow phrase hardly covers the vast array of immigration activities undertaken by the federal government today, including but not limited to: the admission and regulation of temporary workers and tourists, the granting of permanent residency status (a green card) to close relatives of U.S. citizens and lawful permanent residents, and the temporary admission of foreign sports stars and entertainers into the United States. Although textual support for an exclusive national power to regulate immigration is limited, in practice and by constitutional tradition, the federal government has in fact expanded its immigration power to cover large areas of policy far beyond naturalization.

HISTORY OF THE DIVISION OF LABOR BETWEEN THE NATIONAL GOVERNMENT, STATES, AND LOCALITIES

It is a myth that the United States ever had open borders. As the immigration law expert Gerald Neuman notes, it is a historical inaccuracy that people were free to come and go into the United States prior to the national government's assumption of primary control over immigration regulation. Before 1882, first the colonies and later the states had an array of immigration control and screening measures. These qualitative restrictions were not based on national origins, as the federal restrictions to come in the 1920s would be, but they excluded intended immigrants from the colonies and states based on poverty, illnesses, and lack of good moral character (e.g., convicted felons).

Prior to the Civil War, there was little disjuncture between subnational and national immigration policy. Indeed the national government endorsed and supported colonials and state immigration restriction policies, thereby making it difficult to distinguish between a federal immigration policy and a state immigration policy. The states, led by New York and Massachusetts, which had the busiest ports of entry, initially provided the frontline manpower, physical spaces (hospitals, almshouses, Castle Island landing depot), and funding required to provide services to the immigrant poor, convicts, and those with contagious diseases. The funding for these bureaucracies and services was obtained by head taxes on all arriving immigrants and bonds on shipmasters that brought sick or poor immigrants to the country. By 1875 these taxes were invalidated by the Supreme Court, leaving the states with no funding stream to replace the invalidated taxes and bond. As a result, New York, Boston, and other seaports became overwhelmed with the financial burden of caring for indigent and sickly immigrants in the age of mass migration. These states asked the federal government to provide funding via a federal head tax. Ironically, it was the state of New York's threat to withdraw from the business of immigration regulation entirely that finally persuaded the national government to take a more active role.

Most scholars mark the beginning of federal immigration control in 1882, even though there were a few pieces of federal immigration legislation prior to that date. The year 1882 saw the passage of the Chinese Exclusion Act, the first piece of immigration control legislation to single out a race for exclusion. The passage of that act required enforcement, and only the national government was capable of the necessary staffing for such a far-flung bureaucratic mechanism. Prior to the Civil War, the national government lacked the administrative capacity to manage immigration, while the eastern seaboard states, out of necessity, had to build up these administrative structures.

In a federal system, disputes between the national and subnational governments over jurisdiction and divisions of labor in policy areas is often settled by the U.S. Supreme Court. At different points in time, the national government and states offered different legal and political rationales for why they should be in control of immigration policy. It has been up to the Supreme Court to serve as tiebreaker, weigh these competing arguments, and make a decision. One other important reason why the national government assumed control over immigration regulation from the states in 1882 is that a series of Supreme Court cases essentially handed the national government this control.

Before 1876 there existed a space in the development of legal precedent that allowed for states and localities to carve out a space to regulate immigrants. The Supreme Court's interpretation of the commerce clause, which gave the national government the power to regulate interstate commerce, still allowed states to preserve their right to regulate the entry of sickly, criminal, or indigent immigrants as a proper exercise of the police, health, and safety powers that, by constitutional tradition, were reserved to the states. The constitutional space for state and local regulation subsequently closed with the plenary power cases *Chae Chan Ping v. United States* (1889) and *Fong Yue Ting v. United States* (1893), two landmark cases not just in immigration law but also in U.S. constitutional law. These cases presented challenges to the Chinese Exclusion Act and extensions to that act, respectively. Both cases shifted the rationale for federal control over immigrants toward national sovereignty and congressional plenary power and away from the commerce clause justification of immigration as a part of interstate commerce. This shift in rationale is important because the effect on the division of labor between the national and subnational governments has been profound. When the Supreme Court ruled in 1889 and 1893 that, as an incident of any sovereign nation's power, that nation must be able to regulate its borders by being able to determine who may enter and remain in the nation, the hand of the national government was strengthened. In those two cases, and in subsequent cases, the Court also reiterated that the judicial branch would assume a deferential posture toward the actions of the national government, particularly Congress, because the legislative branch has congressional plenary power over this area of law and policy. The ideas of national sovereignty and plenary power that guided the reasoning of the Supreme Court in many immigration cases placed the states and localities at a distinct disadvantage. These cases illustrated the Supreme Court's belief that, given the nature of immigration and its implications for national security and national sovereignty, this area was properly the province of the elected branches of government, especially Congress.

Since the time of the earliest plenary power cases, the federal authorities have been charged with enforcing the civil aspects of the 1952 Immigration and Nationality Act (INA) that stipulates the controlling of aliens who may enter the United States, whether they may remain in U.S. territory, and under what conditions they may enter and stay in the country. The states have restricted themselves to enforcing only the criminal elements of the INA, through the policing of criminal aliens. Beginning in 2000, states and localities got into the business of regulating noncriminal aspects of immigration. In 2006, for example, Hazelton, Pennsylvania, passed the Illegal Immigration Relief Act, which (among other provisions) would have fined landlords for renting to undocumented immigrants and revoked the business licenses (for 5 years) of business owners who hired undocumented immigrants. According to one federal district court judge and another panel of judges on the Third Circuit Court of Appeals, although not directly aimed at undocumented immigrants themselves, the Hazelton law, by going after landlords and employers, infringed upon the Congress's exclusive authority to regulate who can come and go and remain in the United States, thus undermining the intent of congressional immigration laws. The spate of immigration policymaking by the states and localities that began in 2000 has obliterated the parsimonious division of labor between the national and subnational governments over immigration that held for many decades.

IMMIGRATION SETTLEMENT PATTERNS AND FINANCIAL CONSEQUENCES TO STATES AND LOCALITIES

What has caused the entry of localities and states into immigration policy? One answer is the population of approximately 10 million undocumented immigrants that currently reside in the United States. These undocumented immigrants are in the United States because the federal government has either failed to stop them from surreptitiously crossing a land border with the U.S, or because the federal government has failed to locate and deport those immigrants who arrived on temporary visas and have overstayed the expiration dates of their visas. While the federal government has put billions of dollars of resources and personnel into securing the nation's southwest border with Mexico, it has devoted only a fraction of those resources to interior enforcement and worksite enforcement to catch U.S. employers who violate immigration laws by hiring the undocumented. These policies have not been effective in deterring undocumented immigrants from entering the country, or in removing those who are in the country illegally, as evidenced by the 10 million undocumented persons living in the United States (as of 2012). Meanwhile, states and localities, not the federal government, are on the frontlines of managing the documented and undocumented immigration phenomenon. Although immigration is a national political issue and phenomenon, a 2011 Migration Policy Institute report based on census data shows that a large percentage of documented and undocumented immigrants continue to settle in the metropolitan areas of six states: California, Texas, New York, Illinois, Florida, and New Jersey, each of which is home to more than 1.7 million or more foreign-born persons.

With respect to undocumented immigrants in particular, a 2010 Pew Hispanic Trust report showed that, in 2009, 59 percent of unauthorized immigrants resided in California, Texas, Florida, New York, Illinois, and New Jersey. Pew reports that this marked a decline from the high of 80 percent of undocumented immigrants living in these six states in 1990, a result of undocumented immigrants having spread out to new settlement areas beyond these states. Even though the number of the undocumented began declining by mid-2000, surely due to the economic recession that hit the United States, it is still true that the government and citizens of these states (and a growing number of others) must shoulder the bulk of the financial and social cost of a failed federal immigration enforcement policy.

Since the early 1990s, all these states have repeatedly sued the federal government for financial reimbursement for services provided to immigrants. From these states' point of view, they have been conscripted into providing health care (including expensive emergency room care), a free public education, and incarceration of undocumented criminals in state and county jails. The states view these requirements as "unfunded mandates" in which the federal government has unfairly asked state taxpayers to pick up the tab for a failed federal immigration enforcement policy. Unfortunately for these states, these lawsuits have all been dismissed in U.S. district courts, for a variety of reasons. In dismissing the states' suits, some federal courts have viewed the issue as a political question, and therefore the proper province of Congress and not the federal courts, while other courts have stated that the federal government may dictate how it spends its own resources. Still other courts believe that the federal government is protected by sovereign immunity; that is the federal government cannot be sued by the states unless the federal government consents to the suit first.

Under pressure from the states, the federal government began reimbursing the states through various programs, including a program called the State Criminal Alien Assistance Program (SCAAP), which reimburses states for the incarceration of the undocumented. According to an April 11, 2009, article in the *Los Angeles Times,* however, this program has been underfunded by the federal government. Similarly, a 2007 report by the National Conference of State Legislatures details a provision in a 2003 federal law that aids in the reimbursement to hospitals for the emergency care of the undocumented. These funds do not, however, cover the need in a state like Texas. This is because the federal law is very narrowly written to cover only the period from a patient's arrival in the emergency room up until the patient is stabilized.

Many hospitals keep patients beyond the point that they are stabilized, however, and they have to pick up the cost of that extra care. In general, federal funding for these types of reimbursement programs has been sparse and rare because of divisions within the federal government about how best to spend federal funds—whether to use the funds for state reimbursement, or use them for immigration enforcement.

States and localities bristle at the thought of having to provide services for undocumented immigrants, or persons who are illegally in the country, because the federal government has failed to prevent them from entering. By federal law, undocumented immigrants, and even lawful permanent residents (persons legally in the United States with a green card), are not eligible for many government services within their first 5 years in the country, including Medicare, Medicaid, TANF (Temporary Assistance for Needy Families), food stamps, Supplemental Security Income, public housing assistance, and job opportunities for low-income persons. However, undocumented immigrants do qualify for other government programs, including a K–12 public school education, emergency medical care, substance abuse services, mental health services, immunizations, and children with special health-care needs. Most states incur the heaviest cost of caring for undocumented immigrants in the areas of education, incarceration of criminals, and health care.

Many states have undertaken economic assessments of the cost of immigrants to their state and localities, especially the cost of undocumented immigrants. These studies are estimates because of the difficulty of detecting a person's immigration status, especially of someone trying to conceal their undocumented status. Furthermore, as a 2006 report by the Texas Office of the Comptroller acknowledges, most studies of the costs of undocumented immigration are necessarily estimates and educated guesses, given that federal policies prohibit public schools from asking for students' immigration status (Strayhorn, 2006). In higher education, meanwhile, qualification for in-state tuition is based on the length of time the student has lived in the state, not on his or her immigration status. Similarly, most hospitals do not ask for or record a patient's immigration status.

Even with these statistical limitations, most states, especially states that are home to large numbers of documented and undocumented immigrants, have undertaken academic studies to assess the financial cost to their state and localities of immigration, particularly undocumented immigration. As a March 17, 2009, National Conference of State Legislatures summary points out, these state studies are tricky to compare head to head because some studies focus on health, education, and enforcement, while others only focus on educational costs. With regard to consideration of the revenues brought in by immigrants, some states look only at income, sales tax, and property taxes, while other states also focus on the "multiplier effects of immigrants in the labor force and economy." Given the differences in methodology and research design of these studies, it is not surprising that the results are mixed. Robin Baker, a senior analyst at the Bell Policy Center, notes, for example, that in 2005 the amount of sales, income, and property taxes paid by undocumented immigrants in Colorado was equal to 70 to 86 percent of the $225 million per year in K–12 education, emergency medical care, and incarceration costs that these immigrants cost the state. Thus, the tax revenue brought in by the undocumented was not enough to cover the price of the care of the undocumented, and that deficit was passed on to the other Colorado taxpayers. Similarly, a 2006 study by two researchers at the University of North Carolina showed that Hispanics contribute about $756 million each year in taxes and cost the state budget about $817 million annually for the cost of K–12 education, health care, and corrections leaving, the state with a net cost of $61 million that was not covered by incoming revenue (Kasarda & Johnson, 2006).

By contrast, a 2006 report by the Texas Comptroller's Office (Strayhorn, 2006) showed that the revenues collected from the undocumented population exceeded the amount the state spent on services to this population. In Texas, then, the state had a surplus of $427.7 million, even after paying for the services to the undocumented. However, this same report notes that localities incurred $1.44 million in health-care and law enforcement for the undocumented that were not reimbursed by the state. The situation in Texas shows that even when a state is showing an overall surplus in funds from the undocumented population, individual counties and townships may still be taking a financial hit.

A select handful of states and localities are on the frontlines of dealing with a failed federal immigration enforcement policy that cannot keep illegal immigrants out of the country, and that cannot locate and remove those who have overstayed their temporary visas. The financial cost to the taxpayers of these states is substantial and runs into the millions of dollars. While there is some controversy in various state studies over whether the tax revenues generated by undocumented immigrants is enough to offset the costs of educating undocumented children, providing health-care services, and incarcerating the undocumented, a more basic issue of fairness remains. Why do the states and localities have to shoulder the financial consequence of an ineffective federal immigration policy? If the federal government wishes to claim exclusive jurisdiction for immigration policy, it should also be exclusively liable for the costs of the undocumented population. Since the federal courts have repeatedly dismissed or blocked attempts by border states to recoup the financial cost from the federal government, the states should be allowed to fashion their own immigration policies. Indeed, it seems strange that the federal government has gone to court to stop states from identifying and removing undocumented immigrants, or from otherwise carrying out enforcement of the federal government's own immigration laws that it itself declines to enforce or has under-enforced.

PREVAILING ASSUMPTIONS NEED TO BE CHALLENGED

Within the immigrant advocacy community, there seems to be a prevailing belief that the idea of states undertaking immigration policy is an all-around bad idea, and that federal centralized policy brought forth by comprehensive immigration reform is far preferable. This assumption is wrong on two levels. First, states have not engaged in a race to the bottom by competing with each other to come up with the most draconian immigration policies. Second, a comprehensive immigration reform bill may not be a silver bullet that will solve the nation's immigration problem. The federal system ensures that there can be variations in policy as states and localities craft policies that are suitable to their needs, instead of being straitjacketed into a one-size-fits-all national policy. The immigration laws passed in Arizona and Alabama, and the many similar pieces of legislation that target immigrants and those who help them with draconian penalties, have given state immigration policymaking a bad name. Lost in the front-page headlines are the many efforts by other states to ease the difficult lives of both documented and undocumented immigrants, including making undocumented students eligible for in-state tuition rates at public colleges and universities, and allowing undocumented immigrants to obtain driver's licenses.

According to the 1982 Supreme Court decision in *Plyler v. Doe,* all students, regardless of their immigration status, and including undocumented students, have a right to a free public education. In that decision, which has been criticized for its lack of legal substance and unabashed foray into policymaking, the Court majority noted that to deny undocumented minors a free public education would punish innocent children for the actions of their parents, as well as creating a "permanent underclass" of the undocumented who would be locked into their low education and wage status. Critics of this decision view it as rewarding lawbreakers at the expense of state taxpayers. The diverse state responses have also reflected this debate.

The *Plyler* decision pertained only to secondary education, however, and immigrant advocates and a bipartisan group of members of Congress have fought hard to pass a national DREAM Act that would, among other provisions, allow undocumented students to receive in-state tuition benefits. At the federal level, this act has stalled, due in large part to the economic recession that began in late 2007 and the political nonviability of any legislation that appears to aid undocumented immigrants. While the national DREAM Act has not gained passage, individual states have made headway on some of its provisions. Although only the federal government can legalize undocumented immigrants, which is the centerpiece of the proposed DREAM Act, and states cannot normalize someone's undocumented status, some states have successfully enacted other provisions of the DREAM Act, particularly the granting of in-state tuition benefits to undocumented students.

According to the National Conference of State Legislatures, as of fall 2011, while Arizona, Colorado, Georgia, South Carolina, and Indiana have passed laws banning undocumented immigrants from receiving in-state tuition benefits at public universities, many other states have gone the completely opposite route. On their own initiative, states as diverse as Texas, California, New York, Washington, Oklahoma, Illinois, Kansas, New Mexico, Nebraska, Wisconsin, and Connecticut have passed laws offering in-state tuition benefits for undocumented students who can prove 2 to 3 years of residency in the state, graduate from high school, and apply to a state college or university. These states have provided this benefit because their policymakers and citizens realize that undocumented students are not returning to their home country anytime soon, and that the federal government lacks the political will to seriously enforce immigration laws via interior enforcement. Since the undocumented reside in their state, the only question left is how to manage this population. Some states have taken a punitive approach, but far more states have taken the more pragmatic approach and have decided to help willing and talented students who happen to be undocumented obtain a college education, which, in the long run, will benefit those states and their residents by reducing the number of social problems that come along with a lack of education and poverty.

One should not assume comprehensive immigration reform would be desirable, given the wide ideological range among Republican politicians. Going forward, depending on whether the presidency is held by a Democrat or Republican, and considering the differences between liberal and centrist Democrats and Republicans, it is uncertain what a "comprehensive immigration reform" package would look like. President Obama flatly opposes a constitutional amendment that would strip birthright citizenship from children born on U.S. soil to undocumented immigrants. He also supports the passage of the DREAM Act, which would give undocumented students financial access to higher education and give them a path to citizenship if they stay in school or join the military. None of the GOP presidential candidates in the lead-up to the 2012 election supports the DREAM Act, although Rick Perry of Texas has supported the extension of in-state tuition benefits to undocumented students in public colleges and universities. Among Republicans, however, there is a huge range of opinions on immigration. Among the various early contenders for the 2012 Republican nomination, these views range from that of John Huntsman, who would allow undocumented immigrants to have driver's licenses, to that of Michele Bachmann, who would like to amend the constitution to strip automatic birthright citizenship for undocumented immigrants. Speaking at a Tea Party–sponsored rally in Tennessee on October 15, 2011, Herman Cain, then an aspiring candidate, joked that the United States should build an electrified fence along the southwestern border with Mexico, adding that he would support putting a military presence on the southwestern border, armed with "real guns and real bullets," to stop the undocumented immigrants. Depending on who is in the White House and which party is in control of Congress, comprehensive immigration reform can mean very different policies.

The fifty states vary widely in their political culture and their views toward immigration. Even among the states that receive a high volume of documented and undocumented immigration, there is a dramatic variation in their views and approaches to immigration, variations caused by a number of factors, including the history of immigration to that state and the political culture of the state. The draconian immigration laws passed in Arizona and Alabama would never pass in Texas or California because of the large numbers of multigeneration Latinos well integrated into all levels of local government in those states. To paint all the state attempts to create immigration policy with a broad brush as either all negative or all positive glosses over the diversity in state politics. In a federal system, there will be variation among the states. While some states are passing punitive immigration policies, other states have passed versions of laws beneficial to immigrants that the national government has not managed to pass. In addition, a centralized federal response to immigration in the form of a comprehensive immigration bill would look very different depending on the occupant of the White House and the makeup of Congress.

CONCLUSION

A federal system recognizes that, in terms of policies, one size may not always fit all, and it allows for states to tailor policies to their needs. Immigration, in its effects, is still a regional phenomenon, with documented and undocumented immigrants clustering in a handful of states, thereby affecting these states more than others. It is predominantly the taxpayers of the border states that have shouldered the economic and social costs of a federal policy that has failed to meaningfully control undocumented immigration. Although some of the rhetoric and intentions of recent state immigration legislation has been tinged with racism and xenophobia, it is not an anti-immigrant position for states to wish to be compensated for caring for undocumented immigrants. Instead, this position reflects the reality of states and localities struggling with serious fiscal crises. These states should be allowed to create policies in the face of federal abdication in this policy area.

Moreover, while the critics of state immigration policy are right to be concerned about some of the negative consequences that may flow from local enforcement of immigration laws, they are wrong to leap to the conclusion that state and local immigration policy is always detrimental to immigrants, or that federal policy is always better for immigrants. One cannot assume a "race to the bottom" when many states have, on their own initiative, provided benefits to immigrants. The federal system allows at least that state-level DREAM acts like those passed in California and Illinois are possible, even when the national government has failed to pass similar legislation. By contrast, the chances are remote that any version of a federal DREAM Act would pass under a Republican administration. Indeed, it is more likely that a Republican would seek a federal law that would trump and effectively wipe out any state-based DREAM Act legislation. At least with the states allowed to contribute to immigration policy, there exists the possibility that legislation beneficial to the undocumented could exist. The federal system is not perfect, and one is forced to take the good with the bad, but given the complexity of the immigration issue, the flexibility provided by state immigration policies is necessary.

References and Further Reading

Baker, R. (2006, August 29). *Concerning the untold stories of Colorado immigration: Testimony to the alternative hearing on immigration.* Retrieved from The Bell Policy Center website: http://www.thebell.org/PUBS/testimony/2006/08-29immigration.pdf

Gabriel, T., & Wyatt, E. (2011, October 15). At rallies, two candidates deliver blistering attacks on immigration. *The New York Times.* Retrieved from http://www.nytimes.com/2011/10/16/us/politics/bachmann-and-cain-deliver-blistering-attacks-on-illegal-immigration.html

Gans, J. (2007). *Immigrants in Arizona: Fiscal and economic impacts.* Retrieved from Udall Center for Studies in Public Policy website: http://udallcenter.arizona.edu/immigration/publications/impactofimmigrants08.pdf

Kasarda, J. D., & Johnson, J. H., Jr. (2006, January). *The economic impact of the Hispanic population on the state of North Carolina.* Retrieved from University of North Carolina, Frank Hawkins Kenan Institute of Private Enterprise website: http://www.ime.gob.mx/investigaciones/2006/estudios/migracion/economic_impact_hispanic_population_north_carolina.pdf

Mehta, C., & Ali, A. (2003). *Education for all: Chicago's undocumented immigrants and access to higher education.* Retrieved from the Center for Urban Economic Development, University of Illinois at Chicago website: http://www.urbaneconomy.org/node/53

National Conference of State Legislatures. (2009, March 17). *A summary of state studies on fiscal impacts of immigrants.* Retrieved from http://www.ncsl.org/IssuesResearch/Immigration/StateStudiesOnFiscalImpacts/tabid/17271/Default.aspx

Neuman, G. (1993). The lost generation of American immigration law (1776–1875). *Columbia Law Review, 93*(8), 1833–1901.

Passel, J. S., & Cohn, D. (2010, September 1). *U.S. unauthorized immigration flows are down sharply since mid-decade.* Retrieved from Pew Hispanic Center website: http://pewhispanic.org/reports/report.php?ReportID=126

Plyler v. Doe, 457 U.S. 202 (1982).

Simon, R. (2009, April 11). State seeks more federal aid for cost of keeping illegal immigrant inmates. *Los Angeles Times.* Retrieved from http://articles.latimes.com/2009/apr/11/local/me-illegal-felons11

Spencer, A. C. (2007, April 16). Federal law reimburses hospitals for treating undocumented immigrants: A primer on Section 1011. *National Conference of State Legislatures Report, 28*(489). Retrieved from http://www.ncsl.org/default.aspx?tabid=14201

Strayhorn, C. K. (2006, December). *Undocumented immigrants in Texas: A financial analysis of the impact to the state budget and economy* (Special Report). Retrieved from Texas Office of the Comptroller website: http://www.window.state.tx.us/specialrpt/undocumented/undocumented.pdf

Anna O. Law

U.S. Border Control

POINT: Border controls have not proven effective at discouraging unauthorized flows. New efforts to enhance the border fence and to implement other barriers along the border would be costly, ineffective, and increase the vulnerability and victimization of border crossers.

Melysa Sperber, George Washington University Law School

COUNTERPOINT: It is true that current border control strategies are of questionable effectiveness in curtailing unauthorized immigration. However, evidence suggests that increasing border enforcement seems to be effective at deterring repetitive illegal border crossings, which represent a sizeable component of overall border apprehensions.

Catalina Amuedo-Dorantes, San Diego State University
Cynthia Bansak, St. Lawrence University

Introduction

The border between the United States and Mexico spans some 2,000 miles and crosses four states. Policing this massive expanse is the job of the U.S. Border Patrol, which made nearly 2,000 apprehensions per day in 2010. Nevertheless, people come across that border illegally by the millions, and many cross back and forth repeatedly—there is little debate about the idea that the U.S. Border Patrol is currently overwhelmed. In this chapter, Melysa Sperber, Catalina Amuedo-Dorantes, and Cynthia Bansak debate the question of whether or not an intense focus on border control would have a chance at reducing illegal immigration—and if it does, is it worth the cost?

Most people discussing border control agree that, to be effective, it has to be, as Melysa Sperber writes in the Point section of this debate, "comprehensive and balanced." The two sides here address two different issues of border control: Sperber addresses the cost and the effectiveness and finds both aspects wanting, while Amuedo-Dorantes and Bansak present original research on the effectiveness of increased border control on deterring repetitive border crossings.

While both present evidence that border control measures have reduced border apprehensions—Amuedo-Dorantes and Bansak with their original data and Sperber with data from the Department of Homeland Security—they do not agree on the wisdom of enhancing border control.

Sperber argues that the resources poured into the nearly singular focus of apprehending people at the border are not worthwhile—they impede trade while creating congestion and environmentally damaging traffic at the border. She further argues that focusing exclusively on border crossings can actually threaten national security by distracting law enforcement from more pressing cases, such as cross-border gangs, organized crime syndicates, or narco-trafficking rings. It is important that we not lose our focus on eliminating the "pull" of illegal migration caused by criminal enterprises such as the drug trade. As an example, she notes that the Mérida Initiative, begun in 2008, has funneled nearly $1 billion toward combating drug trafficking and human smuggling in Central American countries.

In addition, Sperber worries that forcing immigrants to return to their countries with little or no due process (and often time spent in detention facilities) potentially violates the principle of non-refoulement, which prohibits removal of refugees and asylum seekers who have a fear of future persecution on account of race, religion, nationality, political opinion, or membership in a particular social group. "Restrictive border policies . . . " she writes, "threaten to undermine the standing of the United States as a haven for victims of persecution and torture."

Amuedo-Dorantes and Bansak's Counterpoint essay focuses on a different question: do border control enforcement efforts work as well as their proponents say they do? Because the overall volume of unauthorized immigration is so hard to measure, the authors take a slightly different approach. Using data from interviews with migrants in 1993 and 2003, collected in eight cities along the U.S.-Mexico border, they find that increased linewatch hours (the hours spent monitoring the border) do deter repetitive illegal border crossings. "In sum," they state, "an average yearly increase of a half million linewatch hours, characteristic of the 1990 to 2003 period, could reduce undocumented migrants' willingness to cross again into the U.S. anywhere between 6.5 and 7.5 percentage points." Amuedo-Dorantes and Bansak believe that since research shows that repetitive border crossings are a large percentage of "overall crossings and apprehension costs," it is worth the expense to monitor the border closely.

While reading these essays, ask yourselves whether you agree that the cost of enhanced border control is worth whatever reduction in illegal immigration might be gained, and whether the tradeoffs (spending money for border control often means not spending money for something else, such as legal representation) are acceptable. Is apprehending people at the border the best way to control immigration? Why or why not?

POINT

In 2005, then Arizona Governor Janet Napolitano responded to Congress's restrictive border policies in an interview with the Associated Press, stating, "If you build a 50-foot-high wall, somebody will find a 51-foot ladder." Less than 6 years later, as Secretary of the Department of Homeland Security (DHS), Napolitano announced that the agency was abandoning efforts to complete the virtual fence, after an investment of $1 billion. The incomplete fence represents the failure of restrictive, and notably more expensive, border control policies. It should also be an instructive experience and should mark a turning point toward comprehensive approaches to border security and away from misguided monuments to our security ambitions.

Along the nearly 2,000-mile southern border, both the size of and the scale of activity are expansive. Spanning four states, the border encompasses treacherous terrain and protected environmental habitats. Daily economic activity between Mexico and the United States is conservatively estimated at $800 million per day, much of it in goods and services crossing the border. Over 10,000 trucks cross the border every day, and 500,000 pedestrians and passengers cross daily. Most of the Border Patrol's activity is along the southwest border, where in 2010, 97 percent of border apprehensions occurred—close to 2,000 apprehensions daily (Sapp, 2011). Furthermore, the journey itself is increasingly more dangerous, with hundreds of recorded deaths due to dehydration and exposure.

In evaluating the effectiveness of efforts to enhance control on the border, it is important to put those efforts in context, and to closely consider the legal, fiscal, and national security ramifications of policies, especially since the track record of the "zero tolerance" approach to enforcement is mixed. What is abundantly clear from the U.S. experience is that a singular focus on any one tactic, such as establishing physical barriers or raising criminal penalties, to resolve unauthorized migration will eventually jeopardize the entire system's integrity. Effective border control policies must be comprehensive and balanced. When implemented, the policies should protect national security by minimizing the risk of genuine threats at the border while also addressing the root causes of undeterred border migration. In other words, efforts must encompass policies that minimize pull factors such as job opportunity as well as alleviate push factors such as civil unrest and environmental degradation.

BORDER POLICY: THE HISTORY AND CONTEXT OF RESTRICTIVE ENFORCEMENT APPROACHES

According to Dr. Susan F. Martin, the United States follows an "island" model that focuses enforcement efforts on the border. Other followers include Canada, the United Kingdom, Australia, New Zealand, and Ireland. The island model nations invest heavily (but not exclusively) in keeping undocumented migrants out of the country. In contrast, an interior model approach focuses on finding undocumented migrants after their entry. This model favors investments in oversight of undocumented work through tough worksite compliance sanctions. It also tends to impose stricter identification requirements to prevent unlawful hiring (Martin, 2011). Countries in continental Europe best exemplify the interior approach because they are likely to implement stronger measures to enforce nonborder areas and to focus on the identification of unauthorized migrants already in the country.

The U.S. government's efforts to stem the tide of unauthorized entrants along the southern border date back to the early 1900s. Since the mid-1990s, legislative reforms aimed at enhancing control over the border have demonstrably improved the government's success at reaching ambitious law enforcement benchmarks: there are more physical barriers on the border (299 miles of vehicle barriers and 350 miles of pedestrian barriers), a higher number of law enforcement agents are patrolling the border (over 20,000 in fiscal year 2010), and over 100 manned and unmanned aircraft are monitoring the southwest border. According to the DHS, from 2005 to 2010 these border security enhancements directly contributed to the reduction of border apprehensions, from 1,189,000 to 463,000 (Sapp, 2011). Fortifying the border to reduce undocumented entries demands a constant flow of resources. The Customs and Border Patrol (CBP) budget expanded rapidly in the late 2000s, with a total increase of 32 percent in 2007, to $7.7 billion; and then another

20 percent increase in 2008, to $9.3 billion. The same is true for Immigration and Customs Enforcement (ICE): its budget grew 44 percent in 2007, followed by another 8 percent increase the next year (Batalova & Terrazas, 2010).

Effective border policies necessarily entail a delicate web of coordination among those agencies controlling the ebb and flow of commerce and migration. For this reason, cross-border activities such as migration, trade, and environmental protection are regulated by a spectrum of federal agencies, including the Departments of Homeland Security, State, Justice, Treasury, and Interior. For migration, whether authorized or unauthorized, enforcement authority rests with the DHS, particularly with the CBP and ICE. The Executive Office for Immigration Review (EOIR), under the direct regulation of the attorney general, is responsible for adjudicating immigration cases, including removal proceedings, appellate matters, and other administrative hearings. While the federal government's control over immigration matters is a longstanding power derived from its constitutional mandate over naturalization, foreign affairs, and commerce, border security efforts have not only encompassed reforms to federal activities, but to state and local ones as well.

For nearly two decades, border enforcement has experienced a transformation of both policy and practice along the border. In the early 1990s, then Border Patrol Chief Sylvester Reyes, now a congressman from Texas, implemented Operation Blockade and Operation Hold the Line, initiatives designed to introduce overwhelming force at the border—human, financial, and technological. These operations were grounded on a "border security first" approach to law enforcement related to immigration, and they garnered attention from the media, policymakers, and political elites. Renewed interest in enhanced border security efforts fit squarely in the Clinton administration's law and order agenda. It was in this context that border security became an important priority for then–U.S. attorney general Janet Reno. Under Reno's leadership, the Department of Justice (DOJ) embraced a restrictive approach that has since been adopted and expanded by every subsequent administration and Congress.

At the outset, the transformation of border security involved a comprehensive overhaul of the framework used by the Office of Management and Budget (OMB) to allocate resources for law enforcement across the federal government. Once OMB accepted a new budget approach, policymakers had greater flexibility to change the dynamics on border enforcement. Whereas old budgets focused primarily on human resources, not infrastructure, new budgets allocated support to equipment, technology, support, and vehicles, as well as to new Border Patrol agents. With the restructured budget framework in place, law enforcement implemented a border enforcement approach with several key characteristics: (1) rely on personnel and enforcement efforts as close to the line of the border as possible to achieve greater deterrence through the prevention of unlawful entries; (2) concentrate resources in the corridors with the highest rates of unlawful crossings; (3) heavily invest in personnel, equipment, and advanced technology; (4) mobilize resources throughout the DOJ to complement Border Patrol's leadership; (5) undertake outreach to ensure continuous communication and coordination among law enforcement agencies; and (6) increase attention on safety measures to prevent unnecessary injuries and deaths as undocumented migration shifts to more dangerous terrain.

As a result of the build-up along the border, as well as the passage of several restrictive immigration measures in the mid-1990s, border security underwent a dramatic transformation. At that time, the projected outcomes remained unclear, and the escalating costs raised questions about the sustainability of indefinite fortification of the border. After 9/11, fewer questions remained. Border security assumed even greater importance as an element of counterterrorism strategy. Most prominently, border security was featured in the Enhanced Border Security and Visa Entry Reform Act of 2002. This law provided resources for additional personnel, upgraded technology, and addressed systematic improvements to curtail the use of fraudulent identity documents. Importantly, the law also required information sharing among law enforcement and intelligence agencies.

The next significant milestone reached was the establishment of DHS in early 2002, when President Bush signed the Homeland Security Act into law. The sweeping bureaucratic reform—the largest federal reorganization in over 50 years—merged parts of 22 agencies and affected 170,000 employees. Since DHS assumed authority over border enforcement, it has amassed more legal mandates and absorbed even more resources. In 2006, the passage of the Secure Fence Act led to the goal of "operational control" over the border, thereby requiring the prevention of all unlawful entries into the United States. Implementing a zero tolerance policy on the border required an ambitious investment of resources. Over 5 years the CBP budget grew from $1.67 million in 2005 to $3.58 million in 2010, enabling the agency to quintuple the number of Border Patrol agents on the southwest border.

Two decades of border fortification successfully upended the undeterred flow of undocumented migration. According to the Center for American Progress, only one person succeeds in crossing the border without documentation for every three or four apprehensions—a stark difference from the early 1990s, when projections claimed two or three migrants succeeded for each apprehension.

FENCE AS POLICY: UNINTENDED CONSEQUENCES AND LEGAL CONCERNS

Singular policies premised on total control of the border are flawed and will result in undermining U.S. security, U.S. standing in the world, and even the nation's physical environment. Data demonstrates that "zero tolerance" enforcement policies are ineffectual and unrealistic without the balance provided by interior enforcement and without meaningful reforms to curtail the push and pull factors that fuel unauthorized migration.

Appreciation for the laudable gains in border security does not negate that implementing total operational control is unrealistic and leads to an ineffectual, singular mission that threatens national security in the long term by detracting attention from comprehensive strategies that address the root causes of insecurity along the border (Fitz, 2011; Koslowski, 2011; Martin, 2011). Senior law enforcement officials echo this concern. In 2011, Terry Goddard, a former attorney general of Arizona, responded forcefully to a state senator's solicitation of private donations to complete construction of a border fence. According to Goddard, "The idea that any glowering structure could confound the smuggling efforts of transnational criminal organizations . . . is just naïve. . . . We will only achieve border security when we cut off the flow of money to the cartels, arrest and prosecute their leaders and dismantle their criminal organizations."

Blindly focusing only on reductions in apprehensions obscures a more complex reality: unauthorized migration does not stop, it simply shifts to new geography and adapts with new tactics to evade detection. For example, from 1992 to 2000, apprehensions dropped by 350,000 in the San Diego corridor. During the same period, regions east of San Diego experienced a relative increase in unlawful entries. As migrants moved east, they faced harsher conditions that heightened safety concerns. In southern Arizona's Pima County alone, the medical examiner has reported an average of almost 200 border deaths annually since the early 2000s. Additionally, migrants are increasingly vulnerable to smugglers, who cite the heightened risks of crossing the border as justification for exploiting migrants, charging excessive fees, and coercing victims by threatening family members' safety.

The counterproductive dynamic of shifting geography and tactics at the border is not the only problematic trend—stringent border controls have done nothing to resolve the status of over 10 million people who reside in the United States without authorization. Some estimates suggest that up to 3.5 percent of the national population is undocumented. This population is largely made up of families who have lived in the United States for many years, working, paying taxes, and sending their children to school. According to the Center for American Progress, the cost of removing the entire undocumented population over a 5-year period would exceed $280 billion—a per person cost of $23,148.

Prioritizing border security has resulted in a risky lack of attention on the growing undocumented population living in the shadows of American society. Further, while fortifying the border has deterred unlawful entries, the long-term impact is untested. As economic conditions improve and criminal syndicates adopt more sophisticated techniques to evade detection, border security cannot rely on outdated tactics and excessive physical barriers.

INTEGRITY MUST BE RESTORED TO IMMIGRATION ADJUDICATION

Despite the past decade's achievements in border security, the flow of unauthorized migration continues: at least 5 percent of the American workforce is undocumented, expensive detention centers house almost 35,000 immigrant detainees on a daily basis, and removals have increased 18 percent since 2007, without proportional investments in the capacity of the under-resourced immigration adjudication system. Immigration courts face escalating backlogs, and now federal courts also manage increasing caseloads due to reforms that redirected unlawful entry cases from administrative proceedings to federal criminal prosecutions. According to the Transactional Records Access Clearinghouse at Syracuse University, data from the EOIR show that the court with the longest decision times during the first 6 months of fiscal year 2011 was in Los Angeles, where cases averaged 745 days. Nationwide, there are approximately 275,000 cases awaiting resolution, with an average duration of over 300 days—an increase of almost 30 percent over the average waiting period in fiscal year 2009 (Transactional Records Access Clearinghouse, 2011).

One example of how restrictive policies have undermined the integrity of how U.S. courts administer justice in immigration matters is Operation Streamline, a policy implemented in 2005 to strengthen the punishment for undocumented entry. Under Operation Streamline, federal courts have a fast-track process for bringing criminal charges—misdemeanors for first-time offenders and felonies for repeat offenders—against migrants who cross the border without proper documentation. By redirecting prosecutorial attention from complex criminal litigation against cross-border gangs, organized crime syndicates, and narco-trafficking rings to minor cases akin to civil infractions in complexity and profile, Operation Streamline diverted the law enforcement engagement from meaningful efforts to increase long-term border security. The strain on the federal criminal system was substantial, and it demonstrated that tapping into the limited resources of federal courts is not a policy solution for an overtaxed immigration court system. In March 2011, the U.S. Court of Appeals for the Ninth Circuit took the dramatic step—for only the third time in as many decades—of declaring a judicial emergency in the district of Arizona to suspend time limits under the Speedy Trial Act for bringing accused criminals to trial. Chief Judge Kozinski explained the court's actions as follows:

> The addition of what sometimes seems to be an inexhaustible number of law enforcement agents and federal prosecutors in Tucson division has now produced a tsunami of federal felony cases far beyond the management capacity of the four active district judges in Tucson division. The influx of felony cases also requires physical space in the DeConcini Courthouse exceeding current space availability. Without the possibility of relief from a declaration of judicial emergency, Tucson division is simply unable to absorb the enormous increase in felony cases being scheduled for trial while remaining compliant with the time limits set by the Speedy Trial Act.

This demonstrates that federal courts cannot and should not serve as a safety net for the inadequacy of the under-resourced administrative legal framework that handles civil immigration cases. Instead, policy must focus on supplementing resources for and implementing reforms to the immigration court system.

Enhanced border patrol policies and tactics raise serious legal concerns about whether the United States is in compliance with its international obligations. Vulnerable populations of refugees and torture survivors are protected under international treaties and by international customary law. As a signatory to the 1967 Protocol to the UN Convention Relating to the Status of Refugees (Refugee Convention), the United States must adhere to the principle of non-refoulement that prohibits the removal of refugees and asylum seekers with a well-founded fear of future persecution on account of race, religion, nationality, political opinion, or membership in a particular social group. The principle of non-refoulement is a mandatory obligation of states under the Refugee Convention not to return or expel bona fide refugees from their shores and borders. The United States also ratified the UN Convention Against Torture and Other Cruel, Inhuman or Degrading Punishment (CAT, or Torture Convention) to protect individuals who flee to the United States where there is a substantial likelihood they will be tortured if removed. These treaties prohibit the criminalization of refugees and victims of torture. Due process is a basic right enumerated in the conventions, and is recognized as prevailing custom under international law. However, zero tolerance border controls jeopardize vulnerable populations' access to protection by subjecting bona fide refugees and torture victims to inhumane conditions of confinement without adequate access to legal representation. Further, as a result of streamlining reforms implemented in the 1990s, the adjudication process is expedited, inhibiting many claims for protection from ever being heard.

Judges, prosecutors, and public defenders have spoken in unison about the strains placed by zero tolerance border policies on the federal criminal justice system. The devotion of federal prosecutors' attention, time, and resources to non-violent crimes in uncomplicated, low-profile cases is wasteful and ineffective. In many circumstances, local authorities must compensate for the loss of federal resources, yet local and state authorities have limited expertise and few resources to tackle complex criminal litigation involving multi-count, multi-jurisdictional charges. Restrictive border policies also threaten to undermine the standing of the United States as a haven for victims of persecution and torture. Unless due process is afforded to asylum seekers and torture survivors, the United States cannot meet its international obligations under the Refugee Convention and the Torture Convention.

BORDER FENCE CONSTRUCTION THREATENS SOUTHWESTERN ECOSYSTEMS

Policymakers literally cleared the way for the construction of the border fence. In 2005, provisions of the Emergency Supplemental Appropriations Act for Defense, the Global War on Terror, and Tsunami Relief, provided the secretary of DHS with unfettered authority to waive legal requirements under federal environmental regulations, state laws, and local ordinances if those laws obstruct efforts to complete the fence. As many as 37 federal statutes have been waived, including the Endangered Species Act, the National Environmental Policy Act, and the Religious Freedom Restoration Act.

The waiver of fundamental environmental protections has placed delicate ecosystems along the border in jeopardy. Generally, the border fence is built in regions with high numbers of vulnerable species, including wildlife with small populations that exist in isolated, specialized habitats. Barriers now block the ranges of several species in southern California by as much as 75 percent. Undertaken by scientists from Yale University and the University of Texas at Austin, the first comprehensive environmental analysis of the border concluded that fence construction jeopardized at least four species that are classified as threatened globally. Professor Tim Keitt, one of the biologists who authored the assessment, has warned, "The U.S.-Mexico border spans regions of extraordinary biological diversity as well as intense human impacts. Loss of biological diversity can have negative impacts on the ecosystem services that are the basis of our life-support system."

The loss of endangered species and habitats is incalculable from a monetary or an environmental perspective. When viewed in light of the soaring direct expenses related to the construction and maintenance of the border fence, the suspension of seminal environmental protections appears misguided.

RECOMMENDATIONS: POLICY REFORMS THAT ACHIEVE SUSTAINABLE, COST-EFFECTIVE BORDER SECURITY

No country should rely solely on the island or the interior model to frame its border enforcement policies. Sustainable progress stemming the tide of undocumented migration will only be achieved when reform is undertaken on a comprehensive basis to ensure that restrictive border policies do not undermine trade opportunities, impede legitimate labor migration, or needlessly obstruct the reunification of binational families.

Restrictive border policies alone cannot adequately or efficiently address heightened pressure on the immigration system that will inevitably result from stronger push and pull factors that are respectively driving migrants away from home and luring them across the border. Enhanced border security undoubtedly reduced unlawful entries, but the success rested on economic conditions in the United States and in Mexico that markedly reduced the incentive to migrate without documentation. Entrants from Mexico represent over 80 percent of those apprehended on the southwest border, so "push" factors specific to Mexico are an important consideration. Since the mid-2000s, socioeconomic conditions in Mexico have differed from those in the United States, where the economic crisis has reduced demand for labor and caused a spike in unemployment. In Mexico, the unemployment rate is lower, the middle class is growing, and the business climate is improving. Once economic conditions in the United States or in Mexico change, the dynamics of unauthorized migration will respond accordingly.

Comprehensive immigration reform will not be a panacea, but it is necessary to protect American economic interests and to restore the rule of law. Legally, there are two main vehicles that comprehensive immigration reform must establish to overcome the intractable strain that will be placed on U.S. economic, political, and legal interests if restrictive border policies are implemented without strengthening the integrity of the legal framework regulating immigration. The first vehicle will be a pathway to lawful residency for the more than 10 million people who reside in the United States without authorization. Formalizing the residency of unauthorized immigrants will prevent the specter of a permanent underclass living in the shadows.

Second, comprehensive immigration reform encompasses the establishment of rational avenues for future economic migrants to enter the United States to pursue legitimate work opportunities. Studies demonstrate that it is in the interest of the United States to ensure the flow of labor across the border. The data suggest that comprehensive immigration reform will generate significant economic gains, whereas enforcement-only immigration policies will jeopardize economic growth. For example, a 2010 study by the Immigration Policy Center and the Center for American Progress estimated a difference in GDP growth of $1.5 trillion gained versus $2.6 trillion lost if, respectively, comprehensive immigration reform were implemented compared to singular, restrictive policies focused on border security (Fitz, Martinez, & Wijewardena, 2011). In 2009, the Cato Institute commissioned a study to evaluate the impact of comprehensive immigration reform on the U.S. economy. Relying on an economic model developed for the U.S. International Trade Commission, the study concluded that comprehensive immigration reform would likely result in an annual gain of $261 billion for American households. In comparison, restrictive border enforcement policies are estimated to cost nearly $80 billion annually (Dixon & Rimmer, 2009). To leverage these potential economic gains, comprehensive immigration reform would include the establishment of viable, authorized mechanisms for people to enter the United States for purposes of legitimate work.

The importance of comprehensive immigration reform cannot be understated. It is necessary to protect economic interests because it will contribute to economic growth and respond to fluctuations in demand for labor, an essential element of a prosperous economy. It is a cost-effective decision because it will protect scarce resources by preventing the costly removal of millions who present little risk to national security. It is advantageous for the United States' global standing because it strengthens its adherence to universal legal norms protecting vulnerable populations from persecution and torture.

DIPLOMACY AND RESEARCH TO SUPPORT CROSS-BORDER LAW ENFORCEMENT COORDINATION

Stability at the border requires cross-border cooperation, particularly among law enforcement agencies. To prevent the escalation of violence and to protect public safety in the United States and in Mexico, the United States should continue to prioritize developing a rapport between law enforcement counterparts, cultivating mechanisms to share information, and undertaking joint operations.

The United States has entered into several agreements to formalize its engagement with Mexican officials, and it has also invested heavily in initiatives that have built the capacity of Mexican law enforcement through technical assistance, training, and technology transfers. For example, in 2002, Secretary of State Colin Powell signed the U.S.-Mexico Border Partnership Agreement that covered policies related to the flow of people, the exchange of goods, and the strengthening of infrastructure. The partnership is credited for enhancing collaboration and proactive information sharing, including the discussion of topics previously considered taboo in law enforcement circles, including corruption, impunity, and the frequent exploitation of migrants for purposes of forced labor or sex. Another example is the Mérida Initiative. Launched in 2008 as a 3-year program, Mérida has directed close to $1 billion to countries in Central America and the Caribbean for activities, training, and resources to combat organized crime, drug trafficking, and human smuggling. With major investments in equipment, personnel, and information technology, border security is a major component of Mérida.

Despite the notable success achieved in building solid professional relationships between American and Mexican law enforcement counterparts, the pace and direction of cross-border diplomacy to secure the border has raised important questions. Congestion at the border continues to impede trade, inconvenience legitimate travelers, and cause environmentally damaging traffic. Further, the border agreements and efforts to build law enforcement capacity do nothing to address the root causes of border insecurity, namely the push and pull factors that are unresponsive to zero tolerance policies. The next step for diplomacy must be to tackle the long-term challenges of supporting stable economic growth, to dismantle violent criminal syndicates, and to design sophisticated intelligence systems that empower law enforcement with timely information on emerging threats and opportunities to intervene.

To inform diplomatic and development efforts, more research is necessary to examine the impact of restrictive border policies on economic growth, crime, and the rule of law. Rigorous analysis will involve the collection of quantitative and qualitative data that assesses the relative success of criminal prosecutions, the length and conditions of detention, the reliability of measures to protect vulnerable populations, and the influence of border policy on trade and economic growth. Research will uncover whether systemic weaknesses in the administrative and law enforcement structure regulating immigration are undermining the gains made by border security enhancements.

In Mexico and in the United States, a deeper understanding of the dynamics underlying alternative policy approaches will inform the improvement of law enforcement tactics to secure the border. Long-term border security will depend on the ability of the United States and Mexico to work cooperatively to respond to imminent crises as well as entrenched challenges. Meaningful collaboration will rest not only on established trust, but also on timely access to data and information on systemic weaknesses, emergent threats, and the interventions most likely to succeed in protecting national security, rule of law, and economic interests.

CONCLUSION

Measured by any metric, the border is less porous than ever before. Unlawful entries are at historic lows, and border apprehensions are at historic highs. Border cities have been experiencing declining crime at rates well below the national average for almost a decade.

Undoubtedly, the success of enhanced border security measures should be applauded. However, the importance of examining and addressing the weaknesses and unintended consequences of the border security build-up cannot be underestimated, particularly as economic conditions improve, creating demand for employment that will strain today's unbalanced immigration enforcement framework. Singular approaches are rarely sustainable in any policy arena, and immigration enforcement is no different. Comprehensive legal reform must be undertaken, and it should be guided by in-depth research that examines and evaluates the strengths and weaknesses of border security enhancements, not only considering the impressive national security implications of border fortification, but the related legal, fiscal, and environmental concerns as well. Just as the United States must diversify its efforts internally, it should also continue to cultivate new cross-border endeavors to improve cooperation between American and Mexican law enforcement as a means of strengthening safety and security on both sides of the border.

References and Further Reading

Batalova, J., & Terrazas, A. (2010, December). *Frequently requested statistics on immigrants and immigration in the United States.* Retrieved from Migration Policy Institute website: http://www.migrationinformation.org/Feature/display.cfm?ID=818

Bon Tempo, C. J. (2008). *Americans at the gate: The United States and refugees during the Cold War* (pp. 133–207). Princeton, NJ: Princeton University Press.

Dixon, P. B., & Rimmer, M. T. (2009, August). Restriction or legalization? Measuring the economic benefits of immigration reform. *Cato Institute Trade Policy Analysis, 40.* Retrieved from http://www.cato.org/pubs/tpa/tpa-040.pdf

Fitz, M. (2011, August). *Safer than ever: A view from the U.S.-Mexico border: Assessing the past, present, and future.* Retrieved from Center for American Progress website: http://www.americanprogress.org/issues/2011/08/pdf/safer_than_ever_report.pdf

Fitz, M., Kelley, A. M., & Garcia, A. (2011, March). The *"border security first"* argument: A red herring undermining real security. Retrieved from Center for American Progress website: http://www.americanprogress.org/issues/2011/03/pdf/border_security.pdf

Fitz, M., Martinez, G., & Wijewardena, M. (2011, March). *The costs of mass deportation: Impractical, expensive, and ineffective.* Retrieved from Center for American Progress website: http://www.americanprogress.org/issues/2010/03/pdf/cost_of_deportation.pdf

Goddard, T. (2011, July). *Arizona's latest border fence initiative yet another obstacle to fighting.* Retrieved from Immigration Impact website: http://immigrationimpact.com/2011/07/27/arizona's-latest-border-fence-initiative-yet-another-obstacle-to-fighting-crime

Hoefner, M., Rytina, N., & Baker, B. C. (2009, February). *Estimates of the unauthorized immigrant population residing in the United States: January 2008.* Retrieved from DHS Office of Immigration Statistics website: http://www.dhs.gov/xlibrary/assets/statistics/publications/ois_ill_pe_2008.pdf

Koslowski, R. (2011, February). *The evolution of border controls as a mechanism to prevent illegal immigration.* Retrieved from Migration Policy Institute website: http://www.migrationpolicy.org/pubs/bordercontrols-koslowski.pdf

Lasky, J. R., Jetz, W., & Keitt, T. H. (2011, July). Conservation biogeography of the U.S.-Mexico border: A transcontinental risk assessment of barriers to animal dispersal. *Diversity and Distributions, 17*(4), 673–687. Retrieved from http://www.utexas.edu/news/2011/07/12/border_wildlife

Legomsky, S., & Rodríguez, C. M. (2009). *Immigration and refugee law and policy* (5th ed.). New York, NY: Foundation Press.

Martin, S. F. (2011). *A nation of immigrants.* New York, NY: Cambridge University Press.

Meyers, D. W. (2003). Does "smarter" lead to safer? An assessment of the US border accords with Canada and Mexico. *International Migration, 41*(4), 5–44.

Migration Policy Institute. (2010, February). *Mexico: A crucial crossroads.* Retrieved from http://www.migrationinformation.org/Profiles/display.cfm?ID=772

Moore, S. (2009, January 12). Push on immigration crimes is said to shift focus. *The New York Times.* Retrieved from http://www
.nytimes.com/2009/01/12/us/12prosecute.html?pagewanted=1

Sapp, L. (2011, July). *Apprehensions by the U.S. border patrol: 2005–2010.* Retrieved from DHS Office of Immigration Statistics website:
http://www.dhs.gov/xlibrary/assets/statistics/publications/ois-apprehensions-fs-2005-2010.pdf

Transactional records access clearinghouse. (2011). Syracuse University. Retrieved from TRAC Immigration website: http://trac.syr
.edu/immigration

Melysa Sperber

COUNTERPOINT

Over the past several decades, a variety of policies have been implemented with the intent to reduce the level of unauthorized immigration, particularly from Mexico, into the United States. For instance, through increased border enforcement, the imposition of sanctions on employers who knowingly hire unauthorized workers, and two amnesty programs, the Immigration Reform and Control Act (IRCA) of 1986 aimed to stem the flow of increased undocumented immigration into the United States. A variety of border enforcement operations and policies have had the same purpose, such as Operation Gatekeeper in California (1994), Operation Hold-the-Line in Texas (1993), Operation Safeguard in Arizona (1999), the Secure Border Initiative launched in 2005, the Secure Fence Act of 2006, and the Secure Communities program from 2008. Employer enforcement has also grown, including large-scale worksite enforcement raids. More recently, the Obama administration has focused on promoting the use of E-Verify—a voluntary, online database system that allows employers to validate whether new hires are eligible to work in the United States. Overall, efforts to secure the U.S.-Mexico border are unlikely to stop. Yet, researchers have been unable to confirm that these policies have a significantly large impact on unauthorized immigration.

Instead of focusing on the hard-to-measure volume of unauthorized immigration or on the aggregate and event-based measures of apprehensions, this essay looks at the potential for border enforcement to reduce repetitive illegal border-crossing attempts by undocumented Mexican migrants. Using a rich but not well-known dataset, the essay explores whether increased border enforcement has helped lower the likelihood of repetitive illegal border-crossing attempts on the part of undocumented migrants.

The analysis of returnees, whether they are back in Mexico temporarily to visit family or permanently, is of particular interest for a couple of reasons. First, although long-term illegal immigration appears to be increasingly common (Cornelius, 2005), the vast majority of Mexican immigrants in the United States still return to their home country at some point during their migration spell, possibly owing to the proximity of the two countries. Second, a large fraction of overall apprehensions by border patrol officers are of undocumented migrants attempting to repetitively cross into the United States. Indeed, the vast majority of apprehended migrants attempt to enter again the next evening or within a couple of days (Cornelius, 1998; Sherry, 2004; Spener, 2001). If border enforcement serves as an effective tool in reducing illegal border crossings, one should be able to see a reduction in repetitive illegal border crossings. Therefore, it is of utmost importance to gain a better understanding of the effectiveness of border enforcement and, in general, of other factors driving the repetitive and persistent nature of illegal border crossings.

PREVIOUS RESEARCH ON BORDER ENFORCEMENT: MIXED EVIDENCE AND SHORTCOMINGS

Most immigration scholars have arrived at the conclusion that border enforcement does not have a significant impact on illegal immigration, at least in the long-run, after conducting analyses that rely on aggregate data and (often) apprehension statistics, and by looking at the change in the series before and after an increase in border enforcement. Most of this literature exploits variations in apprehension rates. For most of the time period examined herein, apprehensions showed relatively steady growth, reaching an all-time peak of more than 1.8 million in 2000 (Migration Policy Institute, 2005). Apprehensions then dropped by 42 percent between 2000 and 2003, and went back up by 25 percent border-wide between 2003 and 2004 (Cornelius, 2005). Thomas Espenshade (1994) found that the total undocumented flow is unaffected by variations in the intensity of Border Patrol enforcement activity, although Immigration and Naturalization Service (INS) border control may still exert a less visible deterrent influence. Dávila and colleagues (2002) found that enforcement effects are short-lived, as undocumented migrants seemingly adjust to new information. In a specific study of the impact of border enforcement and amnesty introduced by the 1986 IRCA, Pia Orrenius and Madeline Zavodny (2003) found that apprehensions of persons attempting to cross the U.S.-Mexico border illegally declined immediately following passage of the law, but returned to normal levels during the period when undocumented immigrants could file for amnesty, and in the years thereafter. Most recently, Stephen Devadoss and Jeff Luckstead (2011) concluded that tighter border control curbed illegal farm workers by only 8,147 from 1994 to 2007. Only a few studies find a sizable deterrent effect, such as that by White and colleagues (1990), who found the effects of IRCA reduced apprehensions by nearly 700,000 in the 23-month period following the enactment of the law, and that the reduction in the number of illegal border crossings may be up to 2 million.

As noted by many others in the literature, apprehension statistics present important limitations in the analysis of the impacts of border enforcement, for various reasons. First, apprehension data represent events rather than persons, when in fact there is some evidence that apprehended migrants tried to cross repeatedly until successfully entering into the United States during the second half of the 1970s. In that regard, apprehension data may overstate illegal immigration. Yet apprehension data do not incorporate any information on any other illegal immigrants who manage to enter into the United States without detection, which could underestimate illegal immigration. As a result, analyses based on apprehended migrants could lead to either upward or downward estimates of illegal immigration. Indeed, White and colleagues (1990) point out that the relationship between apprehension statistics and the number of illegal entries is unknown.

Finally, apprehension data provide an aggregate measure of migration and, as such, fail to distinguish between the differential impacts of border enforcement on migrants depending on their personal characteristics. For instance, as noted by Katherine Donato, Jorge Durand, and Douglas S. Massey (1992), border enforcement may have a stronger impact on first-time migrants than on their more experienced counterparts, who may be able to rely on an already existing network from previous migration spells to lower their migration costs and, overall, increase their likelihood of successfully entering the United States.

Another strand of literature has examined the effectiveness of border enforcement using individual-level data. Within this category of studies, two groups are distinguished. One group consists of studies that rely on small or local samples from specific Mexican communities at certain periods of time (e.g., Bustamante, 1990; Chavez, 1990; Cornelius, 1990; Kossoudji, 1992; Massey et al., 1990). While informative, these studies are limited in their ability to provide a representative picture of the effects of border enforcement along the Mexican-U.S. border, and, by focusing on specific periods of time, they are unable to capture their long-run impacts on migration behavior.

The other group of studies within this category use individual-level data collected from a large number of Mexican communities over an extended period of time. For instance, Donato and colleagues (1992) and Pia Orrenius (2001) rely on data from the Mexican Migration Project (MMP) to examine changes in the likelihood of a variety of events—such as taking a first illegal trip, repeat migration, being apprehended, employing a border smuggler ("coyote"), and changes in smuggling costs or border-crossing sites—before and after, as well as over time. Manuela Angelucci (2005) also relies on MMP data to assess the impact of border enforcement on net flows (i.e., coming into and exiting the United States) of unauthorized Mexicans. Susan Ritcher, Edward Taylor, and Antonio Yunez-Naude (2007), on the other hand, use data from the *Encuesta Nacional a Hogares Rurales de Mexico* (ENHRUM) to examine the impact of three policies: IRCA, NAFTA, and increased border enforcement expenditures on migration. All these studies run into various limitations. First, they rely on time breaks (e.g., before and after IRCA) or the usage of dummy variables indicative of the passage of a particular policy to assess its impact on illegal immigration. Yet such time variables may be capturing other confounding changes in the economy, and, as such, one runs into the possibility of making erroneous inferences. Other times, they rely on data from returnees and a small snowball nonrepresentative sample of stayers to assess the impact of border enforcement on the flows of Mexicans going into the United States as well as returning from the United States. Lastly, other studies aggregate the individual-level data to examine migration flows at the village level, running into similar limitations to studies using aggregate data, such as the inability to account for migrant heterogeneity and only producing results for a subset of the population that may not be representative of all individuals or of the overall group as a whole.

This essay is an attempt to add to the body of literature on the impact of border enforcement by examining the following questions: Is border enforcement effective at deterring undocumented migrants from repetitively attempting to cross the border? What factors are driving these migrants' persistent behavior in more recent years? To address these questions and avoid some of the shortcomings from the earlier literature, a large database is used, with individual-level data on migrants interviewed between 1993 and 2003, and whose last migration experiences expand from 1980 to 2003. In this manner, it is possible to observe individual migrating behavior (versus overall crossing events) and account for personal characteristics crucially shaping their migrating behavior over an extended period of time. Additionally, the focus is on a group of migrants for whom there is representative data, and for whom the question of repetitive and persistent illegal border-crossing behavior makes sense, such as undocumented migrants returning, temporarily or permanently, to Mexico.

DATA

Information collected by the *Encuesta sobre Migración en la Frontera Norte de México* (EMIF) is used here. This survey is administered by the Colegio de la Frontera Norte (COLEF) in eight different cities along the U.S.-Mexico border: Tijuana, Mexicali, Nogales, Ciudad Juárez, Piedras Negras, Nuevo Laredo, Reynosa, and Matamoros. These cities account for more than 90 percent of the migration flux from Mexico to the United States, and vice versa (Consejo Nacional de Población, 1998). The EMIF's primary objective is to gain a better understanding of labor migration towards the northern U.S.-Mexico border and to the United States. The survey methodology is designed to constantly update the data flow to obtain a sample that properly represents where and when migrants cross the border into Mexico.

For the purpose of this analysis, data from eight consecutive waves of the EMIF, from 1993 to 2003, is used. Each wave includes four quarterly surveys administered separately to four groups of migrants in the border regions: (1) migrants coming from the South to the northern Mexican border region, (2) migrants in northern border cities originating from another northern border community, (3) migrants returning from the United States to or through the Mexican northern border region, and (4) Mexican migrants deported from the United States. Some migrants in groups 1 and 2 have crossed the border in the past; however, due to the lower incidence of that event among immigrants in group 2, they are not directly inquired about their intent to return to the United States. Due to the interest in assessing the effectiveness of border enforcement in deterring repetitive illegal crossings, the sample consists of all undocumented Mexicans with previous U.S. migration experience in groups 1, 3, and 4. Specifically, the focus is on individuals who are 12 years old or older, not born in the United States, and who migrated to the United States with the purpose to visit family or friends, to complete some business, or to work for more than one month. Additionally, because the vast majority of migrants in the sample are male, the analysis is restricted to men.

Table 9.1 displays the means for the variables used in the analysis separately for deported and nondeported migrants based on supporting evidence from Chow tests that these two groups of undocumented migrants should be examined independently. (The Chow test is a test used to determine whether the independent variables have different impacts on different subgroups of the population, such as deported and nondeported migrants in this case.) Of special interest is whether the migrant indicates an intention to cross to the United States in the near future. Approximately 63 percent of deported immigrants express the intent of returning to the United States in the near future, relative to 38 percent of nondeported returnees. Our key independent variable is linewatch hours (in millions)—"linewatch" refers to the process of monitoring the border in order to observe and prevent the illegal entry of immigrants; "linewatch hours" are the amount of hours devoted to high security level observation of borders to prevent illegal immigration. Linewatch hours serve as a proxy measure of resources devoted to border enforcement. They are considered by the sectors where migrants reported crossing, and averaged around 7 million over the time period under analysis. Table 9.1 also summarizes some of the personal and migratory characteristics of immigrants in the sample. On average, voluntary returnees are more likely to be older, making them also more likely to be married and household heads than deported migrants. Additionally, relative to their deported counterparts, voluntary returnees have more border-crossing experience and are more likely to have crossed through Baja, California, to have traveled alone, and to have used (and paid more for) a coyote on their last trip. Finally, voluntary returnees spent more time in the United States, were more likely to have worked while in the United States, and were more likely to have remitted money back home. Yet, both groups have relatively similar educational attainment and exhibit similar Mexican/U.S. wage gaps.

Table 9.1 Descriptive characteristics of voluntary returnees and deported migrants

Variables	Non-deported returnees (app. 11,000)	Deported migrants (app. 46,500)
Dependent variable		
Intent to Cross	0.38	0.63
Independent variables		
Linewatch hours (millions)	6.93	7.04
Age: Less than 19 years old	0.08	0.19
Age: 20 to 24	0.24	0.29
Age: 25 to 34	0.39	0.36
Age: 35 plus	0.30	0.16
Married	0.59	0.46
Household head	0.66	0.52
Educational Attainment		
No education	6.53	5.56
Primary education	48.77	48.30
Secondary education	27.92	35.04
Preparatory education	11.09	9.07
Higher education	5.70	2.03
First-time crosser	46.13	62.13
State of crossing last trip		
Baja California	37.73	22.97
Sonora	19.46	23.29
Chihuahua	0.92	12.15
Coahuila	19.29	10.72
Tamaulipas	12.07	23.62
Other	10.52	7.26
Traveled accompanied	0.19	0.41
Use of a coyote last trip	0.33	0.15
Coyote cost (in 2000 U.S. dollars in 100s)	6.55	5.32
Border wait (days)	6.17	7.42
Days in U.S. last trip	428.15	77.32
Wage gap (Mexican wage/U.S. wage)	0.19	0.14
Remitted money home	0.57	0.47
Instrumental variables		
Customs user fee (ad valorem import duty in percent)	0.20	0.20
Drug seizures by Border Patrol (in millions of 2000 U.S. dollars)	27310.44	26850.40
Yearly boat arrivals at the Los Angeles–Long Beach international port	5525.76	5524.62

CONCEPTUAL FRAMEWORK AND METHODOLOGY

As is standard in the literature, it is assumed that Mexican migrants come to the United States when the present value of lifetime earnings in the United States exceeds the present value of lifetime earnings in Mexico, net of migration costs. Therefore, in order to model the likelihood that a return migrant might be willing to go back to the United States, information was gathered on wages earned in the United States in the past relative to wages last earned in Mexico. Most immigrants worked in the United States; however, a large number of immigrants have missing information regarding the wages they last earned in Mexico. In those instances, the average wage reported by other migrants of the same age and with the same educational attainment has been used as a proxy for their last wage in Mexico.

To proxy for migration costs, information is provided on the crossing location as well as whether the migrant crossed alone or was accompanied by others, as these characteristics may affect the degree of difficulty involved in the crossing. Additionally, the study incorporates individualized information on explicit and implicit costs to migrating. Explicit costs are captured by the smuggling fees migrants paid in their last crossing. Implicit costs are captured by the border wait (measured in days) in preparation for their last crossing.

The analysis also controls for a wide range of individual and macroeconomic characteristics acting as pull and push factors in the migration decision. Individual-level characteristics include age, marital status, family size, household head status, educational attainment, time spent in the United States during the last migration spell (a proxy for assimilation to the United States), and information on whether the individual remits money back home—often a key motive for migrating. Macroeconomic characteristics include information on per capita GDP in the United States and Mexico, as measures of the health of both the U.S. and Mexican economies possibly influence the migration decision. Of particular interest here is the information on border enforcement as captured by millions of linewatch hours. This variable is used by most researchers as a measure of the intensity of border control efforts. Finally, the analysis includes a variety of time controls—specifically, time trend and time period binary variables—to purge out estimates from any time effects or macroeconomic factors not accounted for with the other regressors.

Using the aforementioned data, the likelihood that a return migrant might be willing to go back to the United States in the near future is estimated using a probit model specification. (A probit model is a model for binary responses where the response probability is the standard normal cumulative density function evaluated at a linear function of the explanatory variables.) Our interest rests on the coefficient estimate for linewatch hours in such a model, which measures the impact of border enforcement on undocumented migrants' willingness to repetitively cross the border. Yet there exists a complication in interpreting the coefficient estimates for linewatch hours as the impact of border enforcement on undocumented migrants' willingness to repetitively cross the border. Linewatch hours can be endogenous: they may be correlated with unobserved events that, in turn, are correlated with the individual decision to remigrate. For instance, an economic slowdown in Mexico, such as the peso devaluation of the 1980s, may induce a larger number of Mexicans to migrate to the United States. The U.S. government may, in turn, enhance border controls in response to the expected increase in migration.

To address this problem, instrumental variable methods are used. The method of instrumental variables (IV) allows analysts to derive estimates of causal relationships when circumstances make controlled experiments impossible. In this specific case, researchers identified various instrumental variables that are highly correlated with linewatch hours but not directly correlated with the probability of reentering the United States illegally. Variations in such instrumental variables allow the identification of the potential impact of increased linewatch hours on undocumented immigrants' willingness to repetitively cross the border. Following Gordon Hanson, Raymond Robertson, and Antonio Spilimbergo (2002), the instruments used include the value of the U.S. Customs user fee, the estimated value of illegal drug seizures by the U.S. Border Patrol in the given fiscal year, and yearly boat arrivals at the Los Angeles–Long Beach international port as instruments for linewatch hours. What is the rationale behind these instruments? The customs user fee is ad valorem duty—a duty based on the value of imports. The higher the duty is, the greater the likelihood of smuggling on the part of individuals wanting to avoid the import tax and, therefore, the greater resources that the Border Patrol may have to shift toward catching smugglers and away from apprehending illegal migrants. Likewise, more illegal drug seizures by Border Patrol agents and more boat arrivals imply a greater shifting of resources away from apprehending illegal migrants at the Mexican-U.S. border.

DOES BORDER ENFORCEMENT SERVE AS AN EFFECTIVE DETERRENT TO REMIGRATION?

Table 9.2 displays the marginal effects from estimating the probit models of the likelihood of return migration separately for deported and nondeported migrants. The first test is for the exogeneity of linewatch hours in each of the models, using the Durbin-Wu-Hausman test. The Durbin-Wu-Hausman test allows for checking for a variable's endogeneity by comparing IV estimates to ordinary least squares estimates. The results from such a test indicate that linewatch hours seem to be endogenous to the likelihood of remigration for all returnees. Therefore, the model is reestimated using instrumental variables. The instrumental variables are inspected to ascertain their validity as instruments from an econometric standpoint. In checking that they are significantly correlated with linewatch hours, the joint F-statistic suggests that they are. Additionally, the Basmann's and Sargan's overidentification tests are used to examine the exogeneity of the instruments. Both tests indicate that the instruments are uncorrelated with the error term—one of the requirements for valid instruments.

Table 9.2 Likelihood of a repetitive border-crossing attempt

	Deported Migrants		Nondeported Migrants	
	Probit w/out IV	IV-Probit	Probit w/out IV	IV-Probit
Variables	M.E.	M.E.	M.E.	M.E.
Linewatch hours (mill)	-0.053***	-0.131***	-0.122***	-0.154***
Wage gap (MX/U.S.)	-0.294***	-0.292***	0.060	0.058
Coyote cost (in $100)	-0.008***	-0.008***	-0.004***	-0.004***
Border wait (days)	-4.7E-05	-4.5E-05	-1.0E-04	-1.0E-04
Sonora	-0.058***	-0.057***	-0.085***	-0.085***
Chihuahua	-0.171***	-0.170***	-0.169***	-0.169***
Coahuila	-0.140***	-0.139***	0.082***	0.083***
Tamaulipas	-0.127***	-0.125***	0.050***	0.051***
Other	-0.185***	-0.180***	-0.067***	-0.066***
Traveled accompanied	0.125***	0.124***	0.147***	0.146***
Days in U.S. last trip	-6.4E-06	-6.3E-06	2.0E-04***	2.0E-04***
Remitted money home	-0.146***	-0.144***	0.077***	0.078***
Regression Fit Statistics				
Observations	39475		10634	
Wald Chi-square	$Chi^2(28)$=1761.46	$Chi^2(28)$=1837.80	$Chi^2(28)$=906.83	$Chi^2(28)$=1113.46
	Prob>Chi^2=0.000	Prob>Chi^2=0.000	Prob>Chi^2=0.000	Prob>Chi^2=0.000
Specification Tests				
Chow Test	F(30, 50077)=160.84		Prob>F=0.000	
Durbin-Wu-Hausman Test	$Chi^2(1)$=0.206		Prob>Chi^2=0.650	
Basmann/Sargan Tests	$Chi^2(2)$=1.110		Prob>Chi^2=0.5740	

Notes: The regressions include a constant term as well as a set of migrant personal characteristics (e.g., age, marital status, household head status, educational attainment) and country level characteristics (e.g., per capita GDP in U.S. in 2000 U.S. dollars and per capita GDP in Mexico in 2000 pesos), possibly acting as pull and push factors influencing the likelihood of remigration, a time trend and period dummies. Standard errors were clustered at the state-of-crossing level. *** Signifies statistically different from zero at the 1 percent level or better, ** at the 5 percent level or better, and * at the 10 percent level or better.

Is border enforcement an effective deterrent of remigration? According to the figures in Table 9.2, it is. When not accounting for the endogeneity of border enforcement, it is found that an additional 1 million linewatch hours would reduce the willingness to repetitively attempt to cross the border by 5 percentage points among deported migrants and by 12 percentage points among their nondeported counterparts. The estimated effect of an additional 1 million linewatch hours in reducing the likelihood of remigration among deported migrants increases (in absolute value) to 13 percentage points, and among their nondeported counterparts to 15 percentage points when one instruments for linewatch hours. In sum, an average yearly increase of a half million linewatch hours, characteristic of the 1990 to 2003 period, could reduce undocumented migrants' willingness to cross again into the United States anywhere between 6.5 and 7.5 percentage points, depending on whether they have been previously deported.

Table 9.2 also reports estimated relationships of other important determinants of the likelihood of remigration in the deported and nondeported samples. For instance, an increase in smuggling costs of $1000 reduces the likelihood of remigration by about 8 percentage points among deported migrants and by 4 percentage points among their nondeported counterparts. For both groups of migrants, traveling with other people or having a longer United States stay during their last trip is associated with a higher likelihood of remigration, perhaps signaling that they crossed with family and friends who stayed in the United States and their greater assimilation to the United States, respectively. However, a 10 percent increase in the Mexican to U.S. relative wages lowers the likelihood of remigration among deported migrants by 3 percentage points, but not among voluntary returnees. To the extent that this group of migrants returned to Mexico voluntarily, this finding is not that surprising, and instead signals the existence of other motives for remigrating, such as, possibly, the presence of family members in the United States.

CONCLUSION

This essay explored the following question: Has increased border enforcement helped lower the likelihood of repetitive illegal border-crossing attempts on the part of undocumented migrants? To answer that question, linewatch hours were used to capture the intensity of border enforcement and consider the possibility that linewatch hours may be endogenous. It was found that increasing border enforcement seems to deter repetitive illegal border crossings—a sizeable component of overall apprehensions. This finding may, to some extent, help explain the recent declines in border apprehension rates noted by government officials and the media. Additionally, it supports one of the unintended consequences of stepped-up border enforcement noted by previous authors—as is the case with the decision of many undocumented migrants to stay longer periods of time in the United States, given the difficulty to reenter the country if they go back home (Cornelius 2005; Massey, Durand, & Malone, 2002). Finally, some may interpret the result as one that encourages putting aside funds for border enforcement purposes.

However, it is important to keep in mind certain limitations of this analysis. First, the data are informative only of migrants' intentions to cross. Secondly, the study addresses only one facet of the impact of border enforcement. If increased border enforcement induces some undocumented migrants who successfully make it into the United States to permanently settle there and never go back to Mexico, increased border enforcement may actually backfire and increase the overall magnitude of the undocumented population in the United States (Massey, 2003). Yet gaining a better understanding of the role played by border enforcement in deterring repetitive border-crossing attempts by undocumented migrants on the Mexican side of the border is still of great interest, given that repetitive border crossings are a large component of overall crossings and apprehension costs.

REFERENCES AND FURTHER READING

Angelucci, M. (2005). *U.S. border enforcement and the net flow of Mexican illegal migration* (Discussion Paper No. 1642). Retrieved from IZA website: http://ftp.iza.org/dp1642.pdf

Bean, F. D. (2001). Circular, invisible, and ambiguous migrants: Components of difference in estimates of the number of unauthorized Mexican migrants in the United States. *Demography, 38*(3), 411–422.

Bean, F., Edmonston, B., & Passel, J. S. (Eds.). (1990). *Undocumented migration to the United States: IRCA and the experience of the 1980s.* Washington, DC: Urban Institute.

Bean, F. D., Espenshade, T. J., White, M. J., & Dymowksi, R. F. (1990). Post-IRCA changes in the volume and composition of undocumented migration to the United States: An assessment based on apprehension data. In F. D. Bean, B. Edmonston, & J. S. Passel (Eds.), *Undocumented migration to the United States: IRCA and the experience of the 1980s* (pp. 111–158). Washington, DC: Urban Institute.

Bustamante, J. A. (1990). Measuring the flow of undocumented immigrants: Research findings from the Zapata Canyon Project. In F. D. Bean, B. Edmonston, & J. S. Passel (Eds.), *Undocumented migration to the United States: IRCA and the experience of the 1980s* (pp. 211–226). Washington, DC: Urban Institute.

Chavez, L. R., Flores, E. T., & Lopez-Garza, M. (1990). Here today, gone tomorrow? Undocumented settlers and immigration reform. *Human Organization, 49*(3), 193–205.

Consejo Nacional de Población. Mexico D.F. (1998). *Encuesta sobre Migración en la Frontera Norte de México 1993–1994.*

Cornelius, W. A. (1989, December). Impacts of the 1986 U.S. immigration law on emigration from rural Mexican sending communities. *Population and Development Review, 15*(4), 689–705.

Cornelius, W. A. (1990). Impacts of the 1986 U.S. immigration law on emigration from rural Mexican sending communities. In F. D. Bean, B. Edmonston, & J. S. Passel (Eds.), *Undocumented migration to the United States: IRCA and the experience of the 1980s* (pp. 227–250). Washington, DC: Urban Institute.

Cornelius, W. A. (1992). From sojourners to settlers: The changing profile of Mexican immigration to the United States. In J. A. Bustamente, C. W. Reynolds, & R. A. Hinojosa (Eds.), *U.S.-Mexico relations: Labor-market interdependence* (pp. 155–195). Stanford, CA: StanfordUniversity Press.

Cornelius, W. A. (1998). The Structural embeddedness of demand for Mexican immigrant labor: New evidence from California. In M. Suárez-Orozco (Ed.), *Crossings: Mexican immigration in interdisciplinary perspective* (pp. 114–144). Cambridge, MA: Harvard University Press/David Rockefeller Center for Latin American Studies.

Cornelius, W. A. (2005). Controlling 'unwanted' immigration: Lessons from the United States, 1993–2004. *Journal of Ethnic and Migration Studies, 31*(4), 775–794.

Dávila, A., Pagán, J. A., & Soydemir, G. (2002). The short-term and long-term deterrence effects of INS border and interior enforcement on undocumented immigration. *Journal of Economic Behavior & Organization, 49*(4), 459–472.

Department of Homeland Security. (2005, November). *Fact sheet: Secure border initiative.* Retrieved from http://www.dhs.gov/xnews/releases/press_release_0794.shtm

Devadoss, S., & Luckstead, J. (2011, July). Implications of immigration policies for the U.S. farm sector and workforce. *Economic Inquiry, 49*(3), 857–875.

Donato, K. M., Durand, J., & Massey, D. S. (1992). Stemming the tide? Assessing the deterrent effects of the Immigration Reform and Control Act. *Demography, 29*(2), 139–157.

Espenshade, T. J. (1990). Undocumented migration to the United States: Evidence from a repeated trials model. In F. D. Bean, B. Edmonston, & J. S. Passel (Eds.), *Undocumented migration to the United States: IRCA and the experience of the 1980s* (pp. 159–182). Washington, DC: Urban Institute.

Espenshade, T. J. (1994). Does the threat of border apprehension deter undocumented U.S. immigration? *Population and Development Review, 20*(4), 871–892.

Espenshade, T. J. (1995). Using INS border apprehension data to measure the flow of undocumented migrants crossing the U.S.-Mexico frontier. *International Migration Review, 29*(2), 545–565.

Global Security. (2011). *Military: Operation gatekeeper, operation hold-the-line and operation safeguard.* Retrieved from http://www.globalsecurity.org/military/ops/gatekeeper.htm

Gonzalez de la Rocha, M., & Latapi, A. E. (1990). *The impact of IRCA on the migration patterns of a community in Los Altos, Jalisco, Mexico* (Working Paper No. 41). Washington, DC: Commission for the Study of International Migration and Cooperative Economic Development.

Hanson, G. H., Robertson, R., & Spilimbergo, A. (2002). Does border enforcement protect U.S. workers from illegal immigration? *The Review of Economics and Statistics, 84*(1), 73–92.

Hanson, G. H., & Spilimbergo, A. (1999). Illegal immigration, border enforcement, and relative wages: Evidence from apprehensions at the U.S.-Mexico border. *American Economic Review, 89*(5), 1337–1357.

Kossoudji, S. A. (1992). Playing cat and mouse at the U.S.-Mexican border. *Demography, 29*(2), 159–180.

Lindstrom, D. P. (1996). Economic opportunity in Mexico and return migration from the United States. *Demography, 33*(3), 357–374.

Lowell, L. B. (1992). Circular mobility, migrant communities, and policy restrictions: Unauthorized flows from Mexico. In C. Goldscheider (Ed.), *Migration, population structure, and redistribution policies* (pp. 137–157). Boulder, CO: Westview.

Massey, D. (2003). *Beyond smoke and mirrors: Mexican immigration in an era of economic integration.* New York, NY: Russell Sage Foundation.

Massey, D. S., Donato, K. M., & Liang, Z. (1990). Effects of the Immigration Reform and Control Act of 1986: Preliminary data from Mexico. In F. D. Bean, B. Edmonston, & J. S. Passel (Eds.), *Undocumented migration to the United States: IRCA and the experience of the 1980s* (pp. 182–210). Washington, DC: Urban Institute.

Massey, D. S., Durand, J., & Malone, N. J. (2002). *Beyond smoke and mirrors: Mexican immigration in an era of economic integration.* New York, NY: Russell Sage Foundation.

Migration Policy Institute. (2005). *Immigration facts: Immigration enforcement spending since IRCA* (No. 10). Retrieved from http://www .migrationpolicy.org/ITFIAF/FactSheet_Spending.pdf

Orrenius, P. M. (2001). Illegal immigration and enforcement along the U.S.-Mexico border; an overview. *Economic and Financial Policy Review, 1*(2–11). Retrieved from at Federal Reserve Bank of Dallas website: http://dallasfed.org/research/efr/2001/efr0101a.pdf

Orrenius, P. M., & Zavodny, M. (2003). Do amnesty programs reduce undocumented immigration? Evidence from IRCA. *Demography, 40*(3), 437–450.

Richter, S. M., Taylor, J. E., & Yunez-Naude, A. (2007). Impacts of policy reforms on labor migration from rural Mexico to the United States. In G. J. Borias (Ed.), *Mexican immigration to the United States.* National Bureau of Economic Research Conference Report, pp. 269–288). Chicago, IL: University of Chicago Press.

Sherry, A. (2004). *Foundations of U.S. immigration control policy: A study of information transmission to Mexican migrants and the role of information as a deterrent at the border* (Working Paper No. 95). San Diego: University of California, San Diego, Center for Comparative Immigration Studies. Retrieved from http://www.ccis-ucsd.org/PUBLICATIONS/wrkg95.pdf

Singer, A., & Massey, D. S. (1988). The social process of undocumented border crossing among Mexican migrants. *International Migration Review, 32*(Fall), 561–592.

Spener, D. (2001). Smuggling migrants through South Texas: Challenges posed by Operation Rio Grande. In D. Kyle & T. Snyder (Eds.), *Global human smuggling: Comparative perspectives* (pp. 129–165). Baltimore, MD: Johns Hopkins University Press.

U.S. Immigration and Customs Enforcement. (n.d.). *Secure communities.* Retrieved from http://www.ice.gov/secure_communities

White, M. J., Bean, F. D., & Espenshade, T. J. (1990). The U.S. 1986 Immigration Reform and Control Act and undocumented migration to the United States. *Population Research and Policy Review, 9*(2), 93–116.

The White House. (2006). *Fact sheet: The Secure Fence Act of 2006.* Retrieved from http://georgewbush-whitehouse.archives.gov/news/releases/2006/10/20061026-1.html

Catalina Amuedo-Dorantes and Cynthia Bansak

Immigrant Detention and Deportation Under the Obama Administration

POINT: The Obama administration must pursue thorough immigration enforcement strategies in the interest of political compromise and comprehensive immigration reform. By focusing agency detention and deportation efforts on immigrant criminals, Obama has relieved pressure on noncriminal immigrants while making the country and our communities safer.

Kathryn Miller, University of Oregon

COUNTERPOINT: Staunch partisanship in Congress has rendered comprehensive reform highly unlikely, drawing into question the logic of using mass deportation as a tool of political compromise. The Obama administration's detention and deportation policies have served to further entrench existing systemic injustices rather than making our communities safer by taking criminals off the streets.

Kathryn Miller, University of Oregon

Introduction

In a May 2011 address in El Paso, Texas, President Barack Obama argued, "Being a nation of laws goes hand in hand with being a nation of immigrants" (Obama, 2011). As a country for which immigration occupies a place of almost mythical importance, contention over the content and sentiment of immigration policy remains ever present. With such a large population of people living in the shadows, the stakes of this policy debate are high. Between 2000 and 2010, the estimated number of unauthorized immigrants in the United States ranged from 8.5 million to 12 million, peaking in 2007 (Passel & Cohn, 2011). During President Obama's first 3 years in office, his administration deported a record 1.2 million people, at a rate of nearly 400,000 per year. Hundreds of thousands of those deported had spent time in a nationwide network of immigration detention facilities, which have been the site of endemic prisoner abuse and systemic failures to ensure due process. This chapter examines two aspects of what is a broad and multifaceted immigration debate through the lens of the Obama administration's immigrant detention and deportation policies.

The Point section of this chapter makes a case for the Obama administration's detention and deportation policies, arguing that while these policies are not perfect, they have served to uphold the law and make U.S. communities safer. By focusing deportation efforts on the "worst of the worst" immigrant criminals, rather than noncriminal immigrants, the administration has been able to make the best of a flawed system of immigration laws. Enforcement has been both tough and fair, removing criminals from the streets while also relieving pressure on unauthorized immigrants brought to the United States as children and immigrant families that might have been separated under the less careful policies of previous administrations. President Obama has also used his limited administrative flexibility to signal his party's willingness to compromise with congressional Republicans on comprehensive immigration reform.

The Counterpoint section contests the administration's position, arguing that these policies have ultimately reinforced systemic injustice while failing to increase public safety or inspire comprehensive immigration reform. When deflecting criticism of the administration's policies, officials have downplayed the extent of their discretion in enforcing immigration laws. Yet the administration's Secure Communities initiative is demonstrative of exactly the kind of discretion it purports not to have. While the administration claims to be focusing enforcement efforts on the most serious criminal offenders, only a small fraction of those deported under the Secure Communities initiative have been criminal immigrants. Moreover, the administration has failed to use its authority to address widespread abuse in detention facilities and racial profiling in local arresting practices.

In reading this chapter, there are a few recurring questions to consider. What is the role of any president's administration in making and enforcing immigration policy, and to what extent do administrative obligations and limitations define its responsibility for problematic immigration laws? What constitutes an adequate administrative response to systemic maltreatment of immigrants? Partisan politics have appeared front and center in this debate. What is, and what should be, the role of partisan politics in shaping immigration policy? What is the extent of the national obligation to unauthorized immigrants in the United States, particularly given the circumstances under which many of them are forced to leave their home countries? Under what conditions should this obligation take precedence over existing legal institutions? Lastly, how does the United States' immigrant heritage inform, and sometimes obscure, the current immigration policy debate?

POINT

Both sides of the debate agree that the system of immigration laws in the United States is in disrepair. Not surprisingly, Barack Obama, both as a candidate for president and then as president, has also maintained that the system is broken. However, as the chief executive and head of the administrative branch of government, he is obliged to enforce the system of immigration laws, whether or not he agrees with them in substance or in sentiment. In his efforts to push Congress to pass comprehensive immigration reform, President Obama has attempted to show, by taking a tough stance on enforcement, that he and the Democrats are willing to compromise with congressional Republicans (Obama, 2011). He has drawn fire from many of his supporters for these enforcement policies, but the administration argues that Immigration and Customs Enforcement (ICE) has used what discretion it does have in its application of the law to focus its efforts on arresting and deporting the worst immigrant criminals (Muñoz, 2011). The Department of Homeland Security (DHS) has also demonstrated that it can respond to community concerns regarding who is being targeted for prosecution and deportation, issuing guidelines for the use of prosecutorial discretion as a means of refocusing agency enforcement efforts on criminals who pose public safety or national security risks (U.S. Immigration and Customs Enforcement, 2011a).

THE LEGACY OF IMMIGRATION AND THE AMERICAN DREAM

The United States has a long and rich relationship with immigration that stretches continuously from the time of the nation's founding to the present day. This relationship has often been one of contestation, conflict, inequality, and discrimination; but it has also been one that welcomes diversity. In many ways, President Obama embodies the American experience. He was born to a black African and a white woman from Kansas, in the middle of the civil rights movement, and at a time when antimiscegenation laws were still the norm in the United States. His life is a paradigmatic example of the promise of the American Dream, which has informed his commitment to ensuring that Americans and immigrants to the United States alike enjoy that promise for generations to come. Yet, as President Obama stressed in a May 2011 policy speech, the United States is a nation that upholds the rule of law, just as it is a nation that upholds and honors its immigrant heritage. There is no inherent or fundamental contradiction between these two foundational American precepts. President Obama argues that it is only in the reconciliation of these values that we, as a nation, will be able to honor either of them. He sees a healthy, fair, and just immigration system as an essential part of that commitment, and because of this, he has made comprehensive immigration reform a priority.

POLITICAL COMPROMISE AND COMPREHENSIVE IMMIGRATION REFORM

The system of laws currently in place to deal with immigration in the United States is deeply flawed. On a fundamental level, it is a system that fails to control immigration; hundreds of thousands of people migrate to the United States illegally each year, some for work and a shot at the American Dream, and others for nefarious reasons. As President Obama stressed in his 2012 State of the Union address to Congress, it also fails on an ethical level, undermining some of the most fundamental American values. Young people who were brought into the United States by parents without legal authorization to be in the country face discrimination, hardship, stunted opportunity, and the constant threat of deportation, in spite of the fact that they have spent most of their lives in the United States, and have grown up as Americans. Congress failed to address this when Republicans blocked the so-called DREAM Act, which would have created a path to citizenship for young people who were brought to the United States as children. Unauthorized immigrants who come to the United States each year to work in the agricultural sector, to do back-breaking jobs that U.S. citizens have shown little interest in doing, are subject to exploitation and abuse that no human being should have to endure. They are forced to endure this because current U.S. immigration law is incapable of protecting them. Mothers and fathers are being separated from their children when they get swept into immigrant detention facilities and deported. These kinds of practical and ethical failures are unacceptable in a country that prides itself on its commitment to notions of justice, fairness, freedom, and opportunity. Yet, as President Obama has often mentioned, it is also unacceptable for some people to bypass legal immigration proceeding while others, unwilling to break the law, are left to wait in line. The Obama administration has used these lines of reasoning in justifying its use of administrative discretion in shaping immigration law enforcement and in its vigorous attempts to persuade Congress to again take on a comprehensive reform of U.S. immigration law.

President Obama argues that what is at stake in the debate over immigration reform is not simply who is allowed into the country and who is kept out, but the very essence of our national character. What it means to be an American is a question of rights and responsibilities, but it is also one of character and morality. To fail to create a just and fair system of immigration laws is not just a practical failure; it is a failure of national integrity. Comprehensive immigration reform has been one of President Obama's stated priorities since he was a candidate. Yet he and his administration understand that complicated and high-stakes legal overhauls are impossible without political compromise. They also understand that, while the authority to make immigration law lies with Congress, the president can exert considerable political pressure on the legislature, and he can signal the willingness of his party to compromise on controversial issues. This is important on its own terms, but it is also important in understanding why the administration has adopted many of the immigration enforcement strategies that it has. Congressional Republicans have made it clear that they will not consider a comprehensive immigration reform package that is soft on unauthorized immigration or border enforcement. Although they have been less clear on the substance of these demands, the need for political compromise has never been in question. Given staunch partisanship in the 111th and 112th Congresses, it has fallen to the Obama administration to rise above the fray and signal its willingness to compromise. However, President Obama has only a limited amount of administrative flexibility with which to shape an enforcement strategy that signals his willingness to compromise on a reform package.

Implementation of a congressional mandate: Enforcing the law. As defined in the Constitution, the administration of laws passed by Congress falls to the executive branch. It is not the prerogative of any given president or presidential administration whether or not to enforce the law. President Obama and his administration are constitutionally bound to uphold, and therefore enforce, federal laws, whether or not they agree with the substance or the sentiment of those laws. This means that President Obama is obliged to faithfully enforce immigration laws, in spite of any objections he may have to them. This is the burden of the executive branch. However, given the often vague nature of congressional action, presidential administrations do in fact have some say in how laws are actually enforced. It is in this gray area of implementation that the Obama administration has found the political space to signal its willingness to compromise in the name of comprehensive immigration reform, as well as the administrative space to implement its own vision regarding enforcement priorities. One of the major outlets for this vision has been the Department of Homeland Security's Secure Communities program.

Secure communities and the prioritization of criminal offenders. The Secure Communities initiative, which has become a considerable point of contention between President Obama and many of his supporters on the left, is arguably the most important, though not the only, program with which the Obama administration has attempted to enforce immigration law while still exercising administrative discretion. The origin of the Secure Communities initiative can be traced back to the George W. Bush administration. The program, which was started in 2008, is intended to facilitate immigration enforcement by increasing cooperation between state and federal officials through a data-sharing program. Initially, individual counties could voluntarily sign on to the program, but it has since been made mandatory by the DHS. As of 2012, all counties are required to participate. Secure Communities has ushered in an unprecedented level of cooperation and communication between local and federal law enforcement agencies on issues of immigration law enforcement. Under the program, the fingerprints of all those arrested by participating local law enforcement agencies are automatically run through the FBI and ICE databases to determine the person's criminal history (if applicable), and whether or not she or he is deportable (i.e., an unauthorized immigrant). In the decade since the September 11 attacks, Congress has put considerably more emphasis on the importance of data and intelligence sharing between federal agencies, and it has also mandated DHS to find and deport immigrant criminals, with a particular emphasis on anyone who poses a national security risk. The Secure Communities program allows DHS to combine these two congressional mandates.

Secure Communities has taken on new prominence under the Obama administration. Immigration and Customs Enforcement has touted the success of Secure Communities in finding and deporting high-priority unauthorized immigrants based on the agency's deportation prioritization scheme. Directed by President Obama, ICE has stated its priorities as follows (in order of decreasing importance): (1) immigrants convicted of crimes, including homicide, sexual offenses, drug offenses, and driving offenses; (2) repeat unauthorized entrants—those who reenter the country without authorization after having already been removed one or more times; (3) unauthorized entrants apprehended at the border, and immigrant fugitives who fail to leave the country after having been ordered to do so by an immigration court; and

(4) other deportable immigrants, including violators ranging from those suspected of being a security risk to noncriminals known to be present without authorization, including those who overstay visas (ICE, 2011, Removal Statistics).

Administration officials stress the fact that this strategy strongly emphasizes the detention and deportation of hardened criminals—the worst of the worst. They have simultaneously de-emphasized noncriminal unauthorized immigrants, and officials have expressed a commitment to avoiding unnecessary separation of families (Muñoz, 2011; Obama, 2011). However, the administration acknowledges that, as hard as they may try, some families are going to be separated. Officials argue that this is a problem inherent in the immigration laws themselves, rather than a result of flawed enforcement strategies, and thus it is a problem that can only be taken up by Congress (Muñoz, 2011; Obama, 2011). The administration is exercising the discretion it has to focus its enforcement efforts on immigrant criminals, rather than deporting people at random as they come into contact with the system. As part of ongoing efforts by the administration to limit the number of noncriminal unauthorized immigrants that are deported, DHS director John Morton issued a memo to ICE personnel (U.S. Immigration and Customs Enforcement, 2011a) emphasizing the need to exercise prosecutorial discretion in deciding who to apprehend and detain, and which deportation cases to pursue, in accordance with the agency's stated priorities. The memo was intended predominantly to clarify and reiterate existing policies and procedures regarding the latitude of federal law enforcement agencies to decide which cases to pursue, but it was also meant to address concerns put forward by community members, immigrant rights activists, and others regarding perceived problems with enforcement outcomes. The administration has cited the memo as a demonstration of flexibility and responsiveness in the face of criticism. Yet only Congress can undertake comprehensive revisions.

PUBLIC SAFETY AND NATIONAL SECURITY

Public safety and national security are central themes of the Obama administration's enforcement policies. This is particularly true of Secure Communities, which enables unprecedented communication between local and federal law enforcement agencies. The result has been a dramatic increase in the numbers of immigrant criminals identified, removed from local communities, and deported. According to the Department of Homeland Security, 54.6 percent of those detained and deported under Secure Communities in fiscal year 2011 were criminals, and that percentage is expected to rise as ICE improves the use of prosecutorial discretion in focusing enforcement efforts on high-priority targets. The administration has succeeded in removing tens of thousands of criminals, including murderers, sex offenders, drug dealers, and traffickers. This emphasis on public safety and the removal of dangerous criminals has made communities around the country safer, and it has also made the country as a whole more secure. Drug smugglers, human traffickers, and violent gang members are not just a problem for local communities; they also pose a national security risk. The United States shares a nearly 2,000-mile-long border with Mexico, rendering total control of the border nearly impossible. The United States has a sovereign right to control immigration, and given that illegal border crossings are inevitable, deportation is a necessary tool of immigration enforcement. Obama administration officials argue that their deportation and detention policies are a legitimate and well-reasoned exercise of this kind of sovereign authority.

RESPONDING TO CRITICISM

As the number of unauthorized immigrants in detention has grown, so too has the backlog in immigration courts. According to *The New York Times,* as of early 2012 there were approximately 300,000 cases languishing in the dockets of immigration courts across the country (Preston, 2012). Critics of the administration's handling of immigration policies have taken this up as fodder, arguing that this massive backlog is proof-positive of an excessive deportation policy. In an attempt to address this problem, President Obama has ordered a review of several thousand cases, instructing officials to drop cases against low-priority nonviolent offenders. If DHS succeeds in extending this program to all jurisdictions, *The New York Times* estimates, the agency might drop as many as 39,000 cases against unauthorized immigrants, and although they will not be granted a status adjustment, those individuals will not be deported (Preston, 2012). If successful, this administrative shift would partially address the issue of family separation by allowing noncriminal immigrants to remain in the United States.

In June 2012, the Obama administration amended its prosecutorial prioritization scheme in order to address ongoing concerns regarding the deportation of young people who were brought to the United States as children. If passed, the Development, Relief, and Education for Alien Minors (DREAM) Act would allow this demographic to permanently change their immigration status. Presidential administrations lack the authority to make these kinds of changes. Instead, Secretary of Homeland Security Janet Napolitano issued a memo to all DHS immigration agents stating that unauthorized immigrants under the age of 30 who were brought to the United States as children 16 years of age or younger will be eligible for a deferral of enforcement action, subject to renewal every 2 years. Those granted deferment would then be able to apply for temporary work visas. The administration stressed that that the policy would not incentivize new immigration, because only immigrants already in the country as of June 15, 2012, would be eligible to apply. Immigrants will only be eligible for deferment if they have lived in the United States for at least 5 years, have not been convicted of a crime, do not pose a risk to national security, have graduated from high school or are currently enrolled in school, or have served in the armed forces (U.S. Department of Homeland Security, 2012).

The policy shift is consistent with the Obama administrations ongoing prioritization of immigrant criminals. The policy attempts to address certain injustices within existing immigration law, but stringent criteria ensure that only those young immigrants most likely to make significant positive contributions to the country will be allowed to stay. While this use of prosecutorial discretion does not diminish the need for legislative reform, it does allow the Obama administration to provide a certain degree of protection for some of the least culpable and most vulnerable unauthorized immigrants (Obama, 2012b; U.S. Department of Homeland Security, 2012).

CONCLUSION

The Obama administration is in the difficult position of having to enforce a system of laws that is deeply flawed. The democratic structure of the U.S. government obliges the executive branch to carry out the mandates of Congress, regardless of whether the executive agrees with those laws. Yet, as the Obama administration has demonstrated, there is some degree of flexibility in the enforcement of those laws that has allowed President Obama to administer a certain vision of what immigration enforcement should look like. However, the administrative discretion that the president does have is not nearly enough to overcome the systemic flaws of the laws themselves. Knowing this, President Obama has used what discretionary authority he has to signal to congressional Republicans that he and the Democrats are willing to compromise in pursuit of comprehensive immigration reform. Under Obama, Immigration and Customs Enforcement has focused enforcement efforts on the "worst of the worst" criminal offenders in order to promote public safety in local communities. The Secure Communities program has ushered in an unprecedented level of cooperation between local and federal authorities, which has served to further the goal of rooting out the most dangerous immigrant criminals. The administration's use of deportation and detention has been both reasonable and focused, but officials have also demonstrated a willingness to respond to criticism and amend the program in the interest of justice and fairness.

REFERENCES AND FURTHER READING

Muñoz, C. (2011, October 18). Cecilia Muñoz: "Even broken laws have to be enforced" [*Frontline: Lost in detention*]. Retrieved from http://www.pbs.org/wgbh/pages/frontline/race-multicultural/lost-in-detention/cecilia-munoz-even-broken-laws-have-to-be-enforced

Obama, B. (2011, May). *Remarks by the President on comprehensive immigration reform in El Paso, Texas.* Retrieved from http://www.whitehouse.gov/the-press-office/2011/05/10/remarks-president-comprehensive-immigration-reform-el-paso-texas

Obama, B. (2012a, January). [State of the Union Address]. Speech presented to a Joint Session of Congress, House of Representatives, Washington, DC. Retrieved from http://www.whitehouse.gov/the-press-office/2011/01/25/remarks-president-state-union-address

Obama, B. (2012b, June). *Remarks by the President on immigration in Washington, D.C.* Retrieved from http://www.whitehouse.gov/the-press-office/2012/06/15/remarks-president-immigration

Passel, J. S., & Cohn, D. (2011). *Unauthorized immigrant population: National and state trends, 2010.* Washington, DC: Pew Research Center.

PBS Investigative Reporting Workshop, & *Frontline.* (2011). *Lost in detention.* Retrieved from http://www.pbs.org/wgbh/pages/frontline/lost-in-detention

Preston, J. (2012, January 19). In deportation policy test, 1 in 6 offered reprieve. *The New York Times.* Retrieved from http://www.nytimes.com/2012/01/20/us/in-test-of-deportation-policy-1-in-6-offered-reprieve.html

U.S. Department of Homeland Security. (2012). *Memorandum: Exercising prosecutorial discretion with respect to individuals who came to the United States as children.* Retrieved from http://www.ice.gov/doclib/about/offices/ero/pdf/s1-certain-young-people.pdf

U.S. Immigration and Customs Enforcement. (2009). Secretary Napolitano and ICE Assistant Secretary Morton announce new immigration detention reform initiatives. Immigration and Customs Enforcement, News Release. Retrieved from http://www.ice.gov/news/releases0910/091006washington.htm

U.S. Immigration and Customs Enforcement. (2011). *Frequently asked questions on the administration's announcement regarding a new process to further focus immigration enforcement resources on high priority cases.* Retrieved from http://www.ice.gov/doclib/about/offices/ero/pdf/immigration-enforcement-facts.pdf

U.S. Immigration and Customs Enforcement. (2011). *Removal statistics.* Retrieved from http://www.ice.gov/removal-statistics

U.S. Immigration and Customs Enforcement. (2011). *Secure communities.* Retrieved from http://www.ice.gov/secure_communities

U.S. Immigration and Customs Enforcement. (2011a, June 17). *Memorandum: Exercising prosecutorial discretion consistent with the civil immigration enforcement priorities of the Agency for the Apprehension, Detention, and Removal of Aliens.* Retrieved from http://www.ice.gov/doclib/secure-communities/pdf/prosecutorial-discretion-memo.pdf

U.S. Immigration and Customs Enforcement. (2011b, June 17). *Prosecutorial discretion: Certain victims, witnesses, and plaintiffs.* Retrieved from http://www.ice.gov/doclib/secure-communities/pdf/domestic-violence.pdf

Kathryn Miller

COUNTERPOINT

President Obama has argued that his deportation and detention policies are setting the stage for comprehensive immigration reform, but the uncompromisingly partisan climate of the 112th Congress makes such legislation politically improbable. Even if reform were a viable political prospect, the Obama administration's sacrifices regarding deportation and detention are too high a price to pay. The administration has demonstrated considerable discretion in its execution of congressional mandates, in spite of President Obama's insistence that he is constitutionally bound to enforce even bad laws as they are written. Under the auspices of the Secure Communities initiative, Immigration and Customs Enforcement (ICE) has arrested hundreds of thousands of nonviolent and noncriminal immigrants while claiming to be focusing its efforts on the "worst of the worst" hardened criminals (ICE, 2011, Removal Statistics). The design of the Secure Communities program is problematic in part because it undermines the ability of federal officials to account for and prevent racial profiling that occurs at the time of arrest. Moreover, the enforcement mechanisms at the heart of the Secure Communities program pollute the relationship between local law enforcement and immigrant communities, leading to mistrust and fear that ultimately hamper everyday policing efforts and undermine public safety.

The vast system of immigrant detention facilities is itself the site of considerable injustice. Immigrants awaiting hearings and deportation are regularly denied due process and habeas corpus, and the majority lack legal representation of any kind (Kohli, Markowitz, and Chavez, 2011). The nature of this system, combined with the sheer numbers of immigrants detained by ICE under President Obama, has produced dangerous conditions for immigrant detainees. Serious accusations of physical, verbal, and sexual abuse of detainees by guards have been surfacing, but corrupt officials and a lack of access to counsel or the media act to silence the victims of these crimes (American Civil Liberties Union, 2011; Organization of American States, 2010; Rentz, 2011). Overall, the administration's deportation and detention policies make unacceptable compromises, which have led not to comprehensive reform or safer communities, but instead to enduring systemic injustice.

POLITICAL COMPROMISE AND COMPREHENSIVE IMMIGRATION REFORM

During the first 3 years of Barack Obama's presidency, his administration has deported a record number of people—nearly 1.2 million—at an annual rate that surpasses that of the George W. Bush administration. In a May 2011 speech, President Obama attempted to justify the large number of deportations during his term in office, citing the need for his administration to demonstrate its willingness to make political compromises. He argued that his administration must vigorously enforce immigration law both at and within the nation's borders in order to win Republican support for comprehensive immigration reform. However, comprehensive immigration reform legislation has repeatedly failed to gain traction in the face of staunch opposition by congressional Republicans. As President Obama pointed out in his May 2011 speech, despite their insistence that heightened enforcement would enable reform, Republican opponents have, by and large, given no indication that they are satisfied with the Obama administration's redoubled enforcement efforts.

The political climate in which President Obama and congressional Democrats repeatedly pitched comprehensive immigration reform was one of entrenched partisanship. During the first 2 years of the Obama presidency, the Democrats controlled both houses of Congress. For many congressional Republicans, however, compromise with the Democrats was off the table. The 2010 midterm election saw a shift in power, as Republicans won a sizable majority in the House of Representatives. While divided government is often ripe for political compromise, prospects for comprehensive immigration reform still seem dim. Senate Bill 1258—the Comprehensive Immigration Reform Act of 2011—proved no exception, as Senate Democrats failed to inspire bipartisan support for the measure.

In the face of this kind of intractable congressional partisanship, it is difficult to see political compromise in the name of comprehensive reform as a legitimate justification for the Obama administration's enforcement policies, regardless of the content of those proposed reforms. Justifications based on the need for compromise have been especially unsatisfying for critics of the deportation and detention policies of the Secure Communities initiative. While political compromise will almost certainly be an essential component of future reform, any reform seems unlikely to be imminent, given intractable partisanship. The Obama administration needs to reconsider its priorities and place more emphasis on the ethical and legal dilemmas arising from current policies.

ADMINISTRATIVE POLICYMAKING: IMPLEMENTATION OF A CONGRESSIONAL MANDATE

It is the responsibility of the Office of the President to administer and execute congressional mandates, but to what extent does the administrative branch have discretion in this regard? The Obama administration maintains that it must enforce immigration laws irrespective of whether or not they are good laws, and that to do otherwise would be to compromise the integrity of the American system of government itself. However, as one presidential administration after another has shown, congressional mandates inevitably leave room for executive interpretation. Policymaking does not only happen in the halls of Congress—administrative agencies too have the de facto authority to make policy in their interpretation and application of the often vague laws passed by Congress.

So what of the Obama administration's claim that its hands are tied with respect to immigration law enforcement? In an October 2011 interview with the PBS series *Frontline*, Cecilia Muñoz—an adviser to President Obama on immigration issues—defended the administration's use of large-scale deportation, arguing that "even broken laws have to be enforced." Yet the Obama administration has exercised exactly the kind of considerable discretion that it claims not to have in how and to what extent it enforces the congressional action to which Muñoz is referring. It is certainly true that when Congress passes a law rendering certain forms of immigration illegal, enforcement of that law falls to the executive. However, Congress rarely allocates sufficient resources to fully enforce a law as written. In this case, as UCLA law professor Hiroshi Motomura points out, the monetary resources that would be required for the Obama administration to fully enforce immigration law outstrip the allocated funds by many billions of dollars (Motomura, 2012, p. 1831). Therefore, the administration is not merely able to exercise discretion; it is forced to do so with respect to how, when, and where it enforces immigration law, knowing that it cannot be fully enforced with the allocated funds.

Administration officials have repeatedly used Muñoz's line of reasoning to defend deportation policies, yet even Muñoz is quick to tout the administration's liberal exercise of discretion in exactly how the law is being enforced. The Secure Communities program is one example of this kind of administrative policymaking. Secure Communities was not part of a congressional mandate, and no funds were specifically allocated to the program. Instead, the Department of Homeland Security, in conjunction with the FBI, developed Secure Communities for the purpose of executing a broader mandate. Given the reality of administrative policymaking, it is incoherent for administration officials to defend deportation and detention policies on the grounds that they have no choice but to execute a congressional mandate.

DEPORTATION AND DETENTION AS STRATEGIES FOR MANAGING UNAUTHORIZED IMMIGRATION

The Obama administration maintains that the U.S. government has the right to defend its national sovereignty and territorial integrity by making and enforcing immigration laws. This is, of course true: a sovereign nation should have the right to regulate the inward flow of people as it sees fit. However, while this may indeed validate the existence of immigration law in the first place, it does not justify any given immigration policy. In evaluating particular policies, the extent to which officials properly consider the complexities associated with immigration is centrally important. The

United States embraces the notion that this is a nation of immigrants, and the American Dream has become engrained in the national narrative. It is taken for granted that people who migrate to the United States do so because this is the land of opportunity, where hard work and perseverance are the only obstacles along the road to freedom and prosperity. No doubt there are many who are pulled to the United States in pursuit of this dream, but there are many other reasons that people immigrate. Many are forced to migrate from their homes on account of economic hardship, environmental degradation, civil conflict, and other forms of violence. Still others, particularly women and children, are forced to leave their homes in order to escape domestic and other forms of gendered violence. Most of these migrants would be unable to obtain refugee status or asylum, as visas are few, and the criteria are difficult to meet.

With so many of those deported for administrative offenses never afforded due process, access to counsel, or any other means of challenging their deportation, the circumstances of immigration are too often given inadequate consideration, if any at all (Kohli et al., 2011). DHS claims to be addressing these problems, issuing memos to ICE field agents and prosecutors instructing them to use discretion, particularly in cases where the immigrant in question is the victim of a crime (U.S. Immigration and Customs Enforcement, 2011, Memorandum). However, according to a report compiled by the American Immigration Council (AIC) and the American Immigration Lawyers Association (AILA), the DHS memos have been largely ineffective, going mostly unheeded by ICE agents (Alonzo, Chen, Kim, & Lawrence, 2011). While the DHS memos may reflect that the Obama administration has heard the critics of the policies in question, insofar as it remains a symbolic gesture, it is an inadequate administrative response.

In addition to overlooking the often-dangerous circumstances that compel people to emigrate from their home countries, the Secure Communities initiative fails to adequately account for the damage that deportation can do to immigrant families already living in the United States. According the Pew Hispanic Center, around 5 million unauthorized immigrants (just under half) have families with minor children, while only about 1 million of those children are themselves immigrants (Passel & Cohn, 2011). In addition, Pew estimates there are around 4.5 million U.S.-born children with one or more unauthorized immigrant parents. The approximately 9 million people living in these "mixed-status" families are particularly vulnerable, given the possibility that either or both parents could be deported at any given time. An Applied Research Center (ARC) study estimates that, as of the end of 2011, there were around 5,100 children living in foster care because one or both of their parents had either been deported or were being detained for immigration violations. ARC anticipates that this number will rise dramatically if deportations continue at their current rate (Wessler, 2011). Obama administration officials have repeatedly expressed their desire to keep the families of unauthorized immigrants together whenever possible, and some efforts in that regard have been made. However, families are still being torn apart unnecessarily. Unauthorized immigrants arrested and detained under Secure Communities are quickly transferred to ICE detention facilities, often without being reunited with their children.

The ARC study also found that victims of domestic violence are particularly vulnerable in this regard. Victims are sometimes arrested when law enforcement officers arrive on the scene of a domestic violence incident, regardless of whether or not they have committed a crime (Wessler, 2011). Under Secure Communities, if these women are also out of legal immigration status, they are likely to be detained by ICE and subsequently deported. Director of Homeland Security Janet Napolitano has assured Congress and the public that DHS has instructed ICE officials to do everything they can to de-prioritize these cases, and to disseminate information about U visas—visas available to some crime victims—as a way of addressing this problem. However, as the AIC and AILA report shows, these directives have had little tangible impact.

REMOVAL DEFERMENT FOR IMMIGRANTS BROUGHT TO THE UNITED STATES AS CHILDREN

President Obama touted his administration's June 2012 policy change, intended to offer relief to young people brought to the United States as children, as both just and fair (Obama, 2012). He rightly argued that it is a miscarriage of justice to punish young people for choices made for them when they were minors. However, the new policy is deeply problematic in its own right. This new scheme institutionalizes a notion that young immigrants who are out of legal status by no fault of their own can still be discriminated against based on, among other things, their level of education. That is, while we might all agree that these young immigrants are not morally culpable for being in the United States without authorization, under the new policy they still must prove their moral worth before being granted reprieve. Only those young people determined to be "good" or desirable immigrants will be granted deportation deferment and the chance to apply for a work permit. Those without the requisite level of education or delineated patriotic sacrifice and those with a criminal record are deemed undesirable and unworthy of this consideration, irrespective of the fact that they, too, are not to blame for their immigration status. This reinforces a good immigrant/bad immigrant dichotomy. The institutionalization of these kinds of narratives ultimately reinforces systems of discrimination and injustice rooted in stereotypes about immigrants.

This policy also poses another set of problems for young, unauthorized immigrants. Applying for this temporary deferment of removal requires the immigrants in question to make their presence in the country know to immigration officials and to reapply for a continuance of deferment every 2 years. However, given that this is an administrative policy, there is no guarantee that it will continue under future presidential administrations. If the policy is discontinued in the future, former beneficiaries who revealed themselves to immigration officials will likely find that they are at even greater risk of deportation than before. President Obama (2012) said, "This is a temporary stopgap measure that lets us focus our resources wisely while giving a degree of relief and hope to talented, driven, patriotic young people." But it is precisely the temporary nature of this policy that renders it fraught with danger for the young people it is intended to help.

PRIORITIZATION OF CRIMINALS UNDER SECURE COMMUNITIES: CIVIL VERSUS CRIMINAL VIOLATORS

While immigration is often framed as a criminal issue, it is not actually a federal crime to be in U.S. territory without authorization. Approximately 40 percent of all unauthorized immigrants in the United States came to the country with a visa (e.g., tourist visas, student visas) and then subsequently overstayed the terms of that visa. A person who overstays her or his visa is considered to be out of legal status and unlawfully present, which is a deportable administrative offense, but not a crime. The other estimated 60 percent of unauthorized immigrants, referred to as entrants without inspection (EWI), have entered the country without going through the proper channels, which is a misdemeanor offense under federal law (Motomura, 2012, p. 1828). Multiple entries without inspection is considered to be a more serious crime under immigration law. As the Obama administration is keen to point out, drug smugglers, human traffickers, and other violent offenders are among those likely to be repeat offenders in this regard. However, migrant laborers make up the majority of repeat offenders. This distinction is important for a number of reasons in the context of the administration's declared emphasis on the deportation of immigrant criminals. The categories of "criminal" and "violent offender" are often conflated in defense of the administration's large-scale deportation policies. However, while many of those deported as "criminals" are indeed violent offenders, many more are actually migrant laborers who came to the United States for work.

According to numbers produced by the Department of Homeland Security, 90.5 percent of those deported in fiscal year 2011 fell into the first three categories of the ICE prioritization scheme—immigrants convicted of crimes, repeat unauthorized entrants, and unauthorized border crossers and immigrant fugitives—though only 54.6 percent of those removed were convicted criminal offenders. Of the 216,698 people deported for criminal offenses in fiscal year 2011, only 6,967 were convicted of homicides or sexual offenses, 44,653 were convicted of drug offenses (broadly categorized), and an additional 35,927 were convicted of driving under the influence. Those categorized as "drug offenders" range from traffickers and dealers to small-scale pushers and addicts, not all of whom ought to be classified as the "worst of the worst." According to ICE Removal Statistics from fiscal year 2010, those convicted of entering without inspection one or more times, violating a deportation order, committing certain traffic offenses, or committing some form of identity fraud are all classified as convicted criminal offenders. While the "worst of the worst" may indeed be the highest priority cases for the Obama administration, they by no means make up the majority of those deported. It is misleading for the administration to tout the number of "criminals" deported without distinguishing between nonviolent and violent criminals, as officials have done in many agency reports and in interviews with the news media. This is particularly true given that the official justification for the increase in deportations has been a supposed focus on public safety and national security.

STATE INVOLVEMENT IN THE ENFORCEMENT OF FEDERAL IMMIGRATION LAW

The notion of security, be it national security or community-level public safety, has been a mainstay justification for a panoply of immigration policies. The Obama administration has used this kind of rhetoric as well, citing a need to focus immigration enforcement efforts on hardened immigrant criminals of all stripes in the name of national security and public safety. However, this position overlooks one very important aspect of public safety: the level of trust between law enforcement agencies and the communities they serve. An unintended consequence of the Secure Communities initiative is that it has fostered suspicion and mistrust, driving a wedge between immigrant communities and local law enforcement agencies (Gavett, 2011b).

When immigrants see local police as enforcers of immigration law, rather than as protectors of the community, they will be much less likely to reach out to the police for help when they need it. Even if Secure Communities were successful in removing violent immigrant criminals, this kind of fear and mistrust between immigrant communities and the local police ultimately hampers law enforcement efforts and decreases public safety (Gavett, 2011b). The disintegration of this relationship results in increased crime in these communities, and in an increased vulnerability of these communities.

ALLEGATIONS OF ABUSE IN IMMIGRANT DETENTION FACILITIES

Hundreds of thousands of immigrants pass through the nationwide network of publicly and privately operated immigrant detention facilities each year. A report filed by the Inter-American Commission on Human Rights, and a series of investigative reports by PBS *Frontline*, the American Civil Liberties Union (ACLU), Amnesty International, *The New York Times*, and others have made clear that detainee abuse and maltreatment in U.S. immigration detention facilities is endemic. A document request filed by the ACLU and others under the Freedom of Information Act in 2011 revealed that there were roughly 170 formal complaints of sexual abuse in immigrant detention facilities between 2008 and 2011. According to a PBS *Frontline* investigation into the abuse reports, few were ever thoroughly investigated, and fewer still led to disciplinary action or criminal charges. It is well known that sexual abuse is an underreported crime, so it is safe to assume that there have been more cases of sexual violence than have been reported through official channels. The reports also conclude that there have been hundreds of allegations of physical and verbal abuse, including racially motivated violence committed against detainees. Evidence compiled in these reports suggests that officials have, in some instances, attempted to cover up detainee abuse by rushing the deportation process for the victim in question.

When questioned on the matter during a hearing of the Senate Judiciary Committee in October 2011, Secretary of Homeland Security Janet Napolitano stressed that DHS was working on improving oversight of the facilities and spreading information about U visas, which are sometimes issued to crime victims in exchange for their cooperation in the prosecution of those crimes (Gavett, 2011a). However, there has been no sustained effort to address the institutionalized nature of the violence, which is at least partially enabled by the failure of the state to ensure due process and access to counsel for detainees. The problem is compounded by the fact that immigrant detention facilities are not required to comply with the Prison Rape Elimination Act, which was specifically designed to address widespread issues of sexual abuse in the U.S. prison system (Rentz, 2011).

RACIAL PROFILING IN IMMIGRATION LAW ENFORCEMENT

According to an October 2011 study conducted by scholars at the Warren Institute on Law and Social Policy at the University of California, Berkeley Law School, there are other reasons to be concerned about the Obama administration's enforcement policies. The study found that, while Latinos constitute only about 77 percent of the total population of unauthorized immigrants in the United States, they make up 93 percent of those arrested under Secure Communities (Kohli et al., 2011). This raises questions regarding how local law enforcement and ICE officials are targeting those suspected of being unauthorized immigrants. Racial profiling is a documented problem in immigration enforcement. In a particularly high-profile example, the Maricopa County Sheriff's Department—under the infamous Sheriff Joe Arpaio—was investigated by the U.S. Justice Department for targeting Latinos in its policing efforts.

Given the way in which the Secure Communities program operates, even if a person is arrested under false pretenses, they can be funneled into ICE custody and deported without ever being given the opportunity to challenge their original arrest. The Berkeley study also estimates that Secure Communities has so far led to the arrests of about 3,600 U.S. citizens. Once arrested by ICE, a person must demonstrate that they have authorization to be in the country, which is information that should theoretically be in the agency's databases already. However, DHS records are not always up to date, which is problematic for recently naturalized citizens, especially if they do not happen to have proof of citizenship with them at the time of arrest (Kohli, Markowitz, & Chavez, 2011). In the United States, citizens are not required to carry proof of citizenship, or any other kind of identification, with them at all times, and they cannot be deported regardless of where they were born. However, as a result of racial profiling, recently naturalized Latinos have reason to fear that they may still be subject to detention and deportation simply because they are Latino.

Racial profiling is unconstitutional, and the Obama administration has responded to the Arizona case by revoking the Maricopa County Sheriff's Office's authority to check the immigration status of prisoners (Lacey, 2011). While this is an appropriate punitive reaction in this case, it fails to address the larger systemic problem. With 93 percent of those arrested under Secure Communities being Latino, it is fair to say that Maricopa County is not the only place where Latinos are being targeted. This raises larger questions about the method by which suspected unauthorized immigrants are coming into contact with ICE. As UCLA law professor Hiroshi Motomura argues, under Secure Communities, the most important opportunity for discretion is at the time of arrest (Motomura, 2011), but the program fails to account for the reality of racial profiling on the part of some local law enforcement officers. That is, as long as the decision as to whether or not to arrest a given individual lies with local law enforcement, ICE will be unable to adequately address issues of racial profiling.

Similarly, administration efforts to enable immigration prosecutors to exercise discretion regarding when they do or do not pursue deportation also fail to account for racial profiling in local arrest procedures, particularly in cases where the immigrant in question is denied legal representation. This line of reasoning draws into question the basic mechanism by which the Secure Communities program brings suspected unauthorized immigrants into contact with federal immigration authorities. While the administration may find racial profiling unethical and unconstitutional, it lacks the ability to account for it under this program.

CONCLUSION

None of the challenges presented in this Counterpoint section assume that immigration law per se is incompatible with embracing the United States as a "nation of immigrants." Law, as a broader concept, is indeed compatible with immigration; one could even argue that the category of "immigrant" would not exist without the legal frameworks that define it. However, this does not mean that any given law is just or ethical. Individual laws should not, therefore, be taken for granted, without critical examination, as either constitutional or compatible with American national values. While the United States may be a nation of immigrants and a nation of laws, it is to the benefit of neither the nation nor its legal institutions to allow any given law to exist unscrutinized. The deportation and detention policies of the Obama administration are no exception, and to say that they are deserving of scrutiny is to show respect for both the immigrants subject to these laws and the constitutional and societal values of the United States.

While laws as such are not incompatible with the United States' values and immigrant heritage, the same cannot be said of the specific deportation and detention policies of the Obama administration. Comprehensive reform is necessary to address deep systemic issues with U.S. immigration law, but the administration's attempts to signal its willingness to make political compromises in this regard do not make sense in light of intense political partisanship in the 112th Congress. The administration's hard-line deportation and detention policies, meant in part as a concession to congressional Republicans, have hampered local public safety and contributed to systemic injustice.

References and Further Reading

Alonzo, A., Chen, G., Kim, S., & Lawrence, B. (2011). *Holding DHS accountable on prosecutorial discretion.* Retrieved from http://www .aila.org/content/default.aspx?docid=37615

American Civil Liberties Union. (2011). *Documents obtained by ACLU show sexual abuse of immigration detainees is widespread national problem.* Retrieved from http://www.aclu.org/immigrants-rights-prisoners-rights-prisoners-rights/documents-obtained-aclu-show-sexual-abuse

Department of Homeland Security. (2010). *Immigration enforcement actions: 2010.* Retrieved from http://www.dhs.gov/files/statistics/ publications/immigration-enforcement-actions-2010.shtm

Gavett, G. (2011a, October 20). Sec. Napolitano questioned about "Lost in Detention" [PBS *Frontline*]. Retrieved from http://www.pbs .org/wgbh/pages/frontline/race-multicultural/lost-in-detention/sec-napolitano-questioned-about-lost-in-detention

Gavett, G. (2011b). Why three governors challenged secure communities [PBS *Frontline*]. Retrieved from http://www.pbs.org/wgbh/ pages/frontline/race-multicultural/lost-in-detention/why-three-governors-challenged-secure-communities/?utm_campaign=vide oplayer&utmmedium=fullplayer&utm_source=relatedlink

Kohli, A., Markowitz, P. L., & Chavez, L. (2011). *Secure communities by the numbers: An analysis of demographics and due process.* Berkeley, CA: The Chief Justice Earl Warren Institute on Law and Social Policy at the University of California, Berkeley Law School. Retrieved from http://www.law.berkeley.edu/files/Secure_Communities_by_the_Numbers.pdf

Lacey, M. (2011, December 15). U.S. finds pervasive bias against Latinos by Arizona sheriff. *The New York Times.* Retrieved from http://www.nytimes.com/2011/12/16/us/arizona-sheriffs-office-unfairly-targeted-latinos-justice-department-says.html

Motomura, H. (2011). The discretion that matters: Federal immigration enforcement, state and local arrest, and the civil-criminal line. *UCLA Law Review, 58,* 1819–1858.

Obama, B. (2011, May). *Remarks by the President on comprehensive immigration reform in El Paso, Texas.* Retrieved from http://www.whitehouse.gov/the-press-office/2011/05/10/remarks-president-comprehensive-immigration-reform-el-paso-texas

Obama, B. (2012, June). *Remarks by the President on immigration in Washington, D.C.* Retrieved from http://www.whitehouse.gov/the-press-office/2012/06/15/remarks-president-immigration

Organization of American States: Inter-American Commission on Human Rights. (2010). *Report on immigration in the United States: Detention and due process.* Retrieved from http://cidh.org/pdf%20files/ReportOnImmigrationInTheUnited%20States-DetentionAndDueProcess.pdf

Passel, J. S., & Cohn, D. (2011). *Unauthorized immigrant population: National and state trends, 2010.* Washington, DC: Pew Research Center.

PBS. (2011, October 18). Cecilia Muñoz: "Even broken laws have to be enforced" [*Frontline: Lost in detention*]. Retrieved from http://www.pbs.org/wgbh/pages/frontline/race-multicultural/lost-in-detention/cecilia-munoz-even-broken-laws-have-to-be-enforced

PBS Investigative Reporting Workshop, & *Frontline.* (2011). *Lost in detention.* Retrieved from http://www.pbs.org/wgbh/pages/frontline/lost-in-detention

Preston, J. (2012, January 19). In deportation policy test, 1 in 6 offered reprieve. *The New York Times.* Retrieved from http://www.nytimes.com/2012/01/20/us/in-test-of-deportation-policy-1-in-6-offered-reprieve.html?_r=1

Rentz, C. (2011). How much sexual abuse gets "lost in detention?" *Frontline*/PBS. Retrieved from http://www.pbs.org/wgbh/pages/frontline/race-multicultural/lost-in-detention/how-much-sexual-abuse-gets-lost-in-detention

Taylor, P., Lopez, P. M., Passel, J., & Motel, S. (2011). *Unauthorized immigrants: Length of residency, patterns of parenthood.* Washington, DC: Pew Research Center.

U.S. Immigration and Customs Enforcement. (2011). *Memorandum: Exercising prosecutorial discretion consistent with the civil immigration enforcement priorities of the Agency for the Apprehension, Detention, and Removal of Aliens.* Retrieved from http://www.ice.gov/doclib/secure-communities/pdf/prosecutorial-discretion-memo.pdf

U.S. Immigration and Customs Enforcement. (2011). *Prosecutorial discretion: Certain victims, witnesses, and plaintiffs.* Retrieved from http://www.ice.gov/doclib/secure-communities/pdf/domestic-violence.pdf

U.S. Immigration and Customs Enforcement. (2011). *Removal statistics.* Retrieved from http://www.ice.gov/removal-statistics/

U.S. Immigration and Customs Enforcement. (2011). *Secure communities.* Retrieved from http://www.ice.gov/secure_communities/

Wessler, S. F. (2011). *Shattered families: The perilous intersection of immigration enforcement and the child welfare system.* Retrieved from http://act.colorlines.com/acton/form/1069/0041:d-0001/0/index.htm

Kathryn Miller

11

Arizona's S.B. 1070

POINT: S.B. 1070 provides an important tool for law enforcement in a state that is currently overwhelmed with illegal immigrants; with proper training, police will be able to use this law to identify and detain illegal aliens without infringing on the rights of others.

Calvin L. Lewis, Texas Tech University School of Law

COUNTERPOINT: S.B. 1070 fails as a model for immigration control. The law invites discrimination, harassment, and racial profiling, while also being expensive and ineffectual.

Roberto Suro, University of Southern California

Introduction

Perhaps no piece of recent immigration legislation has received as much press—and as much controversy—as has Arizona's Senate Bill 1070, also known as S.B. 1070 or the "Support Our Law Enforcement and Safe Neighborhoods Act." The law, passed on April 23, 2010, gave local police the authority to check the immigration status of people during routine arrests (such as traffic stops) and to detain or arrest people who were found to be undocumented. S.B. 1070 immediately drew accusations that it would lead to widespread racial profiling and was parodied in the media as the "show me your papers" act.

But as Calvin Lewis writes in the Point essay, the law specifically prohibits "illegal consideration of race, color, or national origin," and technically only attempts to penalize crimes that are already recognized as such under federal law. S.B. 1070, according to its supporters, is only doing what the federal government has either been unable or unwilling to do.

Lewis summarizes the major sections of the law and makes an argument for why the law is reasonable: illegal immigration has a negative impact on the United States; Arizona disproportionately suffers from illegal immigration; federal enforcement laws have been inadequate; and federal authorities have less at stake than state authorities. He responds to the complaints of racial profiling and violations of civil rights and to the claim that federal immigration law "preempts" S.B. 1070. He also looks to history, finding much evidence that immigration regulation has often been a mix of federal and local control. Finally, he addresses the claims that S.B. 1070 will deter crime reporting among Hispanics fearful of being interrogated about their immigration status, and the claims that S.B. 1070 will damage U.S. relations with other countries and will take resources from other important police responsibilities. Lewis comes down firmly on the side that S.B. 1070 is a good and reasonable law and that it is possible to follow it and still avoid, for instance, racial profiling.

Roberto Suro, on the other hand, writes in the Counterpoint section that the law is flawed in three ways: 1, it shifts responsibility for regulation of immigration from Washington, D.C. to the states; 2, it makes it relatively easy for police officers and other government officials to commit civil rights violations; and 3, it would be costly and ineffective policy.

Suro finds that S.B. 1070 wrongly—and perhaps dangerously—preempts federal law. He feels that it "hinders Washington's immigration policies." As an example, he points to how the "sheer volume" of information requests regarding immigration status to the federal authorities would cause those agencies to shift their priorities—possibly from something as critical as looking at human smuggling operations or false employment documents and instead looking at the immigration status of people arrested for driving while intoxicated. He argues that it is vastly more efficient to focus energies on the first type of problem than on the second.

Suro also argues that Arizona's role as a border state must be considered when looking at this policy—the United States currently has relatively good relationships with Mexico, but Arizona's law, Suro believes, could "impede the federal government's ability to conduct foreign policy on behalf of the entire country."

On June 25, 2012, the Supreme Court struck down three of the four major provisions of S.B. 1070 but kept in place the most controversial part: the right of local law enforcement to check immigration status of those suspected of being in the country illegally, even if the initial reason for the police encounter itself is unrelated to immigration. This, of course, begs the question of who would be suspected of being here illegally and thus continues to inspire accusations that racial profiling will result. Tellingly, both Republican Governor Jan Brewer and President Obama have found elements of the decision to criticize and celebrate, despite the fact that the Supreme Court largely ruled on behalf of federal interests. Indeed, the majority of the Supreme Court expressed strong skepticism about whether local officers in the field would apply judgments in an egalitarian and legal way. As other states gear up to pass their own Arizona-like laws, future judicial review seems inevitable.

When you read this chapter, consider: What is the potential for civil rights violations, whether or not they are prohibited by S.B. 1070? Also consider the issue of state supremacy versus federal laws: How might the law cause ripple effects from state agencies to federal ones? What might be the unintended consequences of this law, even as amended by the Supreme Court's recent decision? Given the failures of the federal government to agree upon a nationwide solution, what can states that bear an unfair burden of undocumented immigrants do to combat this problem?

POINT

Notwithstanding the Supreme Court's June 2012 decision invalidating portions of this law (*Arizona v. United States*, 2012), the Support Our Law Enforcement and Safe Neighborhoods Act, commonly known as S.B. 1070, is a reasonable and measured approach to the problems caused by illegal immigrants within the state of Arizona. As a border state, Arizona suffers disproportionately from the social and economic problems caused by illegal immigration. S.B. 1070 was enacted in direct response to these problems and out of frustration at the federal government's failure to adequately respond to the problems. Claims by opponents that S.B. 1070 will lead to racial profiling are misplaced. The law specifically prohibits illegal consideration of race, color, or national origin, and Governor Jan Brewer signed an executive order directing that law enforcement officials receive training to ensure they avoid illegal racial profiling. Similarly, claims that S.B. 1070 encourages the abuse of civil liberties, conflicts with existing federal law, discourages crime reporting by illegal immigrants, interferes with international relations, and takes law enforcement resources away from more important police responsibilities are all without merit. S.B. 1070 simply penalizes what are already crimes under federal law, crimes that the federal government has been unable or unwilling to enforce. As one of the states most affected by illegal immigration, Arizona was more than justified in passing S.B. 1070.

SUMMARY OF THE LAW

Essentially, S.B. 1070 has six major sections.

1. *Purpose of the law.* Section 1 states simply the purpose of the law, which is to discourage and deter illegal immigrants from entering Arizona, remaining in the state, or engaging in economic activity within the state.

2. *Enforcement of federal immigration law.* Section 2 requires law enforcement officers to make a reasonable attempt, when practicable, to determine an individual's immigration status during the course of any police stop, detention, or arrest. Such a determination requires "reasonable suspicion" that the person is unlawfully present in the United States. Section 2 also requires that all persons who are arrested have their immigration status verified prior to release, and that state officials contact immigration enforcement officials whenever an unlawfully present alien is discharged or assessed a fine after being convicted of a crime. This provision was not invalidated by the Supreme Court's ruling in *Arizona v. United States*, although the provision is subject to further litigation to determine its constitutionality.

3. *Failure to carry alien registration document.* Section 3 makes it a state crime to willfully fail to complete or carry an alien registration document. Such willful failure will only be a crime if it also violates federal law. This provision was declared unconstitutional by the *Arizona v. United States* decision on the grounds that it is preempted by federal law.

4. *Human smuggling.* Section 4 makes it a state crime to smuggle humans into the United States for profit or commercial purposes. Human smuggling has long been a federal crime.

5. *Unlawfully picking up passengers for work and unlawfully transporting or harboring unlawful aliens.* Section 5 makes it a crime for the occupant of a vehicle that is stopped on the street to attempt to hire or pick up passengers for work at a different location if that vehicle blocks or impedes traffic, and it makes it a crime for a person to enter such a vehicle. Section 5 also makes it a crime for illegally present aliens to solicit work in a public place, knowingly apply for work, or otherwise perform work in the state. In addition, Section 5 makes is illegal to transport or harbor unlawfully present aliens within the state. Subsection 5(C) of this provision was invalidated by the Supreme Court in *Arizona v. United States* on the grounds that it is preempted by federal law.

6. *Authority to make arrests without a warrant.* Finally, Section 6 authorizes a police officer to make an arrest without an arrest warrant if the officer has probable cause to believe the person has committed a crime that makes the person deportable under federal immigration law. "Deportable" means that the person may be involuntarily removed from the United States. This provision was also invalidated by the Supreme Court's *Arizona v. United States* decision.

Collectively, the provisions of S.B. 1070 represented a very aggressive state scheme to enforce immigration laws by discouraging and deterring illegal immigrants from entering or remaining in Arizona.

WHY S.B. 1070 IS REASONABLE

Illegal immigration has a negative impact on the United States. Few would argue that illegal immigration does not have a negative impact on the United States. According to the Department of Homeland Security, as of January 2010, 10.8 million unauthorized immigrants were living in the United States (Hoefer, Rytina, & Baker, 2010). Certainly, many of these illegal immigrants are hardworking, law-abiding, tax-paying members of society who contribute to the welfare and economic vitality of this country. At the same time, many live in poverty and use social welfare programs such as food stamps and Medicaid; many attend public schools; and others commit crimes, often resulting in costly incarceration in state or federal penal institutions. Robert Rector, a noted economist, estimated that in 2007 alone the net fiscal cost imposed on all levels of government by illegal immigrants was approximately $90 billion a year (Rector, 2007). These costs are borne by the taxpayers and add to the economic woes already besetting the United States. For these reasons and others, federal law has long regulated the flow of noncitizens into the country. These regulations impose strict limits on the number, categories, and conditions for admission of noncitizens into the United States. This ensures that the nation can absorb these new individuals without any adverse impact. Individuals who enter the country illegally undercut this well-designed system of regulating the flow of noncitizens into the United States. For this reason, illegal immigration is a violation of federal law and is the basis for a robust federal law enforcement structure that involves agencies such as the Department of Homeland Security and the Department of Justice.

Arizona disproportionately suffers the impact of illegal immigration. As a border state, Arizona has one of the fastest growing illegal immigrant populations in the nation. The Department of Homeland Security estimates that the illegal immigrant population in Arizona increased from 330,000 in 2000 to 470,000 by 2010, a 42 percent increase in a mere 10 years (Hoefer et al., 2010). Statistics from 2007, compiled by the Center for Immigration Studies, revealed the following information regarding illegal immigrants and their U.S.-born children who live in Arizona: (1) 73 percent lived in or near poverty, (2) 32 percent used one or more of the major welfare programs (cash assistance, food assistance, or Medicaid), (3) they constituted 37 percent of uninsured individuals in the state, (4) they constituted 16 percent of the school-age population in the state, and (5) they constituted 11.1 percent of the prison population. Clearly, these figures demonstrate the adverse impact that illegal immigration has on the state of Arizona, resulting in state expenditures ranging from law enforcement to education costs to emergency medical care. Not surprisingly, the biggest expenditure is the cost of providing K–12 education for children from illegal immigrant households (Rector, 2007). All told, the estimated costs of providing public services to illegal immigrants in Arizona is $1.3 billion a year, a fiscal burden that falls predominantly on the state of Arizona, giving the state a tremendous incentive to discourage and deter illegal immigration. S.B. 1070 is a response to this problem.

Federal enforcement of immigration laws has been inadequate. Notwithstanding a robust federal law enforcement structure that includes the substantial resources of the Department of Homeland Security and the Department of Justice, the problem of illegal immigration has proved difficult to control. Both sides of the political spectrum in Congress seem to agree that the immigration system is broken. Unfortunately, consensus appears to stop at this point, as Congress has been unable to agree on just how to address the problem, leaving the individual states to shoulder the socioeconomic burden of illegal immigration. This congressional inactivity is particularly frustrating for border states like Arizona that absorb the lion's share of the costs of this problem.

Federal authorities have less at stake than state authorities. Congressional inaction can be explained at least in part by the fact that the federal government and state governments have different interests when it comes to immigration. The federal government's interest in immigration is essentially about retaining central control over admission into this country (Chin, 2011). Centralized federal control provides the efficiency and uniformity needed in the formal admissions and removal process (Rodriguez, 2008). Without such unifying control, each state could enact its own laws controlling immigration, resulting in a patchwork of laws and procedures that would be unworkable in determining admission into the United States. Centralized federal control also allows consideration of international and diplomatic aspects of immigration law, and permits the federal government to mitigate the consequences of any discriminatory practices or undue influence by state and local governments (Chin, 2011). Economically speaking, illegal immigration means the federal government enjoys the addition of scores of unauthorized younger workers who underpin the retirement system by paying an estimated $7 billion a year into Medicare and Social Security, the majority of which will go unclaimed, resulting in a "fiscal windfall" for the federal government (Cunningham-Parmeter, 2011).

The states, on the other hand, have different compelling interests in immigration. Unlike the federal government, states are tasked with providing expensive public services to the illegal immigrant community, including emergency health care, law enforcement assistance, public education, and municipal services. For example, federal law requires that the children of illegal immigrants be provided a public education for grades K–12 (*Plyler v. Doe,* 1982), and federal law requires hospitals to provide emergency medical care to everyone seeking such services (Emergency Medical Treatment and Labor Act, 1986). Moreover, there is the economic and social impact that criminal activities have on state and local communities when committed by illegal aliens. Peter Schuck (2000), a leading commentator on this subject, explains the inequality between federal and state interests as a "fiscal mismatch," wherein the tax revenues generated by immigrants flow to Washington while the costs of illegal immigration are borne mainly by the states. As a result, states do not share in the same fiscal bounty as the federal government, and thus have a more pressing need to act in order to limit or control the draining effects of the illegal community.

Considering the differing interests of the federal and states government, the states sued the federal government to compel federal action to relieve some of the pressure (Rau & Rough, 2011). Unfortunately, the states lost the case, and S.B. 1070 is the follow-on action by the state of Arizona to identify illegal immigrants, remove them from the state, and discourage their return. Not surprisingly, many other states have followed Arizona's example by adopting similar legislation aimed at discouraging illegal immigration (Immigration Policy Project, National Conference of State Legislators, 2011). At least one state, Alabama, has adopted legislation that is even more aggressive that S.B. 1070.

RESPONDING TO THE CRITICISM

Violation of civil rights: Racial profiling. Perhaps the most frequent concern voiced by opponents of S.B. 1070 is that it will result in racial profiling; that is, that Hispanic residents of Arizona will be disproportionately targeted for interrogation, detention, and arrest on suspicion of being unlawfully present in the United States or not having proper immigration paperwork. This concern is raised in part because the vast majority of illegal immigrants in Arizona come from Mexico and other Spanish-speaking countries in South and Central America. With Hispanics making up the bulk of illegal immigrants, the fear is that S.B. 1070 could lead to wrongful interrogation and detention of U.S. citizens of Hispanic origin, as well as other Hispanics lawfully in the country.

Fortunately, this has been addressed in several ways so that it is no longer a valid concern. First and foremost, Arizona House Bill 2162, passed within a week of S.B. 1070, explicitly prohibits consideration of race, color, or national origin except as permitted by the United States and Arizona Constitutions. In interpreting the extent to which race may be considered, the United States and Arizona Supreme Courts have held that race may be considered in enforcing immigration laws, but race alone is not a sufficient basis to stop or arrest individuals (*United States v. Brignoni-Ponce,* 1975; *State v. Graciano,* 1982). Hence, Arizona law enforcement officials are forced to consider factors other than race as indicators of immigration violations and are prohibited by law from making unlawful stops and arrests when race is the only basis for the action (*United States v. Martinez-Fuerte,* 1976).

Second, police may only investigate immigration status incident to a "lawful stop, detention or arrest." In other words, there must be some other lawful reason for the initial stop other than the suspected immigration status of the individual detained. Hence, even if a police officer suspects an individual of being in the country illegally, the officer may not inquire about the person's immigration status unless there has been some other lawful basis for the stop. Third, in signing S.B. 1070 into law, Governor Brewer vowed that law enforcement officials would be properly trained to ensure they know what racial profiling is and how to avoid it, and she signed an executive order requiring law enforcement officials to receive training on how to implement S.B. 1070 to avoid such racial profiling. Finally, the risk of racial profiling has always existed within the criminal justice system, especially in illegal drug cases, and there is no absolute way to prevent it. That the risk of racial profiling exists does not justify invalidating S.B. 1070, especially given the proper and reasonable measures taken by S.B. 1070 and H.B. 2162 to minimize its existence. To invalidate S.B. 1070 on this basis alone would imperil the legitimacy of all criminal laws where racial profiling is possible.

Significantly, the Supreme Court refused to invalidate Section 2(B) of S.B. 1070, which was the primary basis for complaints of racial profiling (*Arizona v. United States,* 2012). While the issue may resurface in a future case, this argument against S.B. 1070 has failed for now.

Violation of civil rights: Requirement to carry immigration papers. A second objection often made to S.B. 1070 is that Section 3 of the law violates the civil rights of Arizona residents by requiring them to produce proof that they are lawfully within the state. Actually, the text of the law simply makes it a misdemeanor to willfully fail to carry an alien registration document when required to do so by federal immigration law. Importantly, federal law requires noncitizens 14 years of age or older who are in the country for more than 30 days to register with the federal government and to carry these registration documents with them at all times (8 U.S.C. 1302 and 1304e). S.B. 1070 merely restates the federal law and makes it a misdemeanor under state law for an alien to be in the state without such documents. In response to those critics fearful that ordinary citizens and persons lawfully in the country would be subject to arrest and detention for failure to show proof of legal status, S.B. 1070 makes it extremely easy to establish one's legal status. In fact, the law presumes a person to not be an alien unlawfully present in the United States if the person provides any of the following to the law enforcement official: a valid Arizona driver's license, a valid Arizona nonoperating identification license, a valid tribal enrollment card or other tribal identification, or any valid federal, state, or local government-issued identification. Granted, it is possible that a personal lawfully present in the United States could be found without any of these documents, but the likelihood of such an occurrence is rare, and the individual could still establish legal residency by other methods. In any event, Section 3 of S.B. 1070 mirrors federal law and is therefore no more onerous than federal law already on the books.

Nevertheless, the Supreme Court ruled in *Arizona v. United States* that Congress regulates this field so comprehensively that it leaves no room for states to regulate. Accordingly, Section 3 was struck down, notwithstanding its obvious merit in the fight against illegal immigration.

Federal preemption. A third claim made by critics is that S.B. 1070 is "preempted" by federal immigration law. In other words, opponents of S.B. 1070 argue that it conflicts with federal law because *only* the federal government may regulate immigration. Hence, they claim, S.B. 1070 is an illegal attempt by the state of Arizona to regulate an area exclusively within the authority of the federal government and outside the power of state governments to regulate. The concept of preemption derives from the supremacy clause of the U.S. Constitution, which states that federal law is the supreme "law of the land," and individual states cannot enact laws that supersede federal laws, nor can they have the intent or the effect of overriding federal laws. In the case of S.B. 1070, the issue is whether this state immigration law is preempted by the federal Immigration and Nationality Act, which is a comprehensive set of federal statutes that control immigration.

The Supreme Court has conclusively stated that the power to regulate immigration is unquestionably exclusively a federal power (*Fong Yue Ting v. United States,* 1893). However, the Court has never held that every state enactment that in any way deals with aliens is a regulation of immigration and thus preempted by the supremacy clause (*De Canas v. Bica,* 1976). States can and have promulgated laws in the area of immigration without being preempted by federal immigration regulation. One such example is the Legal Arizona Workers Act, an Arizona statute requiring employers to use the federal E-Verify program to confirm that all new hires are legally employable in the United States or face harsh penalties for noncompliance. Controversial and groundbreaking when it was initially passed, this Arizona state law has withstood multiple court challenges.

In addition, a review of immigration regulation reveals a rich history of laws favoring a mix of federal and local control. In the past, partnerships between local and federal agencies authorized local law enforcement personnel to investigate and detain persons suspected of violating selected provisions of federal immigration law, assisting in their transfer to federal facilities and commencement of removal proceedings. Indeed, section 287(g) of the federal Immigration and Nationality Act expressly authorizes cooperative agreements between the federal government and state and local officials in enforcing federal immigration regulations.

This federal preemption argument was the main thrust of the federal government case in *Arizona v. United States,* and this argument prevailed on all of the issues except with respect to Section 2(B). Very importantly, it was Section 2(B) that raised the most rancor among opponents of S.B. 1070. Section 2(B) is the provision that requires law enforcement officers to make a reasonable attempt, when practicable, to determine an individual's immigration status during the course of any police stop, detention, or arrest. It was this provision that brought forth claims that S.B. 1070 would lead to racial profiling and other civil rights violations. Yet it was this provision that the Supreme Court refused to invalidate absent a greater showing of unconstitutionality.

Deterrence of crime reporting. Another criticism of S.B. 1070 is that it will discourage Hispanics from reporting crimes or serving as crime witnesses in court. Specifically, the concern is that Hispanics will fear that reporting crimes or serving as witnesses in court will subject them to interrogation regarding their immigration status, or cause them to be detained under the provisions of S.B. 1070 (Cooper, 2010). There is particular concern that S.B. 1070 will make women more vulnerable to domestic abuse because they will fear that reporting the abuse to law enforcement authorities will lead to deportation (Montini, 2010). While this is a valid concern, it is the same concern that any crime victim or witness will have if such person has violated the law. For example, an assault victim high on illegal drugs who has been seriously injured must decide whether or not to seek medical attention for the injuries at an emergency room, and thereby risk being arrested for illegal drug use. Given the high likelihood that law enforcement authorities will discover the illegal drug use, the victim is caught on the horns of a dilemma not unlike that of the illegal immigrant who is the victim of domestic abuse. While this dilemma is regrettable, it is not the role of government to provide a safe haven for illegal immigrants, even when the illegal immigrant is a crime victim.

Interference with international relations. S.B. 1070 has also been criticized as damaging U.S. relations with other countries in the region. This criticism emanates from concerns expressed by government officials in Mexico and several other countries in South and Central America that their citizens living in Arizona would be subject to harassment and human rights violations (Booth, 2010). These claims, of course, have no merit. No provision of S.B. 1070 involves harassment or a violation of human rights. S.B. 1070 merely enforces federal immigration law, about which the foreign officials have not complained. Interestingly, Mexico has a law that is very similar to S.B. 1070, and its enforcement is reported to involve racial profiling, harassment, and shakedowns (Hawley, 2010).

Taking law enforcement resources from more important police responsibilities. A final recurring criticism of S.B. 1070 is that it diverts critically needed law enforcement resources from combating more serious crimes (Cooper, 2010). The simple response to this criticism is that Arizona officials have the discretion to decide the priority of resources to be given to enforcing S.B. 1070 and other crimes. If resources are insufficient to combat both serious crimes and immigration violations, officials can simply shift resources to more serious crimes. When and if resources allow, Arizona officials have the discretion to shift resources back to immigration enforcement. What is important is that the two are not mutually exclusive. Given the number of crimes committed by illegal immigrants, law enforcement resources allocated toward identifying and removing illegal immigrants from the state will logically have the added benefit of lowering the number of serious crimes.

CONCLUSION

When Governor Jan Brewer signed S.B. 1070 into law on April 23, 2010, it was a reasonable and measured approach to the problems caused by illegal immigrants within the state of Arizona. It was in direct response to the failure of the federal government to adequately address the problems caused by illegal immigrants, problems that substantially threaten the social and economic welfare of the state, which labors under the burden caused by 470,000 illegal immigrants. In total, the estimated cost of providing public services to illegal immigrants in Arizona is $1.3 billion a year, a fiscal burden that falls predominantly on the state. Notwithstanding the nationwide firestorm of controversy surrounding the law's enactment, it merely enforces federal immigration laws already on the books.

The predominant objection to S.B. 1070—that it will encourage racial profiling—is completely without merit, given the fact that Arizona subsequently passed a law specifically banning illegal racial profiling, and Governor Brewer signed an executive order requiring law enforcement officials to receive training on how to implement S.B. 1070 to avoid illegal racial profiling. Other complaints voiced by opponents against S.B. 1070 are similarly without merit. And while the Supreme Court in *Arizona v. United States* struck down three of the four provisions at issue, it left intact the provision most objected to by opponents and most important to the Arizona law: the requirement that police officials make a reasonable attempt, when practicable, to determine an individual's immigration status during the course of any police stop, detention, or arrest. Although Arizona would have preferred to keep all provisions of S.B. 1070 in its arsenal of options to combat illegal immigration, it was able to preserve the most important provision. Given the compelling need by Arizona to police its own borders, this was a significant victory.

References and Further Reading

8 U.S.C. § 1304: Forms for registration and fingerprinting.

8 U.S.C. § 1302: Registering of aliens.

Arizona v. United States, U.S. 11-182. Decided June 25, 2012. Retrieved from http://www.supremecourt.gov/opinions/slipopinions .aspx?Term=11

Booth, W. (2010, April 27). Mexican officials condemn Arizona's tough new immigration law. *The Washington Post.* Retrieved from http://www.washingtonpost.com/wp-dyn/content/article/2010/04/26/AR2010042603810.html

Camarota, S. A. (2010). *Center for immigration studies on the new Arizona immigration law, SB1070.* Retrieved from Center for Immigration Studies website: http://www.cis.org/Announcement/AZ-Immigration-SB1070

Chin, R. T. (2011). Moving toward subfederal involvement in federal immigration law. *UCLA Law Review, 58,* 1859–1912.

Cooper, J. J. (2010, May 17). Ariz. immigration law divides police across U.S. *The Associated Press.* Retrieved from http://readingeagle .com/article.aspx?id=220664

Cunningham-Parmeter, K. (2011). Forced federalism: States as laboratories of immigration reform. *Hastings Law Journal, 62*(6), 1673–1708.

De Canas v. Bica, 424 U.S. 351 (1976). Retrieved from http://supreme.justia.com/cases/federal/us/424/351

Emergency Medical Treatment and Labor Act (EMTALA), 42 U.S.C. § 1395dd (1986). Retrieved from http://www.law.cornell.edu/ uscode/text/42/1395dd

Fong Yue Ting v. United States, 149 U.S. 698 (1893). Retrieved from http://supreme.justia.com/cases/federal/us/149/698/case.html

Hawley, C. (2010, May 25). Activists blast Mexico's immigration law. *USA Today.* Retrieved from http://www.usatoday.com/news/ world/2010-05-25-mexico-migrants_N.htm

Hoefer, M., Rytina, N., & Baker, B. C. (2010). *Estimates of the unauthorized immigrant population residing in the United States: January 2010.* Retrieved from Department of Homeland Security website: http://www.dhs.gov/xlibrary/assets/statistics/publications/ ois_ill_pe_2010.pdf

Immigration Policy Project. (2011). *Immigration-related laws and resolutions in the states (January 1–December 31, 2010).* Retrieved from National Conference of State Legislators website: http://www.ncsl.org/default.aspx?tabid=21857

Kobach, K. (2010). *The Arizona immigration law: What it actually does, and why it is constitutional.* Lecture #1173. Retrieved from The Heritage Foundation website: http://www.heritage.org/research/lecture/2010/12/the-arizona-immigration-law-what-it-actually-does-and-why-it-is-constitutional

Montini, E. J. (2010, June 27). Will S.B. 1070 hinder help for abuse victims. *The Arizona Republic.* Retrieved from http://www.azcentral .com/news/articles/2010/06/27/20100627montini-arizona-immigration-law.html

Plyler v. Doe, 457 U.S. 202 (1982). Retrieved from http://caselaw.lp.findlaw.com/cgi-bin/getcase.pl?court=us&vol=457&invol=202

Racial profiling, S.B. 1070 will go hand in hand [editorial]. (2010, April 16). *Arizona Star Daily.* Retrieved from http://azstarnet.com/ news/opinion/editorial/article_a10573e6-03dd-5c13-b345-a84a74fb47ed.html

Rau, A. B., & Rough, G. (2011, February 11). Arizona sues feds over border security. *The Arizona Republic.* Retrieved from http://www .azcentral.com/arizonarepublic/news/articles/2011/02/11/20110211arizona-to-sue-federal-government-over-border-security.html

Rector, R. (2007, May 21). *The fiscal cost of low-skill immigrants to state and local taxpayers.* Statement before the Subcommittee on Immigration of the Committee on the Judiciary of the United States House of Representatives. Retrieved from The Heritage Foundation website: http://www.heritage.org/research/testimony/the-fiscal-cost-of-low-skill-immigrants-to-state-and-local-taxpayers

Registering of Aliens, 8 U.S.C. § 1302. Retrieved from http://www.law.cornell.edu/uscode/text/8/1302

Rodriguez, C. M. (2008). The significance of the local in immigration regulation. *Michigan Law Review, 106,* 567–572.

Schuck, Peter H. (2000). Law and the study of migration. In C. B. Brettell & J. F. Hollifield (Eds.), *Migration theory: Talking across disciplines* (pp. 187–204). New York, NY: Routledge.

State v. Graciano, 653 P.2d 683 (Ariz. 1982).

United States v. Brignoni-Ponce, 422 U.S. 873 (1975).

United States v. Martinez-Fuerte, 428 U.S. 543 (1976).

Calvin L. Lewis

COUNTERPOINT

Did Arizona create a new model for controlling illegal immigration in 2010 by enacting legislation that creates new state crimes and enforcement mechanisms? The answer is no. The Arizona immigration law is flawed in three regards. One, it unwisely shifts responsibility for the regulation of immigration from Washington to the states. Two, it creates conditions for potential civil rights violations by law enforcement personnel and other government employees. And three, if implemented, it would be bad policy—both costly and ineffective. These issues provoked lawsuits that in turn led to court action blocking implementation of the law.

In a decision issued June 25, 2012, the U.S. Supreme Court nullified key provisions of the law on constitutional grounds. By a 5–3 vote, the Court found that Arizona impinged on the federal government's superior prerogatives to set immigration policy and that state actions would interfere with the work of federal immigration agencies. The Court did not, however, take up the civil rights questions and, in fact, let stand the one provision of the Arizona law most likely to produce unlawful racial profiling—a measure requiring local police to check an individual's immigration status when there is a suspicion that person might be in the country unlawfully. Despite the Court's clear ruling on key aspects of the Arizona law, the constitutional disputes will continue to resonate in political and policy debates over immigration.

Several states have adopted or are planning to adopt copycat laws, while others envision even more aggressive action against unauthorized migrants. So long as there is dissatisfaction with the federal government's management of immigration, state and local governments will continue to seek their own means to regulate the arrival of newcomers. Meanwhile, opposition to restrictive state-level policies will serve as a rallying cry for proponents of federal legislation that would offer legalization and a path to citizenship for unauthorized migrants.

ARIZONA'S S.B. 1070: ITS ORIGINS AND ITS IMPACT

Widely known by its listing on the legislative docket, Senate Bill 1070, or more simply, S.B. 1070, the immigration law enacted in Arizona in 2010 was designed to give the state government unprecedented authority and a range of new policy tools to combat illegal immigration (National Conference of State Legislatures, July 2011). It came after more than a decade of political agitation in the state based on claims that the federal government was failing to control the border with Mexico (Doty, 2007). Whether or not those claims are valid is less relevant to this debate than the law's origins in the argument that the state government must take action because Washington is unwilling or unable to fulfill its responsibilities. Thus, the question is not whether new immigration policies are necessary or not. Politicians on all sides of the political spectrum agree that the current system is broken and a new one should take its place. They disagree fiercely over what that new system should be, however. So this debate is not over whether action is needed to control illegal immigration. Instead, the issue is whether the Arizona legislature in 2010 devised a good set of immigration policies, policies that should be implemented in Arizona and replicated elsewhere.

Arizona's S.B. 1070, the Support Our Law Enforcement and Safe Neighborhoods Act, received final legislative approval on April 19, 2010 and Governor Jan Brewer signed it into law four days later. The basic provisions created state violations and imposed tough new penalties on a range of actions related to illegal immigration that are already prohibited under federal law, such as harboring, transporting, or employing unauthorized migrants. Going a step further, S.B. 1070 would, for the first time, apply trespassing statues to any person present anywhere in the state without proper immigration status. One of its most controversial innovations requires "a reasonable attempt" to determine an individual's immigration status during any encounter with any state and local official, if "a reasonable suspicion" exists that the individual is unlawfully present in the country. As stated in the legislation, it is intended to promote "attrition through enforcement," which is to say that the state intends the strict implementation of harsh immigration laws to lead to a decline in migration, both in the resident population of irregular migrants as well as a decline in new arrivals (Arizona Senate Research, 2010).

In 1994, California voters passed a ballot proposition, Proposition 187, which sought to deny state-funded social services and public education to unauthorized immigrants in order to induce them to leave the state. It was the first notable measure in more than a century that sought to use state law to control immigration. Proposition 187 was successfully challenged in the federal courts and was never implemented. However, the idea that governments beyond Washington should attempt to restrict illegal immigration never went away. While Washington remained deadlocked on the issue of immigration reform in the 2000s, and the unauthorized population continued to grow, state and local officials proposed a great many measures to fill the void (Rodriguez, 2011). In 2011, the National Conference of State Legislatures counted 300 bills on immigration introduced in state legislatures in 2005, and by 2009 the number was more than 1,500.

Arizona's S.B. 1070 was not only the culmination of a long process but also a significant legislative achievement. It stands out because of the breadth and originality of its provisions and the strong views it produced among supporters and opponents alike. Moreover, it provoked legal challenges that address key constitutional issues in the enactment and enforcement of immigration policies, and those challenges are almost certain to produce important judicial precedents (Chin et al., 2010). The law was intended to be a standard setter, and indeed it has spawned multiple imitations, most notably a law enacted in Alabama in 2011 that expanded on the Arizona law and competed for designation as the toughest immigration law enacted by a state (Johnson, 2011).

THE FEDERAL PREEMPTION ARGUMENT

"The legislature finds that there is a compelling interest in the cooperative enforcement of federal immigration laws throughout all of Arizona." So begins the text of S.B. 1070, and the power and legitimacy of the law hinges on the validity of that statement. Supporters insist that the law merely enhances Arizona's ability to cooperate with Washington. But a close examination of the law and its likely consequences shows that it would instead supplant federal immigration policy and indeed hinder its effectiveness. That fatal flaw renders S.B. 1070 unconstitutional. This issue has been a subject of court decisions regarding the Arizona law, but before delving into those specifics it is important to take a broader view and look back in history (Varsanyi, 2010).

The supremacy clause of the U.S. Constitution (Article VI, Clause 2) established what has come to be known as the doctrine of preemption. The clause reads: "This Constitution, and the Laws of the United States which shall be made in pursuance thereof; and all treaties made, or which shall be made, under the authority of the United States, shall be the supreme law of the land; and the judges in every state shall be bound thereby, anything in the constitution or laws of any state to the contrary notwithstanding." Under this principle, federal law should take precedence over a state law on the same subject. So, for example, if Washington declares that certain types of banking activities are illegal, a state government cannot turn around and make a law that permits those activities. But the situation has not always been this clear, either because there were disputes about congressional intent or about whether a state measure suborned that intent. In other cases, like that of the Arizona law, states have proposed their own mechanisms to accomplish the goals laid out in a federal law. Time and again the courts have had to decide who got the last word on an issue, and those judicial decisions reflect the nation's long and ongoing disputes over the balance of power between Washington and the states. On the subject of immigration, like much else, the application of the supremacy clause has varied over time as the tides have shifted.

During the nation's first hundred years, state and even local governments played a big role in immigration, sometimes with their own policies to recruit and screen newcomers (Zolberg, 2006). New York City secured its right to exclude potential paupers in a landmark Supreme Court decision in 1837. That position was reversed by the Court in an 1875 ruling, also involving New York City, which for the first time established federal supremacy in determining who was allowed to enter the country from abroad. Starting in the 1880s and through to the present, the federal government has taken an assertive role in enacting statutes, establishing regulations, and maintaining enforcement and administrative agencies to control immigration. Meanwhile, the states largely ignored the issue until the recent wave of activity that began in the mid-1990s (Manheim, 1995).

One reason there has been so much state-level activity in recent years is the lack of a definitive precedent from the U.S. Supreme Court prior to its ruling in the Arizona case. Until then the most recent decision governing preemption in the area of immigration had come in 1976 in the *De Canas v. Bica* case. In that ruling the Court concluded that the preemption doctrine did not apply to a section of the California Labor Code prohibiting the knowing employment of an unauthorized migrant. In the recent debate over preemption's role in immigration policy, both sides have found language in the ruling to support their view. Opponents of state initiatives like S.B. 1070 emphasize a passage that cites numerous precedents for the unambiguous conclusion that "power to regulate immigration is unquestionably exclusively a federal power" (Herndon, 2006). Supporters of the state initiatives emphasize the Court's finding that there is no evidence "that Congress intended to preclude harmonious state regulation touching on aliens in general or the employment of illegal aliens in particular" (Kobach, 2010).

California's Proposition 187 was successfully challenged on the grounds of preemption, with a federal district court judge finding in 1997 that the state was "powerless to enact its own legislative scheme to regulate immigration" or "to regulate alien access to public benefits" (McDonnell, 1997). After a governor opposed to the proposition was elected in 1999, the state dropped its defense of the initiative and the case became moot, unable to produce an appellate opinion let alone a Supreme Court decision. As such, although Proposition 187 focused attention on the preemption argument and provoked a great deal of political activity, that episode did not resolve the ambiguity left by the 1976 *De Canas* ruling. It is in this context that supporters of S.B. 1070 championed the idea that the Arizona law would lead to a new precedent favorable to states. Indeed, the law was written with the idea of a court battle in mind. The challenge came soon enough, and the controversy provoked by S.B. 1070 will determine whether power to regulate immigration belongs to the states or to Washington.

Very soon after S.B. 1070 was enacted, the U.S. Department of Justice and several civil rights organizations filed suits to block its implementation (Markon, 2011). Essentially, S.B. 1070 spent nearly 2 years stuck in court before the U.S. Supreme Court decided that elements of the law could never go into effect. Although numerous objections were aired and litigated, it was the Justice Department's case, focused on the preemption doctrine, that made it all the way to Washington.

In his majority opinion, Justice Anthony Kennedy wrote: "The Government of the United States has broad, undoubted power over the subject of immigration and the status of aliens.... The federal power to determine immigration policy is well settled.… Federal governance of immigration an alien status is extensive and complex" (*Arizona v. United States*, 2012). Ending all ambiguity, the Court produced a sweeping affirmation of the federal role in immigration under the supremacy clause and was unequivocal in finding specific grounds for federal preemption of state initiatives that attempt to create and enforce laws against unauthorized migration. It is therefore worthwhile to spend a minute considering why S.B. 1070 raised such a fundamental challenge to the way immigration is managed in the United States.

As Justice Kennedy suggested, there should be little doubt that the federal government has intended to position itself as the "supreme law of the land," as the Constitution puts it, on all matters related to immigration. There are stacks of laws, resolutions, regulations, and procedures issued in Washington going back for more than a century on this issue (Zolberg, 2006). The federal government has taken measures to decide what kinds of people are admitted into the country, in what numbers, and from what countries. It has rules on how long people can stay, for what purposes, and what they need to do to become citizens. It has an entire structure of immigration courts to adjudicate disputes as well as punishments for those who violate the rules. There are several federal law enforcement agencies whose sole purpose is to police the movement of people in and out of the country and to investigate violations of immigration law. Thus, it can hardly be argued that Washington has failed to exert its authority over immigration. Many people rightfully argue about whether these are the best laws and policies, and whether they are implemented effectively, but there is no justifiable argument over whether the federal government has exercised its supremacy. Every shred of policy could be misguided and every action undertaken could fail to accomplish its purpose, but once Congress and the executive branch have imposed themselves so thoroughly for so many years, the Constitution grants supremacy to the federal government over the states.

So, the question raised by the Arizona law is not whether this piece of state legislation can or should replace the federal effort. Federal supremacy is clear. Rather the primary issue is whether any given state law potentially impedes or supports the federal effort. Simple supremacy might be sidestepped if a law could be shown to be merely enhancing the enforcement of federal laws, as supporters of S.B. 1070 and its spinoffs claim. The evidence runs to the contrary. Even if they do not challenge federal supremacy, laws like S.B. 1070 fail the preemption challenge because they will hinder Washington's immigration policies.

The Arizona law, for example, created a broad requirement for state and local authorities to check the immigration status of individuals suspected of being in the country unlawfully. In the case of police officers, for example, immigration status would be fully checked and verified with federal authorities if necessary before someone could be released after an arrest. Merely having an Arizona driver's license would not satisfy the requirement, according to Judge Bolton, who concluded that potentially thousands of people who otherwise would have merely received a citation and been released—people who might never have seen the inside of a jail or even a police station—would have to be detained until their immigration status could be ascertained. Since the state does not keep immigration records, the police would constantly be turning to federal authorities.

If the Arizona model became widely adopted, the sheer volume of information requests would cause federal immigration agencies to shift their priorities, according to S.B. 1070's opponents, including the U.S. Department of Justice (Preston, 2010). Instead of being out investigating human smuggling operations or big employers who were ignoring their workers' false documents, federal agents would be running down information about people Arizona police had arrested at a DUI checkpoint or during a domestic disturbance. Judge Bolton correctly judged that this would impede the enforcement of federal immigration policy (*United States v. Arizona*, 703 F. Supp. 2d 980, 992 [2010]). Federal agents run a lot of checks to determine if individuals are authorized to be in the country, and they run a lot of checks at the request of local police. But an essential aspect of law enforcement strategy is to prioritize the use of resources. Therefore, instead of running checks on everyone who is arrested and is suspected of being an unauthorized migrant, it is more efficient to focus on people who are arrested for a felony, or who already have been arrested several times in the past, or who have actually been convicted of a prior crime. In effect, Arizona was trying to set priorities for agencies of the federal government in order to achieve its own ends, and that is unconstitutional regardless of whether those ends are justified or not.

Several aspects of the Arizona law would conflict with the federal government's ability to determine the conditions under which legal immigrants can live and work in the United States. In Arizona, a legal immigrant could be subject to questioning, requests for identity papers, as well as arrest and detention under several different circumstances. The U.S. Supreme Court found that these are burdens that only the federal government has the authority to impose, but there is a broader argument here as well. Federal immigration policies do not merely regulate entry; they are also designed to encourage settlement by individuals that Washington views as beneficial to the national interest. This might be by virtue of employment or family connections. It might be because of investments the individual is making or because of special talents, skills, or knowledge. In addition, millions of legal residents have been admitted as refugees, exiles, or asylum seekers because of foreign policy interests. Unduly imposing burdens on these individuals at the state level, let alone making them objects of suspicion and ill treatment, impedes the effective functioning of federal immigration policy.

The Arizona law presented a special violation of the preemption doctrine because the state borders Mexico, and because by far the largest share of illegal immigrants—the stated targets of the law—are from Mexico. Immigration has been a major topic of U.S.-Mexico relations for many decades, and it has been a topic of constant discussion between the two governments since immigration from Mexico reached massive proportions in the 1990s. Although successive U.S. presidents have held that immigration flows will be regulated by the United States alone and are not subject to international negotiation, that does not preclude immigration from being a diplomatic issue as well. American officials work with Mexican counterparts on a number of practical matters, such as law enforcement efforts against migrant smugglers, the movement of temporary workers, and the repatriation of individuals deported from the United States.

Moreover, U.S. immigration policies play an important role in the overall relationship between the two nations. Given that 1 out of every 10 persons born in Mexico now lives in the United States, it should not be surprising that their treatment is a major concern for the Mexican government. As such, a state government could unnecessarily complicate and even impede the federal government's ability to conduct foreign policy on behalf of the entire country. That would constitute yet another usurpation of federal supremacy.

Arizona claimed special standing to develop its own immigration law because it sits on the border with Mexico and serves as a major transit area for illegal migration. However, it enacted a law, and pursued a defense of that law in the federal courts, that sought to establish precedents that would favor all states seeking their own immigration measures. A simple mental exercise illustrates the value of preserving federal supremacy on immigration. Imagine that all 50 states had their own immigration laws. Some states could be exceedingly welcoming and would allow unauthorized migrants to take up residence, get identification documents, work, and receive state-funded social benefits. Other states would follow Arizona's example and would impose state sanctions on all sort of activities, such as signing a housing lease, as Alabama has done. The result would be an exceedingly uneven landscape that would impede some of the core national functions that the federal government was created to protect, such as efficient interstate commerce and well-coordinated national security.

Despite these arguments, Arizona appealed Judge Bolton's injunction on April 11, 2011, and the Ninth Circuit Court of Appeals upheld the ban on certain sections of the law. The majority opinion, written by Judge Richard A. Paez, supported Judge Bolton's assessment that the state had intruded upon federal prerogatives. On August 10, 2011, Arizona filed a petition with the Supreme Court seeking a reversal of the lower court and appellate decisions on the grounds that Washington cannot claim exclusive domain over immigration policy, and that S.B. 1070 falls within the bounds of legitimate state action. On December 12, 2011, the U.S. Supreme Court agreed to hear the case. In summing up the Court's opinion, Justice Kennedy wrote: "Arizona may have understandable frustrations with the problems caused by illegal immigration while that process continues, but the State may not pursue policies that undermine federal law."

THE POTENTIAL FOR CIVIL RIGHTS VIOLATIONS

On purely legal grounds, the future of S.B. 1070 was decided on the doctrine of preemption, but much of the political action surrounding the Arizona law—and certainly most of the public outcry against it—has focused on claims that it would create conditions ripe for widespread civil rights violations. Those concerns appear to be justified. There is a broad and longstanding debate over when it is appropriate for government at any level to consider race or ethnicity in its deliberations. While some, mostly conservative thinkers, argue that we should aim for a colorblind society, others, mainly on the progressive side of the political spectrum, argue that government should take race and ethnicity into account as much as necessary to combat discrimination or to ensure equal access to opportunity (Edsall & Edsall, 1991; Krauthammer, 2009). This is a debate often fought in shades of gray, with settlements designed to balance contradictory imperatives. The U.S. Supreme Court has claimed a middle ground with decisions like the one in the 2003 *Grutter v. Bollinger* case upholding an affirmative action policy at the University of Michigan (Perry, 2007). That decision held that the constitution allows for the consideration of race so long as it is "narrowly tailored" and advances a "compelling interest" on behalf of the general public.

Arizona's S.B. 1070 opens the door to a consideration of race by state officials that is virtually unbounded, rather than narrowly tailored, and that does not advance any public interest but is actually detrimental to the public interest. It is a government action that runs afoul of the barriers that are constitutionally erected to prevent discriminatory action by public officials. The law inevitably promotes the use of race and ethnicity as criteria for police action, and as a result it will produce tangible, hard, and yet avoidable indignities for many individuals.

At the heart of the controversy are the law's requirements for immigration status checks by state and local officials who have a "reasonable suspicion" that an individual might be in the country without permission. Although the state insisted that it would take measures to prevent racial profiling, it seems inevitable that race and ethnicity will come into play, even unconsciously, when an official is deciding who seems suspicious. In litigation going back decades now, law enforcement officers have been found guilty of racial profiling when race became a factor in forming suspicions, unless it was part of a description of a specific suspect (Harris, 1999). Even if Arizona police officers consider race among several factors in forming a suspicion, S.B. 1070 virtually instructs them to march into constitutionally questionable territory.

Imagine that two drivers are driving cars with broken taillights and that both are going to be stopped by a police officer. Both are driving identical, slightly beat-up, down-market automobiles, and both are wearing jeans and a t-shirt. One driver is a blond, light-skinned woman with her hair in a ponytail. The other is a brown-skinned man with black hair and some of the *mestizo* features common in Mexico. Neither is carrying a driver's license. Both are going to be cited. At that point, however, S.B. 1070 requires the officer to decide whether there is a reasonable suspicion that the drivers are in the United States without authorization. It is not hard to imagine which of the two will be questioned about immigration status. Both could be native-born U.S. citizens, and neither would be carrying a birth certificate, a passport, or some other proof of citizenship. One will go home groaning about a ticket. The other will be headed to a jailhouse.

Law enforcement officers today already face a considerable burden to ensure that they do not give undue weight to race and ethnicity. At the very least, S.B. 1070 would further complicate that decision making. At worst, it would consistently influence an officer in favor of stopping someone whose race or ethnicity most resembles the officer's image of an unauthorized immigrant. Because the law's instructions are so broad and so ill defined, it increases the likelihood that police officers will act unconstitutionally at multiple points along the spectrum of interaction between law enforcement and an individual, from the decision to initiate an encounter, to adding a layer of scrutiny, and all the way to detention.

According to estimates for 2010 by the Pew Hispanic Center, Mexicans make up 58 percent of the unauthorized immigrant population, and other nations in Latin America account for an additional 23 percent. Thus, the fact that a majority of unauthorized migrants are Mexican (and the share is undoubtedly higher in Arizona than in the nation as a whole) only increases the danger posed by S.B. 1070. Arizona law enforcement officers reasonably could be expected to harbor a stereotypical image of the undocumented migrant based on a conception of Mexican ethnicity. It is a misconception, in fact, but the law encourages police to act on it. Arizona is home to between 250,000 and 500,000 unauthorized migrants, according to the Pew estimates, with 400,000 as the likeliest number. Meanwhile, Arizona is also home to nearly 1.7 million people who describe themselves as being of Mexican origins, according to the 2010 census. That means that about a million and half people in Arizona who are U.S. citizens or legal immigrants—a quarter of the total population—are in the pool of people who might be suspected of being in the country without authorization based on their ethnicity.

In weighing S.B. 1070's potential civil rights impact, two additional factors need to be considered. First, the framers of the law and those implementing it can be utterly blameless of any willful discrimination. The issue is not whether the law has a discriminatory intent, but whether it might have discriminatory effects. So, for example, the Arizona legislature rushed to supplement S.B. 1070 with statutory language that condemns racial profiling. However, unintended consequences can be just as harmful as the intended ones if the result is a violation of constitutional rights.

Second, the harm itself need not be something so obvious as a denial of service or a prohibition from utilizing a public accommodation. Being subject to increased scrutiny by law enforcement by virtue of race or ethnicity can meet the test of a civil rights violation even if that scrutiny produces no more than a mere inconvenience. S.B. 1070 creates conditions in which hundreds, perhaps thousands, of full-blooded Arizonans will be stopped and questioned by police every year because they share the physical features of many unauthorized Mexican migrants.

The June 2012 Supreme Court decision allowed Arizona to implement the so-called show-me-your-papers provisions of S.B. 1070. Police will be required to check the immigration status of anyone they detain, and they will be able to stop and detain anyone suspected of being an illegal alien. The Court, in effect, chose not to decide on this aspect of the Arizona law, concluding that it was not clearly preempted by federal prerogatives. Regardless of their standing on constitutional grounds, however, these provisions—and others like them in other states—are certain to produce civil rights violations, and those violations will lead to a new wave of court challenges. Once the effects are evident, this kind of policing should be struck down.

BAD POLICY

The final argument against S.B. 1070 rests on simple practicality: It will be expensive, and yet it will not accomplish its stated objectives. As noted above, on the very controversial topic of immigration, there is near unanimous agreement that current policies are ineffective (Suárez-Orozco et al., 2011; Tichenor, 2009). Washington has undertaken a variety of measures over the course of the past 30 years with the aim of controlling illegal immigration, with notable expenditures on border controls dating back to the mid-1990s. Nonetheless, until the beginning of the Great Recession in 2008, the unauthorized population grew until it reached an estimated total of 11 million people in 2007 (Passel & Cohn, 2010). Again, it is important to underscore that this debate is not over whether illegal immigration is a problem or whether the country needs new immigration policies. Rather, the sole issue is whether the Arizona legislation offers an effective way forward.

"The legislature declares that the intent of this act is to make attrition through enforcement the public policy of all state and local government agencies in Arizona." So states Section 1 of S.B. 1070. The objective of an attrition strategy is to make life so difficult for unauthorized migrants already living in the United States that they will gradually pack up of their own accord and return to their countries of origin. Proponents of restriction first articulated this strategy as a basis for federal policy in the early 2000s. Since then, attrition has often been argued to counter proposals for legalization programs that would allow the unauthorized to remain in the country. Opponents of legalization have seized on attrition as an alternative to a more aggressive enforcement strategy that would attempt to locate, detain, and deport the whole population of unauthorized immigrants. The prospect of aggressive action on that scale has never drawn much political support. Legislation passed by the Republican-led House of Representatives in 2005 embodied the attrition strategy, but the proposal died in the face of opposition by Senate Democrats, and it was never actively pursued at the federal level. It remains an untested means of reducing the number of persons living in the country without proper immigration status.

The effects of the Great Recession showed the limits of the attrition strategy. Studies by the Migration Policy Institute (Papademetriou et al., 2011), the Pew Hispanic Center (Passel & Cohn, 2010) and the Department of Homeland Security (Hoefer et al., 2011) all point to the same results in unauthorized migration. On the one hand, as jobs disappeared the flow of newcomers declined drastically to the point that the net flow from Mexico had reached zero by 2010, down from an estimated half a million a year when the economy was booming in 2005. On the other hand, there was no mass exodus homeward of those already here. Indeed, contrary to most expectations, there was no notable return flow at all.

The economic hardship thus had vastly different effects on unauthorized migrants already settled here and those who were in Mexico considering the journey. A fourfold increase in the number of Border Patrol agents, the construction of hundreds of miles of fence and barriers, and a campaign of workplace raids—all measures undertaken since 2001—failed to staunch the flow of newcomers, but the recession shut it down. Meanwhile, the existing population—the ostensible targets of an attrition strategy—stayed put. Even without jobs, they decided to ride out the storm where they had made homes and communities and where their children were born. The most severe economic downturn experienced in the United States since the 1930s convinced hundreds of thousands of potential unauthorized immigrants to stay in Mexico, but the pain was not great enough to make those already here leave.

The question for this debate is: How much pain would it take for an attrition strategy to be effective? Judging from what happened during the Great Recession, the answer is more pain than could be effectively administered under the Arizona law, and probably more pain than the American people would be willing to inflict.

At a time when government budgets at every level are being cut, and when Arizona faces an especially severe fiscal crisis, new duties or services can only be added by cutting existing missions. An aggressive pursuit of the unauthorized population by Arizona's law enforcement agencies would necessarily mean that other police activities would be curtailed (Martinez, 2011). There is no surplus of law enforcement resources, and so attrition through enforcement would need to take precedence over crime prevention, investigations, and other public safety efforts. The displacement would be significant because an aggressive, resource-heavy effort will be necessary to inflict sufficient pain on the unauthorized immigrants who have already weathered the Great Recession.

A serious effort to push out the estimated 400,000 unauthorized migrants in Arizona would need to go beyond passive measures such as inquiring about immigration status after an individual has been stopped for another reason. Effective attrition would require proactive enforcement that sought out and detained unauthorized migrants, and this effort would need to be maintained on a consistent basis for an extended period of time. In addition to sacrificing other law enforcement missions, an attrition campaign would require a variety of additional expenses, most notably the costs of detaining everyone picked up as a suspected illegal migrant while they are being definitively identified, and holding those deemed liable for deportation until federal immigration authorities can take custody of them. The funds for these additional expenses would have to be drawn from other state and local government programs, such as education, transportation, and health.

Imagine that the measures enacted in S.B. 1070 were sufficiently effective to convince 50,000 migrants a year to leave the state. Attrition through enforcement would then require an 8-year effort. Even if the rate of effectiveness was double that, it would still require an extended, multiyear commitment. Taken together, the displacement of law enforcement missions and the shifting of funds would add up to a significant reprioritization of state and local government. Whatever harm might be caused by the presence of unauthorized migrants would be outweighed by the crimes that would go uninvestigated and the school programs that would be cancelled, all in pursuit of an immigration control strategy that offers no clear promise of success. Even taken on its own terms, the Arizona law fails to meet the most basic tests of cost-effectiveness. If the people of Arizona, other states, or the nation as a whole want a solution to persistent high levels of illegal migration, they will have to look elsewhere.

References and Further Reading

Amici curiae brief of Members of Congress and the Committee to Protect America's Border in Support of Petitioner in Arizona v. United States. (2010). Supreme Court of the United States, No. 11-182. Retrieved from http://www.americanbar.org/content/dam/aba/publications/supreme_court_preview/briefs/11-182_petitioner_amcu_moc_etal.authcheckdam.pdf

Arizona Legislature. (2010). Senate Bill 1070. Forty-ninth Legislature, Second Regular Session. Retrieved from http://www.azleg.gov/legtext/49leg/2r/bills/sb1070s.pdf

Arizona Senate Research. (2010, January 15). *Fact Sheet for S.B. 1070.* Retrieved from http://www.azleg.gov/legtext/49leg/2r/summary/s.1070pshs.doc.htm

Arizona v. United States, U.S. 11-182. Decided June 25, 2012. Retrieved from http://www.supremecourt.gov/opinions/slipopinions.aspx?Term=11

Chin, G. J., Hessick, C. B., Massaro, T. M., & Miller, M. L. (2010). A legal labyrinth: Issues raised by Arizona Senate Bill 1070. *Georgetown Immigration Law Journal, 25*(1), 47.

Doty, R. L. (2007). States of exception on the Mexico–U.S. border: Security, "decisions," and civilian border patrols. *International Political Sociology, 1,* 113–137.

Edsall, T. B., & Edsall, M. D. (1991). *Chain reaction: The impact of race, rights, and taxes on American politics.* New York, NY: Norton.

Guizar, M. (2007, June). *Facts about federal preemption.* Retrieved from National Immigration Law Center website: http://www.nilc.org/immlawpolicy/locallaw/federalpreemptionfacts_2007-06-28.pdf

Harris, D. (1999, June 7). *Driving while BLACK: Racial profiling on our nation's highways.* Retrieved from American Civil Liberties Union website: http://www.aclu.org/racial-justice/driving-while-black-racial-profiling-our-nations-highways

Herndon, J. J. (2006). Broken borders: *De Canas v. Bica* and the standards that govern the validity of state measures designed to deter undocumented immigration. *Texas Hispanic Journal of Law & Policy, 12,* 31–121.

Hoefer, M., Rytuna, N., & Baker, B. C. *Estimates of the unauthorized immigrant population in the United States: January 2010.* Washington, DC: Department of Homeland Security, 2011.

Johnson, K. R. (2010). How racial profiling in America became the law of the land: *United States v. Brignoni-Ponce* and *Whren v. United States* and the need for truly rebellious lawyering. *Georgetown Law Journal, 98*(4), 1005–1077.

Johnson, K. R. (2011, December 5). Sweet home Alabama? Immigration and civil rights in the "New" South. *Stanford Law Review Online, 64,* 22. Retrieved from http://ssrn.com/abstract=1971803

Kobach, K. (2010). *The Arizona immigration law: What it actually does, and why it is constitutional* (Lecture No. 1173). Retrieved from the Heritage Foundation website: http://www.heritage.org/research/lecture/2010/12/the-arizona-immigration-law-what-it-actually-does-and-why-it-is-constitutional

Krauthammer, C. (2009, July 3). Ricci decision moves toward equal protection. *The Washington Post.* Retrieved from http://www.washingtonpost.com/wp-dyn/content/article/2009/07/02/AR2009070202685.html

Manheim, K. (1995). State immigration law and federal supremacy. *Hastings Constitutional Law Quarterly, 22,* 939.

Manuel, K. M., Garcia, M. J., & Eig, L. M. (2011, June 7). *State efforts to deter unauthorized aliens: Legal analysis of Arizona's S.B. 1070* (Congressional Research Service Report R41221). Retrieved from Congressional Research Service website: http://fpc.state.gov/documents/organization/166827.pdf

Margolis, J. R. (1994). Closing the doors to the land of opportunity: The constitutional controversy surrounding Proposition 187. *University of Miami Inter-American Law Review, 26*(2), 363–401.

Markon, J. (2011, September 29). Obama administration widens challenge to state immigration laws. *The Washington Post.* Retrieved from http://www.washingtonpost.com/politics/obama-administration-widens-challenges-to-state-immigration-laws/2011/09/28/gIQA8HgR7K_story.html

Martin, P. (1995). Proposition 187 in California. *International Migration Review, 29*(1), 255–263.

Martinez, G. (2011, January 24). *Unconstitutional and costly: The high price of local immigration enforcement.* Retrieved from Center for American Progress website: http://www.americanprogress.org/issues/2011/01/unconstitutional_and_costly.html

Martinez, G., & Kelley, A. M. (2010, July 8). *Taking action against Arizona: Federal lawsuit against Arizona protects people and the constitution.* Retrieved from Center for American Progress website: http://www.americanprogress.org/issues/2010/07/arizona_lawsuit.html

McDonnell, P. J. (1997, November 15). Prop. 187 found unconstitutional by federal judge. *Los Angeles Times.* Retrieved from http://articles.latimes.com/1997/nov/15/news/mn-54053

National Conference of State Legislatures. (2011, January 5). *2010 immigration-related laws and resolutions in the States.* Retrieved from http://www.ncsl.org/default.aspx?tabid=21857

National Conference of State Legislatures. (2011, July 28). *Analysis of Arizona's immigration laws.* Retrieved from http://www.ncsl.org/default.aspx?tabid=20263

Papademetriou, D. G., Sumption, M., & Terrazas, A. (Eds.). (2011). *Migration and the great recession: The transatlantic experience.* Washington, DC: Migration Policy Institute.

Passel, J. S., & Cohn, D. (2010, September 1). *U.S. unauthorized immigration flows are down sharply since mid-decade.* Retrieved from Pew Hispanic Center website: http://www.pewhispanic.org/2011/02/01/unauthorized-immigrant-population-brnational-and-state-trends-2010/

Perry, B. A. (2007). *The Michigan affirmative action cases.* Lawrence, KS: University Press of Kansas.

Preston, J. (2010, July 6). Justice dept. sues Arizona over its immigration law. *The New York Times.* Retrieved from http://www.nytimes.com/2010/07/07/us/07immig.html

Rodríguez, C. M. (2011). The integrated regime of immigration regulation. In M. M. Suárez-Orozco, V. Louie, & R. Suro (Eds.), *Writing immigration: Scholars and journalists in dialogue* (pp. 44–61). Berkeley, CA: University of California Press.

Suárez-Orozco, Marcelo M., Louie, V., & Suro, R. (Eds.). (2011). *Writing immigration: Scholars and journalists in dialogue.* Berkeley, CA: University of California Press.

Tichenor, D. J. (2009). Navigating an American minefield: The politics of illegal immigration. *The Forum, 7*(3) doi: 10.2202/1540-8884.1325.

United States v. Arizona, 9th Cir., No. 10-16645, 4/11/11. Retrieved from http://www.ca9.uscourts.gov/datastore/opinions/2011/04/11/10-16645.pdf

United States v. Arizona, 703 F. Supp. 2d 980, 992 (D. Ariz. 2010). Retrieved from http://www.azcentral.com/ic/pdf/0729sb1070-bolton-ruling.pdf

U.S. Census Bureau. (2011). *Profile of general population and housing characteristics: 2010—Arizona.* Retrieved from http://factfinder2.census.gov/faces/tableservices/jsf/pages/productview.xhtml?pid=DEC_10_DP_DPDP1&prodType=table

Varsanyi, M. W. (2010). Immigration policy activism in U.S. states and cities: Interdisciplinary perspectives. In M. W. Varsanyi (Ed.), *Taking local control: Immigration policy activism in U.S. cities and states.* Palo Alto, CA: Stanford University Press.

Zolberg, A. R. (2006). *A nation by design: Immigration policy in the fashioning of America.* New York, NY: Russell Sage Foundation.

Roberto Suro

12

Driver's Licenses

POINT: Lawful immigration status should not be a requirement to obtain a driver's license. In fact, providing driver's licenses will help law enforcement agencies identify otherwise unknown persons. It also is likely to make the roads safer, promote auto insurance coverage, and discourage the amount of phony documents in circulation.

Michele Waslin, American Immigration Council, Immigration Policy Center

COUNTERPOINT: Individuals who are in the United States illegally should not be able to obtain driver's licenses or other official government identification, because the mere presence of these persons in the country is a violation of law. Permitting them to obtain driver's licenses increases risks of fraud and criminal activity. Any "benefits" that could be obtained from permitting them to obtain driver's licenses are outweighed by the harm that this causes.

Julie Myers Wood, ICS Consulting

Introduction

Prior to the terrorist attacks of September 11, 2001, few states explicitly stated that illegal immigrants could not obtain driver's licenses. However, because many states required a social security number in order to obtain one, driver's licenses were *de facto* unavailable to illegal immigrants in most states. After it was revealed that the 19 hijackers on 9/11 had, among them, a total of 37 domestically obtained identity documents, including eleven state driver's licenses, many states rushed to change their laws to require proof of lawful immigration status. Although all licenses obtained by the hijackers were legal—issued by state Departments of Motor Vehicles—some had been obtained with other fraudulent documents. (Some of the hijackers had misrepresented their state residency but not their identities or their legal status.)

After 9/11, states were understandably concerned with tightening up their systems, particularly with those involved in proving residency. A debate over the wisdom of granting driver's licenses to illegal immigrants ensued. (It is important to note, however, that the hijackers had entered the country legally, though several had overstayed their visas.)

In the Point essay, Michele Waslin argues that limiting immigrants' access to licenses undermines—rather than enhances—national security and that it has an "unintended harmful impact on legal immigrants and U.S. citizens." She further argues that denying driver's licenses to illegal immigrants is a poor way to identify terrorists; does not reduce undocumented immigration; makes our roads less safe; and makes local law enforcement duties more difficult because immigrants will fear being reported to authorities and so will not report crimes to police and/or will clog local courts with a barrage of cases of the relatively minor crime of driving without a license. Waslin is firmly on the side that restricting driver's licenses is bad public policy.

In the Counterpoint essay, however, Julie Myers Wood argues that since illegal immigration itself is a violation of the law, undocumented persons should not be allowed the privilege of a driver's license. She holds firmly to the view that granting licenses to undocumented people "increases risks of fraud and criminal activity." She bases much of her argument on one key fact: driver's licenses are not used solely for driving, but are used as primary documents that often "breed" other documents such as passports, birth certificates, firearms carry permits, hunting licenses, and school or daycare employment eligibility. While Waslin argues that the hijackers' possession of driver's licenses aided in the 9/11 investigation, Wood counters that they made it easier for the hijackers to commit their atrocities.

The REAL ID Act, discussed by both Wood and Waslin, was passed after 9/11 and requires people seeking a license to prove residence in their state, their identity, and their lawful presence in the country. Neither author denies that proving these three things can sometimes be accomplished with fraudulent documents, often relatively easily obtained.

When you read through this chapter, consider if you believe there is more evidence to support Waslin's view that giving driver's licenses to undocumented immigrants increases our safety, or whether you believe the evidence that Wood presents that granting these licenses to undocumented persons only gives tacit approval of illegal activity and further undermines our national security. If you were a policymaker, would you give licenses to undocumented persons? Why or why not?

POINT

One of the ways states have attempted to create immigration policy and control illegal immigration is by limiting immigrant eligibility for driver's licenses and state-issued identification documents. Some believe that restricting unauthorized immigrants from obtaining driver's licenses will enhance national security and reduce illegal immigration. However, state and federal restrictions on immigrants' access to driver's licenses fail to meet the goals of enhancing national security and controlling illegal immigration. Furthermore, denying licenses to a group of people undermines national security and law enforcement efforts, erodes public safety, and has an unintended harmful impact on legal immigrants and U.S. citizens.

Prior to the terrorist attacks of September 11, 2001, very few state statutes contained language explicitly denying driver's licenses to unauthorized immigrants or requiring lawful presence in the country. However, some state driver's license requirements, such as the requirement to provide Social Security numbers (SSNs), or limitations on the types of documents that could be used to prove identity or residency, resulted in a de facto ineligibility for certain immigrants who could not provide the necessary documentation to obtain a license (Waslin, 2002). Because of this, there were concerted efforts in many states to pass more expansive driver's license laws that would allow residents to acquire licenses and identification documents regardless of immigration status.

After the tragic events of 9/11 and revelations that several of the terrorists had obtained state-issued driver's licenses, there was renewed debate over immigrants' access to driver's licenses and state identity documents. Many states rushed to change their driver's license laws by placing restrictions on the documents accepted as proof of identity and state residency, and by requiring proof of lawful immigration status. In 2011, 30 states explicitly required proof of lawful presence to receive a license. Eighteen more states have de facto lawful presence requirements created by agency policy or the combination of documents required to obtain a license. Only two states—New Mexico and Washington—do not have lawful presence requirements. Utah currently allows applicants unable to prove lawful presence to receive a "driving privilege card," which allows the individual to drive but is not acceptable as identification (National Immigration Law Center, 2009).

In 2005 the federal government stepped into the driver's license issue, and the REAL ID Act was passed by Congress and signed into law. It is important to note that the REAL ID Act repealed the Intelligence Reform Act, which was enacted in December 2004. The Intelligence Reform Act contained detailed and comprehensive federal standards on state-issued driver's licenses and IDs to improve security and reduce fraud, which were recommended and endorsed by the 9/11 Commission.

The REAL ID Act requires state Departments of Motor Vehicles (DMVs) to follow specific driver's license issuance rules and regulations, and it provides that, beginning 3 years after enactment, driver's licenses that are not compliant with the act cannot be accepted by federal agencies for any "official" purpose. The date has subsequently been pushed back multiple times. In 2011 the Department of Homeland Security (DHS) announced that they had extended the date by which all states must be in full compliance until January 2013. Under the REAL ID Act, only certain noncitizens are eligible for a REAL ID–compliant license. Unfortunately, the list of eligible immigrants fails to include several groups of legal immigrants who will not be able to obtain a compliant license, despite the fact that they are lawfully present in the country. The law also states that the only acceptable foreign document that can be accepted by state DMVs is a foreign passport, which could severely limit the ability of certain persons who do not have foreign passports to obtain a license. Additionally, the REAL ID Act requires that certain noncitizens be given a temporary license that is valid only for the period of the applicant's authorized stay in the United States or for 1 year; if there is no definite end to the authorized stay, the license must clearly state that it is temporary (Tatelman, 2008).

Despite passage of the REAL ID Act, the issue of driver's licenses and other forms of identification continues to be a key area of legislation in the states. According to the National Conference of State Legislatures (NCSL), 171 immigration-related driver's license/ID bills were introduced in 40 states in the first quarter of 2011 alone. Of course, not all of these bills were driver's license bills, but there were bills to restrict the types of documents that can be used to obtain a driver's license, and some create time limits for driver's licenses for legal permanent residents. Other driver's license/ID–related bills affecting immigrants include proposals to require proof of citizenship for handgun licenses and for licenses for work in certain trades. Other identification bills require proof of citizenship for fishing and hunting licenses, business licenses, and marriage certificates. The number of driver's license/ID bills was surpassed only by immigration-related law enforcement, health, and employment bills introduced in the states.

DRIVER'S LICENSE RESTRICTIONS DO NOT ENHANCE NATIONAL SECURITY OR PREVENT TERRORISM

While driver's license restrictions have been proposed in the name of national security, these restrictions are inefficient and ineffective measures to prevent terrorism. Immigration restrictionists continually remind us that the September 11 terrorists had state-issued driver's licenses. While that is true, it does not follow that restricting immigrant access to driver's licenses will prevent terrorism.

According to *9/11 and Terrorist Travel: A Staff Report of the National Commission on Terrorist Attacks Upon the United States* (2004), the 19 hijackers had a total of 37 domestically obtained identity documents, including 31 issued by state DMVs, and six obtained from a private company that sells identification documents. Eleven terrorists had state driver's licenses and, of these, five had duplicate licenses. One terrorist had two separate driver's licenses from two different states. Eleven terrorists had state identification cards. One hijacker did not have a state ID or a driver's license, and boarded the plane with his Saudi passport.

While several were out of status on 9/11 because they had overstayed their temporary visas, it is important to note that the hijackers came to the United States with visas, although some of those visas may have been obtained using fraudulent documentation. Furthermore, the driver's licenses they obtained were all legal (i.e., not forged) and issued by state DMVs. It is true that the identification documents were not all obtained legally, because seven hijackers used fraudulent statements of state residency to acquire legitimate identification documents. In other words, they misrepresented their state residency in order to get a license, but they did not misrepresent their identities or legal status (9/11 Public Discourse Project).

States have tightened up the requirements for proving residency. However, the restrictions implemented regarding proof of legal status would have done nothing to stop those 19 terrorists from committing their heinous acts. Sophisticated terrorists with substantial financial resources have proven that they have the will and the ability to obtain driver's licenses and other documents in one way or another when they find them necessary. Furthermore, the terrorists did not need U.S.-issued driver's licenses to board planes on September 11; they had foreign passports that allowed them to board. It is also important to note that restricting driver's licenses to immigrants does nothing to address the issue of domestic terrorist threats.

Experts have stated that the fact that the terrorists had valid driver's licenses actually helped the investigation into the terrorist acts. Driver's license records of the hijackers proved to be invaluable to law enforcement following 9/11. The October 2003 report of the American Association of Motor Vehicle Administrators (AAMVA) entitled *Access to Drivers License and Identification Card Data by Law Enforcement* stated,

> Law enforcement agencies, federal, state and local, use the driver license image on a frequent basis to identify victims, criminal suspects, missing children, and the elderly. Digital images from driver records have significantly aided law enforcement agencies charged with homeland security. The events of September 11, 2001 clearly demonstrate the value of the driver record photograph. The 19 terrorists obtained driver licenses from several states and federal authorities relied heavily on those images for the identification of the individuals responsible for the horrific criminal acts on that fateful day.

According to Margaret Stock, former associate professor of law at the U.S. Military Academy at West Point, in a 2005 article,

> Rather than trying to deny licenses and state identification cards to illegal immigrants, we should be encouraging every adult present in America to get a license or identification card. In fact, to enhance law enforcement and security efforts, immigration status should be irrelevant. People should be required to prove their identity, using secure documents that can be verified. In turn, the driver license or state identification document should be a secure document that can be verified easily.

The fact remains that the hijackers obtained lawful identification documents, and they would still be able to obtain those documents even with the new laws and restrictions that have been put in place. If one wants to deny driver's licenses to terrorists, one would have to have a way to identify terrorists. Simply denying licenses to certain groups of immigrants is an ineffective way to target terrorists.

DRIVER'S LICENSE RESTRICTIONS DO NOT DETER ILLEGAL IMMIGRATION

Some have argued that allowing immigrants to obtain driver's licenses encourages unauthorized immigration, and that it also provides unauthorized immigrants with the documentation necessary to obtain the benefits of membership in U.S. society. While our immigration system is broken and Congress must pass comprehensive reforms, the fact is that restricting driver's licenses does not accomplish immigration policy goals such as reducing undocumented immigration. Illegal immigrants will not be deterred by the knowledge they cannot obtain a driver's license, and undocumented immigrants will not simply "go home" if they are denied licenses. There is no evidence that the unauthorized immigrant population in any state has decreased due to the implementation of driver's license restrictions.

While appearing tough on immigration may attract some notoriety and perhaps even some votes, these measures do little, if anything, to fix the nation's broken immigration system.

DRIVER'S LICENSE RESTRICTIONS DO NOT PREVENT ACCESS TO PUBLIC BENEFITS OR UNAUTHORIZED WORK

Driver's license restrictions do not prevent unauthorized work or the receipt of public benefits. Having a driver's license does not allow undocumented immigrants to access any government benefits for which they are otherwise ineligible. Federal law requires all employees to complete an I-9 form, which requires both proof of identity and eligibility to work, so presenting an employer with a driver's license alone is not sufficient. Public benefits programs also require additional proof of identity and immigration status, and studies show that these programs are generally not used by people who are not legally in the country.

ADDITIONAL CONSEQUENCES

Certain legal immigrants will not be able to obtain licenses. Current driver's license laws effectively deny driver's licenses to many people who are authorized to live in the United States, but who cannot provide the required documentation for a variety of reasons. Immigration law is incredibly complex, there are many types of legal status, and there are many types of immigration documents that legal immigrants may possess as proof of legal status. State legislators are often not qualified to write laws in a way that will ensure that people that should be eligible for a license will actually be able to meet the law's requirements. Similarly, the federal government's list of acceptable documents for the REAL ID Act does not include all lawfully present immigrants.

Furthermore, a state DMV staff is not qualified to make judgment calls about immigration status or documents. As a result, various persons will be denied driver's licenses even though they are lawfully present, including persons who have been given temporary protected status due to civil conflict or natural disaster in their countries, abused women who are in the process of petitioning for legal residency under the provisions of the Violence Against Women Act, and individuals whose visas have been approved but not processed. Furthermore, refugees, asylees, and others who have fled persecution without proper identification documents from their countries of birth could also be denied driver's licenses because they cannot produce the documents on the list of acceptable documents (Waslin, 2002).

Immigrant families will be impacted negatively. Even restrictions targeted exclusively on undocumented immigrants extend well beyond that sector because, according to the Pew Hispanic Center, approximately 1 in 10 children in the U.S. lives in a "mixed-status family," in which at least one parent is a noncitizen and one child is a citizen (Passel & Taylor, 2010). Twenty-three percent of U.S. children live with at least one foreign-born parent. There are approximately 4 million children in the United States who have at least one parent who is an unauthorized immigrant, and the majority of those children were born in the country and are U.S. citizens. Thus, driver's license restrictions inevitably have spillover effects because family members and other community members are deprived of mobility, regardless of their immigration status. Parents' ability to provide for their families is compromised if they are unable to drive, and U.S. citizen children may be unable to go to the doctor or to school if their parents are unable to drive. This lack of mobility can result in economic, social, and health ramifications that eventually affect everyone. The economic and social impact of uneducated youth extends far beyond the immediate family, and the lack of proper health care has public health consequences for entire communities.

Driver's license restrictions can result in violations of civil rights. Increased restrictions on immigrant driver's licenses are also likely to result in racial profiling, vigilantism, and other forms of discrimination. For example, under the REAL ID Act, certain noncitizens may only receive temporary licenses, which must clearly state that they are temporary. In other words, the license will look different, and people will be able to single out these noncitizens, which may leave them vulnerable to discriminatory treatment (Johnson, 2004). Similarly, those who carry a license that is not REAL ID compliant (if a state chooses to issue them) or a Utah "driving privilege card" can also be identified as "different," opening them up to discrimination and abuse.

When documents such as driver's licenses are believed to be linked to immigration status, history has shown that Latinos and other ethnic minorities, as well as all people who look or sound "foreign," are the primary targets of document verification. For example, people believed to be "foreign" or who look like they might be "undocumented" because they fit a certain profile may be stopped for the sole purpose of being asked to provide documents, an enforcement activity that clearly leads to racial profiling. It is likely that merchants, restaurant owners, and others will request documentation before services will be provided (Waslin, 2002).

Furthermore, many of the individuals who are asked to show documentation and are suspected of being "undocumented" are often U.S. citizens and legal immigrants, resulting in civil rights violations. Reports of discrimination and racial profiling have already been documented. Puerto Ricans, who are U.S. citizens, have been the targets of such discrimination and have been asked to show proof of citizenship, or even worse, their green cards. Naturalized citizens have also been asked to produce additional documentation. In several cases, the driver's licenses of naturalized citizens, U.S.-born citizens, refugees, and others have been confiscated when the individuals failed to present green cards or other proof of legal immigration status.

Driver's license restrictions result in unsafe roads and high insurance rates. Being ineligible for a driver's license does not mean that unauthorized immigrants will cease driving. Rather, driver's license restrictions result in more unlicensed drivers operating vehicles on U.S. roads. Currently, there are an estimated 11.2 million undocumented immigrants in the United States, many of whom have to drive on U.S. roads in order to work, to go to school, or go to the doctor, whether or not they have a driver's license. As a result of immigrant restrictions, these drivers will not take drivers' classes or pass driving tests, will not be able to get insurance, and may be more likely to flee the scene of an accident for fear of immigration consequences unrelated to the accident.

The AAA Foundation for Traffic Safety has described unlicensed drivers as "among the worst drivers on the road," and it found that unlicensed drivers are almost five times more likely to be in a fatal crash than properly licensed drivers (Scopatz, Hatch, DeLucia, & Tays, 2003). In fact, when California's hit-and-run accidents increased by 19 percent between 2001 and 2003, law enforcement officers pointed to "an abundance of unlicensed drivers" and "drivers driving without auto insurance" as two key reasons for the increase. Nationally, more than 14 percent of all accidents are caused by uninsured drivers, resulting in $4.1 billion in insurance losses per year, according to the Insurance Research Council. High losses mean licensed drivers must pay higher premiums to cover accidents and injuries caused by uninsured drivers (National Immigration Law Center, 2008).

States that allow persons to get driver's licenses regardless of their immigration status have fewer uninsured motorists. In 2003, New Mexico passed a law allowing unauthorized immigrants to obtain driver's licenses, and between 2002 and 2007, uninsurance rates in the state dropped from 33 percent to 10.6 percent (National Immigration Law Center, 2008). When New York considered allowing undocumented immigrants to obtain driver's licenses, the State Department of Insurance estimated that premiums would be reduced by 34 percent, and the measure would have saved New York drivers $120 million a year (Bernstein, 2007).

In 2003, Austin, Texas, Assistant Chief of Police Rudy Landerso testified before the state legislature, stating, "we strongly believe it would be in the public interest to make available to these communities the ability to obtain a drivers license. In allowing this community the opportunity to obtain drivers licenses, they will have to study our laws and pass a driver's test that will make them not only informed drivers but safe drivers" (National Immigration Law Center, 2004).

Driver's license restrictions hamper law enforcement efforts. Security experts have pointed out that it may be counterproductive to deny identification documents to unauthorized immigrants, because denying them identification makes it even more difficult for law enforcement officers to do their jobs. Margaret Stock (2005) puts it this way:

> Refusing to give driver licenses to illegal immigrants means taking illegal immigrants out of the largest law enforcement database in the country. Thus, denial of licenses is a policy prescription that hampers law enforcement far more than it enhances it. If those who oppose granting driver licenses and state identification documents to illegal immigrants have their way, only U.S. citizens and legal aliens will be in the largest law enforcement database in the country. Thus, when a law enforcement official needs to find someone who happens to be an illegal immigrant, she will have no government database in which to look.

Restricting driver's licenses can also interfere with other law enforcement mechanisms. For example, law enforcement officials point out that the current child support enforcement and criminal warrant tracking functions of driver's licenses are less useful if large proportions of the population are excluded from the driver's license databases. Sacramento, California, Chief of Police Albert Najera wrote in the *Sacramento Bee* in 2004, "I have been in the public safety business for 33 years. In my experience, I would rather have a foreign national with reliable identification, a registered name, and photo and fingerprints that my officers can check while in the field than the information we have now, which is nothing" (National Immigration Law Center, 2004).

Furthermore, restricting immigrant access to driver's licenses erodes community trust, because driver's license restrictions result in a situation in which immigrants fear being reported to the immigration authorities, and therefore avoid contact with law enforcement. If immigrants are unwilling to step forward as witnesses to or victims of crime, and if they are fearful of assisting local law enforcement in fighting criminal and terrorist activity, the entire community is less safe. Kansas City, Kansas, Chief of Police Ronald Miller stated in a letter to the Kansas Senate Judiciary Committee in 2003 that "expanding opportunities to obtain drivers' licenses is not incongruent with homeland security considerations; on the contrary, allowing law enforcement to positively identify individuals within our state will help law enforcement to identify potential threats and reduce vulnerability and raise the feeling of security of citizens and non-citizens alike" (National Immigration Law Center, 2004).

There is another aspect of restrictive driver's license laws that has an impact on local law enforcement as well as federal law enforcement and the criminal justice system generally. Driver's license restrictions on immigrants may result in numerous arrests for driving without a license. At the local level, a large number of arrests for this relatively low-level offense could have the effect of clogging the public courts and diverting the limited time and resources of law enforcement officers, which would be better used investigating serious crimes.

Driver's license restrictions have taken on a new level of gravity because local police are increasingly partnering with federal immigration law enforcement agencies. This takes place through official programs like the 287(g) program (which deputizes certain local police officers to enforce federal immigration laws) and the Secure Communities program (which shares fingerprints taken at booking with federal immigration enforcement agencies), or through informal mechanisms, such as local police calling Immigration and Customs Enforcement (ICE) or Customs and Border Patrol (CBP) when they suspect a person they have detained is illegally present. Because federal immigration law enforcement agencies are notified, an arrest for driving without a license can result in the deportation of the unlicensed and unlawfully present immigrant. Immigrant advocates are concerned that this gives local police officers the ability, if not the incentive, to engage in racial profiling and target persons they suspect may be unlawfully present for violating minor traffic laws. Multiple reports show that local police have stopped immigrant drivers for broken taillights, broken license plate lights, or other minor infractions—or for no apparent violation—so that they could ask for documentation and bring the immigrant to the attention of ICE.

In addition to the obvious civil rights violations, this practice has the impact of filling local jails with minor offenders, at the expense of local taxpayers. It also puts ICE in a position of taking enforcement action against immigrants who are not serious criminals, pose no threat to the community, and do not fall high within ICE's enforcement priorities. In other words, ICE spends scarce resources detaining, transporting, and deporting low priority, noncriminal immigrants encountered because they were driving without a license, rather than focusing resources on its own stated priorities (Waslin, 2011).

Driver's license restrictions increase the market for fraudulent documents. Finally, the production and sale of falsified documents is likely to increase if large numbers of immigrants are denied driver's licenses (Waslin, 2002). Excluding individuals from legal driver's licenses creates conditions in which false documents and false identities will proliferate. While many have argued that there is increased need for increasing the integrity of documents for security reasons, and have pointed to driver's license restrictions as a way to do so, if such restrictions actually increase the proliferation of false documents, the government will have less accurate information about who is currently in the country.

CONCLUSION

Restricting immigrant access to driver's licenses is bad public policy that does not result in the desired outcome, but rather creates greater problems, sending the message that immigrants are not welcome, and further equates immigrants and minorities with national security and terrorist threats. This is one of a series of measures aimed at denying immigrants' rights, as well as access to basic benefits of membership in society. This will further marginalize already vulnerable populations, and otherwise pull back America's welcome mat.

Allowing maximum access to state-issued ID cards and driver's licenses through legitimate means ensures that all drivers are properly trained, licensed, and insured. It provides all residents of the United States with documentation, increasing the government's knowledge of who is in the country at any given time and preventing large segments of the population from living clandestinely, using fraudulent documents, and avoiding contact with law enforcement and other government and private agencies.

Safety and security goals are not mutually exclusive and can be accomplished through measures that carefully combine effectiveness, accuracy, explicit civil rights protections, and prevention of discriminatory effects. Steps must be taken to ensure that policies intended to control immigration and increase public safety and national security are effective and truly make the country safer, rather than simply make some people feel better at the expense of other members of the population.

REFERENCES AND FURTHER READING

American Association of Motor Vehicle Administrators. (2003). *Access to drivers license and identification card data by law enforcement.* Retrieved from http://www.aamva.org/aamva/DocumentDisplay.aspx?id=%7BAF5A6C98-EC8A-409E-9ADF-00089F59A2B6%7D

Bernstein, N. (2007, September 22). Spitzer grants illegal immigrants easier access to driver's licenses. *The New York Times.* Retrieved from http://www.nytimes.com/2007/09/22/nyregion/22licenses.html?pagewanted=1&_r=1&ref=nyregion

Eldridge, T. R., Ginsburg, S., Hempel, W. T., II, Kephart, J. L., & Moore, K. (2004). *9/11 and terrorist travel: A staff report of the National Commission on Terrorist Attacks Upon the United States.* Retrieved from http://govinfo.library.unt.edu/911/staff_statements/911_TerrTrav_Monograph.pdf

Johnson, K. R. (2004). Driver's licenses and undocumented immigrants: The future of civil rights law? *Nevada Law Journal, 5,* 218–220.

Lee H. Hamilton 9/11 Public Discourse Project. (n.d.). *Fact sheet: Driver's licenses, 9-11, and intelligence reform.* Retrieved from http://v2011.nilc.org/immspbs/DLs/PDPfactsheet_DLs_9-11&intel_reform.pdf

National Immigration Law Center. (2004). *Driver's licenses for all immigrants: Quotes from law enforcement.* Immigrants & Driver's Licenses Index. Retrieved from http://www.nilc.org/immspbs/DLs/DL_law_enfrcmnt_quotes_101404.pdf

National Immigration Law Center. (2008). *Why denying driver's licenses to undocumented immigrants harms public safety and makes our communities less secure.* Retrieved from http://www.immigrationpolicy.org/just-facts/why-denying-drivers-licenses-undocumented-immigrants-harms-public-safety-and-makes-our-co

National Immigration Law Center. (2009). *Overview of states' driver's license requirements.* Retrieved from http://www.nilc.org/immspbs/DLs/state_dl_rqrmts_ovrvw_2009-04-27.pdf

Passell, J., & Taylor, P. (2010). *Unauthorized immigrants and their U.S.-born children.* Pew Hispanic Center. Retrieved from http://www .pewhispanic.org/2010/08/11/unauthorized-immigrants-and-their-us-born-children/

Scopatz, R. A., Hatch, C. E., DeLucia, B. H., & Tays, K. A. (2003). *Unlicensed to kill: The sequel.* Retrieved from AAA Foundation for Traffic Safety website: http://www.aaafoundation.org/pdf/unlicensedtokill2.pdf

Stock, M. (2005, March 1). Driver licenses and national security. *Bender's Immigration Bulletin, 422.* Retrieved from http://www.drivers .com/article/971

Tatelman, T. B. (2008). *The REAL ID Act of 2005: Legal, regulatory, and implementation issues*, CRS report for Congress. Congressional Research Service. Retrieved from http://www.fas.org/sgp/crs/misc/RL34430.pdf

Waslin, M. (2002). Safe roads, safe communities: immigrants and state driver's license requirements. *Issue Brief*, No. 6. Retrieved from National Council of La Raza website: http://issuu.com/nclr/docs/1393_file_ib6_saferoads_driverlicense

Waslin, M. (2011). *The secure communities program: Unanswered questions and continuing concerns.* Immigration Policy Center Special Report. Retrieved from http://immigrationpolicy.org/sites/default/files/docs/Secure_Communities_112911_updated.pdf

Michele Waslin

COUNTERPOINT

Driver's licenses are a de facto national identity card for obtaining a job, opening a bank account, and accessing the vast majority of governmental institutions and critical infrastructure facilities. To allow the issuance of state driver's licenses or identity cards to persons who are present in the United States in violation of law would undermine numerous federal programs as well as diminish many national security–related programs that have been implemented since the terrorist attacks of September 11, 2001.

DRIVER'S LICENSES ARE "BREEDER DOCUMENTS" AND MUST BE PROTECTED FROM ABUSE

When considering whether driver's licenses should be provided to illegally present immigrants, it is important to recognize that driver's licenses (and state identification cards) are not used solely for driving. They are the de facto national identification card, and are used on a routine basis to establish identity. The fact that driver's licenses are used as a primary identification document is apparent from their use as "breeder documents." Breeder documents are documents that, once issued, allow individuals to obtain further documents based on the original document. Some examples of other supplemental documents obtained using driver's licenses include passports, birth certificates, firearms carry permits, hunting licenses, commercial licenses, building access identification, school or daycare employment, and medical facility access.

The importance of driver's licenses and state identification cards as breeder documents is apparent by reviewing the use of driver's licenses and state identification cards by a number of the 9/11 terrorists. After obtaining those documents, the terrorists used those breeder documents to obtain other documents and hide their identities for purposes of their criminal activities.

For this reason, the 9/11 Commission Report stressed the importance of providing secure identification and eliminating this gap. As the commission noted,

> Secure identification should begin in the United States. The federal government should set standards for the issuance of birth certificates and sources of identification, such as driver's licenses. Fraud in identification documents is no longer just a problem of theft. At many entry points to vulnerable facilities, sources of identification are the last opportunity to ensure that people are who they say they are and to check whether they are terrorists. (National Commission on Terrorist Attacks Upon the United States, 2004, p. 390)

Some argue that driver's licenses should be issued to individuals who are in the United States in violation of law because the 9/11 hijackers could have used their foreign passports to board the aircraft. This argument fails on many fronts. First, the 9/11 hijackers primarily used U.S. identification documents to help disguise their status and ease their boarding process. Next, foreign passport issuing standards are also growing more secure to help prevent fraud in their issuance. Finally, merely because terrorists can use many means to commit their crimes does not mean that the United States should make it easier for them to do so.

In some respects, the question of whether illegal immigrants should obtain driver's license is a closed issue. Almost all states currently require individuals seeking a driver's license to prove residence in the state, prove their identity, and prove their lawful presence in the United States. Many of these requirements were implemented as a direct result of legislation called the REAL ID Act. REAL ID was passed to address the significant vulnerabilities in the country's identification issuances, and in direct response to the 9/11 Commission Report. The theory behind REAL ID was that baseline application requirements and security features were necessary to reduce the vulnerabilities in the de-facto national identification cards. The act relies on state and local governments to handle the bulk of government identity document issuance, but it mandates common standards that make the cards secure. The act has been criticized as an unfunded mandate to states. However, despite full funding, most states and territories have moved to make their identification more secure and are REAL ID–compliant (Center for Immigration Studies, 2012).

PROMOTING FRAUD

To obtain a driver's license, the proof for residency for some states still consists of utility bills or property records, which are easy to forge. However, the majority of states require more secure documents to prove identity and lawful presence. These documents include a U.S. Passport, Social Security Card, Certificate of Naturalization, U.S. birth certificate, foreign passport with U.S. entry stamp, resident alien card, or employment authorization document issued by the Department of Homeland Security. The common thread linking all of these documents is that the local issuing authority has some means by which they can validate the documents presented. To allow unauthorized aliens to obtain driver's licenses would allow them to present foreign-issued documents, which state agencies have no way of validating. This would not only allow for unauthorized aliens to present fraudulent documents with any name they choose, but would also create a significant vulnerability that would allow criminals a much easier means by which to secure false identification.

Permitting illegal immigrants to obtain driver's licenses will also increase fraud in the license process, not only for illegal aliens but for any individual who seeks to hide his or her identity. Persons wanted on outstanding warrants would need only to go into a licensing bureau and claim to be an unauthorized alien and get a new identity issued.

Some argue that criminals would not bother to get driver's licenses to disguise their identity. The result of one recent law enforcement investigation, involving the bribery of state licensing officials, shows the fallacy of this argument (Immigration and Customs Enforcement, 2010; Immigration and Customs Enforcement, 2011). The investigation first targeted a known immigration consultant who was assisting aliens to enter and reside in the United States in violation of the law. The consultant would arrange their travel, transportation, and initial settling in the United States. The consultant would then take the individuals to a local Department of Motor Vehicles (DMV) facility, where he had a prearranged appointment with a licensing officer who would issue a driver's license without a road test for a bribe of several hundred dollars. The investigation identified several other DMV employees who also took bribes from the consultant. Once the corrupt DMV employees were indicted and arrested, several gave statements and evidence so that all of the individuals who were illegally issued licenses could be identified and have their licenses revoked. What was noted during the targeting of the recipients of the licenses was that they were not all unauthorized aliens. Many were U.S. citizens who had obtained a license in another name for a nefarious purpose. Several of these citizens were convicted felons who had also been arrested for narcotics trafficking, firearms possession, and other serious crimes. This shows the vulnerability created by insecure identification.

Another example of criminal use based on insecure identification involves the purchase of firearms. In order to purchase a firearm, a background check must be conducted to ensure the purchasing individual is not a convicted felon, illegal alien, or otherwise barred from possessing a firearm (such as being convicted for the crime of domestic violence). However, fingerprints are not taken, so the checks are solely biographical, not biometric, resulting in results that are a "hit or no hit." If an individual creates a fictitious name and is able to obtain a license in that name, then that person will not be flagged from the firearms purchase. This can be as easy as buying a foreign identity document online. Since the local DMV has no training in foreign documents and no ability to verify the document with the foreign government, then the individual will appear to have a clean identification and be authorized to purchase the firearm.

Another critical aspect of security related to state driver's licenses is the requirement to produce government identification to make certain banking transactions such as opening an account, conducting a wire transfer, and cashing a check. Financial institutions have certain requirements to obtain information about their customers before conducting business with them, and driver's licenses are a key method banks accept in this regard. Individuals, legal or not, who would like to commit bank fraud or wire transfer illicit income would have a much easier time obtaining false identities to facilitate their illegal activity.

INCENTIVIZING ILLEGAL IMMIGRATION

Providing driver's licenses to individuals who are not in the country legally potentially provides another incentive for individuals to come here and stay here illegally, rather than going through the appropriate legal means to immigrate. For example, knowing that the major draw to illegally enter the United States is employment, it would only make life easier for unauthorized workers if they could easily obtain a driver's license and cash their paychecks at the local bank, rather than if they had to use check-cashing services or maintain only foreign accounts. This country needs to ensure that disincentives are created to make it harder for individuals to reside illegally in the United States, rather than incentivize their illegal activity.

INCONSISTENCY WITH FEDERAL LAW AND FEDERAL PROGRAMS

Providing driver's licenses to individuals who are not in the country legally would be inconsistent with other federal government programs and federal policies. For example, the federal government uses a program called Secure Communities to ensure that individuals who are arrested by state and local law enforcement are identified through a federal enforcement agency, U.S. Immigration and Customs Enforcement (ICE). It makes no sense to have state and local authorities working to identify illegal aliens through Secure Communities, and then giving them documents to aid their stay.

ICE also enforces the laws relating to the hiring of illegal workers. Employers have obligations to complete what are known as I-9 Forms and certify that the documents provided by the employee appear to be genuine and reasonably relate to the employee. Issuing driver's licenses to unauthorized aliens would completely subvert the I-9 process, as a driver's license is a commonly used identity document. Employers would have no way to know whether the individual who provided the driver's license really is who he says he is. Unauthorized aliens would then only need to buy an inexpensive but fraudulent Social Security card to subvert the entire I-9 employment eligibility process.

The National Voter Registration Act of 1993 ("Motor Voter Act") requires states to provide individuals with an opportunity to register to vote when they obtain or renew their driver's licenses. At a minimum, there is potential for enhanced fraud in this area. Enabling millions of unauthorized aliens in the ability to vote in local and federal elections could undermine the electoral process.

SUBVERTING TRADITIONAL LAW ENFORCEMENT

Currently, law enforcement officers are able to build reasonable suspicion of someone's unlawful status if they encounter individuals who lack state identification documents. In many cases, if the officers cannot otherwise verify an individual's identity through database checks, some departments notify federal law enforcement agencies like Immigration and Customs Enforcement of their possible unlawful status. Many criminal aliens have been encountered and identified through these interactions. Issuing driver's licenses to unauthorized aliens would only diminish this law enforcement tool and allow many criminal aliens to go free.

DRIVER'S LICENSES WILL NOT MAKE THE ROADS SAFER

One argument in support of providing driver's licenses to undocumented individuals is that doing so would "make the roads safer." Although all share in the goals of keeping roads safe, there is no evidence to support the argument that issuing documentation to illegal individuals will materially aid this process. Most automobile accidents are caused by individuals that hold driver's licenses, not by illegally present immigrants. A report from the AAA Foundation for Traffic Safety found that only 5 percent of drivers in fatal car accidents were unlicensed.

Many individuals who are driving in the United States illegally have learned to drive in their home countries and had driver's licenses issued in those countries. To the extent that they desire to learn more about driving in the United States, there are several options available to them. Currently, unauthorized aliens can read their state's driver instruction manuals (some of which are printed in multiple languages), take driving lessons, and attend driver education classes. None of these are prohibited, and they have been found to make people better drivers and the roads safer without providing a government endorsement of illegal activity.

Some argue that restricting driver's licenses will keep illegal immigrants from obtaining insurance. Regrettably, there is no guarantee that having a license will compel any individual to obtain insurance. If this were true, then there wouldn't be the high number of lawful residents who currently drive every day without insurance. Additionally, there have been countless instances of unauthorized aliens getting auto insurance without having a valid driver's license.

CONCLUSION

As demonstrated above, there is no basis to grant driver's licenses to individuals who are in the United States illegally. Their mere presence in the country is a violation of law. Permitting them to obtain driver's licenses increases risks of fraud and criminal activity, and any "benefits" that could be obtained from permitting them to obtain driver's licenses are outweighed by the harm that this causes.

REFERENCES AND FURTHER READING

AAA Foundation for Traffic Safety. (2011). *Unlicensed to kill*. Retrieved from http://www.aaafoundation.org/pdf/2011Unlicensed2Kill.pdf

Center for Immigration Studies. (2012). *Real ID implementation annual report*. Retrieved from http://cis.org/real-id-implementation-report

Department of Homeland Security. (2011). *Minimum standards for driver's licenses and identification cards acceptable by federal agencies for official purposes* [Final REAL ID rule, with extension of deadline date]. Retrieved from http://edocket.access.gpo.gov/2011/2011-5002.htm

Eldridge, T. R., Ginsburg, S., Hempel, W. T., II, Kephart, J. L., & Moore, K. (2004). *9/11 and terrorist travel: A staff report of the National Commission on Terrorist Attacks Upon the United States*. Retrieved from http://govinfo.library.unt.edu/911/staff_statements/911_TerrTrav_Monograph.pdf

Frosch, D. (2012, January 18). A new fight on licenses for illegal immigrants. *The New York Times*. Retrieved from http://www.nytimes.com/2012/01/19/us/in-new-mexico-a-fight-anew-over-drivers-licenses-for-illegal-immigrants.html

Immigration and Customs Enforcement. (2010, July 14). *ICE press release: New Jersey man sentenced in cash scheme for driver's licenses*. Retrieved from http://www.ice.gov/news/releases/1007/100714philadelphia.htm

Immigration and Customs Enforcement. (2011, January 13). *ICE press release: Two more defendants plead guilty in licensing examiners bribe scheme*. Retrieved from http://www.ice.gov/news/releases/1101/110113philadelphia.htm

National Voter Registration Act of 1993 (Motor Voter Act), Pub. Law No. 103-31. (1993).

9/11 Commission. (2004). *9/11 Commission final report: Final report of the National Commission on Terrorist Attacks Upon the United States*. Available online at http://www.gpoaccess.gov/911/index.html

Numbers USA Education and Research Foundation. (n.d.). *Rewards for illegal aliens*. Retrieved from http://www.numbersusa.com/PDFs/DriversLicenses.pdf

Office of the Comptroller of the Currency, U.S. Department of the Treasury. (n.d.). *Answers about identification*. Retrieved from http://helpwithmybank.gov/get-answers/bank-accounts/identification/faq-bank-accounts-identification-02.html

OpenCongress for the 112th United States Congress. S.1261–PASS ID Act. Retrieved from http://www.opencongress.org/bill/111-s1261/show

Real ID Act, Pub. Law No. 109-13 (2005).

Sifuentes, E. (2009, August 22). Lack of driver's license, no bar to getting insurance. *North County Times*. Retrieved from http://www.nctimes.com/news/local/sdcounty/article_259b0930–198d-5c9f-a56d-ce63ed039670.html

Julie Myers Wood

13

Crime

POINT: Immigrants, especially illegal ones, are responsible for rising crime rates in border areas, as well as drug problems, gang problems, and other crime-related issues.

Trista R. Chaney, Federation for American Immigration Reform (FAIR)

COUNTERPOINT: The statistics, according to some, do not bear an increased crime rate due to immigrants, despite some headline-grabbing incidents; overall, immigrants are no less law-abiding than U.S. citizens.

Walter A. Ewing, American Immigration Council

Introduction

Some political debates are animated by differing interpretations of facts. At other times, however, the very facts themselves are at issue. The Point section of this chapter, by Trista R. Chaney, argues that immigrants—particularly those here illegally—are responsible for rising crime rates in border areas, as well as drug and gang problems. Chaney cites a study claiming that almost 1 in 20 incarcerated persons is a "deportable alien." In contrast, the Counterpoint half of the chapter, by Walter A. Ewing, presents statistics on crime that suggest that immigrants are *not* more prone to crime that U.S. citizens. Ewing cites a study that came to the exact opposite conclusion of the one cited by Chaney: that immigrant men between the ages of 18 to 39 are significantly less likely to be incarcerated than native-born men of the same age group. Which set of facts is true?

Chaney begins by arguing that the rule of law is "routinely" disregarded in foreign countries, and that illegal immigrants bring a "disrespect for the law" when they come to the United States. Chaney notes that, by definition, illegal immigrants break the law by overstaying visas or coming to the country through unauthorized channels. She argues that this law breaking demonstrates that such individuals are already prone to disregarding rules and regulations and will continue to break laws—such as those for driving or working in this country—without concern. Chaney also sees a trend of dangerous criminals, people who were forced to leave their countries precisely because of illegal activities, seeking refuge in the United States. Although she admits that the "precise relationship between illegal aliens and criminality is . . . nearly impossible to establish," she still maintains that there are four types of crimes primarily committed by illegal immigrants: immigration crimes themselves, drug- and gang-related crime, human smuggling and human trafficking, and identity theft and document fraud.

Ewing's Counterpoint starts at a very different place: he states that "get tough" policies on immigration are ineffective because "the overwhelming majority of immigrants are neither criminals nor terrorists." He says evidence conclusively shows that both illegal and legal immigrants are less likely than the native-born to commit crimes. Ewing shows that although immigration rates in the United States have gone up, crime rates have actually gone down; violent crime declined more than 40 percent between 1990 and 2000, while illegal immigration tripled during the same decade. He also shows that the states with the most immigrants have the lowest crime rates.

Ewing admits that unauthorized immigrants may, out of necessity, commit minor crimes (such as falsifying documents in order to get driver's licenses), but he says that the idea that they are more likely than U.S. citizens to commit violent crimes is not borne out by the facts. In addition, Ewing points out that many immigrants in federal prison are there for immigration violations and nothing more; he believes that the best way to improve public safety is by improving the U.S. immigration system rather than by focusing on crimes that, arguably, only a few commit. "Lumping unauthorized gardeners and janitors into the same category as murderers and thieves makes no sense," Ewing argues. "Yet that is exactly what many anti-immigrant activists do."

When reading this chapter, ask yourself what the primary reason is behind the different views of Chaney and Ewing. Is it ideological? It is because they focus on different *types* of crimes? Is the data for one side more compelling than the other? Why or why not?

POINT

The United States is at a period in history when concerns about the safety of its citizens are at the forefront of national security policy debates. In order to maintain a free and democratic society, respect for the rule of law by government and individuals is crucial. In foreign countries, however, the rule of law is routinely disregarded, and illegal aliens coming from those countries bring traditions of disrespect for the rule of law with them to the United States. This has become a serious problem. In *Illegal, but not Undocumented* (2009), Ronald W. Mortensen writes, "The culture of corruption is reinforced when illegal aliens are offered special benefits such as in-state tuition, drivers licenses, financial services, and religious offices and privileges in spite of their multiple, ongoing violations of civil and criminal law."

Advocates for tolerance of illegal immigration rationalize the commission of criminal acts rather than supporting the rule of law. Yet it defies logic to think that individuals who break the laws of the United States by coming into this country illegally or by staying in this country in violation of immigration laws would develop a greater respect for other American laws once they are within the nation's borders. The Immigration and Nationality Act sets out the requirements for lawful admission and continuing presence in the country. Those who blatantly disregard those laws are unlikely to then follow others, when they continue to break the law in order to perform certain tasks, such as driving and working within the country, without authorization.

Illegal immigration advocates argue that these individuals are being "forced" to break the law in order to live in the United States. They studiously disregard the innocent victims of illegal alien crimes, which include fraud and identity theft, to name a few. In October 2006, the Majority Staff Report of the House Committee on Homeland Security stated, "Not all illegal aliens are crossing into the United States to find work. Law enforcement officials indicate that there are individuals coming across the border who are forced to leave their home countries because of criminal activities. These dangerous criminals are fleeing the law in other countries and seeking refuge in the United States." Additionally, "sanctuary cities" such as Los Angeles, Houston, Chicago, and Miami, to name a few, are providing practical refuge to these criminals through policies that prohibit law enforcement officers from verifying citizenship and immigration status.

This half of the essay will discuss the character and scope of illegal alien criminality and the problems related to data collection on this topic, particularly whether immigrants, especially illegal immigrants, are more or less likely than U.S.-born citizens to commit crimes. It will be argued that illegal aliens, as a class, are more likely than native-born citizens to commit crimes.

GENERAL STATISTICS

The southern border of the United States extends for nearly 2,000 miles and spans four states: Arizona, California, New Mexico, and Texas. According to reports, a majority of illegal alien crime is committed within the vicinity of the southwestern border, with a significantly lower incidence near the 4,000-mile northern border between the United States and Canada. But the incidence of illegal alien crime is not limited to the border states. Statistical reports of illegal alien populations and crime rates are both very difficult to ascertain. This absence of a generally accepted statistical basis makes reliable measurements of the connection between the two data sets extremely difficult. Further, research in the area of crime and its connection with immigration in general has been limited. The inaccuracies of research on the topic were discussed extensively by Jack Martin, director of special projects for the Federation for American Immigration Reform (FAIR), in a 2007 study. Using the federal State Criminal Alien Assistance Program (SCAAP), which is designed to reimburse states and localities for costs associated with the incarceration of illegal criminal aliens, FAIR found that SCAAP offered the "only reliable data for a valid assessment of the share of prisoners who are deportable aliens." The FAIR study also found that 1 of every 21 prisoners nationwide is a deportable alien, while 1 of every 31 U.S. residents is an adult illegal alien, concluding that "the likelihood that an illegal alien will be among those incarcerated (1 in 21) is significantly greater than the share of adult illegal aliens in the country (1 in 31). It is this greater likelihood of being incarcerated that clearly demonstrates that illegal aliens are disproportionately involved in criminal activity."

PROBLEMS WITH QUANTIFICATION OF RESEARCH DATA

The precise relationship between illegal aliens and criminality is nearly impossible to establish. Among the more significant reasons for this is the fact that the data collected uses the broader categories of "foreign-born" and "U.S.-born" criminals, and does not separately break out criminal activity by illegal aliens. Factors within the criminal justice system also cannot be controlled, which may also lead to incomplete or inaccurate data. Critics argue that criminal processing differences result in illegal aliens being overrepresented in prison populations. They also argue that illegal aliens are "law-abiding" because it is in their interest not to draw attention to their illegal immigration status and unlawful presence in the United States. This same logic leads to yet another reason that information on illegal alien crime statistics is so difficult to collect: There may be underreporting of crimes committed by illegal aliens when illegal aliens are also the victims. Each of these arguments will be discussed in turn.

The March 2007 FAIR study, *Illegal Aliens and Crime Incidence,* explains why data from studies regarding the criminality of aliens is often misleading. These studies often focus on "foreign-born" criminals versus U.S.-born criminals. Data for illegal aliens is not accurately represented by the category of "foreign-born." As the FAIR study suggests, these individuals include legal immigrants and long-term nonimmigrants. These individuals have been "screened for any previous criminal activities before they can get a green card, . . . screened for criminal activity before they can become U.S. citizens, and . . . [are] required to state under oath whether they have any criminal history before they can get a visa." Jack Martin, the author of the FAIR study, notes, "something would be very wrong with our visa screening process if research did not reveal that the foreign-born were less likely to have committed crimes in the United States than the native-born population."

INCOMPLETE DATA ON CRIMINAL ACTIVITIES

Another reason for inaccurate data regarding the criminal activities of illegal aliens is that state or local government sanctuary policies, which prohibit law enforcement officers from inquiring into citizenship and immigration status, can distort data collection. The studies that have analyzed the prevalence of illegal alien crime often differ, too, in their classification of criminals. Some analyze populations of aliens who were merely detained, but never tried; others review only records of convictions; and yet others use arrests of illegal aliens as their baseline.

Finally, another possible reason for the lack of accurate data is that illegal alien crime is arguably underreported within illegal alien communities. Some analysts argue that because victims of crime in illegal alien communities fear apprehension and deportation, the crime rates of these communities remains higher than reported. Controlling for these factors creates very difficult technical problems, which is yet another reason that peer-reviewed research in this area has been so sparse.

TYPES OF CRIMES

There are four types of crimes that best represent the broader prevalence of illegal aliens in criminal activity: (1) immigration crimes, (2) drug- and gang-related crime, (3) human smuggling and trafficking, and (4) identity theft and document fraud.

Immigration crimes. Some violations of law are committed only by immigrants, by definition. For example, only an immigrant can illegally enter or remain in the country or perform work in the country without a valid visa. An illegal alien living in the United States without authorization is typically in violation of civil law, though a large number of these illegal aliens commit a smorgasbord of other crimes in the process, as well as certain immigration criminal offenses that are ongoing. Critics often forget that some violations of immigration laws are crimes. For example, the reentry of a previously removed alien is punishable as a crime under federal law (Title 8, Section 1326 of the U.S. Code).

Drugs and gangs. Data suggests that criminal aliens in border states are involved with high levels of crime, especially drug smuggling. In 2009, Randal C. Archibold, reporting for *The New York Times,* stated, "Arizona appears to be bearing the brunt of smuggling-related violence. Some 60 percent of illicit drugs found in the United States—principally cocaine, marijuana and methamphetamine—entered through the border in this state."

But problems with illegal aliens and drugs are not limited to border states. According to the U.S. Drug Enforcement Administration and National Drug Intelligence Center report, the increase in drug-trafficking activity in North Carolina during the period from 1990 to 2000 was directly related to a record influx of foreign nationals into the state. In 2005, the House Committee on Homeland Security reported that 1.1 to 2.2 million kilograms of cocaine and 5.8 to 11.6 kilograms of marijuana were smuggled into the United States at the Mexican border. In the words of the committee, Mexican drug cartels have effectively taken control of the U.S.-Mexico border and "operate with military grade weapons, technology and intelligence and their own respective paramilitary enforcers." These Mexican drug trafficking cartels "represent the greatest organized crime threat to the United States," according to a threat assessment report by the National Drug Intelligence Center (2008).

Mexican cartels continue to engage in violent battles against each other, as well as with the Mexican and U.S. governments along the border. They present a serious threat to public safety, due to their history of violence and involvement in transnational crime. Studies, including a 2005 report published by the North Carolina Governor's Crime Commission, suggest that up to 66 percent of Hispanic/Latino gang members in North Carolina are illegal aliens. Similarly, federal authorities estimate that approximately 90 percent of members of the MS-13 gang, one of the most violent and powerful gangs in the United States, are foreign-born illegal aliens that rely on routine unauthorized entry across the southern U.S. border to sustain their criminal operations in this country.

Human smuggling and human trafficking. Another crime often closely associated with illegal aliens is human smuggling and human trafficking. According to the 2006 report *A Line in the Sand,* by the Majority Staff of the House Committee on Homeland Security, Subcommittee on Investigations, the border between Texas and Mexico "has been experiencing an alarming rise in the level of criminal cartel activity, including drug and human smuggling, which has placed significant additional burdens on Federal, state, and local law enforcement agencies." Human smugglers and human traffickers often coordinate their efforts with the drug cartels and gangs discussed above in order to use roadways and other routes under their respective control.

According to the Violent Crimes Institute, "Mexico is the number one source for young female sex slaves in North America." In an attempt to enter illegally into the United States, many aliens become involved with human smugglers and traffickers. In the report *Human Trafficking,* U.S. Immigration and Customs Enforcement (ICE) points out that "human smuggling and human trafficking are two of the most heinous crimes [that it] investigates." Illegal immigrants pay smugglers and traffickers to be illegally transported into the interior of the United States, and these immigrants frequently become prostitutes, sell drugs, or find themselves in other forms of servitude to pay their debts. The U.S. House Committee on Homeland Security reports that illegal aliens commonly pay between $2,000 and $60,000 to be illegally trafficked and smuggled across the border. The committee also notes the following:

> Prosecutions for human smuggling are abysmally low. Typically, groups of illegal aliens apprehended attempting to cross the border will not identify the smuggler in the group. For those smugglers that are identified and captured, most are simply returned to their country of origin. Thus, there is a revolving door for the smugglers. Since it is unlikely the smuggler will be prosecuted he or she can opt for voluntary removal, face no criminal penalties and smuggle again.

While it is not a federal crime for an illegal alien to allow himself to be smuggled across the border, some states, such as South Carolina, have passed laws that would make it a state felony for illegal aliens to allow themselves to be transported, moved, concealed, harbored, or sheltered within the state with the intent to further their unlawful entry into the United States.

Identity theft and document fraud. A final set of crimes strongly associated with illegal immigration status involves document fraud and identity theft. These crimes are most often committed by aliens for purposes of gaining employment, which often requires paperwork that undocumented people, by definition, do not legitimately possess. With modern advancements in technology, the incidences of identity theft and document fraud have continued to increase. According to Ronald Mortensen of the Center for Immigration Studies, "identity theft is one of the fastest-growing crimes in the United States and impacts millions of American citizens and legal residents each year. . . . U.S. law enforcement agencies have observed that identity theft and immigration 'go hand in hand.'" Mortensen further notes that studies have shown that states with the highest rates of illegal immigration also have the highest level of job-related identity theft. Eight of the 10 states with the highest incidence of identity theft are also among the 10 states where illegal aliens are the largest percentages of the total population. These states are Arizona, California, Colorado, Florida, Georgia, Nevada, New York, and Texas.

The federal criminal penalties for felony document fraud, in particular Title 18, Section 1546 of the U.S. Code, include imprisonment for up to 25 years. The crime of document fraud is also punishable at the state level, with each state having its own individual laws sanctioning identity theft. There is, however, a higher standard of proof required in order to establish that a person has committed aggravated identity theft under federal law. In its online document, *About Identity Theft,* the Federal Trade Commission defines identity theft as being "when someone uses your personally identifying information, like your name, SSN, or credit card number, without your permission, to commit fraud or other crimes." Under federal and most state statutes, a person must "knowingly" use another person's Social Security number or other information in order to be convicted of the crime of aggravated identity theft. In the 2009 case of *Flores-Figueroa v. United States,* the U.S. Supreme Court held that prosecutors must prove that an illegal alien is knowingly using another person's Social Security number in order to convict the illegal alien of identity theft under the federal statute, 18 U.S.C. § 1028A(a)(1), leaving prosecutions on behalf of the victims of these serious and devastating crimes with a high hurdle to clear.

A June 2009 study by Ronald W. Mortensen found that "75 percent of working-age illegal aliens use fraudulent Social Security cards to obtain employment." Common types of identity and document fraud include the use of counterfeit Social Security cards, driver's licenses, green cards, and birth certificates in order to gain unlawful employment. These illegal aliens using fake documents will have also committed identity theft felonies by perjuring themselves on I-9 forms and other official applications.

The correlation between the size of the illegal alien population and the incidence of identity theft is undeniable and somewhat predictable. The victims of illegal alien identity theft are frequently children. Crime statistics for Arizona illustrate this correlation, as Arizona ranks number one nationally in identity theft complaints per capita; child identity theft in Arizona is four times the national rate, impacting an estimated 1.1 million children.

Critics of effective law enforcement seek to justify illegal alien document fraud, perjury, and identity theft by arguing that unauthorized aliens are forced to commit crimes in order to obtain jobs. This view turns the criminal justice system on its head, transforming criminals into victims and encouraging broad societal disregard for the rule of law. In fact, the proximate cause for these categories of immigrant crime is the decision of these individuals to enter the country without inspection and remain in it illegally.

CONCLUSION

The lackadaisical nature of the current enforcement of U.S. immigration laws threatens public safety and national security. As discussed, the prevalence of criminal behavior among illegal aliens in the country is undeniable. The problems with research regarding the correlation of criminality and illegal immigration make it difficult to accurately analyze the results. The use of data that is not ideal or often incomplete leads to incorrect conclusions regarding the character and scope of illegal alien criminality.

The four crimes previously discussed (immigration crimes, gang- and drug-related crimes, human trafficking and human smuggling, and identity theft) by no means provide an all-encompassing list of crimes for which illegal aliens have been convicted. However, these crimes, given their nature and relation to illegal immigration, are committed by overwhelming numbers of aliens. Those who blatantly disregard the laws of the United States by entering illegally are less likely to follow other laws of the nation once inside its boundaries.

References and Further Reading

Archibold, R. C. (2009, March 23). Mexican drug cartel violence spills over, alarming U.S. *The New York Times,* p. A1. Retrieved from http://www.nytimes.com/2009/03/23/us/23border.html?pagewanted=all

Committee on Homeland Security, Subcommittee on Border and Maritime Security. (2011). Subcommittee hearing: "Securing our borders—Operational control and the path forward." Retrieved from http://homeland.house.gov/hearing/subcommittee-hearing-%E2%80%9Csecuring-our-borders-%E2%80%93-operational-control-and-path-forward%E2%80%9D

Federal Trade Commission. (2010). *About identity theft.* Retrieved from http://www.ftc.gov/bcp/edu/microsites/idtheft/consumers/about-identity-theft.html#Whatisidentitytheft

Feere, J., & Vaughan, J. (2008). *Taking back the streets: ICE and local law enforcement target immigrant gangs.* Retrieved from Center for Immigration Studies website: http://cis.org/ImmigrantGangs

Identity theft 911 report blames illegal immigration, government inaction for state's top ranking. (2008, March). *Phoenix Business Journal.* Retrieved from http://www.bizjournals.com/phoenix/stories/2008/03/03/daily17.html

Martin, J. (2007). *Illegal aliens and crime incidence.* Report by the Federation for American Immigration Reform. Retrieved from http://www.fairus.org/site/DocServer/crimestudy.pdf?docID=2321

McCaul, M. T. (2006, October). *A line in the sand: Confronting the threat at the southwest border.* Prepared by the Majority Staff of the House Committee on Homeland Security, Subcommittee on Investigations. Retrieved from http://www.house.gov/sites/members/tx10_mccaul/pdf/Investigaions-Border-Report.pdf

Mortensen, R. W. (2009). *Illegal, but not undocumented: Identity theft, document fraud, and illegal employment.* Retrieved from Center for Immigration Studies website: http://cis.org/IdentityTheft

National Drug Intelligence Center. (2008). *National drug threat assessment 2009.* Retrieved from http://www.justice.gov/ndic/pubs31/31379/index.htm#Contents

National Drug Intelligence Center, & Drug Enforcement Administration. (2003). *North Carolina drug threat assessment.* Retrieved from http://www.usdoj.gov/ndic/pubs3/3690/3690p.pdf

Rhyne, A., & Yearwood, D. (2005). *The nature and scope of Hispanic/Latino gangs in North Carolina.* Department of Crime Control and Public Safety/N.C. Governor's Crime Commission. Retrieved from http://www.ncgccd.org/pdfs/pubs/HispanicGangs.pdf

Schurman-Kauflin, D. (2006). *Profiling sex trafficking: Illegal immigrants at risk.* Violent Crimes Institute. Retrieved from http://www.drdsk.com/articles.html#SexTrafficking

South Carolina Senate Bill 20, passed June 2011. Retrieved from http://www.scstatehouse.gov/sess119_2011-2012/prever/20_20110615.htm

U.S. Immigration and Customs Enforcement. (n.d.). *Human trafficking.* Retrieved from http://www.ice.gov/human-trafficking

Trista R. Chaney

COUNTERPOINT

Anti-immigrant activists are fond of telling scary stories. When it comes to the subject of immigration, crime, and terrorism, these stories are typically about individual immigrants—especially unauthorized, or "illegal," immigrants—who planned or committed heinous crimes or terrorist acts. Such stories are presented as proof that the U.S. government should restrict immigration and "get tough" on *all* immigrants to save the lives of U.S. citizens. These kinds of anecdotes may be emotionally powerful, but they are highly misleading. Obviously, dangerous criminals and terrorists must be punished, and immigrants who are dangerous criminals or terrorists should be locked up. But harsh immigration policies are not effective in fighting crime or terrorism, simply because the overwhelming majority of immigrants are neither criminals nor terrorists. In fact, numerous studies over the past 100 years have shown that high rates of immigration are not associated with higher rates of crime. Moreover, immigrants are less likely to commit criminal acts or be behind bars than the native-born. This holds true for both legal immigrants and the unauthorized, regardless of their level of education or country of origin. In other words, most immigrants are not a threat to public safety or national security. But outdated U.S. immigration policies—which spur unauthorized immigration and channel it into the hands of smugglers—undermine both safety and security.

CRIME RATES HAVE FALLEN AS THE IMMIGRANT POPULATION HAS GROWN

If immigration actually fueled more crime, then one would expect crime rates to go up during times when the immigrant population grows larger. In reality, though, crime rates in the United States have fallen at the same time that millions of immigrants have come to the country. The number of immigrants in the country doubled between 1990 and 2009, rising from 19.8 million to 38.5 million, according to data from the U.S. Census Bureau. The share of the U.S. population composed of immigrants rose from 7.9 percent to 12.5 percent (see Figure 13.1), or one out of every eight people.

Figure 13.1 Immigrant share of U.S. population (1990, 2000, 2009)

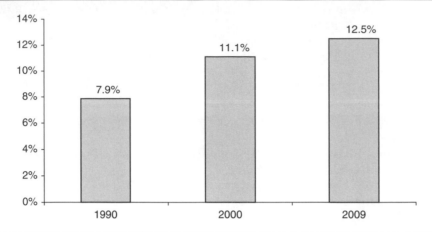

Sources: From *The Foreign-Born Population: 2000* (p. 3), by N. Malone et al., December 2003, Washington, DC: U.S. Census Bureau; *Nativity Status and Citizenship in the United States: 2009* (p. 1), by T. A. Gryn and L. J. Larsen, October 2010, Washington, DC: U.S. Census Bureau.

Figure 13.2 Number of unauthorized immigrants in the United States (1990, 2000, 2010)

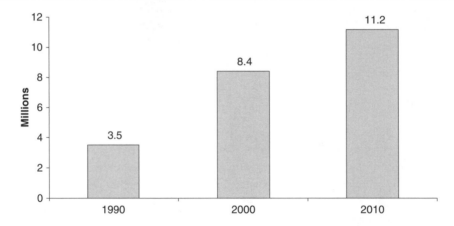

Source: From *Unauthorized Immigrant Population: National and State Trends, 2010* (p. 23), by J. S. Passel and D. Cohn, February 1, 2011, Washington, DC: Pew Hispanic Center.

At the same time, the number of unauthorized immigrants tripled, from 3.5 million in 1990 to 11.2 million in 2010 (see Figure 13.2), according to estimates by the Pew Hispanic Center. By 2010, unauthorized immigrants accounted for more than one out of every four immigrants in the country (Passell & Cohn, 2011, p. 10).Yet while immigration surged, the violent crime rate declined by more than 40 percent, dropping from 729.6 violent crimes per 100,000 people in 1990 to 429.4 in 2009, according to FBI data (see Figure 13.3). Violent crime rates also declined in cities with large immigrant populations, including El Paso, San Diego, Los Angeles, Chicago, New York, and Miami.

Given the weight of this evidence, it is not surprising that even some conservative analysts have come to the conclusion that immigration is unrelated to crime. For instance, a 2008 report from the Americas Majority Foundation concluded that crime rates are lowest in states that have the highest immigration growth rates (Nadler, 2008). From 1999 to 2006, the total crime rate declined by 13.6 percent in the 19 highest-immigration states, compared to a 7.1 percent decline in the other 32 states. In 2006, the 10 "high influx" states—those with the largest recent increases in immigration—had the lowest rates of crime in general and violent crime in particular.

Figure 13.3 Violent crime rate in the United States, 1990–2009

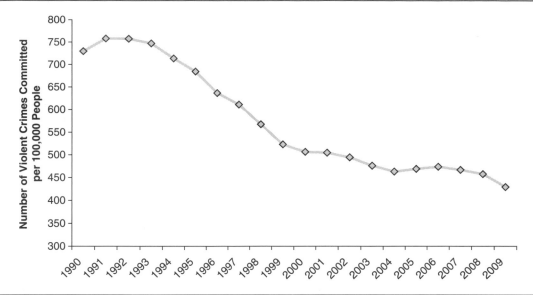

Source: From *Uniform Crime Reports*, by Federal Bureau of Investigation, prepared by the National Archive of Criminal Justice Data, accessed June 13, 2011.

Figure 13.4 Incarceration rates for immigrant and native-born men ages 18–39 in 2000

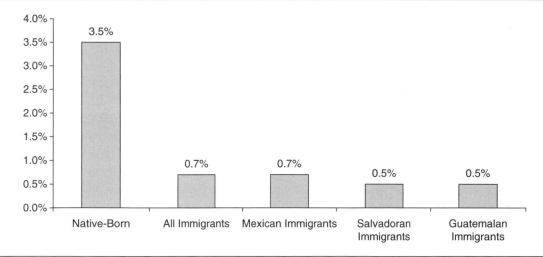

Source: From *The Myth of Immigrant Criminality and the Paradox of Assimilation: Incarceration Rates Among Native and Foreign-Born Men* (p. 6), by R. G. Rumbaut and W. A. Ewing, Spring 2007, Washington, DC: Immigration Policy Center, American Immigration Law Foundation.

IMMIGRANTS ARE FAR LESS LIKELY TO BE IN PRISON THAN THE NATIVE-BORN

Not only does immigration not cause crime, but immigrants are much less likely than the U.S.-born to end up behind bars. This holds true for immigrants of all nationalities and education levels—even less-educated Mexicans, Salvadorans, and Guatemalans, who account for most unauthorized immigrants in the country. A 2007 study by the sociologists Rubén G. Rumbaut and Walter Ewing demonstrated this by examining incarceration rates among men age 18–39, who make up the bulk of the U.S. prison population. Using data from the 2000 census, Rumbaut found that 3.5 percent of native-born men were in prison, compared to only 0.7 percent of immigrant men. The lower rate of incarceration for immigrant men held across nationalities. Only 0.7 percent of Mexican immigrant men, and 0.5 percent of Salvadoran and Guatemalan immigrant men, were in prison in 2000 (see Figure 13.4). The lower rate of incarceration for immigrant men also held when examining only the least educated. Among men without a high school diploma, 9.8 percent of natives were behind bars in 2000, compared to 1.3 percent of immigrants.

Other analyses have yielded similar results. For instance, a 2008 report from the Public Policy Institute of California concluded that foreign-born adults in California have lower incarceration rates than native-born adults. Based on data from 2005, the report found that the incarceration rate for foreign-born adults was only 297 per 100,000 people, compared to 813 per 100,000 for native-born adults. Immigrants accounted for 35 percent of California's adult population, but constituted only 17 percent of the state's prison population. Similarly, a 2008 analysis by New Jersey's *Star-Ledger* of data from the U.S. Census Bureau and the New Jersey Department of Corrections found that U.S. citizens were twice as likely as immigrants to end up in the state's prisons. According to the *Ledger*'s Brian Donohue, non-U.S. citizens accounted for 10 percent of New Jersey's population, but only 5 percent of the 22,623 inmates in prison as of July 2007.

DEFINING ALL UNAUTHORIZED IMMIGRANTS AS "CRIMINALS" IS HIGHLY MISLEADING

The evidence has long been overwhelming that there is no link between immigration and crime (Rumbaut & Ewing, 2007, p. 12–14). However, anti-immigrant activists often attempt to bypass this evidence through word games, arguing that all unauthorized immigrants are "criminals" by definition, because they are in the country without permission, or "illegally." There are two problems with this line of thinking. First, as many as half of unauthorized immigrants came to the United States on valid visas, then stayed once their visas expired—which is a civil violation of immigration law, not a criminal offense. Second, and even more important, someone residing in the country without authorization is not a "criminal" in any meaningful sense of the word. Unauthorized immigrants are not harming anyone by being here. In fact, they contribute to the U.S. economy through their labor, their consumer spending, and their tax payments. Their unauthorized status does lead them to commit certain kinds of minor crimes once they are here, such as buying false identity documents in order to get a job or driving without a license. But these crimes are fundamentally different from crimes that involve attacks upon persons or property. Lumping unauthorized gardeners and janitors into the same category as murderers and thieves makes no sense. Yet that is exactly what many anti-immigrant activists do.

IMMIGRATION VIOLATIONS, NOT VIOLENT ACTS, ACCOUNT FOR MANY OF THE IMMIGRANTS IN FEDERAL PRISON

In an attempt to get around low immigrant incarceration rates, many anti-immigrant activists turn to a frequently cited estimate that just over one-quarter of inmates in federal prisons are "criminal aliens." This estimate, taken from a 2005 report by the U.S. Government Accountability Office, is highly misleading for two reasons. First, many of the immigrants in federal prison are being criminally charged with an immigration violation and nothing more. In other words, they may be in federal prison even though they have not committed a violent crime or even a property crime. Their only crime might be entering the country without permission. The federal government has chosen to prosecute more and more unauthorized immigrants for "unlawful entry" rather than simply deporting them, which means that they end up in federal prison. Second, the federal prison population is a very small share of the total prison population. According to the Bureau of Justice Statistics, only 9 percent of the U.S. prison population was in federal prisons as of 2009. At the state and local level, where the other 91 percent of U.S. prisoners are held, the incarceration rates for immigrants are lower than for the native-born.

A CENTURY'S WORTH OF EVIDENCE HAS DEMONSTRATED THAT IMMIGRATION IS NOT ASSOCIATED WITH HIGHER CRIME

Studies demonstrating that immigration does not fuel crime, and that immigrants are less likely than natives to end up behind bars, are not new. In fact, there have been many such studies over the past century. The economists Kristin Butcher and Anne Morrison Piehl, for instance, analyzed data from the 1980 and 1990 censuses and, like Rumbaut, found that immigrants had lower incarceration rates. Butcher and Piehl also used data from the 1980, 1990, and 2000 censuses to demonstrate that the lower incarceration rate for immigrants could not be explained away with the argument that there are so few immigrants in prison because so many of them are deported, or by the argument that harsher immigration laws are deterring immigrants from committing crimes because they are afraid of getting deported. Instead, Butcher and Piehl (2005) conclude that, during the 1990s, "those immigrants who chose to come to the United States were less likely to be involved in criminal activity than earlier immigrants and the native born."

Other researchers have also gone beyond the question of how often immigrants are being imprisoned for crimes, asking instead how often immigrants are committing crimes. For example, the sociologist Robert J. Sampson and his colleagues studied 180 Chicago neighborhoods from 1995 to 2002 and found that Latin American immigrants were less likely than the U.S.-born to commit violent crimes, even when they lived in crowded and impoverished neighborhoods. Moreover, the likelihood of committing violent crimes increased steadily from generation to generation. It was lowest among the "first generation" (immigrants), higher for the "second generation" (U.S.-born children of immigrants), and higher still for the "third generation and higher" (the U.S.-born children of U.S.-born parents). First-generation immigrants were 45 percent less likely to commit violent crimes than third-generation Americans. Second-generation Americans were 22 percent less likely to commit violent crimes than the third generation and higher.

The sociologists Ramiro Martínez and Matthew Lee also found no link between being an immigrant and being a criminal when they studied homicides in San Diego, El Paso, and Miami, or when they studied drug violence in Miami and San Diego. Several other studies have examined homicide rates among the Cuban refugees who arrived in Miami during the "Mariel Boatlift" of 1980. Although the Mariel Cubans frequently were portrayed in the media as violent criminals, they were in fact no more likely than natives to commit homicides. In addition, after a short period of time in the United States, they were less likely to commit crimes than Cubans who arrived in Miami before the Mariel Boatlift. Miami, and South Florida in general, experienced a spike in homicides before the Mariel Cubans arrived. But homicide rates declined throughout the 1980s, despite a steady stream of immigrants from Latin America.

Other researchers have taken a different approach to the subject of immigrants and crime by drawing upon data from the National Longitudinal Study of Adolescent Health (Add Health). Add Health is a survey of adolescents in the United States that has been conducted in several waves since 1994. The sociologists Kathleen Mullan Harris, Hoan Bui, and Ornuma Thingniramol tapped Add Health data and found that immigrant adolescents were significantly less likely than second- or third-generation adolescents to engage in "risk behaviors" such as violence, delinquency, and substance abuse. In fact, immigrant youth of every nationality engaged in fewer risk behaviors than native-born non-Latino whites.

When it comes to the topic of immigration and crime, history has a way of repeating itself. During the first 3 decades of the twentieth century, in the midst of a previous era of large-scale immigration to the United States, three federal commissions asked many of the same questions about immigration and crime as today's researchers—and they came to the same conclusions. The Industrial Commission of 1901, the Dillingham Immigration Commission of 1911, and the Wickersham National Commission on Law Observance and Enforcement of 1931 each tried to measure how immigration fueled an increase in crime. And each commission found that immigrants were less likely than the native-born to be involved in crime. As the report of the Dillingham Commission concluded a century ago,

> No satisfactory evidence has yet been produced to show that immigration has resulted in an increase in crime disproportionate to the increase in adult population. Such comparable statistics of crime and population as it has been possible to obtain indicate that immigrants are less prone to commit crime than are native Americans (p. 1).

Nearly a century later, the U.S. Commission on Immigration Reform would also ask if immigration is associated with higher crime and would conclude, in a 1994 report, that it is not, and that crime rates generally were lower in border cities like El Paso.

ANTI-IMMIGRANT RHETORIC VERSUS REALITY: THE CASE OF ARIZONA

Arizona is a case study in what happens when the myth takes hold that unauthorized immigrants are dangerous criminals. On April 23, 2010, Arizona governor Jan Brewer signed into law the Support Our Law Enforcement and Safe Neighborhoods Act, also known as S.B. 1070. As its name suggests, this is a law built upon the assumption that unauthorized immigrants are criminals, and that removing them from Arizona will therefore reduce crime. S.B. 1070 declares its intent to "make attrition through enforcement the public policy of all state and local government agencies in

Arizona"—meaning that the law was designed to force unauthorized immigrants out of the state by involving state and local police in the enforcement of immigration laws that should be the responsibility of the federal government. Among many other provisions, S.B. 1070 would require police in Arizona to ask people about their immigration status during any lawful stop, detention, or arrest, and it would authorize police to arrest anyone they believed to be "removable from the United States." In other words, the law would have targeted anyone who looked or sounded "foreign." On July 28, 2010, the day before S.B. 1070 was scheduled to go into effect, a federal district court issued a preliminary injunction against these and several other controversial provisions of the law.

The author of S.B. 1070, Republican State Senator Russell Pearce of Mesa, confidently predicted that the law would result in "less crime" and "safer neighborhoods." What Senator Pearce and other supporters of S.B. 1070 overlook is

Figure 13.5 Number of unauthorized immigrants in Arizona (1990, 2000, 2010)

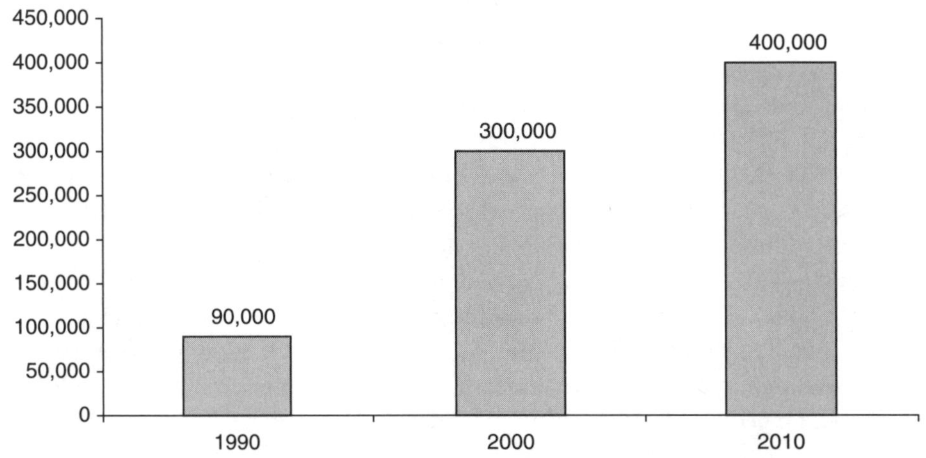

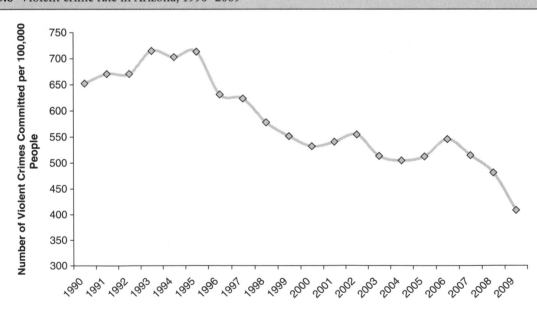

Source: From *Unauthorized Immigrant Population: National and State Trends, 2010* (p. 23), by J. S. Passel and D. Cohn, February 1, 2011, Washington, DC: Pew Hispanic Center.

Figure 13.6 Violent crime rate in Arizona, 1990–2009

Source: From *Uniform Crime Reports*, by Federal Bureau of Investigation, prepared by the National Archive of Criminal Justice Data, accessed June 13, 2011.

that crime rates in Arizona have been falling for years, at the very same time the unauthorized-immigrant population has increased dramatically. Between 1990 and 2010, the number of unauthorized immigrants in Arizona more than quadrupled, increasing from roughly 90,000 to 400,000 (see Figure 13.5). Yet the violent crime rate in the state began a downward slide in the early 1990s, dropping from a high of 715 violent crimes per 100,000 people in 1993 to 408.3 in 2009 (see Figure 13.6). These trends cast serious doubt on the claims of S.B. 1070 supporters that the law is a crime-fighting tool.

TURNING POLICE INTO IMMIGRATION AGENTS MAKES IT *HARDER* TO FIGHT CRIME

Not only do laws such as S.B. 1070 fail to fight crime; they undermine actual crime fighting. Police cannot effectively fight crime unless they have the trust of the communities they serve. People report crimes and serve as witnesses only if they view the police as allies and not enemies. It is for this reason that cooperative, trust-building forms of "community policing" have played such a large part in the decline in crime rates since the early 1990s. But in communities with large numbers of immigrants, crime victims and witnesses will not come forward to the police if doing so will get them deported. Many U.S. citizens and legal immigrants will also avoid contact with the police if a family member, a neighbor, or a friend might be deported as a result.

That is exactly the situation that laws like Arizona's S.B. 1070 create. Police are transformed into immigration agents, and they are viewed with fear and suspicion by entire communities. Crimes go unreported, witnesses to crimes do not come forward, and tips are not provided to police. Moreover, police spend more time and resources on finding unauthorized immigrants, and less on finding actual criminals. This is precisely what happened in Arizona's Maricopa County, where Sheriff Joe Arpaio turned his police officers into immigration enforcement agents, diverting their attention away from the solving of actual crimes (Gabrielson & Giblin, 2008). While Maricopa County diverted more resources to immigration enforcement, thousands of felony warrants were not served, arrest rates dropped, and response times to 911 calls increased. It is just these kinds of negative repercussions that led the International Association of Chiefs of Police and the Major Cities Chiefs Association to publicly oppose policies that force state and local police to become enforcers of federal immigration law (Tramonte, 2011, p. 6). Likewise, a 2010 report from the Police Executive Research Forum stated flatly that police "officers should be prohibited from arresting or detaining persons for the sole purpose of investigating their immigration status" (Hoffmaster et al., 2010, p. 62). The reason is simple: if unauthorized immigrants are afraid of the police, then they will not report crimes or testify against criminal suspects. Moreover, unauthorized immigrants are targeted by criminals who know that unauthorized victims are unlikely to go to the police for fear of deportation (Hoffmaster et al., 2010, pp. xvi–xviii).

IMMIGRATION ENFORCEMENT WITHOUT IMMIGRATION REFORM DOES NOT STOP UNAUTHORIZED IMMIGRATION

The federal government may be the appropriate enforcer of federal immigration law, but federal attempts to control unauthorized immigration have been spectacularly unsuccessful—and misplaced. Unauthorized immigration occurs when the existing legal limits on immigration to the United States do not match the economic and social realities that actually draw immigrants to the country. Yet, rather than keep the broken immigration system in sync with reality, the federal government has tried to enforce that broken system and stem the flow of unauthorized immigrants to the United States with various immigration enforcement initiatives: deploying more and more agents, fences, flood lights, aircraft, cameras, and sensors along the southwest border with Mexico; raiding more and more worksites to arrest unauthorized workers; and expanding detention facilities to accommodate the hundreds of thousands of unauthorized immigrants apprehended (and then deported) each year. The result: an unauthorized population that has tripled in size over two decades.

Anti-immigrant activists sometimes claim that the number of unauthorized immigrants in the country has grown because the federal government has not devoted enough resources to immigration enforcement. Federal budget figures, however, do not bear that out. The annual budget of the U.S. Border Patrol stood at $3.0 billion in fiscal year (FY) 2010—a nine-fold increase since FY 1992 (see Figure 13.7), according to the Border Patrol's Office of Public Affairs. The number of Border Patrol agents stationed along the southwest border with Mexico grew to 16,974 in FY 2010—an almost fivefold increase since FY 1992 (Figure 13.8). The budget of U.S. Customs and Border Protection (CBP), the

Figure 13.7 U.S. Border Patrol budget, FY 1992–2010

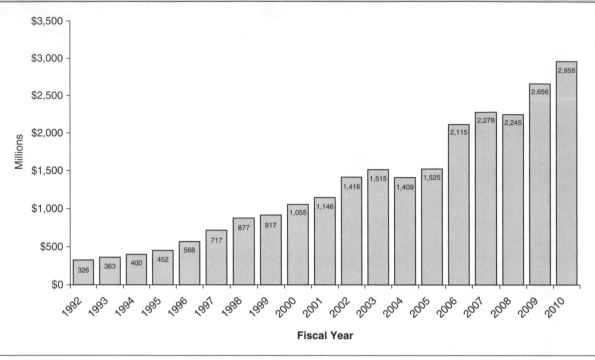

Source: U.S. Border Patrol Headquarters, Office of Public Affairs, April 26, 2010, and September 25, 2009.

Figure 13.8 U.S. Border Patrol agents stationed on southwest border, FY 1992–2010

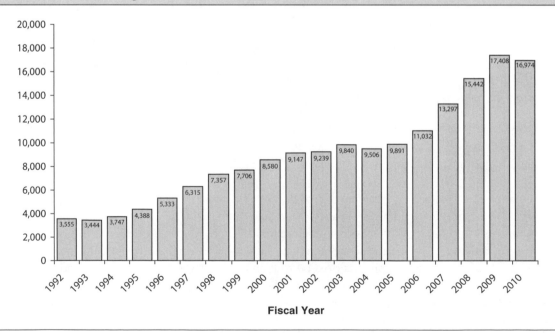

Source: U.S. Border Patrol Headquarters, Office of Public Affairs, April 26, 2010, and September 25, 2009.

Figure 13.9 CBP and ICE budgets, FY 2003–2010

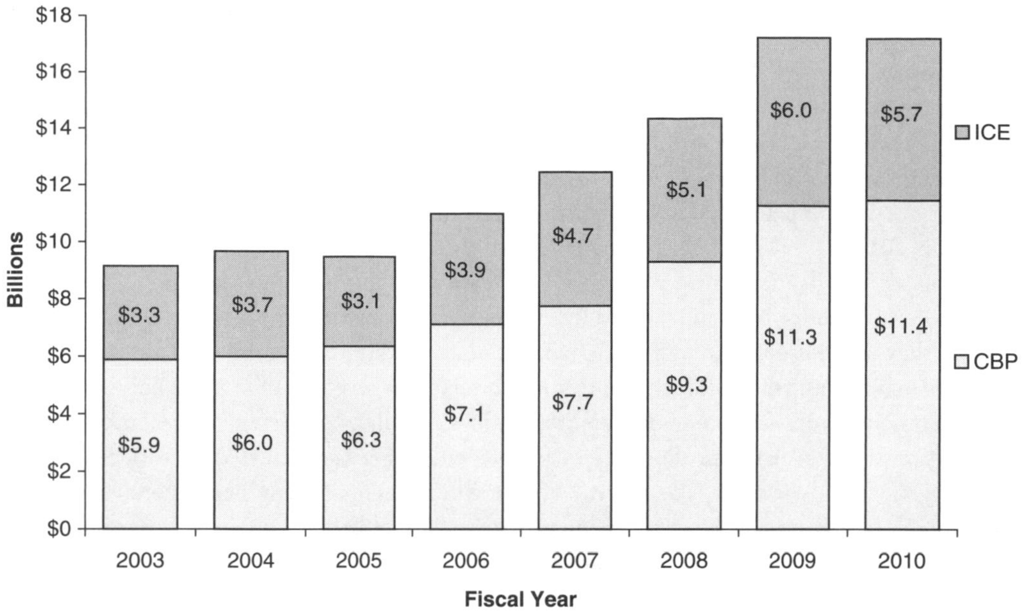

Source: From *Budget-in-Brief*, by U.S. Department of Homeland Security, for fiscal years 2005 through 2011.

parent agency of the Border Patrol within the Department of Homeland Security (DHS), increased from $5.9 billion in FY 2003 (when DHS was created) to $11.4 billion in FY 2010 (Figure 13.9), according to DHS figures. And the budget of U.S. Immigration and Customs Enforcement (ICE), the DHS agency that enforces immigration laws in the interior of the country, grew from $3.3 billion in FY 2003 to $5.7 billion in FY 2010 (Figure 13.9).

These tens of billions of dollars in immigration enforcement spending have done little to hinder unauthorized immigration. Surveys conducted among Mexican immigrants from 2005 through 2009 by the sociologist Wayne Cornelius and a team of researchers at the Center for Comparative Immigration Studies at the University of California, San Diego, found that immigration enforcement had little impact on the chances that an unauthorized immigrant would make it across the border. Due to increased reliance upon smugglers, well over 90 percent of unauthorized immigrants from sending communities in Mexico eventually made it into the United States, although it sometimes took two or three tries.

Rather than lessen unauthorized immigration, the federal government's enforcement-only strategy has wasted federal resources on the pursuit of unauthorized immigrants who are not a threat to anyone, and who were drawn here by the labor demands of the U.S. economy and the natural human desire to join family members already in the United States. The federal enforcement-only immigration strategy has also fueled the growth of increasingly profitable, sophisticated, and violent businesses in human smuggling, which are far more dangerous than the unauthorized immigrants they smuggle. Yet federal immigration authorities continue to spend most of their time and energy chasing unauthorized bus boys through the desert. From a law-enforcement perspective, this is a failed strategy.

IMMIGRATION ENFORCEMENT WITHOUT IMMIGRATION REFORM UNDERMINES NATIONAL SECURITY

Even most anti-immigrant activists would agree that the vast majority of unauthorized immigrants entering the country from Mexico are interested in finding jobs and reuniting with their families, not in launching a terrorist attack. But, since 9/11, concern has grown among policymakers and law enforcement authorities that foreign terrorists might try to enter the United States from Mexico, relying on the same people-smuggling networks that unauthorized immigrants use and becoming lost in the unauthorized flow. Some anti-immigrant politicians have claimed that terrorists are already among the unauthorized immigrants from countries other than Mexico who cross the southern border. Even though most non-Mexican immigrants come from Central and South American nations that are not a security threat to the United States, these politicians point to the extremely small number of Arabs and Muslims apprehended at the border, acting as if they constitute a threat to national security simply because they are Arab or Muslim. In fact, there is no evidence that a foreign terrorist has crossed the southern border into the United States (Leiken & Brooke, 2006). Nevertheless, safeguarding the country from a terrorist attack has become one of the principal justifications for calls to further fortify the border by deploying the military or building a 2,000 mile-long fence from the Pacific Ocean to the Gulf of Mexico (Mehta, 2011; National Public Radio, 2011).

If the recent history of U.S. border enforcement is any indication, measures such as building a fence or calling in soldiers are not likely to drain the sea of unauthorized immigrants within which terrorists could hide, or to eliminate the smuggling networks they could use. Federal efforts to stop unauthorized immigration have succeeded primarily in redirecting it through isolated terrain where border enforcement is relatively weak—and into the hands of people smugglers. In order to circumvent new border-enforcement measures, many smuggling networks have become more technologically savvy in their operations. The growing profitability of people smuggling has attracted the interest of the exceedingly violent Mexican drug cartels. As a result, the current border-enforcement strategy has fostered greater sophistication (and violence) in the illicit pathways by which a foreign terrorist might cross the southern border into the United States.

Yet sealing the U.S.-Mexico border against unauthorized entry is not impossible. The demilitarized zone between North and South Korea demonstrates that this could, in theory, be done. With enough troops, cameras, fencing, razor wire, motion detectors, surveillance aircraft, and land mines, the federal government could prevent any immigrants, smugglers, or terrorists from walking across, flying over, or digging under the U.S.-Mexico border in an unauthorized location. However, these measures are not going to be effective security tools unless they also are implemented along the 4,000 miles of border with Canada and the 5,000 miles of Pacific, Atlantic, and Gulf coastline where unauthorized entry can occur by airplane, boat, or submarine. Otherwise, immigrants, smugglers, and terrorists will simply go around a fortified southern border. In fact, Mexican smugglers are already ferrying boatloads of immigrants (and drugs) to the coast of southern California by way of the Pacific Ocean. But even if the federal government spent the many tens of billions of dollars required to "seal" the entire perimeter of the United States, the country would not be protected against an attack by native-born terrorists, like the Oklahoma City bombing in 1995.

The central policy question, when it comes to national security and border enforcement, is not whether U.S. borders can be sealed, but whether this is the best way to catch terrorists. Border enforcement is a needle-in-a-haystack means of intercepting terrorists from abroad. Catching a terrorist depends on the gathering of intelligence indicating that a particular person is a threat to national security and is either planning to enter the country or is already here. Foreign terrorists can come to the United States legally—on airplanes, with valid visas—if intelligence and law-enforcement agencies have not identified them as threats, or have not shared what they know with each other or the overseas consulates that issue visas (which is what happened in the case with the 9/11 hijackers). Attempting to locate a terrorist by sifting through every immigrant who enters the country—hoping that one of them confesses to being a terrorist—is not an effective means of foiling a terrorist plot.

CONCLUSION

The best available evidence indicates that crime in the United States is not caused or worsened by immigrants, whether they are legal or "illegal." This fact should not be that surprising. Immigrants come here for economic and educational opportunities that are not available in their home countries, and to build better lives for their families. They have much to lose and little to gain by breaking the law. Unauthorized immigrants, in particular, have even more reason to not run afoul of the law, given that they can be deported for not having legal immigration status. It is ironic indeed that unauthorized immigrants are often incorrectly portrayed as hardened criminals by anti-immigrant activists.

The best way to improve both public safety and national security through immigration policy would be to overhaul the U.S. immigration system. Unauthorized immigrants already living in the United States should be given an opportunity to earn legal status. In the process, they would register with federal authorities and undergo background checks, meaning that the federal government would finally know who is in the country. Limits on future employment-based immigration, both permanent and temporary, should rise and fall with U.S. labor demand, within a system that ensures livable wages and working conditions for all workers, regardless of where they were born. And the random caps and endless delays that characterize the family-based immigration system should be eliminated, allowing families to reunite.

Reforms such as these would result in far fewer immigrants trying to enter the United States without permission. The market for people smugglers would be undercut. As a result, criminals and terrorists trying to get across the border without being noticed would not have a large pool of unauthorized immigrants to hide among, or an extensive smuggling infrastructure to aid their entry into the country. And the U.S. Border Patrol could focus more on finding criminals and terrorists, and less on apprehending jobseekers.

REFERENCES AND FURTHER READING

Bui, H. N., & Thingniramol, O. (2005). Immigration and self-reported delinquency: The interplay of immigrant generations, gender, race, and ethnicity. *Journal of Crime and Justice, 28*(2), 79–100.

Butcher, K. F., & Morrison Piehl, A. (1998). Recent immigrants: Unexpected implications for crime and incarceration. *Industrial and Labor Relations Review, 51*(4), 654–679.

Butcher, K. F., & Morrison Piehl, A. (2005). *Why are immigrants' incarceration rates so low? Evidence on selective immigration, deterrence, and deportation.* Working Paper 2005-19. Federal Reserve Bank of Chicago. Retrieved from http://www.chicagofed.org/webpages/publications/working_papers/2005/wp_19.cfm

Donohue, B. (2008, April 12). Citizens twice as likely to land in NJ prisons as legal, illegal immigrants. *The Star-Ledger.* Retrieved from http://www.nj.com/news/index.ssf/2008/04/citizens_twice_as_likely_to_la.html

Ewing, W. A. (2007). Beyond border enforcement: Enhancing national security through immigration reform., *Georgetown Journal of Law and Public Policy, 5*(2), 427–446.

Gabrielson, R., & Giblin, P. (2008, July 8). MCSO evolves into an immigration agency. *East Valley Tribune.*

Harris, K. M. (1999). The health status and risk behavior of adolescents in immigrant families. In D. J. Hernández (Ed.), *Children of immigrants: Health, adjustment, and public assistance* (pp. 286–347). Washington, DC: National Academy of Sciences Press.

Hoffmaster, D. A., Murphy, G., McFadden, S., & Griswold, M. (2010). *Police and immigration: How chiefs are leading their communities through the challenges.* Police Executive Research Forum. Retrieved from http://www.policeforum.org/library/immigration/PERFImmigrationReportMarch2011.pdf

Lee, M. T. (2003). *Crime on the border: Immigration and homicide in urban communities.* New York, NY: LFB Scholarly Publishing.

Lee, M. T., Martínez, R., Jr., Rosenfeld, R. B. (2001). Does immigration increase homicide? Negative evidence from three border cities. *Sociological Quarterly, 42*(4), 559–580.

Leiken, R. S., & Brooke, S. (2006). The quantitative analysis of terrorism and immigration: An initial exploration. *Terrorism and Political Violence, 18*(4), 503–521.

Martínez, R., Jr., & Lee, M. T. (2000). On Immigration and crime. In National Institute of Justice, *Criminal justice 2000: The nature of crime* (Vol. 1, pp. 485–525). Washington, DC: U.S. Department of Justice, Office of Justice Programs.

Martínez, R., Jr., Lee, M. T., & Nielsen, A. L. (2004). Segmented assimilation, local context and determinants of drug violence in Miami and San Diego: Does ethnicity and immigration matter? *International Migration Review, 38*(1), 131–157.

Martinez R., Jr., & Valenzuela, A., Jr. (Eds.). (2006). *Immigration and crime: Race, ethnicity, and violence.* New York, NY: New York University Press.

Mehta, S. (2011, October 15). Michele Bachmann vows to finish Mexico border fence. *Los Angeles Times.* Retrieved from http://articles.latimes.com/2011/oct/15/nation/la-na-bachmann-immigration-20111016

Nadler, R. (2008). *Immigration and the wealth of states.* Retrieved from Americas Majority Foundation website: http://www.amermaj.com/ImmigrationandWealth.pdf

National Public Radio. (2011, October). Illegal immigration a central issue in GOP race. *Talk of the Nation.* Transcript available at http://www.npr.org/2011/10/18/141473380/illegal-immigration-a-central-issue-in-gop-race

Passel, J. S., & Cohn, D. (2011). *Unauthorized immigrant population: National and state trends, 2010.* Retrieved from Pew Hispanic Center website: http://www.pewhispanic.org/2011/02/01/unauthorized-immigrant-population-brnational-and-state-trends-2010

Public Policy Institute of California. (2008, June). *Just the facts: Immigrants and crime.* Retrieved from http://www.ppic.org/content/pubs/jtf/JTF_ImmigrantsCrimeJTF.pdf

Reports of the Immigration Commission, 61st Congress, 3rd Session. (1911). Washington, DC: Government Printing Office, pp. 159–221.

Rumbaut, R. G., & Ewing, W. A. (2007). *The myth of immigrant criminality and the paradox of assimilation: Incarceration rates among native and foreign-born men.* Washington, DC: Immigration Policy Center, American Immigration Law Foundation.

Sampson, R. J., Morenoff, J. D., & Raudenbush, S. (2005). Social anatomy of racial and ethnic disparities in violence. *American Journal of Public Health, 95*(2), 224–232.

Tonry, M. (Ed.). (1996). *Ethnicity, crime, and immigration: Comparative and cross-national perspectives.* Chicago, IL: University of Chicago Press.

Tramonte, L. (2011). *Debunking the myth of "sanctuary cities": Community policing policies protect Americans.* Washington, DC: Immigration Policy Center, American Immigration Council.

U.S. Commission on Immigration Reform. (1994). *U.S. immigration policy: Restoring credibility.* Washington, DC: U.S. Government Printing Office.

Walter A. Ewing

Economic, Labor, and Demographic Debates

Introduction

Two concepts inform the debates over the economic impacts of immigrants. The first is the widely accepted notion that the net effects of these impacts provide the key metrics for determining the structure of the immigration system—that the purpose of the system should be to maximize its net economic benefit to the United States. The second underpinning relates to the driving force behind cultural debates over immigration: the reality that immigrants are outsiders in the imagined American community, or the perception that they are strangers among us. Immigrants' status as outsiders is what makes the debates about their economic impacts salient. If this were not the case, there would be an equivalent focus on the net economic and fiscal impacts in states and regions resulting from internal migration by American citizens.

Immigrants' Economic and Fiscal Impacts Have Been Widely Studied

There is a rich economics literature on the methodology and proper assumptions involved in measuring the wage and other economic consequences of immigration. And, not surprisingly, the results of these measurements differ based on the assumptions and methodology used. The consequences of immigration for public finances—its fiscal impacts—are also widely discussed in the economics literature. These impacts are much more difficult to measure because they occur at the federal and state levels, and because the state impacts are different in each state, reflecting varying tax structures and differing provision of social service. Because public finances involve taxing people to fund government services, the issue of immigration's fiscal impacts is deeply colored by two things: the status of immigrants as outsiders in America's imagined community, and the fact of illegal immigration.

Low-skilled immigrants generate the greatest focus and controversy in the debates over immigration's fiscal impacts. But it is important to remember that these fiscal impacts are not the result of a person's immigration status per se. They derive from the fact that any low-skilled worker, regardless of immigration status, tends to use more in social services than he or she pays in taxes. Both sides of the fiscal impacts equation are involved. Lower-wage workers pay lower income and sales taxes because they earn and consume less than do higher-wage workers. And, lower-wage workers are more likely to need support from the social safety net. In addition, the fact that the current legal structure of the U.S. immigration system specifically limits immigration by low-skilled workers means that a large proportion of low-skilled immigrants are living and working in the United States illegally. Thus, debates over the fiscal impacts of (low-skilled) immigrants are conflated with public outrage over illegal immigration and are centrally tied to opposition to immigration in general.

Demographics Shape Immigration Impacts and Debates

There are important demographic forces at work in the United States with regard to immigration. These demographic forces affect immigration in two ways: they contribute to the number and types of immigrants that come to the United States, and they powerfully shape the economic and fiscal impacts of these immigrants once they are in the country. Large incentives for immigrant workers to come to the United

States result from the fact that the native-born population in the United States is growing slowly and aging. One in two new workers—50 percent of the growth in the labor force—since 1990 has been an immigrant, and immigrants are affecting the size, age structure, and skill mix (measured by educational attainment) of the U.S. population.

Immigrants affect the size of the U.S. population in two ways: by coming to the United States in the first place, and by having children once they are here. Approximately 12.5 percent of the U.S. population is foreign-born. But while immigrants are 12.5 percent of the overall population, a full 23 percent of native-born children under the age of nine, and 16 percent of native-born children between the ages of 10 and 19, have one or more foreign-born parents. Table 1 details the number of native-born and foreign-born persons in 10-year age cohorts, with details on the number of native-born with one or more foreign-born parents.

Table 1   Immigration's impacts on population growth

| | Native-born | | | | Foreign-born | |
| | With 2 native parents | | With 1+ foreign parents | | | |
Age group	Number	Percent	Number	Percent	Number	Percent
0 to 9	30.4	75	9.2	23	1.0	2
10 to 19	31.7	78	6.6	16	2.5	6
20 to 29	30.4	74	4.2	10	6.3	16
30 to 39	27.9	71	2.9	7	8.4	21
40 to 49	33.6	78	2.3	5	7.3	17
50 to 59	32.0	82	1.8	5	5.2	13
60 to 69	20.9	82	1.6	6	3.1	12
70 to 79	12.0	76	1.8	12	1.9	12
80+	6.8	70	1.8	19	1.0	11
U.S. Total	**225.6**	76.6%	**32.2**	10.9%	36.8	12.5%

Source: U.S. Census Bureau's American Community Survey, 2007–2009 (numbers in thousands).

Figure 1   Immigration's impacts on population growth

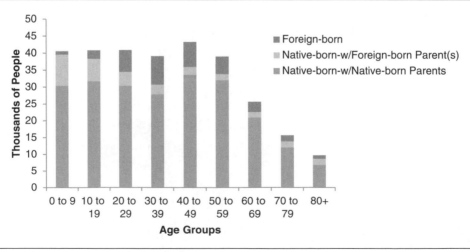

Source: U.S. Census Bureau's American Community Survey, 2007–2009.

Because immigrants are, on average, younger than the native-born population, they also affect the age structure of the U.S. population. Figure 1 depicts the data in Table 1 graphically and illustrates the extent to which immigrants have shaped the number of people who are working age or younger.

Immigrants' effect on the educational attainment profile of people in the United States is also significant. Table 2a, provides comparative data on the educational attainment of immigrants and natives in the United States age 25 and older. Among native-born Americans, only 4 percent have just 0–8 years of education, and another 8 percent have some high school. This means that only 12 percent of native-born Americans are low-skilled when skill is measured by educational attainment. Among the foreign-born, 21 percent of immigrants have just 0 to 8 years of education, and another 12 percent have only completed some high school.

Table 2b examines the share of each educational attainment cohort that is foreign-born, and one sees that immigrants are 52 percent of those with 0 to 8 years of education and 21 percent of those who have completed some high school. The foreign-born share of other educational attainment categories—except for the 26 percent of PhDs who are immigrants—is relatively small. In other words, immigrants are having the greatest impact in the lowest educational attainment category.

When one looks a little more closely at this 0–8 years of schooling cohort, it is clear that the age profile of the very low-skilled differs dramatically for native-born Americans and immigrants. Figure 2 reveals that the majority of native-born persons with 0–8 years of education are 55 and older, while the majority of immigrants in this education cohort are under 55.

The age differences in this educational cohort mean that natives and immigrants are filling very different roles in labor markets and do not compete as directly as some fear. It means that immigrants have been a critical source of young, low-skilled workers in the U.S. economy. And it means that concerns about labor-market competition among low-skilled immigrants and natives may be less than many imagine.

Table 2a Educational attainment of adults age 25 and older by nativity

(Numbers, 000s)	0–8 years	Some HS	HS grads	Some college	College grads	Master's or prof. degrees	PhDs	Total
Number of natives	6,014	13,794	50,732	50,491	29,984	15,196	1,687	167,899
Number of immigrants	6,565	3,683	7,200	5,780	5,115	2,919	596	31,858
Total	12,579	17,477	57,932	56,271	35,099	18,115	2,283	199,756
Percent of nativity cohorts								
Percent of natives	4	8	30	30	18	9	1	100
Percent of immigrants	21	12	23	18	16	9	2	100
Total	6	9	29	28	18	9	1	100

Source: U.S. Census Bureau's American Community Survey, 2007–2009.

Table 2b Nativity share of educational attainment cohorts

	0–8 years	Some HS	HS grads	Some college	College grads	Master's or prof. degrees	PhDs	Total
Percent of educational attainment cohorts								
Native-born	48	79	88	90	85	84	74	84
Immigrants	52	21	12	10	15	16	26	16
Total	100%	100%	100%	100%	100%	100%	100%	100%

Source: U.S. Census Bureau's American Community Survey, 2007–2009.

Figure 2 Age profile of people with 0–8 years of education

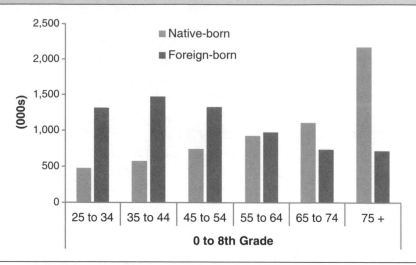

Source: U.S. Census Bureau's American Community Survey, 2007–2009.

These demographic data are important for a number of reasons. First, immigration's impacts on the size and growth of the U.S. population are a matter of concern among some environmentalists, and calls to restrict immigration as a mechanism for slowing population growth is a topic that is debated in this volume. They are also important because they directly affect the economic consequences of immigration. The economic benefits of immigration are maximized when immigrant workers are very different from native workers, although the fiscal impacts are increased when immigrants are low-skilled workers. Finally, they are important because they significantly affect what, if anything, the economy "needs" from the immigration system. To the extent that there are relatively few young, low-skilled people in the native-born population *and* there is significant economic growth in sectors that need these types of workers, immigration is likely to fill the gaps. To the extent that there are relatively few workers in the native-born population with science, technology, engineering, and mathematics skills (so-called STEM workers) *and* there is significant economic growth in sectors that need these types of workers, immigration is likely to fill the gaps. This exactly characterizes the interaction between immigration and demographics in the United States in recent decades; however, low-skilled workers have largely entered the country illegally, while high-skilled STEM workers have been granted H-1B visas to enter the country.

Economic Impacts of Immigration

The theoretical frameworks for understanding the economic impacts of immigration are relatively straightforward and uncontested, although measurement of these impacts is tricky, requiring sophisticated mathematical techniques. Immigration affects the economy through a number of mechanisms. Certainly changes to the supply of labor arising from immigration result in wage consequences. Further, the presence of great numbers and different types of workers affects the mix of what is produced in the economy. Immigration benefits owners of businesses and farms by allowing them to use these productive assets more efficiently. Immigrants benefit consumers through the lower prices that their impacts on wages and productivity make possible.

The immediate effect of immigration for native workers whose skills are similar to those of immigrants is to see their wages fall as a result of competition with immigrants for employment. But for native workers whose skills are different from and complementary to those of immigrants, the effect of immigration is an expansion of their employment opportunities and wages because immigrants expand the productive capacity in industries where these native workers are employed. This theory is uncontested among economists, but the appropriate techniques for measuring these impacts are a subject of much debate. Estimates of the wage impacts of immigration vary depending on the time frame of analysis and the statistical mechanisms used for representing how goods are produced, and on the extent of substitution between native and immigrant workers. For example, the economists Gianmarco Ottaviano and Giovanni Peri estimated that between 1990 and 2006, immigration lowered the wages of native workers without a high school degree by between -0.1 and +0.6 percent, and that immigration had a small positive effect on overall average wages of +0.6 percent. Their analysis concluded that, over the long run, the people most affected by new immigration were previous immigrants who saw their wages decline by 6 percent. Economist George Borjas estimated larger negative impacts on wages as a result of immigration. His analysis indicates that immigration between 1980 and 2000 increased the supply of male workers by 11 percent and resulted in lowering the wages of the average native-born worker by 3.2 percent. Borjas further estimates that the wages of native high school dropouts were lowered by 8.9 percent as a result of immigration, that native college graduates saw their wages fall by 4.9 percent, and that the wages of native workers with some college were essentially unchanged (Borjas, 2003).

Accurate measurement of immigration's fiscal impacts is hampered by data limitations. There is scant accurate data on illegal immigrants, and most social service systems were designed to be means-tested. Federal and state laws attempting to limit access to social services by immigrants—legal or illegal—are state- and program-specific, and it is extremely difficult to get comprehensive, accurate data on immigrant use of social services. This means attempts to quantify these costs rely on drawing inferences from indirect measures, and consensus does not exist on either methodology or results.

Typically, the conceptual approach to understanding the fiscal impacts of immigration involves calculating the difference between the direct taxes paid by immigrants and the cost of social services used by immigrants. But another consideration should be included as well. To the extent that immigrants are filling gaps in the labor force—to the extent that immigrant workers are *different* from native workers—they are making possible economic activity that would not otherwise occur. And this expanded economic activity also has tax consequences, as it expands the tax base. In this case, there are indirect impacts of immigration on public finances. While they are difficult to measure, they are worth keeping in mind.

In fact, attempts to estimate the fiscal impacts of immigration have produced widely differing results, depending on the assumptions involved. These estimates are used in the political arena by advocates on various sides of immigration debates and are one of the central reasons put forth for advocating limits to immigration.

It is easy to get lost in the weeds of the various debates over immigration's economic and fiscal impacts. The economist Gordon Hanson provides perspective by pointing out that distributional effects of immigration—who benefits and who bears the costs—inform much of the political debate over immigration. The net economic gains to the United States from immigration appear to be fairly small as a share of gross domestic product, but the costs and benefits of immigration are quite unevenly distributed—the distributional effects are quite large. Owners of capital and land as well as employers reap the largest benefits. Workers who compete with immigrants experience lower wages and taxpayers in high-immigration states bear most of its fiscal burden. These distributional consequences significantly shape public opinion about immigration policy (Hanson, 2005).

The Political Difficulty of Determining the "Best" Immigration System

Any immigration system must answer two basic questions: how many immigrants should be admitted, and what types of immigrants should be admitted. The various debates over the economic, labor, and demographic impacts of immigration elaborated in this volume relate directly to these two questions. But these questions must be understood in the context of immigration's distributional effects. Debates over the structure of the immigration system, impacts on wages and public finances, and immigration enforcement certainly result from public alarm over illegal immigration, and these three areas are explored in this section of the book. The structure of the system is discussed by Jeffrey Gower and Norman Matloff in the H-1B chapter, while Nik Theodore and Eric Ruark debate temporary worker programs. The economic and fiscal effects are discussed by Sarah E. Bohn and Magnus Lofstrom in the chapter on depression of wages, and by Marshall Fitz, Philip Wolgin, and Ann Robertson in the chapter on the cost to taxpayers. Kristin Johnson and Jack Martin debate the impact of remittances sent by immigrants to home countries. Enforcement issues are considered by Jessica Vaughan, Marielena Hincapié, and Maura Ooi in the chapter on worksite versus border enforcement, which is more specifically considered by Mark Krikorian, Clarissa Martínez-De-Castro, and Laura Vazquez in a debate on worksite raids. Other enforcement concerns are covered here by James Edwards Jr. and Lillie Coney in the chapter on secure ID cards. Rounding the discussion out is a debate surrounding the effect of immigration on the environment, covered by Philip Cafaro, Winthrop Staples, III, and Andrew Light, and debates regarding population growth, put forth by Susan Brown, Frank Bean, Lissette Piedra, Shinwoo Choi, and Hye Joon Park.

As these chapters testify, the various debates reflect a range of perspectives and views. Indeed, the multifaceted and conflicting discussions presented here reveal the competing legitimate interests that arise from the winners and losers created by the uneven distribution of the costs and benefits of immigration. This uneven distribution means that enacting an immigration system that maximizes its net benefit to the United States is politically complicated, for the very reason that maximizing its net benefit to the country as a whole means creating winners and losers.

REFERENCES AND FURTHER READING

Borjas, G. (2003). The labor demand curve is downward sloping: Reexamining the impact of immigration on the labor market. *Quarterly Journal of Economics, 118*(4), 1335–1337. Retrieved from http://www.borjas.com

Hanson, G. (2005). *Why does immigration divide America? Public finance and political opposition to open borders.* Washington, DC: Institute for International Economics. Available at http://irps.ucsd.edu/assets/022/8793.pdf

Ottaviano, G. I. P., & Peri, G. (2006). *Rethinking the effect of immigration on wages.* National Bureau of Economic Research, working paper #12497. Retrieved from http://www.nber.org/papers/w12497.pdf

Judith Gans
Udall Center for Studies in Public Policy, University of Arizona

14

Cost to Taxpayers

POINT: Ultimately, the economic contributions made by immigrants more than offset the amount of resources they consume.

Marshall Fitz and Philip E. Wolgin, Center for American Progress

COUNTERPOINT: The costs for education, incarceration, medical care, and so on far outweigh whatever tax contributions immigrants may make.

Ann Robertson, Independent Scholar

Introduction

Any discussion of the economic impacts of immigrants—of whether immigration is a net gain or loss to the U.S. economy—is especially thorny because it is difficult for debaters to even agree on the basic facts. The debate is intensi-fied, and also muddied, by the reality of illegal immigration and informed by ideas like those expressed by economist Milton Friedman, who said in a Stanford University lecture titled "What Is America?":

> [I]t is one thing to have free immigration to jobs. It is another thing to have free immigration to welfare. And you cannot have both. If you have a welfare state, if you have a state in which every resident is promised a certain minimal level of income, or a minimum level of subsistence, regardless of whether he works or not, produces it or not. Then it really is an impossible thing.

In approaching this topic, there are three broad issues related to immigrants' fiscal impacts that must be discussed. First, as mentioned, accurate *measurements* are very difficult to obtain even if the theoretical framework is clear. Second is the question of what should be included as "costs." This relates specifically to the cost of educating immigrant chil-dren—education is the largest category of fiscal expenditure, but at the same time it is clearly an investment whose return is realized over the life of the immigrant. Third, we should consider the indirect as well as the direct fiscal impacts from immigration. The direct impacts are obtained by subtracting the value of social services used from the amount of taxes paid by immigrants. (The extent to which illegal immigrants may be working "off the books" and avoiding payroll taxes is impossible to measure accurately and further complicates matters.) In any event, to the extent that immigrants are filling gaps in the labor force, they are making possible economic activity that wouldn't otherwise occur, and that economic activity has fiscal consequences. The intuition here is that we are better able to meet our fiscal obligations with a more robust economy.

Theoretically, three things determine a person's fiscal impacts: their educational attainment, where in the United States they live, and their immigration status. With regard to educational attainment, assuming that education results in higher wages, generally a higher wage results in more taxes paid and fewer social services needed. An immigrant's state of residence matters because social service benefits vary widely from state to state, and many Federal benefits have devolved to states. Tax structures also vary widely by state; some states rely heavily on sales taxes, which everyone pays. Other states rely more heavily on progressive income taxes, which lower-skilled legal immigrants pay less of and which illegal immigrants working in the cash economy don't pay at all, though those working with forged documents do pay income and other payroll taxes. Finally, a person's immigration status is a major determinant of fiscal impact. Legal immigrants are barred from most Federal social service programs and naturalized citizens face a 5-year ban in accessing such services. Additionally, most social safety net programs are means-tested, and the extent to which there is a citizenship test for access to these services varies widely by state. Many states have laws that explicitly prohibit illegal immigrants from accessing state social service programs.

Much of the hyperbole surrounding the fiscal impacts derives from misuse of statistics. For example, consider the following scenario: *68 percent of low-skilled (or illegal) immigrants don't have health insurance while only 14 percent of native born don't have health insurance. Therefore the problem of uncompensated care in hospitals is due to immigrants using emergency rooms to get health care.* But while those statistics may be accurate, the reality is that when one applies the percentages to the number of immigrants and native-born in the country, it is clear that there are 3 times as many uninsured native-born people than there are uninsured immigrants. Put simply, a large percentage of a small number is still a small number. The lesson from this example is that claims and counterclaims with regard to the dollar amount of fiscal impacts of immigrants should be greeted with a measure of skepticism as to their accuracy.

There is widespread acceptance of the idea that we should be admitting skilled immigrants because their net fiscal impacts are positive. But when considering the fiscal impacts of low-skilled immigrants, the issue of relatively scarce labor is important. Eliminating low-skilled immigrant workers has the potential of shrinking industries such as leisure and hospitality, agriculture, and a wide variety of service industries. This, in turn has the potential to reduce overall tax collection from those industries as a result of the reduced output, and those losses can offset or even outweigh the gains in savings from eliminating the direct fiscal impacts of low-skilled immigrants.

In the Point essay below, Marshall Fitz and Philip Wolgin take a long-term view of immigrants' contributions to and economic impact on the country's economy, and conclude that the overwhelming evidence shows that these impacts have been powerful and positive. In the Counterpoint essay, on the other hand, Ann Robertson argues that the value of social-service benefits used by often-unauthorized immigrants and their families far outweigh the amount they contribute to the government and infuse into the economy and have the effect of driving up taxes, increasing health care and education costs, and either displacing native workers from their jobs or increasing dependence on government services.

Whatever one's views on the debate regarding the tax burden that immigrants represent to American taxpayers, the fact remains that the issue involves real-world, nuts-and-bolts policy issues at both the state and federal levels. As you read the two sides of this debate, consider the policies in place that the authors refer to and whether you think they should be changed—strengthened, reversed, dropped—in order to maximize immigrant contributions to the American economy and enhance the benefits they bring to it.

POINT

Immigration has been an engine of economic dynamism and a wellspring of economic vitality in the United States. America has depended on immigrants not only for their labor, but also for their personal characteristics—such as their entrepreneurial spirit and willingness to sacrifice to make a better life for themselves. The diversity of skills they infuse into the economy yields dividends that no other country can claim. This is an economic reality as old as the country itself.

The overwhelming evidence is that immigration's economic impacts have been, and continue to be, powerful and positive. This does not mean that the costs and benefits of immigrants are spread evenly throughout the economy or across time. Immigrants are not monolithic—they have different skills, different educational levels, and different cultural backgrounds that affect their net impacts. The extent of their integration into society and the speed at which they become English proficient affects their economic contributions.

Further complicating any analysis of the costs and benefits of immigrants is the fact that the costs and contributions of immigrants change over time, both as immigrants age (from children to workers and from workers to retirees) and as they further settle into the country. In addition, many of the fiscal costs of immigration fall onto the individual states, which end up bearing the burdens of paying for things like education and health care. But the difference in cost structure between federal and state expenditures is true for all residents, not just for immigrants. Likewise, any cost-benefit analysis has to include not simply the use of services and the tax revenue generated, but also other factors such as business and job creation and the revitalization of formerly depressed areas.

The example of Lewiston, Maine, is instructive. This small city of around 42,000 people experienced a sudden surge in immigration around the turn of the new millennium. As often happens, this generated a certain amount of anxiety, and in 2002 the city's mayor argued that the new Somali immigrants had overtaxed the city's resources. Since 2002, however, the evidence from Lewiston has been positive. Lewiston's population had been on the decline for half a century, but with the influx of new immigrants, the city's shopping districts have boomed, tax revenues are up, and the immigrants have opened a significant number of new businesses in the city. Lewiston is a prime example of a postindustrial area revitalized economically by immigration (see Jones, 2004).

Despite evidence that the aggregate fiscal and economic benefits of immigration are positive, restrictionists and nativists use three methods to distort the picture: (1) identifying costs without acknowledging accompanying economic benefits; (2) inflating the calculation of costs that all immigrants impose; and (3) depicting costs as snapshots in time. Instead of using the wide-angle lens needed to capture the full range of economic impacts, immigration restrictionists tend to arrange a series of these narrow snapshots on a broad canvass to construct a highly negative economic portrait. Rather than calculating the full set of costs and benefits that careful analysis demands, they present only the large and immediate costs.

Although these efforts to skew the economic picture do not stand up to scrutiny, immigration restrictionists are not trying to win an economic debate, but are instead disguising a political point of view as economic analysis. Their intention is to fuel a political argument. The skewed economic picture produced by nativists is used to sow doubt about immigrants' contributions, create fear about immigrants' intentions, and generate political support for restrictive immigration policies. Charges that immigrants steal jobs, are a welfare burden, and do not pay taxes tap in to deep-seated fears, especially when leveled during times of great economic uncertainty. Assertions that "immigrants aren't paying their fair share," or that "they are getting something for nothing," reinforce legitimate anxieties about personal and national financial security, as well as providing a villain to shoulder the blame. Americans want a level playing field, and when they think some group isn't pulling its weight, it triggers indignation.

What follows is a rebuttal of the emotionally laden assertions about the drain immigrants place on the nation's fiscal health. This may be a slightly quixotic endeavor, as using data crunching to battle fear mongering is like bringing a butter knife to a gunfight. But the facts will hold after the fear has passed, and a clear presentation of the evidence will show that such fears are unfounded.

This presentation involves a number of steps. First a broader basis for understanding both the revenues generated by immigrants and the costs they impose will be provided. It will then be shown how, at both the federal and state levels, immigrants pay more into the system than they take out of it. There will then be a focus on the fiscal implications of undocumented immigrants, as well as a discussion of the contributions to economic growth from the taxation, consumption, and labor output of all immigrants, beyond simple cost-benefit fiscal analyses. Finally, there will be a look at how the economic contributions of immigrants can be maximized through practical, sensible reforms.

TAKING THE WIDER, LONGER VIEW

Measuring the economic and fiscal impacts of any group in an economic system as complex as the U.S. economy presents obvious challenges. The wider the scope of inquiry, the more complex the cost-benefit calculations become. The result of this is that only one major study over the last 15 years has attempted a comprehensive analysis of the economic and fiscal impact of immigrants. That study by the National Research Council (Smith & Edmonston, 1997) did more than take a snapshot of immigrants in one place at one time; it tracked the economic impact of immigrants over time and projected their gains into the future, concluding that immigrants are a net fiscal benefit to the country.

As President George W. Bush's White House Council of Economic Advisers argued in 2007, "careful studies of the long-run fiscal effects of immigration conclude that it is likely to have a modest positive influence." The 1997 National Research Council report found that immigrants contribute $80,000 more in taxes (in 1996 dollars) over their lifetime than they receive in public services (or over $111,000 in 2010 dollars). In other words, they paid significantly more into the system than they took out of it.

Range of revenues contributed. The most basic charge leveled by restrictionists is that immigrants "do not contribute their fair share." This claim is asserted in a variety of ways with differing degrees of nuance. The most blunt (and most obviously false) expression is that "immigrants do not pay taxes." This statement contains three fundamental assumptions or misrepresentations about immigrant contributions: (1) it loosely conflates undocumented immigrants with *all* immigrants; (2) it assumes that the only taxes of consequence are income-related taxes; and (3) it misrepresents the income-related tax contributions made by undocumented immigrants.

The claim that immigrants do not pay taxes derives from a conflation of undocumented immigrants and legal immigrants. Some undocumented immigrants (and their employers) do not pay employment-related taxes because their lack of work authorization has forced them into the underground cash economy. Many others though, even when working with false documents, do work in the formal economy, and therefore pay employment-related taxes. Conflating that subset of undocumented immigrants with all immigrants is a gross misrepresentation. There is no basis for asserting that lawfully present immigrants have a lower rate of tax compliance than native-born citizens. What's more, the vast majority of immigrants living and working in the United States are doing so lawfully.

So it is probably safe to conclude that a more precise formulation of the restrictionists' claim is that "*undocumented* immigrants don't pay taxes." Implicit in that statement, however, is another inaccurate assumption: that the only taxes worth counting are those paid in relation to earning an income, namely state and federal personal income tax and FICA taxes (for Social Security and Medicare). However, it is indisputable that all individuals' tax payments reach far beyond those income-related taxes.

While it varies from state to state and county to county, everyone—immigrants included—pays a variety of taxes related to daily living. These include taxes on property (homes, vehicles, etc.) that is owned, leased, or rented. Most states have sales taxes or excise taxes on food, clothing and other purchases, and on a variety of activities. These "consumption" or "living" taxes are substantial, accounting for hundreds of billions of dollars in state and local revenues each year. Everyone in the country, regardless of immigration status, contributes to this revenue stream. A study by the Iowa Policy Project (Pearson & Sheehan, 2007) of the state's undocumented immigrants found that even an undocumented family sending remittances abroad will pay more than $1,300 into the state coffers each year in property, sales, and excise taxes.

Thus, the restrictionist claim should be refined still further. Perhaps the intended assertion is really that "*undocumented* immigrants don't pay *income-related* taxes." This assertion, of course, bears little resemblance to the sweeping claim that immigrants don't pay taxes. But even this claim is false. As detailed more thoroughly below, virtually all studies show that significant percentages of undocumented workers—typically estimated at more than half—pay both income and FICA (Social Security and Medicare) taxes.

Scope of costs: The fallacies of snapshot accounting. A more refined formulation of the "immigrants do not pay their fair share" claim acknowledges some revenue generation by immigrants, while maintaining that those revenues are drastically outweighed by costs that immigrants impose on the system. The calculations produced in support of this conclusion rely on two flawed accounting assumptions. The first and most significant problem with these analyses is that they register the large costs that children impose on the system but ignore the even larger returns they deliver as adults. All children—excluding child actors and entertainers—represent a significant fiscal cost to state and local governments. They consume government services (primarily public schooling and sometimes, subsidized, health care) while contributing zero to tax revenues. This is true irrespective of a child's immigration status. As a society, however, these "costs" are viewed as "investments" because over their lifetime, children will generally return more to the system than they received from it before becoming adults.

The second accounting sleight of hand used to inflate the cost side of the ledger involves an overly expansive view of who should be counted. Analyses that estimate high costs of undocumented immigrants typically include the cost of educating their children in the United States. The problem with that is that many of those children are U.S. citizens. Of course, immigration restrictionists (quixotically) want to repeal the Constitution's guarantee of citizenship to those born on American soil. But unless and until they do, it is disingenuous to argue that a cost of undocumented immigration is the education and other services to which the citizen child is entitled. Those children are no more of a burden to society than every other American born in this country.

IMMIGRANTS PAY MORE THAN THEIR FAIR SHARE OF TAX

Federal revenue and immigration. That the foreign-born are a net-positive for the federal government stems both from tax revenue collections and restrictions on noncitizen usage of social services. The Personal Responsibility and Work Opportunity Reconciliation Act (PRWORA) of 1996 bars most noncitizens from federal welfare benefits, severely limiting the number of federal programs noncitizens can access. These restrictions significantly lower federal government expenditures on immigrants. With few exceptions (such as refugees), people who are not citizens or legal permanent residents (green card holders) are barred from receiving social security or unemployment insurance. All working individuals—including noncitizens and legal permanent residents—in the U.S. must contribute to these two programs through employer-paid payroll taxes. Most noncitizens are also ineligible for means-tested federal programs such as Supplemental Security Income (SSI). Thus, not only do immigrants generally cost the federal government less in social services than the native-born, their taxes help support social services from which they cannot receive benefits.

These payments into the welfare system are not trivial. According to a report from the National Foundation for American Policy (Anderson, 2005), legal immigrants will add, net of what they take out, $611 billion to America's Social Security system over the next 75 years. If these payments were to be lost, native-born workers would be required to shoulder the increase in payroll taxes to cover the gap. Alternatively, the Social Security Administration estimates that an increase in immigration of 264,000 people per year (roughly a 33% increase from current levels) would reduce the projected deficit in the Social Security Trust Fund by 10 percent over the next 50 years. This change would save the average family around $600 in payroll taxes over the next 10 years. The inverse is also true: cutting immigration by 264,000 people per year (a 33 percent decrease) would raise the deficit in the Trust Fund by 10 percent over 50 years, and cost the average family $600 in payroll taxes over 10 years.

Immigrant contributions in individual states. Studies analyzing the revenue impacts of all immigrants (regardless of legal status) on individual states point in a positive direction as well. It is important to note that some social service costs, chief among them health care, are born by the states without compensation from the federal government. Still, as on the federal level, fiscal impacts are not a one-way street of costs. Rather, immigrants create economic benefits for states, beyond outlays for social services.

A 2008 study from the Udall Center for Studies in Public Policy at the University of Arizona, for example, found that immigrant workers in Arizona generated roughly $2.4 billion in total tax revenue in fiscal year 2004, while costing the state only $1.4 billion, netting close to $1 billion (Gans, 2008). The study's cost estimates account for a robust variety of costs to the state, including education, health care, and some law enforcement costs, and concludes that immigrants contribute close to $1 billion more than the costs of these services.

Foreign-born persons make up 15 percent of Arizona's population, but even states with far fewer immigrants have experienced a positive effect from immigration. For example, a study for the Winthrop Rockefeller Foundation of

Arkansas's immigrants—where only 4 percent of the population is foreign-born—found that immigrants generated a net tax surplus of $19 million dollars in fiscal year 2004, once all costs were taken into account (Capps et al., 2007). Other states, from New Jersey to Nevada, have also found net positive revenue contributions from their immigrant populations.

Foreign-born versus native-born. Some state studies have gone beyond simply calculating the net revenue from their foreign-born residents, and have compared the contributions of immigrants to those of the native-born population. Here the data is even more conclusive: immigrants' net contributions are consistently higher than those of the native-born population. A 2008 study by the California Immigrant Policy Center, for example, found that households headed by an immigrant contribute a net of $2,679 annually to the Social Security system, $539 more than the average household headed by a native-born person. In terms of social services utilized, the average native-born California resident receives $1,212 each year in Social Security, Supplemental Security Income, Temporary Assistance for Needy Families, and other social services, while the average noncitizen receives less than half of that—only $474 annually.

A 2007 study by Florida International University found that immigrants in Florida paid $10.5 billion in federal taxes and $4.5 billion in Florida state and local taxes annually between 2002 and 2004, and that immigrants received on average $1,619 worth of public assistance. By contrast, native-born Floridians received, on average, $2,217 of public assistance, a difference of almost $600. When Medicare and Medicaid are taken into account, the researchers found that immigrants in Florida contribute close to $1,500 per year *more* than they receive. With significant foreign-born populations in both California and Florida, 27 and 19 percent respectively, these contributions add up quickly.

Similarly, in Massachusetts, a 2009 study by the Immigrant Learning Center found that immigrant-headed households contributed 14.5 percent of sales and excise tax payments, even though they constituted only 14.1 percent of the population (Clayton-Matthews, Karp, McCormack, & Watanabe, 2009). And while 22.3 percent of Massachusetts's natives received public assistance such as food stamps, Supplemental Security Income, and Social Security, at an average of $10,453 annually, only 16.4 percent of immigrants received any of these benefits, at an average of only $8,674. Thus, in Massachusetts, immigrants used welfare at lower rates than the native-born, and at lower costs as well. Clearly then, both on their own and by comparison with the native-born, the published data finds immigrants to be fiscally beneficial to America.

Undocumented immigrants. Calculating the fiscal impact of all foreign-born residents yields a different picture than one produced by examining only undocumented immigrants. Still, although the data on fiscal impacts of undocumented immigrants at the state and local level are mixed, a conservative reading of the data suggests that the costs and benefits are close to a wash.

With states and localities shouldering the costs of immigrants in their communities, one might assume that while foreign-born residents as a whole are a net positive for the nation, undocumented immigrants have deleterious fiscal effects. A 2007 report by the nonpartisan Congressional Budget Office, for example, surveyed a number of fiscal impact studies and concluded that unauthorized immigrants pay slightly less in state and local taxes than it costs these localities to provide services. The report cautioned that most of these studies found that spending on unauthorized immigrants was less than 5 percent of the total state and local outlay for public services, and that, at most, undocumented immigrants cost states and localities a small amount.

A close reading of studies of individual state studies illustrates that these costs can be minimal. On the negative side, in Colorado a 2006 study by the Bell Policy Center concluded that the tax payments of undocumented immigrants were between 70 and 86 percent of what the state and local governments paid to provide public services for the undocumented population (Baker & Jones, 2006). A 2007 study of Iowa's undocumented immigrants by the Iowa Policy Project found that these residents paid approximately 80 percent of the taxes paid by a family with legal status. At the same time, the report concluded that "undocumented families in Iowa may very well have a more favorable ratio of taxes paid to cost of state services accessed" than documented families, because these families are ineligible for state services (Pearson & Sheehan, 2007). Here again, simply looking at either services used or taxes paid into the system does not show the entire picture.

On the positive side, two states with large numbers of undocumented immigrants, New Mexico and Texas, with an estimated 85,000 undocumented immigrants and 1,650,000 undocumented immigrants respectively, found a net positive gain from their undocumented populations. A 2006 report by the New Mexico Fiscal Policy Project, for example, found a net revenue of $1.25 to $1.81 million after educational expenditures (the largest overall cost to a state from undocumented immigrants) are taken into account, while a 2006 report by the Texas Office of the Comptroller found that, overall, undocumented immigrants in Texas "generate more taxes and other revenue than the state spends on them," and this from a state with no income tax (Strayhorn, 2006). To be sure, these states do not take into account health care and law enforcement costs in their overall assessment, though the Texas study also discounts the local taxes that immigrants pay into the system. All in all, in Texas, the comptroller's office estimates that the state collected $425 million more from undocumented immigrants in 2005 than it spent. Even if one were to include health care and law enforcement, these are significant sums of money.

At the federal level, the revenue calculus for undocumented immigrants also tips firmly to the positive. According to the chief actuary of the Social Security Administration, by 2007, unauthorized immigrants working with forged documents had paid $120 billion to $240 billion into the Social Security Trust Fund, including a net $12 billion in 2007. Since these immigrants may never be eligible for Social Security, this is a direct contribution to the system, and one that has helped keep the fund solvent.

The path to fiscal balance. Even if there is a small negative cost of undocumented immigrants on the state and local levels, the most fiscally responsible way to increase those revenues and enhance growth is to make unauthorized immigrants legal by requiring them to pay a fine and earn citizenship. A comprehensive immigration reform that legalized all of the estimated 11.2 million unauthorized immigrants currently living in the United States would add a cumulative $1.5 trillion to the nation's gross domestic product (GDP) over 10 years, according to a joint Center for American Progress and Immigration Policy Center study titled "Raising the Floor for American Workers" (Hinojosa-Ojeda, 2010). The study also found that bringing unauthorized immigrant workers out of the shadows would raise the wages for native-born and immigrant workers, which would contribute billions of dollars in additional tax revenue.

With all undocumented workers part of the legal workforce, tax receipts would rise significantly. Most studies of unauthorized immigrants and taxation assume that only 50 percent of these immigrants work in the formal economy, and as such have taxes withheld from their wages. While all immigrants pay consumption taxes like sales tax, as well as property tax, legalization would increase income and payroll-related state and local tax revenue. Again, these gains are not trivial. According to the Institute for Taxation and Economic Policy and the Immigration Policy Center, unauthorized immigrants nationwide paid $1.2 billion in state income tax, and $11.2 billion in total state revenue in 2010 when property and sales taxes are taken into account. Legalization would also allow the federal government to eliminate the fiscal costs of large-scale expenditures on efforts to catch and detect unauthorized immigrants, ultimately freeing up more government revenue.

The gains from legalization would be felt at the state and local level as well. In California, for example, the Center for American Progress and Immigration Policy Center found that full legalization of the state's undocumented population (which, at an estimated 2.5 million people, is just under 7 percent of the population) would create over 600,000 jobs, and increase tax revenues by $5.3 billion (Hinojosa-Ojeda & Fitz, 2011). In Los Angeles County alone, legalization would add over 200,000 jobs and generate close to $2 billion in additional tax revenue.

A separate report from the University of Southern California's Center for the Study of Immigrant Integration found that in 2009, California's unauthorized Latino population lost $2.2 billion in wages due to their legal status. The best way to help grow the economy is to increase the demand for goods and services. The math is simple: A person buying more products translates into job creation and economic growth. In addition to bolstering the purchasing power of these immigrants, the legalization of all of California's undocumented immigrants would add an additional $2.2 billion in tax revenue to the Medicare and Social Security systems.

On the flip side, if the United States were to deport all of its unauthorized immigrants, the country would lose $2.6 trillion in cumulative GDP over 10 years. This loss primarily reflects the fact that immigrants, even undocumented immigrants, do pay taxes and work in positions that support other workers (known as "upstream jobs"). In addition to the lost GDP, which would significantly decrease government revenues, the actual cost to the government to accomplish this deportation would be $285 billion over 5 years—quite a hefty sum.

IMMIGRATION DRIVES SIGNIFICANT ECONOMIC GROWTH

Beyond fiscal analyses that compare the amount of taxes paid by foreign-born residents—including immigrants with and without legal status—against the amount of social services they receive, any study of the impact of immigrants must take into account the large-scale economic effects that immigrants have on the country's and the states' GDP and labor output. As the White House Council of Economic Advisers pointed out in its 2007 report, immigration is a benefit to the native-born because immigrants typically do not compete for jobs with native workers, but instead complement their skills. The economic gains from immigration are thus an added benefit to the nation, not a revenue stream that could be easily replaced with native workers.

Job creators.   Immigrants are more likely than the native-born to be business owners, and as such generate significant revenues for the nation as a whole. According to the Small Business Administration (SBA), in the 2000 census, immigrants were slightly more represented as business owners (12.5 percent) than in the total workforce (12.2 percent). The SBA found that immigrant business owners generated $67 billion in revenue, roughly 12 percent of all business income.

In addition, according to a 2011 report from the Partnership for a New American Economy, companies founded by immigrants represented 18 percent of the 2010 Fortune 500 businesses. This number rises to 40 percent when it includes companies founded by the children of immigrants. Companies founded by immigrants generated revenues of $1.7 trillion in 2010, and businesses founded by immigrants and their children generated $4.2 trillion in revenue that year. Indeed, according to the same report, "the newest Fortune 500 companies are more likely to have an immigrant founder" than a native-born founder.

Positive state impacts.   The economic gains from immigrants accrue to states with both large and small foreign-born populations. A 2007 study of Arkansas's immigrant population by the Winthrop Rockefeller Foundation, for example, found that without the immigrant labor force, the state's $16.2 billion manufacturing industry would lose about $1.4 billion, or 8 percent of its value. In Nebraska, a state whose foreign-born residents represent only 5.5 percent of the population, still saw $1.6 billion in total output added to its economy in 2006 from immigrant spending, according to a University of Nebraska study (Gouveia & Doku, 2010).

States with larger immigrant populations see even greater gains. A 2004 study from the Progressive Leadership Alliance of Nevada, a state whose foreign-born population is close to 19 percent of the population, found that Hispanic immigrants contributed just under $20 billion to the economy, more than a quarter of the gross state product (Ginsburg & Moberg, 2004). In New Jersey, another state with a high percentage of foreign-born residents (19.7 percent), a 2008 study by Rutgers University found that immigrants represented close to one-quarter of all state earnings, and that immigrants owned one-fifth of all businesses in the state (Gang & Piehl, 2008). In neighboring New York, immigrants contribute 22.4 percent of the state's GDP, for a whopping $229 billion in economic output, slightly more than their 21.3 percent of the state's population (Fiscal Policy Institute, 2007).

Finally, as consumers, immigrants add significantly to the income of states. In Arizona, a 2008 study by the Udall Center for Studies in Public Policy at the University of Arizona found that naturalized citizen households in 2004 contributed $6.1 billion in spending, supporting 39,000 full-time jobs. Immigrant households spent $4.4 billion and supported 28,000 full-time jobs (Gans, 2008). In Washington State, Asian and Hispanic residents alone totaled $28 billion in consumer spending in 2007, roughly 11.5 percent of the total (Jayapal & Curry, 2009).

CONCLUSION

Immigrants are drawn to the United States by the promise of economic opportunity and a desire to create a better life for themselves and their families. They seize this opportunity through hard work and raise their quality of life through consumption. As workers and consumers, they become taxpayers, job creators, and engines of economic growth. The literature paints a clear and consistent picture of the positive economic and fiscal impacts produced by this timeless dynamic.

It is time to move beyond the debate about whether immigrants are an economic benefit or burden. It is clear that immigrants produce net fiscal and economic benefits to the nation. The legitimate question policymakers must now tackle is how to enhance and maximize the contributions that immigrants make while diminishing short-term costs where possible. Addressing this question advances the nation's economic interests, while debating a discredited claim only obscures those interests.

REFERENCES AND FURTHER READING

Anderson, S. (2005, February). *The contribution of legal immigration to the Social Security system.* Retrieved from National Foundation for American Policy website: http://www.nfap.net/researchactivities/studies/SocialSecurityStudy2005.pdf

Baker, R., & Jones, R. (2006, June). *State and local taxes paid in Colorado by undocumented immigrants.* Retrieved from the Bell Policy Center website: http://www.thebell.org/PUBS/IssBrf/2006/06ImmigTaxes.pdf

Borjas, G. J. (1995). The economic benefits from immigration. *Journal of Economic Perspectives, 9*(2), 3–22.

California Immigrant Policy Center. (2008, January). *Looking forward: Immigrant contributions to the Golden State.* Retrieved from http://www.caimmigrant.org/contributions.html

Capps, R., Henderson, E., Kasarda, J. D., Johnson, J. H., Jr., Appold, S. J., Croney, D. L., Hernandez, D. J., & Fix, M. (2007, April 3). *A profile of immigrants in Arkansas.* Retrieved from Winthrop Rockefeller Foundation website: http://www.urban.org/UploadedPDF/411441_Arkansas_complete.pdf

Clayton-Matthews, A., Karp, F., McCormack, J. W., & Watanabe. P. (2009, June). *Massachusetts immigrants by the numbers: Demographic characteristics and economic footprint.* Retrieved from Immigrant Learning Center website: http://www.sabes.org/resources/research/mass-immigrant-demographics-2009.pdf

Coffey, S. B. (2006, January). Undocumented immigrants in Georgia: Tax contribution and fiscal concerns. Retrieved from Georgia Budget and Policy Institute website: http://www.gbpi.org/documents/20060119.pdf

Congressional Budget Office. (2007, December). *The impact of unauthorized immigrants on the budgets of state and local governments.* Retrieved from http://www.cbo.gov/ftpdocs/87xx/doc8711/12–6-Immigration.pdf

Fairlie, R. W. (2008, November). *Estimating the contribution of immigrant business owners to the U.S. economy.* Retrieved from Small Business Administration Office of Advocacy website: http://archive.sba.gov/advo/research/rs334tot.pdf

Fiscal Policy Institute. (2007, November). *Working for a better life: A profile of immigrants in the New York State economy.* Retrieved from http://www.fiscalpolicy.org/publications2007/FPI_ImmReport_WorkingforaBetterLife.pdf

Fitz, M., Martinez, G., & Wijewardena, M. (2010, March). *The costs of mass deportation: Impractical, expensive, and ineffective.* Retrieved from Center for American Progress website: http://www.americanprogress.org/issues/2010/03/pdf/cost_of_deportation.pdf

Gang I. N., & Piehl, A. M. (2008, December). *Destination, New Jersey: How immigrants benefit the state economy.* Retrieved from Eagleton Institute Program on Immigration and Democracy, Rutgers University: http://epid.rutgers.edu/eagleton-program-on-immigration-democracy/academics/reports-from-epid/destination-jersey-how-immigrants-benefit-state-economy

Gans, J. (2008, June). *Immigrants in Arizona: Fiscal and economic impacts.* Retrieved from Udall Center for Studies in Public Policy website: http://udallcenter.arizona.edu/immigration/publications/impactofimmigrants08.pdf

Ginsburg, R., & Moberg, D. (2004, September). *The economic contribution of non-native (immigrant) Hispanics to Nevada.* Retrieved from Progressive Leadership Alliance of Nevada website: http://planevada.files.wordpress.com/2010/07/non-native-hispanics.pdf

Gouveia, L., & Doku, Y. (2010, January). *Nebraska's foreign-born and Hispanic/Latino population: Demographic trends 1990–2008.* Retrieved from Office of Latino/Latin Studies (OLLAS) at the University of Nebraska–Omaha website: http://www.unomaha.edu/ollas/Data%20Series/Demographic%20Trends%20%20FINAL%20version%202010.pdf

Heet, J., Burkey, C., Clark, J., & Vanderstel, D. G. (2009, February). *The impact of immigration on Indiana.* Retrieved from the Sagamore Institute for Policy Research website: http://www.sagamoreinstitute.org/mediafiles/impact-of-immigration.pdf

Hinojosa-Ojeda, R. (2010, January). *Raising the floor for American workers: The economic benefits of comprehensive immigration reform.* Retrieved from Center for American Progress website: http://www.americanprogress.org/issues/2010/01/pdf/immigrationeconreport.pdf

Hinojosa-Ojeda, R., & Fitz, M. (2011, April). *Revitalizing the Golden State: What legalization over deportation could mean to California and Los Angeles County.* Retrieved from Center for American Progress website: http://www.americanprogress.org/issues/2011/04/pdf/ca_immigration.pdf

Immigration Policy Center. (2011, April 18). *Unauthorized immigrants pay taxes, too.* Retrieved from http://www.immigrationpolicy.org/just-facts/unauthorized-immigrants-pay-taxes-too

Jayapal, P., & Curry, S. (2009). *Building Washington's future: Immigrant workers' contributions to our state's economy.* Retrieved from One America website: http://weareoneamerica.org/sites/default/files/Immigrant_Contributions_to_Our_State_Economy.pdf

Jones, M. (2004, March/April). The new Yankees. *Mother Jones.* Retrieved from http://motherjones.com/politics/2004/03/new-yankees

New Mexico Fiscal Policy Project. (2006, May). *Undocumented immigrants in New Mexico: State tax contributions and fiscal concerns.* Retrieved from http://www.nmvoices.org/fpp_attachments/immigrant_tax_rpt_fact_sheet_5–06.pdf

Partnership for a New American Economy. (2011, June). *The "new American" Fortune 500.* Retrieved from http://www.nyc.gov/html/om/pdf/2011/partnership_for_a_new_american_economy_fortune_500.pdf

Passel, J. S., & Cohen, D. (2011, February). *Unauthorized immigrant population: National and state trends, 2010.* Retrieved from Pew Hispanic Center website: http://pewhispanic.org/files/reports/133.pdf

Pearson, B., & Sheehan, M. F. (2007, October). *Undocumented immigrants in Iowa: Estimated tax contributions and fiscal impact.* Retrieved from the Iowa Policy Project website: http://www.iowapolicyproject.org/2007docs/071025-undoc.pdf

Rector, R. (2007, May 17). *The fiscal costs of low-skilled immigrants to state and local taxpayers* (Testimony before the Subcommittee on Immigration of the Committee on the Judiciary of the United States House of Representatives). Retrieved from Heritage Foundation website: http://www.heritage.org/research/testimony/the-fiscal-cost-of-low-skill-immigrants-to-state-and-local-taxpayers

Smith, J. P., & Edmonston, B. (Eds.). (1997). *The new Americans: Economic, demographic, and fiscal effects of immigration.* Washington, DC: National Academy Press. Retrieved from http://www.nap.edu/openbook.php?isbn=0309063566

Strayhorn, C. K. (2006, December). *Undocumented immigrants in Texas: A Financial analysis of the impact to the state budget and economy.* Retrieved from Texas Office of the Comptroller website: http://www.window.state.tx.us/specialrpt/undocumented/undocumented.pdf

Wasem, R. E. (2009, August 20). *Unauthorized aliens' access to federal benefits: Policy and issues.* Retrieved from Congressional Research Service website: http://www.policyarchive.org/handle/10207/bitstreams/19520.pdf

White House Council of Economic Advisers (CEA). (2007, June 20). *Immigration's economic impact.* Retrieved from http://georgewbush-whitehouse.archives.gov/cea/cea_immigration_062007.html

Marshall Fitz and Philip E. Wolgin

Note: The authors would like to thank Center for American Progress colleagues Sarah Jane Glynn, Policy Analyst, Ann Garcia, Research Assistant, and Maya Edelstein, Intern, for their assistance.

COUNTERPOINT

The U.S. government regulates the number of visas ("green cards") issued each year and prioritizes applicants who will contribute to the U.S. economy while not disproportionately consuming social-service benefits. Legal immigrants tend to be skilled workers. The United States welcomes them because the country will benefit from their skills and knowledge without having to bear the cost of their education. Skilled immigrants are also less likely to need taxpayer-provided services. Unskilled immigrants are a far different story. Based on the results of the 2010 census, the U.S. Census Bureau estimated that 11.2 million people had entered the United States illegally.

As the global economy entered a prolonged recession in the late 2000s, unemployment reached record levels in the United States. Many Americans lost their jobs and have been unable to find employment. Many formerly middle-class families lost their homes and turned to the government's social safety net to feed their families. A major factor keeping Americans unemployed is the large pool of unskilled, often illegal, immigrants willing to work at low rates. Unskilled illegal workers take jobs from legal residents, who then turn to government-provided services. Unskilled, underpaid illegal workers often struggle to stay above the poverty line themselves, and their families, which often include U.S. citizens, also use social safety nets. Even if these immigrants pay taxes, their contributions fall short of the level of services they use. Many localities have been forced to borrow funds to meet the demand for benefits.

Given the multiple strains on local, state, and the federal governments, the fiscally responsible action is to prioritize the needs of citizens rather than subsidizing migrants. The costs for education, medical care, incarceration, and other services far outweigh whatever tax contributions low-skilled illegal immigrants may make.

The Heritage Foundation examined this issue in a detailed study released in 2007. The authors tallied up the various forms of revenue and benefits: "the total annual fiscal deficit for all [low-skill immigrant households] together equaled $89.1 billion. . . . Over the next ten years, the net cost (benefits minus taxes) to the taxpayer of low-skilled immigrant households will approach $1 trillion" (Rector & Kim, 2007). On a per capita basis, native-born Americans paid a $330 subsidy to low-skilled immigrant households every year. In 2010, the Federation for American Immigration Reform (FAIR) raised that price tag to $1,117 per year.

TYPES OF COSTS AND EXPENDITURES

Immigrant needs are more a function of education than legal status. Numerous studies indicate that illegal immigrants are far more likely to be low-skilled workers than are legal immigrants. Lower skills earn lower salaries and, often, a higher need for safety-net services. As Robert Rector of the Heritage Foundation told ABC News in 2007, "Each immigrant who does not have a high school degree over his lifetime costs the taxpayer about $1.2 million, and that's all the benefits his family would receive minus the taxes he pays in."

Low-income working families, both legal and illegal, consume three types of government-funded benefits. First, they benefit from a variety of social services, which are direct payments to low-income households to cover basic needs, such as food, shelter, and health care. Welfare, unemployment insurance, Medicaid, food stamps, and WIC (the special supplemental nutrition program for pregnant and postpartum women, breastfeeding women, infants, and children up to the age of 5 years) are all examples of social service programs. With higher fertility levels among women in unskilled households, these families make greater use of WIC.

Second, children of immigrants stress the current U.S. education system. A 1982 Supreme Court ruling established that states must provide free K–12 education to all children, whatever their legal status. Already tight school budgets have to add English language acquisition programs, additional teachers, larger schools, and expanded bus routes to accommodate students who may only stay a few months. Higher than average birth rates among many segments of the undocumented population further increase demand for education and nutrition support.

Third, immigrants increase congestion of common goods such as infrastructure and public safety. It is difficult to measure how one additional person—legal or not—affects how many miles of paved roads or how many firefighters are needed, and some studies deliberately ignore this aspect of population increases. The Urban Institute and other research and policy institutions measure this demand in terms of public safety, by looking at crime and incarceration levels. States from North Carolina to New Jersey and Arizona have reported skyrocketing numbers of criminal aliens in tandem with the rising population of alien workers. Undocumented immigrants made up one-fourth of the federal prison population in 2007. In addition to the costs of incarceration, governments have to pay police to apprehend criminal aliens, pay attorneys to prosecute (and often defend) them, and then arrange for foster care for their U.S.-born children.

The cost of immigrants to taxpayers is thus significant and likely to increase further. In 2007 the U.S. Senate considered adopting an immigration policy that would have granted all immigrants—documented and undocumented—a "Z-visa," immediate legal provisional residency status, and eventual permanent residency. Critics blasted the notion, calculating that it would cost taxpayers $17,000 per undocumented alien to cover the resulting costs of Social Security, Medicare, and other social service benefits, not only of undocumented workers in the country in 2007 but also for the resulting influx of immigrants over the next 2 decades. The total bill: at least $2.6 trillion.

The low-skill immigrant population is younger than high-skilled immigrants or the native-born population. The longer these individuals stay in the United States, the more claims they will make for tax-funded subsidies. As they age, they will eventually claim Social Security and Medicare benefits, but their lower incomes mean they will have contributed less to the government. Furthermore, because current U.S. immigration policy emphasizes family reunification, not education and skill levels, these immigrants will be allowed to bring more and more distant relatives into their U.S. households.

WHO PAYS?

The costs of supporting low-income immigrants are spread across local, state, and federal jurisdictions. In California alone, more than half (56 percent) of households headed by a legal immigrant who did not finish high school use at least one welfare program—a rate triple that of U.S. citizens.

It is difficult to determine how many illegal immigrants pay taxes, much less the amount they pay. Few undocumented workers are going to voluntarily disclose their status to the Internal Revenue Service (IRS). The primary contribution channel for any worker in the United States is through federal payroll taxes (Social Security and FICA), which by law are withheld from paychecks. These funds are retained at the federal level, leaving states, cities, and towns to shoulder unreimbursed expenses.

Illegal immigrants are not eligible for Social Security numbers (SSNs), but their income can be estimated using two sources. First, illegal aliens may obtain fraudulent SSNs, or simply give their employer a random series of nine numbers, resulting in mismatched numbers and employer-reported earnings, typically clustered in immigrant-dense states. Second, there are patterns in tax returns that suggest many persons with Individual Taxpayer Identification Numbers (ITINs) take advantage of certain tax credits for low-income households. The IRS issues these alternative tax-processing numbers to persons not eligible for SSNs. Both resident and nonresident aliens are eligible for ITINs, so the IRS does not check immigration status when issuing ITINs. Possible illegal workers can be flagged by following ITIN filers who claim Earned

Income Tax Credits (EITC) (for low-income households), Child Tax Credits, and Additional Child Tax Credits ACTC (for households with many children under 18). In 2010, 72 percent of ACTC claims were by taxpayers using ITINs, for a total of $4.2 billion.

Even with payroll and other tax contributions, few illegal immigrants fully reimburse the government for the services they use. Workers paid in cash, "off the books," avoid automatic payroll deductions for taxes and Social Security. Those who do file tax returns usually report such small gross incomes that any withheld wages are returned after special tax credits are applied.

For 2011, families with three or more qualifying children could receive as much as a $5,751 in EITCs toward any tax obligation, plus up to $1,000 per child in ACTCs. If their tax obligation was less than this amount, the filer effectively received a bonus. Federal law explicitly prohibits illegal aliens from receiving such federal benefits, but there are ways to sidestep those restrictions, such as forged residency documents, and enforcement is minimal.

The 2009 American Recovery and Reinvestment Act increased the rebate amounts, triggering a huge increase in claims and payments. The Treasury Department's Office of Inspector General (OIG) analyzed the jump in claims, and its 2011 report suggested that one reason for the increase was that illegal immigrants were claiming benefits for ineligible children, such those who still lived outside the United States. The Inspector General's Office criticized the IRS for failing to verify suspicious claims, adding, "The payment of Federal funds through this tax benefit appears to provide an additional incentive for aliens to enter, reside, and work in the United States without authorization" (Treasury Inspector General for Tax Administration, 2011). Further, the report called for clarification of the IRS's ability to disallow ineligible claims. "Based on claims made in Processing Year 2010," the report states, "disallowance of the ACTC to filers without a valid SSN would reduce Federal outlays by approximately $8.4 billion over 2 years." The OIG report also noted that the IRS has a unique opportunity to uncover cases of stolen SSNs by matching W-2 forms with persons submitting claims. However, the IRS has not taken action to pursue identity theft cases, much less notify taxpayers with compromised SSNs.

SOCIAL SERVICES

Social service benefits are immediate, provided at the point of service. Immigrants may use these benefits, and citizens who lose their job to lower-paid immigrants may turn to the social safety net themselves. By law, naturalized citizens must wait 5 years before they become eligible for federal social service benefits, such as Social Security and Medicare. Immigrants can bypass these restrictions by unlawfully acquiring Social Security numbers, but in many cases there is little need to do so. Hospitals and schools are not allowed to ask patients, parents, or students their immigration status, and Medicaid will pay for emergency medical care for uninsured immigrants.

Undocumented aliens can access government-issued benefits if at least one member of their household is a legal resident. Any child born in the United States automatically receives citizenship, and illegal families may produce so-called anchor babies—young children born in the United States—to secure benefits. A 2009 report by the Pew Hispanic Center found that 73 percent of children of illegal aliens were born in the United States (Passel & Cohen, 2009). As Senator Lindsey Graham (R-SC) explained, mothers "come here to drop a child. . . . It's called drop and leave." As of 2007 there were 3 million anchor babies in the country. When these children turn 21, they can request their parents be granted legal permanent residency.

Most social services are now funded and distributed at the local level, and states regulate the types of assistance provided, the amount of this assistance, and the eligibility requirements. States that have traditionally had higher levels of illegal immigrants (California, Texas, New York, and Florida) have borne the highest fiscal costs. Available services and regulations vary from state to state and while immigrants might not intentionally gravitate toward more generous localities, they will avoid stricter jurisdictions. Georgia, North Carolina, Tennessee, and Arkansas have become immigrant destination states, with their undocumented population jumping 500 to 600 percent in the 1990s. Colorado, another new destination, spent $217 million to $225 million on education, Medicaid, and correctional expenses for unauthorized workers in 2005, but collected only $159 million to $194 million in taxes. At the same time, low-skilled native-born workers may be pushed to seek better-paying jobs in states with fewer competing immigrants, creating an expanding ripple of consequences from high numbers of low-skilled, noncitizen residents.

Citizens pay for immigrants' social service benefits in the form of higher taxes and reduced services for themselves. The Heritage Foundation study revealed that low-skill immigrant households paid approximately $10,573 each in taxes in 2004 but used $30,160 worth of taxpayer-funded services, "largely because of the higher level of means-tested welfare benefits received by low-skill immigrant households" (Rector & Kim, 2007). In fact, the fiscal deficit for low-skill immigrant households is double the amount of taxes paid.

Illegal immigrants without private health insurance resort to using hospital emergency rooms (ERs) for medical care. By law, hospital ERs cannot turn away indigent patients, but the influx of uninsured patients increases wait times for insured patients and leaves hospitals with millions of dollars in unreimbursed expenses, driving up the cost for paying patients. The American Hospital Association reports that its members provided $40 billion in uncompensated care in 2009. The "Medicare Modernization Act" of 2003 provided $250 million in federal money for hospitals treating the highest volume of undocumented patients, but that funding expired in 2008. Many hospitals are struggling to stay afloat, particularly hospitals located along the border with Mexico.

U.S.-born children of immigrants often qualify for state-sponsored health coverage, but those plans are still taxpayer-funded. Some localities provide health care to all low-income children as a matter of public health policy. New York, Illinois, Washington, and parts of California are among those extending coverage to illegal immigrant children. San Francisco pays for illegal immigrant adults from the city budget, while New York City and other large municipalities provide free or low-cost clinics that are available to everyone. New York City hospitals have hundreds of illegal immigrant patients who have essentially become boarders at the hospital, because they cannot provide proof of insurance or proof of residence, which are preconditions for discharge. One city health official estimated the city has 300 patients in this type of limbo and that they typically stay in this status for 5 years or more, at $100,000 or more per patient, per year.

EDUCATION

Education is the largest expenditure for states, counties, and cities, and educating children with limited English proficiency costs 20 to 40 percent more than educating native speakers. These same states, counties, and cities spend millions of dollars to educate the children of legal and illegal immigrants—dollars raised through taxes. The 2007 Heritage Foundation report emphasizes that, as a result of these programs, "U.S. taxpayers must sacrifice income and forgo the wants and needs of their own families. . . . The taxpaying family has less income for its own needs as a direct result of the presence of the low-skill immigrant household in the U.S." (Rector & Kim, 2007).

These governments—and taxpayers—will not see returns on these investments in education, such as higher taxable salaries, for decades, if ever. Children brought into the United States by their undocumented parents leave school without the right to work in this country, join the U.S. military, or receive federal loans for college educations. Those children that do legally work would have to make extremely high salaries to have a large enough tax bill to pay back the current $19,588 net annual benefits used by their families. U.S. jurisdictions may never benefit from their investment if the children return to their parents' homeland or do not join the legal economy.

Since the early 2000s, both the U.S. House of Representatives and the U.S. Senate have considered legislation that— although it has taken various forms over the years—is currently referred to as the Development, Relief, and Education for Alien Minors (DREAM) Act. If passed, the law would essentially provide amnesty to foreign-born children whose parents brought them to the country illegally. The DREAM Act would grant legal residency for 6 years to high school graduates who were younger than 15 years old when they moved to the United States and who have lived continuously here for at least 5 years. After 6 years, they could earn citizenship if they had attended college or served in the military for at least two of those 6 years. Opponents of the act say it will encourage yet more illegal immigration. Senator Jeff Sessions (R-AL) has denounced the legislation; a September 18, 2010, article in *The Wall Street Journal* quoted Sessions as saying, "When you take a policy that says you are going to reward people who have entered our country illegally with a guaranteed pathway to citizenship, and with billions of dollars of financial aid or benefits they would not otherwise be entitled to, what message are we sending?" Seventy-five percent of the estimated 825,000 youth eligible for DREAM benefits live in just 10 states, including California, Texas, Florida, New York, and Arizona, imposing an additional burden on their economies.

Immigration-rights groups argue that the children of illegal immigrants should not only have free primary and secondary education, they also should be allowed to attend public universities at in-state tuition rates. But public universities have been hard hit by the economic recession, and state governments are sharply reducing their contributions to university budgets. Public universities are increasingly encouraging admission by out-of-state students who will pay much larger tuition bills. Institutions of higher education cannot afford to drop rates for students whose families are not in the country legally, and critics warn that offering discounted rates will encourage more undocumented families to arrive.

California offers a good case study on many factors related to immigration costs. With the highest number of immigrants in the country, California is home to a full 24 percent of all illegal migrants in the United States. Forty-one percent of California's undocumented population lives in Los Angeles County, and all are heavy users of government services. Thirty-eight percent of adult immigrants in the state lack a high school diploma, their families make up half of the state's uninsured population, and their children account for half of the enrollment in public schools. Unauthorized families in California earned an average of $29,700 in 2004, barely half of the $54,000 average of native-born Californians. A 2004 study by the Federation for American Immigration Reform (FAIR) calculated that California paid over $10 billion per year ($1,183 per household) to heal ($1.4 billion), educate ($7.7 billion), or incarcerate ($1.4 billion) illegal residents. Announcing these results, FAIR president Dan Stein said, "California's addition to 'cheap' illegal alien labor is bankrupting the state and posing enormous burdens on the state's shrinking middle class tax base."

Immigration advocates argue that foreign workers play a vital role in the economy, filling low-skilled jobs that do not interest citizens. Supporters of tougher immigration laws claim the opposite, that not only do unskilled foreign workers take jobs from low-skilled citizens, they also depress hourly rates for everyone in that labor pool, especially African American men without a high school diploma. Lower wages, in turn, depress income tax contributions and sales tax receipts. Testifying before the U.S. Commission on Civil Rights in 2008, Urban Institute Senior Fellow Harry J. Holzer suggested that some employers actively discriminate against African American men and favor Hispanic immigrants of any status for their perceived stronger work ethic and informal network of other job seekers.

WHO ELSE BENEFITS?

Three very different groups also benefit from undocumented workers. First, companies can hire illegal immigrants, pay them below-market wages, and increase profits. Second, skilled workers in migrant-heavy sectors will see new opportunities open up. Construction projects, for example, tend to attract undocumented workers. Their lower pay requirements make construction more affordable, increasing the need for architects and contractors. Third, immigrants usually send money to family and friends in their home country. These remittances remove the funds from U.S. markets, thus reducing consumption, sales tax receipts, and property taxes. Mexico, for example, received $23 billion in remittances in 2011, primarily from workers in the United States. The country has a "Three for One" program that matches émigré remittances with local, state, and federal funds to build schools, clinics, and other types of infrastructure.

CONCLUSION

The immigration-related fiscal deficit can be solved in four ways. First, the government could impose stricter limits and enforcement regarding how many low-skilled immigrants are allowed to enter the country, legally or illegally. Second, government subsidies to poor households could be reduced. Third, immigrants could be denied access to all social-service programs if even one member of the household is undocumented. Fourth, the government could end automatic U.S. citizenship for children born in the United States to an undocumented parent. Anchor babies are guaranteed citizenship under the Fourteenth Amendment to the Constitution. But because low-skilled immigrants are a fiscal drag, primarily on states, lawmakers have called for the creation of state citizenship categories that would bar citizenship and state benefits to anchor babies and their families. "It is fiscally unsustainable," according to the Heritage Foundation, "to apply [our] system of lavish income redistribution to an inflow of millions of poorly educated immigrants."

Frustrated by a perceived failure by the U.S. government to enforce immigration restrictions, many states have enacted stiff laws to weed out unlawful, costly residents. Arizona started the trend, passing Proposition 200 in 2004, the Arizona Legal Workers Act in 2007, and the 2010 Support Our Law Enforcement and Safe Neighborhoods Act, which requires individuals to provide proof of legal residency if detained by police. Governor Jan Brewer touted the 2010 law as a vital step to eliminate drop houses, kidnappings, and "the murderous greed of drug cartels" caused by illegal immigration.

Other states, including Georgia, Mississippi, Nebraska, Oklahoma, Pennsylvania, and South Carolina, quickly adopted and adapted their own versions of this bill.

The new laws have created a "can't live with 'em, can't live without 'em" problem. States are experiencing a fiscal backlash for trying to eliminate illegal government payments to foreign-born workers. Pro-immigration groups called for a boycott of Arizona-based companies, driving away tourists, conventions, and national sporting events. The Center for American Progress calculated the toll from the first year the law was in place: "These losses have already totaled at least $141 million, including $45 million in hotel and lodging cancellations, and $96 million in lost commercial revenue" (Wolgin & Kelley, 2011). In addition, the tourism industry lost 2,761 jobs, $253 million in economic output, and $9.4 million in tax revenue.

At the same time, Arizona's new immigration policies have been effective. In January 2012, FAIR reported a drop in the number of illegal aliens in the state from 560,000 in 2008 to 460,000 in 2009. Similarly, the number of Arizona families living in poverty dropped 5.5 percent between 2005 and 2008. Other sectors registered significant changes, including declining rates for birth, enrollment in limited English proficiency (LEP) classes, as well as violent and property crimes.

The United States is a powerful country with a rich tradition of freedom and entrepreneurship. For centuries it has attracted immigrants from all corners of the world. But at a time of economic crisis and competition for limited fiscal resources, the country needs to pull back its open arms and put the needs of its legal residents, and its citizens, first.

References and Further Reading

Borjas, G., Grogger, J., & Hanson, G. (2006). *Immigration and African-American employment opportunities: The response of wages, employment, and incarceration to labor supply shocks* (NBER Working Paper No. 12518). Retrieved from National Bureau of Economic Research website: http://www.nber.org/papers/w12518

Camarota, S. A. (1998, Fall). Does immigration harm the poor? *Public Interest, 133*. Retrieved from http://www.cis.org/node/303

Camarota, S. A. (2007, December 15). *Immigration, both legal and illegal, puts huge strain on the country.* Retrieved from Center for Immigration Studies website: http://www.cis.org/node/464

Congressional Budget Office. (2007, December). *The impact of unauthorized immigrants on the budgets of state and local governments.* Retrieved from http://www.cbo.gov/publication/41645

Federation for American Immigration Reform. (2012, January). *Recent demographic change in Arizona: Anatomy of effective immigration reform legislation.* Retrieved from http://www.fairus.org/site/News2/1773826781?page=NewsArticle&id=24725

Fortuny, K., Capps, R., & Passel, J. S. (2007, March). *The characteristics of unauthorized immigrants in California, Los Angeles County, and the United States.* Retrieved from Urban Institute website: http://www.urban.org/uploadedpdf/411425_characteristics_immigrants.pdf

Gans, J. (2008, June). *Immigrants in Arizona: Fiscal and economic impacts.* Retrieved from Udall Center for Studies in Public Policy, University of Arizona: http://udallcenter.arizona.edu/immigration/publications/impactofimmigrants08.pdf

Jordan, M. (2010, September 18). A route to citizenship in defense bill. *Wall Street Journal.* Retrieved from http://online.wsj.com/article/SB10001424052748704858304575498072319915164.html

Newman, K. (1999). *No shame in my game: The working poor in the inner city.* New York, NY: Knopf.

Passel, J. S. (2006, March 7). *The size and characteristics of the unauthorized migrant population in the U.S.* Pew Hispanic Center. Retrieved from http://pewhispanic.org/files/reports/61.pdf

Passel, J. S., & Cohen, D. (2009, April 14). *A portrait of unauthorized immigrants in the United States.* Retrieved from Pew Hispanic Center website: http://www.pewhispanic.org/files/reports/107.pdf

Rector, R., & Kim, C. (2007). *The fiscal cost of low-skill immigrants to the U.S. taxpayer.* Retrieved from Heritage Foundation website: http://www.heritage.org/research/reports/2007/05/the-fiscal-cost-of-low-skill-immigrants-to-the-us-taxpayer

Reed, D., & Danziger, S. (2007). The effects of recent immigration on racial/ethnic labor market differences. *American Economic Review, 97*(2), 373–377.

Smith, J. P., & Edmonston, B. (Eds.). (1997). *The new Americans: Economic, demographic and fiscal effects of immigration.* Washington, DC: National Academy Press. Retrieved from http://www.nap.edu/openbook.php?isbn=0309063566

Treasury Inspector General for Tax Administration. (2011, July 7). *Recovery Act: Individuals who are not authorized to work in the United States were paid $4.2 billion in refundable credits.* Retrieved from http://www.treasury.gov/tigta/auditreports/2011reports/201141061fr.pdf

Wolgin, P. E., & Kelley, A. M. (2011, July). *Your state can't afford it: The fiscal impact of states' anti-immigrant legislation.* Retrieved from Center for American Progress website: http://www.americanprogress.org/issues/2011/07/state_immigration.html

Ann Robertson

15

Depression of Wages and Price Levels

POINT: Immigration creates a depression in wages that can disadvantage native-born workers. However, the effects are not uniform across all workers. Further, lower wages make goods and services more affordable, leading to a net benefit for consumers.

Sarah E. Bohn and Magnus Lofstrom, Public Policy Institute of California

COUNTERPOINT: Immigration does not negatively affect wages. In fact, it enhances economic growth through capital investments.

Sarah E. Bohn and Magnus Lofstrom, Public Policy Institute of California

Introduction

One of the most fraught debates concerning immigration is about its effects on labor markets, in particular the wages of native-born workers. A correlated concern is the corresponding effect on prices in the U.S. economy. While empirical studies conflict in the conclusions they draw concerning these issues, the economic theory surrounding this question is surprisingly straightforward. If the supply, or quantity, of a given economic input—in this case labor—goes up, prices—in this case wages—go down, all other things being equal.

The theory relies on two critical assumptions. The first revolves around *substitutability*. Being substitutes in labor markets means having equivalent skills, such as the ability to speak English; equivalent levels of educational attainment, age, or work experience; and technical or job-specific knowledge. Immigrants and native workers must be substantially perfect substitutes for each other, and therefore compete directly in labor markets, in order for the increasing supply–decreasing wage relationship to apply.

The second key assumption relates to the phrase "all other things equal" that economists frequently use. For the purposes of this debate, "all other things equal" means that the number of employers stays essentially the same—that immigrants and natives are competing for the same number of jobs. While this may initially be true, arguing that immigration results in a permanent reduction in wages is equivalent to arguing that lower wages and higher profits do not trigger new capital investment in an industry. Over time, there generally *is* capital investment as a result of an expanded labor force, which in turn creates more jobs. This investment, in turn, puts upward pressure on wages. These dynamic effects tend to counteract each other over time and create real challenges to measuring the relative magnitude of these effects and determining which effect is larger.

Another theoretically straightforward issue further complicates this debate. To the extent that the skills of immigrants and native-born workers are different, immigration can actually increase the wages of some native-born workers. The intuition in this case relates to the key notion of *complementarity*. Immigrant newcomers with skills that are different from those of existing workers are bringing new capabilities to the economy, expanding what is possible. When the newcomers' skills complement those of existing workers, the expanded possibilities can actually increase the demand for, and wages of, native-born workers.

Both the Point and Counterpoint essays here, written by Sarah E. Bohn and Magnus Lofstrom, use similar examples to illustrate this phenomenon. In the construction industry, for example, as more immigrant laborers enter into the market and induce capital to invest in new projects, needs arise for workers whose skills complement those of these new entrants. Bilingual English-speakers with enough skill might be needed as job-site supervisors and, further up the labor supply chain, new positions may be created for architects, engineers, and skilled craftsmen.

This scenario raises one concern pointed out in the Point essay: that while immigrant labor may help increase productive capacity and create new outlets for capital, pressure may be put on the wages of native-born workers who are close to being substitutes for immigrants. Indeed, it is this set of native workers—low-skilled workers with minimum education—that are most frequently considered to be affected by low-skilled, often illegal, immigrant labor.

One problem clouding the discussion surrounding these debates is the difficulty of empirically examining and isolating the factors involved in determining wage levels. Various studies may support different conclusions, depending on the exact labor market considered or its specific features. In a review of a sizeable group of studies that analyzed these questions, the National Academy of Science Panel on Immigration concluded in 1997 that immigration had only a minor adverse impact on native worker employment and wages. Most of this early work dealt with "cross-area" studies, considering the effects of immigration within specific geographic locales, studied as closed markets. Such narrow studies, as discussed in the Point section, don't take migration into account, ignoring the effects of native-born workers moving in response to an increase in immigrant labor in their community.

More recent work (especially that of the Harvard economist George Borjas) has attempted to take migration of native-born workers—and nonnative workers for that matter—into account by designing studies in terms of nationwide labor markets defined by skill set, not locale. Borjas's recent work, described in both the Point and Counterpoint sections, estimates that a 10 percent increase in the labor force from immigration will result in a 3 to 4 percent decrease in wages on average, more than double the effect in previous literature, and a 9 percent decline for native-born high school dropouts. Some, however, are concerned about this methodology. Using a skills-based group as a closed market, whether its geographic reach is broad or not, ignores potential mobility. Critics of this approach suggest that U.S. labor markets are typified by more mobility than that accorded such closed skill-defined markets.

Other analysts, including Patricia Cortes and Giovanni Peri, have found less downward pressure on wages than Borjas. As described in the Counterpoint essay, these researchers have found the substitutability of low-skilled immigrant and low-skilled native-born labor to be less than perfect. In fact, some research suggests that the biggest pressure on wages from immigrant labor is on previous immigrants. Additionally, as many observers claim, the lowest-skilled of native-born workers—college dropouts, in particular—are the most compromised when competing with immigrants.

Despite the statistical uncertainty and methodological problems, it appears that the deleterious effects of immigration on native-born wages are not at all clear, and likely to be minimal, or at least not the cataclysmic effect many claim. Nevertheless, a perception exists that immigrant workers are not good for the economy, depressing wages for the American work force. In reading through this debate, it would be useful to sift carefully through the evidence to arrive at a reasoned and informed judgment.

POINT

Controversies over immigration touch on numerous important issues, including but not limited to who should be let in, how the border should be protected, what public services immigrants should have access to, and how to handle the substantial population that resides and works in the country without the legal right to do so. At the heart of most immigration-related controversies, however, is the following question: How does immigration impact native-born Americans and, most importantly, the labor market opportunities of American workers?

The large number of immigrants who have come to the United States over the last decades may have negatively affected labor market opportunities for American workers. Although simple economic theory predicts that an increase in the labor force will result in a depression of wages, assessing the actual impact of immigration on the wages of American workers is a challenging task for a number of reasons. First of all, immigrants are most likely to settle in areas with high wages and good job opportunities, resulting in an observed positive relationship between immigration and wages that is not necessarily caused by immigration. The possibility that American workers may react to immigration by relocating also complicates the matter. Another challenge lies in determining to what extent immigrants compete for the same kinds of jobs as native-born workers. As a result of the difficulty of the task, reputable economists are in considerable disagreement about the overall impact immigrants have on the American labor market. Although a number of researchers have investigated the question, the immigration scholar providing some of the most compelling evidence of immigration's negative impact on wages is the Harvard economist George Borjas; his work and the contributions of several other economists will be discussed below.

THE UNITED STATES HAS EXPERIENCED A LARGE AND SUSTAINED INFLOW OF IMMIGRANTS

U.S. immigration policy itself plays an important role in immigration's impacts on the labor market. Current immigration policy, which allows for the allocation of permanent visas (legal permanent status, or "green cards") derives from 1965 amendments to the Immigration and Nationality Act. Before 1965, the law emphasized national origin as a basis for immigration. The amended law prioritizes family reunification, and only allows for limited employment-based immigration.

It is worth taking a moment to consider statistics on how green cards are allocated in the United States. In 2009, 1.1 million immigrants were admitted to the country as legal permanent residents (LPRs). Of these, 47 percent were sponsored by immediate relatives (spouses, unmarried minor children, and parents) who were U.S. citizens. Unlike all other categories, immigrants who are sponsored by immediate relatives are not subject to any numerical quotas. Admissions of extended family members are also common: 19 percent of the 1.1 million immigrants who entered in 2009 were sponsored by immediate relatives of LPRs or non-immediate relatives (married and/or non-minor children and siblings) of U.S. citizens. Another large group is composed of refugees or those granted asylum from political persecution, representing another 16 percent, while 4 percent were admitted through a diversity lottery. Only a relatively small number, 13 percent, were admitted for reasons of employment.

One of the unintended consequences of the current immigration policy's emphasis on family reunification is that a large number of immigrants are relatively low-skilled workers. (It should also be noted that the change in the skill composition of immigrants has to do with the fact that the 1965 policy did away with national origin quotas, which opened up immigration from countries characterized by comparatively low educational attainment.) The largest group of immigrants, family-based immigrants, are predominantly in low-skilled occupations and have relatively low schooling levels. In 2010, for example, 29.7 percent of immigrants age 25 and above had less than a high school diploma, according to the U.S Census Bureau, as compared with 9.6 percent of native-born persons. By contrast, employment-based immigrants are largely college educated and in high-skill occupations.

Thus, immigrants represent an increasingly large share of the country's low-skilled workers. A large share of the U.S. workforce is foreign-born. U.S. Census data show that in recent years approximately 17 percent of the U.S. workforce has been foreign-born, a proportion that more than doubled since its 7 percent share in 1980. Although many immigrants are highly educated and skilled, the number of less-educated immigrants is growing faster relative to the native population.

While the immigrant proportion of the college-educated workforce increased from slightly more than 7 percent in 1980 to over 15 percent in recent years, the immigrant share of skilled workers remains roughly equal to the overall proportion of immigrants in the U.S. workforce. However, over this period the share of immigrants in the low-skilled segment of the labor force more than tripled, from 6.7 percent to 20.4 percent, making low-skilled immigrants considerably overrepresented among the least educated workers. One serious concern is that this increase has led to stiffer competition for jobs for America's workers, particularly the economically vulnerable low-skilled population.

THEORY: IMMIGRATION DRIVES DOWN WAGES OF NATIVE WORKERS

Any predictions derived from a simple economic model quite clearly show that an increase in immigration will lower the wages of native-born workers. This can be illustrated with a demand and supply framework. The starting prevailing wage rate, say W_0, can be found at the intersection of the downward sloping labor demand curve and upward sloping supply curve. An inflow of immigrant workers will increase the size of the U.S. labor force, and hence pushes the labor supply curve outward (there are now more workers at any given wage rate). With no changes to labor demand, at the wage level W_0 there are now more workers wanting jobs than employers are willing to hire. The competition will put downward pressure on wages, which in turn will induce firms to hire more workers, but will also lead to some workers leaving the labor market (since the wages are not sufficiently high to entice them to work). The new intersection between labor demand and supply will be at a lower wage than W_0; call it W_1. While employment is higher at W_1, some workers on the margin are not willing to work at this lower wage rate. That is, employment increases by a lower factor than labor supply increases due to immigration. Thus, in addition to the decreased wage, there is also job loss for the marginal worker who would have been employed at W_0. This could include native and immigrant workers who would have been willing to work at W_0. However, immigrants are more likely than natives to be willing to work at W_1, given their, on average, much lower wage opportunities in their home countries.

Theory also predicts positive effects of the inflow of immigration. Immigration has helped expand the size of the economy by increasing employment, and it has increased the income of the owners of firms (or more precisely, the owners of the capital used in production) by not only increasing the size of the economy but also reducing the cost of labor.

However, the above simple theory of the impact of immigration relies on a number of assumptions that might alter the conclusions. One especially significant assumption is that immigrants and natives are perfectly substitutable. In other words, the model described above assumes that employers can perfectly substitute the average immigrant worker for the average native worker. However, immigrants and natives differ along a number of dimensions that are likely of importance to employers. Immigrants tend to have less formal education, on average, with levels of educational attainment particularly low among Hispanic immigrants and many Southeast Asian immigrants. Immigrant and native-born workers are also likely to differ in terms of their ability to converse in English. In addition, immigrants tend to be younger than natives, which suggests that the average immigrant worker may have less labor market experience than the average native-born worker.

Given such difference in skills, it is more likely that immigrants and natives are what economists refer to as "imperfect substitutes" in production—in other words, substituting immigrant for native workers is possible, but limited by differences in skills. The native workers who are most similar to immigrants are more likely to face direct competition for jobs, while natives with very different skills are unlikely to be negatively affected. Given that a substantial share of immigrants to the United States have low schooling levels, the negatively affected are likely to be low-skilled American workers. Previously arrived immigrants are also likely to face competition from relatively newly arrived immigrants.

Moreover, the substitution possibilities are likely to vary between jobs, according to the skill content of various occupations. In some instances, certain subgroups of natives are likely to complement immigrant labor in production. That is to say, certain native workers are likely to be hired in conjunction with the hiring of immigrant workers. For example, Spanish-speaking laborers on a construction site may increase the demand for native-born bilingual Hispanics with enough education to serve in supervisory positions. As another example, an increase in the supply of low-skilled construction labor may increase the demand for architects, structural and civil engineers, skilled craftsmen, and workers in other such occupations, whose labor constitutes important inputs in the construction industry.

In sum, simple economic theory points out that immigration increases national output, harms substitute native labor (and potentially helps complementary native labor), but enriches the owners of capital (that is to say, employers). Stated in the language of labor economists, immigration harms the "factors of production" with which it directly competes, while benefiting those factors that it tends to complement. However, the reality of the situation may be more complex.

EMPIRICAL STUDIES SUPPORT NEGATIVE WAGE EFFECTS OF IMMIGRATION

Economists have turned to data on immigration and wages in order to test the predictions of the theory described above. While on paper the theory is a relatively simple matter of supply and demand, uncovering the true impact of immigration has proven to be a difficult and controversial empirical exercise.

Early studies relied on the geographic dispersion of immigrants to estimate the impact of immigration on wages, and they found no (or relatively small) negative effects. These studies used a so-called cross-area empirical approach that compares the number of immigrants in a particular area (e.g., a metropolitan area, or city), or the changes in the number of immigrants in the area, to the wage levels in the same area. Reviewing a large set of papers that analyzed the effect of immigration on the wages of native-born workers in the United States, the National Academy of Sciences Panel on Immigration concluded in its 1997 report that "there is only a small adverse impact of immigration on the wage and employment opportunities of competing native groups" (National Research Council, 1997, p. 236). These early findings, therefore, seem to run counter to the theoretical predictions.

However, these early empirical approaches were unlikely to expose the true impact of immigration, because they did not fully account for offsetting effects of migration. First, it may be that immigrants choose to move to areas with high wages and high wage growth, and to avoid areas with relatively poorer economic opportunities. In fact, these are indeed generally believed to be the primary decision factors behind migrant location choice. Thus, the correlation between immigration and wages may be biased upwards because immigrants choose cities that already offer higher wages on average, or that have specific job opportunities associated with them. For example, some immigrants are directly recruited to fill job openings, especially in certain industries such as medical services (nursing, in particular) and agriculture (e.g., harvesting crops).

Second, because migration within the United States may diminish local wage differentials, the effects estimated in early studies are generally understated. For example, early studies made the assumption that local labor markets were "closed," meaning that native workers do not relocate in the face of worsening labor market conditions. The question of native worker mobility in response to immigration is thus an empirical challenge in studies that compare how wages across cities change with respect to immigrant inflows. Ignoring these shortcomings biases wage estimates towards zero if the migration of natives equalizes wages across cities. Once researchers account for this bias, they find much larger negative impacts of immigration on native wages—a finding more consistent with economic theory.

In addition, one must recognize that outflows from cities are only half of the migration story—if native-born workers respond to increased immigration by choosing to relocate elsewhere, immigration may also slow population *inflows* to cities. Studying this aspect of immigration is complicated by the fact that native-born workers tend to be attracted to the same robust labor markets that attract immigrants.

Both of these internal migration effects can lead to misidentifying the impact of immigration on native wages. However, there is little consensus on the degree to which natives migrate (or choose not to migrate) due to local immigration influxes. For this reason, there is little agreement on the size of the bias in results that rely on local labor market variation in the immigrant share. Generally, results in most cross-area studies of the impact of immigration on native wages show zero to small negative impacts on wages, even among the less educated population.

However, as discussed above, the substitutability of workers is relevant to economic theory's predictions and early area-based studies of immigration's effects did not account for this complication. To address the fact that immigrant and American workers differ with respect to a number of skill-related factors, researchers have defined more disaggregated labor markets, breaking them down by criteria such as education, experience, and occupation.

In his studies of the issue, George Borjas uses these markets defined by skill and finds a much larger negative impact of immigration on wages. He attempts to circumvent some of the problems in the cross-area approach by analyzing immigration within skill markets rather than geographic markets. Borjas addresses these problems by using a novel kind of "closed market," first presented in his 2003 paper, "The Labor Demand Curve Is Downward Sloping." He uses skill groups (defined by education and labor market experience) in the national labor market, rather than local areas, as his "closed market." In either approach, one must assume some well-defined market is "closed." Here, Borjas trades markets closed by geography for those closed by skill.

Both this and the cross-area approach are subject to the criticism that the given market is not actually closed. But Borjas assumes that workers in different education-experience groups are imperfect substitutes, and thus compete in essentially independent labor markets, and also that they do not "migrate" between groups. The importance of experience found in the literature on human capital is provided as evidence that workers are less than perfectly substitutable, even when they have the same level of education. In addition, he compares the occupational distributions across skill groups and finds they are different enough to suggest that skill groups are not substitutable. However, the degree of substitutability across skill groups is to some extent an open empirical question.

The idea of closed skill markets allows researchers to exploit the differences between education-experience groups and the variation in immigrant shares within these groups nationally over time. Using this strategy, Borjas estimates quite a much larger effect: A 10 percent increase in the supply of workers due to immigration causes a 3 to 4 percent decrease in the wage of the average American worker, more than double the largest effects estimated in previous literature. This effect translate to a decline in earnings of between $1,300 and $1,800 for the median native-born worker in 2009 if immigration suddenly increased the labor supply of workers by 10 percent. A 10 percent increase in labor supply is quite large. For comparison, immigration did increase the labor supply of workers by approximately 10 percent, but over 2 full decades, from 1980 to 2000. The impact, however, is not the same for workers with different schooling levels. (This rough earnings loss estimate is calculated as a range between a 3 percent and 4 percent decline in median income for native-born workers in 2009. Median income is calculated by the U.S. Census Bureau from the *Current Population Survey: 2010*, for full-time, year-round workers age 25 and over.)

Low-skilled workers are estimated have been hurt the most. The wages of high school dropouts are estimated to have dropped by close to 9 percent due to the increase in immigration between 1980 and 2000. The immigrant influx is believed to have reduced the wages of the average native high school graduate by about 2.6 percent, while the wages of U.S. workers with some college education, but no college degree, do not appear to have been negatively affected. The negative impact is not simply one where the least skilled American workers were hurt the most. Borjas estimates that the wages of native college graduates declined by almost 5 percent as a result of the immigration inflows experienced in the United States between 1980 and 2000.

In their 2007 paper, "Does Immigration Affect Wages? A Look at Occupation-Level Evidence," economists Pia Orrenius and Madeline Zavodny also provide evidence that immigration has hurt America's less-skilled workers, but to a lesser degree than George Borjas found to be the case. Utilizing a different approach, they studied the effect of immigration inflows on wages within occupational groups, and they estimate a 1 to 5 percent decrease in American low-skilled blue-collar workers' wages due to legal immigration. The low end of their estimate is not unlike the early estimates using the area approach. However, Orrenius and Zavodny note that if illegal immigration was fully accounted for, the impact on less-skilled native workers would likely be found to be greater.

These recent studies suggest that there is likely to be a negative impact of less-skilled immigration on the wages of similar natives. These range from a 1 to 9 percent decrease in wages of less-skilled natives. This wide range, applied to median earnings among natives without a high school diploma, would translate to a decline in annual earnings between about $250 and $2,400 in 2009 (according to U.S. Census Bureau data, for native-born, full-time workers 25 and older with no high school diploma).

The studies differ on the impacts they estimate on more educated workers. Orrenius and Zavodny do not find any indication that wages of more skilled U.S. workers are hurt by immigration. Interestingly, they also find evidence that suggests that the process of assimilation makes immigrants more substitutable for natives, which indicates that wage competition increases as immigrants spend more time in the United States. In addition, theory suggests that the wages of more skilled U.S. workers might even increase in response to low-skilled immigration to the extent that their skills are complementary. Theory and empirical evidence on this is presented in the following Counterpoint article.

GAINS FROM IMMIGRATION'S NEGATIVE IMPACT ON WAGES

A common way to characterize (and simplify) a controversial issue is to say that there are "winners and losers." As mentioned above, although some are hurt by immigration, some benefit from it. For example, although immigration may have lowered the wages of some American workers, business owners employing these workers are better off because production costs are now lower and there are more potential buyers for their goods and services. It is also possible that the lower immigration-induced wages have a more widespread economic benefit: the prices of goods and services may also have gone down, and hence the cost of living may have gone down.

Recent evidence provided by economist Patricia Cortes, in a 2008 study titled "The Effect of Low-Skilled Immigration on U.S. Prices: Evidence From CPI Data," supports previous work finding lower wages among low-skilled American workers, but it also supports the finding that low-skilled immigration benefits the native population by decreasing the price of some goods. Cortes found that the price of services predominantly produced by immigrants, such as housekeeping and gardening, decreased by about 2 percent in response to a 10 percent increase in low-skilled immigration. Of course, the consumption of immigrant-intensive services and goods varies across income groups of the population: relatively wealthier American families are more likely to purchase such goods than their less fortunate counterparts.

Given that immigration affects both wages and prices differently, depending on skill level, the impact of immigration on the purchasing power of American workers also varies across different skill levels. Cortes's research indicates that among workers living in the 30 largest cities in the United States, the low-skilled immigration wave of the period from 1980 to 2000 increased the purchasing power of high-skilled workers slightly, by an average of about 0.3 percent, but decreased the purchasing power of the average American high school dropouts by as much as 1 percent. The largest negative effect was found among those workers most likely to compete with low-skilled immigrants: U.S.-born Hispanics, whose purchasing power declined by slightly more than 4 percent. Cortes concludes that "through lower prices, low-skilled immigration brings positive net benefits to the U.S. economy as a whole but also generates a redistribution of wealth" (p. 414).

CONCLUSION

Economic research provides empirical support for the theoretical prediction that large-scale immigration lowers wages of American workers. However, the evidence consistently shows that the wage effect differs depending on the skill level of native workers. The large inflow of low-skilled immigrants has reduced the wages of America's least skilled workers, possibly by as much as 9 percent, although most estimates suggest smaller negative effects. Research also consistently shows that any negative effects have been smaller for native high-skilled workers. Although the reduction in wages provides benefits for some American consumers in terms of lower prices and increased purchasing power, low-skilled workers and their families are less likely to reap this benefit.

References and Further Reading

Bohn, S., & Schiff, E. (2011). *Just the facts: Immigrant and the labor market.* Retrieved from Public Policy Institute of California website: http://www.ppic.org/main/publication_show.asp?i=823

Borjas, G. J. (1987, April). Immigrants, minorities, and labor market competition. *Industrial and Labor Relations Review, 40,* 382–392.

Borjas, G. J. (1994, December). The economics of immigration. *Journal of Economic Literature, 32,* 1667–1717.

Borjas, G. J. (2003). The labor demand curve is downward sloping: Reexamining the impact of immigration on the labor market. *Quarterly Journal of Economics, 118,* 1335–1374.

Borjas, G. J. (2006). Native internal migration and the labor market impact of immigration. *Journal of Human Resources, 41*(2), 221–258.

Borjas, G. J., Freeman, R. B., & Katz, L. F. (1992). On the labor market effects of immigration and trade. In G. J. Borjas & R. B. Freeman (Eds.), *Immigration and the work force: Economic consequences for the United States and source areas* (pp. 213–244). Chicago, IL: University of Chicago Press.

Borjas, G. J., Freeman, R. B., & Katz, L. F. (1996). *Searching for the effect of immigration on the labor market* (Working Paper No. 5454). Retrieved from National Bureau of Economic Research website: http://www.nber.org/papers/w5454

Card, D. (2001). Immigrant inflows, native outflows, and the local labor market impacts of higher immigration. *Journal of Labor Economics, 19*(1), 22–64.

Card, D., & DiNardo, J. (2000). Do immigrant inflows lead to native outflows? *American Economic Review, 90*(2), 360–367.

Cortes, P. (2008). The effect of low-skilled immigration on U.S. prices: Evidence from CPI data. *Journal of Political Economy, 116*(3), 381–422.

Friedberg, R. M., & Hunt, J. (1995). The impact of immigration on host country wages, employment and growth. *Journal of Economic Perspectives, 9*(2), 23–44.

Jaeger, D. A. (2007). *Skill differences and the effect of immigrants on the wages of natives* (Working Paper 273, revised). Retrieved from http://www.djaeger.org/research/wp/blswp273.pdf

National Research Council. (1997). *The new Americans: Economic, demographic, and fiscal effects of immigration.* Washington, DC: The National Academies Press.

Orrenius, P., & Zavodny, M. (2007). Does immigration affect wages? A look at occupation-level evidence. *Labour Economics, 14,* 757–773.

Sarah E. Bohn and Magnus Lofstrom

COUNTERPOINT

Simple economic theory predicts that, all other factors being equal, an increase in the supply of workers due to immigration will decrease wages. However, empirical evidence does not support this theory. In fact, average wages in the United States have generally increased during periods of large immigration. The key to understanding the impact of immigration on wages lies in the concepts of substitutability and complementarity of workers. Immigrant workers tend not to compete with native-born workers because, on average, they differ substantially in education, experience, and language ability. The presence of immigrant workers allows native-born workers to specialize in productivity-enhancing tasks and allows firms to invest in productivity-enhancing capital.

SIMPLE ECONOMIC THEORY ON WAGE EFFECTS

"Demand curves slope down." This is perhaps the best-understood principle in all of economics. Economists believe this principle applies in a wide variety of contexts, and the demand for labor is no exception. Just as with any other good, an increase in the supply of labor should reduce labor's equilibrium price. Immigration, which is an increase in the supply of labor to a country, should in theory reduce the wages of all workers in the market.

Despite this simple prediction, the hypothesis of immigration's effect on wages is one of the most hotly debated topics in labor economics. The bulk of the literature on the wage effects of immigration finds little adverse effect of immigration on wages of natives, despite strong theoretical predictions to the contrary. In fact, a simple correlation between wages and number of immigrants by city reveals the opposite of theory's prediction: cities with more immigrants tend to have higher average wages. For example, New York City and San Francisco, two cities with the highest concentration of immigrants in the population, have among the highest average wage rates in the country. Does this mean that immigrants drive up the wages in cities where they live, the opposite of the theory's prediction? No, but this correlation leads to a refinement of the understanding of immigration's effect on wages.

First, one must consider the decision to migrate from the perspective of the immigrant. Economic opportunity is one of the primary motivations for immigration to the United States. For this reason—again, all else being equal—immigrants are more likely to choose to move to a city with higher demand for workers and, thus, higher wages. Migration to U.S. cities is therefore not random, but is instead related to local labor market conditions. The correlation between wages and immigration at the city level is likely to be positive, then—not necessarily because immigrants increase wages, but because they choose cities with higher wages. That is, they tend to choose places with higher demand for labor. Thus, to sort out immigration's effect on wages (the supply effect), one must account for the demand side of the model.

EVIDENCE FROM NATURAL EXPERIMENTS

The ideal test of theory's prediction would be to run an experiment where one randomly locates immigrants in a city, and then observes what happens to wages both there and in an otherwise identical city with no new immigrants. The difference would reveal the impact of immigration on wages in the labor market. Obviously, this is not feasible. Instead, what economists have done is look for a "natural experiment," or "quasi-experiment," where something similar happened in the real world.

Probably the most influential such natural experiment occurred in Miami in the 1980s, following the Mariel Boatlift. In 1980, Fidel Castro announced that Cubans wishing to leave their country could do so via the port of Mariel. About 125,000 persons left for Miami. This caused a 7 percent increase in the Miami labor force—a sizeable shock—and a 20 percent increase in Cuban workers in Miami in particular. David Card, an economist, analyzed the impact of this labor supply shock to wages in Miami in a 1990 paper titled "The Impact of the Mariel Boatlift on the Miami Labor Market" and found basically no impact on the wages of native-born workers. The Miami labor market appeared to have absorbed the new immigrants rapidly. Similar studies have examined natural experiments of migration to Israel and France, with similar findings. These experiments suggest that labor markets are well situated to absorb immigrants, even potentially rapidly, without adversely affecting the wages of native workers.

IMMIGRANTS AND NATIVE WORKERS ARE NOT PERFECTLY SUBSTITUTABLE

The apparent discrepancy between theory and empirical evidence is assuaged by looking more closely at the functioning of labor markets, and at the characteristics of U.S. and foreign-born workers. There are reasons one might expect a supply shock due to immigration to lead to no overall decrease in wages. First, if immigrants and native-born workers are not perfectly substitutable for each other—that is, if they have very different skill levels—then they are unlikely to compete for the same jobs. Indeed, recent immigrants to the United States tend to be, on average, younger and less educated than the native-born population.

To establish the education disparity between immigrants and the native-born, Figure 15.1 shows the percentage of immigrants relative to native-born persons in four major education categories: less than high school diploma, high school graduates, those with some college, and college graduates. If immigrants and native-born individuals are equally represented in a given education group, then the bars should be approximately the same height. However, in 2010, a higher proportion of immigrants were located in the lowest educated group than were natives. Nearly 30 percent of immigrants did not have a high school diploma, compared to nearly 10 percent among native-born.

Native-born persons are more likely to have a high school diploma or some college experience than immigrants. At the highest skill level described in Figure 51.1, native-born persons and immigrants are almost equally likely to have a college degree. However, almost the same percentage of immigrants have a college degree as have no high school degree. This evinces the long-term trend: immigration to the United States is bifurcated by skill.

The bifurcated education distribution of immigrants is tied to immigration policy. Since the 1960s, federal policy has favored immigrant admission based on family reunification rather than on skill level. This has had the effect of increasing the less-skilled immigrant population, as described in the preceding Point article. At the same time,

Figure 15.1 Education levels of immigrants and native-born, 2010

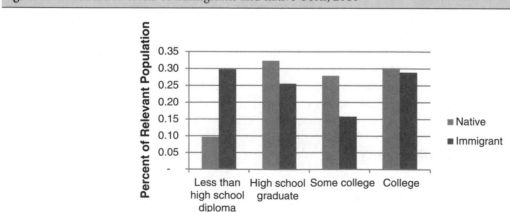

Source: Author's calculations, derived from U.S. Census Bureau's *Current Population Survey: Annual Social and Economic Supplement,* 2010.
Note: The height of each bar represents the number of native-born persons (or immigrants) in the education group relative to the total number of native-born persons (or immigrants). The population includes only people age 25 and older.

increasing numbers of highly educated immigrants are admitted to fill the labor demands of industry through visa programs such as the H-1B, which is a particular type of visa that allows employers to hire high-skilled workers in specific fields. Because high-skilled immigrants are often recruited to fill excess demand for high-skilled labor, the wage impacts of these immigrant workers are generally of less concern to policymakers. Indeed, they are often seen as providing a clear benefit to the economy because of the much-needed skills they can provide.

Most of the policy focus centers on the economic impacts of low-skilled immigrants. In addition to legal routes for admission, there is a large and growing presence of undocumented immigrants in the United States, estimated at 11 million in 2009 and comprising over 5 percent of the labor force. While not all less-educated immigrant workers are undocumented, a majority of nonnaturalized immigrant workers with less than a high school diploma are.

This only highlights further the marked differences in human capital between immigrant and native-born populations. Thus, the effects of immigration on labor market outcomes of native-born persons may not be as clear as expected from the predictions of a simple supply and demand theory. A recently arrived young immigrant with no high school diploma, who is likely undocumented and may not speak English well, is unlikely to directly impact the labor market opportunities of a U.S.-born individual with a degree in engineering, for example.

So, it is clear that one should try to identify a wage impact on native-born workers with similar skill levels. When David Card (1990) examined the impact of the Cuban immigrants to Miami—who were, on average, younger and less educated—on similar native-born workers, he still found no strong evidence of any adverse impact on the wages of similar native-born workers. Other studies have reached similar conclusions: estimates of the wage impact of immigrants on less-educated native-born workers hover around zero. Using a wide variety of data sources and methodologies, when economists evaluate the impact of low-skilled immigration on low-skilled, native-born workers, they tend to find zero or small negative impacts. The largest impact that has been estimated is a 9 percent decline in the wages of high school dropouts due to the large influx in immigration from 1980 to 2000, as found by George Borjas in his 2003 paper, "The Labor Demand Curve Is Downward Sloping" (using income statistics from the U.S. Census Bureau's *Current Population Survey: 2010* for full-time, year-round workers age 25 and over).

Note that this result is from a single study using a different methodology than most. Indeed, reviewing research on the impact of immigration on wages, the National Academy of Sciences Panel on Immigration concluded in 1997 that "there is only a small adverse impact of immigration on the wage and employment opportunities of competing native groups" (National Research Council, 1997, p. 236).

One potential explanation for such scant evidence of a significant negative impact on similar workers is that, even within an education group, immigrants may not be closely substitutable with natives, for many reasons. Differences in language, culture-specific human capital, institutional knowledge, and perhaps even preferences for types of work inhibit perfect substitutability of otherwise similar workers. For example, the more language ability matters in a particular industry or occupation, the less substitutable are immigrants for natives. Thus, the expected effect of immigration on the wages of natives is lessened for workers with otherwise similar skill levels.

A few economists have recently conducted research to determine whether this sort of imperfect substitutability of immigrants and natives is at play. Giovanni Peri and Patricia Cortes have found empirical evidence of the imperfect substitutability of otherwise similar immigrants and natives based on skill. In her 2008 paper titled "The Effect of Low-Skilled Immigration on U.S. Prices: Evidence From CPI Data," Cortes notes that even where there is evidence of a small negative wage effect of less-skilled immigration on less-skilled natives, the wage effect on previous immigrants is even larger, suggesting imperfect substitutes. Peri, in many papers, but exemplified in the 2009 article "Rethinking the Area Approach: Immigrants and the Labor Market in California, 1960–2005," estimates the substitutability of immigrant and native workers within a skill group directly, and finds empirical evidence suggesting they are not perfectly substitutable.

Geography is another factor that inhibits the substitutability of immigrants and native-born workers. Immigrants have traditionally settled in relatively few cities, often referred to as "traditional" destinations or "immigrant gateways," such as New York City, Los Angeles, Chicago, and Miami. Since roughly the mid-1990s, immigrants have ventured beyond these traditional destinations, and cities with little history of receiving immigrants are now home to sizeable numbers of them, particularly cities in the Southwest and Southeast regions of the country. Still, there remain areas that have virtually no presence of immigrants in the labor market. Unless local labor markets are intricately connected and differentials are perfectly arbitraged, the immigrants to one city are likely to have little impact on native-born wages in a city far away. A new immigrant to Atlanta, for example, is unlikely to affect the wages of a native-born worker in Boise.

The imperfect substitutability of immigrant and native workers provides a possible hypothesis for the observation of virtually no negative wage impact of immigrants on natives, despite strong predictions of such findings. While there is some empirical support for the imperfect substitutability hypotheses, more research needs to be done to determine if this is a true causal explanation. It is clear, however, that simple theory rarely can fully capture the complex functioning of labor markets, and the imperfect substitutability of immigrants and natives is one intuitive example of this.

IMMIGRANT SKILLS MAY BE COMPLEMENTARY TO NATIVE WORKERS

Rather than being harmed by immigration, native-born workers may actually gain labor market opportunities to the extent that they are complements for immigrants in production. This complementarity can operate through capital investments, firm creation, and task specialization. Consider, for example, the construction industry, which employs both highly educated workers, such as engineers, and less educated workers, such as carpenters and plumbers. An increase in the supply of the latter due to immigration may increase the demand for the former. Either construction firms can expand their businesses, or new firms can arise to utilize the influx of workers due to immigration. Such expansions require the complementary hiring of high-skilled workers, such as engineers, or individuals in managerial positions. In this way, complementary native-born workers may find increased labor market opportunities, in the form of employment and wages, due to immigration.

Some economists estimate that this complementarity between native and immigrant workers actually yields a positive impact on the wages of native-born. As noted in their 2011 paper, "Rethinking the Effects of Immigration on Wages," Gianmarco Ottaviano and Giovanni Peri found that, on average (across education groups), native workers gained 1.8 percent in wages due to immigration from 1990 to 2004. In related work, Peri and Francesc Ortega (2011) found that an inflow of immigrants equaling 1 percent of the population generates a 1.5 percent increase in total employment, meaning that immigrants provide skills complementary to the native-born population.

In addition, even for native and immigrant workers with similar skill levels, there is reason to expect some degree of complementarity. Returning to the construction industry example, consider laborers on a job site with similar skill levels. If immigrant workers on the site do not speak English well, native-born workers are likely to take on the task of communicating with the owner or builder. In this way, the native-born worker with otherwise identical skill to the immigrant worker steps into a more specialized, in-demand, and thus more highly paid, position. In this example, the communication skills of native-born workers are particularly valuable relative to the more manual tasks of the job. In general, however, a variety of specialized tasks may be taken on by a native-born worker to complement immigrant workers. To the extent that these specialized tasks are more valuable to production, native-born workers who specialize due to an influx of immigrants may earn higher wages.

Economists have used this concept of complementarity of labor to explain labor market phenomena among American workers. Empirical evidence also documents complementarity between immigrant workers and American workers. For example, Giovanni Peri and Chad Sparber, in their 2009 article, "Task Specialization, Immigration, and Wages," note an increase in the supply of communication-skilled tasks among native-born, less-educated workers due to an increase in foreign-born workers. They then use that relationship to predict changes in wages for these native-born workers. When task specialization is not accounted for, the impact of immigration on native-born wages is negative. But after accounting for native task specialization, they find much smaller wage impacts (0.3 percent decline nationwide) or even positive impacts in some local labor markets (0.9 percent gain in New York, for example).

Complementarities can exist across immigrants and natives with very different skill levels (manual laborers to engineers) as well as with more similar, but differentiated skill levels (Spanish-speaking laborers to English-speaking ones). Counterintuitive to simple supply-and-demand theory, these researchers have found evidence that immigrants may benefit native workers in terms of labor market opportunities.

IMMIGRANTS ARE MORE LIKELY TO IMPACT WAGES OF PREVIOUS IMMIGRANTS

Thus far, only the impact of immigration on native-born workers has been considered. However, growing evidence suggests that the primary wage impacts of immigration are on the wages of previous immigrants. This is consistent with the theory that immigrants and native-born workers tend not to compete for the same jobs. Because they have similar skill levels as well as similar socioeconomic characteristics, it is plausible that new immigrants will compete most directly with previous, similar immigrants.

In his study of the Mariel Boatlift, David Card looked at competition among immigrants in Miami in the 1980s. He found little evidence of any effect of the new Cuban immigrants on either previous Cuban immigrants or on non-Cubans. However, in more recent studies covering more time and geography, a number of economists have identified negative effects on immigrants. Ottaviano and Peri (2012), estimate that immigrant workers lost on average 19 percent of real wages due to immigration to the United States broadly between 1990 and 2004. Cortes (2008) likewise notes a negative wage effect of new immigration on previous immigrants. Her estimates suggest that for a 10 percent increase in the share of less-skilled immigrants, the wages of previous less-skilled immigrants fall between 2 and 4 percent.

IMPACT OF IMMIGRATION ON FIRMS

The presence of immigrant workers is likely to impact the decisions of firms in the United States. To the extent that immigrants and native-born persons do not compete for the same jobs, as argued above, new immigrants to the United States constitute a new, unique source of labor for firms. Given this source of labor, firms can adjust their production inputs in order to optimize profits.

In particular, a key decision that firms face is the amount of labor to employ relative to capital. In local areas that receive large immigrant flows, firms may lean toward the production of labor-intensive goods. Alternatively, firms may produce the same goods but switch to more labor-intensive production methods, given the increasing relative cost of capital versus labor due to immigration. Most of the current research suggests that the latter outcome is much more likely than the former. Ethan Lewis, in his 2011 paper, "Immigration, Skill Mix, and Capital Skill Complementarity," found that there is slower adoption of manufacturing production technologies requiring high levels of skill in markets with large increases in unskilled immigrant labor. In addition, Peri (2012) found that the overall capital employed decreased relative to labor in states with larger immigration inflows.

While the evidence is somewhat mixed, it may be that these capital and labor adjustments by firms create an increase in productivity. In this way, native-born workers and the overall economy may gain from immigration due to productivity-enhancing choices of firms.

Finally, an increase in the overall supply of workers due to immigration may allow new firms to enter the market. For example, an immigrant-owned business employing other immigrants creates brand new goods or services, increasing the overall scale of economic activity in a market. In some industries, a new firm may rely heavily on immigrant labor but also require complementary native-born workers. As such, the scale effect would depend on the availability of complementary workers.

CONCLUSION

The majority of economic studies have found little to no impact of immigration on wages in the United States over the last few decades. This evidence is contrary to economic theory, which predicts a significant negative effect on wages due to a large inflow of immigrants. This puzzle is explained by the fact that the average recent immigrant to the United States is very different than the average U.S.-born worker in terms of education, skill, and even place of residence. While some immigrants are highly skilled, the average immigrant arrives with a high school diploma at most, as well as limited proficiency in English. Further, immigrants tend to cluster in a few cities, whereas U.S.-born workers are more dispersed across the country. For this reason, immigrants are not equal substitutes for native-born workers in most jobs. In fact, they tend to complement native-born skills and allow native-born workers to specialize in more highly paid job tasks. Further, the availability of less-skilled immigrant labor allows firms to shift toward lower-cost, labor-intensive production.

REFERENCES AND FURTHER READING

Bohn, S. (2010). The quantity and quality of new immigrants in the U.S. *Review of Economics of the Household, 8*(1), 29–51.

Borjas, G. J. (2003). The labor demand curve is downward sloping: Reexamining the impact of immigration on the labor market. *Quarterly Journal of Economics, 118,* 1335–1374.

Borjas, G. J., Freeman, R. B., & Katz, L. F. (1992). On the labor market effects of immigration and trade. In G. J. Borjas & R. B. Freeman (Eds.), *Immigration and the work force: Economic consequences for the United States and source areas* (pp. 213–244). Chicago, IL: University of Chicago Press.

Borjas, G. J., Freeman, R. B., & Katz, L. F. (1996). *Searching for the effect of immigration on the labor market* (Working Paper No. 5454). Retrieved from National Bureau of Economic Research website: http://www.nber.org/papers/w5454

Borjas, G. J., Grogger, J., & Hanson, G. (2011). *Substitution between immigrants, natives, and skill groups* (NBER Working Paper No. 17461). Retrieved from National Bureau of Economic Research website: http://www.nber.org/papers/w17461.pdf

Card, D. (1990). The impact of the Mariel Boatlift on the Miami labor market. *Industrial and Labor Relations Review, 43*(2), 245–257.

Card, D. (2001). Immigrant inflows, native outflows, and the local labor market impacts of higher immigration. *Journal of Labor Economics, 19*(1), 22–64.

Card, D., & DiNardo, J. (2000). Do immigrant inflows lead to native outflows? *American Economic Review, 90*(2), 360–367.

Cortes, P. (2008). The effect of low-skilled immigration on U.S. prices: Evidence from CPI data. *Journal of Political Economy, 116*(3), 381–422.

Friedberg, R. M. (2001). The impact of mass migration on the Israeli labor market. *Quarterly Journal of Economics, 116*(4), 1373–1408.

Friedberg, R. M., & Hunt, J. (1995). The impact of immigration on host country wages, employment and growth. *Journal of Economic Perspectives, 9*(2), 23–44.

Lewis, E. (2011). Immigration, skill mix, and capital skill complementarity. *Quarterly Journal of Economics, 126,* 1029–1069.

National Research Council. (1997). *The new Americans: Economic, demographic, and fiscal effects of immigration.* Washington, DC: The National Academies Press.

Ottaviano, G., & Peri, G. (2012). Rethinking the effects of immigration on wages. *Journal of the European Economic Association, 10*(1), 152–197.

Peri, G. (2007). How immigrants affect California employment and wages. *California Counts: Population Trends and Profiles, 8*(3). Retrieved from http://www.ppic.org/content/pubs/cacounts/CC_207GPCC.pdf

Peri, G. (2009). Rethinking the area approach: Immigrants and the labor market in California, 1960–2005. *Journal of International Economics, 84*(1), 1–14.

Peri, G. (2012). The effect of immigration on productivity: Evidence from the U.S. states. *Review of Economics and Statistics, 94*(1), 348–358.

Peri, G., & Ortega, F. (2011, March). *The aggregate effect of trade and migration: Evidence from OECD countries* (IZA Working Paper No. 5604). Retrieved from Institute for the Study of Labor website: http://ftp.iza.org/dp5604.pdf

Peri, G., & Sparber, C. (2009). Task specialization, immigration, and wages. *American Economic Journal: Applied Economics, 1*(3), 135–169.

Sarah E. Bohn and Magnus Lofstrom

16

Remittances

POINT: Remittances are a vital part of the global economy, offering prospects for development and providing key resources that contribute to the alleviation of poverty for the families of migrant workers.

Kristin Johnson, University of Rhode Island

COUNTERPOINT: Foreign remittances are a drain on the U.S. economy and should be curtailed.

Jack Martin, Federation for American Immigration Reform (FAIR)

Introduction

Remittances are monies sent by immigrants (and some U.S. citizens) to family members in foreign countries, and they have a large impact on the economies of receiving countries. While the volume of remittances fluctuates with economic conditions, they approximate $400 billion per year worldwide and dwarf the amount of foreign aid to developing countries. For individuals, the ability to send remittances can be central to the decision to migrate, and these monies are important to the economic survival of recipients. From the standpoint of national economies, remittances can be a key source of foreign currency and a significant percent of gross domestic product.

Remittance flows between sending and receiving countries closely mirror migration patterns. According to the World Bank's *Migration and Remittances Factbook 2011,* the largest migration corridor in the world is between the United States and Mexico, with 11.6 million Mexicans in the United States as of 2010. By way of context, the next largest migration corridor is between the Russian Federation and the Ukraine, with 3.7 million Russians in the Ukraine and 3.6 million Ukrainians in Russia as of 2010. Other significant corridors are shown in Table 16.1.

According to the World Bank, the United States is the largest remittance-sending country in the world, measured in dollar volume. Remittances are, however, a relatively small share of U.S. gross domestic product (GDP). Table 16.2 shows the volume of remittances and share of GDP for top sending countries.

There are two aspects to debates about remittances. One relates to the economic consequences of remittances in terms of both family income and national economies. The second relates to whether it is appropriate, in a free society, for government to intrude on how individuals spend their money.

Table 16.1 Selected top migration corridors, 2010 (millions of migrants)

Mexico–United States	11.6
Russian Federation–Ukraine	3.7
Ukraine–Russian Federation	3.6
Turkey–Germany	2.7
China–Hong Kong SAR, China	2.2
China–United States	1.7
India–United States	1.7
Philippines–United States	1.7
Puerto Rico–United States	1.7
India–Saudi Arabia	1.5
Vietnam–United States	1.2
El Salvador–United States	1.1
Republic of Korea–United States	1.1
Pakistan–Saudi Arabia	1.0
Cuba–United States	1.0

Economic Impacts of Remittances in the United States and Internationally

Consumer spending makes up between 65 and 70 percent of U.S. GDP, and is therefore a key determinant of economic performance. Concerns about remittances derive from the idea that monies sent out of the country could have been spent on domestic consumption to the benefit of the overall economy. The earnings of remittance senders, therefore, are seen to have a less beneficial economic impact than earnings of people who do not remit money overseas by directly reducing consumption and foregoing the multiplier effect of that consumption (see sidebar).

Conceptually, remittances are analogous to personal savings, which also take money out of circulation, reducing consumption. Thus, as an analytic matter, the immediate economic impact of remittances depends on the difference, if any, between the percent of personal income that senders remit overseas and the percent of personal income that those who do not remit money overseas actually save. One important caveat to the analogy between remittances and savings is that savings are deferred consumption—money saved will, in the vast majority of cases, ultimately be spent. By contrast, remittances do represent a reduction in potential future consumption.

Internationally, remittances are matter for a number of reasons. They are an important source of foreign currency in senders' home countries. They are also key sources of income to the families receiving them and have been credited with impacts ranging from subsistence survival, the emergence of consumer banking services in some countries, and higher educational attainment rates in families receiving them. Remittances thus constitute a form of poverty alleviation that circumvents intermediaries by going directly to those who need it, diminishing the amount of funds lost to government corruption.

Table 16.2 Top remittance-sending countries, 2009 (billions of U.S. dollars, and share of sending country GDP)

Sending country	Estimated remittances	Share of GDP
United States	$48.3	0.35%
Saudi Arabia	26.0	6%
Switzerland	19.6	4%
Russian Federation	18.6	2%
Germany	15.9	0.54%
Italy	13.0	7.5%
Spain	12.6	0.94%
Luxembourg	10.6	20%
Kuwait	9.9	8%
Netherlands	8.1	1.2%

What is the "multiplier effect"?

Consumer spending flows through the economy with what is known as a "multiplier effect." This spending generates income for producers of consumer goods, which, in turn, generates income for the suppliers of inputs to those goods, and so forth. The result is that a dollar of consumer spending generates more than a dollar of GDP.

Should Remittances Be Regulated?

Taxing or otherwise regulating remittances inherently involves government intrusion on private spending decisions, an intrusion on personal liberties that would be highly contentious if directed at U.S. citizens. As newcomers, however, immigrants—especially noncitizen immigrants—have outsider status, which can result in an impulse to limit their civil, political, and social rights. For immigrants, these rights are often seen as conferred by government; the notion, embedded in the Declaration of Independence, that people possess "certain inalienable rights, among them life, liberty, and the pursuit of happiness" does not necessarily apply to immigrants. Particularly in the case of illegal immigrants, many argue that the American conception of inalienable rights does not apply. Consequently, taxing or otherwise regulating remittances is seen as an appropriate, punitive step justified by illegal presence in the United States.

The debate over whether to regulate remittances is therefore informed by differences in views on the extent to which immigrants are properly viewed as outsiders warranting different standards as to rights, the extent to which remittance senders are equated with illegal immigrants, and the extent to which it is appropriate to formulate U.S. immigration policy according to the economic interests of the United States.

POINT

Many immigrants in the United States and around the world support their families by sending, or remitting, a portion of their income to family members living in their home countries. Remittances, as broadly defined by the U.S. Department of Commerce's Bureau of Economic Analysis, include personal income sent by foreign-born individuals to their families abroad, wages earned by temporary workers, and earnings and wealth accumulation by foreign-born workers who return to their home countries. Personal remittances have grown significantly over the past 2 decades; according to the World Bank, in 2009 remittances exceeded $400 billion. These personal transfers have eclipsed official development assistance (ODA) and are nearing levels of foreign direct investment (FDI) in total capital transfers from developed to developing countries.

Remittances sent from the United States comprise between one-third and one-quarter of the total amount of global remittances; conservative estimates place the value of remittances sent from the United States at over $100 billion. The World Bank estimates that nearly $48.3 billion in remittance's dollars were sent from the United States to Mexico in 2009. The U.S.-Mexico remittance corridor is the largest in the world, and Mexico ranks third globally, behind India and China, in terms of remittance receipts. While remittances are typically thought of as transfers from wealthy to poor countries, France and Germany each place in the top 10 global remittance-recipient countries.

It is unsurprising that remittances have become a point of contention in recent immigration debates. A common assumption ties remittances to illegal immigration, yet immigrants with both legal and illegal status are responsible for remittance flows. Remittances are a critical survival resource for many individuals in developing countries. Remittance dollars contribute to the health and well-being of populations with few other resources, and offer a unique form of microfinance that contributes to the creation of small businesses abroad through the extension of credit, resulting in more jobs and higher wages. While remittance dollars sent and spent abroad likely reduce consumer spending in the U.S. economy; remittances are analogous in the short term to personal savings, and they are sensitive to economic downturns and periods of hardship.

REMITTANCES AND POVERTY

According to the International Monetary Fund, in 2010, remittances accounted for nearly a third of national income in Tajikistan and Laos, a fifth in El Salvador and Honduras, and 12 percent in the Philippines. Even before the devastating 2010 earthquake in Haiti, the World Bank reported that over 55 percent of Haitian households identified remittances as their sole source of income. The ratio of remittances to national income is likely underreported for a number of countries, such as Somalia. Remittances are a critical resource for individuals in the poorest countries. A 2005 study of 71 developing countries by Richard Adams and John Page found that a 10 percent increase in remittances resulted in a 3.5 percent decline in populations living at what the United Nations defines as absolute poverty, or less than a dollar a day. Remittances decrease the severity, depth, and pervasiveness of poverty in a population, having the largest effects in the poorest areas. Remittances allow households to shift from a reliance on subsistence production to the purchase of market goods. While definitions of poverty vary across societies and depend on levels of income inequality within a society, a substantial number of studies establish that remittances do, either directly or indirectly, influence the level of poverty within societies. The direct effect of remittances includes increased resources to support basic household needs, as outlined above. The indirect effect of remittances includes increasing infrastructure and employment opportunities throughout communities where remittance recipients reside.

Critics of remittances contend that remittances do not support substantive changes in the standards of living among populations, and that these monetary transfers are often spent on status goods (e.g., flashy watches or imported name-brand clothing) instead of rent, household goods, food, education, or transportation expenses. Surveys completed in Mexico, the Philippines, and China by World Bank researchers indicates that this view is not borne out by the facts. A case in point is Mexico, where, according to the Federal Reserve Bank of Dallas (2004), nearly 80 percent of remittances are spent on food, clothing, and household expenses. The less wealthy southern Mexican states are particularly impacted by remittances, and a shift that is occurring for the poorest 30 percent of the population, where household expenditures are approaching national averages, is due in large part to remittance contributions. This indicates a shift away from subsistence production to participation in the purchase of household goods. In a 2011 study of Mexico's 2,438 municipalities, Claire Adida and Desha Girod found that remittances were used for the expansion of public services, such as utilities and potable water, when the government was unable to provide these services to poorer subsets of the population. In terms of improving health and access to basic needs, remittances are critical to eliminating debt that traps poor populations into cycles of poverty.

The Nobel laureate Amartya Sen argues in a 1999 book that remittances enhance the number of substantive choices for populations living in poverty, increasing the ability of individuals to control their lives. As the largest source of "bottom-up" redistribution and resource transfer, remittances also avoid a number of challenges accompanying development assistance and poverty alleviation efforts. First, resource transfers are largely person-to-person, with an increasing number of remittances sent via wire transfer. By 2003, nearly 86 percent of remittances sent from the United States to Mexico were electronic money transfers, according to the World Bank. This means that remittances are insulated from diversion by corrupt officials, at least in terms of inflows. Second, remittances do not require substantial bureaucracy or expertise in order to be distributed, as most development and aid projects do. Monetary transfers sent to individuals are typically sent in response to assessed need. Extreme economic hardship, conflict, or emergencies often elicit an increase in remittance inflows for a country, making them an immediate resource.

Individuals living under conditions of extreme poverty are also often the most vulnerable in cases of emergency or natural disaster. The 2010 earthquake in Haiti is again a case in point. Extreme and widespread poverty amplified the scope of the disaster; the collapse of concrete block and semipermanent building structures coupled with a lack of individual and government resources left an already poor population with few resources and little capacity to respond. With 72 percent of the population already living on under $2 a day, and with challenges ranging from food in security to a lack of health care and unsafe drinking water, the humanitarian crisis following the 2010 earthquake was dire. The World Bank estimates that in 2010–2011, the 200,000 Haitian workers granted temporary protected status in the United States were responsible for an increase of $360 million in remittances to Haiti, for a total of over $1.4 billion. Remittances are the first resources to reach individuals in times of crisis and can be used to assist in procuring scarce resources expeditiously. In Haiti, remittances were lauded as one of the most important facets of economic survival and recovery.

Richard Brown and Eliana Jimenez, in a 2008 study that examined the substantial influences of remittances in the South Pacific island nations of Tonga and Fiji, note that remittances are not only motivated by the level of poverty in a household. Through substantial survey efforts, they ascertained that remittances also increased when family members experienced health problems exceeding 30 days, when an elderly individual resided in a home, and when weddings, funerals, or other culturally significant events occurred. The logical conclusion of this evaluation is that remittances serve an informal social protection function in very poor societies.

One important issue should be acknowledged: remittances are not evenly distributed across populations. In some countries, emigration is available only to high-skilled and well-educated workers, resulting in remittance flows concentrated among already relatively privileged subpopulations. Thus, the prospects for an increase in inequality are evident. However, this merely indicates that remittances should be viewed as just one of many tools that can assist in combating poverty. It also belies the stereotype that immigrants who choose to remit are undocumented, low-skilled workers.

Several top migration corridors, such as between the United States and Mexico, between western Europe and Egypt, or between the Middle East and South East Asia, have substantial guest worker programs or large populations of undocumented low-skilled workers, who are more likely to remit resources to poorer populations.

REMITTANCES AND DEVELOPMENT

"Development" is a term fraught with diverse interpretations and debate. Most interpretations of the term include the accumulation or increase in economic and human resources for an identified population. Remittances can contribute to each of these ends for recipients. First, remittances can essentially bring people into markets by transitioning them from subsistence production to being able to purchase household goods. This increase in the purchase of household goods increases the demand for services, generating increases in revenue and economic opportunity. As long as an increase in demand is not too sharp, the consequence of price increases created by shortage should not be overwhelmingly substantial. A large number of remittances are spent on household construction, making remittances an important factor in improving sanitation and security for recipients. An additional benefit can also be found, as construction can employ large numbers of unskilled laborers, resulting in additional resource dissemination throughout the community in which remittance recipients reside.

HUMAN DEVELOPMENT

With the success of microfinance efforts in increasing production and providing small business opportunities—begun first by the Grameen Bank, and subsequently by other microfinance organizations—remittances came to be viewed by many as organic opportunities for microfinance. The Mexican government went so far as to increase access to banking and incentives for individuals to invest remittance dollars in small businesses and entrepreneurial efforts, although this has had limited results to date.

Longer-term investments made possible by remittances are not limited to housing improvements. Additional household resources can provide the necessary funds for families choosing to keep their children in school and out of the labor force for a longer period of time. The benefits of these transfers become multigenerational, with increases in human capital passed onto the next generation. Numerous studies of the effects of remittances—including a 2006 World Bank Report authored by Caglar Ozden and Maurice Schiff—suggest that remittances are related to increased household expenditures on education, higher school enrollment rates, and improved health indicators, including anthropomorphic measurements (e.g., child stunting), lower infant mortality rates, and declining illiteracy rates. Health and education are critical facets in increasing human capital, a necessary element in increasing individual earning capabilities.

INFRASTRUCTURE AND ECONOMIC DEVELOPMENT OPPORTUNITIES

The increase in the use of formal remittance channels, primarily electronic money transfers, has resulted in increased access to savings and credit for a number of individuals who otherwise would have limited access to these services in developing countries. Largely a consequence of the globalization of capital, money transfers are an increasingly large part of a package of services offered by banks and credit unions, and the presence and scope of money transfer companies represents a growing industry.

The expansion of financial institutions and services creates substantial benefits for populations. Initially, remittance fees can provide funding for rural microfinance institutions, allowing the expansion of banking services where they would otherwise be relatively nonexistent. Formal channels of money transfer also increase transparency. Fees, and increasingly exchange rates, are published and available, and the risk of diversion in money orders sent through the mail or carried across the border is lower than with other methods of transfer. However, costs, in the form of acquiring formal identification and reaching a money transfer office, are borne by remittance recipients receiving formal transfers.

The most obvious salient benefit to an expansion of remittance service providers and formal remittance channels is the expansion of banking and credit to populations otherwise unlikely to have access to these services. For example, the harmonization and formalization of the remittance corridor between Ecuador and Spain has resulted in a cooperative partnership between Bank Solidario in Ecuador and La Caixa in Spain. Individuals in Ecuador are increasingly able to access services such as personal credit, mortgage financing, dual-use ATM cards, and small business loans as a consequence of this cooperative model. Banks and credit unions in developed countries are increasingly leveraging remittances as services to entice emigrants to become customers, viewing migrant populations as a resource worthy of recruitment.

Accompanying these benefits are some shortcomings. Despite the increased formalization and competition among remittance service providers, fee structures vary substantially by location and the number of companies in a region involved in providing money transfer services. Most remittances comprise small frequent transfers; the World Bank reports that the average transfer to Mexico ranges between $200 and $300 and occurs approximately once a month. Regressive fee structures, including flat fees rather than percentage-based fees, impose burdens on poor migrant families. In response to this phenomenon, the World Bank has begun publishing and collecting information on money transfer fees and corridors in an effort to increase transparency and encourage remittance service providers to offer affordable and progressive scales for transfers.

REMITTANCES AND MACROECONOMIC BENEFITS

Remittances are capital inflows that can serve to decrease existing external constraints on economic growth. The relationship between remittances and growth, however, is context dependent, with the impact of economic growth dependent on the monetary policy and fiscal structures of the recipient country. The first cross-sectional time-series study of the effects of remittances on growth, published by the International Monetary Fund in 2008, revealed no consistent statistical relationship between short-term GDP growth and remittances levels; however, the poverty alleviation accompanying remittance inflows may result in small long-term domestic productivity and increases in wealth accumulation (see Chami et al., 2008).

In part, this lack of an effect may be explained by evidence that remittances can result in exchange rate appreciation, particularly in smaller countries. For countries reliant on exports, exchange rate appreciation results in decreased trade competitiveness and possibly trade deficits. As many remittance-receiving countries have been encouraged to pursue export-oriented development strategies by international actors such as the World Bank and International Monetary Fund, there may be increased susceptibility to exchange rate appreciation that decreases domestic revenues. However, countries where the currency is tied or pegged to the dollar, such as Panama, Belize, or El Salvador, and where remittances are largely received in dollars, this effect is absent due to the exchange rate regimes.

Remittances do yield some real and substantial macroeconomic benefits. Perhaps most importantly, remittances can increase the revenue base for governments, particularly in the form of indirect taxation. Government attempts to levy taxes directly on remittances or on labor demand created by increases in remittances tend to be unsuccessful in increasing tax revenue because remittances functionally drive both monetary transfers and labor into the informal market. However, governments choosing to indirectly tax the increased consumption accompanying remittance receipts can increase revenues and their ability to provide basic services to their populations.

Similar to the response to natural disasters, the amount of money remitted to families residing in home countries is often responsive to the economic performance of those countries at a given point in time. In other words, remittance levels are counter-cyclic to the economic performance of a country. For example, in a 2009 study of Mexico and Central American countries for the period 1990–2005, Eliseo Díaz González found that the amount of money remitted to family members corresponds roughly to economic performance. When economies are strong, remittance receipts decline; however, when an economic contraction or crisis occurs, remittance levels increase. In addition, recent evidence indicates that remittances are sensitive to economic performance in the migrant's new country of residence as well.

REMITTANCES AND THE U.S. ECONOMY

The view that remittances represent a net loss to the U.S. economy relies centrally on the assumption that monies transferred to family members abroad would otherwise be spent on the consumption of domestic goods. The identified trade-off, however, requires a substantial leap of logic. First, little to no research has been conducted on the "opportunity cost" of remittances. Existing surveys of populations choosing to remit focus on the motivation prompting remittances, such as poverty or natural disaster, rather than alternatives to remitting. Second, remittances, functionally, are not substantially different from the choice to put resources into savings. Simply because monies are sent abroad does not mean that those monies would be immediately spent on domestic consumption rather than saved. Savings are typically spent in the long term, however any long-term net loss for consumption created by remittances remains difficult to estimate and does not represent the short-term consumption trade-offs identified above. Remitting income, similar to the choice to save or purchase consumer goods, remains a personal decision regarding the use of individual resources. Consequently, arguments to restrict remittances should similarly consider the appropriateness of mandates on household expenditures and savings.

A second and indirect effect of remittances includes cultural transfer. Migrant populations, particularly those who return home or impart information, create a demand for U.S. culture and goods. While the immediate effect may not be evident, this cultural transfer can contribute to a long-term demand for U.S. consumer and brand-name goods. Further, in some instances, particularly in very poor countries with low productive capacity such as Haiti, remittances enable the purchase of imported U.S. food. A recent report by the World Bank estimated that over 50 percent of food purchased in Haiti consisted of imports from the United States. While this does not paint a secure picture of food acquisition for Haiti, it does represent a market for U.S. exports. An indirect consequence of remittances can also be an improved trade balance and increased trade competitiveness for the United States, particularly with countries where labor is substantially cheaper.

The empirical record from the 2008–2009 recession and economic downturn provides the most compelling answer to the assertion that remittances harm the U.S. economy. Globally, remittances declined an estimated 25 to 35 percent during this period. Based on survey data, the World Bank reported that up to 40 percent of workers chose not to remit, and instead fulfilled their financial obligations in their new country of residence. Of those that chose to remit, the amount remitted declined. This demonstrates fairly compellingly that remittances have not been a contributing factor in the existing economic downturn.

REFERENCES AND FURTHER READING

Adams, R. H., Jr., & Page, J. (2005). The impact of international migration and remittances on poverty. In S. M. Maimbo & D. Ratha (Eds.), *Remittances: Development impact and future prospects* (pp. 277–306). Washington, DC: World Bank.

Adida, C. L., & Girod, D. M. (2011). Do migrants improve their hometowns? Remittances and access to public services in Mexico, 1995–2000. *Comparative Political Studies, 44*(1), 3–27.

Brown, R. P. C., & Jimenez, E. (2008). Estimating the net effects of migration and remittances on poverty and inequality: Comparison of Fiji and Tonga. *Journal of International Development, 20*(4), 547–571. Retrieved from http://www.ciprd.org/content/general/Working%20Papers/Brown_Remittances_May07.pdf

Chami, R., Barajas, A., Cosimano, T., Fullenkamp, C., Gapen, M., & Montiel, P. (2008). *Macroeconomic consequences of remittances* (Occasional Paper No. 259). Retrieved from International Monetary Fund website: http://www.imf.org/external/pubs/ft/op/259/op259.pdf

Díaz González, E. (2009, December). *The impact of remittances on macroeconomic stability: The cases of Mexico and Central America* (CEPAL Review No. 98). Retrieved from Economic Commission for Latin America and the Caribbean website: http://www.eclac.org/cgi-bin/getProd.asp?xml=/revista/noticias/articuloCEPAL/0/38070/P38070.xml&xsl=/revista/tpl-i/p39f.xsl&base=/celade/tpl-i/top-bottom.xslt

Federal Reserve Bank of Dallas. (2004). Workers' remittances to Mexico. *Business Frontier, 1.* Retrieved from http://dallasfed.org/research/busfront/bus0401.html

International Monetary Fund. (2010). *International financial statistics yearbook, 2010.* Washington, DC: Author.

Ozden, C., & Schiff, M. (Eds.). (2007). *International migration, economic development and policy.* Washington, DC: World Bank.

Ratha, D., Mohapatra, S., & Silwal, A. (2009, July 13). *Outlook for remittance flows 2009–2011: Remittances expected to fall by 7–10 percent* (Migration and Development Brief 10). Retrieved from World Bank website: http://siteresources.worldbank.org/INTPROSPECTS/Resources/334934-1110315015165/Migration&DevelopmentBrief10.pdf

Sen, A. (1999). *Development as freedom.* New York, NY: Knopf.

U.S. Department of Commerce, Bureau of Economic Analysis. http://www.bea.gov/index.htm

World Bank. (2006). *Global economic prospects: Economic implications of remittances and migration.* Retrieved from http://www-wds.worldbank.org/servlet/WDSContentServer/WDSP/IB/2005/11/14/000112742_20051114174928/Rendered/PDF/343200GEP02006.pdf

World Bank. (2011). *Migration and remittances factbook 2011.* Retrieved from http://data.worldbank.org/data-catalog/migration-and-remittances

Kristin Johnson

COUNTERPOINT

Remittances sent home to support family members left behind by foreigners working in the United States are to be expected. While the choice by foreign workers to provide financial support to family members abroad is understandable, it is nevertheless important to recognize that remittances undermine the local economies where the remittance money is earned when it is not spent locally. An issue for policymakers to consider is whether the current volume of remittances—which is closely related to the size of the unauthorized immigrant population—constitutes a major economic drain on the U.S. economy, and is therefore a reason for adopting measures to reduce the foreign worker population, especially those working illegally, in order to correspondingly reduce the remittance flow out of the country.

THE SIZE OF THE REMITTANCE OUTFLOW

While the dollar amount of remittances flowing out of the United States is small in comparison to the annual gross national product (GNP), it is, nonetheless, substantial. A 2006 survey of Latin American and Caribbean residents (legal and illegal) in the United States, authored by Bendixen and Associates and commissioned by the Inter-American Development Bank (IDB), found that remittances to Latin American and Caribbean countries totaled $45.3 billion. (The IDB remittance estimate does not include remittances to Cuba, Haiti, or to English-speaking countries of the region.) Subsequent estimates by the IDB indicate that remittances to that region increased in 2007 and 2008, dropped in 2009, and in 2010 recovered to 2008 levels.

Estimates of remittances vary depending on the source of the information. International organizations, such as the World Bank or the United Nations, collect data from member countries on foreign currency flows through their central banks. These data are likely to miss remittance flows that come through informal systems of money transfers. The polling data among foreign workers used in the IDB estimate cited above suggest that some of the international agency estimates are missing a significant amount of remittance flows.

If the IDB estimate is accurate, the worldwide outflow is necessarily greater. According to a report by the Pew Hispanic Center, slightly over half of the U.S. foreign-born population is from Latin America and the Caribbean, while the remaining 46.5 percent come from elsewhere, with South and East Asia accounting for nearly one-fourth (23.6%) of the total. The share of the foreign-born population that is illegally in the country is more skewed toward the United States' hemispheric neighbors. The Pew Hispanic Center has estimated that the share of this population from Latin America and the Caribbean is 81 percent of the approximately 12 million persons residing illegally in the United States. This estimate is very close to a Census Bureau estimate, based on the 2000 Census, that the illegal alien population—then estimated at 7 million—was about 83 percent from Latin American and Caribbean countries.

If the flow of remittances is proportional to the regional representation in the U.S. foreign-born population, that would suggest that the flow of remittances to elsewhere in the world could be roughly the same as the estimated flow to Latin America and the Caribbean, or a total of roughly double the flow to countries in this hemisphere, totaling some $90 to $100 billion annually. If, however, the flow is more proportional to the representation of foreign nationals in the illegal alien population, that would suggest remittances to the rest of the world would be about one-fourth of the flow to Latin America and the Caribbean, or an additional $9 or $10 billion on top of the $45 billion IDB estimate. The possible range of the total remittance flow then appears to be between from about $55 to $100 billion annually.

WHO ARE REMITTANCE SENDERS?

The survey data on remittances sent from the United States do not distinguish whether the senders are naturalized U.S. citizens, legal permanent residents, guest workers, or illegal aliens. It is likely that individuals in all of those categories, as well as some native-born U.S. citizens, send remittances to family members in other countries. However, demographic data on the senders suggests that a large share of remittances are likely sent by persons living in the country illegally. This may be seen in the finding of the IDB survey that only 7 percent of households sending remittances had household income of more than $50,000. That household income level is close to the median income of immigrant families, according to the Kids Count Data Center. Slightly more than half of all U.S. households had income of over $50,000 in 2007, according to the Census Bureau's American Community Survey.

Legal immigrants are entitled to bring their immediate family members with them, and in that respect they differ from those who come into the country illegally. Yet, according to survey data reported by the Pew Hispanic Center, "The one characteristic that clearly distinguishes remittance receivers from the general population in all the countries studied is that a majority are women" (Suro, 2003). This suggests that a prime motivation of the flow is to support spouses and children left behind. That motivation could apply to both illegal aliens and to temporary legal workers. However, the number of legal temporary low-wage workers coming to the United States—at less than 200,000 per year—is small compared to the size of the estimated unauthorized immigrant population.

Other data that support the conclusion that the remittance flow is closely linked to illegal immigration relate to the youth and mobility of the remittance senders. A 2006 survey conducted for the IDB's Multilateral Investment Fund found that Latin American migrants are not clustering in traditional U.S. immigrant communities, but are increasingly going to wherever jobs become available. A similar finding was reported by researchers at the Pew Hispanic Center: "These very large amounts of money are coming from one of the least prosperous segments of American society. Remittance senders tend to be young immigrants who have relatively little education compared to the rest of the U.S. population and who are employed predominately as laborers for low wages" (Suro, Bendixen, Lowell, & Benavides, 2002).

This, too, points to an unsettled population that has many members who are unburdened by families in this country and moving to take seasonal and casual labor jobs. Finally, the survey done for IDB established estimates of the remittance flow state by state, and these are compatible with estimates of the location of the majority of the undocumented population in the United States:

> States that have long had large Hispanic populations (California, Texas, New York and Florida) still are the biggest sources of remittances to Latin America, but some of the largest increases in volume of transfers took place in other parts of the country. Georgia, Virginia, Maryland, Pennsylvania, Tennessee, Indiana, Wisconsin, South Carolina, Arkansas, Kansas, Kentucky, Nebraska, and Iowa saw increases of more than 80 percent over the past two years. (Inter-American Development Bank, 2006)

The indication that a major portion of the remittances is being sent by illegal aliens suggests that the total flow is probably closer to the smaller of the estimates above discussed, or closer to $55 billion rather than $95 to $100 billion.

WHAT IS THE IMPACT OF THE OUTFLOW OF REMITTANCES?

Why should one care whether foreign-born workers send money abroad rather than spending it where it is earned? The obvious answer is that if the money were spent locally it would benefit the local economy by generating increased sales of goods and services. This would generate greater production of those goods and services and, therefore, greater employment. The increased local expenditure would also generate greater tax collection at the local and national levels.

The cost to the local economy resulting from an outflow of remittances does not stop with the funds remitted abroad. Studies of the impact of remittances on the receiving economies have shown that there is a multiplier effect as the money is spent and circulates through additional hands. A 2008 article by the agricultural economist Phillip Martin and Gottfried Zurcher describes this effect: "Through a multiplier effect, migrants increase spending in their home countries when they send money back to buy materials and hire workers to improve their housing." The size of the multiplier effect may vary depending on the structure of the economy in the receiving country, but it has been estimated for some countries to be as high as four times the amount of the remittances received. More conservative estimates put the multiplier effect at about double the amount of the remittances.

What tends to be overlooked in a discussion of remittances and the multiplier effect in the receiving economy is that there is a corresponding and opposite effect on the sending economy. The remittances are removed from circulation in the local economy. The estimated magnitude of the multiplier effect in receiving countries make it reasonable to assume that a similar negative impact on the U.S. local economy would likely be not just the $55 billion to $100 billion sent abroad, but instead closer to $100 to $200 billion annually.

The total economic effect of remittances may not register as a significant problem for national policymakers because most of the economic impact occurs at the local level. Billions of dollars that, if spent locally, would benefit local economic conditions in cities and towns across America are being sent to foreign countries. Some argue that the economic contributions of illegal aliens offset remittances and other costs associated with illegal immigration. However, given their generally low wages, the money left over after paying for food, rent, utilities, transportation, and other costs, as well as remittances sent back to their home countries, illegal aliens and family members in the United States represent a major fiscal burden, especially at the state and local levels of government, according to a study titled "The Fiscal Burden of Illegal Immigration on Unites States Taxpayers" (Martin & Ruark, 2010). Remittances take cash permanently out of local economies in the United States, and there is no offset to this loss.

Furthermore, the argument that remittances help stimulate the economy in the receiving country, creating jobs and reducing the flow of illegal aliens to the United States, is at best an exaggeration. Mexico is a good example of how remittances do not stimulate the economy in the receiving country. In 2006 alone, an estimated $25 billion in remittances was sent from the United States to Mexico, making it that country's third highest source of foreign exchange. However, rather than investing in economic development and the creation of jobs, a 2005 economic study by Benjamin Rempell found that 70 percent of remittances to Mexico go towards subsistence expenses, with only 1 percent going to business investment.

Remittances sent back to an immigrant's home country can also mask the underlying problem with immigration, particularly, illegal immigration, to the United States. Most unauthorized immigrants in the United States are of working age and had jobs in their home countries before they left to come to the United States. This finding with regard to Mexicans—a majority of the illegal alien population—resulted from a Pew Hispanic Center study of Mexicans applying at Mexican consulates in the United States for consular ID cards. The survey assumed that because these Mexicans were seeking an identity document, they were "undocumented." This migration of workers costs the sending country the ability to harness this labor in its economic development. The flow of remittances also furthers the economic dependency on the United States by foreign countries, as well as undercutting wages and job opportunities for American workers and burdening U.S. taxpayers.

While some of the remittance flow undoubtedly results from legal guest worker programs, one cannot simply ignore the fact that much, and probably most, of the current remittance flow results from the earnings of illegal workers. While this is only one aspect of a full discussion of the negative effects of illegal immigration, it is largely unrecognized in policy discussions of immigration law enforcement.

THE FOREIGN RELATIONS ASPECT

It has already been noted that remittances are welcomed by the governments of countries into which they flow. As a consequence, any threat of disruption to the flow is seen as something to be opposed by those governments.

Foreign countries have actively appealed to the U.S. government for the adoption of a general amnesty for illegal aliens, as well as for other measures that permit their nationals in the United States to work. This may be seen in decisions by the U.S. administrations regarding the designation of Temporary Protected Status (TPS). This is a provision in U.S. immigration law that allows the federal government to confer Temporary Protected Status on foreigners in the United States when political instability or a natural disaster in a foreign country, such as an earthquake or hurricane that disrupts governmental services, makes it temporarily unsafe to return to the country. TPS is granted by the Department of Homeland Security for periods of between 6 and 18 months, but usually for a year, and it can be renewed for similar periods. The Congressional Research Service reported in November 2010 that there were an estimated 217,000 Salvadoran and 3,000 Nicaraguan TPS beneficiaries who had been residing with work permits in the United States since the end of 1998, when Hurricane Mitch hit those countries. Each time that the TPS authorization has been about to expire, the governments of those countries have appealed to the United States to extend the status.

An EFE news service report from Tegucigalpa reported on April 24, 2003, that Honduran president Ricardo Madura planned to travel to the United States to request a TPS extension for the fifth time. It noted, in translation, that the "cancelation of [TPS status] would leave the covered 82,000 immigrants under the risk of deportation." Madura's visit tacitly recognized that the TPS beneficiaries would be in the United States illegally if their TPS status lapsed. The Immigration and Nationality Act (INA) specifies, in Section 244(a)(5), that "nothing in this section shall be construed as authorizing the Attorney General to deny temporary protected status to an alien based on the alien's immigration status." Because TPS status does not distinguish between legal or illegal status of the foreign nationals who may apply for that status, many, if not most, of those who gain legal work permits as the result of a TPS declaration may have entered the country illegally and have no intent of leaving the United States to return to their homeland as soon as conditions in that country allow.

Clearly, the conditions of destruction from the 1998 hurricane do not persist today, yet the affected foreign governments continue to lobby Washington to extend ad infinitum the "temporary" stay of their nationals with Honduras, the supplicants for extended TPS status include Nicaragua, El Salvador, and Haiti. While the governments of these countries argue that jobs are not available for their nationals covered by TPS, the remittance flow from these TPS beneficiaries surely is an important motivation for the importuning for the extension of TPS.

This same concern over the possible forced departure of illegal aliens, and the end to their flow of remittances to their home countries, also suggests why Argentina, Brazil, Chile, Colombia, Costa Rica, El Salvador, Guatemala,

Honduras, Mexico, Nicaragua, and Peru joined a lawsuit in the U.S. federal court system in an effort to block implementation of a new law in Georgia designed to deny jobs to illegal aliens. The court filing includes the following statement: "Mexico respectfully submits that, if HB 87 [Georgia's law] is allowed to take effect, it will have a significant and long-lasting adverse impact on U.S.-Mexico bilateral relations, and on Mexican citizens and other people of Latin American descent present in Georgia." This is not the first instance of Latin American countries— led by Mexico—becoming involved in the U.S. court system in an effort to block state-based restrictions on illegal immigration. The same was also true, for example, in court challenges to restrictive laws enacted in Arizona and other states.

WHAT CAN BE DONE TO REDUCE THE REMITTANCE OUTFLOW?

In 2009, Oklahoma enacted legislation that taxes remittances $5 for each transfer, plus an added 1 percent on amounts over $500. There have been similar proposals in other states. These measures are not designed to reduce remittances but, rather, to recapture some of the money that is lost in taxes when the earnings are not spent where they are earned. There have also been proposals in receiving countries to tax arriving remittances.

Taxing remittances, however, is a Band-Aid response to the negative local economic effects of remittances. A more direct approach to reducing the negative effects of remittances leaving local economies is to focus on reducing the population of those sending the remittances. This could involve reducing the level of legal immigration, as recommended by the U.S. Commission on Immigration Reform in its 1994 report, *U.S. Immigration Policy: Restoring Credibility*, as well as reducing the size of the illegal alien population. The latter focus does not imply some form of massive roundup and deportation program—described as a logistical impossibility by both President George W. Bush and President Barack Obama. Rather, it entails a comprehensive approach to deterring new illegal immigration and diminishing the existing illegal alien population through a process of attrition. The key to that process is the effective denial of jobs in the United States to persons unauthorized to take those jobs.

Opponents of enforcement measures against illegal aliens, such as those who oppose the adoption of a mandatory work authorization requirement using the federal government's E-Verify system, argue that the existing illegal alien population is here to stay and must be accommodated, perhaps by giving them legal status through some form of amnesty, a process often described as bringing them "out of the shadows." The assessment that illegal residents will not leave voluntarily is belied by estimates by the Department of Homeland Security (DHS) and others, such as the Pew Hispanic Center, that the size of the illegal alien population has declined as a result of increased enforcement and fewer available jobs. Notably, the estimated reduction in this population was much higher in Arizona, the state that has been at the forefront of increased enforcement measures against illegal aliens, than in any other state. The DHS estimated that the U.S. illegal alien population declined by 7.3 percent between 2008 and 2009. In Arizona the estimated drop in the illegal alien population was 18 percent.

Adoption of the E-Verify system as a national mandatory system for all new employees would not only reduce the incentive to enter the country illegally, it would also reduce the incentive for those who have entered temporarily with visas to seek a job and stay illegally. In addition, comprehensive verification of the work eligibility of new employees would also reduce job possibilities for existing illegal workers as they lose currently held jobs. The rise to the 11 million to 12 million illegal aliens in the country in 2011 occurred over an extended period of time, following the amnesty enacted in 1986. It should be anticipated that the process of attrition will be similarly protracted.

CONCLUSION

Regardless of how long the process of reducing the illegal alien population takes, there can be no doubt that it is a realistic scenario. Similarly, there can be no doubt that as the illegal alien population decreases, the remittance flow from the illegal alien population will similarly diminish. While it must be acknowledged that this will have a negative effect in the countries that are currently benefiting from remittances as a result of the movement of their surplus labor to the United States, it will have a corresponding positive effect on the local U.S. economies that are now losing the benefit of the local spending of earnings from local jobs. The prospect of this occurring gradually will facilitate economic adjustments in both the United States and abroad.

REFERENCES AND FURTHER READING

Bendixen and Associates. (2006, October 18). *Public opinion research study of Latin American remittance senders in the United States.* Washington, DC: Inter-American Development Bank. Retrieved from http://idbdocs.iadb.org/wsdocs/getdocument .aspx?docnum=35063903

Dockerman, D. (2009, March 5). *Statistical portrait of the foreign-born population in the United States, 2007.* (See Table 3 for origin of the foreign-born by region.) Retrieved from Pew Hispanic Center website: http://www.pewhispanic.org/2009/03/05/statistical-portrait-of-the-foreign-born-population-in-the-united-states-2007

Federation for American Immigration Reform. (2009, July). *Remittances to Mexico.* Retrieved from http://www.fairus.org/site/News2? page=NewsArticle&id=20897&security=1601&news_iv_ctrl=1007

Georgia and Alabama spark lawsuits over immigration laws. (2011, June 17). *The Americano.* Retrieved from http://theamericano .com/2011/06/17/georgia-alabama-spark-lawsuits-immigration-laws

Inter-American Development Bank. (2006, October 16). *Migrant remittances from the United States to Latin America to reach $45 billion in 2006, says IDB.* Retrieved from http://www.iadb.org/en/news/news-releases/2006-10-18/migrant-remittances-from-the-united-states-to-latin-america-to-reach-45-billion-in-2006-says-idb,3348.html

Martin, J., & Ruark, E. A. (2010). *The fiscal burden of illegal immigration on United States taxpayers.* Retrieved from Federation for American Immigration Reform website: http://www.fairus.org/site/DocServer/USCostStudy_2010.pdf?docID=4921

Martin, P., & Zürcher, G. (2008). Managing migration: The global challenge. *Population Bulletin, 63*(1). Retrieved from http://www .prb.org/Publications/PopulationBulletins/2008/managingmigration.aspx

Mohapatra, S., Ratha, D., & Silwal, A. (2010, November 8). *Outlook for remittance flows 2011–12: Recovery after the crisis, but risks lie ahead* (Migration and Development Brief 13). Retrieved from World Bank website: http://siteresources.worldbank.org/ INTPROSPECTS/Resources/334934-1110315015165/MigrationAndDevelopmentBrief13.pdf

Passel, J. S., & Cohn, D. (2008, October 2). *Trends in unauthorized immigration: Undocumented inflow now trails legal inflow.* Retrieved from Pew Hispanic Center website: http://www.pewhispanic.org/2008/10/02/trends-in-unauthorized-immigration

Pew Hispanic Center. (2005, December 6). Pew Hispanic Center report: Unemployment plays small role in spurring Mexican migration to U.S. [News release]. Retrieved from http://www.prnewswire.com/news-releases/pew-hispanic-center-report-unemployment-plays-small-role-in-spurring-mexican-migration-to-us-55351762.html

Rempell, B. (2005, November). Leveraging migrant remittances to Mexico: The role for sub-national government. *Journal of Development and Social Transformation, 2.* Retrieved from http://www.maxwell.syr.edu/uploadedFiles/moynihan/dst/rempell8 .pdf?n=9442

Social Science Research Council. (2009, March). *Remittances and multiplier effects* (Topic 12). Retrieved from http://www.ssrc.org/ publications/view/CE1C5540-D255-DE11-AFAC-001CC477EC70

Suro, R. (2003, November 24). *Remittance senders and receivers.* Retrieved from Pew Hispanic Center website: http://www.pewhispanic .org/2003/11/24/remittance-senders-and-receivers

Suro, R., Bendixen, S., Lowell, B. L., & Benavides, D. C. (2002, November 22). *Billions in motion: Latino immigrants, remittances and banking.* Retrieved from Pew Hispanic Center website: http://pewhispanic.org/files/reports/13.pdf

U.S. Commission on Immigration Reform. (1994). *U.S. immigration policy: Restoring credibility.* Retrieved from http://www.utexas .edu/lbj/uscir/exesum94.html

Jack Martin

H-1B Visas

POINT: U.S. industries, particularly high-tech firms, need highly trained people in order to stay competitive; there is a shortage of native-born people with the necessary skills.

Jeffrey L. Gower, University at Buffalo–State University of New York

COUNTERPOINT: There is no labor shortage in the tech field. Instead, the H-1B visa is used by employers, large and small, throughout the industry as a means to access low-wage labor.

Norman Matloff, University of California, Davis

Introduction

The H-1B visa is a nonimmigrant (i.e., temporary) visa that allows U.S. companies to hire a foreign "specialty" worker for up to 6 years. H-1B workers must be sponsored by an employer, and if the visa holder either quits or is dismissed by that employer, he or she has three options: to find another sponsoring employer, to apply for and receive a change of status to another nonimmigrant status, or to leave the United States. As of 2012, the number of H-1B visas was capped at 65,000 per year.

While widely used in the U.S. computer industry, H-1B visas are also used to fill a variety of other specialty occupations. Requiring theoretical or technical expertise, specialty occupations are understood to be those requiring at least a bachelor's degree. Employers have used these visas to sponsor workers in occupations such as computer programming, engineering, medicine, higher education, and even fashion modeling.

Political support for H-1B visas results from the widespread perception that high-skilled immigrants benefit the economy directly by providing key, relatively scarce, knowledge. Perceived benefits also derive from an understanding that higher-skilled immigrants are unlikely to make demands on the social safety net, and are therefore seen as a net fiscal benefit to the country. Further, public concern about shortcomings of the U.S. education system in producing students proficient in science, technology, engineering, and mathematics (STEM subjects), creates a sense of urgency for acquiring these needed skills from immigrants.

While the features and factors underlying the H-1B program may seem benign to many, debates do surround its use. First is the issue of competition in the labor market. In the Counterpoint essay, Norman Matloff argues that the visa program is used by employers—particularly in technology industries—to hire lower-wage workers. Using computer-related industries as his main example, he disputes claims of a labor shortage in computer fields. He also suggests that certain features of the H-1B program encourage guest workers to accept lower wages. For example, according to the rules of the visa program, foreign-born workers must be sponsored by a U.S. company; given this rule, foreign workers are not highly mobile in the job market as they must rely on the company that sponsored them for legal status, and this undermines their ability to seek higher-paying jobs with other employers.

The wage effects of the relative immobility of the H-1B worker are compounded by details of the law concerning setting wages. According to the program, employers are required to pay the "prevailing wage," based on job type, geographic location, and experience level, but they are not required to take into account specific skills, such as those necessary for working with a new programming language. As Matloff describes it, not having to factor in premiums for such special skills allows employers to hire H-1B workers at wages frequently 10 percent below the market rate.

These types of objections, however, don't address the perceptions of those who want to ensure that the U.S. labor markets include a highly skilled workforce that can compete on the global stage. As discussed by Jeffrey L. Gower in the Point section, there is a concern that restricting highly skilled labor migration (HSLM) may lead to the outsourcing of tech jobs to foreign labor markets. Ironically, he argues, many H-1B visa holders are educated in the United States and the idea that U.S. taxpayers should educate them, then send them home to use that valuable, cutting-edge education to benefit another country's economy seems shortsighted at best.

The concern goes beyond the immediate employment effects of outsourcing. In an environment where technology is changing rapidly, skills can quickly become obsolete. Capping the number of H-1B visas restricts the ability of companies to respond to needs arising from this kind of innovation. The issue of long-term competitiveness is made more urgent—and more complex—by economic globalization. In a world where capital flows freely, talent follows capital, and vice versa. Therefore, making it difficult to bring this talent to the United States, according to Gower and other analysts, could foster the emergence of high-growth technology-based industries in other countries. Agglomeration effects are an important dynamic in economic development. Industries tend to concentrate in specific areas—such as the computer industry in Silicon Valley—because efficiency and synergistic benefits arise from clustering in this way. Proponents of expanded H-1B visas worry that a failure to attract "the best and the brightest" and people trained in the latest technological developments will result in the emergence of industry clusters based on the latest technologies in other countries, and that the United States will lose its innovative edge.

However, relying on nonnative labor to deal with this potential long-term problem raises concerns about the responsibility the U.S. government has to its own citizens. To the extent that the ability to "import" so-called STEM talent lowers the consequences of the failure of the U.S. education system to produce such talent within the United States, H-1B visas may result in a form of "moral hazard" that lowers the urgency of doing so. Thus, reliance on H-1B visas is a double-edged sword. There are risks in doing so, but there are also real risks in not taking advantage of the talent these workers bring to the United States.

POINT

In a January 6, 2010, speech at the White House honoring STEM (science, technology, engineering, and mathematics) teachers, President Barack Obama made the following remarks:

> Whether it's improving our health or harnessing clean energy, protecting our security or succeeding in the global economy, our future depends on reaffirming America's role as the world's engine of scientific discovery and technological innovation. And that leadership tomorrow depends on how we educate our students today, especially in math, science, technology, and engineering. But despite the importance of education in these subjects, we have to admit we are right now being outpaced by our competitors. One assessment shows American 15-year-olds now ranked 21st in science and 25th in math when compared to their peers around the world. Think about that—21st and 25th. That's not acceptable. . . . So make no mistake: Our future is on the line. The nation that out-educates us today is going to out-compete us tomorrow.

President Obama later gave a speech, on June 13, 2011, on technology education in Durham, North Carolina, to promote his "Educate to Innovate" campaign. As part of this initiative, Obama promised to join with industry and universities as part of a $500 million program to spur the development of an additional annual 10,000 U.S. graduates in the STEM fields. Upon hearing the president's pronouncement, Lawrence Jacobson, the executive director of the National Society of Professional Engineers, remarked,

> The issue for the U.S. is not meeting the new expectation per se, but putting greater emphasis on STEM training and education. The number 10,000 is arbitrary. We're going to need a lot more than that. I totally agree, we need more engineers and more innovation. The country really needs this not to just compete, but to also replace the baby-boomer population. (Herring, 2011)

The connection between technological innovation and growing economies is well documented. Innovation, often as a result of major investments into research and development (R&D), is a knowledge-intensive process that requires extensive education in the STEM fields. The inherent structure of technological innovation offers few remedies for countries such as the U.S. that want to create jobs and grow their economies, but are either unable or unwilling to produce sufficient numbers of graduates in the STEM fields.

One "quick fix" has been to encourage highly skilled labor migration (HSLM), where "highly skilled" refers to migrants with the equivalent of a college degree or more (Salt, 1997). As of 2011, the United States allowed an annual entry of 65,000 workers in specialty occupations under its H-1B visa program (the majority of whom are employed in high-technology fields), plus an additional 20,000 visas for holders of advanced academic degrees. However, this is much fewer than the 195,000 annual visas allowed in the early 2000s. Because domestic hiring firms must sponsor all H-1B visa applicants, these professionals enter the country with support. They also often have an existing social network of previous migrants from their sending countries. For several years during the 2000s, domestic firm applications for H-1B visas greatly exceeded the annual quota for such visas, indicating that these firms could not bring in many of the educated foreign professionals that they wanted to hire.

The generally accepted view is that HSLM are a net benefit to receiving countries, because they experience the effects of a "brain gain" as employed educated and skilled persons interact within communities (Betts & Cerna, 2011). Receiving countries also benefit economically, because employment gaps are filled and migrants contribute to the economy by consuming goods and paying taxes.

The intent here is to elucidate the argument in favor of increased HSLM into the United States. Importing foreign educated professionals allows a country to reap economic and social gains with few costs. It is difficult to imagine coherent policy reasons for erecting barriers to domestic firms importing this type of labor—a type that the domestic education system is not supplying in adequate numbers. The United States is alone among developed countries in restricting HSLM, purportedly for reasons of internal labor development. By reducing the number of H-1B visas, the government's shortsighted policy restricting HSLM has had the opposite of its intended effect, leading indirectly to an increase in the outsourcing of technology work to foreign firms.

GLOBAL COMPETITIVENESS REQUIRES HIRING THE BEST MINDS

American business interests face increasing difficulties as they attempt to compete with global science and technology (S&T) industries. As the U.S. educational system produces relatively few technology workers, many U.S. firms look to foreign talent pools from India, China, and other countries that have educated and skilled professionals willing to migrate to the United States. Immigration by foreign skilled professionals, however, has come under intense scrutiny from U.S. government officials, domestic labor interests, and media commentators, who argue that hiring foreign professionals increases competition in local labor markets and depresses wages. Technology employers counter that many of the skills they require are not readily available in the domestic workforce. Further, the short product life cycles in the high technology industries does not allow waiting for domestic workers to upgrade their skills. Domestic technology firms also argue that the limited availability of H-1B visas means they are often unable to hire the best innovative minds in the global marketplace. The consequent lack of skilled workers causes technology firms to outsource work, often to foreign firms that employ those workers that the domestic firm would have hired but could not, due to lack of an H-1B visa.

By lowering the availability of H-1B visas, U.S. immigration policy has had two unintended consequences that curtail national competitiveness. First, arbitrary H-1B visa caps limit the movement of foreign intellectual capital to the United States, an action referred to here as "brain blocking." This precludes the potential brain gain that might have been realized through agglomeration and spillover effects resulting from innovation. Second, the arbitrary H-1B cap enriches foreign countries with less restrictive HSLM policies that compete in technology industries, because intellectual capital that could have benefited the United States locates elsewhere, an action referred to here as "brain diversion." As educated and skilled foreign professionals are diverted to foreign competitors or foreign subsidiaries of U.S. firms, the benefits of brain gain flow to other countries and firms that compete against U.S. companies.

GLOBAL COMPETITIVENESS AND INNOVATION

Sovereign countries use political power through their legal institutions to regulate flows across their borders. These flows take a variety of different forms, such as trade and financial flows, flows of information, or flows of human and intellectual capital. Flows of human and intellectual capital involve the movement of labor from one country to another through migration. Of course, migration between some countries is freer than others as a result of differing national immigration policies. Countries that have immigration and labor policies that deter free cross-border movement add friction to the flow of human capital.

Globalization has evolved an integrated system of arrangements between nations and multinational businesses that move large volumes of manufactured goods, services, and information over international borders (Arthurs, 2001). Globalization is shaped by the legal systems of various countries and is constrained by the willingness of some countries to eliminate protectionist trade barriers and bring their regulatory and national investment protection laws into harmony with those of its trading partners. One key to furthering globalization is the development of agreements that allow for easy movement of human and intellectual capital.

Migration of educated S&T workers to the United States is different from migration of unskilled laborers. Innovation within technology industries has been a major factor in keeping the United States at the leading edge of globalization, and the migration of foreign intellectual capital to the United States has been a driving force of this innovation. (Held, McGrew, Goldblatt, & Perraton, 1999; Sassen & Appiah, 1999). Thus, public policy that restricts HSLM into the United States works against goals of growing the domestic economy through innovation in technology sectors.

The U.S. technology industries are not alone in trying to attract educated foreign IT professionals. Germany, the United Kingdom, Australia, Canada, France, the Netherlands, Ireland, and New Zealand have also created expedited special visas to attract foreign educated professionals in the "Battle for the Brains" (Doomernik, Koslowski, & Thränhardt, 2009). The current selective immigration system in the United States for foreign science and technology workers, the H-1B visa program, is criticized by IT employers, who characterize it as outdated and failing to address industry needs. In 2007, reacting to reductions in the availability of H-1B visas, Craig Barrett, the CEO of Intel, remarked, "With Congress gridlocked on immigration [H-1B visa reform], it's clear that the next Silicon Valley will not be in the United States."

Globalization created a time-space compression that has removed many spatial barriers around the world (Harvey, 1990). Innovations in computer technology, global communications systems, long-distance transportation, international cargo movement, and global financial networks have made physical location less important to the design, manufacturing, and distribution of new products and services. For example, computer hardware and software design, once found only in Silicon Valley and Boston, is now shared with South and East Asia and Europe (Engardio & Einhorn, 2006). A Dell Computer product may be designed in the United States and Taiwan (with programming from India), manufactured in Taiwan, then returned to the United States for distribution.

Many large firms (often multinational corporations, or MNCs) possess first-mover advantages due to a new product or an innovation of a previous product, and thus receive at least an initial majority of a dominant market share, if not profits. These firms will invest large sums of money in their R&D divisions, with the intent of innovating the "next big thing" within their industry and capturing some of the spillover and agglomeration effects from this first-mover advantage (VanderWerf & Mahon, 1997). Some patents generated by R&D departments can become the financial building blocks of an entire firm, creating a cash flow that subsidizes future R&D efforts (Griliches, Hall, & Pakes, 1991; Pakes, 1985). Maximization of shareholder value, one of the main reasons for the existence of a firm, therefore relies on constant invention and innovation within a firm. It should come as no surprise, then, that a firm would want to employ the best and brightest minds within the industry, regardless of their nationality or location.

In response to the employment needs of S&T firms, many governments of industrialized countries attempt to create greater competitive advantages for their national economies through various forms of HSLM legislation. Although talented employees are sought by firms rather than countries, government policies and their attendant legislation play an important role in the recruitment of educated S&T professionals (Krugman, 1994).

STEM EDUCATION IN THE UNITED STATES

Another factor related to the importance of recruiting foreign S&T talent is that the United States may not be training enough people in the STEM fields to meet present and future demand. In his book *Is America Falling Off the Flat Earth?* (2006), Norman Augustine documents the following potential employment problems for U.S. technology industries:

1. In 2002, Asian countries awarded 636,000 bachelor's degrees in engineering, and European countries awarded 370,000 similar degrees, while the United States only awarded 122,000.

2. The United States ranks 17th among all nations over the last 20 years in the number of science and engineering bachelor's degrees awarded, and 23rd overall in the number of mathematics bachelor's degrees awarded.

3. The number of PhDs in STEM subjects awarded to U.S. citizens by U.S. universities declined by 23 percent from 1996 to 2006.

4. Although only 13 percent of U.S. high school students study calculus, it is a required subject for graduation from Chinese high schools.

Where the United States was once the main destination for STEM talent, other countries have closed the gap. Higher salaries and new opportunities are no longer found solely in the United States. Further, difficulties such as H-1B visa uncertainty and long citizenship waits make it difficult for domestic technology firms to recruit needed talent, and may result in the loss of foreign talent that is already here (Paral & Johnson, 2004).

ECONOMIC MULTIPLIERS FROM HSLM

Many domestic technology firms insist that without expanded H-1B visas, their firms cannot be competitive and must take other measures to ensure a competitive advantage. Anne Mulcahy, the CEO of Xerox, speaking at a Silicon Valley Tech Policy Summit gathering in March 2008, argued the following:

> You have to raise the [H-1B visa] quotas. It gets worse each year because our needs are greater. We have just been stuck on inaction in this country. It's not pros or cons. Its inaction, it's the political polarization in this country that has made for extraordinary problems. Having access to international talent is a big part of what has fueled our technology industry. The statistics about new companies that have started up by founders who came from outside the country. I mean, this is just dumb. (Cooper, 2008)

Jonathan Schwartz, the CEO of Sun Microsystems, added, "We're not dumb. You put a quota here, we'll go hire there" (Cooper, 2008).

Multinational companies now have access to technology that allows instant communication around the world, and domestic technology employers have opted to send work offshore rather than hire unqualified or untrained local workers. And rather than displacing domestic professionals, several studies make the case that the H-1B visa holder complements the local workforce.

In 2008, the National Foundation for American Policy (NFAP) issued a policy brief that outlined several of the benefits related to H-1B visas and domestic job creation. Among the study's findings were the following:

1. For every H-1B visa requested, U.S. technology companies created five jobs.

2. In technology companies with less than 5,000 employees, for every H-1B visa requested, there was an increase of employment of 7.5 jobs.

3. Because decisions to hire H-1B visa workers and domestic workers are specific to the business opportunities of the firm, the addition of H-1B visa workers is complimentary to the hiring of domestic workers and does not displace them.

4. Even in periods of decline in technology hiring, domestic workers are still hired over H-1B visa workers by 7 to 1 in firms over 5,000 employees, and 5 to 1 in firms with less than 5,000 employees.

5. Seventy-four percent of firms responding to the NFAP survey thought that the inability to fill a technical position because of a lack of H-1B visas made their company less competitive against foreign companies.

UNINTENDED CONSEQUENCES OF LOW H-1B VISA CAPS: BRAIN BLOCKING AND BRAIN DIVERSION

H-1B visa numbers that are not high enough to meet the needs of domestic technology firms reduce an industry's competitive capacities. Numbers that are too low have two unintended consequences: (1) the entry of foreign intellectual capital is reduced, causing the United States to forgo the potential agglomeration effects and expansion of social networks from that intellectual capital, and (2) foreign intellectual capital that cannot enter the country to work in technology industries is diverted elsewhere. With intellectual capital being blocked or diverted, U.S. technology sectors and the country as a whole fail to capitalize on potential brain gain.

"Unintended consequences" refers to unforeseen effects that result from intervention into a complex system. Unintended consequences may be positive (such as Adam Smith's invisible hand), but they are often negative despite the fact that they may result from well-intended legislation and regulation. These negative effects are often not readily apparent. Often cited examples include protectionist steel import tariffs that reduced industry competition but raised consumer prices in products that used steel, or wage and hiring legislation that reduced the number of available jobs for those the legislation intended to help.

It is doubtful that any member of Congress desires that the nation suffer harm from the unintended consequences of well intended but ultimately misguided selective immigration legislation. However, since the country does not have enough domestic skilled technology workers to meet the needs of its firms, legislation is needed to allow foreign workers to fill these jobs in the United States rather than working for competitors.

In addition to a direct economic benefit, HSLM also produces indirect economic and social benefits. One of these indirect benefits is brain gain, which arises from educated foreigners bringing intellectual capital into the country. A country receiving educated immigrants who add to its national intellectual storehouse of knowledge is said to benefit from brain gain (Beine, Docquier, & Rapoport, 2001; Bhagwati & Hamada, 1974). Studies show that the H-1B visa program does add to a brain gain of technology knowledge in the United States. In a 2005 article, Sami Mahroum noted that many skilled foreign technology professionals seek to work at the geographic core of their profession, wherever it is, and that core regions benefit more than other areas where workers might go. There are additional benefits from brain gain when the receiving country does not have to pay for the education of the foreign worker. The H-1B visa cap for foreign technology workers, therefore, means that U.S. immigration policy is constructing a ceiling on brain gain into the country.

As H-1B visa caps are tightened by partisan legislative action and other anti-immigration acts, Congress engages in "brain blocking" or "brain diversion," which diminish additional knowledge gains for the United States. A foreign educated professional applicant turned away from the United States for lack of an H-1B visa does not have the opportunity while in the United States to share knowledge, create professional networks, or participate in any of the agglomeration and spillover effects that drive knowledge clusters such as Silicon Valley.

There are concrete examples of science and technology jobs leaving the United States or being diverted to a third country's technology sector as a result of H-1B visa caps. Ironically, these jobs are often with foreign subsidiaries of U.S. firms that were intended for the United States. Microsoft, the largest historical user of H-1B visas, in response to the lack of sufficient H-1B visas, announced in 2007 that it would build a new software development center in Vancouver, Canada, 150 miles from its Redmond, Washington headquarters (Perelman, 2007). As of 2010, Microsoft's Vancouver location employed approximately 1,000 software developers, most of whom were denied an H-1B visa into the United States. Another large software developer, Oracle, has also opened a software development center in Vancouver (Mills, 2008).

Brain diversion may also result in fewer science and technology jobs in the long run, as new technology firms may not be created at all. H-1B visa workers that eventually become U.S. citizens regularly start technology companies once they develop local networks of suppliers and potential customers. These downstream start-ups further contribute to the U.S. economy with additional gains in domestic innovation and job creation. AnnaLee Saxenian (2006) found that 30 percent of Silicon Valley companies in the 1990s were headed by ethnic Indian or Chinese engineers. Her research also estimated that these companies added an estimated $20 billion yearly to the U.S. economy, and accounted for 70,000 high-technology jobs. The U.S. economy risks missing out on these potential entrepreneurial activities when it limits H-1B visas.

CONCLUSION

Shortsighted public policy decisions on HLSM, particularly through the lowering of H-1B visa caps, decreases U.S. competitiveness in high-technology industries. Technology firms that have been unable to hire qualified persons domestically, and that face uncertainty in obtaining sufficient quantities of H-1B visas, have found themselves needing to outsource jobs to foreign companies or set up U.S. subsidiaries in other countries to accomplish work that could have been completed in the United States.

Studies prove that HLSM does not displace domestic technology workers but, rather, are complimentary in nature, often creating new domestic jobs. Further benefits of HLSM include an increase in national brain gain, expansion of intellectual capital and social networks, and an increase in entrepreneurial activity. To rectify this misguided public policy on HSLM, Congress should act to lift, if not eliminate, the current level of H-1B visas quotas. Through this action, the U.S. technology industry would no longer face uncertainty about whether it can recruit the brightest minds and continue its competitive advantage in the global marketplace.

REFERENCES AND FURTHER READING

Arthurs, H. (2001). Reinventing labor law for the global economy. *Berkeley Journal of Employment and Labor Law, 22,* 271–291.

Augustine, N. (2006). *Is America falling off the flat Earth?* Washington, DC: National Academies Press.

Barrett, C. (2007, December 23). A talent contest we're losing. *The Washington Post,* p. B07.

Beine, M., Docquier, F., & Rapoport, H. (2001). Brain drain and economic growth: Theory and evidence. *Journal of Development Economics, 64,* 275–289.

Betts, A., & Cerna, L. (2011). High-skilled labour migration. In A. Betts (Ed.), *Global migration governance* (pp. 60–77). Oxford, UK: Oxford University Press.

Bhagwati, J., & Hamada, K. (1974). The brain gain, international integration of markets for professionals and unemployment. *Journal of Development Economics, 1,* 19–42.

Cooper, C. (2008, March 7). Schwartz, Mulcahy: When will Uncle Sam get a clue on H-1Bs? *CNET News.* Retrieved from http://news.cnet.com/8301-10787_3-9888863-60.html?tag=contentMain;contentBody;1n

Doomernik, J., Koslowski, R., & Thränhardt, D. (2009). *The battle for the brains: Why immigration policy is not enough to attract the highly skilled.* Retrieved from German Marshall Fund website: http://dare.uva.nl/document/186515

Engardio, P., & Einhorn, B. (2006). Outsourcing innovation. In D. Mayle (Ed.), *Managing innovation and change* (3rd ed.). London, UK: Sage.

Galama, T., & Hosek, J. (2008). *U.S. competitiveness in science and technology.* Santa Monica, CA: RAND Corporation.

Griliches, Z., Hall, B., & Pakes, A. (1991). R & D, patents, and market value revisited: Is there a second (technological opportunity) factor? *Economics of Innovation and New Technology, 1,* 183–210.

Harvey, D. (1990). *The conditions of postmodernity.* Malden, MA: Blackwell Press.

Held, D., McGrew, A., Goldblatt, D., & Perraton, J. (1999). *Global transformations: Poitics, economics, and culture.* Palo Alto, CA: Stanford University Press.

Herring, M. (2011, June 14). Obama calls for 10,000 more engineers. *Technician* [online]. Retrieved from http://www.technicianonline .com/news/obama-calls-for-10-000-more-engineers-1.2600544

Krugman, P. (1994, March/April). Competitiveness: A dangerous obsession. *Foreign Affairs.* Retrieved from http://www.foreignaffairs .com/articles/49684/paul-krugman/competitiveness-a-dangerous-obsession

Mahroum, S. (2005). The international policies of brain drain: A review. *Technology, Management, and Strategic Management, 17,* 219–230.

McInnis, L. (2011). *Obama launches technology partnership to spur jobs.* Reuters. Retrieved from http://uk.reuters.com/article/ 2011/06/24/us-obama-manufacturing-idUKTRE75N1EI20110624

Mills, E. (2008). Will H-1B visa caps force the next Google to open in Vancouver? *CNET News.* Retrieved from http://www.news.cnet .com/8301-1078_3-9908117-7

National Foundation for American Policy. (2008). *H-1B Visas and job creation* [Policy brief]. Retrieved from http://www.nfap.com/ pdf/080311h1b.pdf

Ó Tuathail, G. (1996). *Critical geopolitics.* Minneapolis, MN: University of Minnesota Press.

Obama, B. (2010). Honoring educators in math and science (Remarks by the president on the "Educate to Innovate" campaign and Science Teaching and Mentoring Awards). Retrieved from http://www.whitehouse.gov/photos-and-video/video/honoring -educators-math-and-science

Obama, B. (2011, June 13). Educate to innovate (Remarks by the President at Cree, Inc., in Durham, North Carolina). Retrieved from http://www.whitehouse.gov/the-press-office/2011/06/13/remarks-president-cree-inc-durham-north-carolina

Pakes, A. (1985). On patents, R & D, and the stock market rate of return. *Journal of Political Economy, 93*(2), 390–409.

Paral, R., & Johnson, B. (2004). *Maintaining a competitive edge: The role of foreign-born and U.S. policies in science and education* (Immigration Policies in Focus 3). Washington, DC: Immigration Policy Center.

Perelman, D. (2007). Hiring frenzy for Microsoft Vancouver [Web log post]. Retrieved from http://www.blogs.eweek.com/careers/ content001/outsourcing/hiring_frenzy_for_microsoft_vancouver.hml

Salt, J. (1997). *International movements of the highly skilled* (OECD Occasional Paper 3). Retrieved from Organisation for Economic Co-operation and Development website: http://www.oecd.org/dataoecd/24/32/2383909.pdf

Sassen, S., & Appiah, K. (1999). *Globalization and its discontents: Essays on the new mobility of people and money.* New York, NY: New Press.

Saxenian, A. (2006). *The new Argonauts: Regional advantage in a global economy.* Cambridge, MA: Harvard University Press.

VanderWerf, P., & Mahon, J. (1997). Meta-analysis of the impact of research methods and findings of first-mover advantage. *Management Science, 43*(11), 1510–1519.

Jeffrey L. Gower

COUNTERPOINT

The H-1B work visa has been popular among technology industry employers since its inception in 1991. The visa is good for up to 6 years, during which time the worker is typically sponsored by the employer for a green card, (i.e., U.S. immigrant status). For the sake of brevity, this essay will focus on the H-1B visa, although the green card issue is equally important.

The tech industry claims that H-1B is crucial to American technological competitiveness in STEM (science, technology, engineering, and math) fields. They assert a tech labor shortage, caused by an insufficient number of American college students majoring in STEM subjects. (The discussion here will simply use the term *Americans* to refer to U.S. citizens and permanent residents.) This situation is in turn due, they say, to a "Johnnie Can't Do Math" problem.

It will be shown here, however, that the industry's interest in the H-1B visa stems from a desire for cheap, compliant labor. The "shortage" claims will be shown to be unwarranted, and instead it will be argued that H-1B law has built-in loopholes that enable employers to hire foreign workers at below-market wages.

DEMOGRAPHICS

First, who are the H-1B visa holders? A key issue is that the H-1B visa holders (or "H-1Bs") are much younger than their coworkers. Figure 17.1 depicts the age distributions of H-1Bs in computer science and electrical engineering, in the 2003 National Survey of College Graduates.

Although the discussion here refers to the tech industry in general, computer-related H-1Bs—software developers, database administrators, and the like—predominate. During 2000–2009, 46 percent of H-1Bs were in this category, far more than in the second-largest category, university employment, which comprised 7 percent of the total. Electrical engineers formed only 4 percent of the H-1Bs. Thus, the focus here will be primarily in the computer fields.

Computer-related H-1Bs are predominantly from India, with Indian nationals forming 64.8 percent of this group. H-1Bs from China are a distant second, at 8.2 percent, followed by Filipinos, at 2.3 percent (Hoefer, personal communication, 2001). About half of the PhD students in U.S. computer science programs are foreign (Computing Research Association, 2011), and most do receive H-1B visas after they graduate, en route to an employer-sponsored green card. However, they form only a small portion of computer-related H-1Bs generally, as only 1.6 percent of them had a PhD in 1999–2000 (Hoefer, personal communication, 2001).

CLAIMS OF A TECH LABOR SHORTAGE

During the dot-com boom of the late 1990s, the rapid growth of technology industries made the labor shortage claims plausible to Congress. Yet, other than one survey conducted by the Information Technology Association of America (ITAA), an industry trade group, in 1997, no study at that time or since has confirmed such a shortage. The Department of Commerce, a university computer science consortium known as the Computing Research Association, the Urban Institute's Robert Lerman, and the National Research Council have all conducted studies, and each failed to confirm the ITAA claim of a technology labor shortage.

In 2011, the "shortage" rhetoric picked up again. And again, such rhetoric was at odds with the actual data. Starting salaries of new computer science graduates were up only 3 percent from the year before. This is hardly consistent with claims of a shortage. For experienced workers, wages in Silicon Valley were up only 3 percent since 2009. The mismatch between rhetoric and actual data was especially remarkable in a report by Dice, the large online jobs board (Dice Resource

Figure 17.1 Age distributions of H-1Bs in computer science and electrical engineering

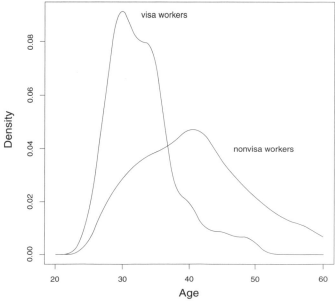

Source: Scientists and Engineers Statistical Data System, National Center for Science and Engineering Statistics (http://sestat.nsf.gov/datadownload).

Center, 2011), which gave a lot of anecdotal evidence of a shortage but then conceded that tech salaries had risen less than 1 percent in the past year.

Further, industry claims that an insufficient number of American college students earn STEM degrees were refuted in an extensive 50-page report by the Urban Institute (Lowell, 2007). The authors found that U.S. universities graduate more than enough STEM students each year to meet the demands of the economy. Indeed, in testimony before the U.S. House Immigration Subcommittee in 2011, Darla Whitaker of Texas Instruments stated that the firm does not sponsor foreign workers at the bachelor's degree level for H-1B visas, because the company has plenty of qualified American applicants. In short, the data do not confirm the shortage claims of the industry lobbyists.

FOREIGN STUDENTS IN U.S. PHD PROGRAMS

There is one aspect of this debate that must be discussed separately. Industry lobbyists point out that international students are a large fraction of enrollments in U.S. STEM departments at the postgraduate level. (Foreign enrollment in STEM departments is low in undergraduate programs.) Employers then cite this as a major factor driving the hiring of foreign workers under the H-1B program.

The industry's enrollment data is correct, but their reasoning is not. On the contrary, industry hiring of H-1B visa holders is the *cause* of the high number of foreign students in U.S. doctoral programs, not the *result* of it. During the late 1980s, an internal report at the National Science Foundation, a key government agency, opined that STEM PhD wages were too high, and the authors of the report proposed, as a remedy, the admission of large numbers of foreign students to U.S. universities. This would expand the labor pool of PhDs and thus suppress wages. Remarkably, this report also noted that the resulting stagnant wages would discourage American students from enrolling in doctoral programs, while the foreign students would be attracted to the programs as a stepping-stone to immigration. The phrasing of the report is noteworthy:

> A growing influx of foreign PhD's into U.S. labor markets will hold down the level of PhD salaries to the extent that foreign students are attracted to U.S. doctoral programs as a way of immigrating to the U.S. . . . [The Americans] will select alternative career paths . . . by choosing to acquire a "professional" degree in business or law, or by switching into management as rapidly as possible after gaining employment in private industry . . . [as] the effective premium for acquiring a PhD may actually be negative. (quoted in Weinstein, 1998)

That last point on the "negative" salary premium is key. By foregoing an industry-level salary for the 5 years or so of doctoral study, the student actually incurs a net lifetime loss in wages, according to calculations in a 2011 congressionally commissioned report by the National Research Council. Moreover, the influx of students from abroad also keeps graduate student stipends low, rendering graduate study even less financially attractive to domestic students.

Whether the NSF planned it or not, the result was exactly as forecast: slow wage growth for workers with graduate degrees, large increase in enrollments of international students, and major reductions in domestic enrollments. By 2009, the Berkeley economists Clair Brown and Greg Linden would write, concerning those with bachelor's degrees in electrical engineering, "the earnings premium for a domestic BSEE who pursues a graduate degree [is] relatively low. For foreign BSEEs, however, the financial incentive to pursue a U.S. graduate degree is much greater. A U.S. graduate degree opens the door for these students to high-paid jobs both in the United States and at home"(p. 164).

These financial disincentives against pursuing a PhD were also reflected in the 2011 testimony of Darla Whitaker mentioned earlier. When a member of Congress asked why the American students tended to stop at a bachelor's degree, rather than pursuing graduate study, Whitaker replied that the Americans are anxious to start earning money. This and other NSF reports were cited heavily by Congress in justifying the H-1B program they enacted in 1990. Very few computer industry jobs actually require a PhD, however, and, as noted earlier, only 1.6 percent of the computer-related H-1Bs have a doctorate. However, if one takes the position that there is a "shortage" of doctorates, then the above suggests that the H-1B visa is the cause, not the remedy.

H-1B VISA HOLDERS AS CHEAP LABOR

There are structural reasons why H-1B workers accept lower salaries. First, workers being sponsored for a green card are essentially immobile, and thus unable to allow other employers to compete for their services. During the lengthy period of the green card process, often 6 years or more, workers dare not switch to other employers, as that would entail starting the green card process over again. The employer may, therefore, not give raises as large or as frequent as those American workers receive (National Research Council, 2001). (The employer needs to pay a worker's legal fees, but the amount is much less than the employer saves by paying a lower salary over the years the worker is employed.)

One may ask, "Don't employers at least compete for a foreign worker at the time he or she is hired?" Yes, but they can still can pay the foreign worker less. As pointed out above, immigrant status (i.e., a green card) is a form of highly valued nonmonetary compensation for foreign workers. Even those who do not stay permanently in the United States gain American work experience, which itself has a high value when they return home. Foreign workers are thus willing to work for lower pay—in economics terms, they have a lower *reservation wage.*

In the discussion below of H-1B workers as cheap labor, the reader should keep in mind the following central points:

- Most employers who use H-1Bs for cheap labor do so in full compliance with the law, through the use of loopholes. The problem lies not in fraud or violation of the law, but in the law itself.

- The use of H-1B visas to reduce labor costs pervades the computer industry, including mainstream U.S. firms. It is not limited to the Indian-owned IT staffing firms.

There are (at least) two ways that employers save money via the H-1B program: *Type I savings,* which involves paying H-1Bs less than comparable U.S. citizens and permanent residents; and *Type II savings,* which involves hiring younger H-1Bs in lieu of Americans over the age of 35.

TYPE I WAGE SAVINGS

Employers are required to pay H-1B workers, and those being sponsored for a green card, the prevailing wage for the given occupation at the given experience level, in the given geographical region. The problem, however, is that the legally defined prevailing wage is typically well below the true market wage. This creates a huge loophole in the law. (The law also requires that the employer pay the higher of the prevailing wage and what is known as the "actual wage," but there are loopholes in the latter as well. It is not necessary to detail those here, as the actual wage is not relevant to the discussion.)

As mentioned earlier, employers underpay H-1B workers not out of fraud, but in full compliance with the law, due to a number of loopholes. Employers claim that they hire such workers because they have special value in some way, such as experience in a scarce technological skill or extraordinary talent. In the free market, employers would have to pay a premium for such special value, but this is not the case for the H-1B visa holders, as the prevailing wage is only defined in terms of the wage of an *average* worker. In other words, the employer gets a special-value worker for the price of an average one, and thus for less than what a similar special-value American would be paid.

The problems arise from a number of factors. First, the statute defines "prevailing wage" in terms of the *job,* not in terms of the *worker.* Second, the statute, in dealing with broad occupational categories, does not take into account specific technical skill sets or other special values that command a premium in the open labor market. The employer of an H-1B has a choice of several methods for determining prevailing wage. The "safe harbor" method involves querying the Department of Labor (DOL) Online Wage Library. This online tool asks the user for the occupational title or code, the geographical region, and one of four experience levels. The employer is not asked to input special skill sets and the like, as the legally defined prevailing wage does not account for these.

As an example, say the employer prefers a worker with experience in a "hot" new programming language. Since the legal prevailing wage does not (and cannot) take this skill into account, the employer can hire an H-1B worker with this skill at the wage of generic programmers lacking the skill. This is very important to employers, as they state that they hire H-1Bs with experience in skills that Americans lack (Duffy, 2003; U.S. General Accounting Office, 2011). "Hot" skills often command a wage premium of 20 percent or more on the open market if taken singly (Matloff, 2003). In many cases an employer will hire an H-1B worker with multiple special skills, so the wage premium should go up even further, yet the legal prevailing wage does not. In other words, based on the skills issue alone, the prevailing wage is easily undervalued by 20 percent. In a similar manner, an employer can hire a foreign worker with a master's degree at a bachelor's-level price, if it would be a "plus" but not a hard requirement for the job.

The fact that the legally required wage is below the real market wage has been occasionally recognized by government. An employer survey conducted in 2003 by the U.S. General Accounting Office (GAO) found that some employers readily admitted to paying H-1Bs less than Americans, but noted that they were nevertheless paying the legally required wage, thereby illustrating that the latter is indeed below the market wage. Representative Zoe Lofgren of California has remarked that the Department of Labor found that the average wage for computer systems analysts in her district was $92,000, while the legal prevailing wage was $52,000 (Thibodeau, 2011).

TYPE II SAVINGS

The Type II category is actually the one of prime interest to many employers in the H-1B program. While discussions of underpayment of H-1Bs almost always focus on Type I salary savings, the type of larger importance to employers is actually Type II, the hiring of young H-1Bs in lieu of older (age 35+) Americans. As noted earlier, H-1Bs tend to be markedly younger than their American colleagues. This makes the H-1Bs cheaper to hire.

To see the scale involved, Table 17.1 presents a comparison of wage distributions among new computer graduates and all software engineers, as of 2005. Clearly, the potential for labor cost reduction via H-1B is even greater for Type II than for Type I.

Industry lobbyists acknowledge that H-1Bs tend to be younger, but they claim that this is because only new graduates have the latest skills, which older workers could acquire only after undergoing training. Yet there have been a number of instances in which U.S. firms—such as Pfizer, Nielsen, Wachovia, and the Bank of America—have reportedly laid off American tech workers, replacing them with foreign workers, and forcing Americans to train their foreign replacements (Hira, 2010). This clearly indicates it was the foreign workers that lacked the skill set, not the Americans. In other words, the skills issue is merely a pretext to avoid hiring the older, that is, more expensive workers. This issue is treated in detail by Norman Matloff (see Matloff, 2003, 2006).

UNWARRANTED FOCUS ON THE INDIAN IT STAFFING FIRMS

A major theme here will involve the Indian IT staffing firms, which hire H-1Bs and then rent them to other companies. (Here the term "Indian" will be shorthand for "Indian and Indian-American.") It is common among analysts of the H-1B workforce to refer to the market as *segmented*, referring to two segments: U.S. mainstream firms and Indian IT staffing firms. The claimed nature of the segmentation is that the U.S. firms use the H-1B visa properly while the Indian firms abuse it.

This claim eventually made its way into Congress. During a controversial speech in the Senate in 2010, Senator Charles Schumer claimed that the majority of employers who use H-1B visas for cheap labor were the Indian IT staffing firms. The Indian community took offense and accused him of scapegoating, especially since he referred to the Indian firms as "chop shops" (Cha, 2010). Although the criticism centered on Senator Schumer, his view that the Indian firms are the principal problem with the H-1B visa is widely held in Washington. It was mentioned a number of times at a 2011 workshop attended by leading government policymakers, and led to introduction of a bill being introduced in 2011 by Representative Zoe Lofgren. Lofgren's district includes Silicon Valley, and she has consistently been Congress's staunchest supporter of the H-1B program. Close inspection of the bill revealed that many of its provisions were aimed at the Indian IT staffing firms.

Because of this view of Indian IT staffing firms, the analysis here will separate the Indian and U.S. firms, focusing specifically on U.S. firms. It will be shown that abuse is commonplace among the mainstream U.S. firms as well. These firms do tend to hire workers of much higher quality, but they still often pay them less than Americans of the same

Table 17.1 Wage distribution comparison

Worker cohort	25th wage percentile	Median wage	90th wage percentile
New computer graduates	$45,000	$50,664	$61,500
All software engineers	$65,070	$82,120	$120,410

Source: The data for all software engineers are from May 2005 Occupational Employment and Wage Estimates from the Bureau of Labor Statistics, while the data for new workers are from the National Association of Colleges and Employers survey.

quality would command in the open market. Thus, legislation targeting the Indian firms would not be justified. The question of the Indian IT staffing firms should not be conflated with the fact that Indians are the dominant nationality among H-1Bs. Indian IT staffing firms account for only 12 percent of the H-1Bs (Cha, 2010), yet, as noted previously, they form 64.8 percent of the computer-related H-1Bs.

USE OF H-1B VISAS FOR CHEAP LABOR: STATISTICAL ANALYSES

Now, armed with this background, the main issue will be looked at: the use of H-1B visas as a mechanism for reducing labor costs. Most studies of this issue are based solely on statistical regression analysis. This is a valuable tool that will also form part of the analysis, but it is also a very fragile tool that must be used properly. The focus therefore will be on the simplest, most directly interpretable analyses. The analysis of green card data below should fit that description. On the other hand, one should not rely on a single data set, so an analysis based on a second, regression-based, data set is also presented.

The green card data. The analyses in this section were conducted on the Program Electronic Review Management (PERM) data, which consists of Department of Labor records of all employer-sponsored green cards (see U.S. Department of Labor, Foreign Labor Certification Data Center). Note that each record corresponds to an actual foreign worker, unlike the H-1B Labor Condition Application records. As with the H-1B visa, workers being sponsored for a green card are subject to the prevailing wage requirement.

Professor Ron Hira, who has studied the Indian IT staffing firms extensively, has found that these employers rarely sponsor their foreign workers for green cards (Hira, 2007). The point here is not that lack of green card sponsorship is "bad"; rather, the point is that this means that analyses of the PERM data effectively remove the Indian IT staffing firms from consideration, and thus these analyses provide a view of U.S. mainstream firms.

This analysis of PERM data involves the ratio between wages paid and the employer's reported prevailing wage, a ratio known as WR (wage ratio). By law (after 2004), WR must be at least 1.00. Table 17.2 provides the median values of the WR for the years 2005–2010.

Since the median of a data set is the point at which half the data is higher and half is lower, it can be seen here that 50 percent of the foreign workers were being paid exactly the prevailing wage. Since, as seen earlier, the prevailing wage is below the market wage, this means that at least 50 percent of the foreign workers are paid below-market wages. Again, since the PERM workers are almost all in mainstream U.S. firms, it is clear that underpayment of H-1Bs is common in the mainstream. Recall, too, that this is fully legal, not a matter of fraud.

There are also, obviously, a number of cases in the data in which the wage paid was well above prevailing wage. However, this does not imply that they were paid fairly. Suppose, for instance, that a foreign worker had a WR value of 1.15 but had a combination of skills that would have been worth 1.30 had the worker been an American. The foreign worker would still be underpaid, even though his WR value is larger than 1.00. Thus, the statement that at least 50 percent of the foreign workers are underpaid is just a lower bound. The actual figure could be much higher, and it likely is, in view of the point made earlier that the foreign workers have lower reservation wages.

As noted earlier, this underpayment stems from a major loophole in the legal definition of "prevailing wage," under which the required wage is defined in terms of the job, not the worker. These data suggest that employers are well aware of this loophole, and that they aggressively exploit it. To make this point even clearer, another loophole will be examined.

Before 2005, it was legal to pay 5 percent below prevailing wage. While this 5 percent savings is quite minor, the point of the data presented as follows is that the mainstream firms are indeed keenly aware of the loopholes,

Table 17.2 Wage ratio (WR) for software engineers and electrical engineers, 2005–2010

Worker category	Median wage ratio
Software engineers	1.01
Electrical engineers	1.00

Source: Program Electronic Review Management, U.S. Department of Labor, Foreign Labor Certification Data Center.

Table 17.3

Worker category	Percent of cases less than the prevailing wage
All Software Engineers	33.1%
All Electrical Engineers	34.6%
Individual companies	
Cisco	50.5%
Intel	25.0%
Microsoft	10.2%
Motorola	14.6%
Oracle	20.2%
Qualcomm	70.9%

Source: Program Electronic Review Management, U.S. Department of Labor, Foreign Labor Certification Data Center.

so much so that they take advantage of even the minor ones. The situation is no different from exploiting every loophole in the tax code. Using PERM data, Table 17.3 examines how widespread usage of this loophole was during 2001–2004 for software engineers and electrical engineers.

Clearly, these household-name U.S. firms know the loopholes quite well. (When reading Table 17.3, one should not read too much into the interfirm variation in the data; that is, one should not assume that Intel is "worse" than Microsoft. Each firm has its own method of calculating prevailing wage, as the government gives employers the choice of using a private survey instead of the Department of Labor's Online Wage Library.)

Regression analysis. The data set here is again the 2003 National Survey of College Graduates (NSCG). This survey was used because it includes data on visa type. The methodology used is statistical regression, and the analysis is very narrowly targeted. In order to directly compare H-1Bs to Americans, age was limited to 29 or under. The professions were software engineers and electrical/electronic engineers. Only full-time, nonmanagement workers in nonacademic positions were analyzed.

Some of the variables here are *indicator* variables, which have a value of 1 and 0, indicating the presence or absence of a trait. The MS variable, for example, is 1 if the worker has a master's degree (but not a PhD), otherwise it is 0. The analysis also excluded all workers who first entered the country on a work visa, examining instead the H-1Bs who first came under a student visa. This effectively excludes workers in the Indian IT staffing firms (though it also excludes some of the U.S. mainstream firm workers). There is an indicator variable for the student visa (F-1) type of initial entry (note that an American would have the 0 for this value). In other words, it is this variable that will be used to compare the H-1Bs to Americans.

A *regression equation* expresses, or "explains," the mean of one variable in terms of other variables. It is used to estimate relations between variables (and also for prediction). Here is the regression equation used in the statistics to be presented below:

$$\text{mean wage} = \beta_0 + \beta_1 \text{ age} + \beta_2 \text{ MS} + \beta_3 \text{ PhD} + \beta_4 \text{ origF1} + \beta_5 \text{ highCOL}$$

This mathematical notation is read as follows: β_0 is a constant; β_1 is the impact on income from each year of age, using age as a proxy for work experience; β_2 is the effect on income from earning a Master of Science degree; β_3 is the impact on income from earning a PhD degree; β_4 is the effect on income of entering via a student visa; and β_5 is the impact on income of working in an area with a high cost of living. Table 17.4 shows the results of this regression analysis.

With age, degree, and region held constant, the H-1B group's wages were on average $7,153 lower than those of comparable Americans. The analysis shows that foreign workers with a master's degree make less than Americans with just a bachelor's. (A master's adds $6,855, but foreign student origin subtracts $7,427, a net loss.) This is especially of interest in view of the industry's claim, discussed earlier, that it hires under the H-1B program because an insufficient number of American students pursue graduate study. Again, note that almost all workers in this group are at the mainstream U.S. firms, not the Indian IT staffing companies. Accordingly, one can see that use of H-1B visas for cheap labor is indeed common among mainstream firms.

LANGUAGE ISSUES

The lower wages of the H-1B workers are not due to weak English skills. This can be seen in several ways. First, recall that most of the computer-related H-1Bs are from India, where English is the language of instruction in education. (Indeed, those who teach foreign graduate students from India often find that their English is richer and more expressive than those of the Americans.)

Second, the tech industry is famously meritocratic for engineering workers. (The managerial side is considered by some to be less meritocratic.) If you produce, you are rewarded. In her book *Doing Engineering* (2000), Professor Joyce Tang found that language skills were not a barrier even to Asian immigrant engineers who wished to obtain academic positions.

Finally, a regression analysis was run on the 2000 U.S. census data, in an effort to determine the impact, if any,

Table 17.4 Regression analysis of H-1B workers and U.S. workers

Explanatory variable	Estimated beta (β) ± marg. err.	Statistically significant?
Constant	21164 ± 37881	no
Age	1342 ± 1336	yes
Master of Science	6855 ± 3922	yes
PhD	29715 ± 17493	yes
Enter on a student visa	-7427 ± 5125	yes
High cost-of-living area	7153 ± 3067	yes

of English facility on the probability of having a high salary among Chinese engineers in Silicon Valley. No statistically significant relation was found. Instead, the real factor underlying the lower wages earned by H-1B workers is their lower reservation wage, and their relative immobility, as discussed earlier.

THE INDIAN FIRMS, AGAIN

The above analyses, by excluding the Indian IT staffing firms, show that use of H-1B visas to reduce labor costs is common among U.S. mainstream firms. Needless to say, the Indian firms engage in the same behavior, but the above methods cannot be used to show it. However, Mann and Kirkegaard, in *Accelerating the Globalization of America* (2006), present charts that are similar to the PERM analyses above but are instead based on the Labor Condition Application (LCA) data, which are for H-1B visas rather than green cards. An LCA is simply an application by an employer for permission to hire H-1B workers (whether the employer has a specific worker in mind or not). Note that the authors' analysis combines all occupations, in contrast to the computer-related focus in the analyses above.

Mann and Kirkegaard essentially plot WR against prevailing wage, for various specific Indian and U.S. firms. They point out that the Indian firms' prevailing wage levels tend to be much lower than those of the U.S. employers; this reflects the point made earlier that the Indian firms tend to hire lower-level (e.g., less experienced) workers. However, they go further than that, making the key assumption that the prevailing wage is equal to the market wage. As seen earlier, this is not a valid assumption, but on that basis Mann and Kirkegaard concluded that the primary abusers of H-1B are the Indian firms. This finding became the academic basis for Congress's focus on the Indian firms. By contrast, Ron Hira, cited earlier for his work on the Indian firms, explicitly opposes targeting the Indians in legislation (Hira, 2010). As noted, Hira has been critical of U.S. firms such as Bank of America in their abuse of foreign worker programs.

THE BEST AND THE BRIGHTEST

Supporters of the H-1B program assert that H-1Bs, especially those hired from U.S. universities, tend to be outstanding talents. This, they say, is crucial to the industry's ability to innovate. But while all sides of the H-1B controversy agree that the United States should be welcoming the immigration of outstanding talents, the question is whether the H-1Bs are typically in this league. The industry has done little to support such assertions. While it has pointed to some famous immigrant success stories in the field, in most cases the people cited never held either H-1B or F-1 (foreign-student) visas. Google cofounder Sergey Brin is frequently cited, for instance, but he immigrated to the United States with his parents at the age of 6.

Actually, the data show that most H-1Bs are, for the most part, ordinary people doing ordinary work. For instance, the researcher David North, a former U.S. assistant secretary of labor, found that the foreign doctoral students in engineering are disproportionately in the lower-ranked U.S. universities, relative to domestic students (North, 1995). North shows that the lower the ranking of an engineering school, the larger its percentage of foreign students.

A forthcoming paper by Norman Matloff compares former foreign students who are now U.S. citizens or permanent residents, and who are working as software engineers or electrical engineers, to their American colleagues. The study finds that the former foreign students are of the same quality as, instead of better than, the Americans, in terms of wages, awards, and patent applications. It is also shown that the former foreign students are less likely than the Americans to be working in research and development positions, contrary to the industry's claim that it needs H-1Bs to keep its technological edge. The industry's portrayal of the H-1Bs as being especially innovative is thus not borne out.

Much has been made of immigrant entrepreneurship in the tech field. However, while simple probabilities suggest that, with many immigrants in the industry, there will also be many immigrant-founded businesses, a methodological difficulty arises in that one doesn't know what kind of business is involved. The Berkeley researcher AnnaLee Saxenian found that 36 percent of the Chinese-immigrant-owned firms are in the business of "computer wholesaling," meaning that they are simply assemblers of commodity PCs, with no engineering or programming work being done (Saxenian, 1999). In addition, many Indian-owned tech firms are in the offshore outsourcing businesses, again not the type of entrepreneurship that is relevant here.

THE INTERNAL BRAIN DRAIN

Still, is it not good to have as many engineers as possible, even if they aren't geniuses? The answer is no, because the H-1B and green card programs have been causing an *internal brain drain* of tech talent in the United States. The internal NSF report mentioned earlier (and quoted in Weinstein, 1998) called for flooding the STEM PhD market with international students in order to suppress wages in that market. The report also projected that the resulting stagnant wages would drive away domestic students from STEM doctoral programs, and into more lucrative fields such as business and law. This was an accurate projection, as it turned out.

The influx of tech workers in general has caused similar limitations on wage growth beyond the PhD market. A Berkeley study found that "high-tech engineers and managers have experienced lower wage growth," and that "[the large influx of] foreign students [is] an important part of the story" (Brown, Campbell, & Pinsonneault, 1998). This is causing many students at the nation's most elite institutions to flee STEM for more lucrative fields. Graduates of MIT enter the financial services field at a rate of almost 25 percent, and Harvard graduates enter that field at far higher rates than in the pre–H-1B era (Schramm, 2011).

OTHER STUDIES

There have been numerous studies of the H-1B visa's impacts, in terms of wages, patents, and so forth. An extensive bibliography is given in Hunt's 2011 article, "Which Immigrants Are Most Innovative and Entrepreneurial?" However, readers wishing to pursue this topic further, perhaps even conducting their own statistical analyses, should keep in mind the numerous pitfalls that can entrap the unwary analyst. Consider, for instance, a 2010 *Management Science* paper that found that the H-1Bs actually earn higher wages than comparable Americans (Mithas & Lucas, 2010). The data source here consisted of a reader survey of the magazine *InformationWeek*. The problem with this data source is the readership, which the magazine itself characterizes as "business technology executives"—not engineers and programmers. Moreover, those H-1B respondents in the survey had an average of 11.23 years of experience, quite a contrast to the median of less than 2 years of experience among computer-related H-1Bs in general. Thus, the survey was not representative.

Above all, one must ask whether an analysis meets the "common sense" test. Do the findings jibe with what is known qualitatively? As discussed earlier, foreign workers are typically willing to work for lower wages than those enjoyed by American workers with the same education, experience, skills, and so on.

CONCLUSION

Industry assertions that they hire H-1Bs because the foreign workers possess "hot" technological skills or have outstanding talent are not borne out by careful statistical analysis. Instead, it is seen that the H-1Bs are sought as a pool of inexpensive labor. The use of the H-1B program to reduce labor costs is usually done in full compliance with the law, due to gaping loopholes in the law. Although the "conventional wisdom" in Congress is that such abuse occurs mainly among the Indian IT staffing firms, the data show that mainstream U.S. firms know the wage loopholes and make use of them. Reform should thus apply to the entire industry. In addition, reform should take into account the adverse impact of both H-1B visas and green cards on American workers over the age of 35.

One simple, easily implemented solution has been proposed by the Department of Professional Employees, AFL-CIO. It would set the prevailing wage at the 75th percentile of the occupation and region, without breaking things down into experience levels. As noted by Paul Almeida, president of the Department for Professional Employees, AFL-CIO, "If guest workers are the best and the brightest, as supporters claim, then they should command a greater premium than their U.S. counterparts" (Almeida, 2011).

REFERENCES AND FURTHER READING

Almeida, P. (2011). *Immigration and the science and engineering workforce: A Labor perspective* (Remarks at Workshop on Dynamics of the Science and Engineering Labor Market, at Georgetown University). Retrieved from http://dpeaflcio.org/wp-content/uploads/Immigration.pdf

Brown, C., Campbell, B., & Pinsonneault, G. (1998). *The perceived shortage of high-tech workers.* Berkeley, CA: University of California, Berkeley, Department of Economics. Retrieved from http://heather.cs.ucdavis.edu/ClairBrown.html

Brown, C., & Linden, G. (2008). Semiconductor engineers in a global economy. In The Committee on the Offshoring of Engineering, *The offshoring of engineering: Facts, unknowns, and potential implications* (pp. 149–178). Washington, DC: The National Academies Press.

Brown, C., & Linden, G. (2009). *Chips and change.* Cambridge, MA: MIT Press.

Cha, A. E. (2010, August 10). Indian government calls H1B visa fee hike "discriminatory." *The Washington Post.* Retrieved from http://voices.washingtonpost.com/political-economy/2010/08/indian_government_calls_h1b_vi.html

Computerworld Skills Survey: Part 2. (1998, November 16). *Computerworld.*

Computing Research Association. (2011, April 5). *Taulbee Survey Report, 2009–2010.* Retrieved from http://www.cra.org/uploads/documents/resources/taulbee/CRA_Taulbee_2009-2010_Results.pdf

Dice Resource Center. (2011). *America's tech talent crunch.* Retrieved from http://marketing.dice.com/pdf/Dice_TechTalentCrunch.pdf

Duffy, P. (2003, September 16). *Examining the importance of the H-1B visa to the American economy* (Testimony of Patrick Duffy, Human Resources Attorney, Intel Corporation, before U.S. Senate Committee on the Judiciary). Retrieved from http://www.gpo.gov/congress/senate/pdf/108hrg/93082.pdf

Foreign Labor Certification Data Center Online Wage Library. http://www.flcdatacenter.com/OesWizardStart.aspx

Foreign Labor Certification Data Center Online Wage Library. (n.d.). *Permanent program data.* Retrieved from http://www.flcdatacenter.com/CasePerm.aspx

Hira, R. (2007, March 28). *Outsourcing America's technology and knowledge jobs* (EPI Briefing Paper No. 187). Retrieved from Economic Policy Institute website: http://www.epi.org/publication/bp187

Hira, R. (2010). *The H-1B and L-1 visa programs out of control* (EPI Briefing Paper No. 280). Retrieved from Economic Policy Institute website: http://www.epi.org/publication/bp280

Hunt, J. (2011, July). Which immigrants are most innovative and entrepreneurial? *Journal of Labor Economics, 29*(3), 417–457.

Information Technology Association of America. (1997). *Help wanted: The IT workforce gap at the dawn of a new century.* Arlington, VA: Author.

Kirkegaard, J. F. (2005). *Outsourcing and skill imports: Foreign high-skilled workers on H-1B and L-1 visas in the United States* (Institute for International Economics Working Paper No. 05-15). Retrieved from Peterson Institute website: http://www.petersoninstitute.org/publications/wp/wp05-15.pdf

Lowell, B. L., & Salzman, H. (2007). *Into the eye of the storm: Assessing the evidence on science and engineering education, quality, and workforce demand.* Retrieved from Urban Institute website: http://www.urban.org/publications/411562.html

Mann C., & Kirkegaard, J. (2006). *Accelerating the globalization of America: The role for information technology.* Washington, DC: Peterson Institute.

Martin, S. (2002). U.S. immigration policy: Admission of highly skilled workers. *Georgetown Immigration Law Journal, 16,* 619–628.

Matloff, N. (2003, Fall). On the need for reform of the H-1B nonimmigrant work visa in computer-related occupations. *University of Michigan Journal of Law Reform, 36*(4), 815–914.

Matloff, N. (2006, August). On the adverse impact of work visa programs on older U.S. engineers and programmers. *California Labor and Employment Law Review.*

Mithas, S., & Lucas, H. C., Jr. (2010, May). Are foreign IT workers cheaper? U.S. visa policies and compensation of information technology professionals. *Management Science, 56*(5), 745–765.

National Research Council, Committee on Workforce Needs in Information Technology. (2001). *Building a workforce for the information economy.* Washington, DC: National Academies Press. Available from http://www.nap.edu/catalog.php?record_id=9830

North, D. S. (1995). *Soothing the establishment: The impact of foreign-born scientists and engineers on America.* Lanham, MD: University Press of America.

Saxenian, A. (1999). *Silicon Valley's new immigrant entrepreneurs.* Retrieved from Public Policy Institute of California website: http://www.ppic.org/content/pubs/report/R_699ASR.pdf

Schramm, C. (2011, April 13). Is the financial sector gobbling up the U.S.' would-be entrepreneurs? *Forbes.*

Tang, J. (2000). *Doing engineering: The career attainment and mobility of Caucasian, black, and Asian-American engineers.* Lanham, MD: Rowman & Littlefield.

Thibodeau, P. (2011). H-1B pay and its impact on U.S. workers is aired by Congress. *Computerworld.* Retrieved from http://www.computerworld.com/s/article/9215405/H_1B_pay_and_its_impact_on_U.S._workers_is_aired_by_Congress

U.S. General Accounting Office. (2003, September). *H-1B foreign workers: Better tracking needed to help determine H-1B Program's effects on U.S. workforce* (GAO-03-883). Retrieved from http://www.gao.gov/new.items/d03883.pdf

U.S. General Accounting Office. (2011, January). *H-1B Visa Program: Reforms are needed to minimize the risks and costs of current program* (GAO-11-26). Retrieved from http://www.gao.gov/products/GAO-11-26

U.S. Immigration and Naturalization Service. (2002, July). *Report on characteristics of specialty occupation workers (H-1B): Fiscal year 2001.* Retrieved from http://www.ilw.com/immigrationdaily/News/2002,0815-h1b.pdf

Weinstein, E. (1998). *How and why government, universities, and industry create domestic labor shortages of scientists and high-tech workers.* Retrieved from National Bureau of Economic Research website: http://www.nber.org/~peat/PapersFolder/Papers/SG/NSF.html

Whitaker, D. (2011, October 5). *STEM the tide: Should America try to prevent an exodus of foreign graduates of U.S. universities with advanced science degrees* (Testimony of Darla Whitaker, Senior Vice President, Worldwide Human Resources, Texas Instruments, on behalf of the Semiconductor Industry Association, before the U.S. House of Representatives Committee on the Judiciary, Subcommittee on Immigration). Retrieved from http://judiciary.house.gov/hearings/pdf/Whitaker%2010052011.pdf

Norman Matloff

Temporary Worker Programs

POINT: Temporary worker programs are necessary to provide a legal mechanism for increased immigration of low-skilled workers. Certain industries, such as agriculture and construction, rely heavily on low-skilled workers, and the absence of legal mechanisms for these workers is a key cause of illegal immigration.

Nik Theodore, University of Illinois at Chicago

COUNTERPOINT: There is nothing more permanent than a temporary worker, and there are already legal mechanisms for foreign workers, such as H-2A visas for seasonal agricultural workers and H-2B visas for other seasonal workers. Low-skilled immigration creates a fiscal burden that the country cannot afford.

Eric A. Ruark, Federation for American Immigration Reform (FAIR)

Introduction

Temporary worker programs allow U.S. employers to sponsor non-U.S. citizens as laborers for approximately 3 years. Though these programs are generally popular with employers, they have been strongly opposed by various groups, including immigrant rights organizations, labor unions, and opponents of expanded immigration. These groups cross ideological boundaries, and thus the debate over temporary worker programs cannot be divided cleanly along partisan lines. When it comes to temporary workers, both Republicans and Democrats must manage competing interests within their parties.

The GOP is split between business interests, who want access to less expensive or scarce labor, and social conservatives, who are concerned about the (negative, in their view) impacts of immigrants on the United States. When asked a question about temporary worker programs at a Republican presidential debate on December 10, 2011, Newt Gingrich said, "We ought to have an effective guest worker program with very severe penalties for those employers who hire people illegally"—essentially crafting his answer to appeal to both business interests (i.e., we should indeed have a guest worker program) as well as the social, law-and-order conservatives (i.e., punishments for lawbreakers should be severe). Likewise, in an interview with NPR on September 5, 2011, Gingrich gave a response that attempted to please both social conservatives and the business community: "We need a guest-worker program to ensure that guest workers pay taxes, get driver's licenses, buy auto insurance, abide by the law, and that filters out criminals and potential terrorists. The program should not be an automatic qualification for citizenship, though eventual citizenship should be held out as an opportunity." In theory, the temporary worker program lets Republicans speak to both sets of interests by expanding admissions temporarily for work while limiting social rights by limiting immigrants' full participation in society.

Democrats, on the other hand, are split between labor interests, who want to limit competition from foreign workers, and progressives, who are sympathetic to the plight of poor migrants seeking a better life in a tough world. Theoretically, the numbers of workers allowed to enter the country under a temporary worker program can be adjusted to reflect economic conditions and thereby lessen labor market competition while letting people migrate legally for employment. In 2007, then-Senator Barack Obama voiced his support for a guest worker program while emphasizing the need to address the concerns of American workers regarding wages and working conditions: "We must also replace the flow of undocumented immigrants coming to work here with a new flow of guest workers. Illegal immigration is bad for illegal immigrants and bad for the workers against whom they compete. Replacing the flood of illegals with a regulated stream of legal immigrants who enter the United States after background checks and who are provided labor rights would enhance our security, raise wages, and improve working conditions for all Americans."

In the Point section below, Nik Theodore argues that temporary worker programs play an important role in managing migration and remedying supply-demand imbalances in local labor markets. He goes on to say that in the twenty-first century, the United States needs to implement a "rights-based approach" to temporary worker migration so that absolute authority over worker entry and terms of employment do not reside solely with employers. A switch to this type of approach would reduce the control employers have over the allocation of labor, enhance worker mobility and, thus, both protect the interests of the domestic work force and strengthen labor markets.

Eric Ruark argues in the Counterpoint essay that the adjective "temporary" is a misnomer, since "there is nothing as permanent as a temporary worker." Ruark argues that the temporary worker program is essentially all about U.S. employers' desire for foreign workers as a source of cheap labor, and that the system must be reformed so that the interests of the American people are prioritized over the needs of American businesses. Furthermore, Ruark says, these programs are almost wholly unnecessary—and even detrimental—to the U.S. economy, as they lead to an oversupply of low-skilled workers that have a negative impact on wages and working conditions. Indeed, employers in some industries often depend on a steady supply of low-wage foreign workers and routinely petition Congress for increased numbers of guest workers. The problem is exacerbated by the large number of low-skilled illegal workers who are competing for the same jobs, a phenomenon that has, with the consent of state and federal governments, led to the most deplorable working conditions since the Industrial Revolution over a century and a half ago—thanks to the exploitative practices of business vis-à-vis labor.

The debates about the issue of temporary worker visas underscore the deeply political nature of immigration policy. In economics, a "free market" for labor would suggest allowing labor to move freely around the world in a similar way that capital moves. Consider in reading this chapter how the idealized notion of the free market collides with domestic political realities. How does the fact that the world is organized around social groups called "nation states" complicate the ideal of labor mobility? Is it possible to design a temporary worker program that balances the agendas of various interests, be it business owners and workers, or progressives and social conservatives?

POINT

This chapter considers whether temporary worker programs (also known as guest worker programs) are a necessary and effective mechanism for managing the migration of low-skilled workers to the United States. The answer to this question depends on several factors, including whether these programs are able to meet domestic industry needs, whether they return income and wealth to labor-exporting countries, and whether they can be designed in a way that safeguards the well-being of migrant workers and the domestic workforce. Temporary worker programs have been used by the United States and other high-income countries to recruit workers into a range of occupations when labor shortages have restricted employers' ability to fill vacant positions. Although generally popular with employers, these programs have been vigorously opposed by labor unions, immigrant rights organizations, and opponents of expanded immigration.

WHAT ARE TEMPORARY WORKER PROGRAMS?

One of the most controversial and vexing immigration policy challenges facing countries that attract large numbers of migrants is how to align rules and mechanisms for admitting migrant workers with conditions within domestic labor markets. In many immigrant-receiving countries, governments seek to manage migration through a battery of temporary worker programs that are designed to meet employers' needs for workers without undermining the job prospects and wages of the domestic workforce, and without increasing permanent immigration.

As suggested by their name, temporary worker programs are visa programs that, in most cases, allow employers to recruit a specified number of migrant workers into specified occupations where unfilled vacancies are placing the employers at a competitive disadvantage. Labor recruitment is not for workers to fill positions on a permanent basis, but instead to assist the employer in fulfilling a labor need on a seasonal or short-term basis until the processes of labor market adjustment improve the supply of labor over time.

When establishing employment visa programs, governments must balance several considerations, including determining how many migrants to admit, how those workers should be selected, what rights and privileges they should receive, and whether they should have the opportunity to become permanent residents or citizens. Additional considerations include the likely impacts of migration on the employment opportunities available to local workers, and the ability of employers to recruit workers for job vacancies. One approach is to have employers attest to the presence of labor shortages before recruiting foreign workers for vacancies that could not be filled by local workers. Another approach is to use a labor market test by which a government agency certifies that an employer has been unable to fill a vacancy with workers in the local labor market.

Unfortunately, the task of establishing whether a labor shortage actually exists is far from straightforward (see, e.g., Anderson & Ruhs, 2011; Martin & Ruhs, 2011; Veneri, 1999). Employers may be prone to asserting that they are unable to recruit and hire suitable workers for a given position, but since recruitment is contingent on the wage being offered the putative labor shortage may merely reflect employers' unwillingness to raise wages sufficiently to meet the market rate. In fact, economic theory suggests that in the long run there is no such thing as a labor shortage, since wage rates should rise to a level at which jobseekers will accept employment, thereby eliminating the "shortage" through processes of labor market adjustment. However, as a practical matter, the speed at which wages may need to rise and the time it takes for workers to adjust to wage signals means that, depending on the industry and occupation, temporary labor shortages may exist.

TEMPORARY WORKER PROGRAMS IN THE UNITED STATES

During the 1990s, the U.S. implemented a new set of guest worker programs that remain in effect as of this writing. These programs target different sectors and skill levels, and each is governed by complex rules and various labor market tests. Most programs share a number of characteristics: they are employer-driven, meaning that employers must request that foreign workers fill job vacancies; they are time-limited; and they contain certification criteria that require employers to demonstrate the existence of a labor shortage in a particular occupation by advertising the position in newspapers, along with a wage rate for that occupation set by the U.S. Department of Labor. The failure to find suitable job candidates is taken as prima facie evidence of a labor shortage. The United States has implemented more than 20 visa programs that allow individuals from foreign nations to enter and work in the country. Several large visa programs are briefly described below.

The H-1B program is the largest employment visa program in the United States. It allows employers to recruit high-skilled foreign workers who have earned a bachelor's degree (or other advanced degree) to fill jobs requiring that level of education. The program was authorized in 1990 to assist employers in coping with shortages of scientists and engineers in the defense sector, as well as specialists in the computer industry (Martin, Abella, & Kuptsch, 2006). The U.S. Department of Labor establishes prevailing wage rates for a range of occupations. When hiring a worker through the H-1B program, employers must meet or exceed the wage rate that has been established for the occupation in question. After a foreign national has been hired through the program, the employer attests that the prevailing wage rate has been met or exceeded, and the worker signs a contract that ties him/her to the position with that employer. The number of visas is capped at 65,000 (for fiscal year 2012), according to the U.S. Citizenship and Immigration Services (2011b).

The H-2A program is designed to manage the migration of workers to fill temporary or seasonal vacancies in agricultural production, provided that U.S. workers are not available. Employers who wish to hire farmworkers through the H-2A program must receive a certification by the U.S. Department of Labor indicating that there is not a sufficient supply of local workers who are available and qualified to fill the job vacancies, and that the employment of guest workers in the industry will not undermine the wages and working conditions of U.S. workers in the industry. To receive certification, employers must (1) have unsuccessfully attempted to hire U.S. workers, (2) cooperate with state workforce development agencies in the latter's efforts to recruit workers to fill vacancies in the industry, and (3) pay guest workers and other workers holding the same position at rates above the minimum wage, adverse effect wage rate, or prevailing wage rate, whichever is higher. (The adverse effect wage rate is the minimum pay rate for U.S. and H-2A workers employed in agricultural production, as determined by the U.S. Department of Labor, and the prevailing wage rate is the rate of pay that has been determined by the U.S. Department of Labor for a given class of labor in a particular geographic area and for a particular type of project.) In addition, workers must be provided with housing, transportation, tools, and work-related benefits such as workers' compensation insurance for cases of on-the-job injury or illness. Workers' continuous participation in the program is limited to 3 years or less. There are no limits on the number of H-2A visas that may be issued.

The H-2B program allows for the admission of foreign workers for temporary employment in nonagricultural industries, provided that U.S. workers are not available. Employers who wish to hire foreign workers through the program must first receive certification from the U.S. Department of Labor indicating that U.S. workers are not available to perform the work, and that the employment of guest workers will not undermine the wages and working conditions of U.S. workers. Program rules stipulate that for a job to qualify as "temporary," the worker must be filling a seasonal, peak-load, or intermittent need, or a one-time occurrence. Employers of H-2B workers must pay above the prevailing wage rate. Initial H-2B visas are valid for up to 1 year, and workers' participation may not exceed 3 consecutive years. The program was capped at 66,000 workers in fiscal year 2012 (U.S. Citizenship and Immigration Services, 2011a).

The L-1 program allows employers to transfer managers and professionals from their foreign operations to companies in the United States. Employers are not required to satisfy any labor market test before initiating an employee transfer, though workers must have been employed with the company for at least 1 year prior to the transfer. Workers holding an L-1 visa are prohibited from moving to other firms while they are in the United States. There is no limit on the number of L-1 visas that may be issued.

WHY MANAGE MIGRATION?

Large-scale, transnational migration of labor has significant implications for the functioning of the economies of both labor-sending and labor-receiving countries, as well as for the employment prospects of workers in these countries. This section reviews the perspectives of labor-exporting countries and receiving countries, as well as the migrant workers themselves, regarding the suitability of temporary worker programs.

Sending-country perspectives. Uneven global development has placed severe pressures on low- and moderate-income countries and their workforces. Employment declines in core industries as a result of international trade, deindustrialization, mechanization, and technological change have meant that unemployment and underemployment are systemic problems that have undermined the livelihoods of billions of people worldwide. The years since 1990 have been especially difficult for workers in many low-income countries, as they have been forced to contend with large-scale economic restructuring, due to globalization rising unemployment, and the growth of informal economies. Entrenched unemployment combined with underemployment in informal sectors has meant that large shares of the working-age population in these countries are unable to find gainful employment (International Labour Office, 2011). As a result, during the 2000s, international organizations, such as the World Bank and the United Nations, began to actively promote the idea that low-income countries could achieve net positive benefits from the out-migration of working-age adults to high-income countries. Workers abroad would likely send a portion of their earnings back to their country of origin in the form of remittances, which would support the needs of family members and stimulate economic activity. There are several potential downsides to such an approach to development, however, including that a resulting "brain drain" could negatively impact the long-term growth prospects of labor-exporting countries.

Receiving-country perspectives. Several factors have contributed to the appeal of temporary worker programs in high-income countries, such as those in North America and western Europe. Many countries are contending with an aging population, low birth rates, and rising employer demand for workers employed on a temporary or flexible basis. Crucially, however, for large-scale flows of migrant workers to be sustained, labor market conditions in receiving countries must be such that foreign workers can be readily incorporated into economic activities. A focus on migration "push" factors in sending countries greatly underplays the importance of labor demand in high-income countries (Sassen, 1988).

Industries and sectors such as agriculture, child care, construction, food processing, and hospitality are increasingly reliant on foreign workers to fill key positions, typically at relatively low wages. In the United States, employers in these industries have remade workforce systems in ways that are reliant on the availability of low-wage labor, leading to processes of "occupational closure" as jobs come to be regarded as "immigrant jobs" for which U.S. workers need not apply (Waldinger & Lichter, 2003). This, in turn, has led to rising demand for foreign workers, in large part as a strategy to contain product costs, boost profits, and enhance competitiveness. There is a danger, then, that migrants will become the workers of choice in low-wage industries as employers discover that these workers can be easily exploited.

Worker perspectives. Contrary to the dominant migration narrative that has characterized immigration policy debates since the 1980s, not all migrant workers—even those from countries experiencing tremendous economic hardships—would like to permanently relocate to the United States. Rather, they see work-related migration as a way to improve their economic circumstances, and they retain strong attachments to family and community in their country of origin. Many migrant workers who come to hold low-skill, low-wage jobs in the United States enter the labor market as unauthorized migrants. This lack of legal status places them at a severe disadvantage in the labor market, and it often relegates them to industries and occupations where labor standards are routinely violated (Bernhardt et al., 2008; Waldinger & Lichter, 2003). In addition, lack of legal status greatly restricts their mobility, since unauthorized migrants are often reluctant to risk apprehension by changing jobs or visiting their country of origin. A well-functioning temporary worker program might better meet these workers' needs by facilitating temporary migration to the United States, enhancing workers' rights in the workplace, and enabling workers to travel back and forth to their countries of origin without fear of apprehension by immigration authorities.

CRITICISMS OF TEMPORARY WORKER PROGRAMS

In principle, it seems that a temporary worker program could meet the varied needs of labor-exporting countries, migrant workers, and the U.S. economy. However, in the United States, temporary worker programs increasingly have come under fire because they are said to distort wages and patterns of employer recruitment, because they have been associated with widespread violations of labor standards, and because they do not appear to curtail unauthorized migration. Research has documented how guest workers have routinely suffered the nonpayment of wages; been forced to pay inordinate sums of money to secure low-wage, temporary jobs; had their freedom of movement denied by employers or labor brokers who confiscate their documents; and been denied basic labor protections, including medical benefits when they have been injured on the job (Bauer, 2007; Griffith, 2006; Marshall, 2007; Ness, 2011).

Furthermore, employer reliance on migrant workers who can be deployed on a flexible basis, without adequate employment rights, and at the sole whim and discretion of the employer is damaging to migrant workers, to U.S. workers who compete with them for jobs, and to the workings of local labor markets and the economy in general. Under the present rules, temporary work programs confer multiple advantages to the employers who hire guest workers, but these advantages come at the expense of the workers themselves. In many respects, the adage "there is nothing as permanent as a temporary worker" is apt, because employers come to depend on migrant workers upon whom second-class status has been conferred.

The question, then, is whether temporary worker programs can be overhauled in such a way that they defend the rights of migrant workers while also meeting domestic demand for labor.

TOWARD A RIGHTS-BASED APPROACH

Admittedly, the historical record of low-skilled temporary worker programs in the United States has been poor, leading some critics to argue that the H-2A and H-2B programs should be scrapped completely. At a minimum, the abuses documented by researchers and advocates suggest that temporary worker programs need to be thoroughly reconceived and redesigned. This section takes a step in that direction by presenting a policy framework for a rights-based approach to temporary worker migration.

Currently, temporary worker programs to fill low-skilled jobs, although requiring certification by the U.S. Department of Labor, place ultimate authority over worker entry in the hands of employers. The employer is able to design the position, determine the minimum length of the job, and dismiss the worker at any time. With little recourse against the employer, and completely dependent on the employer for continued earnings while in the United States, guest workers are in an unenviable situation. They often must accept the terms of employment as dictated by their employer, or else risk reprisals.

Unfortunately, certain components of temporary worker programs that are designed to protect the interests of the domestic workforce actually undermine both their interests and those of guest workers. Take, for example, provisions that restrict the movement of migrant workers from one job to another.

Because low-skilled temporary worker programs are specifically created to recruit workers into unfilled jobs, migrant workers' movement within the labor market is restricted by design. But this inability to freely change jobs eliminates an important mechanism for safeguarding labor standards: the threat of exit. If employers have little reason to worry that workers will leave when confronted with substandard working conditions, incentives to improve conditions are dampened, and substandard practices may go unchecked. Furthermore, because the employer can unilaterally terminate the employment of a worker or group of workers, employers may be emboldened to degrade working conditions further, creating a set of perverse incentives that rewards employment downgrading.

The law professor and immigration expert Jennifer Gordon has succinctly summarized why "mobility matters" for well-functioning labor markets. In *Free Movement and Equal Rights for Low-Wage Workers? What the United States Can Learn From the New EU Migration to Britain* (2011), Gordon offers three related reasons why migrant workers should be provided opportunity for greater mobility in the labor market:

> When migrants are able to *change employers* at will, they are better able to claim their rights, because they can look elsewhere if they are being abused in their current position, and they need not fear deportation if they complain. This should make it harder for exploitative employers to find employees or hide from government officials, reinforcing the floor on wages and working conditions for all workers. When migrants can *shift between industries and regions,* they should be able to move to wherever unemployment is lowest and residents are least interested in doing the work, filling an economic need while minimizing competition. Finally, when migrants can *travel to and from the destination country* at will, they have the ability to move to take advantage of new opportunities as they arise. (pp. 5–6, italics in original)

This suggests that one way to improve the conditions facing guest workers is to allow mobility between employers and regions. But what should be done about the reciprocal concern for the interests of U.S. workers who might face heightened competition from migrant workers who are moving between jobs?

Labor market tests are a means for determining the presence of labor shortages in particular industries, occupations, and places, and they have been a feature of contemporary low-skilled temporary worker programs in the United States. However, the measures that have been used—principally whether an employer reports being able to recruit local workers along with current wage rates for the identified occupations–are inadequate for the task of accurately assessing the mismatch between labor supply and demand. More robust measures could both safeguard the interests of the domestic workforce and those of migrant workers who could be granted the right to mobility within the U.S. labor market. Labor market tests to determine if employers reporting labor shortages should be allowed to recruit foreign workers on a temporary basis should include additional measures, such as the presence of (1) rising employment levels in the industry and occupation in question, (2) rising wages, and (3) low and falling unemployment rates (Martin & Ruhs, 2011). These indicators are a reflection of wider processes of labor market adjustment. To the extent, for example, that employment levels and wage rates are rising in an industry, while unemployment rates in the locality remain low, a case could be made that migrant mobility between jobs could offer net benefits to employers and the local economy, while also granting migrant workers greater scope for exiting substandard workplaces.

The above discussion suggests that temporary worker programs should not be driven entirely by the needs of any individual employer, nor should workers be tethered to a given employer, as historically has been the case. Instead, there is scope for various workers' rights organizations—including labor unions and worker centers (nonprofit organizations that engage in labor organizing, service delivery, policy advocacy, and other supports for low-wage workers)—to assume the role of migrant-worker sponsor. Workers' rights organizations play a meaningful role in the operation of local labor markets, and they are well positioned to deliver a rights-based approach to migrant worker programs. First, as worker representatives they have intimate knowledge of the inner workings of the sectors and industries where they are active. This knowledge can be important in ensuring that employment laws are abided by and enforced. In this sense they provide a means of enforcing labor standards from within the labor market. Second, workers' rights organizations can facilitate migrant worker incorporation into local communities and regional economies. Through their connections with community groups and government agencies, these organizations can be a bridge between newcomers and established community institutions. Third, these organizations can build worker solidarity, educate workers about their rights, and partner with government enforcement agencies to ensure that employment and labor laws are not violated. In this way the rights of all workers can be strengthened. In the United States, examples of these organizations include the affiliates of the National Domestic Workers Alliance (organizing household workers) and the National Day Laborers Organizing Network (organizing construction laborers and other day workers).

Finally, some temporary migrant workers may, over time, establish enduring roots in the United States and may wish to adjust their immigration status. Including a mechanism for becoming a permanent resident with a path toward citizenship might be seen as an important component of a rights-based migrant worker program. Workers' rights organizations could document workers' time in the United States and otherwise verify claims toward permanent residency.

Temporary worker programs have a role to play in managing migration and remedying supply-demand imbalances in local labor markets, but not in the form they have taken at the beginning of the twenty-first century. It is argued that a rights-based approach that reduces the control of employers in allocating labor, enhances worker mobility, strengthens labor market tests, and, most importantly, relies on unions and other workers' rights organizations as sponsors of migrant workers could dramatically improve the functioning of these programs, as well as safeguard the rights of U.S. and migrant workers.

References and Further Reading

Anderson, B., & Ruhs, M. (2011). Migrant workers: Who needs them? A framework for the analysis of staff shortages, immigration, and public policy. In M. Ruhs & B. Anderson (Eds.), *Who needs migrant workers? Labour shortages, immigration, and public policy* (pp. 15–52). Oxford, UK: Oxford University Press.

Bauer, M. (2007). *Close to slavery: Guestworker programs in the United States.* Montgomery, AL: Southern Poverty Law Center.

Bernhardt, A., Milkman, R., Theodore, N., Heckathorn, D., Auer, M., DeFilippis, J., Gonzalez, A. L., Narro, V., Perelshteyn, J., Polson, D., & Spiller, M. (2008). *Broken laws, unprotected workers: Violations of employment and labor laws in America's cities.* Report sponsored by Center for Urban Economic Development, National Employment Law Project, and UCLA Institute for Research in Labor and Employment. Retrieved from http://www.unprotectedworkers.org/index.php/broken_laws/index

Fine, J. (2006). *Worker centers: Organizing communities at the edge of the dream.* Ithaca, NY: Cornell University Press.

Gordon, J. (2011). *Free movement and equal rights for low-wage workers? What the United States can learn from the new EU migration to Britain.* Berkeley, CA: Chief Justice Earl Warren Institute on Law and Social Policy, University of California, Berkeley Law School.

Griffith, D. (2006). *American guestworkers: Jamaicans and Mexicans in the U.S. labor market.* University Park, PA: Pennsylvania State University Press.

International Labour Office. (2011). *Global employment trends 2011: The challenge of a jobs recovery.* Geneva, Switzerland: Author.

Marshall, R. (2007). *Getting immigration reform right.* Washington, DC: Economic Policy Institute.

Martin, P., Abella, M., & Kuptsch, C. (2006). *Managing labor migration in the twenty-first century.* New Haven, CT: Yale University Press.

Martin, P., & Ruhs, M. (2011). Labor shortages and U.S. immigration reform: Promises and perils of an independent commission. *International Migration Review, 45*(1), 174–187.

Ness, I. (2011). *Guest workers and resistance to U.S. corporate despotism.* Champaign, IL: University of Illinois Press.

Sassen, S. (1988). *The mobility of labor and capital: A study in international investment and labor flow.* Cambridge, UK: Cambridge University Press.

Sassen, S. (1999). *Guests and aliens.* New York, NY: The New Press.

Theodore, N., Valenzuela, A., Jr., & Meléndez, E. (2009). Worker centers: Defending labor standards for migrant workers in the informal economy. *International Journal of Manpower, 30*(5), 422–436.

United Nations Conference on Trade and Development. (2010). *Maximizing the development impact of remittances.* Retrieved September 12, 2011 from http://www.unctad.org/en/docs/ciem4d2_en.pdf

U.S. Citizenship and Immigration Services (2011a). *Cap count for H-2B nonimmigrants.* Retrieved from http://www.uscis.gov/portal/site/uscis/menuitem.5af9bb95919f35e66f614176543f6d1a/?vgnextoid=356b6c521eb97210VgnVCM100000082ca60aRCRD&vgnextchannel=d1d333e559274210VgnVCM100000082ca60aRCRD

U.S. Citizenship and Immigration Services (2011b). *H-1B fiscal year (FY) 2012 cap season.* Retrieved from http://www.uscis.gov/portal/site/uscis/menuitem.5af9bb95919f35e66f614176543f6d1a/?vgnextoid=4b7cdd1d5fd37210VgnVCM100000082ca60aRCRD&vgnextchannel=73566811264a3210VgnVCM100000b92ca60aRCRD

Veneri, C. M. (1999). Can occupational labor shortages be identified using available data? *Monthly Labor Review, 122*(3), 15–21.

Waldinger, R., & Lichter, M. I. (2003). *How the other half works: Immigration and the social organization of labor.* Berkeley, CA: University of California Press.

World Bank. (2006). *Global economic prospects 2006: Economic implications of remittances and migration.* Washington, DC: Author.

Nik Theodore

COUNTERPOINT

Temporary guest workers are seldom temporary and almost wholly unnecessary to the U.S. economy. Guest worker programs have contributed to a massive oversupply of low-skilled workers in America that has driven down wages and working conditions. Employers in some industries have increasingly come to depend on a constant supply of low-wage foreign workers and they routinely petition Congress for increased numbers of guest workers. Exacerbating the problem is the large number of low-skilled illegal workers who compete for the same jobs. Not since the Industrial Revolution over a century and a half ago, when state and federal governments were willing to overlook the exploitative practices of businesses in the "national interest" of economic growth, has the United States seen such deplorable working conditions.

In order to understand why today's low-skilled guest worker programs are harmful, one must have a fuller under-standing of why the overall U.S. immigration system is dysfunctional. As it stands now, a very small percentage (only 6% in 2009, according to the U.S. government) of immigrants are admitted for employment reasons. Annually, approximately three quarters of all immigrants—or legal permanent residents, as they are officially referred to—are admitted because of familial ties to persons already in the country. The result is that immigration is adding to a massive glut of low-skilled native workers who are struggling to compete for a limited number of jobs; jobs that have become increasingly scarce since the onset in 2007 of what many economists refer to as the "Great Recession."

Compounding the problem is the large illegal alien population (11–13 million), 7 million of whom are estimated to be working in the United States, almost all of them in low-skilled occupations. (This estimate is based on projections by the U.S. Census Bureau's *Current Population Survey,* the Pew Hispanic Center, and the Center for Immigration Studies; See Passel & Cohn, 2009, and Camarota & Jensenius, 2009, for more information.) Employers who follow the law and refrain from illegally employing foreign workers should be commended, but just because an employer uses legal guest workers does not mean that native workers are not available and willing to work. While the United States has historically welcomed immigrants, and should continue to do so, it cannot allow employers in the United States to use foreign workers to put Americans at a disadvantage. The evidence overwhelmingly proves that there is no shortage of available and willing American workers.

JOBS AMERICANS *ARE* DOING

Many business owners, and entire industries in some cases, have come to depend on a low-wage workforce, and they rely on immigration to furnish these workers. In order to justify this practice, employers and their political allies have continually put forth the proposition that there are jobs that can only be filled by foreign workers. This is simply not true. There is no such thing as an "immigrant" job, and there is no job that Americans will not do. No academic or economic research has ever been able to demonstrate that not enough American workers are available to fill low-wage jobs, or that Americans are unwilling to perform certain jobs. There are, however, jobs that Americans are less likely to take because employers are offering poverty wages and little or no benefits. In the words of Jared Bernstein, the former chief economic advisor to Vice President Joe Biden, "Employers are very quick to raise the specter of a labor shortage, but often it's another way of saying they can't find the workers they want at the price they're paying.... They are unwilling to meet the price signal the market is sending, so they seek help in the form of a spigot like immigration" (quoted in Herbst, 2007).

According to the Economic Policy Institute, in June 2011 there were 4.5 job seekers for every available job—a tough market for job seekers, but a substantial improvement from the previous year. In the low-skill sector, however, the ratio remains much worse, with often more than 10 job seekers for every job. Unemployment is at a 30-year high, yet employers are calling for more unskilled workers. As immigration, particularly illegal immigration, has increased, the economic opportunities for low-skilled, native-born workers have steadily decreased. The negative impact on low-skilled Americans by foreign workers is the one consensus upon which economists agree. The larger debate is over *how much* low-wage workers are affected by immigration, with some economists downplaying the impact by assuming that native workers do not compete with foreign workers, but rather that the two groups "complement" one another in the labor market (Ruark & Graham, 2011). As it stands now, the unemployment rate for those without a high school diploma is over three times that of those who have a college degree. In addition, the wages for those in low-skilled occupations have stagnated since the 1970s, in large part because of immigration, widening the income gap considerably.

Jobs that once provided a means of support for middle-class American families are becoming difficult to find for those without college degrees. Construction work is now increasingly considered a job for foreign workers, despite the fact that 65 percent of construction laborers are native-born. The meatpacking industry is another good example of how immigration has reshaped the economic landscape in the United States, much to the detriment of America's working-class. In 1960, meatpacking workers earned 15 percent more than the average wage for manufacturing workers. Over the succeeding decades, foreign workers (often illegal) began to make up a larger percentage of workers in meatpacking, and by 2002, industry workers were earning 25 percent less than the average manufacturing wage, and real wages for meatpacking workers had dropped 45 percent (Kammer, 2009). The argument that Americans refuse to work in meatpacking facilities has also been proven false. In 2006, approximately 1,700 illegal workers were terminated from six Swift & Co. plants as a result of federal law enforcement actions. Within five months, however, all the plants had resumed operations by hiring local workers, and the average hourly pay had increased by 8 percent (Ruark, 2010).

The unemployment rate during the first three months of 2011 for U.S.-born adults without a high school diploma was 22 percent. For native-born Americans with only a high-school diploma the unemployment rate during that period was 20 percent. There is a total of 21 million native-born Americans with a high school diploma or less between the ages of 18 and 65 who are not in the labor force. These are the individuals that compete most directly with low-skilled immigrants for jobs. Despite there being millions of Americans out of work, there is a constant call for more foreign workers because Americans supposedly are unwilling to take many of the jobs necessary for the U.S. economy (Camarota, 2011).

Table 18.1 shows that native-born workers are the majority of those who fill jobs that some argue are "jobs Americans won't do." The fact that Americans have always done these jobs, and continue to do them in large numbers, belies the notion that foreign workers are needed to fill them.

Table 18.1 Some jobs Americans are doing (Native-born share of sector workforces)

Food prep and service (including fast food): 86%

Janitors: 75%

Cooks: 71%

Dishwashers: 69%

Parking lot attendants: 67%

Grounds maintenance workers: 65%

All construction laborers: 65%

Painters (construction & maintenance): 63%

Butchers and meat processing workers: 63%

Roofers: 61%

Taxi drivers and chauffeurs: 58%

Maids and housekeeping workers: 55%

Agricultural workers: 50%

Source: Camarota & Jensenius (2009), pp. 3–12.

Note: Percentages represent the native-born share of each occupation.

A strong correlation exists between low-skill foreign labor and native low-skilled unemployment, because these two groups do compete for the same jobs. It is true that if every job held by a foreign worker were vacated, some would not be filled by native workers. In some cases that job would be automated, outsourced, or cease to exist altogether. It is also true that some Americans choose not to work, despite opportunities available to them. However, it is totally implausible to argue that there are not enough native-born workers who could fill jobs that are vital to the American economy.

A NATIONAL CRISIS

Unemployment numbers are abstract and may not always convey the seriousness of the situation facing Americans. The failure of the U.S. immigration system over the last three decades to accord with the economic needs of the country has led to depressed wages and deteriorated working conditions. There are severe consequences that result from the expansion of the labor pool and many Americans being systematically unemployed. It is becoming increasingly difficult for low-skilled workers to earn a living wage, and fewer Americans can now find entry-level jobs, which provide valuable work experience for teenagers and young adults. According to Steven Camarota's "A Need for More Immigrant Workers?" (2011), U.S.-born teens have an unemployment rate of 28 percent; for black teens the rate is 48 percent. The numbers are staggering. Even more troubling, a study by the Center for Labor Market Studies found that young people who are not in the job market are likely to remain systematically unemployed throughout much of their adult lives, and to earn lower wages when they do work (Sum & Khatiwada, 2004). Unemployed teens are more likely to drop out of high school and have higher rates of teen pregnancy and criminal activity.

As the level of low-skill immigration has increased, so too has income inequality in the United States. Rising income inequality is a problem that few politicians seem to want to confront, and even fewer wish to acknowledge the role that immigration has played in it. While immigration is not the sole cause of stagnating wages for low-skilled workers, it is certainly a major factor in this long-term trend. Figure 18.1 shows that wages paid to noncitizen workers are lower than those paid to native workers. This discrepancy drives overall wages down and incentivizes employers to discriminate against hiring native workers.

NEEDED REFORMS

> *"Basically . . . there is a massive labor surplus in the United States . . . and the working class is getting crushed."*
>
> —*Andrew Sum, Professor of Economics, Northeastern University (quoted in Reuters, October 23, 2009)*

The interest of some employers has trumped the interest of the American people, and the federal government has failed in its responsibility to prioritize the welfare of American workers. Technically, there are safeguards that are supposed to

Figure 18.1 Wage and salary earnings per year in high-illegal-immigrant industry categories, 2008

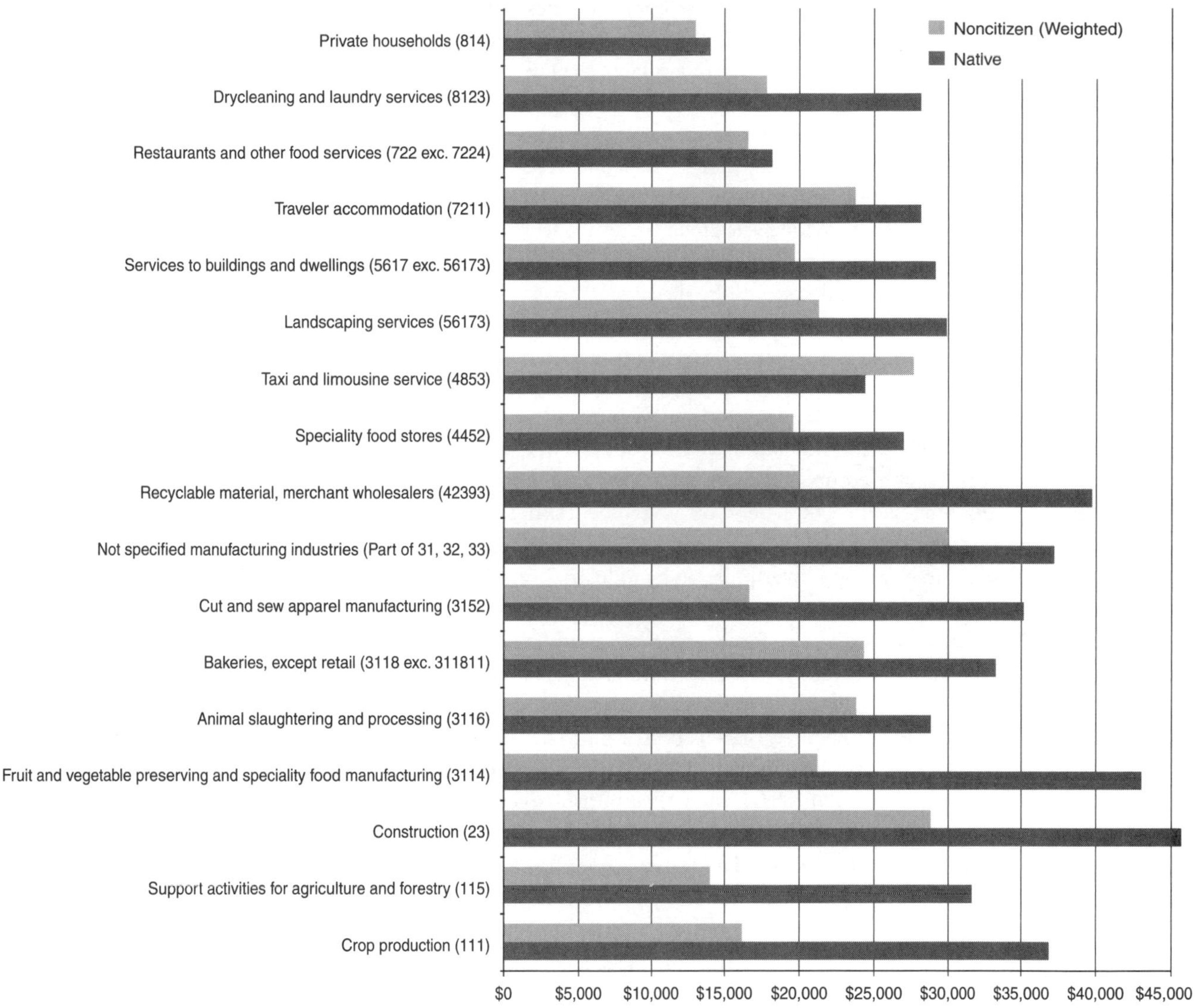

Source: Ruark and Graham (2011).

ensure that Americans are not displaced by foreign workers. According to rules for foreign labor certification laid out by the U.S. Department of Labor (DOL), an employer who wants to hire a guest worker must "show that there are insufficient qualified U.S. workers available and willing to perform the work at the prevailing wage paid for the occupation" in order to receive a labor certification from the DOL. But this process is little more than a formality, with the DOL doing very little to ensure that employers are abiding by the guidelines set forth by Congress. One of the most important reforms that could be made to the U.S. immigration system would be to drastically reduce the number of low-skilled guest workers admitted each year. That could be done by eliminating the H-2B visa program that brings in 66,000 seasonal, low-skilled, nonagricultural workers each year, with most H-2B visa holders already in the country not counted against the cap; and by enforcing the provisions of the H-2A visa program, which is supposed to provide farmers with seasonal labor needs.

The H-2B program has allowed employers to sidestep local workers in order to bring in cheaper foreign workers who have little bargaining power and are not likely to complain about poor treatment. Employers have so abused the H-2B program that the Department of Labor was successfully sued in federal court and had to recalculate wage rates for H-2B (seasonal, nonagricultural) guest workers to better align wages with "marketplace realities." A 2011 article in the *Daily*

Press, "Seafood Industry, Congress Members Fight Migrant Worker Pay Boost," stated that wages paid to H-2B workers were far below the fair market wage, at least 30 percent lower than other seafood workers in the Chesapeake Bay region.

Farmers, or more accurately, large agribusiness conglomerates, often contend that there are not enough available native workers to do farm labor, and that foreign workers are therefore needed. But a 2009 report by the Congressional Research Service found that there is no shortage of available farm workers in the United States, and many Americans who are jobless and collecting welfare benefits expressed the desire to take farm jobs. This does not mean that there might not be labor shortages in some localities at a particular time, but the H-2A program allows for an *unlimited* number of agricultural workers to meet any temporary shortages. However, only around 5 percent of all farm workers are H-2A visa holders, while close to 50 percent are illegal aliens (Ruark & Moinuddin, 2011). The reason for this is that the H-2A program requires that employers provide basic amenities to the workers, such as a fair wage rate, access to sanitary living quarters, and transportation to the worksite. Large commercial farms can maximize their profits by not abiding by the conditions of the H-2A program and instead hire illegal workers.

THE UNITED STATES IS A COUNTRY, NOT AN ECONOMY

The major argument used to justify the importation of foreign low-skilled workers is that these workers contribute to the gross domestic product (GDP) and help raise the economic output of the United States. This is true, but what is also true is that native workers, as a group, add more on a per capita basis than do foreign workers, and households headed by native-born persons are less likely to depend on government programs than those headed by foreign-born individuals (Camarota, 2011). Furthermore, the GDP only measures total spending, whether it's the money being spent to pay factory workers or money spent to clean up a river polluted by industrial runoff. GDP has little to do with economic equality or quality of life for the average citizen.

Another argument put forward is that foreign workers create jobs for native workers, but the research cited as proof actually shows a paltry number of jobs created in relation to jobs occupied by foreign workers. (The most widely cited research, by the Perryman Group in 2008, found that 8.3 million illegal aliens held jobs, while their economic impact only supported 2.8 million jobs.) Further, there is no reason to believe that any job supposedly created by the presence of a foreign worker goes to an American. In fact, the Pew Hispanic Center has shown that from June 2009 to June 2010, foreign-born workers gained 665,000 jobs while native-born workers lost 1.2 million jobs. A major reduction in the foreign-born workforce could cause the economy to contract and the GDP to shrink, but that does not mean that there would be negative economic contributions. The feeble economic contributions of low-skilled foreign workers and the enormous costs of so many unemployed and underemployed Americans far outweigh any economic benefit from guest worker programs.

Those few who benefit from the importation of low-skilled foreign workers are very economically powerful, and therefore able to exert political influence, but what is good for a narrow economic elite is not good for the country as a whole. Increased economic output and higher profit margins for large corporations are not necessarily congruent with the economic health of a nation and its citizens. Yes, a vital national economy is the goal of any government and its people, but one must not forget that an economy should serve the needs of a nation and its people, not the other way around. Those who argue that guest worker programs are necessary in the United States seem to have forgotten this. Foreign low-skilled workers have distorted labor markets in the United States and contribute to the idea that economic growth is always desirable and beneficial, and the faster the growth the better, no matter the long-term costs.

CONCLUSION

The case made for the importation of low-skill, low-wage foreign workers is usually based on economic (Americans won't work) or humanitarian (immigrants are only seeking a better life) reasons. But the truth is that Americans will do the work and there is already a massive oversupply of unemployed, low-skilled Americans, who are being denied opportunities to find gainful employment. The population is growing much faster than the growth in jobs created in the United States. That was true even before the start of the current recession, yet the call for increased low-skilled immigration and expanded guest workers programs continues unabated—now under the guise of an "economic stimulus." The enormous fiscal and social costs associated with low-skilled immigrants will only increase if more low-skilled immigrants are admitted.

The operation of America's guest worker programs has nothing to do with need and everything to do with U.S. employers seeking foreign workers as a source of cheap labor at the expense of tens of millions of American workers. The United States is a twenty-first-century postindustrial society continuing to abide by nineteenth-century immigration practices. Jobs that require low-skilled workers are increasingly limited, and there are more than enough Americans to fill these jobs many times over. Increasing the low-skill labor pool through immigration or guest worker programs only makes it more difficult for any worker to earn a decent living in these occupations. It is far past the time for the immigration system to be reformed, with the interest of the American people—all of the American people—put first.

While it is true that many foreigners do come to the United States in search of a better life, the interests of foreigners are not, nor should they be, the goal of the U.S. immigration system. The United States has the most generous immigration policy of any country in the world, admitting more than one million immigrants every year. As pointed out above, most of these immigrants come into the country irrespective of any educational or occupational skills they may possess. This is not a system that works in the interest of American workers or American taxpayers. No one has the inherent right to come to the United States, no matter their education or skill level, although the United States should favor those who can make contributions to the U.S. economy. As it stands now, there is a profound disconnect between the needs of U.S. labor markets and the supply of foreign labor, which is increasing exponentially with each passing year.

REFERENCES AND FURTHER READING

AFL/CIO. (n.d.). *Exporting America: What are the broader impacts?* Retrieved from http://www.aflcio.org/issues/jobseconomy/exportingamerica/outsourcing_problems.cfm

Borjas, G. J. (2004, May). *Increasing the supply of labor through immigration* [Backgrounder]. Retrieved from Center for Immigration Studies website: http://www.cis.org/articles/2004/back504.pdf

Cafaro, P. (2009, December). *The economic impacts of mass immigration into the United States and the proper progressive response* (Policy Brief No. 09-2). Retrieved from Progressives for Immigration Reform website: http://www.progressivesforimmigrationreform.org/wp-content/uploads/2009/12/cafaro.pdf

Camarota, S. A. (2011, April). *Welfare use by immigrant households with children: A look at cash, Medicaid, housing, and food programs* [Backgrounder]. Retrieved from Center for Immigration Studies website: http://www.cis.org/articles/2011/immigrant-welfare-use-4-11.pdf

Camarota, S. A. (2011, June). *A need for more immigrant workers? Unemployment and underemployment in the first quarter of 2011* [Memorandum]. Retrieved from Center for Immigration Studies website: http://www.cis.org/articles/2011/need-more-immigrant-workers-q1-2011.pdf

Camarota, S. A., & Jensenius, K. (2009, August). *Jobs Americans won't do? A detailed look at immigrant employment by occupation* [Memorandum]. Retrieved from Center for Immigration Studies website: http://www.cis.org/illegalImmigration-employment

Camarota, S. A., & Jensenius, K. (2009, December). *A huge pool of potential workers: Unemployment, underemployment, and non-work among native-born Americans* [Memorandum]. Retrieved from Center for Immigration Studies website: http://www.cis.org/articles/2009/q3-2009-u6.pdf

Herbst, M. (2007, August 21). Labor shortages: Myth and reality. *BusinessWeek.* Retrieved from http://www.businessweek.com/bwdaily/dnflash/content/aug2007/db20070821_451283.htm

Job seeker to job ratio a stat mashup. (2010, July 15). *San Francisco Chronicle.* Retrieved from http://articles.sfgate.com/2010–07–15/business/21983904_1_labor-turnover-survey-job-seekers-job-market

Kammer, J. (2009, November). *Labor market effects of immigration enforcement at meatpacking plants in seven states* (Forum testimony: American jobs in peril). Retrieved from Center for Immigration Studies website: http://www.cis.org/node/1577

Levine, L. (2009, January 29). *Immigration: The effects on low-skilled and high-skilled native-born workers* (Congressional Research Service Report 95-408). Retrieved from http://assets.opencrs.com/rpts/95-408_20091105.pdf

Levine, L. (2009, November 9). *Farm labor shortages and immigration policy* (Congressional Research Service Report RL30395). Retrieved from National Agricultural Law Center website: http://www.nationalaglawcenter.org/assets/crs/RL30395.pdf

Martin, P. (2009). *Importing poverty? Immigration and the changing face of rural America.* New Haven, CT: Yale University Press.

Passel, J. S., & Cohn, D. (2009, April) *A portrait of unauthorized immigrants in the United States.* Retrieved from Pew Hispanic Center website: http://pewhispanic.org/files/reports/107.pdf

Perryman Group. (2008, April). *An analysis of the economic impact of undocumented workers on business activity in the US with estimated effects by state and by industry.* Retrieved from http://americansforimmigrationreform.com/files/Impact_of_the_Undocumented_Workforce.pdf

Pew Hispanic Center. (2010, January 21). *Statistical portrait of the foreign-born population in the United States, 2008.* Retrieved from http://pewhispanic.org/factsheets/factsheet.php?FactsheetID=59

Ruark, E. A. (2010). *Amnesty and the American worker: A look at how illegal immigration has harmed working class Americans and how amnesty would make it worse.* Retrieved from Federation for American Immigration Reform (FAIR) website: http://www.fairus.org/site/DocServer/amnesty_and_workers.pdf?docID=4581

Ruark E. A., & Graham, M. (2011, May). *Immigration, poverty, and low-wage earners.* Retrieved from Federation for American Immigration Reform (FAIR) website: http://www.fairus.org/site/DocServer/poverty_rev.pdf?docID=5621

Ruark, E. A., & Moinuddin, A. (2011, April). *Illegal immigration and agribusiness: The effect on the agriculture industry of converting to a legal workforce.* Retrieved from Federation for American Immigration Reform (FAIR) website: http://www.fairus.org/site/DocServer/agribusiness_rev.pdf?docID=5541

Seafood industry, Congress members fight migrant worker pay boost. (2011, August 10). *Daily Press.* http://www.dailypress.com/news/science/dead-rise-blog/dp-seafood-industry-congress-members-fight-migrant-worker-pay-boost-20110810,0,7745777.story?track=rss

Seminara, D. (2010, February). Dirty work: In-sourcing American jobs with H-2B guestworkers [Backgrounder]. Retrieved from Center for Immigration Studies website: http://www.cis.org/articles/2010/h-2b.pdf

Shierholz, H. (2011, August 10). *Two-and-a-half years of a job-seeker's ratio above 4-to-1.* Retrieved from Economic Policy Institute website: http://www.epi.org/publications/entry/7441

Sum, A., & Khatiwada, I. (2004, January). *Still young, restless, and jobless: The growing employment malaise among U.S. teens and young adults.* Boston, MA: Center for Labor Market Studies, Northeastern University. Retrieved from American Youth Policy Forum website: http://www.aypf.org/publications/stillyoungrestlessandjoblessreport.pdf

Swain, C. (Ed.). (2007). *Debating immigration.* New York: Cambridge University Press.

U.S. blue collar army chases few vacancies. (2009, October 23). *Reuters.* Retrieved from http://www.reuters.com/article/idUSTRE59M3CT20091023

U.S. Citizenship and Immigration Services. (n.d.). *H-2A temporary agricultural workers.* Retrieved from http://www.uscis.gov/portal/site/uscis/menuitem.eb1d4c2a3e5b9ac89243c6a7543f6d1a/?vgnextoid=889f0b89284a3210VgnVCM100000b92ca60aRCRD

U.S. Citizenship and Immigration Services. (n.d.). *H-2B temporary non-agricultural workers.* Retrieved from http://www.uscis.gov/portal/site/uscis/menuitem.eb1d4c2a3e5b9ac89243c6a7543f6d1a/?vgnextoid=d1d333e559274210VgnVCM100000082ca60aRCRD&vgnextchannel=d1d333e559274210VgnVCM100000082ca60aRCRD&vgnextchannel=889f0b89284a3210VgnVCM100000b92ca60aRCRD

U.S. Department of Labor, Office of Foreign Labor Certification. http://www.foreignlaborcert.doleta.gov

Eric A. Ruark

Secure ID Cards

POINT: In order to assure a lawful workforce, employers in the United States need reliable mechanisms for ensuring that a potential employee is legally eligible to work in the United States. Present ID cards must be made more secure and harder to falsify.

James R. Edwards Jr., Center for Immigration Studies

COUNTERPOINT: A "secure" ID card is nothing more than a national ID card and would be a violation of Americans' right to privacy. It would be an expensive and complicated new system that we can't afford, and it would likely involve too much opportunity for clerical error.

Lillie Coney, Electronic Privacy Information Center

Introduction

The debate over secure ID cards revolves around questions of security and enforcement, on the one hand, and civil liberties and privacy, on the other. The tension between the need for effective identification of individuals legally authorized to work in the country and the very American belief in freedom from state intrusion into citizens' everyday lives animates the discussion. Two initiatives related to identity confirmation—the E-Verify program and the REAL ID Act— brought into focus the arguments of both sides.

E-Verify is a federal electronic verification system that employers can use to confirm that a person is authorized to work in the United States. To confirm this eligibility, it compares information from the prospective employee's Form I-9 (Employment Eligibility Verification Form) to data from the Department of Homeland Security (DHS) and Social Security Administration records. The program is voluntary, and states can participate at no cost. E-Verify has shown its usefulness at spotting identity fraud but not identity theft, which is why DHS has plans for the program to include biometric information, thereby making identity theft more difficult.

The REAL ID Act was enacted by Congress in 2005, and it called for state identification (ID), in particular driver's licenses, documents to meet certain federal standards recommended by the 9/11 Commission and the American Motor Vehicle Administrators. The act was an attempt to address ID weaknesses in the aftermath of the 9/11 terrorist attacks. REAL ID is the closest the government has come to creating a national ID card, but it is not currently tied to employment verification.

This debate is part of a larger question about focusing enforcement at the worksite, as opposed to the border. There is widespread understanding that as long as illegal immigrants can find employment once they are inside the country, they will continue to come. If, on the other hand, immigrants doubted their ability to find a job if they are in the country illegally, this doubt would take a great deal of pressure off of the border.

The 1986 Immigration Reform and Control Act (IRCA), for the first time, made it illegal to "knowingly" hire an illegal immigrant. Employers are required by IRCA to complete an I-9 form for all new hires. The I-9 requires documents to (a) establish a person's identity, and (b) establish their authorization to work. Some documents (a passport, for example) meet both requirements. In other cases the job applicant has to provide two documents to meet both requirements. Many of these documents are easily forged, so employers can comply with the law and still hire illegal immigrants. The use of forged documents became widespread after IRCA.

A secure ID card is an attempt to fix this problem so that employers can more reliably know that a new hire is in the country legally and authorized to work. But it immediately raises the specter of a "national ID card," which many civil libertarians deeply object to as a federal intrusion into state governance.

In the Point essay, James Edwards argues that E-Verify and the REAL ID Act have made great strides in achieving a reliable, secure way to confirm someone's identity and authorization to work in the United States. They have, Edwards maintains, effectively addressed the problems of, among other things, employer accountability, ID falsification, identity theft, and IRCA's I-9 system, which has suffered from loopholes easily exploited by illegal aliens and unscrupulous employers. These programs have proven reliable and cost-effective, and they have delivered tangible results.

In the Counterpoint essay, Lillie Coney presents a libertarian argument against the drift toward acceptance of a national ID card. National identification systems, she argues, have far more often been abused than used for the benefit of societies, as evidenced by such programs in South Africa, the former Soviet Union, and elsewhere. Coney argues that we must be constantly vigilant against the potential for such abuses in the United States, paying close attention to the rationalizations for the need to track or monitor private citizens. Security and privacy, she argues, are not incompatible, as privacy and civil liberties can assure greater security by promoting transparency, accountability, and oversight over those government and private entities that promote and control the use of a national ID.

In reading the debate, consider Benjamin Franklin's famous quote, "They who can give up essential liberty to obtain a little temporary safety, deserve neither liberty nor safety." Does that sentiment apply to a debate on the overlapping topics of immigration, Americans' economic security, and identity authentication? Is the optimum balance between security and privacy different when the issue of immigration intersects with the issue of terrorism?

POINT

An overriding concern about immigration is its impact on citizens' economic well-being, particularly the effect immigrants have upon labor markets. Since the nation's founding, there has been widespread support for the principle that immigrants should be economically self-sufficient, contribute positively toward the nation's economic goals, and cause no economic dislocation to the nation's citizens. Concerns about job competition, the possibility of depressed wages, and other negative impacts of immigration are widely held with regard to legal immigrants. These concerns are greatly magnified in the face of illegal immigration and raise the question of how to eliminate access to jobs in the United States as a way of reducing the incentives for illegal immigration.

This essay examines the history of attempts to reduce the hiring of illegal immigrants through the use of common documents, and it describes how U.S. policy has moved toward achieving a reliable, secure way to confirm someone's identity and U.S. work authorization. It focuses on employer sanctions and two initiatives relating to ID documents and verification of identity: the E-Verify program and the REAL ID Act.

BACKGROUND

The United States has a vibrant economy that typically rebounds quickly from economic downturns. It has created jobs at a more dynamic rate than other countries, with jobs that tend to pay better than those in many countries. In addition, the U.S. standard of living is higher than that of many other nations. High per-capita income, a larger middle class, and other measures of economic success are all distinguishing features of the U.S. economy.

While the U.S. economy has generally expanded and created jobs over time, the American labor market is less regulated than those of other wealthy countries. Nonetheless, U.S. laws do regulate who may work in the country. For example, child labor laws protect young Americans from exploitation; otherwise, children could face 12-hour days 6 or 7 days a week, toiling under grueling or dangerous conditions, as was once the case. Most temporary foreign visitors, such as students or tourists, may not lawfully seek employment in the United States. The terms of their visas disallow it. Lawfully eligible aliens receive a U.S.-issued employment authorization permit, and U.S. citizens over 16 may, of course, look for a job.

A number of factors have combined to lower the cost and risks of illegally migrating to the United States. Proximity to the United States, with the steady improvement and affordability of telecommunications, transportation, and other "modern conveniences," has increased knowledge of and the viability of illegally migrating from Latin American and other nations, where income is vastly unequal, corruption is endemic, and the standard of living lags behind America's. Thus, the prospect of finding a job in the United States that pays significantly more than one might earn in one's home country becomes a great attraction. The reality may be harsher than the myths that lure people to the United States, however. Migrants find significantly higher costs of living and the challenges of overcoming large distances between where they can afford to live and where they can find work.

Employers are legally responsible for verifying the employment eligibility of new hires. This is easier in a smaller community, where the person applying for a position is often known to the employer. In large cities and large companies, however, most employment situations do not lend themselves to an informal trust model.

Over time, state and federal laws have required an expanded role for employers in enacting labor laws, such as the deductions and filings relating to taxation for each worker and verification of each worker's identity. The decades following the 1950s have seen a growing employer role in worker eligibility verification as Congress has quadrupled legal immigration levels from those of the early 1960s. Meanwhile, laws that prohibit employment discrimination on the basis of race, ethnicity, and national origin have also been enacted. These civil rights laws combine with an expanding segment of job seekers who are themselves, or whose relatives are, immigrants to create real compliance challenges for employers of all sizes across the nation. Employers may inadvertently find themselves breaching civil rights protections in trying to be diligent in verifying an employee's work eligibility or identity. Thus, the need has grown for reliable mechanisms that employers can use to verify, in a nondiscriminatory manner, new workers' identity and employment eligibility.

Identification documents in the United States range from certain federally issued documentation, primarily a Social Security number and card, to state-issued documents, such as a birth certificate and a driver's license. A birth certificate and Social Security card have been referred to as "breeder documents," because they serve as the basis for obtaining other forms of ID such as a driver's license or for entering into contracts such as a mortgage or opening a bank account. For lawful aliens, valid IDs in the United States include a visa, home-country-issued passport, or U.S.-issued employment authorization permit. A number of these various forms of ID serve as accepted identification for other purposes, as well.

For illegal immigrants, obtaining employment has required providing needed documents for the I-9 form, and document fraud has posed a challenge since enactment of the Immigration Reform and Control Act (IRCA) in 1986. Further, the growth of illegal immigration has added to the problem of identity fraud. High incidence of ID theft and fraud correlate with a large illegal alien population in a given state (Mortensen, 2009). ID theft and fraud have become significant problems that cause innocent Americans to suffer tremendous grief, economic stress and even financial ruin, and they cost both individuals and the financial sector billions of dollars each year, even when the ID crime is motivated by wanting to secure a U.S. job. Mexico now issues an ID called a Matricula Consular. This card is available at U.S.-based consulates and is readily available to Mexican aliens in the United States unlawfully. Though of primary usefulness to illegal aliens, Matricula IDs may be accepted by banks to establish new accounts. The Internal Revenue Service now issues an Individual Taxpayer Identification Number (ITIN), which operates for certain foreign residents similarly to a Social Security number for citizens. However, the ITIN, too, has become subject to fraud and abuse.

Thus, a combination of factors have created challenges for verifying a person's authorization to work in the United States. These include the growth of immigration (including illegal immigration), the number of available forms of identification, the reality of identity fraud and identity theft, and the array of worksite discrimination laws through which employers must tiptoe. A further barrier is Americans' resistance to an approach taken in some countries: adoption of a national ID card. A national ID card faces deep opposition in American political culture. A single ID issued by the federal government raises the specter of federal control over people's activity and constraints on their liberty, and is thus objectionable to a people whose history rests upon ordered liberty, hard-won independence from tyrannical government, and a belief that states and localities serve as a check upon potential excesses of the federal government. In addition, Americans recognize the stark contrasts between the individual liberties of U.S. citizens and the abusive controls of totalitarian regimes ranging from Nazi Germany to Soviet Russia to Red China to Islamist Iran. Thus, a unique solution is required in the face of the legitimate need to block unauthorized foreign workers from the American workplace.

THE "JOBS MAGNET"

The term "jobs magnet" refers to the availability of employment at wages higher than similar work would provide workers in their home countries, and it is widely believed that the jobs magnet draws people from other countries to the United States, whether lawfully or unlawfully. The prospect of a relatively well-paying job entices many aliens (the legal term for noncitizens) to venture to this country illegally.

A country's immigration laws generally establish measures for regulating the inflow of foreigners. One objective of immigration laws is to serve as a check on the potentially adverse impact of immigration on domestic labor markets. The number of visas a nation issues is often specified according to certain characteristics of aliens (e.g., high-technology skills, nursing degrees), and safeguards may be established to ensure that temporary foreign workers return home when their visas expire. A legal immigration regime allows a nation an orderly flow of visitors and new residents at volumes deemed to be in the nation's best interest, and on grounds and conditions that can be enforced. Visas can be withdrawn should an individual abuse the immigration privileges afforded by the host nation.

With illegal immigration, however, aliens circumvent the normal, legal channels for entering and living within a sovereign state. In the case of illegal alien workers, the consequences may be to disadvantage citizens and disrupt the normal functioning of the labor market. For example, estimates based on Census data indicate that in 2010 between 7 million and 8 million illegal immigrants held jobs in the United States (out of an estimated 11 million total illegal foreign residents). These individuals typically compete for jobs in the same sectors as Americans with lower skill levels and at best a high school education (Camarota, 2007; Passel & Cohn, 2009). The occupations where economically vulnerable Americans and immigrants (particularly illegal aliens) vie for employment include cooks, janitors, farming, construction laborers, and grounds maintenance. Native-born unemployment and underemployment tends to be higher in these sectors, and wages tend to lag those in other sectors. Further, the presence of illegal workers, whom employers may underpay and otherwise exploit, also provides the businesses that hire them an unfair competitive advantage over those who do not employ illegal workers. Their competitors who are law-abiding may not be able to stay in business, harming the economy and consumers alike.

EMPLOYER SANCTIONS

The pivotal recommendations of the 1981 Hesburgh Commission (officially, the Select Commission on Immigration and Refugee Policy), named for Father Theodore Hesburgh, president of the University of Notre Dame, who chaired it, included the institution of employer sanctions. The commission found that both unscrupulous employers and unlawful foreign workers shouldered blame for the jobs magnet and its adverse impacts on job-seeking Americans who compete with illegal immigrants. The 1986 Immigration Reform and Control Act, which embodied the Hesburgh Commission's proposals, enacted a system intended to reduce the ability of illegal aliens to secure jobs in the United States and to hold the employers who were hiring them accountable. The new sanctions policy relied upon employers checking new hires' identification documents and workers' completion of a new federal form, the I-9.

For the first time, employers who knowingly hired illegal foreign workers faced fines and possible imprisonment. They had to check the identities of new employees and keep completed I-9 forms on file. This requirement applied to all new hires in order to diminish potential employment discrimination on account of one's race or ethnicity or national origin. Employers could not just check individuals they might suspect of being illegal immigrants, but had to gather ID information on every new employee. Employees who used false documents to obtain employment faced penalties. Thus, a new system for depriving law-skirting employers from hiring illegal workers and would-be illegal workers from obtaining U.S. jobs took effect. This policy added administration of the I-9 form and scrutinizing ID documents proffered by new employees to other employer responsibilities, such as filing federal and state tax forms.

This approach to reducing the pull of the jobs magnet as a contributor to illegal immigration rested upon a few key elements. First, employers played the central role in carrying out the process of collecting forms and checking IDs. Second, identification documents, some of which were issued by the federal government and others by states, served as verification of one's identity for employment purposes. This meant that some forms of identification, such as driver's licenses, were serving increasingly broad purposes beyond their initial intent. For instance, driver's licenses might be shown when cashing a check at a bank, checking into a hotel, or buying certain controlled products. In light of political resistance to a national ID card, building incrementally upon existing IDs and practices seemed sensible with respect to the employer sanctions regime.

The initial system was not without shortcomings. Law-abiding employers bore additional government paperwork requirements yet could not exercise diligence if some IDs looked somewhat questionable. Employers could accept any ID an employee presented from among a range of ID documents, and they could not question its validity unless the document was obviously falsified. IRCA even created a special counsel in the Justice Department to handle allegations of immigration-related employment discrimination. In most cases, I-9 forms remained in employees' files without federal authorities ever checking them—there would never be enough federal agents to audit enough workplaces to give businesses realistic expectations of facing accountability for failing to abide by this law, or to give those using forged documents realistic expectations of ever being caught. Thus, there was plenty of room for illegal aliens to obtain employment in the United States and for employers to hire them, either unwittingly or because they were inclined to do so.

ELECTRONIC VERIFICATION

"Demagnetizing" the jobs magnet has proven a sizeable challenge. Congress contemplated adding a verification component to the employer sanctions/I-9 system as well as creating a counterfeit-proof Social Security card during the IRCA debates, but ultimately these were not made part of the IRCA law. Thus, despite the establishment of an employer sanctions system that includes the possibility of prison or fines, fraudulent IDs and identity theft have made it relatively easy to evade the legal barriers against illegal alien employment.

Provisions for employer sanctions, promised border security, and mass legalization of the illegal population were the legs of the "three-legged stool" enacted with IRCA in 1986. Yet, despite what was promoted as a one-time amnesty of some 3 million illegal aliens, the illegal immigrant population replenished itself within a decade. By 1996 an estimated 5 million illegal aliens resided in the United States. The promised enforcement measures and resources did not immediately materialize, but the amnesty did go into effect, and the employer sanctions system—lacking ID verification or meaningful accountability—fell short of policymakers' promises to the American public.

Congress eventually revisited the idea of giving employers a meaningful way to verify workers' identity. The 1996 Illegal Immigration Reform and Immigrant Responsibility Act, or IIRIRA, called for pilot programs to evaluate more effective ways of verifying employment eligibility. This provision of IIRIRA was based on a recommendation of the bipartisan Commission on Immigration Reform, then chaired by Congresswoman Barbara Jordan of Texas.

Pilot projects would establish a toll-free telephone verification system and a computer-based system. Proponents noted that this would bridge the accountability gap missing from the 1986 I-9 regime. Now, an individual's information provided on the I-9 form would be confirmed against government records instead of relying solely on employers scrutinizing different forms of identification. As with the I-9, employers participating in the pilot programs would use the system to verify every new hire, not just those who might not appear to be U.S. citizens, in order to remove discretion, avoid discrimination, and ensure uniform treatment of all new workers in this respect.

E-VERIFY

The electronic verification system now known as E-Verify was developed under IIRIRA and was first known as the "Basic Pilot" program. Initially operating in a handful of states where illegal immigrants were most prevalent, private employers could participate voluntarily starting in 1997. Congress expanded Basic Pilot, by then renamed E-Verify, in 2004 to all employers nationwide for voluntary participation. Employers choosing to participate in the program can do so at no cost. Additionally, an employer who relies on an E-Verify determination with regard to an individual's eligibility for U.S. employment gains legal protections in any resulting litigation.

The program works as follows. Once a new worker is hired, an employer has three days to verify the worker's information on a Form I-9. That information is entered into an online form on a Department of Homeland Security (DHS) website. For U.S. citizens, their Social Security number, name, birth date, and citizenship are validated, usually instantaneously, against Social Security Administration records. Noncitizens' information is confirmed against Social Security and DHS immigration databases.

Most inquiries receive a reply about work authorization within 24 hours. If discrepancies in records do not allow confirmation within that time frame, businesses receive a tentative nonconfirmation (TNC). Employers double-check the accuracy of the data input, looking for such errors as misspelled names or incorrect numbers. Businesses advise employees whose verification checks generate a TNC, and employees have 10 days to rectify the situation. Many TNCs involve circumstances such as a name change that occurred since taking one's previous job, or immigration databases that are either inaccurate or not up to date. Corrected data can be resubmitted or an employee whose record is in question may be referred to the appropriate government agency to resolve the matter.

A worker who contests a TNC may not be fired while the contestation is under way. Contesting employees must be treated in the same way as workers who receive work confirmation. Eventually, either one's employment eligibility is confirmed or the agency issues a final nonconfirmation notice. Employees who do not receive employment verification and do not contest initial nonconfirmation are regarded as receiving final nonconfirmation after 10 days. At that point the employee must be dismissed.

Businesses that do not terminate a finally nonconfirmed worker must notify the Department of Homeland Security that they have retained such an employee. Failing to advise DHS of nonconfirmed workers remaining on the payroll subjects the business to fines between $500 and $1,000 per failure to notify the agency.

Independent analysis of Basic Pilot/E-Verify's performance has shown that the system is effective, and that its quality is steadily improving. A 2002 report conducted by the Institute for Survey Research, at Temple University, and Westat found that the verification program reliably identified illegal immigrants using false Social Security or immigration documents. The researchers also found that employers' usage of electronic employment verification itself deterred illegal aliens from applying for work. In the 2000s, about 1 in 10 screened workers at participating businesses were illegal aliens, according to the report. Some 64 percent of Basic Pilot/E-Verify users reported seeing a drop in illegal job applicants.

Furthermore, participating employers spoke positively about electronic verification. Ninety-six percent of employers told the independent analysts that the program effectively checks work status. Ninety-three percent of employers regarded electronic verification as easier than the I-9 process, while 92 percent reported the system was not a burden on their staff. Less than 50 percent incurred appreciable costs in beginning to use Basic Pilot/E-Verify.

A 2007 independent evaluation by Westat for DHS found improvements in E-Verify's performance, with reductions in employers' inquiry processing times. The program also had increased the accuracy of databases so there were fewer tentative nonconfirmation cases resulting from inaccurate Social Security or DHS records. For noncitizens, E-Verify now provides employers with aliens' digital photographs in their employment authorization file. DHS has scaled up the photo tool as available and is working to eliminate ID theft through the use of photos and other biometric identifiers. This photographic identification increases the accuracy of verifications and decreases the chances of an illegal alien being able to "borrow" someone else's identity or documents. A weakness of E-Verify had been its difficulty in detecting identity theft, where worker data are legitimate but are illegitimately used by another person.

The Government Accountability Office (GAO) has confirmed that E-Verify functions at a high level of accuracy (Stana, 2011). The number of TNCs fell from 8 percent in 2004–2007 to 2.6 percent in 2009. E-Verify instantly confirmed the work eligibility of 97.4 percent of the 8.2 million new hires queried in the system in 2009. Of the 2.6 percent of nonconfirmed workers (about 211,000 people), 0.3 percent contested the TNC and were later deemed eligible for U.S. employment. The remaining 2.3 percent of nonconfirmed persons who did not contest the nonconfirmation are presumably illegal aliens who attempted to gain unlawful employment.

In 2011, a DHS official told Congress that more than 246,000 employers with 850,000 locations participated in E-Verify, with 1,300 new businesses enrolling every week (Bertucci, 2011). Queries had skyrocketed from 3.27 million in fiscal year 2007 to 16.4 million in 2010. More than 98 percent of verification checks that year resulted in automatic confirmation. Independent evaluation found that employers got an accurate initial result for eligible workers more than 99 percent of the time. A 2010 customer satisfaction survey gave E-Verify an index of 82 percent out of 100, compared with the federal government's general satisfaction index of 69 percent.

According to a GAO report, from October 2009 to August 2010, employers viewed alien workers' photos using E-Verify 393,574 times. This led to 1,569 incidents of no-matches of workers by photo. Only one person contested the resulting TNC. These statistics indicate that the photo feature of E-Verify has helped to reduce identity fraud, improve accuracy, and deter ineligible employment by illegal aliens.

Thus, the E-Verify program has grown from a pilot project in 1997 to a robust, reliable system for employers nationwide to confirm someone's work authorization. Its convenience, ease of use, and added measure of certainty in workforce decisions benefits employers, lawful workers, and immigration enforcement officials.

ID DOCUMENT SECURITY

Forms of identification have steadily proliferated and come to serve numerous functions in American society. IDs must be shown in connection with one's work, entertainment, official business, and personal business. In the employment sanctions context, Congress developed a list of documents acceptable for use by newly hired employees for the Form I-9. Two of these forms of identity—the federally issued Social Security number and the state-issued driver's license—now serve functions well beyond their initial purposes. In short, proving one's identity has become a routine requirement in modern society.

The fact that many forms of identification, including those issued by the government, are subject to counterfeiting has contributed to efforts to improve document quality and security. When IRCA was being crafted in the 1980s, Congress debated how to improve the security of Social Security numbers, including ways of making Social Security cards tamperproof.

That debate was repeated during enactment of the 1996 immigration law, when Congress considered mechanisms for rendering Social Security cards and immigration-related documents resistant to counterfeiting. At that time, differing standards for state-issued documents—principally the driver's license and birth certificate—were recognized as contributing to fraud and abuse in that these state documents plus a Social Security card that appeared legitimate could facilitate many kinds of crimes, including immigration and employment deceptions and identity theft and fraud. Thus, improving document security without creating a national ID card was an integral part of debates over immigration and employment verification.

IIRIRA's passage in 1996 directed the creation of federal standards for driver's licenses and birth certificates, although each state retained flexibility in designing these documents. The law required states either to put an individual's Social Security number on his or her driver's license or to check the validity of the number before issuing someone a license. It also created a grant fund to help states meet the costs of compliance to IIRIRA. After IIRIRA was passed, various legal challenges and legislative counteraction prevented enactment of the law's federal standards provisions.

Yet document fraud has long been a criminal activity, and its connection to gaining employment as an illegal alien has steadily risen. ID fraud, identity theft, counterfeit document production, and similar crimes have facilitated illegal immigration, financial crimes, and other illicit behavior, including perjury on the Form I-9's attestation of employment eligibility. One form of identity crime has enabled illegal aliens to establish a seemingly valid identity (Mortensen, 2009). Supplied with "breeder documents," illegal aliens obtain access to other legitimizing documentation and to obtaining employment. Such employment-connected identification may involve a fabricated identity, a stolen identity, an identity shared with someone else (or many others), or some combination thereof.

REAL ID

The terrorist attacks on the United States that occurred on September 11, 2001, were a catalyst for addressing identity document security. The 9/11 Commission investigated how the perpetrators carried out their plot (Eldridge et al., 2004; National Commission, 2004). The commission reported that all except one of the September 11 hijackers had obtained U.S. IDs. The 19 terrorists had about 30 forms of ID among them, including 17 American driver's licenses and 13 state-issued identification cards. They exploited loopholes in the ID issuance process and in some instances committed fraud to obtain them. Their American IDs allowed them to board airplanes, rent automobiles, and otherwise present a seemingly legitimate presence in the United States. The reality that domestic ID documents enabled foreign terrorists to execute an act of aggression on American soil against innocent civilians created widespread support for addressing the problem of ID weaknesses.

In 2004, the 9/11 Commission recommended federal standards for identification documents, including driver's licenses. The official report also called for tighter standards for issuing IDs, in order to ensure that applicants are who they purport to be and to verify ID applicants' true identity. In 2005, Congress passed the REAL ID Act, which enacted provisions of the 1996 immigration reform law relevant to government-issued IDs.

The REAL ID Act called for state ID documents to meet certain federal standards. Those standards followed the 9/11 Commission's recommendations, as well as those of the American Association of Motor Vehicle Administrators. The law left driver's license and other state-issued ID standards up to each state; however, if a state did not comply with REAL ID, that state's IDs would not be acceptable for federal purposes. For example, the bearer of a driver's license out of compliance with REAL ID standards would not be able to enter a federal building or board a federally regulated airline flight.

This law includes a number of provisions. Each REAL ID–qualified ID card must have the bearer's full name, birth date, sex, address, driver's license or ID number, signature, and a photograph; birth records must be digitized; information submitted when applying for a license must be authenticated. For aliens on temporary visas, a license must be set to expire when the visa length of stay is over. REAL ID–qualified cards must contain certain tamper-resistant security features. State licensing agencies must verify that an applicant does not hold licenses in other states. This verification uses a REAL ID–required network of state records. States must develop security plans detailing how they will meet the law's security and privacy requirements. States may seek funds under a federal grant program in order to defray the implementation costs.

In spite of delays won by opponents of REAL ID, states have progressed toward REAL ID compliance. Groups such as the National Governors Association (2006) have claimed implementation would run to $1 billion or more. However, for all states together the total costs appeared closer to between $350 million and $750 million. By 2011, some 11 states had fully complied with REAL ID standards, while more than 40 states had demonstrated they were within reach of meeting the legal requirements (Kephart, 2011).

Opponents have continued to level charges against the REAL ID Act. However, proponents point out that REAL ID is not an unfunded federal mandate. Federal funds are available to offset compliance costs. Further, states are free to choose not to meet the law's standards. However, there are consequences for their residents who try to use their state's noncompliant IDs for federal purposes.

The REAL ID Act did not create a national ID card. Rather, this law established minimum standards for IDs and their issuance. No federal database was created, and no federal ID was established. Individual privacy was not compromised. A requirement called for states' driver's license and birth certificate records systems to be able to cross-check information. However, the information remains in state control, and no communication is made with the federal government, other than to verify federal records, such as Social Security numbers or immigrant records. However, even then the data are not aggregated.

However, the REAL ID Act has injected accountability into the ID process by requiring verification as part of the process, thus weeding out false identity claims. It has improved the quality, security, and authenticity of basic forms of identification. It has left the states' central role intact while achieving a national goal of security where IDs are concerned. It has protected individuals from being victimized by identity theft and fraud, while leaving their privacy and personal confidentiality intact.

CONCLUSION

Securing American jobs just for lawful workers has presented a challenge. As U.S. employers have faced a larger role in achieving this goal of a lawful workforce, their role has been made easier with the addition of new tools and better IDs. The problems with employer sanctions before E-Verify and REAL ID involved the lack of employers' accountability, unworkable restrictions on employers' scrutinizing the documents presented by workers and the ease of falsifying IDs or fraudulently obtaining these documents. The fake ID industry enabled a rise in identity theft and identity fraud, leaving many Americans victimized by such crimes. IRCA's I-9 system has suffered from loopholes easily exploited by illegal aliens and unscrupulous employers.

E-Verify has proven to be highly reliable and cost-effective. This verification system is easy for employers to use, and it takes the guesswork out of employment eligibility and document checking. The program has reduced the number of illegal aliens seeking jobs where E-Verify is used, and has singled out the majority of illegal foreign workers trying to sneak through the process. The program has caused minimal harm to U.S. citizens, as it allows anyone the system does not instantly confirm to keep his or her job while contesting a nonconfirmation. The high satisfaction ratings participants have given E-Verify could serve as a model for other government programs.

REAL ID is tangibly raising the level of security and authenticity of the most commonly used forms of identification in the United States. The law's requirements will make IDs used in connection with employment, including for employment eligibility verification, less vulnerable to fraud and abuse. All states now verify the Social Security numbers of ID applicants. By 2011, all but two states checked driver's license applicants' legal presence.

Together, E-Verify and REAL ID give employers a reliable means of verifying new employees' identity and eligibility to work in the United States. These programs already appear to have begun demagnetizing the jobs magnet. The legitimate workers and employers in America are the ultimate beneficiaries of this new, better paradigm of secure IDs.

More can be done. Congress should consider allowing employers greater discretion to question IDs they suspect of being fraudulent, without facing the hammer of the Justice Department's special counsel's office. When nearly all states have complied with the REAL ID standards for identification documents, only REAL ID–compliant IDs should be acceptable with I-9s. Federal prosecutors should take I-9 felonies tied to worker attestation seriously and take up those cases. Congress should make E-Verify usage mandatory for all U.S. employers, including those using subcontractors or day laborers in employment sectors having a disproportionate share of illegal aliens in their workforces.

REFERENCES AND FURTHER READING

Bertucci, T. C. (2011, February 10). *E-Verify: Preserving jobs for American workers* (Testimony before the U.S. House Committee on the Judiciary, Subcommittee on Immigration Policy and Enforcement). Retrieved from http://judiciary.house.gov/hearings/printers/112th/112-4_64405.PDF

Borjas, G. J. (1999). *Heaven's door: Immigration policy and the American economy.* Princeton, NJ: Princeton University Press.

Borjas, G. J. (2003, November). The labor demand curve is downward sloping: Reexamining the impact of immigration on the labor market. *Quarterly Journal of Economics, 118*(4), 1335–1374.

Camarota, S. A. (2007, November). *Immigrants in the United States, 2007: A profile of America's foreign-born population* [Backgrounder]. Retrieved from Center for Immigration Studies website: http://www.cis.org/immigrants_profile_2007

Eldridge, T. R., Ginsburg, S., Hempel, W. T., II, Kephart, J. L., Moore, K., Accolla, J. M., & Falk, A. (2004, August 21). *9/11 and terrorist travel: A staff report of the National Commission on Terrorist Attacks Upon the United States.* Franklin, TN: Hillsboro Press.

Gimpel, J, G., & Edwards, J. R., Jr. (1999). *The congressional politics of immigration reform.* Needham Heights, MA: Allyn & Bacon.

Hoefer, M., Rytina, N., & Baker, B. C. (2011, February). *Estimates of the unauthorized immigrant population residing in the United States: January 2010.* Retrieved from Office of Immigration Statistics, U.S. Department of Homeland Security website: http://www.dhs.gov/xlibrary/assets/statistics/publications/ois_ill_pe_2010.pdf

Institute for Survey Research, Temple University, & Westat. (2002, January 29). *INS Basic Pilot evaluation: summary report* (Report submitted to U.S. Department of Justice). Retrieved from http://www.essentialestrogen.com/pdf/temple_westat_2002_eval_basic_pilot.pdf

Kephart, J. L. (2007, February). *Identity and security: Moving beyond the 9/11 staff report on identity document security.* Retrieved from Center for Immigration Studies website: http://www.cis.org/articles/2011/REAL-ID-White-Paper-FINALv2.pdf

Kephart, J. L. (2009, June). *Repealing REAL ID? Rolling back driver's license security* [Backgrounder]. Retrieved from Center for Immigration Studies website: http://www.cis.org/realid

Kephart, J. L. (2011, January). *REAL ID implementation: Less expensive, doable, and helpful in reducing fraud* [Backgrounder]. Retrieved from Center for Immigration Studies website: http://cis.org/real-id

Mortensen, R. W. (2009, June). *Illegal, but not undocumented: Identity theft, document fraud, and illegal employment* [Backgrounder]. Retrieved from Center for Immigration Studies website: http://www.cis.org/IdentityTheft

National Commission on Terrorist Attacks Upon the United States. (2004, July 22). *The 9/11 Commission Report.* Washington, DC: U.S. Government Printing Office. Retrieved from http://www.9-11commission.gov/report/index.htm

National Governors Association, National Conference of State Legislatures, & American Association of Motor Vehicle Administrators. (2006, September). *The REAL ID Act: National impact analysis.* Retrieved from http://www.ncsl.org/print/statefed/Real_ID_Impact_Report_FINAL_Sept19.pdf

Passel, J. S., & Cohn, D. (2009, April 14). *A portrait of unauthorized immigrants in the United States.* Retrieved from Pew Hispanic Center website: http://www.pewhispanic.org/2009/04/14/a-portrait-of-unauthorized-immigrants-in-the-united-states

Select Commission on Immigration and Refugee Policy. (1981). *Immigration policy and the national interest: The final report and recommendations of the Select Commission on Immigration and Refugee Policy.* Washington, DC: U.S. Government Printing Office.

Stana, R. M. (2011, February 10). *Employment verification: Federal agencies have improved E-Verify, but significant challenges remain* (Testimony before the U.S. House Committee on the Judiciary Subcommittee on Immigration Policy and Enforcement). Retrieved from http://www.gao.gov/assets/130/125481.pdf

U.S. Commission on Immigration Reform. (1994). *Immigration policy: Restoring credibility.* Washington DC: U.S. Government Printing Office.

Westat. (2007, September). *Findings of the Web Basic Pilot Evaluation* (Report submitted to U.S. Department of Homeland Security). Retrieved from http://www.uscis.gov/files/article/WebBasicPilotRprtSept2007.pdf

James R. Edwards, Jr.

COUNTERPOINT

A "secure" ID card was proposed as a response to September 11, 2011, but the terrorist attack was not the sole inspiration for the development of a national ID document. It is true that the climate regarding proof of identity changed dramatically after 9/11. However, the George W. Bush administration resisted calls for a national ID card until conflict occurred with Republican congressional leadership over language in the Intelligence Reform and Terrorism Prevention Act of 2004. The compromise bill that passed the House on December 7, 2004, allowed states the discretion to issue driver's licenses to undocumented persons. The House Republican leadership fought to keep language in the final bill that would ban the issuance of driver's licenses to noncitizens, but they lost that fight.

As reported in *The Washington Post* on January 28, 2005, the House Republican leadership was not completely pleased with the compromise version of the bill. Key members of the House Republican majority felt they could not vote in support of the bill, while those that did support it found the pro-immigration stance regarding the issuance of driver's licenses disquieting. The history of bill sponsorships for the 108th Congress on House Resolution 10 and Senate Bill 2845, as recorded by Library of Congress THOMAS system as well as, the work in the 109th Congress on House Resolution 418—the REAL ID Act—reflects how strongly the delegation felt about the unsatisfactory outcome of Senate Bill 2845, which had become Public Law 108-458.

On February 2, 2005, the *New York Sun*'s Daniela Gerson reported on some of behind-the-scenes struggle over immigration and the issuance of driver's licenses to undocumented persons. H.R. 10 was reintroduced in the 109th Congress as H.R. 418, the REAL ID Act of 2005. The REAL ID Act had over 115 original Republican sponsors, including the bill's lead sponsor and chair of the House Judiciary Committee, Representative James Sensenbrenner of Wisconsin. The REAL

ID Act included much of the language of H.R. 10, but additional specifics were added regarding unauthorized residents' ability to obtain state-issued driver's licenses. HR 418 specified that a digital photo would be stored on the document, and it removed a role for states in the development of secure driver's licenses and state-issued ID cards.

In May 2005, the REAL ID Act became law as part of a bill to address tsunami relief efforts and emergency military supplemental appropriations for the wars in Afghanistan and Iraq. The supplemental bill was a "must pass" piece of legislation, meaning the addition of the REAL ID Act would not stop its passage. It would thereby create a national ID card while avoiding debate regarding its privacy and civil liberties implications. The REAL ID Act did not have formal hearings, nor did either the House or Senate debate it prior to its becoming law. The REAL ID Act mandates that states adopt technical standards and verification procedures for all state-issued identification documents. Further, federal agencies are prohibited from accepting state-issued identification documents that do not meet the standards and verification requirements of the REAL ID Act.

HISTORY OF NATIONAL ID IN THE UNITED STATES

Unfortunately, the history of identification systems in the United States is marked by a pattern of forgery, co-option by insiders providing documents to those not permitted to hold them, theft of documents of legitimate ID holders, and modifications of documents in order to achieve a benefit or service associated with the document.

Fundamentally, identification systems are mechanisms for controlling access by a subset of the population to societal rights, privileges, benefits, or freedom of movement. Understanding the reason for a proposed identification system begins with defining the problem that the system intends to solve. Historically, various mechanisms were used to identify individuals for purposes of exclusion from rights in society on the basis of ethnicity, race, gender, and conditions of employment—such as the type of work that a person could perform, the ability to rise to higher positions, where one could work, and what wage would be paid.

By way of example, Christian Parenti, in *The Soft Cage: Surveillance in America from Slavery to the War on Terror* (2003), explains that during the colonial period, Native Americans were prevented from entering colonial territories. Indentured servants could not leave the Virginia Colony without written permission from the governor. From the late 1600s to the mid-1800s, a race-based identification system was deployed to control the movement of persons of African descent. From the late 1800s into the early 1900s, the Chinese Exclusion Act and its amendments limited the movement and immigration of persons from China. Various systems of identification were used.

From the colonial era to the industrial age, the primary forms of identification were based on three characteristics: something you *were,* something you *had,* or something you *knew.* The "something-you-are" form of identification was based on ethnicity, tribe, race, and sometimes gender. Two phenomena affected this form of identification. First, the need for "something-you-are" forms of identification changed when the size of the targeted group changed relative to the nontargeted population. Second, the effectiveness of "something-you-are" forms of identification was compromised when persons in the targeted group became indistinguishable from nontargeted persons. An example of a change in need for this type of identification occurred when the Native American population shifted as a result of their voluntary and involuntary relocations to other regions of the country and, later, their transitions from tribal communities to larger cities. These changes altered social and cultural reactions to Native Americans and reduced the perceived need for tribal identification systems. Further, while the perceived need for a Native American identification system declined in some regions of the country, it increased in those areas where indigenous persons were settled.

The effectiveness of this type of identification was undermined when indentured servants were ethnically indistinguishable from the general population, making them hard to identify if they refused to complete the conditions of their indentured servitude. In addition, the introduction of slavery as a racially unique source of cheap labor made indentured servants less cost-effective. Later, former slaves who became freed persons, either through self-emancipation or release by former owners, added another source of complexity for the identification system. The lines between freed persons and slaves were further blurred as interracial births increased and, over time, the hue of a person's skin ceased to be the only reliable factor for determining a person's heritage. All of these events combined to make the "something-you-are" form of identification inadequate as an identification system.

A "something-you-have" form of identification was first introduced in the form of a written pass system. It became popular because reading and writing were skills available only to intellectual elites and the wealthy, and it was against the law in much of the South to teach writing to slaves or persons of color. However, when writing skills became more common among the target group, the written pass was easily forged or gotten around.

According to Parenti, the written pass was replaced by tin ID tags, which were stamped with identifying information about the person wearing the tag. Freed persons of color as well as slaves were required to carry these tags. The tags were premade and recorded in city records, making then the first registered ID documents used in the United States. This system broke down when individual states banned the ownership of human beings, creating a destination for those escaping slavery. This identification system was further eroded by a significant evolution in social and cultural attitudes toward a rejection of slavery.

Finally, the "something-you-know" form of identification relies on passwords or phrases that individuals must know to obtain access to something. This has been a popular means of communicating private messages for millennia, dating to the time of Egypt's Old Kingdom. The popularity of this form of communication in the United States emerged during the American Revolution and became more popular during the Civil War.

RISKS OF IGNORING CIVIL LIBERTIES

The central concerns about the establishment and use of a government identity document revolve around the possible undermining of civil liberties. Threats to privacy include the potential for loss of individual control over personal information. Civil liberty threats include the potential for a continued expansion of the number of everyday situations requiring use of a national ID card, as well as the potential for unbounded use of state power to expand the criteria for successful acquisition of such a card. Thus, because requiring personal information encroaches on privacy, implementing a national and secure identification system has costs in privacy, civil liberties, and dollars. Recent proposals for a national ID system have focused attention on possible tradeoffs between security and privacy.

The cost to privacy is measured by the degree to which an individual's societal rights are negatively impacted by not having a specific form of identification, especially in cases where an activity or right did not formerly require proof of identity. It is possible that the conditions for obtaining identification documents will be weighted in favor of those who are better off physically or financially. For example, the right to vote without a state-issued ID in most states was not questioned until the passage of the Help America Vote Act of 2002 (P.L. 107-252). The law mandated that individuals who register to vote in a federal election for the first time had to produce one of several forms of identification to cast a ballot. New voters could provide a state or federally issued identification document, a utility bill, a bank statement, or a payroll stub—provided the document had the name and home address of the voter on it. These requirements favored people with greater financial means, and enactment of this law, as reported by the National Conference of State Legislatures, triggered a wave of states passing enhancements to voting and ID requirements that continued through 2011.

An important guard against identification document abuse is the ability to exercise discretion regarding when, where, how, and for what purpose personally identifiable information (PII) held on secure IDs is collected, retained, or used by others. The ability of individuals to exercise effective control over the circumstances in which proof of identification may be required could become more difficult as specific rights are joined to the presentation of a particular document.

The costs to civil liberties are determined by any expansion in the conditions under which a national identity document may be demanded, and by whom, as well as the consequences for noncompliance. The authority of the federal government to demand a national identity document could extend to every arena in which the government determines it serves society to do so. These might include management of monuments and parks, dealing with the U.S. Postal Service, receipt of prescription and nonprescription medication, entitlement programs such as Social Security, federally backed student loans, and assistance following natural disasters. Privacy and civil liberties are also further undermined when private sector entities mimic the actions of federal government and impose their own list of situations in which a national ID document is required to engage in a private-sector transaction. Possible examples include checking into a hotel, registering for a library card, or voting. Converting a government issued identity document from a choice to a requirement for daily living facilitates a power shift from the individual to the state.

A final area with implications for civil liberties and privacy is the power of the state to have an open-ended list of criteria that applicants must meet in order to obtain a required identity document. The potential for an ever-increasing list of barriers to successfully obtaining a national identity document would further erode individual rights and civil liberties. In addition, the federal government may allow individual states discretion in the issuance of identity documents or in altering already-issued documents to communicate that they are noncompliant or should not be accepted as a national identity document. In the case of the Help America Vote Act, states were given the power to increase voter identification requirements, and many have considerably limited the number of approved forms of identification. For example, in the state of Texas a driver's license, election identification certificate, Department of Public Safety personal ID card, U.S. military ID, U.S. citizenship certificate, U.S. passport, and a license to carry a concealed handgun issued by the Department of Public Safety are the only forms of identification that will be accepted for voting.

On June 20, 2011, *USA Today* reported that a record number of states had passed a record number of laws that require a photo ID to vote. State legislatures will ultimately have control over the training that state Department of Motor Vehicle (DMV) employees will receive regarding the issuance of driver's licenses and state ID documents. They will have the latitude to establish new requirements regarding the issuance of those documents, which could exceed the regulations established by the Department of Homeland Security. Ultimately, it is the decision of each DMV office to make, a determination regarding the acceptability of documents presented by applicants for state-issued driver's licenses. There are few assurances that each person seeking a driver's licenses or state ID document will have the same experience when either receiving a document or being rejected for receipt of a document.

SECURITY CHALLENGES WITH A SECURE ID

The more uses that are made of a single identity document, the greater its value. This, in turn makes it a target for theft, abuse, and misuse. As a consequence, the cost of producing the document increases because it will need to be made more secure to protect its associated benefits or services from fraud, waste, or abuse. Identity theft for the purpose of obtaining a service or benefit has been on the rise for several years, with instances of medical identity theft and theft of IRS tax return funds being just two examples. The more trust there is in a form of identification, the less likely it is that systems that are in place to catch fraud will take into consideration the possible breaching of the security of an identity document.

In *Beyond Fear* (2003), Bruce Schneier argues that the cost in dollars to taxpayers, document users, and the commercial sector can be unbounded, because the cost of addressing forgery, compromise, or abuse of a specific type of document cannot be fully calculated before any of the documents are issued. There is always the possibility that a "secure" ID document will not be as secure as advertised. The fundamental problem with issuing "secure" ID documents to about 150 million potential users is the security of that document once it is issued. There are real-world problems that occur when secure IDs are lost, stolen, or damaged, which can compromise the "security" of the identification document. Schneier describes this as the "bank vault problem." A bank vault is not really designed to prevent break-ins; instead, it is designed to take a minimum of 72 or more hours to breach. This is because a bank, by law, can only be closed for 3 consecutive days. This means that to protect the contents of the bank vault, it is important that thieves are not given enough time to break in and escape.

For this reason, security calculations are based on a threshold. A number of questions must be addressed: What is a level of acceptable risk for what is being protected? How secure will the ID be? Are the goals to create a secure ID that is completely impossible to forge, requiring a great deal of specialized equipment and expertise to make, and therefore to forge; or that is reliant upon screening systems designed to catch forgeries, such as "smart ID readers"? There are costs associated with the real-world problem of what happens if a forgery is successful. Does the government recall all secure IDs, apply a fix of some type to "secure" the IDs, deploy new technology or techniques to catch forgeries that exploit the vulnerability, or none of the above? Each decision regarding the purpose, design, and use of a secure ID can lower security while lowering the cost of issuance, but also raise the cost of post-issuance failures of the ID to remain secure. An increase in security for an ID will not protect against all threats, because they cannot all be known, but it can offer a measure of protection against certain threats, while also raising costs related to issuance and management. It is, of course, impossible to have a 100 percent secure ID.

In other words, the way to think about security is not in absolute terms, but in degrees or probabilities of success in preventing a particular negative outcome. Wisdom regarding security claims is found in listening for those that promise the impossible: absolute security.

WHAT IS PRIVACY?

The right to privacy is defined by the degree to which an individual has control over when, why, and how another may collect, retain, or use "personally identifiable information" (PII), as well as who may do so. Privacy is a foundation upon which other fundamental rights rest, such as freedom of religion, freedom of association, political beliefs, ownership rights, location privacy, family privacy, and freedom of expression.

A legal and policy framework for privacy originated in the United States with an 1890 *Harvard Law Review* article by Samuel Warren and Louis Brandeis titled, "The Right to Privacy." The article, which successfully argued for the concept of a legal right of privacy, captured the attention of legal scholars, legislators, and the public. According to *Privacy and Human Rights 2006: An International Survey of Privacy Laws and Developments,* a report by the Electronic Privacy Information Center, this work has been cited and debated for over a century, and it has guided the establishment of laws not only in the United States but around the world. Central to the right to privacy is the right and ability to control one's personal information, often referred to as PII.

"Personally identifiable information" (PII) encompasses information about who one is, what one has, where one lives, what one believes, and what one knows. PII may include one's name, addresse, Social Security number, date of birth, mother's maiden name, home town, high school, birthmarks, tattoos, phone number, e-mail address, biometrics such as DNA, voice identification, and photographs, as well as mundane information, such as hobbies, clubs, and favorite restaurants. It may also include more intimate details of one's life, including medical conditions, phobias, fears, personal relationships, conversations, worries, musings, words spoken in frustration or joy, fantasies, hopes, and dreams.

All of the PII from a single lifetime can include millions of details that no one person could recall, but the power of technology to record and replay this information can be abused. For example, a photo may suggest that a person has consumed too much alcohol—but is that interpretation of the photo accurate? What was the context of the photo: was it taken in college at a dorm party, or just before a medical procedure? Depending on how the image is interpreted, it could damage a person's ability to get a job, retain a job, obtain a promotion, retain respect among colleagues, or gain trust from those seeking one's services.

In *Privacy on the Line* (2007), Whitfield Diffie and Susan Landau note that the arrival of the "digital information age" was accompanied by a much-needed expansion of the definition of privacy. During the 1960s and 1970s, interest in the protection of privacy rights increased with the arrival of the information technology revolution. Congress and many state legislatures acted proactively to address the real threats posed by powerful computer systems.

Computers greatly enhanced the capability of government agencies to collect PII and to search, sort, and retrieve records maintained by government agencies. The Federal Privacy Act, the Freedom of Information Act, updates to the Fair Credit Reporting Act, and new laws like the Family Educational Rights and Privacy Act combined to strengthen privacy protections in several ways. They established the right of citizens to be free from government abuse and misuse of personal information, and they provided protection from credit reporting agencies by requiring that consumers have the right to access credit reports and to correct errors.

Today, computing coupled with telecommunication systems can mean that millions of details of a person's life, from before birth until death, can be recorded, stored, reviewed, analyzed, or judged by nearly anyone. Birthdays, holidays, school events, family vacations, graduations, first cars, play, rest, and intimate moments can be captured and filed away, and include information about where you were, who you were with, what you were doing, and for what reason. And this can be done not just by you, but by friends, acquaintances, and even strangers. The market for this data is hidden from consumers, but the consequences can include forgone employment, education, and other opportunities.

Privacy is not explicitly mentioned in the U.S. Constitution or its amendments. However, legal decisions by the Supreme Court have found privacy to be a living part of the Constitution. For the purpose of this Counterpoint essay, only the right of privacy found in the First and Fourth Amendments will be addressed. The First Amendment protects the freedoms of speech, assembly, and religion. The Fourth Amendment protects Americans' right "to be secure in their persons, houses, papers, and effects, against unreasonable search and seizures."

Key to privacy protection are laws, policies, and rules that protect PII. These are called fair information practices, or FIPs. FIPs comprise a list of conditions that must be met when PII is collected, retained, or used. The most basic list was developed as part of a 1973 report produced by the U.S. Department of Health, Education and Welfare. This Code of Fair Information Practices includes the following principles:

- There must be no personal data record-keeping systems whose very existence are secret.

- There must be a way for a person to find out what information about that person is in a record and how it is used.

- There must be a way for a person to prevent information about that person that was obtained for one purpose from being used or made available for other purposes without the person's consent.

- There must be a way for a person to correct or amend a record of identifiable information about the person.

Any organization creating, maintaining, using, or disseminating records of identifiable personal data must ensure the reliability of the data for it intended use and must take precautions to prevent misuses of the data.

WHAT ARE CIVIL LIBERTIES?

Civil liberties are the privileges enjoyed by members of a society based on a set of enumerated laws. In the United States, civil liberties are defined by the nation's Constitution and the Bill of Rights. Although the Bill of Rights guarantees individuals many rights and privileges, society does reserve authority to limit the time, location, or conditions under which these rights may be exercised.

The Fourth Amendment protects "the right of people to be secure in their persons, houses, papers, and effects, against unreasonable searches and seizures." This right is very important in the context of a national ID document. A National ID, in fact, is the equivalent of a person's papers. The history of U.S. law in this area sets a high standard for when a person may be asked for their identification. Prior to September 11, 2001, there were only a handful of exceptions to this high standard. These included purchasing alcohol and tobacco, or matters related to the operation of a motor vehicle. Since September 11, 2001, details of the attackers ability to function in society centered on the issuance of state IDs. The 9/11 Commission recommended increased security for state-issued Ids, but recognizing the potential threats to privacy and civil liberties, it rejected the creation of a national identity document.

CIVIL LIBERTIES AND NATIONAL IDENTITY DOCUMENTS

As stated above, the costs to civil liberties of identity documents are measured by the conditions under which that document may be demanded, and by whom, as well as by the consequences for noncompliance. Another way that civil liberties can be affected is through the potential for an ever-expanding list of purposes for which the document may be required. People currently need IDs to board a commercial flight, ride an Amtrak train, or enter a federal building. This could easily expand to include requiring an ID to use public transportation, such as city buses, commuter trains, or subways. Currently, states must establish minimum ages for alcohol consumption in order to receive federal dollars for roads and highways. It would not be too big of leap for the federal government to require the registration of E-Z Tags, or to require the use of a national identify document, for a state to receive certain federal funds related to highway construction.

The federal government's theoretical right to demand a national identity document includes every function it serves in society, including the management of monuments, parks, and the Postal Service; benefits programs like Social Security; and the provision of federally backed student loans or assistance before or during disasters. The power to demand a national identity document could become a requirement for applying for or retaining employment under E-Verify, a rapidly expanding government-operated employment eligibility program.

An ever-increasing list of barriers to successfully obtaining a national identity document further erodes individual rights and civil liberties. In addition, the federal government may dictate to states the discretion to deny the issuance of an identity document, or to alter the document in order to communicate that it is noncompliant or should not be accepted as a national identity document. This can be more burdensome than actually not receiving a document, because on its face it carries the equivalent of the "scarlet letter." In commercial exchanges, identification is required for transactions such as purchasing alcohol or tobacco, as well as purchasing tickets for certain movies (those rated NC-17). It is not difficult to imagine that merchants might be unwilling to accept such a document. States may also follow the lead of the federal government and pass laws that prohibit persons with a federal noncompliant ID from engaging in a host of activities. Public and private records could make note of the person's ID status, which in turn could have implications for access to housing, getting loans, or accessing any number of private opportunities. Neither private- nor public-sector entities would be barred from sharing information regarding the ID status of individuals. By spreading the notice of a deficiency regarding its use for federal matters, there may also be detrimental outcomes for nonfederal use.

A final consideration of the civil liberties implications of a national identity document is the reality that, over time, there would be diminished resistance to the requirement for such a document. Identity states of the past, including apartheid-era South Africa and former Soviet bloc countries, succeeded in operating identity management and control systems for their populations by making their use routine. Public cooperation in this very essential aspect of a police state is fundamental to creating urgency regarding the papers a person has and making sure they are present when in public. The existence of status levels in the type of papers issued, and thus what people could expect regarding treatment based on the document, also nurtures human desires to be seen as someone special. When expectations for presenting identification documents shift from unexpected to something that is not questioned, a critical shift occurs in the power of the individual and the power of the state. Another aspect of a "your papers please" society involves the consequences for those who do question the practice, which could include public suspicion, censure, or fines. "They only want to keep us safe," and "If you have nothing to hide you have nothing to fear," are two of the routine replies from codependent enablers of the identity state.

REAL ID AND CIVIL LIBERTIES

National identification systems can be designed based on how they will be used, which will be decided by society, the government, and businesses. These decisions may be made for a variety of purposes, which may or may not support the need for a more "secure" ID.

The passage of the REAL ID Act gave the federal government increased control over who is and, more importantly, who is not eligible to receive a state-issued identification document. Prior to the REAL ID law, the Intelligence Reform Act of 2004 created a process to develop secure driver's licenses, which included state participation in the planning process.

The major difference between the approaches found in the REAL ID Act and the Intelligence Reform Act is the role that the states play in the design and implementation of the new identity document. The Intelligence Reform Act included a role for states in the planning process for a new, more secure ID. The REAL ID Act removed the states from this decision-making process. The Department of Homeland Security had a role in both bills regarding developing guidance to states on the security features for a secure ID. However, REAL ID greatly enhanced the agency's ability to dictate to the states. This expanded authority included design requirements for driver's licenses, documents required from applicants, collection and retention of copies of primary documents provided by applicants as proof of identity, obligations to retain those documents in electronic form for a number of years, and provision of remote access to federal government agencies and state identification databases.

The first rule for privacy and civil liberties protection is that the collection, retention, and use of personal information establishes the right of individuals to control when, where, and why they provide PII to another entity. The collection of PII should be for an enumerated purpose, and its use should be limited to that purpose. The power to exercise autonomy as it relates to personal information is a fundamental test of a free society.

The establishment of a national identity document erodes PII autonomy in three ways. First, increased federal requirements for government-issued photo identification documents will, over time, decrease the number and type of acceptable documents. Second, these requirements will increase the demands on citizens who seek to obtain such a document. Third, state, local, and private entities will follow the federal government's lead by establishing conditions and circumstances under which the federally sanctioned identification document will be required. Ultimately, civil liberties will be curtailed for no other reason than failing to possess a REAL ID or national identity document. (The Identity Project's "Papers Please: A Real Story about REAL ID," provides a good example.)

Federal government agencies such as the U.S. Postal Service, Social Security Administration, Internal Revenue Service, and Department of Veterans Affairs maintain databases containing millions of PII records that are protected by the Federal Privacy Act. REAL ID, when fully operational, will create a new database in every jurisdiction that issues state IDs.

The reaction to the REAL ID process has been very negative, with 19 states passing some form of legislation opting out of participation. Further, there are serious doubts regarding the feasibility of developing the system in a way that protects civil liberties. The final rule for REAL ID allows private entities to create new databases using the information stored on the "machine readable zone of the card." By swiping the card in a reader, the information stored would be transferred to the computer connected to the secure ID card reader.

Commercial establishments that routinely request driver's licenses for identification are going one step further by collecting information stored on the magnetic strip on the back of the card. This is, in fact, a collection of PII that was initially collected in order to issue the driver's license, but under the conditions of a retail purchase this would be a privacy violation. This form of collecting PII is not equivalent to asking a customer under a required statue to present a driver's license or state-issued identification card to verify the age of a customer prior to completing a sale of alcohol or tobacco. One swipe of a driver's license will allow the collection of a set of PII that can be added to a database.

Private and public databases, if held in secret, can cause problems for data subjects. Secret databases are nearly impossible for the data subject to amend or correct, because one has no way of knowing that they even exist. There are some government databases that are known such as the Terrorist Center Screening Database, but an individual does not have the right to know whether he or she is in one of them.

In 2011, the Wegmans grocery store chain provided an example of the privacy and security problems associated with the implementation of REAL ID in how it issued loyalty cards at a new store in Abingdon, Maryland. Customers were asked for their state-issued driver's licenses or identity cards so that they could be swiped and the data on the cards' magnetic strip accessed. The data from the cards was used to fill in the data on the e-form for the store's loyalty card. The store now has a copy of the data on each person's driver's license, creating a point of vulnerability for the security of these documents.

This type of data collection violates the first privacy rule of FIPs: No secret databases. The data collected must be for the stated purpose of the collection. The Wegmans case brings up a number of questions. First, what is collected and what is actually needed in order to issue a loyalty card to a customer? Second, how much of the driver's license information is retained by the store, and for how long? Third, what is the information used for, and can the customer know or have access to information regarding those uses? Unfortunately, the Drivers Privacy Protection Act of 1994 does not protect the driver's license information collected by Wegmans, because the data did not come from the DMV, but was voluntarily given to the store by the holder of the document. Questions can be raised regarding whether holders of Maryland state-issued identification documents understand that the information on the card is not protected, and whether they know what the consequence of allowing others to swipe the card to collect or read the data might be.

THE COMPLEXITY OF IMPLEMENTING REAL ID

The REAL ID Act requires each state, tribal authority, and territory to restructure how they approve and issue driver's license and identification cards. Each state's Department of Motor Vehicles (DMV) must collect proof of lawful residence, either by obtaining an original version of a birth certificate with the state seal or, in cases of persons born abroad, an official record of their birth, naturalization documents, visas, or other records that establish lawful residence. The DMV may collect the documents and return them later by mail. This requirement presents challenges to obtaining birth records that raise the cost of getting a state-issued identification document. It also presents problems for persons who provide the only means of proving lawful presence in the country to state DMV staff. DMV's are required to retain copies of the documents for up to 5 years or more. This creates an additional security burden for state DMVs, which will have to safeguard that data from internal misuse, abuse, or external theft.

Meanwhile, states are required to provide remote access to their DMV records. This opens the door to the types of security threats now faced by large institutions with information warehouses containing less valuable data. The cost to states for creating interoperable databases and facilitating remote access means that each DMV becomes a point of vulnerability for all state DMV databases. A thief would only need to breach one system to potentially gain access to others.

As part of the REAL ID Act, "the Department of Homeland Security is establishing minimum standards for State-issued driver's licenses and identification cards that Federal agencies would accept for official purposes on or after May 11, 2008, in accordance with the REAL ID Act of 2005." Further, the REAL ID law "prohibits Federal agencies . . . from accepting a driver's license or personal identification card for any official purpose unless the license or card has been issued by a

State that is meeting the requirements set forth in the Act." The original date for compliance with this provision of the act was September 2009, but the Department of Homeland Security extended this to January 15, 2013, as of March 7, 2011.

CONCLUSION

National identification systems are neither cheap nor easy to deploy. Any promotion of a national ID document that is rationalized by a need to control, track, or monitor the activities of a minority group for the purpose of increasing security for the overall society should be scrutinized. National ID systems fail because the methods of creating them rest on existing identity systems that are not typically about security, but rather about a particular person's competence in something such as operating a vehicle or being a member of a trained profession, such as a doctor, lawyer, accountant, or dentist.

Security and privacy are not incompatible, but if the method that defines greater security is linked to diminishing privacy or civil liberties, then one is equated with the other. Privacy and civil liberties can assure greater security by creating transparency, accountability, and oversight over those government and private entities that promote and control the use of a national ID. This approach supports greater public education, which can better inform the debate process from the beginning. Knowledge is the key to better policymaking and an efficient use of limited taxpayer dollars by making decisions based on the facts and not shying away from admitting what can be done well and what may need greater reflection for the best outcome.

National identification systems have far more often been abused than used for the benefit of societies: South Africa, East Germany, the former Soviet Union, and Rwanda are the most recent examples of national ID systems that were abused.

A nation that wishes to deploy a national identification system should proceed with caution, promote public debate, engage in sound policymaking, and avoid actions that target a group of people within its larger population and do not address specific problems. When the problem is defined, then the range of solutions may be more cost-effective than what would otherwise have been considered.

REFERENCES AND FURTHER READING

Department of Homeland Security. (2008, January 29). Minimum standards for driver's licenses and identification cards acceptable by federal agencies for official purposes, 73 FR 5271, FR 5-08. Retrieved from http://edocket.access.gpo.gov/2008/08-140.htm

Diffie, W., & Landau, S. (2007). *Privacy on the line: The politics of wiretapping and encryption* (Updated ed.). Cambridge, MA: MIT Press.

Electronic Privacy Information Center. (n.d.). *The Drivers Privacy Protection Act (DPPA) and the privacy of your state motor vehicle record.* Retrieved from http://epic.org/privacy/drivers

Electronic Privacy Information Center. (n.d.). *National ID and the REAL ID Act.* Retrieved from https://epic.org/privacy/id_cards

Electronic Privacy Information Center. (2006). *Privacy and human rights 2006: An international survey of privacy laws and developments.* Washington, DC: Author.

Electronic Privacy Information Center. (2008, May). *REAL ID implementation review: few benefits, staggering costs: Analysis of the Department of Homeland Security's National ID Program.* Retrieved from http://epic.org/privacy/id_cards/epic_realid_0508.pdf

Finney, M. (2010, May 13). *More retailers requiring driver's license swipes.* ABC 7-KGO-TV, San Francisco. Retrieved from http://abclocal.go.com/kgo/story?section=news/7_on_your_side&id=7441118

Gerson, D. (2005, February 2). Immigration bill opponents claim it derails bush plan. *New York Sun.* Retrieved from http://www.nysun.com/national/immigration-bill-opponents-claim-it-derails-bush/8602

The Identity Project (2011, October 1). Papers please! A real story about REAL-ID [Web log post]. Retrieved from http://www.papersplease.org/wp/2011/10/01/a-real-story-about-real-id

Intelligence Reform and Terrorism Prevention Act of 2004, Pub. L. 108-458, 118 Stat. 3638. Retrieved from http://www.gpo.gov/fdsys/pkg/PLAW-108publ458/html/PLAW-108publ458.htm

National Commission on Terrorist Attacks Upon the United States. (2004, July 22). *The 9/11 Commission Report.* Washington, DC: U.S. Government Printing Office. Retrieved from http://www.9-11commission.gov/report/index.htm

National Conference of State Legislatures. (2012). *Voter identification requirements.* Retrieved from http://www.ncsl.org/default.aspx?tabid=16602#Legislation

Parenti, C. (2003). *The soft cage: Surveillance in America from slavery to the war on terror.* New York, NY: Basic Books.

REAL ID Act, Pub. L. 109-13, 119 Stat. 231, 302. (May 11, 2005). Retrieved from https://epic.org/privacy/id_cards/real_id_act.pdf

Schneier, B. (2003). *Beyond fear: Thinking sensibly about security in an uncertain world.* New York, NY: Copernicus Books.

U.S. Department of Health, Education and Welfare, Secretary's Advisory Committee on Automated Personal Data Systems. (1973, July). *Records, computers, and the rights of citizens: Report of the Secretary's Advisory Committee on automated personal data systems.* Retrieved from http://aspe.hhs.gov/datacncl/1973privacy/tocprefacemembers.htm

Warren, S., & Brandeis, L. (1890). The right to privacy. *Harvard Law Review, 4*(5), 193–220.

Lillie Coney

Worksite Enforcement

POINT: Enforcement of immigration laws at the workplace is an essential element in gaining control of illegal immigration and addressing the most significant negative effects of immigration, namely the displacement of legal workers and the deterioration of wages for those who must compete with illegal workers. Workplace enforcement is as important as securing the border itself, and policies of strict enforcement of the laws against illegal employment have been shown to be effective.

Jessica M. Vaughan, Center for Immigration Studies

COUNTERPOINT: Immigration worksite enforcement drives undocumented immigrants into the cash economy, costing taxpayers billions of dollars in lost tax revenue. This lowers the wages and degrades the working conditions of all workers, without stopping unauthorized employment.

Marielena Hincapié, National Immigration Law Center
Maura Ooi, Georgetown University Law Center

Introduction

The number of immigrants has ballooned in recent years. According to the U.S. Census Bureau, the United States saw an influx of 13 million immigrants during the first decade of the twenty-first century, the highest number of any decade in U.S. history. As a result, much attention has focused on how to curtail the flow of undocumented individuals who make up a sizeable portion of that figure. Some strategies to reduce illegal immigration focus on what might be called the "supply" side, meaning cutting off the ability of people to get across the border. Worksite enforcement, by contrast, is understood to be a "demand" side solution, in the sense that the more difficult it is to find work, the less likely it becomes that people will seek to work illegally in the United States. This chapter, by Jessica Vaughan, Marielena Hincapié, and Maura Ooi, contemplates whether or not the worksite solution is an effective response.

Several enforcement tools have been developed to be used at the worksite level. These include not only raids—a practice discussed more specifically in another chapter in this section of this book—but also methods of documenting and verifying the status of workers, such as the online system called E-Verify, a federally administered database developed in the 1990s. Despite a growing focus on worksite enforcement, however, concerns exist. Is the worksite the best place for enforcement? Or should securing the borders be the focus of the nation's policy?

This debate, to some extent, involves an empirical question about the most effective way to prevent illegal entry of immigrants to the United States. The evidence strongly suggests that border enforcement is ineffective when immigrants have strong economic incentives to enter the United States illegally. According to an analysis done by the Migration Policy Institute, the 2002 border enforcement budget for the Immigration and Naturalization Service, replaced by Immigration and Customs Enforcement (ICE) in 2003, reached $2.8 trillion. Only $458,000 was budgeted for interior investigations that same year, and only 2 percent of the interior investigation cases in 2002 were focused on the workplace. Meanwhile, according to estimates by Pew Hispanic Center, illegal immigrants were entering the country at a rate of 850,000 per year between 2000 and 2004. More recently, enforcement has continued to focus on the border under the Department of

Homeland Security (DHS). The DHS budget for Customs and Border Patrol (CBP) grew to $5.7 billion in 2010, and the ICE budget grew to $11.4 billion. While worksite enforcement by ICE has increased in recent years, it remains a small percentage of ICE's budget. In spite of the United States having spent billions of dollars on enforcement at the border, the number of undocumented immigrants in the country grew to an estimated 11.8 million in 2010.

To the extent that worksite enforcement makes it difficult for illegal immigrants to find work once they are inside the country, it reduces their incentive to enter illegally. According to Vaughan in the Point essay, following the highly publicized adoption of the E-Verify system as an enforcement tool by several states (including Arizona, Colorado, Georgia, and Oklahoma), anecdotal and indirect evidence (such as school enrollment and tenancy rates) support the claim that this type of worksite enforcement—or perhaps simply the threat thereof—helps to reduce undocumented workers in the specific locales that adopt it.

There is an important distinction, however, between unauthorized employment (of people already here) and unauthorized immigration (bringing new people in). Reducing or eliminating illegal entry is only one aspect of the consequences of worksite enforcement. It will also impact immigrants who are already inside the United States illegally. Proponents of increased worksite enforcement argue that it will help induce this population to "self-deport" themselves (to go home). However, this will depend on the extent to which illegal immigrants are embedded in American society, or on the extent to which they have American citizen spouses and children. It will also depend on whether they have opportunities in the informal economy.

There is a real concern that increased worksite enforcement will simply push illegal immigrants currently in the United States further underground, resulting in an expansion of the informal economy. As described by Hincapié and Ooi in the Counterpoint essay, the effects of expanding the informal economy are fairly deleterious; more workplaces go underground, taking more jobs for all workers with them. This can result in a deterioration of working conditions, giving unscrupulous employers more power over their workers.

Furthermore, growth in the informal economy would have significant implications for tax collections, as these kind of underground jobs are not easily taxed. One example described in the Counterpoint essay is that of Arizona, one of the states that adopted E-Verify. In 2008, the first year of the program, income tax revenue dropped by 13 percent. However, sales tax revenue dropped only by 2.3 percent for food and 6.8 percent for clothing, indicating to some analysts that undocumented workers were being absorbed into the underground economy; that is, they were still consuming, but not paying income tax.

The authors of the Counterpoint essay suggest that the best alternative to enforcement at the worksite is comprehensive immigration reform. They propose measures that are familiar to many in the reform debate, including legalizing the undocumented workers currently in the United States and strengthening the mechanisms for legal immigration in a way that supports the needs of the economy. Many analysts agree that starting from a clean state and remaking the system anew is an attractive alternative. However, many question whether this kind of approach is politically possible. Whatever the answer, the efficacy of various enforcement tools would likely be improved if they were part of an immigration system that reflected current economic realities. For many in this debate, the comprehensive answer is the holy grail.

POINT

The decade from 2000 to 2009 saw the highest levels of immigration in U.S. history. According to the U.S. Census Bureau, more than 13 million immigrants (legal and illegal) settled in the United States during that period. This was more immigration than any other 10-year period in American history, including the decade at the start of the twentieth century, and even more than in the 1990s, now the second highest decade of immigration in U.S. history. According to an analysis of Census Bureau data by Steven Camarota of the Center for Immigration Studies, about one in three immigrants is in the country unlawfully, and about half of all post-2000 immigrants are estimated to be in the country unlawfully.

Unlike previous waves of immigration, this one occurred in a decade of very little net job growth in the United States. In the 2000s, according to the Bureau of Labor Statistics, the U.S. economy experienced a net loss of about 400,000 jobs and became mired in a recession. This is in stark contrast with the situation in the 1990s, when the United States received nearly as many immigrants but the economy added about 22 million jobs.

Recent high U.S. unemployment has focused public attention on the labor market effects of illegal immigration, along with the fiscal, national security, and public safety effects that have long been of concern. While there is broad agreement that immigration laws should be enforced, there is some debate over whether the emphasis should be on border security in order to prevent illegal entry, or whether it should be on the workplace, with the emphasis on preventing employers from hiring illegal workers. The former can be called a "supply-side" approach to enforcement, while the latter focuses on employer "demand" for workers. Clearly, both approaches are necessary for effective immigration control, but experience has shown that federal efforts that are focused on the workplace and on employers will be more effective than enforcement efforts directed at the physical borders.

THE JOB MAGNET

Most observers agree that the main reason that individuals migrate to the United States is to work. There are other reasons, of course, such as joining family members, escaping oppression or violence, or to participate in criminal activity, but the principal motivation is employment.

A Pew Hispanic Center analysis based on Census data estimates that in March 2010 there were approximately 8 million illegal immigrants holding jobs in the United States. The presence of this number of illegal workers causes certain labor market distortions that have adverse effects on U.S. workers. These include an increase in the supply of unskilled labor (since most illegal immigrants are less educated than the native population), and downward pressure on the wages and working conditions of native workers and legal immigrants in those same occupations. The workers most affected are those at the bottom of the wage scale, who are already struggling to be self-sufficient.

Since the principal reason illegal aliens come to the United States is employment, and since the key effects of illegal immigration are the displacement of U.S. workers and the degradation of wages and working conditions, it makes sense that enforcement efforts should be focused at the workplace, and especially on those employers who choose to hire illegal workers over U.S. workers.

WHY NOT JUST SEAL THE BORDER?

With more than six million employers in the United States, how can authorities possibly police every workplace and hiring decision? Why not simply seal the border to prevent the illegal workers from coming? While this sounds simple, it is not.

The United States' land borders together are more than 10,000 miles long, with varied physical features and challenges, including deserts, rivers, canyons, and extreme weather conditions. Some sections run through urban centers, such as San Diego, El Paso, and Detroit, while others are in remote areas, Indian reservations, national parks, and wilderness areas. There is no one-size-fits-all infrastructure, technology, or staffing pattern of border patrol agents that can secure the border.

Increasing control over the physical border is costly. Doing so is important for reasons of national security and public safety, as well as preventing illegal immigration, and is a worthy investment of taxpayer dollars. Federal government spending on border security increased from $900 million per year in the mid-1990s to about $10 billion in 2010. Yet the size of the illegal population grew from 3.8 million to 10.8 million during that same period, peaking at about 12 million around 2006.

Not all illegal immigrants enter the United States surreptitiously. It is estimated that 35 to 45 percent of illegal immigrants arrived with a legal visa and stayed beyond the time allowed by that visa. This type of illegal immigrant is called an "overstayer." Further, with improvements to border security, it appears that an increasing number of illegal migrants are crossing the border through legal ports of entry as imposters using genuine documents, such as a U.S. passport or a bona fide visa, or they are smuggled in cargo trucks or other vehicles. No fence, agent on horseback or all-terrain vehicle, drone, or sensor can stop all methods of illegal entry. Controlling illegal immigration will require a combined strategy of increasing the risks and costs of attempting illegal entry through stronger border enforcement together with reducing the perceived benefits of living in the United States illegally through increased enforcement and compliance at the worksite.

WORKPLACE ENFORCEMENT IS DOABLE AND COST-EFFECTIVE

Currently, control of the border is more of an aspiration than an achievement. The Government Accountability Office (GAO) reported in February 2011 that the Department of Homeland Security (DHS) had achieved partial, or "operational" control of only about 44 percent of the Southwest border and only about 15 percent of that was deemed to be fully controlled. While there is certainly more that can be done, at some point there will be diminishing returns to additional investments in infrastructure and staffing.

In contrast, the DHS has barely scratched the surface of workplace enforcement, and there are many ways to improve on this effort. There are a number of proven tools that can bring about increased compliance at relatively little cost to the federal government. These include the federal systems to electronically verify the status of workers (E-Verify and the Social Security Number Verification System) and robust enforcement of identity theft, labor, tax, and wage reporting laws at the state and federal level. When combined with effective enforcement of the laws against egregious employers and removal of workers, authorities will increase job opportunities for U.S. workers and simultaneously address a root cause for illegal immigration, thereby creating a deterrent effect against future illegal immigration.

HISTORY OF WORKSITE ENFORCEMENT

While this essay discusses workplace enforcement in general terms, it is important to distinguish between the concepts of *compliance* and *enforcement*, as both play a role in the general mission of preventing illegal hiring. Compliance efforts refer to the tools that help employers avoid hiring illegal workers, thus reducing the pool of immigration law violators. Enforcement efforts are actions taken by the Immigration and Customs Enforcement (ICE) division of the Department of Homeland Security against those employers who are suspected of or found to be violating the laws. Examples of enforcement efforts would include raids, fines, or criminal charges.

Congress has established a system of enforcement and compliance that aims to hold employers accountable for knowingly hiring illegal workers. There is no law against working illegally per se, except for those who work in violation of the terms of a tourist or other nonwork visa. Most illegal aliens who are caught working are charged with violations of illegal entry or identity fraud offenses, if they are charged at all.

The statutes on illegal hiring were enacted by Congress in 1986, as one of the main features of the Immigration Reform and Control Act (IRCA). For the first time, it became expressly illegal to knowingly hire, recruit, or refer for a fee someone who was not authorized to work in the United States. Employers were required to check documents presented by new hires to establish that they were authorized to work and to record the information on a form now known as the I-9. The law created sanctions in the form of fines and possible prison time for the act of illegal hiring and for not properly checking the status of new employees.

Since the implementation of laws prohibiting knowingly hiring foreign nationals who are not authorized to work in the United States, immigration authorities have directed only a small percentage of their investigative resources toward worksite caseloads each year. Worksite enforcement has never been a top priority for the immigration agency, and worksite arrests have made up only a small share of enforcement activity. In the 1990s, criminal investigations, fraud, and smuggling were the immigration agency's top priority, and worksite enforcement represented only about 6 percent of the immigration agency's caseload, producing roughly 14,000 arrests per year. ICE no longer publishes information on the percentage of its resources devoted to worksite enforcement, but according to the agency's enforcement statistics, the number of worksite arrests dropped by more than half from 2008 to 2010.

One of the major problems with the IRCA is that, while it requires employers to ask new hires for documentation, it does not require them to verify the information; nor has there been an easy way for them to do so. Many employers are able to avoid sanctions by claiming, sometimes honestly, sometimes dishonestly, that they could not detect that the documents presented by illegal workers were false. In addition, out of concern for the potential for discrimination, the law forbids employers from asking workers to present different documents if they suspect fraud. The law allows for more than a dozen different forms of identification as proof of work authorization. As a result, illegal workers simply began providing false documents, and a booming trade in false identification for employment purposes was born. Still, the immediate effect of the IRCA on illegal immigration was noticeable; in the first year after the IRCA was enacted, the number of apprehensions of illegal aliens dropped significantly. Many observers believe that this was an indication that prospective illegal aliens living in Mexico and Central America were deterred from attempting illegal entry by the new law, because they thought jobs were no longer available.

TOOLS FOR EMPLOYER COMPLIANCE

Government agencies at all levels have tools to help ensure that employers comply with the laws against hiring illegal workers. The most efficient and cost-effective tool is a system developed by the Immigration and Naturalization Service in the mid-1990s that enables employers to electronically submit certain key pieces of information—name, date of birth, Social Security number, and immigration identification number, if applicable—to the government for verification. Those employees who cannot be confirmed as work-authorized must be fired. Now known as E-Verify, this system addresses one of the key weakness of the IRCA—the false documents problem. As of June 2011, about 270,000 employers were using it at over 900,000 hiring sites, including all federal agencies and large government contractors. Several states require all employers to use E-Verify, and more than a dozen states plus a number of municipalities require public agencies and government contractors to use it.

While E-Verify is not without problems, most employers who use it indicate that it helps them avoid hiring illegal workers without discriminating against legal immigrants. The law has specific guidelines for employers regarding when to verify, what information can be requested, and how to handle cases in which the employee is not confirmed. E-Verify does a good job of confirming employees who are U.S. citizens and legal immigrants. Nearly all authorized workers are confirmed within a few seconds. E-Verify also does a good job at catching employees using false documents. But E-Verify cannot automatically detect those employees who are using the identity of a legal worker. Both employers and immigration agents report that as the use of E-Verify has grown over the years, more illegal workers have resorted to committing identity theft to evade the confirmation process.

Under current law, the use of E-Verify is limited to checking the status of newly hired workers, except for federal contractors, who must use it to verify certain employees already on the payroll. Many employers also make use of another system, the Social Security Number Verification System (SSNVS), to check that all employees on the payroll are correctly matched to a valid Social Security number. This system is not intended for immigration status verification, but immigration authorities recommend that it be used to help detect illegal workers using fake, borrowed, or stolen Social Security numbers. A number of state governments have mandated use of this program to ensure payroll integrity. In addition, the Social Security Administration periodically sends out notices to employers, known as "no-match letters," when it detects that a number is possibly being used fraudulently or by a number of different people.

ENFORCEMENT TOOLS AND METHODS

ICE has two main ways that it enforces the laws against illegal hiring: worksite raids and audits. The two are not necessarily mutually exclusive. A raid on a workplace is usually the result of an investigation that might have started as the result of a tip, a referral from another government agency, or as a spin-off of another investigation. Agents seize personnel and other files to examine and possibly use them as evidence in building a case that an employer has been knowingly hiring illegal workers, or that the employer failed to properly screen and keep records on workers. The raids usually result in arrests of illegal workers, and these workers may be key witnesses in the case against the employer. Illegal workers usually are charged with immigration violations and possibly with other offenses such as identity fraud. Employers can be charged with various violations, such as knowingly hiring illegal workers, labor law violations, and harboring or transporting illegal workers, or they can be fined for paperwork or other violations.

The other main tool ICE uses is the worksite audit. Employers are selected to be audited based on various criteria, such as whether they are part of the critical infrastructure, whether the industry traditionally has relied on illegal labor, or other information known to the agents through investigations or referrals. The auditors examine I-9s and other information in personnel files to verify work authorization and check for identity fraud. Typically, ICE has no contact with most of the workers, so no arrests of illegal workers occur. Employers can be fined or warned for paperwork violations, and they sometimes settle for large fines if ICE sees indications of other wrongdoing. In other cases, employers who made relatively minor mistakes or were duped by identity fraud receive warnings and training on how to avoid hiring unauthorized workers in the future. They are required to terminate the illegal workers, and they sometimes reach a settlement that requires enrollment in E-Verify and SSNVS.

There are advantages, disadvantages, and trade-offs to raids and audits, and the most effective approach is probably a combination of the two. Raids are effective at penalizing both workers and employers. Both employers and workers are caught red-handed, making it easier both to apprehend and remove the illegal workers and to prosecute the employers, in large part because the workers can testify against the employer. In addition, the negative publicity associated with a raid can deter future illegal hiring. On the other hand, some consider these raids to be excessively intimidating to both workers and employers, as ICE agents will use customary law enforcement procedures in order to maintain order and prevent escape or violence. The raids are costly to the U.S. government because, depending on the size of the operation, they may require hundreds of agents, months of preparation, and complex logistics.

Audits, on the other hand, are largely a paperwork exercise that enables ICE to examine the practices of a much larger number of employers than is possible through raids. Audits might be part of a full investigation that culminates in a raid, but it is also possible to perform an audit without the business disruption of a raid. The auditors can, for the most part, easily determine which employees lack authorization using the standard verification tools. On the other hand, the audits may not detect employees working under the table. The audits also offer no opportunity for ICE to apprehend the illegal workers. The employer is required to terminate any unauthorized workers discovered through the audit, but the worker is free to find employment elsewhere. In general, the audits result in lesser sanctions on employers found to be violating the law. Without the testimony of the workers, it can be very difficult for ICE to make a case or press charges on an employer for knowingly hiring illegal workers.

WORKSITE ENFORCEMENT WORKS

After a lull in the late 1990s and early 2000s, worksite enforcement was stepped up at the federal level beginning in 2006 as a result of funding increases and political pressure to step up immigration law enforcement across the board. In addition, a number of states became frustrated with the inadequacy of federal efforts and decided to enact mechanisms for immigration law enforcement using state authorities. A handful of states, including Arizona, Colorado, Georgia, and Oklahoma adopted state-level mandates for E-Verify use, either for all employers in the state or for state agencies and contractors. By 2011, 15 states had adopted E-Verify requirements for some or all employers, either through legislation, executive order, or regulation. These states were joined by a number of municipalities that passed E-Verify ordinances.

The public debate and enactment of this legislation typically received a great deal of media and public attention. These states and localities came to be perceived as less welcoming to illegal immigrants. As a result, a significant number of illegal immigrants left those places, either to return home or to migrate to states without these tougher laws. This phenomenon has been reported anecdotally in news media stories and confirmed through a number of other indices, such as school enrollments, tenancy rates, loss of customers at businesses catering to foreign nationals, requests for consular services to return home, and, eventually, Census Bureau counts. A 2009 analysis of monthly Census Bureau data by the Center for Immigration Studies identified a drop in the illegal population of nearly 14 percent from 2007 to 2009, after many years of annual growth.

The decline in the illegal immigrant population resulted from several factors including the weak U.S. economy and high unemployment, but it is clear that laws aimed at preventing illegal employment also played an important role. One study by the Public Policy Institute of California found that Arizona's universal mandatory E-Verify law reduced the population of unauthorized workers by 17 percent from 2008 to 2009. With respect to employment, the study found that employment opportunities for illegal workers were significantly reduced, although some unauthorized workers did move into underground or self-employment.

It is likely that local efforts to enforce immigration laws and to cooperate with federal authorities on immigration law enforcement also contributed to the exodus of illegal aliens from Arizona. At the same time that lawmakers passed the E-Verify law, several sheriffs' departments began to participate in federal cooperative enforcement programs, including one program that enables local officers to charge illegal aliens with immigration violations, and also a number of locally-initiated workplace raids.

WORKPLACE ENFORCEMENT CREATES JOBS FOR U.S. WORKERS

The purpose of workplace enforcement is not just to expel, drive out, or deter illegal workers, even though there are legitimate policy reasons for doing so. Enforcement of the laws against illegal hiring is also intended to prevent employers from bypassing U.S. workers. Researchers have convincingly demonstrated that there are several kinds of unhealthy labor market distortions that result from high levels of illegal employment.

First, consistent with the laws of supply and demand, an increase in the number of illegal workers causes wages to decrease for those native-born workers who compete with them for employment in occupations such as construction, food processing, restaurant workers, and custodial work. Numerous studies have shown that wages in these occupations have remained stagnant or declined in recent decades, corresponding to periods of high illegal immigration. A 2003 study by the Harvard economist George Borjas found that wages for unskilled native workers declined by more than 7 percent as a result of immigration (as opposed to international competition, trade agreements, or other factors), and the decline was even larger for unskilled black native workers. The effects are even higher in the industries that are most associated with illegal employment. For example, wages for workers in the meatpacking industry declined 45 percent from 1985 to 2007 (adjusted for inflation), according to government data. While other factors may have contributed to this decline, such as de-unionization, it cannot be argued convincingly that the increase in illegal hiring that took place in this industry would have been helpful or put any upward pressure on wages for U.S. workers in this field.

In addition, the presence of a large number of illegal workers in an occupation can drastically reduce opportunities for U.S. workers seeking those jobs. Sometimes this happens because employers deliberately restrict hiring to illegal workers. For example, employers may contract out cleaning or certain facets of construction work to labor contractors who recruit abroad or within their own circles. Some employers do so for convenience or legitimate business reasons, but others may do so to attempt to establish a buffer layer of deniability for illegal hiring, while also enabling them to pay lower wages. In addition, the mere presence of a large supply of illegal workers who will accept lower wages can, over time, displace U.S. workers. Some researchers have traced the noticeably declining levels of teen employment to this problem.

The clearest evidence of how workplace enforcement helps U.S. workers came after some of the highly visible workplace raids of the late 2000s. In the last quarter of 2006, several large meatpacking plants in the Midwest lost about 1,700 workers, or 23 percent of their workforce, over the course of several months, following the implementation of stricter verification of worker authorization and raids by immigration agents. All the facilities returned to full production within a few months, and the illegal workers were replaced with U.S. citizens and legal immigrant workers who were recruited with increased wages, bonuses, and better transportation options. This resulted in a negligible, if any, impact on consumer prices, as labor accounts for only a tiny share of consumer costs in the meat industry.

CONCLUSION

Enforcement of immigration laws at the workplace is not a substitute for border enforcement, but it is ultimately a more effective approach. Since a significant number of illegal aliens enter legally on visas, in addition to illegally crossing land borders, any strategy to control illegal immigration must operate beyond the border and disrupt the magnet of employment that causes most illegal immigrants to settle in the United States. Workplace enforcement accomplishes this by targeting and deterring the employers of illegal workers and by penalizing workers who are apprehended at the workplace. Workplace enforcement is flexible, with a variety of aspects that include both voluntary compliance by employers and sanctions against egregious or knowing violators. Finally, workplace enforcement provides a direct benefit to U.S. workers by opening up job opportunities and improving wages and working conditions as a direct result of the enforcement action.

References and Further Reading

Borjas, G. J. (2003, November). The labor demand curve is downward sloping: Reexamining the impact of immigration on the labor market. *Quarterly Journal of Economics, 118*(4), 1335–1374.

Camarota, S. A. (2011, October). *A record setting decade of immigration: 2000–2010.* Retrieved from Center for Immigration Studies website: http://cis.org/2000-2010-record-setting-decade-of-immigration

Camarota, S. A., & Jensenius, K. (2009, July). *A shifting tide: Recent trends in the illegal immigrant population.* Retrieved from Center for Immigration Studies website: http://www.cis.org/IllegalImmigration-ShiftingTide

Kammer, J. (2009, July). *Immigration raids at Smithfield: How an ICE enforcement action boosted union organizing and the employment of American workers.* Retrieved from Center for Immigration Studies website: http://www.cis.org/SmithfieldImmigrationRaid-Unionization

Krikorian, M. (2011, January 26). *Worksite enforcement: Audits are not enough* (Testimony before the U.S. House of Representatives Judiciary Committee, Subcommittee on Immigration Policy and Enforcement). Retrieved from Center for Immigration Studies website: http://cis.org/node/2548

Lofstrum, M., Bohn, S., & Raphael, S. (2011, March). *Lessons from the 2007 Legal Arizona Workers Act.* Retrieved from Public Policy Institute of California website: http://www.ppic.org/main/publication.asp?i=915

Mortensen, R. W. (2009, June). *Illegal but not undocumented: Identity theft, document fraud, and illegal employment.* Retrieved from Center for Immigration Studies website: http://cis.org/IdentityTheft

Passel, J. S., & Cohn, D. (2011, February 1). *Unauthorized immigrant population: National and state trends, 2010.* Retrieved from Pew Hispanic Center website: http://pewhispanic.org/reports/report.php?ReportID=133

Sum, A., Harrington, P., & Khatiwada, I. (2006). *The impact of new immigrants on young native-born workers, 2000–2005.* Retrieved from Center for Immigration Studies website: www.cis.org/articles/2006/back806.html

U.S. Department of Homeland Security, Office of Immigration Statistics. (2011). *2010 yearbook of immigration statistics.* Retrieved from http://www.dhs.gov/xlibrary/assets/statistics/yearbook/2010/ois_yb_2010.pdf

Vaughan, J. M. (2010, November 29). *Hearing on immigration issues facing Colorado: Statement of Jessica M. Vaughan* (Testimony before the Republican Study Committee of Colorado). Retrieved from Center for Immigration Studies: http://cis.org/node/2603

Jessica M. Vaughan

COUNTERPOINT

This essay will describe how enforcement of immigration law at the worksite does not eliminate employment opportunities for undocumented workers, but rather lowers the wages and working conditions of all workers. U.S. enforcement of immigration law at the worksite emanates from the Immigration Reform and Control Act (IRCA) of 1986. Before IRCA was implemented, the Government Accountability Office (GAO, formerly the General Accounting Office) studied 19 countries with worksite immigration enforcement polices and found that, in those countries, worksite enforcement of immigration law did not, on balance, curtail unauthorized employment. Since IRCA's implementation, it has become clear that worksite enforcement has not reduced unauthorized employment in the United States either. Immigration enforcement at the worksite may result in a slight initial reduction in job opportunities for undocumented workers. This "reduction," however, is more aptly deemed a "relocation" of job opportunities that moves undocumented workers from one jobsite to another but does not eradicate their presence in the job market. Additionally, as undocumented workers face immigration enforcement at the worksite, they become desperate for employment and more willing to accept illegally low-paying or dangerous jobs.

In addition to not deterring unauthorized employment, increases in worksite enforcement have had significant negative consequences for U.S. workers and the economy. More jobs have moved into the underground economy, the wages and working conditions of all workers have worsened, and unscrupulous employers have increased their tools to coerce and control workers. Instead of focusing blindly on enforcement of immigration law at the worksite, policymakers should adopt a broader approach that includes legalizing the workers already in the country, reforming the immigration system to adjust the channels for legal immigration to the country's current needs, expanding and vigorously enforcing worker protections, and ensuring that immigration enforcement does not trump labor law. With a shift in perspective, immigration enforcement at the worksite can be a tool that actually supports and creates higher wages and better working conditions for all workers.

UNDOCUMENTED WORKERS IN THE U.S. ECONOMY

Undocumented immigrant workers are a core part of the U.S. economy. Recent worksite enforcement efforts, myopically focused on ridding the U.S. of undocumented immigrants, ignore this reality. In 2010 there were an estimated 8 million undocumented workers in the country, representing 5.2 percent of the U.S. labor force, according to the Pew Hispanic Center. For example, 12 percent of Nevada's workforce comprises undocumented workers, the highest proportion of any state. In fact, the number of undocumented immigrants in states such as Kentucky and Mississippi, where the percentage of immigrant workers in the workforce has traditionally been relatively low, increased by 300 and 350 percent, respectively, from 2000 to 2010.

Undocumented workers labor in a variety of industries, but they are a core part of the workforce in agriculture, construction, manufacturing, and the service and restaurant industries. The U.S. economy is highly dependent on labor provided by undocumented workers and would suffer significantly if these workers were suddenly to leave the workforce. For example, California accounts for approximately 13 percent of U.S. gross domestic product (GDP), according to the Department of Commerce. In California, undocumented immigrants account for about 9 percent of the workforce and gross state product and make up 22 percent of the agriculture, forestry, and fishing/hunting workforce; 17 percent of the leisure and hospitality workforce; and 15 percent of the construction workforce, according to a 2010 report by the Center for American Progress and the Immigration Policy Center. Removing undocumented workers from the aboveground workforce in California alone would thus have a significant impact on the U.S. economy as a whole.

Figure 20.1 Share of undocumented workers by industry in the United States

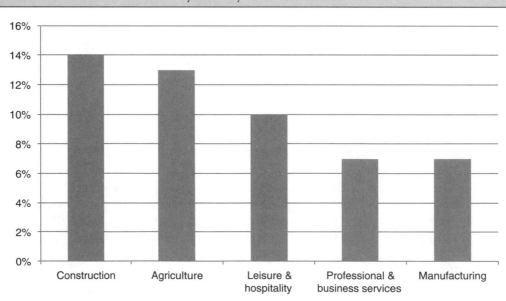

Source: Data from *A Portrait of Unauthorized Immigrants in the United States,* by J. Passel and D. Cohn, April 14, 2009, Washington, DC: Pew Hispanic Center, http://pewhispanic.org/files/reports/107.pdf.

Not only would the economy be injured if undocumented workers left the labor force, but thousands of jobs held by U.S. workers would be directly affected. For example, *The Washington Post* reports that 50 to 75 percent of the U.S. agricultural labor force is composed of undocumented workers. The U.S. Department of Agriculture reports that for every on-farm job there are about 3.1 upstream and downstream jobs in America—jobs that support and are created by the growing of agricultural products. The vast majority of these complementary jobs are held by U.S. citizens and work-authorized immigrants who would face unemployment if on-farm jobs were eliminated or moved out of the country.

Moreover, groups like the Cato Institute have found that immigrants and native-born workers with similar educational attainment and experience possess unique skills that lead them to specialize in different occupations. This means that even if all undocumented workers were suddenly deported, American workers would not move into those jobs and fill in those gaps. Rather, many jobs currently filled by undocumented workers would cease to exist, and businesses would go under. Additionally, according to data provided to the Immigration Policy Center by Rob Paral & Associates (2009), there is no statistically significant relationship between unemployment and recent immigration. In fact, this data further shows that unemployment rates among native-born workers are actually lower in areas with higher levels of immigration, because immigrants in the workforce create a need for jobs in supervisory and middle-income positions, and spending by immigrants as consumers stimulates the economy and creates additional jobs.

THE 1986 IMMIGRATION LAW

In 1986, the IRCA made it unlawful for employers to "knowingly" hire individuals ineligible to work in the country and created civil and criminal penalties (known as "employer sanctions") for violations. IRCA requires employers to verify the employment authorization of workers using the I-9 form (Employment Eligibility Verification Form) and to certify on the form that documents presented by workers as proof of identity and employment eligibility reasonably appear genuine on their face. Penalties range from civil fines of $250 per undocumented worker to criminal fines of $3,000 per undocumented worker. IRCA also authorized the Immigration and Naturalization Service (now U.S. Immigration and Customs Enforcement, or ICE, a bureau within the U.S. Department of Homeland Security, or DHS) and the U.S. Department of Labor (DOL) to inspect I-9 forms. This drastic change in immigration law was intended to discourage illegal immigration by removing the U.S. "job magnet."

IRCA has been in place for 25 years, and worksite enforcement of immigration law has reached unprecedented levels. In fiscal year 2010, Congress appropriated $135 million to DHS for worksite enforcement, up from just $10 million in 2006. Between 2003 and 2007, ICE was granted a sixfold increase in new officers dedicated to worksite enforcement. Yet the population of undocumented immigrants and undocumented workers is at an all-time high. According to the Pew Hispanic Center, in 2010 there were an estimated 11.2 million undocumented immigrants in the United States, up from 8.4 million in 2000, with an estimated 8 million in the labor force, an increase from 5.5 million in 2000.

Figure 20.2 Undocumented immigrant population in the United States (in millions)

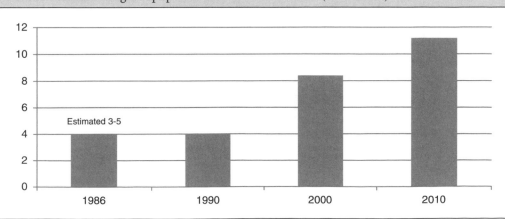

Sources: Passel and Cohn (2011); Lowell & Suro (2002).

The high population of undocumented workers in the U.S. is the result of several factors. Currently, undocumented workers are a much-needed segment of the national economy. Their crucial labor has, in many instances, driven job creation and economic vitality. This reality, coupled with official immigration policies that make it extremely difficult for workers considered "low-skilled" to immigrate legally to the United States, has resulted in an antiquated immigration system that is out of step with the needs of the U.S. labor market. Worksite enforcement does not address the complicated facets of this reality.

ICE WORKSITE ENFORCEMENT TOOLS

Effective March 1, 2003, ICE took over worksite enforcement responsibilities from its legacy agency, the former Immigration and Naturalization Service (INS). Under the George W. Bush and Barack Obama administrations, the ICE's four primary tools for enforcing immigration law at the worksite have included worksite raids, audits of I-9 forms, E-Verify, and Social Security Administration (SSA) "no-match" letters.

Worksite enforcement in the aftermath of IRCA has ebbed and flowed. According to the GAO, use of I-9 audits declined significantly, from nearly 10,000 in fiscal year 1990 to fewer than 2,200 in fiscal year 2003, then increased again in 2006. Beginning in 2006, the Bush administration announced a new interior enforcement strategy that resulted in increased worksite enforcement, including military-style raids. The Bush administration also expanded the use of E-Verify, an electronic employment eligibility verification system, and sought to use notices issued by SSA as an enforcement tool.

In 2009, the Obama administration announced a worksite enforcement strategy that prioritizes prosecuting employers instead of taking punitive actions against workers. This new enforcement strategy resulted in a shift from military-style raids to large-scale I-9 audits. Like the Bush administration, the Obama administration supports expansion of E-Verify.

WORKSITE RAIDS

During the Bush administration, military-style raids were the main tool used to enforce immigration law in the workplace. From 2003 to 2008, the number of workers arrested in worksite raids increased tenfold. In a worksite raid, ICE agents arrive unannounced at places of employment, often brandishing weapons, and detain workers who cannot immediately produce documentation of their legal immigration status. Often, detained workers are quickly moved out of state, away from their families, support networks, and access to attorneys. This tactic triggers fear and panic throughout the raided worksites as well as in the broader community, as families are traumatized by the sudden disappearance of their parents or spouses and businesses are shuttered due to the loss of customers and workers. From 2006 to 2008, numerous high-profile worksite raids led to the apprehension of thousands of workers and the detention of more than 9,000 individuals.

Under the Bush administration, worksite raids generally focused on penalizing undocumented workers, while the employers who hired them often received lenient treatment. For example, in 2007, ICE raided a New Bedford,

Figure 20.3 Recent trends in worksite enforcement

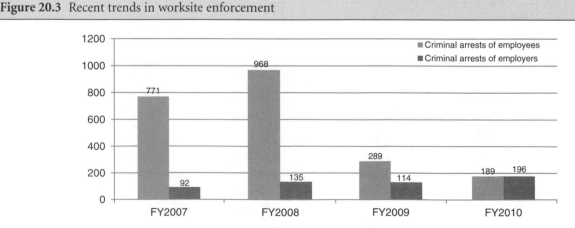

Sources: Bruno (2011); Chertoff (2008); Kibble (2010).

Massachusetts, leather factory that manufactured vests and backpacks for the U.S. military and detained 361 immigrant workers, most of whom were transferred almost immediately to detention centers in Texas. In contrast, the factory owner was released on the day of the raid, production resumed uninterrupted the following day, and a federal judge permitted the owner to travel to Puerto Rico on business two days later. In 2008, only 2 percent of apprehensions made by ICE during worksite raids were of employers or their agents. The use of worksite raids has been widely condemned by immigrant rights' advocates, labor unions, and the faith community as inhumane. Operations are characterized by a disregard for workers' civil rights, including unlawful detention, denial of bond hearings, racial profiling, denial of access to attorneys, denial of food and water, and failure to advise workers of their Miranda rights.

I-9 AUDITS

Under the Obama administration, there has been an increase in worksite enforcement under a worksite enforcement strategy based on the use of I-9 audits, or "silent" raids. In an I-9 audit, ICE serves an employer with a Notice of Inspection, which informs the employer that ICE will review and inspect employee I-9 forms and other documents to determine whether the employer is employing undocumented workers. Under the law, employers have the right to receive notice three days prior to an audit. Employers may not refuse or delay presenting employees' I-9 forms; doing so is a violation of federal law. In the first 2 years of the Obama administration (2009–2010), ICE collected over $8 million in employer fines, compared with $879,679 over 5 years (2003–2008) of the Bush administration. In fiscal year 2010, ICE conducted I-9 audits of 2,196 companies, an increase from 503 in fiscal year 2008. Although the majority of the Obama administration's worksite enforcement takes the form of audits, ICE continues to carry out smaller-scale worksite raids, although in much fewer numbers than during the Bush administration.

Although I-9 audits represent a different approach than military-style raids, they still have a devastating impact on immigrant workers, communities, and local economies. Despite President Obama's asserted strategy of targeting abusive or exploitative employers, there is no indication that audits have, in fact, focused on these employers. I-9 audits lead to the termination of thousands of workers and promote a climate of fear in the workplace. According to the Migration Policy Institute, low-skilled immigrant workers' wages and working conditions are generally worse than those of U.S.-born workers. I-9 audits create a chilling effect, as workers become even more afraid to report discrimination, wage-and-hour violations, or safety and health violations (reported anecdotally in a report from the National Commission on ICE). Ultimately, I-9 audits can make workers fear that if they complain, their employer will retaliate by contacting ICE. Additionally, these audits merely churn the workforce, sending workers to jobs in the same town and industry, but for lower pay and under worse working conditions. In turn, this gives employers a large new pool of easily pliable workers and allows them to lower labor and production costs, thereby producing a competitive advantage over the recently audited business.

E-VERIFY

E-Verify is an Internet-based system used to verify the employment eligibility of workers by matching information they present with information held in DHS and SSA databases. The mostly voluntary system was created in 1996 by the Illegal Immigration Reform and Immigrant Responsibility Act of 1996 (IIRIRA) as a pilot program in five states with the highest population of undocumented immigrants. Since then, the program has been repeatedly reauthorized and expanded for voluntary use in all states. Following Congress's failure to pass comprehensive immigration reform in 2007, President Bush made E-Verify mandatory for most federal government contractors. Several states have also passed laws mandating use of E-Verify by some or all employers in those states. Nonetheless, by mid-2011, the system was used by only 4 percent of employers in the country.

E-Verify is widely criticized by immigrant rights' organizations, privacy groups, and labor unions as being unreliable, error-prone, expensive, and bad for workers and the economy. The system also provides inadequate due process for workers who lose their job because of a database error, nor are there penalties for employers who misuse it. E-Verify has not successfully served its intended purpose of ensuring that employers hire only authorized workers, but instead has resulted in thousands of authorized immigrant workers and U.S. citizens wrongfully losing their jobs. Further, according to a report by Westat, Inc., 54 percent of unauthorized workers for whom E-Verify checks were run were erroneously confirmed as being work-authorized. In Arizona, where state law requires that all employers in the state use E-Verify, the system has been ineffective at reducing unauthorized employment. The *Arizona Republic* reported that, despite stiff state penalties, nearly 50 percent of employers simply are not complying with the law (Gonzalez, 2008). Further, ICE officials report that among the 50 percent of Arizona employers who do comply with the mandate to use E-Verify, some unscrupulous employers coach employees on ways to get around the system.

SSA NO-MATCH LETTERS

Each year, employers file a Wage and Tax Statement (Form W-2) with the SSA and the Internal Revenue Service (IRS) to report how much they paid their employees and how much they deducted from employee wages in taxes throughout the year. An SSA "no-match" letter is a letter sent by the SSA when the names or Social Security numbers listed on the employer's W-2 forms do not match SSA records. The purpose of the SSA no-match letter is to notify workers and their employers of the discrepancy and inform them that employees are not receiving proper credit for their earnings, which can affect future retirement or disability benefits administered by SSA.

Soon after the 2007 comprehensive immigration bill failed in the Senate, the Bush administration announced that it would use SSA no-match letters as a tool to identify undocumented workers. The administration issued a rule that effectively would have forced employers to either fire any worker unable to resolve discrepancies in SSA's records or risk being held liable for immigration law violations. After a coalition of labor unions and immigrant and civil rights organizations filed a lawsuit challenging the rule, a federal judge blocked its implementation until the court made a final ruling on the legality of the rule. In the summer of 2009, DHS secretary Janet Napolitano announced that DHS would rescind the rule, and SSA halted sending out no-match letters.

While no-match letters themselves are not proof of immigration law violations, many employers mistakenly believe that the letter indicates that a person named in it is unauthorized to work, and the receipt of no-match letters often has resulted in workers being summarily fired without first having a chance to correct their records. This is confirmed by results of a national survey conducted by the University of Illinois Center for Urban Economic Development. Unscrupulous employers have also used the letters to stymie organizing campaigns by ignoring the letters when they first receive them, then later using them as a pretext for firing workers who participate in efforts to improve working conditions and wages.

THE CONSEQUENCES OF WORKSITE ENFORCEMENT

More worksite enforcement is not the key to eliminating the employment of undocumented workers. Immigrant workers are essential to the U.S. economy and have become a part of local communities. Increased enforcement will simply result in undocumented workers moving off the books into the cash economy, where they will suffer more exploitation at the hands of unscrupulous employers. It will also result in billions of dollars of lost tax revenue at the federal and state levels, increased opportunities for unscrupulous employers to use threats of immigration enforcement to coerce and control workers, and a degradation of working conditions for all workers.

The U.S. economy will lose out on billions of dollars in tax revenue. Because undocumented workers make up 5 percent of the workforce, employers have a strong incentive to keep them, including moving into the underground economy, misclassifying workers as independent contractors, and simply not participating in employment eligibility verification systems. In analyzing a 2008 bill that would have made use of E-Verify mandatory (without also providing for legalization of undocumented workers), the Congressional Budget Office (CBO) determined that such a requirement would decrease federal revenue by more than $17.3 billion over 10 years, because it would increase the number of employers and workers who would resort to the black market, outside of the tax system.

Arizona, the first state to require all employers in the state to use E-Verify, provides a window into the economic consequences of increasing worksite enforcement where there is a high population of undocumented workers. In 2008, the first year the law was in effect, the *Arizona Republic* found that income tax collection dropped 13 percent from the previous year. Sales taxes, however, dropped by only 2.5 percent for food and 6.8 percent for clothing. The article concluded that workers were not paying income taxes, but were still spending money—indicating that the underground economy was growing (Gonzalez, 2008). The timing of this loss in tax revenue was particularly harmful, as it occurred while the state was already facing a $3 billion budget gap. Similarly, the Public Policy Institute of California found that the Arizona law resulted in shifting undocumented workers into less formal work arrangements. Moreover, a 2010 report prepared jointly by the Center for American Progress (CAP) and the Immigration Policy Center (IPC) states that deporting the entire undocumented population of the United States would cause a $2.6 trillion cumulative loss in gross domestic product (GDP) over 10 years, not including the actual costs of deportation. Additionally, the chief actuary of SSA has stated that without undocumented immigrants' contributions to the Social Security Trust Fund, the SSA would have faced a short-fall of tax revenue to cover payouts starting in 2009. The trust fund received a net benefit between $120 billion and $240 billion from undocumented immigrants in 2007, representing 5.4 percent to 10.7 percent of the trust fund's total assets. CAP and IPC found that a legalization program would amount to a cumulative $1.5 trillion in additional GDP and would also boost wages for both native-born and authorized immigrant workers.

Wages and working conditions for all workers will be lowered. The goal of IRCA was to protect jobs and wages of U.S. workers. The theory was that if employers could not hire undocumented immigrants, they would be unable to pay below-market wages, which would drive down wages for all workers and make undocumented workers more appealing to hire. This goal has not been realized, however, and unions like the AFL-CIO argue that employer sanctions have instead resulted in lower wages and working conditions. IRCA gave employers the power to police immigration at the worksite by permitting them to determine the legitimacy of documents that workers present. This gave unscrupulous employers a powerful new tool for coercing workers: the threat of deportation with the assurance that they could be easily replaced by other similarly vulnerable workers.

When some workers are easy to exploit, the conditions of all workers suffer, because abusive employers who pay less gain a competitive advantage over high-road employers. For example, after a high-profile audit of ABM, a janitorial services company in Minnesota, a worker was dismissed from his well-paying job after working 6 years for the company. He subsequently found a 7-days-a-week janitorial job where he earned only $25 a night in cash, sometimes at an hourly rate as low as $5. Sequences of events such as this, in turn, give the new—exploitative—employer an advantage over employers who comply with the law and pay workers legal wages.

Making programs such as E-Verify mandatory will exacerbate this phenomenon. Unless the existing workforce is provided a way to gain work authorization, undocumented workers and their employers will simply move into the cash economy to get around the system. For workers in the underground economy, working conditions are abysmal: lawbreaking flourishes and a parallel labor system is created that is characterized by underpayment of wages, nonexistent overtime pay or breaks, and generally unsafe working conditions. Furthermore, when workers are working "off the books," they have no access or recourse to safety nets designed to protect low-income workers, such as Social Security, workers' compensation, and minimum wage laws. This creates an even greater economic incentive to hire undocumented workers: companies benefit if they hire such workers because they perceive them as carrying reduced liability for labor law violations, since the workers are too fearful to report violations.

Enforcement of immigration law will come at the expense of labor law protections. When unscrupulous employers threaten workers with deportation under the guise of complying with immigration law, it undermines the enforcement of labor and employment law. Abusive employers will hire undocumented immigrants with the intent of exploiting their labor by, for example, placing them in unsafe working conditions, paying them lower-than-market wages, or not paying them at all. If workers do file a labor complaint or join with their fellow workers to form a union, the employer will either threaten workers with deportation or actually call ICE to have the workers deported. Oftentimes, the workers are whisked into detention or out of the country before they have a chance to seek remedies for the labor violations, and employers pay no monetary penalty for their actions. These actions send a strong signal to other undocumented workers that they must silently accept deplorable working conditions or risk being sent home.

In addition, workers' opportunities for collective action are undermined. For example, an I-9 audit of Fresh Direct, an online grocer in New York City, was deliberately carried out before a union election in order to disrupt the workplace and break up organizing efforts. The timing of the action made it clear to workers that the audit was tied to the election's outcome, and that workers could face termination and deportation. Many workers left their employment at the company and others refused to vote for the election of a union they had supported just weeks before.

In 2011, DOL and DHS entered into a revised memorandum of understanding (MOU) in an attempt to ensure that the two agencies' worksite-based enforcement activities do not conflict. This 2011 MOU updates a 1998 MOU agreed to by DOL and the former INS. The MOU establishes a process for both agencies to coordinate their workplace enforcement activities by limiting the worksite enforcement power of ICE when a DOL investigation is pending, and requiring DOL to communicate with ICE concerning worksite investigations. It also outlines the agencies' commitment to protecting workers against retaliation and intimidation by employers and other parties who use threats of immigration enforcement. This is a necessary step in ensuring that immigration enforcement does not undermine the enforcement of labor laws.

ALTERNATIVE STRATEGIES

The past 25 years have demonstrated that an enforcement-only approach has failed to reduce employment of undocumented immigrants or curb unauthorized immigration. A real solution to this issue includes three components: (1) legalizing the status of undocumented workers currently in the United States; (2) creating adequate legal mechanisms for workers to enter the country and contribute to the economy; and (3) ensuring the protection of all workers' rights. Instead of single-mindedly focusing resources on immigration enforcement at the worksite, official policy should be to devote resources to vigorously enforcing labor and employment laws. This would eliminate employers' incentives to hire and exploit undocumented workers, and it would remove employers' incentives to adopt substandard employment practices designed to evade their obligations under the core tax, social benefit, and regulatory systems.

Instead of layering more enforcement on top of a broken immigration system, policymakers need to fix the system and ensure that all workers are protected. This can be done through the following actions:

1. *Legalize the current undocumented workforce.* Deporting 8 million undocumented workers and their families is unrealistic, and having a legal workforce is essential to the success of any worksite enforcement system. Drawing workers out of the shadows will eliminate incentives for employers to circumvent employment eligibility verification laws and will improve wages and working conditions for all workers.

2. *Increase mechanisms for legal migration of workers.* The immigration system should be reformed to allow willing workers more legal channels to immigrate to the United States. In its framework for comprehensive immigration reform, the labor movement recommends an independent commission to study and regulate a worker visa system to ensure that there is a close match between the number and types of visas available and the needs of the economy.

3. *Prevent unscrupulous employers from using immigration law to avoid their obligations under labor law.* Holding employers liable for labor law violations and precluding them from being able to use immigration law to get rid of perceived "troublemakers" is essential to reducing employers' economic incentive to seek out workers who are vulnerable to exploitation because they are undocumented. It would also prevent the churning of the workforce that degrades jobs and working conditions generally. Innovative legislation such as the proposed POWER (Protect Our Workers from Exploitation and Retaliation) Act, introduced in 2011 by Senator Robert Menendez (D-NJ), addresses this complex dynamic. The bill would lessen employers' incentive to use the threat of immigration enforcement as a means to keep wages low and workplaces unsafe, and it would help create just and decent workplaces for all workers.

4. *Expand and vigorously enforce labor law.* Labor and employment laws, first, must be enforced to ensure protection of all workers, regardless of immigration status, to remove any incentive for unscrupulous employers to seek out and exploit undocumented workers. Second, existing labor and employment laws should be strongly enforced to ensure that employers cannot evade their responsibilities to maintain a safe workplace, pay lawful wages, and withhold payroll taxes by exploiting legal loopholes or by outright lawbreaking. Experience shows that voluntary compliance works best where there is vigorous enforcement against the worst offenders, and is unlikely to work if there is lax enforcement.

5. *Require coordination between ICE and DOL to target labor law violators for I-9 audits.* Rather than randomly audit employers, ICE should instead identify and target labor lawbreakers for I-9 audits based on intelligence from DOL and state departments of labor. Any audit, however, must not interfere with a labor dispute or organizing campaign. ICE coordination with DOL would not only be consistent with its stated priorities of targeting egregious employers who break labor laws, it would also allow limited worksite enforcement resources to be devoted to the shared goal of improving conditions at workplaces.

CONCLUSION

For more than two decades, the federal government's approach to dealing with unauthorized employment has been "enforcement-only," and this approach has not worked. Increasing worksite enforcement, in the absence of fundamental, comprehensive reform the immigration system, undermines American jobs and ultimately will impose new burdens on the economy, workers, and businesses. Congress and the administration must consider an approach to immigration worksite enforcement that does not rely solely on employer sanctions. Instead, the approach must ensure that ICE enforcement efforts do not trump workers' ability to vindicate their basic labor rights and are not used as a tool to deny workers' earned wages or benefits. The country needs stronger enforcement of labor, employment, and civil rights laws, rather than the current churning of the workforce, where undocumented workers are preferred over documented workers because they are easier to hire, fire, and exploit. This reality only results in further downward pressure on wages and working conditions for all U.S. workers. The goal of immigration enforcement at the worksite should be to create higher wages and better conditions for all workers.

REFERENCES AND FURTHER READING

Bruno, A. (2011, March 1). *Immigration-related worksite enforcement: Performance measures* (Congressional Research Service Report R40002). Retrieved from Congressional Research Service website: http://assets.opencrs.com/rpts/R40002_20110301.pdf

Center for American Progress, and Immigration Policy Center. (2010, January 14). *The economic benefits of comprehensive immigration reform.* Retrieved from http://www.americanprogress.org/issues/2010/01/pdf/cir_factsheet.pdf

Chertoff, M. (2008, April 2). *Testimony of the Honorable Michael Chertoff, Secretary, Department of Homeland Security, before the U.S. Senate Committee on the Judiciary.* Retrieved from U.S. Senate Committee on the Judiciary website: http://judiciary.senate.gov/hearings/testimony.cfm?id=e655f9e2809e5476862f735da1373a5c&wit_id=e655f9e2809e5476862f735da1373a5c-1-1

Gonzalez, D. (2008, November 30). Illegal workers manage to skirt Arizona employer-sanctions law: Borrowed identities, cash pay fuel an underground economy. *Arizona Republic.* Retrieved from http://www.azcentral.com/news/articles/2008/11/30/20081130underground1127.html

Griswold, D. (2011, January 26). *ICE worksite enforcement: Up to the job?* (Testimony before the Subcommittee on Immigration Policy and Enforcement, Committee on the Judiciary, U.S. House of Representatives). Retrieved from the Cato Institute website: www.cato.org/pub_display.php?pub_id=12730

Hincapié, M., Moran, T., & Waslin, M. (2008, May). *The Social Security Administration no-match program: Inefficient, ineffective, and costly.* Retrieved from Immigration Policy Center website: http://www.immigrationpolicy.org/special-reports/social-security-administration-no-match-program-inefficient-ineffective-and-costly

Kerwin, D. M., & McCabe, K. (2011, July). *Labor standards of enforcement and low-wage immigrants: Creating an effective enforcement system.* Retrieved from Migration Policy Institute website: http://www.migrationpolicy.org/pubs/laborstandards-2011.pdf

Kibble, K. (2010, January 26). *Statement of Kumar Kibble, Deputy Director, U.S. Immigration and Customs Enforcement, regarding a hearing on worksite enforcement* (Testimony before the House Subcommittee on Immigration Policy and Enforcement). Retrieved from U.S. Immigration and Customs Enforcement website: http://www.ice.gov/doclib/news/library/speeches/012611kibble.pdf

Lowell, B. L., & Suro, R. (2002, March 21). *How many undocumented: The numbers behind the U.S.-Mexico migration talks.* Retrieved from Pew Hispanic Center website: http://pewhispanic.org/files/reports/6.pdf

National Commission on ICE Misconduct and Violations of 4th Amendment Rights. (2006, December 12). *Raids on workers: Destroying our rights; A comprehensive analysis and investigation of ICE raids and their ramifications.* Retrieved from http://www.ufcw.org/docUploads/UFCW%20ICE%20rpt%20FINAL%20150B_061809_130632.pdf?CFID=10629926&CFTOKEN=75705750

National Immigration Law Center. (2009, November). *Overview of key issues facing low-wage immigrant workers.* Retrieved from http://www.nilc.org/dc_conf/flashdrive09/Worker-Rights/empl_emp-issues-ovrvw-2009-11-05.pdf

Passel, J., & Cohn, D. (2011, February 1). *Unauthorized immigrant population: National and state trends, 2010.* Retrieved from Pew Hispanic Center website: http://pewhispanic.org/files/reports/133.pdf

Rob Paral and Associates. (2009, May). *Immigration and native-born unemployment across racial/ethnic groups: Untying the knot* (Part II of III). Retrieved from Immigration Policy Center website: www.immigrationpolicy.org/sites/default/files/docs/Part%202%20-%20 Unemployment%20Race%20Disconnect%2005-19-09.pdf

Stana, R. M. (2005, July 21). *Immigration enforcement: Preliminary observations on employment verification and worksite enforcement efforts; Statement of Richard M. Stana, Director, Homeland Security and Justice* (Testimony before the Subcommittee on Immigration, Border Security, and Claims, Committee on the Judiciary, House of Representatives). Retrieved from Government Accountability Office website: http://www.gao.gov/new.items/d05822t.pdf

Marielena Hincapié and Maura Ooi

21

Worksite Raids

POINT: Worksite raids are a legitimate part of immigration law enforcement. High-profile raids on businesses that employ large numbers of undocumented workers are more efficient than smaller operations, and the publicity serves as a deterrent to other companies. Until it is possible to prevent undocumented immigrants from working, it will be difficult to stop illegal immigration.

Mark Krikorian, Center for Immigration Studies

COUNTERPOINT: Dramatic raids at the workplace lead to an atmosphere of paranoia and fear that is dehumanizing and undermines productivity. Furthermore, because undocumented immigrants often live in mixed-status families, such raids are harmful to children and families. While undocumented workers are violating immigration laws, they are not dangerous criminals who warrant these dramatic raids.

Clarissa Martínez-De-Castro and Laura Vazquez, National Council of La Raza

Introduction

Two basic issues animate the debate over worksite raids of employers who hire illegal immigrants. One has to do with the punitive nature of worksite enforcement—who gets "punished," in other words. Worksite raids result in arrests of workers, most of whom (but not all) are undocumented, while employers are much less likely to be arrested or be the focus of the enforcement action. There may be follow-up investigations of how the undocumented workers were hired, with subsequent consequences for employers (usually human resources personnel, not company owners), but the visible and de facto target of raids are the workers themselves. With audits, some would argue, the process is more systematic, employers are held more accountable, and legal Hispanic workers are less likely to be caught in the crossfire.

The other issue has to do with public sensibilities. The deportation hawks among us like the "red meat" aspect of seeing the heavy hand of the law engaged in enforcement action—indeed, for many raid supporters, the dramatic nature of the action is itself part of its value as a deterrent. On the other hand, more moderate sensibilities prefer the administrative approach that involves a more structured, quieter process.

While the administration of George W. Bush focused on headline-grabbing raids that led to the arrests of immigrant workers, the Obama administration has charted a different course. Believing that employers who hire unauthorized workers create the demand that drives most illegal immigration, the Obama administration has instead placed an emphasis on going after employers with I-9 audits undertaken by U.S. Immigration and Customs Enforcement (ICE). That said, it is worth noting that ICE deported a record number of out-of-status immigrants in the first 3 years of the Obama administration—more than 400,000 per year—surpassing Bush's record.

Audits primarily target employers, while raids primarily target workers, but the stakes are high for both parties. Business owners trying to follow the law must accept seemingly legitimate forms of documentation required by the I-9 form. If they don't, they could be exposed to charges of employment discrimination. And even employers who have followed the rules can be devastated by an audit that forces them to fire valuable, long-time employees after it is discovered that these employees could not produce authentic documents attesting to their authorization to work in the United States. Meanwhile, after an audit, ICE does not round up the affected workers for deportation. This means that these workers are free to seek employment elsewhere—including with competitors, putting the employer at an additional disadvantage. As for the immigrants who live under the threat of a raid, there is, of course, the sudden surprise of being arrested without any chance to put one's affairs in order. This is especially problematic in mixed-status families with children who are U.S. citizens.

In the Point essay, Mark Krikorian asserts that the Obama administration should reinstate the Bush-era emphasis on worksite raids, in tandem with audits, because they are the best way to get control of the illegal immigration problem, protect the rights and raise the wages of American workers, and keep the country secure. Raids, Krikorian believes, serve as a general deterrent—both to illegal workers entering the country seeking jobs and to employers illegally hiring them, and they should be part of what Krikorian calls "full spectrum enforcement."

In the Counterpoint essay, Clarissa Martínez-De-Castro and Laura Vazquez argue that worksite raids are costly and socially and economically disruptive, and that they do not create a sufficient deterrent against the employment of unauthorized workers. What must happen, they contend, is complete reform of the country's immigration laws, without which increased workplace enforcement alone will remain ineffective. They point out that the resources devoted to removing undocumented workers from the workplace have steadily increased, yet the core problem remains untouched. Rather, what is needed is to strengthen the efficiency of the country's *legal* immigration system, which would encourage people to go through it rather than around it, thus increasing legal immigration, shoring up the economy, and protecting the rights of all workers.

POINT

In April 2009 the administration of President Barack Obama announced a worksite enforcement strategy that prioritizes audits of employers over taking action against employees. This change in strategy resulted in a shift from worksite raids to large-scale audits of I-9 forms (the Employment Eligibility Verification forms that employers use to confirm that employees are legally eligible to work in the United States). The vast majority of the Obama administration's worksite enforcement takes the form of these audits (or "silent" raids).

The administration has been working hard to treat all violations of immigration law as secondary offenses, so that only those illegal immigrants guilty of some additional crime will be deported. Indeed, the administration is seemingly more comfortable targeting employers rather than also scrutinizing the illegal workers themselves. The result of this backtracking is that, although in its first 2 years the Obama administration continued the steady increase in deportations that has occurred since the administration of Bill Clinton, as of 2010 the pace of deportations has been essentially flat, increasing at less than 1 percent per year. This flattening has occurred in the context of an economic recession. This unbalanced approach to immigration enforcement—audits over raids, rather than audits in concert with raids—not only hampers the effectiveness of the country's tackling of the illegal immigration problem; it also leaves American workers worse off and puts American security at risk.

NECESSITY OF ENFORCEMENT

According to the Pew Hispanic Center, in 2010 there were an estimated 11.2 undocumented immigrants in the United States, a number that reflects an increase of 2.8 million since 2000. An estimated 8 million of these undocumented immigrants were in the labor force, an increase from 5.5 million in 2000. According to the Bureau of Labor Statistics, the average unemployment rate for calendar year 2011 was 8.9 percent. Between 2007 and 2010, the U6 unemployment rate, which includes underemployed and discouraged workers, stood at a whopping 16.7 percent. This represents nearly 26 million Americans, and the rates are even higher for young workers and minorities (Camarota, 2010a).

Yet immigration policymakers take no note of these facts. In the first decade of the twenty-first century, 13.1 million immigrants (legal and illegal) arrived in the United States, while there was a net decline of 1 million jobs over the same period (Camarota, 2010b). The disconnect between immigration and employment was even more stark in 2008–2010. According to a report from Northeastern University's Center for Labor Market Studies (reported by Reuters), U.S. household employment declined by 6.26 million, but 1.1 million new immigrants got jobs during this period (Stoddard, 2011).

The author of that Northeastern University report estimated that about one-third of the new immigrant jobholders were illegal aliens. That means, of course, that most of the immigration-employment disconnect is caused by legal immigration. Changing the levels and selection criteria for legal immigration is a long and complicated matter, and outside the scope of this essay. It is also not a matter any presidential administration can address on its own.

But the one-third of new immigrant workers who are illegal immigrants are a different matter altogether. In this case the problem is not a badly designed immigration system but a lack of enforcement of existing laws by the executive branch. As part of the Obama administration's April 2009 worksite enforcement strategy, real worksite enforcement declined significantly, with administrative arrests down by more than half compared with 2008. Criminal arrests are down by more than half, as are indictments and convictions. What have increased in this area are audits of employee I-9 forms and the number and total dollar amount of fines against employers (although the recent statistics include settlements from cases that may be several years old). Such audits and fines are by no means a bad thing, as far as they go. But they don't go very far.

By limiting worksite enforcement to the personnel office, the current strategy foregoes the benefits of full-spectrum enforcement that includes both audits and raids, and both fines and arrests—in short, what is needed is a focus on both the employers and the employees. The current focus by U.S. Immigration and Customs Enforcement (ICE) on audits is as effective as the FBI doing gang suppression by just giving talks at high schools, without actually arresting any gang members.

Other law enforcement agencies prioritize the targets of enforcement all the time, without completely halting random enforcement. The benefit of such enforcement is a general deterrence: people will know there is a danger of being caught if they break the law. Tax audits, for example, do not focus only on money-launderers, drug dealers, and corporate crooks, but also on a random selection of ordinary taxpayers. The same is true for enforcement of occupational safety and health laws, traffic laws, hunting regulations, and every other kind of enforcement—except immigration.

FULL-SPECTRUM ENFORCEMENT

The benefits of full-spectrum enforcement are clear from recent experience. First, it opens up jobs for Americans. The Smithfield pork plant in Tar Heel, North Carolina, was raided in January 2007, and later that year more arrests were made at the homes of illegal workers (Kammer, 2009a). As a result of the departure of more than 1,500 mostly Hispanic illegal workers, local black Americans were able to find jobs at the plant, as they had when it opened in 1992, before they were slowly but steadily replaced with illegal workers from Latin America. *The New York Times* reported that the African American share of the workforce at the plant climbed from just 20 percent before the raids to 60 percent afterwards.

The Pulitzer Prize–winning journalist Jerry Kammer, who visited the Smithfield plant in the wake of the raids, observed that these raids had positively affected the job prospects for African Americans (as well as a few whites) who gathered in the company's employment office. One new employee was a woman who had been let go from a Fayetteville cafeteria due to a business slowdown; she was finishing her paperwork before starting work at the plant. Another new employee, a 20-year-old who had lost his $8.50-an-hour job at a Red Lobster in Fayetteville, told Kammer he would be making $4 an hour more at Smithfield: "That's pretty good money around here," he said (Kammer, 2009a).

Another benefit of comprehensive worksite enforcement over the current selective, almost tentative, approach is that it raises wages for blue-collar American workers. Consistent with the laws of supply and demand, an increase in the number of illegal workers causes downward pressure on wages for those native-born workers competing with them for employment in occupations such as construction, food processing, restaurants, and custodial work. Many studies have shown that wages in these industries have either stagnated or declined in recent decades, and this corresponds to periods of high illegal immigration.

At the Smithfield plant, after the raid took place, attempts to unionize in order to bargain for better wages were successful. Because they were afraid of deportation, many Hispanic workers were afraid to show support for a union. The *Charlotte Observer* reported that the raids "may have finally sealed the union's victory," while the *Fayetteville Observer* reported that "the new black majority proved to be the difference."

There is direct evidence of increased compensation that has resulted from a series of other raids. In December 2006, 1,300 illegal workers were arrested at six meatpacking plants owned by Swift & Company in the largest-ever worksite enforcement action, generating more arrests of illegal workers in one day than the current administration arrested in all of fiscal year 2010 (Kammer, 2009a). All of the plants resumed production the same day, and all were back to full production within five months, despite the fact that nearly one-quarter of the total workforce had been illegal aliens. Most importantly, at the four facilities where information was available, wages and bonuses rose an average of 8 percent after the departure of the illegal workers—that's an 8 percent raise virtually overnight due to vigorous worksite enforcement.

A third benefit of full-spectrum enforcement that includes arrests of illegal employees is that it is necessary to gather evidence against crooked employers. Despite the current Worksite Enforcement Strategy's claimed focus on targeting bad-actor employers, the number of criminal arrests of employers actually dropped from fiscal year 2008 to 2009, and the number in 2011 was only slightly higher than 2 years before. One reason for this is that if agents can't arrest or even speak to illegal workers, it's very difficult to gather evidence on their employers' illegal activities. The Agriprocessors, Inc. kosher meatpacking plant in Postville, Iowa, for instance, had been the target of investigations by state officials for health and safety violations even before the May 2008 raid that resulted in the arrest of nearly 400 illegal aliens for identity theft and related charges. But only after the arrests was the curtain torn away and the squalor and mass illegality exposed. Management personnel were arrested for criminal child labor and immigration violations. What's more, the raid also exposed financial crimes committed by the plant's chief executive. Merely auditing the plant's personnel records, while scrupulously avoiding any arrests of illegal workers, could well have meant that Agriprocessors would still be abusing underage workers today.

Finally, full-spectrum worksite enforcement is necessary to successfully turn off the jobs magnet that attracts illegal immigrants to the United States in the first place, and also enables them to remain. While the goal of worksite enforcement is not to try to actually arrest and deport every illegal worker, every illegal worker does need to know that he could be arrested at any time. Likewise, the goal is not to fine or arrest every employer of illegal aliens, but rather to ensure that employers are aware that there's a realistic chance that they could be arrested. This is the only way to create an environment where illegal aliens are unable to find work and self-deport—an approach called "attrition through enforcement." In the absence of across-the-board enforcement, neither illegal workers nor their employers have much to fear from law enforcement; on the contrary, they get the impression that what they are doing isn't really all that illegal after all. Under such lax conditions, the decline in the illegal immigrant population that occurred before the recession began as a result of enhanced enforcement would not have taken place (Camarota & Jensenius, 2009). In fact, if and when the job market significantly improves, the current constrained and limited approach to worksite enforcement virtually ensures that the illegal population will start growing again.

Jerry Kammer's reporting on the Smithfield pork plant provides another example of how proper enforcement of immigration laws helps neutralize the magnetic force that attracts illegal immigrants to American jobs. Two Mexican maintenance workers expressed their wish to leave the jobs they currently held tending the grounds outside the plant, which they obtained through a contractor and which only paid an hourly wage of $6.50, for a job at Smithfield. The problem was that this was not an option for them because the company was insisting on proper documentation. As a result, the two men told Kammer, they would probably soon be moving on to look for better pay elsewhere.

Illegal immigrants like any other people respond to the signals they are given. When the government indicates through real worksite enforcement that illegal employment is not tolerated, these workers move on. When, as occurs today, the opposite signal is sent, they make different choices.

Finally, in July 2011, *USA Today* reported that the American towns on the Mexican border are not "war zones" and have relatively low crime rates, proving that the border is better policed than in the past. Indeed, there are far more Border Patrol agents in the area than there were a decade ago. The importance of this report cannot be overstated: The U.S. government can control the border, even if has not yet been totally successful in this effort. American taxpayers would get more bang for the next buck spent on immigration enforcement by concentrating on interior enforcement, using tools like mandatory E-Verify, enforcing policies that jail illegal aliens for identity theft, and, yes, continuing the policy of worksite raids. Such raids are as necessary as speed traps or IRS audits. It's a question of prioritizing the country's resources. The alternative is to downgrade immigration law itself. Because immigration control is one of the most important security priorities for the government, failure to control the border compromises the rule of law. More importantly, it compromises our nation's safety and economic well-being.

References and Further Reading

Camarota, S. A. (2010a). *From bad to worse: Unemployment and underemployment among less-educated U.S.-born workers, 2007 to 2010.* Retrieved from Center for Immigration Studies website:http://cis.org/bad-to-worse

Camarota, S.A. (2010b). *Immigration and economic stagnation: An examination of trends 2000 to 2010.* Retrieved from Center for Immigration Studies website: http://cis.org/highest-decade

Camarota, S. A., & Jensenius, K. (2009). *A shifting tide: Recent trends in the illegal immigrant population.* Retrieved from Center for Immigration Studies website: http://cis.org/IllegalImmigration-ShiftingTide

Greenhouse, S. (2008, December 12). After 15 years, North Carolina plant unionizes. *The New York Times.* Retrieved from http://www.nytimes.com/2008/12/13/us/13smithfield.html

Kammer, J. (2009a). *Immigration raids at Smithfield: How an ICE enforcement action boosted union organizing and the employment of American workers.* Retrieved from Center for Immigration Studies website: http://cis.org/SmithfieldImmigrationRaid-Unionization

Kammer, J. (2009b). *The 2006 Swift raids: Assessing the impact of immigration enforcement actions at six facilities.* Retrieved from Center for Immigration Studies website: http://cis.org/2006SwiftRaids

Stoddard, E. (2011). Over a million immigrants land U.S. jobs in 2008–10. *Reuters.* Retrieved from http://www.reuters.com/article/idUSTRE70J37P20110120

U.S. Department of Homeland Security. (2009). *Worksite enforcement strategy: Factsheet.* Retrieved from http://www.ice.gov/doclib/news/library/factsheets/pdf/worksite-strategy.pdf

Mark Krikorian

Note: This essay was adapted from Mark Krikorian's "Worksite Enforcement: Audits Are Not Enough," text of testimony given before the Committee on the Judiciary, Subcommittee on Immigration Policy and Enforcement, January 26, 2011. Available online at http://www.cis.org/node/2548.

COUNTERPOINT

The last time there was a significant overhaul of the country's immigration system, Ronald Reagan was president, DVDs were not around, cell phones were two-pound contraptions beyond the reach of the vast majority of American households, and most of today's college undergrads had not been born. The year was 1986. The U.S. economy has changed a great deal since then, but its immigration system has not.

In 1986, President Ronald Reagan signed the Immigration Reform and Control Act into law. Among other things, the act provided a path to legal status for unauthorized immigrants who met certain requirements, and it created, for the first time, requirements for employers to verify the eligibility of their employees to work lawfully in the United States. On the one hand, these policy prescriptions acknowledged that the main factor driving unauthorized immigration flows into the country was the lure of jobs. On the other hand, the prescription dealt with the symptoms, rather than the cause of the problem, which still has much to do with the deficiencies in the legal immigration system surrounding the issue of workforce supply and demand.

In the past, particularly in times of economic growth, employers seeking workers, and workers seeking jobs, met each other outside of the legal channels provided by an immigration system ill equipped to respond to economic and workforce needs. The result was a wink-and-a-nod system where many employers were able to hire undocumented workers to maintain and expand their operations, many politicians helped redirect enforcement operations aimed at employers in their districts, and the undocumented population grew. The 1986 law sought to wipe the slate clean by creating a vetting process for undocumented workers to legalize their status, and by establishing some mechanisms to attempt to regulate employment practices. However, it did not deal with the core challenge that would address both of those issues: recasting the employment-based legal immigration system to meet the needs of the economy and the U.S. workforce. Congress missed an opportunity to create a system with sufficient elasticity and adequate regulations that would expand legal channels and therefore disincentivize unauthorized flows; a system where needed workers could come to the U.S. legally vetted under regulations that would prevent their exploitation and prevent the undermining of American workers.

Instead, Congress adopted the theory that punishing employers for hiring undocumented workers would reduce the lure of jobs for unauthorized immigrants and, over time, reduce the number of people coming in illegally. The reality was that employers and politicians exerted influence to divert punishment, mostly to undocumented workers. When worksite raids were carried out, they largely focused on workers and did not succeed in changing the hiring practices of the industries, or in penalizing the employers they targeted. In the end, worksite raids were not a sufficient deterrent to override the powers of supply and demand in the marketplace. A growing economy had created a demand for more workers, and unauthorized immigrants were part of the supply that met that demand. Because the United States failed to modernize its legal immigration system, supply and demand were meeting in the black market.

There are two principal mechanisms for immigrating legally to the United States: family visas and employment visas. These are the pillars of the country's immigration system. The vast majority of visas are family-based. On the employment-based side, there are approximately 140,000 available visas per year for permanent workers, with a number of additional visa categories available for seasonal and temporary workers. Most employment categories are for high-skilled workers, with a cap on low-skilled permanent workers of 5,000. These numbers have proved to be insufficient over the decades, particularly in the face of growth of the service, construction, and similar sectors. This mismatch between legal supply channels and demand fueled the growth of a labor black market. With these transactions taking place outside legal channels, American labor laws and protections proved harder to enforce, often to the detriment of immigrant and native workers alike.

Fast-forward to the present, and the problem still has not been solved. The result is another, larger group of unauthorized workers who helped the country thrive during a strong economy. Estimates for 2008 put the undocumented population at nearly 11 million, including in its ranks over 8 million workers who made up approximately 5 percent of the American workforce. Two-thirds of the immigrants in the country illegally have lived here for over 10 years, and half of them now live in mixed-status families with children. Most of those children, about 4 million of them, are U.S. citizens. This population of unauthorized workers is the one most directly targeted by worksite raids, although the effect of such raids is felt far beyond these workers.

THE ESCALATION OF WORKSITE RAIDS

Congress has made several attempts, particularly between 2005 and 2007, to address the problems with the immigration system. As a result, the nation continues to experience the systemic failure of its immigration policies. The breakdown—particularly in the legal immigration arena, where existing channels have been inadequate to meet family reunification needs or the demand for workers during a strong economy—fueled the growth of the undocumented population and introduced pressures in other areas of the system. Since the multiple components of the U.S. immigration system are designed to work in tandem to achieve a legal and orderly process, the lack of federal action to address ongoing policy breakdowns has had a deep impact on multiple levels. This inaction affects the ability of the system to (1) achieve a legal and regulated flow, (2) implement enforcement measures that prioritize national security and public safety and help ensure that employers maintain a legal workforce, (3) support the successful integration of immigrants into society, and (4) conduct itself in way that upholds the nation's values and traditions respecting the legal and civil rights of America's diverse community.

While a needed policy overhaul has remained elusive, public frustration over inaction and the political vitriol around the issue have intensified. Thus, absent meaningful immigration reform, the response has been increasingly aggressive enforcement tactics that deal with the symptoms of the problem, with little examination of their impact on its core causes or of their unintended consequences. In this environment, worksite raids increased, providing a high-visibility show of force meant to indicate a change from the low priority historically given to workplace enforcement in the 1990s. Widely described as heavy-handed, these raids captured headlines and catered to political calls for heightened enforcement as the way to prevent illegal immigration. However, after a period of escalation between 2006 and 2008, and despite their ability to grab headlines, worksite raids have largely been discredited as an effective strategy.

The costs. Between 2006 and 2008, large-scale worksite raids were used to round up workers and put those found to be unauthorized into deportation proceedings. A 2011 statement by the National Immigration Law Center to the U.S. House of Representatives reported that Immigration and Customs Enforcement (ICE) detained over 9,000 workers in worksite raids during fiscal years 2007 and 2008. Some of the better-documented examples of worksite raids during that period included a December 2006 raid of six pork processing plants operated by Swift & Company in several states, during which ICE arrested 1,282 workers. It is described as the largest immigration raid on a single company in U.S. history. In 2008, the largest single-site raid was conducted at an electrical equipment plant in Laurel, Mississippi, resulting in the arrests of 595 immigrant workers. And in 2008 in Postville, Iowa, a town with a population of 2,273, approximately 900 ICE agents raided the Agriprocessors meat packing plant, arresting 389 workers.

Worksite raids have included SWAT-style teams with several hundred armed personnel in full gear securing all exits of a workplace, helicopters hovering overhead, and all workers, regardless of their immigration status, detained for hours while ICE agents interrogated everyone. Given the nature of these operations, worksite raids carry a high price tag that has not been justified by the outcomes. The raid of Agriprocessors in Postville was estimated to have cost $5.2 million, putting the cost to taxpayers at an average of $13,396 for each of the 389 undocumented immigrants taken into custody. This cost may be low, since workers in the Postville raid were put in fast-tracked court proceedings and charged en masse, even though some of the workers did not understand the proceedings or the charges. Based on 2008 data, the Center for American Progress calculated that it would cost between $200 billion and $285 billion over 5 years to deport the nearly

11 million undocumented immigrants estimated to be in the United States at the time—which would put the cost between $18,000 and $26,000 per deportee.

In addition, were such policies to be successful, by some estimates the mass deportation of nearly 11 million people—a population the size of Ohio—would result in $2.6 trillion in cumulative lost gross domestic product (GDP) over 10 years.

The impact on families and communities. In many instances, the zeal with which ICE agents carried out worksite raids led to violations of the rights and civil liberties of workers, including U.S. citizens and lawful residents. According to a 2009 analysis of the raids at the Swift & Company plants by the United Food and Commercial Workers union, U.S. citizens working in the plants, including a Korean War veteran, were subjected to ridicule, threats, and intimidation by ICE agents. U.S. citizens and lawful workers were handcuffed, searched, and deprived of their ability to contact their families for hours even after having informed agents of their lawful status.

Clearly, the impact was more acute among unauthorized workers and their families, but it is important to note that U.S. citizens were also affected. In 1999, the Urban Institute estimated that approximately 1 in 10 families in the United States was a mixed-status family, meaning that its members include U.S. citizens as well as legal and undocumented immigrants. In the immediate aftermath of the raids, workers were put on buses and detention times ranged from a few hours to months. Following detention, some unauthorized workers were immediately deported and others were released to wait for a hearing before an immigration judge. Some of the workers were sent to detention facilities in states far from the site of the raid, away from their families, social workers, and attorneys working on their cases. Family members were unaware of what was happening to loved ones, and parents were separated from their children, causing long-lasting impact. Women who were breastfeeding their children were separated from their newborns. In one case, an emergency room physician treating a newborn for dehydration appealed to ICE to free the 8-month-old infant's mother, citing medical reasons for which the child needed to continue breastfeeding. Not only did children suffer from the fear of the initial separation, but they continued to suffer from the financial instability in their homes that led to food shortages and increased economic hardship. Negative emotional and mental health consequences for these children also ensued. Children displayed symptoms of depression and other psychological problems, such as sleep disturbance, loss of appetite, fearfulness, mood swings, and feelings of abandonment by one or both parents—since in some cases both parents were removed. A study by the Urban Institute of three communities where large-scale worksite raids occurred revealed that for every two immigrants detained as a result of worksite raids, approximately one child is left behind.

In addition to the workers and their families, worksite raids also impact the broader communities where they occur. A federal court interpreter assigned to work in the Agriprocessors case likened the raid to a manmade disaster. Schools and local agencies had to act as first responders, making arrangements for children whose parents were detained and unable to contact them. School officials had to instruct school bus drivers to drop off children only at residences where there was an adult present. Teachers were requested to stay late to help care for children, and they coordinated mental health services. After the chaos of the raids, school personnel held community meetings to assure parents that the schools were safe places and urge students to return to school. The principal of the school stated that the American children who returned to school also were traumatized, feeling as if their classmates who didn't return to school had died. The Postville City Council declared the town a humanitarian and economic disaster area. Agriprocessors ultimately filed for bankruptcy in 2008. A report on the aftermath of the 2006 Swift & Company plant raid in Marshalltown, Iowa, documented that demand for goods and services suffered and the city experienced an economic downturn. The city's tax revenues saw a decline of 3.2 percent in retail sales in the fiscal year when the raids occurred. Businesses lost not only valuable workers but also customers. Schools lost students, and tenants lost renters. Swift & Company was sold to a Brazilian company. The report concluded that the town suffered from a localized economic recession for 6 months to a year after the raid.

The impact on jobs. Some proponents of worksite raids and similar measures argue that these actions are essential to free up jobs for native-born and legal immigrant workers—although some would exclude the latter as well. It is not unusual to hear arguments that draw a direct line between jobs undocumented immigrants may have and the number of unemployed American and legal immigrant workers, particularly during the current economic recession. But this presupposes a perfect match between the location of jobs and the ability of the unemployed to relocate, and between the type of jobs that would theoretically become available and the willingness of the unemployed to take them. Indeed, there may be workers willing to relocate for a job and willing to take a job they would not consider in better economic times. But to argue that removing the estimated 8 million undocumented workers from the workforce would translate to putting 8 million unemployed Americans back to work is simplistic. It assumes, for example, that a laid-off American telecommunications worker would take a job made available by deporting an undocumented farm worker or dishwasher.

There has also been much debate about the impact of undocumented workers on wages. The conclusions are mixed and paint a more complicated picture than the simple assertion often made that these workers depress wages. Evidence indicates that those most affected by competition with low-skilled unauthorized workers are recent legal immigrants, while the aggregate impact on the economy ranges from neutral to positive, because these workers operate in sectors that complement the American workforce. According to a report from the Fiscal Policy Institute, the unemployment rates of native-born workers are lower in areas with higher rates of immigration because immigrants stimulate the economy with their spending. This helps to create jobs. The report shows that in the combined 25 largest metropolitan areas of the United States—which represent 42 percent of the country's overall population, 66 percent of the national immigrant population, and half of the national gross domestic product—immigrants are 20 percent of the population and generate 20 percent of the economic output (Kallick, 2009).

A more local example of this phenomenon comes from Georgia, which passed a restrictive immigration law in 2011. This law is a copycat of a 2010 Arizona law that generated national condemnation and boycotts and raised concerns about racial profiling and jurisdiction over enforcement of immigration laws. As with the Arizona law, the courts enjoined Georgia's law on constitutional grounds. But confusion and fear about its ramifications made many migrant farm workers—legal and undocumented—decide to avoid the state. As a result, the agricultural sector in the state started seeing labor shortages that led to an inability to pick crops, some of which were left to rot in the fields. State agriculture commissioner Gary Black surveyed farm employers, who reported a shortage of approximately 11,000 workers. Potential losses to the industry were estimated to be between $300 million and $1 billion in 2011. These are, unquestionably, punishing jobs. They are also seasonal. Even with an unemployment rate of nearly 10 percent, these agricultural jobs have been hard to fill, moving the governor to propose recruiting people on probation, though early attempts to do so indicate this will not solve the shortage.

A job does not exist in isolation. The consequences of a worker shortage in the fields, for example, have ripple effects throughout the industry at various levels, such as packaging, distribution, marketing, and management. The U.S. Department of Agriculture states that there are 3.1 related jobs off the farm for every job on the farm. Seeking to deport the 800,000 to 1 million undocumented immigrants who work in the agricultural sector would impact jobs held by native-born workers as well.

Finally, it is not clear that worksite raids are effective in improving job quality and working conditions in sectors where undocumented workers hold jobs. In several cases, worksite raids disrupted investigations of labor abuses that were already underway. For example, Iowa authorities were investigating the Agriprocessors meat packing plant for child labor abuses, hour and wage violations, and harassment when the ICE raid took place. A dozen children, including one as young as 13 years old, were poised to provide information assisting the investigation, but they were instead detained for several days by ICE authorities. ICE had knowledge of the egregious labor violations occurring at the Agriprocessors plant, but they did not coordinate with labor investigators to ensure that the investigation could continue and citations of labor violations could be filed. In New Bedford, Massachusetts, ICE had knowledge of egregious conditions at the Michael Bianco plant, but it conducted a raid and arrested 361 workers without coordinating with labor investigators. One week after the raid, Occupational Safety and Health Administration inspectors arrived after many of the workers who could attest to those conditions had been removed to detention facilities outside of the state. As a result, federal authorities missed an opportunity to prosecute abuse of workers, including minors, and thereby help protect the rights of all workers. Worksite raids failed to send the message that exploiting workers and skirting U.S. labor laws would not be tolerated. During the height of these raids, relatively few businesses were fined or had their executives held liable. Instead, employees and their families bore the full brunt of these tactics.

ADDING NEW INGREDIENTS TO AN OLD PRESCRIPTION

The mixed record of worksite raids, and a growing understanding of their detrimental effects, led President Barack Obama to announce in 2009 that his administration would focus worksite enforcement resources on places where there was evidence of widespread abuses and violations of criminal statutes. They would look for signs of abuse of workers and evidence of trafficking, smuggling, harboring, visa fraud, document fraud, and money laundering. Instead of conducting costly worksite raids, ICE would audit employers using, as the point of departure, the I-9 form established in 1986 to verify worker eligibility. The I-9 form requires that employers examined certain forms of personal identification, such as a driver's license, Social Security number, or passport, at the time of hire. But this process has turned out to be a formality. A market for fake documents has grown and the I-9 form has not actually prevent the hiring of unauthorized workers. Using audits, the Department of Homeland Security (DHS) checks the completed I-9 forms against federal databases. According to testimony submitted by ICE to the House Judiciary Committee in January 2011, in fiscal year 2010, ICE more than doubled the number of worksite investigations compared to fiscal year 2008 by initiating 2,746 worksite enforcement investigations. ICE issued 237 final orders requiring employers to stop violations of the law, and fining them nearly $7 million, in contrast with the 18 final orders issued in fiscal year 2008, which resulted in $675,209 in fines. This was the highest number of final orders issued since the creation of ICE in 2003.

In theory, this approach could be used to help eliminate unfair advantages enjoyed by unscrupulous employers who choose to hire more vulnerable undocumented workers over authorized workers. So far, however, the strategy has not clearly focused on employers who are abusing the immigration system to depress wages or game labor standards. Several of the high-profile I-9 audits have been conducted at worksites where employers paid above the minimum wage and treated workers fairly. While very different in nature and designed to avoid some of the social chaos unleashed on communities by huge, SWAT-style worksite raids, the audits—also known as desktop raids or "silent" raids—have affected employers in various sectors, including garment makers, fruit growers, building service contractors, and fast food restaurants. This underscores the extent to which unauthorized immigrant workers are intertwined in the U.S. economy.

There are many honest employers who are trying to comply with the law but describe being faced with having to fire long-time employees as a result of the ICE audits. One nursery owner in Visalia, California, told *The New York Times* that telling 26 of his employees that they were fired was "probably the worst day of my life." The employees had worked for him between 5 and 10 years and had reliably provided a specialized service. Since the audit, he estimates that his expenses have increased about 10 percent, and he has had difficulty finding replacement workers. In the meantime, he believes some of his old workers have gone to work for competitors that pay less than he does. Similarly, in October 2009, ABM Janitorial Services laid off about 1,250 employees after ICE audited the company. ABM, in Minnesota, provided benefits and good wages, and workers had union representation. A survey of 50 of the ABM workers who lost their jobs after the audit showed that most of the workers remained in Minnesota. The unintended effects of desktop raids seem to be that these workers are being pushed deeper into the underground economy. Data show they are not leaving the country, but rather shifting to other sectors where employers are willing to find ways around the system. As a result, the workers become more vulnerable and can be forced to accept unsafe conditions and lower wages by unscrupulous employers, who now compete with the honest employers that had to fire the workers in the first place.

Another mechanism that has been used to increase compliance with hiring laws has been DHS's E-Verify online verification system. E-Verify is still largely a voluntary program, although federal contractors are mandated to use it, and several states are now requiring its use. E-Verify began as a pilot program in 1997 as a way for employers to enter the information submitted by an employee on the I-9 form and receive a quick response as to whether the information provided by the employee matched the information in Social Security and DHS databases. The system sends a response to the employer as to whether the employee is authorized to work or whether there may be an error preventing the system from confirm automatically that the employee is authorized to work. According to the DHS website, more than 238,000 employers are currently enrolled in the E-Verify program, and about 1,200 new businesses enroll each week. While there have been improvements to the E-Verify program since its inception, and it is seen as a useful tool to aid employers in verifying worker eligibility, stakeholders from various sectors have voiced concerns and pushed for changes to the system. For example, E-Verify is 30 times more likely to incorrectly flag naturalized U.S. citizens as ineligible to work than native-born workers, while it confirms nonauthorized workers as eligible to work over 50 percent of the time. Additionally, it has been documented that concern about immigration enforcement and confusion about the system have led some employers to simply not consider any workers they deem to be "foreign." This disproportionately affects Latino and Asian workers, among others, regardless of immigration status. The existing system has yet to prevent subjecting many lawful workers to intentional or inadvertent discrimination.

CONCLUSION

Worksite raids are not an unambiguously good strategy for solving the immigration situation. Costly, as well as socially and economically disruptive, they do not create a sufficient deterrent to unauthorized employment and have been replaced by other workplace enforcement strategies. The real lesson behind worksite raids is that the systemic failure of our immigration policies requires strategies that go beyond a "force them out" approach, and should start with a functioning legal immigration system that aims to shrink the black market for labor.

Large-scale worksite raids, desk audits, and E-Verify are different iterations of a similar prescription—an approach that deals with the consequences, not the cause, of the problem. Resources devoted to securing the border have exceeded the targets set in all recent immigration proposals. There are more agents at the border than ever before, and deportations have reached historic levels, with approximately 1 million immigrants being deported in the first 2 years of the Obama administration, through a combination of workplace enforcement and other tactics. Yet at current rates it would take 20 years to remove the unauthorized population if no other workers joined their ranks.

In the absence of a complete reform of U.S. immigration laws, it is difficult to argue that increased workplace enforcement alone can be effective. The resources devoted to removing undocumented workers from the workplace have steadily increased, but the core problem remains. It is necessary to strengthen the efficiency of the legal immigration system, which would encourage people to go through it rather than around it. During the past 2 decades, in spite of tremendous increases in worksite enforcement and expenditures on border security, the number of undocumented immigrants in the country has roughly tripled. The one factor that has definitively slowed illegal immigration has been the economic recession. Ironically, while the current partisan environment in Congress has eroded the bipartisan coalition needed to advance comprehensive immigration reform legislation, from an economic perspective this is the most propitious time to enact measures to restore law and order to the system. In light of reduced demand for workers due to the state of the economy and the reduction in immigrant flows, this is the moment to overhaul the system in a way that responds to the future needs of the country.

History has pointed to ways to reduce illegal immigration. A weak economy with high unemployment is extraordinarily effective, but not desirable. Increasing legal immigration is also extremely effective, and if managed effectively can help build the economy while protecting the rights of all workers.

REFERENCES AND FURTHER READING

Alba, R. (2009). Paradoxes of race and ethnicity in America today. In R. Alba, *Blurring the color line: The new chance for a more integrated America* (pp. 1–20). Boston, MA: Harvard University Press.

Alba, R. (2010). Achieving a more integrated America. *Dissent, 57*(3), 57–60. doi: 10.1353/dss.0.0175

Archibold, R. C. (2010, April 23). Arizona enacts stringent law on immigration. *The New York Times.* Retrieved from http://www.nytimes.com/2010/04/24/us/politics/24immig.html

Asia-Pacific Human Rights Information Center. (2008). *South Korea; Support for Multicultural Families Act enacted.* Retrieved from http://www.hurights.or.jp/archives/newsinbrief-en/section1/2008/10/south-korea-support-for-multicultural-families-act-enacted.html

Barrett, A. N. (2010). *Acculturative stress and gang involvement among Latinos: U.S.-born versus immigrant youth* (Unpublished psychology honors). Georgia State University, Georgia.

Capps, R., Fix, M. E., Murray, J. O., Passel, J. S., & Hernandez, S. H. (2005). *The new demography of America's schools: Immigration and the no child left behind act.* Retrieved from The Urban Institute website: http://www.urban.org/publications/311230.html

Chapa, J. (2005). Affirmative action and percentage plans as alternatives for increasing successful participation of minorities in higher education. *Journal of Hispanic Higher Education, 4*(3), 181–196.

Children in the United States of America: A statistical portrait by race-ethnicity, immigrant origins, and language. (2011). *Annals of the American Academy of Political and Social Science, 633*(1), 102. doi:10.1177/0002716210383205

Cohn, D. V., & Taylor, P. (2010). *Baby boomers approach age 65 glumly: Survey findings about America's largest generation.* Retrieved from Pew Research Center website: http://pewresearch.org/pubs/1834/baby-boomers-old-age-downbeat-pessimism

Dickson, M. C. (2004). *Latina teen pregnancy: Problems and prevention.* Retrieved from Population Resource Center website: http://www.prcdc.org/files/Latina_Teen_Pregnancy.pd

Dinan, K. A. (2006). *Young children in immigrant families the role of philanthropy: Sharing knowledge, creating services, and building supportive policies.* Retrieved from National Center for Children in Poverty webiste: http://www.nccp.org/publications/pdf/download_24.pdf

Duncan, G. J., & Brooks-Gunn, J. (Eds.). (1997). *Consequences of growing up poor.* New York, NY: Russell Sage Foundation.

Elmelch, Y., McCaski, K., Lennon, M. C., & Lu, H. (2002). *Children of immigrants: A statistical profile (September 2002).* Retrieved from The National Center for Children in Poverty website: http://www.nccp.org/publications/pdf/text_475.pdf

Engstrom, D. W. (2006). Outsiders and exclusion: Immigrants in the United States. In D. W. Engstrom & L. M. Piedra (Eds.), *Our diverse society: Race and ethnicity—implications for 21st century American society* (pp. 19–36). Washington, DC: NASW Press.

Fortuny, K., Hernandez, D. J., & Chaudry, A. (2010). Young children of immigrants: The leading edge of America's future. Retrieved from The Urban Institute website: http://www.urban.org/UploadedPDF/412203-young-children.pdf

Fry, R. (2003). *Hispanic youth dropping out of U.S. schools: Measuring challenge.* Retrieved from Pew Hispanic Center website: http://www.pewhispanic.org/files/reports/19.pdf

Fry, R., & Gonzales, F. (2008). *One-in-five and growing fast: A profile of Hispanic public school students.* Retrieved from Pew Hispanic Center website: http://pewhispanic.org/reports/report.php?ReportID=92

Fry, R., & Passel, J. S. (2009). *Latino children: A majority are U.S.-born offspring of immigrants.* Retrieved from Pew Hispanic Center website: http://pewhispanic.org/files/reports/110.pdf

Garcia, M., & Nury, M. (2011, October, 12). Hey Alabama, take a hint from California. Retrieved from *Huffington Post* Latino Politics LatinoVoices website: http://www.huffingtonpost.com/monica-garcia/hey-alabama-take-a-hint-f_b_1005772.html

Grieco, E. M., & Trevelyan, E. N. (2010, October). Place of birth of the foreign-born population 2009. *American Community Survey Briefs.* Retrieved from U.S. Census Bureau website: http://www.census.gov/prod/2010pubs/acsbr09-15.pdf

Grubel, H., & Grady, P. (2011). *Immigration and the Canadian welfare state 2011* (Immigration and Refugee Policy Report). Retrieved from Fraser Institute website: http://www.fraserinstitute.org/research-news/display.aspx?id=17546

Hernandez, D. J. (2004). Demographic change and the life circumstances of immigrant families. *Future of Children, 14*(2), 17–47.

Hernandez, D. J., Denton, N. A., & Macartney, S. E. (2008). Children in immigrant families: Looking to America's future. *Society for Research in Child Development, 22*(3), 3–22.

Immigration Works USA. (2012). *Fact sheet: Bottom line. The economic consequences of state immigration law.* Retrieved from http://www.immigrationworksusa.org/uploaded/file/IW%20bottom%20line.pdf

Jiménez, T. R. (2007). From newcomers to Americans: An integration policy for a nation of immigrants [Policy paper]. *Immigration Policy in Focus, 5*(11).

Kallick, D. D. (2009). *Immigrants in the economy: Contribution of immigrant workers to the country's 25 largest metropolitan areas.* New York: Fiscal Policy Institute. Retrieved from http://www.fiscalpolicy.org/ImmigrantsIn25MetroAreas_20091130.pdf

Ku, L., & Matini, S. (2010). Left out: Immigrants' access to health care and insurance. *Health Affairs, 20*(1), 247–256.

Kurtzleben, D. (2010, December, 14). U.S. Hispanic population is booming. *U.S. News.* Retrieved from http://www.usnews.com/news/articles/2010/12/14/us-hispanic-population-is-booming

Leach, M. A., Brown, S. K., Bean, F. D., & Hook, J. V. (2011). *Unauthorized immigrant parents: Do their migration histories limit their children's education?* Retrieved from http://www.scribd.com/doc/70242186/Unauthorized-Immigrant-Parents-Do-Their-Migration-Histories-Limit-Their-Children-s-Education

Lee, S. (2011). Racial variations in major depressive disorder onset among immigrant populations in the United States. *Journal of Mental Health, 20*(3), 260–269.

Lee, R., & Jang, S. (2010). Analysis of immigrant support policies in multicultural societies: Case studies of the U.S. and Canada (S. Choi, Trans.). *International Community Research, 14*(1), 179–208.

Martin, P., & Midgley, E. (2010). Immigration in America 2010. *Population Bulletin.* Retrieved from http://www.prb.org/Publications/PopulationBulletins/2010/immigrationupdate1.aspx

Massey, D. (1995). The new immigration and ethnicity in the United States. *Population and Development Review, 21*(3), 631–652.

Mather, M. (2009). Children in immigrant families chart new path. *Population Reference Bureau Report.* Retrieved from http://www.prb.org/pdf09/immigrantchildren.pdf

McLoyd, V. C. (1998). Socioeconomic disadvantage and child development. *American Psychologist, 53*(2), 185–205.

Montero-Sieburth, M., & Melendez, E. (Eds.). (2007). *Latinos in a changing society.* Boston, MA: Greenwood.

Morales, R., & Bonilla, F. (1993). *Latinos in a changing U.S. economy: Comparative perspectives on growing inequality* (Vol. 7). Newbury Park, CA: Sage.

Nasser, H. E., & Overberg, P. (2010). Kindergartens see more Hispanic, Asian students. *USA Today.* Retrieved from http://www.usatoday.com/news/nation/census/2010-08-27-1Akindergarten27_ST_N.htm

Obama, B. (2008, March 18). Barack Obama's speech on race, Transcribed speech. *The New York Times.* Retrieved from http://www.nytimes.com/2008/03/18/us/politics/18text-obama.html

Passel, J., & Cohn, D. (2009). *A portrait of unauthorized immigrants in the United States.* Retrieved from Pew Hispanic Center website: http://www.pewhispanic.org/files/reports/107.pdf

Perez, R. (2011). Latino mental health: Acculturation challenges in service provision. In L. P. Buki & L. M. Piedra (Eds.), *Creating infrastructures for Latino mental health* (pp. 31–54). New York, NY: Springer.

Pew Hispanic Center. (2010). *Statistical portrait of the foreign-born population in the United States, 2008.* Retrieved from http://pewhispanic.org/factsheets/factsheet.php?FactsheetID=59

Portes, A. (1997). Immigration theory for a new century: Some problems and opportunities. *The International Migration Review, 31*(4), 799. doi:10.2307/2547415

Portes, A., & Rumbaut, R. G. (2001). School achievement and failure. In A. Portes & R. G. Rumbaut (Eds.), *Legacies: The story of the immigrant second generation* (pp. 233–268). New York, NY: Russell Sage Foundation.

Ridings, J. W., Piedra, L. M., Capeles, J., Rodríguez, R., Freier, F., & Byoun, S. (2011). Building a Latino youth program: Using concept mapping to identify community-based strategies for success. *Journal of Social Service Research, 37*(1), 34–49.

Robertson, C. (2011, October 3). After ruling, Hispanics flee an Alabama town. *The New York Times.* Retrieved from http://www.nytimes.com/2011/10/04/us/after-ruling-hispanics-flee-an-alabama-town.html?pagewanted=all

Schneider, B., Martinez, S., & Owens, A. (2006). Barriers to educational opportunities for Hispanics in the United States. In M. Tienda & F. Mitchell (Eds.), *Hispanics and the future of America* (pp. 179–221). Washington, DC: National Academies Press.

Sullivan, T. A. (2006). Demography, the demand for social services, and the potential for civic conflict. In D. Engstrom & L. M. Piedra (Eds.), *Our diverse society: Race and ethnicity—implications for 21st century American society* (pp. 9–18). Washington, DC: NASW Press.

Suro, R. (2006). A developing identity: Hispanics in the United States. *Carnegie Reporter, 3*(4). Retrieved from http://lrc.salemstate.edu/hispanics/other/A_Developing_Identity_Hispanics_in_The_United_States_by_Roberto_Suro.htm

Taylor, P., Lopez, M. H., Passel, J., & Motel, S. (2011). *Unauthorized immigrants: Length of residency, patterns of parenthood.* Retrieved from Pew Hispanic Center website: http://www.pewhispanic.org/files/2011/12/Unauthorized-Characteristics.pdf

Tienda, M. (2011). Hispanics and U.S. schools: Problems, puzzles and possibilities. In M. T. Hallinan (Ed.), *Frontiers in sociology of education* (pp. 303–310). New York, NY: Springer.

Tienda, M., & Sullivan, T. A. (2009). The promise and peril of the Texas uniform admission law. In M. Hall, M. Krislov, & D. L. Featherman (Eds.), *The next twenty-five years? Affirmative action and higher education in the United States and South Africa* (pp. 155–174). Ann Arbor, MI: University of Michigan Press.

Tumlin, K. C., & Zimmerman, W. (2003). *Immigrants and TANF: A look at immigrant welfare recipients in three cities.* Retrieved from The Urban Institute website: http://www.urban.org/uploadedpdf/310874_op69.pdf

Urban Institute. (2006). *Children of immigrants: Facts and figures* [fact sheet]. Retrieved from http://www.urban.org/publications/900955.html

U.S. Department of Education. (2002). *Executive summary: The No Child Left Behind Act of 2001.* Retrieved from http://www2.ed.gov/nclb/overview/intro/execsumm.html

U.S.-Mexico Border and Immigration Task Force. (2008). *U.S.-Mexico border policy report: Effective border policy; security, responsibility, and human rights at the U.S.-Mexico border.* Retrieved from http://www.utexas.edu/ . . . /humanrights/borderwall/ . . . /municipalities-US-Me

Clarissa Martínez-De-Castro and Laura Vazquez

Population Growth

POINT: Population growth and economic growth are linked. Immigration in the face of declining birth rates of native-born Americans has been an important source of new workers, especially young workers. Further, immigrants contribute to both the supply and the demand aspects of the U.S. economy.

Susan K. Brown and Frank D. Bean, University of California, Irvine

COUNTERPOINT: Although population growth and economic growth are linked, the fact that the United States remains socially and economically stratified should temper unrestrained optimism that dividends generated by such growth will be realized. Unless population growth spurred by immigration is met with federal policies to incorporate immigrants into the American mainstream, negative outcomes will prove to be unavoidable.

Lissette M. Piedra, Shinwoo Choi, and Hye Joon Park, University of Illinois at Urbana-Champaign

Introduction

Debates about immigration and population growth result from consideration of how best to respond to important demographic realities in the United States. First among these is that the native-born population is aging and the birthrate has plateaued for several decades and has actually decreased since the recent "Great Recession" in the late 2000s. Figure 22.1 shows the change in the number of native-born and foreign-born persons in each age group between 1990 and 2006, making clear how important immigrants have been to the growth in the labor force.

Because many immigrant-sending countries in the world have relatively young populations compared to the United States, immigration from these countries is seen as a way to alleviate these demographic trends.

The next graph of Census Bureau data (Figure 22.2) shows the projected change in various age cohorts of the U.S. population between 2010 and 2030. Note that these projections include the assumption that current immigration levels of about 1 million legal immigrants per year will continue throughout the projected period. Further, the elderly population is projected to grow from 40 to 88 million people between 2010 and 2050. In 2010 there were 59 dependents (defined as either children or elderly people) per 100 people of working age. By 2050, there are projected to be 76 dependents per 100 people of working age.

To meet projected workforce needs in the face of these fundamental demographic shifts, Susan Brown and Frank Bean argue in the Point essay below that the United States will require both higher- and lower-skilled foreign-born workers. These workers, they contend, both provide and use additional services, adding both supply and demand to the economy. Acting as a complement to native workers, they enhance the economy and slightly raise the wages of natives who have at least a high school diploma. Moreover, these immigrants have proven a long-term benefit, since, over time, they and their descendants have strengthened the fabric of American society. In making their case, Brown and Bean address changes in both the age and the socioeconomic structures of the country, and they touch on the erroneous assumption that employment is a zero-sum game—what is known as the "lump-of-labor fallacy."

Those opposed to looking to immigration as a solution to these demographic realities have two fundamental concerns. First, what are the environmental implications of the population growth caused by increased immigration? (This topic is

Figure 22.1 Change in the number of native- and foreign-born persons per age group, 1990–2006

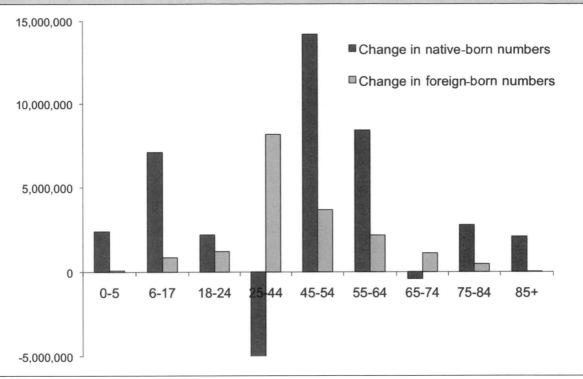

Source: U.S. Census Bureau's *Current Population Survey.* Available at http://www.census.gov/cps.

Figure 22.2 Population change projections, 2010–2030 (millions of people)

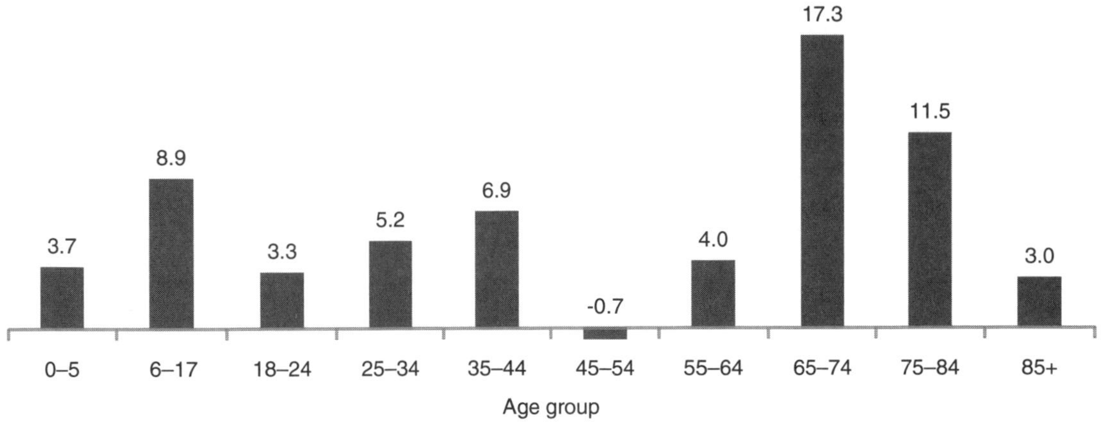

Source: U.S. Census Bureau Population Projections, 2008. Available at http://www.census.gov/population/www/projections/2009downloadablefiles .html.

addressed in a separate chapter.) Second, does the United States have the ability and the political will to create the needed social infrastructure to facilitate the integration of young, often low-skilled and poor immigrants into society? Failure to do so could exacerbate already growing social inequality in the country, create social fragmentation, and further strain the education system.

The Counterpoint essay by Lissette Piedra, Shinwoo Choi, and Hye Joon Park argues that the federal government needs to first deal with the huge number of unauthorized immigrants that are already in the country by putting together an immigration reform package that avoids the thrust of the growing number of reactionary policies seeking to promote "attrition by choice." The authors contend that such policies erode the economic dividends that can be derived from a youthful population. Immigration reform, they argue, will facilitate the incorporation of immigrants into the wider American society and ensure the success of their native-born children. Immigrants are, after all, a highly diverse group: they hold varying levels of human capital and require different investments. If such reform is not achieved, continued immigration could yield a generation not fully incorporated into the American mainstream economy, thus handicapping future labor forces.

POINT

The United States has needed and will continue to need immigrants for its workforce and for other reasons. The baby boomers, born in the 2 decades after World War II and highly educated, are already retiring, portending a rise in the elderly population and increased use of Social Security and Medicare. The U.S. birthrate has plateaued for several decades and fallen since the recent "Great Recession" in the late 2000s. To meet projected workforce needs in the face of such fundamental demographic shifts, the United States will require foreign-born workers, both higher- and lower-skilled (with the latter defined as people whose formal education consists only of a high school diploma or less). Although the extent to which immigrants take existing jobs and create new ones remains a subject of dispute, the fact remains that, at a concrete level, more workers both provide and use additional services. That is, rather than subtracting, they add both supply and demand to the economy. From a social perspective, immigrants have proven a long-term benefit; over time, they have not merely acculturated, but their descendants have strengthened the American fabric (Hirschman, 2005).

Immigration began to rise in the United States after Congress revised the immigration law in 1965 and did away with national-origins quotas. By 2010, the foreign-born consisted of 40 million people, or nearly 13 percent of the total population. Almost all of these are immigrants. While many immigrants are unskilled laborers, in the nation's largest cities an even greater number now are college graduates. Of the immigrant adults who are 25 and older, one in eight holds a degree in science or engineering. In all, 27 percent of foreign-born have a bachelor's degree or higher, and the proportion of highly educated immigrants continues to rise (Gambino & Gryn, 2011; Hall, Singer, De Jong, & Graefe, 2011). The number of unauthorized immigrants appears to have peaked at about 12 million in 2007 and fallen by nearly a million since then (Passel & Cohn, 2011).

CHANGES IN THE U.S. AGE STRUCTURE

The age structure of a population has enormous implications for national vitality. The lower the dependency ratio—that is, the ratio of children and retirees to people of working ages—the less a country needs to spend on care giving and social services, and the more it can invest in economic growth. One reason often cited for the massive development in East Asia in recent decades is its favorable dependency ratio (Bloom & Williamson, 1998). In the United States, the dependency ratio has been falling since 1965, as the postwar baby boomers began to join the labor force. But with the retirement of the boomers, this ratio is expected to begin to rise by 2013.

The baby boom was an era of high fertility, but this era ended by the mid-1960s, when the total fertility rate (TFR) fell below 3.0. From the height of the baby boom to the mid-1970s, fertility in the United States dropped by about half, as measured by TFR, or the average number of children a woman would be expected to have if her lifetime childbearing followed the fertility age pattern shown during that year. In the 1970s, the TFR fell below 2.1, the point at which the population replaces itself. After the 1970s, fertility rates rose slightly and hovered around 2.0–2.1 children per woman (National Center for Health Statistics, 2010). But the TFR fell during the Great Recession and was only slightly higher in 2011 than in the 1970s. Among the native-born, the fertility rate is even lower: below 1.9 for many years and recently about 1.7, or nearly 20 percent below replacement level.

Thus, over the past 30 years, the size of new native-born birth cohorts in the United States has been shrinking slowly. This means that the numbers of natives available to meet workforce needs and fund the social safety net is now in both relative and absolute decline, on account of diminished fertility alone. The continuation of current immigration trends can help alleviate some of the severity of a rising dependency ratio (Meissner, Meyers, Papademetrious, & Fix, 2006).

LABOR FORCE EXPECTATIONS

Including both legal and unauthorized immigration, the U.S. population has been growing, though rarely more than 1 percent annually since 1980. Since 2000, population growth has fallen below even this level. To keep up with this population expansion, the economy must add 1.3 to 1.5 million jobs each year (Bean & Stevens, 2003). Generally, it has done this. Until the Great Recession, the annual percentage change in gross domestic product (GDP) averaged more than

3 percent per year (see Figure 22.3). Even with periods of economic contraction included in the statistics, each decade averaged job growth at or well above the levels needed to absorb population growth. For example, during the 1970s, economic growth generated more than 1.9 million new jobs on average each year or about 50 percent *more* than the number required to absorb immigrants and the baby boomers then coming of age. During the 1980s, job growth was almost as high, at about 1.8 million new jobs per year. In the 1990s, job growth was even higher, averaging more than 2.1 million jobs per year (Bureau of Labor Statistics, 2011). During the 2000s and the recession of 2001, job growth matched the levels needed to absorb new native and immigrant workers up through 2007.

What about the future? Every 2 years the Bureau of Labor Statistics releases 10-year projections for employment. The most recent set, for 2008–2018, projects generally modest net growth of roughly 15.3 million jobs, or 10.1 percent more jobs overall. A full 96 percent of these new jobs are expected to be in service-providing industries, most notably professional and business services (4.2 million) and health care and social assistance (4.0 million). But consider the projected job growth in light of population projections leaving out immigration. At zero net migration, the Census Bureau projects the U.S. population between the ages of 18 and 64 to fall by 0.6 percent between 2010 and 2020 (U.S. Bureau of the Census, 2009). Absent migration, those 15.3 million projected new jobs would have to be filled entirely from the ranks of the unemployed, the underemployed, those out of the labor force, and those 65 and over.

In sum, the United States cannot realistically provide enough natives to fill those jobs. In December 2011 the Labor Department reported 13.3 million unemployed people, for an unemployment rate of 8.6 percent. Not all of the unemployed can be absorbed at once into jobs, however, because the search process for a job and geographical mismatch create "frictional" unemployment. With an unemployment rate of 4 percent, which economists consider natural, only about 7.1 million unemployed realistically are available to be hired. In addition, in 2011 the Bureau of Labor Statistics counted nearly 6.6 million people outside the labor force who said they would like to work. In reality, though, not all would. In the late 1990s, labor-market shortages emerged after about 3 years of strong job growth induced by the high-tech boom. Those shortages suggest that the nonimmigrant supply of unskilled labor among the elderly, minorities, and teenagers can be rather quickly exhausted (Freeman, 2007).

Since the 15.3 million projected new jobs represent all types of work at all skill levels, jobs requiring special skills, particularly those in science and engineering, would be even more likely to go begging if they had to be filled only by the native population. Among the fastest-growing sectors of the economy are niches that are already largely filled

Figure 22.3 Percentage change in growth of U.S. GDP and population, 1950–2010

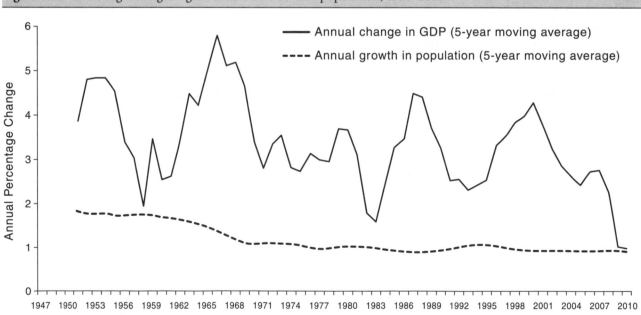

Sources: U.S. Bureau of the Census; U.S. Bureau of Economic Analysis.

by immigrants. As of 2000, 45 percent of the medical scientists, 27 percent of the computer software engineers, and 17 percent of the postsecondary teachers were foreign-born. In 2004, half of the graduate students in engineering were foreign-born, as were 41 percent of the graduate students in physics. By contrast, native-born students are more likely to gravitate toward education and business (Meissner et al., 2006). Even if some foreign workers were substitutes for similar natives (thus driving down wages), economists have found little evidence for competition among natives and immigrants among skilled workers. Indeed, the slowdown in the rate of increase in college completion in the United States since 1980 (Goldin & Katz, 2008) implies that natives are unlikely to be able to fill any growth in the demand for scientists and engineers. Moreover, skilled immigrants are an immediate gain to the economy (Smith & Edmonston, 1997).

CHANGES IN THE SOCIOECONOMIC STRUCTURE

The numbers of natives available to fill less-skilled jobs over the past 30 years have also been influenced by factors other than demographic shifts. The expansion of educational access in the early and middle decades of the twentieth century has reduced the proportion of the population that is lower-skilled. Despite current debates about reasons for slowdowns in the tendency to finish college (Goldin & Katz, 2008), the fraction of the population with some postsecondary schooling has steeply risen during most of the past 60 years, and recently more so for women than men. For example, the percent of adults (persons age 25 and over) with more than a high school education rose from 5.3 percent in 1950 to nearly 60 percent in 2010. The flip side of this picture, of course, is relatively and absolutely fewer persons with high school diplomas or less. Particularly striking is the decline in the percentage of the population with less than a high school education. In 1950, over 87 percent of the U.S. adults fell into this category. By 2010, only 12.9 percent did. And the concomitant decline in absolute numbers was from about 80 million to 25.7 million. In short, by 2010 there were 68 percent fewer low-skilled persons in the country than in 1950, if "low-skilled" refers to persons without a high school diploma or its equivalent. The magnitude of this drop is all the more remarkable given that this is a figure for the entire adult population. That is, it makes no allowance for the millions of immigrants who received little education in their countries of origin.

The key question for the workforce is whether the availability and skill level of jobs has shifted in equivalent fashion. Manufacturing jobs have disappeared. From 1970 until 2010, the share of manufacturing jobs in the economy more than halved, dropping from more than one in four to about one in eight. The drop-off in the share of manufacturing jobs held by persons with a high school diploma or less has been similarly precipitous (also falling from about one in four in 1970 to about one in eight in 2010). Interestingly, during this same time, the overall number of manufacturing jobs remained around 21 million. But because of overall job growth, manufacturing holds a smaller *share* of jobs today. Also, many of today's manufacturing jobs require at least some college. Thus, the relative demand for lesser-skilled workers in manufacturing has declined. However, during this same period, the share of the lesser-skilled workforce in service jobs has grown considerably (Freeman, 2007). Since 1980, the number of nonmanufacturing jobs held by less-skilled younger males (regardless of nativity or ethno-racial background) has held fairly steady at about 45 percent of the less-skilled workforce.

If the demand for unskilled work remains strong, how are immigrants filling this need? And how likely is it that immigrants are getting jobs at the expense of natives? Young unskilled native males are the group most likely to have to compete for jobs with immigrants, many of whom are also young unskilled males. The number of foreign-born males with low education has increased from a very small presence in the workforce in 1970 to about 2.7 million today. Since 1990, the increase for foreign-born males ages 25 to 34 was about 1.7 million. However, the comparable native workforce in this age range *lost* 2.8 million workers. In other words, the native male workforce shrank more than the immigrant workforce expanded, thanks in part to declining fertility and the expansion of education.

In every decade since the 1970s, the number of native males who never finished high school has declined, sometimes substantially, for a cumulative drop of 1.6 million. The rise in the number of comparable foreign-born males offsets this drop only by about 1 million, for total drop of about 600,000. The number of native males earning only a high school diploma did not drop until the 1990s, but since then the absolute number of natives whose education stops with a diploma has continued to decline.

These dramatic demographic and social changes miss part of the greater story affecting the availability of a low-skilled native labor force. Low-skilled native workers are more likely to live in job-poor areas, to engage in alcohol and drug usage, to suffer from poor health and physical limitations, and to have been arrested, convicted, and imprisoned.

Regarding the first of these, for example, the correlation across cities between where either less educated whites and blacks live or where less-educated Latino immigrants live is negative (about –0.4 to –0.5, based on American Community Survey (ACS) data cited in Ruggles et al., 2009). Given that most Latino immigrants are labor migrants—that is, they migrate to where the jobs are—it is reasonable to conclude that less educated natives are more likely than Latino immigrants to live in areas with weak employment prospects for unskilled workers. Employers seeking less-skilled native workers in areas with strong economies may have trouble finding them, because they tend not to live there.

Further, lesser-educated natives and whites are more likely to have problems with alcohol and drug usage than immigrants, and to have health and physical limitations. For example, among those with less than a high school diploma, young Hispanic males (data are not available by nativity) have, for more than a decade, been less likely to report usage of alcohol than their white counterparts, and for even longer they have been much less likely to report usage of illicit drugs. Similarly, among males who did not finish high school, whites are substantially more likely than Hispanics to report health impairments and involvement with the criminal justice system. Thus, not only are relatively fewer natives with low education available now to hold low-skilled jobs than there were four decades ago, those who are available often do not live where the jobs are, and many are less able to work or are less desirable to employers because of substance abuse, poor health, or criminal involvement.

OBJECTIONS TO INCREASED IMMIGRATION

Thus, it seems reasonable to expect that once the economy recovers, the United States will face labor shortages. Some caveats are necessary, however. Many baby boomers are likely to remain in the labor force longer (Myers, 2007). Some evidence exists that age of retirement, which declined among men for the first three-quarters of the twentieth century, has already ticked upward, in part because of the rise of the age of eligibility for Social Security (Gustman & Steinmeier, 2009). The government is forecasting that among workers age 65 to 74, the labor force participation rate will rise from 26.3 percent in 2010 to 30.5 percent by 2018 (Bureau of Labor Statistics, 2011). Yet even if the baby boomers delay retirement on average a full 3 years, Richard Alba (2009) argues that their presence in the workforce is likely to reduce the availability of jobs in 2030 by only about 5 percent. By then, inevitably, the vast majority of baby boomers will have retired.

Some may further argue that many of these potential jobs will be relocated offshore, thus reducing any need for both native and immigrant labor. The economist Alan Blinder (2009) has estimated that about a quarter of all U.S. jobs, both high-skilled and low-skilled, are potentially vulnerable to being moved offshore because they are not tied to a specific locale. The measurement of such locale-based ties is subjective, however. Proximity to related firms can still reduce average costs of production, through what urban economists refer to as "economies of agglomeration"; these have long been used to explain the rise of central business districts (Anas, Arnott, & Small, 1998). Further, while many jobs may not require daily interpersonal contact, high-skilled jobs often require face-to-face interaction to develop and maintain trust with customers or clients (Alba, 2009), and low-skilled service jobs generally require a physical presence. As more jobs are contracted out, human interaction may become more important, not less so. Case studies of Silicon Valley suggest that entrepreneurial success depends on social networks that both extend globally and cluster at the local level (Saxenian, Motoyama, & Quan, 2002). Thus, offshoring on such an enormous scale is not necessarily inevitable, though it is impossible to know for sure. Overall, one might conclude that although pessimistic forecasts cannot be dismissed, neither is there reason to argue for a significant shift from past labor needs.

Opponents of immigration also point to the rise of chronic underemployment or unemployment among low-skilled Americans, especially men, as a reason to curtail immigration. Certainly, chronic underemployment is a real issue. The precariousness of work has become "the dominant feature of the social relations between employers and workers" (Kalleberg, 2009, p. 17). According to the U.S. Government Accountability Office, nearly a third of the U.S. workforce has "contingent" employment rather than permanent jobs. Between 2000 and 2009, men's employment rates dropped by 12.6 percentage points for those in their early 20s, and by 11.3 percentage points for those in their late 20s, with the severest declines among the least educated. Between 1979 and 2007, median real annual earnings for employed men in their 20s dropped by nearly 18 percent, with gains going only to those with a bachelor's degree or higher (Sum & McLaughlin, 2011).

THE LUMP-OF-LABOR FALLACY

The argument that jobs taken by low-skilled immigrants are jobs forgone to native-born Americans rests on the erroneous assumptions that immigrant labor can easily substitute for native labor and that employment is a zero-sum game. The fallacy, known as the "lump of labor," was popularized in 1891 by the economist David Schloss, who described it as the erroneous belief that the amount of work was fixed and could be parceled out in various ways. Advocates of shorter work weeks still defend the lump-of-labor idea as a way to expand employment. Such a viewpoint presumes that newly arrived immigrants must necessarily be taking jobs from natives. Similarly, it also assumes that immigrant labor inevitably substitutes for native labor rather than complementing it.

Instead, immigrants often make jobs, sometimes as a result of supply creating its own demand, as predicted by Say's Law. Immigrant workers themselves consume, and thereby increase aggregate demand. The very availability of workers may create demand for certain kinds of services for which demand is elastic. In addition, insofar as immigrant labor complements that of natives and increases the productivity of natives, immigration can foster growth and employment (Cortes, 2008), such as when immigrants care for children or the elderly. And, of course, some immigrant work involves tasks which could probably be carried out with either current or new technology, such as certain manufacturing and agricultural jobs (Lewis, 2005; Martin, 2009).

What does research actually show about the tenability of the "lump of labor" idea, or the notion that any immigrant worker is taking a job away from some native? In particular, what does research indicate about the effects of immigrants on less-skilled workers? While analysts generally agree that higher-skilled workers benefit the economy overall (and thus other workers) (Bertelsmann Stiftung and Migration Policy Institute, 2009; Freeman 2007), less consensus exists about the effect of less-skilled immigrants. On balance, research appears to show only small negative consequences on the labor market for natives (Holzer, 2011). To be sure, some less-skilled natives may lose their jobs through competition with newly arrived immigrants. But these losses are mostly offset by positive labor market effects for other natives. Most important, this same research literature also shows that less-skilled immigrants exert substantial downward pressure on the employment and wage prospects of one important category of workers, namely other lesser-skilled immigrants (Cortes, 2008).

Why does so little competition appear to exist between lesser-skilled immigrants and natives? One possibility is that immigrants do the dangerous and dirty jobs that natives refuse to do (Cornelius, 1998; Cornelius & Tsuda, 2004). Some further argue that if such jobs paid more, natives might be more willing to do them (Martin, 1997, 2009). But both of these possibilities beg the question of the shrinking number of lower-skilled native workers. Not only is the absolute number of native workers declining, the number of low-skilled natives with good health and unblemished backgrounds is lower still, and at levels decidedly below the need for such workers.

CONCLUSION

In broad outline, without immigrants, the working-age population of the United States would be declining. The United States would not have enough skilled labor for some of its fastest-growing and most energetic science and engineering sectors. It would not even have enough unskilled labor, at least in the long run. To the extent that immigrants complement the labor of natives, they enhance the economy and slightly raise the wages of natives who have at least a high school diploma (Ottaviano & Peri, 2011). But even though the United States does in fact need and benefit from immigrant workers of all skill levels, the country may not need as many low-skilled workers as it has been receiving. The fact that labor-market impact studies show a negative effect of low-skilled immigrant workers on the wages of other low-skilled immigrants, if not those of native workers, implies that crowding or competition among low-skilled immigrants could be occurring. But the lower wages could also result from the relative income declines generally in the bottom half of the population. The concentration of immigrants on each end of the income distribution may also be contributing slightly toward overall wage inequality (Card, 2009).

One reason immigrants are not more appreciated is that it is hard to discern how they can raise the productivity of native workers. Because immigration's consequences and benefits are diffuse and not readily experienced, it is not easy to see the broad positive implications of immigration for the economy. As a result, many observers see only that more less-skilled immigrants, especially unauthorized migrants, seem to be coming to their communities than are needed.

They also worry about the fiscal repercussions of such workers and their families, which even though positive at the national level in the short run, are often negative at the state and local governmental levels (Smith & Edmonston, 1997).

Nonetheless, on balance, it seems that the United States does in fact "need" immigrants, even less-skilled ones. So do many other more-developed countries, whose birth rates are even lower than those in the United States (Harris, 2006). In the last two decades, the United States and other countries have dealt with such labor needs largely by resorting to temporary workers or unauthorized migrants, usually without acknowledging that this is the case (Cornelius et al., 2004). Skilled workers seeking legal permanent residency in the United States often must wait years, and unskilled labor often has no legal means of entry at all. As developed countries eventually will have to compete further for labor, they will need explicit immigration and economic growth policies to cope with both the need for immigrant workers and rising economic inequality and social insecurity.

REFERENCES AND FURTHER READING

Alba, R. (2009). *Blurring the color line: the new chance for a more integrated America.* Cambridge, MA: Harvard University Press.

Anas, A., Arnott, R., & Small, K. A. (1998). Urban spatial structure. *Journal of Economic Literature, 36,* 1426–1464.

Bean, F. D. (1983). The baby boom and its explanations. *The Sociological Quarterly, 24*(Summer), 353–365.

Bean, F. D., Lowell, B. L., & Taylor L. (1988). Undocumented Mexican immigrants and the earnings of other workers in the United States. *Demography, 25*(1), 35–52.

Bean, F. D., & Stevens, G. (2003). *America's newcomers and the dynamics of diversity.* New York, NY: Russell Sage Foundation.

Bertelsmann, S., & Migration Policy Institute. (Eds.). (2009). *Talent, competitiveness and migration.* Gütersloh, Germany: Bertelsmann Stiftung.

Blinder, A. (2009). How many U.S. jobs might be offshorable? *World Economics, 10*(2), 41–78.

Bloom, D. E., & Williamson, J. G. (1998). Demographic transitions and economic miracles in emerging Asia. *The World Bank Economic Review, 12*(3), 419–455.

Brown, S. K., Bachmeier, J., & Bean, F. D. (2009). Trends in US immigration: A shift toward exclusion? In J. Higley & J. Nieuwenhuysen (Eds.), *Nations of immigrants: Australia and the USA compared* (pp. 442–455). Cheltenham, UK: Edward Elgar.

Bureau of Labor Statistics. (2011). *Current population survey.* Retrieved from http://www.bls.gov/cps/#data

Card, D. (2009). Immigration and inequality. *American Economic Review, 99*(2), 1–21.

Centers for Disease Control and Prevention. National Center for Health Statistics. (2010). *VitalStats.* Retrieved from http://www.cdc.gov/nchs/vitalstats.htm

Cornelius, W. A. (1998). The structural embeddedness of demand for Mexican immigrant labor: New evidence from California. In M. M. Suárez-Orozco (Ed.), *Crossings: Mexican Immigration in Interdisciplinary Perspective* (pp. 113–144). Cambridge, MA: Harvard University Press.

Cornelius, W. A., & Tsuda, T. (2004). Controlling immigration: The limits of government intervention. In W. A. Cornelius, T. Tsuda, P. L. Martin, & J. F. Hollifield (Eds.), *Controlling immigration: A global perspective* (2nd ed., pp. 3–48). Stanford, CA: Stanford University Press.

Cornelius, W. A., Tsuda, T., Martin, P. L., & Hollifield, J. F. (Eds.). (2004). *Controlling immigration: A global perspective* (2nd ed.). Stanford, CA: Stanford University Press.

Cortes, P. (2008). The effects of low-skilled immigration on US prices: Evidence from CPI data. *Journal of Political Economy, 116*(3), 381–422.

Crook, C. (2011, May 16). Fixing America's immigration mess. *Financial Times,* p. 9.

Freeman, R. B. (2007). *America works: Critical thoughts on the exceptional U.S. labor market.* New York, NY: Russell Sage Foundation.

Gambino, C., & Gryn, T. (2011). *The foreign born with science and engineering degrees: 2010.* Washington, DC: U.S. Bureau of the Census. Accessed December 4, 2011, from http://www.census.gov/prod/2011pubs/acsbr10–06.pdf

Goldin, C., & Katz, L. F. (2008). *The race between education and technology.* Cambridge, MA: Belknap Press of Harvard University Press.

Gustman, A. L., & Steinmeier, T. (2009). How changes in social security affect recent retirement trends. *Research on Aging, 31*(2), 261–290.

Hall, M., Singer, A., De Jong, G. F., & Graefe, D. R. (2011). *The geography of immigrant skills: Educational profiles of metropolitan areas.* Washington, DC: Brookings Institution.

Harris, F. R. (Ed.). (2006). *The baby bust: Who will do the work? Who will pay the taxes?* Lanham, MD: Rowman & Littlefield.

Hirschman, C. (2005). Immigration and the American century. *Demography, 42*(4), 595–620.

Holzer, H. J. (2011). *Immigration policy and less-skilled workers in the United States: Reflections on future directions for reform.* Washington, DC: Migration Policy Institute.

Kalleberg, A. (2009). Precarious work, insecure workers: Employment relations in transition. *American Sociological Review, 74*(1), 1–22.

Krugman, P. (2003, October 7). Lumps of labor. *The New York Times.* Retrieved from http://www.nytimes.com/2003/10/07/opinion/lumps-of-labor.html

Lee, M. A., & Mather, M. (2008, June). U.S. labor force trends. *Population Bulletin.* Retrieved from Population Reference Bureau website: http://www.prb.org/Publications/PopulationBulletins/2008/uslaborforce.aspx

Lewis, E. (2005). *Immigration, skill mix and the choice of technique.* Working Paper. Philadelphia, PA: Federal Reserve Bank of Philadelphia.

Martin, P. (1997). Do Mexican agricultural policies stimulate emigration? In F. D. Bean, R. O. de la Garza, B. R. Roberts, & S. Weintraub (Eds.), *At the crossroads: Mexico and U.S. immigration policy* (pp. 79–116). New York, NY: Rowman and Littlefield.

Martin, P. (2009). *Importing poverty? Immigration and the changing face of rural America.* New Haven, CT, and London, UK: Yale University Press.

Meissner, D., Meyers, D. W., Papademetrious, D. G., & Fix, M. (2006). *Immigration and America's future: A new chapter. Report of the independent task force on immigration and America's future.* Washington, DC: Migration Policy Institute.

Myers, D. (2007). *Immigrants and boomers: Forging a new social contract for the future of America.* New York, NY: Russell Sage Foundation.

Ottaviano, G. I. P., & Peri, G. (2011). Rethinking the effect of immigration on wages. *Journal of the European Economic Association.* doi: 10.1111/j.1542–4774.2011.01052.x

Passel, J., & Cohn, D. (2011). *Unauthorized immigrant population: National and state trends, 2010.* Washington, DC: Pew Hispanic Center. Retrieved from http://www.pewhispanic.org/2011/02/01/unauthorized-immigrant-population-brnational-and-state-trends-2010

Reed, D., & Danziger, S. H. (2007). The effects of recent immigration on racial/ethnic labor market differentials. *American Economic Review, 97*(2), 373–377.

Ruggles, S., Sobek, M., Alexander, T., Fitch, C. A., Goeken, R., Hall, P. K., King, M., & Ronnander, C. (2009). Integrated public use microdata series: Version 4.0. Machine-readable database. Produced and distributed by Minnesota Population Center, Minneapolis.

Saxenian, A., Motoyama, Y., & Quan, X. (2002). *Local and global networks of immigrant professionals in Silicon Valley.* San Francisco, CA: Public Policy Institute of California.

Smith, J. P., & Edmonston, B. (1997). *The new Americans: Economic, demographic, and fiscal effects of immigration.* Washington, DC: National Academy Press.

Sum, A., & McLaughlin, J. (2011, September). *Changes in the weekly and annual earnings of young adults from 1979–2010: Progress and setbacks amidst widening inequality* (CDF Policy Brief no. 3). Retrieved from http://www.childrensdefense.org/child-research-data-publications/changes-in-the-weekly-and.pdf

Susan K. Brown and Frank D. Bean

COUNTERPOINT

An unusual opportunity lies ahead to advance the racial integration of American society. . . . As the baby boomers leave the work force between now and the early 2030s, when the youngest of them turn seventy, the young Americans entering the labor market will be much more diverse in ethno-racial terms than the old Americans exiting it.

—Richard Alba (2010, p. 57)

We do need to remind ourselves that so many of the disparities that exist in the African-American community today can be directly traced to inequalities passed on from an earlier generation that suffered under the brutal legacy of slavery and Jim Crow.

—Barack Obama (2008 speech on race)

There are now more illegal migrants living in the United States than there were blacks living under Jim Crow in the states of the old Confederacy at the time of the Brown v. Board of Education *decision in 1954—and this cohort represents a sizeable portion of the Hispanic population. About one-out-of-every-five Latinos is undocumented, including about one half of all foreign-born Hispanics. Nearly one-out-of-every-three Latinos lives in a family with at least one undocumented relative.*

—Roberto Suro (2006, p. 30)

These three passages set the parameters for the argument that population growth through immigration will translate into economic growth for the nation. Two major population trends will define the United States for the next 50 years. On January 1, 2011, the first of the American baby boomers started retiring. Over the next 2 decades, an average of 10,000 baby boomers per day will reach retirement age (Cohn & Taylor, 2010). As retirees exit the workforce, a much more diverse group of young Americans will be poised to assume these jobs. However, much of this future diversity comes from the largely nonwhite children of immigrants (Sullivan, 2006). Consider, for example that in 2010, one in four kindergartners was Hispanic (U.S. Census Bureau, 2010, as cited in Kurtzleben, 2010). Although the United States has had a sizable population increase through immigration, much of the future population growth will come from the native-born offspring of immigrants. These two demographic trends are destined to intersect, and the future economic and social outcomes will largely depend on economic policies that support the social mobility and inclusion of a future, ethnically diverse, generation. Unfortunately, such policies are related to the dire need for immigration reform.

The United States leads the world in its annual receipt of immigrants (Martin & Midgley, 2010). According to statistics from the U.S. Department of Homeland Security, the United States takes in somewhere around one million legal immigrants each year. Such a population flow will have consequences for current and future generations. As of 2010, about 39 million foreign-born people lived in the country, making up roughly 12 percent of the population, and there is widespread dissatisfaction with the current immigration system.

Although immigrants are a highly diverse group, much contention centers on the presence of a sizeable population of unauthorized residents, predominately of Mexican origin, and on the costs of immigration to the states that attract large numbers of new arrivals. Among the total foreign-born population, roughly 11 million are estimated to be unauthorized persons (Martin & Midgley, 2010). Although the undocumented are technically prohibited from working, ineligible to receive most public services, and banned from seeking citizenship, many do find employment in marginal labor sectors, and they manage to live in the country undetected (Suro, 2006). However, their presence evokes consternation in the general public that sometimes even extends to legal immigrants as well.

Immigration policy is the purview of the federal government, but the consequences of inadequate and antiquated policies are felt directly at the local level. Immigrants, even those who are unauthorized, frequently work in low-paying jobs and pay federal taxes, but they use public services that are funded by state and local taxes. Often perceived as usurpers of jobs and community resources by established residents frustrated by the lack of immigration reform, which can only occur at the federal level, several states have enacted laws to further curtail access to public services to noncitizens in an effort to promote "self-deportation." Such policies and their consequences raise particular concerns for the well-being of future generations, and they provide the caveat in any answer to the question, "Will population growth through immigration bring economic growth to the United States?"

The counterpoint essay offered in this chapter considers the current population trends in the context of a sizeable unauthorized population, exploring the potential consequences of continued neglect of immigration reform by the federal government. Appropriate policies will be considered that facilitate the incorporation of immigrants and to ensure the success of their native-born children. Such policies would need to consider that immigrants, a highly diverse group, hold different levels of human capital and require differential investments (Fortuny, Hernandez, & Chaudry, 2010). Otherwise, the inevitable population growth spurred by immigration could yield a generation not fully incorporated into the American mainstream economy.

THE PROBLEM OF EXCLUSION

The legal status of immigrants has become a defining feature for new arrivals. Numerous scholars express concern about the current exclusionary policies, which create unsupportive societal institutions for the immigrants' incorporation into U.S. society (Engstrom, 2006; Jiménez, 2007; Perez, 2011; Suro, 2006). Such policies draw a sharp distinction between citizens and noncitizens by limiting various rights, legal protection, labor market opportunities, access to educational and health-care institutions, and other social benefits for the latter (Engstrom, 2006). Roberto Suro (2006) draws a frightening parallel between the role of immigration status in modern-day American and that of race in the Jim Crow–era South. In this post–civil rights era, Suro argues, immigration status operates as a new legal boundary that works as an "insuperable barrier to full inclusion and participation in American society."

Like race under Jim Crow laws, the limiting effect of immigration status on the individual has radiating effects on families and communities. Nearly half of unauthorized adult immigrants are parents of minor children (Taylor, Lopez, Passel, & Motel, 2011). They are about a decade younger than legal immigrants and native-born adults, and they are more likely to be of childbearing and child-rearing age. Consequently, there is a growing population of children born to unauthorized immigrant parents. Recent estimates suggest 4.5 million native-born minors live with at least one undocumented immigrant parent, a figure that has doubled since 2000 (Taylor et al, 2011). Taken together, at least 9 million people live in "mixed status" families that include at least one unauthorized adult and at least one US-born child, or roughly 54 percent of the 16 million people in families that can be categorized as "mixed status" (Taylor et al., 2011).

Both past and recent state policies have sought to discourage immigration at the local level through the denial of benefits and policies that promote "attrition through enforcement." In 1998, California's Propositions 187 and 227 were created out of fear of growing immigrant populations (Montero-Sieburth & Melendez, 2007). Proposition 187 denies public services to undocumented immigrants, and Proposition 227 limits the time students can attend bilingual classes and the role that parents can have in making such decisions. These two exclusionary laws negatively impact important life domains: welfare and education.

More recent examples can be found in Arizona and Alabama. After President George W. Bush's failed effort to reform immigration law in 2004, the immigration reform issue laid dormant until Arizona passed the "most stringent immigration law in the nation" in April 2010 (Archibold, 2010). Senate Bill (S.B.) 1070 made Arizona the first state to demand that immigrants comply with federal requirements to carry identification documents that demonstrate the legality of their presence on American soil. However, critics contend that the real intent of the law was to discourage illegal immigrants from entering or remaining in the state. The law makes it a state crime or a misdemeanor if immigrants fail to carry immigration papers, and it gives more authority to local policemen to inspect, detain, and deport suspected illegal aliens. Moreover, it allows people to sue local governments they think are not properly implementing the law. After the law's enactment, numerous nationwide demonstrations against it were held because of the potential inequalities such a law created and the implicit permission it granted to authorities to engage in discriminatory behavior. For instance, Judge Susan Bolton in Phoenix expressed that there is a "substantial likelihood that [police] officers will wrongfully arrest legal resident aliens" (Archibold, 2010).

Despite the nationwide criticism of Arizona's immigration law, Alabama followed suit by enacting H.B. 56 in October 2011. In this case the legal impact was more far-reaching than Arizona's S.B. 1070. H.B. 56 not only gives police the authority to conduct random inspections on people, it also mandates schools to screen illegal immigrant children to be registered. The law had a chilling effect on school attendance statewide: 1,988 Hispanic students—5 percent of the entire Hispanic population in the school system—were absent on an average day (Robertson, 2011), a particularly troubling occurrence given that many native-born children of immigrants reside in mixed-status households. Legislation that so negatively affects the educational prospects of children ultimately endangers the long-term economic gain of population growth through immigration.

Although some would say that Arizona and Alabama's immigrant laws undermine "basic notions of fairness that [we] cherish as Americans" (Archibold, 2010), they have been effective in curtailing the presence of illegal immigrants in their respective states. In what some call Alabama's Hispanic Exodus, thousands of Hispanic families have fled the state, leaving work, abandoning houses, and removing their children from school. While one can imagine the fear and chaos of those directly affected by such laws, the rapid flight of these immigrants has destabilized communities (Archibold, 2010).

Ironically, these exclusionary policies have also had negative consequences for the native-born. Since immigrants, especially Mexican immigrants, make up a critical part of the less-skilled labor force, the economies of states such as Alabama, Arizona, and Georgia have suffered from worker shortages. For instance, in the first year after strict immigration provisions went into effect (in 2011), 56 percent of Georgia farmers reported labor shortages, resulting in a $75 million loss of unharvested crops (Immigration Works USA, 2012). In Alabama, the state's business-friendly reputation has been tarnished by incidents involving legally present foreign-born employees working for Mercedes-Benz and Honda being detained by local police officers who were enforcing state law (Immigration Works USA, 2012). Estimates of Arizona's economic loss if all unauthorized immigrants left the state are predicted to be severe: a loss of $11.7 billion in gross state product, and the loss of more than 140,000 jobs (Immigration Works USA, 2012). Such laws thwart economic gains that population growth through immigration has the potential to provide.

UNINTENDED CONSEQUENCES: FUTURE PROSPECTS FOR THE CHILDREN OF IMMIGRANTS

Twenty-five percent of school-aged children in the United States are either immigrants or children of immigrants (Capps, Fix, Murray, Passel, & Hernandez, 2005), representing the fastest growing segment of the child population. Second-generation Latinos (i.e., the native-born of at least one immigrant parent) account for the majority of such children (Fry & Passel, 2009). From 1990 to 2006, the number of Latino students in the nation's public schools nearly doubled (Fry & Gonzales, 2008). This increase represented 60 percent of the total growth in the nation's public school enrollments over this period. Among preschoolers, Latino representation is even higher. In 2010, Latinos accounted for one in four of the cohort of kindergartners who will graduate from high school in 2023 (Nasser & Overberg, 2010). In the context of an aging society, these numbers call attention to the important role of Latino youth in future labor markets. However, if U.S. society is to reap benefits from these demographic trends, there must be a larger public investment in their education. Yet the exclusionary legislation discussed in the previous section undermines the educational opportunities of native-born children of immigrants.

For children, membership in a mixed-status family can negatively affect their development and integration into the U.S. society, because their parents' fear of deportation stymies their ability to access the services they are entitled to (Ku & Matini, 2001). Such barriers compound common risk factors associated with poor outcomes for children: parents with low levels of education, ongoing economic hardships, residence in an overcrowded households, living in a linguistically isolated household in which no one over the age of 14 speaks English only or speaks it "very well" (Hernandez, 2004). The deleterious effect of parental citizenship status on children's academic and psychological development has recently come under scrutiny (Leach, Brown, Bean, & Van Hook, 2011). Children of unauthorized parents average 2 fewer years of schooling than their counterparts with legal resident or citizen parents. Significantly, the amount of schooling a child receives increases substantially if at least one parent obtains legal status (Leach et al., 2011). Another study suggests that the negative psychological consequences associated with immigration status contribute to higher levels of stress and anxiety, which inhibit the learning and cognitive development of children of unauthorized immigrants (Yoshikawa, 2011, as cited in Leach et al., 2011).

Even among those with legal resident status, poverty presents a greater threat to children's development than the parents' level of education or living in a single-parent household (Duncan & Brooks-Gunn, 1997; McLoyd, 1998). Compared to the children of the native-born, poverty rates for children of immigrant families are much higher (21% vs. 17%) (Mather, 2009). Among Latinos, the children of immigrants fare worse. Of the 6.1 million Latino children in the nation who live in poverty, more than two-thirds (4.1 million) are the children of immigrants.

Randolph Capps and Michael Fix have identified four major hardships for children living in poverty: living in crowded housing, having one or more food-related problems, paying rent greater than 50 percent of family income, and suffering from poor health. The percentage of children experiencing each hardship was assessed by their immigrant status, and children of immigrants were found to be more likely to suffer the four hardships than their counterparts in the native-born population (Capps & Fix, 2006, as cited in Dinan, 2006). Moreover, parental educational status, which usually works as a buffer against poverty, was not found to be a significant protective factor for the children of immigrants.

Such children were still more likely to live in poverty, even if their parent had graduated from high school (Elmelech, McCaskie, Lennon, & Lu, 2002).

Children's well-being and educational success are significantly correlated with their parents' levels of education and employment opportunities (Hernandez, 2004). Unfortunately, one study found that children of immigrants had parents with lower education levels compared to their native-born counterparts. Twenty-five percent of immigrant parents had less than a high school degree, while only 8 percent of native-born parents did (Fortuny et al., 2010). Because of these factors, immigrant children have more difficulty in gaining academic and social resources than children of native-born parents. In particular, considering that most immigrant families come from non-English-speaking countries, these children have more difficulty achieving a higher academic level because of the language barriers they encounter (Mather, 2009). Furthermore, immigrant children are less likely to be enrolled in early childhood education services (child-care centers, preschools) than native-born children (Hernandez, 2004).

Data from 2008 show that most of the adult foreign-born population (72%, or 11.9 million people) have limited English proficiency (LEP) (Pew Hispanic Center, 2010). As with many demographic trends, the rates of LEP raise concerns for the children of immigrants. A quarter of preschool-age children are English language learners (ELL), which is another way to say LEP, and more than half have at least one parent who is an ELL (Fortuny et al., 2010). Among children of Mexican and Central American origin, the rate of having at least one ELL parent jumps to 81 percent and 71 percent, respectively.

Because so many children of immigrants come from economically disadvantaged households, they are more likely to attend ethnically segregated, under-resourced schools. These schools are known for overcrowded classrooms, low-quality textbooks, and marginal instructional quality. Furthermore, limited family resources for enrichment experiences, books, exam preparatory courses, and computers widen the achievement gap (Schneider, Martinez, & Owens, 2006).

LACK OF A COMPREHENSIVE IMMIGRATION POLICY

Despite a long history of immigration in this country, which has shaped and transformed the nation by altering its demographic composition and affecting its political, social, and economic institutions, it still lacks a consistent and coherent policy for incorporating immigrants into American society (Engstrom, 2006; Jiménez, 2007). Compared to other countries with immigrants, this laissez-faire approach to incorporation is itself an act of exclusion (Engstrom, 2006).

Most of the countries with a high immigrant population have a set of policies to support their successful incorporation process in various domains, such as job training, free language courses, and health care. South Korea, which has gradually received immigrants and foreigners since the turn of the century, has developed a comprehensive immigration policy through its Support for Multicultural Families Act of 2008 (Asia-Pacific Human Rights Information Center, 2008). This law specifies support and resources available for the target population in various social institutions, such as education, welfare, and health care. Although this law does not cover all immigrants (such as temporary migrant workers), it at least seeks to distribute resources in concert with demographic changes.

The lack of a comprehensive immigrant integration policy at the federal level is reflected by the presence of policies that clearly misunderstand the needs of the immigrant population. Take, for example, the No Child Left Behind (NCLB) Act of 2001, which was developed to improve American students' academic performance on the standardized exams (U.S. Department of Education, 2002). Under this policy, schools with low scores are penalized through reduced funding. A number of studies have determined the negative impacts of NCLB on immigrant or ELL students. According to research done by linguistics, it usually takes 7 years for ELL students to master English, but schools are encouraging students to move out of ELL class and learn with native speakers as early as just 1 year after their immigration (U.S. Department of Education, 2002).

A second example can be found in the Temporary Assistance for Needy Families (TANF) program, which protects families in poverty from falling into worse situations. Although many poor families use this program, after 1996 the Personal Responsibility and Work Opportunity Reconciliation Act (PRWORA) sharply curtailed noncitizens' eligibility for welfare and other major federal benefits (Tumlin & Zimmerman, 2003). Intended to decrease welfare dependency and encourage recipients to be self-sufficient, this policy negatively affects beneficiaries by imposing strict working requirements, and it reduced the eligibility of legal immigrants. Research indicates that for those immigrants who remained in the TANF program, the negative impacts of PRWORA were more detrimental than on their American counterparts (Tumlin & Zimmerman, 2003). For instance, immigrants had a harder time finding a rewarding job, due to their lower educational level and LEP, so they took menial jobs to fulfill the work requirement. However, such work took time away from learning English and engaging in activities that would lead to greater self-sufficiency in the long run.

In contrast, Canada provides systematic support for its newcomers. Under the Immigration and Refugee Protection Act of 2001, the Canadian government developed four supportive programs for the immigrant population to assist with acclimation and integration (Lee & Jang, 2010). First, the Immigrant Settlement and Adaptation Program (ISAP) provides a general orientation and referral system for the newcomers to local social, educational, and health-care services; job-related training; or other necessary services, such as translation and interpretation (Lee & Jang, 2010). Second, Language Instructions for Newcomers (LINC) provides free English or French classes to immigrants for a certain period of time after their arrival by contracting with local community colleges. Third, the HOST program connects Canadian families with immigrant families on a one-on-one basis so that immigrant families can be supported as they adapt to a local community. Lastly, Settlement Workers in Schools (SWIS) is an outreach program where workers from each ethnicity and language group reach out to local public schools to make sure that the new immigrant students are adjusting well to the new school environment (Lee & Jang, 2010).

Since the above supports are mandated by federal policy, it is comprehensive and holistic. In other words, every province in Canada needs to make sure that immigrants are being protected and supported under this law. According to Grubel and Grady (2011), immigrants in Canada are receiving sufficient welfare benefits in domains such as education, housing, and other social services.

CONCLUSION

Although the United States is a nation of immigrants, the country has long been and continues to be ambivalent about the presence of immigrants themselves. This ambivalence is reflected in the lack of comprehensive immigration reform and a growing number of reactionary policies that seek to promote "attrition by choice." Such policies erode the economic dividends that can be derived from a youthful population that is growing, mainly through natural increase. The hostile environments created by such policies promote communities with a high concentration of poverty and low access to formal institutions, which stifles social mobility. Indeed, the opportunity for economic gain is present. But to reap the benefits, more policies are needed to facilitate the incorporation of immigrants into society and reduce exclusionary practices that can potentially handicap the abilities of future members of the labor force.

References and Further Reading

Alba, R. (2009). Paradoxes of race and ethnicity in America today. In *Blurring the color line: The new chance for a more integrated America* (pp. 1–20). Boston, MA: Harvard University Press.

Alba, R. (2010). Achieving a more integrated America. *Dissent, 57*(3), 57–60. doi: 10.1353/dss.0.0175

American Community Survey. (2009). *Place of birth of the foreign-born population 2009*. Retrieved from http://www.census.gov/prod/2010pubs/acsbr09-15.pdf

Archibold, R. C. (2010, April 23), Arizona enacts stringent law on immigration. *The New York Times*. Retrieved from http://www.nytimes.com/2010/04/24/us/politics/24immig.html

Asia-Pacific Human Rights Information Center. (2008). *South Korea: Support for multicultural families act enacted*. Retrieved from http://www.hurights.or.jp/archives/newsinbrief-en/section1/2008/10/south-korea-support-for-multicultural-families-act-enacted.html

Barrett, A. N. (2010). *Acculturative stress and gang involvement among Latinos: U.S.-born versus immigrant youth* (Unpublished Psychology Honors). Georgia State University, Atlanta, GA.

Capps, R., Fix, M. E., Murray, J. O., Passel, J. S., & Hernandez, S. H. (2005). *The new demography of America's schools: Immigration and the No Child Left Behind Act*. Retrieved from The Urban Institute website: http://www.urban.org/publications/311230.html

Chapa, J. (2005). Affirmative action and percentage plans as alternatives for increasing successful participation of minorities in higher education. *Journal of Hispanic Higher Education, 4*(3), 181–196.

Children in the United States of America: A statistical portrait by race-ethnicity, immigrant origins, and language. (2011). *Annals of the American Academy of Political and Social Science, 633*(1), 102. doi:10.1177/0002716210383205

Cohn, D. V., & Taylor, P. (2010). *Baby boomers approach age 65, glumly survey findings about America's largest generation*. Retrieved from Pew Research Center website: http://pewresearch.org/pubs/1834/baby-boomers-old-age-downbeat-pessimism

Dickson, M. C. (2004). *Latina teen pregnancy: Problems and prevention*. Retrieved from Population Resource Center website: http://www.prcdc.org/files/Latina_Teen_Pregnancy.pdf

Dinan, K. A. (2006). Young children in immigrant families the role of philanthropy: *Sharing knowledge, creating services, and building supportive policies*. New York, NY: National Center for Children in Poverty; Columbia University Mailman School of Public Health. Retrieved from http://www.nccp.org/publications/pdf/download_24.pdf

Duncan, G. J., & Brooks-Gunn, J. (Eds.). (1997). *Consequences of growing up poor* (1st ed.). New York: Russell Sage Foundation.

Elmelech, Y., McCaskie, K., Lennon, M. C., & Lu, H.-H. (2002, September). *Children of immigrants: A statistical profile*. Retrieved from National Center for Children in Poverty website: http://www.nccp.org/publications/pdf/text_475.pdf

Engstrom, D. W. (2006). Outsiders and exclusion: Immigrants in the United States. In D. W. Engstrom & L. M. Piedra (Eds.), *Our diverse society: Race and ethnicity—implications for 21st century American society* (pp. 19–36). Washington, DC: NASW Press.

Fortuny, K., Hernandez, D. J., & Chaudry, A. (2010). *Young children of immigrants: The leading edge of America's future*. Retrieved from The Urban Institute website: http://www.urban.org/UploadedPDF/412203-young-children.pdf

Fry, R. (2003). *Hispanic youth dropping out of U.S. schools: Measuring challenge*. Retrieved from Pew Hispanic Center website: http://www.pewhispanic.org/files/reports/19.pdf

Fry, R., & Gonzales, F. (2008). *One-in-five and growing fast: A profile of Hispanic public school students*. Retrieved from Pew Hispanic Center website: http://pewhispanic.org/reports/report.php?ReportID=92

Fry, R., & Passel, J. S. (2009). *Latino children: A majority are U.S.-born offspring of immigrants*. Retrieved from Pew Hispanic Center website: http://pewhispanic.org/files/reports/110.pdf

Garcia, M., & Nury, M. (2011, October 12). *Hey Alabama, take a hint from California*. Retrieved from Huff Post Latino Politics LatinoVoices website: http://www.huffingtonpost.com/monica-garcia/hey-alabama-take-a-hint-f_b_1005772.html

Grubel, H., & Grady, P. (2011). *Immigration and the Canadian welfare state 2011* (Immigration and Refugee Policy Report). Retrieved from Fraser Institute website: http://www.fraserinstitute.org

Hernandez, D. J. (2004). Demographic change and the life circumstances of immigrant families. *Future of Children, 14*(2), 17–47.

Hernandez, D. J., Denton, N. A., & Macartney, S. E. (2008). Children in immigrant families: Looking to America's future. *Society for Research in Child Development, 22*(3), 3–22.

Immigration theory for a new century: Some problems and opportunities. (1997). *The International Migration Review, 31*(4), 799. doi:10.2307/2547415

Immigration Works USA. (2012). *Fact sheet: Bottom line. The economic consequences of state immigration law*. Retrieved from http://www.immigrationworksusa.org/uploaded/file/IW%20bottom%20line.pdf

Jiménez, T. R. (2007). From newcomers to Americans: An integration policy for a nation of immigrants [Policy Paper]. *Immigration Policy in Focus, 5*(11).

Ku, L., & Matini, S. (2001). Left out: Immigrants' access to health care and insurance. *Health Affairs, 20*(1), 247–256.

Kurtzleben, D. (2010, December 14). U.S. Hispanic population is booming. *U.S. News & World Report*. Retrieved from http://www.usnews.com/news/articles/2010/12/14/us-hispanic-population-is-booming

Leach, M. A., Brown, S. K., Bean, F. D., & Van Hook, J. (2011, October). *Unauthorized immigrant parents: Do their migration histories limit their children's education?* Retrieved from http://www.russellsage.org/blog/r-mascarenhas/new-us-2010-report-unauthorized-immigrant-parents-do-their-migration-histories-li

Lee, R., & Jang, S. (2010). Analysis of immigrant support policies in multicultural societies: Case studies of the U.S. and Canada (S. Choi, Trans.). *International Community Research, 14*(1), 179–208.

Martin, P., & Midgley, E. (2010). Immigration in America 2010. *Population Bulletin*. Retrieved from http://www.prb.org/Publications/PopulationBulletins/2010/immigrationupdate1.aspx

Massey, D. (1995). The new immigration and ethnicity in the United States. *Population and Development Review, 21*(3), 631–652.

Mather, M. (2009, February). *Children in immigrant families chart new path* (Population Reference Bureau Reports on America). Retrieved from http://www.prb.org/pdf09/immigrantchildren.pdf

McLoyd, V. C. (1998). Socioeconomic disadvantage and child development. *American Psychologist, 53*(2), 185–205.

Montero-Sieburth, M., & Melendez, E. (Eds.). (2007). *Latinos in a changing society* (1st ed.). Boston, MA: Greenwood.

Morales, R., & Bonilla, F. (1993). *Latinos in a changing U.S. economy: Comparative perspectives on growing inequality* (Vol. 7). Newbury Park, CA: Sage.

Nasser, H. E., & Overberg, P. (2010). Kindergartens see more Hispanic, Asian students. *USA Today*. Retrieved from http://www.usatoday.com/news/nation/census/2010-08-27-1Akindergarten27_ST_N.htm

Obama, B. (2008, March 18). Barack Obama's Speech on Race, Transcribed speech. *The New York Times*. Retrieved from http://www.nytimes.com/2008/03/18/us/politics/18text-obama.html

Passel, J., & Cohn, D. (2009). *A portrait of unauthorized immigrants in the United States*. Retrieved from Pew Hispanic Center website: http://www.pewhispanic.org/files/reports/107.pdf

Perez, R. (2011). Latino mental health: Acculturation challenges in service provision. In L. P. Buki & L. M. Piedra (Eds.), *Creating Infrastructures for Latino Mental health* (pp. 31–54). New York, NY: Springer.

Pew Hispanic Center. (2010). *Statistical portrait of the foreign-born population in the United States, 2008.* Retrieved from http://pewhispanic.org/factsheets/factsheet.php?FactsheetID=59

Portes, A., & Rumbaut, R. G. (2001). School achievement and failure. In *Legacies: The story of the immigrant second generation* (pp. 233–268). New York, NY: Russell Sage Foundation.

Racial variations in major depressive disorder onset among immigrant populations in the United States. (2011). *Journal of Mental Health, 20*(3), 260.

Ridings, J. W., Piedra, L. M., Capeles, J., Rodríguez, R., Freier, F., & Byoun, S. (2011). Building a Latino youth program: Using concept mapping to identify community-based strategies for success. *Journal of Social Service Research, 37*(1), 34–49.

Robertson, C. (2011, October 3). After ruling, Hispanics flee an Alabama town. *The New York Times.* Retrieved from http://www.nytimes.com/2011/10/04/us/after-ruling-hispanics-flee-an-alabama-town.html?pagewanted=all

Schneider, B., Martinez, S., & Owens, A. (2006). Barriers to educational opportunities for Hispanics in the United States. In M. Tienda & F. Mitchell (Eds.), *Hispanics and the future of America* (pp. 179–221). Washington, DC: National Academies Press.

Sullivan, T. A. (2006). Demography, the demand for social services, and the potential for civic conflict. In D. Engstrom & L. M. Piedra (Eds.), *Our diverse society: Race and ethnicity—implications for 21st century American society* (1st ed., pp. 9–18). Washington, DC: NASW Press.

Suro, R. (2006). *A developing identity: Hispanics in the United States.* Retrieved from http://lrc.salemstate.edu/hispanics/other/A_Developing_Identity_Hispanics_in_The_United_States_by_Roberto_Suro.htm

Taylor, P., Lopez, M. H., Passel, J., & Motel, S. (2011). *Unauthorized immigrants: Length of residency, patterns of parenthood.* Retrieved from Pew Hispanic Center website: http://www.pewhispanic.org/files/2011/12/Unauthorized-Characteristics.pdf

Tienda, M. (2011). Hispanics and U.S. schools: Problems, puzzles and possibilities. In M. T. Hallinan (Ed.), *Frontiers in sociology of education* (pp. 303–310). New York, NY: Springer.

Tienda, M., & Sullivan, T. A. (2009). The promise and peril of the Texas uniform admission law. In M. Hall, M. Krislov, & D. L. Featherman (Eds.), *The next twenty-five years? Affirmative action and higher education in the United States and South Africa* (pp. 155–174). Ann Arbor, MI: University of Michigan Press.

Tumlin, K. C., & Zimmerman, W. (2003). *Immigrants and TANF: A look at immigrant welfare recipients in three cities.* Retrieved from The Urban Institute website: http://www.urban.org/uploadedpdf/310874_op69.pdf

The Urban Institute. (2006). *Children of immigrants: Facts and figures* [fact sheet]. Retrieved from http://www.urban.org/publications/900955.html

U.S. Department of Education. (2002). *Executive summary: The no child left behind act of 2001.* Retrieved from www.nlts2.org/reports/2005.../nlts2_report_2005_03_execsum.pdf

U.S.-Mexico Border and Immigration Task Force. (2008). *U.S.-Mexico border policy report: Effective border policy; security, responsibility, and human rights at the U.S.-Mexico border.* Retrieved from www.utexas.edu/.../humanrights/borderwall/.../municipalities-US-Me

Lissette M. Piedra, Shinwoo Choi, and Hye Joon Park

Environment and Immigration

POINT: A serious commitment to environmentalism entails slowing America's population growth by implementing a more restrictive immigration policy.

Philip Cafaro, Colorado State University
Winthrop R. Staples III, Independent Scholar

COUNTERPOINT: The issue of climate change is the most urgent issue of our time, but the U.S. border is neither an appropriate nor useful place to tackle it.

Andrew Light, Center for American Progress

Introduction

Debates about immigration understandably center on human concerns. Whether argued from the right or the left, questions about who should be a citizen of the United States—whether immigration improves our culture or weakens it, whether it aids our economy or not—center around what is good for us as a people. But Americans do not live in a vacuum, and the planet is profoundly impacted by the choices we make. In this chapter, Philip Cafaro, Winthrop R. Staples III, and Andrew Light debate whether restricting immigration to the United States is a necessary step toward protecting the environment.

The argument that the planet is better off if immigration to wealthy countries is restricted has some appeal to environmentalists. Consumption levels are higher in wealthy countries, and these countries tend to have a larger carbon footprint. Absorbing new immigrants into wealthier populations will likely increase the carbon footprints of these populations still further. In light of Americans' high levels of consumption relative to those of people in developing countries, Cafaro and Staples argue that moving people from lower-consumption to higher-consumption countries will have a deleterious effect on the global environment.

Because of high levels of fossil fuel use in the United States, the country has one of the world's highest per capita greenhouse gas emissions. Reducing emission levels will be a large task, and Cafaro and Staples suggest that it will become an insurmountable one if population increases from immigration is not drastically slowed.

In the Counterpoint essay, Light points out that there are other factors affecting a country's environmental impact. While economically developed countries contribute more emissions to the planet's atmosphere, the maturity and effectiveness of regulatory and legal structures typical of such countries help them address environmental problems. This does not just apply to carbon emissions. Other dimensions of a growing population's impacts on the environment—things like overfishing, lax or ineffective regulation of natural resource extraction, protection of endangered species, deforestation, and disposition of toxic materials—depend on the strength of a country's legal and regulatory infrastructure and environmental regulations. Wealthy countries are generally better equipped, by virtue of their economic resources and the strength of their political institutions, to enact environmental protections.

These institutional assets are the mechanisms by which the United States deals with the environmental consequences of a growing population as it continues to absorb immigrants. In the Counterpoint essay, Light discusses the example of sprawl. He questions the assertion that sprawl is a necessary side effect of population growth. Rather, it is the factors that policymakers have programmatic control over, such as the building of freeways, zoning and tax policies, and infrastructure planning and development, that affect population density and determine the extent of sprawl.

Some, however, note that despite its relatively sophisticated policymaking and regulatory framework, the United States has failed to stop sprawl or lessen its effects in the past. With growth in the immigrant population projected by the U.S. Census Bureau and other institutions, it seems unlikely to some that the United States will ameliorate the negative effects of such population growth in the future.

There are additional practical and moral issues to consider. First, deforestation is a by-product of subsistence living in many developing countries in the tropical and subtropical regions from which many U.S. immigrants come. Deforestation pressures are reduced by out-migration from these regions, and by economic development. At the same time, rising carbon emissions are closely linked to economic development, to increased standards of living, and to the expanded automobile use that comes with rising incomes. Proposing to control carbon emissions by limiting immigration to wealthy countries is equivalent to condemning would-be immigrants to live in poverty, and such an approach only works if these immigrants remain poor. If developing countries succeed in raising the standards of living of their citizens—an objective sought by most officials and citizens of the world community—per capita carbon emissions will inevitably increase.

Thus, limiting immigration to the United States appears to be centrally about protecting its own environment, rather than protecting the planet. However, since many environmental problems ignore national boundaries, protecting the United States can only go so far.

There are certainly important environmental challenges and policy decisions facing the United States and countries around the world, and many of them result from population growth. In the long run, however, especially with regard to carbon emissions, the environmental challenges derive more from the number of people on the planet rather than where people live. Linking immigration policy to controlling carbon emissions seems to confound this reality. It puts wealthy countries in the position of diverting attention from difficult internal tradeoffs with regard to carbon emissions, and instead suggests that much of the world's population remain in poverty as a mechanism for controlling carbon emissions.

It is obvious from these considerations that these issues are both technically complex and fraught with value-laden considerations, not the least of which is the role that the United States should play in the world. These issues raise a number of questions. How does the United States best serve its own environmental needs and those of the planet? Given the size of its environmental footprint, is it possible that the country can best serve the planet by first taking care of its own house, which might mean limiting immigration in an effort to curb population growth? Or, given the physical interconnectedness across countries, are environmental considerations even relevant to immigration policy?

POINT

The environmental argument for reducing immigration to the United States is relatively straightforward. Immigration levels are at a historic high, and immigration is now the main driver of U.S. population growth. Population growth contributes to environmental problems within the United States, and increases both America's large environmental footprint beyond U.S. borders and the country's disproportionate role in stressing global environmental systems. In order to seriously address environmental problems at home and become good global environmental citizens, U.S. population growth must be curtailed. There is a moral obligation for Americans to address the country's environmental problems and become good global environmental citizens. Therefore, immigration to the United States should be limited to the extent needed to stop U.S. population growth. This conclusion rests on a commitment to mainstream environmentalism, easily confirmed empirical premises, and logic.

POPULATION GROWTH AND THE ENVIRONMENT

From 1880 to the mid-1920s, America experienced an immigration boom, known as "the Great Wave," during which immigration averaged 600,000 people annually. U.S. population numbers grew rapidly in these years, due to a combination of high birth rates and high levels of immigration. For the next 40 years, from 1925 to 1965, the United States had a relatively restrictive immigration policy, which allowed 200,000 people into the country annually, on average. The U.S. population grew substantially during this time, as well, from 115 million to 194 million, primarily due to high rates of natural increase. During the 1950s, for example, American women had an average of 3.5 children each, far above the 2.1 total fertility rate (TFR) necessary to maintain the population of a nation with modern health care and sanitation.

By the 1970s, American women were averaging fewer babies—in 1975 the TFR stood at an all-time low of 1.7—and the United States was well positioned to transition from a growing to a stable population. One study found that without post-1970 immigration, the U.S. population would have leveled off below 250 million in the first few decades of this century. That didn't happen, however, because in 1965, and several times thereafter, Congress greatly increased immigration levels. Between 1965 and 1990, immigration averaged 1 million people annually, 5 times the average in the previous 4 decades. Between 1990 and the great recession of the late 2000s, immigration increased even more, to approximately 1.5 million annually (1 million legal and half a million illegal immigrants)—the highest rate in history. For these reasons, the U.S. population continued to grow, resulting in a missed opportunity to get one key aspect of sustainability—human numbers—under control. The U.S. population stood at over 308 million people in 2010, and it continues to grow rapidly.

Population growth contributes significantly to a host of environmental problems within the United States. Since 1990, for example, sprawl, defined as new development on the fringes of existing urban and suburban areas, has come to be recognized as an important environmental problem in the United States. Between 1982 and 2001, the United States converted 34 million acres of forest, cropland, and pasture to developed uses, an area the size of Illinois. The average annual rate of land conversion increased from 1.4 million acres to 2.2 million acres over this time, and it continues on an upward trend. Sprawl is an environmental problem for a lot of reasons, including increased energy consumption, water consumption, air pollution, and habitat loss for wildlife. Habitat loss is by far the number one cause of species endangerment in the United States; unsurprisingly, some of the worst sprawl centers (such as southern Florida and the Los Angeles basin) also contain large numbers of endangered species.

What causes sprawl? Transportation policies that favor building roads over mass transit appear to be important sprawl generators. So are zoning laws that encourage "leapfrog" developments far out into the country, and tax policies that allow builders to pass many of the costs of new development on to current taxpayers rather than new home buyers. Between 1970 and 1990, these and other factors caused Americans' per capita land use in the hundred largest metropolitan areas to increase 22.6 percent. In these same areas during this same period, however, the amount of developed land increased 51.5 percent.

What accounts for this discrepancy? Population growth. This is the number one cause of sprawl, by far. New houses, new shopping centers, and new roads are being built for new residents. In recent decades, cities and states with the highest population growth rates have also shown the most sprawl. The most comprehensive study to date on the causes of sprawl in the United States, *Outsmarting Smart Growth: Population Growth, Immigration, and the Problem of Sprawl* (2003), by

Roy Beck, Leon Kolankiewicz, and Steven Camarota, analyzed several dozen possible factors. Grouping together all of the factors that can increase per capita land use, and comparing these with the single factor of more "capitas," the authors found that in America between 1982 and 1997, 52 percent of sprawl was attributable to population increase, while 48 percent was attributable to misguided policies that increased land use per person.

On the other hand, cities with growing populations sprawled even more. Several states that managed to decrease their per capita land use during this period also sprawled, due to high rates of population growth. From 1982 to 1995, Nevada decreased its per capita land use 26 percent while sprawling 37 percent, due to a whopping 90 percent population increase. Arizona, meanwhile, decreased per capita land use 13 percent while its population increased 58 percent, generating 40 percent sprawl. This shows that population growth also causes sprawl (Beck, Kolankiewicz, & Camarota, 2003).

The bottom line is that stopping sprawl requires changing the transportation, tax, zoning, and *population* policies that encourage it. To simply accept as inevitable the factor (population increase), that the best research shows accounts for over half of the problem, will obviously not solve the problem. Nor will the nation's other major domestic environmental problems be solved.

Beyond domestic issues, an expanding U.S. population increases the country's already large environmental footprint beyond U.S. borders. Consider global warming. Nothing mortifies American environmentalists more than the country's failure to show leadership in dealing with this, the most important environmental challenge facing the world in the 21st century. As the world's largest economy, and historically the largest greenhouse gas emitter, the United States has a moral obligation to lead the world in meeting this challenge. A good start would be striving to stabilize greenhouse gas emissions at 1990 levels (the Kyoto Protocol, rejected by the United States, calls for an initial reduction of 5 percent below 1990 levels). Meeting even this modest objective will prove difficult, however, if the population continues to grow.

The United States' CO_2 emissions increased 20.4 percent between 1990 and 2005, from 4,991 to 6,009 million metric tons. That means emissions would have to decrease by 20.4 percent per person to get back to 1990 levels, *at the current population level.* But if the U.S. population doubles, as it is on track to do in six or seven decades, per capita emissions will have to decrease 58.5 percent in order to reduce CO_2 emissions to 1990 levels—almost three times as great a per capita reduction. Such reductions will be much more expensive and demand greater sacrifice from Americans, and they are thus less likely to happen.

Critics may respond that the technologies to cut carbon emissions exist, and that the real problem is Americans' hoggish overconsumption. Indeed, limiting consumption must play an important role in addressing global warming. American environmentalists should work to enact policies that reduce fossil fuel consumption as much as possible. However, reengineering the world's largest economy and changing the consumption patterns of hundreds of millions of people are immense undertakings that will be difficult and expensive, and they therefore will be (one may assume) only partly successful at best. If Americans are serious about doing their part to limit global warming, the "multiplier effect" of population growth is too important to ignore.

Between 1990 and 2003, U.S. per capita CO_2 emissions increased 3.2 percent, while *total* U.S. CO_2 emissions increased 20.2 percent. Why the discrepancy? During that same period, America's population increased 16.1 percent. More people drove more cars, built more houses, and so on. Population growth greatly increased total emissions, and it is total emissions, not per capita emissions, that quantify the full U.S. contribution to global warming.

SUSTAINABILITY

The claim here is not that halting U.S. population growth by itself will solve the sprawl problem or meet the nation's global warming responsibilities. On the contrary, Americans must reduce their per capita consumption of land and energy in order to meet these challenges. On the other hand, the evidence clearly shows that recent population growth has increased Americans' total land and energy consumption and made these problems even worse. Americans must address both overconsumption and overpopulation if they hope to create a sustainable society and contribute to a sustainable world.

Given the difficulties of getting 300 million Americans to curb their consumption, there is no reason to think sustainability can be achieved with two or three times that number. Environmentalists sometimes assume an infinite elasticity in the ability to reduce environmentally harmful consumption. This might have made sense 30 years ago, when the paradigm for such consumption was burning leaded gasoline or spraying deodorants that contained ozone-depleting CFCs. Americans could spend some money, remove lead or CFCs from those particular products, and continue happily consuming, minus the negative environmental effects.

Today, as human beings cook the earth and cause the sixth great extinction episode in the planet's history, environmentally harmful consumption is measured in terms of carbon footprints and the hectares of land necessary to sustain consumption choices (land which is then *not* available as habitat for other species). Such personal impacts can and should be reduced. But because carbon emissions and basic resource use are implicated in almost all consumption acts, they cannot be reduced to zero. As the cost of greener substitutes increases, the general public, and then environmentalists themselves, refuse to pay them. As people move beyond *changing* consumption patterns in ways that perhaps more efficiently provide the benefits they want, and instead are asked to *reduce* consumption of goods and services that they desire or enjoy, sustainability becomes a much harder sell.

American environmentalists need to remember that future consumption levels will be set both by government policies and by many billions of individual consumption decisions. These policies and decisions will be made not just by environmentalists, but also by people who are relatively unmoved by environmental considerations. Any reasonable scenario for creating a sustainable society must take this into account. Furthermore, even environmentalists tend to fade to a lighter shade of green when consuming less would seriously harm what they consider their quality of life.

In other words, one can imagine Americans living and consuming at the levels of western European or Japanese citizens. As a goal, this is worth striving for politically. One cannot, however, imagine Americans (or western Europeans or Japanese, for that matter) voluntarily living and consuming at the levels of the average Mexican citizen, much less the level of the average citizen of Nigeria or Bangladesh. Barring universal enlightenment or dire catastrophe, these are not realistic political options (regardless of whether a few thousand or even a few million hard-core environmentalists succeed in creating ultra-low-consumption lifestyles in the midst of a high-consumption culture). Nevertheless, it is urgent that the United States move toward creating a sustainable society.

Of course, population stabilization would not guarantee sustainability, but it would make it possible. In philosophical terms, stabilizing the population is a necessary but not a sufficient condition for creating a sustainable society.

A PROPOSAL—AND THE ALTERNATIVES

It is proposed here, then, that the United States reduce immigration by taking the following measures: (1) cut legal immigration from one million to 200,000 per year (the level allowed during the middle of the last century); (2) reduce illegal immigration by strictly enforcing sanctions against employers who hire illegal workers (it is fruitless to try to lower legal immigration levels while ignoring or condoning illegal immigration); (3) rework trade agreements, and increase and better target development aid, to help people live better lives in their own countries.

Such policies would allow some of the benefits of immigration to continue (providing asylum for political refugees, allowing small influxes of workers with special skills, etc.) while helping the United States move toward population stabilization. Because the current TFR of 2.05 is right around the "replacement rate" (2.1), and because reducing immigration would likely help drive the TFR even lower, such stabilization is no wild eco-fantasy. The United States is nearly there, if the government is willing to limit immigration (this also holds true for other developed nations, whose TFRs tend to be even lower than that in the United States).

Many readers will instinctively recoil from this proposal. But paeans to sustainability, or talk of nonhuman beings having an intrinsic value that people need to respect, or reminders that God calls us to be good stewards of his creation, or earnest expressions of strong environmental feelings—these are all mere cant when coupled with a blithe acceptance of the doubling or tripling of America's human population. The second half of this essay will address some of the main objections that might be raised against this proposal. But at a minimum, readers unwilling to reduce immigration into the United States must own the demographic and environmental implications of their position. Supporting the immigration status quo of 1.5 million immigrants annually also means supporting increasing America's population to over 700 million by 2100. Supporting an immigration policy along the lines of the Bush/Kennedy/McCain bill of 2007, which might have increased immigration to 2.25 million people annually, also means supporting a near tripling America's population to over 850 million by 2100.

To support these scenarios, or anything like them, means that one does not just support drastically increasing America's human population. It also means support for more cars, more houses, more malls, more power lines, and more concrete and asphalt. It means support for less habitat and resources for wildlife; fewer forests, prairies, and wetlands; and fewer birds and wild mammals (except perhaps for house sparrows, rats, and a few other human commensals). And it means support for replacing these other species with human beings and the economic support systems they require.

OBJECTIONS

Moral arguments: Rights. Perhaps the most important objections raised against restrictive immigration policies are that they are unjust, because they are unfair to potential immigrants. One concise way of stating this is to say that would-be immigrants have a *right* to live and work in the United States. While some immigrants' rights proponents argue for abolishing national borders altogether, most assert a general human right to freely move and settle without regard to national borders, subject to reasonable state restrictions to keep out criminals and prevent gross harms to receiving societies.

Clearly this right does not exist in American law. The Constitution names no right to immigrate, and the Supreme Court has consistently upheld the federal government's right to regulate immigration into the country. Neither does such a right exist in international law. The U.N. Universal Declaration of Human Rights does not assert a general human right to immigrate into the country of one's choice, nor do other major framework international rights treaties. Proponents, then, claim first the existence of a *moral* right to immigrate freely across borders, and second that national laws should be amended accordingly. What arguments do they provide for creating this new and important legal right?

The political theorist Chandran Kukathas (2003) gives the following "liberal egalitarian" argument for open borders. From a proper universalistic moral point of view, he maintains, citizens of rich countries have no special claims to the resources and opportunities into which they have been born. "Egalitarianism demands that the Earth's resources be distributed as equally as possible," he writes, "and one particularly effective mechanism for facilitating this is freedom of movement" (pp. 571–572). Egalitarians want to equalize not just resources, but opportunities. Allowing people to migrate from poor, overcrowded countries with high unemployment and little chance for economic advancement to wealthier, less crowded countries equalizes opportunities.

This is a powerful argument, since it rests on egalitarian values that many people share. It also relies on a common thought: "What right do I have to 'shut the door' on people who are just as good as I am and who, through no fault of their own, have been born into less happy circumstances?" Kukathas's argument may speak particularly strongly to people who feel some sympathy with egalitarianism, but not enough to do anything about it personally. For it says to wealthy Americans, "You don't have to give up anything yourself to help poor people overseas live better lives. You can fulfill any moral obligations you may have toward them by allowing them to come here and cut your grass, cook your food, and diaper your children."

As noted above, current high levels of immigration into the United States are leading to a larger population, which makes it much harder to share the landscape generously with nonhuman beings. Allowing a general right to immigrate into the United States would greatly accelerate this process. With "open borders," the interests of nonhuman nature would be sacrificed completely to the interests of people. The economic interests of would-be immigrants would trump the very existence of many nonhuman organisms, endangered species, and wild places in the United States.

Kukathas (and most immigrants' rights advocates) can accept this trade-off. As the previous quotes illustrate, Kukathas sees nature essentially as "the Earth's resources." The only question to ask about these resources, therefore, is how people may divide them up fairly and efficiently. But those who reject this anthropocentric perspective must consider the interests of the nonhuman beings that would be displaced by an ever-increasing human presence. Many believe that the human appropriation of natural landscapes has progressed so far in America that any further appropriation is unjust. Some readers might not be willing to go that far (although if that is the case, one wonders what they are waiting for). But it is important to realize that accepting a general right to immigrate leaves *no* room to take nature's interests seriously, in the United States or elsewhere, since it undermines any possibility of limiting the human appropriation of nature. For this reason alone, it must be rejected by anyone committed to sustainability.

This is not to deny the importance of human rights. On the contrary, the authors presuppose them. Rights allow us to protect important human interests and create egalitarian societies that maximize opportunities for people to flourish. Rights are justified ultimately *because* they contribute to such human flourishing. But when rights are pressed so far as to undermine human or nonhuman flourishing, they should be rejected.

Moral arguments: Welfare. Even if no general right to immigrate exists, however, there might still be good moral reasons for upholding the permissive immigration status quo. Consider the following welfare-based argument. Approximately 1.5 million people immigrate into the United States each year, and clearly the majority believe they will improve their own or their families' welfare by doing so. Otherwise they wouldn't come. Immigrants may find educational, vocational, or other personal opportunities in the United States that they would otherwise be denied. Immigrants coming from some countries may significantly improve their own or their families' health and longevity. All else being equal, the potential improvements in would-be immigrants' welfare seem to make a powerful argument for continuing to allow mass immigration.

Of course, all else is *not* equal, as has already been shown. Whatever may once have been the case, continued mass immigration into the United States threatens the very existence of many nonhuman beings and species. It compromises future generations' right to a decent environment, both here and abroad. It makes it easier for common citizens and wealthy elites in other countries to ignore the conditions that are driving so many people to emigrate in the first place. In addition, economists have shown that mass immigration drives down the wages of working-class Americans and increases economic inequality in the United States.

Still, immigration's benefits to new immigrants remain substantial, and welfare arguments of the sort just canvassed cannot be ignored. They point to a responsibility, not to immigrants per se, but to people around the globe who live in poverty, insecurity, and injustice. Even the most generous immigration policies will not help most of them, since only a small percentage can conceivably emigrate from their home countries, and the worst off rarely have the resources to do so. The wealthy people of the world—including not just citizens of "the West," but hundreds of millions of people in the developing world—owe the world's poor people something. Not the lucky few millions who manage to immigrate to the West, but the billions who will have to sink or swim where they are. It is hoped that most people will agree that wealthy people—West and East—have a prima facie duty to share some of their wealth and help the world's poor people live better lives. Rather than try to justify this duty, however, three brief comments on its proper scope and pursuit will be presented.

First, mass immigration is neither a sufficient nor an efficient means of meeting it. Inviting the world's poor to America is a poor substitute for helping them create safe, just, flourishing societies where they live. Even taking the most positive view possible of its effects on immigrants, mass immigration does nothing for the vast majority of the world's poor.

Second, serious environmentalists will not allow efforts to help poor people run roughshod over their environmental commitments. Serious and immediate human needs may sometimes overrule prima facie duties to protect wild nature and preserve a healthy environment. But committed environmentalists cannot interpret our social duties in ways that make our environmental duties impossible to fulfill.

Third, fortunately, our prima facie duty to help the world's poor may be pursued in ways that do not undermine efforts to meet our prima facie environmental duties. The U.S. government should be much more generous and intelligent with development aid to poor countries. (America ranks near the bottom among Western democracies in per capita foreign aid, and much of this comes as military aid that actually harms poor people.) It should fully fund international family planning efforts, which help both nature and the poor. It should set trade policies to benefit poor workers and protect nature, rather than to maximize trade. All these efforts, and more, may be taken up without embracing mass immigration, which is not a substitute for such efforts.

Environmental arguments. Environmentalists sometimes give specifically environmental reasons for supporting—or at least tolerating—high levels of immigration. One common argument says that the focus should be on *consumption, not population,* as the root cause of the nation's environmental problems. This argument is appealing because it seems to put the responsibility for change where it belongs: not on poor immigrants but on average Americans, who do consume too much and who could consume less without harming their quality of life. But, as noted above, it is Americans' *overall* consumption that determines their environment impact. Overall consumption equals per capita consumption multiplied by population. So if high consumption is a problem, population growth must be a problem, too.

Indeed, a strong case can be made that the nation is overpopulated right now. Signs of stressed ecosystems and lost biodiversity abound. A way has not yet been found to bring air and water pollution within limits acceptable to human health, the loss of productive farmlands and wildlife habitat has not been stemmed, and no more than a handful of the hundreds of speciesth humans have endangered have been recovered. When considering global warming, a large and growing population makes it much harder for Americans to live up to their environmental responsibilities as global citizens.

Advocates for international action are correct that wealthy countries should help poor countries stabilize their populations. However, "think globally, *don't* act locally" is terrible advice. It is possible and necessary to work on multiple levels at once.

Environmentalists should think long and hard before advocating anything that weakens this "local focus," because a passionate connection to places that are "near and dear" is how environmentalism works, whether in Boston or Beijing. This doesn't involve believing American (or Chinese) landscapes are more valuable than others. It involves acting *as if* they are the most important landscapes in the world, and using the most accessible political levers to protect them. Although questions about the justice of moral particularism are vexing a large degree of "environmental particularism" is justified, on both ethical and pragmatic grounds.

However, cosmopolitan ethical universalists who reject a parochial concern for protecting America's native species and unique landscapes should still support the proposal to reduce immigration into the United States, since doing so would also benefit the rest of the world. This is because moving people to America, far from being environmentally benign or neutral, increases overall global resource consumption and pollution. This in turn threatens to weaken the already stressed global ecosystem services that all people depend upon—with the world's poorest people facing the greatest danger from possible ecological failures.

Compare the average American's "ecological footprint" with averages from the nation's 10 largest immigration "source" countries: Mexico, China, the Philippines, India, Cuba, El Salvador, Vietnam, Korea, Canada, and the Dominican Republic. On average, immigrating from 9 of these 10 countries greatly increases an individual's ecological footprint—and the ecological footprints of his or her descendants—by 100 percent to 1,000 percent or more. In the case of Mexico, which accounts for nearly a third of all immigration to America, immigration increases an individual's consumption and pollution by approximately 350 percent. There probably are cases where immigrants consume more but do less ecological damage than they would have had they remained in their countries of origin (e.g., slash-and-burn agriculturalists inhabiting biologically rich forests), but clearly these are the exceptions. More Americans is bad news for America's native flora and fauna. But given global warming, it is also bad news for poor people living in the Sahel or in the Bhramaputra Delta.

If emigration helped America's source countries get their own demographic houses in order, or if it opened up an ecological space that they then used to create more sustainable or just societies, a case might be made for continuing to allow mass immigration into the United States. Instead, America's permissive immigration policies appear to enable demographic and ecological irresponsibility and continuing social injustice. As an example, consider Guatemala. About 10 percent of adult native-born Guatemalans now live and work in the United States (and a recent poll showed that most young Guatemalans hope to do so in the future). The TFR of Guatemalan women averaged 4.6 children in 2005, resulting in an annual population growth rate of 2.4 percent. The Guatemalan government outlaws abortion (except when a mother's life is at risk) and does little to encourage contraception. Guatemala has high deforestation rates and an unjust, highly inequitable distribution of wealth. But there is little effort to change any of this, perhaps because the negative effects of local overpopulation are lessened through emmigration and counterbalanced, for many individuals, by the positive incentives of receiving remittances from family members in the United States.

Economic arguments. Many pro-business proponents praise mass immigration for increasing economic growth. Immigration brings in poor unskilled workers willing to work physically demanding jobs for less money than native-born Americans, as well as highly trained professionals with the specialized skills needed by high-tech companies. It thus helps businesses meet their needs and grow. Immigration creates more domestic consumers, which is why *The Wall Street Journal,* the U.S. Chamber of Commerce, and other important business interests strongly support mass immigration (and in the case of the *Journal,* "open borders").

On the other hand, focusing on whether mass immigration is "good for the economy" ignores the fact that any immigration policy creates economic winners and losers. According to Harvard economist George Borjas, "immigration induces a substantial redistribution of wealth, away from workers who compete with immigrants and toward employers and other users of immigrant services" (1999, p. 13). This is because, compared to other industrialized nations, the United States imports a much higher percentage of less-educated, lower-skilled workers. Borjas notes that "between 1980 and 1995, immigration increased the number of high school dropouts by 21 percent and the number of high school graduates by only 4 percent." During this same period, the wage disparity between these two groups increased 11 percent, with perhaps half of that disparity a result of mass immigration. Borjas calculates that between 1980 and 2000, immigration reduced the average annual earnings of high school dropouts by 7.4 percent, or $1,800 on an average salary of $25,000. For these workers, who could least afford it, real wages actually declined during this period.

While the economic effects of immigration are complex and the details are open to debate, it appears that over the past few decades high immigration levels have contributed to increased economic growth, lower wages for the poorest Americans, and increased economic inequality in the United States. Continued high levels of immigration will likely further these trends.

Economic considerations also support the immigration policy proposal presented here—with a proper understanding of "economy." Eighty-five years ago, in a talk to the Albuquerque Chamber of Commerce (which he once headed), environmentalist Aldo Leopold asked, "What, concretely, is our ambition as a city? '100,000 by 1930'—we have blazoned it forth like an army with banners. . . . Can anyone deny that the vast fund of time, brains, and money now devoted to making our city big would actually make it better if diverted to betterment instead of bigness?" Civic-mindedness *may* be a force for good, Leopold added, but he went on to ask his "boosters," somewhat plaintively, "Is it too much to hope that this force, harnessed to a finer ideal, may some day accomplish good as well as big things? That our future standard of civic values may even exclude quantity, obtained at the expense of quality, as not worth while?"

No, this is not too much to hope. Without such a society-wide "revaluation of economic values," environmentalism will not succeed. "The good life" must be redefined in less materialistic terms, and economies must be designed to sustain a finite number of such good lives, not to grow indefinitely. These are daunting tasks, but they are not optional for serious environmentalists. In America, where people habitually mistake bigness for goodness and quantity for quality, these tasks are even more urgent. And as Leopold understood, population growth is an important part of the overall picture.

CONCLUSION

A number of reasons for limiting immigration into the United States have been presented here, as well as responses to the most common and consequential objections to this proposal. Simply put, immigration is now the main driver of American population growth, and continued American population growth is incompatible with sustainability, nationally or globally. Therefore, environmentalists committed to sustainability should support reducing current high levels of U.S. immigration. Not just on pain of contradiction, but on pain of failure. Americans must choose between sustainability and continued population growth. They cannot have both.

REFERENCES AND FURTHER READING

Beck, R., & Kolankiewicz, L. (2000). The environmental movement's retreat from advocating U.S. population stabilization (1970–1998): A first draft of history. *Journal of Policy History, 12*(1), 123–156.

Beck, R., Kolankiewicz, L., & Camarota, S. (2003). *Outsmarting smart growth: Population growth, immigration, and the problem of sprawl.* Washington, DC: Center for Immigration Studies.

Borjas, G. (1999). *Heaven's door: Immigration policy and the American economy.* Princeton, NJ: Princeton University Press.

Borjas, G. (2004). *Increasing the supply of labor through immigration: Measuring the impact on native-born workers* [Backgrounder]. Retrieved from Center for Immigration Studies website: http://www.cis.org/articles/2004/back504.pdf

Bouvier, L. (1998). *The impact of immigration on United States' population size: 1950–2050.* Washington, DC: Negative Population Growth.

Cafaro, P. (1998). Less is more: Economic consumption and the good life. *Philosophy Today, 42,* 26–39.

Cafaro, P. (2002). Economic consumption, pleasure, and the good life. *Journal of Social Philosophy, 32*(4), 471–486.

Camarota, S. (2005). *Birth rates among immigrants in America: Comparing fertility in the U.S. and home countries.* Retrieved from Center for Immigration Studies website: http://www.cis.org/articles/2005/back1105.html

Czech, B. (2000). Economic growth as a limiting factor for wildlife conservation. *Wildlife Society Bulletin, 28,* 4–15.

Daly, H. (1996). *Beyond growth: The economics of sustainable development.* Boston, MA: Beacon Press.

Energy Information Administration, U.S. Department of Energy. (2006, November). *Emissions of greenhouse gases in the United States 2005.* Retrieved from ftp://ftp.eia.doe.gov/pub/oiaf/1605/cdrom/pdf/ggrpt/057305.pdf

Kukathas, C. (2003). Immigration. In H. LaFollette (Ed.), *The Oxford handbook of practical ethics* (pp. 571–586). Oxford, UK: Oxford University Press.

Leopold, A. (1991). A criticism of the booster spirit. In A. Leopold (Ed.), *The river of the mother of God and other essays.* Madison, WI: University of Wisconsin Press.

Macedo, S. (2007). The moral dilemma of U.S. immigration policy: Open borders vs. social justice? In C. Swain (Ed.), *Debating immigration* (pp. 63–81). New York, NY: Cambridge University Press.

Natural Resources Conservation Service, U.S. Department of Agriculture. (2003). *National resources inventory 2001: Urbanization and development of rural land.* Retrieved from http://www.nrcs.usda.gov/technical/land/nri01/nri01dev.html

Pevnick, R., Cafaro, P., & Risse, M. (2008). An exchange: The morality of immigration. *Ethics & International Affairs, 22*(3), 241–259.

Pimentel, D., & Pimentel, M. (1990). *Land, energy and water: The constraints governing ideal U.S. population size* (NPG Forum Series paper). Retrieved from Negative Population Growth website: http://www.npg.org/forum_series/LandEnergyWater ContraintsGoverningIdealUSPopSize018.pdf

President's Council on Sustainable Development. (1996). *Sustainable America: A new consensus for prosperity, opportunity, and a healthy environment for the future.* Retrieved from http://clinton2.nara.gov/PCSD/Publications/

Rolston, H., III. (1998). *Environmental ethics.* Philadelphia, PA: Temple University Press.

Singer, P. (2002). *One world: The ethics of globalization.* New Haven, CT: Yale University Press.

Thoreau, H. D. (1962). *Journal* (Vol. VIII). New York, NY: Dover Press. (Original published in 1856)

Wilcove, D. S., Rothstein, D., Dubow, J., Phillips, A., & Losos, E. (1998). Quantifying threats to imperiled species in the United States: Assessing the relative importance of habitat destruction, alien species, pollution, overexploitation, and disease. *BioScience, 48*(8), 607–615.

Philip Cafaro and Winthrop R. Staples III

Note: This essay was adapted from the essay "The Environmental Argument for Reducing Immigration" by Philip Cafaro and Winthrop R. Staples III (Center for Immigration Studies, 2009).

COUNTERPOINT

The need for immigration reform in the United States is beyond question; the nation's broken immigration system undermines core national values as well as U.S. economic and security interests. Reforming the immigration system is also an important element in successfully addressing other key issues, such as health care and the economy. The relationship between immigration and health care is fairly self-evident: Adding more people potentially without insurance to an already overstressed health care system will only serve to further increase health care costs. Some might ask, however, how immigration reform can possibly be related to the environment and climate change. One answer, as Philip Cafaro and Winthrop Staples III put it in the preceding essay, has to do with population growth. This claim follows closely from a lingering history of concern in the environmental movement with regard to population growth, which has faded from the top of most environmentalists' agendas for some years now.

At this point in the twenty-first century, the environmental movement has been primarily focused on global warming and climate change, rather than population growth, but this has not always been the case. As early as the late eighteenth century, Reverend Thomas Malthus warned of the dangers of population growth, describing a "Malthusian" world in which population growth would outstrip food production, resulting in human beings being relegated to subsistence living characterized by "misery and vice." In 1968, Paul Ehrlich published *The Population Bomb*, which warned of imminent environmental and human disaster as a consequence of population growth. This book brought widespread attention to the issue of population growth and raised concerns about the world's capacity to feed an ever-increasing number of people.

The problem, of course, is that the "bomb" Ehrlich warned about didn't go off and most of his dire predictions didn't come true, due to forces such as increased urbanization (which drove down family size in developing countries), AIDS, increased crop yields, and other factors. Meanwhile, population growth has slowed (though not as much as was expected in a major 2004 UN assessment), and the medium range of estimates is that global population is on a path to reach 9.3 billion in 2050, and then rise and likely stabilize at 10.5 billion people in 2100. That being said, population should not be taken off the agenda of environmentalists completely. If average fertility rates increase by half a child over the medium variant from the most recent UN estimates, then global population would reach 10.6 billion in 2050 and 15.8 billion by 2100. A fertility rate of half a child below the medium variant would result in a population of 8.1 billion by 2050 and 6.2 billion by 2100 (United Nations, 2011). Continuation of family planning and women's education initiatives—considered to be the strongest drivers of fertility rates—is needed to keep the Malthusian scenarios at bay.

From an environmental and climate perspective, though, global population is not the only concern. Population of individual countries is also a concern. In the United States, fertility rates have slightly increased, but immigration has clearly contributed to population growth. And even though immigration has been steadily decreasing since its peak in the 1990s and is projected to continue a downward slide out to 2050, some environmentalists, like Cafaro, have argued that immigration into the United States should be strictly limited in order to reduce the negative impact that increased population growth has on the environment. The negative impacts cited include local issues like urban "sprawl," regional problems such as decreasing biodiversity, and global problems such as climate change. On the more extreme end of the spectrum, Cafaro suggests that U.S. immigration be limited to 200,000 people a year. This would be a dramatic drop from the more than 1 million people a year who legally are granted permanent resident status. (According to the Pew Hispanic Center some 300,000 arrive illegally each year.)

Given these current statistics and absent any principled and defensible policies justifying draconian policies to reduce population, a singular focus on population in environmental circles seems overwrought. Nonetheless, for the purposes of this essay, it is given that population considerations should be a factor in environmental policy. Thus, the issues of urban sprawl and climate change will be addressed, to see if the environmentalist calls to limit immigration hold up as population-related solutions to these problems. It will be argued that debates over the security of U.S. borders or immigration policy in general are not the appropriate focus for solving these environmental problems.

URBAN SPRAWL

Some who favor immigration reduction as an antidote to environmental problems in the United States point to the role that growing populations play in increased urban sprawl, and particularly to the costly environmental damage caused by cities that move away from the environmentally beneficial density that can accompany urban life. For example, denser cities are overwhelmingly more energy efficient than cities that have spread out, and denser cities usually benefit as well from greater use of public transportation (Light, 2001).

But it is difficult to make the case that immigration is the strongest, or even a meaningful, driver of urban sprawl. Sprawl exists throughout the United States, and its extent in any region is not correlated to any significant degree with either legal or illegal immigration to a particular place. Sprawl is certainly a problem in places like Atlanta and Miami, where the population is increasing. But it is also a problem in places where population is decreasing, such as St. Louis. Urban sprawl is driven by complex factors such as zoning, city planning, transportation policy, and the building of freeways, and not simply by population growth. Solutions to urban sprawl and its attendant problems lie in comprehensive regional planning and policy changes in a variety of arenas, not simply in limiting population growth by limiting immigration. Even so, it is very interesting to note that, according to a study by the Brookings Institution, the 10 highest carbon-emitting cities have an average immigrant population below 5 percent—such as Louisville, Indianapolis, and Cincinnati—while the cities with the lowest carbon footprints have immigrant populations of 25 to 40 percent—such as Los Angeles, El Paso, and New York City (Madrid, 2010). Is this a correlation, or is there a causal connection here? Though a correlation is sufficient to cast doubt on the immigration case for urban sprawl, a causal explanation could be at hand. These same studies show that immigrants are more likely to use public transportation and overall consume less than nonimmigrants.

Of course, where there are more people, there are going to be increases in what economists refer to as "congestion costs." Population growth generally coincides with economic growth—and with the need for increased capacity in public infrastructure (roads, schools, housing, and so forth). But sprawl is not an inevitable consequence of meeting these needs. Good planning and careful use of resources that accrue from economic growth can avoid these problems. This is made clear by the fact that there is sprawl in cities with decreasing populations as well as in those where the population is growing. The solution, then, is not to focus simplistically on limiting population growth in order to tackle the challenge of urban sprawl. Rather, it is to focus on the specific causes of sprawl and address them directly.

CLIMATE CHANGE

The issue of climate change is arguably the most urgent environmental issue of our time, and one of the biggest challenges humanity has ever faced. The question of how immigration to the United States impacts climate change should be taken seriously, given that the United States is the largest major per-capita emitter of greenhouse gases in the world. The core concern is that when people immigrate to the United States from countries with a lower carbon footprint their individual contribution to global warming increases, further exacerbating an already complex problem.

This is the reasoning behind a 2008 paper from the Center for Immigration Studies, titled *Immigration to the United States and World-wide Greenhouse Gas Emissions*. The authors, Steven Camarota and Leon Kolankiewicz, argue that immigration "significantly increases world-wide CO_2 emissions because it transfers population from lower-polluting parts of the world to the United States, which is a higher-polluting country." The study found that when immigrants come to the United States, on average, their carbon footprint increases by a factor of four. Based on this analysis, Camarota and Kolankiewicz determined that some 637 million tons of the U.S.'s annual CO_2 emissions are due to immigrants—more than the emissions of Great Britain and Sweden combined. Those emissions are 482 million tons more than these immigrants would have contributed had they remained in their countries of origin. In this analysis, 83 percent of these emissions are estimated to come from legal immigrants, and 17 percent from illegal immigrants.

Anyone concerned about climate change would find these facts compelling on first glance and worth a closer look. But if one considers where the world is headed with respect to annual emissions, as well as where it needs to go, eliminating that 482 million tons per year by ending immigration would not make much of a difference against the backdrop of overall U.S. emissions and overall emission reduction goals. Further, it is highly unlikely that a slight benefit to the U.S. emissions profile would offset such a radical change to U.S. immigration policy as decreasing immigration to 200,000 people per year. There are better and more direct ways to reduce U.S. emissions, and a rational climate policy would look to reducing the emissions of all Americans, not simply the minority immigrant population. Consider the following five objections.

First, to get some perspective on the relative reductions in emissions that would be generated by eliminating the contribution made by all immigrants to the United States, consider where experts want emissions to go in order to make an adequate contribution to overall greenhouse gas reductions. Admittedly, considering the value of eliminating all emissions by immigrants is an even more radical policy than that proposed in the last essay, but the thought experiment will help to better understand the significance of the claim.

The most ambitious greenhouse gas mitigation target articulated by the United States was in the final communiqué of the 2009 G8 meeting in Italy. There the Obama administration endorsed the idea that developed countries should reduce emissions by 80 percent by the year 2050. Emissions in the United States in 2009 were 6,576 million tons (though this was a drop from 2008, since it was a temporary reduction due to the economic recession; see USEIA, 2011). An 80 percent reduction would require the United States to lower its annual CO_2 emissions to approximately 1,315.20 million tons per year from 2009 levels (and even more from today's levels, since emissions have gone up since then). While the United States is the second largest emitter in the world behind China, the gap between the United States and the third-largest emitter is several thousand million metric tons, making this emissions target, though ambitious, still a larger reduction than most of the top 20 carbon polluters.

Nonetheless, suppose that, hypothetically, the country could magically eliminate the entire carbon impact created by immigrants in the United States. This would only amount to a 7.32 percent decrease in U.S. emissions in a good year, and even less otherwise. This should put the figure offered by the Center for Immigration Studies into perspective. While the idea that the total emissions by immigrants in the United States—taking into account the amount they would have emitted had they stayed home—would create a country with a carbon footprint larger than Sweden and Great Britain sounds like a lot, it really isn't, given how big an emitter the United States is and how small the emissions of these countries have become. Further, reductions garnered through population reductions do not have the same aggregating capacity as reductions achieved through structural improvements in energy efficiency or transition to renewable energy. If the United States were to set and achieve a target to generate sufficient solar or wind power to substitute for 482 million tons of CO_2 emissions annually, then increasing this capacity would be a matter of adding capacity to a system already set to integrate this power into the overall grid system. Savings achieved by stopping immigration are not additive in the same way. If immigration were stopped completely, the reductions from future people who would have never been allowed to immigrate to the United States could not be counted. At best one could only continue population reductions as a mechanism for emission reductions by finding a way to reduce birth rates in the United States, but it is highly unlikely there would be sufficient motivation to proceed with such a policy given the modest birth rates already in effect. It is simply not a problem that people appear interested in taking on.

Second, while it might currently be the case that immigration from developing to developed countries increases the average immigrannt's carbon footprint, this could change in the future. Right now, developing countries like China, India, and Mexico do not have any mandatory constraints on their emissions with respect to any standing international climate treaty. These countries can continue to increase emissions as their economies grow. And their economies are growing:

- According to the World Bank, China's gross domestic product (GDP) has grown an average of 10.1 percent per year since 1990, and its per capita CO_2 emissions in 2005 were 210 percent higher than they were in 1990.

- India's GDP has grown an average of 6.6 percent per year since 1990, and its per capita CO_2 emissions in 2005 were 153 percent higher than they were in 1990.

- Mexico's GDP has grown an average of 2.8 percent per year since 1990, and its per capita CO_2 emissions in 2005 were 108 percent higher than they were in 1990.

While the United States is not currently party to a binding agreement either, other developed countries, such as the countries of the European Union, are party to such international agreements, and they are required to reduce their emissions. At present all countries are working on creating a new binding international climate treaty under the auspices of the United Nation's Durban Platform for Enhanced Action. And while the expectation is that it will be binding for all countries, it will nonetheless place higher mitigation targets on developed countries than developing countries.

If developing countries with high out-migration continue to experience economic growth, with its attendant increased carbon emissions, their per capita emissions may approach those in the United States over the long run. At current economic and emissions growth rates, China's per capita CO_2 emissions will exceed those of the European Union by the middle of this decade, and they are on target to equal those of the United States in 12 to 15 years. As early as 2030, China may have the largest cumulative emissions on the planet. In this respect, from the perspective of moving people around the world—or rather halting their movement or redirecting it by radically decreasing immigration to the United States—it may soon be the case that the restriction of immigration to developed countries increases the emissions of some in developing countries.

Third, this last point helps us see how misguided is the idea of moving people around the world in order to mitigate greenhouse gas emissions. If one were to accept all of Cafaro's and Staples's assumptions (as well as those of the Center for Immigration Studies report mentioned earlier), then, from the point of view of the atmosphere and the future of the planet, there should be a forcible movement of people from high per-capita carbon countries to low per-capita carbon countries. Since the United States is the highest per capita emitter, a policy of "directed migration" of Americans to lower carbon-emission countries could lower cumulative global emissions by hundreds if not thousands of millions of tons. One could reverse this reasoning as well. Given that the largest accumulation of biomass and biodiversity on the planet is at the equator, and given that these areas will be more susceptible to climate change than areas further north, one could make a parallel case that the best way to make these places les vulnerable would be by directing more people from the equatorial regions to the north, say from Central America to North America. If such a position sounds absurd, it's because it is absurd. But it follows from the reasoning offered in the climate case for immigration restrictions.

Fourth, to argue that people should stay in lower-polluting parts of the world in order to minimize global CO_2 emissions is to argue that people who were unlucky enough to be born in poor countries should continue to live in poverty. This is a not a morally defensible approach to minimizing global carbon emissions in its present form. A principal reason CO_2 emissions are higher in the United States than they are in out-migration countries is that people in the United States enjoy higher standards of living than people in out-migration countries. Suggesting that people should remain poor in order to effect lower greenhouse gas emissions is not morally justifiable. Rather than using immigration restrictions as a mechanism for controlling greenhouse gases, the focus should be on policies that reduce per capita CO_2 emissions in the United States and simultaneously promote growth in poorer parts of the world in ways that are sustainable and less reliant on carbon, and thus pull people out of poverty in an environmentally friendly way.

Finally, a purely political point must be made. Immigration reform is clearly one of the most highly politicized issues in American public life today. It is becoming increasingly difficult to have a rational conversation about immigration reform, given the political stakes. Would it help either debates over immigration or debates over climate change to conflate them? This seems an imprudent move at best, especially in light of the fact that there is of an active debate over the reality of climate change itself. The last thing that proponents of energy transformation in the United States need is to tar these efforts with a hot button issue like immigration reform.

CONCLUSION

The most rational choice with regard to climate change is for a country like the United States to move as quickly as possible to reduce emissions for everyone, rather than selectively reducing emissions for those who were not born in the country. U.S. efforts have so far fallen very short of what is necessary to put the nation on a sustainable track of lower emissions. In many respects, the United States should have an easier time taking on this challenge than other places because its development needs are not as great as other parts of the world. China provides an interesting example. China is a country whose population is increasing, but one that is also addressing concerns about its expanding carbon footprint. It is ahead of the United States in terms of adapting renewable electricity standards, adopting better fuel efficiency standards, and even in terms of experimenting with regional cap and trade systems as a prelude to a national program. China spent a bigger percentage of its last stimulus package on moving to alternative energy than the United States did in its 2009 stimulus package.

China's reasons for this strategy go beyond simply environmental concerns. They are also determined to dominate clean energy markets around the world. In this respect the Chinese government's support of developing renewable energies is a strategy the United States can and should learn from. Even if primarily driven by self-interest, China's strategies will no doubt help to move it toward greater sustainability in the face of a growing population.

The argument that the best way, even a viable way, to resolve environmental concerns—most importantly climate change—is by decreasing U.S. immigration is misguided. The primary focus should be to decrease the carbon footprint of all those living in the United States, regardless of where they were born. If one wants to pursue a connection between population shifts and climate change, a much more fruitful avenue of research is the potential forced migration that will occur as populations in one part of the world need to move elsewhere because of the additional stressors placed on already unstable conditions in their countries by climate change. Rather than risking using climate change as a stalking horse for other motivations for immigration reform, this line of inquiry would directly address the potential impacts of climate change and seek to understand them on their own terms.

References and Further Reading

American Association for the Advancement of Science. (2001). *Atlas of population and the environment*. Berkeley, CA: University of California Press.

Camarota, S., & Kolankiewicz, L. (2008). *Immigration to the United States and world-wide greenhouse gas emissions*. Retrieved from Center for Immigration Studies website: http://cis.org/GreenhouseGasEmissions

International Organization for Migration. (2008). *Climate change and migration: Improving methodologies to estimate flows* (Migration Research Series 33). Retrieved from http://publications.iom.int/bookstore/index.php?main_page=product_info&products_id=85

Light, A. (2001). The urban blind spot in environmental ethics. *Environmental Politics, 10,* 7–35.

Lovejoy, T. E., & Hannah, L. (Eds.). (2005). *Climate change and biodiversity.* New Haven, CT: Yale University Press.

Madrid, J. (2010, October). *From a "green farce" to a green future: Refuting false claims about immigrants and the environment.* Retrieved from Center for American Progress website: http://www.americanprogress.org/issues/2010/10/pdf/immigration_climate_change.pdf/

United Nations. (2011). *World population prospects: The 2010 revision.* Retrieved from http://esa.un.org/unpd/wpp

U.S. Energy Information Administration. (2011, March). *Emissions of greenhouse gases in the United States, 2009.* Retrieved from http://www2.hmc.edu/~evans/EIAEGG.pdf

Vorosmarty, C., et al. (2000). Global water resources: Vulnerability from climate change and population growth. *Science, 289,* 284–288.

White, G. (2011). *Climate change and migration: Security and borders in a warming world.* Oxford, UK: Oxford University Press.

Andrew Light

Note: This essay was adapted from statements by Andrew Light at the panel discussion, "Immigration, Population and the Environment," hosted by the Center for Immigration Studies, August 2009.

Social and Cultural Debates

Introduction

As Elaine Replogle and Dan Tichenor discussed in their introduction to the Politics section, there is broad public perception that the U.S. immigration system is in need of reform, and this perception has resulted in several recent attempts to change the system. Senators Ted Kennedy and John McCain introduced the Secure America and Orderly Immigration Act (S.1033) in May of 2005; Senators John Cornyn and Jon Kyl introduced the Comprehensive Enforcement and Immigration Reform Act of 2005 (S. 1438) in July of 2005; an Senator Arlen Specter introduced the Comprehensive Immigration Reform Act (S. 2611) in May of 2006. The Comprehensive Immigration Reform Act (S. 1348) was proposed in May of 2007 as a result of an agreement reached by Senators Ted Kennedy, Jon Kyl, and John McCain that incorporated many of the provisions of the earlier proposals.

All of these attempts to change the U.S. immigration system failed, and subsequent efforts to introduce such legislation have been largely symbolic. This political failure has resulted from a number of specific disputes about immigration policy. It also reflects, in larger part, cultural divisions over immigration and notions of what it means to be an American. The debates in this section explore some of the cultural divides that exist in the current immigration debate, animated by themes such as antipathy toward immigrants by some Americans and unease over immigration's impact on national identity.

Immigration Affects National Identity

Animosity in the United States toward immigrants is not new, and Americans are not unique in this sentiment. Human beings form groups, or communities, based on perceptions of shared identity, shared interests, shared values or ideals, and other perceived commonalities. Benedict Anderson, in his seminal book *Imagined Communities* (1983), coined the title phrase of his book to distinguish "imagined" communities from "actual" communities. Imagined communities are communities where everyday face-to-face interactions between its members are not possible, yet a perceived common bond exists. Anderson posited that nations are imagined political communities, sovereign and inherently bounded in size and membership. An individual cannot know all or even most of his fellow citizens in even the smallest nations, yet, Anderson points out, "in the minds of each lives the image of their communion." What it means to be "American" or "French" or "Mexican" likely differs for individuals within these nations, yet there exists a degree of affinity among members of each of these countries.

Immigration necessarily affects a nation's imagined community. It increases the number of people within a country's physical borders and, more importantly, it brings people of different backgrounds and cultures, who usually speak different languages, into that community. Without immigration, these (immigrant) strangers are distant members of *another* imagined community. Their presence in the United States means that *they* are now inside *our* country's physical boundaries, but *they* may not yet "belong." For America's imagined community to survive—to remain cohesive—in the face of immigration, there exists a two-sided requirement. The immigrant must *join* the new imagined community—must become "American"—and Americans must *accept* the immigrant as a member of society.

A chapter by Francisco Alatorre on social integration addresses the first part of the equation, the *joining*, as Alatorre explores whether or not some immigrants are equipped to become a part of the American fabric. In a separate chapter on cultural integration, Morris Onyewuchi seems to share this concern, arguing that immigrants' attachment to their own cultures, and particularly their own languages, works against their assimilation to the fabric of American life. Meanwhile, Elizabeth Hull takes the opposite side in her debate with Onyewuchi, arguing that culture in America is a living, evolving thing that can adapt to whatever its new members bring to it.

Hull is in effect discussing the second part of the above equation, the *joining,* as she argues that "American culture" should become whatever the current crop of Americans decides it is. The *accepting* part of the equation is also touched upon by Donald Kerwin, who explores the this aspect of the debate as it relates to the Catholic Church. Is the church compelled, due to its tenets about assisting the stranger, to safeguard the rights of immigrants? Or can that ideal be taken too far, to the point of turning the other cheek to illegal activity?

Historically, Cultural Integration Has Been Contentious

The conditions for being accepted as a member of America's imagined community are complex and have evolved over time. Seventeenth-century political philosopher Alexis de Tocqueville and others argued that a sufficient condition for becoming American is adherence to a set of classic liberal democratic political values based in individual liberty and equality. Yet political scientist Rogers Smith (*Civic Ideals,* 1997) points out that the United States has, throughout much of its history, limited citizenship—membership—based on a host of ascriptive traits rooted in race, gender, and class. Benjamin Franklin's imagined community clearly did not include Germans, as was made evident by his famous reference to "swarthy Germans" who were "too stupid to learn English," and therefore a political threat to the nation. The first law limiting immigration to the United States was the Chinese Exclusion Act, which, along with other related restrictions targeting Asians, passed in response to the emergence of nativist antipathy to Chinese immigrants in the western United States in the mid-1800s. The term "yellow peril" underscored the racial threat that white Americans perceived with regard to immigration from Asia, and the term made it clear that the imagined community of most Americans did not then include immigrants from Asia. Chinese immigrants, partly in response to this evident hostility, clustered in enclaves in San Francisco and other cities, and for some this segregation reinforced stereotypes of Chinese as unwilling or unable to "assimilate."

At the turn of the nineteenth century, relatively high levels of immigration from southern and eastern Europe and from Ireland once again raised questions of national identity, and once again challenged the cohesiveness of the United States' imagined community. In this case, animus toward immigrants was based on ethnicity and religion. Many of these new immigrants were Catholic, and many Americans saw the United States as a Protestant nation. Nativist passions were once again stirred, eventually resulting in passage of national origins quotas laws, which greatly reduced total immigration and effectively limited it to immigrants from northern (Protestant) Europe. These laws remained in effect until the mid-1960s.

The decade of the 1960s was a period of great cultural change in the United States. The sensibilities that defined the American imagined community, as well as attitudes towards immigration, changed. The 1964 Civil Rights Act prohibited discrimination on the basis of race, color, religion, or national origin. Multiculturalism—respect for cultural differences that promotes their coexistence within society—emerged during the late 1960s and early 1970 as a natural outgrowth of the civil rights movement, and these societal and legal changes also shaped immigration policy. A new era of migration to the United States from new source-countries began in 1965 with enactment of the Hart-Cellar Act, which created an immigration system based on family reunification. In this section, a debate between David Koelsch and Carol Cleaveland addresses the family reunification policy, exploring whether or not the current focus on uniting immigrant families is the best approach to choosing new citizens.

A New Era of Immigration

The Hart-Cellar Act expanded the number of immigrants admitted each year, and the immigrant share of the U.S. population increased steadily in ensuing years. Immigrants were 4.7 percent of the U.S. population in 1970 and grew to 12.9 percent by 2010. Much of this immigration was from Asia and from Spanish-speaking countries, with relatively few immigrants coming from Europe.

Initially, this shift in the national origins of immigrants did not engender a widespread reaction in the native-born population, and the diversity of these new immigrants combined with multicultural sensibilities to effect passage of the Bilingual Education Act in 1968. Over time, however, the Bilingual Education Act set the stage for renewed debates over the role of English in American society and resulted in calls by some to make English the official language of the United States. Each of these language debates is explored in its own chapter here—Rosalie Pedalino Porter and Karen Manges Douglas debate whether or not English instruction should be a top priority in the schools, while K.C. McAlpin and Alida Lasker debate the symbolic value of English being declared the official language of the United States.

Other dimensions of nativism remained relatively dormant through much of the 1970s and 1980s, although these years did see increasing public concern about illegal immigration. The most significant immigration-related legislation to be enacted during this period was the 1986 Immigration Reform and Control Act (IRCA), which granted amnesty to some 3 million illegal immigrants. But family reunification has remained the cornerstone of U.S. immigration policy up to the present. And this cornerstone tends to reinforce the current diverse country-of-origin mix of immigrants and to magnify its attendant questions of culture and national identity.

The world has changed dramatically since the 1960s. The Cold War ended, and globalization became a major focus of international diplomacy during the final decades of the twentieth century. The 9/11 terrorist attacks in 2001 added a national security dimension to public consciousness about immigration. Technological innovation combined with globalization to foster migration and profoundly change the employment landscape in the United States in ways that created both tremendous opportunity and tremendous displacement. Income inequality increased, and along with it came a distinction between "elite" views and "mass opinion." The political scientist Deborah Schildkraut notes, in her study of American reaction to the terrorist attacks of September 11, 2001, that social elites have a more inclusive view of American identity than is evident in mass opinion, and that the 9/11 attacks reawakened ascriptive norms in mass opinion. This phenomenon has had direct implications for attitudes toward immigration and immigrant integration to society (Schildkraut, 2002). Deep divisions have emerged along religious, political, and educational lines in arenas unrelated to immigration. America's imagined community is decidedly fragmented and immigration debates are occurring in this fragmented environment.

Illegal Immigration Complicates Matters

Today's immigration debates are further complicated by the fact of significant illegal immigration to the United States since the 1960s. In 2010, an estimated 28 percent of all foreign-born persons in the United States could be described as "illegal immigrants"—although even the terminology itself is open to debate, as described in a chapter by Eric Ruark and Shoba Sivaprasad Wadhia. Ruark argues that people who remain in the United States without permission are, by definition, breaking the law ("illegal") and are "alien" in the sense of being non-citizens. Thus, he argues, there should be no stigma attached to "illegal alien" as a designation, noting that the term is technically correct. Wadhia counters that the term is one designed to alienate and divide, as it emphasizes the "illegality" of an entire being rather than referring to a specific act.

Public concern about illegal immigration inevitably leads to debates over how best to prevent it. Because many illegal immigrants are Hispanic, controversies have arisen over whether it is appropriate to use racial profiling to identify and arrest illegal immigrants. Peter Schuck, in the Point essay on this topic, argues that racial profiling is a legitimate law-enforcement tool that, when properly used, enhances law enforcement effectiveness without violating individuals' civil rights. Karin Martin and Jack Glaser, in the Counterpoint essay on this topic, argue that the practice necessarily violates civil rights and is actually counterproductive for law enforcement purposes. Andrew Parr and Matthew Tabor articulate two sides of the debate over whether granting in-state tuition at public colleges and universities to illegal immigrant children brought to the United States by their parents has the effect of encouraging further illegal immigration by others. And RAND Corporation scholars Jessica Saunders, Carl Matthies, and Nelson Lim explore the pros and cons of involving local law enforcement in immigration enforcement.

The presence of large numbers of legal and illegal immigrants in the United States has renewed the focus on issues of culture and national identity and inflamed nativist passions among those who see immigration, especially illegal immigration, as harmful. Advocates for restricting overall immigration argue that legal (Hispanic) immigration is itself a cause of illegal immigration (Edwards, 2006). The fact that many Americans are themselves recent immigrants or have immigrant parents means that sensibilities about immigration are split along cultural, racial, and ethnic lines. For example, a study conducted in North Carolina showed that native residents are more likely to have positive views of immigration if they have prolonged contact with immigrants, and that they are more likely to have negative opinions if the contact is only superficial. These findings are independent of political orientation, educational attainment, and attitudes toward diversity (O'Neil & Tienda, 2010). Thus the complexities of today's immigration landscape are contributing to and interacting with the current fragmented imagined community in America.

Immigrant Integration and Social Cohesion

The social and cultural debates elaborated in this section directly reflect immigration's impacts on this fragmentation of America's imagined community. The late political scientist Samuel Huntington, in his book *Who Are We? The Challenges to American National Identity* (2005), articulated the view that the current large number of diverse immigrants, combined with a public embrace of multiculturalism, poses a serious threat to American national identity. Not surprisingly, multiculturalists widely disagreed with Huntington's thesis, while political and cultural conservatives who view American culture as Anglo-Protestant widely praised it. Fundamentally, the book brought into sharp focus the debate about who "belonged" in the American imagined community, and it underscored the challenge of incorporating newcomers to that community.

This challenge is further complicated by the fact that the extent of illegal immigration has caused the terms "immigration" and "illegal immigration" to be conflated in public discourse. Illegal immigration has fueled anti-immigrant sentiment, particularly toward Hispanics, because a large percentage of illegal immigrants are Hispanics from Mexico, and because, as is discussed in the chapter on racial profiling, it is difficult to distinguish between legal and illegal Hispanic immigrants.

Further, the phenomenon of Hispanic immigrants clustering in Spanish-speaking enclaves contributes to the impression that today's immigrants are, in keeping with multiculturalism, choosing to maintain separate identities rather than joining mainstream American society. Economist George Borjas, among others, argues that this concentration of Hispanic immigrants in Spanish-speaking enclaves works against immigrant economic integration, risks Balkanization of American society, and threatens English as the de facto official American language. Researchers have found that Anglo attitudes toward immigration and English language policies are significantly related to the size of the Latino population and to the extent that Anglos live in segregated communities. Anglos are less hostile to Latinos when they speak English and were born in the United States (Rocha & Espino, 2009). There has been much analysis of the extent of worksite competition between native-born and immigrant workers, and political economists argue that political opposition to immigration is highly correlated with the economic benefits and costs of immigration (Hanson, 2005). But economic impacts are not the sole determinants of attitudes toward immigration. As is explored in several of the chapters in this section, research has also found that support for restricting immigration is associated with the view that immigrants should shed their native cultures and that English should be the official language of the United States (Cummings & Lambert, 1998).

At one level, three questions animate the social and cultural dimensions of immigration debates: (1) to what extent are immigrants integrating to as opposed to changing mainstream society and American cultural identity, (2) how should illegal immigration best be dealt with, and (3) what values should be the organizing principle of U.S. immigration policy? At a deeper level, each of these topics is controversial precisely because immigrants are newcomers to the imagined community.

The presence of newcomers—strangers—inevitably triggers such questions as "Who are they?" "What are their values?" "Do they belong?" and "Are they a threat to me?" Illegal immigration triggers such questions as "Why did they break our laws?" "Are they trying to take advantage of us?" and "How do we stop illegal entry?" Fundamentally, these questions relate to what is required to form a nation—a cohesive imagined community—that incorporates newcomers within a geographical boundary in an orderly fashion, and the topics debated in these chapters are specific aspects of these fundamental questions.

REFERENCES AND FURTHER READING

Anderson, B. (1983). *Imagined communities.* London, UK: Verso.
Borjas, G. (1999). *Heaven's door: Immigration policy and the American economy.* Princeton, NJ: Princeton University Press.
Cummings, S., & Lambert, T. (1998). Immigration restriction and the American worker: An examination of competing interpretations. *Population Research and Policy Review, 17*(6), 497–520.
Edwards, J. R. (2006). *Two sides of the same coin: The connection between legal and illegal immigration.* Retrieved from Center for Immigration Studies website: http://www.cis.org/articles/2006/back106.html
Hanson, G. (2005). *Why does immigration divide America? Public finance and political opposition to open borders.* Washington, DC: Institute for International Economics. Available at http://irps.ucsd.edu/assets/022/8793.pdf
Huntington, S. (2005). *Who are we? The challenges to American national identity,* New York, NY: Simon and Schuster.
O'Neil, K., & Tienda, M. (2010). A tale of two counties: Natives' opinions toward immigration in North Carolina. *International Migration Review, 44*(3), 728–761.

Rocha, R. R., & Espino, R. (2009). Racial threat, residential segregation, and policy attitudes of Anglos. *Political Research Quarterly, 62*(2), 415–426.

Schildkraut, D. J. (2002). The more things change . . . American identity and mass and elite responses to 9/11. *Political Psychology, 23*(3, Special Issue: 9/11 and its aftermath, September 2002), 511–535.

Smith, R. (1997). *Civic ideals.* New Haven, CT: Yale University Press.

Judith Gans
Udall Center for Studies in Public Policy, University of Arizona

Family-Based Immigration

POINT: Immigration is a tool for economic development and should not be disproportionally squandered on family-based immigration, which offers relatively fewer economic advantages compared to employment-based immigration. In light of prolonged slow economic growth in the United States, priorities should be reallocated in the realm of immigration law and policy to maximize the economic benefit of immigration.

David C. Koelsch, University of Detroit Mercy School of Law

COUNTERPOINT: Family unification should continue to be the cornerstone of U.S. immigration policy, not only for humanitarian reasons but also for economic ones.

Carol L. Cleaveland, George Mason University

Introduction

When a country sets out to regulate immigration, it must address two questions: First, *how many* immigrants to admit over a specific time period (usually a year), and second, *which* immigrants to admit. The answers to these questions are determined by the underlying objectives of the immigration system, and these objectives derive from political processes that distill the country's cultural, economic, and political crosscurrents. These crosscurrents, in turn, reflect salient geopolitical and diplomatic sensibilities of the time.

Current immigration debates are informed by the reality that global economic integration has been a key driver of recent migration. Many of the immigration-related controversies in the United States have focused on immigration's economic costs and benefits and how the immigration system can be tweaked to optimize them. Thus, the debate over family-based immigration is centrally about whether the U.S. immigration system should be explicitly structured to maximize its economic benefit to the United States rather than keeping its focus on uniting families.

Under the current family-based system, approximately 1 million persons receive a green card each year and are thereby granted legal permanent resident (LPR) status. Over 60 percent of green cards are issued to family members of U.S. citizens, and only 150,000 persons, or 12–15 percent of all LPRs, immigrate through employment-based preferences. Details are provided in Table 24.1.

The workforce-related skills that these immigrants happen to bring to the United States are the result of the education and work experience each immigrant happens to have received in his or her home country, and the economic implications of this education and work experience are largely irrelevant to obtaining LPR status. Table 24.2 details the occupations of immigrants to the United States in 2010.

The U.S. immigration system also provides for temporary admission to the United States, and there is much greater provision for economic-based admission on a temporary basis. In 2010, temporary visas were granted to almost 3 million persons and their families to come to the United States for work, compared to only 148,000 green cards issued through employment-based preferences shown in Table 24.2. Table 24.3 provides details on the basis for temporary admissions in 2010, and it reveals that most temporary employment visas are issued to high-skilled workers.

Table 24.1 Persons receiving legal permanent residence status by class of admission

	2008		2009		2010	
	Number	**Share**	**Number**	**Share**	**Number**	**Share**
Immediate relatives of U.S. citizens	488,483	44%	535,554	47%	476,414	46%
Family-sponsored preferences	227,761	21%	211,859	19%	214,589	21%
Employment-based preferences	164,741	15%	140,903	12%	148,343	14%
Asylees, refugees, & parolees	169,440	15%	180,601	16%	138,517	13%
Diversity	41,761	4%	47,879	4%	49,763	5%
All other	14,940	1%	14,022	1%	14,999	1%
Total	1,107,126	100%	1,130,818	100%	1,042,625	100%

Source: Department of Homeland Security Immigration Statistics, available at http://www.dhs.gov/files/statistics/immigration.shtm.
Note: Includes Nicaraguan Adjustment and Central American Relief Act (NACARA) and Haitian Refugee Immigration Fairness Act (HRIFA).

Table 24.2 Persons receiving legal permanent residence status, by occupation

	2010	**Percent**
Students or children	273,331	26%
Unknown	264,203	25%
Homemakers	146,587	14%
Management, professional, and related occupations	103,375	10%
Unemployed	93,639	9%
Service occupations	52,853	5%
Production, transportation, and material moving occupations	41,584	4%
Sales and office occupations	36,275	3%
Farming, fishing, and forestry occupations	14,042	1%
Retirees	10,136	1%
Construction, extraction, maintenance, and repair occupations	6,551	1%
Military	49	0.005%
Total	1,042,625	

Source: Department of Homeland Security Immigration Statistics, available at http://www.dhs.gov/files/statistics/immigration.shtm.

The extent of illegal immigration to the United States underscores flaws in the current system. Key reasons cited by experts for illegal immigration include limited provision for low-skilled immigration and the demographics of an aging, slow-growing population. It is not difficult to argue that the current U.S. immigration system is fundamentally out of alignment with large economic and demographic forces driving immigration to the United States and proposals to reform the system focus on correcting this misalignment.

The debate over how to effect that reform—over whether family relationships should continue to be central to the U.S. immigration system—reflects the reality that *any* immigration system creates winners, losers, and their associated interest groups. Under the current system, 31 percent of green cards in 2010 were issued to people from Latin America (Mexico, Central America, and South America), and 24 percent were issued to people from Asia. Thus, geography and family-based social networks tied to countries of people with U.S. citizen relatives currently determine who immigrates

Table 24.3   Temporary admissions to the United States by class of visa

	2010	Percent		2010	Percent
Temporary visitors for pleasure	35,131,310	76	All temporary workers and families	2,816,525	100
Temporary visitors for business	5,205,980	11	High-skilled temporary workers	1,153,326	41
Temporary workers and families	2,816,525	6	Intra-company transferees	702,460	25
Students and exchange visitors	2,138,413	5	Treaty traders and investors	383,700	14
All other temporary admissions	799,047	2	Low-skilled temporary workers	211,983	8
Diplomats and other representatives	380,241	1	Families of temporary workers	199,551	7
			Specialty and religious workers	117,272	4
Total I-94 admissions	46,471,516	100	Representatives of foreign media	48,233	2

Source: Department of Homeland Security Immigration Statistics, available at http://www.dhs.gov/xlibrary/assets/statistics/publications/ni_fr_2010.pdf.

to the United States. Changing, for example, to a point-based immigration system tied to the labor-market needs of the U.S. economy and focused on maximizing the net economic benefits of immigration would mean that professional and economic networks, rather than family-based social networks, would determine who immigrates to the United States. Not surprisingly, recent immigrants, who often have family members in their countries of origin, and people with cultural ties to Asia and Latin America tend to advocate for maintenance of the current family-based system, while businesses and other economic interests tend to advocate for a system that explicitly attempts to maximize the economic and fiscal benefits from immigration.

Finally, it is important to note that *both* sides of this debate—advocates for social/family networks and advocates for professional/economic networks—are advancing alternatives based in political or economic self-interest rather than approaches grounded in notions of basic human rights.

POINT

This essay makes the case for new objectives of U.S. immigration law and policy. Central to these new objectives are restrictions on traditional family-based immigration and a countervailing easing of limits on immigrants— family- and employment-based—who offer the most in terms of economic output and consumption of consumer goods. The United States remains a magnet for immigration and needs to use that attractive force to its best advantage.

To be clear, the crux of this debate is not merely how immigration can be used as a driver of economic growth; rather, the benefits of economic growth also need to be weighed. The social contract in the United States depends the principle of paying taxes with the expectation of receiving benefit from the government in the form of good schools, safe roads and bridges, Social Security, and other amenities and programs. People also pay taxes so that members of society who are in distress due to job loss or disability are not destitute. Greater economic growth yields greater tax revenues, and the simple truth is that higher-skilled immigrants earn more and pay more in taxes than less-skilled low-wage immigrants, the majority of whom arrive in the United States based on family sponsorship. A computer programmer with an advanced degree earns five times what a cashier at Dunkin' Donuts earns, and is thus less likely to require government assistance to make ends meet. The computer programmer also pays nearly eight times in taxes what the cashier pays. Simple math dictates that a greater proportion of skilled immigrants than unskilled immigrants is needed to preserve the social contract.

Reasonable minds can disagree about the best way to use immigration to promote economic growth, but nearly all observers of the family-based immigration system agree that it is dysfunctional. This approach does not address the needs of the families it claims to serve, nor does it promote economic growth as well as it could. Proponents of increased family-based immigration call for an end to lengthy waiting periods for family members of lawful permanent residents (LPRs), clearing the backlog of pending family-based claims, and eliminating per-country caps on family-based immigrants. The rationales for such actions are to reunite family members and allow anchor relatives in the United States to exercise a nearly unlimited ability to sponsor their family members, without regard to their family members' age, education, or anticipated ability to succeed in the United States.

Unfettered family-based immigration ignores several central tenets of the U.S. immigration model, namely that immigration is not merely a numbers game or driven solely by family reunification, but is also intended to promote economic growth or, at the least, be cognizant of domestic economic conditions. The family-based immigration system should be dramatically restructured to tap into that self-motivated and entrepreneurial zeal rather than simply rewarding would-be immigrants for their biological connections to LPRs and U.S. citizens. After exploring both the fallacy of broader family-based immigration and the efficacy of a more prudent, growth-oriented approach to immigration, this essay offers several practical prescriptions to realign U.S. immigration laws with renewed focus on growth-oriented objectives.

This essay makes a broad assumption: immigration is critical to sustain and grow the U.S. economy. While family reunification is important, a principal goal of the U.S. immigration system should be to promote the immigration of the best and brightest immigrants, who have many productive, revenue-producing years still ahead of them. Immigrating to the United States remains a goal of millions of people across the planet, and they are willing to learn new skills and work hard to achieve their dreams. The U.S. government would do well to tap into that innate desire for advancement and tailor its immigration laws and policies to reward high achievers with residency in the United States.

This approach is unabashedly Darwinian and based on a capitalist model of economic growth and production. This is the world in which we all now live, but it does not mean that a desire for economic growth should blindly steer all immigration laws and policies. In fact, the more the United States welcomes those able to earn higher wages, the more federal, state, and local governments can collect in tax revenues, both from income and sales taxes. As a result, governments are able to provide additional services. Increased high-skilled immigration allows the government to serve its primary role in the nurturing of the populace to be productive and care for those segments of the population at the end of their economically productive lives.

CLEAR OBJECTIVES FOR U.S. IMMIGRATION LAW AND POLICY

Immigrants come to the United States through two primary means: family- or employment-sponsorship. Under current laws and regulations, the U.S. immigration system is heavily skewed in favor of family-based immigration to the detriment of employment-based immigration. For example, as Pia M. Orrenius, an economist and research officer at the Federal Reserve Bank of Dallas, notes, 85 percent of all green cards (i.e., Lawful Permanent Resident status) granted by the United States each year go to family-sponsored immigrants and only 15 percent go to higher-skilled employer-sponsored immigrants (Orrenius et al., 2011). Among Western industrialized nations, only the United States gives such a high preference to family-sponsored immigrants.

The U.S. government needs to articulate clear and consistent objectives for immigration in order to spark economic growth. Any discussion of objectives is incomplete, of course, without a critical examination of current U.S. policies, which, in their present form, run counter to the objectives and, accordingly, the objectives are followed by a critique of the current family-based immigration model. That said, the following is a short list of proposed objectives:

- A greater number of employment-based immigrant visas should be offered to persons with advanced technical degrees, English proficiency, and high prospects for economic success.

- Family-based immigrant visas should be allocated based, in large part, on education levels and wage-earning potential, rather than solely on shared DNA.

- Country-specific numerical caps on family-based immigrant visas should be eliminated to promote equity in the immigration process.

- Bureaucratic processing times for immigrant visas—both employment- and family-based—should be reduced significantly.

CRITIQUE OF FAMILY-BASED IMMIGRATION

Family-based immigration is not inherently negative, nor is employment-based immigration intrinsically positive. To the contrary, families are a key element of any society, and the value of families are difficult to overstate. Families pool capital and provide a ready supply of workers for family businesses. Families raise children collectively and allow parents to maximize their productive years of employment. Families pass along values, faiths, and traditions that both help guide their adherents and enrich American society in general. And, on a personal note, as an immigration attorney there are few more satisfying experiences than playing a critical role in preserving family unity by avoiding deportation of a family member or reuniting long-separated families after a successful visa petition. Yet, despite all of the attributes of family-based immigration, it does not currently optimally serve the broader interest of the United States in economic growth.

There is broad agreement that the U.S. system for family-based immigration is far from perfect. Indeed, the system of family-based immigration in the United States is deeply flawed. The process takes too long, is patently discriminatory against potential immigrants from certain countries, and does not allow important factors—other than a biological or marital relationship—to be used to vet potential immigrants. In a sense, family-based immigration is a blunt instrument solely used to promote family unification without any nuance, limitations or alternative objectives.

The base of the U.S. immigration structure is the family relationship. Certain U.S. citizens and LPRs, known as "petitioners," can sponsor certain family members, known as "beneficiaries," to obtain lawful permanent resident status. The classes of eligible petitioners and beneficiaries vary based on their family relationship. U.S. citizens can petition for their spouses, parents, children, and siblings, and LPRs can petition for their spouses and unmarried children. No other family relationships are eligible for family-based immigration. All petitioners must have a sufficient income, and they are legally bound to financially support their beneficiaries in the event they cannot support themselves.

The second level of the structure is more complicated. Per-country limits on immigration apply to certain beneficiaries, such as married children and siblings of U.S. citizens, as well as minor children of LPRs. The per-country limits are equal for all countries, regardless of their population or historic patterns of immigration to the United States. Iceland and Mexico, for example, have the same annual per-country limit. The limits have dramatic practical consequences: a female LPR must wait 5 years for her minor child to also become an LPR, while a U.S. citizen must wait over 20 years for his or her brother (should he live so long) from the Philippines to immigrate to the United States, and a U.S. citizen must wait 16 years for his or her married daughter to be admitted to the United States. The limits also have unintended consequences for beneficiaries from countries with long waits, as some beneficiaries will attempt to enter the United States illegally or overstay visitor visas.

PRACTICAL FIXES TO THE U.S. IMMIGRATION SYSTEM

Increase employment-based visas. The first fix acknowledges the priority shift noted above: more immigrant visas should be offered to persons who have the greatest capacity for economic success in the United States. There are two primary means to accomplish this objective. Either the total number of immigrant visas—family- and employment-based—available each fiscal year could be increased and a greater share of such visas could be set aside for employment-based immigrants, or the number of visas could remain at current levels and employment-based visas would be issued at the expense of family-based visas. In other words, the United States could increase the size of the immigration pie and ensure it is divided equitably, or the immigration pie could stay the same size but a greater share of employment-based visas would be allocated. Increasing the size of the pie has two benefits: It allows for increased employment-based visas, and it mitigates criticism from family-based immigration advocates that their interests are being shortchanged.

Institute human capital factors into family-based immigration. Human capital is the most important commodity in a modern economy, in which mass production of durable consumer goods has been largely replaced by service-related and technology-intensive occupations. The United States already includes human capital considerations in the context of employment-based immigration by vetting prospective immigrants based on their education, work history, and record of performance. Similar factors could be applied as a further aspect of family-based immigration and would be aimed at not only maximizing the ability of immigrants to succeed economically, but also to integrate successfully into American society (Schoellman, 2009). The U.S. government should impose similar human capital criteria on prospective family-based immigrants, such as a bachelor's or associate's degree or their equivalent, English language proficiency, and the ability to integrate based on an evaluation of specific metrics. In effect, the United States could develop a point system, similar to the point systems in use for decades in many countries, including Canada, New Zealand, and Australia (Ochel, 2001). A point system, obviously, has limitations when applied in the context of family-based immigration, and exceptions and waivers could be judiciously granted. The point of human capital factors is not to impose an Orwellian vision of a future in which family-based immigrants are selected solely based on their productive value; rather, the use of broad human capital factors would allow the United States to differentiate between immigrants who would be a net economic gain and those who would likely take more than they give.

The accurate assessment of human capital factors is critical and, fortunately, the United States can look to Canada's point system as a model. Certain metrics, such as age, skills, education, and profession, can be easily assessed, but others, such as hardship or other less-quantifiable criteria, require careful review. Consular officers, assisted by staff of the U.S. Citizenship and Immigration Services (USCIS), are well qualified to perform such evaluations, and in fact already do so in the context of waivers of admissibility. The imposition of human capital factors would lead to difficult decisions for families, and while it may not ease that heartache, potential immigrants should recognize that immigration to the United States is a privilege—not a right—and that privilege may be granted judiciously.

Restrict eligible family relationships. Along with including human capital criteria is the need to limit the degree of family relationship eligible for sponsorship and the number of persons that may be sponsored. Beyond the economic implications, the current structure of family-based immigration has consequences for family relationships. For example, larger families with multiple siblings benefit disproportionately compared to smaller families with fewer siblings, because there are no limits to the number of siblings a U.S. citizen can sponsor to immigrate. There is no practical reason for this disparity, and mere biological relationship should not be used to justify the expanded immigration of large families. In addition, the current structure increases the waiting periods for the closest family relationship: between parents and children. Sibling-based visas use up a slice of a finite "visa pie," and as a result, the slice of pie for children of LPRs and children of U.S. citizens who are married or over 21 is smaller. A better strategy is to reslice the pie to increase visas for the unmarried children of LPRs and U.S. citizens and decrease visas for siblings and parents of U.S. citizens.

It may appear severe or unfair—certainly to the beneficiaries currently patiently waiting to immigrate to the United States—to change which family relationships qualify for sponsorship. Yet some incremental change is needed to address the policy goals of economic growth and more efficient immigration of close family members. For example, there is no practical reason that a U.S. citizen with six siblings should be allowed to sponsor each sibling (together with their spouses and minor children) to immigrate to the United States regardless of their age or ability to be productive. Similarly, it is not in the national economic interest for a U.S. citizen to sponsor a married child when that child is legally independent, or, absent a showing of need, to sponsor an elderly parent to immigrate.

To be clear, a limit on the number of siblings and parents who may be sponsored would cause families to make difficult decisions about who would be selected as a beneficiary and who would not. Changing qualifying relationships would also need to be phased-in to avoid undue hardship on those already in line. The second prescription described previously—to include age, education, and skill criteria—may make such choices easier and thus ameliorate some of the hardships. For example, suppose a U.S. citizen has two siblings, one of whom has a graduate degree in engineering while the other dropped out of high school. With the institution of human capital factors, the die has already been cast, so that the higher-achieving sibling will get an immigrant visa while the other sibling will not. Similarly, if a sibling of a U.S. citizen ages out of eligibility for an immigrant visa, the law has winnowed the list of eligible immigrants and no blame can be ascribed to the sponsor.

Is this social Darwinism? Yes, to a degree, but not with entirely negative consequences. Nor is this a novel approach. New Zealand, for example, limits sibling beneficiaries to those 55 years of age and younger, and it does not allow married children of citizen or permanent resident parents to immigrate. First, limiting the numbers and age of siblings, in particular, allowed to immigrate to the United States would reinforce the fabric of the sending country's society. If a sibling of a U.S. citizen is waiting for eventual immigration to the United States, he or she is less likely to invest in a future in their home country. That person may not buy a home in the home country or maintain bank deposits and invest in the home country. In a sense, an intending sibling or, to a lesser degree, parental immigrant has one foot in the country of his or her birth and one foot (figuratively) in the United States. This is not good for the home country.

The difficulty in this process is that it fails to take into account cultural and social norms and economic realities in certain sending countries and, to a degree, the United States. For example, if an extended family with a U.S. citizen sponsor has to choose which family members will receive an education—a precious and expensive undertaking in many countries—in order to maximize their chances of immigrating to the United States, the family may choose male siblings rather than female siblings, the presumption being that male siblings will be able to earn a higher wage and provide greater remittances to send back to the family. This is a hard reality, and one that U.S. policymakers could perhaps address by placing gender parity limits on sibling-based immigrant visas. Are gender parity limits also a form of social Darwinism that may not respect the traditional values of a sending country? Yes, but again, the United States can use its attractive force to attain positive results in the United States and globally.

Eliminate country-specific numerical caps. Scrapping per-country numerical caps would decrease waiting periods for qualifying beneficiaries from countries that have high rates of immigration to the United States. In other words, the trade-off for a U.S. citizen not being able to sponsor all of his or her siblings to immigrate would be a much shorter waiting period for the siblings that could be sponsored. In practical terms, that would mean that a U.S. citizen could sponsor a sibling from Mexico, and that sibling need only wait 3 years to immigrate to the United States, rather than the 15 to 20 years currently needed. Reduced fourth-preference-sibling waiting periods could also discourage siblings from entering the United States illegally, as there is less to gain from illegal entry if the waiting period to legally immigrate is shorter.

Of course, while the per-country numerical caps should be eliminated, this should only be done in tandem with restrictions on family-based relationships qualifying for immigration and the institution of human capital factors. If numerical caps are loosened without the concomitant limiting of eligibility for immigration, then increased numbers of immigrants will enter the United States, particularly from countries that are large sending countries, such as Mexico, the Philippines, and India. As noted above, the per-country caps would become less significant than closeness of the family relationship and the education and skills of intending immigrants. In this manner, while such changes would be a dramatic shift in U.S. immigration policy, enacting them as a package would impact as few intending immigrants as possible.

Eliminate bureaucratic processing backlogs. Not all of the delay in visa issuance is due to per-country caps, broad familial sponsorship categories, or the absence of human capital standards. Bureaucratic inefficiency, shifting priorities, and inadequate staffing levels can add years to the process. In particular, the USCIS processing centers dedicated to adjudication of family-based petitions and the National Visa Center should be fully staffed, and processing targets should be set and enforced. In addition, consular staff should be directed to expedite interviews and medical screenings for intending immigrants. If additional revenue is needed to enhance service, then visa and immigrant petition fees could be increased. Because the United States is such a draw for family-based immigrants, it seems likely that the families of eligible immigrants will find the needed funds. Indeed, dramatic and across-the-board fee increases at USCIS in 2008 did not reduce the filing of petitions and applications.

CONCLUSION: A GROWTH-ORIENTED IMMIGRATION POLICY IS NEEDED AND FEASIBLE

Changes to immigrant policies do not occur in a vacuum. Each change, no matter how slight, may have far-reaching and unintended consequences. As noted above, changes in per-country numerical limits, coupled with changes in the sponsorship eligibility and addition of human capital factors, will likely have a greater impact on Mexicans than Indians. That would be a consequence with short-term negative results for, in particular, Mexican fourth-preference beneficiaries. Over the long-term, Mexicans could see greater educational gains, driven by a desire to gain parity with prospective immigrants from other sending countries. In so doing, Mexicans would benefit themselves, increase the odds of securing a visa, and create a basis for a successful life in the United States. Further, even if they do not obtain a visa, their education would benefit Mexico.

As noted above, family-based immigration has positive aspects that should be preserved. Several tweaks to the family-based structure would help the system function more efficiently and better serve key goals of U.S. immigration policy. Each change would bring some degree of hardship, particularly for individuals and families who have relied upon assumptions that the system could never change. Each change, however, would also reap rewards in terms of economic growth and greater stability for immigrants and the native-born U.S. population. In addition, changes can be phased-in through grandfathering persons already in the queue or fixing sunset dates for current visa categories.

There are doubtless other consequences of these proposed changes, but overall the effect of these changes would be a net positive. They would need to be phased in, and allowances and exceptions would need to be carefully crafted to avoid undue hardship to intending immigrants and their families. These few changes would help reform an anachronistic immigration system based on family structures and economic needs from the early twentieth century. Family dynamics have changed, global travel is viable and relatively affordable, and the economic needs of the United States are vastly different today than when the current policies were created. Some of the changes may appear to be bitter medicine, but they are good for all concerned: the U.S. economy, sponsoring families, sponsored immigrants, and sending countries.

REFERENCES AND FURTHER READING

Furchtgott-Roth, D. (2011, August 25). *Getting real on immigration.* Retrieved from Manhattan Institute for Policy Research website: http://www.manhattan-institute.org/html/miarticle.htm?id=7399

Hall, J. C., VanMetre, B. J., & Vedder, R. K. (2012, Winter). U.S. immigration policy in the 21st century: A market-based approach. *Cato Journal, 32*(1), 201–220. Retrieved from http://www.cato.org/pubs/journal/cj32n1/cj32n1-13.pdf

Hanson, G. H. (2012, Winter). Immigration and economic growth. *Cato Journal, 32*(1), 25–34. Retrieved from http://www.cato.org/pubs/journal/cj32n1/cj32n1-3.pdf

Hinojosa-Ojeda, R. (2012, Winter). The economic benefits of comprehensive immigration reform. *Cato Journal, 32*(1), 175–199. Retrieved from http://www.cato.org/pubs/journal/cj32n1/cj32n1-12.pdf

Hunt, J. (2011, July). Which immigrants are most innovative and entrepreneurial? Distinctions by entry visa. *Journal of Labor Economics, 29*(3), 417–457.

Legrain, P. (2007). *Immigrants: Your country needs them.* Princeton, NJ: Princeton University Press.

Ochel, W. (2001). Selective immigration policies: Point system versus auction model. *CESifo Forum 2*(2), 48–52. Retrieved from http://www.cesifo-group.de/portal/pls/portal/docs/1/1208147.PDF

Orrenius, P. M., Wadhwa, V., Jacoby, T., Bowles, J., Dixon, P., Rimmer, M. T., & Rawlins, A. (2011, March 14). *Expert roundup: Immigration and U.S economic performance.* Retrieved from Council of Foreign Relations website: http://www.cfr.org/immigration/immigration-reform-us-economic-performance/p24358

Papademetriou, D. G., & Sumption, M. (2011, June). *Eight policies to boost the economic contribution of employment-based immigration.* Retrieved from Migration Policy Institute website: http://www.migrationpolicy.org/pubs/competitivenessstrategies-2011.pdf

Peri, G. (2012, Winter). Immigration, labor markets, and productivity. *Cato Journal, 32*(1), 35–53. http://www.cato.org/pubs/journal/cj32n1/cj32n1-4.pdf

Powell, B. (2010). *An economic case for immigration.* Retrieved from Library of Economics and Liberty website: http://www.econlib.org/library/Columns/y2010/Powellimmigration.html

Schoellman, T. (2009, July 14). *The occupations and human capital of U.S. immigrants* (Research Paper Series 19). Retrieved from Economics and Econometrics Research Institute website: http://www.eeri.eu/documents/wp/EERI_RP_2009_19.pdf

Shapiro, R., & Vellucci, J. (2010). *The impact of immigration and immigration reform on the wages of American workers.* Retrieved from New Policy Institute website: http://www.immgrationworksusa.org/uploaded/file/NPI_Report_Shapiro_5_26_10.pdf

Terrazas, A. (2011, July). *The economic integration of immigrants in the United States: Long- and short-term perspectives.* Retrieved from Migration Policy Institute website: http://www.migrationpolicy.org/pubs/EconomicIntegration.pdf

David C. Koelsch

COUNTERPOINT

Proponents of an education or skills-based immigration system argue that current immigration policy should be overhauled so that potential immigrants with specific needed skills or educational qualifications have priority in obtaining permission to live and work in the United States. Such a change would mark a departure from current immigration policy, which is designed to facilitate the unification of families that might otherwise be divided if only some family members are given permission to immigrate. Advocates of employment-based immigration argue that it promises relatively high earnings for immigrant workers, and that it abets the quest by certain industries to fill jobs that might otherwise remain unstaffed by providing for certain types of scarce labor. Though the idea of privileging immigrants with specific skills or educational backgrounds may seem appealing, there exists substantial evidence in favor of maintaining family-based immigration policies. This essay will argue that family unification should continue to be the cornerstone of U.S. immigration policy for more than humanitarian reasons alone.

Key among these considerations is the fact that family-based immigration fuels economic growth by providing the nation with entrepreneurs and the labor to staff their businesses. In addition, immigrant labor is helping pay for critical social insurance programs such as Social Security (federally guaranteed support for the elderly and disabled) and Medicare (government-funded medical care for the elderly). As will be discussed in what follows, however, the backlog of immigration petitions is detrimental to American families, communities, and the economy as a whole. It would, in fact, be in the best interest of the United States not only to de-emphasize education or skills-based immigration in favor of family unification, but to attend to the backlog of family-based petitions to support community and economic development.

Family reunification became the guiding principle for U.S. immigration in 1965, when federal officials eliminated quotas designed to limit the numbers of 'undesirable' immigrants, a category that included Jews, Greeks, Italians, and other non-northern Europeans. The nation's immigration laws were again overhauled in 1990 to de-emphasize family-based immigration and to create more visas for immigrants with selected occupational or educational backgrounds. As noted in a recent address to the Senate, former NAACP president Julian Bond argued that while the family-based immigration system has deep flaws, it provides the basis for 85 percent of legal immigration to the United States. Bond and other civil rights leaders argue that with some families waiting as long as 23 years for the government's permission to allow a relative to immigrate legally, more visas should be made available to clear the backlog. Though family visas now constitute the path of legal entry for the majority of the nation's immigrants, many continue to wait, despite having "legal" relatives—including siblings and children—in the United States.

This discussion begins with an acknowledgment that the current immigration system suffers from a dire need for reform. A 2009 Carnegie Foundation analysis of Department of Homeland Security data found that more than 4 million prospective immigrants are now backlogged on waiting lists to join family in the United States. A legal resident from the Philippines who petitions to have his or her sibling immigrate legally typically waits more than 20 years before receiving permission, as noted by the Carnegie Foundation. Nonetheless, some advocates insist that the United States should base its immigration system solely on immigrants' skills or on labor market demand. During a period punctuated by high unemployment and marginal economic growth, this argument may seem compelling, in that it would allow authorities to limit immigration during periods of low labor market demand. Yet, as will be described below, immigrants who enter the United States through familial networks continue to generate economic growth through entrepreneurship, providing low-cost labor, and developing human capital for the future.

Before proceeding to the core arguments, it is imperative to acknowledge that wage growth and job creation for all immigrants, as well as native-born Americans, are subject to fluctuation in periods of economic duress. The effects of the October 2008 "Great Recession," followed by 3 years of stymied economic growth and a high unemployment rate, could conceivably be problematic for either category of immigrant. Future research will be necessary to gauge the effect of the current economy on immigrant wage growth and entrepreneurial efforts, though some analysts already suggest that the net impact of immigration benefits even a struggling economy over the long term.

In any event, considerable evidence suggests that even during recessions, immigrants help foster economic growth in all sectors and contribute to the economy as a whole by paying sales, income, and property taxes, as well as contributing to two key programs for the nation's elderly: Medicare and Social Security. Thus, while the idea of skills-based immigration may be appealing during a period of economic duress, jobs performed by immigrants who enter through family unification immigration quotas contribute to economic growth as well as the revitalization of communities where they settle in large numbers.

SOCIAL SECURITY

Immigrant wage growth is vital to the U.S. economy as a whole, in part because of its potential for helping ensure Social Security's financial viability in the future. Numerous studies have found that despite having higher poverty rates than native-born Americans, immigrants have lower rates of welfare receipt and higher rates of employment. In addition, demographic analyses have found that immigrant workers are, on average, 11 years younger than their native counterparts. By entering the workforce substantially ahead of retirement age, and by being employed at higher rates than native-born Americans, immigrants help maintain the viability of Social Security, a social insurance program dating back to the New Deal that provides supports for the elderly and people who are disabled. A 2010 demographic analysis by Stewart Anderson of the National Foundation for American Policy (NFAP) concluded that a moratorium on legal immigration would force native-born Americans to pay $407 billion more in Social Security taxes over the next 50 years to keep pace with those now paid by immigrants. For an American who earned $60,000 in 2004, that would mean a Social Security tax increase of more than $1,800 over the next 10 years. By comparison, the same study noted that if the United States were to permit a one-third increase in legal immigration, those same Social Security costs would be reduced by $600 over the next 10 years.

A further gauge of the contribution of immigrants to Social Security's solvency comes from consideration of the role that undocumented immigrants play in stabilizing that program. As noted in a 2006 policy briefing by the National Immigration Law Center, the Social Security Administration reports that even undocumented immigrants contribute $8.5 billion annually to Social Security and Medicare—costs that would otherwise be born by native-born Americans and legal immigrants. Federal policies such as the "welfare reform" legislation of 1996 prohibit all immigrants (legal and undocumented) from obtaining Medicaid (federal health-care funding for low income families), as well as cash assistance and subsidized housing—despite the fact that immigrants pay into these programs through both federal and state taxes. One financial analysis firm, The Perryman Group, estimated that if all undocumented workers and consumers were deported, the United States would lose $551.6 billion in spending on consumer goods ranging from clothing to food to furniture. Along with that loss would be unpaid sales taxes, property taxes, and federal and state income taxes. As noted by Perryman, contrary to public perception, from one-half to three-quarters of undocumented immigrants pay federal and state taxes. Having more avenues for occupational advancement than their undocumented counterparts, legal immigrants who enter the United States through family-based visas have been found to advance relatively quickly in the economy, a fact that bodes well for the solvency of Social Security and Medicare.

ENTREPRENEURIAL EFFORTS

Entrepreneurial efforts of immigrants who enter the United States through family visas merit examination. The Kauffman Foundation, a think tank that tracks entrepreneurial activity in the United States, reported that immigrants launch new businesses at a rate of 530 per 100,000 people each month. That compares to 280 for every 100,000 native-born Americans. A 2006 case study by Padma Rangaswamy of Dunkin' Donuts ownership and management in the Midwest illustrates how immigration promotes economic growth. South Asian men (immigrants from India and Pakistan) began purchasing Dunkin' Donut stores in the late 1980s, often using loans from family and friends as well as financing from Indian banks—some of which were willing to help the entrepreneurs without collateral. According to this study, conducted by the Chicago-based South Asian American Police and Research Institute, 95 percent of Dunkin' Donuts stores in the Chicago area are owned by South Asians, a process facilitated to great measure by family-based immigration. Though the initial establishment of the franchise ownership was due in part to immigration by educated, highly-skilled South Asians, its growth came by virtue of the family reunification law, which permitted the early immigrants to sponsor relatives and employ them in the business. As noted in the case study, one strategy adopted by this cohort was to purchase failing Dunkin' Donuts stores and make them profitable through bulk purchases of supplies, controlling labor costs (including hiring family members), and reducing waste. A failed, closed store in a neighborhood brings little in the way of property tax revenue, while a thriving small business contributes to the region's tax base. Store owners admitted to the frequent use of undocumented immigrant labor, a fact that controlled costs. Though the issue of undocumented immigrant labor raises concerns about exploitation and work without benefits such as medical insurance, store owners insisted that demand for labor forced them to rely on this population. During testimony before the Senate Subcommittee on Immigration in 2007, the sociologist Jimy M. Sanders argued that a large majority of immigrant-owned businesses in the United States rely heavily on family labor. Sanders (2007) said his research found that immigrant small businesses depended on family participation. In fact, the family can be the main social unit supporting the establishment and ongoing operation of a small business.

Though the entrepreneurial efforts of South Asians in this niche endeavor might seem of relatively little consequence to native-born Americans (except for those who like donuts), it is important to consider the supply chain that keeps the donuts, bagels, and coffee available. Franchise owners must purchase ingredients for the donuts fried in their stores, as well as boxes, napkins, and other supplies. All of these are transported by trucks, providing jobs that may well be held by native-born and possibly even union-represented workers.

The drudgery and low-wage nature of jobs frying donuts and serving coffee at a drive-thru window motivates many immigrants, particularly those who are "legal" and able to access education and training, to acquire skills for better jobs. A recent Brookings Institution analysis of the Philadelphia region's growth credits immigrants with helping to revitalize moribund neighborhoods through entrepreneurial efforts. Much of that growth came in the last decade. As noted in the Brookings study, a distinctive feature of immigrant workers is that they are much more likely than their native-born American counterparts to engage in entrepreneurial activities. Eleven percent of Philadelphia's immigrants were found to be self-employed, compared to 8 percent of the native-born population. Self-employment in small businesses has been a traditional pathway to relative prosperity for immigrants. Retail stores, contracting firms, and service providers such as dry cleaners become avenues into the labor market for new immigrants; in addition, these businesses often serve a customer base in immigrant communities where consumers want certain types of food, clothing, or services. By opening businesses, buying houses or even renting properties, immigrants help replenish a city's tax base eroded in previous decades by large-scale movement to suburban areas.

The economist Harriet Duleep, who has conducted extensive studies of immigrant contributions to the economy, argued before a House of Representatives subcommittee in 2007 that family-based immigrants contribute to the economy by investing in human capital, as evidenced by comparatively high earnings growth. Though kinship-based immigrants from developing nations may enter the workforce earning very low wages, they experience higher wage growth than their native-born counterparts. "Because of their propensity to invest in human capital, kinship-based immigrants provide the U.S. economy a highly malleable resource that promotes a vibrant economy in the long run," Duleep said. In recent research, Duleep has also weighed the opportunity costs for kinship-based immigrants. Opportunity costs refer to the expected gains from pursuing schooling or vocational training. Workers earning low wages have less to lose by investing time in training in comparison to those who are already earning relatively high wages. "Empirical evidence supports the theoretical expectation that family-based admissions are associated with a high propensity to invest in human capital. Earnings growth is a sign that human capital investment is taking place," Duleep told the House subcommittee.

CONTRIBUTORS TO COMMUNITIES

Theologians, psychotherapists, politicians, and teachers venerate the idea of family as critical for its individual members for support, and for ensuring the healthy development and raising of children. By allowing more immigrants to enter with family visas, the nation as a whole will benefit by the incorporation of families into the national fabric. Research has found that extended family helps facilitate immigrant incorporation into the United States. Children of immigrants with extended family in the country experience less isolation and more familial support, factors that research has found to promote healthy cognitive development and to be keys in helping them succeed academically, accumulating human capital for the future. As Julian Bond told the Senate Committee on the Judiciary during hearings on immigration reform, unified immigrant families help further the success of new immigrants by helping them learn the language and understand the laws and customs of the United States, as well as providing guidance on such endeavors as buying houses.

A 2011 study by Harvard University's Hirokazu Yoshikawa compared developmental outcomes of young children in various immigrant groups. Yoshikawa found that children growing up in homes without legal status suffered developmentally in comparison to children with extended families residing in the United States with legal status. Children with "legal" extended families enjoyed the presence of doting grandparents, aunts, and uncles, who visited, brought gifts, held them, and read to them. Such nurturance is critical for future school performance as it abets cognitive development. By comparison, hardships borne by families without legal status included isolation, fear, overcrowded housing and, at times, weathering utility shut-offs. Ethnographic field observation with families found that children of Dominican parents who had large networks of family were able to receive care from grandparents when their parents worked. Thus, opening channels for family-based immigration helps to support young children as they enter schools and acquire the skills that will one day contribute to the nation's human capital. Though skills-based immigrants might enter the United States with spouses and children, family visas would ensure the support of extended family.

One sociological study of Filipina workers in Canada—a nation that privileges skills over family in granting visas—found that women suffered long separations from their husbands and children (Cohen, 2000). Filipinas who obtain visas to work as domestic servants for privileged Canadian families experience prolonged separations from their spouses, often resulting in divorce and estrangement from children. If they are granted the right to bring their immediate families to Canada for reunification, the skills-based program tends to preclude the legal entry of siblings and parents, who could help stabilize a family during the rigors of immigration and acculturation.

Sadly, given the backlog in the United States of applications for family-based immigrant visas, the prolonged separation of families is not unique to Canada. Cecelia Menjívar (2006), a sociologist who studies immigration, has detailed the experiences of immigrants from Guatemala and El Salvador. Many families from these countries suffered prolonged separations while awaiting family reunification visas. During these separations, immigrants and their family members endure anxiety and uncertainty. Menjívar notes that parents and children sometimes have difficulty even recognizing one another after more than a decade of separation. When family reunification visas are virtually impossible to obtain, desperate families resort to unauthorized immigration. One El Salvadoran woman recounted hugging and kissing her son after not having seen him for years, only to find out that she had showered such affection on a stranger. She could not recognize her own son when she arrived at the house where a smuggler of illegal immigrants, known as a "coyote," had led a group of undocumented immigrants across the border. The fact of their meeting through a coyote illustrates the fact that she could not arrange to have her son immigrate here legally; thus, the family was forced to arrange his passage through paying a criminal syndicate to bring him to the United States. The very fact of the desperation of families to reunite costs the United States money to police borders, inevitably with little success, and by extension means the funneling of money to criminal cartels, many of which are engaged in drug as well as human smuggling.

Still, once across the border safely, the presence of immigrant communities facilitates immigrant economic incorporation as well as inclusion in other aspects of civil society, such as church membership, political activism, and artistic expression. As noted by Menjívar, Central Americans have worked together to lobby city councils to legalize street vending, as well as to organize formal day labor sites that ensure the orderly hiring of workers. The presence of family members who have legal immigration status proves invaluable to undocumented immigrants, many of whom struggle for years with the assistance of attorneys and community service organizations to secure legal status themselves.

Immigrant communities containing extended families not only provide support for immigrants themselves, but also help foster stability for the larger community, as illustrated in a 2011 study of Kennett Square, Pennsylvania by the folklorist Debra Lattanzi Shutika. Kennett Square had long been the site of migration by Mexican workers who harvest mushrooms, a critical component of the area's economic base. Prior to the Immigration Reform and Control Act of 1986, which granted undocumented immigrants an amnesty and offered pathways to work legally in the United States, migrant laborers lived in trailers or in low-income housing on the outskirts of town. After their incorporation legally, Mexican men brought their families to live with them. A decade later, in part to stem opposition to their presence by the dominant, white residents, a community-based nonprofit organization developed a low-income housing complex of townhouses with a community center. Settled into their own homes, families purchased furniture, plants, food, and clothing, all of which contributed to the overall well-being of the community. Lattanzi Shutika details the incorporation of a mushroom laborer and his family into the community. His daughter was admitted to Penn State University after graduating from the local high school. A decade later, several Mexican businesses had opened in the town center. Thus, the Kennett Square experience illustrates the advantages of family-based immigration. "Low-skilled" mushroom workers achieved financial stability and, in turn, benefited the community by opening businesses.

CONCLUSION

Research has found that family-based immigration facilitates entrepreneurship including the establishment of small businesses, as well as providing unskilled workers an opportunity to contribute to the economy. In addition, many "unskilled" immigrant workers take jobs that Americans are unwilling to accept. Though new immigrants may initially lag behind their U.S. counterparts in earnings and employment, research has found those gaps are quickly closed as immigrants are incorporated into the economic system. Family-based immigration helps foster overall economic growth by providing labor for jobs eschewed by native-born Americans or their more skilled immigrant counterparts. In addition, family-based immigration helps build the economy through the entrepreneurial efforts of family members. As immigrants establish new businesses and bring family members to the country to help in their operations, they purchase goods ranging from houses to food to clothing, all of which contributes to the nation's prosperity.

As has been detailed above, immigrants—even those who are undocumented—are proving important to maintaining Social Security and Medicare, two social insurance programs that protect older Americans from poverty by providing a monthly payment and ensuring that their health-care costs are covered. Without the contribution of immigrants, Americans would be forced to bear a greater share of the burden for maintaining these programs. The evidence presented here suggests that it would be in the nation's best interest to make family-based visas more readily available so that immigrants can more readily enter via legal means, thus proffering the nation an opportunity to benefit from their contributions.

REFERENCES AND FURTHER READING

Anderson, S. (2010). *Family immigration: The long wait to immigrate.* Retrieved from National Foundation for American Policy website: http://carnegie.org/fileadmin/Media/Publications/NFAP_Policy_Brief_Family_Immigration.pdf

Asian American Justice Center. (n.d.). *The economic impact of family-based immigration: Family-based immigration is vital to economic growth.* Retrieved from http://www.advancingequality.org/attachments/wysiwyg/7/FamilyImmigrationEconomy.pdf

Asian Pacific American Legal Center. (2008). *A devastating wait: Family unity and the immigration backlogs.* Retrieved from http://www.advancingequality.org/attachments/files/117/APALC_family_report.pdf

Cohen, R. (2000). "Mom is a stranger": The negative impact of immigration policies on the family life of Filipina domestic workers. *Canadian Ethnic Studies, 32,* 76–88.

Duleep, H. O. (1998). The family investment model: A formalization and review of evidence from across immigrant groups. *Gender Issues, 16,* 84–104.

Duleep, H. O. (2007, May 8). Testimony, Subcommittee on Immigration, Citizenship, Refugees, Border Security, and International Law, Committee on the Judiciary, U.S. House of Representatives. Retrieved from http://judiciary.house.gov/hearings/May2007/Duleep070508.pdf

Duleep, H. O., & Dowhan, D. J. (2008). Research on immigrants earnings. *Social Security Bulletin, 68,* 31–50.

Duleep, H. O., & Regets, M. C. (1996). Social Security and immigrant earnings. *Social Security Bulletin, 59,* 20–30.

Duleep, H. O., & Regets, M. C. (1997). Measuring immigrant wage growth using matched CPS files. *Demography, 34,* 239–249.

Duleep, H. O., & Regets, M. C. (1999). Immigrants and human-capital investment. *American Economic Review, 89,* 186–191.

Green, D. A. (1999). Immigrant occupational attainment: Assimilation and mobility over time. *Journal of Labor Economics, 17,* 49–79.

Guillermina J., & Rosenzweig, M. R. (1995). Do immigrants screened for skills do better than family reunification immigrants? *International Migration Review, 29*(1), 85–111.

Hinojosa-Ojeda, R. (2010, January). *Raising the floor for American workers: The economic benefits of comprehensive immigration reform.* Retrieved from Center for American Progress website: http://www.americanprogress.org/issues/2010/01/raising_the_floor.html

Immigration Policy Center. (2005). *Economic growth and immigration: Bridging the demographic divide.* Retrieved from http://www.immigrationpolicy.org/special-reports/economic-growth-immigration-bridging-demographic-divide

Lattanzi Shutika, D. (2011). *Beyond the borderlands: Mexican migration and belonging in the US and Mexico.* Berkeley, CA: University of California Press.

Lawrence, S. J. (2007). *Divided families: New legislative proposals would needlessly restrict family-based immigration.* Retrieved from Immigration Policy Center website: http://www.immigrationpolicy.org/special-reports/divided-families-new-legislative-proposals-would-needlessly-restrict-family-based-im

Martin, P. L. (2010). *Migration's economic tradeoff: Farmworker wages and food costs.* Retrieved from Population Reference Bureau website: http://www.prb.org/Articles/2010/usfarmworkersfoodprices.aspx

Menjívar, C. (2006). Liminal legality: Salvadoran and Guatemalan immigrants' lives in the United States. *American Journal of Sociology, 111,* 999–1037.

National Immigration Law Center. (2006). *Paying their way and then some: Facts about the contributions of immigrants to economic growth and public investment.* Retrieved from http://v2011.nilc.org/immspbs/research/research003.htm

Rangaswamy, P. (2006). South Asians in Dunkin' Donuts: Niche development in the franchise industry. *Journal of Ethnic and Migration Studies, 33,* 671–686.

Sanders, J. (2007). Social underpinnings of ethnic/informal economies. In G. Ritzer (Ed.), *The Blackwell encyclopedia of sociology: Volume III* (pp. 1459–1463). Malden, MA: Blackwell.

Sanders, J., Nee, V., & Sernau, S. (2002). Asian immigrants' reliance on social ties in a multiethnic labor market. *Social Forces, 81,* 281–314.

Suárez-Orozco, C., Bang, H. J., & Kim, H. Y. (2010). I felt like my heart was staying behind: Psychological implications of family separations and reunifications for immigrant youth. *Journal of Adolescent Research, 26,* 222–257.

Yoshikawa, H. (2011). *Immigrants raising citizens: Undocumented parents and their young children.* New York, NY: Russell Sage.

Carol L. Cleaveland

25

Cultural Assimilation

POINT: There is no such thing as an essential "American culture." American culture has been constantly created and re-created by the people who live in the United States, most of whom are descended from immigrants. As immigrants integrate in to society, culture evolves.

Elizabeth Hull, Rutgers University

COUNTERPOINT: The cultural diversity of current immigrants works against their joining the "melting pot" of American society in the way that earlier generations did. The existence of largely separate immigrant communities, and particularly their resistance to linguistic assimilation, erodes the fundamental "American culture" and works against social cohesion.

Morris I. Onyewuchi, Attorney-at-Law

Introduction

Recent high levels of immigration to the United States from a wide variety of countries has inevitably raised questions about how many different kinds of people can be absorbed by society in a short period of time. As of 2010, there were over 37 million immigrants in the United States from over 200 countries around the world:

- 12 percent from Europe,

- 27 percent from Asia,

- 54 percent from Central America, South America, and the Caribbean, and

- 7 percent from the remaining regions of the world.

As an accommodation to this diverse immigration, many in the United States (and other Western countries) embraced multiculturalism during the latter half of the twentieth century. But multiculturalism—as well as the immigration itself—reignited divisions over culture, identity, and what it means to be American. These divisions are characterized by animus toward those who are seen as unwilling to assimilate, to join the national dominant culture.

Social groups have been central to human survival for centuries, and the many ways that people form and participate in these groups is the subject of a rich body of research by sociologists, anthropologists, and social psychologists. Every social group defines itself relative to "others" and creates boundaries around this definition. Citizenship is a key mechanism for defining membership in a nation's social group (its society) and immigration directly confronts a country's terms for citizenship and for belonging.

The United States has a long history of integrating, or assimilating, a wide variety of immigrants. The motto "e Pluribus Unum" on the Seal of the United States speaks to that history. But each new wave of immigrants generates unease about whether they will, like those of earlier times, fully integrate into society. The metaphor that is widely used to describe the process of integration is that of a "melting pot," whereby new immigrants "melt" into and become indistinguishable from the larger society. Multicultural sensibilities have fostered use of a different metaphor, that of a "salad bowl," which conveys the idea of a diverse whole made up of distinct, individual elements. These dueling metaphors reflect a visceral concern that immigration generates in the form of the question, "Whose society is this, anyway?" Americans who see themselves as *most* different from immigrants feel this concern most strongly. Whatever the metaphor, immigrant integration fundamentally means that immigrants come to "belong," that they see themselves as full members of the society and that they are accepted as such.

It is not surprising that visible aspects of these perceived differences themselves—the ability to speak English, the concentration of immigrants in ethnic neighborhoods, different cultural practices, and race, to name a few—become contentious and are key benchmarks for measuring immigrant integration. English language acquisition is the first among equals of these measures. It is a key determinant of economic success, and many see English as central to American cultural identity. Perceptions that immigrants "refuse" to learn English generate strong negative reactions and foster anti-immigrant sentiment. To the extent that immigrants living in ethnic neighborhoods works against learning English, immigrant "ghettos" foster the sense that immigrants are a separate group out of mainstream society. The evidence that English language proficiency rates increase with the length of time immigrants are in the country, and that the children of immigrants overwhelmingly speak English, does not eliminate debates over English acquisition.

Ultimately, the process of immigrant integration occurs over time and across generations, and it is important to note that the rich cultural diversity that immigrants have brought to the United States throughout its history points to an important distinction in this debate. Cultural practices that reflect an individual's personal heritage are part of the *private* realm whereby individuals live in a free society. These are distinct from the civic and political ideals that define the United States (the right to free speech and freedom of religion, separation of church and state, civil and political liberties, civic engagement, participatory democracy, individual responsibility, private property, and so forth), and it is these ideals that are the basis of American cohesiveness in the *public* sphere. These are the ideals that define American citizenship and that constitute the American polity. Immigrants' embrace of these ideals has been, and is likely to continue to be, the basis of immigrant integration into American society.

POINT

American society has been shaped by every language and culture, drawn from every end of this Earth.

—President Barack Obama, Inaugural Address, 2009

According to a familiar adage, there are only two things one can count on in life: death and taxes. In the United States, at least, one could add a third: Every new group of immigrants entering the United States will trigger fears that its members will never assimilate. Historically, however, immigrants have integrated so well into the larger society that they themselves eventually become among part of the chorus bemoaning the hordes of newcomers who are too poor, alien, dark-skinned, or otherwise different from real Americans to ever fit in, and there is no reason to think recent entrants will not do so as well.

It is true that over the last 4 decades more immigrants have settled in the United States than at any other time in its history. It is also true that over 50 percent of today's immigrants are Asian or Hispanic, resulting in a country that is more racially diverse than at any other period in its history. Before tolling the alarm bells, however, concerned citizens should keep two points in mind: First, according to the Census Bureau, in 2010 only 12.9 percent of the U.S. population was foreign-born. Many other countries exceed that percentage, as did the United States itself every year between 1860 and 1920. Second, this country's own history provides ample grounds for optimism. As the sociologist Charles Hirschman (2006) observes,

> While it is not possible to predict the role of immigration in America's future, it is instructive to study the past. The current debates and hostility surrounding immigrants echo throughout American history. What is most surprising is that almost all popular fears about immigration and even the judgments of "experts" about the negative impact of immigrants have been proven false by history. Not only have almost all immigrants (or their descendants) assimilated over time, but they have broadened American society in many positive ways.

More than 2 centuries ago, Benjamin Franklin illustrated this "hostility surrounding immigrants" when he pilloried the "Palatine Boors" from Germany who refused to learn English, and would, he feared, swamp America's then-dominant British culture. Irish immigrants were scorned in the mid-1800s as lazy drunks and, worse, Roman Catholics. Later in the century, as the historian John Higham (1988) notes, the Immigration Restriction League advocated a literacy test to prevent southern and eastern Europe from spewing forth an "alarming number of illiterates, paupers, criminals, and madmen who endangered American character and citizenship" (p. 103).

In the early twentieth century, "new immigrants"—Poles, Italians, and Russian Jews—were deemed so incapable of assimilating that in 1924 the country adopted national origin quotas intended to exclude altogether almost everyone from Asia and Africa and sharply limit arrivals from southern and eastern Europe. These national quotas reflected eugenic principles influential at the time that supposedly proved the inferiority of the new immigrants relative to old stock Americans. In hindsight, of course, it's clear such doomsayers were completely wrong. Daniel Griswold (2002) has observed that immigration, "far from undermining the American experiment, is an integral part of it." "Successive waves of immigrants," he points out, "have kept our country demographically young, enriched our culture and added to our productive capacity as a nation, enhancing our influence in the world."

IMMIGRANT CONTRIBUTIONS

Imagine how bland and impoverished American society and culture would be without the contributions of its immigrants: The United States would have lost Levi Strauss, who first manufactured blue jeans, and the dynamos who created Google, Yahoo, Intel, and eBay. It would have forfeited both the greatest mind of the twentieth century (Albert Einstein), fully one-third of its Nobel Prize winners, and many of the world's athletes and creative geniuses, including Irving Berlin, Frank Capra, Bob Hope, Greta Garbo, Al Jolson, Mikhail Baryshnikov, Zubin Meta, Hakeem Olajuwon, I. M. Pei, Sidney Poitier, and Oscar de La Renta. It would also have forfeited the sons and daughters of these first-generation immigrants. Imagine how diminished American culture would be without the contributions of George and Ira Gershwin, Richard

Rodgers, Lorenz Hart, Jerome Kern, Harold Arlen, and Leonard Bernstein. More recently, had its welcome mat been removed, the United States would have excluded a whole new generation of immigrants who are similarly weaving gold into its national tapestry, such as the hockey player Wayne Gretzky, basketball star Patrick Ewing, actor Michael Fox, singer Gloria Estefan, Aids researcher David Ho, and the model Iman.

The New York Times columnist Thomas Friedman wrote an article in March 2010 commemorating this new generation, in particular the 40 high school students who were finalists in the 2010 Intel Science Search. He listed some of their names, including Linda Zhou, Alice Wei Zhao, Sunanda Sharma, Sarine Gayaneh Shahmirian, David Chienyun Liu, Ruoyi Jiang, Otana Agape Jakpor, Peter Danming Hu, Yuval Yaacov Calev, Levent Alpoge, and John Vincenzo Capodilupo. What these names have in common is obvious: they are all either immigrants themselves or the descendants of immigrants, as were the majority of other Intel winners. These outstanding young people will go on to capture other prestigious awards, make scientific breakthroughs, and bring further pride to their adopted country.

IMMIGRANT TIDES

Simply because past waves of immigrants successfully assimilated does not guarantee, of course, that current immigrants will, but there are reasons for optimism. Today, no less than in the past, many newcomers bear little resemblance to the northern European whites that once made up the bulk of America's population. Today, however, to the extent there is a typical American, he or she could as easily be Asian or Hispanic or of African descent. Upon reaching the United States, moreover, new arrivals from China, El Salvador, or Nigeria find large immigrant enclaves that welcome compatriots, socialize them in their new country's strange ways, and provide employment and social service networks. New arrivals can also benefit from the same institutions that in the early twentieth century actively encouraged assimilation, such as labor unions, political parties, and the military. Even during economic slowdowns, they can still find the same kind of low-skilled, entry-level jobs that awaited earlier generations of immigrants.

There are, in addition, many recent developments that facilitate assimilation, including the network of social and legislative reforms brought about by the civil rights movement of the 1950s and 1960s. Today, both state and federal laws, and in particular the 1964 Civil Rights Act, prohibit employers from discriminating on the basis of race or national origin. Long gone are the days when newspaper ads could warn, "no Irish need apply."

Most successful firms now resemble the United Nations, with their employees representing almost every country on the planet. Most CEOs actively foster an atmosphere of tolerance and fair play—as much to reduce the racial and ethnic tensions that could impair productivity as to comply with the law. The sociologist Victor Nee points out, for example, that Microsoft, whose workforce is 25 percent nonwhite, enforces a zero tolerance policy with respect to racism (Nee & Waldinger, 2003).

Technological change is also bolstering assimilation. New arrivals find it easier to learn English than did their counterparts in the late 1800s and early 1900s because of the ready availability of foreign language programs, television, and the Internet. While it is easier today than in the past to live in an ethnic enclave, it is also harder to avoid mainstream media. *The Washington Post* writer Karin Brulliard (2007) points out that the globalization of American culture enables immigrants to arrive here already half-assimilated, munching McDonald's burgers and sporting baseball caps and sneakers. As a result, as the policy analysts Heather Craigie and Marina Moses (2006) note, there has been a reduction from three generations to two between arrival and assimilation.

ASSIMILATION CAN CAUSE CONFLICT

Immigrants themselves are a self-selecting group who possess character traits assuring their assimilation: resilience, optimism, resourcefulness, and industry. As sociologist Rubén G. Rumbaut has pointed out, commenting on immigrants' strong work ethic, "couch potatoes don't emigrate" (Schulte, 2008). Those lacking such traits are unlikely to abandon all that is familiar and comfortable in order to seek opportunity in an alien land.

Still, the process of assimilation is often rife with conflict and misunderstanding. Longitudinal studies by political scientists Bruce Cain and Roderick Kiewiet indicate that this results from "varying expectations" of first-, second-, and third-generation immigrants (Skerry, 2000). Members of the first generation are relatively content, considering themselves vastly better off than they were in their native land. Their American-born children and grandchildren, however, often have considerably higher expectations and chafe under any perceived cultural or linguistic restraints that impair their mobility.

Assimilation can also strain relationships across generations among family members. Peter Skerry (2000), who conducted field research in South Texas's impoverished Rio Grande Valley, recalls a conversation he had with a Mexican-American physician and Democratic Party activist who was dismayed by the fact his grown children "think like Dallas Republicans."

BENCHMARKS OF ASSIMILATION

Analysts measure assimilation using a variety of benchmarks, including citizenship, acquisition rates English language proficiency, income, and educational attainment. Although there is significant variation among different immigrant groups, most are doing well in several of these categories. They are, for example, acquiring English at impressive rates. Rubén Rumbaut observes that although adult immigrants generally have a hard time learning English, their children are commonly bilingual, noting, "By the third generation, it's over. English wins" (Brulliard, 2007).

The scholar Jacob Vigdor notes in an authoritative 2009 study, moreover, that in 2009 "immigrants in America continue[d] to assimilate strongly along economic lines," indicating that in terms of economic well-being "they quickly closed in on native-born Americans." Most are also making notable educational strides. Rumbaut found that the dropout rate among immigrant children is half that of their native counterparts, and according to educational scholars Wendy Erisman and Shannon Looney, new immigrants are twice as likely as native-born citizens to have completed at least some postbaccalaureate education.

Educational attainment tends to improve over time: Among first-generation immigrants the dropout rate is 27 percent, but among their grandchildren it drops to 8.6 percent. College completion rates among immigrants have been rising steadily, moreover, and these newcomers go on to earn twice as many PhDs as their native counterparts.

Why, then, do so many people question whether assimilation is in fact taking place? Because skeptics seldom reside in communities where immigrants settled decades ago, and whose foreign roots are thus scarcely recognizable by now. Rather, it is those dwelling in states with sizeable populations of new immigrants who doubt whether these new neighbors will ever fit in. They will indeed fit in, but only over time: assimilation is a process that requires two and even three generations. Policy analysts Dowell Myers and John Pitkin (2010) argue that Americans frequently "fall prey" to the presumption "that immigrants are like Peter Pan—forever frozen in their status as newcomers, never aging, never advancing economically, and never assimilating." They point out that examining the data on immigrant advancement can help dispel this fallacy.

Assimilation not only takes time, but its path is uneven and multidimensional. In his research on immigration, the sociologist Milton Gordon (1964) discovered that newcomers can make great progress economically but lag behind culturally or politically, or they can make political inroads but have difficulty securing an economic foothold. That newcomers rarely advance in all categories at the same rate does not necessarily indicate a lack of assimilation, but only that they take a course that another sociologist, Herbert J. Gans (1992), describes as "bumpy" rather than a "straight line."

Historian Marcus Lee Hansen described this "bumpy" course as a phenomenon that is particularly evident among immigrant families, noting in a 1938 essay, "What the son wishes to forget the grandson wishes to remember." Assimilation is not necessarily a straightforward or even irreversible process, but rather one that starts, stalls, and moves backward and forward among the generations. The children and grandchildren of immigrants occasionally choose to de-assimilate. Upon reaching young adulthood, for instance, many linguistically assimilated Mexican Americans reassert the importance of Spanish in their lives. The political scientist Peter Skerry observes, ironically, that Selena, the Latina pop singer who was raised in Corpus Christi as an English speaker, was later forced to learn Spanish in order to become a Tejano star.

MUSLIMS AND MEXICANS

There are two immigrant groups that, for a variety of reasons, are facing particular scrutiny in their attempts to integrate into American life: Muslims and Mexicans. Even so, both groups are doing considerably better than media headlines suggest.

There are over 2 million Muslim immigrants in the United States, or slightly less than one percent of the population. Most are integrating well. This includes girls from Muslim (and other traditionally patriarchal) families, who are excelling in school and joining the workforce in sizeable numbers. A majority of Muslims also report being optimistic about their futures. The following statistics provide interesting context. Seven percent of Muslim immigrants living in Italy have become citizens. In Switzerland, the figure is 10 percent, and in Spain it is 25 percent. In the United States, fully 48 percent of Muslim immigrants are naturalized citizens. This relatively high percentage is not surprising in light of a 2011 Gallup poll finding that two-thirds of American Muslims identify strongly with the United States.

Mexican Americans also identify with the United States, although perhaps because of their proximity to their homeland this attachment often takes a generation longer to ripen than it does for other new arrivals. Like other first- and even second-generation immigrants, Mexicans often continue to honor symbols and holidays they associate with their native land—-by waving the Mexican flag, for instance, or celebrating Cinco de Mayo, even while they are undergoing social, political, and civic integration into American society. These celebrants are the same people, Myers and Pitkin observe, "who will enlist in the U.S. Army and be proud about it." (They compare this behavior to New York transplants now living in Los Angeles who continue to root for the Yankees.)

That Muslims and Mexican Americans are in the process of assimilating is not to say that there aren't hurdles as they attempt to integrate to American society. After the terrorist attacks of September 11, 2001, Muslim Americans were subjected to widespread public suspicion and occasional violence. Mexican Americans, on the other hand, have been handicapped by their relative poverty and, some researchers maintain, their sheer numbers. Since there are more than 30 million Mexican Americans living in the United States, many scholars, including the economist Stephen Trejo and historian Samuel Huntington, predict that their assimilation will be particularly difficult because they can live in self-sufficient ethnic ghettos that largely eliminate the need to interact with the larger community.

A 2009 report by Duke University professor Jacob Vigdor largely debunks this hypothesis. Vigdor concludes that Mexican immigrants are assimilating in ways "remarkably similar" to those of earlier Irish, Jewish, and Italian immigrants—and that Mexican immigrants are likely ultimately to fit into American society just as comfortably as these earlier immigrant groups. If Vigdor's prognosis is correct, Mexicans, too, will in time be largely indistinguishable from their neighbors, buying houses, going on picnics, and complaining about taxes just like everyone else.

UNDOCUMENTED ALIENS

There is one group of noncitizens that is not assimilating well: the approximately 11 million undocumented aliens. Vigdor does not find this surprising. He notes many factors working against assimilation, including barriers to taking most decent jobs, becoming a citizen, receiving the loans that might make a college education possible, qualifying for subsidized housing or affordable health care, and even, in some places, securing a driver's license or walking down the streets without being asked by police officers to produce identification. Vigdor concludes that assimilation would be facilitated by expanding undocumented immigrants' civil and economic rights in order to broaden opportunities for their integration into the larger society.

MELTING POT OR TOSSED SALAD?

Americans take great pride in the notion that the United States is a "melting pot" in which immigrants gradually absorb American customs and values, forging a country that makes "one out of many." According to this narrative, the sociologist Roger Waldinger wryly observes, they "learn English, buy a barbeque, and within a generation or two can't be separated from Europeans who came over on the Mayflower" (Nee & Waldinger, 2003). A 1909 Broadway play by Israel Zangwill first eulogized the ideal of the melting pot. Its leading man delivers an impassioned soliloquy in which he declaims that "America is God's Crucible, the great melting-pot where all the races of Europe are melting and reforming! . . . German and Frenchman, Irishman and Englishman, Jews and Russians—into the Crucible with you all. God is making the American." President Theodore Roosevelt, attending the play's premiere, reported afterwards that its message confirmed his steadfast conviction that "the man who becomes completely Americanized . . . is doing his plain duty to his adopted land."

John Higham (1988) points out that by virtue of the melting pot ideal, newcomers felt enormous pressure to blend in by becoming 100 percent American. New arrivals were urged to forsake their native language, religious customs, values, dietary and cooking habits, and notions of child rearing and personal hygiene—all on the assumption that only by repudiating their former ways could they assimilate into American society. Such thorough adaptation facilitated assimilation, to be sure, but as many historians have observed, including Higham and John Isbister, it also left many immigrants feeling guilt-ridden, ashamed, and estranged from their family. Moreover, while the melting pot's emphasis on conformity to dominant cultural norms was relatively easy to accommodate when newcomers were overwhelmingly white and Protestant, it became decidedly more problematic once they arrived with darker skin or clasping a rosary.

For these exotic newcomers, assimilation in the United States historically conformed in practice less to the melting pot than to a pluralist and more multicultural integration model. Horace Kallen first extolled this model in a 1915 magazine article in which he implored the United States to become a "democracy of nationalities, cooperating voluntarily and autonomously in the enterprise of self-realization [utilizing] a common language, English" (Meyer, 2008). Kallen compared America to a symphony orchestra—just as various performers, each playing their separate instruments, together produce a beautiful composition, so, too, a multiplicity of immigrant groups, each with its own culture and habits, together produce a splendid and harmonious country.

Ironically, as the sociologist Vincent Parrillo (2009) observed, Kallen may have been among the first to embrace pluralism, but he himself rarely invited people of color to join his celebrated orchestra. As the multicultural movement evolved, however, its adherents abandoned Kallen's Eurocentric focus and, at least since the 1960s, have labored to honor and preserve the norms and cultural practices valued by minority groups. By virtue of their efforts, educational curriculums now reflect this country's diversity and pay tribute to the many ways non-European civilizations have influenced its history, culture, and values.

Today most Americans are multiculturalists—whether they know it or not. They revel in their country's variety, celebrate the way continuous immigrant flows have revitalized and strengthened its culture; and, as journalist Steven Roberts observes, take pride in the elasticity of America's "self-definition." No matter where people are from, they can define themselves as American. It is not possible for immigrants anywhere else in the world to identify in this way with a new country.

Roberts pays homage to this cultural elasticity when he reflects on the transformation of his old neighborhood of Bayonne, New Jersey. Today, he says, "the Italian church has masses in Spanish. The old bus station is a Coptic Christian church. All the stores on Broadway that used to be owned by Jews are now owned by Indians." Indeed, he says, "the winner of the annual award given by the Jewish community for an essay about the Holocaust is a Muslim woman from Pakistan."

Americans' willingness to forbear, and ultimately to celebrate, its multicultural society—for all the Sturm und Drang this involves—distinguishes it from many other countries that insist as a condition of membership that newcomers adopt their own national habits and mores. For example, there have been very different reactions in the United States and France to Muslim schoolgirls wearing hijabs, their traditional religious headscarf, to school. In the United States, many—although certainly not all—tolerate this practice as one that does not threaten, and may even enrich, civic culture (and which is, at any rate, protected by the free exercise clause of the Constitution's First Amendment). The French, in contrast, interpret the wearing of the hijab as a divisive and even unpatriotic act at odds with their secular society, and as a consequence the government has forbidden students from wearing a headscarf or anything else that is identifiably religious to class.

During a 2011 television interview, French president Nicolas Sarkozy articulated his country's disdain for immigrants who refused to accept the customs of their adopted country: "If you come to France, you accept to melt into a single community, which is the national community, and if you do not want to accept that, you cannot be welcome in France." Many thoughtful Americans, illiberal as they might find Sarkozy's declaration, nevertheless sympathize with his concern that excessive diversity could unduly strain or even fragment the United States. They fear that to the extent members of the public emphasize their differences, rather than their commonalities, they render assimilation increasingly difficult to achieve. These individuals become not simply Americans, but Italian Americans, Arab Americans, and Mexican Americans.

Arthur Schlesinger captured these misgivings in his 1992 book, *The Disuniting of America,* when he averred that such an emphasis on group identity promotes a "cult of ethnicity," which in turn encourages the "Balkanization of society," or the fraying of the social fabric that inevitably occurs when group identity supersedes individual or societal identity. "The bonds of cohesion in our society are sufficiently fragile," he wrote, "that it makes no sense to strain them by encouraging and exalting cultural and linguistic apartheid" (p. 137).

CONCLUSION

That the United States is headed for ethnic or linguistic apartheid is a worry many citizens dismiss as unlikely, given its history. Many of these same people, however, are troubled by something else: that by admitting too many newcomers who lack Judeo-Christian roots, this country will overwhelm its own assimilative capacities; that if it embraces too many foreigners from regimes alien to its own—from despotisms, say, where notions of limited government or civic involvement or the rule of law have never been allowed to take root—it could undermine its own institutional strength. Indeed, in sufficient numbers, immigrants who espouse the subordination of women, for example, or who don't believe in the separation of church and state or the imperative of mutual toleration could ultimately imperil this country's entire way of life. By opening its gates too wide, the country may even be inviting the urban unrest and violence that has convulsed many European cities.

These concerned citizens sometimes wonder whether their disillusioned brethren in Europe might even be right, that the United States has been willing to tolerate sharp cultural and religious differences only because it has not yet endured the intense ethnic and religious strife that has beleaguered so many other liberal democracies. By retaining such generous admission policies, is the United States making such strife inevitable? If so, might the public end up agreeing not only with President Sarkozy, but also with Chancellor Angela Merkel of Germany and Prime Minister David Cameron of Great Britain, who in separate interviews declared that their countries' "longstanding policies of multiculturalism had been failures." (Cameron's *cri de coeur* was uttered well before August 2011, when England experienced the worst urban rioting in its modern history.) What then would become of the vaunted pluralist society in the United States?

These worries merit respect, of course, especially given the experiences of this country's European allies, but those who harbor them underestimate the durability of their culture. American culture has been strengthened, challenged, enriched, strained, occasionally even whiplashed by each new immigrant wave, but in spite of this its defining values have remained remarkably robust. These defining principles include a commitment to freedom and equality, reverence for the Constitution and the rule of law, and a profound dedication to the values of fair play and tolerance. Find anyone who has been in this country one or two generations, and look beneath his skull cap, her hijab, his kufi, or her mantilla, and there will be men and women whose devotion to these principles has made them Americans in the truest sense of the word.

REFERENCES AND FURTHER READING

Batalova, J., & Terrazas, A. (2010, December). *Frequently requested statistics on immigrants and immigration in the United States.* Retrieved from Migration Policy Institute website: http://www.migrationinformation.org/Feature/display.cfm?ID=818#1

Brown, S. K., & Bean, F. D. (2006, October 1). *Assimilation models, old and new: Explaining a long-term process.* Retrieved from Migration Information Source website: http://www.migrationinformation.org/feature/display.cfm?id=442

Brulliard, K. (2007, August 7). At odds over immigration policy. *The Washington Post.* Retrieved from http://www.washingtonpost.com/wp-dyn/content/article/2007/08/06/AR2007080601581.html

Cabrera, A. (2004, November). *Pathways for Latino youth.* Retrieved from Wisconsin Center of Education Research website: http://www.wcer.wisc.edu/news/coverstories/pathways_for_latino_youth.php

Caruba, A. (2011, February 7). Multicultural suicide. *The Bear.* Retrieved from The Absurd Report website: http://www.theabsurdreport.com/2011/multicultural-suicide-by-alan-caruba

Center for the Study of Immigrant Integration (CSII), University of Southern California. (2001, September 1). *Assimilation today—New evidence on the advancement of immigrants in America's culture and economy.* Retrieved from http://csii.usc.edu/assimilation_today.html

Craigie, H., & Moses, M. (2006, September 21). *Soup or salad: Immigrant assimilation, separatism, and multiculturalism.* Retrieved from Migration in the Americas website: http://unschooler.org/marina/essays/souporsalad

Dannheisser, R. (2007).

Dockterman, D. (2011, February 17). *Statistical portrait of Hispanics in the United States, 2009.* Retrieved from Pew Hispanic Center website: http://www.pewhispanic.org/2011/02/17/statistical-portrait-of-hispanics-in-the-united-states-2009

Erisman, W., & Looney, S. (2007, April). *Opening the door to the American dream: Increasing higher education access and success for immigrants.* Retrieved from: http://www.sunywcc.edu/cccie/pdfs/OpeningTheDoor%20Inst%20Higher%20Ed.pdf

Friedman, T. L. (2010, March 21). America's real dream team. *The New York Times.* Retrieved from http://www.nytimes.com/2010/03/21/opinion/21friedman.html

Gans, H. J. (1992, Fall). Ethnic invention and acculturation: A bumpy-line approach [Comment]. *Journal of American Ethnic History, 11*(1), 42–52.

Gordon, M. (1964). *Assimilation in American life: The role of race, religion, and national origins.* New York, NY: Oxford University Press.

Griswold, D. T. (2002, February 18). *How Immigrants have enriched American culture and enhanced our influence in the world.* Retrieved from Cato Institute website: http://www.cato.org/research/articles/griswold-020218.html

Hanson, G. H. (2005, December). *Why does immigration divide America? Public finance and political opposition to open borders* (Working Paper No. 129). San Diego, CA: University of California; Cambridge, MA: National Bureau of Economic Research. Retrieved from http://irps.ucsd.edu/assets/022/8793.pdf

Higham, J. (1988). *Strangers in the land: Patterns of American nativism, 1860–1925* (2nd ed.). New Brunswick, NJ: Rutgers University Press. (Originally published 1955)

Hirschman, C. (2006, July 28). *Impact of immigration on American society: Looking backward to the future.* Retrieved from Border Battles website: http://borderbattles.ssrc.org/Hirschman

Hudson, J. H. (2001, August 2). U.S. Muslims Say they're patriotic and optimistic about future. *Atlantic Monthly.* Retrieved from http://www.theatlanticwire.com/politics/2011/08/us-muslims-say-theyre-patriotic-and-optimistic-about-future/40717

Isbister, J. (1996). *The immigration debate remaking America:* West Hartford, CT: Kumarian Press.

Jensen, R. (2002). No Irish need apply: A myth of victimization. *Journal of Social History, 36*(2), 405–429. Retrieved from http://tigger.uic.edu/~rjensen/no-irish.htm

Kirkwood, R. C. (2011, February 14). Sarkozy joins Cameron, Merkel, condemns multiculturalism. *New American.* Retrieved from http://www.thenewamerican.com/world-mainmenu-26/europe-mainmenu-35/6289-sarkozy-joins-cameron-merkel-condemns-multiculturalism

Laurence, J., & Vaisse, J. (2011, March 28). The dis-integration of Europe. *Foreign Policy.* Retrieved from http://www.foreignpolicy.com/articles/2011/03/28/the_dis_integration_of_europe

Levine, R. A. (2004, July). *Assimilating immigrants: Why America can and France cannot.* Retrieved from RAND Corporation website: http://www.rand.org/pubs/occasional_papers/OP132.html

McClymer, J. (1982). The Americanization movement and the education of the foreign-born adult, 1914–1925. In B. Weiss (Ed.), *American education and the European immigrant: 1880–1940* (97f). Urbana, IL: University of Illinois Press.

Meyer, G. (2008, November). The cultural pluralist response to Americanization: Horace Kallen, Randolph Bourne, Louis Adamic, and Leonard Covello. *Journal of the Research Group on Socialism and Democracy Online.* Retrieved from http://sdonline.org/48/the-cultural-pluralist-response-to-americanization-horace-kallen-randolph-bourne-louis-adamic-and-leonard-covello

Myers, D., & Pitkin, J. (2010, September 1). *New evidence shows the latest immigrants to America are following in our history's footsteps.* Retrieved from Center for American Progress website: http://www.americanprogress.org/issues/2010/09/pdf/immigrant_assimilation.pdf

Nee, V., & Waldinger, R. (2003, February 7). *Are "new immigrants" to the United States assimilating?* [Debate, moderated by Janet Reno]. Retrieved from Center for the Study of Inequality website: http://inequality.cornell.edu/events/papers/Contorversies%20About%20Inequality%20Debate%20Series/CAIDebate1.PDF

Parrillo, V. N. (2009). *Diversity in America.* Thousand Oaks, CA: Pine Forge Press.

Passel, J. S., & Cohn, D. (2011, March 3). *How many Hispanics? Comparing Census counts and Census estimates.* Retrieved from Pew Hispanic Center website: http://pewhispanic.org/reports/report.php?ReportID=139

Portes, A., & Rumbaut, R. G. (1996). *Immigrant America: A portrait* (2nd ed.). Berkeley, CA: University of California Press.

Rivera, G. (2008). *His panic: Why Americans fear Hispanics in the U.S.* New York, NY: Celebra.

Roberts, S. (2009). *From every end of this earth: 13 families and the new lives they made in America.* New York, NY: HarperCollins.

Rumbaut, R. G. (1999). Assimilation and its discontents: Ironies and paradoxes. In C. Hirschman, J. DeWind, & P. Kasinitz (Eds.), *The handbook of international migration: The American experience* (pp. 172–195). New York, NY: Russell Sage Foundation.

Schlesinger, A. M., Jr. (1990, April 23). When ethnic studies are un-American. *The Wall Street Journal.*

Schlesinger, A. M., Jr. (1990, Fall). Against academic apartheid. *The Social Contract, 1*(1). Retrieved from http://www.thesocialcontract.com/artman2/publish/tsc0101/article_8.shtml

Schlesinger, A. M., Jr. (1992). *The disuniting of America.* New York, NY: Norton.

Schulte, B. (2008, May 15). Mexican immigrants prove slow to fit in. *U.S. News and World Report.* Retrieved from http://www.usnews.com/news/national/articles/2008/05/15/mexican-immigrants-prove-slow-to-fit-in

Sheen, D. (n.d.). Famous American immigrants [Web log post]. Retrieved from http://immigrationupdate.wordpress.com/famous-american-immigrants

Skerry, P. (2000, March/April). *Do we really want immigrants to assimilate?* Retrieved from Brookings Institution website: http://www.brookings.edu/articles/2000/03immigration_skerry.aspx

U.S. Census Bureau. (2011). *State and county QuickFacts.* Retrieved from http://quickfacts.census.gov/qfd/states/00000.html

Venugopal, A. (2011, May 24). *Immigrants assimilate more successfully in the U.S. than in Europe: Report* [WNYC News]. Retrieved from http://www.wnyc.org/articles/wnyc-news/2011/may/24/immigrants-assimilate-more-successfully-us-europe-according-report

Vigdor, J. L. (2009, October). *Measuring immigrant assimilation in the United States* (Civic Report No. 59). Retrieved from Manhattan Institute for Policy Research website: http://www.fas.org/sgp/crs/row/RL32934.pdf; http://www.manhattan-institute.org/html/cr_59.htm

Villarreal, M. A. (2011, February 24). *U.S.-Mexico economic relations: Trends, issues, and implications.* Retrieved from Congressional Research Service website: http://www.fas.org/sgp/crs/row/RL32934.pdf

West, D. M. (2011, January 13). *Creating a "brain gain" for U.S. employers: The role of immigration* (Brookings Policy Brief No. 178). Retrieved from Brookings Institution website: http://www.brookings.edu/papers/2011/01_immigration_west.aspx

Elizabeth Hull

COUNTERPOINT

The debate about cultural assimilation of immigrants into the "American melting pot" is ubiquitous. Because immigrants come to the United States from every region of the world with different cultural experiences, examining the issue of cultural assimilation is vital for determining the effects of the diversity of recent immigrants on core values Americans understand as fundamental to national identity and cohesiveness. However, this question of cultural assimilation cannot be properly addressed without understanding what constitutes "culture."

Unfortunately, "culture" is a nebulous concept, and what is considered a cultural norm in one country can be taboo in another. For example, polygamy is a cultural norm in many African and Middle Eastern countries, but it is taboo in many European and North American countries, including the United States. In effect, a polygamist immigrating to the United States must abide by the cultural norms of the United States, where polygamy is illegal. In such a scenario, one must wonder what it means for such an immigrant to be assimilated into the American culture. Is cultural assimilation complete once an immigrant who is predisposed to polygamy chooses to accept monogamy in order to comply with the U.S. laws and cultural norms? Is monogamy even a cultural norm of the United States? Better yet, considering the diverse racial, ethnic, and religious cohorts in the country, is there such a thing as an "American culture"? These questions are not simple ones, because there are many aspects of culture, making it difficult to pin down what constitutes the "essential American culture" into which immigrants are expected to assimilate. For the purposes of this essay, however, in order to discuss cultural assimilation, it is necessary to have a working knowledge of what constitutes the "culture of a society."

WHAT IS CULTURE?

According to Carroll Quigley's 1966 history, *Tragedy and Hope,* the "culture of a society" can be divided into six arbitrary aspects: military, political, intellectual, economic, social, and religious (p. 33). Each of these aspects of culture is interrelated with, and inseparable from, the others. It is reasonable to assume that these aspects of culture take different forms in every country from which immigrants to the United States originate. These cultural differences inculcate and cultivate certain worldviews in immigrants based on the accepted cultural norms of their respective societies of origin. This means that the interrelationship among different aspects of culture in the United States may differ from their interrelationships in other countries. However, despite these interrelationships and differences, an immigrant's complete cultural assimilation envisions an ability to fully function in both the public and private realms of society.

In the public realm, one political aspect of U.S. culture is grounded in the idea of "one person, one vote," whereas an immigrant's country of origin may have been a dictatorship, where this democratic ideal did not exist. In the private realm, certain types of violence against women, such as honor killing and female genital mutilation, are cultural norms in some societies, where they are considered family matters. An immigrant coming to the United States from any of these societies must be willing to abandon the practices of honor killing and female genital mutilation in order to assimilate and fully function in the United States; otherwise, that immigrant, though acting according to the private realm of his old culture, would run afoul of U.S. criminal laws. Thus, whether dealing with political or social aspects of cultural practices, cultural assimilation in both the public and private realms is necessary for an immigrant to fully function in the larger, mainstream society. Consequently, keeping in mind Quigley's aspects of culture, it is appropriate to examine in detail what "cultural assimilation" means for an immigrant in the United States.

WHAT IS CULTURAL ASSIMILATION?

Based on the diversity of immigrants and their cultural experiences, what then is the appropriate measure of when an immigrant has assimilated culturally? Cultural assimilation means different things to different people. In this author's view, it means embracing the "positive" American ideals that are essential to American culture; ideals that are encompassed by notions of human rights, democracy, equality of opportunity, economic prosperity through hard work and personal sacrifices, individual responsibility and accountability, the rule of law, civic responsibility, respect for the rights of others, national cohesiveness, abiding patriotism, and the country's English linguistic heritage. While this list is not exhaustive, it is a starting point in evaluating what it means to say that immigrants who come to the United States should assimilate into American culture.

As one examines the cultural assimilation of immigrants, it is important to recognize that cultural assimilation is a multifaceted process; that does not happen automatically or immediately once immigrants enter the country. In fact, some immigrants may never be able to achieve assimilation into every aspect of American culture, despite their sincere desire to do so. Likewise, some immigrants may not be interested in some aspects of the culture and still be considered sufficiently assimilated by embracing other aspects considered fundamental to American nationhood. For example, an immigrant who enters the United States as an atheist, soccer enthusiast, or couscous connoisseur may not be interested in becoming a Christian, watching baseball, or baking an apple pie. But this person could still be considered assimilated if he or she is making meaningful contributions to society, such as serving in the military and embracing core beliefs in freedom, democracy, and the rule of law.

As another example, in some countries from which immigrants originate, there may be no, or very lax, traffic laws compared to the United States, where traffic laws are strictly enforced for obvious safety and economic concerns. In order for an immigrant coming from one of those countries to assimilate culturally, embracing American notions of the rule of law, by respecting and abiding by our traffic laws, is imperative. As one may extrapolate from these few examples, there are many facets of cultural assimilation that make it difficult to have a finite number of ways assimilation is achieved. But what, then, is the American culture into which immigrants should assimilate? Is there even an essential American culture?

ENGLISH AS THE ESSENTIAL AMERICAN LINGUISTIC CULTURE

Arguably, there is no such thing as an essential "American culture." For example, within the United States, cultural norms differ from region to region. The cultural norms in New York are different from those in Alabama. Although patterns of cultural exchanges in every society are different, a common language is an essential bond that holds a society together as one people. As such, English is the primary embodiment of the linguistic cultural heritage and identity of the United States (Brooks, Carrasco, & Selmi, 2005, p. 923). As the Irish leader Eamon de Valera aptly pointed out in 1966, "Language is a chief characteristic of nationhood-the embodiment, as it were, of the nation's personality and the closest bond between its people" (p. 136). Any doubt that English is the unspoken personification of nationhood of the United States is dispelled by Theodore Roosevelt's assertion, "We have room for but one language here, and that is the English language, for we intend to see that the crucible turns our people out as Americans, of American nationality, and not as dwellers in a polyglot boarding house." Roosevelt added, "We must have but one flag. We must also have but one language. That must be the language of the Declaration of Independence, of Washington's Farewell address, of Lincoln's Gettysburg speech and second inaugural" (quoted in King, 1997).

The first step in any meaningful cultural assimilation is linguistic assimilation, because irrespective of any specific immigrant's personal attributes and adaptability to other aspects of culture, assimilation inheres in the ability to interact and function within the mainstream dominant culture. In order to interact, the immigrant must be able to communicate in the dominant language of the host culture. Using Quigley's six aspects of culture as a guidepost in contextualizing linguistic assimilation, communication, as a social aspect of culture, is of utmost importance in the cultural assimilation of immigrants.

WHAT IS LINGUISTIC ASSIMILATION AND WHY IS IT NECESSARY?

In the United States, linguistic assimilation means the ability to communicate in the English language, and language is a vital aspect of national identity. Immigrants arrive with different life experiences and cultural perspectives, irrespective of ethnic, racial, national, political, or religious similarities. Cultural assimilation in the United States involves the desire to form relationship bonds with the mainstream English-speaking culture. Forming such relationships may not be possible without the ability to speak English, because English is the de facto cultural language of communication in politics, security, commerce, and other interethnic cultural exchanges that sustain the bond between Americans. Without being able to speak English, it is difficult to fathom how an immigrant can meaningfully interact socially, politically, intellectually, or economically with the mainstream culture. Showing interest in the communication medium of the host country and taking steps to learn the language is vital to cultural assimilation. Even expressing a simple "thank you" in English will arouse interest that may lead to establishing a common linguistic bond. As Judge Emillio M. Garza of the U.S. Court of Appeals for the Fifth Circuit correctly observed in *Fisher v. University of Texas* (2011),

> Life experiences differ significantly if a Hispanic student's ethnicity originates in Mexico as opposed to Spain, or, for that matter, any of various Central and South American countries. Likewise, an African-American student whose roots come from Nigeria would be distinct in culture and ethnicity from a student whose ancestry originated in Egypt or Haiti. . . . [Likewise], second-generation students from English, Irish, Scottish, or Australian ancestry would come with very different cultural experiences.

Consequently, the ineluctable linguistic diversity resulting from the arrival of immigrants from different cultures necessitates requiring them to learn English as a "linguistic common ground," if we are to maintain a national cohesiveness. A sure means of destroying and eroding the nation's core values is to fail to demand the linguistic assimilation of immigrants who opt to maintain separate linguistic cultural identities that are in tension with U.S. Society, in order to remain connected to their respective countries of origin.

Consider the case of Flushing, New York, where immigrants speak nearly 120 foreign languages. As reported by Dan Bilefsky for *The New York Times* in 2011, a Chinese American member of the City Council, Peter Koo, himself an immigrant, spearheaded a measure that would mandate that all storefront signs and displays contain at least 60 percent English, or the store owners would face fines. Mr. Koo commented about the unintended consequence of alienating English speakers when immigrants erect business signs in their respective native languages. He further noted the discomfort he would feel if he were to go to a business in New York and the signs were written in a foreign language he did not understand.

It is true that the mere ability to communicate in English does not necessarily mean that cultural assimilation is complete; however, social, political, economic, and intellectual assimilation is not complete without it. Based on the sheer number of Hispanic immigrants in the United States, Spanish is likely, and will continue to be, the second most spoken language in the United States after English; however, English, spoken by about 95 percent of the U.S. population, is not likely to be displaced as the dominant, essential American linguistic culture (King, 1997). Commentator James Fallows made this point in 1983 in an essay in *The Atlantic,* when he noted that even though Spanish will outlive any other alternative language to English, the dominance of English as the de facto mainstream language in the United States was "inescapable."

In addition, there are continuing debates on immigration reform; making English our official language; and recent immigrants' intransigence to linguistic assimilation into the English-speaking culture of the United States. Tom Tancredo, then a member of Congress from Colorado, addressed this intransigence in a speech he gave on cultural assimilation in 2006. He suggested that recent immigrants mainly come for economic advantage, without any desire to disconnect from their previous political, linguistic, or familial cultures, as did those who came through Ellis Island in the early nineteenth century did. Tancredo described this lack of desire to assimilate as "a dangerous thing" to fundamental American values. While this author does not subscribe to some of Tancredo's extreme views on immigration, Tancredo is clearly correct in his assessment that resistance to cultural assimilation is dangerous to both societal cohesion and the potential integration of immigrants into the American "melting-pot," in a way that is beneficial both to the immigrant and the mainstream society.

As these debates on immigration and making English the official language of the United States continue at state and federal levels, legal immigrants with valid immigrant visas and immigrants without valid immigrant visas (commonly called "illegal immigrants") continue to stream into the United States from every corner of the globe in search of economic advantage and physical security, among other reasons. (For simplicity and coherency, despite the legal definition of an "immigrant visa" in Section 101(a)(16) of the United States Immigration and Nationality Act, both legal immigrants who enter the United States with valid "immigrant visas" and those who enter and remain in the country without valid "immigrant visas" will be collectively referred to here as "immigrants.") Unfortunately, the tenor of these debates often devolves into political and ideological rhetoric, steeped in accusations and counteraccusations of sinister motives among those who advocate for or against mandating recent immigrants to learn English as a condition of legal immigration status in the United States. Such a climate of suspicion and political rhetoric masks the existential reality that, if the linguistic diversity of current immigrants continues in combination with immigrant resistance to assimilating into the common language that makes Americans one people, it will undermine the fundamental cohesiveness of American culture in many ways.

Despite the ideological rhetoric common in immigration debates, complete fluency in English is not being asked of immigrants; however, acquiring a certain level of proficiency with the language should be required in order for them to function in an English-speaking culture in a meaningful way. Research quoted by David Solar in a 1990 article in the *Los Angeles Times* indicates that achieving complete fluency in English can require more than 15 years of progressively studying all aspects of the language. Immigrants are not being asked to achieve complete fluency in English, nor are they being asked to abandon their native tongues or completely disconnect from their old cultures. Such a requirement would be a violation of U.S. law. (See, for example, the 1993 EEOC decision in *Garza v. Department of the Army.*) In fact, immigrants should grapple their cultural experiences, including their respective native tongues, to their souls with, to borrow a phrase from Shakespeare, "hoops of steel." At the same time, they should be embracing and learning English, the language of their new culture, in order to both succeed and exchange their respective rich cultural experiences with members of their new host society. Even though the United States is a nation of immigrants, English provides a way for different ethnic groups to communicate and cultivate relationship bonds that engender societal cohesion.

LINGUISTIC ASSIMILATION AND OTHER ASPECTS OF CULTURAL ASSIMILATION

Despite the political and ideological rhetoric surrounding the cultural assimilation of immigrants, the deleterious economic, social, legal, political, civic, health, and safety implications of maintaining separate languages by the various immigrant communities cannot be taken lightly. Some political rhetoricians and pro-immigrant activists may find it extreme to require immigrants to assimilate linguistically in order to become legal permanent residents in the United States. However, if there is no requirement for linguistic assimilation, how can immigrants participate in commerce, discharge their civic rights and obligations, vindicate their legal rights through the legal process, engage in an exchange of ideas with other ethnic groups, or leverage the educational opportunities available to them. Only if they can communicate in the common language of the nation will they be able to do these things.

As noted above, cultural assimilation is multifaceted and interrelated. Immigrants cannot assimilate culturally with just a desire to enjoy the benefits that come with lawful residence in the United States without a parallel desire to fulfill the attendant obligations. The following sections illustrate the reasons that compel mandatory linguistic assimilation of any immigrant who wishes to partake in all the nation has to offer.

Linguistic assimilation and economic and intellectual aspects of culture. Outside a particular immigrant's insular cohort, which may not have the resources to sustain the economic needs of its community, lack of English proficiency can negatively impact upward economic mobility into the mainstream society. Economic prosperity and intellectual development are vital to the survival of individuals and the nation. Without education, a person's economic prosperity is limited; with limited education and limited financial resources, the immigrant becomes a burden on the society by turning to the public fisc for survival. Since university education in the United States is normally conducted in English, immigrants who do not speak English are limited in their ability to leverage the vast educational opportunities that could be instrumental in achieving economic success. It would be detrimental for immigrants who wish to succeed economically and educationally in the United States to circumscribe themselves within self-imposed limits by choosing not to assimilate linguistically.

In fact, even in the international arena, English is the language of business. As Eugene Jackson and Antonio Rubio (1990) point out, French was once the sole language of diplomacy and the preferred foreign language among educated persons in Europe, until it was displaced by English. Today, English is the most useful language for those traveling in

Europe for business or tourism. Therefore, when an immigrant does not assimilate linguistically by learning English that immigrant is likely to be locked into perpetual economic and intellectual underclass status. While every honest labor is admirable and respectable, an immigrant is unlikely to leverage the vast opportunities available in the mainstream employment arena without English. It is difficult to imagine any language other than English dominating the U.S. white-collar labor and employment environment, unless the specific foreign language is a bona fide occupational qualification, such as in the case of foreign-language court interpreters.

Linguistic assimilation and the socio-legal aspects of culture. From a socio-legal perspective, the last thing the United States needs is to create a situation of "benign linguistic neglect," such that the nation's "unity is gravely imperiled by language and ethnic conflicts" (King, 1997). An immigrant's inability to communicate with members of the larger community outside of that immigrant's cohort fosters separateness and stymies cohesion. More importantly, the question arises as to which immigrant community's language should be preferred over others if English is not accepted as the sole national language? Should immigrants who have already learned English as a second language in order to assimilate or integrate into the American linguistic culture be required to learn yet another language that is imposed on them to accommodate a specific immigrant community's desire to remain linguistically separate? The legal implications could mean liability against employers who would deny native-born and other immigrant English speakers employment for a lack of ability to speak a language other than English for profit-driven reasons rather than as a bona fide occupational qualification.

In fact, a group called Concerned Citizens instituted an Internet-driven petition in 2011 titled "End Unfair Treatment of Legal Immigrants" on this issue based on complaints about employment discrimination because of people's inability to speak Spanish. The petition stated the following:

> There are many people who come to America (legally) from countries that are not Spanish speaking. When they get here and learn English, teach their children English, and then lose their jobs due to the fact that they cannot speak Spanish, that is an outrage. If we are not going to require Spanish-speaking people (many of whom are not here legally) to learn English, then we should not be requiring anyone to learn English. It is not fair to require some to learn two new languages, while others never have to learn one. That is discrimination. . . . Either we are an English speaking country, or we are not. It is not fair to pick one Non-English speaking sect of the population over another.

As this petition illustrates, many immigrants come to the United States already equipped with two and in some cases three languages, including English. Some bilingual and trilingual non-Spanish-speaking immigrants complain that they are being marginalized in favor of Spanish-speaking immigrants even after they have learned English in order to assimilate. Consider one of the oft posed questions respecting linguistic cultural assimilation: Why should bilingualism be coterminous with the ability to speak both English and Spanish as opposed to English and any of the various foreign languages spoken by other non-Spanish-speaking immigrant communities? If some immigrants are complaining that they are being marginalized for not speaking Spanish, the potential for interethnic conflict and resentment becomes a reality. The Concerned Citizens petition drives home the point that immigrants must learn English as a "linguistic common ground" in order to engender societal cohesion. In fact, it may constitute unlawful employment discrimination under Title VII of the Civil Rights Act of 1964, as the petitioners correctly point out above, to prefer one linguistic group over another, whether the preferred language is Arabic, French, Spanish, Chinese, or any other.

Although the Concerned Citizens petition targets Spanish speakers, the need to embrace English is not a Hispanics-only problem—it is an assimilation problem. It should be recognized that, according to a 2006 survey conducted by the Pew Hispanic Center, a majority of Hispanic survey participants "believe that immigrants have to speak English to be a part of American society and even more so that English should be taught to the children of immigrants." Of course, based on recent immigration patterns, Spanish-speaking (Hispanic) immigrants numerically overwhelm other immigrant groups who speak first languages other than English; Hispanics are not the only immigrant group who must assimilate linguistically. However, linguistic assimilation of all immigrants would eliminate the potential erosion of societal cohesiveness, which may result from interethnic conflicts. Because of the social disharmony and legal liability that may result from preferring one immigrant group over another, no immigrant should be denied employment on the basis that he or she does not speak an alternative language to English. (Of course, jobs where knowing a language other than English is a bona fide occupational qualification are an exception to this statement.) Moreover, linguistic separatism is antithetical to cultural assimilation and should not be rewarded.

Linguistic assimilation and the political and military aspects of culture. On the political front, the question is: How can a person choose his or her leaders or participate in the electoral process if the person is disconnected from the events that shape his or her environment? In fact, even native-born citizens who lack English proficiency face obstacles in fully participating in the political arena.

Lack of facility with the English language is not only an issue of cultural assimilation. It is also a national security issue, which cannot be masked with political and ideological rhetoric. A strong case can be made that resistance to linguistic assimilation is tantamount to rejection of one's obligations of citizenship. Cultural assimilation, to some, also includes full participation in fulfilling the obligations of citizenship, such as jury duty and voting. These obligations would be impossible for non-English-speaking immigrants to fulfill without facility with the English language. For example, serving on juries often requires missing work and accepting compensation below one's salary. Immigrants who do not speak English are not required to make the same sacrifices in order to fulfill their civic obligations. Should immigrants be exempt from these obligations absent a recognized physical or mental disability or age limitation? It is likely that most Americans would reject any such exemption.

On the military front, military readiness includes the ability to have a fighting force that can communicate in English. Although the U.S. military is a volunteer force, the possibility of a draft is not far-fetched. An immigrant who is not assimilated linguistically cannot be ready to defend the country when duty calls, whether that duty is military service, jury duty, or some other form of public service.

Linguistic assimilation and health and safety considerations. The time-sensitive nature of health and safety emergencies that may arise cannot be effectively and efficiently addressed if the first responders, such as firefighters and police officers, cannot communicate with the victims during critical moments when communication can make the difference between life and death. "If you see something, say something" is a Department of Homeland Security community awareness campaign slogan. But how can a non-English-speaking immigrant say something if he or she sees something but is unable to read the announcement or communicate what is seen due to a language barrier? The health and safety implication of immigrants not learning English affect immigrants, other members of the community, and the nation as a whole. The immigrants and other inhabitants of that community and the nation. The possible dangers include mishandling hazardous materials at places of employment due to the inability to read the labels; driving on roads without understanding traffic signs written in English; becoming a victim of a crime but not being able to help law enforcement officers apprehend the assailant; or endangering children by administering the wrong dosage of prescription medicines due to inability to read the instructions.

In fact, Peter Koo, the member of the New York City Council mentioned earlier, recognized these safety concerns in the legislation he proposed requiring that English be the dominant language on storefront signs. According to Koo, "the legislation was needed so that police officers and firefighters could quickly identify stores in case of an emergency" (Bilefsky, 2001). As another example, if a non-English-speaking immigrant is the victim of a crime, he or she will not be able to help law enforcement officers effectively. If an immigrant is the plaintiff or defendant in a court trial but cannot speak English, it will be difficult to participate in the administration of justice without interpreters to fill the language gap. In a criminal trial context, non-English speakers are exempt from being summoned to perform jury duty due to lack of facility with the English language (Brooks et al., 2005, p. 921).

CONCLUSION

As noted above, arguably, there is no one thing that is identifiable as the "essential American culture." However, in examining the cultural assimilation of immigrants, English is a key embodiments of our nationhood that represents the essential American culture. Based on Quigley's guidepost regarding what constitutes the "culture of a society," it is clear that cultural assimilation of any kind in the United States is impossible without the ability to communicate in English. Therefore, linguistic assimilation is critical if an immigrant is to be deemed to have assimilated into the American melting pot.

No level of political or ideological rhetoric can diminish the fact that when police officers or other first responders are called in times of an emergency, they ought to be able to read the address when they arrive at their destination, and they ought to be able to discharge their duties without the need for interpreters. Because language is the chief embodiment of nationhood, and because a common language engenders societal cohesion, one must question whether the nation should devolve into a chaotic "Tower of Babel" mentality, accommodating every immigrant group that wishes to carve out its own linguistic enclave within the United States without any desire to assimilate or interact with the English-speaking mainstream culture. Should the nation not demand linguistic assimilation from those who consciously choose to come to this country as permanent sojourners, whether for economic advantage or physical security or any other reason? English proficiency should be required as a condition of permanent residency or citizenship for any immigrant who wishes to benefit from the advantages of living in the United States, because it is only the ability to communicate in English that can pave the meaningful cultural assimilation in other aspects of U.S. culture and society.

Those who encourage immigrants, to treat the need to learn and speak English in the United States as adopting an ephemeral medium of communication that would cede its mainstream nature to the person's native language, do a disservice to both the immigrant and the nation. In matters of cultural assimilation, it is the sojourner who should adjust to the linguistic culture of the host, not the host who should adjust to the linguistic culture of the sojourner. This is where the adage, "When in Rome, do as the Romans do," is most apt. As Fallows (1983) points out, "those who do come to the United States are . . . those who have attained the necessary knowledge of America and how to get here, and who have accumulated or been able to borrow the funds they need to pay for their airline tickets or to pay their smugglers." Naturally, therefore, those who emigrate from countries where English is not spoken, but who wish to become an integral part of U.S. society, should not be surprised if they are expected to learn English when they arrive. Cultural assimilation begins when an immigrant can communicate with the members of the mainstream culture of which the immigrant wishes to become an integral part.

References and Further Reading

Arrieta, O. (1994). Language and culture among Hispanics in the United States. In T. Weaver (Ed.), *Handbook of Hispanic cultures in the United States: Anthropology* (pp. 168–190). Houston, TX: Arte Público.

Bayan, R. (n.d.). Bilingualism [Blob post]. Retrieved from http://newmoderate.com/the-issues/bilingualism

Bilefsky, D. (2011, August 1). In neighborhood that's diverse, a push for signs to be less so. *The New York Times.* Retrieved from http://www.nytimes.com/2011/08/02/nyregion/queens-councilman-wants-english-to-dominate-store-signs.html?_r=2

Bower, D., & Bower, C. (n.d.). *Learn Spanish: Why Americans don't.* Retrieved from Language Learning Advisor website: http://www.language-learning-advisor.com/learn-spanish-why-americans-dont.html

Brooks, R. L., Carrasco, G. P., & Selmi, M. (2005). The rights of language minorities. In *Civil rights litigation: Cases and perspectives* (3rd ed.). Durham, NC: Carolina Academic Press.

Childress v. Department of the Air Force, EEOC DOC 01842814, 1986 WL 635306 (July 7, 1986).

Citizenship and Immigration Canada. (2011). *The citizenship test.* Retrieved from http://www.cic.gc.ca/english/citizenship/cit-test.asp

Cooper, H., & Stokes, J. (2008, July). Immigrants should learn English: The U.S. should require people to learn and speak English before they can attain citizenship. Pro or con? *BusinessWeek.* Retrieved from http://www.businessweek.com/debateroom/archives/2008/07/immigrants_shou.html

de Valera, E. (2005). "These were all men": Speech on the fiftieth anniversary of the Easter Rising, 10 April 1966. In *Speeches that changed the world: The stories and transcripts of moments that made history* (pp. 136–139). London, UK: Quercus Publishing.

Deputies should not have to learn Spanish; let immigrants learn English [Letters]. (2009, October 25). *Tampa Bay Times.* Retrieved from http://www.tampabay.com/opinion/letters/deputies-should-not-have-to-learn-spanish-let-immigrants-learn-english/1046711

English Language Unity Act of 2009, H.R. 997, 111th Congress (2009–2010). Retrieved from http://www.govtrack.us/congress/bill.xpd?bill=h111-997

Fallows, J. (1983, November). Immigration: How it's affecting us. *Atlantic Monthly.* Retrieved from http://www.theatlantic.com/magazine/archive/1983/11/immigration/5928/3/?single_page=true

Fisher v. University of Texas, 631 F.3d 213, 256 n.12 (5th Cir. 2011).

Garza v. Department of the Army, EEOC DOC 01924360, 1993 WL 1505080 (October 1993).

Gutierez, G. (2011, June 10). *Texas senator calls Spanish speech "insulting," urges man to speak English.* KHOU 11 News. Retrieved from http://www.khou.com/news/texas-news/Texas-senator-calls-Spanish-speech-insulting-urges-man-to-speak-English-124076709.html

Jackson, E., & Rubio, A. (1990). *French made simple*. New York, NY: Doubleday.

King, R. D. (1997, April). Should English be the law? *The Atlantic Monthly*. Retrieved from http://www.theatlantic.com/past/docs/issues/97apr/english.htm

Lipka, S. (2002, December 11). The battle over bilingual education. *The Atlantic Monthly*. Retrieved from http://www.theatlantic.com/past/docs/unbound/flashbks/bilingual.htm

Lopez, R. (2009, April). "U.S. Hispanics need to learn to speak English!" Says who? [Blog post]. Retrieved from http://www.latinoopinion.com/2009/04/%E2%80%9Cus-hispanics-need-to-learn-to-speak-english%E2%80%9D-says-who/

Nevaer, L. E. V. (n.d.). *"Hispanic" versus "Latino" versus "Latin."* Retrieved from Hispanic Economics website: http://www.hispaniceconomics.com/overviewofushispanics/hispaniclatinolatin.html

Pew Hispanic Center. (2006, June 7). *Hispanic attitudes toward learning English* [Fact Sheet]. Retrieved from http://pewhispanic.org/files/factsheets/20.pdf

Pew Hispanic Center. (2010, April 29). *Hispanics and Arizona's new immigration law*. Retrieved from http://pewresearch.org/pubs/1579/arizona-immigration-law-fact-sheet-hispanic-population-opinion-discrimination

Quigley, C. (1966). *Tragedy and hope: A history of the world in our time*. New York, NY: Macmillan.

Solar, D. (1990, November 23). Immigrants learn the write stuff at UC's ESL classes. *Los Angeles Times*. Retrieved from http://articles.latimes.com/print/1990-11-23/local/me-5024_1_esl-class

Tancredo, T. (2006, October 27). Immigration and "cultural assimilation" (Speech given at Tattered Cover Bookstore, Denver, Colorado). Retrieved from http://www.youtube.com/watch?v=ZSTdGC4z6io

Torrens, C. (2011, May 11). Some immigrants forced to learn Spanish. *Associated Press*. Retrieved from http://www.nwherald.com/2011/05/28/some-immigrants-forced-to-learn-spanish/ama661b/

Valette J.-P., & Valette, R. M. (1989). *Contacts: Langue et culture françaises* (4th ed.). Boston, MA: Houghton Mifflin.

Morris I. Onyewuchi

Social and Political Integration

POINT: Immigrants are attracted by the core American principles of democracy, religious freedom, the rule of law, and the protection of the rights of the individual, but political and social integration occur gradually over time. Today's immigrants are integrating into American society just as earlier generations did.

Francisco J. Alatorre, New Mexico State University

COUNTERPOINT: Many contemporary immigrants come from countries with political, social, and religious traditions that are at odds with American society. Further, the diversity of immigrants' countries of origins and their attendant cultural differences result in fragmented communities and strain social and political cohesion. These strains are exacerbated by the reality that immigrants tend to cluster in communities with fellow immigrants and often have difficulty integrating into mainstream American society.

Francisco J. Alatorre, New Mexico State University

Introduction

The question of whether immigrants are integrating into American society has been a topic of public controversy in recent years. This controversy is fostered by the extent and diversity of current immigration. In this regard, there is an important distinction between private cultural practices and the social and political ideals that define American society. Public civic principles and ideals such as freedom of speech, freedom of religion, separation of church and state, freedom of the press, freedom from unreasonable search and seizure, equal protection under the law, and so forth, are enshrined in the U.S. Constitution, and a body of laws and practices give definition to these principles that govern U.S. society. This legal framework shapes public social and political life in myriad ways, and immigrant social and political integration means adopting these various social and political practices in a public arena as part of a broader process of coming to "belong" and of being accepted as "belonging."

Adjusting oneself to these social norms does not necessarily mean abandoning one's private cultural practices. The United States has a long history of absorbing many different cultures, and there is evidence of this absorption throughout the country—from Chinese New Year's parades in San Francisco, to people of Swedish heritage in Wisconsin lighting candles at Advent and honoring a white-clad Lucia with a crown of candles in her hair, to people of Mexican heritage in Arizona celebrating El Día de los Muertos. These private cultural practices can easily coexist with integration into American political and social life in the public sphere. Of course, some cultural practices, such as polygamy or honor killings, are directly at odds with specific American civic and political ideals, and in these cases assimilation requires abandoning them. But in the vast majority of situations, immigrant integration relates to public social and civic virtues rather than private practices.

Having said all of this, immigrant integration is fundamentally about acquiring a sense of "belonging" and of being accepted as such. This is a complex process, and the receiving community is not neutral in this. How immigrants are welcomed by Americans matters to their integration. If there is widespread hostility to immigrants (say, as a result of illegal immigration that catches all Hispanic immigrants in its wake), this works against both sides of the "belonging" equation.

Communications technology, together with relatively inexpensive travel that allows immigrants to stay in close touch with social networks in their countries of origin (their "imagined communities"), can undermine social integration in the face of an unwelcoming reception in the United States.

The reality of hostility to illegal immigration and illegal status itself, for those who have it, complicates the nature of the "welcome" to Hispanic immigrants, which, in turn, complicates their integration to society. Hostility can result in a cultural and ethnic "banding together" that can appear to be a resistance to integration to broader society when it is, in fact, self-protective. But even if this "banding together" results in more overtly holding to cultural practices, it does not necessarily mean failure to adopt the public civic and social ideals that define being "American." The distinction between private cultural practices and public civic and social ideals is important.

In the case of low-skilled illegal immigration, poverty (class issues) and illegal status combine to complicate the process of integration. If poverty and illegal status affect children's educational success and levels of educational attainment, full integration to society of this population will take longer across generations.

The Point essay below offers a quantitative and qualitative study of immigrant families living and working in Maricopa County, Arizona, to determine their level of integration. All of these families came to the United States primarily to seek a better life rather than for political reasons or the pursuit of personal or emotional freedom. These families' lives in the United States were made difficult by the downturn of the economy and police and legal pressure, but the difficulties they faced instilled in them an understanding of the value of education and the power of the economic opportunities around them. Their integration, the author concludes, is ongoing as they continue to learn English, work, pay taxes, and seek improvement for themselves and their children.

The Counterpoint essay, through a study of nine undocumented families receiving assistance from a faith-based organization, examines the various threats to resiliency that immigrant families must endure in a new country. Resiliency is defined as the degree to which people are productive and healthy despite hardships, traumas, and obstacles in their environment. Sometimes threats to resiliency are successfully endured, but not always. This essay argues that many contemporary immigrants come from countries with political, social, and religious traditions that are at odds with American society, and that these immigrants do not necessarily seek social and political integration as previous generations did. Instead they cluster in communities in which they may adapt and live, allowing the cultural differences that separate them from mainstream American society to intensify their already difficult situations. This state of affairs leads to broken families, educational underachievement, social and political isolation, acculturation issues, and segregation from the host society, as well as fosters hatred, resentment, and hostility on both sides.

POINT

Immigrants to the United States seek not only accommodation with but also integration into the country's social, political, and cultural values. According to the Pew Research Center, in 2009 a "record 12.7 million Mexican immigrants lived in the United States, a 17-fold increase since 1970; Mexicans now account for 32% of all immigrants living in this country." Research has found, both quantitatively and qualitatively, that Hispanic immigrants living and working in Maricopa County, Arizona, seek to find a place in mainstream society by working, sending their children to school, learning English, learning computer skills, and taking advantage of opportunities offered by relief agencies and the government (Marsiglia et al., 2002). These immigrants find the strength and resiliency to adapt and persevere by means of their own cultural heritage, "symbolic interaction" with the host society, and the concept of the "imagined community."

Twenty-first-century immigrants integrate into the American society because they are attracted by core American principles, such as democracy, religious freedom, rule of law, and protection of the rights of the individual. The desire for integration is observed in the "gestures" immigrants make toward the mainstream society, such as working hard, paying taxes, and taking care of children and sending them to school. These gestures toward the host society are created and fostered by the immigrants' resiliency, which is defined and measured by the degree to which people are productive and healthy despite hardships, traumas, and obstacles in their environment. Resiliency in this sense is determined partly by the following factors: (1) the family context, (2) a strong sense of cultural identity, (3) notions of an "imagined community," and (4) gestures of "symbolic interaction."

The family provides cultural transmission of values, beliefs, traditions, and practices that are passed from elders to children. The generally healthy, supportive immigrant family may proffer protection from risk. Yvonne Kingon and Ann O'Sullivan (2001) note that open family communication can be an asset by offering expressions of concern for all the members of the family. Moreover, members of families with better communication are more likely to resist depression than those in families with poor communication. Also, the higher the level of family cohesion, the less likely adolescents are to exhibit distress or deviance (Kumper, Karo, Olds, Alexander, Zucker, & Gary, 1998). Marsiglia et al. (2002) describe the family context as a protective factor, noting that among Hispanic immigrants, familism is an important source of resiliency. The family of origin is of primary importance, even after marriage. Hispanic families tend to have strong family pride, family closeness, respect for parents, and a sense of mutual obligation, trust, and cohesion. Traditional Mexican norms, such as parental monitoring and involvement with children, as well as the tendency of married couples to settle close to their parents and other family members, provide children with a greater number of caring adults and a more cohesive community. Despite the challenges associated with immigration and acculturation, family context remains a vital factor in resiliency.

Although this may seem counterintuitive, a strong sense of cultural identity helps when seeking integration. Immigrant families, both with and without legal documentation, frequently exert greater protectiveness over their family members as they seek to protect their cultural integrity. Rosario Ceballo (2004) has established that despite general trends in the underachievement of racial minority youths, some children from impoverished immigrant families do succeed against the odds. Adolescents are motivated to do well in school by a sense of obligation to repay their immigrant parents for the sacrifices the parents made in coming to the United States (Bacallo & Smokowski, 2007). A Mexican family's cultural traditions and practices give family members a cultural identity and sense of belonging based on a sense of *nosotros* (we-ness) that comes from having common values, beliefs, and traditions (Castro, Boyer, & Balcazar, 1998). In many immigrant families, religious beliefs and their own unique practices contribute to a strong sense of family unity, which involves family identification, attachments, obligations, and loyalty (Castro et al., 1998). Such cultural factors give families and individuals the strength and confidence to seek integration.

More abstract resources for resiliency include the "imagined community" and gestures toward "symbolic interaction" with the host or dominant society. Benedict Anderson's classic work, *Imagined Communities* (1983; revised 2006), examines the creation and global spread of "imagined communities of nationality." Although Anderson does not specifically address the case of the immigrant, his reflections detail how a communal sense of people allegiant to a nation, itself an abstract entity, binds people in a deep horizontal comradeship that transcends the truly imaginary borders that separate nation from nation and creates distinct national identities. The community that Anderson defines is "imagined" because "members of even the smallest nation will never know most of their fellow-members, meet them, or even hear of them, yet in the minds of each lives the image of their communion." In this way, a nation (which is truly a concept), with borders defined by lines on a map, becomes a community because the people dwelling within it know they belong to this community. This belief, as Anderson writes, "makes it possible . . . for so many millions of people, not so much to kill, as willingly to die for such limited imaginings" (p. 7).

Immigrants who have disengaged from their original imagined community in order to try to live in another learn that crossing a border is not a simple physical act, but also a conceptual one, with both physical and abstract consequences. Moreover, their imagined community of success in the United States is frequently challenged, if not shattered. Nonetheless, this idea of an imagined community can prove to be a positive force for immigrants. They can be encouraged to imaginatively reach out to other members of their community—that is, the community of immigrants from the same country living in the United States—and see themselves as a nation of sorts, bound together by language, general background, customs, beliefs, experiences (such as legally or illegally crossing a border), religion, and even the familial, domestic, and political challenges that test their resiliency. To a degree, this community exists in physical reality, as immigrants contact each other through social service agencies, e-mail, work, and neighborhoods. This is the foundation of the full extent of an imagined community that gives people a sense of identity, a set of objectives, and the emotional resources to keep going.

Leo R. Chavez, in "The Power of the Imagined Community: The Settlement of Undocumented Mexicans and Central Americans in the United States" (1994), seeks a sense of community that contributes to the immigrant's decision to pass from "sojourning" to "settling" in the United States. He reflects on "how immigrants perceive their relationships to the communities in which they live; and . . . the relative importance of the imagined community on the intentions of the immigrants to stay in the United States" (p. 52). Chavez feels that a sense of fixed community has receded in the twentieth century, as travel and media have dissolved certain barriers. Instead, he believes that migrants have the ability to "develop feelings of belonging to multiple communities"—feelings that don't depend on physical locations. Immigrants can belong to two communities at once, as is the case with members of the Aguililla community living in Redwood City, California. "Immigrants from Mexico and Central Americans," Chavez argues, "can, and often do, develop social linkages, cultural sentiments, and economic ties that result in imagining themselves to be part of their communities in the United States" (p. 56). The immigrants Chavez profiles in his study feel themselves to belong to some kind of community. This feeling arises from adaptation to, or at least from becoming accustomed to, a sense of concern about the immediate community, and about the country. Whatever the source of this feeling, Chavez does not call it resiliency but rather a feeling of belonging: "Feeling like you are part of the community appears to be related to overcoming feelings of isolation, developing a network of family and friends in the local community, acquiring local cultural knowledge, and reconciling yourself to the possible threat of becoming unsuccessful in the United States" (p. 62).

Some immigrants gain a sense of belonging to a community by having "paid their dues" in one way or another. Other links come from a shared heritage, either recent (immigration from Mexico and Central America for either political or social reasons) or at a distance, such as the rich history of Latinos in the American Southwest. Chavez concludes, "Although some segments of the larger society may like to imagine immigrants to be rootless, unattached, and temporary residents in U.S. society, the evidence here suggests many immigrants perceive themselves as part of the community and intend to become . . . permanent settlers" (p. 68). Notably, for the immigrant families considered in this work, legal immigration status "is but one of many factors contributing to a migrant's sense of belonging to a community" (p. 68).

This mental conceptualization of an imagined community (and seeking accommodation with another imagined community) can be strengthened and made practical by means of the fourth quality, that of "symbolic interaction." Interaction is the foundation "out of which human beings and their conduct originate" (Adler & Adler, 1980, p. 40). The human being is an "actor" and, as an actor, is a "perceptive creature," both within the world and within himself or herself. Human beings are capable of reflecting on their actions, reassessing their actions, and constantly adjusting their behavior. "Human beings, as highly complex organisms, continually re-assess their situation and behave as best they can in a world that cannot be depended upon to remain simple and constant . . . instead of reacting, the individual puts forward lines of action that amount to instant innovations" (Adler & Adler, 1980, p. 40).

Sandstrom, Martin, and Fine's *Symbols, Selves, and Social Reality* (2006) is particularly insightful about how the outsider, or the sidelined person in a community, can make symbolic gestures toward the dominant society in order to deal with it, survive, and make some kind of sense of objects, groups, events, and structures. The authors write about symbolic interaction in terms that human beings act toward things on the basis of the meanings those things have for them, and that meaning is derived from social interaction. The meaning of things is not inherent; it is a social construct, and thus depends on the environment, the situation, and, of course, the individual's interpretation. Social definitions therefore guide people's actions. However, the individual does not make or reflect actions—rather, "when we find ourselves in a situation, we must decide which of the many things present in that situation are relevant.... Moreover we must figure out which of the many meanings that can be attributed to a thing which are the appropriate ones in this context" (p. 8). This is not always easy, and "when we find ourselves in some situations, particularly new and ambiguous, we discover that no established meanings apply. As a result, we must be flexible enough to learn or devise new meanings" (p. 8).

In Marko Valenta's "Immigrants' Identity Negotiation and Coping with Stigma in Different Relational Frames" (2009) the author considers the case of Bosnian and Iraqi immigrants in Norway, whose circumstances and responses to circumstances parallel those of Hispanic immigrants in the United States. With his focus on how they seek integration into the prevailing society, Valenta studies how immigrants deal with exclusion by impression management, passing and covering, and "disidentifiers." He writes that "the primary focus of this study is on the meanings immigrants themselves attach to different interactions and relationships." He seeks out not only the steps the immigrants take to interact more successfully, but also why such steps are taken. Immigrants project "dynamic integration strategies to manage and construct new identities that can help them deal with chronic and acute discrimination" (p. 354).

The strategies Valenta examines included the ones mentioned above, but certain strategies are of particular relevance to the Hispanic immigrant, such as "passing," and showing by their behavior that the host citizens' stereotyped conceptions are wrong. Another particularly relevant observation that Valenta makes is how immigrants create and maintain a hybrid identity, and thus "juggle" minority and majority behavior. Valenta quotes a 2001 study by Brekke, who observes that migrants may also fight stigma by separating their ethnic identity from other immigrants. Valenta describes how a Bosnian woman was embarrassed when in the company of other Bosnians, whose inept actions could "be ascribed to a shared cultural background" (p. 367). In other words, she felt tarred by the same brush by her collective identity with all other Bosnians. Such immigrants "are anxious that the team's performance may disturb and undermine each individual's self-presentation" and they seek ways of compensating. In the cases described below, undocumented immigrants seek to mimic the values of the majority: they work hard, send their children to school, and try to avoid all contact with police. This is more than mere self-identifying behavior, because such symbolic interaction maintains households, ensures children's future, and reduces possibilities of trouble.

To summarize, there are four factors by which one can more sensitively consider the strengths of the immigrant seeking integration into the host society: resiliency, cultural identity, the concept of "imagined community," and symbolic interaction. All contribute to an intensely human process by which individuals thrust into different circumstances continually alters themselves while maintaining an identity, which helps immigrants seek closer integration within the mainstream society.

METHODOLOGY

For this study, a mixed-method approach, combining quantitative and qualitative approaches, was used to carry out the ethnographic research, because it deals with human beings facing difficult circumstances. Quantitative methodology is characterized by being objective and assertive, but is at the same time cold. However, qualitative means alone may be too subjective. Therefore, a mixed-method is best suited to this type of study, because this approach takes advantage of both the representativeness and generalizablity of quantitative findings and the in-depth, contextual nature of qualitative findings (Hanson et al., 2005). Simply stated, a mixed-methods approach allows both methodologies to complement each other.

The intent of quantitative analysis is to descriptively summarize the participant characteristics in order to understand the population being analyzed and gain insight into key variables that could help provide a more effective interpretation of the qualitative results. In this case, measures of central tendency and dispersion were used to summarize continuous data, and measures of frequency were used to summarize categorical data. The population in this quantitative design was located in Maricopa County, Arizona, and the participants were drawn from a group of first-generation Hispanic immigrants who received social services from a faith-based agency during the year 2009. This group belonged to a program intended to assist families with housing and other financial assistance, as well with financial literacy classes, English classes, computer classes, and legal assistance with immigration issues. The research design took into account socioeconomic factors relevant to the study, including income status (family income), level of education, and composition of the household (e.g., family size, single-parent family, or both parents in the household). Also considered were any relevant risk characteristics, such as criminal records (e.g., parole or probation) and family welfare system records (e.g., Department of Economic Security, or federal assistance), which were accessed through the archival data from the agencies' files (Flay et al., 2005). This population was chosen due to the convenience of the researcher having access to the files.

This design used a qualitative sample of nine undocumented families drawn from a relevant program from a faith-based organization. This program, developed with the intention of promoting resiliency among undocumented immigrant families in the United States, was composed of these nine participant families, so there was no need for sampling. The qualitative analysis was conducted by naturalistic perspective, as described by Sandstrom et al. (2003). In the second stage of the qualitative analysis, a systematic inspection of the substantive data, created by interviews, structured the exploration and analysis in four sections: a description of the family; the reasons and motivations for the family to cross the border into the United States; a description of a typical day in their lives; and specific issues and obstacles that they confront. The narrative concluded with their thoughts about the recent enforcement of immigration laws. The conclusions of the qualitative analysis sought to develop generalizations, as described by Wengraf (2001), of the common threads of resiliency and the common threats of problematic situations, which include personal and political issues.

ANALYSIS AND DISCUSSION OF RESULTS OF THE QUANTITATIVE STUDY

The intent of the quantitative analysis was to create a descriptive overview of the participant characteristics in order to understand the population and recognize key variables that could help provide a more effective interpretation of the qualitative results. Any missing values encountered in the data were excluded by deleting cases from the analysis of the variable on which they had missing values.

The participant characteristics in the sample included the following *categorical* variables: sex, employment status, source of income, felony offense, drug and alcohol addiction, domestic abuse, assistance variables, skill-building variables, level of English, and mode of transportation. Frequency measures (n and percent) were used to summarize the distribution of the data across the various categories. The participant characteristics in the sample also included the following *continuous* variables: age, level of education, monthly income, years living in the United States, and number of individuals in the household. The mean and standard deviation were used to summarize the central tendency and dispersion of these data. To perform cross-tabulations, these continuous variables were transformed into categorical variables.

Table 26.1 shows a summary of the participant characteristics. Continuous variables that were transformed into categorical variables are shown in italics.

The population of participants in this research (see Table 26.1) was on average approximately 35 years old, had an average level of education of sixth grade, and had an average monthly income of approximately $1,220 for an average household size of four. The majority were females (68%), a small proportion were employed full-or part-time (31%), and only 14 percent received welfare aid as a source of their income. These findings suggest that a typical profile for a first-generation Hispanic worker who seeks social services in Maricopa County, Arizona, is a young adult with no more than elementary school education, has a family of four, and struggles to find a job but earns less than the federal poverty line of $22,050 (in 2009).

From the population of participants (see Table 26.1), only a small proportion acknowledged having a felony offense (18%) or suffering from drug or substance addictions (14%) or domestic abuse (33%). Since this is self-reported data, it is possible that these findings underrepresent reality. Interestingly, the majority of the participants requested assistance with securing identification (75%) as well as help with medical (95%), financial (99%), immigration (99%), identity (99%), and transportation (98%) costs. In addition, the vast majority of participants also requested assistance with skill-building classes, such as computer (100%), English as a second language (99%), and parenting (99%) classes. These findings seem to indicate that first-generation Hispanic immigrant workers who seek social services in Maricopa County have a resolute desire to improve. They probably see this improvement as a means to upgrade the sometimes mistaken perceptions of others, and to help them ultimately succeed in this country. The fact that only a small proportion of the participants requested assistance for mortgage or rent (15%), clothing (12%), school (26%), and finding a safe place to sleep (11%), seems to indicate that these needs are, for the most part, satisfied. This perhaps reflects the more collective (versus individualistic) idiosyncrasy of Hispanics, among whom groups of individuals help each other with the basic needs for housing.

Table 26.1 Participant characteristics

Demographic	**N=100**
Age—mean (SD)	35.2 (9.1) range: 18–78
Age-group—no. (%)	
-Young adult (<40 years)	73 (73%)
-Older adult (≥40 years)	27 (27%)
Sex—no. (%)	
-Male	32 (32%)
-Female	68 (68%)
Socioeconomic	**N=100**
Level of education—mean (SD)	6.0 (2.9) range: 2–12
Education-group—no. (%)	
-Elementary (≤6th grade)	65 (65%)
-Middle/high (>6th grade)	35 (35%)
Employment status—no. (%)	
-Full/Part-time	31 (31%)
-No/Seasonal	69 (69%)
Monthly income—mean (SD)	1220.3 (556.7) range: 0–3000
Income-group—no. (%)	
-Low (<$1000)	42 (42%)
-Medium/high (≥$1000)	58 (58%)
Source of income—no. (%)	
-Work	86 (86%)
-Welfare/aid	14 (14%)
Risk	**N=100**
Felony offense (Yes)—no. (%)	18 (18%)
Drug test (Yes)—no. (%)	95 (95%)
Drug/alcohol addiction (Yes)—no. (%)	14 (14%)
Domestic abuse (Yes)—no. (%)	33 (33%)
Assistance	**N=100** (exceptions noted)
Help with medical issues (Yes)—no. (%)	95 (95%)
Financial assistance (Yes)—no. (%)	99 (99%)
Help with getting identification (Yes)—no. (%)	75 (75%)
Immigration legal assistance (Yes)—no. (%)	98 (99%) **N=99**
Help with creating identity in U.S. (Yes)—no. (%)	99 (99%)
Help with mortgage or rent (Yes)—no. (%)	15 (15%)
Help with clothing (Yes)—no. (%)	12 (12%)
Help with school issues (Yes)—no. (%)	25 (26%) **N=98**
Help finding safe place to sleep (Yes)—no. (%)	11 (11%)
Help with bus pass or gas money (Yes)—no. (%)	98 (98%)
Skill-building	**N=100**
Help with parenting skills (Yes)—no. (%)	99 (99%)
Help with computer classes (Yes)—no. (%)	100 (100%)
Help with English classes (Yes)—no. (%)	99 (99%)

Table 26.1 (continued)	
Acculturation	**N=100**
Level of English—no. (%)	
-None	40 (40%)
-Some	23 (23%)
-Regular/Fluent	37 (37%)
Years living in the US—mean (SD)	5.8 (3.1) range: 1–15
Duration-group—no. (%)	
-Short (≤3 years)	25 (25%)
-Long (>3 years)	75 (75%)
Household and Transportation	**N=100** (exceptions noted)
No. individuals in household—mean (SD)	4.2 (1.4) range: 2–8 **N=99**
Household-size-group—no. (%)	
-Small (≤4 people)	62 (63%)
-Large (>4 people)	37 (37%)
Mode of transportation—no. (%)	
-Car	97 (97%)
-Bus	3 (3%)

The majority of the participants also had no or very limited knowledge of English (63%), despite an average duration in the United States of almost 6 years. This may be a function of the profile of individuals who come to faith-based social service agencies seeking help. It can also reflect that, over time, individuals get exposed to norms and customs of the new culture but continue to struggle with the English language. This lack of command of the English language likely accentuates incorrect perceptions of others and contributes to exclusion and criminalization patterns that form a vicious cycle which perhaps only immigrant resiliency and citizen education efforts can break.

In summary, the major findings of this mixed approach are the following: data reveal that immigrants do not fit a general media-created profile of a criminal population seeking welfare. Most are working and seek to learn English and computer skills and attend parenting classes, revealing a desire to improve in skills both inside and outside the home. A lesser percentage request help with rent, clothing, and food; a higher percentage request assistance with identification and transportation. The statistics overall reveal a population that is more interested in seeking assistance for personal and family safety, that wishes to improve itself, and for the most part avoids criminal activities. This profile, created by statistics, will be more thoroughly examined and understood by means of the analysis of case histories of nine undocumented immigrant families.

RESULTS OF THE QUALITATIVE STUDY

The nine families that were interviewed have highly similar experiences, concerns, and acts of resiliency that allow them to survive in the United States. These families clearly demonstrate that there is no such thing as a "typical" immigrant currently residing in the United States. Their backgrounds, reasons for coming to the United States, personal and social experiences, family composition and unity, and reasons to seek integration can all differ.

One of the women interviewed reported a history of prior contact with the United States. The woman's father successfully entered and reentered the United States over a period of years. Each time he found work and then returned home after the work was finished. The money her father brought back from the United States then assisted other families in their pueblo. The daughter and her husband decided to immigrate to the United States for monetary reasons. They made a 10-year plan, which involved making money and then returning to Mexico to open businesses. They chose Phoenix over Los Angeles and for a while were successful, but the economic downturn forced them to change their plans and demonstrated the need for integration. Yet they seem to be successfully persisting and surviving despite their disappointments.

One reason for this may be that the woman feels an emotional kinship with the United States because her father had been successful here. Their decision to remain in the United States may be more a financial than a political one, but they have remained and seek a degree of integration by improving their language and computer skills. In addition, their son is an A+ student in school, and perhaps they sense that his future lies in the United States.

Another fairly similar story is that of a family whose border crossing was expedited by a grandmother being a United States citizen. Her daughter, who was already divorced and is apparently an extremely capable worker, brought three children with her. Lacking an education, she engages in heavy physical work, and she wants to become a painter. Though living in somewhat difficult circumstances, the family helps and supports each other: the grandmother looks after the children and the house, and the older son has a job. Family relations seem cordial despite many stresses. The mother, despite having troubles with the law regarding drug possession, is confident enough to think about starting her own business here in the United States. The family may have had a strong sense of "belonging" in the United States, despite the illegal status of most family members, because of this woman's mother's previous experiences of being in the United States in the "Bracero program" and being a citizen. This woman seems to seek "freedom" in the United States, engaging in work that might not be considered appropriate for a woman in Mexico. Dedicated to integrating, she seeks help for her legal problems, sends her children to school, and looks forward to opening her own painting business.

There are three particularly strong examples of women and their families seeking integration following failed marriages. Their "symbolic gestures" toward the mainstream society are different from those made by most men. These women see little future back in Mexico, and they seem to realize they must become part of the host society to benefit their children—and possibly themselves. The women have self-perception issues caused by husbands who abused or abandoned them. One of the women interviewed endured an abusive 20-year marriage that ended on a bizarre note. Then an attempted new alliance went sour when the boyfriend deserted her, leaving her with an enormous mortgage. She is close to her children, however, and commits herself to them by being the breadwinner, but she also seeks outside sources to assist her, particularly counseling, which helps her with self-doubts and fears. She is improving her English, learning computer skills, and improving her reading and writing, which gives her more skills and the confidence to realize that her future lies in integration.

Yet another woman has found personal power in seeking to make it on her own following her failing marriage. Though she and her two children are living in an office space rather than a conventional apartment, she declares it is "good enough" and works hard to support her children. She also takes advantage of available resources by sending her son to a neighborhood Head Start program. She is planning to learn about adolescent and teenage issues before her children enter these difficult years. This desire is perhaps inspired by her brother-in-law, who finds help at Alcoholics Anonymous rather than dealing with his alcoholism on his own.

Another woman's husband left her, but he continues to seek sexual favors by paying bills for her. The woman feels like a prostitute, but she persists by working, sending her children to school, and counseling them on their own future relationships. Another woman is unmarried and has children from several fathers. Social service providers detected her stress and recommended counseling and therapy, which she took advantage of, and she has begun to regain a degree of calm and control.

In these cases of undocumented Hispanic women, all made a unique symbolic gesture toward the mainstream society. In doing so, they alleviated embedded cultural notions that women are to be dominated and protected, and they sought a degree of independence and personal freedom in the United States, which offers a relatively more accepting atmosphere for the unmarried or divorced woman.

DISCUSSION

Qualitative and quantitative results indicate that many immigrants, despite problems and hardships, seek integration within the mainstream society. The quantitative results help confirm the outcomes of the qualitative results. For instance, the quantitative study found that most recent immigrants in the United States seek integration by searching for work, seeking improvement with English and computer skills, and avoiding criminal activities. Such motivations do not clearly indicate that immigrants are seeking the political and social ideals of the United States. That said, their desire to live peaceably within U.S. society, and to contribute by working and paying taxes, indicates that they appreciate a country that idealizes principles of democracy, freedom of religion, and the rule of law. Moreover, the immigrant community profiled in this study seeks integration for various reasons, ranging from monetary reasons to personal desires for freedom and independence. This is particularly notable among the Hispanic women who at first were forced to seek their own way, and then came to enjoy, or at least appreciate, the greater degree of independence they achieved.

In summary, the immigrants depicted in this essay did not necessarily come to the United States seeking a new society for their political beliefs or personal and emotional freedom. In all nine cases, the prospect of a better life (jobs, home-owning, luxury items) seems to have been the first attraction, but subsequent living in the United States—sometimes a result of the downturn of the economy and police and legal pressure—has underscored the attraction of education, more opportunities, and, for women, the chance to live in a less male-dominated society. Their integration, which in most cases has not been pursued systematically, is still being pursued as they learn the language, work, pay taxes, and seek improvement for themselves and for their children. Their paths may not be deliberate, but their integration continues as they live and work in the United States.

REFERENCES AND FURTHER READING

Adler, P. A., & Adler, P. (1980). The gloried self. *Social Psychology Quarterly, 52*(4), 229–310.

Anderson, B. (2006). *Imagined communities.* London, UK: Verso.

Bacallo, M. L., & Smokowski, P. R. (2007). The cost of getting ahead: Mexican family system changes after immigration. *Family Relations, 56*(1), 52–66.

Blumer, H. (1969). *Symbolic interactionism: Perspective and method.* Englewood Cliffs, NJ: Prentice Hall.

Castro, F. G., & Alarcon, H. E. (2002). Integrating cultural variables into drug abuse prevention and treatment with racial/ethnic minorities. *Journal of Drug Issues, 32*(3), 783–810.

Castro, F. G., Boyer R. G., & Balcazar, H. G. (1998). Healthy adjustments in Mexican American and other Hispanic adolescents. In R. Montemayor, G. R. Adams, & T. P. Gullota (Eds.), *Adolescent diversity in ethnic, economic and cultural context* (pp. 141–178). Thousand Oaks, CA: Sage.

Ceballo, R. (2004). From barrios to Yale: The role of parenting strategies in Latino families. *Hispanic Journal of Behavioral Sciences, 26*(2), 171–186.

Chavez, L. (1994). The power of the imagined community: The settlement of undocumented Mexicans and Central Americans in the United States. *American Anthropologist, 96*(1), 52–73.

Flay, B. R., Biglan, A., Boruch, F., Castro, F. G., Gottfredson, D., Kellam, S., Mosciki, E. K., Schinke, S., Valentine, J. C., & Ji, P. (2005). Standards of evidence: Criteria for efficacy, effectiveness and dissemination. *Prevention Science, 6*(3), 151–175.

Hanson, W. E., Creswell, J. W., Clark, V. L. P., & Creswell, J. D. (2005). Mixed methods research designs in counseling psychology. *Journal of Counseling Psychology, 52*(2), 224–235.

Kingon, Y. S., & O'Sullivan, A. L. (2001). The family as a protective asset in adolescent development. *Journal of Holistic Nursing, 19*(2), 102–121.

Kumpfer, K. L., Karo, L., Olds, D. L., Alexander, J. F., Zucker, R. A., & Gary, L. E. (1998). Family etiology of youth problems. In R. S. Ashery, E. B. Robertson, & K. L. Kumpfer (Eds.), *Drug abuse prevention through family interventions* (NIDA Research Monograph No. 177, pp. 42–76). Washington, DC: U.S. Government Printing Office. Retrieved from http://archives.drugabuse.gov/pdf/mono graphs/monograph177/042-077_Kumpfer.pdf

Marsiglia, F. F., Miles B. W., Dustman, P., & Sills, S. (2002). Ties that protect: An ecological perspective on Latino/a urban pre-adolescent drug use. *Journal of Ethnic and Cultural Diversity in Social Work, 11*(3/4), 191–220.

Pew Research Center. (2009, April 15). *Mexican immigrants in the United States, 2008* (Fact Sheet). Retrieved from Pew Hispanic Center website: http://www.pewhispanic.org/2009/04/15/mexican-immigrants-in-the-united-states-2008

Sandstrom, K., Martin, D., & Fine, G. A. (2006). *Symbols, selves and social reality: A symbolic interactionist approach to social psychology and sociology* (2nd ed.) Los Angeles, CA: Roxbury.

Valenta, M. (2009). Immigrants' identity negotiation and coping with stigma in different relational frames. *Symbolic Interaction, 32*(4), 351–371.

Wengraf, T. (2001). Concepts and approaches to depth interviewing. In T. Wengraf (Ed.), *Qualitative research interviewing* (pp. 1–60). Thousand Oaks, CA: Sage.

Francisco J. Alatorre

COUNTERPOINT

Many contemporary immigrants come from countries with political, social, and religious traditions that make it difficult to adapt to American society. For instance, recent immigrants do not necessarily seek social and political integration, as perhaps former generations did, but they nevertheless seek to cluster in communities in which they may adapt and live. Cultural differences between communities of recent immigrants and mainstream American society exacerbate an already difficult situation leading to broken families, isolation, segregation, health threats, and so on.

The aim here is to describe the various threats to resiliency that immigrant families must endure. For today's immigrants, continual threats to resiliency divert or ruin their ideas of success and possible integration into mainstream society. To understand the critical aspect of resiliency and how the lack of it threatens integration into mainstream society, the ecological risk and resiliency approach will be used. Such an approach indicates that "risk factors" influence behavioral outcomes.

Resiliency is defined and measured by the degree to which people are productive and healthy despite hardships, traumas, and obstacles in their environment. Individual and family resiliency, which is critical to the immigrant's survival when living in an environment of risk, is created and built by personal attributes and influenced by cultural factors (Marsiglia et al., 2002). Certain risks derail resiliency, though both strengths and risks can come from the same source. Researchers studying family structure have discovered contradictory and inconsistent findings on the effects of family function. Much of their work is based on the recognition that a structured family cannot be a proxy for effectiveness, and that a more traditional or normative family structure is no guarantee of an emotionally healthy, well-supervised family environment (Amey & Albrecht, 1998; Castro et al., 1998).

If there is no guarantee of how an emotionally healthy family develops, then it is important to look at specific patterns of risk that reduce resiliency. For instance, immigrant parents who have received very little formal schooling can negatively impact their children's academic performance if they lack an understanding of the importance of education. Their lack of reading and writing skills also puts them at risk of failure in a variety of ways (Punklett & Bamaca, 2003). Another potential risk that challenges this community arises because children from poor immigrant families tend to display lower levels of cognitive functioning, social development, psychological well-being, and self-esteem. The educational performance of many immigrant children is marked by a consistent pattern of underachievement (Ceballo, 2004). Thus, immigrant families are put at risk by many factors beyond their own beliefs and ideals of success, integration, or even nonintegration. In the descriptions of immigrant families below, various factors that threaten their stability, their future, and their desire to be successful, as well as their ability to successfully integrate into society, are identified.

METHODOLOGY AND ANALYSIS

The design of this study used a qualitative sample of nine undocumented families drawn from a relevant program from a faith-based organization. This program, developed with the intention of promoting resiliency among undocumented immigrant families in the United States, was composed of these nine participant families, so there was no need for sampling. The qualitative analysis was conducted by naturalistic perspective, as described by Sandstrom, Martin, and Fine (2003). These nine families were selected because they were accessible and were willing to participate in interviews. Also, these immigrants exemplify in their experiences the risks that damage resiliency, affect their attitudes, and perhaps derail attempts at integration (Wengraf, 2001).

All nine families that were interviewed have highly similar experiences, concerns, and acts of resiliency that allow them to survive in the United States. These families clearly demonstrate that there is no such thing as a "typical" immigrant currently residing in the United States, for their backgrounds, reasons for coming to the United States, personal and social experiences, family composition and unity, and degrees of resiliency have a varied widely. As undocumented immigrants, however, these families exist in a community that is more abstract than concrete, and they do not actively seek integration because doing so might draw attention to their presence. Some suffer a lack of acculturation that damages their families and possibly their future. There are three common threats to resiliency that can be tracked across all nine families: ironically, familism, or a form of it; a lack of acculturation; and alcohol and drugs.

THREATS TO RESILIENCY

As suggested by Cheryl Amey and Stan Albrecht (1998), familism, or the family, may prove a threat to resiliency, and even a source of destruction. The most obvious example is that eight out of the nine families interviewed were affected by death, desertion, and divorce. These family situations were not necessarily the fault of the host society, but the stress of immigration, combined with cultural concepts of male-female relationships, create many problems. In these families, generally speaking, the husband has dominated the wife and the family, frequently resorting to threats and violence. The wife, in an effort to protect her children and maintain some kind of family while dealing with their illegal status, loses self-esteem, is fearful, and suffers even more stress. This stress causes her children stress, which may lead into problems at school, and possibly to criminal activity. Even when a husband is not in the picture, feelings of abandonment or residual anger can destroy or damage a woman's confidence, and thus her resiliency.

In one case, a seemingly successful and family-oriented mother still neglects her children. The mother is a widow, and she did not suffer from any known abuse from her husband, save for the stress of his being put in prison for drug trafficking. She strengthened her family by bringing her two now-divorced daughters and their children back into her home, and by taking care of her boyfriend by helping him to save money and find work. This woman is by all accounts hardworking and capable, but she may depend too much on money to keep herself and her family resilient, and she does not find the time to tend to her two youngest children, who are in need of her attention. Her lack of acculturation causes her youngest daughter to be contemptuous of her mother and act out in school, as well as running with a gang and possibly doing drugs. The girl's singular problems are exacerbated by her mother being unable to effectively communicate with teachers, and perhaps being unable to explain to the girl the realities of being illegal, including what they can do to better the situation. Lacking her own sense of acculturation, the girl can't help her mother very much, and the mother avoids acculturation by working and spending perhaps too much time with family and friends speaking Spanish and listening to Spanish-language music. The girl is close to getting into trouble with the law, which would probably bring authorities down on the family. The younger boy requires services to overcome motor dysfunction, but his mother is too busy working to see to his needs. She does not seem to understand how failing to correct his dysfunction will lead to greater problems later on since an industrialized, money-based economy wants citizens who can read and write well.

Another woman is separated from her abusive husband but still continues to put up with his demands for sex in exchange for bills being paid. Illegal, and not well educated, she cannot seek better-paying work, and thus must continue to deal with her husband in order to maintain a home. She knows that her children are being affected by this, both positively, as his money keeps a roof over their head and services paid, and negatively, in that this is a great source of distress. She places the children first, and is even thinking of returning to Mexico, where they would not be in fear of detention and deportation. The children are currently doing well, and they seem to be avoiding any behavior that would attract law enforcement. However, she is taking care of her family at the expense of her good self-opinion, and while her family is serving her in return, this support is not enough to heal her and maintain her emotional and mental well-being.

Another woman was married to an abusive husband who, when she declared she was leaving him, set up a bizarre revenge plot, and the police had to be called in. Although she was not arrested at that time, she now has a police record, which will work against her legal bid for citizenship. She also became involved with a boyfriend, and together they bought a house, which they then lost when mortgage payments soared. She works and takes care of her children, insists on them attending school, and counsels her daughters about relationships with men. But she is depressed and needs counseling to help her with her problems.

Drugs (and alcohol) are another threat to resiliency. Children engaging in drugs and alcohol are endangering their families with the threat of arrest. In the above case of the woman taking care of her boyfriend and helping him with his finances, her efforts are undermined by his drinking and posing a threat to her children. Another woman's husband was a hardworking man and respectful husband until he became involved with drug trafficking. He ended up exposing his children to weapons, alcohol, and drugs. When fleeing the law, he took her and the children back to Mexico. She finally fled from his threats, leaving Mexico again, but with only two of the four children. In other cases, parents are constantly seeking to learn if their children are on drugs.

These types of challenges can lead to depression, which creates yet another challenge. In one case, a woman with four children, each from a different man, immigrated to the United States. She found work and was maintaining her family, but she then lost her employment and had to seek assistance. Though being able to house her family again, she has grown depressed over her past history with men, her oldest daughter's pregnancy by a man who deserted her, and the future of her three other children.

DISCUSSION

The picture that emerges from these cases is that immigration is always a difficult challenge, whether the immigrant seeks integration or simply seeks to survive and persist. Families create problems as family pressures create conflict, drugs and alcohol pose further threats, and a lack of acculturation increases these threats because the immigrant does not always know what to do or how to seek help.

Although many immigrant families adapt successfully to the new host society, many others can't or won't adapt because of problems arising from social and cultural differences with the host society. The immigrant families profiled here suffer from family problems and acculturation issues, and for the immigrants with illegal status there are additional legal problems to deal with. These problems exacerbate the relationship between the mainstream society and the immigrants, who may not have the knowledge or the resources to resolve their status and lives. This creates a fragmented community, which may have severe consequences for the immigrants and for the host society. Hatred, resentment, and hostility may occur on both sides, and this can affect both sides economically, socially, and politically.

REFERENCES AND FURTHER READING

Amey, C. H., & Albrecht, S. L. (1998). Race and ethnic differences in adolescent drug use: The impact of the family structure and the quantity and quality of parental interaction. *Journal of Drug Issues, 28*(2), 283–298.

Castro, F. G., & Alarcon, H. E. (2002). Integrating cultural variables into drug abuse prevention and treatment with racial/ethnic minorities. *Journal of Drug Issues, 32*(3), 783–810.

Castro, F. G., Boyer, R. G., & Balcazar, H. G. (1998). Healthy adjustments in Mexican American and other Hispanic adolescents. In R. Montemayor, G. R. Adams, & T. P. Gullota (Eds.), *Adolescent diversity in ethnic, economic and cultural context* (pp. 141–178). Thousand Oaks, CA: Sage.

Ceballo, R. (2004). From barrios to Yale: The role of parenting strategies in Latino families. *Hispanic Journal of Behavioral Sciences, 26*(2), 171–186.

Marsiglia, F. F., Miles, B. W., Dustman, P., & Sills, S. (2002). Ties that protect: An ecological perspective on Latino/a urban pre-adolescent drug use. *Journal of Ethnic and Cultural Diversity in Social Work, 11*(3/4), 191–220.

Petersilia, J. (2003). *When prisoners come home: Parole and prisoner reentry.* New York, NY: Oxford University Press.

Phinney, S. J., Ong, A., & Maden, T. (2000). Cultural values and intergenerational value discrepancies in immigrant and non-immigrant families. *Child Development, 71*(2), 528–539.

Plunkett, S. W., & Bamaca, G. M. Y. (2003). The relationship between parenting, acculturation, and adolescent academics in Mexican-origin immigrant families in Los Angeles. *Hispanic Journal of Behavioral Sciences, 25*(2), 222–239.

Sandstrom, K., Martin, D., & Fine, G. (2003). *Symbols, selves and social reality.* Los Angeles, CA: Roxbury.

Wengraf, T. (2001). Concepts and approaches to depth interviewing. In T. Wengraf (Ed.), *Qualitative research interviewing* (pp. 1–60). Thousand Oaks, CA: Sage.

Francisco J. Alatorre

Catholic Church and Immigration

POINT: The Judeo-Christian tradition and Catholic social teaching call persons of faith to work to safeguard the rights of migrants and newcomers, including those who entered the country illegally or who otherwise lack immigration status.

Donald M. Kerwin Jr., Center for Migration Studies

COUNTERPOINT: The Christian mandate to love one's neighbors and welcome the stranger does not require endorsing lawlessness or ignoring the consequences of illegal immigration for the "national family."

Donald M. Kerwin Jr., Center for Migration Studies

Introduction

Controversy over the Catholic Church's stance on immigration is, at its core, a debate about what should be the guiding principles defining U.S. immigration policy: moral and ethical considerations or transient pragmatic considerations. This is not a new debate. In any age, there is tension over whether immigration policy should be informed by moral values and political ideals, or whether it should derive from the national self-interested sensibilities of the time.

The Catholic Church advocates immigration policies based on Christian teaching rooted in human rights and the dignity of every human being. And while the United States is a pluralistic society whose constitution requires a separation of church and state, it is also a predominantly Christian nation. A 2007 survey by the Pew Research Center's Forum on Religion and Public Life found that 78.4 percent of Americans are Christians and 23.9 percent are Catholic. And while the mandate to "welcome the stranger" is a central tenet of Christianity, this imperative also exists in other religious traditions. Further, these religious traditions resonate with the "self-evident" ideal enshrined in the Declaration of Independence and rooted in the Enlightenment that "all men are created equal, that they are endowed by their Creator with certain inalienable Rights, that among these are Life, Liberty, and the pursuit of Happiness." In other words, it is not surprising that a tension exists between moral values and self-interest in relation to U.S. immigration policy, and it is difficult to imagine a policy arena with more relevance to national identity and to the meaning of citizenship.

As U.S. immigration policy grew more restrictive over time, pragmatic self-interested considerations increasingly displaced moral values or political ideals in its formation. It became a *political* decision by the early twentieth century, and U.S. immigration laws now derive from complex interactions between domestic politics, international diplomatic, and political imperatives, as well as the place of the United States in the larger world order. Public sensibilities about immigration evolve in subtle ways with global diplomatic and economic trends, and these shifts in turn shape changes to immigration laws. While there is generally a lag between this evolution and changes to immigration law itself, it is instructive to examine U.S. immigration policy and public sentiment about immigration during the second half of the twentieth century.

The end of World War II and the start of the Cold War marked the emergence of the United States as the leader of the free world. This role complicated maintenance of then-extant highly restrictive immigration laws that discriminated against the majority of the world's population on the basis of race. Thus, while the 1952 McCarran-Walter Immigration Act continued the national origins provisions of 1920s immigration legislation, it did eliminate a color bar in naturalization. The Cold War also increased public awareness of the diplomatic importance of winning the hearts and minds of people around the world with regard to freedom and democracy. People fleeing Fidel Castro's Cuba and entering the United States outside of normal immigration processes were not treated as illegal immigrants. Instead, they were welcomed as refugees from a tyrannical dictatorship and, more importantly, as people who were rejecting communism in favor of freedom and democracy. Immigrants were understood to have embraced American ideals, in effect endorsing capitalism and rejecting communism. This Cold War sentiment and the civil rights movement of the 1960s combined to effect a replacement of national origins quotas laws with the 1965 Hart-Cellar Act, an immigration regime based on family reunification.

With the end of the Cold War in the 1980s, the ideological battle between capitalism and communism ended. The United States was the world's remaining super power and capitalism the ascendant economic paradigm. The diplomatic importance of advancing the virtues of freedom and democracy and of winning the hearts and minds of people around the world waned. Global economic integration became the post–Cold War focus of U.S. international leadership. Globalization saw the elimination of most trade barriers, the reduction or elimination of barriers to direct foreign investment, and technology-driven changes in how goods were manufactured, distributed, and consumed around the world. These changes stimulated an increase in global migration as people moved in response to the dislocations and opportunities wrought by globalization.

But this global economic integration occurred in *everything except labor*. Countries, especially wealthy countries, maintained immigration regimes that restrict labor mobility. In the United States, the legal immigration system proved to be ill suited to the changed economic conditions and to the demographics of an aging population. The result was an increase in both legal and illegal immigration that has fostered heated debate about controlling illegal immigration and about how much and what kind of legal immigration to allow. These debates focus on immigration's impacts on the economy and on native-born Americans.

It is not surprising that current immigration debates focus on whether immigrants are good for the economy, whether they are a fiscal drain on public coffers, and what immigration means to national identity. This focus on the economic and social costs and benefits of immigration reflects sensibilities that derive from today's global economic and political realities. In a world characterized by global economic competition, raw economic self-interest is of utmost salience. There is a vast economics literature attempting to measure immigration's impacts on wages, economic output, economic growth, and technological innovation. Moral imperatives, human rights considerations, and founding political ideals are not generally on the radar screen in these discussions.

The Catholic Church, in articulating its values with regard to immigration, extends the discussion beyond the current era's sensibilities of economic self-interest as the appropriate arbiter of immigration policy. It reminds participants in these debates that they are rooted in current transient economic and political conditions, and that ideals related to the rights of the greater human family are also relevant.

POINT

In Hebrew scripture, the Jewish people endure deportation, Exodus, exile, and dispersion. Based on their long history as migrants and dispossessed people, they learn to love and to empathize with the "stranger." In the Gospels, Jesus enters the world in the midst of a journey, carries out an itinerant public ministry, and personally identifies with migrants and newcomers. He teaches that on judgment day God will assemble the nations and separate people based on whether they have welcomed the stranger and embraced the dispossessed. Catholic social teaching—the 130-year-old body of authoritative church documents on social questions—views migration as a way to unify diverse peoples on the basis of their shared values. It recognizes the right of persons to migrate in order to realize their God-given rights, the corresponding responsibility of sovereign states to accept them, and the moral imperative that newcomers be allowed to participate fully in their adopted communities and country. Drawing from these principles, the U.S. Catholic bishops lead a coalition of Catholic dioceses and agencies that support the following:

- An "earned legalization" for the nation's 11 million unauthorized immigrants

- Reform of the U.S. legal immigration system to expedite family reunification and to admit necessary workers

- Strong refugee protection policies and due process for persons at risk of removal (deportation)

- A concerted push to integrate the nation's 38 million foreign-born persons and their children

While people of good faith can differ on immigration issues, the policy positions and strategies advocated by some in the U.S. immigration debate offend Catholic teaching. These include opposition to humanitarian assistance to unauthorized immigrants, invocation of the "rule of law" to justify the denial of human rights, use of the language of illegality and criminality to marginalize and demean self-sacrificing people, scapegoating unauthorized immigrants, and exploiting animus towards immigrants to pursue policies at odds with Catholic teaching.

IDENTITY AND THE HUMAN FAMILY

In the Judeo-Christian tradition, migration is a mystery in plain view. It consistently provides the occasion for God's self-revelation to human beings. Hebrew scripture describes the Jewish people's long saga of uprooting, deportation, Exodus, exile, persecution, dispersion, and return to the Promised Land. Migration provides the backdrop to Jesus's birth in Bethlehem. The wise men follow the star on their sojourn to the newborn. The Holy Family flees to Egypt to escape wicked King Herod. Jesus journeys from God to man, so that human beings might return to God. In his public ministry, he moves from place to place, laments having nowhere to lay his head (Luke 9:58), and refers to himself as "the way" (John 14:16). The apostles encounter the resurrected Lord on the road to Emmaus. St. Paul experiences conversion on the road to Damascus. The earliest Christians referred to themselves as *pároikois*, which roughly means "resident aliens." The word "parish" derives from *pároikois*. True to their etymology, the world's parishes have been populated—and the reach of the Christian faith extended—through migration.

Migration occupies such an exalted place in the Judeo-Christian tradition that the journey has become its central metaphor for the lives of the faithful, who are never truly at home in the world, but are always en route to their final, spiritual home. In St. Augustine's formulation, Christians are pilgrims on a journey to the City of God. In this journey, they can turn away and reject their brothers and sisters, or they can walk with them.

What lessons can be drawn from this tradition? In the Pentateuch, the first five books of the Bible, the injunction to love the stranger appears more than 30 times. God calls the Jewish people to remember their own experience of migration and exile, to love resident aliens and to treat them no differently than natives (Lev. 19:33). Jesus takes the themes of hospitality, compassion, and empathy to a new level by personally identifying with the stranger. He preaches that salvation depends on how truly Christians welcome the stranger and serve the dispossessed (Matt. 25:35). In pursuing the Christian mission to gather together God's scattered children (John 11:52), distinctions between people diminish in importance: "There is neither Jew nor Greek, there is neither slave nor free man, there is neither male nor female" (Gal. 3:28).

To Christians, migration should not be seen as a cause for division, but as an opportunity to build the "human family." In Catholic social teaching, cultural diversity need not be a barrier to national unity. Because the values of immigrants invariably find expression in their native cultures, migration can be the means to unify peoples based on their deepest values. Of course, culturally embedded values may be life-giving or not, and the Catholic Church seeks to "evangelize" the cultures of both immigrant communities and receiving states. At the same time, it urges that host communities be open to the positive values of immigrants, and that newcomers embrace the positive values of their new communities.

It might be argued that this body of teaching speaks to religious or personal commitments, and does not have public policy implications. However, the very purpose of Catholic social teaching is to apply enduring Christian values and principles to pressing social questions or "signs of the times." On immigration, it asks: how can public policies reflect the God-given dignity of immigrants, our "brothers and sisters"?

HUMAN RIGHTS AND RESPONSIBILITIES

Mary Ann Glendon argues that human rights language has been used so promiscuously in public policy discourse that its effectiveness has been compromised. In her view, the rhetoric of rights has become less a way to express the core protections and conditions that apply to all human beings, and more an instrument to pursue an expanding list of causes. Moreover, rights claims have increasingly taken on an absolutist cast. If partisans can articulate a desired social outcome in the language of rights, they seem to believe that this should curtail dialogue and end debate.

Catholic teaching uses the language of rights in a different way. To the Catholic Church, rights derive from the radical equality of all people as the children of God. They speak to individual and collective responsibilities, grounded in love of God and neighbor. They are not a tool to attain socioeconomic or political advantage, but a way to speak about and to honor our duties to each other. As such, rights serve the "common good," defined as the minimal conditions that allow *all* members of a community to flourish.

From this perspective of Catholic social teaching, a purely instrumental view of human rights reflects an impoverished sense of rights and the common good. Conversely, a diminished sense of the shared good of the community lays the groundwork for denying the God-given rights to marginal populations, who are invariably the persons most likely to be excluded from the "goods" of the community. Furthermore, it does not suffice to recognize or honor rights in the abstract. Christians have the responsibility to restore people whose rights have been violated to full membership in the human family. Beyond simply respecting juridical rights, they are called to love their neighbors, to act justly, and to extend hospitality to them.

How does this sense of rights and responsibilities apply to the phenomenon of migration? According to Catholic social teaching, migration should be a matter of choice, not necessity. People have a right not to have to migrate, and states have a responsibility to provide the minimal conditions that would allow their residents to flourish and realize their God-given rights at home. However, when states fail to meet this responsibility, persons have a right and responsibility to seek conditions that will allow them to live in dignity and support their families.

The Catholic principle of "subsidiarity" holds that decisions should be made by the competent authority closest to a particular issue or problem. Migrants and their families are typically in the best position to decide whether sustaining themselves requires one or more of their members to migrate. In fact, these wrenching decisions are often made as part of a family survival strategy. In these circumstances, migration is an act of self-sacrifice and even an act of self-realization. In giving of themselves, migrants are becoming who God calls them to be.

According to Catholic social teaching, the right to migrate creates a corresponding moral responsibility on the part of states to receive and to welcome immigrants. The Catholic Church has been criticized for its alleged support of "open border" policies. In fact, it recognizes the right and the responsibility of nations to regulate immigration. Yet it teaches that this responsibility must be tempered by a commitment to safeguard rights and to promote the common good, which it sees as the very purpose of states. In Catholic thought, a state's responsibilities to its own residents does not relieve it of the responsibility to defend the rights of the greater human family. This concept—known as the universal or "borderless" common good—starts from the premise that certain minimum "goods" (including rights) apply to all people and must be afforded to all, even if doing so requires states, individually or collectively, to reach beyond their borders.

Immigrants, in turn, have a right and a responsibility to contribute to the good of their new communities. Beyond their labor and family commitments, immigrants should embrace the life-giving values of their host nations. Receiving communities, in turn, have a responsibility to allow newcomers to participate fully in their communities. Catholic teaching uses the terms "social justice" and "contributive justice" synonymously. The latter term conveys the idea that just relations between people turns on the ability of all members of a community to contribute. For this reason, the United States Conference of Catholic Bishops (USCCB) has decried the creation of a dual society, with the rights of some of its members honored and the rights of others denied.

PUBLIC POLICY IMPLICATIONS

The bishops in the United States have developed several principles for immigration reform in light of Catholic social teaching. They have created the Justice for Immigrants (JFI) campaign to pursue public policies that are rooted in these principles. First, the bishops support policies and programs designed to mitigate the need to migrate and to allow persons to live in dignity in their home countries. Thus, the USCCB and other Catholic entities advocate in favor of generous foreign aid, just trade agreements, and debt relief, and agencies like Catholic Relief Services (CRS) fund development and self-help initiatives that seek to facilitate economic opportunities in migrant-sending communities.

Second, the bishops support reform of the legal immigration system of the United States, with a particular focus on the insufficient number of low-skilled permanent work visas available (5,000 per year) and multiyear delays in granting visas to the close family members of U.S. citizens and lawful permanent residents (LPRs). The U.S. legal immigration system has not been significantly modified since 1990, and it has not been overhauled since 1965, despite immense changes in the U.S. labor market and the global economy. This outdated system has contributed significantly to the growth of the unauthorized population in the country.

Third, the bishops support allowing certain unauthorized residents to earn legal status over many years through work, good character, and English language proficiency. They have been particularly vocal in favor of legalizing young people who were brought to the United States as children, and who are American in every way but immigration status. The Development, Relief, and Education for Alien Minors Act (the DREAM Act)—though defeated in the waning days of the 111th Congress in 2010—would provide conditional legal status to unauthorized persons who entered prior to age 16, have been present for at least 5 years, have been admitted to an institution of higher education or have earned a high school diploma or a General Education Development (GED) degree, and have not reached age 35. After 6 years, applicants would be able to become full LPRs if they have (1) obtained a degree from an institution of higher education, completed at least 2 years in a program for a bachelor's degree (or higher), or honorably served at least 2 years in the U.S. military; (2) demonstrated good moral character; and (3) not become inadmissible or deportable on specified grounds.

Fourth, the bishops support strong refugee protection policies for those at risk of persecution, torture, or death in their home countries. They also support due process for immigrants who are facing removal from the United States. For many years, the Catholic Church has sponsored the nation's largest refugee resettlement and immigrant legal service networks. Its public policy positions have arisen out of its intimate knowledge of the needs and aspirations of these populations.

Fifth, the bishops recognize the need to integrate the record number of U.S. immigrants—roughly 38 million, with about an equal number of children of immigrants—to mainstream society. The foreign-born represent roughly one in every eight U.S. residents, one in every seven workers, one in every five low-wage workers, and (adding their children) perhaps one in every two Catholics. While crucial to integration, legal status should be viewed as a step on the way to full incorporation into U.S. society. Like natives, immigrants need educational opportunities, jobs that pay a living wage and have an upward trajectory, and the ability to participate fully in the political life of their communities and nation. Since the nation's prospects increasingly depend on the contributions of its historic number of immigrants and their children, particular attention needs to be paid to these core integration needs.

POLICY STANCES AND STRATEGIES AT ODDS WITH CATHOLIC SOCIAL TEACHING

Catholic teaching views migration from the perspectives of God-given human dignity and promotion of the common good. In practice, respect for rights and the common good go hand in hand. Educating immigrant children and youth benefits them as well as the larger society. Extending police protection to immigrants increases public safety. Providing public and emergency health services to immigrants improves public health and safeguards the community.

Catholic teaching provides broad principles that can frame and inform complex public policy issues. However, it would be inconsistent with the church's view of the nature of human beings, as imbued with reason and conscience, if its teaching did not permit a range of views on complex policy questions. At the same time, certain arguments and strategies that have emerged in the bitter U.S. immigration debate offend Catholic social teaching.

First, attacks on institutions and individuals that provide humanitarian assistance to migrants are inimical to Catholic teaching. Along these lines, the U.S. bishops furiously opposed legislation in 2005 that would have made it a crime "to assist" unauthorized immigrants. A protestor outside a church in Tucson, whose members leave water for desperate migrants along the U.S.-Mexico border, carried a placard that read "Good Samaritans, Bad Americans." In Catholic teaching, however, the very purpose of sovereign states is to protect God-given human rights. It cannot be unpatriotic to meet the basic human needs of desperate people.

Nor can Catholic social teaching be used to justify the personal rejection of immigrants who have settled in communities throughout the United States. In a town hall meeting in northern Virginia, a supporter of a restrictive legal ordinance made the point to his immigrant neighbors that he did not hate them personally. Rather, he did not welcome them. Yet in the Christian faith, it is not enough not to hate one's neighbors. Christians believe that their lives will be judged by how truly they love God and neighbor, particularly the "stranger" and persons from other marginal groups (Matt. 25:35).

Second, Catholic teaching supports the "rule of law." This ancient concept initially spoke to the need for rulers to be bound by the law. In more recent years, a stronger sense of this concept has emerged, which requires democratically sanctioned legal systems that safeguard human rights and that apply their laws even-handedly. The "rule of law" is often misused in the public debate to support the notion that people without immigration status have no rights. It is true that the federal government possesses broad power to regulate immigration—to determine who can enter, who can stay and on what terms, and who must leave—and that it can exercise this power in ways that might otherwise be deemed to violate constitutional rights. At the same time, U.S. constitutional rights extend to persons, including those without status in matters that do not implicate the immigration power. The federal government could not, for example, deny indigent immigrants (without status) government-appointed legal counsel in a criminal trial, or take their property without compensation, or suppress their speech, or torture them.

The "rule of law" is often invoked to support legislative proposals that would further marginalize immigrants. However, attempts to criminalize work or mere presence in the United States by persons without immigration status, or to deny citizenship to U.S.-born children with unauthorized parents, do not honor the rule of law. If successful, these initiatives would create a permanent underclass without rights, security, or prospects—precisely the kind of dual society that Catholic social teaching deplores. The assault on birthright citizenship also runs squarely against the plain language of the Fourteenth Amendment's citizenship clause, its legislative history, and the Supreme Court's ruling in *United States v. Wong Kim Ark* (1898), which affirmed that the amendment applies to the children of immigrants.

Many states have also passed legislation that seeks to regulate immigration through an explicit strategy of "deportation by attrition." These laws seek to force unauthorized immigrants and their families to leave their communities by denying them housing, schooling, work, police protection (in effect), and other basic rights. Part of this strategy has been aimed at overturning the U.S. Supreme Court's decision in *Plyler v. Doe* (1982), which extended public education through high school to all children, regardless of their immigration status. Such strategies, in the guise of a bedrock commitment to the rule of law, seek to deny rights as a means to an end, which is inimical to Catholic teaching on God-given rights and on the role of sovereign states.

The emphasis on absolute adherence (by others) to ever-stricter rules and laws, coupled with disdain for the hopes and aspirations of immigrants, evokes a pharisaical mind-set. The defining sin of the Pharisees, who persistently treated Jesus as a lawbreaker, was that they idolized the law while hardening their hearts to Jesus's message. Christianity calls for conversion—to love God and neighbor—which cannot be reconciled with the steady drumbeat of attacks against "illegals," "aliens," and "criminal aliens" by politicians, media, and anti-immigrant groups.

The U.S. and Mexican bishops addressed this trend in their 2003 pastoral statement, *Strangers No Longer: Together on the Journey of Hope.* Faith in God's presence in migrants, they said, should lead to a conversion of heart and mind and a sense of solidarity with immigrants. Time and again, Jesus urges his followers not to condemn others, but to examine their own flaws and consciences.

Third, Catholic social teaching argues against categorizing people in ways that fail to recognize their full dignity, that give preeminence to relatively superficial aspects of identity, or that expose them to ridicule and hatred. Yet politicians and advocacy groups consistently label person without immigration status "illegal aliens" or "criminal aliens." In the Catholic tradition, persons can break the law, but it is sacrilegious to call God's children "illegal." Moreover, there is nothing "alien" about immigrants in a church that reveres and identifies with immigrants and that has become a "universal" church through migration.

In 1920, 75 percent of U.S. Catholics were foreign-born. All of the defining institutions of the Catholic Church in the United States arose in response to the needs and aspirations of successive waves of immigrants. At different points in U.S. history, Catholics faced sharp bigotry and well-organized opposition. Nativists viewed Catholics as inherently unpatriotic and unassimilable, just as some today view Muslim Americans in this way. An 1876 cartoon by Thomas Nast depicted a swarm of bishops crawling onto U.S. soil, their mitres open like crocodile jaws waiting to devour American schoolchildren, while their followers led off Lady Liberty. Anti-Catholic sentiment may not be so explicit today, but the rhetoric directed against immigrants, most of whom are Catholic, rivals that of earlier periods in U.S. history.

Fourth, an age-old feature of anti-immigrant movements, including those that historically targeted Catholic immigrants, has been to blame immigrants for whatever social problems happen to be prominent at the time. In recent years, persons without immigration status have been collectively blamed for terrorism, the health-care crisis, mortgage defaults, the "Great Recession," high unemployment, displacement of U.S. workers, federal and state budget shortfalls, and the return of leprosy to the United States. The phenomenon of scapegoating—with its roots in the ritual of Yom Kippur of symbolically laying the communal sins of a people on a goat and casting it into the wilderness (Lev. 16:5, 7–10)—undermines the Christian commitment to build the human family.

A related tactic has been to ascribe the offenses of individual immigrants, particularly high-profile crimes, to all unauthorized immigrants. Yet noncitizens are sentenced for violent crimes and, excluding federal immigration-related offenses, commit crimes at far lower rates than natives. More to the point, lack of status does not cause crime anymore than U.S. citizenship does. If a citizen commits a crime, that person might be categorized as pathological, mean, immoral, disturbed, crazy, or simply bad. If an unauthorized immigrant commits a crime, it is attributed by many to their immigration status. Blaming a highly diverse group for the crimes of individual members is a smear tactic and a textbook example of stereotyping.

More recently, alternative "faith" voices have criticized immigrants for their purported greed and selfishness in coming to the United States. This criticism cannot be squared with Catholic teaching, the Catholic Church's long experience of migration, and the lives of millions of self-sacrificing, hard-working immigrants. Jesus held out the despised foreigner of his day, the Good Samaritan, as the model of Christian charity and generosity. Many of today's immigrants follow in that same path and should be seen as a source of hope for the United States.

Finally, anti-immigrant measures often mask underlying public policy agendas. Many restrictionist agencies, for example, arose in response to environmental concerns related to population control. As a result, these activists oppose both illegal immigration and current rates of legal immigration. Occasionally, this agenda surfaces in the immigration debate in ways that conflict with Catholic teaching. For example, a scholar at a restrictionist think tank opined in early 2011 that U.S. immigration policy should prioritize the admission of immigrants who promise not to have children or to petition for family members to join them. Under his "fantasy proposal," immigrants who violated this pledge would be summarily removed. The proposal offends Catholic teaching on life and family, as well as the church's core conviction that human beings should never be treated as a means to an end.

The 2003 pastoral letter of the U.S. and Mexican bishops squarely addressed the tension between the authority of sovereign states to regulate immigration and the right of persons to seek fully human lives in other countries. Rather than balancing sovereignty and rights, the bishops reconciled these two concepts through an understanding of the common good that encompasses the rights of migrants: "While the sovereign state may impose reasonable limits on immigration, the common good is not served when the basic human rights of the individual are violated." Furthermore, the bishops presumed that due to rampant "global poverty and persecution, . . . persons must migrate in order to support and protect themselves." According to Catholic social teaching, development does not refer solely to economic well-being. It must be "integral," encompassing the fulfillment of each person and the "whole" person. A nation is underdeveloped if it cannot provide the basic necessities of life to its residents. However, nations can also be underdeveloped if, despite their immense wealth, they exclude and reject human beings who are seeking conditions that are consonant with their dignity as the children of God.

REFERENCES AND FURTHER READING

Batalova, J., & McHugh, M. (2010, July). *DREAM vs. reality: An analysis of potential DREAM Act beneficiaries.* Retrieved from Migration Policy Institute website: http://www.migrationpolicy.org/pubs/DREAM-Insight-July2010.pdf

Edwards, J. R., Jr. (2009, September). *A Biblical perspective on immigration policy.* Retrieved from Center for Immigration Studies website: http://www.cis.org/ImmigrationBible

Glendon, M. A. (1991). *Rights talk.* New York, NY: Free Press.

Groody, D. G., & Campese, G. (2008). *A promised land, a perilous journey: Theological perspectives on migration.* Notre Dame, IN: University of Notre Dame Press.

Hake, B., & Hake, J. (2010, January 1). What the Bible *really* says about immigration policy: An analysis of "A Biblical Perspective on Immigration Policy" and "And You Welcomed Me: Immigration and Catholic Social Teaching." *Bender's Immigration Bulletin, 15,* 6–20. Retrieved from http://www.theimmigrantsjournal.com/Hake_BIB_1-1-10.pdf

Kerwin, D. (2009). Toward a Catholic view of nationality. *Notre Dame Journal of Law, Ethics & Public Policy, 23*(1), 197–207.

Kerwin, D. (2011, May). The faltering US refugee protection program: Legal and policy responses to refugees, asylum seekers, and others in need of protection. Retrieved from Migration Policy Institute website: http://www.migrationpolicy.org/pubs/refugeeprotection-2011.pdf

Kerwin, D., & Gerschutz, J. M. (Eds.). (2009). *And you welcomed me: Migration and Catholic social teaching.* Lanham, MD: Lexington Books.

Kerwin, D., Meissner, D., & McHugh, M. (2011, March). *Executive action on immigration: Six ways to make the system work better.* Retrieved from Migration Policy Institute website: http://www.migrationpolicy.org/pubs/administrativefixes.pdf

Morris, C. R. (1997). *American Catholic: The saints and sinners who built America's most powerful church.* New York, NY: Vintage Books.

National Conference of Catholic Bishops. (1986). *Together a new people: Pastoral statement on migrants and refugees.* Washington, DC: National Conference of Catholic Bishops, Committee on Migration.

North, D. (2011, February 4). *The "one-off" immigrants: A proposed fantasy immigration policy.* Retrieved from Center for Immigration Studies website: http://www.cis.org/north/one-off-migrants

Passel, J. S., & Cohn, D. (2009). *A portrait of unauthorized immigrants in the United States.* Retrieved from Pew Hispanic Center website: http://pewhispanic.org/files/reports/107.pdf

Passel, J. S., & Cohn, D. (2011). *Unauthorized immigrant population: National and state trends, 2010.* Retrieved from Pew Hispanic Center website: http://pewhispanic.org/files/reports/133.pdf

Pope John XXIII. (1963, April 11). *Pacem in terris* [Peace on Earth (Encyclical)]. Retrieved from http://www.vatican.va/holy_father/john_xxiii/encyclicals/documents/hf_j-xxiii_enc_11041963_pacem_en.html

Pope John Paul II. (1995, July 25). *Message for World Migration Day, 1996.* Retrieved from http://www.vatican.va/holy_father/john_paul_ii/messages/migration/documents/hf_jp-ii_mes_25071995_undocumented_migrants_en.html

Pope Paul VI. (1964, November 21). Dogmatic constitution on the church, *Lumen gentium* [Light of the world]. Retrieved from http://www.vatican.va/archive/hist_councils/ii_vatican_council/documents/vat-ii_const_19641121_lumen-gentium_en.html

Pope Paul VI. (1965, December 7). Pastoral constitution on the church in the modern world, *Gaudium et spes* [Joy and hope]. Retrieved from http://www.vatican.va/archive/hist_councils/ii_vatican_council/documents/vat-ii_cons_19651207_gaudium-et-spes_en.html

Pope Paul VI. (1967, March 26). *Populorum progression:* On the development of peoples (Encyclical). Retrieved from http://www.vatican.va/holy_father/paul_vi/encyclicals/documents/hf_p-vi_enc_26031967_populorum_en.html

Rocha, J. L. (2003, July). Why do they go? Theories on the migration trend. *Revista Envio, 264,* 34–48. Retrieved from http://www.envio.org.ni/articulo/2105

Rosenblum, M. R., & Kandel, W. A. (2011, October 21). *Interior immigration enforcement: Programs targeting criminal aliens* (CRS Report for Congress). Retrieved from Congressional Research Service website: http://www.fas.org/sgp/crs/homesec/R42057.pdf

Tamanaha, B. (2004). *On the rule of law: History, politics, theory.* Cambridge, UK: Cambridge University Press.

United States Conference of Catholic Bishops, & Conferencia del Espiscopado Mexicano. (2003). *Strangers no longer: Together on the journey of hope.* Retrieved from http://www.usccb.org/mrs/stranger.shtml

Donald M. Kerwin Jr.

COUNTERPOINT

Religious touchstones can provide common ground for a more productive dialogue on immigration. Catholic social teaching recognizes the authority and responsibility of sovereign states to regulate migration in furtherance of the common good. It teaches that states exist to safeguard the rights and to promote the good of all of their members. The "common good," which serves as the linchpin to Catholic teaching on migrants and newcomers, speaks to the minimal conditions that allow all persons in a (local or national) community to flourish and live fully dignified lives. This begs the question of how membership should be determined. Catholic teaching provides support for aspects of "civic nationalism," particularly the notion that membership should turn on the shared "civic values" that constitute the "American creed." However, this generous view of membership raises a dilemma for pro-legalization activists, since for many "the rule of law" represents a defining feature of the "American creed."

Catholic teaching does not require supporting reforms as extensive as those proposed by the Catholic bishops in the United States. The "common good" would best be served by allowing far fewer low-skilled immigrant laborers to enter the country, by prioritizing the needs of the native working poor, and by enforcing labor standards in industries with substantial numbers of unauthorized immigrants. It also argues for making the U.S. legal immigration system more responsive to the supply and demand characteristics of the labor market, and for allowing immigrant families to reunify in a timely way. The United States should abandon large-scale legalization proposals in favor of proposals to legalize discrete, worthy groups of unauthorized persons. Finally, Catholic teaching supports prioritizing the integration of lawful immigrants and strictly enforcing the law, both as a good in itself and as a way to educate newcomers on the value that the nation places on the rule of law.

RELIGIOUS TOUCHSTONES AND THE U.S. IMMIGRATION DEBATE

The U.S. immigration debate is highly polarized and will not be satisfactorily resolved if partisans continue to speak past one another and exclusively to their own constituents. The often unrealized promise of religious language, and of Catholic teaching in particular, is that it allows persons of diverse viewpoints to speak to each other from common touchstones. In the immigration debate, religious conviction has the potential to serve as common ground for a genuine dialogue. A central tenet of Catholic teaching is that all human beings are created in the image and likeness of God. For this reason, all are entitled to respect. None should be vilified, and nobody has a corner on wisdom, particularly when it comes to passionately contested, complex social issues like immigration.

A good midcourse correction in the immigration debate would be to attribute good motives to one's opponents and to recognize that they may be approaching the issue from a place of values, rather than bad faith, selfishness, or even hatred. This approach may prove to be naive, and it will not be successful in addressing the pathologically aggrieved, dishonest, or angry. However, to appeal to what are assumed to be shared values, and to try to convince fellow citizens of how society falls short of them, is a precondition to democratic dialog. It is also the legacy of the civil rights movement, whose mantle pro-immigrant activists claim. More importantly, this approach respects the God-given dignity of those with whom we disagree.

CATHOLIC TEACHING

The touchstones of Catholic teaching on migrants and newcomers cannot be contested. But the Hebrew scripture passages on offering hospitality and succor to the stranger do not prove the merits of particular public policy positions. Rather, their timeless themes and lessons infuse the Judeo-Christian tradition, calling on people to respect and empathize with migrants and newcomers. They are a reminder that all peoples have been unsettled, driven from their homes, and needful of compassion and acceptance.

The Catholic Church is, at its heart, the community of believers that comprises what St. Paul called the mystical body of Christ. As such, the church does not see migrants in "them versus us" terms: instead, it emphasizes a shared humanity and recognizes that all have been, are, and will again be migrants and newcomers.

These core themes have been drawn on to produce the body of authoritative texts known as "Catholic social teaching," or simply "Catholic teaching." Its lessons can be inspiring, challenging, and maddeningly broad. It leaves abundant room for disagreement on particular policy positions.

SOVEREIGNTY

According to Catholic teaching, sovereign states possess the authority and responsibility to regulate immigration. The Catholic bishops in the United States have criticized particular enforcement programs and strategies, but they have never disputed the need for effective enforcement of the law. Another tenet of Catholic teaching is that states must provide the conditions that allow their members to live with dignity and to realize their God-given rights. Human beings, in turn, bear the responsibility to fulfill their potential, according to God's plan. If states fail to meet this fundamental duty, persons have a right to improve their situations, either through migration or other means.

People who migrate because they cannot survive or sustain themselves or their families—whether the very poor, victims of natural disaster, or refugees—must be accepted and embraced by host nations, consistent with the common good of those nations. While something of an amorphous concept, the "common good" does not allow the rejection of needy migrants for purely economic reasons. Instead, the goods of the earth belong to all, have a "universal destination" and are held in a "social mortgage." In short, private property must serve the good of society. As a matter of justice—defined as the "right relations" between peoples—newcomers must also be allowed to participate in the life of their new community. It is not acceptable for societies to benefit from the labor of immigrants but prevent them from participating in other aspects of community life. What does this teaching mean and how should it be applied in the context of the U.S. immigration debate?

It has become more commonplace to view the notion of sovereign nation-states, widely credited as coming into being in the Peace of Westphalia (1648), as an anachronism. Some have argued that globalization has diminished the relevance and viability of nation-states. Others have questioned the salience of the idea of sovereignty in light of international human rights.

Catholic teaching rejects the totalitarian view of sovereignty as an expression of absolute state power. In Catholic thought, natural law and divine law limit the power of states. At the same time, Catholic social teaching places on states an immense responsibility: to defend rights and to promote the common good of their citizens. Hannah Arendt argued in the *Origins of Totalitarianism* (1951) that persons not deemed to belong to a state have nobody to defend their inalienable rights. In the current era, the importance of sovereign states has been further dramatized by the threats to rights posed by terrorist organizations in failed states and ungoverned territories. Finally, the Catholic Church recognizes civil and political rights (to vote and to practice one's religion, for example), socioeconomic rights (to sustenance, clothing, housing, education, work, and family life), and other rights that are necessary to live a fully human life. As a practical matter, such an expansive array of rights could not be realized absent local communities and sovereign states.

While often criticized, U.S. immigration policies exemplify the vital role states can play in safeguarding rights. Immigrants and their children represent a full one-fourth of the U.S. population, the largest total in U.S. history. Between 2000 and 2010, the United States granted lawful permanent resident (LPR) status to more than 11 million persons. Since 1975, it has admitted and resettled nearly 3 million refugees. Each year, it also awards political asylum to tens of thousands of persons and "temporary protected status" to thousands more who would face refugee-like conditions if returned home.

As Catholic teaching documents have frequently urged, the United States has adopted the relevant international protocols and conventions to protect refugees and persons at risk of torture. In 1968 the United States ratified the 1967 United Nations Protocol relating to the Status of Refugees. In doing so, it became bound by the 1951 United Nations Convention relating to the Status of Refugees. As a result, it cannot "expel or return" a refugee to territories "where his life or freedom would be threatened on account of his race, religion, nationality, membership of a particular social group or political opinion." In 1994 the United States ratified the UN Convention against Torture, which prevents the return of persons to countries where they are more likely than not to be tortured.

NATIONAL MEMBERSHIP

It does not follow from the idea that nations exist to honor God-given rights and to promote the common good that they cede the authority to determine who can belong. The question of the common good mostly speaks to the shared good of members in a local or national community. In addition, Catholic teaching views humans as social beings, with circles of association that begin with their families and extend to neighbors, local communities, and nations. The Catholic organizational principle of subsidiarity holds that the competent body closest to an issue should be vested with the authority to address it. This principle assumes coherent, engaged, and viable communities, not amorphous groupings to which anybody could chose to belong or could abandon at their convenience. Honoring the national common good—that is, providing the conditions that allow established residents (much less newcomers) in a community to flourish—presents real challenges for even wealthy nations. This point need not be belabored at a time of high unemployment and (involuntary) part-time employment.

A relatively recent development in Catholic teaching has been the idea of a universal or "border-less" common good that encompasses the broader international community. This concept gives states the responsibility to defend the rights of citizens of other states, including social and economic rights that involve complex distributive decisions. Yet, as world events regularly prove, the ability of one state to influence another's treatment of its own nationals can be very limited. In addition, even with the best of intentions, meaningful social change requires a long-term commitment to sound educational systems, laws and legal systems that honor the rule of law, robust democratic institutions, and broadly inclusive social and economic policies. For these reasons, the notion of a universal common good should be seen as highly aspirational and, thus, less credible as a guide to state behavior or as a tool to influence state action. In fact, it might best be viewed as a simple affirmation that nations—as their resources, proximity, and capacity permit—should attempt to provide some level of support or protection to vulnerable persons in other nations. The scope, shape, and urgency of foreign intervention would also depend on the level of privation or repression involved.

What does the Catholic Church teach about how nations should constitute themselves or decide who can belong? Its criteria for membership cannot be divorced from the issue of national identity, broadly understood to mean how a nation understands or views itself. While the Catholic Church decries racism and nationalism, its teaching on political membership is relatively underdeveloped. In U.S. history, there have been three, often overlapping views on national identity and membership.

Nativists, or "ethnocultural" nationalists, believe that membership should turn exclusively on characteristics that noncitizens cannot change, such as ancestry, national origin, race, ethnicity, or religion. To nativists, nothing but these characteristics matter—not the contributions of immigrants, not their character, hard work, time in the country, U.S. families, military service, or reasons for having come to the United States. Of course, the people behind the labels are precisely who *does* matter in Catholic teaching. Fortunately, only a small percentage of U.S. citizens can accurately be labeled nativist, though this term has been unfairly used to describe all persons who support further restrictions on immigration and oppose legalization of the nation's 11 million unauthorized immigrants.

Conservative "civic nationalists" believe that memberships should be defined by a core national culture. The late Harvard political scientist Samuel Huntington, for example, argued that the United States is primarily a Christian country, but with a strong tradition of respect for religious minorities. According to Huntington, the defining U.S. culture encompasses Anglo-Protestant values, the work ethic, the rule of law, the English language, a European artistic and philosophical heritage, and the principles of the American creed.

Although Huntington endorsed a multiracial, multiethnic nation, his emphasis on religion as a defining cultural characteristic could be criticized as nativist. At the same time, many of the characteristics he posited—hard work, respect for the rule of law, and the English language—would be accessible to persons of different races, creeds, and religions.

Under the more "liberal" form of civic nationalism, membership should turn on a shared commitment to democratic political institutions and civic ideals such as freedom, equality, rights, liberty, justice, and opportunity. This does not mean that all persons who accept what might be seen as universal values should be able to become U.S. citizens. It does mean that a precondition of membership should be acceptance of the "American creed," and that the response to immigrants who embrace and embody these values should be one of openness and generosity.

In his first inaugural speech, President George W. Bush drew heavily on the language and principles of Catholic social teaching to set forth a vision of membership not bound by ancestry or by birth on U.S. soil (the traditional criteria for citizenship), but rather by ideals that "move us beyond our backgrounds" and "lift us above our interests." In Bush's formulation, these ideals are that "everyone belongs," "everyone deserves a chance," and "no insignificant person was ever born." President Barack Obama, in his January 2010 State of the Union speech, struck a similar theme, arguing that ideals and values "built America" and "allowed us to forge a nation made up of immigrants from every corner of the globe; values that drive our citizens still." However, Obama appropriately conditioned equal treatment and protection under the law to adherence to the law and to shared values. "No matter who you are or what you look like," he said, "if you abide by the law you should be protected by it; if you adhere to our common values you should be treated no different than anyone else."

The Catholic Church views itself as a symbol—a "sign and instrument"—of unity that is not based on ethnicity, ancestry, or race. Nativism conflicts with this vision. On the other hand, Catholic teaching recognizes the responsibility of immigrants to contribute to the good of their adopted communities and nation, to embrace its positive values, and to obey its laws. Thus, it offers support for certain aspects of civic nationalism.

The "rule of law" presents a challenge for pro-immigrant groups that subscribe to this generous understanding of membership, but that also favor legalizing the nation's 11 million unauthorized immigrants. Laws presumably reflect the defining ideals of "creedal" nations. This may be why the "rule of law" plays a prominent role in the immigration debate, both in the United States and globally. A 2010 survey found that respondents in many European states viewed "respecting political institutions and laws" as a more important precondition to citizenship than even U.S. respondents did. For many U.S. natives, persons who break the law in entering or in using fraudulent documents start their lives in their new nation by defying its core values. To this way of thinking, lack of status creates a presumption that unauthorized immigrants do not value obedience to the law, do not want to belong, and perhaps even chose to be "illegal" as a way to enjoy the benefits of national membership without the responsibilities. This presumption can be overcome through contact with hard-working, law-abiding immigrants, whether neighbors, coworkers, employees, or coreligionists. However, even then, many natives distinguish the "good" immigrants they know from the mass of undifferentiated lawbreakers to whom they would not award legal status.

Some Catholics have responded to their bishops' support for a massive legalization program with incredulity. When earlier waves of Catholic immigrants faced hostility, the church responded with a two-pronged strategy. First, it took every opportunity to promote, encourage, and publicize the patriotism of Catholics. Second, it created a "cradle to grave" set of institutions to serve Catholics that included parishes, grade schools, high schools, universities, labor schools, charities, hospitals, insurance companies, and fraternal and sororal societies. This "parallel" society helped to ensure that Catholics received the services and support they needed in a hostile nation and could integrate into the larger society from a position of acceptance and strength.

In recent years, the Catholic Church has adapted many of the institutions that arose in response to earlier waves of immigrants to the needs of today's immigrants. However, these programs and ministries are not well known outside of immigrant communities. Thus, to many, the Catholic Church does not appear to be taking on the hard and important work of integrating immigrants as it did in the past. However, the Church has been quite public in its support for the legalization of 11 million unauthorized residents, a position that many long-settled Catholics view as unpatriotic.

PUBLIC POLICY IMPLICATIONS

If immigrant restrictionists negatively stereotype unauthorized immigrants, pro-immigrant advocates—including faith communities—idealize them. In fact, not all immigrants reinvigorate U.S. culture, reflect emblematic U.S. ideals, or even want to remain permanently. As with any group, U.S. immigrants include violent criminals, substance abusers, and troubled persons of every variety. In addition, not all migrants seek to support their families; in fact, some have abandoned their families abroad and started new families in the United States. Fortunately, Catholic teaching does not condition love of neighbor on the virtue or merits of our neighbors. The Catholic Church is a church of self-acknowledged sinners. Yet, for whatever reason, this most worldly of churches fails to recognize the following inconvenient truths about immigration and the policy implications that flow from them. If its public policy positions reflected these facts, these policies would enjoy greater support.

First, the ability of receiving nations to influence migrant-producing conditions in sending nations can be very limited. In most situations, the "right not to have to migrate" can best or only be realized by the sending nation itself. However, it may be possible to develop programs that would create modest economic opportunities in communities that have been decimated by emigration.

Second, the most desperate people generally lack the resources, support structures, and wherewithal to migrate to the United States. Most of those who enter illegally are poor compared to most Americans, but not abjectly so. U.S. residents benefit from lower-cost goods and services as a result of low-wage immigrant workers. However, immigration has a negative impact on the wages of less-educated U.S. workers, a group that ought to be of primary concern to the Catholic Church in the United States. It undermines the common good of the United States, particularly in difficult economic times, to admit high numbers of low-skilled immigrants or to fail to stop them from entering illegally.

In addition, certain employers prefer unauthorized workers because they can pay them less and treat them more unfairly than other workers. In this way, these employers drive down wages and working conditions for all workers, thus gaining an unfair competitive advantage over their law-abiding competitors. For this reason, the enforcement of labor standards in industries that hire substantial numbers of unauthorized workers should be a high priority.

Third, the United States increasingly finds itself in competition for entrepreneurs and highly skilled workers, who can help create jobs for others. It needs to attract more of these immigrants and should be particularly open to persons who have attended graduate school and been trained in the United States. Mostly, however, it needs a legal immigration policy that is flexible and supple enough to identify and admit the kinds of workers that the nation needs, when and where it needs them. In setting admissions categories and numbers, it needs information on unemployment rates, labor market needs, demographic trends, and immigrant integration. The Migration Policy Institute has proposed the creation of a Standing Commission on Immigration and Labor Markets that would make recommendations to Congress and the president on admissions policies based on the best, most current research on these kinds of issues. Congress should act on this recommendation.

Fourth, Catholic teaching sees the family as the fundamental building block of society. Thus, U.S. legal immigration policies should ensure that immediate family members of U.S. citizens and LPRs can immigrate in a timely matter. On the other hand, Congress should review and limit admissions under the immigration categories for more distant family relations, such as the adult brothers and sisters of U.S. citizens. Finally, the Catholic Church should acknowledge that just as deportations have divided immigrant families in the United States, so has immigration itself divided families in sending communities.

Fifth, not all unauthorized immigrants have equal claims to remain in the United States. The major flaw of large-scale legalization proposals is that they do not sufficiently distinguish groups that have the strongest claims to remain, whether based on their length of residence, family ties, potential to contribute, willingness to fill certain jobs, or their entry as children. The unauthorized comprise the following:

- The parents of 4.5 million U.S. citizen children

- 2.1 million residents who would be *prima facie* eligible for legal status under the DREAM Act

- Several million persons whose family-based visa petitions have been approved, but who have not yet received them

- Roughly 6 million residents who have resided in the United States for 10 years or more, and 1.4 million who have lived in the United States for at least 20 years

- More than 5 percent of the U.S. labor force

Deportation does not represent an acceptable or proportional solution for many persons who fall into these categories. Yet a "path to citizenship" represents an equally unfitting, and politically unrealistic, alternative for many authorized immigrants.

Since its first systemic restrictions on immigration in the 1920s, the United States has regularly seen the need to extend permanent legal status to discrete populations without immigration status and to certain temporary residents. Unauthorized persons with the following characteristics, particularly those who fit into more than one group, should be considered for legalization under the principles of Catholic social teaching:

- Young people brought to the United States as children who lack legal status and who have shown that they wish to contribute to their adopted country

- Certain unauthorized farm workers, guest workers, and other workers demonstrably in short supply in the U.S. labor market, as well as their spouses and minor children

- Immediate family members of LPRs who have not yet received family-based visas due to multiyear delays and other barriers in the visa process

- Persons repeatedly granted "temporary protected status" (based on untenable conditions in their homelands) who have built their lives in the United States

- Very long-term residents (in excess of 15 years) with strong family and equitable ties in the United States

Sixth, Catholic teaching strongly supports and values immigrant integration policies. Integration takes place through (1) civics classes, citizenship programs, and English language instruction; (2) job-training programs; (3) school, work, and other commitments; (4) mediating institutions such as churches, labor unions, political parties, and the armed services; and (5) participation in self-help groups and community-based organizations. Public and private institutions need to commit themselves to expanding these services and promoting immigrant integration in whatever ways they can.

However, the essential preconditions for integration are the capacity of communities to accommodate newcomers while preserving the positive aspects of their identity, and the willingness of immigrants to become full members of their new communities. In a nation defined by civic values, "patriotic" assimilation assumes a particular significance. Immigrants will not be bound by ideals that they fail to understand or to which their new nation pays only lip service. Catholic teaching recognizes the authority of sovereign states to regulate immigration in furtherance of the common good. Aggressive enforcement of U.S. immigration laws, combined with these other reforms, would send an important message about core U.S. values to newcomers and persons who are considering entering the country illegally or overstaying a visa.

References and Further Reading

Arendt, H. (2004). *The origins of totalitarianism.* New York: Schocken Books. (Originally published 1951)

Batalova, J., & McHugh, M. (2010, July). *DREAM vs. reality: An analysis of potential DREAM Act beneficiaries.* Retrieved from Migration Policy Institute website: http://www.migrationpolicy.org/pubs/DREAM-Insight-July2010.pdf

Bush, G. W. (2001, January 20). *Inaugural address.* Retrieved from http://www.bartleby.com/124/pres66.html

German Marshall Fund of the United States. (2010). *Transatlantic trends: Immigration 2010.* Retrieved from http://trends.gmfus.org/immigration/doc/TTI2010_English_Key.pdf

Groody, D. G., & Campese, G. (2008). *A promised land, a perilous journey: Theological perspectives on migration.* Notre Dame, IN: University of Notre Dame Press.

Holzer, H. J. (2011). *Immigration policy and less-skilled workers in the United States.* Retrieved from Migration Policy Institute website: http://www.migrationpolicy.org/pubs/Holzer-January2011.pdf

Kerwin, D. (2009). Toward a Catholic view of nationality. *Notre Dame Journal of Law, Ethics & Public Policy, 23*(1), 197–207.

Kerwin, D. (2010, December). *More than IRCA: US legalization programs and the current policy debate.* Retrieved from Migration Policy Institute website: http://www.migrationpolicy.org/pubs/legalization-historical.pdf

Kerwin, D., & Gerschutz, J. M. (Eds.). (2009). *And you welcomed me: Migration and Catholic social teaching.* Lanham, MD: Lexington Books.

Kerwin, D., with McCabe, K. (2011, July). *Labor standards enforcement and low-wage immigrants: Creating an effective enforcement system.* Retrieved from Migration Policy Institute website: http://www.migrationpolicy.org/pubs/laborstandards-2011.pdf

Kerwin, D., Meissner, D., & McHugh, M. (2011, March). *Executive action on immigration: Six ways to make the system work better.* Retrieved from Migration Policy Institute website: http://www.migrationpolicy.org/pubs/administrativefixes.pdf

Meissner, D., Meyers, D. W., Papademetriou, D. G., & Fix, M. (2006). *Immigration and America's future: A new chapter.* Retrieved from Migration Policy Institute website: http://www.migrationpolicy.org/ITFIAF

Morris, C. R. (1997). *American Catholic: The saints and sinners who built America's most powerful church.* New York, NY: Vintage Books.

Obama, B. (2010, January 27). *State of the Union Address.* Retrieved from http://www.nytimes.com/2010/01/28/us/politics/28obama.text.html?pagewanted=all

Passel, J. S., & Cohn, D. (2009). *A portrait of unauthorized immigrants in the United States.* Retrieved from Pew Hispanic Center website: http://pewhispanic.org/files/reports/107.pdf

Passel, J. S., & Cohn, D. (2011). *Unauthorized immigrant population: National and state trends, 2010.* Retrieved from Pew Hispanic Center website: http://pewhispanic.org/files/reports/133.pdf

Pope John XXIII. (1963, April 11). *Pacem in terris* [Peace on Earth (Encyclical)]. Retrieved from http://www.vatican.va/holy_father/john_xxiii/encyclicals/documents/hf_j-xxiii_enc_11041963_pacem_en.html

Pope John Paul II. (1995, July 25). *Message for World Migration Day, 1996.* Retrieved from http://www.vatican.va/holy_father/john_paul_ii/messages/migration/documents/hf_jp-ii_mes_25071995_undocumented_migrants_en.html

Pope Paul VI. (1964, November 21). Dogmatic constitution on the church, *Lumen gentium* [Light of the world]. Retrieved from http://www.vatican.va/archive/hist_councils/ii_vatican_council/documents/vat-ii_const_19641121_lumen-gentium_en.html

Pope Paul VI. (1965, December 7). Pastoral constitution on the church in the modern world, *Gaudium et spes* [Joy and hope]. Retrieved from http://www.vatican.va/archive/hist_councils/ii_vatican_council/documents/vat-ii_cons_19651207_gaudium-et-spes_en.html

Pope Paul VI. (1967, March 26). *Populorum progression:* On the development of peoples (Encyclical). Retrieved from http://www.vatican.va/holy_father/paul_vi/encyclicals/documents/hf_p-vi_enc_26031967_populorum_en.html

Spiro, P. J. (2008). *Beyond citizenship: American identity after globalization.* New York, NY: Oxford University Press.

United States Conference of Catholic Bishops, & Conferencia del Espiscopado Mexicano. (2003). *Strangers no longer: Together on the journey of hope.* Retrieved from http://www.usccb.org/mrs/stranger.shtml

Donald M. Kerwin Jr.

English as Official Language

POINT: America is an English-speaking country, and people who come here should be proficient in it or become so quickly; it is wasteful and culturally divisive to provide forms in so many languages.

K.C. McAlpin, ProEnglish

COUNTERPOINT: Establishing English as the official language of the United States will only cause harm to both non-English speakers and the nation as a whole.

Alida Y. Lasker, Cleary Gottlieb Steen & Hamilton

Introduction

Immigration brings into sharp focus issues of social cohesion and membership in the "imagined community" of nationhood. One of the attributes of American nationhood has been use of the English language, not just as a de facto practice but also deriving from the nation's history as a former British colony.

Earlier waves of immigrants have understood integration into American society as requiring the learning of English. In the twenty-first century, however, the existence of large Spanish-speaking immigrant enclaves has been interpreted by some as a "refusal" to learn English by these immigrants. This perceived refusal has led some to make the leap from "they should" learn English in order to be fully integrated to the idea that English should be the "official language" of the United States. In the debate that follows, K.C. McAlpin provides a window into the evolution of the pro-official English movement, which resists what its supporters see as the Balkanization of American culture.

In the Counterpoint essay, Alida Lasker argues that, as a practical matter, it's not clear what this would mean. Freedom of speech would make it impossible to require that people only speak English in the United States. Making English the "official language of government," as Newt Gingrich—the former Speaker of the House of Representatives and a 2012 candidate for the Republican nomination for president—has advocated, raises myriad issues, including concerns over equal protection, public safety (as a result of the problems that could arise if people can't read emergency instructions in government buildings), and access to government benefits, to name just a few.

Some equate making knowledge of English a precondition of citizenship with making English the country's official language. This isn't the case. English can be a requirement of citizenship without making it an "official" language. Thus, this is really a symbolic debate that touches on a number of sensitive and complex problems, such as resentments over illegal Hispanic immigration; visceral reactions to the number of "other" immigrants from strange and foreign lands who have not or, in some people's opinions, will not assimilate or integrate into American society; frustration from equating the difficulty of learning a new language as an adult with a "refusal" to learn English; and fundamental questions such as "Whose country is this, anyway?"

There are also occasional concerns raised about the expense of printing official documents in multiple languages and about the fairness of catering to Spanish-speakers at the expense of other immigrant groups, but these are largely side issues in the overall debate.

In the Point essay below, McAlpin asserts that unless the United States takes steps to preserve its linguistic unity and immigration continues at current levels, the United States is in danger of transforming itself into a linguistically divided society. It is also noted that the history of linguistically divided societies is not a peaceful one. McAlpin traces the history of the U.S. government's movement away from policies that place a premium on learning English—such as mandating English in schools and requiring English for public office as a condition for statehood—toward the current prevailing policies that, to the detriment of the country's cultural cohesion, encourage multilingualism and discourage linguistic assimilation. Making English the official language of the United States, in McAlpin's view, would have symbolic as well as practical importance.

In contrast, Lasker argues that there is no compelling reason the United States should designate English as the official language of the country. In fact, doing so would not only be inconsistent with the country's history of a generally tolerant attitude towards immigration and multilingualism, it would seriously abridge the rights of millions of people, many of whom are, in fact, citizens of this country. Indeed, even the Founding Fathers were not unanimous in their opinions on the role of language—whose should be spoken and with what official status. Over the course of American history, such opinions are often inextricably linked to political sentiments and attitudes toward an influx of immigrants that are non-English speakers. "The Constitution itself," Lasker notes, "when it was signed in 1787, made no mention of the establishment of an official language for the nation."

Indeed, although some Americans believe that returning to the core convictions of the Founding Fathers is the best way to approach the complex problems of American governance, in the case of the debate over language and its importance for the social, cultural, and political cohesion of the country, seeking the counsel of the Founders leads to just as many questions as answers.

POINT

When men cannot communicate their thoughts to each other, simply because of difference of language, all the similarity of their common human nature is of no avail to unite them in fellowship.

—St. Augustine, The City of God, *Book XIX, Chapter 7*

As St. Augustine's fifth-century observation illustrates, the critical role language plays as either a bridge or a barrier between peoples has been known for centuries. When Augustine was writing, in the twilight days of the Western Roman Empire, Latin was the tongue that bound the empire together and made Rome's rule over its vast collection of tribes and peoples possible.

The western part of the empire collapsed not long after St. Augustine's death. But thanks to the Roman Church's monopoly on education, the linguistic unity the empire ushered in persisted throughout the western Mediterranean and Europe for another 1,300 years, through wars, migrations, plagues, and political upheavals, and well into the modern era. Until Francis Hutcheson started teaching in the local Scots-English dialect at the University of Glasgow in 1730, every university student from Lisbon to St. Petersburg had to be fluent in Latin because all classes and exams were conducted in the classic tongue.

Thus, when one reads that the Dutch-born theologian Erasmus traveled to England, where he befriended Sir Thomas Moore in the early sixteenth century, or that they each traveled to Rome and spoke to the pope, it was Latin they used to communicate. It may be more than an accident of history that the rise of European nationalism that so devastated Europe in successive wars during the nineteenth and twentieth centuries coincided with the disappearance of Latin as the lingua franca of Europe's educated elite.

Throughout history, empires and nation-states exercising political dominion over disparate linguistic groups have sought to unite their territories with a common language. Often, this has meant the systematic suppression of minority languages and the imposition of a dominant tongue. At other times, the imperative manifested itself in a more benign policy of official multilingualism. But the goal was always the same: to forge a linguistic bond between dissimilar peoples and facilitate efficient communication, administration, a degree of cultural unity, and thereby strengthen the state's power against outsiders.

HISTORY OF ENGLISH AS THE COMMON LANGUAGE OF THE UNITED STATES

Viewed in the context of European empires and nation-states, the United States is an anomaly. Except for scattered German-speaking settlements, the 13 colonies that occupied its original territory were overwhelmingly English-speaking. John Jay, the first president of the Continental Congress and a coauthor of the Federalist Papers, observed that one of the American colonists' great strengths was that they were "one united people speaking the same language."

English's role as the nation's unifying and virtually universal tongue did not go unchallenged. Nineteenth-century territorial expansion and conquest, especially the acquisition of vast sparsely populated territories as a result of the Louisiana Purchase and the U.S.-Mexican War, added significant French- and Spanish-speaking minorities to the population. But U.S. government policies such as mandating English in schools and requiring English for public office as a condition for statehood in territories like Oklahoma, Arizona, and New Mexico, together with an influx of English-speaking settlers, succeeded in absorbing these minorities into the larger English-speaking community over time.

English's role as the national tongue was challenged again by the great wave of immigration from mostly non-English-speaking European countries during the last decade of the nineteenth century and first two decades of the twentieth century. The rapid growth of the non-English-speaking population and the natural tendency of new immigrants to settle among people speaking the same tongue created large and flourishing linguistic ghettos in many northern industrial cities. These ghettos had the critical mass necessary for English to be virtually displaced as the common language of the local population. Over time, they gave rise to foreign-language newspapers, churches, synagogues, schools, and numerous community-based organizations.

Yet once again the country succeeded in meeting the challenge of linguistic assimilation into America's English-speaking community. This occurred for four main reasons. First, the prevailing, almost universal view of American intellectuals and cultural elites at the time was that learning English was essential. It was necessary both for the successful assimilation of new immigrants and to enable these newcomers to join unions, fend for themselves, and free themselves from the power of the industrial magnates. Institutionally, the impulse was expressed in things like the Settlement House movement, in which civic associations, churches, and progressive activists taught English as well as American government, traditions, and civic culture to new arrivals. Conceptually, it found expression in the ideal of the "melting pot" society in which dissimilar ingredients melted to form a more uniform whole. The task was made easier by the fact that the immigrant flow was far more linguistically diverse then, and no one language dominated among immigrants as Spanish has in recent decades.

Second, government policy favored English. Scant public resources were devoted to accommodating the linguistic needs of new immigrants. The prevailing government view was expressed by political leaders like Theodore Roosevelt and Woodrow Wilson, who made no bones about immigrants' responsibility to learn English, assimilate, and reassign their political loyalty to their adopted country. The Naturalization Act of 1906, signed into law by President Theodore Roosevelt, required immigrants to learn English to become naturalized citizens.

Third, although many immigrants failed to adapt, and did eventually return to their native countries, the large majority who remained were determined to learn English or make sure their children did. They were eager to adopt a new identity as Americans, and to cast off the social, class, and ethnic identities that had barred or limited upward mobility in their homelands.

The fourth and decisive blow to the linguistic Balkanization of the country was the government's decision in the early 1920s to sharply curtail immigration. This cut the flow of new arrivals to a trickle. Deprived of new additions, the large, non-English-speaking ghettos of Italians, Germans, Poles, Jews, Ukrainians, and other mostly eastern European nationalities ceased to grow. As time passed, successive generations learned English in public school, joined the armed forces, or took jobs in government or business. As they gained affluence, they married or moved outside their communities. It did not happen overnight, but eventually the old ghettos faded away. Most of what remains today are cultural rather than linguistic markers, such as foods, architecture, festivals, and religious affiliations.

In the 1970s, however, things began to change. Propelled again by mass immigration from non-English-speaking countries, English's place as the unifying and almost universally spoken language in the United States began to erode. In 1980 the U.S. Census Bureau reported 11 percent of U.S. residents spoke a language other than English at home, but by 2007 the figure had risen to 20 percent, representing 55.4 million people. More ominously for the nation's linguistic unity, of those 55.4 million, 62 percent, or 34.5 million people, spoke a single language at home, Spanish. The rapid increase in the non-English-speaking population had once again created large linguistic ghettos and the critical mass necessary for English to be virtually displaced as the common language of the local population.

These demographic trends and the reemergence of linguistic diversity and linguistic-cultural segregation have been reinforced and facilitated by other trends. One has been a decided shift in the attitudes of most American intellectuals and cultural elites away from assimilation into the prevailing American culture and the ideal of the "melting pot" and toward "multiculturalism" with its closely related manifestation of multilingualism, in which maintaining group identity is the overriding goal. Metaphorically, the competing ideal is described as the "salad bowl," in which different ingredients are mixed, but instead of blending retain their separate identities and distinctiveness.

This shift in elite opinion was accompanied by a gradual but pronounced shift in government policy. Before the 1970s, government policy had discouraged multilingualism, but by 2000 this had changed and the use of foreign languages is now encouraged and even demanded. In August 2000, for example, President Bill Clinton issued Executive Order 13166. The order mandated that all recipients of federal funds, including state and local governments, provide translation and interpreter services for their non-English-speaking clients in many instances and circumstances, or else face the loss of federal funds and the threat of civil rights prosecution.

Another change occurred in education policy starting in the early 1970s. The 1968 Bilingual Education Act required schools to give special help to children lacking English language ability. The new approach the act called for was to teach such children core subjects in their native language while giving them supplemental help in learning English. This approach, called bilingual education, was promoted as a way to help children keep from falling behind their peers while they strove to learn English. In the words of the law's sponsor, Senator Ralph Yarborough of Texas, its purpose was "not to create pockets of different languages throughout the country . . . but to make these students fully literate in English" (Porter, 1998). Federal money was appropriated and although the federal government never mandated bilingual education, many states passed strict laws requiring bilingual education in their public schools.

Despite the expenditure of hundreds of billions of dollars, these programs failed to teach English effectively and ultimately lost support from natives and immigrants alike. This was reflected in an April 2007 McLaughlin & Associates poll of 1,000 likely voters and 300 likely Hispanic voters that found an identical 88 percent of both groups in favor of placing limited English proficient children in English-immersion classrooms. The attitude of many Hispanic parents toward bilingual education was best expressed by the South Texas ranch foreman Ernesto Ortiz, who said, "My children learn Spanish in school so they can grow up to be busboys and waiters. I teach them English at home so they can grow up to be doctors and lawyers" (Silber, 1989, p. 25).

In 1975, Congress amended the Voting Rights Act to mandate the provision of bilingual ballots in political jurisdictions in which certain thresholds were met. Because the 1952 Immigration and Naturalization Act requires knowledge of English for naturalization, the justification the amendment's sponsors used was that the change was necessary to remedy the unequal access to education experienced by certain minority-language groups. Thus, American Indian, Spanish, and Asian languages were included, but not others such as Middle Eastern, African, or eastern European languages. The threshold for providing bilingual ballots is that the number of voting-age citizens speaking one of the protected languages exceeds 5 percent of the total number of citizens, or 10,000 citizens, in a particular jurisdiction, whichever is less.

An example of the government bureaucracy's bias in favor of multilingualism occurred early in the implementation of the bilingual ballot laws. Counterintuitively and with little credible justification, the Census Bureau chose to include citizens who describe themselves as speaking English "well" in the group of citizens needing language assistance to vote. By doing so, Census Bureau bureaucrats tripled the number of jurisdictions subject to the law.

Supporters of bilingual ballots said the provisions were only temporary remedial measures. A 1986 report by the U.S. General Accounting Office found that the ballots were rarely used, and polls indicated widespread public opposition. A March 2006 Zogby International poll of 1,007 likely voters found 63 percent favored ballots in English alone. Despite this finding, Congress lacked the political will to let them expire, and bilingual ballots were renewed for the third time in 2007, extending the "temporary" measure for another 25 years.

Under pressure from various ethnic interest groups and advocates, government agencies increasingly act on their own and without specific authorization to provide signage, translations, and interpreters in foreign languages, especially Spanish. So, for example, the Social Security Administration makes information available online not only in English, but in sixteen other languages.

The Equal Employment Opportunity Commission (EEOC) provided more evidence of the bureaucracy's ideologically driven determination to transform the United States into a multilingual/multicultural utopia, even at the expense of fundamental civil rights. In 2002 the EEOC filed suit against the owners of a family-owned drive-in restaurant in Page, Arizona, charging them with "national origins" discrimination for implementing an English-on-the-job policy to stop some of their Navajo employees from sexually harassing other Navajo employees in the Navajo language. The EEOC continues to investigate and file suit against employers with English-on-the-job policies, notwithstanding the fact that the courts have ruled repeatedly that employers have the right to have such workplace policies and have told the EEOC that its actions are *ultra vires,* or outside the scope of its legal authority.

Nonetheless, the widespread and often unauthorized about-face in the direction of government language policy did not satisfy multilingual advocates. In 1999, Thomas E. Perez, a high-ranking official in the Health and Human Services (HHS) Department, held a private meeting with a number of leaders of multilingual advocacy organizations, who wanted to force health-care providers to provide interpreter services and translations for non-English-speaking patients. The meeting led to a letter signed by 16 advocacy groups urging HHS to "strengthen and enhance" its language policy guidance to require health-care providers to provide language assistance to patients regardless of the size of the language group involved.

The legal theory put forward by the interest groups was to equate language with a person's national origin, and thereby make the failure to provide multilingual services a violation of federal civil rights law. To most observers, however, it is self-evident that the language someone speaks often says nothing about that person's national origin. Spanish, French, and Chinese, for example, are the principal languages of dozens of different nations. Conversely, a native of India could speak any one of dozens of different tongues. It also did not matter that the effort to equate national origin with language under the 1964 Civil Rights Act had been rejected in numerous court decisions at the federal and state level for 30 years. The groups wanted action.

What they got exceeded their expectations. On August 11, 2000, President Clinton signed Executive Order 13166 (E.O. 13166) which claimed to merely "interpret" existing civil rights law instead of creating new law, which is exactly what E.O. 13166 did. The order applied the disputed "language equals national origin" formula to all recipients of federal funds including federal, state, and local government agencies, government contractors, and medical providers such as doctors and hospitals participating in the Medicaid or Medicare programs. (Fearful that a new administration would rescind the order, the Justice Department ordered federal agencies to begin implementation within 120 days, light-speed by government standards. They need not have worried. Soon after President George W. Bush was sworn into office in January 2001, his administration signaled that it would not revoke E.O. 13166, which remains in effect.)

E.O. 13166 gave ideologically minded government bureaucrats an extraordinarily powerful new tool to advance their multicultural agenda, notwithstanding the opposing views of the vast majority of U.S. citizens, or the order's suspect legal authority. (A Rasmussen Reports poll of 1,000 adults in May 2010 found 87 percent of respondents in favor of making English the official language of the country.) In 2001 the Supreme Court vacated *Sandoval v. Alexander,* the solitary case that had upheld the language equals national origin formula. However, federal courts in the Fourth and Ninth Circuits subsequently shielded Executive Order 13166 from direct legal challenge by subjectively and inconsistently applying Department of Justice procedural objections to avoid a trial.

The wholesale change in the prevailing views of intellectual elites and government policy was greatly assisted by technological advances. The computerization of communications technology, for example, made it far more feasible for a whole range of institutions—from government agencies to medical providers, businesses, and social welfare organizations—to provide multilingual services either in person, via telephone translation services, or over the Internet. A common example of this technology is the ubiquitous automatic teller machine (ATM) that offers services in multiple languages. Yet there could hardly be an example in a democratic society of a more unpopular policy being imposed on the majority by a willful, ideologically driven minority. Not surprisingly, it has led to popular resistance.

THE RISE OF THE OFFICIAL ENGLISH MOVEMENT

The late U.S. Senator S. I. Hayakawa, a Canadian-born naturalized U.S. citizen of Japanese descent and former professor of English and president of San Francisco State University, who was elected to the U.S. Senate in 1976, is widely acknowledged as the "father" of the Official English movement in the United States. In 1981, alarmed by the drift toward linguistic Balkanization and segregation he saw taking place in his home state of California, the senator introduced the first Official English legislation ever introduced in the U.S. Congress: a constitutional amendment declaring English the official language of the United States. The Senate failed to take up the legislation, but after retiring from the Senate in 1983, Senator Hayakawa continued the battle and cofounded U.S. English, the first national organization dedicated to making English the official language of the United States.

The senator's action capitalized on growing concerns among members of the U.S. public. When he introduced his amendment, only five states (Hawaii, Illinois, Louisiana, Massachusetts, and Nebraska) had made English their official language of government. But beginning in the 1980s, successive citizen petition campaigns succeeded in passing Official English laws by overwhelming margins, despite determined opposition from business, political, and media elites. More and more states joined the bandwagon until, in 2009, 31 states had adopted Official English laws of various descriptions.

The move to adopt Official English laws spread to cities and counties. In 2006 the city of Hazleton, Pennsylvania, made national headlines following its adoption of an Official English ordinance. The city's action inspired a flurry of copycat efforts by cities, towns, and counties across the country.

A similar manifestation of the public's opposition to the government's undeclared policy in favor of multilingualism was the movement to get rid of bilingual education programs, long considered a sacred cow in the field of education, notwithstanding their 30-year record of failure. The movement started in 1996 when a group of Hispanic immigrant parents in Los Angeles, outraged that their children were being placed in Spanish language classrooms year after year, organized a boycott of a Los Angeles County elementary school.

The boycott attracted national attention and led Silicon Valley entrepreneur Ron Unz to bankroll a petition campaign that succeeded in putting a referendum on the California ballot in 1998. Proposition 227 called for the elimination of bilingual education programs and replacing them with assisted English-immersion style classrooms. Despite opposition from the two major political parties, newspapers, unions, business leaders, religious leaders, ethnic interest groups, and a lavishly funded media campaign to defeat it, Proposition 227 passed with 60 percent of the vote.

Overnight, the nation's largest state, home to over 27 percent of the country's foreign-born population, had resolved to eliminate bilingual education. Rising test scores for non-English-speaking school children transferred to English-immersion classrooms convinced even some former opponents, and California's example was followed by Arizona in 2000 and Massachusetts in 2002.

Nonetheless, a 2002 statewide referendum to eliminate bilingual education in Colorado failed by 49 percent to 50 percent, following a multimillion dollar media campaign by opponents. They warned that if the referendum passed, majority white suburban school districts would be overrun by non-English-speaking Hispanic children. The opposition's race-baiting campaign and misleading TV ads were so egregious they were condemned by the state's major newspapers, even though the newspapers opposed the measure.

At the national level, legislation to make English the official language of the United States has been introduced in every Congress since Senator Hayakawa first introduced his amendment. Proponents succeeded in passing bills in the House of Representatives in 1996 and in the Senate in 2006 and 2007. But each time the legislation failed to be taken up by the other chamber before Congress adjourned.

WHAT OFFICIAL ENGLISH MEANS

Making English the official language simply makes it the standard language of government operations, so that whenever government acts in its official capacity, it has to use English. It would not prevent government from using other languages whenever there is a general public interest in doing so. Exceptions would include things like teaching foreign languages; printing documents or taking actions necessary for national security; foreign relations; or the promotion of commerce, tourism, and international trade. Protecting public health and safety would be exempted, for example, in the distribution of information to warn people about the dangers of diseases like HIV/AIDS. An Official English law also would have no effect on how the Census Bureau gathers information, on actions that protect the rights of victims of crimes or criminal defendants, or on many other common-sense needs for which government has to use other languages.

On the other hand, if properly implemented, Official English laws would bar driver's license exams in multiple languages, taxpayer-paid interpreter services in civil lawsuits, foreign-language signs in government offices, and numerous other instances in which no public interest is being served for the wider community.

OPPOSITION ARGUMENTS

Dismayed by the overwhelming success of Official English initiatives and bans on bilingual education, opponents of Official English have tried to counter with a variety of arguments including harsh rhetoric and outright distortion.

Initially, the opposition sought to downplay the size of the problem, citing data to prove the United States is overwhelmingly monolingual and asserting that immigrants are indeed learning English. But these arguments have been undermined by Census Bureau reports revealing a sharp rise in the number of "linguistically isolated" households, as well as the day-to-day experience of ordinary Americans who come into contact with increasing numbers of non-English-speaking residents in their local communities.

Opponents have therefore turned to distortions and inflammatory rhetoric. For example, Official English laws are unfairly accused of criminalizing the use of other languages, not only when used informally by government officials, but also when used by ordinary people in their private conversations. Such characterizations are false. None of the 31 states with Official English laws prohibits the use of other languages by private individuals or businesses, or for many legitimate public needs. Yet opponents continue to make such unfounded charges.

If anything, government officials in states with Official English laws already on the books err on the side of being too lax in enforcing them. For example, Alabama, which has a constitutional amendment making English the official language, and that specifically directs state officials to "take all steps necessary to insure that the role of English as the common language of the state of Alabama is preserved and enhanced," continues to offer driver's license exams in 13 other languages. Despite these examples, opponents continue to spread totally unfounded fears, especially in non-English-speaking communities, about the impact of Official English.

A more subtle form of distortion is frequent use of the term "English only" by the media and others to characterize Official English laws. In addition to being false, this description conveys a sense of linguistic exclusivity that is entirely alien to the leadership of the Official English movement, many of whom, like the late Senator S. I. Hayakawa, are multilingual first-generation immigrants. Indeed, the two major national organizations dedicated to making English the official language are chaired by bilingual and trilingual, first-generation immigrants.

Opponents also have resorted to the age-old strategy of ad-hominem attacks, demonizing supporters of Official English, using guilt by association, and similar smear tactics. Senator Harry Reid, the Democratic Majority Leader, even went so far as to say on the Senate floor that he thought an Official English amendment being offered by Senator James Inhofe of Oklahoma, a Republican who speaks fluent Spanish, was "racist," notwithstanding the fact that 11 of Reid's Senate Democratic colleagues later voted for the amendment. Polls show that the American people do not accept Senator Reid's characterization. In 2010, when Rasmussen Reports asked if Official English is a form of racism or bigotry, the public disagreed 84 percent to 10 percent.

WHY OFFICIAL ENGLISH IS NECESSARY

The history of linguistically divided societies is not a peaceful one. As an anonymous philosopher is reputed to have said, religion and language are the two great dividers of mankind. In the past decade countries as diverse as Belgium, Canada, Sri Lanka, Kenya, and the Ukraine have been torn by linguistic-cultural conflict that often resulted in murderous intercommunal violence.

Today, the United States is one of the few countries in the world without at least one official language (along with fewer than 15 percent of 193 United Nations member states). Fifty-four countries, located mainly in Africa, Asia, and the Caribbean, have made English an official language, including 27 that have designated English as their sole official language. Many of those countries were created with numerous language groups within their boundaries and have deliberately chosen English as a neutral ground in the hope—unfortunately, often a vain hope—of avoiding intercommunal strife and conflict. As the educator and author E. D. Hirsch Jr. (1988) notes, "multilingualism enormously increases cultural fragmentation, civil antagonism, illiteracy, and economic-technological ineffectualness" (p. 92).

In contrast, unless it takes intentional steps to preserve its linguistic unity, and if immigration continues at current levels, the United States may be the only nation in history to deliberately transform itself into a linguistically divided society. De facto government policies that encourage multilingualism and discourage immigrants from assimilating into a common American culture mean that U.S. policymakers are effectively abandoning the formula that enabled it to become the most successful, multiethnic country in the history of the world, and replacing it with a balkanized model of society that endangers social cohesion and national unity wherever it exists.

As the late Barbara Jordan, a former member of Congress and civil rights leader, who chaired the U.S. Commission on Immigration Reform, observed when she testified to Congress on June 28, 1995, "Cultural and religious diversity does not pose a threat to the national interest *as long as public policies insure civic unity* [emphasis added]. Such polices should help newcomers learn to speak, read, and write English effectively."

Making English the official language would have the practical effect of stipulating that while government could act in other languages, for its actions to be legally binding and authoritative, they would have to be communicated in the English language. It would also clarify that whenever a conflict in meaning occurs between laws, regulations, or government communications in more than one language, the English language version is the authoritative meaning. Adopting Official English would align federal government agencies with other government institutions, like the armed services and the federal court system, which for practical reasons have decided to conduct official business in English alone.

Such an action would also save money. Providing translations and interpreter services in even a handful of the 322 languages now spoken in the country adds significantly to the cost of government operations. The Office of Management and Budget (OMB) estimated in 2002 that the cost of providing language assistance services was as much as $1 to $2 billion annually. However, the OMB says its estimate may not reflect the full cost, because government agencies are not required to account for the cost of such services. A more accurate estimate might be derived from Canada. Although it has roughly one-tenth the population of the United States, Canada spends an estimated $1 billion annually to provide the translation and interpreter services it needs to conduct government business in two official languages.

Barring translations and interpreters for standard government services would also encourage immigrants to learn English. This would not only save the government money in the short run, it would help immigrants to become self-sufficient by improving their job skills and raising their incomes. Research from the U.S. Department of Education shows immigrants with a low degree of English fluency earn only half as much as those with moderate fluency and only a third as much as those who are highly fluent. So encouraging immigrants to learn English strengthens the economy, boosts tax revenue, and helps the U.S. remain competitive in the global economy. Government policy that provides incentives rather than disincentives for immigrants to learn English is a win-win situation for both the United States and the immigrant.

Symbolically, declaring English the official language of the United States would send this important message to new arrivals: If you aspire to avail yourselves of all the opportunities in this society, you have a responsibility to make learning English your first priority. At the same time, it would reassure native-born English-speaking Americans that immigration is not going to transform the United States into a country they do not recognize and where they no longer feel at home. It would signal that the United States intends to remain unified as an English-speaking country and not plunge headlong down the path of a linguistically divided society, with all the dangers and conflicts that entails.

Finally, such a decision would be responsive to the principles of democracy and the will of the American people, overwhelming majorities of whom, according to polls, want English to be the official language of the United States. This desire cuts across all lines and reflects a degree of unanimity not known to exist on any other major policy issue. A 2007 Harvard University poll of 2,923 young adults, ages 18 to 24 found 72 percent favored making English the official language of the country, including majorities of Hispanic and Asian young adults. To preserve the incredibly successful "melting pot" society and protect the opportunity the United States offers to people from every country on earth, it is important to make English the official language of the nation.

REFERENCES AND FURTHER READING

Caravantes, E. (2006). *Clipping their own wings: The incompatibility between Latino culture and American education.* Lanham, MD: Hamilton Books.

Education Testing Services. (2004, March). *A human capital concern: The literacy proficiency of U.S. immigrants.* Retrieved from http://www.ets.org/Media/Research/pdf/PICHUMAN.pdf

Geyer, G. A. (1996). *Americans no more: The death of citizenship.* New York, NY: Atlantic Monthly Press.

Hayakawa, S. I. (1978). *Language in thought and action* (4th ed.). New York, NY: Harcourt Brace Jovanovich.

Hirsch, E. D., Jr. (1988). *Cultural literacy: What every American needs to know.* New York, NY: Vintage.

Huntington, S. P. (2004). *Who are we? The challenges to America's national identity.* New York, NY: Simon & Schuster.

National Center for Educational Statistics. (2001, August). *English literacy and language minorities in the United States: Results from National Adult Literacy Survey.* Retrieved from http://nces.ed.gov/pubsearch/pubsinfo.asp?pubid=2001464

Porter, R. P. (1996). *Forked tongue: The politics of bilingual education.* New York, NY: Basic Books.

Porter, R. P. (1998, May). The case against bilingual education. *The Atlantic Monthly, 281*(5), 28–39.

Porter, R. P. (2001). *American immigrant: My life in three languages.* New Brunswick, NJ: Transaction.

Schlesinger, A. M., Jr. (1998). *The disuniting of America: Reflections on a multicultural society* (2nd ed.). New York, NY: W. W. Norton.

Silber, J. (1989). *Straight shooting: What's wrong with America and how to fix it.* New York, NY: HarperCollins.

U.S. Bureau of the Census. (2010, April). *Language use in the United States: 2007* (American Community Survey Report). Retrieved from http://www.census.gov/prod/2010pubs/acs-12.pdf

U.S. Commission on Civil Rights. (2011, July). *English only policies in the workplace: A briefing report.* Retrieved from http://www.usccr.gov/pubs/Re_EOPWORK_10-03-11.pdf

U.S. General Accounting Office. (1986, September). *Bilingual voting assistance: Costs of and use during the November 1984 general election* (Briefing report to the Honorable Quentin N. Burdick, U.S. Senate). Retrieved from http://gao.gov/products/GGD-86-134BR

U.S. Office of Management and Budget. (2002, March 14). *Assessment of total benefits and costs of implementing Executive Order No. 13166: Improving Access to Services for Persons with Limited English Proficiency* [Report to Congress]. Retrieved from http://www.justice.gov/crt/about/cor/lep/omb-lepreport.pdf

K.C. McAlpin

COUNTERPOINT

The United States has never designated English—or any other language—the official language of the nation. Nor is there any compelling reason it should do so now. In fact, establishing English as the official language of the United States would not only be inconsistent with this nation's history and generally tolerant attitude toward immigration and multilingualism, it would also seriously abridge the rights of millions of people, many of whom are citizens of this country. As of the 2000 U.S. Census (the last census for which linguistic data are available), more than 300 languages are spoken in the United States, and approximately 4.2 percent of people living in the United States are not proficient in English. Translated into population numbers from early 2012, this means that as many as 13 million people would be affected by Official English laws, which would undermine their rights to education, a fair trial, voting, and a workplace free of discrimination. Therefore, as elaborated below, the United States should not establish English as its official language.

HISTORICAL BACKGROUND

The United States is now, and has always been, a nation of people that hail from many different countries and speak many different languages. That is why there is truth to the expression that, with the exception of the Native Americans, the United States is quite literally a country of immigrants. At the time of the American Revolution, at least six European languages were widely spoken in the United States, with German being the most frequently spoken after English. As part of an effort to enlist the assistance of German speakers in the Revolutionary War, the Continental Congress published documents in German. Moreover, the Articles of Confederation, which founded the first incarnation of the United States in 1781, were printed in official French, German, and English versions.

Given the nation's history of immigration and multilingualism, it is not surprising that debates concerning the role and status of languages in the United States date back to even before the founding of this nation. The Framers of the Constitution themselves differed on the role of the English language in this multilingual nation. John Adams was in favor of English as the official language of the fledgling nation, while Thomas Jefferson was an advocate of multilingualism. In 1780, prior to the drafting of the Constitution, John Adams proposed that Congress establish a National Academy for "refining, improving, and ascertaining the English Language"—an act that, if undertaken, would have codified English as the official language of the United States (Perea, 1992, p. 295). Adams's proposal died in a congressional committee before being debated by Congress, and according to the legal scholar Juan F. Perea (1992), the proposal was "doomed to failure" because it "was inconsistent with principles of individual liberty, and it had the taint of monarchist association" (p. 297). For his part, Benjamin Franklin had long feared the impact of the German speaking population in Pennsylvania, observing as early as 1751 that "unless the stream of their importation could be turned from this to other Colonies . . . they will soon outnumber us [and] all the advantages we have will not (in My Opinion) be able to preserve our language, and even our Government will become precarious" (Perea, 1992, p. 288). Thus, one can see that, as early as the founding of this nation, conflicts over the role of language (whose should be spoken and with what official status) have been inextricably linked to political sentiments and attitudes toward the influx of immigrants who are non-English speakers.

Significantly, however, the Constitution itself, when it was signed in 1787, made no mention of the establishment of an official language for the nation. Was this an oversight? Probably not, considering that, as described above, the Founders had strong views on this matter. Although it is not known whether language debates arose at the Constitutional Convention (because the discussions were held in secret), some scholars believe that the view that language choices should be left to individuals prevailed, and that the Founders made "a deliberate choice of a *policy not to have a policy*" on the issue of language (Crawford, 1990, quoting Heath, 1976 [emphasis in original]). Whatever the case may be, it is clear that the Constitution itself is silent on the question of an official language, strongly suggesting that there was no consensus among the Framers that making English the official language of the United States was an essential provision of the nation's foundational document.

Despite ongoing immigration in the nineteenth century, it was not until 1906 that a federal law was enacted related to the official status of the English language, and it came in the form of the first requirement that applicants for naturalization must "speak the English language," in the Naturalization Act of 1906 (repealed 1940). Not surprisingly, this law was enacted in the first two decades of the twentieth century, a period marked by public and political opposition to the swells of immigration from eastern and southern Europe. In 1911, a federal report on immigration "accused these so-called 'new immigrants'—Italians, Jews, and Slavs—of failing to learn English as quickly as the Germans and Scandinavians of the Nineteenth Century" (Crawford, 1990).

However, after the United States entered World War I against Germany, attention shifted away from Italians, Jews, and Slavs and back to the German speakers in America, out of fear that they were not loyal to the United States in the war. The consequences of this included state laws banning the speaking of German on the street, at religious services and—most significantly for this discussion—in schools. In the 1920s immediately after the war 15 states made English the official language of school instruction. When Nebraska went so far as to make instruction in a language other than English prior to the eighth grade a crime, a teacher was criminally charged for teaching reading in German to a child who had not yet reached that grade. Significantly, the ancient languages of Latin, Greek, and Hebrew were exempt from this law, suggesting that the law was aimed at the languages of non-English-speaking immigrants. The case wound its way to the Supreme Court, where proponents of the law argued, in *Meyer v. Nebraska* (1923), that its purpose "was to promote civic development by inhibiting training and education of the immature in foreign tongues and ideals before they could learn English and acquire American ideals, and 'that the English language should be and become the mother tongue of all children reared in this State.' It is also affirmed that the foreign born population is very large, that certain communities commonly use foreign words, follow foreign leaders, move in a foreign atmosphere, and that the children are thereby hindered from becoming citizens of the most useful type, and the public safety is imperiled."

In finding the Nebraska law unconstitutional under the due process clause of the Fourteenth Amendment, the Supreme Court observed: "The protection of the Constitution extends to all, to those who speak other languages as well as those born with English on the tongue. Perhaps it would be highly advantageous if all had ready understanding of our ordinary speech, but this cannot be coerced by methods which conflict with the Constitution—a desirable end cannot be promoted by prohibited means."

At around this same time, in 1924, Congress enacted a strict immigration law, based on quotas for people from different countries and designed to exclude groups deemed inferior. The number of people from a particular national origin permitted to enter was calculated as 2 percent of the people with that heritage already in the United States as of 1890. It was aimed at limiting the influx of people from southern and eastern Europe and entirely excluding immigrants from Asia, the Middle East, and South Asia. With fewer immigrants entering the United States speaking non-English languages, movements to make English the official language of the United States also dissipated. Then, in 1950, amid the hysteria of the Cold War, Congress enacted a new English language literacy test for naturalization. Tellingly, the provision was included in the Subversive Activities Control Act of 1950, suggesting that the new literacy requirement was imposed to counteract a perceived threat from immigrants.

The modern movement for the establishment of English as the official language of the United States began in the 1980s with Senator S. I. Hayakawa's establishment of a group called U.S. English. Not surprisingly, the 2 decades prior to the 1980s had seen an increase in immigration, as Congress had repealed the quota system in 1965 and, at more or less the same time, the Cuban Revolution and Vietnam War caused a significant increase of Cuban and Southeast Asians coming to the United States. U.S. English's first noteworthy act was to seek an amendment to the U.S. Constitution declaring English the official language of the United States. Although committees of both the House and Senate debated the proposal, it was never passed. Likewise, since the 1980s, numerous constitutional amendments and over 50 bills have been introduced in Congress seeking to make English the official language of the United States; none of them has succeeded. The last failed attempt occurred in 2007, when the English Unity Act of 2007 died in committee. Thus, the history of this nation plainly shows that the United States does not want—or need—the establishment of English as its official language.

CURRENT LANDSCAPE

Although the movement to designate English the official language has failed at the federal level to date, the English Language Unity Act of 2011, which would declare English to be the official language of the United States, was introduced into Congress in March 2011. Not surprisingly, this bill was introduced at a time when immigration had once again become a hot item. Under the Obama administration, the federal government has increased enforcement of its immigration laws, continued to build massive walls along much of the border between Mexico and the United States, while at the same time talking about the need for "comprehensive immigration reform." And pro-immigration organizations are pushing for less rigid immigration laws that would allow immigration judges more discretion in granting relief from deportation, while anti-immigrant organizations are advocating harsher federal laws. Moreover, the states themselves have enacted laws relating to immigration, making it a crime, for example, to hire undocumented immigrants or rent homes to them. In 2011, the Alabama legislature passed—and the Alabama governor signed into law—an act that is, as of early 2012, viewed as the toughest immigration-related law in the country. Parts of the Alabama law (the Beason-Hammon Alabama Taxpayer and Citizen Protection Act) were temporarily enjoined in October 2011 by a federal appeals court so that the constitutionality of some of its provisions could be assessed including whether a state can in fact enact immigration legislation, an area that has been historically regarded as being within the exclusive purview of the federal government. One controversial provision that was not blocked by the federal court requires police to enquire as to a person's immigration status during a "lawful stop, detention or arrest" if police suspect the person is "an alien who is unlawfully present in the United States," a suspicion that might arguably (though not justifiably) arise from a person's facility with English. Another provision of the Alabama law that was temporarily blocked by the court would allow officials to check the immigration status of children in public schools, and would also require schools to report to the legislature data regarding students suspected of being undocumented immigrants and students enrolled in English as a second language (ESL) classes. These provisions are clear examples of language being used a proxy for immigration status.

As of early 2012, 31 U.S. states had instituted Official English laws. However, it is important to note that there are essentially two types of Official English laws: those that are intended to be "merely" symbolic (such as designating a state flower) and do not carry any legal ramifications; and those that impede the rights of non-English speakers to engage in government or receive the benefits of government. An example of the latter are laws advocated by U.S. English that would end the practice of offering government services in multiple languages. The organization's position is that "it is not the responsibility of the government to provide services in 322 different languages spoken in the United States. It is the responsibility of each individual either to learn English or to find a friend or family member to translate." However, under Title VI of the Civil Rights Act of 1964 and Executive Order No. 13166 (signed by President Clinton in 2000), states cannot receive federal funding unless they comply with laws requiring public entities that are the recipient of federal funds to make available all vital documents in every language that their clients speak. Thus, in order to gain any meaningful ground with respect to Official English, the movement must—as it has consistently been trying to do—change the law on a federal level by way of a constitutional amendment or a federal law establishing English as the official language of the United States.

ARGUMENTS AGAINST ENGLISH AS THE OFFICIAL LANGUAGE OF THE UNITED STATES

This leads to the central question in this debate: Why should the federal government not establish English as its official language? The answer is that this designation is wrong for the United States because, to paraphrase James Crawford, director of the Institute for Language and Education Policy, Official English is (1) unnecessary and self defeating, (2) punitive, (3) pointless as a practical matter, (4) divisive, and (5) inconsistent with American values, laws, and Constitutional requirements (Crawford, 2006). We will now consider each of these arguments in turn.

Official English is unnecessary and self-defeating. As discussed above, more than 200 years of U.S. history have shown that this country does not want or need the establishment of English as its official language. Likewise, because America is by and large a nation of immigrants, language has not been central to American identity in the same way that, for example, the Russian language is central to Russian identity. Immigrants have not come to this country because they share a common language or ethnicity with Americans; they have come to enjoy the freedoms afforded by the Constitution and to seek better lives for themselves and their families. These are the common bonds that unite Americans, not the speaking of English. At any rate, demographic research shows that non-English speakers in the United States are acquiring English more rapidly than ever before (Crawford, 2006). According to the 2000 Census of the Population, 82.1 percent of the country's residents speak only English; 17.9 percent are bilingual; 9.8 percent speak English "very well"; 3.9 percent speak English "well"; 2.9 percent speak English "not well"; and only 1.3 percent speak English "not at all" (Crawford, 2006, quoting 2000 Census data). Similarly, 95 percent of first generation Mexican Americans are proficient in English, and nearly 90 percent of Latinos 5 years old or older speak English in their homes (American Civil Liberties Union, 2009, p. 11).

As such, any arguments expounded by Official English proponents that non-English speakers are somehow a threat to the ongoing viability of the English language are simply unfounded. Non-English speakers are not a threat to English; by and large their goal—as evidenced by the demand for ESL courses—is to acquire English in order to participate fully in their new country. Moreover, despite U.S. English's claim that declaring English the official language of the United States will "encourage immigrants to learn English in order to use government services," there is no data suggesting that non-English speakers are deciding not to learn English because of the availability of multilingual services. As James Crawford stated before Congress, "Official English is truly a solution in search of a problem" (Crawford, 2006, p. 3).

Official English is punitive. Official English laws threaten the rights and welfare of millions, many of whom are citizens who happen not to be proficient in English. In fact, because naturalization law exempts people over 50 years of age from the English literacy requirement, there are many American citizens who simply do not speak English proficiently. Should a 60-year-old Chinese citizen be denied the right to vote simply because he cannot read the ballot? Putting aside the issue of citizenship, should a mother with a green card who does not speak English be precluded from advocating for her child because the school administration may only speak to her in English? Should an Iraq War veteran be unable to seek VA benefits because he cannot read the English language pamphlet outlining the benefits he is due? These are just a sampling of the practical consequences that could follow from a federal Official English law that overrides Title VI of the Civil Rights Act of 1964 and Executive Order 13166.

Official English is pointless as a practical matter. Official English laws offer no practical assistance to people trying to learn English. The U.S. English website suggests that the "money formerly spent on multi-lingual services can instead provide immigrants with the assistance they really need—classes to teach them English." The 2007 and 2011 bills designed to make English the official language of the United States did not include provisions for funding of ESL courses, despite the fact that these classes are in high demand and chronically underfunded. According to the American Civil Liberties Union (ACLU), in Los Angeles in 2009 there were over 40,000 people on the waiting list for adult English classes.

Official English is divisive. Advocates of Official English argue that a common language would increase national unity and that the provision of "multilingual government benefits actually encourages the growth of linguistic enclaves . . . [and] contributes to racial and ethnic conflicts" (U.S. English). This argument is precisely backwards. In fact, Official English laws are divisive, marginalizing, and, as a result, they exacerbate tensions among diverse communities. In part this is because Official English laws are viewed by many non-English speakers as a proxy for hostility toward immigration in general and their minority groups in particular—particularly Hispanics and Asians, who are among the more recent immigrants. According to legal scholar Antonio J. Califa (1989),

> While the English-speaking community may see English-Only proposals as benign, minority language communities view such legislation as stigmatizing and as an expression of xenophobia. One prominent Hispanic leader likened English-Only laws to the Jim Crow laws faced by blacks. The emotional reaction to these laws is so intense that it united Hispanic communities which otherwise differ in many important respects, including race and national origin. (pp. 323–324)

Laws that restrict the rights of non-English speakers send a message of intolerance that constitutional protections do not apply to you if you do not speak English or if you are an immigrant. So-called merely symbolic laws, while seemingly ineffectual, are also problematic. Even if they do not actually affect individual rights, these laws send a message to non-English speakers that they are marginalized and stigmatized by their inability to speak English. In short, even "merely symbolic" laws establishing English as the official language leave non-English speakers feeling that they are second-class citizens.

Moreover, Official English policies, symbolic or otherwise, can incite individuals to act antagonistically toward non-English speakers: consider the uproar that occurred when Geno's Steaks, a famous cheesesteak shop in Philadelphia adopted an English-only policy, placing a sign in its window reading, "This Is America: When Ordering Please Speak

English" (Corsaro, 2009). Or consider an incident where a police officer in Yonkers ticketed a Cuban American when he was unable to answer questions in English (Crawford, 2006, p. 5).

Official English is inconsistent with American values, laws, and constitutional requirements. Not only are Official English laws contrary to the American values of tolerance and acceptance of different cultures, these laws pose serious legal and constitutional problems. Indeed, many Official English laws have been found unconstitutional under the First Amendment's right to freedom of speech, as well as the due process and equal protection provisions of the Fifth and Fourteenth Amendments. For example, in 1998 the highest court in Arizona (in *Ruiz v. Hull*) held that a state constitutional amendment requiring state and local governments to act in English-only violated the freedom of speech clause of the First Amendment and the equal protection clause of the Fourteenth Amendment. Likewise, in 2007 the highest court in Alaska held that a law requiring all government employees in all government functions to speak only English was unconstitutional under the freedom of speech clause of the First Amendment. Thus, from a legal perspective, Official English laws relating to education, criminal proceedings, voting, and employment are particularly problematic.

The federal 1976 Bilingual Education Act expressly provides for bilingual education for students lacking proficiency in English. Specifically, this approach "involves the use of two languages, one of which is English, as mediums of instruction to assist children of limited English Speaking ability. Both languages are used for the same student population—not as an isolated effort, but as a key component of a program embracing the total curriculum" (Senate Report No. 763, 93rd Cong., Sess. 42 [1974]). As such, the 1976 act ensures that students with limited English language ability have equal access to public education. Any attempt to eliminate bilingual education would not only require rescission of this act, but would also raise serious constitutional questions under the clause of the Fourteenth Amendment that requires equal protection under the law. It is unlikely that such a law could survive constitutional scrutiny.

An Official English law that eliminated courtroom interpretation for a criminal defendant would have serious ramifications under the Fifth and Sixth Amendments to the Constitution. Under the Fifth Amendment, a criminal defendant has a right to due process of law, meaning that each person has a right to fundamental fairness and justice. But how could a trial be fundamentally fair if a criminal defendant is unable to understand the case being made against him or her? How could one understand and participate in one's own defense under those circumstances? Similarly, under the Sixth Amendment, a criminal defendant has a right to "be informed of the nature and cause of the accusation [and] to be confronted with the witnesses against him." Again, how could a criminal defendant be informed of the charges or confront the witnesses if that person cannot understand the language of the proceedings?

Congress amended the Voting Rights Act in 1975 to include bilingual provisions because Congress had found that voters were discriminated against on the basis of language and that the discrimination was "pervasive and national in scope" (Califa, 1989, p. 305). Bilingual (or multilingual) ballots are therefore available in languages that are spoken by at least 5 percent of the voting age citizens in a jurisdiction of at least 10,000 people (U.S. Department of Justice, 2012). Similar to the law requiring bilingual education, eliminating bilingual and multilingual ballots would entail rescinding the bilingual provisions of the Voting Rights Act and would present serious questions about its constitutionality under the equal protection clause of the Fourteenth Amendment.

An important guideline issued by the Equal Employment Opportunity Commission (EEOC) provides that rules requiring employees to speak only English are a "burdensome condition of employment" unless an English-only rule is justified by a bona fide business necessity (Califa, 1989, pp. 310–311). An Official English law that reversed this guideline would likely lead to widespread discrimination for minorities in the workplace, and it could allow an employer to fire a person for simply speaking his or her own native language while on the job.

CONCLUSION

Establishing English as the official language of the United States would prove harmful to non-English speakers and to the nation as a whole. Indeed, for more than 200 years, this country has thrived without an official language, and with the exception of certain anti-immigrant movements, it has acted with a spirit of tolerance and acceptance of people who hail from other nations and speak other languages. Making English the official language of the United States would undermine these fine national qualities of tolerance and acceptance and would seriously undermine the equal rights of non-English speakers and those with limited English abilities. As noted by the ACLU (2009), "The bond that unites our nation is not linguistic or ethnic homogeneity but a shared commitment to democracy, liberty and equality." The United States should not eviscerate this bond by establishing English as its official language.

REFERENCES AND FURTHER READING

Aka, P., & Deason, L. (2009, Fall). Culturally competent public services and English-only laws. *Howard Law Review, 53*(1), 53–132.

Aka, P., Deason, L., & Hammond, A. (2010, Fall). Measuring the impact of political ideology on the adoption of English-only laws in the United States. *Scholar: St. Mary's Law Review on Minority Issues, 13*(1), 12–28.

American Civil Liberties Union. (2009). *English only* (Briefing Paper No. 6). Retrieved from http://www.lectlaw.com/files/con09.htm

Beason-Hammon Alabama Taxpayer and Citizen Protection Act, H.B. 56. (2011). Retrieved from Alabama State Legislature website: http://alisondb.legislature.state.al.us/acas/searchableinstruments/2011rs/bills/hb56.htm

Califa, A. (1989). Declaring English the official language: Prejudice spoken here. *Harvard Civil Rights-Civil Liberties Law Review, 24*(2), 293–348.

Corsaro, R. (2009, June 18). Rudy visits controversial cheesesteak shop. *CBS News Online.* Retrieved from http://www.cbsnews.com/stories/2007/10/01/politics/main3316410.shtml

Crawford, J. (n.d.). *Language legislation archives.* Retrieved from http://www.languagepolicy.net/archives/leg-arc.htm

Crawford, J. (1990). Language freedom and restriction: A historical approach to the official language controversy. In J. Reyhner (Ed.), *Effective language education practices and Native language survival.* Choctaw, OK: Native American Language Issues. Retrieved from http://jan.ucc.nau.edu/~jar/NALI2.html

Crawford, J. (2006, July 26). *Official English legislation: Bad for civil rights, bad for America's interests and even bad for English* (Testimony before the House Subcommittee on Education Reform). Retrieved from http://users.rcn.com/crawj/Crawford_Official_English_testimony.pdf

Gilman, D. (2011). A "bilingual" approach to language rights: How dialogue between U.S. and international human rights law may improve the language rights framework. *Harvard Human Rights Journal, 24*(1), 101–170. Retrieved from http://harvardhrj.com/wp-content/uploads/2009/09/1-70.pdf

Heath, S. B. (1976). A national language academy? Debate in the new nation. *International Journal of the Sociology of Language, 11,* 9–43.

King, R. D. (1997, April). Should English be the law? *The Atlantic Monthly.* Retrieved from http://www.theatlantic.com/past/docs/issues/97apr/english.htm

Lamborn, R. (2005). The fiber of the common bond. *George Mason Law Review, 13*(2), 367–410. Retrieved from http://www.georgemasonlawreview.org/doc/13-2_Lamborn.pdf

Meyer v. State of Nebraska, 262 U.S. 390 (1923). Retrieved from http://www.law.cornell.edu/supct/html/historics/USSC_CR_0262_0390_ZO.html

Nicolino, N. (2007, Spring). ¿Por qué no podemos leer en la biblioteca? Questioning the application of Official English legislation to public libraries. *Journal of Gender, Race and Justice, 10*(3), 531.

Perea, J. (1992). Demography and distrust: An essay on American languages, cultural pluralism, and Official English. *Minnesota Law Review, 77*(2), 269–374.

Ruiz v. Hull, 191 Ariz. 441 (1998).

Schroth, P. (1998). Language and law. In G. A. Bermann & S. C. Symeonides (Eds.), *American law at the end of the 20th century: U.S. national reports to the XVth International Congress of Comparative Law* (pp. 17–40). New York, NY: American Society of Comparative Law.

Somerstein, M. B. (2006). Official language A, B, Cs: Why the Canadian experience with official languages does not support arguments to declare English the official language of the United States. *University of Miami Inter-American Law Review, 38*(1), 251–277.

U.S. Department of Justice. (2012). *About language minority voting rights.* Retrieved from http://www.justice.gov/crt/about/vot/sec_203/activ_203.php

U.S. English. http://www.us-english.org

Alida Y. Lasker

English Instruction in the Classroom

POINT: For children entering U.S. schools without full fluency in English, there is no more urgent need than the rapid learning of the English language for equal educational opportunity. Whether newly arrived immigrants or native-born residents, these students need immediate and focused English language instruction, which is essential for academic progress in learning school subjects, for inclusion in school and community, and for integration and success in mainstream society.

Rosalie Pedalino Porter, READ Institute

COUNTERPOINT: An increasingly globalized world is no place for monolingual curricula. Voters in states such as California, Arizona, and Massachusetts, motivated by state budget shortfalls, have legally restricted bilingual education. In the long run, these myopic restrictions, which continue the long-standing monolingual tradition that characterizes U.S. culture, will hamper U.S. students' ability to compete in an intertwined world.

Karen Manges Douglas, Sam Houston State University

Introduction

At first glance, the debate over English language instruction in schools involves a dispute about how best to teach English to immigrant children and the children of immigrants who do not speak English at home. It is also part of the larger question about how best to integrate newcomers and their children into the fabric of American society. Learning English is understood by most to be a prerequisite for that integration, and English language acquisition by immigrant children is crucial to their academic achievement, their subsequent economic success, and their integration into mainstream society as adults.

One would think that this relatively straightforward pedagogical question could be resolved through empirical research on the relative effectiveness of the two major approaches to teaching English: bilingual education or structured English immersion. But, as with many debates involving immigration, it is not that simple. The debate over English language instruction is multilayered and informed by different sensibilities reflecting broader cultural divisions in American society. And, because larger issues are at stake, the result is a dynamic where ceding ground on the specific pedagogical question risks ceding ground on the larger issues as well.

Again, there are multiple layers to this debate, and a little historical perspective is useful. Bilingual education programs were established in response to an influx of Spanish-speaking immigrants that coincided with the civil rights movement of the 1960s and its attendant embrace of multiculturalism. But as immigration has increased in recent years, multiculturalism itself has become controversially linked with concerns about immigrant integration, social fragmentation, and questions of national identity, such as whether English will remain the lingua franca of the United States.

In other words, the debate over how best to teach English to immigrant children is multifaceted. Its elements include the following:

1. A pedagogical disagreement over the relative merits of the two approaches to teaching English to students lacking English proficiency

2. Concern about immigrant integration that views multiculturalism with suspicion and as undermining of American identity

3. Reaction to the reality that, according to the U.S. Department of Education, during the 2007–2008 school year, 10.7 percent of the children (or 5.3 million) enrolled in pre-K–12 public schools in the United States were classified as English language learners

4. Controversy related to allocation of limited educational funding to the historically underfunded schools attended by many immigrant children

5. Concern about the broader fiscal impacts of low-skilled (illegal) immigrants.

Thus, this debate has become, in part, a debate about immigration itself, and about differing visions of American society.

Attitudes about multiculturalism are a key aspect of this debate. On one side, critics of multiculturalism decry the use of terms such as "African American," "Mexican American," and "Hispanic American" instead of simply "American," and they argue that the role of English in American society is threatened by Spanish-speaking immigrants. On the other side, cultural progressives continue to promote proud maintenance of different cultural identities, pointing to increased English language proficiency across generations of Hispanic immigrants as a reason to be unconcerned about multiculturalism. By way of example, according to a 2006 paper published in *Population and Development Review* by Rubén Rumbaut, Douglas Massey, and Frank Bean ("Linguistic Life Expectancies: Immigrant Language Retention in Southern California"), among people of Mexican ancestry in Los Angeles age 25 and older, 25 percent of the second generation prefer to speak Spanish at home, while just 4 percent of the third generation and 3 percent of the fourth generations had this preference. Each side remains unconvinced by the other's point of view, however, and multiculturalism remains a point of contention that animates this debate.

There is also a fairness question related to funding for bilingual education. According to the Migration Policy Institute's National Center on Immigrant Integration Policy, for the United States as a whole, Spanish-speaking English language learners (ELLs) vastly outnumber all other language groups. Table 29.1 illustrates the dominance of Spanish as well as the range of other languages spoken by immigrant children.

Opponents of Bilingual Education convincingly point out that school systems could not possibly provide an equivalent bilingual education to Spanish speakers and to the students who speak all of these other languages. They argue that this results in unequal educational opportunity for different immigrant groups. Further, to the extent that bilingual programs are synonymous with multiculturalism, they are seen to work against immigrant integration into society.

A question of basic economics also informs this debate because bilingual education is more expensive than structured English immersion programs. But funding for bilingual education is intertwined with overall funding for schools attended by immigrant children and provides additional resources for these schools—schools that are typically in poor neighborhoods and are resource-constrained in the face of the host of challenges associated with poverty. Efforts to eliminate bilingual education programs are de facto efforts to

Table 29.1 Top ten languages of English language learner students

Language	Percent
Spanish	73.1
Chinese	3.8
Vietnamese	2.7
French or Haitian Creole	2.1
Hindi & Related	1.8
Korean	1.5
German	1.5
Arabic	1.2
Russian	1.1
Miao or Hmong	1.1
All other languages	10.1
Total	**100**

reduce funding for these schools. Thus proponents of bilingual education are, in part, arguing to protect an overall source of funding for beleaguered school systems. In the face of tight state and local government budgets, the number of immigrant children in public schools inevitably connects with broader concerns about the fiscal impacts of immigrants.

The pedagogical argument also has different emphases. Proponents of structured English immersion point to studies that measure English language acquisition rates and argue that this approach obtains faster and better results in students learning to speak English. Proponents of bilingual education point to broader measures of academic achievement that include performance in subject areas, measures of cognitive development, and so forth. The substantive arguments are not yet resolved, in part because the sensibilities of each side inform the research design of the various studies. Proponents of structured English immersion are specifically focused on English language acquisition, are philosophically opposed to multiculturalism, and suspect the other side's agendas with regard to protecting budgets and disregard for American culture. Proponents of bilingual education are focused on broader measures of academic performance and cognitive development, and they suspect the other side's agenda with regard to budgets and hostility to immigrant (Hispanic) culture. These debates are difficult to resolve in the face of this underlying mistrust.

POINT

Dramatic increases in the influx of immigrants into the United States since the 1960s, and a growing population of native-born children in families speaking any of 300 languages other than English, present a growing challenge for U.S. public schools: how to provide equal educational opportunities to children who do not have a sufficient knowledge of the English language to do regular classroom work in English. English language learners (ELLs, formerly designated limited English proficient, or LEP, students) now number 5 million children and constitute the fastest growing segment in U.S. public schools. Providing these students with the most effective type of special help is a serious priority in states with a high enrollment of ELLs, such as Arizona, California, Florida, Illinois, New Mexico, New York, and Texas, though there are now ELLs in every state.

Earlier generations of immigrant children, from the late nineteenth century to the 1960s, were generally treated with benign neglect if not consigned to the "dummy" class when they did not understand the language of the classroom. Neither state nor federal laws required special help for these students, and low expectations prevailed. Given the high poverty rate of most immigrant families, children often left school as early as permitted and took up unskilled labor on farms and in factories. The late Albert Shanker, founder of the American Federation of Teachers, once remarked that in his New York Jewish-immigrant neighborhood in the 1930s, people celebrated a child who graduated from grammar school (i.e., from the eighth grade) (Porter, 1996, p. 16).

The tectonic shift in education priorities began in the mid-1960s, when, exacerbated by a sudden influx of refugees from Cuba, as well as the growing presence of Puerto Rican and Mexican children, Congress passed the first federal law to address the language problem. Texas Representative Henry Yarborough of Texas sponsored the Bilingual Education Act, Title VII of the Elementary and Secondary Education Act of 1968. The aim of this act was to help disadvantaged Spanish-speaking children, "not to keep any specific languages alive" or "create pockets of different languages throughout the country . . . but just to try to make these children fully literate in English" (Chavez, 1991, pp. 11–12). However, this has not been the effect of this and other mandates to help English language learners.

THE PROPOSED REMEDIES

Taking a leaf from the pages of the civil rights movement for the integration of African American students with their white peers, the lobby advocating for Spanish-speaking children claimed a new right—instruction in two languages, with the child's native language predominating for a period of years and English gradually added. This experimental program, labeled "transitional bilingual education" (TBE), quickly became the default solution. Since most education laws, as well as federal and state funding, favored this bilingual teaching idea, the political power of the Spanish-speaking community gave it political correctness, thereby short-circuiting the public dialogue about alternative educational approaches. Public advocacy groups such as Multicultural Education, Training and Advocacy (META), the Puerto Rican Legal Defense and Education Fund (now LatinoJustice PRLDEF), La Raza, and others strongly support Spanish bilingual programs. In some cases these groups have sued school districts to impose this teaching model, but there is a real division in the opinions of parents. Among Cuban, Mexican, and Puerto Rican parents of English language learners, there have always been substantial numbers who prefer intensive English in the classroom rather than an overreliance on Spanish. But for at least 3 decades after 1968, states with bilingual laws did not allow what was then known as English as a second language (ESL) as a program choice.

Educators divided into camps favoring these different options. The most contentious and highly politicized arena in public education may well be the niche occupied by "bilingual education." Evidence from 4 decades of research on the achievement of students both in learning the English language and the learning of school subjects, either through bilingual or structured English immersion (SEI), is now available. This research examined a number of questions: Which approach generates superior results for students: teaching mostly in the student's native language for the first few years, or the immediate focus on teaching the English language? Has the experiment called "bilingual education," strongly promoted since 1968, achieved its stated goals? Or are "structured English immersion" programs the preferred model for successful student outcomes? This author's conclusions on these questions are informed by over three decades of experience in the field, as a teacher, program administrator, researcher, and adviser to school districts, states, and the U.S. Congress.

THE BILINGUAL EDUCATION DESIGN AND EXPECTED RESULTS

The stated goal of all federal legislation in this field has been broadly defined as providing students with English language skills for classroom work on a level comparable to native English speakers. State laws, however, beginning in 1971 with Chapter 71-A in Massachusetts and copied by other states, immediately imposed the bilingual education model as the sole legal option. The Massachusetts law required any school district enrolling 20 limited-English students of the same language background to start a full program of bilingual instruction—no matter what the ages of the students. Hypothetically, if the 20 children were scattered across grades from Kindergarten to grade 12, bilingual instruction classrooms could be required at each grade level for just one or two children per grade. The TBE model requires all teaching in all subjects, including reading and writing, to be done in the students' native language. English lessons are provided for just up to an hour of the school day. A 3-year plan supposes that each year more of the instruction will be done in English and native language instruction will be reduced, thereby achieving a full transition to English language competency while allowing students to keep up with subject matter learning. An auxiliary benefit is the high self-esteem these children develop from having their native tongue valued in the classroom, which leads to higher academic achievement.

It is important to dispel one myth. The idea that bilingual education was meant for speakers of the 328 different languages represented in U.S. public schools is completely inaccurate. From its inception to the present, it has been prominently used by the Spanish language community, and has served as a symbol of ethnic solidarity. There are no true bilingual programs in any language other than Spanish. Textbook publishers translated schoolbooks into Spanish for use in bilingual programs, curriculum guidelines were developed in Spanish in various school districts, and reading and math tests were created in Spanish. Nothing near the level of this activity was ever done in Japanese or Vietnamese or any dialect of Chinese. Bilingual advocates pay lip service to the other-than-Spanish speakers, but everyone in the field knows this to be a thinly veiled charade. Spanish speakers make up 75 percent of all ELLs and are the only recipients of true bilingual programs. Children whose first language is Khmer or Arabic or any other language may be taught by a teacher who knows their language and, at best, may use it minimally while teaching the English language and school subjects.

Since the TBE model has been the most widely implemented, the question arises as to whether the expectations first predicted in 1971 have been met. In the early years, the understanding was that it would take a few years to train teachers, create a curriculum, buy books and tests, and plan school schedules to incorporate a separate new program. Accountability for student performance had to wait. In other words, for the first decade the focus was on the "in-puts" of program development, such as student-teacher ratio, availability of books and materials, and the presence of certified bilingual teachers—not on the outputs of student achievement.

Over a 14-year span working as a teacher and administrator, this author observed the annual reporting requirements for special programs for ELL students—how many hours a day were subjects taught in Spanish or English, how much time was given to the students' culture, and so forth. State officials required very little reporting on the rate of English language acquisition for academic and social purposes; on the percentage of students who succeeded in graduating from the bilingual program in 1, 2, 3 or more years; or on what percentage graduated from high school or what percentage went on to higher education. Nor was data collected and reported on whether ELLs, after some period in bilingual classrooms, were able to pass state tests in reading, math, and writing. In the case of Massachusetts, after 23 years of heavily imposed bilingual teaching, a 1994 report by the Massachusetts Bilingual Education Commission found that "adequate and reliable data has never been collected that would indicate whether or not bilingual programs offer language minority pupils a superior educational option" (p. 2).

TWO CRUCIAL COURT RULINGS AND A NATIONAL MOVEMENT

A civil rights lawsuit on behalf of Kinney Lau, a Chinese student in the San Francisco school district, claimed that he was not receiving an equal education because he did not know the language of the classroom. The Supreme Court ruling in *Lau v. Nichols* (1974) placed a clear duty on all schools to provide special help for English learners, stating, "Teaching English to children of Chinese ancestry who do not speak the language is one choice. Giving instruction to the group in Chinese is another. There may be others" (Chavez, 1991, p.15). In this author's considered opinion, had legislators and educators followed the lead of the Supreme Court and promoted *choice*—allowing local school districts to implement their favored program and produce data to show student success—the most effective programs would have been identified without the strife and rancor that has accompanied the growth of a bilingual bureaucracy intent on maintaining its power, funds, and jobs.

The other critical ruling came in *Castañeda v. Picard* (1981), which has had the greatest impact on determining whether a given program for ELL students is legally valid. *Castañeda*, decided by the United States Court of Appeals for the Fifth Circuit, requires three proofs to evaluate program effectiveness:

1. A recognized methodology/theory must be employed (Bilingual, SEI, ESL, or other).

2. Sufficient resources to implement the methodology must be provided, such as trained staff, appropriate materials, and enough time on a task.

3. After a set period of time, objective measures and tests must show student progress through the use of these special methods.

All subsequent court cases challenging the validity of ELL programs, whether brought by advocacy groups, parents, or the Office for Civil Rights, have relied on the three-pronged *Castañeda* proofs.

NO CHILD LEFT BEHIND AND STATE ACCOUNTABILITY INITIATIVES

Since the 1990s, a national movement for accountability in student achievement has resulted in approximately 30 states developing standards for what should be learned in each basic subject at every grade level. These states have pumped new money into public education to develop curricula, train teachers, and create tests to measure how well the essentials are being mastered in reading, writing, and math. The federal government endorsed accountability by crafting the bipartisan No Child Left Behind (NCLB) initiative in 2002, requiring states to demonstrate annually that student progress is actually occurring.

The accountability movement, whatever its imperfections, has, in fact, had a beneficial effect for ELL students. No longer can states hide behind arcane regulations exempting English learners from state tests for several years. California, for example, invested in enormous efforts to improve curriculum and teacher competencies, and the state began requiring testing of all students annually from grade two through high school. Schools that are deemed to be chronically underperforming are allocated extra funding to promote improvements, and if student achievement does not improve, there are consequences for the districts.

States have also mandated high school tests in English and math as a nonnegotiable condition for earning a high school diploma, ending the practice of allowing high school students to graduate without even eighth-grade literacy and math knowledge. A challenge in Texas to the requirement of passing a math and reading test for high school students of African American and Spanish-speaking heritage was dismissed in federal court in *GI Forum v. Texas Education Agency* (2000). The state showed that when large sums of additional money were spent to improve education, the rate of minority student achievement showed improvement each year. These new initiatives provide an important lesson for educators of English learners. Unless students are held to the same standards and measured by the same objective tests as other students, it is difficult to know how well or how poorly English learners are faring, and to focus urgently needed efforts where they are most needed. Exempting English learners in bilingual programs for 3 years or longer did not serve them well.

EARLY BILINGUAL EDUCATION: THE CRITICAL RECEPTION

Bilingual education critics were mostly silent in its first decades. This was partly to give this new idea a chance to prove itself, and partly because the idea was so powerfully protected that few teachers or administrators dared challenge the conventional wisdom. In the late 1980s, this author served on the National Advisory and Coordinating Council on Bilingual Education (NACCBE). Although no federal law has ever required teaching English learners in two languages, the power of the idea was such that 96 percent of the federal money given to states to support teacher training, research, and other activities was allocated to bilingual education. Only 4 percent went to English-teaching programs. NACCBE advised Congress to make the funding formula more equitable, and in 1988 it was changed to a 75–25 percent allocation. Soon after, the council was abolished.

Research studies began to be published questioning the wisdom of native language instruction. In 1978 the prestigious American Institute for Research (AIR) published the first study on bilingual education, coming to two conclusions: ELL students in bilingual programs were having less success learning English than students receiving no special help at all, and ELL students learned math equally well if they were taught in Spanish and English or taught only in English. This was the first bombshell to rock the complacency of the bilingual establishment, and the beginning of a fight for a return to educational common sense. Educators needed to face the reality that the best way for students to learn English rapidly was for it to be immediately and directly taught.

In 1981 the U.S. Department of Education published *Effectiveness of Bilingual Education: A Review of the Literature*, known as the Baker-de Kanter Report, a study that soon became infamous in the field. The researchers Keith Baker and Adriana de Kanter came to the following conclusion: "The case for the effectiveness of transitional bilingual education is so weak that exclusive reliance on this instructional method is clearly not justified" (p. 1). These two researchers would be widely scorned for this analysis, but the reliability and validity of their study could not be faulted. This alone did not change the political climate, but it began to give courage to educators who advocated choice.

A trickle of valid research continued to appear. "Valid" here refers to research studies employing basic elements of good statistical comparisons: two groups of similar students (say, all limited-English speakers, all at the same grade and age on entering school, and of similar socioeconomic background), placed in two identifiably different programs, with comparable resources. Such a study would monitor student outcomes (i.e., subject matter learning, test scores, school attendance, attitudes) over a period of time—generally 3 to 5 years—and report conclusions. A research study not meeting these conditions cannot be considered a reliable measure of the superiority of one approach over another. Over time, studies in Dade County, Florida; El Paso, Texas; Seattle, Washington; and New York City all reported superior results in student learning for English immersion rather than bilingual teaching. In all of these cases, English learners were completely mainstreamed and able to do regular classroom work in English in far fewer years than those in bilingual classrooms. In cases where students were surveyed for attitudes, those in English immersion classes registered higher self-esteem than those in bilingual classes. In many years as a teacher, this author observed the truly motivating factor of early inclusion with English-speaking peers. Students experienced greater pride in becoming quickly fluent in English and no longer being segregated in a special program than they did from hearing Spanish used in a substantially separate classroom.

A large study conducted in 1995 by Professors Virginia Collier and Wayne Thomas at George Washington University illustrates the damaging effects that bad research can have on public opinion. Collier and Thomas claimed to have reviewed the performance of some 40,000 ELL students in elementary and secondary schools for their rate and quality of learning. They received maximum public adulation for their work from bilingual advocates, and for this their major conclusion: children in English immersion classes need 7 to 10 years to learn English well enough to do subject matter work in English, while children in bilingual programs achieve these skills in 5 to 7 years. This finding was a boon to the true believers, who could now argue that bilingual programs should last longer than merely 3 years, and that ELL students should not be required to take state tests until after at least 5 to 7 years of schooling.

Christine Rossell at Boston University reviewed Collier-Thomas in detail in 1998 and reported two serious faults of this research that deem it unreliable. She found that the Collier-Thomas study has serious methodological flaws, and the authors would not allow their data sets to be examined. When the federal government undertook a comprehensive review of bilingual education research (August & Hakuta, 1998) the Collier-Thomas study was not included for these reasons. But the damage this report did is still evident in the ensuing propaganda for the now widely accepted but unexamined magical "5–7 year" idea. Common sense indicates that any child placed in a U.S. public school for 7 to 10 years in an English-speaking environment—without any special help at all—would learn the language long before the Collier-Thomas prediction.

In 1998 the National Research Council of the Institute of Medicine published *Educating Language-Minority Children* (August & Hakuta, 1998), a thorough review of 29 years of bilingual education research. A main conclusion of the report is that there is no evidence for long-term advantages or disadvantages to initial literacy instruction in the primary language as opposed to English. In other words, the absolute cornerstone of bilingual teaching theory did not hold up. As the study stated, teaching children to read and write in English without first developing literacy in their native language *does not have negative effects* [author's emphasis]. It is worth noting that the dozen scholars who collaborated on this report, under the direction of Dr. Diane August and Dr. Kenji Hakuta are recognized to be approving of bilingual education. Had they found even minimal evidence for the benefits of bilingual teaching, they would have trumpeted those claims to the world. But, as Professor Hakuta commented on the lack of such positive evidence, "Someone promised bacon but it wasn't there" (Hakuta, 1986, p. 219).

PARENT REVOLTS INFLUENCE CHANGES IN STATE LAWS

Published research, parent protests, and advocacy by critics of bilingual education laid the foundation for changes in state laws through legislation or popular referenda, as in California, Arizona, and Massachusetts. To the amazement of ethnic loyalists and multiculturalists, it was public protests by groups of Latino parents that sparked the attempts to change state laws. In Los Angeles, Mexican parents of children in the Ninth Street School became disaffected because the school kept their children in Spanish-instruction classes for years, and the resulting parent boycott made the national news. From this small beginning, the 1998 "English for the Children" referendum won the support of 60 percent of California voters and brought about the end of the 25-year bilingual education law, replacing it with structured English immersion. In 2000 the voters of Arizona, who also had many years of bad experience with Spanish bilingual programs, passed that state's English for the Children referendum with 62 percent of the vote, bringing about the same change as in California.

Massachusetts was last to host an English for the Children referendum, in 2002, a gubernatorial election year that brought high voter participation. A reluctant co-chair of this campaign at first, this author dared not dream that the most liberal, politically correct voters in the country would opt to change this education policy. The three chairs—Professor Christine Rossell and Dr. Lincoln Tamayo were the other two—worked mightily, and the measured passed with 68 percent of the vote. The two teachers' unions lobbied heavily against the referendum, outspending the other side, but they could not get a majority vote, even in some urban districts that had the highest proportion of ELL students and the longest experience with bilingual programs (Porter, 2002).

The Massachusetts Department of Education has not done nearly enough since the new law was implemented in 2004 to provide teacher training in new methods, or to chart ELL student progress from year to year. However, the Boston Public Schools reported one bright event in June 2009. Among the valedictorians at the 41 high schools, a total of 17 were born in other countries and learned English on arrival in Boston schools. This is a remarkable record of achievement and gives at least anecdotal evidence that the intensive focus on English teaching for ELLs is having some beneficial effects (Vaznis, 2009).

Parents' efforts to win better educational options for their children, unfortunately, do not always succeed. The Bushwick Parents Organization, in Brooklyn, New York, in 1995 lodged a protest with the New York Department of Education, demanding that the children of this community be allowed to enroll in regular classrooms and opt out of the Spanish instruction classes. Individual members said their children spoke English at home, and many had attended preschool programs in English. Yet when they enrolled their children in Kindergarten, they were automatically assigned to Spanish bilingual classrooms because of the Hispanic family name. Parent objections went unheeded, and some alleged that their children were still in bilingual classes after 6 or 7 years in school. They did not win their lawsuit, *Bushwick Parents Organization v. Richard P. Mills* (1996), though the judge ruled that no law in New York State requires bilingual education. The parents had the right to demand a different assignment for their children, but the schools made it almost impossible.

REPORTS FROM CALIFORNIA AND ARIZONA

After changes in state laws, bilingual program advocates predicted that ELL students would be seriously harmed, that children would become school failures in great numbers, and that their civil rights were being denied. Within a few years, California, home to one-fourth of all the ELL students in the country, began to report success as teachers and administrators observed children learning not only English but rapidly gaining the competency to do all classroom work in English. This was occurring in 1 to 2 years, not in the old "3–6 year" time frame. Two major lawsuits were brought in federal court attempting to invalidate the new law in California. One alleged that teachers should have the right to use any language they wish and must not be required to teach in English. In this case the court ruled that the state's right and responsibility to set curriculum is paramount. The other suit alleged that structured English immersion programs were an infringement on the civil rights of students, but that suit also was dispatched. The California law was affirmed and is still in effect.

A new California English Language Development Test (CELDT), administered annually, provides proof of the rapid acquisition of English language skills through English immersion. The Lexington Institute published a 2006 study of California students in three representative districts that had switched from bilingual to English immersion. In 2001, only 25 percent of these ELL students scored at the top level of the CELDT; in 2005, however, 47 percent of ELL students scored at the advanced level. A 2008 Lexington Institute study reported a growing number of California's highest-performing high school students knew little English when they started kindergarten but had achieved English proficiency early in their elementary school years.

ALL THE WAY TO THE U.S. SUPREME COURT

The state of Arizona, to date, has made admirable improvements in the education of ELL students and done an effective job of reporting accurate data on student performance. Since the legal change in 2002, and especially since 2009, Arizona has invested heavily in redesigning statewide curriculum standards, providing teacher training, and appointing a committee of experts to monitor progress in implementing new initiatives and recommending substantive changes when needed.

In the 1992 *Flores v. Arizona* case against the Nogales, Arizona, Independent School District, the plaintiffs alleged that the state was not spending enough money on the education of ELL students, who are a large proportion of the students in this city on the Mexican border. Initially, the suit may have had merit. However, although the state did invest more funding in improving education for ELL students throughout the state and although these efforts resulted in improved student achievement, the case continued to drag on. Arizona argued that the state had earned relief from court supervision because the lower courts had completely ignored the "changed circumstances" and focused only on funding. The U.S. Supreme Court took up the case (now called *Horne v. Flores*), ruling in June 2009 that in the 17 years since the lawsuit began, circumstances had changed substantially, and that the legal standard for judging an education initiative should be "the quality of education programming and services provided to students, not the amount of money spent on them."

The *Flores* case provides some lessons about how public advocacy law firms tenaciously pursue malefactors (i.e., state and local education authorities), to good and bad effect. One would have expected this case to end once the Supreme Court remanded it to the lower court, but the same plaintiffs restarted the suit with newly invented claims: that the Structured English Immersion programs are spending too much instructional time teaching English, that the interview protocol for enrolling children in school doesn't ask enough questions, and that the Arizona English language test is not rigorous enough. Frankly, it is a novel event to attack a state agency for doing too much and demanding that they do less. In this author's professional judgment, the new complaints are obvious gestures to continue a lawsuit in spite of the present realities. As of December 2011, a ruling had yet to be announced.

A postscript on ELL achievement appeared in a June 2011 report from the Arizona Office of the Auditor General, with the following highlights: since 2008, when 22 percent of ELL students were classified as "English proficient," the rate of success rose to 31 percent in 2010, while the total number of ELL students in Arizona dropped 38 percent between 2008 and 2010, "from 170,000 to 106,000." The number declined in this period "because ELL students became proficient at higher rates" (pp. 1–2). Though Arizona is not perfect, the state is conscientiously monitoring and adjusting its programs and documenting student success.

CONCLUSION

To assess the progress of English language learners, one must address the true barriers to equal education and the reasons for the achievement gap between English learners and native English speakers. Several times since 1990, at the request of members of the U.S. Congress, the U.S. General Accounting Office (GAO, now the Government Accountability Office) has produced studies on the characteristics and needs of limited-English students, citing various factors in addition to a lack of English fluency. These factors include a high incidence of mobility that interrupts school work and the stability of learning, family poverty, and the low level of education of students' parents (Graham, 1997; U.S. General Accounting Office, 1994; Youngblood, 1995).

Has sufficient funding been provided through federal, state, and local sources to help ELL children overcome the barriers to an equal education? This is difficult to determine because of differences in each state's classification of spending data on special programs. Two attempts by the American Legislative Exchange Council (ALEC) to compare state funding for bilingual or English-intensive programs could not reach clear conclusions (ALEC, 1994; Littlejohn, 2001). Such conclusions would be possible if there were uniform reporting rules, and if such rules were enforced. As one small example, the Newton, Massachusetts, Public Schools program (directed by this author for 10 years) routinely compiled all costs directly expended on ELL students and reported that an additional $1,000 was spent per student for these special services, over and above the general per pupil cost.

A common error when reporting on the achievement of ELL students is that they are compared to English speakers even when they do not yet know the language. On state tests of reading, writing, and math, an ELL student will always score lower than English speakers, otherwise he or she would not be classified as an ELL. Apparently, this concept is difficult for some to understand. The time to compare ELL students with other students is *after* they have mastered English. This is precisely the kind of reporting that California and Arizona are providing. When ELL students have been in a U.S. public school for 1 or 2 years, and when they have been provided special help in English, their performance on state tests of reading, writing, and math may legitimately be compared with that of their native-born English-speaking classmates. Lacking English fluency and literacy is not a learning disability but a temporary condition that is surmountable, and the more that well-focused help is available, the more rapidly the barrier to an equal education is removed. Providing English language skills for ELL students as rapidly as possible is a civil right, tied to opportunities in school and community, and to life enhancement.

REFERENCES AND FURTHER READING

American Legislative Exchange Council. (1994). *The cost of bilingual education in the United States 1991–92.* Washington, DC: Author.

Arizona Office of the Auditor General. (2011, June). *Arizona English language learner program* (Report No. 11-06). Retrieved from http://www.azauditor.gov/Reports/School_Districts/Statewide/2011/ELL_Highlights.pdf

August, D., & Hakuta, K. (Eds.). (1998). *Educating language-minority children.* Washington, DC: National Academy Press. Retrieved from http://www.nap.edu/openbook.php?isbn=0309064147

Baker, K. A., & de Kanter, A. A. (1981). *Effectiveness of bilingual education: A review of the Literature.* Washington, DC: U.S. Department of Education.

Bushwick Parents Organization v. Richard P. Mills, Commissioner of Education of the State of New York, 225 A.D.2d 104 (1996).

Chavez, L. (1991). *Out of the barrio: Toward a new politics of Hispanic assimilation.* New York, NY: Basic Books.

Collier, V. P., & Thomas, W.P. (1995). *Research summary of study in progress: Language minority student achievement and program effectiveness.* Washington, DC: George Washington University.

GI Forum et al. v. Texas Education Agency et al., 87 F. Supp.2d 667 (W. D. Tex. 2000).

Graham, T. (1997). The Cost of Bilingual Education: Updating a National Study. *READ Perspectives, 4*(1), 95–102. Retrieved from http://www.unz.org/Pub/Read-1997q1-00095

Hakuta, K. (1986). *The mirror of language: The debate on bilingualism.* New York, NY: Basic Books.

Hart, P. K. (2000, January 8). Judge upholds school exit test in Texas. *The Boston Globe,* p. A5.

Horne v. Flores, 129 S.Ct. 2579 (2009).

Littlejohn, J. (2001). Meeting the needs of students with limited-English proficiency: A critique of GAO's report. *READ Perspectives, 8,* 185–197. Retrieved from http://198.173.245.213/READ/READ%20PERSPECT%20VOL%20VIII.pdf

Massachusetts Bilingual Education Commission. (1994). *Striving for success: The education of bilingual pupils: A report of the Bilingual Education Commission.* Boston, MA: Author.

Mujica, B. (1995). Findings of the New York City Longitudinal Study: Hard evidence on bilingual and ESL programs. *READ Perspectives, 2*(2), 7–36. Retrieved from http://www.unz.org/Pub/Read-1995q2-00007

Porter, R. P. (1995). A review of the U.S. General Accounting Office study on limited-English students. *READ Perspectives, 2*(1), 9–23.

Porter, R. P. (1996). *Forked tongue: The politics of bilingual education* (2nd ed.). Piscataway, NJ: Transaction Publishers.

Porter, R. P. (2001). Educating English language learners in U.S. schools: Agenda for a new millennium. In J. E. Alatis & A. H. Tan (Eds.), *Georgetown University round table on languages and linguistics* (pp. 128–138). Washington, DC: Georgetown University.

Porter, R. P. (2002, November 22). Question 2: How and why it won. *Daily Hampshire Gazette* (Northampton, MA), p. A-6.

Porter, R. P. (2009, August 14). High court case lends support to English language instruction. *Amherst Bulletin*, p. 7.

Porter, R. P. (2009, December 11). Is bilingual education best for English-language learners? *CQ Researcher*. Available from http://library.cqpress.com/cqresearcher/document.php?id=cqresrre2009121100

Porter, R. P. (2011). *American immigrant: My life in three languages.* Piscataway, NJ: Transaction Publishers.

Porter, R. P., & Clark, K. (2004*). Language and literacy for English learners: Grades 7–12 (four programs of proven success).* Longmont, CO: Sopris West.

Rossell, C. H. (1998). Mystery on the bilingual express: A critique of the Thomas and Collier study "School effectiveness for language minority students." *READ Perspectives, 5*(2), 5–32. Retrieved from http://www.unz.org/Pub/Read-1998q2-00005

Rossell, C. H., & Baker, K. (1996, February). The educational effectiveness of bilingual education. *Research in the Teaching of English, 30*(1), 7–74.

Rossier, R. E. (1995). A Critique of California's Evaluation of Programs for Students of Limited-English Proficiency. *READ Perspectives, 2*(2), 27–54. Retrieved from http://www.unz.org/Pub/Read-1995q1-00027

U.S. General Accounting Office. (1994, January). *Limited English proficiency: A growing and costly educational challenge facing many school districts.* Retrieved from http://www.gao.gov/products/HEHS-94-38

Vaznis, J. (2009, June 7). Class acts: 2009 valedictorians—New to the U.S., he blazed a path. *The Boston Globe*, p. B-1.

Youngblood, M. (1995). The cost of bilingual education in the U.S.: A review of the ALEC report. *READ Perspectives, 2*(2), 37–52. Retrieved from http://www.unz.org/Pub/Read-1995q2-00037

Rosalie Pedalino Porter

COUNTERPOINT

While there is debate about the nature and extent to which reforms are needed in American schools, all parties seem to agree that American schools are indeed in need of reform. (Diane Ravitch's article "School 'Reform': A Failing Grade" [2011], provides a nice summary of these debates.) One point that is not being contested is the intransigent correlation between low family income and poor school performance. As education advocate Jonathan Kozol (1985, 1991, 2005) has been arguing for more than 3 decades, the quality of schooling for America's upper-middle-class and wealthy kids compared to the education of the country's poor and minority children is quantitatively and qualitatively different. Bluntly, U.S. schools are failing, both literally and figuratively, many of the children who need it most.

THE CURRENT STATE OF AFFAIRS

What does this debate have to do with bilingual versus English immersion programs? What goes unsaid in most debates about this issue is that these are funding debates involving historically underfunded schools. As in historical times, today's immigrants and their children often enter the country at the bottom rungs of society. (For upper-middle-class immigrant children, assuming these children enter the United States without already possessing English language skills, this is not an issue, because parents have the means to enroll their children in language classes to ensure they are not academically disadvantaged.) Low-income immigrant children are not randomly distributed throughout the United States, nor are they randomly distributed across neighborhoods in the cities and towns they inhabit. Indeed, according to Charles Hirschman (2005) the foreign-born are twice as likely as the native-born to live in the central cities of large metropolitan areas. Many immigrants move into already troubled low-income neighborhoods, thereby further challenging resource-poor neighborhood schools. According to Jennifer Hochschild (2003), these "nested inequalities" ensure the perpetuation of inequality in education between the rich and poor, and between minority and majority. Thus, the debate surrounding bilingualism versus English immersion is centrally a question about whether money and resources should be invested in educating today's poor immigrant children, a significant portion of whom are Latino.

In fact, the debate surrounding English immersion curricula versus bilingual education more often than not pits English speakers against Spanish speakers. This is not surprising, since in 2003 Latinos overtook African Americans as the largest minority group in the United States. Since the 1960s, Latin American and Asian countries have been the largest senders of people to the United States. According to the Migration Policy Institute (2010) there were 11.7 million Mexican-born people living in the United States in 2010, which was 6 times the 1.6 million Chinese-born, the second largest foreign-born population in the country. Further, according to Sáenz and Murga (2011), the Latina/o population more than tripled between 1980 and 2008, growing to 46.9 million. Indeed, as they point out, two out of every five persons added to the U.S. population during this period of time was Latina/o. The impact of this immigration from Latin America can be seen in the state of Texas, where Latina/o children are the numerical majority within the state's elementary schools.

Concurrent with this trend has been a dramatic increase in U.S. households where a language other than English is the primary language spoken in the home. According to Angela Pascopella (2011), the number of children in homes that speak a language other than English increased more than threefold between 1979 and 2008, jumping from 3.8 million to 10.9 million. Given the large number of immigrants from Latin American countries, Spanish is the most common foreign language spoken. According to U.S. Census data, more than 6 in 10 foreign-language speakers in the United States are Spanish speakers (Crawford, 2002).

Thus, the context in which the debates between bilingual and English immersion programs are taking place is extremely important. It is not coincidental that these debates coincide with immigrant population proportions that rival those witnessed at the turn of the twentieth century, when similar English-only language debates dominated the national discourse. Going even further back, in 1751 Benjamin Franklin lamented about the Germans, "Why should Pennsylvania, founded by the English, become a Colony of Aliens, who will shortly be so numerous as to Germanize us instead of our Anglifying them, and will never adopt our Language or Customs, any more than they can acquire our Complexion?" More recently, Samuel Huntington (2004) expressed worries about the immigrant threat to the United States, and the failure of these immigrants to assimilate into mainstream culture. However, this time the threat is the inflow of Latino immigrants (primarily Mexican), rather than German. Huntington wonders if the "United States [will] remain a country with a single national language and a core Anglo-Protestant culture?" Ignoring this question, he warns, is to the peril of the United States and will lead to the "eventual transformation into two peoples with two cultures (Anglo and Hispanic) and two languages (English and Spanish)" (p. 31).

Further, these debates are taking place in settings within the United States that have grown increasingly inhospitable toward the Latino population irrespective of nativity (Crawford [1992] refers to this as "Hispanophobia"). In the absence of comprehensive immigration reform at the federal level, several states—including Arizona, Utah, Georgia, Alabama, and Indiana—have passed their own draconian immigration laws targeted specifically at the (undocumented) Latino population. And while the U.S. Courts have thus far blocked the most egregious aspects of these laws, Latinos remain in the crosshairs in many parts of the United States. This general hostility toward the largest ethnic group in the United States is not irrelevant to the debates pitting English immersion against bilingual programs. Indeed, it speaks to the lower status that Latinos occupy, which extends to the language many of them speak as well (cf. Perea, 2006).

Regarding the efficacy of bilingual education and English immersion programs, Theodore Andersson (1969) cites an early study that found that Spanish-speaking children in bilingual programs outperformed in every category tested the children taught exclusively in English. Twenty years later, the same results were confirmed. In 1991, the Department of Education released the results of an 8-year study which found that students who received instruction in their native language throughout elementary school fared better academically than their English immersion counterparts (Cummins, 1992). In summarizing the research, Crawford states, "a preponderance of the evidence favors the conclusion that well-designed bilingual programs can produce high levels of school achievement over the long term, at no cost to English acquisition, among students from disempowered groups" (Crawford, 1998, p. 50).

There is a growing body of literature that speaks to the intellectual advantages that appear to accrue from bilingual/multilingual ability. Andersson (1971) cites research that found "bilingual readiness was demonstrated to exist alongside other forms of readiness, such as readiness for numbers, music, art, science and literature" (p. 71). Judy Foreman (2002) discusses other advantages, including the ability for abstract thinking and the ability to focus and concentrate. As with learning music, learning a language involves greater brain usage and, consequently, greater brain power. Janice Stewart (2005) confirms these positive benefits associated with foreign language learning, noting, "research shows that foreign language study improves cognitive abilities, positively influences achievement in other disciplines, and results in higher achievement test scores, especially when study of a second language begins in the elementary school years" (p. 11). Amina Khan (2011) notes that neuroscience researchers report that bilingual children are better at multitasking; and that being bilingual seems to help ward off early symptoms of Alzheimer's disease.

However, despite mounting evidence of the cognitive advantages associated with bilingualism, Khan points out that schools are moving away from bilingual programs. And, unfortunately, the absence of bilingual programs has not been beneficial to limited English proficiency students. Angelo Amador (2000), a policy analyst with the Mexican American Legal Defense and Educational Fund (MALDEF), points out that when California terminated its bilingual programs, the performance gap between native English speakers and limited English proficiency (LEP) students widened for nearly all grade levels. When the objective is to transition a child into classes with other native English speakers as quickly and cheaply as possible, it seems plausible that English immersion would perform this task. However, if the objective is to educate students at the same time they are learning English, then without question, bilingual programs are best for accomplishing this purpose.

This is a critical distinction. A 2010 report by the American Psychological Association highlights the fact that early literacy development is critical to later academic success. Children with poor reading skills are more likely to repeat a grade; and the dropout rate for children who repeat grades is significantly higher than for those who are not held back. Prohibiting instruction in languages other than English cannot be in the best interest of non-English-speaking children. But perhaps that is the point, especially in light of considerable evidence that shows that children from non-English-speaking backgrounds *do* learn English (Crawford, 1992). Corroborating this, Sáenz et al. (2007), in their evaluation of U.S. Census data, found that 90 percent of foreign-born Mexicans who entered the United States before 1970 were fluent in English, as were 72 percent of those who entered after 1970.

While there is evidence that dual-immersion language programs can be effective (note this is not a "one language only" immersion, such as English immersion programs), even the efficacy of such programs require that all parties involved (administrators, teachers, parents, and students) consider bilingualism to be a positive attribute rather than a linguistic, cognitive, and academic liability. As Anne Soderman (2010) articulates, "pedagogy must be addressed from a non-deficit model." It is this point that appears lacking among the proponents of English immersion programs.

Certainly, one does not have to search long to find evidence that many Americans perceive Spanish speakers as deficient. For example, John Lillpop (2007), in a web log titled "Illegal Aliens Must Go," is quite clear in stating this: "When English is not spoken in the home, youngsters are at a decided disadvantage and must, therefore, receive intensive English instruction elsewhere." According to Lillpop, instructing non-English speakers in a language other than English is considered "pampering." His disdain for Spanish speakers is clear when he concludes, "English proficiency is required to graduate high school. Spanish proficiency is required to pick fruit and operate leaf blowers." Apparently, only English is acceptable, regardless of where it is spoken.

While some may dismiss Lillpop's views as unrepresentative of most Americans (a debatable point), these expressions are harder to dismiss when the utterances are those of a judge whose job it is to uphold the laws of the land. Such was the case when a state district judge in Texas threatened to take Martha Laureano's child away if she did not begin to speak English to her at home. "If she starts first grade with the other children and cannot even speak the language that the teachers and the other children speak and she's a full-blood American citizen," Judge Kiser told Ms. Laureano, "you're abusing that child and you're relegating her to the position of housemaid. . . . Now, get this straight. You start speaking English to this child because if she doesn't do good [*sic*] in school, then I can remove her because it's not in her best interest to be ignorant. The child will only hear English" (Verhovek, 1995). Perea (2006) confirms the negativity that many teachers and society more broadly hold for Spanish speakers: "It is important to recognize that 'no Spanish' rules and disparaging judgments about native Spanish-speakers are part of a whole system of behavioral controls intended to banish manifestations of 'Mexicanness' or 'Latinoness' from public schools" (p. 102). As Perea points out, Latinos face hostility and discriminatory treatment based on their use of Spanish. Thus, discussions of English immersion versus bilingual curricula are deeply embedded within the discriminatory racial stratification system of the United States.

Ironically, a dueling rhetoric characterizes the foreign language landscape in the United States. On the one hand, political notables such as Defense Secretary Leon Panetta have expressed concerns about the lack of foreign language proficiency of American students. On the other hand, children who speak a language other than English are often negatively labeled (and tracked accordingly) by U.S. school systems and placed in remedial programs. As Charise Pimental (2011) describes, neither her nor her husband's PhDs or university professorships prevented her son from being labeled an "at-risk" student by his school simply because he spoke only Spanish. That he already knew the curriculum requirements seemed not to factor into the decision. Yet, as Crawford (1992) notes, this need not be an "either/or" proposition. Rather than viewing the inability to speak English as a cultural deficit it should be seen as a cultural resource to be cultivated and expanded. Crawford argues that non-English speakers should not forget their native languages when learning English. Indeed, he advocates for what he calls "English plus" policies.

Indeed, Crawford and others, such as Edward Trimnell (2005), point out numerous ways that Americans could be advantaged if the shackles of monolingualism could be lifted. Particularly in the business arena, monolingual Americans have been hamstrung. Most business negotiations involve levels of knowledge and specificity that are beyond most interpreters. And if the level of knowledge is there, this specialization comes at a hefty price. Furthermore, interpreters make it difficult to develop the rapport that is often needed when cultivating business ties.

This author argues that, in this era of globalization, bilingualism should be required for all Americans. However, as this essay suggests, not everyone is convinced of this. As Andersson (1969) points out, many Americans are monoglots who believe that all other Americans should also be monoglots. This insistence that everyone should learn English contradicts another American value, namely freedom. As chronicled next, this tension between freedom and conformity is longstanding and embedded within the language debates in the United States.

FOREIGN LANGUAGE POLICIES IN THE UNITED STATES

Despite repeated attempts to have English declared its official language, the United States does not have a standard national education curriculum, much less a standard language policy. This ambivalence toward language reflects the conflict between competing ideologies. To early Americans, the idea of mandating a national language contradicted the grand experiment based on the principles of liberty and that the young democracy was intent on building.

However, the incorporation and continued immigration of large non-English-speaking populations challenged these high minded ideas. For example, German immigrants resisted speaking and learning English, which alarmed the English-speaking leadership. Southern colonists worried about revolt among slaves if a common language was cultivated within the slave population, and thus passed laws banning their literacy. At various times, significant numbers of non-English-speaking populations came into U.S. territories and seemingly threatened the English-speaking hegemony. A large French-speaking population came with the Louisiana Purchase in 1803, Chinese were recruited as West Coast laborers, and Mexico ceded more than half its territory with the signing of the Treaty of Guadalupe Hidalgo (Crawford, 1992).

The forced assimilation policies embodied in the Native American boarding school programs were developed as one mechanism to remake the Indian in the white man's image. A large part of this transformation involved forcing Indian children to learn English. To facilitate this process, in 1864, Congress prohibited instruction to Native peoples in their own languages. At the other end of the spectrum, and in marked contrast to national policies governing instruction to Native Americans, states and territories began authorizing bilingual schools to educate the large numbers of non-English-speaking people. As Andersson (1971) documents, the state of Ohio, and Cincinnati in particular, was at the forefront in establishing bilingual schools in 1839. Its large German-speaking population found the public schools to be lacking, and they established their own German schools instead. The state of Louisiana quickly followed suit, passing a law similar to Ohio's bilingual education law in 1847. German schools also thrived in Texas. The Texas legislature chartered German schools in San Antonio and Austin in 1858. New Braunfels was established as a German enclave in 1845 and remained a German-speaking community until World War I (Eikel, 1966).

One characteristic of these early bilingual programs is notable. Bilingual programs developed as a result of political pressure applied by interest groups. And while bilingual programs were tolerated, they were "rarely integrated into either the philosophy or the practice of the school or of society" (Andersson, 1971, p. 428). Within decades of their creation, efforts were initiated to dismantle these programs. By 1889, schools in St. Louis, Louisville, and San Francisco had discontinued their German programs.

World War I and growing tensions with Germany marked an end to the rest of the German programs, and language programs more broadly. Anti-German sentiment was so virulent in the United States that mobs organized against the Germans, and German textbooks were burned. Anti-German sentiment was only one part of a growing tide of anti-immigrant sentiment. Use of languages other than English was perceived as disloyal to the United States (Crawford, 1998). What began as a backlash against the German language quickly spread to all minority languages, and by the mid 1920s, laws were in place banning native-language instruction, and bilingual schooling largely disappeared from the American landscape (Andersson, 1971; Crawford, 1998). In keeping with the nativist sentiments of the times, many states adopted English-only provisions, which would remain the guiding philosophy up to the civil rights era of the 1960s.

One glaring exception to the wartime turn to English in the United States involved the armed forces. Ironically, World War I provoked the closure of many bilingual programs in the United States as a patriotic rallying cry, while World War II revealed the downside of this monolingual impulse. Benjamin Rowe pointed this out in 1945: "The war has brought sharply into focus the lack of foreign language skill on the part of many native Americans. This news was by no means startling, for we Americans prided ourselves on the fact that we didn't know a 'foreign tongue'" (p. 136). In an ironic twist of fate, the U.S. government turned to Native Americans—the very people whose language Americans made concerted efforts to extinguish—and their languages to enable secret wartime communication. Native American languages were ideal as a code for a number of reasons, most notably because their complexity and uniqueness of syntax and tonality, coupled with the lack of a written alphabet, rendered them indecipherable to the nation's enemies (Meadows, 2011). In short, the military leaders realized the importance of language skills (and the inadequacy of monolingualism) to the fulfillment of their missions (Bess, 1954).

An understanding of the world's increasing complexity and interconnectedness, which demanded a more adequately prepared and trained population, resulted in passage of the National Defense Education Act of 1958. This act recognized that an educated populace was important for global competitiveness and was resourced accordingly. Foreign language training was specifically included as a skill set that needed fostering, along with science and technology. As described by Flemming (1960), the part of the act known as Title VI "increased curricular opportunities for the study and mastery of the languages of those countries with which the United States has business and diplomatic relations" (p. 136).

The first extensive bilingual program in the United States began in 1963 in Miami, Florida, to educate the large and growing Spanish-speaking Cuban population. Funded in large part by the Ford Foundation, this program offered students the opportunity to continue instruction entirely in English or, instead, to opt for a bilingual program in which half the instruction would be in Spanish. The popularity of the bilingual program was so great that the traditional English-only option was dropped after the first year. For the targeted students, half of the school day was taught in the native language of the student, be it English or Spanish. Subsequent evaluations of the program indicated that instruction was effective for both English and Spanish speakers.

In 1964, the National Defense Act was expanded to include increased funding for English as a second language (ESL) programs. Bilingual programs began to spread to other Spanish-speaking areas, including Texas. Bilingual instruction was first established in the Texas border county of Webb in 1964. Over the next couple of years, bilingual programs spread to about a dozen other locales in Texas, and to other southwestern states, including New Mexico, Arizona, and California. Paradoxically, in order to qualify for federal funds, many states—including California, Texas, and New York—had to revoke their English-only instruction rules for public schools passed after World War I (Burns, 1982).

In the spirit of expanding educational opportunities for all Americans as required by both the landmark Supreme Court decision in *Brown v. Board of Education of Topeka* (1954) and the National Defense Act of 1958, the Bilingual Education Act of 1968 was the first official recognition of the needs of poor students with limited English speaking ability (LESA). Introduced by Senator Ralph Yarborough of Texas in 1967, the bill proposed assistance to school districts in establishing educational programs for LESA students (Stewner-Manzanares, 1988). The bill specifically recognized that children whose first language was not English were being significantly short-changed in their education and sought to remedy this situation. The act passed with overwhelming congressional support.

The Bilingual Education Act also resulted from a recognition of the irony that, on the one hand, the country was making significant investments in teaching adults foreign languages via the Army Specialized Training Programs while, on the other hand, it was extinguishing the foreign language skills that children had acquired by accident of their birth. The Bilingual Education Act encouraged both instruction in languages other than English and cultural awareness (Stewner-Manzanares, 1988). Initially targeted to Spanish speakers, the act was expanded in 1974 to rectify English-language deficiencies of all students. The 1974 amendments also removed the low-income eligibility criteria of the 1968 act, so that coverage was extended to all limited-English speakers, regardless of income.

As with much of the civil rights legislation that emerged out of the 1960s, subsequent decades saw a retreat from the ideals embodied in these progressive reforms. The Bilingual Education Act was no exception. Major newspapers like *The Washington Post* began to write stories questioning whether the federal government should be in the business of financing ethnic identities (Epstein, 1977). In fact, Washington began to retreat in the 1980s. As reported by *The New York Times* (Hunter, 1981), the first major act of President Ronald Reagan's secretary of education, T. H. Bell, was to "revoke proposed regulations that would have required public schools to teach foreign-speaking students in their native languages."

The specter of a federal "intrusion on state and local responsibility" would be invoked multiple times throughout the Reagan-Bush era to roll back civil rights legislation.

The 1980s saw a continued redefining of the original principles of the Bilingual Education Act. While the original act appreciated diversity and multiculturalism, the 1980s reversed course and returned to the assimilation policies that characterized the early decades of the twentieth century. In addition to reducing federal financial commitments, changes to the act allowed for a retreat from instruction in students' native languages. Further, the act was amended to limit a student's participation to 3 years in transitional bilingual education programs (Stewner-Manzanares, 1988). In addition, as a harbinger of budget cuts to come, school districts were being strongly encouraged to develop the capacity to fund bilingual programs independent of federal funds.

During the 1990s the Clinton administration restored the original bilingual function (as opposed to transition to English) of the Bilingual Education Act. Unfortunately, this return to the original intent was short-lived, as the Bilingual Education Act ultimately met its demise under the George W. Bush administration's No Child Left Behind education policies.

INVESTMENTS IN EDUCATION KEY TO FUTURE

In some ways the country has come full circle: in the early days, bilingual education was promoted by key interest groups seeking to advantage (or at least not to disadvantage) their children's futures. The German bilingual education experiment began because German American citizens perceived the public schooling available to their children at the time to be substandard, and they established their own schools. This system was tolerated because the Germans paid for the schools that educated their children while continuing to finance the public education system. German bilingual programs met their demise under a barrage of anti-German sentiment that expanded to encompass all non-English-speaking immigrant groups.

Much has changed in the United States and in the world during the last 100 years. The nation emerged from World War II as a world leader and super power. The United States led the world, not only militarily but intellectually as well. This intellectual capital was deliberately developed. The United States invested heavily in expanding the intellectual capabilities of its population via the National Defense Education Act of 1958. As explained by the former secretary of health, education and welfare Arthur S. Flemming, the National Defense Education Act of 1958 recognized that "the obligations of world leadership, the increasing demands of industry and the armed forces for highly trained personnel, the requirements of foreign trade and international diplomacy for personnel having mastery of languages other than their own, and the increasing complexity of our economic and social arrangements" demanded a considerable investment and commitment at all levels of the U.S. education system to developing a well-trained and educated population to meet these changing demands (Flemming, 1960, p. 133).

But the commitment to these principles was short-lived. Leon Panetta, who became secretary of defense in 2011, was an original member of President Jimmy Carter's Commission on Foreign Language and International Studies. Reporting in 1979, the commission found "a serious deterioration in this country's language and research capacity, at a time when an increasingly hazardous international military, political and economic environment is making unprecedented demands on America's resources, intellectual capacity and public sensitivity" (Panetta, 1999). With globalization, these demands have only increased.

The past 50 years have also witnessed a good deal of change. Beginning in the mid-1960s, immigration to this country began to surge to levels that rivaled those experienced during the turn of the last century. However, instead of originating in Europe, most immigrants were now coming from Latin America and Asia (Hirschman, 2005). At the same time, high levels of immigration combined with low birth rates in the native population have contributed to significant demographic changes in the U.S. population. As Sáenz (2011b) describes, Latinos now account for more than one of every four babies less than 1 year of age, and in Texas and California the figure is one in two babies under 1 year of age. According to Ayala (2011), for the first time ever in U.S. history, over half of U.S. children under the age of two are minorities. Additionally, Latinos are leading the way to college campuses. According to the Pew Hispanic Research Center in 2010, Latinos accounted for the greatest increase in college enrollment among 18- to 24-year-olds (Sáenz, 2011b).

Another significant global change that bears directly on the importance of language learning and bilingualism is the challenge to U.S. global hegemony and the ascendancy of China and India onto the world stage. The United States is finding itself assuming more of a defensive position on this stage. While undeniably still the world's military leader, on the diplomatic and commerce fronts, the United States is now responding to what Schapiro (2007) calls the European Union's "soft power" of diplomacy and regulations. Where the United States once led—in engineering, math, and science, for example—there are now worries about how to increase enrollments of U.S.-born students in these crucial fields. According to a 2005 National Research Council report, in 1966, 78 percent of science and engineering doctorates were awarded to U.S.-born recipients. That figure was down to 61 percent in 2000, and it continues to decline. In 2003, international students earned 58.9 percent of engineering doctorates awarded in the United States. The report's authors reveal that the U.S. strategy has been to rely upon foreign talent to fill these critical human resource needs. And India and China—the largest senders of international students to the United States—have been heeding these calls.

Heckman and LaFontaine (2007) report several other relevant details, including the fact that high school graduation rates peaked in the 1960s, then began to decline, and have fallen 4 to 5 percent over the past 40 years; children born in the late 1940s graduated at higher rates than today's children; and minority graduation rates have shown little improvement since the 1950s.

Today's minority children are tomorrow's future. In Texas and California, the majority of elementary school children are children of color. Unfortunately, it seems, in the area of investing in our minority populations, much has remained stubbornly the same. The United States is riding a wave of anti-immigrant (anti-Latino) sentiment that rivals the xenophobia that engulfed the nation at the turn of the last century. And again, highly punitive legislation is being used to deal with the influx of nonwhite "Others." For example, while Florida once served as the bilingual role model for the rest of the nation, Dade County voters passed an ordinance in 1980 prohibiting the expenditure of county funds for the purpose of utilizing any language other than English. The ordinance also prohibited spending public funds for promoting any culture other than that of the United States. In Alabama, officials are attempting to turn school principals and teachers into immigration officers, sparking massive school absenteeism and fear within the Latino community (Robertson, 2011). According to Crawford (1992), this backlash is a result of the resentment Anglo voters feel about the increasing role that immigrants are having in society.

The disadvantages of the monolingual system in the United States were starkly revealed upon the nation's entry onto the world stage via the two world wars of the twentieth century. The military had to scramble to develop its own intensive language-training programs. Demaree Bess exclaimed in 1954 that the "Army is seeing that its soldiers will never again be caught speechless overseas!" However, following the terrorist attacks of September 11, 2001, the country found itself in just that position again. Military and intelligence officials began scrambling to find sufficient Arabic and Farsi speakers. According to Major John W. Davis (2006), U.S. military forays into the Middle East have exposed the nation's "Achilles' heel" as "spies gain access to our plans because they are skilled in our languages and we are ignorant of theirs. The way into the American fortress is through the open gate of language. No traitor betrays us; our lack of training does" (p. 110).

The costs of serial monolingualism are mounting. Trimnell (2005) reports on a 1987 study that found that more than 200,000 Americans were excluded from job opportunities because they lacked foreign language skills. Twenty-five years later, with a continuing and growing economic commitment to globalization, this figure has certainly increased. The need for an educated citizenry is even more important today than in the past. Unfortunately, the financial commitments to these principles are flagging. As Charles Kolb (2007) explains, "as a country, we have considerable difficulty addressing these 'front end' investment issues. . . . Americans find it extremely difficult to make sound investment decisions now that will yield important payoffs in the future." As did Panetta and Andersson before him, Kolb laments the foreign language deficiency among Americans, which "has serious implications for our economic security, our national security, and the effectiveness of our public diplomacy" (p. 2).

To reverse course, significant investments need to be funneled into retooling U.S. education to meet the needs of the future. However, in the current era of budget austerity, the opposite is happening. For example, the state of Texas, where the elementary school population is already majority-minority, has cut $4 billion from the state's K–12 public education system and $1.4 billion from full-day pre-K and dropout prevention programs (Sáenz, 2011a). Other states are also rolling back their bilingual programs. In general, instruction in foreign languages decreased following passage of No Child

Left Behind, and, according to the National Association of State Boards of Education, both arts and foreign languages are at risk of being eliminated from core curricula (Cutshall, 2004).

Was the commitment to bilingualism, as reflected in the original passage of the Bilingual Education Act, a fleeting fancy? As with much of the civil rights achievements, the optimism that accompanied its passage faded along with the commitment to the ideal. Perhaps the optimism and prescience that oversaw passage of critical pieces of legislation such as the National Defense Education Act and the Bilingual Education Act were simply incidental to the prosperity of the time. More likely, though, these investments were major contributors to the overall prosperity. Continuing to under-resource and undereducate the nation's future workforce and citizenry will not arrest the current economic slump, nor will it reverse the levels of inequality that mimic those at the turn of the last century. Unless the nation begins again to make the necessary investments in its population, including educating in the most effective (not necessarily the most efficient) method that provides the best odds for a prepared and literate workforce and citizenry, a reversal of the alarming trends outlined in this essay is not likely. Passage of the National Defense Education Act and the Bilingual Education Act are indications that, in the not too distant past, the nation recognized this necessity and marshaled the political will to realize it. Can history repeat itself? Zen zen wakarimasen.

REFERENCES AND FURTHER READING

Amador, A. (2000, September 4). Test scores validate bilingual education [Letters to the editor]. *Washington Times.* Retrieved from http://www.washingtontimes.com/news/2000/sep/4/20000904-012019-2439r/print

American Psychological Association. (2010). *Facing the school dropout dilemma.* Retrieved from http://www.apa.org/pi/families/resources/school dropout prevention.aspx

Andersson, T. (1969, March). Bilingual schooling: Oasis or mirage? *Hispania, 52*(1), 69–74.

Andersson, T. (1971). Bilingual education: The American experience. *Modern Language Journal, 55*(7), 427–440.

Ayala, E. (2011, June 24). Ex-Census chief says future is up to minorities. *San Antonio Express-News.* Retrieved from http://www.mysanantonio.com/default/article/Ex-census-chief-says-future-is-up-to-minorities-1437957.php

Bess, D. (1954, December 4). The army's Tower of Babel. *Saturday Evening Post, 227*(23), 22–128.

Burns, M. (1982, May 10). "New Federalism" vs. bilingual education. *Christian Science Monitor,* p. 23.

Cannon, G. (1971, May). Bilingual problems and developments in the United States. *PMLA, 86*(3), 452–458.

Crawford, J. (1992). *Hold your tongue: Bilingualism and the politics of English only.* New York, NY: Addison-Wesley.

Crawford, J. (Ed.). (1992). *Language loyalties: A source book on the official English controversy.* Chicago, IL: University of Chicago Press.

Crawford, J. (1997, March). *Best evidence: Research foundations of the Bilingual Education Act.* Washington, DC: National Clearinghouse for Bilingual Education. Retrieved from http://www.ncela.gwu.edu/files/rcd/BE020828/Best_Evidence_Research_Foundat.pdf

Crawford, J. (1998, Fall). Language politics in the U.S.A.: The paradox of bilingual education. *Social Justice, 25*(3), 50–69.

Crawford, J. (2002). *Census 2000: A guide for the perplexed.* Retrieved from James Crawford's Language Policy Web Site & Emporium: http://www.languagepolicy.net/articles/census02.htm

Cummins, J. (1992, Winter/Spring). Bilingual education and English immersion: The Ramirez Report in theoretical perspective. *Bilingual Research Journal, 16*(1–2), 91–104.

Cutshall, S. (2004, December 1). Why we need "the Year of Languages." *Educational Leadership, 62*(4), 20–23.

Davis, J. W. (2006, March/April). Our Achilles' heel: Language skills. *Military Review, 86*(2).

Eikel, F., Jr. (1966, February). New Braunfels German: Part I. *American Speech, 41*(1), 5–16.

Epstein, N. (1977, June 5). The bilingual battle: Should Washington finance ethnic identities. *The Washington Post,* p. C1.

Flemming, A. S. (1960, January). The philosophy and objectives of The National Defense Education Act. *Annals of the American Academy of Political and Social Science, 327,* 132–138.

Foreman, J. (2002, October 7). The evidence speaks well of bilingualism's effect on kids. *Los Angeles Times.* Retrieved from http://articles.latimes.com/2002/oct/07/health/he-sense7

Heckman, J. J., & LaFontaine, P. A. (2007, December). *The American high school graduation rate* (Discussion Paper No. 3216). Retrieved from Institute for the Study of Labor website http://ftp.iza.org/dp3216.pdf

Hirschman, C. (2005, November). Immigration and the American century. *Demography, 42*(4), 595–620.

Hochschild. J. (2003). Social class in public schools. *Journal of Social Issues, 59*(4), 821–840.

Hunter, M. (1981, April 3). Cuts in U.S. aid to education to have wide impact. *The New York Times,* p. A1.

Huntington, S. (2004, March 1). The Hispanic challenge. *Foreign Policy.* Retrieved from http://www.foreignpolicy.com/articles/2004/03/01/the_hispanic_challenge

Khan, A. (2011, February 26). Bilingualism good for the brain, researchers say. *Los Angeles Times.* Retrieved from http://www.latimes.com/health/la-he-bilingual-brain-20110227,0,59722.story

Kolb, C. (2007, January 4). A continuum of necessary investments for learning. *Education Week, 26*(17).

Kozol, J. (1985). *Death at an early age.* New York, NY: Penguin.

Kozol, J. (1991). *Savage inequalities: Children in American schools.* New York, NY: Crown.

Kozol, J. (2005). *The shame of the nation: The restoration of apartheid schooling in America.* New York, NY: Crown.

Lillpop, J. W. (2007, March 18). English vs. Spanish: A question of racism? [Blog post]. Retrieved from http://illegalaliensmustgo.blogspot.com/2007/03/english-vs-spanish-question-of-racism.html

Meadows, W. C. (2011). Honoring Native American code talkers: The road to the Code Talkers Recognition Act of 2008 (Public Law 110-420). *American Indian Culture and Research Journal, 35*(3).

Migration Policy Institute. (2010). *Ten source countries with the largest populations in the United States as percentages of the total foreign-born population: 2010.* Retrieved from http://www.migrationinformation.org/datahub/charts/10.2010.shtml

National Research Council. (2005). *Policy implications of international graduate students and postdoctoral scholars in the United States.* Retrieved from http://www.nap.edu/catalog/11289.html

Panetta, L. (1999). *Foreign language education: If "scandalous" in the 20th century, what will it be in the 21st century?* Retrieved from Stanford University website: https://www.stanford.edu/dept/lc/language/about/conferencepapers/panettapaper.pdf

Pascopella, A. (2011, February 1). Successful strategies for English language learners. *District Administration.* Retrieved from http://www.districtadministration.com/article/successful-strategies-english-language-learners

Perea, J. F. (2006). *Mi profundo azul:* Why Latinos have a right to sing the blues. In M. Olivas (Ed.), *"Colored men" and "hombres aquí":* Hernandez v. Texas *and the emergence of Mexican-American lawyering.* Houston, TX: Arte Público.

Pimental, C. (2011). The color of language: The racialized educational trajectory of an emerging bilingual student. *Journal of Latinos and Education, 10*(4), 335–353.

Ravitch, D. (2011, September 29). School "reform": A failing grade. *New York Review of Books.* Retrieved from http://www.nybooks.com/articles/archives/2011/sep/29/school-reform-failing-grade

Robertson, C. (2011, October 27). Critics see "chilling effect" in Alabama immigration law. *The New York Times.* Retrieved from http://www.nytimes.com/2011/10/28/us/alabama-immigration-laws-critics-question-target.html?_r=1&pagewanted=all

Rowe, B. (1945, February). Army streamlines language instruction. *Modern Language Journal, 29*(2), 136–141.

Sáenz, R. (2011a, July 11). Texas squandering its future. *San Antonio Express-News.* Retrieved from http://www.mysanantonio.com/default/article/Texas-squandering-its-future-1461850.php

Sáenz, R. (2011b, September 14). Today's young Latinos are nation's future. *San Antonio Express-News.* Retrieved from http://www.mysanantonio.com/default/article/Today-s-young-Latinos-are-nation-s-future-2168925.php

Sáenz, R., Filoteo, J., & Murga, A. L. (2007). Are Mexicans in the United States a threat to the American way of life: A response to Huntington. *Du Bois Review, 4*(2), 375–393.

Sáenz, R., & Murga, A. L. (2011). *Latino issues.* Santa Barbara, CA: ABC-CLIO.

Schapiro, M. (2007). *Exposed: The toxic chemistry of everyday products: Who's at risk and what's at stake for American power.* White River Junction, VT: Chelsea Green.

Soderman, A. K. (2010, May). Language immersion programs for young children? Yes . . . but proceed with caution. *Phi Delta Kappan, 9*(8), 54–61.

Stewart, J. H. (2005, August). Foreign language study in elementary schools: Benefits and implications for achievement in reading and math. *Early Childhood Education Journal, 33*(1), 11–16.

Stewner-Manzanares, G. (1988, Fall). The Bilingual Education Act: Twenty years later. *New Focus: National Clearinghouse for Bilingual Education, 6.* Retrieved from http://www.ncela.gwu.edu/files/rcd/BE021037/Fall88_6.pdf

Trimnell, E. (2005). *Why you need a foreign language and how to learn one* (2nd ed.). Cincinnati, OH: Beechmont Crest.

Verhovek, S. H. (1995, August 29). Mother scolded by judge for speaking Spanish. *The New York Times.* Retrieved from: http://www.nytimes.com/1995/08/30/us/mother-scolded-by-judge-for-speaking-in-spanish.html

Karen Manges Douglas

Higher Education and Immigration Status

POINT: It is in the economic and fiscal interest of the country for young people to become as educated as they can, regardless of immigration status. Further, illegal immigrant children should not be punished for their parents' decisions.

Andrew J. Parr, Nevada Department of Education

COUNTERPOINT: There are not enough slots at universities for citizens, and it is unfair to students who get rejected by these institutions that their spots might be taken by undocumented students. Further, passage of something like the DREAM Act will only encourage further illegal immigration.

Matthew K. Tabor, EducationNews.org

Introduction

The debate over out-of-status immigrant access to higher education is an aspect of deep disagreements over illegal immigration, and is informed by vast differences of opinion about the appropriate conceptual framework for understanding it, and these differences inform the extent to which illegal immigration is seen as a serious violation of the law that warrants severe penalties.

One side argues that giving children brought to the country illegally by their parents the ability to pay in-state tuition is equivalent to rewarding lawlessness. In the parlance of economics, it is a "moral hazard" argument, in the sense that providing this privilege will encourage future illegal immigration. After all, if the objective for immigrating illegally is to seek a better life for one's self and family, giving illegal immigrant children "subsidized" access to higher education is equivalent to giving them a better life, and thus the "moral hazard" of encouraging subsequent lawbreaking by others. When discussed in the context of the proposed DREAM Act, access to in-state tuition also includes gaining legal permanent residency status which is, in turn, a path to citizenship. Those opposed to earned legalization, or amnesty, for illegal immigrants would argue that the DREAM Act simply represents amnesty in a different form.

On the other hand, those who argue in favor of providing in-state tuition to children brought in illegally by their parents are saying that the children should not be punished for the "sins of their fathers," and that basic notions of justice and fairness suggest that children who work hard in school and want to pursue their life goals and dreams should be encouraged in this endeavor by being treated on a par with their classmates. There are also strong pragmatic arguments in favor of allowing illegal immigrant children to pay in-state tuition. Most notably, the more education these children obtain, the less likely they are to become a fiscal burden to the state as adults. Arguments that it's a fiscal drain to allow the lower tuitions are shortsighted and misguided, proponents proclaim, in that they classify expenditures on education as a cost rather than an investment whose return will be realized over the productive life of the student. Keeping children out of college relegates them to a working life in lower-skilled jobs and makes it more likely they will be a fiscal burden.

In the Point essay below, Andrew Parr argues in favor of allowing the children of illegal immigrants access to higher education, pointing out that this would bring economic and labor-market benefits to individual immigrants, to their families, and to the wider society. Passage of the DREAM Act would essentially be a down payment on future substantial and widespread economic growth, which would be achieved through increased consumption, job creation, and collection of additional tax revenue. Additionally, encouraging undocumented people to acquire more education would support long-term community revitalization and the growth of the middle-class. The U.S. government could turn the presence of the children of undocumented immigrants into a net economic benefit for the country by reducing their negative fiscal impacts.

In the Counterpoint essay, Matthew Tabor argues that the claims that states and the federal government will receive net tax benefits from allowing illegal immigrants access to higher education are suspect. The hypothetical revenue increases that might result will only be experienced in the distant future, and these gains are offset by the increased financial burdens that a surge in student enrollment would place in the present on educational institutions. He also alludes to the moral hazard argument when he refers to the "perverse incentives" created by legislation such as the DREAM Act, in that it will act as a magnet for immigrants to enter the country illegally and pursue higher education simply to attain citizenship. He also objects to the artificial relationship between pursuing higher education and military service that the DREAM Act forges, pitting the two choices against each other rather than presenting them as two options to be weighed by individuals, each based on its own merits. It additionally places a premium on these two pursuits at the expense of others.

In short, this debate commingles issues related to immigration policy, the long-term economic security of immigrant children, fairness, and the question of what policies this "country of immigrants" should enact with regard to the children of illegal immigrants.

POINT

Meeting the educational needs of all young people and providing a pathway to higher education for traditionally underserved student populations is vital to the future and is in the economic interest of the country. In addition to the individual economic and social benefits of a college education, the education of each person has the potential to improve the lives of others. It has long been a matter of public policy in America to provide an education for all, and an educated society has long been viewed as an essential element for a democratic and productive society. In reality, however, the doors to the American schoolhouse continue to be open only to some.

Higher levels of educational attainment are highly correlated with higher earnings, which contribute to a healthy economy in two ways. First, individuals earning higher wages indirectly reduce public expenditures because they are far less likely to require public assistance in the form of food programs, unemployment payments, and other social safety net programs. In addition, those who are better educated are far less likely to be incarcerated, thereby further reducing costs to federal, state, and local agencies. Second, higher wage earners increase public revenues by paying higher federal and state income taxes and sales taxes, and they contribute to social programs such as Medicare and Social Security at higher levels.

Children born outside of the United States to undocumented immigrant parents have great difficulty in finding meaningful employment. They are most often required to pay nonresident college tuition rates, and they are ineligible for most forms of federal student aid. These realities make higher education all but inaccessible except in the rarest of cases. The proposed DREAM Act would provide a pathway to higher education and possible citizenship for young undocumented immigrants, which would lead to healthier social conditions by preparing undocumented youth to fully participate in American democratic processes and make meaningful contributions to their communities.

INDIVIDUAL BENEFITS OF HIGHER EDUCATION

Admittedly, some individuals with low levels of education are financially successful throughout their working life, but these people are the exception, not the norm. As a group, individuals completing higher levels of education generally have much higher annual incomes than those with less education. *The Costs and Benefits of an Excellent Education for all of America's Children* (Levin, Belfield, Muennig, & Rouse, 2007) reported that a Hispanic male with a bachelor's degree or higher would be expected to earn nearly $33,000 more each year than a male Hispanic high school dropout. Over a working lifetime, the earnings of the male Hispanic college graduate are likely to be more than double the earnings of the high school graduate.

The financial benefits to the individual are clear, but higher education also improves one's quality of life in other ways. Adults with higher levels of education tend to have better access to health care and live a healthier lifestyle. Those with higher levels of education are also more likely to use preventative health care and visit a physician for less severe ailments (Levin et al., 2007). The smoking rate has declined for all educational groups since 1960, but the smoking rate for individuals with a bachelor's degree or higher has declined more rapidly than for those with lower educational attainment. Finally, those with a bachelor's degree or higher are far more likely to have never smoked than those who attended only some or no college (Baum et al., 2010).

There are demonstrable relationships between educational attainment and both leisure activity exercise and obesity. As levels of educational attainment increase, the percentages of those who regularly exercise increase and rates of obesity decrease. The children of parents who have earned a bachelor's degree or higher also share in the benefits of better health and are themselves more likely to obtain higher education (Baum et al., 2010). In summary, when individuals attain higher levels of education, they can be expected to earn higher wages, have better access to health care, and live healthier lives.

BENEFITS OF HIGHER EDUCATION TO SOCIETY AT LARGE

Society also benefits from individuals' higher education through increased tax revenues and lowered expenditures on social support programs. Higher education provides greater skills and increased knowledge to individuals, who tend to develop an approach to life that benefits all of society. For example, 43 percent of individuals with a bachelor's degree were found to have participated in at least 50 hours of volunteerism per year, which is more than double the volunteerism rate for those with only a high school diploma (Baum et al., 2010).

As earnings increase, so do taxes paid to local, state, and federal governmental agencies. In 2008, individuals holding a bachelor's degree paid almost double the taxes paid by those with only a high school diploma (Baum et al., 2010). Over the course of a 40-year working lifetime, a male Hispanic college graduate would directly contribute nearly $800,000 to the tax base, whereas a male Hispanic high school graduate would pay less than $300,000 in taxes (Levin et al., 2007).

Individuals with higher levels of education are far less likely to participate in or rely upon Medicaid or Medicare during their working years. This is due to the fact that higher incomes preclude qualification for these programs and higher incomes are associated with a healthier lifestyle. The result is that a male Hispanic high school graduate is expected to cost taxpayers approximately $23,000 over a lifetime, compared to only $4,000 for a male Hispanic college graduate. This translates to a savings to the public of over $19,000 (Levin et al., 2007).

Individuals who have attained higher levels of education are far less likely to participate in or rely upon social support programs such as unemployment insurance, welfare, food stamps, or the national school lunch program. The lifetime savings to taxpayers for expenditures attributed to a high school graduate as compared to a high school dropout are substantial but are also dependent on race/ethnicity and gender. Every time a high school student graduates instead of dropping out, taxpayers save an average of at least $3,000 on social programs. The savings are even greater as educational attainment increases (Levin et al., 2007).

Finally, better-educated individuals are less likely to be incarcerated than those with lower levels of education. High school dropouts make up 20 percent of the overall population but over 50 percent of the state prison population (Levin et al., 2007). Over the working life of an average Hispanic male, the government saves an estimated $62,000 in criminal justice expenditures when a Hispanic male earns a bachelor's degree rather than only a high school diploma (Baum et al., 2010).

High school graduation is typically required for an individual to gain access to higher education. For every student who graduates high school instead of dropping out, the American taxpayers save an average of nearly $210,000 over the lifetime of that person (Levin, Belfield, Muennig, & Rouse, 2007). The lifetime savings figure is substantially greater when comparing projected societal costs for a high school dropout to those of a person attending some college, and it increases even further for individuals earning a college degree. When these factors are considered together, the monetary benefits to society are close to $1 million for every person who graduates college instead of dropping out: $800,000 in additional tax payments and $200,000 in reduced expenditures for government-supported social programs.

The monetary benefits of increasing the educational attainment of people in America can be measured in many billions of dollars annually in the form of increased tax collection and reductions in expenditures for public health, criminal justice, and other social assistance programs. Notwithstanding the monetary benefits associated with higher educational attainment, a healthier society with a high rate of employment and reduced crime is simply a better society in which to live. The facts and findings presented thus far strongly suggest that every person should be encouraged to graduate high school, attend college, and graduate from higher education because these achievements benefit all of society as well as the individual. However, some argue that the benefits of higher education should be reserved for some, not all.

EDUCATION FOR SOME, NOT ALL

Maria (not her real name) was born in Mexico and was brought to the United States by her parents when she was only 2 years old. Soon after entering the United States, she was provided with a new name and social security identification without her knowledge. At 18, a very American-like Maria went to the department of motor vehicles to obtain a driver's license, at which time she was arrested for use of a fraudulent identity and a variety of other offenses. In exchange for not implicating her mother, which would have surely led to her mother's deportation or imprisonment, Maria paid a substantial monetary fine, spent some time in the county jail, and successfully completed probation.

Another young lady, Angela, is currently in a similarly difficult and fragile situation. Angela, now 19 years old, was also brought to America when she was very young and has done nothing wrong; Angela graduated from high school and has maintained a high moral character in a community known for an array of social ills. She lives with friends because her mother left the area long ago and her father participates in illicit activities, of which Angela wants no part.

Angela is terrified of being deported to Mexico, where she has no family and no support; the United States is all she has ever known. Angela would like to attend college, but because of her undocumented immigration status, she cannot find work that provides her with a living wage and the means to save for college. She is stranded in an unsettled world bounded by high school graduation on one side and deportation on the other.

Although similar in many ways, the day-to-day experiences of these two young women could not be more different. For Maria, the arguably broken immigration system did provide her a path toward legalization after arrest and incarceration. She now has the ability to work legally, and a chance to earn a living to support her family. But for Angela, there is no path toward legalization, little hope of continuing her education, and few prospects for meaningful or even legal employment.

The U.S. Supreme Court ruled in *Plyler v. Doe* (1982) that children brought into America without proper documentation are entitled to equal protection under the law and may not be discriminated against on the basis of their immigration status regarding public elementary and secondary education. Justice William J. Brennan opined that to deny K–12 education to undocumented children was to create a lifetime of hardship and a permanent underclass of individuals. Brennan's comments came at a time in American history when a high school education was viewed as the minimum education necessary to obtain employment capable of providing a living wage. The ruling explicitly linked education and social mobility, and this issue continues to be debated today.

Foreign-born children brought into the United States by their undocumented parents are sent profoundly conflicting messages. On the one hand, these children are provided with public education and are encouraged to graduate high school for the purpose of contributing to society in a positive manner. On the other hand, undocumented high school graduates find college enrollment and meaningful work nearly impossible to obtain due to their uncertain legal status. At age 18, their future and hopes are handcuffed (figuratively and sometimes literally) through no fault of their own.

EDUCATION FOR THE TRADITIONALLY UNDERSERVED

The U.S. foreign-born population is currently estimated to be slightly less than 40 million people. Approximately 54 percent of all U.S. immigrants come from Mexico and Latin America, 27 percent from Asia, and 15 percent from Canada and Europe. Estimates vary, but approximately 1 to 1.5 million people immigrate to the United States each year and at least one-third of these immigrants enter the United States illegally (Papademetriou & Terrazas, 2009). Current estimates indicate that between 11 and 12 million people reside illegally in the United States and 50 to 80 percent of these undocumented residents came from Mexico or Latin America (Hanson, 2009; Padron, 2008). An estimated 2 million undocumented residents, the majority of whom are Hispanic/Latino, currently enrolled in public schools are younger than 18 (Gonzales, 2009). This means that the discussion about immigration and higher education is really about undocumented residents originating from Mexico and Latin America currently enrolled in the public education system and pursuing the "American Dream."

Educational attainment is highly correlated with wealth. A disproportionate number of Hispanic/Latino children (25 to 30 percent) live below the poverty line. For a variety of reasons unrelated to immigration status, Hispanic students begin their formal schooling with academic skills below those of many others. Without extra academic support, they continue to lag behind their peers academically through high school. The high school graduation rate for Hispanic students was approximately 59 percent (compared to 82 percent for all students) in 2008, and was even lower for foreign-born Hispanic students (Fry, 2010). It follows that a disproportionate share of Hispanic students fails to ever enroll in higher education institutions; 36 percent for Hispanic students as compared to 57 percent for all students (Fry, 2010; Gándara, 2010; Kober et al., 2010).

To be sure, high school graduates with low-income backgrounds, and those of Hispanic or Latino ethnicity, enroll in college at lower rates and attain lower levels of education than other demographic groups (Baum et al., 2010). While other subpopulations have increased their share of college degrees since 1980, Latinos have made little progress to this end. In 2008, all things being equal, Latinos were about half as likely to earn a college degree as African Americans and about one-third as likely to earn a college degree as Caucasians. Reversing this low level of education among Latino youth is necessary to prepare students to participate fully in society and make meaningful contributions to their community (Gándara, 2010).

Both Maria and Angela, the young Hispanic women discussed earlier, have already beaten the odds just by graduating from public high school and seeking the upward social mobility accessible only through higher education. But the educational and employment opportunities available to each are severely limited. Many people would find it ludicrous to prohibit adults from attending college, working legally, and making positive economic contributions after having expended many dollars in educating them as children. Yet this practice is supported by current policy. From a moral or humanitarian perspective, the policy is reprehensible and serves only to maintain a permanent underclass.

BENEFITS OF DREAM ACT PASSAGE

A widely discussed solution to this problem is the Development, Relief, and Education for Alien Minors (DREAM) Act. The DREAM Act would provide undocumented youth who arrived in the United States before the age of 16 a path toward legalization, provided they attend college or serve in the U.S. military for 2 years while maintaining "good moral character." The DREAM Act has the potential to resolve the ambiguous legal status of more than 2 million undocumented youths who have lived in the United States nearly all of their lives. The DREAM Act would produce thousands of college graduates and contribute to the pool of higher income earners required by the national economy (Ojeda, Takash, Castillo, Flores, Monroy, & Sargeant, 2010).

The economic benefits of passage of the DREAM Act were recently addressed in a Migration Policy Institute (MPI) report, *DREAM vs. Reality: An Analysis of Potential DREAM Act Beneficiaries* (Batalova & McHugh, 2010). A North American Integration and Development Center (NAIDC) follow-up report with updated census figures, *No DREAMers Left Behind: The Economic Potential of DREAM Act Beneficiaries* (Ojeda, Takash, Castillo, Flores, Monroy, & Sargeant, 2010) had similar findings. The MPI report conservatively estimates that $1.38 trillion would be generated over a 40-year period by DREAM Act beneficiaries, while the NAIDC report estimates that $3.6 trillion would be generated by DREAM Act beneficiaries over a 40-year period.

Passing the DREAM Act would expand the nation's economy by developing a more highly educated workforce that would contribute trillions of dollars to the U.S. economy. The DREAM Act offers a humanitarian solution to the unenviable trap of being a young, motivated, and undocumented immigrant in the United States, and it would advance the interests of American society. Because many potential DREAM Act beneficiaries have been enrolled in the public K–12 education system at taxpayer expense, passage of the act would represent a practical step toward recouping some of the costs of educating immigrant youths (Ojeda et al., 2010).

Some will argue that taxpayers would bear the burden of billions of tax dollars to "subsidize the college education of illegals"—language meant to provoke outrage. However, this multibillion dollar "subsidy" would not be an excessive burden, considering the payback in increased tax collection. Further, this figure is simply the difference between the cost of out-of-state tuition and in-state tuition rates. One study from a small northeast state found that the in-state tuition paid by each full-time student exceeded the instructional expenses by approximately $2,700 at a Tier 1 university and by $1,800 at a Tier 2 state college. Taking into account the number of students expected to enroll at different institutions of higher education if the DREAM Act were to be enacted, a net increase in tuition-derived revenues is indicated (Mehlman-Orozco, 2011). For another New England state, the net revenues to colleges and universities are estimated to be in the millions of dollars annually (Massachusetts Taxpayers Foundation, 2006).

In 2010 alone, the Immigration Policy Center (IPC) reported that at least half of undocumented workers paid state and federal income taxes, and when combined with other taxes, taxes paid by undocumented residents amounted to an estimated $11.2 billion (IPC, 2010). According to the IPC, undocumented residents account for over $500 billion in economic activity and nearly $250 billion in gross domestic product. Passage of the DREAM Act would simply provide undocumented students with the legal right to pursue educational opportunities they and their families have already paid for and already earned (Gonzales, 2009).

Those opposed to the DREAM Act argue that the addition of approximately 1 million new college students (illegal aliens) over the 15-year period would overburden the nation's college system and force out or deny a commensurate number of "legal" students the opportunity to attend college. Just as there is no evidence that undocumented residents "steal" American jobs, there is no reason to presuppose that DREAM Act beneficiaries would displace American-born citizens in colleges and universities. Since 2001, 10 states have passed laws giving undocumented noncitizens the opportunity to pay in-state tuition while attending college, provided several prerequisites are met. Thus far, none of the states has experienced an influx of immigrant students who have displaced American citizens (Gonzales, 2009). Admittedly, some potential American students may be denied attendance at some colleges and universities, but this is the current practice.

All universities and many state colleges accept some students' and deny other students' applications based on a combination of criteria. To presuppose that the "illegal aliens" will displace the "legal residents" is unsubstantiated, alarmist, and meant to instill fear.

CONCLUSION

Children born outside of the United States and brought to this country at a young age by their undocumented parents have no say on the location of their upbringing. U.S. society faces a choice of either supporting them or, by doing nothing, alienating them and leaving them in limbo. To maintain the status quo is to relegate these young undocumented immigrants to be workers in an underground economy at best, or unemployed, uneducated, and dependent upon government services at worst (Padron, 2008). In writing for the U.S. Supreme Court majority in *Plyler v. Doe* (1982), Justice Brennan opined that a lifetime of hardship and a permanent underclass would be created if public education were denied to undocumented immigrants. This group of people deserves a chance to become productive Americans rather than an oppressed underclass.

In the quest for social justice, it is not only logical but imperative to intervene when, as is the case here, a substantial subpopulation is vulnerable and disenfranchised (Gonzales, 2009). Numerous studies demonstrate that legal status brings economic and labor market benefits to individuals and their families, but it also benefits society in a number of ways. With the ability to attend college, foreign-born children of undocumented parents can improve their education, obtain quality employment, pay more in taxes, and, perhaps most importantly, participate fully and contribute in a positive manner to the communities of which they already are a part.

America was founded by immigrants, and for more than 200 years, immigrants have made positive contributions to the country. It has long been viewed as the land of opportunity, as a place of hope where each person's dreams may be fulfilled with hard work and perseverance. Congress can increase the net benefit to the United States that derives from undocumented immigrants by reducing their negative fiscal impacts. One obvious strategy for reducing negative fiscal impacts is to provide access to an education and work opportunities that do not make immigrants reliant on government services (Hanson, 2009).

Passage of legislation like the DREAM Act would bring economic and labor-market benefits to individual immigrants, to their families, and to society as a whole. Passage of the act would help lay the foundation for substantial and widespread economic growth through increased consumption, job creation, and the collection of additional tax revenue. Encouraging undocumented people to come out of the shadows for the purposes of acquiring more education would support long-term community revitalization and the growth of the middle-class. Undocumented children of immigrants are capable of meeting the challenges of higher education, are prepared to invest in their own futures, and are eager to contribute fully to the future of the nation. It is wrong for the government to keep them from the achievements that they can earn with their ability and hard work in the only country they have ever known.

REFERENCES AND FURTHER READING

Batalova, J., & McHugh, M. (2010). *DREAM vs. reality: An analysis of potential DREAM Act beneficiaries.* Retrieved from Migration Policy Institute website: http://www.migrationpolicy.org/pubs/DREAM-Insight-July2010.pdf

Baum, S., Ma, J., & Payea, K. (2010). *Education Pays 2010: The benefits of higher education for individuals and society.* Retrieved from College Board website: http://trends.collegeboard.org/downloads/Education_Pays_2010.pdf

Camarota, S. (2010). *Estimating the impact of the DREAM Act.* Retrieved from Center for Immigration Studies website: http://www.cis.org/dream-act-costs

Fry, R. (2010). *Hispanics, high school dropouts and the GED.* Retrieved from Pew Hispanic Center website: http://www.pewhispanic.org/2010/05/13/hispanics-high-school-dropouts-and-the-ged

Gándara, P. (2010). *The Latino education crisis: Rescuing the American Dream.* Retrieved from WestEd website: http://www.wested.org/online_pubs/pp-10–02.pdf

Gonzales, R. (2009). *Young lives on hold: The college dreams of undocumented students.* Retrieved from College Board website: http://professionals.collegeboard.com/profdownload/young-lives-on-hold-college-board.pdf

Hanson, G. (2009). *The economics and policy of illegal immigration in the United States.* Retrieved from Migration Policy Institute website: http://www.migrationpolicy.org/pubs/Hanson-Dec09.pdf

Immigration Policy Center. (2010). *Unauthorized immigrants pay taxes, too.* Retrieved from http://www.immigrationpolicy.org/just-facts/unauthorized-immigrants-pay-taxes-too

Kober, N., Chudowsky, N., Chudowsky, V., & Dietz, S. (2010, June 30). *Improving achievement for the growing Latino population is critical to the nation's future.* Retrieved from Center on Education Policy website: http://www.cep-dc.org/displayDocument.cfm?DocumentID=133

Levin, H., Belfield, C., Muennig, P., & Rouse, C. (2007, January). *The costs and benefits of an excellent education for all of America's children.* Retrieved from Center for Benefit-Cost Studies of Education website: http://www.cbcse.org/media/download_gallery/Leeds_Report_Final_Jan2007.pdf

Massachusetts Taxpayers Foundation. (2006). *Massachusetts public colleges would gain millions of dollars from undocumented immigrants.* Retrieved from http://www.masstaxpayers.org/publications/education/20060101/massachusetts_would_gain_millions_dollars_undocumented_immigrants

Mehlman-Orozco, K. (2011). *The effects of in-state tuition for non-citizens: A systematic review of the evidence.* Retrieved from Latino Policy Institute at Roger Williams University website: http://www.rwu.edu/sites/default/files/lpi-report.pdf

Ojeda, R. H., & Takash, P. C. (with Castillo, G., Flores, G., Monroy, A., & Sargeant, D.). (2010). *No DREAMers left behind: The economic potential of DREAM Act beneficiaries.* Retrieved from North American Integration and Development Center website: http://naid.ucla.edu/uploads/4/2/1/9/4219226/no_dreamers_left_behind.pdf

Padron, E. (2008). The DREAM Act, deferred. *Harvard Journal of Hispanic Policy, 20,* 49–52.

Papademetriou, D., & Terrazas, A. (2009). *Immigrants and the current economic crisis: Research evidence, policy challenges, and implications.* Retrieved from Migration Policy Institute website: http://www.migrationpolicy.org/pubs/lmi_recessionJan09.pdf

Andrew J. Parr

COUNTERPOINT

Higher education in the United States is at a historical peak, with more students attending college from more diverse social and economic backgrounds than ever. As institutions of higher learning, states, and the federal government deal both logistically and fiscally with a growing student population, questions have arisen about how each should treat illegal immigrants wishing to attend college. In many states, illegal immigrants are eligible to pay in-state tuition despite their illegal status. Problematic legislative proposals such as the DREAM Act have further compounded an already complex policy issue, and important moral questions have been raised about the role of education in the United States.

The lack of a comprehensive immigration policy in the United States has long-term effects. Social services are strained by populations whose use outpaces their financial support through taxation. Businesses large and small bear the brunt of the federal government's inability to regulate the eligibility of the workforce and the collection of appropriate taxes.

Since the 1980s, a number of towns and cities, from Miami to Minneapolis to San Francisco, have designated themselves as "sanctuary cities." These are municipalities that have decided not to use public funds or resources to police immigration issues in order to call attention to the scope of the immigration problem, and to their unwillingness and inability to deal with such a complex issue. Other states, such as Arizona and Alabama, have decided not to wait for the federal government. These states have passed stringent new laws intended to stop the flow of state resources to illegal aliens.

The education of immigrant children accounts for a substantial portion of the costs of current U.S. immigration policy. K–12 schools, however, have limited flexibility in deciding whether, and to what extent, they must deal with an increasingly complex immigration landscape. The Supreme Court's decision in *Plyler v. Doe* (1982) established that K–12 schools must educate all students, without charging additional tuition, regardless of a student's immigration status. Colleges and universities are in a more complicated position, however, since they are susceptible to political and legal challenges over whether illegal alien students should be admitted, and whether those students, in the case of public colleges, should pay in-state or out-of-state tuition. The recent recession and the uncertain economic future of public colleges and universities have refocused attention on the importance of the question, "What sort of access should illegal aliens have to higher education?"

Immigration reform proposals such as the DREAM Act have offered higher education as a path to citizenship, and along the way have raised important moral and economic questions about the relationship between college and one's role as a citizen, and about whether the act tramples on the educational opportunities for native-born citizens and legal immigrants. The DREAM Act exacerbates ethical issues in immigration policy by, for example, forging an artificial relationship between higher education and military service, and by attaching to debates about higher education some of the larger political issues of our time.

THE IIRIRA AND ITS IMPACT ON HIGHER EDUCATION

In 1996, the Illegal Immigration Reform and Immigrant Responsibility Act (IIRIRA) established that states could not provide postsecondary education benefits to illegal aliens unless lawful United States citizens were eligible for the same benefits. Title 8, Chapter 14, Sec. 1623(a) of the act states,

> An alien who is not lawfully present in the United States shall not be eligible on the basis of residence within a State (or a political subdivision) for any postsecondary education benefit unless a citizen or national of the United States is eligible for such a benefit (in no less an amount, duration, and scope) without regard to whether the citizen or national is such a resident.

However, the legislation provided no language that states could use for guidance in regulation, and the Congressional Research Service has noted that the exact meaning of the relevant sections of IIRIRA have been disputed. State legislatures have taken advantage of that lack of clarity to promote broader access to higher education.

As of July 2011, 13 states had enacted legislation that allows illegal aliens to receive in-state tuition benefits at public colleges and universities. These states are California, Connecticut, Illinois, Kansas, Maryland, Nebraska, New Mexico, New York, Oklahoma, Texas, Utah, Washington and Wisconsin. Oklahoma reversed course in 2008, however, ending in-state tuition policies for illegal immigrants.

While these policies give students who are resident noncitizens large breaks on tuition, the stress on education budgets is tremendous—and taxpayers foot the bill. The difference in tuition can be large; at the University of California, Los Angeles (UCLA) campus, nonresident undergraduate students must pay an additional $22,878 annually in "Nonresident Supplemental Tuition," resulting in total mandatory fees of $36,788 per year. California state residents pay $13,910 for the same education, with the state university system subsidizing their tuition. The cost of college rises for both institutions and consumers each year. The average difference between in-state and out-of-state tuition in California is $17,159 per year, a figure slightly above the national average of about $14,500. With colleges in most states in difficult financial positions due to the weak economy and tighter controls on public spending, the burdens of subsidizing college tuition for illegal aliens further stresses already delicate budgets.

Most illegal aliens looking to study at a postsecondary institution cannot afford fees like those at UCLA, nor can they secure the necessary loans to attend. Because illegal aliens aren't eligible for federal financial aid, few can afford the more expensive campuses and are drawn to community colleges out of financial necessity. Non-flagship campuses in state university systems are often less expensive, and community colleges and 2-year institutions have even friendlier fee and tuition schedules. This combination of accessibility and convenience for illegal immigrants seeking less expensive college degrees has contributed both to congestion and underfunding, particularly at community colleges.

Some have challenged policies that invite illegal aliens to take advantage of subsidized study. According to Kris Kobach—a law professor at the University of Missouri, Kansas City—California taxpayers spend approximately $200 million per year in tuition subsidies for an estimated 25,000 noncitizen students. Kobach represented a group of California students who sued the Regents of the University of California, charging that California legislation (Assembly Bill 540) violated federal IIRIRA law, and argued that by requiring students to submit an affidavit saying they have or intend to file for legitimate immigration status, the institution knowingly abets the violation. After a series of appeals, the U.S. Supreme Court declined to review the ruling against Kobach's party in June 2011.

This has given support to the view that friendly tuition rates serve as a perverse incentive for illegal aliens to bypass the slow-but-lawful paths to legitimate immigration. If an immigrant family brings their children into the United States and remains undetected, or if the family settles in a sanctuary state or city committed to ignoring detection, not only do they receive a free, comprehensive K–12 education, they are also rewarded with significant discounts on higher education (over $85,000 in a case like UCLA) at taxpayer expense. William Gheen of the Americans for Legal Immigration Political

Action Committee put the argument succinctly in a 2008 article in *U.S. News & World Report*: "At a time of economic hardship for so many Americans, we need to worry about American students."

Lawful residents of the United States have objected, charging that providing tuition breaks to illegal aliens while denying them to U.S. citizens in neighboring states constitutes an unfair advantage—one likely prohibited by IIRIRA—and constitutes a moral offense. Brigette Brennan, a graduate of the University of Kansas, sued to receive in-state tuition. Brennan graduated from a Kansas high school, but her family lived just beyond the state border in Kansas City, Missouri. The Brennans were required to pay out-of-state tuition rates, despite Brigette's Kansas education pedigree, while illegal aliens were granted in-state tuition. Her suit was unsuccessful, and U.S. citizens from states bordering Kansas continue to pay out-of-state tuition. Supporters of arguments like Brennan's contend that education funds currently flowing to illegal aliens could better benefit lawful U.S. citizens in nearby states.

Claims that states and the federal government will receive net tax benefits are suspect. First, any revenue increases will be experienced in the far future, as it will take many years for increased earnings to accrue and come back via taxes. Second, these gains may be offset by the increased financial burdens a surge in student enrollment places on institutions.

THE DREAM ACT: PROMISE AND PROBLEMS

The DREAM Act, which was reintroduced in the United States Senate on May 11, 2011, would provide a path to citizenship for illegal immigrants who complete at least 2 years at an accredited institution of higher education or at least 2 years of service in the United States military with an honorable discharge. Though supporters of the DREAM Act argue that it provides a path to citizenship for those who plan a lifetime of residence in the United States, are of "good moral character," and largely came to the United States through no fault of their own, arguments against the act and its implications for higher education are considerable.

The chief objection to the DREAM Act is that it rewards those who knowingly and willingly violate immigration laws to improve life for their families. By awarding citizenship to children of illegal immigrants, the purpose of their immigration violations would be fulfilled in their entirety. Potential immigrants would have little incentive to pursue traditional, lawful paths to immigration when it is clear that their children can receive all the benefits of citizenship while sidestepping the immigration process. Critics of the act suggest that this will encourage unlawful immigration on a grand scale.

The DREAM Act also creates a moral conundrum; do children who were brought to the United States have a responsibility as adults to abide by the law? Some, like Ira Mehlman of the Federation for American Immigration Reform, say yes:

> Many would-be DREAM Act beneficiaries have been dealt a bad hand (by their parents). As difficult (even unfair) as it may be, upon reaching adulthood they have the responsibility to obey the law. When, for example, Jose Antonio Vargas proclaims on the pages of *The New York Times Magazine*, that he knowingly engaged in illegal activities in order to remain and work in the United States illegally, he became culpable in his own right. While he, and others like him, may be more sympathetic than the people who committed the predicate offense, their situation does not excuse their own illegal acts. (Mehlman, 2011)

The unwritten message is this: The United States has laws governing immigration, but they do not intend to uphold them and will provide a host of alternatives and workarounds. The act contains no provisions to regulate illegal immigration in the future, which encourages a never-ending stream of illegal immigration and procurement of citizenship via the provisions of the DREAM Act.

Steven A. Camarota (2010) of the Center for Immigration Studies estimates that 1.03 million illegal immigrants will eventually enroll in public institutions of higher education, which will take seats from lawful U.S. citizens and account for an estimated annual subsidy of approximately $6,000 per student, or a total of $6.2 billion per year. Such burdens on public institutions will be passed down to all students through tuition hikes that the student community can ill-afford, as the DREAM Act does not provide funding for schools to deal with increased enrollment, which would be an estimated 1 million new students.

The federal government has avoided clarity in its immigration initiatives regarding higher education and failed to provide funding for implementation of its decisions, which makes the DREAM Act ripe for fraud. Colleges and universities simply will not have the funds or human resources to examine applications properly. E-Verify, a federal program used to verify the employment eligibility of workers, executes a similar check with an overall accuracy rate of 99.5 percent according to a 2008 Center for Immigration Studies analysis. In June 2001, a Center for American Progress analysis showed that E-Verify would cost the government $247 million per year at a minimum, with businesses shouldering an additional $2.6 billion per year in total costs. A new, more comprehensive system for processing DREAM Act applications—one that verifies all details, including age, residence claims, work histories, and educational plans and enrollments—would necessitate massive increases in government costs or the creation of appropriate, competent departments within higher education institutions to prevent fraud.

Despite the fact that 90 percent of applications were approved, nearly one-third of the 1.3 million applicants for citizenship under the Immigration Reform and Control Act of 1986 were considered fraudulent. A smaller percentage of the additional 1.7 million who were granted general amnesty "raised concerns" about fraud, according to a 2006 *New York Times* interview with Demetrios G. Papademetriou, who studied the 1986 amnesty while working in the Labor Department during George H. W. Bush's administration. Evidence from the 1986 amnesty suggests that improprieties in future processes are a very real concern. Fraud among DREAM Act applicants would present a broader challenge to the Department of Homeland Security, which would likely be required to involve itself in the approval and monitoring process to ensure the safety of both local communities and the nation.

Logistical issues aside, the DREAM Act unintentionally transforms higher education from a meaningful personal or professional enrichment program into a de facto requirement for citizenship. Slogging through 2 years of classes—and paying in-state tuition at community college rates—is a small price to pay for U.S. citizenship. One would be justified in thinking that adding 1 million students, who may or may not be committed to their courses and degree programs, could negatively affect both the seriousness of purpose that drives higher education and its quality. At a time when the real value and utility of a college education is hotly debated—and, for the first time in decades, truly questioned—the DREAM Act presents higher education as an incentive simply to attain citizenship, without even requiring "DREAMers" to attain any sort of degree.

The DREAM Act also sends a perverse message about what is valued in U.S. society. One has two choices with the DREAM Act: sit through 2 years of classes at an accredited institution, or enter the military. The implicit message is that either of those paths is valued by the United States more than any others. One might be a plumber, an artist, a preacher, or a wonderful, committed parent, but the message is clear: Spend 2 years in college or the military, or the United States is not interested in fast-tracking your citizenship. Few would argue that pursuing higher education or military service is not valuable to both the individual or the state, but even fewer would argue that such narrow limits on what value is placed on citizens is anything but a message congruent with the values of American society.

Though a broad range of centrists and conservatives have found fault in the DREAM Act, progressives, too, have raised concerns about creating an either/or dichotomy between higher education and military service. The Committee Opposed to Militarism and the Draft (COMD) has stated objections to the DREAM Act that include coercing young Hispanics into military service: "In a period of an unusually extreme and aggressive U.S. foreign policy, preemptive wars and military interventions, this situation should concern all progressives and counter-recruitment activists."

For years, COMD has advocated for the elimination of the military service clause from the DREAM Act, pointing out that pursuing higher education may not be an option for all illegal immigrants. This could create an undue inducement to enter military service. Thus, for a significant percentage of the illegal immigrant population, military service is artificially pitted against higher education—along with the opportunity costs of each—rather than presenting each as an option to be selected based on the merits of the pursuit.

IMMIGRATION POLICY AND K–12'S EFFECT ON HIGHER EDUCATION

The National Education Association, the largest education-related union in the United States, with over 6 million members, has, in the words of its president, Dennis Van Roekel, supported initiatives such as the DREAM Act, touting the act as recognizing proud immigrant heritage and helping to "lift up immigrant students."

Unfortunately, the U.S. K–12 education system struggles—particularly in urban communities that serve impoverished minority families—to prepare students for postsecondary education. For many, the DREAM Act would provide an incentive to enter higher education without the necessary support from the K–12 education system to prepare those students for success in postsecondary endeavors. Problems in K–12 education with implications for higher education are many, including staff seniority rules (such as "last in, first out" union rules) that discourage the best teachers from teaching in high-need communities; tenure and employment protection systems, including evaluation schemes that keep ineffective teachers in classrooms; and ambiguous legislation and pedagogical approaches for students who need instruction in English as a second language (ESL), a good number of whom are also illegal aliens. The list of improvements needed in K–12 education is depressingly long, and students eager to benefit optimally from the DREAM Act cannot be expected to do so without concurrent support for the educational foundation that is meant to prepare them for college.

According to California's Legislative Analyst's Office (2011), approximately 85 percent of incoming community college students in the state are unprepared for college-level math. The data on reading and writing are not much better: about 70 percent fall short in college-level English skills, despite graduating from high school and successfully passing the California High School Exit Exam. It is not surprising that only 3 out of 10 community college students in California complete a certificate, obtain a 2-year degree, or transfer to a 4-year institution after 6 years.

In 2008 the National Center for Public Policy and Higher Education pointed to California—a bellwether for other states with significant immigrant populations—as sending "mixed signals," and appropriately subtitled their analysis, "A Mismatch Between High Schools and Community Colleges." An EdSource study of course-taking patterns in California's community colleges showed that students who are prepared for basic coursework are more likely to buck California's troubling community college dropout trends. California's case is not unique, and without proper K–12 and developmental support, immigrant populations are set up to fail.

The burden of that failure doesn't just fall on the shoulders of the students discouraged by the difficulty of higher education, or on the colleges who must offer more remediation (up to five semesters in some cases) just to get students up to speed. Businesses also pay. U.S. companies spend approximately $25 billion a year on remediation of employees' basic skills. This money offsets the revenue gains touted by supporters of increased access to higher education for illegal immigrants.

There undoubtedly are, and will be, outliers from this bleak data. High-achieving undocumented students will attain 2-year, 4-year, and graduate or professional degrees and add value to businesses and communities while generating tax revenues, both explicit and implicit, that more than offset the government money spent on their education. But for every inspiring success story, many more illegal immigrant students will spend 13 years in an expensive public K–12 education system, then attend a postsecondary institution with a combination of their own money and significant institutional funds just to drop off the educational map. The system that promised illegal aliens the fulfillment of a dream—a solid, comprehensive education and a life that parlays it into security and prosperity for themselves and their families—is unlikely to deliver without a commitment to the educational foundation that will truly allow their dreams to come true. Instead, the failure of that system limits their personal and professional capabilities while extending expensive entitlements and offering no long-term solutions to underlying problems.

CONCLUSION

It is difficult to balance criticism of increased access to higher education for illegal aliens with the knowledge that so many who would benefit were forced into an unenviable position through no fault of their own. Both proponents of measures like the DREAM Act and those who find it wanting—or flat-out harmful—want to see a sensible, efficient immigration policy that allows those who want to add to the richness of the United States a path forward. But both sides need to recognize that the fulfillment of those hopes and dreams depends on uncomfortable and often inconvenient realities. These include heavy strains on already stressed state and federal budgets and the unintended consequences of legislative, legal, and policy decisions. It is tempting—morally, emotionally and, for some, politically—to advance agendas that provide relief to individual components of a complex problem.

The nation must not, however, put a bandage on a bullet wound and call it good medicine. Increased access to higher education for illegal immigrants must be achieved in a way that is fair to law-abiding citizens. The numbers must balance and financial problems must not be compounded with burdensome regulations and subsidies that do nothing to address seminal issues of current policy problems. The country must protect—and even augment—the integrity of the higher education system without decreasing opportunities for one population as opportunities for another are increased.

The United States needs an immigration policy that expands educational opportunities for immigrant populations while respecting the values of the nation, not policies that leave the nation susceptible to continued fraud, abuse, or liability. That will require a strong, sober commitment to improving the K–12 education system so that immigrants succeed, while also committing to policies that eliminate perverse incentives.

REFERENCES AND FURTHER READING

California Assembly Committee on Higher Education. (2001). *Bill Analysis, AB 540.* Retrieved from http://info.sen.ca.gov/pub/01-02/bill/asm/ab_0501-0550/ab_540_cfa_20010502_124759_asm_comm.html

California Legislative Analyst's Office, Higher Education. (2011). *Are entering freshmen prepared for college-level work?* Retrieved from http://www.lao.ca.gov/sections/higher_ed/FAQs/Higher_Education_Issue_02.pdf

Camarota, S. A. (2010). *Estimating the impact of the DREAM Act.* Retrieved from Center for Immigration Studies website: http://cis.org/dream-act-costs

Cooper, B., & O'Neil, K. (2005). *Lessons from the Immigration Reform and Control Act of 1986.* Retrieved from Migration Policy Institute website: http://www.migrationpolicy.org/pubs/PolicyBrief_No3_Aug05.pdf

H.R.1842, DREAM Act of 2011 (Introduced in House), 112th Congress (2011–2012). Retrieved from http://thomas.loc.gov/cgi-bin/query/z?c112:H.R.1842:

Illegal Immigration Reform and Immigrant Responsibility Act (IIRIRA), Pub. L. 104–208, 110 STAT. 3009 (1996). Retrieved from http://www.gpo.gov/fdsys/pkg/PLAW-104publ208/html/PLAW-104publ208.htm

Madigan, T. (2010, April 5). Should undocumented students get federal support? [Education Expert Blog]. *National Journal.* Retrieved from http://education.nationaljournal.com/2010/04/should-undocumented-students-g.php

Mariscal, J. (2004, November–December). The interpretation of dreams: Covert recruitment strategies in the DREAM Act. *Draft NOtices.* Retrieved from http://www.comdsd.org/article_archive/Dreams11-04.htm

Martinez v. Regents of University of California, 50 Cal. 4th 1277 (2010).

Mehlman, I. (2011). *Five moral arguments against the DREAM Act.* Retrieved from Federation for American Immigration Reform website: http://www.fairus.org/site/News2?page=NewsArticle&id=24257&security=1601&news_iv_ctrl=1742

Mexican Migration Project. http://mmp.opr.princeton.edu

Morse, A., & Birnbach, K. (2011). *In-state tuition and unauthorized immigrant students.* Retrieved from National Conference of State Legislatures website: http://www.ncsl.org/default.aspx?tabid=13100

National Center for Public Policy and Higher Education. (2008). *Mixed signals in California: A mismatch between high schools and community colleges.* Retrieved from http://www.highereducation.org/reports/pa_mixed_signals/mis.pdf

New York City's "Sanctuary" Policy and the Effect of Such Policies on Public Safety, Law Enforcement, and Immigration: Hearing before the Subcommittee on Immigration, Border Security, and Claims, of the Committee on the Judiciary, 108th Cong, 1st Sess. (2003, February 27). Retrieved from http://commdocs.house.gov/committees/judiciary/hju85287.000/hju85287_0f.htm

Plyler v. Doe, 457 U.S. 202 (1982).

Ramirez, E. (2008, August 7). Should colleges enroll illegal immigrants? *US News and World Report.* Retrieved from http://www.usnews.com/education/articles/2008/08/07/should-colleges-enroll-illegal-immigrants

S.952, DREAM Act of 2011 (Introduced in Senate), 112th Congress. (2011–2012). Retrieved from http://thomas.loc.gov/cgi-bin/query/z?c112:S.952:

Swarns, R. L. (2006, May 23). Failed amnesty legislation of 1986 haunts the current immigration bills in Congress. *The New York Times.* Retrieved from http://www.nytimes.com/2006/05/23/washington/23amnesty.html

University of California Los Angeles Registrar's Office. (2011). *Fees: Graduate and undergraduate annual 2011–12.* Retrieved from http://www.registrar.ucla.edu/fees/gradfee.htm

U.S. Citizenship and Immigration Services. (2011). *E-Verify.* Retrieved from http://www.uscis.gov/E-Verify

Washington Legal Foundation. (2008). *Case detail:* Day v. Bond. Retrieved from http://www.wlf.org/litigating/case_detail.asp?id=382

Wolgin, P. E. (2011). *The costs of E-Verify.* Retrieved from Center for American Progress website: http://www.americanprogress.org/issues/2011/06/e_verify_infographic.html

Matthew K. Tabor

Racial Profiling

POINT: Profiling is a legitimate practice if used correctly. It can be an effective and necessary tool for law enforcement.

Peter H. Schuck, Yale University

COUNTERPOINT: Racial profiling is a discriminatory practice that undermines fundamental civil rights while failing to promote law enforcement goals.

Karin D. Martin and Jack Glaser, University of California, Berkeley

Introduction

The practice of racial profiling, which involves singling out a person or persons for special (usually law-enforcement-related) attention based solely on their race or ethnicity, is part of a specific set of issues that the United States has grappled with in protecting the civil rights of minority individuals belonging to a specific group or class. The Fourth Amendment to the U.S. Constitution, protecting against unreasonable search and seizure, and the equal protection provisions of the Fourteenth Amendment make racial profiling per se illegal. But the legal community and law enforcement agencies have worked to define parameters that would allow consideration of race or ethnicity in conjunction with other behaviors or factors.

Given its controversial nature, it is not surprising that definitions of racial profiling vary. The Department of Justice, for example, defines it as "any police-initiated action that relies on the race, ethnicity, or national origin rather than the behavior of an individual or information that leads the police to a particular individual who has been identified as being, or having been, engaged in criminal activity." Far more simply, the General Accounting Office defines it as "using race as a key factor in deciding whether to make a traffic stop." The Office of the Arizona Attorney General, meanwhile, describes it as "use by law enforcement personnel of an individual's race or ethnicity as a factor in articulating reasonable suspicion to stop, question or arrest an individual, unless race or ethnicity is part of an identifying description of a specific suspect for a specific crime."

The issue of racial profiling has been brought into sharp focus in the immigration arena by passage of state laws such as Arizona's S.B. 1070. Although S.B. 1070 specifically forbids racial profiling, critics have widely decried the law as impossible to enforce unless police engage in the practice. The central challenge is that, while the vast majority of illegal immigrants in Arizona are from Mexico and are Hispanics, not all Hispanics of Mexican origin are illegal immigrants. Thus, the probability that S.B. 1070 will result in discrimination by virtue of racial profiling against Hispanics who are either U.S. citizens or foreign nationals legally in the country seems very high.

As in all situations where racial profiling is a concern, there is a power imbalance between law enforcement personnel, who are frequently members of the majority population, and the targets of that enforcement, who are by definition members of a minority population. Proponents of "legitimate" racial profiling argue that it provides law enforcement with a valuable tool. Opponents argue that it is counterproductive and is a fundamental violation of core American values of human rights and dignity.

In the Point essay below, Peter Schuck argues that in the post-9/11 era, and with the issue of illegal immigration becoming more and more pressing, it is important for the country to have a rational discussion about the use of racial profiling. "Government may not treat individuals arbitrarily," he argues, "it must base its action on information that is reliable enough to justify its exercise of power over free individuals." He goes on to say, "Context is everything," and when it is used properly and within defined legal parameters, racial profiling can be a legitimate, useful tool of law enforcement.

In the Counterpoint essay, Karin Martin and Jack Glaser contend there are serious social costs incurred both by the targets of racial profiling and by the broader American society. They consider the effectiveness of racial profiling, determining that, in fact, the evidence shows that racial profiling is both ineffective and inefficient. Finally, they argue that the demonstrated ineffective and unjust nature of racial profiling demands that it be rejected, and that a proactive, enforceable ban on its use be enacted.

In reading this chapter, consider not only whether racial profiling is effective, but also to what extent such a practice is valuable, given the rights to equal protection established by the U.S. Constitution. How much safety can be "bought" through racial profiling, and is the price acceptable? Conversely, given the high expectations placed on law enforcement, is it reasonable to expect that consideration of race and ethnicity *not* be a part of standard investigation techniques?

POINT

Since the terrorist attacks of September 11, 2001, racial profiling has become one of the hottest civil rights issues of the day whose prominence that has only been heightened by the subsequent passage of state laws designed to deter undocumented immigrants from entering or remaining in the state. The issue, however, deserves cooler reflection than it has received thus far. Politicians and pundits, regardless of ideology, reflexively denounce the practice, and nary a word is raised in its defense. Some states have already barred any form of profiling, and it is possible that the U.S. Congress could follow suit. Yet, as Dr. Johnson said of the gallows, the events of 9/11 concentrate the mind wonderfully. The disaster that befell the United States on that day—and those that, on a smaller scale have occurred elsewhere since then, and will probably do so in the future—demands a profiling debate that is clear-eyed and hardheaded, not simplistic or demagogic.

One must be clear about the state laws that opponents believe invite profiling. In the case of Arizona's controversial statute (and some or all of the other similar state laws), the law specifically prohibits consideration of race, color, or national origin in its enforcement. Indeed, Arizona's governor, Jan Brewer, signed an executive order directing that law enforcement officials be trained to avoid illegal racial profiling. Further, the law expressly prohibits officials from making stops and arrests when race is the only basis for doing so. A lawful reason for the initial stop must exist other than the suspected immigration status of the detained person. Indeed, the law tracks the 2003 memorandum issued by the U.S. Department of Justice banning racial profiling in federal law enforcement. Therefore, the "racial profiling" argument against such laws serves only to prevent rational discussion of a screening practice that, when used properly and within defined legal parameters, can be a legitimate, effective tool of law enforcement. There are legitimate reasons to criticize the Arizona legislation, but the false assertion that the law permits racial or ethnic profiling is not one of them.

CONTEXT IS EVERYTHING

The furor over racial profiling is easy to understand. Harassment of those who, as the sayings go, "drive while Black" or "fly while Arab," are emblems of the indignities that law enforcement officials are said to inflict on minorities on the basis of demeaning stereotypes and racial prejudice. This is no laughing matter. The state's coercive power creates special responsibilities for law enforcement officials to screen only in accordance with legal guidelines. Respect for the rule of law means that people must not be singled out for enforcement scrutiny simply because of their race or ethnicity.

Or does it? Much turns on the meaning of "simply" in that sentence. Profiling is not only inevitable, it is in fact sensible public policy under certain conditions and with appropriate safeguards against abuse. After September 11, the stakes in deciding when and how profiling may be used and how to remedy abuses when they occur could not be higher.

A fruitful debate on profiling properly begins with the core values of American society. The most important of these, of course, is national defense, without which no other values can be realized. But one should be wary of claims that ideals must be sacrificed in the name of national security; this means that other ideals remain central to the inquiry. The ideal most threatened by profiling is the principle that all individuals are equal before the law. In most but not all respects, the same entitlements are extended to aliens who are present in the polity, whether they are here legally or illegally. Differential treatment must meet a burden of justification—and in the case of racial classification, a very high one.

This ideal has a corollary: government may not treat individuals arbitrarily. To put this principle another way, government must base its action on information that is reliable enough to justify its exercise of power over free individuals. How good must the information be? The law's answer is that it depends. Criminal punishment requires proof beyond a reasonable doubt, while a tort judgment demands only the preponderance of the evidence. Health agencies can often act with little more than a rational suspicion that a substance might be dangerous. A consular official can deny a visa if, in the official's "opinion," the applicant is likely to become a public charge, and, unlike the previous examples, courts may not review this decision. Information good enough for one kind of decision, then, is not nearly good enough for others. Context is everything.

This brings us to profiling by law enforcement officials. Consider the context in which an FBI agent must search for the September 11 terrorists, or in which a security officer at a railroad or airline terminal must screen for new terrorists. Vast numbers of individuals pass through the officer's line of vision, and they do so only fleetingly, for a few seconds at most. As a result, the official must make a decision about each of them within those few seconds, or be prepared to hold all of them up for the time it will take to interrogate each individual, one by one. The official knows absolutely nothing about these individuals, other than the physical characteristics that can be immediately observed, and learning more about them through interrogation will take a lot of time. The time this would take is costly, and each question that is asked will either allow others to pass by unnoticed or prolong the wait of those in the already long, steadily lengthening line. The time is even more costly to those waiting in line; for them, more than for the official, time is money and opportunity. Politicians know how their constituents hate lines, and security, customs, immigration, and toll officials are constantly pressed to shorten them.

At the same time, the risks of being wrong are dramatically asymmetrical. If everyone is stopped, all of the problems just described may occur, and all of the people (except one, perhaps) will turn out to be perfectly innocent. On the other hand, if the official fails to stop the one person among them who is in fact a terrorist, the result may be a social calamity of immense proportions (not to mention the prospect of the official losing his or her job). In choosing between these competing risks, self-interest and the social interest will drive the official in the direction of avoiding calamity. The fact that society also presses for evenhandedness only adds to the dilemma, while providing no useful guidance as to what to do, given these incentives.

STEREOTYPES ARE OFTEN USEFUL

So what should be done? Each person can get at this question by asking what she or he would do in this situation. To answer this question, one need not engage in moral speculation but can look to our own daily experiences. Each day, we all face choices that are very similar in structure, albeit far less consequential. We all must make decisions very rapidly about things that matter to us. We know that our information is inadequate to the choice, but we also know that we cannot in the time available get information that is sufficiently better to improve our decision significantly. We consider our risks of error, which are often asymmetrical. Because we must momentarily integrate all this uncertainty into a concrete choice, we resort to shortcuts to decision making. Psychologists call these shortcuts "heuristics."

The most important and universal of these tactical shortcuts is the stereotype. The advantage of stereotypes is that they economize on information, enabling us to choose quickly when our information is inadequate. This is a great, indeed indispensable virtue, precisely because this problem is ubiquitous in daily life, so ubiquitous that we scarcely notice it, nor do we notice how often we use stereotypes to solve it. Indeed, few of us live without stereotypes. We use them to predict how others will behave. We may assume that Black people will vote Democratic, for example (though many do not), and we anticipate others' desires, needs, or expectations, perhaps offering help to disabled people (though some of them find this presumptuous). We use stereotypes when we take safety precautions when a large, unkempt, angry-looking man approaches us on a dark street (though he may simply be asking directions), or when we assume that higher-status schools are better (though they often prove to be unsuitable). Such assumptions are especially important in a mass society where people know less and less about one another.

Stereotypes, of course, have an obvious downside: they must sometimes be wrong, almost by definition. After all, if they were wrong all the time, no rational person would use them, and if they were never wrong, they would be indisputable facts, not stereotypes. Stereotypes fall somewhere in between these extremes, but it is hard to know precisely where, because we seldom know precisely how accurate they are. Although all stereotypes are overly broad, most are probably correct much more often than they are wrong; that is why they are useful. But when a stereotype is wrong, those who are exceptions to it naturally feel that they have not been treated equally as individuals, and they are right. Their uniqueness is being overlooked so that others can use stereotypes for the much larger universe of cases where the stereotypes are true and valuable. In this way, the palpable claims of discrete individuals are sacrificed to a disembodied social interest. This sacrifice offends not just them but others who identify with their sense of injustice, and when their indignation is compounded by the discourtesy or bias of bag checkers or law enforcement agents, the wound is even more deeply felt.

This is where the law comes in. When these stereotype-based injustices are viewed as sufficiently grave, they are prohibited. Even then, however, this is only done in a qualified way that expresses a general ambivalence. Civil rights law, for example, proscribes racial, gender, disability, and age stereotyping. At the same time, it allows government, employers, and others to adduce a public interest or business reason strong enough to justify using them. The law allows religious groups to hire only coreligionists. Officials drawing legislative districts may, to some extent, treat all members of a minority group as if they all had the same political interests. The military can bar women from certain combat roles. Employers can assume that women are usually less suitable for jobs requiring very heavy lifting. Such practices reflect stereotypes that are thought to be reasonable in general, though false as to particular individuals.

Can the same be said of ethno-racial profiling? The answer is, "sometimes," but again, context is everything. Most would object to a public college that categorically admitted women rather than men on the theory that women tend to be better students—not because the stereotype is false but because the school can readily ascertain academic promise on an individualized basis when reviewing applicants' files, which it must do anyway. On the other hand, no one would think it unjust for an airport security officer to have screened for Osama bin Laden, who was a very tall man with a beard and turban, by stopping all men meeting that general description. This is so not only because the stakes in apprehending someone like bin Laden are immense, but also because in making instantaneous decisions about whom to stop, the official can use gender, size, physiognomy, and dress as valuable clues. It would be irresponsible and incompetent not to do so, even though every man stopped in this way would likely turn out to be a false positive, and thus feel unjustly treated for having been singled out.

Racial profiling in more typical law enforcement settings can raise difficult moral questions. Suppose that society views drug dealing as a serious vice, and that a disproportionate number of drug dealers are Black men, although of course many are not. Would this stereotype justify stopping Black men simply because of their color? Clearly not. The law properly requires more particularized evidence of possible wrongdoing. Suppose further, however, that police were to observe a Black man engaging in the ostensibly furtive behavior that characterizes most but not all drug dealers, behavior also engaged in by some innocent men. This type of observational deduction is referred to as "behavioral profiling," and of course it is a perfectly legal means of inferring the likelihood that the suspect has committed the crime in question. Here, the behavioral stereotype would legally justify stopping the man. But what if the officer relied on both stereotypes in some impossible-to-parse combination? What if the behavioral stereotype alone had produced a very close call, and the racial one pushed it over the line?

Likewise, imagine a scenario that takes place in an immigrant-dense region such as Arizona, where a large number of Spanish-speaking males are gathered outside a 7-Eleven store in the morning and are eventually approached by a man in a pickup truck looking for workers for the day. The response of a law enforcement officer who observes this scene will be determined by two types of profiling, working in tandem: behavioral (some but not all Spanish-speaking men engaged in this type of activity would be illegal aliens) and ethnic (the vast majority of illegal aliens in Arizona are of Hispanic descent). When the officer pulls into the parking lot, some of the men run away. Is it legally justifiable for an officer to stop these individuals if this decision is reached based partly on ethnic profiling? And should that depend on a subsequent judicial determination of what percentage of such an inference was based on observed behavior and what percentage on ethno-racial generalization (which, again, would be accurate in the vast majority of such cases)?

Although all of these questions cannot be answered with certainty, most critics of ethno-racial profiling do not even ask them. A wise policy will insist that the justice of profiling depends on a number of variables. How serious is the crime risk? How does the public feel about the relative costs of false positives and false negatives? Is it relevant that members of the group being stereotyped would support such profiling in their capacities as citizens equally concerned about security? How accurate is the stereotype? How practicable is it to pursue the facts through an individualized inquiry rather than through stereotypes? If stereotypes must be used, are there some that rely on less incendiary and objectionable factors?

A sensible profiling policy will also recognize that safeguards become more essential as the enforcement process progresses. Stereotypes that are reasonable at the stage of deciding whom to screen for questioning may be unacceptable at the later stages of arrest and prosecution, when official decisions should be based on more individualized information, and when lawyers and other procedural safeguards can be made available. Screening officials can be taught about the many exceptions to even serviceable stereotypes, to recognize them when they appear, and to behave in ways that encourage those being screened not to take it personally.

It is a cliché that September 11 changed the world. Profiling is bound to be part of the new dispensation. With the debate over illegal immigration persisting and growing increasingly heated, clearer thinking and greater sensitivity to the potential uses and abuses of profiling can help produce both a safer and a more just America.

References and Further Reading

Chebel d'Appollonia, A., & Reich, S. (Eds.). (2008). *Immigration, integration, and security.* Pittsburgh, PA: University of Pittsburgh Press.

Glaser, J. (2006). The efficacy and effect of racial profiling: A mathematical simulation approach. *Journal of Policy Analysis and Management, 25,* 395–416.

Heumann, M., & Cassack, L. (2007). *Good cop, bad cop: Racial profiling and competing views of justice.* New York, NY: Peter Lang.

Muffler, S. J. (2006). *Racial profiling: Issues, data, and analyses.* New York, NY: Nova Science.

Schuck, P. H. (2006). *Meditations of a militant moderate: Cool views on hot topics.* Lanham, MD: Rowman & Littlefield.

Stein, D. (2010, April 30). What Arizona's immigration law really says. *Los Angeles Times.* Retrieved from http://articles.latimes.com/2010/apr/30/opinion/la-oe-stein-20100430

Viscusi, W. K., & Zeckhauser, R. J. (2003). Sacrificing civil liberties to reduce terrorism risks. *Journal of Risk and Uncertainty, 26*(2/3), 99–120.

Von Spakovsky, H. (2010). *The Arizona immigration law: Racial discrimination prohibited.* Retrieved from the Heritage Foundation website: http://www.heritage.org/research/reports/2010/10/the-arizona-immigration-law-racial-discrimination-prohibited

Withrow, B. L. (2006). *Racial profiling: From rhetoric to reason.* Upper Saddle River, NJ: Pearson/Prentice Hall.

Peter H. Schuck

Note: This essay was adapted from a chapter in *Meditations of a Militant Moderate* by Peter H. Schuck.

COUNTERPOINT

Racial profiling is law enforcement's use of race, ethnicity, or national origin as a basis for criminal suspicion. Racial profiling is an intuitively appealing idea—target groups with higher offending rates for greater law enforcement—that proves deeply problematic. This essay argues that racial profiling is unjustified because it is discriminatory and unconstitutional, ineffective, and probably counterproductive.

DEFINING RACIAL PROFILING

Racial profiling is the use by law enforcement officials of race, ethnicity, or national origin (or proxies thereof) as a basis of criminal suspicion. This definition is consistent with well-established definitions used at the highest levels of American government. The U.S. Department of Justice, in a 2003 memorandum that specifically banned racial profiling in federal law enforcement, stated, "In making routine or spontaneous law enforcement decisions, such as ordinary traffic stops, federal law enforcement officers may not use race or ethnicity to any degree, except that officers may rely on race and ethnicity if a specific suspect description exists."

Despite many attempts over the last decade, the U.S. Congress has not passed federal legislation on racial profiling. Nevertheless, the leading proposed legislation, the End Racial Profiling Act (ERPA) of 2010, defines it as

> the practice of a law enforcement agent or agency relying, to any degree, on race, ethnicity, national origin, or religion in selecting which individual to subject to routine or spontaneous investigatory activities or in deciding upon the scope and substance of law enforcement activity following the initial investigatory procedure, except when there is trustworthy information, relevant to the locality and timeframe, that links a person of a particular race, ethnicity, national origin, or religion to an identified criminal incident or scheme.

The definition used by the authors of this essay adds two items to the definition of racial profiling. First, including the use of the phrase "proxies thereof" reflects the reality that law enforcement agents typically do not have direct information regarding suspects' race or ethnicity; they are merely making inferences about race or ethnicity based on appearance, name, or other superficial proxy characteristics like clothing and car type. Second, it is also worth elaborating on the use of the phrase "basis of criminal suspicion." This choice of words is deliberately inclusive, so that racial profiling also includes cases where no actual stop, search, or detention is carried out, but where the likelihood of such actions is increased. This wording would include as racial profiling any law enforcement procedures, such as consideration of race in compilation of suspect lists or decisions to patrol certain neighborhoods, because they raise the probability of detention and sanction of minorities. On the whole, these would have the same discriminatory effect as an aggregation of stops and searches each of which was determined, in whole or in part, by the race or ethnicity of the individual suspects.

What racial profiling is not. In defining racial profiling, it is important to distinguish it from two law enforcement practices that bear some resemblance to it, but which are legal and, if carried out correctly, nondiscriminatory. The first is "criminal profiling," which can take two forms. One is the development of a constellation of characteristics that are predictive of a perpetrator of a particular crime. This can be thought of as profiling broadly defined. It is generally a more formal process than racial profiling and can result from either formal agency guidelines (as in the case of early Drug Enforcement Agency drug courier profiles starting in the 1970s) or informal stereotypes of criminals held by individual officers. This practice is also referred to as "behavioral profiling," although the emphasis in behavioral profiling protocols is, as the name indicates, typically not on *trait* characteristics (e.g., age, gender), but rather on *behaviors* such as loitering, avoiding eye contact, and furtiveness (in the case of drug crimes), or purchasing one-way tickets with cash and then traveling without luggage (in the case of terrorism).

The second form of criminal profiling is an older variety that is qualitatively different. Whereas racial profiling involves searching for suspects of crimes (e.g., drugs or weapons possession, terrorism) that are not yet known to have been committed, classical criminal profiling involves narrowing the pool of suspects for a known (already perpetrated or, based on valid intelligence, imminent) crime. For example, investigators seeking to apprehend serial killers have utilized criminal profilers (sometimes forensic psychologists or psychiatrists) who develop a demographic (and possibly psychiatric) profile of the likely perpetrator. There are some remarkable success stories, but on the whole this kind of criminal profiling has had limited success, at best (Silke, 2001; Winerman, 2004).

Another important distinction is between *racial profiling* and the *use of race in suspect descriptions*. Although some legal scholars (e.g., Banks, 2004) argue that use of race in suspect descriptions can, under some circumstances, be a discriminatory practice akin to racial profiling, the two procedures must be kept distinct from one another. Use of race in suspect descriptions necessarily involves a known crime with specific evidence (e.g., a witness report) of a suspect's race, while racial profiling involves as yet unknown crimes with no direct basis for inference about a possible criminal's race.

Racial profiling must be distinguished from these other practices because they are often conflated, with the effect of confusing the issue and, more troublingly, justifying racial profiling. By arguing that use of race to identify suspects in any form is racial profiling, some seek to raise concerns about throwing out a valuable law enforcement tool. However, using race or ethnicity to describe a known suspect of a known crime is a perfectly legitimate and, no doubt, effective investigatory practice. Similarly, criminal profiling and offender profiling are legitimate tools to narrow the pool of suspects for a known crime, although there is only anecdotal support for this approach and no empirical evidence that it is a reliable practice. Behavioral profiling, which by definition focuses on behaviors and not traits like race, has been found to be effective, at least in the case of counterterrorism (Silke, 2011). A precise definition of racial profiling that avoids conflation with other legitimate law enforcement practices affords a meaningful consideration of the subject on its merits.

One other source of definitional imprecision that can undermine a productive consideration of the subject is the tendency for some commentators to define racial profiling as being law enforcement decisions that are based *solely* on race. Legal scholar R. S. MacDonald, for example, uses the race-as-sole-factor characteristic to distinguish between traffic stop profiling and airport security screening profiling, arguing that the latter is based on multiple factors and, for this and other reasons, is acceptable. This type of definition can enable profiling to be either defined away ("nobody does *that*") or promote support for a practice that seems, by comparison, to be innocuous. This misses the basic point that using race as the sole basis for decisions to stop and search is not mere "bias" but full blown racial oppression. It also violates the basic semantics of the terminology—a "profile" is by definition a multifaceted depiction. Perhaps most insidiously, the sole-factor definitional approach fails to appreciate that even if race is only one of many factors, its presence in the profile necessarily has the effect of increasing the probability that one racial group will be subject to disproportionate police attention. If the profile is young, male, and Black, then young, Black men will, for reasons to be elaborated further, bear the brunt of the policy.

The argument presented here against racial profiling operates on several fronts, beginning with a brief review of the relevant case law and subsequent options for legal remedy. The remedies, it will be seen, are meager, even though racial profiling violates basic civil liberties and fundamental American values. This is followed by a discussion of the grave social costs incurred by the targets of racial profiling and by society as a whole. Then the effectiveness and efficiency of racial profiling will be considered, and it will be shown that there is no compelling evidence in this regard; to the contrary, there is evidence that racial profiling is ineffective and inefficient. Finally, it will be argued that the demonstrated ineffective and unjust nature of racial profiling demands not only a lack of support for the practice, but a proactive, enforceable ban on it altogether, and the promotion of policies and practices to remediate it.

CONSIDERATIONS OF LAW AND JUSTICE

Constitutional remedies and case law. The Fourth Amendment to the U.S. Constitution protects citizens against "unreasonable searches and seizures," and the Fourteenth Amendment forbids any state to "deny to any person within its jurisdiction the equal protection of the laws." The vast majority of legal cases seeking remedies for those who allege they have been racially profiled make arguments under these two amendments: the Fourth for its mandate for "probable cause," and the Fourteenth for its prohibition against any action by the state that discriminates on the basis of race. Importantly, the standard of proof is lower for the Fourth Amendment—reasonableness—than it is for the Fourteenth—strict scrutiny for racial discrimination.

As Harris (2002), Withrow (2006), and others have compellingly described, the most relevant case law rests on two cases. In *Terry v. Ohio* (1968), the U.S. Supreme Court ruled that, in order to justifiably detain and search a suspect, a law enforcement officer need only have reasonable suspicion that a person is armed and dangerous, even if this suspicion is not sufficient to be probable cause for arrest. *Whren v. United States* (1996) is probably the most significant court case in terms of leaving open the possibility of legal racial profiling. This case stemmed from an incident in which police officers pulled over a Pathfinder truck, with a young (Black) driver and passenger inside, waiting at a stop sign (for what the police officers claimed was an abnormally long time). After the truck turned and went an "unreasonable" speed, and then stopped at a red light, the police officers pulled it over. One of the officers spotted what appeared to be, and turned out to be, plastic bags containing cocaine, and the truck's occupants were arrested. Several other types of illegal drugs were also found. In *Whren,* the defendants argued that there had been no probable cause or reasonable suspicion of illegal drug activity and that the officers used a pretext of giving a warning about traffic violations.

The Court of Appeals for the District of Columbia Circuit eventually ruled that a traffic stop is permissible as long as another reasonable officer could have stopped the car for a suspected traffic violation, and the Supreme Court upheld the decision. In essence, the Court ruled that the police officers' "subjective intentions" did not matter, even if race was a factor, and validated the use of pretexts—using one reason (e.g., minor traffic violation) to more extensively investigate a more serious offense even in the absence of reasonable suspicion (Withrow, 2006). In the Court majority's words, "We think these [past Supreme Court rulings] foreclose any argument that the constitutional reasonableness of traffic stops depends on the actual motivations of the individual officers involved."

Because it provides wide latitude for these pretextual stops, *Whren* effectively removes the option of Fourth Amendment–based challenges to racial profiling. Legal scholars tend to characterize the Supreme Court's rulings as "race-neutral" *to a fault,* because they fail to address the racial attitudes and tensions of both law enforcement and the victims of racial profiling (e.g., Lyle, 2001). Taken together, current case law puts in place rather high legal hurdles that must be cleared in order to prove racial profiling and its subsequent harm. Indeed, almost all racial profiling constitutional challenges have failed or have ended with out-of-court settlements (Harcourt, 2004, p. 1278).

Threat to civil liberties. The inadequacy of the current legal remedies for racial profiling does not obviate its violation of the core American principles of civil liberty, nondiscrimination, and basic fairness. The violation of these principles is obvious to anyone with a basic American civics education. Yet the persistence of support for racial profiling reflects the perennial tension between the necessity of securing public safety and the constitutional mandate to protect against restrictions of individual liberty. Indeed, there are some liberties that need to be abridged (such as speech that incites violence, or littering) to promote public safety. With regard to intrusions by law enforcement, people must and do submit to surveillance and screening, including relatively invasive procedures like those used on airline passengers. However, because racial profiling involves differentiations among racial and ethnic groups in terms of whose liberties are more or less infringed, it concerns *civil* liberties. It is one thing to expect everyone to relinquish the right to yell "fire" in a crowded theater, or to carry their own beverages through airport security, but it is quite another to deny only one racial or ethnic group that right. Regardless of one's beliefs about the potential effectiveness of racial profiling, even if we were to stipulate that targeted groups have criminal offending rates so high as to pose a threat to public safety, singling them out on the basis of race or ethnicity (as opposed to individual behavior) would violate sacrosanct American constitutional and moral principles.

These principles are enshrined in the statements of America's founders and most respected jurists:

"They who can give up essential liberty to obtain a little temporary safety, deserve neither liberty nor safety" —Benjamin Franklin (1818)

"Civil government cannot let any group ride roughshod over others simply because their consciences tell them to do so" —Justice Robert H. Jackson, *Douglas v. City of Jeannette,* 319 U.S. 157 (1943)

"The greatest dangers to liberty lurk in insidious encroachment by men of zeal, well-meaning but without understanding" —Justice Louis D. Brandeis, dissenting, *Olmstead v. United States,* 277 US 479 (1928)

"History teaches us that grave threats to liberty often come in times of urgency, when constitutional rights seem too extravagant to endure" —Justice Thurgood Marshall, dissenting, *Skinner v. Railway Labor Executives Association,* 489 U.S. 602, 635 (1989)

Despite America's strong tradition of and commitment to liberty, the government has, at several points in its history, succumbed to fear and insecurity to engage in policies that have violated basic individual and civil liberties. The Alien and Sedition Acts, Lincoln's suspension of habeas corpus, the internment of Japanese Americans during World War II, and the Congressional persecution of suspected communists and their associates in the early years of the Cold War—were all rationalized by real or perceived dangers. Although the drug war that inspired racial profiling in traffic and pedestrian stops has not been held up as rising to that level of threat, terrorist threats (and the attendant "war on terror") have, and these threats have subsequently been used to justify racial profiling. It is worth remembering that the historical, liberty-violating policies that preceded racial profiling have been judged extremely harshly by history, after the fog of war has cleared.

Racial profiling clearly falls into the same category as these historical lapses because it is an unmistakable breach of the Fourth and Fourteenth Amendments and the core American principles of fair and equal treatment and liberty that these amendments reflect. The notion that a person who happens to be a member of a racial, ethnic, or religious category that is presumed to be populated with a relatively high proportion of perpetrators of some sort of crime should be subject to greater suspicion and law enforcement intrusion because of that coincidence, is unambiguously in contradiction with American law and values. This is reflected not only in the quotes of influential officials like those provided above, but also in public opinion polls, wherein overwhelming majorities disapprove of racial profiling (e.g., 81% in Gallup Organization, 1999).

Not surprisingly, the post-9/11 "war on terror" appears to have engendered a greater sense of threat—and, consequently, willingness to compromise civil liberties—than has the "war on drugs." In a November 2001 Kaiser Family Foundation poll, 66 percent of Americans surveyed approved of profiling "people who are Arab or of Middle Eastern descent." However, in the same survey, only 21 percent approved when asked about a more generic profiling scenario involving traffic stops—an approval rate comparable to the pre-9/11 response. The majority approval of counterterrorism profiling of Middle Easterners has persisted since 2001 (e.g., Quinnipiac University, 2006). The ability of Americans to maintain these paradoxical views is not new when it comes to the public safety–civil liberties tradeoff, and it is not limited to the public. As the Supreme Court majority articulated in *Hirabayashi v. United States* (1943), "Because racial discriminations are in most circumstances irrelevant, and therefore prohibited, it by no means follows that, in dealing with the perils of war, Congress and the Executive are wholly precluded from taking into account those facts and circumstances which are relevant to measures for our national defense and for the successful prosecution of the war, and which may, in fact, place citizens of one ancestry in a different category from others." Yet the Court also addressed the offensiveness of discrimination: "Distinctions between citizens solely because of their ancestry are by their very nature odious to a free people whose institutions are founded upon the doctrine of equality." Somehow, the court had confidence that the stereotypes causing racial discrimination were "irrelevant" (i.e., spurious) in most domains, but not in the domain of national security. The flaw in this view was laid bare by subsequent revelations that the U.S. government had, in the Hirabayashi trial upholding Japanese-only curfews, suppressed evidence indicating that, in fact, very few Japanese Americans were actually suspected of treason or espionage. Hirabayashi's conviction was, as a result, later overturned.

There is no reason to believe that specious stereotypes are any more reliable in national security than in ordinary law enforcement. One can argue that the stakes are higher, but the error is the same, and the costs borne by the targets of discrimination are at least as severe.

Fairness and social costs. Because it heaps further disadvantage on groups—particularly African Americans and Hispanics—that are historically disadvantaged due to discrimination, racial profiling raises the issue of basic fairness and social costs. Racial profiling is not the sole source of disproportions in the criminal justice system, but it necessarily exacerbates them insofar as it increases the likelihood that certain racial minorities are targets of suspicion. In being disproportionately subject to suspicion, surveillance, and intrusion, members of these groups are inordinately punished and disenfranchised, with the attendant alienation from economic, political, and civic affairs. The magnitude of the racial disparities is striking. The Bureau of Justice Statistics projected that, assuming that 2003 incarceration rates persisted, 5.9 percent of White men born in 2001 would be incarcerated at some point in their lifetime, while for Latinos it would be 17.2 percent, and for African Americans it would be 32.2 percent (Bonczar, 2003). In an analysis of men born between 1965 and 1969, Petit and Western (2004) estimated that 60 percent of African American men who dropped out of high school would spend time in prison (compared to 11 percent of White high school dropouts). These disparities are reflected in the composition of the state prison population: According to the U.S. Department of Justice, in 2008, African Americans comprised 38.1 percent, Whites were 35.5 percent, and Hispanics were 18.7 percent, even though African Americans represent only 12.6 percent of the US population, Whites (non-Hispanic) 63.7 percent, and Hispanics, 16.3 percent (U.S. Census Bureau, 2010). The myriad collateral consequences of imprisonment compound how troublesome these statistics are.

Chief among these consequences is the effect of incarceration on employment and income. In a clever and careful employment audit experiment, Pager (2003) found that having a criminal record significantly decreased the likelihood that a job applicant would be called back by a real employer, and that this effect is even more dramatic for Black applicants. White applicants had their prospects cut in half by a criminal record, from 34 percent to 17 percent. Black applicants fared worse with or without a criminal record, but their prospects were reduced nearly threefold, from 14 percent to 5 percent. It is further noteworthy that Whites with a criminal record still fared better than Blacks without one, a general, pronounced employment discrimination finding replicated by Bertrand and Mullainathan's (2003) large and highly rigorous employment audit study. It is not surprising then that another study found the employment rate of formerly incarcerated men to be 6 percentage points lower than comparable men who had not been incarcerated, and their hourly wage to be between 14 and 26 percent lower (Geller, Garfinkel, & Western, 2006). Given the perennially higher unemployment rates for African Americans and Hispanics (U.S. Department of Labor, 2009), the repercussions of incarceration are even more calamitous, because they further limit the wage-earning capacity of so many people. The effects of incarceration are magnified in these vulnerable populations, making the collateral damage of racial profiling even greater.

To make matters worse, the effects of incarceration extend beyond the individual who serves time. There are also formidable costs to the families of those who are incarcerated in terms of lost income and employment-related benefits, strains on parenting, social stigma, and the emotional toll of having an absent family member. There is recent evidence that paternal incarceration puts children at greater risk for behavioral and mental health problems, and that the racial disparities in incarceration are a factor in the racial disparities in these childhood problems (Wakefield & Wildeman, 2011). There is also evidence that those who have been incarcerated are more likely to suffer from infectious diseases and illnesses related to stress (Massoglia, 2008). Intimates of incarcerated individuals are also at greater risk. For example, Johnson and Raphael (2006) found that higher incarceration rates among Black men are a significant, unique source of the disparity in HIV infection rates between Black women and women of other racial and ethnic groups.

Contact with the criminal justice system results in a significant, negative effect on political and civic engagement, even when socioeconomic status and criminal propensity are taken into account (Weaver & Lerman, 2010). Having a felony conviction also bars individuals from accessing many types of state assistance, such as housing, welfare, and financial assistance for higher education (Finzen, 2005). Moreover, in 48 states, a felony conviction results in either a temporary or permanent loss of the right to vote; as a consequence, 1.4 million African American men (13%) are disenfranchised (Sentencing Project, 2011). The systematic disenfranchisement of one ethnic group undermines the representation of that group's interests in government, and there is direct evidence that some elections would have had different outcomes had ex-felons been allowed to vote (Uggen & Manza, 2002).

As will be discussed further, computational modeling shows how racial profiling necessarily causes targeted groups to be incarcerated at rates that are disproportionate to their offending rates (Glaser, 2006). Racial profiling therefore brings additional burdens on minority populations. That racial minorities already face impediments to well-being should prompt an assiduous assessment of the threat to American ideals and social costs posed by racial profiling.

The clear violation of core constitutional principles and American values of liberty and fairness should be sufficient grounds on which to reject and condemn racial profiling in any domain of law enforcement. Nevertheless, the tipping point for the safety–liberty tradeoff resides at different points on the spectrum for different people. Indeed, discourse over racial profiling often turns to questions of police efficiency and effectiveness, in terms of conserving resources and mitigating crime. Even commentators who oppose racial profiling will sometimes stipulate that it is appealing on efficiency grounds (e.g., Kennedy, 1999). However, there is no evidence that racial profiling actually affords the kinds of efficiency and effectiveness gains that it is presumed to, or that would be necessary to pass even a minimal threshold for compromising civil liberty. In fact, there are good reasons to be concerned that racial profiling, if practiced as its defenders commend, has very modest effects on criminal captures and deterrence, and can even have ironic effects.

EFFECTIVENESS

Efficient use of law enforcement resources. Perhaps the most common and straightforward rationale offered to support racial profiling is that it is efficient. The logic goes that if one group (e.g., a racial group) is more prone to committing a particular kind of crime (e.g., drug possession for sale, terrorism), then targeting police resources at members of that group will (1) net more criminal captures and (2) deter crime among those most inclined to commit it. The argument appears sound. However, when considered carefully, there are serious problems with this logic.

The first problem is that in practice it is rarely known, even by law enforcement agencies, what actual criminal offending rates are within a group for the crimes of interest. Racial profiling is typically targeted at drug and weapons possession, and statistics on perpetrators are based on *known* perpetrators. These statistics are going to be skewed by any prior racial bias in policing. To the extent that police are disproportionally stopping and searching a given group, it is a mathematical reality that they will disproportionally arrest members of that group (as illustrated in the mathematical simulations described below; see Glaser, 2006). Surveys, in fact, indicate that Whites and Blacks in the United States report comparable rates of illicit drug use (U.S. Department of Health & Human Services, 2007), and that among youths rates are considerably lower for Blacks (Johnston, O'Malley, & Bachman, 2001). The implication of not actually knowing what the offending rates of different groups are is that when police profile, they are almost certain to rely on informal stereotypes of unknowable accuracy.

The stereotype problem. A stereotype is a belief about the traits that are disproportionately possessed by members of a group. Beliefs (stereotypes) that Blacks are more likely to be engaged in drug crime and Muslims are more likely to be terrorists drive drug interdiction and counterterrorism profiling. Most people have a sense that judgments of individuals based on stereotypes about their groups are inherently misguided, and are particularly intolerable when they engender discriminatory outcomes such as the undue deprivation of material resources, status, or liberty. Consequently, a recognition of the role of stereotyping is usually a sufficient rationale for rejecting racial profiling. Even those who do not object to stereotype-based law enforcement, however, should have concerns about effectiveness.

One could argue that law enforcement agents develop their own stereotypes regarding race and criminal offending, and that these stereotypes, being based on direct experience (e.g., investigating, searching, and arresting suspects) have a good chance of being reasonably accurate. This does not address the fairness problem, but it does allow for the possibility of effectiveness. There are a number of important reasons, however, why police stereotypes are unlikely to be particularly accurate or effectively applied to suspect identification.

Nearly a century of scientific study of stereotyping has provided the field of social psychology with a deep and broad understanding of the phenomenon. Fundamental discoveries include the fact that stereotypes serve as cognitive shortcuts ("mental heuristics") for making judgments in the absence of complete information (Fiske & Taylor, 1991), and that this can cause people to make dramatically different assessments of the identical behaviors of individuals (Darley & Gross, 1983; Sagar & Schofield, 1980). Research has shown that entirely spurious stereotypes can be formed via "illusory correlation," such as when rare events (like minority status and crime) co-occur (Hamilton & Gifford, 1976); and that stereotypes are resistant to change, even in the face of clearly contradictory evidence (Weber & Crocker, 1983). Stereotypes can, ironically, have even more pronounced biasing effects when one attempts to suppress them (MacRae, Bodenhausen, Milne, & Jetten, 1994). It has also been shown that stereotypes can be formed and perpetuated to serve the psychological function of rationalizing inequities between groups and that they are exacerbated by a phenomenon called "outgroup homogeneity," wherein people tend to overestimate the similarities within groups to which they do not belong (Park & Rothbart, 1982). The mere knowledge of a stereotype, even if it is consciously repudiated, is sufficient to cause stereotype-biased judgments (Devine, 1989). Most recently, scores of studies have shown that stereotypes can operate outside of conscious awareness or control, but nevertheless influence important, discriminatory behaviors (Jost et al., 2009). In other words, there is overwhelming evidence that stereotypes are distortions and, even if based on a "kernel of truth," present serious obstacles to accurate and fair appraisals of others.

As undesirable as stereotyping may be, the research shows that it is entirely normal to human cognition—most, if not all, people do it. Because law enforcement agents are normal humans with normal cognition, they too are vulnerable to the pitfalls of stereotyping, including the flawed judgments of individuals that result from it. Importantly, research conducted on police samples has directly demonstrated this; police possess race-crime stereotypes and these unduly influence their judgments and behaviors toward minorities (Correll et al., 2007; Eberhardt, Goff, Purdie, & Davies, 2004).

Even if stereotypes are directionally accurate (e.g., if Blacks have a higher rate of drug-related criminal offending, or Arabs have a higher rate of terrorism), employment of them in decisions to stop and search can reflect an error akin to the logical fallacy of "affirming the consequent." This error takes the form "if A, then B; B therefore A." In stereotype-based judgments, this translate into, "if criminal, then likely to be Black; Black therefore likely to be criminal." The error is not unlike the common "base-rate fallacy" (Kahneman & Tversky, 1973), where people fail to account for the general prevalence of something when trying to estimate its likelihood based on some indicator. For example, people who obtain a positive result on a test for a rare disease are likely to overestimate the probability that they have the disease, having failed to account for the low overall probability of the disease. If crime and terrorism are rare events (and they are, especially terrorism), even if race or ethnicity is correlated with them, it will have low diagnostic value at the individual level. This is borne out in the statistics on hit (arrest) rates for stop-and-frisk programs (Jones-Brown, Gill, & Trone, 2009; Office of the Attorney General of New York, 1999); these analyses tend to reveal low hit rates, typically around 10 percent, and paradoxical racial disproportions—stop/search rates are higher for minorities, but hit rates among those stopped are higher for Whites.

In short, there are many reasons to be skeptical about the accuracy of the stereotypes that cause racial profiling. Furthermore, even if one stipulates the possibility that officers will have a concrete basis for their stereotypes, one should be very skeptical about their accuracy and practicality when it comes to predicting criminality in individual suspects.

Diminishing returns and self-fulfilling prophecies. Even if respective offending rates of different racial groups were known, and assuming one group actually had a higher rate, the long-term effects of profiling are likely to exhibit diminishing returns that yield modest results in terms of criminal captures—and yet profiling would still create racial disproportions in excess of any real differences in offending. In a series of mathematical simulations (necessitated by the lack of information about actual offending or profiling rates), Glaser (2006) found that sustained profiling (i.e., stopping minorities at proportionally higher rates) yielded only modest gains in criminal captures, unless minority-offending rates were dramatically (and implausibly) higher than the rates of others. In scenarios where stop rates were disproportionate to offending (i.e., minorities were stopped at relative rates that were in excess of their relative offending rates), profiling was particularly ineffective and led to overall capture rates that were lower than those in the absence of profiling. Of particular note was the finding that racial profiling causes incarceration disparities that are in excess of any actual offending disparities. This is, of course, most evident and transparently unjust in scenarios where there are no offending disparities (i.e., minorities offend at the same rate as Whites), but it poses a fairness problem even when targeted groups have higher offending rates. Profiling itself causes or exacerbates racial disparities in criminal sanctions, and this is in addition to the problem of the higher proportions of innocent (non-offending) minorities' lives being disrupted by unwanted contact with police.

Deterrence? The deterrent effect of racial profiling is also dubious. The theory with regard to deterrence is that the increased attention to targeted groups should cause a decrease in offending among those groups, and that this deterrent effect would be especially consequential if those groups had relatively high offending rates. This thesis is consistent with deterrence theory, a key component of criminological canon (Blumstein, Cohen, & Nagin, 1978), which holds that expectations of increased costs of crime (due to increased penalties, increased probability of apprehension, or both) will lead even partially rational criminals to reduce offending, to the extent that they perceive changes in costs.

Racial profiling, however, presents a special case with regard to deterrence because there is no net increase in enforcement, but rather just a shifting of resources from some group or groups to others. As Glaser (2006) and Harcourt (2004) have noted, because profiling necessitates greater focus on one group, there is less focus on other groups. If deterrence works as it is theorized to, with criminals detecting changes in costs of offending, criminals (and marginal criminals) in nonprofiled groups should expect a lower cost, and therefore commit more crime. If the criminality rate in these groups is nontrivial, this could have an upward pressure on crime rates.

Glaser showed in his simulations that, with conservative assumptions about deterrence included in the model, the already modest benefits for criminal captures seen in most racial profiling scenarios are further reduced because the groups receiving the most attention (i.e., minorities) are committing less crime, while groups receiving the least attention (i.e., Whites) are committing more crime. Because nonprofiled groups tend to be larger, this could cause a net increase in crime.

Experimental evidence supports this pattern. Hackney and Glaser (2009) simulated racial profiling in a classroom testing paradigm wherein student cheating could be reliably detected. They found that when White students thought that Black students were being profiled for cheating by the administrator, they cheated *more* than when White students were ostensibly being profiled or in a no-profiling control condition. In contrast, Black students cheated at comparable (low) rates across all three experimental conditions (perhaps not inferring race-based profiling in the Whites-profiled condition because there is no preexisting schema for that). The net effect of profiling, therefore, was an increase in cheating, what Hackney and Glaser call "reverse deterrence." Racial profiling will not necessarily lead to a net increase in crime. If the targeted group is deterred and has an offending rate much higher than other groups, it could yield a net decrease. However, given that targeted groups tend to be numerical minorities, and the oft-targeted crimes (e.g., drug possession) do not appear to have dramatic offending rate differences between groups, there is the very real potential for ironic effects of racial profiling on crime rates and criminal captures. In the realm of counterterrorism, White separatist extremists in the United States, who have a long and deadly history of terrorism, could feel they can act with relative impunity if other ethnic groups are receiving the lion's share of law enforcement attention. The possibility of a more strategic form of reverse deterrence should also be considered, where terrorist groups deliberately exploit and circumvent profiles by recruiting outside of them.

In sum, racial profiling (1) is often targeted at groups that we are not at all confident actually have higher offending rates; (2) yields at best modest gains in criminal incapacitation, but only when targeted groups have higher offending rates; and (3) has the potential to, at best, have moderate aggregate deterrent effects, and at worst, increase crime through reverse-deterrence. Because of these factors, the assumed efficiency of racial profiling is highly questionable.

Crime reduction. The appropriate standard for assessing the effectiveness of any law enforcement strategy is whether or not it reduces crime and its consequences. In arenas where racial profiling might seem compelling—reducing drug trafficking or gun possession, terrorism, illegal immigration—the achievement of ostensible goals is difficult to assess due to the intractable problems with establishing reliable offending base rates, collecting comprehensive data, and conducting reliable analyses. Specifically, in order to determine the ability of racial profiling to capture offenders successfully, the underlying rate of offending by race and ethnicity would need to be known.

With that limitation in mind, it is useful to note that in many jurisdictions studied, targeted groups often yield less evidence of crime (e.g., contraband, weapons) when stopped and searched (see Harris, 2002, citing New Jersey State Police data on turnpike stops; and Center for Constitutional Rights, 2009), while other analyses find approximately equal hit rates (e.g., Harris, 2002, citing evidence from the Maryland State Police). For example, in Gross and Barnes's (2002) analysis of traffic stops in Maryland, the proportion of car searches that yielded drugs was 37.4 percent for White drivers, 30.6 percent for Black drivers, and 11.9 percent for Hispanics. The lower hit rates for Black and Hispanic drivers indicates that they required a lower threshold of suspiciousness to get stopped or searched, and that offending rates may not be any higher for the targeted groups.

Recent assessments of the "stop, question, and frisk" policies of the New York Police Department further indicate that racial profiling is an ineffective crime reduction strategy. After controlling for a variety of factors that are predictive of police activity (e.g., precinct and its racial composition), Fagan (2010) found that Black and Hispanic individuals were stopped at much higher rates, and that the overall hit rate is less than 6 percent (the rate of gun seizures was only 0.15 percent). An analysis of stops made from 2005 through 2008 found that 80 percent of all stops were of Black and Latino individuals, who, respectively, make up 25 percent and 28 percent of the city's population (Center for Constitutional Rights, 2009). Ten percent of stops during the same time period were of White individuals, who were 44 percent of the city's population. The clearest indication of the ineffectiveness of racial profiling is the report's finding that only 2.6 percent of the stops yielded contraband. Similarly, Jones-Brown, Gill, and Trone (2010) found that even though the number of pedestrian stops in New York City more than tripled between 2003 (<150,000) and 2009 (>500,000), the total number of illegal guns found through these searches remained fairly constant during the same time period. The number of stops of White individuals in 2003 was around 20,000 and grew to 50,000 in 2009. The number of stops of Black individuals went from approximately 80,000 in 2003 to nearly 350,000 in 2009. The additional searches in later years appear to have been highly arbitrary, yielding trivial gains in gun seizures over the results obtained from the earlier, smaller numbers of searches.

The U.S. Customs Service provides an apt example of the ineffectiveness of racial profiling that mirrors the findings from New York City. In 1998 the service made a series of reforms to reduce gender and racial bias in the selection of air travel passengers for personal searches. By 2000 the service had conducted 79.3 percent fewer searches, yet while the overall number of seizures of contraband was roughly the same as before, racial disparities in stops, searches, and seizures decreased.

The conclusion to be drawn from this type of evidence is that subjecting African American and Hispanic individuals to a lower threshold for suspicion and an increased likelihood of being stopped and searched by the police will certainly have a discriminatory impact on those minority groups but is unlikely to reduce crime.

Procedural justice. Another reason to doubt racial profiling's effectiveness is the likelihood that this practice is perceived by its targets as a gratuitous violation of procedural justice, thereby eroding the law-enforcement benefits of good police-community relations. Procedural justice concerns the fairness of how (i.e., the mechanisms or processes by which) an outcome is achieved, as opposed to the fairness of the outcome itself (Lind & Tyler, 1988). At its core, racial profiling involves singling out a person for a nonlegal reason (race is not legally relevant). Importantly, the effects of violating procedural justice extend beyond the original target. While the target may experience the violation as a personal affront (Skitka, 2002), friends and family of the target may experience "empathic anger," which occurs when someone one cares about is harmed (as opposed to the anger caused by being harmed personally) (Batson et al., 2007).

Moreover, a negative emotional response to racial profiling can even occur when an observer does not personally know the target. Just seeing someone being harmed can generate intense anger and a sense of injustice (Hafer, 2000). It follows that the repercussions of racial profiling can be understood as radiating out from the target, affecting not just targets of racial profiling but also those who know them or even just know of them. Psychologists Tom Tyler and Yuen Huo discuss such problems in their book, *Trust in the Law* (2002). They find that "people generalize from their personal experiences to their broader views about the law, legal authorities, others in their community, and society" (p. 206) and that breaches of procedural justice negatively influence what people think of the police and their general respect for the law. To wit, public opinion data reveals that 61 percent of White individuals consider the "honesty and ethical standards" of police to be either "very high" or "high," while only 37 percent of Black individuals hold this view (Gallup Organization, 2010). The upshot is that when communities (e.g., racial or ethnic minority groups) do not trust police, they are less inclined to cooperate with law enforcement activities. This is particularly troublesome in the context of police reliance on assistance from community members during crime investigations.

Indeed, a survey conducted by the Consortium for Police Leadership in Equity (CPLE) found that among White and Latino residents (citizens, as well as documented and undocumented aliens), one in three would not report certain serious crimes if police officers had the authority to check citizenship status (Burbank, 2010). This should be a cause for serious concern among lawmakers considering the laws, like those in Arizona and Alabama, that require police departments to enforce immigration law and promote the use of ethnicity in identifying illegal immigrants.

Because it entails an unfair mechanism—using an individual's race or ethnicity as the basis for heightened scrutiny—racial profiling is procedurally unjust. By violating procedural justice, racial profiling is likely to erode trust in the police and results in decreased cooperation with law enforcement officers. In this way, the effectiveness of racial profiling as a crime reduction strategy is further diminished.

CONCLUSION

In using race, ethnicity, or national origin as a basis of criminal suspicion, law enforcement officials engage in a practice that is especially pernicious because it engenders a false sense of effectiveness in the face of substantial harms that may not be readily evident. The goal of policing is to promote public safety. Insofar as it inflicts harm on particular segments of the population, racial profiling contravenes this goal. The objective here has been to explain the harms to both justice and effectiveness. Specifically, we contend that racial profiling not only violates the U.S. Constitution, but it violates core American principles of liberty and nondiscrimination. By subjecting members of historically disadvantaged groups to increased scrutiny, profiling contributes to the striking overrepresentation of African Americans and Hispanics in the criminal justice system. Moreover, proof of the effectiveness of racial profiling is lacking, especially considering the indications that it may increase crime through reverse deterrence and stifle cooperation with law enforcement as a result of procedural injustice. Taken altogether, the evidence presented here indicates that racial profiling falls far short of any reasonable threshold for trumping liberty in the name of public safety.

Indeed, racial profiling is so objectionable that it is insufficient merely to state that it should not be supported. Rather, affirmative policies to ban its practice, monitor its occurrence, and enforce prohibitions against it are warranted. This is imperative because racial profiling likely occurs, in large part, informally, spontaneously, and in many instances unintentionally. Thus, the mere absence of a formal pro-profiling policy or even the existence of an unenforced prohibition are likely to be insufficient for preventing it.

REFERENCES AND FURTHER READING

Ayres, I. (2002). Outcome tests of racial disparities in police practices. *Justice Research and Policy, 4,* 131–142.

Banks, R. R. (2004, January). *The story of* Brown v. City of Oneonta: *The uncertain meaning of racially discriminatory policing under the equal protection clause* (Stanford Law School Research Paper No. 81). Stanford, CA: Stanford Law School.

Batson, C. D., Kennedy, C. L., Nord, L.-A., Stocks, E. L., Fleming, D. A., Marzette, C. M., Lishner, D. A., Hayes, R. E., Kolchinsky, L. M., & Zerger, T. (2007). Anger at unfairness: Is it moral outrage? *European Journal of Social Psychology, 37,* 1272–1285.

Bertrand, M., & Mullainathan, S. (2003). *Are Emily and Greg more employable than Lakisha and Jamal? A field experiment on labor market discrimination.* MIT Department of Economics Working Paper No. 03-22.

Blumstein, A., Cohen, J., & Nagin, D. (Eds.). (1978). *Deterrence and incapacitation: Estimating the effects of criminal sanctions on crime rates, report of the panel of deterrence and incapacitation.* Washington, DC: National Academy of Sciences.

Bonczar, T. P. (2003, August). *Prevalence of imprisonment in the U.S. population, 1974–2001* (Bureau of Justice Statistics Special Report). Retrieved from http://bjs.ojp.usdoj.gov/content/pub/pdf/piusp01.pdf

Burbank, C. (2010, June 17). Testimony of Mr. Christopher Burbank, Chief of Police, Salt Lake City Police Department, to the Subcommittee on the Constitution, Civil Rights and Civil Liberties; Hearing on Racial Profiling and the Use of Suspect Classifications in Law Enforcement Policy. Retrieved from http://www.gpo.gov/fdsys/pkg/CHRG-111hhrg56956/html/CHRG-111hhrg56956.htm

Center for Constitutional Rights. (2009). *Racial disparity in NYPD stops-and-frisks: The Center for Constitutional Rights Preliminary Report on UF-250 data obtained for 2005 through June 2008.* Retrieved from http://www.ccrjustice.org/files/Report_CCR_NYPD_Stop_and_Frisk_1.pdf

Clark, R. (1970). *Crime in America: Observations on its nature, causes, prevention, and control.* New York, NY: Simon & Schuster.

Clayton, S., & Opotow, S. (2003). Justice and identity: Changing perspectives on what is fair. *Personality and Social Psychology Review, 7,* 298–231.

Correll, J., Park, B., Judd, C., Wittenbrink, B., Sadler, M. S., & Keesee, T. (2007). Across the thin blue line: Police officers and racial bias in the decision to shoot. *Journal of Personality and Social Psychology, 92,* 1006–1023.

Council of Economic Advisors. (1999). *Changing America: Indicators of social and economic well-being by race and Hispanic origin.* Retrieved from http://w3.access.gpo.gov/eop/ca/index.html

Darley, J. M., & Gross, P. H. (1983). A hypothesis-confirming bias in labeling effects. *Journal of Personality and Social Psychology, 44,* 20–33.

Devine, P. G. (1989). Stereotypes and prejudice: Their automatic and controlled components. *Journal of Personality and Social Psychology, 56,* 5–18.

Eberhardt, J. L., Goff, P. A., Purdie, V. J., & Davies, P. G. (2004). Seeing black: Race, crime, and visual processing. *Journal of Personality and Social Psychology, 87,* 876–893.

Fagan, J. (2010). *Floyd, et al. v. City of New York, et al.,* Report to the U.S. District Court, Southern District of New York. Retrieved from http://ccrjustice.org/files/Expert_Report_JeffreyFagan.pdf

Finzen, M. E. (2005, Summer). Systems of oppression: The collateral consequences of incarceration and their effects on black communities. *Georgetown Journal on Poverty Law & Policy, 12*(2), 299–324.

Fiske, S. T., & Taylor, S. E. (1991). *Social cognition* (2nd ed.). New York, NY: McGraw-Hill.

Franklin, B., & Franklin, W. T. (1818). *Memoirs of the life and writings of Benjamin Franklin.* London, UK: H. Colburn.

Gallup Organization, Inc. (2010, November 19–21). Respondents' ratings of the honesty and ethical standards of police. In *Sourcebook of criminal justice statistics table online.* Retrieved from http://www.albany.edu/sourcebook/pdf/t2212010.pdf

Geller, A., Garfinkel, I., & Western, B. (2006). *The effects of incarceration on employment and wages: An analysis of the Fragile Families Survey* (Working Paper 2006-01-FF). Princeton, NJ: Center for Research on Child Wellbeing. Retrieved from http://www.safer foundation.org/files/documents/Princeton-Effect%20of%20Incarceration%20on%20Employment%20and%20Wages.pdf

Gelman A., Fagan, J., & Kiss, A. (2007, September 1). An analysis of the New York City Police Department's "stop-and-frisk" policy in the context of claims of racial bias. *Journal of the American Statistical Association, 102*(479), 813–823.

Glaser, J. (2006). The efficacy and effect of racial profiling: A mathematical simulation approach. *Journal of Policy Analysis and Management, 25,* 395–416.

Gross, S. R., & Barnes, K. Y. (2002, December). Road work: Racial profiling and drug interdiction on the highway. *Michigan Law Review, 101*(3), 651–754. Retrieved from http://papers.ssrn.com/sol3/papers.cfm?abstract_id=331260

Gross, S. R., & Livingston, D. (2002). Racial profiling under attack. *Columbia Law Review, 102*(5), 1413–1438.

Hackney, A., & Glaser, J. (2009). *Reverse deterrence in racial profiling: Increased transgressions by the non-profiled group* (Working Paper No. GSPP09-003). Berkeley, CA: Goldman School of Public Policy.

Hafer, C. L. (2000). Do innocent victims threaten the belief in a just world? Evidence from a modified Stroop task. *Journal of Personality and Social Psychology, 79,* 165–173.

Hamilton, D. L., & Gifford, R. K. (1976). Illusory correlation in interpersonal perception: A cognitive basis of stereotypic judgments. *Journal of Experimental Social Psychology, 12,* 392–407.

Harcourt, B. E. (2004). Rethinking racial profiling: A critique of the economics, civil liberties, and constitutional literature, and of criminal profiling more generally. *University of Chicago Law Review, 71.* Retrieved from http://papers.ssrn.com/sol3/papers.cfm?abstract_id=471901

Harris, D. (2002). *Profiles in injustice: Why racial profiling cannot work.* New York, NY: The New Press.

Harris, D. (2003). Racial profiling redux. *St. Louis University Public Law Review, 22,* 73.

Hirabayashi v. United States, 320 U.S. 81, 100 (1943).

Johnson, R. C., & Raphael, S. (2006, June). *The effects of male incarceration dynamics on AIDS infection rates among African American women and men* (Working Paper 22). Ann Arbor, MI: National Poverty Center, University of Michigan. Retrieved from http://www.npc.umich.edu/publications/working_papers/?publication_id=84&

Johnston, D. (1995). Effects of parental incarceration. In K. Gabel & D. Johnston (Eds.), *Children of incarcerated parents* (pp. 59–88). New York, NY: Lexington Books.

Johnston, L. D., O'Malley, P. M., & Bachman, J. G. (2001). *Demographic subgroup trends for various licit and illicit drugs, 1975–2000* (Monitoring the Future Occasional Paper 53). Bethesda, MD: National Institute on Drug Abuse. Retrieved from http://monitor ingthefuture.org/pubs/occpapers/occ53.pdf

Jones-Brown, D., Gill, J., & Trone, J (2010, March). *Stop, question & frisk policing practices in New York City: A primer.* Retrieved from Center on Race, Crime and Justice website: http://www.jjay.cuny.edu/web_images/PRIMER_electronic_version.pdf

Jost, J. T., Rudman, L., Blair, I. V., Carney, D. R., Dasgupta, N., Glaser, J., & Hardin, C. (2009). The existence of implicit bias is beyond reasonable doubt: A refutation of ideological and methodological objections and executive summary of ten studies that no manager should ignore. *Research in Organizational Behavior, 29,* 39–69.

Kahneman, D., & Tversky, A. (1973). On the psychology of prediction. *Psychological Review, 80,* 237–251.

Kennedy, R. (1999, September 13). Suspect policy. *The New Republic,* pp. 30–35. Retrieved from http://www.tnr.com/article/suspect-policy

Knowles, J, Persico, N., & Todd, P. (2001). Racial bias in motor vehicle searches: Theory and evidence. *Journal of Political Economy, 109,* 203–229.

Lind, E. A., & Tyler, T. R. (1988). *The social psychology of procedural justice.* New York, NY: Plenum.

Lyle, P. A. (2001). Racial profiling and the Fourth Amendment: Applying the minority victim perspective to ensure equal protection under the law. *Boston College Third World Journal, 21*(2). Retrieved from http://lawdigitalcommons.bc.edu/twlj/vol21/iss2/2 or http://www.bc.edu/bc_org/avp/law/lwsch/journals/bctwj/21_2/02_TXT.htm

Macrae, C. N., Bodenhausen, G. V., Milne, A. B., & Jetten, J. (1994). Out of mind but back in sight: Stereotypes on the rebound. *Journal of Personality and Social Psychology, 67,* 808–817.

Massoglia, M. (2008, March). Incarceration as exposure: The prison, infectious disease, and other stress-related illnesses. *Journal of Health and Social Behavior, 49*(1), 56–71.

Newport, F. (1999). *Racial profiling is seen as widespread, particularly among young black men.* Retrieved from Gallup website: http://www.gallup.com/poll/3421/racial-profiling-seen-widespread-particularly-among-young-black-men.aspx

Office of the Attorney General of the State of New York. (1999). *The New York City Police Department's "stop & frisk" practices: A report to the people of the State of New York from the Office of the Attorney General.* Retrieved from http://www.nysl.nysed.gov/scandoclinks/ocm43937374.htm

Pager, D. (2003). The mark of a criminal record. *American Journal of Sociology, 108*(5), 937–975.

Park, B., & Rothbart, M. (1982). Perception of out-group homogeneity and levels of social categorization: Memory for the subordinate attributes of in-group and out-group members. *Journal of Personality and Social Psychology, 42,* 1051–1068.

Persico, N. (2002). Racial profiling, fairness, and effectiveness of policing. *The American Economic Review, 92*(5), 1472–1497.

Petit, B., & Western, B. (2004, April). Mass imprisonment and the life course: Race and class inequality in U.S. incarceration. *American Sociological Review, 69,* 151–169.

Quinnipiac University. (2006, August). *Voters back profiling in security checks, wiretaps* [News Release]. Retrieved from http://www.quinnipiac.edu/x1295.xml?ReleaseID=952

Sabol, W. J., & West, H. C. (2011, December 15). *Prisoners in 2009 (Revised)* (Prisoners Series, NCJ 231675). Washington, DC: U.S. Department of Justice, Bureau of Justice Statistics. Retrieved from http://bjs.ojp.usdoj.gov/index.cfm?ty=pbdetail&iid=2232 (See p. 30, Appendix Table 16c; p. 32, Appendix Table 17c.)

Sagar, H. A., & Schofield, J. W. (1980). Racial and behavioral cues in black and white children's perceptions of ambiguously aggressive acts. *Journal of Personality and Social Psychology, 39,* 590–598.

Sanga, S. (2009). Reconsidering racial bias in motor vehicle searches: Theory and evidence. *Journal of Political Economy, 117,* 1155–1159.

The Sentencing Project. (2011). *Felony disenfranchisement laws in the United States.* Retrieved from http://www.sentencingproject.org/detail/publication.cfm?publication_id=15

Silke, A. (2001). Chasing ghosts: Offender profiling and terrorism. In D. P. Farrington, C. R. Hollin, & M. McMurran (Eds.), *Sex and violence: The psychology of crime and risk assessment* (pp. 242–258). London, UK: Routledge.

Silke, A. (2011). The psychology of counter-terrorism: Critical issues and challenges. In A. Silke (Ed.), *The psychology of counter-terrorism* (pp. 1–18). London, UK: Routledge.

Skitka, L. J. (2002). Do the means always justify the ends, or do the ends sometimes justify the means? A value protection model of justice reasoning. *Personality and Social Psychology Bulletin, 28*(5), 588–597.

Tyler, T., & Huo, Y. J. (2002). *Trust in the law: Encouraging public cooperation with the police and courts.* New York: Russell Sage Foundation.

Tyler, T., & Lind, E. A. (1990). Intrinsic vs. community-based justice models: When does group membership matter? *Journal of Social Issues, 46*(1), 83–94.

Uggen, C., & Manza, J. (2002, December). Democratic contraction? Political consequences of felon disenfranchisement in the United States. *American Sociological Review, 67*(6), 777–803.

U.S. Census Bureau. (2010). *State and county QuickFacts.* Retrieved from http://quickfacts.census.gov/qfd/index.html

U.S. Customs Service. (2000, October 19). *Customs releases end-of-year personal search statistics: New data suggest internal reforms are beginning to work* [Press release]. Retrieved from http://www.cbp.gov/hot-new/pressrel/2000/1019-02.htm

U.S. Department of Health and Human Services. (2007). *Results from the 2007 National Survey on Drug Use and Health: National findings.* Retrieved from http://www.oas.samhsa.gov/nsduh/2k7nsduh/2k7Results.pdf

U.S. Department of Labor, Bureau of Labor Statistics. (2009). Labor force characteristics by race and ethnicity, 2008: Table 10. Unemployment rates by sex, race, and Hispanic or Latino ethnicity, 1972–2008 annual averages. Retrieved from http://www.bls.gov/cps/race_ethnicity_2008_10.htm

Wakefield, S., & Wildeman, C. (2011). Mass imprisonment and racial disparities in childhood behavioral problems. *Criminology & Public Policy, 10,* 791–792.

Weaver, V., & Lerman, A. (2010, November). Political consequences of the carceral state. *American Political Science Review, 104*(4), 817–833. Retrieved from http://www.princeton.edu/~alerman/LermanPolCons

Weber, R., & Crocker, J. (1983). Cognitive processes in the revision of stereotypic beliefs. *Journal of Personality and Social Psychology, 45,* 961–977.

Winerman, L. (2004). Criminal profiling: The reality behind the myth. *Monitor on Psychology, 35,* 66.

Withrow, B. L. (2006). *Racial profiling: From rhetoric to reason.* Upper Saddle River, NJ: Pearson/Prentice Hall.

Karin D. Martin and Jack Glaser

State and Local Law Enforcement

POINT: State and local law enforcement is critical to identifying and deporting illegal immigrants because federal law enforcement resources are too limited to work effectively in all communities throughout the country with illegal immigrant populations.

Jessica Saunders and Nelson Lim, RAND Corporation
Carl Matthies, Vera Institute of Justice

COUNTERPOINT: Local police involvement in immigration enforcement generates fear and undermines community-policing efforts in immigrant communities. The courts have repeatedly upheld the principle that enforcement of immigration laws is a federal responsibility, and that state-level immigration laws violate this principle.

Jessica Saunders and Nelson Lim, RAND Corporation
Carl Matthies, Vera Institute of Justice

Introduction

With a population of "illegal" (also described as "out of status") immigrants surpassing 10 million individuals, the federal Immigration and Customs Enforcement (ICE) agency finds itself significantly overwhelmed. As a result, since 2002, a trend has emerged to involve state and local law enforcement in the investigation and detention of illegal immigrants. In this chapter, RAND scholars Jessica Saunders, Carl Matthies (now with the Vera Institute of Justice), and Nelson Lim present two sides of the debate over whether or not state and local enforcement of federal immigration laws is effective and appropriate. This debate about local responsibility in such immigration matters occurs on two levels: one has to do with immigration enforcement, and the other with what constitutes "community" within state and local areas.

In one sense, it is easy to see why state and local officials would feel that immigration issues are well within their jurisdiction: after all, local communities, not the federal entities, are most directly affected by who lives in them. While ICE has just 20,000 employees, only half of whom are directly involved in detaining and removing illegal immigrants, local police forces are over three-quarters of a million in number.

Proponents of local enforcement want to leverage federal immigration resources for controlling illegal immigration with state and local law enforcement resources. For example, according to the ICE website, "The 287(g) program, one of ICE's top partnership initiatives, allows a state and local law enforcement entity to enter into a partnership with ICE, under a joint Memorandum of Agreement (MOA). The state or local entity receives delegated authority for immigration enforcement within their jurisdictions."

Authors' note: The RAND Corporation is a nonprofit institution that helps improve policy and decision making through objective research and analysis. While the authors are presenting the point and counterpoint arguments on involving state and local law enforcement in enforcing immigration laws in these two essays, RAND and the authors take no position on this topic due to the lack of research conducted to support either side. At this time, the arguments on both the point and counterpoint sides are based primarily on anecdotal evidence, audit data, speculation, and political rhetoric. The authors have highlighted where more research is necessary before the real impact of these laws and policies can be evaluated on their objective and empirical merits.

Attempts at bringing immigration enforcement down to the local level have been bolstered by a wide variety of ordinances passed by state legislatures, city councils, and other nonfederal jurisdictions, creating new immigration-related crimes and penalties and clearing the way for an increased involvement by local law enforcement. Arizona's controversial immigration law, S.B. 1070, debated in another chapter in this volume, is just one of many such laws that pulls local law enforcement into the immigration issue. And, indeed, the out-of-status population has begun to drop since its high in 2007. While a variety of factors caused this drop, proponents of local enforcement argue that this improved, up-close monitoring is at least partly responsible.

However, as Saunders, Matthies, and Lim highlight in their Counterpoint essay, there are a number of problems with the local approach. Most obviously, the U.S. Constitution reserves immigration enforcement for the federal government, and the constitutionality of many of these new laws remains an open question.

More pressing, perhaps, is the question of whether or not local law enforcement can effectively pursue all of their other responsibilities while simultaneously chasing illegal immigrants. Although it is true that there are many more law enforcement officials than federal immigration officers, in reality many local precincts are already understaffed and overburdened with other kinds of cases.

Further, pursuing immigration-related cases, especially in the context of a partnership between local police and ICE, may make it much more challenging for local police officers to investigate their non-immigration cases. Criminal investigations, after all, require witnesses and testimony. They require, in other words, the cooperation of the broader community. If an officer needs to interview someone for a robbery investigation, for example, but that individual is out of status, he or she is all the less likely to cooperate, even if the robbery being investigated is unrelated to immigration status. Police officers are charged with protecting the safety of all the residents of a community—can they do this if they are simultaneously charged with rooting out illegal immigrants?

This brings us to another issue at stake in this debate: what constitutes a community? This is a subtler point, and it relates to the extent to which these immigration enforcement programs isolate immigrant neighborhoods within their larger communities, intensifying social divisions in the process. These social divisions largely occur along racial and ethnic lines and create a beleaguered, discriminated-against feeling within immigrant communities, which in turn works against immigrant integration into the larger society. It is also important to remember that many illegal immigrants live in mixed-status families—for example, out-of-status immigrants may have U.S. citizen children, may live with legally-present immigrants, may be married to U.S. citizens, or may have close friends or family who are U.S. citizens.

In reading this chapter, consider what kinds of signals local immigration enforcement might send. Does it, on the one hand, indicate a seriousness toward enforcing the law that is much needed, given the seemingly out-of-control nature of illegal immigration? Or, on the other hand, does it merely send out-of-status immigrants even further into the shadows? Does concern for the immigration status of community members dovetail with the overall focus of local law enforcement, or does it work against it? Does it make local communities more or less safe? And if local law enforcement should not take up this charge, who else can or should?

POINT

Enforcing immigration laws in a country as large and prosperous as the United States is a monumental undertaking, and few would argue that the federal government has been equal to the task over the last half-century. According to the U.S. Department of Homeland Security (DHS), the unauthorized immigrant population in the country was nearly 11 million in 2010, a 27 percent increase over the previous decade. It is unrealistic to expect that this problem can be solved by federal law enforcement alone. U.S. Immigration and Customs Enforcement (ICE) employs only 20,000 people and is vastly underequipped to locate, investigate, and properly process all of these individuals.

Having state and local law enforcement shoulder some of the responsibility for enforcing immigration law is the obvious solution for getting illegal immigration under control, and indeed, there are several immigration enforcement initiatives now in place that do just that. Involving state and local law enforcement in immigration enforcement is a relatively new trend, and rigorous research to evaluate its impact on immigration and crime patterns is still lacking, but anecdotal evidence suggests that these approaches of partnership and shared responsibility may actually work. With assistance from local law enforcement officials, illegal immigrants can be identified effectively through the criminal justice system and then processed by the immigration system.

The size of the illegal immigrant population, or, more technically, the "out-of-status" immigrant population, increased steadily at the beginning of the twenty-first century and peaked in 2007 at an estimated 12 million people. The out-of-status immigrant population consists of a heterogeneous mix of people, not all of who have committed either a civil or a criminal offense. Some are waiting to learn the results of immigration applications and, because the federal immigration system and specialized courts are overburdened, there is often a long delay in rendering decisions about appeals. More often, however, they have violated federal immigration law. These violations fall broadly into two categories: (1) civil offenses, such as living in the country illegally or overstaying a visa, and (2) criminal offenses, such as illegal entry into the country, human smuggling, or ignoring a deportation order. Historically, local law enforcement officers only had the authority to enforce federal criminal offenses, but a memo from the Justice Department in 2002 gave them the authority to enforce both criminal and civil federal immigration law.

As shown in Figure 32.1, the out-of-status immigrant population has begun to decrease, perhaps due to improved border security, amplified interior enforcement, and an economic downturn that has reduced the economic incentive to come to the United States illegally. Since all of these changes occurred more or less contemporaneously, it is difficult to

Figure 32.1 Estimates of out-of-status immigrants residing in the United States

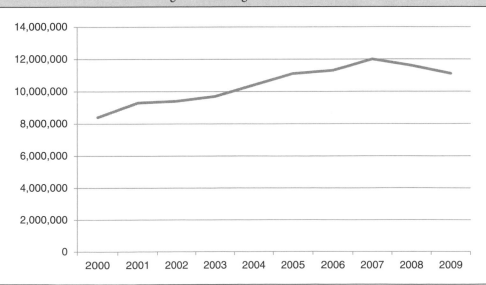

Source: Created by authors from Pew Hispanic Center data.

disentangle the impact each has had individually on the size of the illegal immigrant population. However, some have credited at least part of the decrease to interior immigration law enforcement efforts, which are being augmented by state and local law enforcement officers.

Figure 32.2 illustrates the average cost to deport each illegal immigrant, and it shows that apprehension costs dwarfed all other expenditures by a factor of more than five. At the present rate and budget levels, it would take 15 years and more than $5 billion just to clear the absconder backlog, without addressing new overstays, illegal entries and reentries, and absconders.

The cost of rounding up these 11 million out-of-status immigrants, in a hypothetical 5-year mass deportation scheme, has been estimated at $200 billion: $158 billion for apprehension, $29 billion for detention, $7 billion for legal costs, and $6 billion for transportation.

In recent years the American public has grown increasingly frustrated with the federal government's handling of illegal immigration. Leadership in the Department of Homeland Security have also candidly admitted that it is unrealistic to expect that the immigration problem can be solved by federal law enforcement alone, and that it will require using other resources as well. For example, ICE does not have enough space to house immigration offenders in its own facilities and has outsourced some of this responsibility to the states. In fiscal year (FY) 2010, the State Criminal Alien Assistance Program (SCAAP) provided a total of $324 million to 922 state, county, and local jurisdictions as partial federal reimbursement for incarcerating criminal aliens. This reimbursement program, which requires local collaboration with ICE, has even been implemented in so-called sanctuary cities, which have official policies of noncooperation with federal immigration law. SCAAP's record of partial cost reimbursements suggests that sanctuary policies may have more to do with avoiding unfunded federal mandates than altruistic motives.

There are two ways in which states and localities can assume a greater role in immigration enforcement. One strategy is for states and localities to create and enforce their own immigration laws and statutes. A second option is to form partnerships between federal immigration agencies and local law enforcement agencies so that their combined expertise, manpower, and other resources can be directed to identifying, apprehending, and deporting fugitive aliens. The federal government has favored the latter approach. The Department of Homeland Security has promoted enforcement

Figure 32.2   Average cost per each illegal immigrant deported

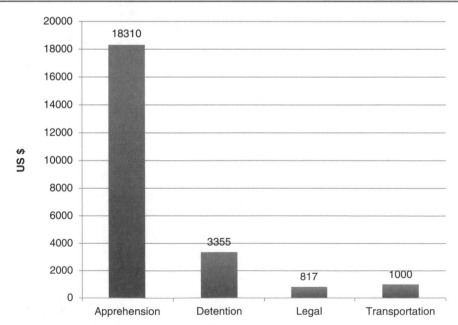

Source: Created by authors using data from U.S. Immigration and Customs Enforcement.

partnerships, while the Department of Justice has filed suits to block many of the recent state immigration laws as preempting federal jurisdiction.

The involvement of local law enforcement officials has the potential to significantly enhance enforcement capabilities, since the nation's local public safety workforce vastly outnumbers federal immigration enforcement officials. ICE currently has approximately 20,000 employees throughout the United States, roughly half of whom are involved in identification, detention, and removal operations. By comparison, the number of sworn, full-time state and local peace officers throughout the country is approximately 800,000. Mobilizing these local law enforcement officers would dramatically increase the manpower available for reducing the backlog of fugitive aliens.

The major concern with involving local law enforcement officers is that gains in immigration enforcement would be offset by a corresponding reduction in the ability to fulfill their core mission to protect and serve all members of the public, whether or not they are citizens. This concern is valid insofar as local law enforcement cannot incorporate immigration enforcement into the course of their normal duties. Currently, there is only one comprehensive research study that directly examines this issue. This study found that the initiative did temporarily damage police-community relationships in the Hispanic community. The study also found that adding immigration enforcement to a local police officer's responsibilities did not impact crime rates—suggesting that their job performance was not negatively affected by the additional duties.

HISTORY OF IMMIGRATION POLICY RELATED TO STATE AND LOCAL LAW ENFORCEMENT: APPROACHES THAT FAVOR STATE AND LOCAL IMMIGRATION ENFORCEMENT

Many state and local governments have opted to assume responsibility for immigration enforcement through enactment of laws and ordinances, and through official arrangements with the federal government called ICE Agreements of Cooperation in Communities to Enhance Safety and Security (ICE ACCESS). The ICE ACCESS initiative was developed to make the various programs or tools that ICE offers available to state, local, and tribal law enforcement agencies. These programs put local law enforcement agencies in contact with ICE to collaborate on projects tailored to meet the needs of the specific communities. There are dozens of such programs, ranging in scope from short term focused enforcement activities to long-term partnerships that become a part of the local policing organizational mission.

The Department of Justice's Bureau of Justice Assistance doles out grants to reimburse partner agencies for costs associated with participating in these programs. A few of these will be highlighted here.

The Law Enforcement Support Center (LESC), operated by U.S. Immigration and Customs Enforcement, provides access to federal, state, and local criminal justice enforcement and corrections agencies (ICE, 2008). It gives law enforcement officers immediate access to 277,000 of the 100 million immigration records that ICE maintains through use of the Immigration Alien Query option within the National Crime Information Center (NCIC). The LESC operates a communications center that can confirm for law enforcement officials whether someone has been charged with a federal immigration offense and verify the individual's current immigration status. If a charge is verified, the LESC can then issue a "detainer notice" so that the police department may hold the individual based on the administrative warrant in the NCIC. The police may run this check on individuals who have been stopped for something as minor as a traffic violation.

According to ICE, the LESC received 728,243 requests for information on the immigration status of suspects from the NCIC database in 2007. Of 676,502 requests from local enforcement agents, 65,000 were confirmed as immigration offenders.

Initially, the LESC was highly prone to error because it contained incomplete or inaccurate records and relied on highly fallible name-based identification. These flaws have largely been addressed, and use of the LESC has grown substantially. Between 2003 and 2010, the LESC responded to over 5,737,800 electronic queries, received almost 950,000 phone queries, and placed 121,734 immigration detainers. Immigration detainers are orders to hold an immigration offender while they are processed through the federal immigration system. In FY 2008, LESC was responsible for placing 16,436 detainers for criminal and immigration violations, and 20,446 such detainers were placed in FY 2010. Agencies from all 50 states and the District of Columbia have used this service to identify and remove immigrants with outstanding federal warrants from their communities.

The Criminal Alien Program (CAP) is another mechanism through which state and local criminal justice agents have participated in immigration enforcement. The primary goal of CAP is to identify incarcerated immigrants within federal, state, and local facilities and secure final orders of removal prior to the termination of their sentences so that they are not inadvertently released back into the community. The program prioritizes those deportable immigrants perceived to pose the largest risk to the community. The program also provides partial federal reimbursement for the cost of incarcerating criminal aliens. An Office of the Inspector General (OIG) audit conducted in 2007 published data on the effectiveness of the CAP program. This audit found that CAP allowed ICE to remove 164,296 criminal aliens from state and local detention and 11,292 from federal detention in FY 2007. These individuals were referred for immigration proceedings and constituted approximately 60 percent of all immigration removals. CAP resulted in the filing of 221,085 charging documents to remove criminal aliens in FY 2008.

Section 287(g) partnerships are perhaps the most controversial of ICE's efforts to secure cooperation from local law enforcement, because they allow ICE to cross-deputize local peace officers to enforce federal immigration law. Section 287(g) was incorporated into the Immigration and Nationality Act as part of the Illegal Immigration Reform and Immigrant Responsibility Act (IIRIRA). This provision authorized the federal government to enter into voluntary Memoranda of Agreement (MOAs) with state, county, and local law enforcement agencies to train their officers to help identify individuals who are in the country illegally.

Although the option to form Section 287(g) partnerships has been available since 1996, it wasn't until 2002 that the state of Florida signed the first agreement, motivated by a post-9/11 national security imperative (some of the hijackers had lived and received flight-training in Florida as out-of-status immigrants). These agreements were slow to take off, with only eight being signed before 2007, but that year another 24 agencies signed up, and currently there are 69 active agreements across 24 states.

These partnerships take three forms: (1) the task force model, in which police officers enforce federal immigration law while going about their regular law enforcement duties; (2) the jail model, in which corrections officers in the jails have the power to enforce federal immigration law; and (3) the joint model, in which both types of immigration enforcement are practiced.

Of the 69 different 287(g) MOAs across 24 states, 40 percent are task force model partnerships, 39 percent are jail model partnerships, and the remaining 21 percent are joint model partnerships. The MOAs mandate a four-week ICE training program, and as of October 2010, more than 1,240 officers had completed this training, effectively increasing ICE's workforce by 6 percent. These partnerships are credited with identifying 200,300 deportable aliens from 2006 to 2010.

STATE AND LOCAL LAWS AND ORDINANCES THAT CRIMINALIZE IMMIGRATION STATUS

Dissatisfaction with the level of federal immigration regulation and enforcement has led state legislatures, county boards of supervisors, and city councils to write laws that greatly expand the role of state and local law enforcement in regulating immigration. These laws define new immigration-related requirements, crimes, and penalties. While these state and local immigration laws permeate every area of public policy, from health care to education, law enforcement and employment are their most common targets, and the clear objective of most of them is to make illegal immigrants *personae non gratae*.

According to the National Conference on State Legislatures, a total of 1,538 such laws were introduced in the first quarter of 2011, representing a 30 percent increase over the first quarter of 2010. The number of law enforcement bills nearly doubled, to 267. Increasingly, states are drafting omnibus bills aimed at simultaneously addressing a wide range of immigration issues, such as law enforcement, employment verification, and access to public services. Over 50 immigration-related omnibus bills were introduced in 30 states in the first quarter of 2011. Predictably, many of these laws have met with legal challenges that have limited or delayed their implementation; however, they continue to be introduced and hotly debated.

Probably the most notorious of these bills is Arizona's controversial S.B. 1070, the Support Our Law Enforcement and Safe Neighborhoods Act, which was enacted in April 2010. S.B. 1070 contains a set of provisions that intensify local law enforcement pressure on undocumented immigrants. It requires state and local law enforcement to make a reasonable attempt to ascertain the immigration status of persons involved in a lawful stop when officers have a reasonable suspicion that an individual is in the country unlawfully, unless doing so hinders another investigation. Under S.B. 1070, harboring, transporting, concealing, or encouraging an alien to come to Arizona are Class 1 misdemeanors subject to fines of at least $1,000 and possible vehicle impounding. Unauthorized aliens who knowingly apply for or solicit work as an employee or independent contractor are similarly guilty of a Class 1 misdemeanor, while failure to have a certificate of alien registration or alien registration receipt in their possession is tantamount to trespassing, which is a Class 1 misdemeanor in most cases but can be a felony for alien absconders. Finally, the Support Our Law Enforcement and Safe Neighborhoods Act prohibits state and local law enforcement from restricting enforcement of federal immigration laws and allows state residents to sue localities that restrict enforcement.

The day before S.B. 1070 was to take effect, a federal judge granted an injunction blocking several key provisions after petitioners, including the Department of Justice, sought to prevent its implementation. The injunction blocked the legal requirement for aliens to apply for and carry registration papers, the prohibition against gainful employment, and the provision allowing police to inquire about a person's immigration status or conduct warrantless arrests of persons suspected of being in the country illegally. Other sections of the legislation, such as employer sanctions and the prohibition of sanctuary cities, were allowed to stand. The state of Arizona appealed the ruling, and the Court of Appeals for the Ninth Circuit denied the appeal in April 2011, However, Governor Jan Brewer subsequently made a direct appeal to have the case heard by the U.S. Supreme Court, which was granted in December 2011.

S.B. 1070 has had a strong ripple effect. Legislatures in at least 22 states have since announced their intention to enact similar laws. A broadly similar law was passed by the Utah legislature in March 2011, albeit with a slightly higher threshold for the circumstances under which police officers could ask for proof of legal residency. That same month the Georgia General Assembly passed H.B. 87, the Illegal Immigration Reform and Enforcement Act. Like S.B. 1070, Georgia's H.B. 87 entitles law enforcement in the state to inquire into the immigration status of suspects and all but mandates use of the E-Verify system to determine worker employment eligibility. But the Georgia statute goes further by making the use of false identification to obtain employment a felony. This new crime—aggravated identity fraud—is punishable by up to 15 years in prison and a fine of $250,000. In June 2011 the Alabama and South Carolina legislatures enacted H.B. 56 and Act 69, respectively. Both are based on Arizona's S.B. 1070, but they feature additional provisions denying undocumented immigrants access to public benefits such as schooling and medical care, under most circumstances.

Opposition to these laws has likewise been forceful, and both sides have been able to claim partial victory. Following lawsuits by multiple civil rights organizations, a federal judge delayed implementation of Utah's H.B. 497 until arguments could be heard in federal court. On June 27, 2011, federal judge Thomas Thrash blocked only those parts of Georgia's H.B. 87 he deemed were preemptive of federal law. These included the requirement that officers check immigration status of persons without identification and the prohibition of transporting and housing illegal immigrants. On September 27, 2011, a federal district court judge in Birmingham upheld most sections of H.B. 56. In a departure from the precedents established in Arizona and Georgia, Judge Sharon Blackburn affirmed Alabama's right to require its law enforcement to verify immigration status during routine traffic stops if officers have a reasonable suspicion the driver or occupants are in the country illegally, as well as the provision criminalizing "willful failure" to carry immigration papers. Blocked were two sections: one that prohibited the transporting and harboring of illegal immigrants, and one that barred illegal immigrants from enrolling in public universities. Both were blocked on the grounds that they preempted federal law.

In cases where state governments are not inclined to adopt tough immigration enforcement laws, some counties and municipalities have sought to enact their own local ordinances. Prince William County, Virginia; Farmer's Branch, Texas; Costa Mesa, California; and Valley Park, Missouri, are a few of the jurisdictions that have passed laws to sanction landlords for renting to illegal immigrants and employers for hiring them. Like the state laws, these ordinances have faced legal opposition, and many have yet to be put into effect.

Even absent full implementation, these laws seem to have had the desired effect of driving illegal immigrants out of the affected jurisdiction or into the margins of society. Farmers in Alabama, Georgia, and South Carolina, who rely heavily on immigrant labor, have reported severe workforce shortages and crop losses, and schools in immigrant communities have seen a sharp drop in enrollment.

STATE AND LOCAL POLICE SHOULD PARTICIPATE IN ENFORCING IMMIGRATION LAW

Illegal immigration is a crime, and each crime committed by an illegal immigrant is preventable. Support for state and local laws to control illegal immigration is often motivated by community outrage over crimes committed by illegal immigrants. These are crimes which could have been prevented if the perpetrators had been kept from entering the county in the first place or, barring that, if they had been deported prior to committing the crime. ICE estimates that

300,000 to 450,000 criminal aliens—aliens who are incarcerated for committing a crime—are identified each year in federal, state, and local correctional facilitites. The current tide of anti-immigrant fervor has been inflamed by real high-profile crimes committed by illegal immigrants, not just by imagined threats (see sidebar).

Crimes committed by illegal immigrants

Denise Mosier was killed and her two companions were seriously injured, in a car accident in Bristow, Virginia on August 2, 2010, at 8:30 a.m. The collision occurred when a southbound vehicle struck a barrier and swerved into the northbound lane. The driver of that car, a 23-year-old Bolivian man in the country illegally, was charged with involuntary manslaughter and his third DUI in 5 years.

On July 8, 2011, Humberto Leal, one of more than 50 Mexican nationals currently on death row in Texas, was executed for the 1994 kidnapping and murder of 16-year-old Adria Sauceda.

Santana Batiz Aceves was arrested on suspicion of rape in January of 2008 and pled guilty after DNA testing linked him to five sexual assaults on 12- to 14-year-old girls in Chandler, Arizona. Aceves was in the country illegally and had twice been deported.

Congressman Gary Condit was a suspect in the 2001 murder of Capitol Hill intern Chandra Levy, and his career was ruined over revelations of an affair with the victim, but the investigation ultimately led to Ingmar Guandique, an illegal immigrant who had attacked two other young women in the park where Levy's body was found.

Angel Maturino Reséndiz, alias Rafael Resendez-Ramirez, was a Mexican national dubbed the Railroad Killer for his reliance on trains to travel around the United States. Over the course of several years, he murdered as many as 15 people in the U.S., mainly in Texas, but also in Illinois, Florida, and Kentucky. After a nationwide manhunt he was finally apprehended in July 1999, convicted of murder, and sentenced to death.

Public support for state and local involvement in immigration enforcement is also driven by the substantial cost of incarcerating illegal immigrants convicted of violent felonies. Illegal immigrants are an estimated 4 percent of the total resident population, but an estimated 29 percent of imprisoned convicted felons are noncitizens. The cost of incarcerating these approximately 630,000 potentially deportable aliens in state and federal prisons for offenses committed in the United States is $1.6 billion annually, which does not factor in the cost of removing them from the country upon release, as required by law.

Criminal aliens are clearly a significant problem for federal, state, and local criminal justice systems, and local police need every tool possible to combat the crime and disorder associated with all of the populations they deal with. Some local government officials have estimated that the illegal immigrant population living in their jurisdiction has a much higher incarceration rate than the incarcertation rates of their native-born and legal immigrant counterparts. Maricopa County, Arizona, estimates that 22 percent of the felons in its prisons are illegal aliens; Lake County, Illinois, found that 19 percent of jailed inmates are illegal immigrants; Collier County, Florida, estimates that 20 to 22 percent of jail inmates and arrestees are illegal immigrants; and Weld County, Colorado, found that 12.8 to 15.2 percent of jail inmates are illegal aliens. In fact, DHS reports that 11 to 17 percent of the jail populations in the country are noncitizens, and that they make up 26.4 percent of inmates in federal prisons.

Cooperative immigration enforcement programs like CAP and 287(g) partnerships have been criticized by media and interest groups as predominantly deporting illegal immigrants arrested for minor offenses, but these reports are somewhat misleading. Many of the most dangerous criminal aliens were convicted and imprisoned for their crimes and will not be deported until they have served lengthy sentences. Thus, as time goes by, the number of criminal aliens convicted of serious crimes may increase although the worst offenders may not be remanded to ICE for decades. In addition, the crimes for which these individuals were arrested and deported are not necessarily the first or worst crime they have committed, nor can we assume it is the last or worst crime they would ever commit if they were allowed to remain in the country. Lastly, these reports count drunk driving as a minor offense. While this offense might lack the malicious intent of first- or second-degree murder, it can be equally deadly.

Research indicating illegal immigrants are no more prone to commit crimes than native-born citizens must also be taken with a grain of salt. To begin with, this is faint praise, as few in law enforcement would describe the offending rates of the native-born population as negligible. More importantly, the problem of undocumented immigrants underreporting crime, often invoked as an argument against local involvement in immigration control, would tend to bias estimates of immigrant criminality downward. Regardless of whether this bias is significant, there is no dispute that the offending rate of this population is well above zero. This underscores a central reality of illegal immigrant crime: every offense criminal aliens commit in the United States was potentially preventable if federal immigration enforcement authorities had identified, apprehended, and deported these criminal aliens before they victimized anyone.

The public supports using police to enforce immigration. When presented with a choice between tighter border security and a crackdown on illegal immigrants within U.S. borders, Americans seem to prefer having the federal government focus on prevention by increasing border security. Fifty-three percent of respondents in a June 2011 Gallup poll said the need for government action to halt the flow of illegal immigrants at the borders was "extremely important," an 11 percentage point increase from the previous year, while another 29 percent said it was "very important." A majority of those surveyed (55 percent) felt it was more important to halt the flow of illegal immigrants than to devise strategies for dealing with illegal immigrants already in the country, and only a minority (21 percent) thought all those residing in the U.S. illegally should be deported.

And yet, when asked specifically about local enforcement of immigration, voters have largely supported Arizona's new immigration law and strongly believe states should be able to fight illegal immigration if the federal government does not effectively do so. A 2010 poll conducted by the Pew Research Center found that 62 percent favored allowing law enforcement to question people they suspect may be in the country illegally, while 73 percent favored requiring people to carry documents proving legal resident status and allowing police to detain people unable to produce acceptable documentation. Republicans viewed the law most favorably (82 percent), but support was still strong among independents (64 percent), and Democrats were split almost evenly, with 45 percent being in favor of the law. S.B. 1070 had the highest approval rating among respondents 65 and older, at 75 percent, and only the youngest age group, 18- to 29-year-olds, had a marginally unfavorable assessment, with only 45 percent supporting the measure.

A more recent Rasmussen Reports national telephone survey found that two out of three eligible U.S. voters think that a state should have the right to enforce immigration laws if its residents believe the federal government is not enforcing them appropriately. Interestingly, 57 percent of unaffiliated voters favor these types of laws, along with 49 percent of Democrats and 77 percent of Republicans. Fifty-seven percent of voters continue to favor passage of an immigration law like Arizona's in their own state. Twenty-eight percent oppose such a law, and 15 percent are undecided about it.

The police are well suited to perform this function. Just as members of the community are well suited to assist local law enforcement with maintaining public safety, local law enforcement is well suited to assist the federal government with immigration control. Peace officers are apt to encounter illegal aliens in the course of everyday criminal investigations and enforcement activities. Surely this is one reason ICE has situated a team of Detention and Removal agents at Phoenix Police Department Headquarters.

Positive identification and verification of criminal alien status can be greatly facilitated by law enforcement's exclusive access to the FBI's biometric database, the largest of its kind in the world. The information technology infrastructure in law enforcement agencies is continually improving to take full advantage of this database. According to the latest Law Enforcement Management and Administrative Statistics (LEMAS) survey, in 2007, 70 percent of local police departments, and more than 90 percent of agencies serving 25,000 or more residents, had access to an Automated Fingerprint Identification System (AFIS), including digitized print files and in-field computers capable of accessing warrants and criminal records.

Anecdotal evidence suggests that state and local partnerships with ICE may be effective at identifying potentially deportable aliens, which is the most costly activity associated with immigration enforcement for ICE. In 2007, Sheriff Joe Arpaio of Maricopa County entered into a 287g partnership with ICE. Over the next 2 years, he provided training to 60 detention officers, who have interviewed 106,000 inmates and identified 16,000 as illegal immigrants. As of April 2008, his deputies had arrested more than 1,000 illegal immigrants for breaking state immigration laws and had turned over an additional 1,000 arrestees who were determined to be in Arizona illegally. While his department no longer participates in the 287(g) program, they continue to enforce state and federal immigration laws.

In Prince William County, the 287(g) partnership has been heralded as a great success, though initially jail capacity posed a problem that had to be worked out with ICE over the first few months. During the first 2 years, there were 2,984 contacts with suspected illegal immigrants, nearly all of which were later confirmed. An independent evaluation of this initiative credited it with a significant decrease of 74,000 illegal immigrants in Prince William County over the 2 years following the policy change. The evaluation also concluded that the 287g agreement did not negatively impact law enforcement's ability to perform their other functions, property crime and most crimes of public disorder were unaffected, there was a reduction in violent crime, and a reduction in hit-and-run accidents.

This can be done responsibly. Many immigrant and civil rights advocacy groups claim that local police cannot engage in immigration enforcement without charges of discrimination and violations of civil rights. But it can be done responsibly. There have been claims of racial bias and discrimination in some jurisdictions, but no charges have been levied against the vast majority of departments engaging in immigration enforcement.

The independent evaluation of the Prince William County 287(g) program "found no evidence of overzealous or inappropriate immigration enforcement actions by the police. The flood of costly racial-profiling litigation that some had feared—under both the original and the current policy—never materialized." Hence, the study's authors conclude, "one implication of Prince William's experience is inescapable: it is indeed possible for a local government to have an impact on its experience with illegal immigration, despite the national scope of the problem and the primacy of the federal government in dealing with the issue" (Guterbock et al., 2010, p. xvii).

Moreover, there are well-established rules of engagement with this type of enforcement. The federal government has already put checks in place to ensure that their programs are implemented in compliance with the law. For example, ICE and the Department of Homeland Security's Office for Civil Rights and Civil Liberties have devised safeguards to prevent their programs from being used irresponsibly, such as (1) retaining a statistician to examine the Secure Communities data to identify indications of racial profiling in the quarterly monitoring report, (2) developing additional trainings, and (3) revising the ICE detainer to emphasize that authorities may not detain someone for over 48 hours. The Office of the Inspector General routinely audits ICE and DHS programs, and their recommendations are consistently accepted to ensure the proper implementation of federal and local law enforcement partnerships in immigration enforcement.

CONCLUSION

Protecting the borders and enforcing immigration laws are essential duties of the federal government. But with the current level of resources committed to these duties, it is unrealistic to expect that the federal government can do this alone. As the effects of uncontrolled immigration are felt across the country, an increasing number of state and local governments have enlisted local law enforcement officials to enforce immigration laws in recent years. They either enforce federal immigration laws in partnership with the federal government, or they create new laws, statutes, and initiatives criminalizing illegal immigration that have been passed in a number of jurisdictions. At present, the latter strategy is largely opposed by the Justice Department.

There are four main arguments in favor of involving state and local law enforcement in federal immigration enforcement. First, since every criminal offense committed by an illegal alien is theoretically avertable, deporting illegal immigrants, some of whom may pose a threat to public safety, will reduce crime and ease the police's workload in the long term. Second, there is widespread public support for increasing immigration enforcement in the interior of the country using state and local law enforcement officers. Third, the thousands of local criminal justice systems are natural partners with the federal government, since they are already enforcing criminal law, cross paths with illegal and criminal aliens in the course of their routine job functions, and outnumber ICE enforcement officers more than 5,000 to 1. Lastly, local immigration enforcement can be done responsibly and without violating anyone's civil rights. While rigorous evaluation of the various enforcement programs is needed, anecdotal evidence so far seems to suggest that they can be effective. Immigration enforcement by state and local law enforcement officers can help identify, detain, and remove illegal immigrants.

REFERENCES AND FURTHER READING

Arizona State Government. (2010). SB 1070, Support Our Law Enforcement and Safe Neighborhoods Act, passed April 23, 2010. Retrieved from http://www.azleg.gov/legtext/49leg/2r/bills/sb1070s.pdf

Chin, G. J., Hessick, C. B., Massaro, T., & Miller, M. L. (2010). A legal labyrinth: Issues raised by Arizona Senate bill 1070. *Georgetown Immigration Law Journal, 25*(1), 47.

Department of Homeland Security. (2011). *Congressional budget justification, fiscal year 2011*. Retrieved from http://www.dhs.gov/xlibrary/assets/dhs_congressional_budget_justification_fy2011.pdf

Georgia State Government. (2011). HB 87, Illegal Immigration Reform and Enforcement Act of 2011, passed April 14, 2011. Retrieved from http://www1.legis.ga.gov/legis/2011_12/pdf/hb87.pdf

Guterbock, T., Vickerman, M., Walker, K., Koper, C., Taylor, B., & Carter, T. (2010). *Evaluation study of Prince William County's illegal immigration enforcement policy: Final report 2010*. Charlottesville, VA: University of Virginia, Center for Survey Research.

Hoefer, M., Tytina, N., & Baker, B. C. (2011). *Estimation of the unauthorized immigrant population residing in the United States: January 2010*. Retrieved from Department of Homeland Security Office of Immigrant Statistics website: http://www.dhs.gov/xlibrary/assets/statistics/publications/ois_ill_pe_2010.pdf

Hoffmaster, D., Murphy, G., McFadden, S., & Griswold, M. (2011). *Police and immigration: How chiefs are leading their communities through the challenges*. Retrieved from Police Executive Research Forum website: http://www.policeforum.org/library/immigration/PERFImmigrationReportMarch2011.pdf

INS/FBI. (2006). *Statistical report on undocumented immigrants*.

Koback, K. W. (2006). *State and local authority to enforce immigration law: A unified approach for stopping terrorists*. Retrieved from Center for Immigration Studies website: http://www.cis.org/articles/2004/back604.pdf

National Conference of State Legislatures. (2011). *2011 immigration-related laws, bills and resolutions in the states: Jan 1–March 31, 2011*. Available online at http://www.ncsl.org

National Conference of State Legislatures. (n.d.). *Issues and research: Immigration*. Retrieved from http://www.ncsl.org/Default.aspx?TabID=756&tabs=951,119,851#951

North Carolina Department of Justice. (n.d.). *View crime statistics*. Retrieved from http://www.ncdoj.gov/Crime/View-Crime-Statistics.aspx

Office of Inspector General. (2011). *U.S. immigration and customs enforcement identification of criminal aliens in federal and state custody eligible for removal from the United States* (OIF-11-26). Retrieved from Department of Homeland Security website: http://www.dhs.gov/xoig/assets/mgmtrpts/OIG_11-26_Jan11.pdf

Parlow, M. (2006). A localist's case for decentralizing immigration policy. *Denver University Law Review, 84*, 1061–1073.

Pew Research Center. (2010, May 12). *Broad approval for new Arizona immigration law*. Retrieved from http://www.people-press.org/2010/05/12/broad-approval-for-new-arizona-immigration-law

Pham, H. (2006). The constitutional right not to cooperate? Local sovereignty and the federal immigration policy. *University of Cincinnati Law Review, 74*, 1382–1384.

Rasmussen Reports. (2011, February 18). *67% say states should be able to enforce immigration laws if feds are not*. Retrieved from http://www.rasmussenreports.com/public_content/politics/current_events/immigration/67_say_states_should_be_able_to_enforce_immigration_laws_if_feds_are_not

Robertson, C. (2011, September 28). Alabama wins in ruling on its immigration law. *The New York Times*. Retrieved from http://www.nytimes.com/2011/09/29/us/alabama-immigration-law-upheld.html

Saad, L. (2011, June 22). *Majority of Americans urge gov't action on border control*. Retrieved from Gallup Politics website: http://www.gallup.com/poll/148160/majority-americans-urge-gov-action-border-control.aspx

Sabol, W. J., Minton, T. D., & Harrison, P. (2007). *Prison and jail inmates at midyear 2006* (NCJ 217675). Washington, DC: Bureau of Justice Statistics.

Seghetti, L. M., Vina, S. R., & Ester, K. (2006, August 14). *Enforcing immigration law: The role of state and local law enforcement* (Congressional Research Service Report for Congress, order code RL32270). Washington, DC: Congressional Research Service.

Su, R. (2010). The significance of Arizona's new immigration law. *Michigan Law Review, First Impressions, 109*(63), 76–79.

Transactional Records Access Clearinghouse. (2010). *TRAC immigration*. Retrieved from http://trac.syr.edu/immigration

U.S. Department of Justice, Office of the Inspector General, Audit Division. (2007, January). *Cooperation of SCAAP recipients in the removal of criminal aliens from the United States* (Redacted—public version). Retrieved from http://www.justice.gov/oig/reports/OJP/a0707/final.pdf

U.S. House of Representatives. (2003). Clear Law Enforcement for Criminal Alien Removal Act of 2003 (H.R. 2671). Retrieved from http://commdocs.house.gov/committees/judiciary/hju89636.000/hju89636_0.HTM and http://immigration.procon.org/sourcefiles/HouseofRepresentativesBillHR2671ClearLawEnforcementforCriminalAlienRemovalActof2003.pdf

U.S. Immigration and Customs Enforcement. (2008). *Law enforcement support center fact sheet*. Retrieved from http://www.ice.gov/news/library/factsheets/lesc.htm

U.S. Immigration and Customs Enforcement. (2011). *Delegation of immigration authority, Section 287(g), Immigration and Nationality Act*. Retrieved from http://www.ice.gov/287g

U.S. Immigration and Customs Enforcement. (2011). *ICE overview*. Retrieved from http://www.ice.gov/about/overview

U.S. Senate. (2003). Homeland Security Enhancement Act of 2003 (S. 1906). Retrieved from http://immigration.procon.org/source files/SenateBillS1906HomelandSecurityEnhancementActof2003.pdf

Utah State Government. (2011). HB 497, Utah Illegal Immigration Enforcement Act, passed March 4, 2011. Retrieved from http:// le.utah.gov/~2011/bills/hbillenr/hb0497.pdf

Venbrux, G. K. (2006). Devolution or evolution? The Increasing role of the state in immigration law enforcement. *UCLA Journal of International Law and Foreign Affairs, 11*, 307.

Williams, A. (2008, October 6). Refuges of crime and terror: How sanctuary cities endanger national security [Op-Ed]. *Washington Times*. Retrieved from http://www.washingtontimes.com/news/2008/oct/06/refuges-of-crime-and-terror

Jessica Saunders, Carl Matthies, and Nelson Lim

COUNTERPOINT

The federal government certainly needs to improve its capabilities to enforce immigration laws. However, enlisting state and local law enforcement to fill this role is a misguided approach. The involvement of state and local law enforcement in immigration control is a relatively recent development, but where police and sheriff's departments have made it a high priority it has created several serious problems. First it has diverted attention away from preventing, deterring, and solving crimes, because there is no direct connection between immigrants and crime. Second, it has further eroded already strained relationships between the police and immigrant communities, which are vital to police functioning. Third, it has added yet another responsibility to already overburdened law enforcement agencies, courts, and correctional facilities. Finally, it has left the state and local police open to charges of racial profiling and discrimination, which can lead to civil rights violations and lawsuits. Thorough evaluation of local immigration enforcement programs is needed, but the available evidence suggests that any gains in immigration control are offset by the problems associated with tasking state and local police to enforce immigration laws.

Protecting national borders and enforcing immigration laws are difficult and essential responsibilities of the federal government. Yet the millions of "out-of-status" aliens (also referred to as "illegal immigrants") living in the country attest to the magnitude of this task and the extent to which the federal government has failed to achieve this objective. According to recent estimates by the Pew Hispanic Center, almost 12 million "out of status" aliens were residing in the United States in 2007, although the numbers had reportedly declined to 11 million by 2009. Out-of-status aliens are actually a heterogeneous group with regard to their immigration status. The group includes (1) individuals who originally entered the country legally and whose visas have expired, (2) individuals who entered illegally, and (3) a subgroup, called "fugitive aliens" or "alien absconders," who have been processed through the immigration system and subsequently ignored deportation orders.

While the federal government is interested in identifying and removing all of these illegal immigrants, they have recently concentrated efforts on locating and removing the population of absconders from the United States. There were approximately 560,000 immigrants in the fugitive alien category in 2008, approximately 5 percent of all out-of-status immigrants. At current rates, given the budgets under which the Department of Homeland Security's Immigration and Customs Enforcement (ICE) is operating, it would take 15 years and over $5 billion—almost as much as its entire annual budget—just to clear the absconder backlog.

It is unrealistic to expect that the immigration problem can be solved by federal law enforcement alone. "The absconder population is exhibit number one," noted Victor Cerda, ICE's former chief of staff and general counsel. "We haven't been able to handle the 600,000-plus who went through the legal system. What's going to lead us to believe we're going to handle the 12 million?"

One response to this challenge has been to encourage the creation of partnerships between federal immigration agencies and state and local law enforcement agencies so that their combined expertise, manpower, and other resources can be directed at apprehending and deporting illegal immigrants. ICE currently has approximately 20,000 employees (not all of whom are law enforcement officers) throughout the United States, compared to the over 800,000 full-time state and local sworn law enforcement officers.

But this solution is not as straightforward as it might seem, and it may not be worth the costs. While including local law enforcement officers could indeed help to identify and detain illegal immigrants by increasing manpower focused on this problem, gains in that area would be offset by a corresponding reduction in the ability of state and local law enforcement officers to fulfill their core mission to protect and serve all members of the public in their immediate jurisdictions.

HISTORY OF IMMIGRATION POLICY RELATED TO ENFORCEMENT: A GRADUALLY INCREASED ROLE FOR STATE AND LOCAL GOVERNMENT

The 1986 Immigration Reform and Control Act (IRCA) was the first comprehensive bill aimed at reducing illegal immigration. Its main provisions included sanctions against employers who knowingly hired undocumented workers, stronger enforcement of immigration law at U.S. borders and inside the country, and the largest program ever conducted to legalize the majority of the unauthorized migrant population.

Over the years, however, illegal immigration continued and concerns mounted that illegal immigrants were taking jobs from U.S. citizens, increasing crime rates, and draining scarce public resources. Thus, in 1996 Congress passed legislation that further constrained immigrants' rights. The Antiterrorism and Effective Death Penalty Act greatly curtailed the rights of illegal immigrants suspected of criminal activity or terrorism and put in place an alien terrorist removal court that accelerated the process of removing criminal aliens. The Personal Responsibility and Work Opportunity Reconciliation Act (PRWORA) restricted unauthorized immigrants' access to essential public services.

The Illegal Immigration Reform and Immigrant Responsibility Act (IIRIRA) of 1996 expanded the range of offenses for which immigrants could be deported and increased penalties for violations. It curtailed immigrants' due-process rights, further reduced their access to public services, and tightened security at the U.S.-Mexico border. Section 642(a) of IIRIRA also expressly prohibited noncooperation policies that would prevent public employees from reporting the immigration status of individuals to ICE.

As part of the IIRIRA legislation, Section 287(g) was incorporated into the Immigration and Nationality Act. Section 287(g) authorized the federal government to enter into voluntary agreements with state, county, and local law enforcement agencies to train officers to help identify individuals who are in the country illegally. The program is supervised by ICE, formerly the Immigration and Naturalization Service (INS).

Originally conceived with a narrow mandate—to arrest unauthorized immigrants already subject to outstanding warrants of deportation (fugitive aliens)—the program has undergone multiple transformations. The first, following the September 11, 2001, attacks, sought to utilize the program as a tool to fight terrorism and promote national security. The second transformation, occurring in 2006, expanded the program's agenda to include broader and more generalized immigration enforcement. A third transformation occurred in July 2009 when Secretary of Homeland Security Janet Napolitano announced that she would standardize all 287(g) Memoranda of Agreement (MOAs) to make policies and procedures surrounding immigration enforcement requirements more consistent at the national, state, and local levels, and to place the focus on identifying, detaining, and removing immigrants convicted of a serious offense, who pose a threat to public safety, or have been ordered removed.

There have been other attempts by the federal government to encourage the participation of state and local jurisdictions in enforcing immigration laws, Such as the Homeland Security Enhancement Act of 2003. No proposal has been more ambitious than the Clear Law Enforcement for Criminal Alien Removal (CLEAR) Acts of 2003, 2005, and 2007, introduced by Congressman Charles Norwood of Georgia's 10th District. These laws proposed giving state and local law enforcement agencies the authority to "investigate, apprehend, detain, transport and remove noncitizens from the United States." This legislation would have made unlawful presence in the United States a felony, and it sought to greatly increase penalties for immigration violations. It would have authorized financial assistance to state and local police agencies that enforce federal immigration law and mandated training for their personnel. It would have required the addition of data related to immigration violations to the National Crime Information Center (NCIC) and mandated that state and local entities participate in the Institutional Removal Program, which identifies removable noncitizens in federal and state correctional facilities, ensures that they are not released into the community, and removes them from the United States after completion of their sentences. Needless to say, these laws would have dramatically redefined the role of state and local law enforcement in immigration control, but each time the legislation stalled in committee, partly due to pressure from civil rights activist groups who asserted that the bills promote racial profiling.

In the absence of immigration reform at the national level, state legislatures, county boards of supervisors, and city councils have begun to enact immigration laws containing immigration enforcement provisions directed at state and local criminal justice systems. There has been a significant increase in the number of bills introduced and laws enacted that regulate immigration at the state level, with almost 1,600 bills introduced and 200 laws enacted in 2011 alone. Some of these require state and local law enforcement's involvement in immigration enforcement, which has spawned a great deal of controversy and backlash from immigrant communities and civil rights groups, not to mention legal challenges from the Justice Department. (These developments are described in more detail in the Point argument.)

As they attempt to regulate and control their jurisdictions, city, county, and state officials are confronted by competing goals with respect to relationships with immigrant populations. Police officers, for example, must balance their obligations to serve and protect all members of the public (whether or not they are citizens) with obligations related to immigration enforcement. The response in some cases has been to adopt a policy of limited cooperation—that is, to support federal efforts to remove illegal immigrants convicted of felonies, but otherwise to decline to identify and remove undocumented aliens with the rationale that this is a federal responsibility. These are sometimes called "sanctuary policies," although most police officials object to the term on the grounds that it misstates the level of protection accorded illegal immigrants. They therefore use the alternative term "separation ordinances."

These limited cooperation policies may be informal or codified. According to the National Immigration Law Center, as of April 2008, states and municipalities had passed 87 laws, resolutions, and policies providing some degree of "sanctuary." These range from local law enforcement refusing to cooperate in the enforcement of immigration offenses to the equivalent of a "don't ask, don't tell" for immigration status. Twenty-three states have at least one such provision passed in their jurisdictions. Indeed, four states—Alaska, Montana, New Mexico, and Oregon—explicitly prohibit the use of state resources for the purpose of immigration enforcement, yet some local agencies within Alaska, Montana, and New Mexico have entered into 287(g) MOAs with the Department of Homeland Security, seemingly in direct violation of state policy.

Some of the largest cities in the United States—including New York, Los Angeles, San Francisco, the District of Columbia, Chicago, Baltimore, Boston, Detroit, Minneapolis, St. Louis, Newark, Philadelphia, Austin, and Seattle—have passed legislation limiting local enforcement of immigration laws. The Police Foundation's 2008 conference proceedings and findings found that most police executives were against cooperation of state and local law enforcement in immigration enforcement unless its ultimate goal was to reduce crime. To further support this position, a national group representing 57 police chiefs from cities with populations greater than 1.5 million stated in 2006 that local enforcement of immigration would "undermine [the] trust and cooperation" necessary for effective policing. The next section enumerates why involving state and local public safety resources in immigration enforcement is a bad idea.

WHY STATE AND LOCAL POLICE SHOULD NOT PARTICIPATE IN ENFORCING IMMIGRATION LAW

There is no relationship between immigrant status and criminal behavior. Every major wave of U.S. immigrants has provoked some social backlash. From populist demagoguery to ostensibly high-minded discussions about their "less-than-desirable" attributes and lack of human capital, immigrants have often been the scapegoats for social ills, especially crime. Sociologists in the early 1900s pondered the relationship between immigrant status and crime, though as early as 1931 the Wickersham Commission Report noted that there was very little empirical basis for blaming urban crime problems on immigrants. Yet the link between crime and immigration has persisted in the public's mind.

Public sentiment against immigration has risen in recent years, paralleling a demographic shift in which children of foreign-born parents have become the fastest-growing segment of the population. As of the 2010 census, over one-fifth of the U.S. population (69.7 million) was foreign-born or had parents who were foreign-born, compared to 55.9 million in 2000. This segment of the population is disproportionately exposed to socio-environmental risk factors for a variety of negative life outcomes, such as low educational attainment, poverty, poor health, and higher criminal involvement or crime victimization. Traditional sociological theories of crime predict that immigrants will be more involved in crime because they are more likely to be living in poverty, to be living in poor urban neighborhoods without much informal social control, to be less skilled and educated, and because they face the added difficulty of adjusting to new sets of cultural norms. Veteran police officers have more mundane explanations: illegal immigrants are attractive targets because they typically don't have bank accounts and are thus more likely to carry cash, and because they're less likely to report crimes for fear of deportation.

However, more recent empirical studies have shown that immigrants are less likely than native-born counterparts to be engaged in criminal behavior. Jeffrey Morenoff and Avraham Astor (2006), for example, found that first-generation immigrants in Chicago had lower violence rates than either second- or third-generation immigrants, using data from the Project on Human Development in Chicago Neighborhoods study. Besides differences in crime rates across immigrant generations, they found that some contextual contributors of crime may actually work in the opposite direction for immigrants. For instance, first generation immigrants were less likely to engage in crime as neighborhood disadvantage increased, whereas this relationship worked in the opposite direction for third-generation immigrants, and there was no relationship in the second immigrant generation, suggesting that neighborhood effects are at least partially dependent on generation status.

Rumbaut and colleagues (2006) also found that incarceration rates among the least educated young immigrant men were significantly lower than those for nonimmigrants with similar educational achievement, but that this gap narrowed over generations, which they ascribed to "downward" assimilation. Assimilation and acculturation into American society may be associated with higher propensity for criminal involvement, such that by the second or third generation the risk of these outcomes becomes equivalent to other natives of similar social status.

These relationships persist among illegal immigrants as well, even in the subset that commit crimes. The only research study that has focused specifically on the public safety threat of illegal immigrants in the state and local criminal justice system found that deportable immigrants released from a local jail did not pose a greater threat to public safety than nondeportable immigrants released at the same time. This RAND study of nearly 1,300 male inmates found that there was no difference in recidivism rates between nondeportable and deportable immigrants, where "deportable immigrants" were defined as those eligible for deportation because they entered the United States illegally, overstayed their visas, or committed other violations. The author stated, "our findings run counter to the notion that illegal immigrants are more likely than other immigrants to cycle in and out of the local criminal justice system."

It will devastate already strained relationships between the police and immigrant communities. Over the past several decades, community policing, which involves forging partnerships in the community to identify problems and solve crimes, has become the dominant model of local law enforcement, and it is credited with markedly improving public safety and police-community relations. Utilizing local police for immigration enforcement would jeopardize the immigrant community's trust in the police, making illegal immigrants reluctant to come forward as victims and witnesses for fear of deportation. Without community cooperation, the community-policing model breaks down, putting immigrants and their communities at higher risk of exploitation and victimization.

Policing research has demonstrated that trust and rapport between the police and the community are essential for effective policing. Community policing differs from traditional policing in how law enforcement perceives the community and in its expanded policing goals. This approach involves police augmenting crime-control tactics with strategies to prevent crime, reduce the fear of crime, and improve the quality of life in neighborhoods. While crime control and prevention remain central priorities, community-policing strategies use a wide variety of methods to address these expanded goals. Because community members are often in a better position than police to identify and observe problems, police and the community become partners in addressing problems of disorder and neglect (e.g., violent crime, gang activity, abandoned cars, and other "broken windows" measures) that may not themselves be criminal but that increase fear of crime and can eventually lead to serious crime. As links between the police and the community are strengthened over time, the partnership becomes more and more proactive in pinpointing and mitigating the underlying causes of crime.

In communities with large immigrant populations, community involvement and trust are severely undermined by police taking on the responsibility for immigration enforcement, as these communities may begin to fear police contact, due to fear of possible deportation. Law enforcement leaders from around the nation, including the Major Cities Chiefs Association, Police Foundation, and International Association of Chiefs of Police, have issued statements expressing a need to maintain focus on public safety and warning about the "chilling effect" of adding immigration enforcement to local police responsibilities. Several police executives, including the Arizona Association of Chiefs of Police, have stated their opposition to S.B. 1070 and laws like it.

Immigrants tend to have less positive attitudes toward the police than native-born citizens, and they are less likely to report crimes or initiate contact with the police. This is a problem for law enforcement because the more legitimacy police have in their communities, the more effective they can be. Widespread police corruption and brutality in many immigrants' countries of origin is one explanation for immigrants' reluctance to cooperate with U.S. police, but the fear of deportation—whether for themselves, family members, or friends—is also seen as the main barrier to building trust and cooperation with the police. According to work by Mark Hugo Lopez and Susan Minushkin at the Pew Hispanic Center, only 45 percent of Latinos have confidence that police officers in their communities treat Latinos fairly. In their 2008 National Survey of Latinos, they found that 81 percent of Hispanics believed that immigration enforcement should be left to federal authorities, and 57 percent reported that they worried about family members, close friends, or themselves being deported. In fact, 10 percent of immigrants and 8 percent of U.S.-born Hispanics reported being stopped and asked about their immigration status in the previous year.

A microcosm of the problems caused by merging immigration enforcement with community policing can be found in the overlapping jurisdictions of Maricopa County, Arizona. Both the cities of Mesa and Phoenix have their own police departments, but they are also within the jurisdiction of the Maricopa County Sheriff's Office (MCSO). The police chiefs of Mesa and Phoenix have implemented policies consistent with community policing in dealing with immigrant populations: inquiries about immigration status are limited to persons placed under arrest and are not to be made of either crime victims, witnesses, or persons stopped for minor infractions. Both agencies have gone to considerable lengths to solicit input from the community in devising these policies and to inform their communities about them. Maricopa County Sheriff Joe Arpaio, however, has taken a much harder stance toward illegal immigrants. His deputies routinely conduct workplace raids and establish traffic checkpoints to arrest undocumented immigrants. On several occasions MCSO has carried out raids in Phoenix and Mesa, in some cases with no advanced notice to the local police departments. According to Phoenix and Mesa police, these raids damaged the trust they had worked hard to establish with members of the immigrant community, who do not necessary distinguish between police officers and sheriff's deputies. In the aftermath of these raids, and in the face of rumors about future raids, many immigrants have gone into hiding. Children have stayed home from school and adults have avoided work, upsetting local commerce. Anecdotally, the raids made immigrants more reluctant to interact with police, not only endangering themselves but the officers who patrol their neighborhoods.

Further evidence of the deleterious effect of local immigration enforcement on community policing comes from the eastern seaboard. Virginia's Prince William County Police entered into a 287(g) partnership with the Department of Homeland Security in 2007, and a research team led by Thomas M. Guterbock at the Police Executive Research Forum and the University of Virginia's Center for Survey Research studied this initiative. They found that the partnership severely impacted police-community relations, especially within the Hispanic community and that there were large differences between Hispanics and non-Hispanics in overall satisfaction with police, police fairness, officer fairness, and with the 287(g) partnership itself. These differences appeared to decrease over time, suggesting that it was perhaps only a temporary change, although another possibility is that the policies drove the more dissatisfied Hispanics from the community. The policy's impact on reporting victimization was not established, but it was found that Hispanics were less likely to report being a victim of a crime both before and after implementation, and both police and community members believed that crime reporting may have been lowered. There is evidence that these negative consequences diminished over time, but at this point the long-term effects are unknown.

Interviews with Hispanics in the 287(g) partnership jurisdiction of Alamance County, North Carolina likewise indicated an erosion of trust in the local authorities and a decreased willingness to report crimes. This finding was mirrored in a 2009 study conducted by the Southern Poverty Law Center on the impacts of the 287(g) partnership in Davidson County, Tennessee. This study showed that over half of Latinos indicated they would not call to report a crime to the police in the future, and one-third indicated that their fear of the police related directly to immigration issues.

Local immigration enforcement will add another responsibility to an already overburdened criminal justice system. At a time when criminal justice systems are facing deep budget cuts, adding responsibility for immigration enforcement may hinder law enforcement's ability to fight crime and further challenge the capacity of courts and jails. Researchers argue that enforcing immigration law is very different from criminal law and, in light of its legal complexity, does not merely add one more task to law enforcement's list. Particularly in jurisdictions that are apt to face a large number of immigration cases, immigration enforcement may be the proverbial last straw.

In addition to the costs associated with training and deploying officers to check on immigration offenses, detaining illegal immigrants can be an issue for already overcrowded detention facilities. According to a detention department in Florida, ICE rarely responds to their requests to have criminal aliens picked up when they are released after completing their prison sentences. The federal immigration system is so overburdened that, due to a lack of equipment, a daily average of 900 to 1,000 detainees are shuffled around Virginia in order to use videoconferencing services for court hearings. These logistical challenges, along with many others, such as inaccurate and missing records, have led to missed court appearances and immigrants being detained for long periods, even after having agreed to voluntarily deportation.

ICE responds to these allegations by claiming they target their limited resources on the worst offenders. And while several localities report successes in their immigration enforcement efforts as a result of the number of illegal aliens identified, there is no empirical measure of whether they are improving public safety by catching the most dangerous criminal aliens, or merely deporting those who were involved in minor violations. Contrary to their supposed purpose, research on 287(g) partnerships shows that some programs have resulted in the identification, detention, and removal of undocumented immigrants who have committed only minor offenses.

There is no direct empirical research that demonstrates whether adding immigration responsibilities impairs local law enforcement's effectiveness. However, there is indirect evidence suggesting that these additional enforcement duties do not advance, and may hinder, the objective of public safety. A report by Dora Schriro, former director of ICE's Office of Detention Policy and Planning, found that the 287(g) program resulted in the detention of a large proportion of undocumented immigrants who were not criminals. In fact, 72 percent were not charged with any non-immigration-related crimes at initial booking in fiscal year (FY) 2008, and 65 percent were similarly not charged in FY 2009.

The Maricopa County Sheriff's Office's (MCSO) aggressive immigration enforcement has come under heavy criticism for its perceived impact on the county's budget and public safety. Although the agency did not establish a formalized agreement with ICE until early in 2007, Sheriff Joe Arpaio began making illegal immigration a high priority in 2005, when Arizona passed the so-called coyote statute prohibiting the transport of human beings in the state for profit or commercial purposes. As interpreted by then—County Attorney Andrew Thomas, the law gave Arpaio the authority to arrest undocumented immigrants for smuggling themselves. Within 3 months of forming the 287(g) partnership, MCSO racked up $1.3 million in debt, and its budget increased 23 percent between 2005 and 2008. The number of violent crimes reported in 2007 was 69 percent higher than in 2004. The clearance rate dropped dramatically, from 10.5 percent of investigations cleared by arrest in 2005 down to 3.5 percent in 2007. Response time also increased substantially. According to Ryan Gabrielson at the *East Valley Tribune,* in 2006 and 2007, patrol cars were late two-thirds of the time for the most serious calls for service. Moreover, a startling number of MCSO cases were designated "cleared exceptionally," meaning investigators knew who the perpetrator was but for some reason could not or did not make an arrest. In 2006 only 25 percent of cleared MCSO cases were cleared by arrest, whereas the Phoenix Police Department cleared 78 percent by arrest the following year.

An assessment of the crime-fighting benefits of 287(g) partnerships in five North Carolina counties also casts doubt on the cost-effectiveness of the program. The vast majority (86.7 percent) of the 10,743 undocumented immigrant arrests were for misdemeanor violations. The Alamance County Sheriff credited the 287(g) partnership with a 38 percent reduction in rape and a 29 percent reduction in armed robbery in the first eight months of implementation. Based on North Carolina Department of Justice crime statistics, however, overall violent crime in Alamance County was down a more modest 14 percent in the 4 years after the 287(g) partnership was formed, as compared to the 4 years prior. This is still a substantial decrease, though it is not known whether some of the apparent decrease might be the result of underreporting, or, as Sheriff Johnson acknowledged, a result of the crackdown shifting the criminal alien burden on to neighboring jurisdictions. Meanwhile, the price tag for processing 386 immigration violations in the program's first year was conservatively estimated at $5 million.

While the available evidence does not definitively demonstrate that the changes in these measures of police effectiveness were due to the diverted focus of the department to immigration enforcement, the statistics do suggest that other police functions suffered, at least in part, as a result of enforcing immigration regulations.

It will leave state and local police open to charges of racial profiling and discrimination. Immigration law enforcement involves a complex and evolving set of rules that require extensive and continual training. A common concern of policing executives voiced by both the Police Foundation and the International Association of Chiefs of Police is that immigration enforcement will leave them open to charges of racial profiling and discrimination. Illegal immigrants are more likely to belong to minority groups, and thus there is a strong potential for civil rights violations if the officers do not have the necessary understanding, preparation, and experience with enforcement. While ICE provides training for officers involved in the 287(g) partnerships, questions have arisen as to the adequacy of intensive training the approximately 2,000 officers have received. Cameron University and Advanced Systems Technology (AST) received a grant from the DOJ's Office of Community Oriented Policing Services (COPS) to develop a Basic Immigration Enforcement Training (BIET) pilot program to provide web-based training to a larger audience. While BIET may make training readily accessible to the nation's approximately one million state and local law enforcement officers, it remains to be seen whether it will improve upon on-site training, and how many agencies will be interested in it.

Police are not allowed to use race or national origin as a factor in their enforcement activities. Yet it is very difficult, if not impossible, to enforce immigration laws without considering race or national origin. In fact, over half of the agencies the Government Accountability Office (GAO) interviewed about their participation in the 287(g) partnerships reported receiving concerns expressed by their community members about the potential for the program to lead to racial profiling and intimidation by police officers. Anecdotal evidence so far demonstrates that these 287(g) partnerships do result in charges of profiling.

An investigation by Arizona's attorney general found that the Chandler, Arizona, police engaged in racial profiling during a five-day joint operation with Border Patrol agents in 1997. Chandler police pulled over vehicles driven by persons of perceived or actual Hispanic heritage and asked them for proof of citizenship, even though they were instructed to stop vehicles based solely on probable cause of a violation of state and local laws. The Chandler City Council settled the subsequent civil rights lawsuit for $400,000.

More recent local law enforcement immigration crackdowns have also spurred allegations of racial profiling. Most notable are the numerous lawsuits accusing the Maricopa County Sheriff's Office of racial profiling in its enforcement of immigration laws. In October 2009, MCSO's 287(g) partnership was terminated, but the sheriff announced he would continue his immigration enforcement activities. This is currently the subject of a lawsuit before the U.S. District Court in Arizona. One lawsuit stemming from an MCSO worksite enforcement raid was settled in July 2011 for $200,000. In March 2009, the Justice Department's Civil Rights Division launched a formal investigation into Sheriff Arpaio's practices to determine if the Maricopa County deputies engaged in "patterns or practices of discriminatory police practices," "unconstitutional searches and seizures," and "national-origin discrimination." The findings, summarized in a December 2011 report, characterize MCSO as having a "pervasive culture of discriminatory bias against Latinos." According to the Justice Department, the Sheriff's practices created a "wall of distrust that has significantly compromised MCSO's ability to provide police protection to Latino residents." The investigation also uncovered sufficient evidence to warrant a separate inquiry into MCSO's alleged lax handling of numerous sex crimes.

Arizona is by no means the only state facing such accusations. In July 2010 the Department of Justice launched an investigation of the Alamance County Sheriff's Office in North Carolina regarding alleged racial profiling. The Cobb County Sheriff's Office in Georgia settled a racial profiling lawsuit in May 2011, which had been brought after Angel Francisco Castro Torres claimed two officers stopped him for no reason, then arrested him for obstructing an officer as a ruse to get him deported. Part of a racial profiling lawsuit settlement reached in July 2011 between the American Civil Liberties Union and authorities in Sonoma County, California, stipulates that deputies will no longer relay information to ICE for persons arrested solely for traffic violations. The Frederick County Sheriff's Office in Maryland was sued, in November 2009, after entering into a 287(g) partnership, as was the Davidson County Sheriff's Office (Tennessee) in January 2011.

Even the programs that seem as if they could be administered in a race-blind manner are turning up evidence of racial profiling. The Criminal Alien Program, in which an immigration check is run only after someone has been detained on criminal charges, seems inherently less prone to discriminatory policing practices. However, a study conducted by the Warren Institute found that when police were allowed to investigate the immigration status of detainees only after they had been detained in the Irving (Texas) Jail, this led to the police arresting more Hispanics for traffic stops, and it meant that police officers may have begun to stop cars and detain traffic violators at least partially on the basis of race.

CONCLUSION

The United States has a broken immigration system, and the enforcement of existing immigration law is vastly inadequate. It is appealing to involve state and local law enforcement officials to supplement federal enforcement efforts as force multipliers. However, enforcing federal immigration law is very different from typical policing duties and could hinder the primary mission of law enforcement, which is ensuring public safety. These additional immigration enforcement responsibilities, whether they arise through partnerships with the federal government or through new state or local laws and ordinances, can lead to four serious problems: (1) the lack of a connection between immigration and crime makes immigration enforcement a cost-ineffective means of crime control, (2) immigration enforcement by state and local police can strain police-community relations and hinder their ability to control crime, (3) adding another task to an already overburdened criminal justice system diverts valuable resources that are needed to promote public safety, and (4) enforcing immigration law leaves state and local law enforcement vulnerable to charges of racial discrimination and profiling. There is limited empirical evidence on which to judge the merits of involving state and local law enforcement in immigration enforcement, but much of the available evidence seems to indicate that, though the impact varies by jurisdiction, this policy shift is associated with the problems just enumerated. The public safety consequences as well as the economic and legal consequences of these practices are far from settled, yet they are potentially dire enough to suggest that state and local law enforcement officers should not be used as "force multipliers" for federal immigration enforcement efforts.

REFERENCES AND FURTHER READING

American Civil Liberties Union. (n.d.). *Immigrants rights: No human being is illegal.* Retrieved from http://www.aclu.org/immigrants-rights

Cecilia, M., & Bejarano, C. (2004). Latino immigrants' perceptions of crime and police authorities. *Ethnic and Racial Studies, 27*(1), 123.

Davis, R. C., (2000). *Perceptions of the police among members of six ethnic communities in central Queens, NY.* New York, NY: Safe Horizon.

Davis, R. C., & Erez, E. (1998). Immigrant populations as victims: Toward a multicultural criminal justice system. *Research in Brief.* U.S. Department of Justice, National Institute of Justice. Retrieved from https://www.ncjrs.gov/pdffiles/167571.pdf

Gabrielson, R. (2008, July 12). Reasonable doubt. *East Valley Tribune.* Retrieved from http://www.eastvalleytribune.com/special_reports/reasonable_doubt

Guterbock, T., Vickerman, M., Walker, K., Koper, C., Taylor, B., & Carter, T. (2010) *Evaluation study of Prince William County's illegal immigration enforcement policy: Final report 2010.* Charlottesville, VA: University of Virginia, Center for Survey Research. Retrieved from http://americansforimmigrationreform.com/files/Impact_of_the_Undocumented_Workforce.pdf#page=69

Hoffmaster, D., Murphy, G., McFadden, S., & Griswold, M. (2011). *Police and immigration: How chiefs are leading their communities through the challenges.* Retrieved from Police Executive Research Forum website: http://www.policeforum.org/library/immigration/PERFImmigrationReportMarch2011.pdf

International Association of Chiefs of Police. (2007). *Police chief's guide to immigration issues.* Retrieved from http://www.theiacp.org/documents/pdfs/Publications/PoliceChiefsGuidetoImmigration.pdf

Lopez, M. H., & Livingston, G. (2009). *Hispanics and the criminal justice system: Low confidence, high exposure.* Retrieved from Pew Research Center website: http://pewresearch.org/pubs/1182/hispanic-confidence-in-criminal-justice-system-low

Lopez, M. H., & Minushkin, S. (2008). *2008 National Survey of Latinos: Hispanics see their situation in U.S. deteriorating.* Retrieved from Pew Research Center website: http://www.pewhispanic.org/2008/09/18/2008-national-survey-of-latinos-hispanics-see-their-situation-in-us-deteriorating-oppose-key-immigration-enforcement-measures

Martinez, R., & Lee, M. (2000). On immigration and crime. In G. LaFree, R. J. Bursik Jr., J. F. Short Jr., & R. B. Taylor (Eds.), *The nature of crime: Continuity and change* (Vol. 1, pp. 485–524). Washington, DC: National Institute of Justice. Retrieved from https://www.ncjrs.gov/criminal_justice2000/vol_1/02j.pdf

Menjivar, C., & Bejarano, C. (2004). Latino immigrants' perceptions of crime and police authorities in the United States: A case study from the Phoenix metropolitan area. *Ethnic and Racial Studies, 27*(1), 120–148.

Morenoff, J. D., & Astor, A. (2006). Immigrant assimilation and crime: Generational differences in youth violence in Chicago. In R. Martinez Jr. & A. Valenzuela Jr. (Eds.), *Immigration and crime: Race, ethnicity, and violence* (pp. 36–63). New York, NY: New York University Press.

National Immigration Forum. (2010). *Deficits, lawsuits, diminished public safety: Your state can't afford SB 1070*. Retrieved from http://www.immigrationforum.org/images/uploads/2010/SB1070Report.pdf

National Immigration Law Center. http://www.nilc.org

Nelson, L., Schlatter, E., & Beirich, H. (2011). *When Mr. Kobach comes to town: Nativist laws and the communities they damage*. Retrieved from Southern Poverty Law Center website: http://www.splcenter.org/sites/default/files/downloads/publication/Kobach_Comes_to_Town.pdf

Nguyen, M. T., & Gill, H. (2010, February). *The 287(g) program: The costs and consequences of local immigration enforcement in North Carolina communities*. Chapel Hill, NC: University of North Carolina at Chapel Hill Latino Migration Project, Institute for the Study of the Americas and the Center for Global Initiatives. Retrieved from http://www.welcometheimmigrant.org/storage/287g_report_final.pdf

Perez, T. E. (2011, December 15). *United States' investigation of Maricopa County sheriff's office*. Retrieved from http://www.azcentral.com/ic/pdf/1215arpaioletter.pdf

Perryman Group. (2008). *An essential resource: An analysis of the economic impact of undocumented workers on business activity in the U.S. with estimated effects by state and by industry*. Waco, TX: Author.

Police Foundation. (2008). *The role of local police: Striking a balance between immigration enforcement and civil liberties*. Washington, DC: Author.

Romero, M., & Serag, M. (2005). Violation of Latino civil rights resulting from INS and local police's use of race, culture and class profiling: The case of the Chandler Roundup in Arizona. *Cleveland State Law Review, 52*(1 & 2), 75–95.

Rumbaut, R. G., Gonzales, R. G., Komaie, G., Morgan, C. V., & Tafoya-Estrada, R. (2006). Immigration and incarceration: Patters and predictors of imprisonment among first- and second-generation young adults. In R. Martinez Jr. & A. Valenzuela Jr. (Eds.), *Immigration and crime: Race, ethnicity, and violence* (pp. 64–89). New York, NY: New York University Press.

Seghetti, L. M., Vina, S. R., & Ester, K. (2006, August 14). *Enforcing immigration law: The role of state and local law enforcement* (Congressional Research Service Report for Congress, order code RL32270). Washington, DC: Congressional Research Service.

Southern Policy Law Center. (2009). *Under siege: Life for low income Latinos in the South*. Retrieved from http://www.splcenter.org/get-informed/publications/under-siege-life-for-low-income-latinos-in-the-south

Tramonte, L. (2011). *Debunking the myth of "sanctuary cities": Community policing policies protect American communities*. Retrieved from Immigration Policy Center website: http://immigrationpolicy.org/special-reports/debunking-myth-sanctuary-cities

U.S. Government Accountability Office. (2009). *Immigration enforcement: Better controls needed over program authorizing state and local enforcement of federal immigration laws*. Washington, DC: Author. Retrieved from http://www.gao.gov/products/GAO-09-109

Villazor, R. C. (2008). What is a "sanctuary"? *SMU Law Review, 61*, 133.

Waslin, M. (2003). Immigration enforcement by local police: The impact on the civil rights of Latinos. *National Council of La Raza Issue Brief*, No. 9. Retrieved from http://www.nclr.org/images/uploads/publications/1390_file_IB9_ImmEnforce_CivRgts.pdf

Wesley, S., & Frydl, K. (Eds.). (2004). *Fairness and effectiveness in policing: The evidence*. Washington, DC: The National Academies Press.

Jessica Saunders, Carl Matthies, and Nelson Lim

Use of the Term "Illegal Alien"

POINT: If someone is not a citizen of this country (an "alien") and not here legally, they are by definition an "illegal alien." Adopting a different euphemism only serves to normalize what is in fact a criminal situation.

Eric A. Ruark, Federation for American Immigration Reform (FAIR)

COUNTERPOINT: The term "illegal alien" is inherently pejorative and serves to criminalize the entire person. Alternative, more accurate terms exist and should be used, such as "unauthorized immigrant" or "undocumented worker."

Shoba Sivaprasad Wadhia, Penn State Law

Introduction

It is telling that, in the midst of broad debates over immigration, there is even a debate over what term to use. What do we call foreign nationals in the United States illegally, either without proper authorization by the federal government or in violation of the terms of a visa? Labeling this debate as a mere semantic argument, however, would belie the serious political and philosophical differences that inform it.

This debate is, at its core, a coded discussion about the appropriate penalty for being in the United States without proper authorization, and it is informed by large differences over the relevant conceptual framework for understanding illegal immigration. These differences, in turn, inform the extent to which illegal immigration is seen as a serious infraction warranting serious penalties.

One side argues that the term "illegal alien" is a proper technical term deriving from federal law, which defines any noncitizen in the United States as an "alien." It follows, therefore, that any "alien" in the country illegally is an "illegal alien." The other side argues that the term "illegal alien" is not defined in federal law, is dehumanizing, and categorizes a person rather than an act. These two points of view are elaborated in this chapter.

Those who argue for the appropriateness of the term "illegal alien" view the decision to be in the United States in violation of its immigration laws as a serious act deserving serious consequences. Illegal immigration is understood to be the result of individual decisions to violate U.S. law; the reasons for that violation are seen as irrelevant in a society governed by the rule of law. The current extent of illegal immigration is understood as a predictable consequence of lax enforcement of immigration laws combined with the aftermath of the 1986 Immigration Reform and Control Act (IRCA). This law provided a one-time mechanism for illegal immigrants to shed that status by meeting certain conditions and embark on a path to citizenship. Opponents refer to this provision as "amnesty" and argue that it only served to foster further illegal immigration. Attempts to use other terms in reference to those in the country in violation of its immigration laws are seen as a deliberate attempt to frame public debate so as to minimize the seriousness of the crime, with the objective of generating public support for another "amnesty" and for revisions to U.S. immigration laws that would allow for expanded immigration.

Those who argue against using the term "illegal alien" believe illegal immigration to be a predictable consequence of flaws in the structure of the U.S. immigration system and of a mismatch between that system and economic and demographic forces on both sides of the border that drive migration. This view implicitly holds the immigration system itself, rather than individual (illegal) immigrants, as primarily responsible for illegal immigration. Further, the plight of impoverished migrants seeking a better life for themselves and their families elicits a compassionate response that tends toward forgiveness of the violation of immigration laws. In other words, this view downplays the seriousness of illegal status per se and views the solution as lying in reforms to the system, which must include enumerated penalties that, once satisfied, result in legal status for the estimated 10–12 million immigrants currently in the United States illegally, thus providing a "path to citizenship."

POINT

The term "alien" means any person not a citizen or national of the United States.

—United States Code, Title 8, Section 1101(a)(3)

An illegal alien . . . is any alien (1) whose most recent entry into the United States was without inspection, or (2) whose most recent admission to the United States was as a nonimmigrant and—(A) whose period of authorized stay as a nonimmigrant expired, or (B) whose unlawful status was known to the Government, before the date of the commission of the crime for which the alien is convicted.

—United States Code, Title 8, Section 1365(b)

It is not difficult to understand why it is not only appropriate but also correct to use the term "illegal alien" to refer to a person in the United States illegally. Under federal law, any non-U.S. citizen is an alien. An alien can either be lawfully admitted or illegally present in the United States. A lawfully admitted alien can be a legal permanent resident (immigrant), a temporary resident (also known as a nonimmigrant, and often a guest worker or student), a refugee, or an individual who has been paroled into the United States under various designations. Aliens who have entered the United States without permission, or who have violated the terms of their admission, are identified under the law as illegal aliens. That is a fact, not an issue for debate.

It is also a fact that, according to U.S. law, it is a crime to enter the United States without permission. The first offense is a misdemeanor, the second a felony. It is true that most violations of immigration law are dealt with in a civil court and not in a criminal court. An immigration judge is really an administrative adjudicator who has authority under the Department of Justice's Executive Office for Immigration Review (EOIR) to determine whether or not an individual is deportable under U.S. law. This procedure for handling immigration cases is designed to speed up the process of deportation; it should not be interpreted as an indication that illegal immigration is not a criminal violation. Because illegal aliens are not U.S. citizens, they are not entitled to the full panoply of rights and privileges under the Constitution as are citizens. Thus, they can be held subject to a nonjudicial ruling instead of a jury trial for their criminal violation of immigration law.

Despite the clarity in the U.S. Code on proper terminology, what is known in legal parlance as the "term of art," a political movement has arisen with the objective of substituting euphemism for precision. A variety of motivations underlie this effort, but regardless of intent, the goal is the same. An insistence on alternate terms, such as "undocumented worker," represents a deliberate avoidance of the central and unavoidable fact that millions of people are illegally residing in the United States, in direct violation of democratically enacted and popularly supported law. It is not that those who seek to replace the term are necessarily arguing that illegal aliens should receive amnesty and remain in the United States; it is rather that they are treating violations of immigration law as wholly irrelevant to the debate. Those who object to the use of the term "illegal alien" appear to believe that if they can convince the American public that illegal immigration is not really illegal, then amnesty is no longer amnesty, and enforcing immigration law is unnecessary.

Advocates of immigration enforcement often ask amnesty proponents, "What part of illegal don't you understand?" This may be simplistic, but it highlights the frustrations that many Americans have when it comes to the immigration debate. No meaningful dialogue can occur if both sides cannot agree on the meaning of certain essential terms. As long as one side in the immigration debate insists on substituting "undocumented" or "unauthorized" immigrant in place of "illegal alien," the discussion will remain at an impasse. Americans, while generous and forgiving, are not about to simply brush aside the fact that millions of foreigners are living and working in the country illegally, and they will not accept another mass amnesty that rewards illegal aliens and the employers who profit from hiring them at the expense of the American people.

HISTORY OF THE TERM

The manufactured controversy over the term "illegal alien" ignores not only U.S. law but also historical precedent. The origin of the term dates back to ancient Rome, which had a highly developed concept of citizenship, and the language to describe it. The modern usage of the term is first found in fourteenth-century France and was incorporated into Anglo-Saxon common law from which the U.S. legal system is descended. The U.S. government has referred to noncitizens as aliens for over two centuries.

The Immigration Reform and Control Act (IRCA) of 1986, that granted amnesty to over 3 million illegal aliens, along with a promise of a secured border and penalties for employers who hire illegal workers, forms the basis of the current immigration enforcement code. While IRCA does mention "unauthorized aliens," this is in reference to non-U.S. citizens who do not have authorization to work in the United States. Aliens may be in the country legally but without permission to work. But as IRCA makes clear, an alien in the country in violation of immigration law is an "illegal alien." As the legal scholar Patrick Charles has pointed out, in Title V of IRCA, which deals with law enforcement, there are five references to "illegal alien," while the terms "unauthorized" or "undocumented" are not mentioned once.

A quarter of a century later, there is no ambiguity in the law over the correct term to apply to a foreign national in the United States illegally. However, there is a political movement afoot for another amnesty, this time covering over 10 million illegal aliens. Part of this effort is an attempt to redefine the terms of the immigration debate, which ends up causing vagueness and confusion. A telling illustration of this occurred when Supreme Court Justice Sonia Sotomayor correctly used the term "illegal aliens" in court proceedings during *Chamber of Commerce of the United States v. Whiting* (2011), and then promptly reverted to "undocumented aliens," which was a departure from her use of the term "undocumented immigrant" in a previous case. Justice Sotomayor may be able to raise a political argument about whether illegal aliens should be referred to as undocumented, but that argument would not be grounded in the law. Creating such ambiguities, especially at the highest level of the justice system, does a great disservice to the rule of law and undermines the public's faith in the institutions of government.

THE CASE AGAINST

There are a few principal arguments made against the use of illegal alien. They are simplistic, transparently flawed, and easily refutable. The first is that no human being is illegal, which one must suppose is tautologically true. It is also a red herring and a straw man argument, because the term is not "illegal human" or "illegal person" but instead a precise legal term that identifies a person who is in violation of democratically enacted, constitutionally authorized, and ethically and morally justified immigration law. To say that because no human is illegal no one can be an illegal alien is illogical. To identify someone as an illegal alien does not banish that person from the human race; it identifies an individual who does not have the legal right to reside in the United States.

Another oft-employed argument is to claim that illegal aliens just lack the proper "papers," and thus are not really illegal but "undocumented." The implication is that a person with documents was lucky enough to have somehow come into possession of a visa or a green card, and not that an alien who received these documents submitted to a process that complies with the requirements of entry into the United States, including a screening to check for health risks, a criminal and national security background check, and a determination that one has the means to avoid becoming a public charge. The term "undocumented" is also patently misleading, because illegal aliens as a group are certainly not lacking identification documents, only legitimate, legally obtained ones relating to their immigration status. Often, an illegal alien will purchase or manufacture false or stolen documents. According to Ronald Mortensen (2009) of the Center for Immigration Studies, as many as 75 percent of illegal aliens in the workforce are using fraudulent Social Security cards.

A sophomoric, but nevertheless popular argument is that aliens are from outer space, whereas most people in the United States "without papers" are from Mexico. An alien may technically come from another planet, which is why science fiction writers have distinguished them as "space aliens," but the correct term is *extraterrestrial*. If an extraterrestrial does enter the United States without permission—hopefully with no malign intentions against us Earth dwellers—it would also be considered an *illegal* alien.

THE "I" WORD

A website maintained by the Applied Research Center (ARC), a self-described "racial justice think tank," is called "Drop the I-Word" and is devoted to a campaign to stamp out the use of the term *illegal alien*. "The racially charged slur and related terms confuse the immigration debate [and] fuel violence," ARC claims, adding that while "people may be out of status for many reasons . . . that doesn't make them 'illegal.' No one should adopt dehumanizing terms that are racially charged, legally innacurate [*sic*] or deny people due process." The ARC suggests "accurate terms" for use in place of illegal alien, such as "undocumented immigrant," "unauthorized immigrant," and "NAFTA refugee."

The assertion that it is not legally accurate to identify a foreign national who is in violation of U.S. immigration law as an illegal alien is wholly false. So is the inference that "NAFTA refugee" is anything other than an invented designation implying that the United States is somehow responsible for illegal immigration as a result of being a co-signatory of the North American Free Trade Agreement (NAFTA) with Mexico and Canada. What's even worse than attempting to spread such blatant disinformation is the charge that those who do use appropriate language are racist and provocateurs of violence against immigrants. Just as genuine racists deserve repudiation, so, too, do those who falsely accuse their political opponents of racism in an effort to discredit and silence them.

This type of inflammatory and defamatory rhetoric is not the work of fringe groups. The ARC is part of an umbrella organization that is funded with millions of dollars from the Ford Foundation, Tides Center, the Annie E. Casey Foundation, and George Soros, as are allied groups such as the Mexican American Legal Defense and Education Fund, National Council of La Raza, Center for America Progress, Southern Poverty Law Center, America's Voice, and National Immigration Forum. These groups are well connected politically to the Obama White House and on Capitol Hill. Whatever position one takes in the immigration debate, coordinated campaigns to stifle legitimate debate over immigration policy are unpardonable.

ILLEGAL IMMIGRATION IS ALSO ABOUT IMMIGRATION

To argue, as some do, that one must enter the United States illegally or remain illegally in the United States because there is not a legal avenue open for immigrants to come to the United States is to ignore the 1.1 million legal permanent residents that the United States has admitted annually over the past decade. According to immigration statistics from the Department of Homeland Security, Mexico, the country that has the most illegal aliens living in the United States, also sends the most immigrants through legal channels. It is true that not everyone who wants to come to the United States is allowed in, but in order to accommodate all who would like to immigrate, the United States would have to admit tens of millions, if not hundreds of millions, of people every year. U.S. immigration policy is very generous; in fact, it is more generous than the rest of the world's countries combined. In order for Americans to continue to be welcoming to immigrants, they must have the assurance that the system has integrity and that foreigners are not coming to the country illegally. The goal of U.S. immigration policy, first and foremost, is to benefit the American people. Advocates for illegal aliens seem not to understand this fundamental principle; they seem to think immigration policy should be recast to benefit those who came to the United States illegally.

One of the main reasons for having an immigration system that limits immigration and a legal system that enforces those limits is that the resources of the United States are not limitless—a point that advocates of mass immigration fail to acknowledge. The population of the United States is growing rapidly because of immigration—directly through the arrival of immigrants themselves, and indirectly through the children born in the United States to immigrants. The population of the United States has grown rapidly since the immigration laws were changed in 1965 to dramatically expand immigration levels. According to the U.S. Census Bureau, between 1970 and 2010 the U.S. population grew by more than 105 million people, or by over 50 percent.

At the same time that the United States was growing so rapidly, native-born women were having children at a rate that would have led to population stability if not for increased immigration. Census Bureau data reveals that a new immigrant is added to the U.S. population every 45 seconds, and immigrant women on average have higher fertility rates than do native-born women, helping grow the overall population by one person every 12 seconds. This rate of population growth is potentially putting the United States on the path to having a population of a billion residents by the end of this century. This is simply too many people, and reducing immigration levels must begin with the enforcement of immigration laws, not rewarding those who have come here illegally, and thus encouraging more illegal immigration. U.S. overpopulation is not something that can be brushed aside as insignificant or irrelevant to the discussion of illegal immigration.

WHY ALL THE FUSS?

In addition to the looming problem of immigration-driven overpopulation, there are other concerns that should disquiet all Americans. The battle to describe illegal aliens as "unauthorized," "undocumented," or simply "immigrants" would have profound consequences if successful. The semantic wrangling over the term illegal alien goes beyond whether these words are proper to use. Underlying the "newspeak" by defenders of illegal aliens is the question of whether the United States will remain a sovereign, independent nation, governed by the rule of law and subject to constitutional constraints. U.S. immigration laws were enacted by Congress, and the executive branch has the responsibility to enforce them, not to implement them as the President sees fit. Those who deny that immigration laws are binding are declaring that there should be inequality under the law, where some groups are not only immune from compliance but should benefit from their offense.

To argue that an illegal alien is not, or should not be, "illegal" is to attack the very foundations of this republic as a nation founded on the principle of respect for the law, and it is a denial of the right to self-determination of the American people. A fundamental principle of sovereignty is that the people of any country have the absolute right to defend their borders and to admit or deny admittance to others according to their discretion. Foreigners have no right to come to the United States unless, under law, they have permission from the U.S. government in the exercise of the power conferred on it by the American people. It is not extremist, racist, or anti-immigrant for Americans to expect their national borders to be secure, or that those who violate immigration laws should be held accountable. Those who challenge the use of the term "illegal alien" to identify those who violate immigration law fail to recognize that borders are more than just lines on a map, and that laws are more than just words on paper.

CONCLUSION

There are many words that can be used to marginalize or demean a person. "Alien" and "illegal alien" are not among them. There is nothing insulting or dehumanizing about using the term *alien* to indicate an individual is a noncitizen. Likewise, it is perfectly fitting to acknowledge that an alien who is residing illegally in the United States has broken the law. It has only been recently, within the political context of the current immigration debate, that proper and unambiguous language has come under attack as inaccurate or derogatory.

What might appear at first glance to be a minor semantic disagreement is crucial to understanding what is at the very heart of the contemporary debate over illegal immigration and "comprehensive immigration reform." The words used in a public discussion determine the framework of that discussion, and the consequence of deliberate ambiguity or reckless provocation is a diminished civic discourse. Referring to an illegal alien as an undocumented immigrant, or any other such euphonious alternative, is ultimately the denial that a foreigner is in the United States in violation of the law. This is the first step in denying that the American people have the right to determine who is admitted and under what conditions.

REFERENCES AND FURTHER READING

Charles, P. J. (2010). Much ado about the Supreme Court using the term "illegal aliens" [Web log post]. Charles Law and History Blog. Available from http://patrickjcharles.wordpress.com/2010/12/10/much-ado-about-about-the-supreme-court-using-the-term-illegal-aliens

Color Lines. (n.d.). *Drop the I-word*. Retrieved from http://colorlines.com/droptheiword

Department of Homeland Security. (2011). *Yearbook of immigration statistics*. Alexandria, VA: National Technical Information Service. Available from http://www.dhs.gov/files/statistics/publications/yearbook.shtm

Hardin, G. (1995). *The immigration dilemma: Avoiding the tragedy of the commons*. Washington, DC: Federation for American Immigration Reform.

Krikorian, M. (2008). *The new case against immigration: Both legal and illegal*. New York, NY: Sentinel.

Martin, J., & Ruark, E. A. (2010). *The fiscal burden of illegal immigration on United States taxpayers.* Retrieved from Federation for American Immigration Reform website: http://www.fairus.org/site/DocServer/USCostStudy_2010.pdf?docID=4921

McCarthy, E. (1992). *A colony of the world: The United States today: America's senior statesman warns his countrymen.* New York, NY: Hippocrene Books.

Mortensen, R. W. (2009, June). *Backgrounder: Illegal, but not undocumented: Identity theft, document fraud, and illegal employment.* Retrieved from Center for Immigration Studies website: http://www.cis.org/articles/2009/back809.pdf

Pevnick, R., Cafaro, P. J., & Risse, M. (2008, Fall). An exchange: The morality of immigration. *Ethics & International Affairs, 22*(3). Retrieved from http://www.carnegiecouncil.org/resources/journal/22_3/exchange/001.html

Ruark, E. A., & Graham, M. (2011, May). *Immigration, poverty, and low-wage earners: The harmful effect of unskilled immigrants on American workers.* Retrieved from Federation for American Immigration Reform website: http://www.fairus.org/site/DocServer/poverty_rev.pdf?docID=5621

Eric A. Ruark

COUNTERPOINT

This essay examines the use of the terms "alien," "illegal," and "illegal alien." It will show that use of the term "illegal alien" is problematic for a number of reasons, not least because it is subject to many definitions that are often inaccurate. Moreover, even if there is agreement on the scope of the term, it cannot be fully understood without studying the individual characteristics of those defined by this term, as well as the role of the government in sustaining an outdated immigration structure that creates powerful incentives for illegal immigration. Finally, this essay will show that the term "illegal alien" is dehumanizing because it modifies not just a single action but the entire person.

BACKGROUND

The legal framework for immigration includes a statute designed by Congress and a lengthy set of regulations and policies created by various units in the executive branch of government. The Immigration and Nationality Act (INA) is the statute passed by Congress in 1952 (and amended many times thereafter) that articulates the technical details and definitions of immigration law. The INA draws lines between those wishing to come to the United States temporarily (student, visitor, scholar, etc.) and those seeking to immigrate permanently, often on the basis of a family or employer-employee relationship. The various visa categories identified in the INA can be confusing, but for the purposes of this essay what is important is that many people seeking permanent residence in the United States are subject to numerical quotas or country-based limitations, which over the years have resulted in long wait times for noncitizens, even when they are legally eligible for a visa. Moreover, the law provides for only 5,000 permanent visas for persons performing essential work such as migrant labor and hospitality services, which means that many noncitizens living in the United States providing this work without specific authorization under the immigration laws live "in the shadows."

Many immigration enforcement functions, including arrest, detention, and deportation, as well as immigration "service" functions, such as the processing of green card applications, asylum applications, and citizenship applications, are housed in different parts of a cabinet level agency known as the Department of Homeland Security (DHS). Individuals who are apprehended by DHS for deportation or "removal" are often repatriated "voluntarily," sometimes removed speedily, and other times placed in "removal proceedings" before the immigration courts. This means that only a fraction of the people facing removal actually see a courtroom or judge before they are physically expelled or granted some form of relief from removal. The immigration court system has lower and appellate levels of review and rests within the Department of Justice. The judges who preside over removal cases do not enjoy unfettered discretion or independence, and in many cases they are required to issue removal orders against people who have compelling personal traits or circumstances, such as a lucrative job or a family member who is a U.S. citizen.

DEFINITIONS IN DICTIONARY AND IMMIGRATION CODE

The *Merriam-Webster Online Dictionary* defines *illegal* as "not according to or authorized by law," or "not sanctioned by official rules (as of a game)." The word *alien* is defined as "belonging or relating to another person, place, or thing," or "relating, belonging, or owing allegiance to another country or government." These terms, as well as "illegal alien," have been used by legislators, judges, government employees, and journalists in meaningful ways, as will be discussed herein.

The Immigration and Nationality Act (INA) defines *alien* as "all people who are not nationals" of the United States, and it goes on to utilize the term fruitfully throughout the code. On the other hand, the term "illegal alien" appears nowhere in the code. The words *alien* and *illegal* appear in the governing regulations that interpret sections contained in the INA and a number of documents created by the agencies responsible for applying the INA. These documents include, but are not limited to, written opinions by the immigration court or Board of Immigration Appeals, policies and news releases posted by the Department of Homeland Security, and decisions published by the Administrative Appeals Office within DHS. For example, the DHS website contains facts about its enforcement activities, including a record number of removals of "illegal aliens" in 2010—over 392,000 removals nationwide. These sources also contain the terms "unauthorized alien," "undocumented alien," "criminal alien," and "fugitive" to describe noncitizens residing in the United States without legal authority.

USE OF THE TERM "ILLEGAL ALIEN" BY THE U.S. SUPREME COURT

The terms "illegal alien," "alien," and "illegal" appear in judicial opinions that involve immigration matters, including many decisions issued by the U.S. Supreme Court. To illustrate, consider the noteworthy case of *Hoffman Plastic Compounds, Inc. v. NLRB* (2002), which involved an immigrant named Jose Castro who relied on a friend's birth certificate to gain employment at a plastics factory called Hoffman Plastic Compounds. Castro and other workers were terminated from their jobs after the company learned about their union activities. Concluding that the factory had violated the law by firing Castro and others "in order to rid itself of known union supporters," the National Labor Relations Board (NLRB) ordered the factory to pay Castro back wages. The Supreme Court disagreed, however, and held that unauthorized workers like Castro were not entitled to back wages. Writing for the majority, Chief Justice William Rehnquist used the terms "illegal workers" and "illegal aliens" several times. The use of the terms was not limited to the majority opinion but was also used multiple times by Justice Stephen Breyer in his dissenting opinion. For example, Justice Breyer remarked, "The Court has recognized these considerations in stating that the labor laws must apply to illegal aliens." Thus, the term "illegal alien" has been used by the Court even when offering a "pro-immigrant" opinion.

Justice Sonia Sotomayor made news when she used the terms "undocumented worker" and "undocumented immigrants" instead of "illegal aliens" or "illegal immigrants" in the 2009 case of *Mohawk Industries v. Carpenter*. As reported by *The New York Times*, a legal database revealed that Justice Sotomayor was the first justice to use the term "undocumented immigrant" in the history of decisions by the Supreme Court. Sotomayor later used the term "illegal alien(s)" several times in the 2011 case *Chamber of Commerce of the United States v. Whiting*, but she was citing previous cases in which the Supreme Court had used the phrase.

USE OF TERM "ILLEGAL ALIEN" BY MEDIA AND SPECIAL INTEREST GROUPS

In light of the regular use of the terms "alien," "illegal," and "illegal alien" in legal documents and by the U.S. Supreme Court, it might seem reasonable for journalists, policy pundits, and the public to use the same terms. In many cases, media outlets make conscious decisions about which phrases to use in their publications. For example, *USA Today* employs the term "illegal immigrants" to describe noncitizens in the United States without authorization. As with many other mainstream papers that use the same term, *USA Today* does not use the words "illegal" or "illegals" as nouns. Similarly, the *Associated Press* uses the term "illegal immigrants" but avoids using "illegal alien" or "illegal" as nouns. *The New York Times* also uses the term "illegal immigrant." Ruben Navarrette, a columnist for the *San Diego Union Tribune*, supports the use of "illegal immigrant" but has written that he believes there are "bigger fish to fry" than the terms used in the immigration debate.

With somewhat different motivations than mainstream journalists, special interest groups, and immigration restrictionists in particular, use the terms "illegal alien" and "illegal" to advance positions that oppose any form of immigration, legal or otherwise. Professor Kris Kobach, a former advisor to Attorney General John Ashcroft and the architect of numerous immigration programs aimed at penalizing immigrants in the name of 9/11 security, relies on a discrete subsection of the U.S. Code to support the use of illegal alien. But most anti-immigration organizations, among them Numbers USA, Federation for American Immigration Reform (FAIR), and the Center for Immigration Studies, defend the term with the catchphrase, "What part of illegal don't you understand?"

THE TERM "ILLEGAL ALIEN" IS INACCURATE

The term "illegal alien" is not defined in the Immigration and Nationality Act, and for this reason alone is considered inaccurate to some scholars and immigration pundits. Beyond this absence, it is difficult to find the right fit or composition of people that accurately fall within the scope of the term. For some, it includes anyone who entered the United States without a valid entry or admission—those who "snuck" over the U.S.-Mexico border for example. Others apply the term to most of the population in the United States that is in violation of the immigration laws. In technical terms, this would include both the unlawful border crossers and those who entered the country with a valid visa or through legal means but then did not maintain their status or let it expire. A third but less popularized segment of the potentially unauthorized population comprises lawful permanent residents (LPRs) or green card holders who engage in conduct that would warrant an immigration charge. Applying the term "illegal alien" to this group is inaccurate in some cases, the government must first prove by *clear and convincing evidence* that the legal permanent resident is in fact deportable. Moreover, the term "illegal alien" is problematic in all three cases because immigration status can change when the noncitizen applies for an immigration benefit or relief from removal under the law.

A related problem is that the label "illegal alien" follows a person even when he or she is technically regularized to a legal status at a point in the future, because those who use the label keep using it even after a person achieves valid status. As the Supreme Court said in *Plyler v. Doe* (1982), "the illegal alien of today may well be the legal alien of tomorrow." For example, a man who enters the U.S. without a valid visa may later be identified as a beneficiary on a valid visa petition filed by his U.S. citizen wife. Similarly, individuals who enter on a business visa from a war-torn country where they face harm could let their visas expire and then pursue refugee protection by applying for asylum. Finally, a green card holder who is placed in removal proceedings because of a past shoplifting conviction might be eligible for a discretionary waiver based on hardship to that person's U.S. citizen family or the date of the crime in question. If a person spends a short period of time without legal justification and then regularizes to a valid immigration status based on a decision by the immigration agency or a judge, it is inaccurate to continue to label the person an illegal alien. It is also inaccurate to describe the entire population of noncitizens living in the United States without authority under immigration laws "undocumented," because many of the individuals described above, namely those who enter the United States and let a visa expire, or green card holders who have a run-in with the law, did enter the United States with "documents."

The term "alien" is formally and broadly described in the immigration code. Consequently, it would be difficult to argue that using the term to describe persons who are not citizens or nationals of the United States is wholly inaccurate. On the other hand, the law specifies that the government bears the burden of proving "alienage" for noncitizens present in the United States without being admitted or paroled. Moreover, looking just at the dictionary definition of "alien," it could be asserted that persons living in the United States without a legal immigration status or pending application for relief belong to an "other place" or owe their allegiances to "another country." On the contrary, many people living in the United States without a legal immigration status have significant ties to the country, live in "mixed" households where a child or spouse may be a U.S. citizen, and contribute to the U.S. society in meaningful ways.

One might argue that people with such intimate ties and family relationships would nevertheless be eligible to apply for some form of legal relief from removal, such as cancellation of removal or a waiver based on hardship to a legal loved one. But the INA contains limited offerings for people who present compelling or equitable reasons. For example, it is possible for Jose, a noncitizen who has lived in the United States for 10 years, is a financial breadwinner to his family, is husband to a U.S. citizen and the father to three U.S. citizen children, and is a regular patron of his local church, to be ordered deported or removed from the United States because he used an irregular social security number to work. Jose may disagree that he owes allegiance to "another country" or that after 10 years of living in the United States he associates with "another place."

EXAMINING INDIVIDUAL CHARACTERISTICS OF THE "ILLEGAL ALIEN" POPULATION

Even if there is agreement regarding who falls within the illegal alien population, it is important to explore why and how they got there. For discussion purposes, "illegal alien" is defined here as any person who is in the United States without a valid immigration status. Roughly, this would include both those who entered the country surreptitiously and those who entered on a valid visa but then let that visa expire. Nonetheless, a level of tension still exists for people like Jose. In his examination of "undocumented immigrants" through the lens of a "lawbreaker" versus a "resident," Stephen Legomsky (2009) found that the vast majority of noncitizens residing in the United States without authorization have been in the country for several years. Relying on social science research, Legomsky concluded that unauthorized immigrants behave far more like other residents than like other lawbreakers.

This tension is even more pronounced when considering the case of "DREAMers," or students who would potentially benefit from the Development, Relief, and Education for Alien Minors (DREAM) Act. The DREAM Act is a piece of legislation that has been introduced in many Congresses and, in a nutshell, would provide a legal gateway for people brought to the United States as children by their parents without a lawful status who pursue higher education or enter the military. The stories of individuals who would benefit from the DREAM Act are compelling, in part because they came to the United States at such a tender age, and only years after growing up in the United States—where they have developed great character and intellectual curiosity—discovered they were in the country "without documents." In many cases, the DREAM Act students have been forced to build campaigns around their immigration story in order to receive a temporary reprieve from the U.S. government.

Consider as an example the case of Mandeep Chahal, a graduate of Los Altos High School in California, where she was voted "Most Likely to Save the World." Eligible for the DREAM Act, Mandeep is an honors pre-med student at University of California–Davis, pursuing a degree in neurology, physiology, and behavior. In a speech before members of Congress and advocates on Capitol Hill in June 2011, Mandeep remarked, "I came to this country at age six knowing nothing but the alphabet and phrases like 'thank you' and 'please' that my mom had taught me. Today, I stand before you as an honors college student on her way to med school. It's been 14 years since I walked into my first grade classroom, and I've come a long way since then." It would be difficult to conclude that Mandeep or the thousands of DREAMers in her shoes are aliens who belong to or owe their loyalties to another country.

WHO IS ACCOUNTABLE? GOVERNMENT INACTION ON IMMIGRATION

The Department of Homeland Security estimated the unauthorized immigrant population to be about 10.8 million in January 2010 (Hoefer, Rytina, & Baker, 2011). This is a legal crisis that requires a congressional response. However, the last time Congress created a legal vehicle for immigrant workers and family members living in the United States in contravention of the immigration laws was in 1990, more than 20 years ago.

To use a simple example, imagine a public university in Virginia operating on a 500-person quota for each incoming undergraduate class in the year 1978. As the population in Virginia, funds at the university, and the number of students in colleges and universities continues to grow, consider the implications of the university maintaining a 500-person quota 25 years later. Like this hypothetical university in Virginia, Congress has not changed the immigration system in more than 20 years, despite significant changes in migration. The frozen quota has created a class of illegal aliens who would have a legal means to transfer their status if Congress formulated an updated immigration system. Consequently, it is inappropriate to classify would-be beneficiaries of a legalization program as illegal aliens simply because of government inaction.

It is also important to examine the extent of resources Immigration and Customs Enforcement (ICE, a division of DHS) has to physically remove the entire "illegal alien" population (which under this definition does not include individuals who are in the process of applying for a waiver or relief from removal). According to the Department of Homeland Security, ICE has monies to remove 400,000 persons, or less than 4 percent of the illegal immigrant population per year. In response to this financial reality, and in the absence of broad congressional reforms, DHS has issued a flurry of memoranda on "prosecutorial discretion." Prosecutorial discretion refers to the immigration employee's decision to target an individual for removal even if he or she is technically without an immigration status or is "illegal." A June 2011 memorandum from the agency suggests that ICE officers and attorneys should refrain from enforcing immigration laws against individuals who are very young, elderly, have maintained long residence in the United States, show intellectual promise at a U.S. college, or are members of the military, among others. The memo was criticized as a "backdoor amnesty" from largely anti-immigrant politicians and ICE union members, who accused the executive branch of circumventing Congress. But the reality is that the immigration agency has provided similar guidance on prosecutorial discretion for more than 30 years, because it recognizes that even when the immigration system is "fixed" there are people who have built their lives and contributed generously to the nation, but nevertheless remain vulnerable to deportation.

Together, the existence of an outdated immigration system, the stated position of ICE on the importance of prosecutorial discretion, and the administration's own support for updating the immigration system really test the appropriateness of identifying potential beneficiaries of an updated immigration design as illegal aliens.

"ILLEGAL ALIEN" IS DEHUMANIZING

Finally, the term "illegal alien" is dehumanizing because it criminalizes the person, not just an action. Some scholars and journalists choose not to include the terms "alien" or "illegal alien" in their discourse because they convey qualities that extend beyond identification (e.g., "noncitizen") or a single act (e.g., entering the country without inspection). Such critics of these terms often draw analogies to driving over the speed limit. This infraction can sometimes result in a ticket and a fine, but people are not treated as second-class citizens for speeding, and the conduct is forgotten once the fine is paid for. Stephen Legomsky (2009) deems the term "illegal immigrant" degrading, and remarks, "You don't call a *person* illegal because he or she has violated a law. It would be like calling someone who speeds on the highway an 'illegal driver,' or even an 'illegal citizen'" (p. 29).

Restrictionists have even converted "illegal" into a noun, usually in the plural ("illegals"), as if one could sum up everything that constitutes a person by calling sole attention to his or her violation of the immigration laws. It's not just imprecise and illogical—it's utterly dehumanizing. Legal scholar and law school dean Kevin Johnson (1996–1997) has identified "illegal aliens" as the most damning term because it implies criminality, "thereby suggesting that the persons who fall in this category deserve punishment, not any kind of legal protection" (p. 8). Similarly, the scholar Gerald Neuman (1995) has criticized the term "illegal alien" because it implies that a person is a criminal, and that no legal duties are owed to him, effectively placing the person outside the scope of the legal system.

Critical of the negative connotations behind the phrase "illegal alien," *New York Times* editorial writer Lawrence Downes (2011) posits that the word "['illegal'] spreads, like a stain that cannot be washed out. It leaves its target diminished as a human, a lifetime member of a presumptive criminal class." The National Association of Hispanic Journalists has instructed journalists as follows: "Except in direct quotations, do not use the phrase illegal alien or the word alien, in copy or in headlines, to refer to citizens of a foreign country who have come to the U.S. with no documents that show they are legally entitled to visit, work or live here. Such terms are considered pejorative not only by those to whom they are applied but by many people of the same ethnic and national backgrounds who are in the U.S. legally."

Emotion behind the word "illegal" was refueled in June 2011 when Jose Antonio Vargas, a 30-year-old Pulitzer Prize–winning journalist, chronicled his immigration story in *The New York Times Magazine*. Vargas wrote about his life as a sixth grader in California, falling in love with his American home and life, and his passion for language. He discovered his immigration status while at the DMV at the age of 16. In the process of applying for his driver's permit, he learned that his green card was "fake." Despite his immigration status, Vargas proceeded to earn high achievements as a student, eminent journalist, and full-fledged American until he declared, "I'm done running. I'm exhausted. I don't want that life anymore." Vargas consciously used the term "undocumented immigrant" throughout his essay, leading to a proliferation of the term "undocumented immigrant" and a tweet from Vargas declaring, "Undocumented Immigrant is trending. So let's drop 'illegal' and 'alien.' No person is illegal or an alien."

Even legal immigrants have been described pejoratively in discussions about exclusionary rules and future migration. In the seminal 1889 Supreme Court case of *Chae Chan Ping v. United States* (the Chinese Exclusion case), Justice Stephen Field held, "To preserve its independence, and give security against foreign aggression and encroachment, is the highest duty of every nation, and to attain these ends nearly all other considerations are to be subordinated. It matters not in what form such aggression and encroachment come, whether from the foreign nation acting in its national character or from vast hordes of its people crowding in upon us." Terms such as "illegal aliens" and "vast hordes" produce negative images of people who are criminal, undeserving, and un-American. It is the repeated use of such terms that block solutions to problems with the legal immigration system. The positions put forth by immigration and race scholars, as well as journalists demonstrate the degree to which "alien," "illegal," and "illegal alien" are dehumanizing terms.

CONCLUSION

The narrative around "illegal alien" needs to change, not only to advance more accurate terminology, but also to build a more politically neutral ground when discussing solutions for fixing the U.S. immigration system. Some possible alternatives include "noncitizen worker," "noncitizens," "unauthorized immigrants," or terms that highlight family relationships, such as "spouse of a green card holder" or "parent of a U.S. citizen child." In the long run, the Supreme Court, lawmakers, and political leaders must change the terms they use to describe noncitizens by using more affirmative terminology and, where appropriate, discussing the lasting nature of a noncitizen's contribution.

REFERENCES AND FURTHER READING

Alexander, A. (2010, January 7). The debate over immigration language. *The Washington Post*. Retrieved from http://www.washing tonpost.com/wp-dyn/content/article/2011/01/07/AR2011010704597.html

Bazar E., & Brown, D. (2009, July 8). News roundtable: How we refer to immigrants. *USA Today*. Retrieved from http://www.usatoday .com/news/2009-07-08-immigration-roundtable_N.htm

Chacon, J. (2007). Unsecured borders: immigration restrictions, crime control and national security. *Connecticut Law Review, 39*, 1827–1891.

Chae Chan Ping v. United States, 130 U.S. 581 (1889).

Cunningham-Parmeter, K. (2011). Alien language: Immigration metaphors and the jurisprudence of otherness. *Fordham Law Review, 79*, 1545–1598. Retrieved from http://fordhamlawreview.org/assets/pdfs/Vol_79/9_Article-Cunningham_Mar.pdf

Downes, L. (2007, October 28). What part of "illegal" don't you understand? *The New York Times*. Retrieved from http://www .nytimes.com/2007/10/28/opinion/28sun4.html

Hoefer, M., Rytina, N., & Baker, B. C. (2011, February). *Estimates of the unauthorized immigrant population residing in the United States: January 2010*. Retrieved from Department of Homeland Security website: http://www.dhs.gov/xlibrary/assets/statistics/ publications/ois_ill_pe_2010.pdf

Hoffman Plastic Compounds, Inc. v. NLRB, 535 U.S. 137 (2002). Retrieved from http://www.law.cornell.edu/supct/html/00-1595 .ZO.html

Johnson, K. R. (1996–1997). "Aliens" and the U.S. immigration laws: The social and legal construction of nonpersons. *University of Miami Inter-American Law Review, 28*, 276–279.

Khan, M. (2011, June 30). Mandeep speaks in Washington [Blog]. Retrieved from America's Voice website: http://americasvoiceon line.org/page/content/Mandeep

Kobach, K. W. (2008). Reinforcing the rule of law: What states can and should do to reduce illegal immigration. *Georgetown Immigration Law Journal, 22*(3), 459–483.

Legomsky, S. H., (2009) Portraits of the undocumended immigrant: A dialogue. *Georgia Law Review, 44*(1), 65–226.

Legomsky, S. H., & Rodriguez, C. (2009). *Immigration and refugee law and policy* (5th ed.). New York, NY: Foundation Press.

Liptak, A. (2009, December 9). Sotomayor draws retort from a fellow justice. *The New York Times*. Retrieved from http://www .nytimes.com/2009/12/09/us/09sotomayor.html?_r=2&adxnnl=1&ref=us&adxnnlx=1311955902-QL3ySPVQgqOCx7DH 0ba85Q

Ly, P. (2011, July 1). *Vargas' essay renews attention to media's use of "illegal" & "undocumented."* Retrieved from Poynter Institute website: http://www.poynter.org/how-tos/newsgathering-storytelling/diversity-at-work/137806/vargas-essay-renews-attention- to-debate-about-medias-use-of-illegal-undocumented

Lyon, B. (2004). When more "security" equals less workplace safety: Reconsidering U.S. laws that disadvantage unauthorized workers. *University of Pennsylvania Journal of Labor and Employment Law, 6*(3), 571–611. Retrieved from http://www.law.upenn.edu/ journals/jbl/articles/volume6/issue3/Lyon6U.Pa.J.Lab.&Emp.L.571(2004).pdf

Morton, J. (2011, June 17). Exercising prosecutorial discretion consistent with the civil immigration enforcement priorities of the agency for the apprehension, detention, and removal of aliens [Memorandum]. Retrieved from U.S. Customs and Immigration Enforcement website: http://www.ice.gov/doclib/secure-communities/pdf/prosecutorial-discretion-memo.pdf

National Association of Hispanic Journalists. (2006). *NAHJ urges news media to stop using dehumanizing terms when covering immigration.* Retrieved from http://www.nahj.org/nahjnews/articles/2006/March/immigrationcoverage.shtml

National Public Radio. (2010, January 7). *Which is acceptable: "Undocumented" vs. "illegal" immigrant?* Retrieved from http://www.npr.org/templates/story/story.php?storyId=122314131

Neuman, G. L. (1995). Aliens as outlaws: Government services, Proposition 187, and the structure of equal protection doctrine. *UCLA Law Review, 42,* 1428.

Vargas, J. A. (2011, June 22). Outlaw: My life as an undocumented immigrant. *The New York Times Magazine.* Retrieved from http://www.nytimes.com/2011/06/26/magazine/my-life-as-an-undocumented-immigrant.html?pagewanted=all

Shoba Sivaprasad Wadhia

APPENDIX

Documents Highlighting Key Moments in U.S. Immigration History, 1924 to 2011

This appendix of documents is meant to give readers a brief overview of milestones in U.S. immigration policy over roughly the last century in U.S. history. Using politics as its lens, it distils the controversies and debates surrounding milestones in this history, including signing statements, political speeches, court opinions, and testimony.

Among the documents included are the text of Justice William Brennan's finding in the key Supreme Court case *Plyler v. Doe* (1982) and the signing statement of Governor Jan Brewer at the signing of controversial Arizona law S.B. 1070 in 2010. You'll also find official testimony from the Federation for American Immigration Reform (FAIR) and from the National Council of La Raza—two major organizations involved in the immigration debate.

The appendix also includes remarks from a number of U.S. presidents on immigration over the years. Interestingly, although the presidents hail from different periods and parties, many of their statements display a similar level of frustration about how to cope with the competing agendas surrounding immigration debates. From the reservations of President Calvin Coolidge at his signing of the Immigration Act of 1924 to President Harry Truman's transparently irritated veto of the McCarran–Walter Act, which he deemed "un-American"; from President George W. Bush's hopeful but doomed attempt to introduce reform in 2006, to President Barack Obama's 2011 assurance to El Paso voters that he will address immigration problems if given a second term, the documents Appendix demonstrates that even the leaders of the free world have long been vexed by the political complexities of American immigration.

★　★　★

President Calvin Coolidge's Statement on Signing the Immigration Act of 1924

The Immigration Act of 1924 set the quota for immigrants entering the United States at two percent of the total of any given nation's residents in the United States as reported in the 1890 census. The law was intended to further restrict immigration from Southern and Eastern Europe, from which people were emigrating in large numbers starting in the 1890s. It also aimed to curb immigration from Middle Eastern, East Asian, and Asian Indians. President Calvin Coolidge appended a statement to the bill upon signing it into law in which he expressed his disapproval of the bill's exclusion of Japanese immigrants.

Washington, DC

May 26, 1924

In signing this bill, which in its main features I heartily approve, I regret the impossibility of severing from it the exclusion provision, which in the light of existing law affects especially the Japanese.

I gladly recognize that the enactment of this provision does not imply any change in our sentiment of admiration and cordial friendship for the Japanese people, a sentiment which has had and will continue to have abundant manifestation.

The bill rather expresses the determination of the Congress to exercise its prerogative in defining by legislation the control of immigration, instead of leaving it to international arrangements. It should be noted that the bill exempts from the exclusion provision Government officials, those coming to this country as tourists or temporarily for business or pleasure, those in transit, seamen, those already resident here and returning from temporary absences, professors, ministers of religion, students, and those who enter solely to carry on trade in pursuance of existing treaty provisions.

But we have had for many years an understanding with Japan by which the Japanese Government has voluntarily undertaken to prevent the emigration of laborers to the U.S. and in view of this history relationship and of the feeling which inspired it would have been much better, in my judgment, and more effective in this actual control of immigration, if we had continued to invite that cooperation which Japan was ready to give and had thus avoided creating any ground for misapprehension by an unnecessary statutory enactment.

Unnecessary and Deplorable

That course would not have derogated from the authority of the Congress to deal with the question in any exigency requiring its action. There is scarcely any ground for disagreement as to the result we want, but this method of securing it is unnecessary and deplorable at this time.

If the exclusion provision stood alone, I should disapprove it without hesitation, if sought in this way at this time. But this bill is comprehensive measure dealing with the whole subject of immigration and setting up the necessary administrative machinery. The present quota act of 1921 will terminate on June 30 next. It is of great importance that a comprehensive measure should take its place and that the arrangements for its administration should be provided at once to avoid hardship and confusion.

I must therefore consider the bill as a whole and the imperative need of the country for legislation of this general character. For this reason, the bill is approved.

Source: Retrieved from http://onlinelibrary.wiley.com/doi/10.1111/j.1747–7379.2010.00844.x/pdf.

Comments on the Immigration and Nationality Act of 1952

The Immigration and Nationality Act of 1952, also known as McCarran–Walter Act, for its sponsors Senator Pat McCarran (D-Nevada) and Congressman Francis Walter (D-Pennsylvania), liberalized immigration from Asia and also increased the government's power to deport immigrants or naturalized citizens engaged in subversive activities or suspected of having Communist sympathies. President Harry S. Truman vetoed the law, considering it discriminatory and "un-American." His veto was overridden by a vote of 57 to 26 in the Senate and 278 to 113 in the House. Below are Truman's veto message followed by Senator McCarran's comments after the law's eventual passage.

President Harry S. Truman's Veto Message

June 25, 1952

Today, we are protecting ourselves as we were in 1924, against being flooded by immigrants from Eastern Europe. This is fantastic. . . . We do not need to be protected against immigrants from these countries, on the contrary we want to stretch out a helping hand, to save those who have managed to flee into Western Europe, to succor those who are brave enough to escape from barbarism, to welcome and restore them against the day when their countries will, as we hope, be free again. . . . these are only a few examples of the absurdity, the cruelty of carrying over into this year of 1952 the isolationist limitations of our 1924 law. In no other realm of our national life are we so hampered and stultified by the dead hand of the past, as we are in this field of immigration.

Senator Pat McCarran

March 2, 1953

I believe that this nation is the last hope of Western civilization and if this oasis of the world shall be overrun, perverted, contaminated or destroyed, then the last flickering light of humanity will be extinguished. I take no issue with those who would praise the contributions which have been made to our society by people of many races, of varied creeds and colors. America is indeed a joining together of many streams which go to form a mighty river which we call the American way. However, we have in the United States today hard-core, indigestible blocs which have not become integrated into the American way of life, but which, on the contrary are its deadly enemies. Today, as never before, untold millions are storming our gates for admission and those gates are cracking under the strain. The solution of the problems of Europe and Asia will not come through a transplanting of those problems en masse to the United States. . . . I do not intend to become prophetic, but if the enemies of this legislation succeed in riddling it to pieces, or in amending it beyond recognition, they will have contributed more to promote this nation's downfall than any other group since we achieved our independence as a nation.

Source: Both documents retrieved from http://www.state.gov/r/pa/ho/time/cwr/87719.htm.

President Lyndon B. Johnson's Speech at the Signing of the Immigration Reform Act of 1965

Known informally as the Hart–Celler Act, the law marked a radical shift in immigration policy, opening up immigration to foreigners from across the globe. Enacted during the height of the civil rights movement, it eliminated the so-called National Origins Formula that had been in place since the 1920s. The old quota system, which restricted immigration on the basis of national origin was replaced with two main criteria that continue to have resonance in our system today, emphasizing family reunification, on one hand, and the skill sets of would-be immigrants on the other. Although Hart–Celler was not perceived as a radical change in course—and indeed, Johnson downplays the significance of the policy shift in his speech—the law led to profound demographic changes in the make-up of the American body politic.

Liberty Island, New York

October 3, 1965

Mr. Vice President, Mr. Speaker, Mr. Ambassador Goldberg, distinguished Members of the leadership of the Congress, distinguished Governors and mayors, my fellow countrymen:

We have called the Congress here this afternoon not only to mark a very historic occasion, but to settle a very old issue that is in dispute. That issue is, to what congressional district does Liberty Island really belong—Congressman Farbstein or Congressman Gallagher? It will be settled by whoever of the two can walk first to the top of the Statue of Liberty.

This bill that we will sign today is not a revolutionary bill. It does not affect the lives of millions. It will not reshape the structure of our daily lives, or really add importantly to either our wealth or our power.

Yet it is still one of the most important acts of this Congress and of this administration.

For it does repair a very deep and painful flaw in the fabric of American justice. It corrects a cruel and enduring wrong in the conduct of the American Nation.

Speaker McCormack and Congressman Celler almost 40 years ago first pointed that out in their maiden speeches in the Congress. And this measure that we will sign today will really make us truer to ourselves both as a country and as a people. It will strengthen us in a hundred unseen ways.

I have come here to thank personally each Member of the Congress who labored so long and so valiantly to make this occasion come true today, and to make this bill a reality. I cannot mention all their names, for it would take much too long, but my gratitude—and that of this Nation—belongs to the 89th Congress.

We are indebted, too, to the vision of the late beloved President John Fitzgerald Kennedy, and to the support given to this measure by the then Attorney General and now Senator, Robert F. Kennedy.

In the final days of consideration, this bill had no more able champion than the present Attorney General, Nicholas Katzenbach, who, with New York's own "Manny" Celler, and Senator Ted Kennedy of Massachusetts, and Congressman Feighan of Ohio, and Senator Mansfield and Senator Dirksen constituting the leadership of the Senate, and Senator Javits, helped to guide this bill to passage, along with the help of the Members sitting in front of me today.

This bill says simply that from this day forth those wishing to immigrate to America shall be admitted on the basis of their skills and their close relationship to those already here.

This is a simple test, and it is a fair test. Those who can contribute most to this country—to its growth, to its strength, to its spirit—will be the first that are admitted to this land.

The fairness of this standard is so self-evident that we may well wonder that it has not always been applied. Yet the fact is that for over four decades the immigration policy of the United States has been twisted and has been distorted by the harsh injustice of the national origins quota system.

Under that system the ability of new immigrants to come to America depended upon the country of their birth. Only 3 countries were allowed to supply 70 percent of all the immigrants.

Families were kept apart because a husband or a wife or a child had been born in the wrong place.

Men of needed skill and talent were denied entrance because they came from southern or eastern Europe or from one of the developing continents.

This system violated the basic principle of American democracy—the principle that values and rewards each man on the basis of his merit as a man.

It has been un-American in the highest sense, because it has been untrue to the faith that brought thousands to these shores even before we were a country.

Today, with my signature, this system is abolished.

We can now believe that it will never again shadow the gate to the American Nation with the twin barriers of prejudice and privilege.

Our beautiful America was built by a nation of strangers. From a hundred different places or more they have poured forth into an empty land, joining and blending in one mighty and irresistible tide.

The land flourished because it was fed from so many sources—because it was nourished by so many cultures and traditions and peoples.

And from this experience, almost unique in the history of nations, has come America's attitude toward the rest of the world. We, because of what we are, feel safer and stronger in a world as varied as the people who make it up—a world where no country rules another and all countries can deal with the basic problems of human dignity and deal with those problems in their own way.

Now, under the monument which has welcomed so many to our shores, the American Nation returns to the finest of its traditions today.

The days of unlimited immigration are past.

But those who do come will come because of what they are, and not because of the land from which they sprung.

When the earliest settlers poured into a wild continent there was no one to ask them where they came from. The only question was: Were they sturdy enough to make the journey, were they strong enough to clear the land, were they enduring enough to make a home for freedom, and were they brave enough to die for liberty if it became necessary to do so?

And so it has been through all the great and testing moments of American history. Our history this year we see in Viet-Nam. Men there are dying—men named Fernandez and Zajac and Zelinko and Mariano and McCormick.

Neither the enemy who killed them nor the people whose independence they have fought to save ever asked them where they or their parents came from. They were all Americans. It was for free men and for America that they gave their all, they gave their lives and selves.

By eliminating that same question as a test for immigration the Congress proves ourselves worthy of those men and worthy of our own traditions as a Nation.

Asylum for Cuban Refugees

So it is in that spirit that I declare this afternoon to the people of Cuba that those who seek refuge here in America will find it. The dedication of America to our traditions as an asylum for the oppressed is going to be upheld.

I have directed the Departments of State and Justice and Health, Education, and Welfare to immediately make all the necessary arrangements to permit those in Cuba who seek freedom to make an orderly entry into the United States of America.

Our first concern will be with those Cubans who have been separated from their children and their parents and their husbands and their wives and that are now in this country. Our next concern is with those who are imprisoned for political reasons.

And I will send to the Congress tomorrow a request for supplementary funds of $12,600,000 to carry forth the commitment that I am making today.

I am asking the Department of State to seek through the Swiss Government immediately the agreement of the Cuban Government in a request to the President of the International Red Cross Committee. The request is for the assistance of the Committee in processing the movement of refugees from Cuba to Miami. Miami will serve as a port of entry and a temporary stopping place for refugees as they settle in other parts of this country.

And to all the voluntary agencies in the United States, I appeal for their continuation and expansion of their magnificent work. Their help is needed in the reception and the settlement of those who choose to leave Cuba. The Federal Government will work closely with these agencies in their tasks of charity and brotherhood.

I want all the people of this great land of ours to know of the really enormous contribution which the compassionate citizens of Florida have made to humanity and to decency. And all States in this Union can join with Florida now in extending the hand of helpfulness and humanity to our Cuban brothers.

The lesson of our times is sharp and clear in this movement of people from one land to another. Once again, it stamps the mark of failure on a regime when many of its citizens voluntarily choose to leave the land of their birth for a more hopeful home in America. The future holds little hope for any government where the present holds no hope for the people.

And so we Americans will welcome these Cuban people. For the tides of history run strong, and in another day they can return to their homeland to find it cleansed of terror and free from fear.

Over my shoulders here you can see Ellis Island, whose vacant corridors echo today the joyous sound of long ago voices.

And today we can all believe that the lamp of this grand old lady is brighter today—and the golden door that she guards gleams more brilliantly in the light of an increased liberty for the people from all the countries of the globe.

Thank you very much.

Source: Retrieved from http://www.lbjlib.utexas.edu/johnson/archives.hom/speeches.hom/651003.asp.

———————————————

Supreme Court Opinion in *Plyler v. Doe* Delivered by Justice William J. Brennan Jr.

One topic that continues to reassert itself in discussions about immigration policy is that of the education of undocumented immigrants. In the 1982 case of Plyler v. Doe, the Supreme Court struck down a Texas statute that denied funding for education to illegal immigrant children (K–12) and that struck down a municipal school district's effort to force illegal immigrants to pay an annual $1,000 tuition fee for each illegal immigrant student as compensation for the loss of state funding. Opposition to this decision continues to be voiced by immigration restrictionists in the 21st century. Justice Brennan's opinion, presented below, explicates the Court's arguments based on the Equal Protection Clause; it also highlights the importance of education as a core American value, one that in the Court's view is critical to the assimilation of immigrants.

Washington, DC

June 15, 1982

The question presented by these cases is whether, consistent with the Equal Protection Clause of the Fourteenth Amendment, Texas may deny to undocumented school-age children the free public education that it provides to children who are citizens of the United States or legally admitted aliens.

I

Since the late 19th century, the United States has restricted immigration into this country. Unsanctioned entry into the United States is a crime, and those who have entered unlawfully are subject to deportation. But despite the existence of these legal restrictions, a substantial number of persons have succeeded in unlawfully entering the United States, and now live within various States, including the State of Texas.

In May, 1975, the Texas Legislature revised its education laws to withhold from local school districts any state funds for the education of children who were not "legally admitted" into the United States. The 1975 revision also authorized local school districts to deny enrollment in their public schools to children not "legally admitted" to the country. These cases involve constitutional challenges to those provisions.

This is a class action, filed in the United States District Court for the Eastern District of Texas in September, 1977, on behalf of certain school-age children of Mexican origin residing in Smith County, Tex., who could not establish that they had been legally admitted into the United States. The action complained of the exclusion of plaintiff children from the public schools of the Tyler Independent School District. The Superintendent and members of the Board of Trustees of the School District were named as defendants; the State of Texas intervened as a party-defendant. After certifying a class consisting of all undocumented school-age children of Mexican origin residing within the School District, the District Court preliminarily enjoined defendants from denying a free education to members of the plaintiff class. In December, 1977, the court conducted an extensive hearing on plaintiffs' motion for permanent injunctive relief.

In considering this motion, the District Court made extensive findings of fact. The court found that neither § 21.031 nor the School District policy implementing it had "either the purpose or effect of keeping illegal aliens out of the State of Texas." Respecting defendants' further claim that § 21.031 was simply a financial measure designed to avoid a drain on the State's fisc, the court recognized that the increases in population resulting from the immigration of Mexican nationals into the United States had created problems for the public schools of the State, and that these problems were exacerbated by the special educational needs of immigrant Mexican children. The court noted, however, that the increase in school enrollment was primarily attributable to the admission of children who were legal residents. It also found that, while the "exclusion of all undocumented children from the public schools in Texas would eventually result in economies at some level," funding from both the State and Federal Governments was based primarily on the number of children enrolled. In net effect, then, barring undocumented children from the schools would save money, but it would "not necessarily" improve "the quality of education." The court further observed that the impact of § 21.031 was borne primarily by a very small subclass of illegal aliens, "entire families who have migrated illegally and—for all practical purposes—permanently to the United States." Finally, the court noted that, under current laws and practices, "the illegal alien of today may well be the legal alien of tomorrow," and that, without an education, these undocumented children,

> [a]lready disadvantaged as a result of poverty, lack of English-speaking ability, and undeniable racial prejudices, . . . will become permanently locked into the lowest socio-economic class.

The District Court held that illegal aliens were entitled to the protection of the Equal Protection Clause of the Fourteenth Amendment, and that § 21.031 violated that Clause. Suggesting that

> the state's exclusion of undocumented children from its public schools . . . may well be the type of invidiously motivated state action for which the suspect classification doctrine was designed,

the court held that it was unnecessary to decide whether the statute would survive a "strict scrutiny" analysis because, in any event, the discrimination embodied in the statute was not supported by a rational basis. The District Court also concluded that the Texas statute violated the Supremacy Clause.

The Court of Appeals for the Fifth Circuit upheld the District Court's injunction. The Court of Appeals held that the District Court had erred in finding the Texas statute preempted by federal law. With respect to equal protection, however, the Court of Appeals affirmed in all essential respects the analysis of the District Court, concluding that § 21.031 was "constitutionally infirm regardless of whether it was tested using the mere rational basis standard or some more stringent test." We noted probable jurisdiction.

No. 8194 In re Alien Children Education Litigation

During 1978 and 1979, suits challenging the constitutionality of 21.031 and various local practices undertaken on the authority of that provision were filed in the United States District Courts for the Southern, Western, and Northern Districts of Texas. Each suit named the State of Texas and the Texas Education Agency as defendants, along with local officials. In November, 1979, the Judicial Panel on Multidistrict Litigation, on motion of the State, consolidated the claims against the state officials into a single action to be heard in the District Court for the Southern District of Texas. A hearing was conducted in February and March, 1980. In July, 1980, the court entered an opinion and order holding that § 21.031 violated the Equal Protection Clause of the Fourteenth Amendment. The court held that

> the absolute deprivation of education should trigger strict judicial scrutiny, particularly when the absolute deprivation is the result of complete inability to pay for the desired benefit.

The court determined that the State's concern for fiscal integrity was not a compelling state interest, that exclusion of these children had not been shown to be necessary to improve education within the State, and that the educational needs of the children statutorily excluded were not different from the needs of children not excluded. The court therefore concluded that § 21.031 was not carefully tailored to advance the asserted state interest in an acceptable manner.

While appeal of the District Court's decision was pending, the Court of Appeals rendered its decision in No. 80–1538. Apparently on the strength of that opinion, the Court of Appeals, on February 23, 1981, summarily affirmed the decision of the Southern District. We noted probable jurisdiction and consolidated this case with No. 80–1538 for briefing and argument.

II

The Fourteenth Amendment provides that

> [n]o State shall . . . deprive any person of life, liberty, or property, without due process of law; nor deny to *any person within its jurisdiction* the equal protection of the laws. [Emphasis added]

Appellants argue at the outset that undocumented aliens, because of their immigration status, are not "persons within the jurisdiction" of the State of Texas, and that they therefore have no right to the equal protection of Texas law. We reject this argument. Whatever his status under the immigration laws, an alien is surely a "person" in any ordinary sense of that term. Aliens, even aliens whose presence in this country is unlawful, have long been recognized as "persons" guaranteed due process of law by the Fifth and Fourteenth Amendments. Indeed, we have clearly held that the Fifth Amendment protects aliens whose presence in this country is unlawful from invidious discrimination by the Federal Government.

Appellants seek to distinguish our prior cases, emphasizing that the Equal Protection Clause directs a State to afford its protection to persons *within its jurisdiction,* while the Due Process Clauses of the Fifth and Fourteenth Amendments contain no such assertedly limiting phrase. In appellants' view, persons who have entered the United States illegally are not "within the jurisdiction" of a State even if they are present within a State's boundaries and subject to its laws. Neither our cases nor the logic of the Fourteenth Amendment support that constricting construction of the phrase "within its jurisdiction." We have never suggested that the class of persons who might avail themselves of the equal protection guarantee is less than coextensive with that entitled to due process. To the contrary, we have recognized that both provisions were fashioned to protect an identical class of persons, and to reach every exercise of state authority.

The Fourteenth Amendment to the Constitution is not confined to the protection of citizens. It says:

> Nor shall any state deprive any person of life, liberty, or property without due process of law; nor deny to any person within its jurisdiction the equal protection of the laws.
> *These provisions are universal in their application, to all persons within the territorial jurisdiction,* without regard to any differences of race, of color, or of nationality, and the protection of the laws is a pledge of the protection of equal laws. [Emphasis added]

In concluding that "all persons within the territory of the United States," including aliens unlawfully present, may invoke the Fifth and Sixth Amendments to challenge actions of the Federal Government, we reasoned from the understanding that the Fourteenth Amendment was designed to afford its protection to all within the boundaries of a State. Our cases applying the Equal Protection Clause reflect the same territorial theme:

> Manifestly, the obligation of the State to give the protection of equal laws can be performed only where its laws operate, that is, within its own jurisdiction. It is there that the equality of legal right must be maintained. That obligation is imposed by the Constitution upon the States severally as governmental entities, each responsible for its own laws establishing the rights and duties of persons within its borders. *Missouri ex rel. Gaines v. Canada,* 305 U.S. 337, 350 (1938).

There is simply no support for appellants' suggestion that "due process" is somehow of greater stature than "equal protection," and therefore available to a larger class of persons. To the contrary, each aspect of the Fourteenth Amendment reflects an elementary limitation on state power. To permit a State to employ the phrase "within its jurisdiction" in order to identify subclasses of persons whom it would define as beyond its jurisdiction, thereby relieving itself of the obligation to assure that its laws are designed and applied equally to those persons, would undermine the principal purpose for which the Equal

Protection Clause was incorporated in the Fourteenth Amendment. The Equal Protection Clause was intended to work nothing less than the abolition of all caste-based and invidious class-based legislation. That objective is fundamentally at odds with the power the State asserts here to classify persons subject to its laws as nonetheless excepted from its protection.

Although the congressional debate concerning § 1 of the Fourteenth Amendment was limited, that debate clearly confirms the understanding that the phrase "within its jurisdiction" was intended in a broad sense to offer the guarantee of equal protection to all within a State's boundaries, and to all upon whom the State would impose the obligations of its laws. Indeed, it appears from those debates that Congress, by using the phrase "person within its jurisdiction," sought expressly to ensure that the equal protection of the laws was provided to the alien population. Representative Bingham reported to the House the draft resolution of the Joint Committee of Fifteen on Reconstruction (H.R. 63) that was to become the Fourteenth Amendment. Two days later, Bingham posed the following question in support of the resolution:

> Is it not essential to the unity of the people that the citizens of each State shall be entitled to all the privileges and immunities of citizens in the several States? Is it not essential to the unity of the Government and the unity of the people that all persons, *whether citizens or strangers, within this land,* shall have equal protection in every State in this Union in the rights of life and liberty and property?

Senator Howard, also a member of the Joint Committee of Fifteen, and the floor manager of the Amendment in the Senate, was no less explicit about the broad objectives of the Amendment, and the intention to make its provisions applicable to all who "may happen to be" within the jurisdiction of a State:

> The last two clauses of the first section of the amendment disable a State from depriving not merely a citizen of the United States, but *any person, whoever he may be,* of life, liberty, or property without due process of law, or from denying to him the equal protection of the laws of the State. This abolishes all class legislation in the States and does away with the injustice of subjecting one caste of persons to a code not applicable to another. . . . It will, if adopted by the States, forever disable every one of them from passing laws trenching upon those fundamental rights and privileges which pertain to citizens of the United States, *and to all person who may happen to be within their jurisdiction.* [Emphasis added]

Use of the phrase "within its jurisdiction" thus does not detract from, but rather confirms, the understanding that the protection of the Fourteenth Amendment extends to anyone, citizen or stranger, who *is* subject to the laws of a State, and reaches into every corner of a State's territory. That a person's initial entry into a State, or into the United States, was unlawful, and that he may for that reason be expelled, cannot negate the simple fact of his presence within the State's territorial perimeter. Given such presence, he is subject to the full range of obligations imposed by the State's civil and criminal laws. And until he leaves the jurisdiction—either voluntarily, or involuntarily in accordance with the Constitution and laws of the United States—he is entitled to the equal protection of the laws that a State may choose to establish.

Our conclusion that the illegal aliens who are plaintiffs in these cases may claim the benefit of the Fourteenth Amendment's guarantee of equal protection only begins the inquiry. The more difficult question is whether the Equal Protection Clause has been violated by the refusal of the State of Texas to reimburse local school boards for the education of children who cannot demonstrate that their presence within the United States is lawful, or by the imposition by those school boards of the burden of tuition on those children. It is to this question that we now turn.

III

The Equal Protection Clause directs that "all persons similarly circumstanced shall be treated alike." But so too, "[t]he Constitution does not require things which are different in fact or opinion to be treated in law as though they were the same." The initial discretion to determine what is "different" and what is "the same" resides in the legislatures of the States. A legislature must have substantial latitude to establish classifications that roughly approximate the nature of the problem perceived, that accommodate competing concerns both public and private, and that account for limitations on the practical ability of the State to remedy every ill. In applying the Equal Protection Clause to most forms of state action, we thus seek only the assurance that the classification at issue bears some fair relationship to a legitimate public purpose.

But we would not be faithful to our obligations under the Fourteenth Amendment if we applied so deferential a standard to every classification. The Equal Protection Clause was intended as a restriction on state legislative action inconsistent with elemental constitutional premises. Thus, we have treated as presumptively invidious those classifications that disadvantage a "suspect class," or that impinge upon the exercise of a "fundamental right." With respect to such classifications, it is appropriate to enforce the mandate of equal protection by requiring the State to demonstrate that its classification has been precisely tailored to serve a compelling governmental interest. In addition, we have recognized that certain forms of legislative classification, while not facially invidious, nonetheless give rise to recurring constitutional difficulties; in these limited circumstances, we have sought the assurance that the classification reflects a reasoned judgment consistent with the ideal of equal protection by inquiring whether it may fairly be viewed as furthering a substantial interest of the State. We turn to a consideration of the standard appropriate for the evaluation of § 21.031.

A

Sheer incapability or lax enforcement of the laws barring entry into this country, coupled with the failure to establish an effective bar to the employment of undocumented aliens, has resulted in the creation of a substantial "shadow population" of illegal migrants—numbering in the millions—within our borders. This situation raises the specter of a permanent caste of undocumented resident aliens, encouraged by some to remain here as a source of cheap labor, but nevertheless denied the benefits that our society makes available to citizens and lawful residents. The existence of such an underclass presents most difficult problems for a Nation that prides itself on adherence to principles of equality under law.

The children who are plaintiffs in these cases are special members of this underclass. Persuasive arguments support the view that a State may withhold its beneficence from those whose very presence within the United States is the product of their own unlawful conduct. These arguments do not apply with the same force to classifications imposing disabilities on the minor children of such illegal entrants. At the least, those who elect to enter our territory by stealth and in violation of our law should be prepared to bear the consequences, including, but not limited to, deportation. But the children of those illegal entrants are not comparably situated. Their "parents have the ability to conform their conduct to societal norms," and presumably the ability to remove themselves from the State's jurisdiction; but the children who are plaintiffs in these cases "can affect neither their parents' conduct nor their own status." Even if the State found it expedient to control the conduct of adults by acting against their children, legislation directing the onus of a parent's misconduct against his children does not comport with fundamental conceptions of justice.

> [V]isiting . . . condemnation on the head of an infant is illogical and unjust. Moreover, imposing disabilities on the . . . child is contrary to the basic concept of our system that legal burdens should bear some relationship to individual responsibility or wrongdoing. Obviously, no child is responsible for his birth, and penalizing the . . . child is an ineffectual—as well as unjust—way of deterring the parent. *Weber v. Aetna Casualty & Surety Co.,* 406 U.S. 164, 175 (1972)

Of course, undocumented status is not irrelevant to any proper legislative goal. Nor is undocumented status an absolutely immutable characteristic, since it is the product of conscious, indeed unlawful, action. But § 21.031 is directed against children, and imposes its discriminatory burden on the basis of a legal characteristic over which children can have little control. It is thus difficult to conceive of a rational justification for penalizing these children for their presence within the United States. Yet that appears to be precisely the effect of § 21.031.

Public education is not a "right" granted to individuals by the Constitution. But neither is it merely some governmental "benefit" indistinguishable from other forms of social welfare legislation. Both the importance of education in maintaining our basic institutions and the lasting impact of its deprivation on the life of the child mark the distinction. The "American people have always regarded education and [the] acquisition of knowledge as matters of supreme importance." We have recognized "the public schools as a most vital civic institution for the preservation of a democratic system of government." We have recognized "the public schools as a most vital civic institution for the preservation of a democratic system of government," and as the primary vehicle for transmitting "the values on which our society rests," and as the primary vehicle for transmitting "the values on which our society rests."

> [A]s . . . pointed out early in our history, . . . some degree of education is necessary to prepare citizens to participate effectively and intelligently in our open political system if we are to preserve freedom and independence. *Wisconsin v. Yoder,* 406 U.S. 205, 221 (1972)

And these historic

> perceptions of the public schools as inculcating fundamental values necessary to the maintenance of a democratic political system have been confirmed by the observations of social scientists. *Ambach v. Norwick,* 441 U.S. 68, 76 (1979)

In addition, education provides the basic tools by which individuals might lead economically productive lives to the benefit of us all. In sum, education has a fundamental role in maintaining the fabric of our society. We cannot ignore the significant social costs borne by our Nation when select groups are denied the means to absorb the values and skills upon which our social order rests.

In addition to the pivotal role of education in sustaining our political and cultural heritage, denial of education to some isolated group of children poses an affront to one of the goals of the Equal Protection Clause: the abolition of governmental barriers presenting unreasonable obstacles to advancement on the basis of individual merit. Paradoxically, by depriving the children of any disfavored group of an education, we foreclose the means by which that group might raise the level of esteem in which it is held by the majority. But more directly, "education prepares individuals to be self-reliant and self-sufficient participants in society." Illiteracy is an enduring disability. The inability to read and write will handicap the individual deprived of a basic education each and every day of his life. The inestimable toll of that deprivation on the social, economic, intellectual, and psychological wellbeing of the individual, and the obstacle it poses to individual achievement, make it most difficult to reconcile the cost or the principle of a status-based denial of basic education with the framework of equality embodied in the Equal Protection Clause. . . . What we said 28 years ago in *Brown v. Board of Education,* (1954), still holds true:

> Today, education is perhaps the most important function of state and local governments. Compulsory school attendance laws and the great expenditures for education both demonstrate our recognition of the importance of education to our democratic society. It is required in the performance of our most basic public responsibilities, even service in the armed forces. It is the very foundation of good citizenship. Today it is a principal instrument in awakening the child to cultural values, in preparing him for later professional training, and in helping him to adjust normally to his environment. In these days, it is doubtful that any child may reasonably be expected to succeed in life if he is denied the opportunity of an education. Such an opportunity, where the state has undertaken to provide it, is a right which must be made available to all on equal terms.

B

These well-settled principles allow us to determine the proper level of deference to be afforded § 21.031. Undocumented aliens cannot be treated as a suspect class, because their presence in this country in violation of federal law is not a "constitutional irrelevancy." Nor is education a fundamental right; a State need not justify by compelling necessity every variation in the manner in which education is provided to its population. But more is involved in these cases than the abstract question whether § 21.031 discriminates against a suspect class, or whether education is a fundamental right. Section 21.031 imposes a lifetime hardship on a discrete class of children not accountable for their disabling status. The stigma of illiteracy will mark them for the rest of their lives. By denying these children a basic education, we deny them the ability to live within the structure of our civic institutions, and foreclose any realistic possibility that they will contribute in even the smallest way to the progress of our Nation. In determining the rationality of § 21.031, we may appropriately take into account its costs to the Nation and to the innocent children who are its victims. In light of these countervailing costs, the discrimination contained in § 21.031 can hardly be considered rational unless it furthers some substantial goal of the State.

IV

It is the State's principal argument, and apparently the view of the dissenting Justices, that the undocumented status of these children *vel non* establishes a sufficient rational basis for denying them benefits that a State might choose to afford other residents. The State notes that, while other aliens are admitted "on an equality of legal privileges with all citizens under nondiscriminatory laws," the asserted right of these children to an education can claim no implicit congressional imprimatur. Indeed, in the State's view, Congress' apparent disapproval of the presence of these children within the United States, and the evasion of the federal regulatory program that is the mark of undocumented status, provides authority for its decision to impose upon them special disabilities. Faced with an equal protection challenge respecting the treatment of aliens, we agree that the courts must be attentive to congressional policy; the exercise of congressional power might well affect the State's prerogatives to afford differential treatment to a particular class of aliens. But we are unable to find in the congressional immigration scheme any statement of policy that might weigh significantly in arriving at an equal protection balance concerning the State's authority to deprive these children of an education.

The Constitution grants Congress the power to "establish an uniform Rule of Naturalization." Drawing upon this power, upon its plenary authority with respect to foreign relations and international commerce, and upon the inherent power of a sovereign to close its borders, Congress has developed a complex scheme governing admission to our Nation and status within our borders. The obvious need for delicate policy judgments has counseled the Judicial Branch to avoid intrusion into this field. But this traditional caution does not persuade us that unusual deference must be shown the classification embodied in § 21.031. The States enjoy no power with respect to the classification of aliens. This power is "committed to the political branches of the Federal Government." Although it is "a routine and normally legitimate part" of the business of the Federal Government to classify on the basis of alien status, and to "take into account the character of the relationship between the alien and this country," only rarely are such matters relevant to legislation by a State.

As we recognized in *De Canas v. Bica,* the States do have some authority to act with respect to illegal aliens, at least where such action mirrors federal objectives and furthers a legitimate state goal. In *De Canas,* the State's program reflected Congress' intention to bar from employment all aliens except those possessing a grant of permission to work in this country. In contrast, there is no indication that the disability imposed by § 21.031 corresponds to any identifiable congressional policy. The State does not claim that the conservation of state educational resources was ever a congressional concern in restricting immigration. More importantly, the classification reflected in § 21.031 does not operate harmoniously within the federal program.

To be sure, like all persons who have entered the United States unlawfully, these children are subject to deportation. But there is no assurance that a child subject to deportation will ever be deported. An illegal entrant might be granted federal permission to continue to reside in this country, or even to become a citizen. In light of the discretionary federal power to grant relief from deportation, a State cannot realistically determine that any particular undocumented child will in fact be deported until after deportation proceedings have been completed. It would, of course, be most difficult for the State to justify a denial of education to a child enjoying an inchoate federal permission to remain.

We are reluctant to impute to Congress the intention to withhold from these children, for so long as they are present in this country through no fault of their own, access to a basic education. In other contexts, undocumented status, coupled with some articulable federal policy, might enhance state authority with respect to the treatment of undocumented aliens. But in the area of special constitutional sensitivity presented by these cases, and in the absence of any contrary indication fairly discernible in the present legislative record, we perceive no national policy that supports the State in denying these children an elementary education. The State may borrow the federal classification. But to justify its use as a criterion for its own discriminatory policy, the State must demonstrate that the classification is reasonably adapted to "*the purposes for which the state desires to use it.*" (emphasis added). We therefore turn to the state objectives that are said to support § 21.031.

V

Appellants argue that the classification at issue furthers an interest in the "preservation of the state's limited resources for the education of its lawful residents." Of course, a concern for the preservation of resources, standing alone, can hardly justify the classification used in allocating those resources. The State must do more than justify its classification with a concise expression of an intention to discriminate. Apart from the asserted state prerogative to act against undocumented children solely on the basis of their undocumented status—an asserted prerogative that carries only minimal force in the circumstances of these cases—we discern three colorable state interests that might support § 21.031.

First, appellants appear to suggest that the State may seek to protect itself from an influx of illegal immigrants. While a State might have an interest in mitigating the potentially harsh economic effects of sudden shifts in population, § 21.031 hardly offers an effective method of dealing with an urgent demographic or economic problem. There is no evidence in the record suggesting that illegal entrants impose any significant burden on the State's economy. To the contrary, the available evidence suggests that illegal aliens underutilize public services, while contributing their labor to the local economy and tax money to the state fisc. The dominant incentive for illegal entry into the State of Texas is the availability of employment; few if any illegal immigrants come to this country, or presumably to the State of Texas, in order to avail themselves of a free education. Thus, even making the doubtful assumption that the net impact of illegal aliens on the economy of the State is negative, we think it clear that "[c]harging tuition to undocumented children constitutes a ludicrously ineffectual attempt to stem the tide of illegal immigration," at least when compared with the alternative of prohibiting the employment of illegal aliens.

Second, while it is apparent that a State may "not . . . reduce expenditures for education by barring [some arbitrarily chosen class of] children from its schools," appellants suggest that undocumented children are appropriately singled out for exclusion because of the special burdens they impose on the State's ability to provide high-quality public education. But the record in no way supports the claim that exclusion of undocumented children is likely to improve the overall quality of education in the State. As the District Court in No. 801934 noted, the State failed to offer any

> credible supporting evidence that a proportionately small diminution of the funds spent on each child [which might result from devoting some state funds to the education of the excluded group] will have a grave impact on the quality of education.

And, after reviewing the State's school financing mechanism, the District Court in No. 80-1538 concluded that barring undocumented children from local schools would not necessarily improve the quality of education provided in those schools. Of course, even if improvement in the quality of education were a likely result of barring some *number* of children from the schools of the State, the State must support its selection of *this* group as the appropriate target for exclusion. In terms of educational cost and need, however, undocumented children are "basically indistinguishable" from legally resident alien children.

Finally, appellants suggest that undocumented children are appropriately singled out because their unlawful presence within the United States renders them less likely than other children to remain within the boundaries of the State, and to put their education to productive social or political use within the State. Even assuming that such an interest is legitimate, it is an interest that is most difficult to quantify. The State has no assurance that any child, citizen or not, will employ the education provided by the State within the confines of the State's borders. In any event, the record is clear that many of the undocumented children disabled by this classification will remain in this country indefinitely, and that some will become lawful residents or citizens of the United States. It is difficult to understand precisely what the State hopes to achieve by promoting the creation and perpetuation of a subclass of illiterates within our boundaries, surely adding to the problems and costs of unemployment, welfare, and crime. It is thus clear that whatever savings might be achieved by denying these children an education, they are wholly insubstantial in light of the costs involved to these children, the State, and the Nation.

VI

If the State is to deny a discrete group of innocent children the free public education that it offers to other children residing within its borders, that denial must be justified by a showing that it furthers some substantial state interest. No such showing was made here. Accordingly, the judgment of the Court of Appeals in each of these cases is

Affirmed.

Source: Retrieved from http://www.law.cornell.edu/supct/html/historics/USSC_CR_0457_0202_ZO.html.

President Ronald Reagan's Statement on Signing the Immigration Reform and Control Act of 1986

President Reagan signed into law the Immigration Reform and Control Act (IRCA) after several years of intense congressional debate. It introduced the most extensive changes to U.S. immigration policy since the Hart-Cellar Act of 1965 and contained two major provisions: The first offered amnesty and the opportunity to obtain legal permanent residency to individuals who could prove they had lived in the United States since 1982 or earlier. The second imposed criminal penalties on employers knowingly hiring illegal immigrants (though there was lax enforcement of these employer sanctions). The IRCA proved controversial among both those opposed to illegal immigration worried about "rewarding" those who break the law and those civil rights organizations concerned about possible discrimination against Hispanic applicants for jobs. The IRCA's implementation failures helped fuel the dramatic expansion of illegal immigration in the ensuing decades.

Washington, DC

November 6, 1986

The Immigration Reform and Control Act of 1986 is the most comprehensive reform of our immigration laws since 1952. In the past 35 years our nation has been increasingly affected by illegal immigration. This legislation takes a major step toward meeting this challenge to our sovereignty. At the same time, it preserves and enhances the Nation's heritage of legal immigration. I am pleased to sign the bill into law.

In 1981 this administration asked the Congress to pass a comprehensive legislative package, including employer sanctions, other measures to increase enforcement of the immigration laws, and legalization. The act provides these three essential components. The employer sanctions program is the keystone and major element. It will remove the incentive for illegal immigration by eliminating the job opportunities which draw illegal aliens here. We have consistently supported a legalization program which is both generous to the alien and fair to the countless thousands of people throughout the world who seek legally to come to America. The legalization provisions in this act will go far to improve the lives of a class of individuals who now must hide in the shadows, without access to many of the benefits of a free and open society. Very soon many of these men and women will be able to step into the sunlight and, ultimately, if they choose, they may become Americans.

Section 102(a) of the bill adds section 274B to the Immigration and Nationality Act. This new section relates to certain kinds of discrimination in connection with employment in the United States. Section 274B(a) provides that it is an "unfair immigration-related employment practice" to "discriminate against" any individual in hiring, recruitment or referral for a fee, or discharging from employment "because of" such individual's national origin or—if such individual is a United States citizen or an alien who is a lawful permanent resident, refugee admitted under INA section 207, or asylee granted asylum under section 208, and who has taken certain steps evidencing an intent to become a United States citizen—because of such individual's citizenship status. Employers of fewer than four employees are expressly exempted from coverage. Discrimination against an "unauthorized alien," as defined in section 274A(h)(3), is also not covered. Other exceptions include cases of discrimination because of national origin that are covered by title VII of the Civil Rights Act of 1964, discrimination based on citizenship status when lawfully required under government authority, and discrimination in favor of a United States citizen over an alien if the citizen is at least "equally qualified."

The major purpose of section 274B is to reduce the possibility that employer sanctions will result in increased national origin and alienage discrimination and to provide a remedy if employer sanctions enforcement does have this result. Accordingly, subsection (k) provides that the section will not apply to any discrimination that takes place after a repeal of employer sanctions if this should occur. In the light of this major purpose, the Special Counsel should exercise the discretion provided under subsection (d)(1) so as to limit the investigations conducted on his own initiative to cases involving discrimination apparently caused by an employer's fear of liability under the employer sanctions program.

I understand section 274B to require a "discriminatory intent" standard of proof: The party bringing the action must show that in the decisionmaking process the defendant's action was motivated by one of the prohibited criteria. Thus, it would be improper to use the "disparate impact" theory of recovery, which was developed under paragraph (2) of section 703(a) of title VII, in a line of Supreme Court cases over the last 15 years. This paragraph of title VII does not have a counterpart in section 274B. Section 274B tracks only the language of paragraph (1) of section 703(a), the basis of the "disparate treatment" (discriminatory intent) theory of recovery under title VII. Moreover, paragraph (d)(2) refers to "knowing an intentional discrimination" and "a pattern or practice of discriminatory activity." The meaning of the former phrase is self-evident, while the latter is taken from the Supreme Court's disparate treatment jurisprudence and thus includes the requirement of a discriminatory intent.

Thus, a facially neutral employee selection practice that is employed without discriminatory intent will be permissible under the provisions of section 274B. For example, the section does not preclude a requirement of English language skill or a minimum score on an aptitude test even if the employer cannot show a "manifest relationship" to the job in question or that the requirement is a "bona fide occupational qualification reasonably necessary to the normal operation of that particular business or enterprise," so long as the practice is not a guise used to discriminate on account of national origin or citizenship status. Indeed, unless the plaintiff presents evidence that the employer has intentionally discriminated on proscribed grounds, the employer need not offer any explanation for his employee selection procedures.

Section 274B(c) provides that the President shall appoint, with the advice and consent of the Senate, a Special Counsel for Immigration-Related Unfair Employment Practices within the Justice Department, to serve for a term of 4 years. I understand this subsection to provide that the Special Counsel shall serve at the pleasure and with the policy guidance of the President, but for no longer than for a 4-year term (subject to reappointment by the President with the advice and consent of the Senate).

In accordance with the provisions of section 274B(h) and (j)(4), a requirement to pay attorneys' fees may be imposed against nonprevailing parties—including alleged victims or persons who file on their behalf as well as employers—if claims or defenses are made that do not have a reasonable foundation in both law and fact. The same standard for the imposing of attorneys' fees applies to all nonprevailing parties. It is therefore expected that prevailing defendants would recover attorneys' fees in all cases for which this standard is satisfied, not merely in cases where the claim of the victim or person filing on their behalf is found to be vexatious or frivolous.

The provisions of new INA section 245A(a)(4)(B) and (b)(1)(C)(ii), added by section 201(a) of the bill, state that no alien would qualify for the lawful temporary or the permanent residence status provided in that section if he or she has been convicted of any felony or three or more misdemeanors committed in the United States.

New INA section 245A(d)(2) states that no alien would qualify for the lawful temporary or permanent residence status provided in that section if "likely to become [a] public charge [ ]." This disqualification could be waived by the Attorney General under certain circumstances. A likelihood that an applicant would become a public charge would exist, for example, if the applicant had failed to demonstrate either a history of employment in the United States of a kind that would provide sufficient means without public cash assistance for the support of the alien and his likely dependents who are not United States citizens or the possession of independent means sufficient by itself for such support for an indefinite period.

New INA section 245A(a)(3) requires that an applicant for legalization establish that he has been "continuously physically present in the United States since the date of the enactment" but states that "brief, casual, and innocent absences from the United States" will not be considered a break in the required continuous physical presence. To the extent that the INS has made available a procedure by which aliens can obtain permission to depart and reenter the United States after a brief, casual, and innocent absence by establishing a prima facie case of eligibility for adjustment of status under this section, I understand section 245A(a)(3) to require that an unauthorized departure and illegal reentry will constitute a break in "continuous physical presence."

New INA section 210(d), added by section 302(a) of the bill, provides that an alien who is "apprehended" before or during the application period for adjustment of status for certain "special agricultural workers," may not under certain circumstances related to the establishment of a nonfrivolous case of eligibility for such adjustment of status be excluded or deported. I understand this subsection not to authorize any alien to apply for admission to or to be admitted to the United States in order to apply for adjustment of status under this section. Aliens outside the United States may apply for adjustment of status under this section at an appropriate consular office outside the United States pursuant to the procedures established by the Attorney General, in cooperation with the Secretary of State, as provided in section 210(b)(1)(B).

Section 304 of the bill establishes the Commission on Agricultural Workers, half of whose 12 members are appointed by the executive branch and half by the legislative branch. This hybrid Commission is not consistent with constitutional separation of powers. However, the Commission's role will be entirely advisory.

Section 304(g) provides that upon request of the Commission's Chairman, the head of "any department or agency of the United States" must supply "information necessary to enable it to carry out [the] section." Although I expect that the executive branch will cooperate closely with the Commission, its access to executive branch information will be limited in accordance with established principles of law, including the constitutional separation of powers.

Section 601 establishes a Commission for the Study of International Migration and Cooperative Economic Development, all of whose members are appointed by the legislative branch. Section 601(d)(1) states that the access to executive branch information required under section 304(g) must be provided to this Commission also. Accordingly, the comments of the preceding paragraph are appropriate here as well.

New INA section 274A(a)(5) provides that a person or entity shall be deemed in compliance with the employment verification system in the case of an individual who is referred for employment by a State employment agency if that person or entity retains documentation of such referral certifying that the agency complied with the verification system with respect to the individual referred. I understand this provision not to mandate State employment agencies to issue referral documents certifying compliance with the verification system or to impose any additional affirmative duty or obligation on the offices or personnel of such agencies.

Distance has not discouraged illegal immigration to the United States from all around the globe. The problem of illegal immigration should not, therefore, be seen as a problem between the United States and its neighbors. Our objective is only to establish a reasonable, fair, orderly, and secure system of immigration into this country and not to discriminate in any way against particular nations or people.

The act I am signing today is the product of one of the longest and most difficult legislative undertakings of recent memory. It has truly been a bipartisan effort, with this administration and the allies of immigration reform in the Congress, of both parties, working together to accomplish these critically important reforms. Future generations of Americans will be thankful for our efforts to humanely regain control of our borders and thereby preserve the value of one of the most sacred possessions of our people: American citizenship.

Source: Retrieved from http://www.reagan.utexas.edu/archives/speeches/1986/110686b.htm.

Introduction to *Becoming an American: Immigration and Immigrant Policy*

The bipartisan U.S. Commission on Immigration Reform was mandated by Section 141 of the Immigration Act of 1990 to review and evaluate the implementation and impact of U.S. immigration policy. The final recommendations were presented to Congress and President Clinton in 1997. The Commission examined provisions of the act related to family reunification, employment-based immigration, and the program to ensure diversity for the sources of U.S. immigration. It also examined: the efficacy of efforts to curb illegal immigration; the influence of immigration on labor needs, employment, and other economic and domestic conditions in the United States; the impact on social, demographic, and natural resources; and its effect on the foreign policy and national security interests of the country.

Report to Congress by U.S. Commission on Immigration Reform

September 1997

Immigration and immigration policy is about immigrants, their families and the rest of us. It is about the meaning of American nationality and the foundation of national unity. It is about uniting persons from all over the world in a common civic culture.

The process of becoming an American is most simply called "Americanization," which must always be a two-way street. All Americans, not just immigrants, should understand the importance of our shared civic culture to our national community. This final report of the U.S. Commission on Immigration Reform makes recommendations to further the goals of Americanization by setting out *immigrant* policies to help orient immigrants and their new communities, to improve educational programs that help immigrants and their children learn English and civics, and to reinforce the integrity of the naturalization process through which immigrants become U.S. citizens.

This report also makes recommendations regarding *immigration* policy. It reiterates and updates the conclusions we reached in three interim reports—on unlawful migration, legal immigration, and refugee and asylum policy—and makes additional recommendations for reforming immigration policies. Further, in this report, the Commission recommends ways to improve the structure and management of the federal agencies responsible for achieving the goals of immigration policy. It is our hope that this final report *Becoming An American: Immigration and Immigrant Policy,* along with our three interim reports, constitutes a full response to the work assigned the Commission by Congress: to assess the national interest in immigration and report how it can best be achieved.

Mandate and Methods

Public Law 101-649, the Immigration Act of 1990 [IMMACT], established this Commission to review and evaluate the impact of immigration policy. More specifically, the Commission must report on immigration's impact on: the need for labor and skills; employment and other aspects of the economy; social, demographic, and environmental conditions; and the foreign policy and national security interests of the United States. The Commission engaged in a wide variety of fact-finding activities to fulfill this mandate. Site visits were conducted throughout the United States. Commission members visited immigrant and refugee communities in California, Texas, Florida, New York, Massachusetts, Illinois, Arizona, Washington, Kansas, Virginia, Washington, DC, Puerto Rico and the Commonwealth of the Northern Mariana Islands. Some Commission and staff members also visited such major source countries as Mexico, the Dominican Republic, Cuba, Haiti, and the Philippines. To increase our understanding of international refugee policy issues, members and staff of the Commission visited Bosnia, Croatia, Germany, and Kenya, and consulted with Geneva-based officials from the U.N. High Commission for Refugees and the International Organization for Migration. We held more than forty public hearings, consultations with government and private sector officials, and expert roundtable discussions.

Today's Immigrants

The effects of immigration are numerous, complex, and varied. Immigrants contribute in many ways to the United States: to its vibrant and diverse communities; to its lively and participatory democracy; to its vital intellectual and cultural life; to its renowned job-creating entrepreneurship and marketplaces; and to its family values and hard-work ethic. However, there are costs as well as benefits from today's immigration. Those workers most at risk in our restructuring economy— low-skilled workers in production and service jobs—are those who directly compete with today's low-skilled immigrants. Further, immigration presents special challenges to certain states and local communities that disproportionately bear the fiscal and other costs of incorporating newcomers.

Characteristics of Immigrants

In FY 1996 (the last year for which data are available), more than 900,000 immigrants came to the United States from 206 nations, for a variety of reasons and with a diverse set of personal characteristics. Not surprisingly, the characteristics of immigrants from different sending countries vary, as do their effects on the U.S. There are also differences between immigrants admitted under different classes of admission. These differences generally reflect the statutory provisions that guide admissions.

Places of Origin. Asia and North America (i.e., Mexico, Canada, the Caribbean, and Central America) remain the sending regions with the largest share of immigrants. Mexico remains the largest sending country and its share of total legal immigrants to the U.S. increased from an average of 12 percent in the 1980s to more than 13 percent in FY 1994 and up to 18 percent in FY 1996. The effects of the Immigration Reform and Control Act of 1986 [IRCA], which resulted in the legalization of about two million formerly illegal Mexican residents, explains this trend. Even though the special admission category for the spouses of legalized aliens' dependents has been discontinued, Mexico benefits from the IMMACT's removal of per-country limits on the numerically limited spouse and children class of admission (FB-2A).

IMMACT established a transitional and a permanent "diversity" category for countries whose admission numbers were adversely affected by the Immigration Act of 1965. The transitional program was in effect from FY 1992 to 1994, but unused visas were carried over through FY 1996. The permanent program went into effect in FY 1995. European countries benefited the most from the transitional program, which mandated that as many as 40 percent of the visas could go to nationals of Ireland. Actual Irish admissions reached only 35 percent, with Polish immigrants accounting for an even larger share (38 percent). Under the permanent diversity program, 42 percent of the immigrants came from European countries and 35 percent came from Africa. The effect on African admissions is particularly noteworthy as Africans account for less than 1 percent of immigrants in other admission categories.

Intended U.S. Destinations. Immigrants in FY 1996 continue to select just a few states as their destinations. About two-thirds intend to reside in California, New York, Texas, Florida, and New Jersey. One-quarter of admissions are to California alone with another one-seventh to New York. New York City retains its place as the pre-eminent immigrant city with 15 percent of immigrants intending to go there. About 7 percent of immigrants intend to go to Los Angeles, and Miami and Chicago are in third place with about 4.5 percent each of the total. There has been little change in these leading destinations since IMMACT. However, some new destinations have emerged in recent years. For example, during the past decade, such midwestern and southern states as Mississippi, Nebraska, Kansas, Georgia and North Carolina saw more than a doubling of the number of immigrants intending to reside there. Although the numbers are significantly smaller than the more traditional destinations, absorbing more new immigrants can be a challenge for these newer destinations that often do not have the immigration-related infrastructure of the traditional receiving communities.

Age. Immigrants in FY 1996 remain young, with the largest proportion being in their later teens or twenties. A little more than one-fifth are children 15 years of age or younger, and another one-fifth are 45 years or older. More than one-half of family-based immigrants are younger than 30 years of age, reflecting the predominance of spouses and children. Because of beneficiaries, employment-based immigrants have just as many minor dependents age 15 years and younger as other groups, but more than two-fifths of these employment-based immigrants themselves are 30–44 years, the experienced and highly productive working ages. Diversity immigrants have a similar, yet somewhat younger, age distribution than other classes of admission. In contrast, and in large part due to those admitted as refugees from the former Soviet Union, humanitarian admissions tend to be somewhat older than other immigrants.

Gender. Females were 54 percent of admissions in FY 1996. There had been an essentially even balance of men and women during the decade of the 1980s. The increased share of females in the 1990s parallels the historical tendency toward more female immigrants throughout much of the post-World War II period. It also reflects the admission of the spouses of legalized aliens who were predominantly male. In FY 1996, family-based admissions were predominantly female (57 percent) and employment-based admissions (including beneficiaries) were evenly balanced by gender. Diversity (45 percent female) and humanitarian (48 percent female) admissions, in contrast, had more male immigrants. That a slight majority of FY 1996 humanitarian admissions were male is somewhat surprising given that worldwide refugee populations are disproportionately female.

English Ability. The Immigration and Naturalization Service [INS] admissions data do not include information on English language ability (or education, as discussed below). The following analysis draws instead on preliminary data from the New Immigrant Survey [NIS], which studied a sample of immigrants admitted in FY 1996. The NIS is a pilot study designed to test the feasibility of a longitudinal immigrant survey. Although the data are not yet published, analysis indicates that it offers promise of providing certain information about immigrants that has not previously been available. The NIS, using the same measure as the U.S. Census, reports on the English language proficiency of adult legal immigrants who are 18 years and older. The initial results show that employment-based immigrants report the greatest English ability—70 percent of employment-based admissions report speaking at least fairly well and less than 10 percent speak very little or no English (the remainder report an "average" speaking ability). About 37 percent of family-based admissions report speaking English at least fairly well and an almost equal proportion report speaking little or no English. The diversity immigrants tend to report even less English ability, despite the requirement that they have at least a high school education. The humanitarian admissions trail the furthest behind in reported English language ability. Only 16 percent report speaking English at least fairly well, while more than 50 percent report speaking little or no English.

Education. The years of schooling completed by immigrants is perhaps one of the most critical measures of skill level. The NIS provides our first indicators of years of education of adult legal immigrants at the time of their admission. As found in studies of foreign-born residents, the immigrants surveyed by the NIS tend to cluster at the higher or lower ends of the educational spectrum and differ significantly in their educational attainment by class of admission. Fully 46 percent of employment-based admissions have completed four years of college or a graduate degree. This figure includes principals and beneficiaries, making it likely that well-educated employment-based immigrants tend to have well-educated spouses. In contrast, just 17 percent of family-based immigrants 25 years and older have completed a college-level education while 42 percent have less than a high school education.

Diversity immigrants are required to have a high school education or two years of skilled work experience. The NIS data show that diversity immigrants tend to be better educated than family-based, but not as well educated as employment-based immigrants. About 14 percent have not completed high school. They may be either principals who meet the work but not the education requirement or the spouses of the principals. Twenty-two percent of diversity immigrants have completed college or done graduate-level education, about the same proportion as among U.S. natives.

The humanitarian classes of admission are less well educated than the employment-based, but are better educated than family admissions. The large number of relatively well-educated persons admitted as refugees from the Soviet Union may partly explain this finding. About 21 percent have less than a high school education, while about 19 percent have college or higher degrees.

Occupation. Ultimately, the English and educational skills that immigrants have are reflected in their occupations. The INS admissions data, which we use here, have only crude occupational classifications. It imperfectly captures the difference between immigrants who adjust into legal permanent resident [LPR] status after working in a U.S. job for several years and those who report an occupation upon admission that tells us more about what the immigrant did at home than what they will do here.

Sixty-five percent of all immigrants in FY 1996 reported no occupation or being a "homemaker," reflecting the fact that children, parents, and spouses are a large share of all admissions and most do not work at the time of entry.

Nevertheless, occupational status faithfully reflects the legal requirements of the admission class—the proportion of all immigrants not reporting an occupation is greater among family and humanitarian admissions, about 70 percent of all immigrants in each category. By way of comparison, only about one-half of all employment and diversity admissions have no reported occupation. The skills which immigrants bring to the United States are reflected in their type of occupations. Family and humanitarian immigrants are primarily blue-collar workers. In contrast, employment-based and permanent diversity immigrants are predominantly white-collar workers. These broad differences between the major classes of admission have changed only slightly over the past three decades.

IMMACT has had an effect on occupational distribution within these broad categories. To gauge its effects, a research paper prepared for the Commission calculated simple linear projections for all of the admission categories now subject to the worldwide ceiling on admissions. Data from FY 1972–1991 were analyzed and the trends identified, then projected forward to FY 1996. This analysis, therefore, paints a "what-if" picture of what today's immigration might have looked like if past trends had continued unaffected by IMMACT.

The actual total number of admissions under the worldwide ceiling in FY 1996 was 720,314 which—compared to the projected figure of 426,929—was 69 percent greater than would have been expected without IMMACT. Admissions were greater than the projected figure because IMMACT increased numerically-limited family, employment, and diversity admissions. The numerically-exempt admissions for the immediate relatives of U.S. citizens would have grown between 1992 and 1996 even without IMMACT. This analysis does not include humanitarian admissions.

Of immigrants who reported an occupation, the actual admissions in FY 1996 were 221,731 which—compared to the projected figure of 165,234—was 34 percent greater than would have been expected if IMMACT had not gone into effect. By contrast, nonworking immigrants experienced a 91 percent increase of actual over projected. This finding is not surprising as FY 1996 family admissions were significantly higher than would have been permissible under previous law. In part this was because IMMACT permitted unused FY 1995 employment-based numbers to be transferred to the FY 1996 family categories. In combination with a growth in immediate relatives (including those who would normally have been admitted in FY 1995 but were caught in processing delays), the additional visas meant more spouses and minor children entered. These immigrants are the least likely to be employed.

As might be anticipated, IMMACT's new emphasis on admitting highly-educated and skilled persons led to growth in professional occupations among those who reported an occupation. As stated above, there was an overall 34 percent increase in persons reporting an occupation. This increase was not evenly distributed, however. The number of health professionals, for example, was projected to be 10,244, but at 18,985 was 85 percent greater. The number of executives also shows a higher than expected increase. Interestingly, projections not shown here indicate that within the employment-based category, family members (beneficiaries) of the principals show the greatest growth in professional occupations. This suggests that when principals with more skills are admitted, they bring with them spouses who are, likewise, more skilled than in the past. Further, projections not shown here indicate that the skill requirement for permanent diversity immigrants makes for more highly-skilled admissions from eligible countries. In short, IMMACT increased both the numbers of more skilled admissions and their share of immigrants admitted.

Most nonprofessional white-collar and blue-collar occupations show very little or no growth over what might have occurred without IMMACT. The one notable exception is a greater-than-expected increase in the number of "Operators, Fabricators, and Laborers." There were 53,936 admissions in these occupations compared to the 37,702 that were projected. As the employment-based access for persons with these occupations is highly limited, it appears that much of this increase is attributable to family-based admissions. It is unclear from the data, however, why this pattern has emerged.

Earnings. According to the NIS survey, the median earnings of all male immigrants admitted in 1996 was $15,600 and for women was $11,960, lower than the median earnings for natives. Compared to the earnings in their last country of residence, male immigrants experienced a 59 percent increase and women a 45 increase in earnings upon admission to the United States. Differences in earnings are, as should be expected, substantial by admission class. Many employment-based immigrants earn a median income of $36,400 on the date of their admission to LPR status, while the sibling or spouse of an LPR earns $11,750 and the spouse of a citizen earns $18,200.

Effects on the Economy

An independent evaluation of immigration by a panel of eminent social scientists at the National Research Council [NRC], sponsored by the Commission, found that immigration has a positive economic impact on the national level. However, the NRC panel's findings confirm the by now commonplace conclusion that there are tangible costs to certain sectors of the labor market and certain communities. This reinforces the Commission's conclusions on the need for a well-regulated system of immigrant admissions, as well as the need for attention to means of improving integration and reducing friction between newcomers and established residents.

The NRC panel estimates that immigrants may add $1–10 billion directly to the national economy each year, a small but positive amount in a $7.6 trillion economy. Many consumers, business owners, and investors benefit from the immigrant labor force. Recent newcomers may be willing to work for lower wages than other U.S. workers, although, with the exception of many immigrants with less than a high school education, most immigrants tend to earn as much as natives after a decade. Many others in the economy benefit, particularly those who do work that is complementary to that performed by immigrants. Immigrants provide the labor that has kept viable entire segments of certain labor-intensive industries, such as garment and shoemaking. Many immigrant entrepreneurs expand trade with foreign countries from which they come, and the language and cultural expertise of many immigrant employees are valuable to U.S. companies doing business abroad.

Immigrants also contribute to the economic revitalization of the communities in which they live. As middle-class natives have left the inner cities, immigrant newcomers have settled, established businesses, bought homes, and otherwise invested in these areas. Gateway cities, such as New York and Los Angeles, have benefited particularly from this urban renewal. At the same time, these cities face new challenges related to immigration. Growing immigrant communities require local school systems (some of which may have otherwise faced declining enrollments) to provide sufficient classroom space and teachers. They must also develop programs to teach children who are without English skills or prior education. Overcrowded housing, drug trafficking, gang violence, sweatshops, and public health problems also may be found in many of these inner-city communities.

Immigration particularly affects certain U.S. workers. The NRC panel finds that workers with less than twelve years of education are the most adversely affected by low-skilled immigrant workers. Immigrants may have reduced substantially the wages of high school dropouts, who are about one-tenth of the workforce, by 5 percent nationwide. This is a sizable impact on a group that was already poorly paid before the loss in real earnings it experienced over the past two decades. Most often it is the foreign-born worker, particularly in labor markets with large numbers of immigrants who experience the greatest competition. While the education and skill level of most U.S. workers differs significantly from those of most immigrants (and therefore they are not competing for the same jobs), the new arrivals are often direct substitutes for immigrants who arrived a short time before them.

The evidence on the impact of immigration on native-born minorities nationwide is less clear. The NRC concluded that in the aggregate, the economic opportunities of African Americans are not reduced by immigration because African

Americans and immigrants tend to be in different labor markets and reside in different cities. Other research finds small, adverse effects on African Americans. These effects are found most strongly when low-skilled minority workers compete with low-skilled immigrant workers in the same industries and the same geographic areas.

The fiscal effects of immigration also are complicated. Generally, the impacts on the federal government are favorable compared to those on state and local governments. Most studies show that at the federal level, the foreign-born pay more in taxes than they receive in services. When spread across all taxpayers, this characteristic represents a very small, but positive, benefit. At the local level, however, immigrants often represent a net fiscal cost, in some cases a substantial one. Research on the resident illegal alien population finds the clearest examples of fiscal costs to states and localities. In general, much of the negative effect is related to school costs that are considerable because of the larger size of many immigrant families. Although funds spent on education may be considered an investment, not just a fiscal burden, the payoff is not realized for many years.

Education affects fiscal impacts in a second way. Ultimately, the economic success and fiscal contributions of immigrants are determined by their educational level. The NRC panel found that immigrants who complete high school and beyond generally represent a more favorable balance of fiscal costs and contributions than do those with little or no education. Even over their lifetimes, immigrants without education are unlikely to contribute sufficient tax revenues to offset their use of services. Both groups of immigrants tend to use public services in a similar fashion, particularly as related to the schooling of their children, but the more educated immigrants tend to earn more and pay higher taxes.

Educational differences also explain why certain states and localities are more adversely affected by immigration than are others. California immigrants represent a sizeable tax burden (estimated at almost $1,200 per native-headed family per year) while New Jersey immigrants represent a more modest tax burden (estimated to be $232 per native-headed family per year). The difference can be explained largely by the differences in the average educational level of the immigrants residing in these states.

English language ability also affects the economic success and fiscal impacts of immigrants. In the 1990 Census, 47 percent of the foreign-born more than 5 years of age reported not speaking English "very well." Individuals with poor English language skills tend to be confined to the lowest levels of the U.S. job market. By contrast, ability in spoken English markedly improves immigrants' earnings, especially for Hispanic and Asian adult immigrants. English reading comprehension also has been found to improve the earnings of young immigrant adults.

Population Growth and Natural Resources

In recent years there have been about 800,000 legal admissions and an additional estimated 200,000 to 300,000 unauthorized entries, but the net annual increase of the foreign-born population is about 700,000 each year due to return migration and mortality. In 1996, the foreign-born population was 24.6 million, 9.3 percent of the U.S. population. Recent arrivals make up a large share of the resident foreign-born population; about 28 percent arrived after 1990, and an additional 35 percent during the 1980s.

It is estimated that international migration makes up somewhere between one-quarter and one-third of net annual population increase. Given current demographic trends and noting that much can happen to alter long-range forecasts, the U.S. Census Bureau projects the population to increase by 50 percent between 1995 and 2050. Immigration is likely to become a larger proportion of the net increase.

The NRC report also presented estimates of population growth. It found that *without* immigration since 1950, the U.S. population would have been 14 percent smaller than its 1995 size of 263 million. The NRC projected the population to the year 2050 after making certain assumptions about mortality, fertility, and rates of group inter-marriage. According to the projection based on these assumptions, the U.S. population would increase by 124 million persons to 387 million, with immigration responsible for two-thirds (82 million) of the increase. Of this 82 million, 45 million are immigrants and an additional 37 million increase is due to their higher assumed fertility.

Immigration affects the age structure as well as the overall population. The NRC panel projected that under current immigration policy, kindergarten through grade eight school enrollment in 2050 would be 17 percent higher than it was in 1995. High school enrollment would rise from 14.0 million in 1995 to 20.3 million in 2050. Immigration also has small effects on the proportion of the population that is elderly. No matter which immigration policies are adopted, according to the NRC, the number of persons aged 65 years and older will double between 1995 and 2050. However, the proportion of older people in the total population will be somewhat smaller with immigration.

The NRC panel's projection of the ethnic distribution of the U.S. population in 2050 shows the Hispanic population increasing from 10 to 25 percent and the Asian population from 3 to 8 percent of the population. These projections are dependent on today's rates of group intermarriage and how persons report their ethnicity. It may be that, like children of immigrants who arrived in the last century, descendents of today's immigrants will choose to report their ethnicity as being different from that of their parents, and that today's ethnic categories will not accurately describe tomorrow's populations.

What broader implications do these growth figures have? Some analysts argue that high immigration levels mean an abundant supply of youthful workers who will be a substantial spur to the economy. From this perspective, population growth is an engine for technological progress and the means to solve environmental problems, effectively spawning change out of necessity. Proponents of this view argue that human resourcefulness has dealt with population growth in the past and the solutions often have left us better off. Adding more people may "cause us more problems, but at the same time there will be more people to solve these problems."

Others are concerned about the negative consequences of population growth, particularly on the environment, infrastructure, and services. They see population growth as imposing pressures on our natural resources and quality of life, raising special concerns in the arid regions of the southwest or sites of industries relocating to the south central states. Those concerned argue that our future wellbeing depends upon both conservation, and stabilizing population growth.

This debate primarily concerns total U.S. population growth, which is strongly influenced by immigration. Still, there is little or no information about whether immigrants have *differential* impacts distinct from the population increase they produce on the U.S. environment.

The Commission did find that rapid inflows of immigrants can pose difficulties for those who must plan for community growth. Schools sometimes receive large numbers of new immigrant students that had not been planned for. Housing and infrastructure development may not be adequate in affected urban and rural communities. New immigrant destinations, sometimes to areas that have not had new immigrants for a century or more, can put particular stress on communities that have experienced rapid growth in the past decade.

Foreign Policy and National Security Interests

Immigration matters frequently are intertwined with foreign policy and national security. Today, migration and refugee issues are matters of high international politics engaging the heads of state involved in defense, internal security, and external relations. International migration intersects with foreign policy in two principal ways. The U.N. Security Council has acknowledged that migration can pose threats to international peace and security through economic or social instability or humanitarian disasters. Migration can also build positive relations with other countries and thereby promote national security. As a consequence, migration itself requires bilateral and international attention to help address the causes and consequences of movements of people.

During the Cold War, a foreign policy priority was the destabilizing of Communist regimes. Refugee policy was often a tool to achieve that strategic goal, for instance, by encouraging the flow of migrants from Eastern Europe or Cuba. Elsewhere, political, economic, and military involvement in Southeast Asia and the Dominican Republic had significant migration consequences, as large numbers of Southeast Asians and Dominicans ended up as refugees and immigrants to the U.S. These foreign policy priorities generally have had significant immigration consequences years later.

Alternatively, immigration concerns sometimes have played a significant role in U.S. foreign policy, especially when mass movements to the U.S. are feared. A stated rationale for U.S. Central-American policy in the 1980s was to prevent a mass movement that would occur if anti-American Marxist dictatorships were established in Central America. One of the explicit reasons for the military intervention in Haiti in 1994 was to restrain the flow of migrants onto U.S. shores. And, although the U.S. does not officially maintain relations with Cuba, migration concerns gained priority over diplomatic ones leading to negotiations on the Cuban Migration Agreement and to a reversal of policy regarding the interdiction of Cuban migrants.

Some observers believe that environmental causes now rival economic and political instability as a major source of forced migration throughout the world. There are estimates that as many as one hundred million people may be displaced, in part, because of degradation of land and natural resources. "That will increase the pressure to migrate to places like the United States." The pervasive deterioration of Mexico's rural drylands may contribute to between 700,000 and 900,000 people a year leaving rural areas. Environmental degradation in Mexico, Haiti, and Central America also are believed to have migration consequences for the U.S. Often environmental problems intersect with other causes. One researcher argues that migrants from Haiti may be considered "environmental refugees" because the root causes of their migrations are land degradation and the Haitian government's unwillingness to act in the interest of the general population.

Stabilizing economic growth and democracy may be an effective means of reducing migration pressures. The Commission for the Study of International Migration and Cooperative Economic Development concluded that, over the long run of a generation or more, trade and investment are likely to reduce migration pressures. Supporters of the North American Free Trade Agreement [NAFTA] argued that NAFTA-related development eventually will reduce unauthorized Mexican migration. The U.S. has provided the reinstalled democratically-elected government of Haiti with a great deal of rehabilitation assistance that should aid the stability of that country.

Conclusion

Properly-regulated immigration and immigrant policy serves the national interest by ensuring the entry of those who will contribute most to our society and helping lawful newcomers adjust to life in the United States. It must give due consideration to shifting economic realities. A well-regulated system sets priorities for admission; facilitates nuclear family reunification; gives employers access to a global labor market while protecting U.S. workers; helps to generate jobs and economic growth; and fulfills our commitment to resettle refugees as one of several elements of humanitarian protection of the persecuted.

Source: Retrieved from http://www.utexas.edu/lbj/uscir/becoming/full-report.pdf.

Speech by President George W. Bush From the Oval Office

Following months of debate within the halls of Congress and demonstrations by immigrants and their supporters, President Bush delivered this televised address to the nation in May 2006. In it he set out a five-point plan intended to reduce illegal immigration, a plan that included a path to citizenship for illegal immigrants that would represent a "middle ground" between mass deportation and automatic granting of citizenship, deployment of National Guard troops to the U.S.–Mexican border, and a "guest worker" program enabling foreigners to work temporarily in the United States. House Republicans balked at the president's plan due to political concerns, and there was no movement on it. The ideas President Bush put forth are still part of the ongoing debate surrounding comprehensive immigration reform.

Washington, DC

May 15, 2006

Good evening. I've asked for a few minutes of your time to discuss a matter of national importance: the reform of America's immigration system.

The issue of immigration stirs intense emotions and in recent weeks, Americans have seen those emotions on display. On the streets of major cities, crowds have rallied in support of those in our country illegally. At our southern border, others have organized to stop illegal immigrants from coming in. Across the country, Americans are trying to reconcile these contrasting images. And in Washington, the debate over immigration reform has reached a time of decision. Tonight, I will make it clear where I stand, and where I want to lead our country on this vital issue.

We must begin by recognizing the problems with our immigration system. For decades, the United States has not been in complete control of its borders. As a result, many who want to work in our economy have been able to sneak across our border and millions have stayed.

Once here, illegal immigrants live in the shadows of our society. Many use forged documents to get jobs, and that makes it difficult for employers to verify that the workers they hire are legal. Illegal immigration puts pressure on public schools and hospitals, . . . it strains state and local budgets . . . and brings crime to our communities. These are real problems, yet we must remember that the vast majority of illegal immigrants are decent people who work hard, support their families, practice their faith, and lead responsible lives. They are a part of American life but they are beyond the reach and protection of American law.

We are a nation of laws, and we must enforce our laws. We're also a nation of immigrants, and we must uphold that tradition, which has strengthened our country in so many ways. These are not contradictory goals. America can be a lawful society and a welcoming society at the same time. We will fix the problems created by illegal immigration, and we will deliver a system that is secure, orderly, and fair. So I support comprehensive immigration reform that will accomplish five clear objectives.

First, the United States must secure its borders. This is a basic responsibility of a sovereign nation. It is also an urgent requirement of our national security. Our objective is straightforward: The border should be open to trade and lawful immigration, and shut to illegal immigrants, as well as criminals, drug dealers, and terrorists.

I was the governor of a state that has a 1,200-mile border with Mexico. So I know how difficult it is to enforce the border, and how important it is. Since I became president, we've have increased funding for border security by 66 percent, and expanded the Border Patrol from about 9,000 to 12,000 agents. The men and women of our Border Patrol are doing a fine job in difficult circumstances and over the past five years, they have apprehended and sent home about six million people entering America illegally.

Despite this progress, we do not yet have full control of the border, and I am determined to change that. Tonight I'm calling on Congress to provide funding for dramatic improvements in manpower and technology at the border. By the end of 2008, we will increase the number of Border Patrol officers by an additional 6,000. When these new agents are deployed, we will have more than doubled the size of the Border Patrol during my Presidency.

At the same time, we are launching the most technologically advanced border security initiative in American history. We will construct high-tech fences in urban corridors, and build new patrol roads and barriers in rural areas. We will employ motion sensors, . . . infrared cameras . . . and unmanned aerial vehicles to prevent illegal crossings. America has the best technology in the world and we will ensure that the Border Patrol has the technology they need to do their job and secure our border.

Training thousands of new Border Patrol agents and bringing the most advanced technology to the border will take time. Yet the need to secure our border is urgent. So I'm am announcing several immediate steps to strengthen border enforcement during this period of transition:

One way to help during this transition is to use the National Guard. So in coordination with governors, up to 6,000 Guard members will be deployed to our southern border. The Border Patrol will remain in the lead. The Guard will assist the Border Patrol by operating surveillance systems, . . . analyzing intelligence, . . . installing fences and vehicle barriers, . . . building patrol roads . . . and providing training. Guard units will not be involved in direct law enforcement activities. That duty will be done by the Border Patrol. This initial commitment of Guard members would last for a period of one year. After that, the number of Guard forces will be reduced as new Border Patrol agents and new technologies come online. It is important for Americans to know that we have enough Guard forces to win the war on terror, to respond to natural disasters, and help secure our border.

The United States is not going to militarize the southern border. Mexico is our neighbor, and our friend. We will continue to work cooperatively to improve security on both sides of the border, . . . to confront common problems like drug trafficking and crime, . . . and to reduce illegal immigration.

Another way to help during this period of transition is through state and local law enforcement in our border communities. So we will increase federal funding for state and local authorities assisting the Border Patrol on targeted enforcement missions. And we will give state and local authorities the specialized training they need to help federal officers apprehend and detain illegal immigrants. State and local law enforcement officials are an important part of our border security resource and they need to be are part of our strategy to secure our borders communities.

The steps I have outlined will improve our ability to catch people entering our country illegally. At the same time, we must ensure that every illegal immigrant we catch crossing our southern border is returned home. More than 85 percent of the illegal immigrants we catch crossing the southern border are Mexicans, and most are sent back home within 24 hours. But when we catch illegal immigrants from other countries, it is not as easy to send them back home. For many years, the government did not have enough space in our detention facilities to hold them while the legal process unfolded. So most were released back into our society and asked to return for a court date. When the date arrived, the vast majority did not show up. This practice, called "catch and release," is unacceptable and we will end it.

We're taking several important steps to meet this goal. We've have expanded the number of beds in our detention facilities, and we will continue to add more. We've have expedited the legal process to cut the average deportation time.

And we are making it clear to foreign governments that they must accept back their citizens who violate our immigration laws. As a result of these actions, we've have ended "catch and release" for illegal immigrants from some countries. And I will ask Congress for additional funding and legal authority, so we can end "catch and release" at the southern border once and for all. When people know that they'll will be caught and sent home if they enter our country illegally, they will be less likely to try to sneak in.

Second, to secure our border, we must create a temporary worker program. The reality is that there are many people on the other side of our border who will do anything to come to America to work and build a better life. They walk across miles of desert in the summer heat, or hide in the back of 18-wheelers to reach our country. This creates enormous pressure on our border that walls and patrols alone will not stop. To secure the border effectively, we must reduce the numbers of people trying to sneak across.

Therefore, I support a temporary worker program that would create a legal path for foreign workers to enter our country in an orderly way, for a limited period of time. This program would match willing foreign workers with willing American employers for jobs Americans are not doing. Every worker who applies for the program would be required to pass criminal background checks. And temporary workers must return to their home country at the conclusion of their stay. A temporary worker program would meet the needs of our economy, and it would give honest immigrants a way to provide for their families while respecting the law. A temporary worker program would reduce the appeal of human smugglers and make it less likely that people would risk their lives to cross the border. It would ease the financial burden on state and local governments, by replacing illegal workers with lawful taxpayers. And above all, a temporary worker program would add to our security by making certain we know who is in our country and why they are here.

Third, we need to hold employers to account for the workers they hire. It is against the law to hire someone who is in this country illegally. Yet businesses often cannot verify the legal status of their employees, because of the widespread problem of document fraud. Therefore, comprehensive immigration reform must include a better system for verifying documents and work eligibility. A key part of that system should be a new identification card for every legal foreign worker. This card should use biometric technology, such as digital fingerprints, to make it tamper-proof. A tamper-proof card would help us enforce the law and leave employers with no excuse for violating it. And by making it harder for illegal immigrants to find work in our country, we would discourage people from crossing the border illegally in the first place. Fourth, we must face the reality that millions of illegal immigrants are already here already. They should not be given an automatic path to citizenship. This is amnesty, and I oppose it. Amnesty would be unfair to those who are here lawfully and it would invite further waves of illegal immigration.

Some in this country argue that the solution is to—is to deport every illegal immigrant and that any proposal short of this amounts to amnesty. I disagree. It is neither wise nor realistic to round up millions of people, many with deep roots in the United States, and send them across the border. There is a rational middle ground between granting an automatic path to citizenship for every illegal immigrant, and a program of mass deportation. That middle ground recognizes that there are differences between an illegal immigrant who crossed the border recently and someone who has worked here for many years, and has a home, a family, and an otherwise clean record. I believe that illegal immigrants who have roots in our country and want to stay should have to pay a meaningful penalty for breaking the law, . . . to pay their taxes, . . . to learn English . . . and to work in a job for a number of years. People who meet these conditions should be able to apply for citizenship but approval would not be automatic, and they will have to wait in line behind those who played by the rules and followed the law. What I've have just described is not amnesty it is a way for those who have broken the law to pay their debt to society, and demonstrate the character that makes a good citizen.

Fifth, we must honor the great American tradition of the melting pot, which has made us one nation out of many peoples. The success of our country depends upon helping newcomers assimilate into our society, and embrace our common identity as Americans. Americans are bound together by our shared ideals, an appreciation of our history, respect for the flag we fly, and an ability to speak and write the English language. English is also the key to unlocking the opportunity of America. English allows newcomers to go from picking crops to opening a grocery, . . . from cleaning offices to running offices, . . . from a life of low-paying jobs to a diploma, a career, and a home of their own. When immigrants assimilate and advance in our society, they realize their dreams, . . . they renew our spirit . . . and they add to the unity of America.

Tonight, I want to speak directly to members of the House and the Senate: An immigration reform bill needs to be comprehensive, because all elements of this problem must be addressed together or none of them will be solved at all. The House has passed an immigration bill. The Senate should act by the end of this month so we can work out the differences between the two bills, and Congress can pass a comprehensive bill for me to sign into law.

America needs to conduct this debate on immigration in a reasoned and respectful tone. Feelings run deep on this issue and as we work it out, all of us need to keep some things in mind. We cannot build a unified country by inciting people to anger, or playing on anyone's fears, or exploiting the issue of immigration for political gain. We must always remember that real lives will be affected by our debates and decisions, and that every human being has dignity and value no matter what their citizenship papers say. I know many of you listening tonight have a parent or a grandparent who came here from another country with dreams of a better life. You know what freedom meant to them, and you know that America is a more hopeful country because of their hard work and sacrifice. As president, I've have had the opportunity to meet people of many backgrounds, and hear what America means to them. On a visit to Bethesda Naval Hospital, Laura and I met a wounded Marine named Guadalupe Denogean. Master Gunnery Sergeant Denogean came to the United States from Mexico when he was a boy. He spent his summers picking crops with his family, and then he volunteered for the United States Marine Corps as soon as he was able. During the liberation of Iraq, Master Gunnery—Master Gunnery Sergeant Denogean was seriously injured. And when asked if he had any requests, he made two: a promotion for the corporal who helped rescue him . . . and the chance to become an American citizen. And when this brave Marine raised his right hand, and swore an oath to become a citizen of the country he had defended for more than 26 years, I was honored to stand at his side.

We will always be proud to welcome people like Guadalupe Denogean as fellow Americans. Our new immigrants are just what they've have always been: people willing to risk everything for the dream of freedom. And America remains what she has always been: the great hope on the horizon, . . . an open door to the future, . . . a blessed and promised land. We honor the heritage of all who come here, no matter where they are from, because we trust in our country's genius for making us all Americans, one nation under God.

Thank you, and good night.

Source: Retrieved from http://georgewbush-whitehouse.archives.gov/news/releases/2006/05/20060515-8.html.

Press Release from the Office of the Governor of New York Announcing New Policy on the State's Driver's License Policy

On September 21, 2007, New York Governor Eliot Spitzer issued an executive order directing that state offices allow illegal aliens to be issued driver's licenses, effective from December of that year. The measure drew intense criticism from both Republicans and Democrats, with critics bristling at a policy that they claimed would open the door for illegal immigrants to receive official documentation and expressing concerns that it would compromise the improvements made in national security since 9/11. Largely as a result of coverage on cable news and talk radio, the issue of driver's licenses for undocumented immigrants entered the national dialogue, with candidates for the 2008 presidential contest being asked for their views on the policy. The measure was finally withdrawn after sustained public and political opposition.

September 21, 2007

Department of Motor Vehicles Changes License Policy to Include More New Yorkers and Implements New Regime of Anti-Fraud Measures to Strengthen the Security of the System

Improves Safety of New York Streets, Lowers Auto Insurance Rates and Brings More New Yorkers into the System

Governor Eliot Spitzer and Department of Motor Vehicles (DMV) Commissioner David Swarts today announced an administrative policy change that will give all New Yorkers the opportunity to apply for state driver licenses without regard to immigration status. Tied to the policy change, the Governor and Commissioner also announced plans to implement a new regime of anti-fraud measures to increase the security of the licensing system as a new population of New Yorkers comes into the system.

The DMV estimates that tens of thousands of undocumented, unlicensed and uninsured drivers are currently on New York's roads, contributing to increased accidents and hit-and-runs as well as higher auto insurance rates. In addition, bringing more New Yorkers into the system will ensure a greater number of people have a license record that, if necessary, can be used to enhance law enforcement efforts.

"I applaud the DMV and Commissioner Swarts for making this commonsense change that deals practically with the reality that hundreds of thousands of undocumented immigrants live among us and that allowing them the opportunity to obtain driver licenses in a responsible and secure manner will help increase public safety," said Governor Eliot Spitzer. "After a comprehensive review, DMV has developed changes that will increase the security of our license system by obtaining better and more verifiable information from applicants, which will decrease the number of uninsured drivers on the roads, lower auto insurance rates for all drivers and, when necessary help law enforcement agencies in their investigations."

Commissioner Swarts said: "This policy change allows the DMV to focus its resources on its core mission—to ensure that every person driving on our roads is fit to drive and can prove his or her identity. Currently, too many drivers are unlicensed and uninsured simply because they do not have a social security number. Rather than bury our heads in the sand and pretend the problem does not exist, today we are choosing to confront it and in doing so greatly improve the safety of our roads."

To ensure a smooth transition without disruption to regular customer service, the implementation of the policy change will take place in two phases:

Phase 1 will begin immediately. Informational letters from DMV will be sent to the approximately 152,000 New Yorkers, who at one point had (or currently have) a New York State license, but are unable to renew it because of the previous administrative policy. DMV will notify these former and current license holders of the policy change and will begin the re-licensing process at the end of 2007. Those affected will still need to prove their identity, date of birth and fitness to drive before being issued a new license.

Phase 2 will begin six to eight months after Phase 1 and will open the application process to all New Yorkers.

The time period between phases will allow the DMV to make the necessary infrastructure and staffing improvements to accommodate the expected increase in customer volume while maintaining the highest level of customer service and anti-fraud security.

The benefits of this policy change include:

- *Safer Streets:* In its report, "Unlicensed to Kill," the AAA Foundation for Traffic Safety found that unlicensed drivers are almost five times more likely to be in a fatal crash than are validly licensed drivers.

- *Lower Insurance Rates:* The State Department of Insurance estimates that expanded license access will reduce the premium costs associated with uninsured motorist coverage by 34% which will save New York drivers $120 million each year. Other states with similar policies have seen their auto insurance rates drop as well.

- *Safer Homeland:* This policy change helps bolster homeland security by bringing more individuals into the system and, when necessary, assisting law enforcement efforts to locate those who present a real security threat.

The new policy will apply to all state-issued licenses that are not governed by certain federal laws that require a social security number, like commercial driver licenses and hazardous materials endorsements. Currently, eight other states—Hawaii, Maine, Maryland, Michigan, New Mexico, Oregon, Utah and Washington—do not require drivers to prove legal status in order to obtain a license. Assembly Speaker Sheldon Silver said: "When the previous Governor changed the requirements for law-abiding immigrant citizens to obtain a driver's license, the Assembly Majority held public hearings and urged the Pataki Administration to change the regulations. But it took a change in the administration to get where we are today. I applaud Governor Spitzer for his actions. To deny law-abiding immigrant New Yorkers access to a driver's license and make it more difficult for hardworking families to get to work, the hospital or even get their children to school is to admit that terrorism has won."

Senate Minority Leader Malcolm A. Smith said: "I am pleased to endorse this very fair and reasonable change in policy by the Spitzer administration. This change will enhance public safety while allowing driver licenses to be granted to those able to meet reasonable standards of proof of identity."

State Police Acting Superintendent Preston Felton said: "DMV's new steps to increase security and validate identification will reduce fraud and increase safety. Ensuring more of our drivers are properly licensed and qualified to drive results in safer streets."

State Insurance Superintendent Eric Dinallo said: "Now, people with insurance pay the costs when people without insurance have accidents. That's not right. Experience in other states makes it clear that when drivers have licenses, they are much more likely to buy insurance. We project that this program will substantially cut the cost of uninsured drivers and that means millions of dollars in savings on auto insurance."

Deputy Secretary for Homeland Security Michael Balboni said: "We have been meticulous in ensuring that this change in policy, and the new security measures we are putting in place, strengthen our homeland security efforts by licensing a population of New Yorkers who previously had no public records."

Margaret Stock, an immigration and national security law expert who is an Attorney and Lieutenant Colonel in the Military Police, US Army Reserve, is currently assigned as a part-time Associate Professor at the US Military Academy at West Point. Ms. Stock, who is also chair of the International Security Affairs Committee of the Association of the Bar of the City of New York, said: "New York State's new policy will enhance the security of New Yorkers and all Americans. Granting driver licenses to all residents of a state who can prove their identity allows law enforcement officials to find persons who may be security threats, and gives law enforcement officials more tools to prevent and solve crimes."

President of the New York State AFL-CIO Denis Hughes said: "We applaud Governor Spitzer for his actions today. Equal access to a driver's license, regardless of immigration status, is essential to the public safety and well-being of all New Yorkers."

Chung-Wha Hong, Executive Director of the New York Immigration Coalition and Co-Founder of the New York Coalition for Immigrants' Rights to Driver's Licenses said: "Our state's new driver's license policy is a win-win for immigrants and for all New Yorkers. Not only does it enable more New Yorkers to get licensed and insured, making our roads much safer, but it's going to make our licensing system far more secure and immune to fraud. We applaud the Governor for developing a smart and fair solution that can serve as a model for the rest of the nation."

Amy Sugimori, co-chair of the New York Coalition for Immigrants' Rights to Driver's Licenses said: "Today's announcement is a huge victory for the immigrant, civil rights and labor movements. For four years, diverse groups from across the state have been working to ensure that all New Yorkers are treated equally by the government. Today our voices are being heard. We applaud Governor Spitzer for his leadership as he sends a strong message to the country that second-class treatment of immigrants is bad public policy."

State law requires license applicants to prove their identity, date of birth and fitness to drive, and to provide a social security number (SSN). The SSN requirement was added in 1995 as part of an effort to punish parents who were not paying child support. In 2002, a state regulation was adopted to allow applicants who are ineligible for a SSN to also apply for driver licenses. Following this step, the DMV then issued an administrative policy that effectively made it impossible for illegal immigrants to obtain driver licenses by stipulating that the only way to define "ineligibility" would be through obtaining a formal letter of ineligibility from the Social Security Administration, a letter that is only obtainable by individuals who have legal immigration status.

It is this last administrative policy that the DMV is changing. Starting in the phases discussed above, license applicants will check a box on the license application that states that the applicant is not eligible to receive a social security number. Instead of presenting a SSN or a letter of ineligibility, individuals instead will provide a current foreign passport and other valid and verifiable documents to prove identity. As such, the DMV will be able to achieve its primary goal in issuing licenses, which is to ensure that the individual who is receiving the license is not misrepresenting themselves to obtain a fraudulent identity card, and controlling who has access to driving motor vehicles.

The DMV's new anti-fraud measures will make the current system even more secure in a number of ways. It will utilize new state-of-the-art document verification technology, including photograph comparison tools and specially-trained staff with expertise in foreign-sourced identity documents, and a proposal to implement a residency requirement for all state license holders.

- The DMV's secure "6-point ID requirement" will be based on an expanded list of valid and verifiable documents. Along with the other identity documents currently on the list, individuals' identities will be verified using this new document verification technology to reduce the potential for fraud.

- The DMV has begun a pilot program to test photo comparison technology, which will prevent a person from obtaining more than one license under more than one name. Currently, 18 states use photo comparison technology as part of their fraud-protection system.

- The DMV will also train personnel in verifying foreign-sourced identity documents.

- Finally, as a further fraud-prevention measure, the DMV will propose to require a license applicant prove his or her New York State residency in order to be eligible for a state-issued license. Currently, 27 states have such residency requirements.

There will be no increase to the current license fee as a result of these changes.

Source: Retrieved from http://web.archive.org/web/20071030132823/http://www.ny.gov/governor/press/0921071.html.

Testimony Before the Subcommittee on Immigration, Citizenship, Refugees, Border Security and International Law Committee on the Judiciary on ICE Detention and Removal Programs

The Federation for American Immigration Reform (FAIR) is a non-profit organization founded in 1972 that advocates for changes in U.S. immigration policy that would result in considerable reductions in both legal and illegal immigration. It also lobbies strongly for vigorous enforcement of current immigration laws, often testifying before Congress on matters such as visa overstays, refugees, and specific legislation currently before Congress. In this testimony from 2008, FAIR president Dan Stein puts forth the organization's stance on how the U.S. Department of Homeland Security's Immigration and Customs Enforcement arm (ICE) is falling short in its administration of the program for detaining and removing illegal aliens.

Dan Stein, President, FAIR

February 13, 2008

A Hearing on Reported Problems with ICE Interrogation, Detention, and Removal Procedures

Madame Chair, members of the subcommittee, thank you very much for the opportunity to testify here today on behalf of the Federation For American Immigration Reform (FAIR). I have included information on FAIR at the end of my statement.

FAIR strongly supports the principle that U.S. immigration law is just as important as any other law in the United States Code, and that the enforcement of these laws is vital to maintenance of a sense of fairness and justice to all Americans who work hard to respect all the laws of this nation. Basic principles of fundamental fairness and respect for law are the cornerstones of citizenship in this highly diverse society. There many who argue that violating an immigration law lacks any negative moral connotation. We disagree. One reason why many immigrants want to come to the United States is because here "the system works."

Congress has passed laws and the Executive Branch maintains a series of procedures governing the arrest, detention and removal of aliens illegally inside the United States. They are under constant review. We support the effective and humane administration of these laws and procedures, consistent with the process that is due at all points of apprehension, detention and removal.

In the administration of these complex laws and procedures, mistakes will occasionally be made. This is especially true given the scope and complexity of these procedures, the demands of limited resources and the fact that human beings are fallible. The effective and judicious administration of all phases of these procedures will require a continued and growing infusion of resources: the management of immigration process is an extremely expensive proposition if it is to be done right.

But when mistakes are made by ICE in the administration of these laws, it is a serious matter. Our nation's commitment to fairness and the rule of law dictate that all instances of misconduct be investigated thoroughly and, where criminal conduct is proved, a full prosecution should invariably follow. Where rules and procedures are not followed, such as in the inappropriate administration of sedation drugs, the willful failure to identify sole caregivers in the course of an interior enforcement operation and similar events, an investigation should follow from the Inspector General to ascertain why procedures were not followed.

Madame Chair, we understand at FAIR that immigration policy involves sensitive and emotional issues—the very real impacts on real people are factors that must be considered in the establishment of any enforcement policy. We must be true to our principles as a people and work to ensure that immigration enforcement—vigorous and effective—nevertheless respects basic human rights and the dignity of all involved.

At present, the Department of Homeland Security's Immigration and Customs Enforcement Program (ICE) program for detaining and removing illegal aliens is undergoing rapid expansion. The Bush Administration's most recent budget request seeks an additional $3 billion for internal enforcement, including work-site raids conducted by Immigration and Customs Enforcement officials. The President will ask for $1.8 billion more to expand ICE's capacity to detain illegal immigrants by providing 1,000 more detention beds.

This rapid funding increase is necessitated by a rapid increase in illegal immigration, by declines in enforcement personnel and funded bed space (which declined by 3 percent and 6 percent, respectively between 2002 and 2004), and by public demands that interior immigration enforcement be dramatically expanded. Despite an increase in overall resources, bed space and personnel levels have failed to keep pace with the growing number of alien apprehensions.

According to a 2006 audit report issued by the Department of Homeland Security's Office of Inspector General, "of the 774,112 illegal aliens apprehended during the past three years, 280,987 (36 percent) were released and largely due to a lack of personnel, bed space, and funding needed to detain illegal aliens while their immigration status is being adjudicated." Further, an astounding 62 percent of the aliens released "will eventually be issued final orders of removal by the . . . Executive Office of Immigration Review (EOIR) and later fail to surrender or abscond." We now have over 600,000 alien fugitives in the United States.

According to DHS, three major problems facing the Detention and Removal Office (DRO) are "(1) the propensity of illegal aliens to disobey orders to appear immigration court; (2) the penchant of released illegal aliens with final orders to abscond; (3) the practice of some countries to block or inhibit the repatriation of its citizens; and (4) two recent U.S. Supreme court decisions which mandate the release of criminal and other high-risk aliens 180 days after the issuance of the final removal order except in "Special Circumstances." DRO says major problems carrying out large-scale removal include lack of "sufficient resources," a lack of "political will, and the [lack of] operation of foreign governments."

FAIR calls on Congress and the national political leadership of this nation to demonstrate the political will to dramatically increase the enforcement of US immigration laws in a manner consistent with credible deterrence. We would also like some broader recognition of the tremendous hidden processing and enforcement costs associated with the administration of laws associated with the use of so-called "inexpensive" foreign labor.

At present, specific problems with individual enforcement operations are properly subject to internal investigations by DHS. Every one of these allegations is worthy of serious consideration, all the while keeping in mind that many of the underlying facts are omitted from news reports. Further, we would suggest that overall policy changes not be made on the basis of one or two isolated instances of agent misconduct. Rather, we should be looking at the entire set of objectives in the aggregate and work to fashion an enforcement strategy that will operate to serve the nation as a whole.

Furthermore, we are concerned that these isolated incidents are being used to try to build political support by those who oppose immigration enforcement generally. The reaction to the recent increases in interior enforcement—welcomed by the overwhelming majority of the American people—has been negative among those organizations traditionally opposed to robust enforcement strategies.

With an estimated population of illegal aliens ranging from 12 to 13 million, one can hardly argue that this nation is too aggressive in its enforcement of immigration law. In 2005, DHS's Immigration Enforcement Actions report 135,610 formal removals—perhaps 1% of the illegal immigrant population in the United States. Clearly, the government has only begun to initiate which promises to be a multiyear effort.

Commonly we hear the red herring, "What you want, mass deportations?" To which I respond that 135,000+ formal removals is already a form of mass deportation. Moreover, the sort of large-scale interior enforcement operations contemplated by the term "mass deportations" are unnecessary. This problem was not created overnight. It will not be solved overnight. Stepped up interior enforcement, when combined with the aggressive enforcement of employer sanctions, dramatically increased detention space, and streamlined removal proceedings will achieve the deterrence that will encourage most illegal aliens to return home.

Madame Chair, we believe it is possible to enforce our immigration laws in a manner that is both effective and consistent with our values. We see the effects of state-based policy changes now: deterrence sets in quickly once it becomes clear that remaining unlawfully in the United States is not a viable option.

Our immigration law enforcement is notoriously lax. While we understand that there are organizations and interests that seek to abolish nearly all forms of immigration enforcement, we believe that is a minority view. Even under today's relaxed standards, the United States deports well over 100,000 aliens from the interior of the country each year. While it will be costly to dramatically increase detention and bed space to bring about true deterrence, such costs can be reduced through expedited removal and similar streamlining techniques. The United States utilized expedited removal to repatriate over 70,000 aliens in 2005, and last year the Administration started using expedited removal for non-Mexicans apprehended near the border.

The administration has more authority to use expedited removal than it has exercised to date. Current law allows the administration to utilize expedited removal for any alien who entered illegally and has been in the United States for less than two years. FAIR has previously supported provisions of the House-passed version of the Intelligence Reform and Terrorism Prevention Act of 2004, which require the use of expedited removal for all aliens who enter the US illegally and have been here for less than five years. This is the sort of creative and innovative thinking we would like to see expanded.

Madame Chair, this nation has allowed its interior enforcement apparatus to atrophy for years. It has happened as a result of the aggressive lobbying of private, special interests in United States who seek to use immigration to control labor costs. We believe it is time to change direction. The simple truth is that vigorously enforcing our immigration laws will have a negative impact on illegal aliens. However, we believe that the basic principles of fairness and justice require that we not provide specific benefits to those who have chosen to jump the line and break the law.

Madame Chair, thank you very much for the opportunity to offer the views of FAIR.

Source: Retrieved from http://www.fairus.org/site/News2?page=NewsArticle&id=16414.

Congressional Testimony at a Hearing on Comprehensive Immigration Reform in 2009: Can We Do It and How?

This hearing took place nearly two years after the failure of the Comprehensive Immigration Reform Act of 2007, which would have provided legal status and a path to citizenship for the estimated 12 to 20 million unauthorized immigrants that were residing in the country. At the time there was no specific piece of legislation before the Committee. Kris Kobach, an opponent of the 2007 legislation, delivered his testimony in person.

Testimony Presented to the U.S. Senate Subcommittee on Immigration, Refugees, and Border Security

Kris W. Kobach, Professor of Law, University of Missouri, Kansas City, Missouri

April 28, 2009

Thank you, Mr. Chairman. I will assume for the sake of this hearing that when we talk about comprehensive immigration reform, we mean reform similar in basic respects to the Senate bill 1348 of 2007, and I will explain with that understanding two basic reasons why pursuing that course of action would be ill-advised: first, the incapacity of the administration of U.S. CIS [Citizenship and Immigration Services], the bureaucratic incapacity to implement the amnesty in the time scale that was anticipated by that bill; and, secondly, the national security concerns that must flow from any large-scale amnesty.

First, looking at the CIS, it simply does not have the resources at this time to effectively implement an amnesty of the scale contemplated by the 2007 bill. To understand this, just consider a few numbers. On top of the 12 million-plus illegal aliens in the country who would be eligible for the amnesty, presumably, there would also be a mass influx of hundreds of thousands or perhaps millions more, which is exactly what happened after the 1986 amnesty, who would present fraudulent documents to apply for the amnesty as if they had already been here. INS reported after the 1986 amnesty that they discovered 398,000 cases of such fraud, and it is reasonable to expect that a similar influx would occur this time.

But let us just assume for the sake of argument that 12 million illegal aliens are eligible and apply for the amnesty. Now, the 2007 bill required everyone to apply within a single year period. There are 250 calendar days that the Government is open for business in a given year. That means that there would have to be an average of 48,000 applications for amnesty every day. As of September 2008, there were only 3,638 status adjudicators at U.S. CIS, and that number cannot be increased quickly because of the difficulty of hiring and training them quickly, and, of course, the attrition of existing adjudicators. Forty-eight thousand applications spread among about 3,600 adjudicators means an average of 13 amnesty applications per adjudicator per day. And, of course, on some days the number might well be double that amount. And under the 2007 bill, with each application the adjudicator had only one business day to determine if there were any national security or criminal reasons why an individual application should not be granted.

Now, that is a bleak picture, but unfortunately it gets worse because that is assuming that those adjudicators are not doing anything right now. Of course, they are. There is a backlog of pending applications of approximately 3 million cases at present, and, of course, on top of that comes the 4 to 6 million applications for things like green cards and other benefits that we currently grant that come in every year.

The GAO [Government Accountability Office] recently reported that U.S. CIS is, accordingly, stretched to the breaking point—so much so that there is so much time pressure that they spend too little time scrutinizing the applications. As a result, the GAO concluded the failure to detect fraud is already "an ongoing and serious problem" at U.S. CIS. They said a high-pressure production environment exists, and it is widely known that at some U.S. CIS offices, there is an informal so-called 6-minute rule in place where an adjudicator has to get through at least 10 applications per hour, and it is a veritable bureaucratic sweatshop.

Well, as a result of this time pressure, U.S. CIS right now is failing to engage in common-sense verification with outside agencies, for example, calling a State DMV to see if two people who allege that they are married are actually living together. And, in fact, in many offices adjudicators are discouraged from making back-up calls like that.

So this agency is already dangerously overburdened and susceptible to fraud. What would an amnesty of the style contemplated by the 2007 bill do? It would more than triple their existing workload. This 6-minute rule might become a 3-minute rule or a 2-minute rule. And it must also be remembered that the much smaller amnesty of 1986 for 2.7 million aliens was extended—or, rather, it took 17 years for that amnesty to be fully implemented. As late as fiscal year 2003, U.S. CIS was still adjudicating applications from the 1986 amnesty. This Committee is now contemplating an amnesty that would be approximately 4 times as large.

Now, in the past U.S. CIS, when presented with a proposal like this, has said that the way it would deal with that surge of applications is by hiring contractors and that that might somehow solve the problem. But that approach is problematic for two reasons.

First of all, it is unlikely that the necessary background checks and training of the contractors could be completed in time. There is already a massive backload at the Office of Personnel Management, which does background checks on U.S. Federal Government employees, of several hundred thousand people. The 2007 bill ignored that problem.

The second problem is that contractors, even if they could be found and quickly put into place, they have to be trained.

Now, one of the benefits of our current status adjudicators is that they are expert in immigration law and they are trained in detecting fraud in the applications for benefits. It is simply critical that in any amnesty the adjudicators be properly trained.

Secondly, I want to talk about some national security concerns. An additional flaw in the 2007 bill is that it would have required any background check, as I mentioned, for the probationary visa to be accomplished within one business day. Now, that might be possible if the U.S. Government had a readily searchable computer database of every terrorist in the world. But, in fact, many of the records are paper records, and many of the records are held by foreign governments. So a 24-hour background check simply is impossible. Indeed, right now the FBI is doing name checks for U.S. CIS for applicants for benefits, and there is a huge backlog of about 60,000 name checks waiting at the FBI right now.

Now, their objective, if all of the problems are solved, is to get to a world where most of the name checks can be done in 30 days and all of the name checks can be done in 90 days. But we are not there yet. So to imagine that we could do something like the 2007 bill and have a thorough name check in 24 hours is simply infeasible.

But even when the Government has as much time as it needs, as much time as it wants to do a name check, terrorist applications can get through. Case in point: Mahmud "the Red" Abouhalima. He was given legal status under the 1986 amnesty as a seasonal agricultural worker even though he was driving a cab in New York. He subsequently was a ringleader in the 1993 plot against the World Trade Center, and his brother Mohammed also got amnesty fraudulently in the 1986 amnesty.

Finally, I would like to conclude by pointing that a terrorist has one other option other than attempting to apply for the amnesty under his real name, and that is to simply invent a clean identity, a fictitious identity. The 2007 bill failed to include any safeguard for this problem, and I would urge you, if a bill is drafted again, it must close this loophole, because the former bill never contained any requirement that a secure, biometric embedded passport be provided to prove that the amnesty applicant is who he says he is.

All it required was two scraps of paper, two easily forged documents, like a pay stub or a bank slip, saying that a person of this name exists. Under that bill, a person could walk into U.S. CIS office, call himself "Rumpelstiltskin," offer two easily forged pieces of paper, and walk out the next day with a Federal Government-issued ID card under that name, which he could then use as a breeder document to get a driver's license, to board airplanes, to do all sorts of things. And that gap can be closed if the bill were to include a requirement that every amnesty applicant provide a passport, a secure passport of the type that has embedded biometrics, which some countries, but not all countries, currently issue today.

In conclusion, there are very large bureaucratic problems, incapacity problems, and there is also the issue of terrorism, which is a very real threat. I am not saying that all or even a very large number of amnesty applicants would be terrorists, but the point is if an amnesty program is created, it has to take into this risk.

Thank you.

Source: Retrieved from http://www.gpo.gov/fdsys/pkg/CHRG-111shrg55034/pdf/CHRG-111shrg55034.pdf.

Written Statement for a Hearing on Comprehensive Immigration Reform in 2009: Can We Do It and How?

The National Council of La Raza is a Hispanic civil rights organization that was founded in 1968. Clarissa Martínez-De-Castro, La Raza's director of immigration campaigns, submitted this written testimony to the Senate Subcommittee on Immigration, Refugees, and Border Security one week following the testimony presented above.

Testimony Submitted to the U.S. Senate Subcommittee on Immigration, Refugees, and Border Security

Clarissa Martínez-De-Castro, Director of Immigration and National Campaigns

National Council of La Raza

May 7, 2009

Introduction

The National Council of La Raza (NCLR) the largest national Hispanic civil rights and advocacy organization in the United States works to improve opportunities for Hispanic Americans. Through its network of nearly 300 affiliated community-based organizations (CBOs), NCLR reaches millions of Hispanics each year in 41 states, Puerto Rico, and the District of Columbia. To achieve its mission, NCLR conducts applied research, policy analysis, and advocacy, providing a Latino perspective in five key areas assets/ investments, civil rights/immigration, education, employment and economic status, and health. In addition, it provides capacity-building assistance to its Affiliates who work at the state and local level to advance opportunities for individuals and families. Founded in 1968, NCLR is a private, nonprofit, nonpartisan, tax-exempt organization headquartered in Washington, DC. NCLR serves all Hispanic subgroups in all regions of the country and has operations in Atlanta, Chicago, Los Angeles, New York, Phoenix, Sacramento, San Antonio, and San Juan, Puerto Rico.

NCLR has a long history in the immigration debate. Our work on this issue is focused on ensuring that we have an immigration system that functions in the best interest of the nation. Immigration in the United States should be orderly and legal, promote economic growth, sustain our families, and be implemented in a way consistent with our nation's values. After more than two decades of neglect, our immigration system, far from achieving those goals, creates conditions that contradict or trample those values. The effects of our failed system have made the need for policy solutions urgent. The consequences of unabated toxic rhetoric around the issue have made progress a moral imperative. And the engagement and message from voters in recent elections have shown that real solutions on immigration are smart politics.

This alignment indicates that the time for comprehensive immigration reform is now, and action can prove an important tool on our path to economic recovery. NCLR, our Affiliates, and our many coalition partners are committed to working with Congress to reform U.S. immigration laws in a way that promotes order, fairness, and above all, legality.

Impact of Inaction on Latino Community

Of the country's 45.5 million Latinos, about 39% are foreign-born, and a significant portion of Latinos live in families with mixed immigration status, making immigration policy an important issue for this community. In addition to an overhaul of the nation's immigration system that would deal effectively and humanely with undocumented immigrants, family reunification, worker protections, immigrant integration, and future flows, Latinos are also interested in forward movement on this issue because of its impact on civil rights.

Failure to reform the nation's immigration system has led to piecemeal state and local measures that are often detrimental to the well-being and safety of Hispanic communities. These measures, combined with the toxic nature of the immigration debate, are contributing to an environment of intolerance against immigrants, regardless of immigration status, and against Latinos, who are often erroneously assumed to be all immigrants. Coinciding with the rise in vitriol in the immigration debate, the FBI has documented a nearly 40% increase in hate crimes targeting Latinos in the last four years, and the Southern Poverty Law Center (SPLC) attributes the 47% rise in hate groups between 2000 and 2007 almost completely to the manipulation of anti-immigrant rhetoric. This rise in intolerance has resulted in tragic consequences for the Latino community, horrifyingly exemplified more recently by the brutal, fatal beatings of Luis Ramirez, Jose Osvaldo Sucuzhañay, and Marcelo Lucero for walking while being Latino.

The harsh tone of the immigration debate galvanized Latino voters in the 2008 election, who turned out in record numbers and supported candidates favoring comprehensive immigration reform over candidates who engaged in anti-immigrant rhetoric. As election results and polling demonstrate, the country as a whole is in a more pragmatic place on this issue than Congress seems to realize. In 2008, reform-minded candidates won 20 out of 22 battleground races against opponents supporting deportation-only or restrictionist approaches, and 66% of voters in swing districts supported an approach that will result in undocumented immigrants becoming legal, tax-paying workers within the system.

A Worsening Status Quo

The nation's immigration system is in urgent need of reform that restores dignity and the rule of law and rejects a deteriorating status quo that does neither. NCLR believes that the United States can and should enforce its immigration laws. As with any set of laws, the nation should enforce them wisely and well. This requires an examination of the costs and benefits of particular enforcement strategies to ensure that the priorities and tactics we choose do not undercut other important laws, values, and goals. A true return to legality calls for a systemic overhaul that addresses problems exacerbated by over two decades of neglect, including:

- A burgeoning undocumented population whose status makes it easier to prey upon and harder to integrate into American society

- Unscrupulous employers ready to exploit undocumented workers to the disadvantage of all workers and good employers

- Obstructed legal channels that keep families apart and legal workers out, as well as foster a black market and smuggling rings

- Hard-line, high-cost enforcement strategies that do little to curb immigration but terrorize communities and decrease national security

- A costly and ineffective patchwork of state and local laws that do little to address these problems but introduce greater chaos into an already broken system

Half-measures will not work. In fact, failure to enact comprehensive immigration reform has left behind a lopsided and ineffective federal system of enforcement that attacks the symptoms but not the problem.

As we have seen in recent years, trying to solve the problems of our broken immigration system through a deportation-only approach does not work. The strategy of using raids and local law enforcement agencies to round up, detain, and deport the undocumented population has been costly and ineffective. There has been a significant increase in interior immigration enforcement operations by the Department of Homeland Security in the form of large-scale worksite raids as well as raids on homes throughout the country. In 2007, according to U.S. Immigration and Customs Enforcement (ICE), more than 4,900 arrests were made in connection with worksite enforcement investigations, representing a 45-fold increase in criminal worksite arrests compared to fiscal year 2001. In 2008, ICE conducted a five-state sweep of Pilgrim's Pride poultry plants, and one year ago this month, it raided Agriprocessors, Inc., a kosher meatpacking plant in Postville, Iowa, a raid which ICE has called the largest in history. While the stated goal of the worksite and home raids has been to focus on unscrupulous employers and the worst of the worst in the undocumented population, the agency has not maintained that focus. The results have led to racial profiling and rounding up anyone who may be undocumented in order to increase the numbers of immigrants in detention. Instead of looking for solutions to our outdated, ineffective immigration system, resources have been allocated toward the expansion of SWAT-like teams that have descended on the homes of families who are suspected of being undocumented. In the ICE Fugitive Operations Program, ICE agents have not focused on immigrants who have criminal convictions, as intended by the program; instead, 73% of the immigrants apprehended from 2003 to 2008 had no criminal convictions.

In addition to worksite and home raids, the rapid proliferation of agreements between local law enforcement agencies and the federal government to enforce complex immigration laws has led to further civil rights violations. U.S. citizens and legal immigrants are being racially profiled because of agreements between the federal government and local law enforcement agencies that allow police officers to question the immigration status of community members. As of March 2009, there are 67 law enforcement entities in 23 states that have signed memoranda of agreement (MOAs) with ICE as part of the 287(g) program. Reports by the government and nongovernmental organizations alike have found numerous problems with these agreements.

As a result of the raids and the indiscriminate rounding up of immigrants (and, in some cases, U.S. citizens), the numbers of people who are in detention facilities has grown tremendously in recent years. As many as 30,000 immigrants are held in detention centers every day, which is a three-fold increase in the number of immigrant detainees from a decade ago. By the end of 2009, the U.S. government will hold more than 440,000 people in immigration custody in approximately 400 facilities at an annual cost of more than $1.7 billion. Immigrants are detained in a variety of facilities ranging from detention centers operated by ICE or private contractors to county jails under contract with ICE. Conditions in detention centers have come under fire after multiple news reports and investigations outlined the substandard conditions that led to the death of more than 80 immigrants in ICE custody since 2002. In one case, an immigrant from El Salvador was detained for 11 months and denied medical care. He was released from detention after being diagnosed with terminal cancer. He subsequently died at the age of 36. The federal government has admitted medical negligence in a lawsuit that his family is pursuing. Cases such as this underscore the need for scrutiny of the standards in detention facilities.

Upon examination, it becomes evident that the government's tactics of rounding up undocumented immigrants through raids and with local law enforcement cooperation have high costs that far outweigh the benefits. While Congress has increased the resources for enforcement efforts, it must ensure that there is oversight of enforcement resources and that the priorities are not lost.

The zeal with which federal and local law enforcement agencies have applied enforcement policies has violated the rights and civil liberties of many in various communities, including legal residents and U.S. citizens. Latinos specifically have been racially profiled, arrested without warrant, detained without counsel, and in some cases even deported out of the country despite being legally present. These concerns over racial profiling and abuse of authority are not new for Latinos. In 1993, a report documented that U.S. citizens, as well as Hispanic immigrants, have been harassed by immigration authorities. More recently, a publication by the Southern Poverty Law Center reported that nearly 50% of respondents to their survey of Latinos in the South knew someone who had been treated unfairly by the police. In one case, a worker who was traveling to Mexico with his earned wages was stopped by a police officer in Alabama for failure to maintain a marked lane. Even though the worker was not arrested or charged with any crime, the officer confiscated his savings and wages of nearly $20,000, claiming it was drug money. Such policy is an abrogation of civil rights, common decency, and human dignity. This is not the way to resolve the problems in our immigration system.

One of the primary concerns with the 287(g) program has been the blatant use of racial profiling, which affects all Latinos. There have been many news stories and investigative reports, as well as pending lawsuits, which suggest that law enforcement officers who are part of the 287(g) program are using race or Latino appearance to make stops and arrests for minor offenses. In Tennessee, where racial profiling data collection is mandated, and where there are two MOAs in place, a study of arrest data shows that the number of arrests of Latino defendants driving without a license in Davidson County more than doubled after the implementation of the 287(g) program. Alarmingly, jurisdictions that have been found to engage or have been accused of engaging in racial profiling have signed or are in the process of entering into 287(g) agreements. In communities like Rogers, Arkansas, community groups and immigrants advocates have strongly opposed the 287(g) agreement because the city was sued for unlawfully targeting Latino motorists for stops, searches, and investigations in 2001. When the City of Rogers applied for 287(g) authority to enforce immigration law, it was still under federal court supervision pursuant to the lawsuit.

Another cost of the tactics that we have seen in recent years is the impact on families. One of the fundamental values we uphold in this country is the importance of family unity. Our broken immigration system has resulted in the degradation of this American value. Nationwide, there are approximately four million U.S. citizen children who have at least one undocumented parent and policies that target their parents have grave effects on these children. A report released by the Urban Institute and commissioned by NCLR in 2007 found that for every two immigrants apprehended in an immigration enforcement operation, one child is left behind. The impact of these operations on children, the most vulnerable group in our society, is significant and long-lasting. In the status quo, these children are victims of a system that disrupts their lives and forces them to bear the distress of being torn apart from their parents and loved ones. In one case, a U.S.-born citizen, Paul, who had been married to his wife, Teresa, since June 2005, is now raising their three-year-old daughter on his own as he waits to find out if his wife will be allowed to reenter the country. At 6:00 a.m. on a mid-November day in 2008, ICE agents pounded on the family's door and took his pregnant wife from their home. A month later, she was deported to Argentina. Paul remains in the U.S. with their daughter while he awaits news from their attorney. The couple was in the process of adjusting Teresa's immigration status. This is only one of many stories of families who are forced apart.

In addition to tearing apart families living in the United States, our outdated immigration system also separates families through its untenable backlogs. In the family immigration system, U.S. citizens and legal permanent residents may file applications for close relatives to join them in the United States. The applications are first processed by the U.S. Citizenship and Immigration Service and, upon approval, are sent overseas for further processing. While the applications are in process, the loved ones of U.S. citizens and legal permanent residents wait for an appointment at the U.S. Consulate's office abroad. Currently, there are three Latin American countries on the State Department's list of top ten countries with the highest number of waiting-list applicants. Mexico alone has nearly one million applicants currently on the waiting list. In the case of one of our family immigration categories, spouses have remained separated from each other for more than a decade. We have neglected the legal avenues that were created to uphold our ideal of keeping families united. These practices chip away at the principle of family unity that has been a part of our immigration policies and strike the very core of our fundamental moral and civic values as a nation.

Not only have failed deportation-only tactics raised concerns about the protection of civil rights, they also threaten the safety of communities throughout the country, evidenced by the chilling effect these agreements have on the relationships between local law enforcement officials and the communities they are responsible for protecting. In fact, local law enforcement agencies have spoken out against the 287(g) program because it goes against their efforts to build strong relationships in their communities, thus hindering their ability to earn the trust of community members. Impacted communities are less likely to report crimes or come forward as witnesses as a result of the wedge that has been driven between police and residents.

Yet we shoulder all of these costs for a system that does not work. From 1990 to 2006, the United States witnessed a large increase in the number of undocumented immigrants entering the country. Over the past decade, billions of dollars have been spent on detention and deportation efforts without making a dent in the problem. The immigration enforcement agencies within the Department of Homeland Security have seen their budgets skyrocket while the number of undocumented immigrants in the United States has grown. The annual budget of the U.S. Border Patrol has increased 332% and the number of Border Patrol agents has increased 276% since fiscal year 1993. Still, the undocumented population has increased threefold. We cannot solve the problems of our immigration system through expensive deportation-only strategies. The current undocumented population is estimated to be approximately 12 million people. If the United States is deporting approximately 250,000 immigrants per year, it would take about 40 years to deport our way out of this situation.

Latinos and the Electorate as a Whole Want to See Solutions

The American people have demonstrated in numerous national polls and multiple election cycles that they want to see a solution to the problem of our broken immigration system. They want to see a comprehensive approach that secures the border, cracks down on employers who hire illegal immigrants, and requires all illegal immigrants to register and meet certain requirements to become legal over an enforcement-only approach that doesn't offer a real solution.

Congress and the administration need to restore the rule of law and enact an immigration system that works for the good of the country. A true return to legality calls for a systemic overhaul that addresses the problems exacerbated by more than two decades of neglect. Given the complex nature of the problems in our immigration system, it is clear that this issue cannot be resolved in a piecemeal fashion. To be effective and achieve a solution that serves the national interest, reform must include measures that bring order to our borders, protect workers, and bring the undocumented out of the shadows.

A part of comprehensive immigration reform includes the ability to secure our borders. From 2001 to 2008, the Bush administration spent billions of dollars to build barriers and increase the number of border patrol agents and other enforcement controls. Border security must be enacted in a fiscally responsible and efficient manner. This requires border enforcement policies that focus on the criminal elements and are developed in collaboration with communities on both sides of the border. Attention must be paid to the ports of entry to ensure that there are sufficient inspectors working in a safe and efficient environment in order to complete screening and inspections of visitors.

Comprehensive immigration reform will restore order by getting approximately 12 million undocumented people in our country to come forward, obtain legal status, learn English, and assume the rights and responsibilities of citizenship. Enforcement agencies need to follow the mandate of their programs and seek out those who have been convicted of committing violent crimes. Comprehensive immigration reform will allow immigrants who have been working, paying taxes, and learning English and who can pass background checks to become a part of the formal economy and work on the books, therefore contributing more to the tax rolls and making it more difficult for corrupt employers to cheat them and, consequently, all Americans.

We recognize that people of goodwill differ on how to address the question of a future flow of potential workers from abroad. Indeed, NCLR itself feels somewhat conflicted because both sides of the argument bring legitimate perspectives to bear. On the one hand, we sympathize with those who have correctly noted the tendency of temporary worker programs to restrict workers rights. They also correctly note that many legal immigrants who enter via the family reunification system also work.

On the other hand, it's hard to disagree with those who point out that virtually every credible, long-term economic projection strongly suggests that once our economy recovers, we will continue to need some number of workers from abroad to maximize economic growth. We also believe that U.S. citizens and legal immigrants wishing to reunite with family members abroad should be permitted to do so lawfully in a reasonable period of time.

Clearly, our future immigration policy must balance these competing interests, and NCLR believes an appropriate balance is possible. Specifically, NCLR supports:

- Increased family-based immigration, which includes reducing backlogs that have made it virtually impossible for all but the closest relatives of U.S. citizens to immigrate lawfully to the United States

- A rational, needs-based process to link the future flow of employment-based visas to independent assessments of U.S. labor market needs

- Full labor rights and protections for employment-based workers, accompanied by vigorous enforcement to ensure that any future flow program does not undercut wages and working conditions of domestic workers

Some of our critics have confused our opposition to ineffective, counterproductive, and harmful enforcement efforts as tantamount to opposition to any form of enforcement. Permit me to disabuse them of that notion in this testimony. For the record, NCLR supports the right of the United States, as a sovereign nation, to control its borders. Furthermore, we believe it is in the interest of the Hispanic community, both substantively and politically, for our country to implement an enforcement system that is fair, effective, and humane. We do not believe any of those adjectives could be used to describe the status quo.

Specifically, we believe that any effective enforcement system must be nondiscriminatory, must actually reduce the undocumented population in the U.S. as well as deter future unlawful entries, and must be implemented in a manner consistent with our highest ideals as a nation. We believe comprehensive immigration reform is the only way to achieve such a system, as described below.

First, by adjusting the status of the bulk of the undocumented population in the U.S., and by increasing avenues for lawful entry, we can ensure that the proverbial front door to our country remains open; among other benefits, this will allow us to concentrate enforcement resources on closing the back door to illegal entries. In a society as free and open as ours, finding lawbreakers has been compared to finding a needle in a haystack. Our previous policy of increasing legal immigration backlogs and growing the criminalization of civil immigration offenses has been, in effect, creating more stacks of hay, making it harder to find the needles, even with greater resources. In this context, creating a path to permanent residence and eventual citizenship for the undocumented who pay taxes, learn English, and pass background checks is an essential part of any enforcement strategy. Simply put, these policies make the haystack smaller and more manageable.

Second, we must recognize that there is no single strategy that will eliminate all forms of unauthorized entry and presence. Even effective elimination of all unauthorized entries, for example, would not affect the estimated 40% of the undocumented population that entered with lawful visas and then overstayed. Similarly, even a perfect employment verification system would not address those who entered the country for purposes other than employment. Thus, NCLR believes any effective enforcement system must consist of a series of layers of enforcement, none of which may in and of itself be 100% successful, but taken together would provide both an effective deterrent and swift and efficient punishment to those who break the law in the future.

The first layer involves smart border enforcement, which provides a reasonable deterrent against unlawful entry of individuals, drugs, and human traffickers without adversely affecting the lawful flow of goods and commerce. It would require more efficient resources and infrastructure developments on ports of entry, allowing well-trained enforcement officers to focus on smugglers and traffickers. It would also require increased deployment of technology and greater cooperation with Mexico to reduce the southern flow of arms and the northern flow of drugs and traffickers.

The second layer should focus on labor law enforcement to deter and punish unscrupulous employers from hiring and exploiting a vulnerable, undocumented labor force. Such a policy would have the salutary additional effect of improving wages, working conditions, and worker safety for the entire low-wage domestic workforce.

The third and probably most important layer is an effective, nondiscriminatory worker verification system. Immigration experts have long recognized that the U.S. labor market is the single strongest incentive for unauthorized migration to the United States. But as this committee knows, the existing systems offer the worst of both worlds they permit widespread hiring of unauthorized workers while subjecting many lawful workers to intentional or inadvertent discrimination. Surely we can do better. NCLR supports the investment of sufficient resources to reduce error rates to reasonable levels and permit maximum access of lawful workers to mechanisms that document their employment status. Moreover, because we recognize that any system will produce some errors, we must insist on effective nondiscrimination provisions and swift redress mechanisms. I would also note that the vast majority of Latinos of my acquaintance want a verification system that permits them to demonstrate and prospective employers to confirm their authorization to work in the U.S. It is not the concept but the execution that raises concerns for most Hispanic Americans.

The fourth layer of enforcement should focus on employers that engage in a pattern and practice of recruiting and hiring unauthorized workers. Any efficient law enforcement effort should target the big fish, yet in recent years it has been individual workers, rather than employers, that have borne the full brunt of immigration enforcement. Part of this involves a simple change of focus, and in this respect we are cautiously optimistic that Secretary Napolitano's recent announcement may reflect a more balanced strategy. But this may also require policy changes, including, for example, addressing loopholes in labor laws that permit employers to evade responsibility by labeling workers as independent contractors.

Finally, we agree with the overwhelming majority of local law enforcement personnel that immigration should be a federal responsibility. Our own assessment, confirmed by independent reviews by the Government Accountability Office, a number of federal courts, and others, is that state and local enforcement has produced little enforcement benefit but resulted in widespread violations of the rights of citizens and lawful permanent residents. One possible exception involves agreements by state and local law enforcement to assess the immigration status of violent criminals, which seems to us a sensible way of reducing the burden on local governments while remaining focused on serious offenders.

Taken together, NCLR believes that these five layers of enforcement would substantially reduce the current population of those who live outside the scope and protection of the law; maintain a credible deterrent at the border; crack down on unscrupulous employers for violations of labor and immigration law; establish an accurate and reliable employer verification system to reduce the scope of unlawful employment; and ensure the swift identification and disposition of violent criminals who have also violated immigration laws.

Federal leadership is required to address the inconsistencies of current policies and ensure that our treatment of immigrants is aligned with America's best values and traditions. Congress and the administration can, and must, achieve comprehensive immigration reform this year because reform will demonstrate that America is true to its best values, not its worst instincts. How lawmakers resolve the immigration debate will say much about who we are as a country and as human beings.

The American people have made it clear that they are interested in solutions to our country's difficult problems. Numerous polls and election results over multiple election cycles have demonstrated that Americans support a realistic solution that is tough but comprehensive, as opposed to half-measures that only focus on deportation. The status quo is unacceptable. We look forward to working with members of the subcommittee, as well as other members of Congress and the administration, to achieve comprehensive immigration reform this year.

Source: Retrieved from http://www.nclr.org/images/uploads/publications/58182_file_NCLR_Testimony_for_the_Record_Final.pdf.

Speech by Arizona Governor Jan Brewer After Signing Senate Bill 1070

Governor Jan Brewer came to national prominence in April 2010 when she signed Arizona's controversial Senate Bill 1070, which required state and local law enforcement officers to determine the immigration status of anyone involved in a lawful stop, detention, or arrest where "reasonable suspicion exists" that the person is unlawfully present in the country. The law immediately kicked up a firestorm on all sides of the immigration debate. Brewer announced the signing of the bill at a press conference, and below are her comments on and defense of the new law.

Phoenix, Arizona

April 23, 2010

Thank you for being here today, to join me as we take another step forward in protecting the state of Arizona.

The bill I'm about to sign into law—Senate Bill 1070—represents another tool for our state to use as we work to solve a crisis we did not create and the federal government has refused to fix . . .

. . . The crisis caused by illegal immigration and Arizona's porous border.

This bill, the Support Our Law Enforcement and Safe Neighborhoods Act, strengthens the laws of our state.

It protects all of us, every Arizona citizen and everyone here in our state lawfully.

And, it does so while ensuring that the constitutional rights of ALL in Arizona remain solid—stable and steadfast.

I will now sign Senate Bill 1070.

For weeks, this legislation has been the subject of vigorous debate and intense criticism. My decision to sign it was by no means made lightly.

I have listened patiently to both sides. I have considered the significance of this new law long into the night. I have prayed for strength and prayed for our state.

I've decided to sign Senate Bill 1070 into law because, though many people disagree, I firmly believe it represents what's best for Arizona. Border-related violence and crime due to illegal immigration are critically important issues to the people of our state, to my Administration and to me, as your Governor and as a citizen.

There is no higher priority than protecting the citizens of Arizona. We cannot sacrifice our safety to the murderous greed of drug cartels. We cannot stand idly by as drop houses, kidnappings and violence compromise our quality of life.

We cannot delay while the destruction happening south of our international border creeps its way north.

We in Arizona have been more than patient waiting for Washington to act.

But decades of federal inaction and misguided policy have created a dangerous and unacceptable situation.

Yesterday, I announced the steps I was taking to enhance security along our border.

Today—with my unwavering signature on this legislation—Arizona strengthens its security WITHIN our borders.

Let me be clear, though: My signature today represents my steadfast support for enforcing the law—both AGAINST illegal immigration AND against racial profiling.

This legislation mirrors federal laws regarding immigration enforcement.

Despite erroneous and misleading statements suggesting otherwise, the new state misdemeanor crime of willful failure to complete or carry an alien registration document is adopted, verbatim, from the same offense found in federal statute.

I will NOT tolerate racial discrimination or racial profiling in Arizona.

Because I feel so strongly on this subject, I worked for weeks with legislators to amend SB 1070, to strengthen its civil rights protections.

That effort led to new language in the bill, language prohibiting law enforcement officers from "solely considering race, color, or national origin in implementing the requirements of this section . . ."

The bill already required that it "shall be implemented in a manner consistent with federal laws regulating immigration, protecting the civil rights of all persons and respecting the privileges and immunities of United States citizens."

While the general protection was already included, I believe the issue is so important, we needed to make it CRYSTAL clear.

And I believe that we need to more than simply inscribe it in statute.

Words in a law book are of no use if our police officers are not properly trained on the provisions of SB 1070, including its civil rights provisions.

Today I am issuing an executive order directing the Arizona Peace Officer Standards and Training Board—AZPOST—to develop training to appropriately implement SB 1070.

Importantly, this training will include what DOES—and DOES NOT—constitute "reasonable suspicion" that a person is not legally present in the United States.

Currently, AZPOST serves approximately 170 law enforcement agencies encompassing over 16,000 sworn peace officers, 9,000 correctional service officers, and 16 training academies.

The AZPOST Board of Directors includes the Arizona Attorney General, the Directors of the Arizona Department of Public Safety, the Arizona Department of Corrections, several county sheriffs, and local police departments.

I am also asking the Board to make recommendations on possible improvements to SB 1070 before the end of the year.

For 28 years in public service, I have worked without fail to solve problems diligently and practically. I have done so always with an eye toward civility, and always with the greatest respect for the rule of law.

This new law is no different: As committed as I am to protecting our state from crime associated with illegal immigration I am EQUALLY committed to holding law enforcement accountable should this statute ever be misused to violate an individual's rights.

Respect for the rule of law means respect for every law. I have led that way every day in every office I have ever held. That will not change.

I have also spent my career in service to Arizona working to bring people together, no matter the color of their skin and no matter the depth of our disagreements.

This bill—and this issue—will be no exception.

While protecting our citizens is paramount, it cannot come at the expense of the diversity that has made Arizona so great. Nor can safety mean a compromise of freedom for some, while we, the many, turn a blind eye.

We must acknowledge the truth—people across America are watching Arizona, seeing how we implement this law, ready to jump on even the slightest misstep.

Some of those people from outside our state have an interest in seeing us fail.

They will wait for a single slip-up, one mistake, and then they will work day and night to create headlines and get the face time they so desperately covet.

We cannot give them that chance.

We must use this new tool wisely, and fight for our safety with the honor Arizona deserves.

We must react calmly.

We must enforce the law evenly, and without regard to skin color, accent, or social status.

We must prove the alarmists and the cynics wrong.

I know in my heart that this great state, my home for more than 40 years, is up to the task.

I believe every one of us wants to be safe, and none of us wants to compromise on the subject of civil rights.

I believe we must love and honor those who fight beside us—just as we must love and honor those who look and believe nothing like we do.

I believe Arizona, like America, is governed by laws.

Good laws . . . well-intentioned laws . . . laws that confer respect and that demand respect in return.

In his third State of the Union address, President Theodore Roosevelt said, "No man is above the law and no man is below it; nor do we ask any man's permission when we require him to obey it. Obedience to the law is demanded as a right; not asked as a favor."

So, let us move forward—ever mindful of our rights . . . —ever faithful to the law . . . and ever conscious of our bond as Arizonans, and the blessing we share together.

Thank you.

Source: Retrieved from http://tucsoncitizen.com/mark-evans/archives/236.

Immigration Speech by President Barack Obama

During the Democratic presidential primary in 2008, President Obama promised Latino voters that in his first year as president he would push for passage of a comprehensive immigration reform bill. This speech in El Paso was an attempt by the president, who was then gearing up for his reelection campaign, to shore up Latino support and address their disappointment at his failure to follow through on his 2008 promise. In the speech he once again asserted his support for comprehensive immigration reform, lauded major increases in security along the U.S.-Mexico border, and contended that in light of the improved security, Republicans had no excuse to continue to block immigration reform.

El Paso, TX

May 10, 2011

Hello, El Paso! It's great to be back here with all of you, and to be back in the Lone Star State. I love coming to Texas. Even the welcomes are bigger down here. So, to show my appreciation, I wanted to give a big policy speech . . . outdoors . . . right in the middle of a hot, sunny day.

I hope everyone is wearing sunscreen.

Now, about a week ago, I delivered the commencement address at Miami Dade Community College, one of the most diverse schools in the nation. The graduates were proud that their class could claim heritage from 181 countries around the world. Many of the students were immigrants themselves, coming to America with little more than the dreams of their parents and the clothes on their backs. A handful had discovered only in adolescence or adulthood that they were undocumented. But they worked hard and gave it their all, and they earned those diplomas.

At the ceremony, 181 flags—one for every nation represented—was marched across the stage. Each was applauded by the graduates and relatives with ties to those countries. But then, the last flag—the American flag—came into view. And the room erupted. Every person in the auditorium cheered. Yes, their parents or grandparents—or the graduates themselves—had come from every corner of the globe. But it was here that they had found opportunity, and had a chance to contribute to the nation that is their home.

It was a reminder of a simple idea, as old as America itself. E pluribus, unum. Out of many, one. We define ourselves as a nation of immigrants—a nation that welcomes those willing to embrace America's precepts. That's why millions of people, ancestors to most of us, braved hardship and great risk to come here—so they could be free to work and worship and live their lives in peace. The Asian immigrants who made their way to California's Angel Island. The Germans and Scandinavians who settled across the Midwest. The waves of the Irish, Italian, Polish, Russian, and Jewish immigrants who leaned against the railing to catch that first glimpse of the Statue of Liberty.

This flow of immigrants has helped make this country stronger and more prosperous. We can point to the genius of Einstein and the designs of I. M. Pei, the stories of Isaac Asimov and whole industries forged by Andrew Carnegie.

And I think of the naturalization ceremonies we've held at the White House for members of the military, which have been so inspiring. Even though they were not yet citizens, these men and women had signed up to serve. One was a young man named Granger Michael from Papua New Guinea, a Marine who deployed to Iraq three times. Here's what he said about becoming an American citizen. "I might as well. I love this country already." Marines aren't big on speeches. Another was a woman named Perla Ramos. She was born and raised in Mexico, came to the United States shortly after 9/11, and joined the Navy. She said, "I take pride in our flag . . . and the history we write day by day."

That's the promise of this country—that anyone can write the next chapter of our story. It doesn't matter where you come from; what matters is that you believe in the ideals on which we were founded; that you believe all of us are equal and deserve the freedom to pursue happiness. In embracing America, you can become American. And that enriches all of us.

Yet at the same time, we are standing at the border today because we also recognize that being a nation of laws goes hand in hand with being a nation of immigrants. This, too, is our heritage. This, too, is important. And the truth is, we've often wrestled with the politics of who is and who isn't allowed to enter this country. At times, there has been fear and resentment directed toward newcomers, particularly in periods of economic hardship. And because these issues touch on deeply held convictions—about who we are as a people, about what it means to be an American—these debates often elicit strong emotions.

That's one reason it's been so difficult to reform our broken immigration system. When an issue is this complex and raises such strong feelings, it's easier for politicians to defer the problem until after the next election. And there's always a next election. So we've seen a lot blame and politics and ugly rhetoric. We've seen good faith efforts—from leaders of both parties—fall prey to the usual Washington games. And all the while, we've seen the mounting consequences of decades of inaction.

Today, there are an estimated 11 million undocumented immigrants in the United States. Some crossed the border illegally. Others avoid immigration laws by overstaying their visas. Regardless of how they came, the overwhelming majority of these folks are just trying to earn a living and provide for their families. But they've broken the rules, and have cut in front of the line. And the truth is, the presence of so many illegal immigrants makes a mockery of all those who are trying to immigrate legally.

Also, because undocumented immigrants live in the shadows, they're vulnerable to unscrupulous businesses that skirt taxes, pay workers less than the minimum wage, or cut corners with health and safety. This puts companies who follow those rules, and Americans who rightly demand the minimum wage or overtime or just a safe place to work, at an unfair disadvantage.

Think about it. Over the past decade, even before the recession, middle class families were struggling to get by as costs went up but incomes didn't. We're seeing this again with gas prices. Well, one way to strengthen the middle class is to reform our immigration system, so that there is no longer a massive underground economy that exploits a cheap source of labor while depressing wages for everyone else. I want incomes for middle class families to rise again. I want prosperity in this country to be widely shared. That's why immigration reform is an economic imperative.

And reform will also help make America more competitive in the global economy. Today, we provide students from around the world with -- to get engineering and computer science degrees at our top universities. But our laws discourage them from using those skills to start a business or power a new industry right here in the United States. So instead of training entrepreneurs to create jobs in America, we train them to create jobs for our competition. That makes no sense. In a global marketplace, we need all the talent we can get—not just to benefit those individuals, but because their contributions will benefit all Americans.

Look at Intel and Google and Yahoo and eBay—these are great American companies that have created countless jobs and helped us lead the world in high-tech industries. Every one was founded by an immigrant. We don't want the next Intel or Google to be created in China or India. We want those companies and jobs to take root in America. Bill Gates gets this. "The United States will find it far more difficult to maintain its competitive edge," he's said, "if it excludes those who are able and willing to help us compete."

It's for this reason that businesses all across America are demanding that Washington finally meet its responsibility to solve the immigration problem. Everyone recognizes the system is broken. The question is, will we summon the political will to do something about it? And that's why we're here at the border today.

In recent years, among the greatest impediments to reform were questions about border security. These were legitimate concerns; it's true that a lack of manpower and resources at the border, combined with the pull of jobs and ill-considered enforcement once folks were in the country, contributed to a growing number of undocumented people living in the United States. And these concerns helped unravel a bipartisan coalition we forged back when I was a United States Senator. In the years since, "borders first" has been a common refrain, even among those who previously supported comprehensive immigration reform.

Well, over the past two years we have answered those concerns. Under Secretary Napolitano's leadership, we have strengthened border security beyond what many believed was possible. They wanted more agents on the border. Well, we now have more boots on the ground on the southwest border than at any time in our history. The Border Patrol has 20,000 agents—more than twice as many as there were in 2004, a build up that began under President Bush and that we have continued.

They wanted a fence. Well, that fence is now basically complete.

And we've gone further. We tripled the number of intelligence analysts working the border. I've deployed unmanned aerial vehicles to patrol the skies from Texas to California. We've forged a partnership with Mexico to fight the transnational criminal organizations that have affected both of our countries. And for the first time we are screening 100 percent of southbound rail shipments—to seize guns and money going south even as we go after drugs coming north.

So, we have gone above and beyond what was requested by the very Republicans who said they supported broader reform as long as we got serious about enforcement. But even though we've answered these concerns, I suspect there will be those who will try to move the goal posts one more time. They'll say we need to triple the border patrol. Or quadruple the border patrol. They'll say we need a higher fence to support reform.

Maybe they'll say we need a moat. Or alligators in the moat.

They'll never be satisfied. And I understand that. That's politics.

But the truth is, the measures we've put in place are getting results. Over the past two and a half years, we've seized 31 percent more drugs, 75 percent more currency, and 64 percent more weapons than before. Even as we've stepped up patrols, apprehensions along the border have been cut by nearly 40 percent from two years ago—that means far fewer people are attempting to cross the border illegally.

Also, despite a lot of breathless reports that have tagged places like El Paso as dangerous, violent crime in southwest border counties has dropped by a third. El Paso and other cities and towns along the border are consistently rated among the safest in the nation. Of course, we shouldn't accept any violence or crime, and we have more work to do. But this progress is important.

Beyond the border, we're also going after employers who knowingly exploit people and break the law. And we are deporting those who are here illegally. Now, I know that the increase in deportations has been a source of controversy. But I want to emphasize: we are not doing this haphazardly; we are focusing our limited resources on violent offenders and people convicted of crimes; not families, not folks who are just looking to scrape together an income. As a result, we increased the removal of criminals by 70 percent.

That is not to ignore the real human toll. Even as we recognize that enforcing the law is necessary, we don't relish the pain it causes in the lives of people just trying to get by. And as long as the current laws are on the books, it's not just hardened felons who are subject to removal; but also families just trying to earn a living, bright and eager students; decent people with the best of intentions. I know some here wish that I could just bypass Congress and change the law myself. But that's not how a democracy works. What we really need to do is keep up the fight to pass reform. That's the ultimate solution to this problem.

And I'd point out, the most significant step we can take now to secure the borders is to fix the system as a whole—so that fewer people have incentive to enter illegally in search of work in the first place. This would allow agents to focus on the worst threats on both of our borders—from drug traffickers to those who would come here to commit acts of violence or terror.

So, the question is whether those in Congress who previously walked away in the name of enforcement are now ready to come back to the table and finish the work we've started. We have to put the politics aside. And if we do, I'm confident we can find common ground. Washington is behind the country on this. Already, there is a growing coalition of leaders across America who don't always see eye-to-eye, but who are coming together on this issue. They see the harmful consequences of this broken system for their businesses and communities. They understand why we need to act.

There are Democrats and Republicans, including former-Republican Senator Mel Martinez and former-Bush administration Homeland Security Secretary Michael Chertoff; leaders like Mayor Michael Bloomberg; evangelical ministers like Leith Anderson and Bill Hybels; police chiefs from across the nation; educators and advocates; labor unions and chambers of commerce; small business owners and Fortune 500 CEOs. One CEO had this to say about reform. "American ingenuity is a product of the openness and diversity of this society. . . . Immigrants have made America great as the world leader in business, science, higher education and innovation." That's Rupert Murdoch, the owner of Fox News, and an immigrant himself. I don't know if you're familiar with his views, but let's just say he doesn't have an Obama bumper sticker on his car.

So there is a consensus around fixing what's broken. Now we need Congress to catch up to a train that's leaving the station. Now we need to come together around reform that reflects our values as a nation of laws and a nation of immigrants; that demands everyone take responsibility.

So what would comprehensive reform look like?

First, we know that government has a threshold responsibility to secure the borders and enforce the law. Second, businesses have to be held accountable if they exploit undocumented workers. Third, those who are here illegally have a responsibility as well. They have to admit that they broke the law, pay their taxes, pay a fine, and learn English. And they have to undergo background checks and a lengthy process before they can get in line for legalization.

And fourth, stopping illegal immigration also depends on reforming our outdated system of legal immigration. We should make it easier for the best and the brightest to not only study here, but also to start businesses and create jobs here. In recent years, a full 25 percent of high-tech startups in the U.S. were founded by immigrants, leading to more than 200,000 jobs in America. I'm glad those jobs are here. And I want to see more of them created in this country.

We need to provide farms a legal way to hire the workers they rely on, and a path for those workers to earn legal status.

Our laws should respect families following the rules—reuniting them more quickly instead of splitting them apart. Today, the immigration system not only tolerates those who break the rules, it punishes the folks who follow the rules. While applicants wait for approval, for example, they're often forbidden from visiting the United States. Even husbands and wives may have to spend years apart. Parents can't see their children. I don't believe the United States of America should be in the business of separating families. That's not right. That's not who we are.

And we should stop punishing innocent young people for the actions of their parents—by denying them the chance to earn an education or serve in the military. That's why we need to pass the Dream Act. Now, we passed the Dream Act through the House last year. But even though it received a majority of votes in the Senate, it was blocked when several Republicans who had previously supported the Dream Act voted no.

It was a tremendous disappointment to get so close and then see politics get in the way. And as I gave the commencement at Miami Dade, it broke my heart knowing that a number of those promising, bright students—young people who worked so hard and who speak to what's best about America—are at risk of facing the agony of deportation. These are kids who grew up in this country, love this country, and know no other place as home. The idea that we would punish them is cruel and it makes no sense. We are a better nation than that.

So we're going to keep up the fight for the Dream Act. We're going to keep up the fight for reform. And that's where you come in. I will do my part to lead a constructive and civil debate on these issues. We've already held a series of meetings about this at the White House in recent weeks. And we've got leaders here and around the country helping to move the debate forward. But this change has to be driven by you—to help us push for comprehensive reform, and to identify what steps we can take right now—like the Dream Act and visa reform—areas where we can find common ground among Democrats and Republicans to begin fixing what's broken.

I am asking you to add your voices to this debate—and you can sign up to help at whitehouse.gov. We need Washington to know that there is a movement for reform gathering strength from coast to coast. That's how we'll get this done. That's how we can ensure that in the years ahead we are welcoming the talents of all who can contribute to this country; and that we are living up to that basic American idea: you can make it if you try.

That idea is what gave hope to José Hernández, who is here today. José's parents were migrant farm workers. And so, growing up, he was too. He was born in California, though he could have just as easily been born on the other side of the border, had it been a different time of year, because his family moved with the seasons. Two of his siblings were actually born in Mexico.

They traveled a lot and José joined his parents picking cucumbers and strawberries. He missed part of the school year when they returned to Mexico each winter. He didn't learn English until he was 12. But José was good at math, and he liked it. The great thing about math was that it's the same in every school, and it's the same in Spanish.

So he studied hard. And one day, standing in the fields, collecting sugar beets, he heard on a transistor radio that a man named Franklin Chang-Diaz—a man with a name like his—was going to be an astronaut for NASA.

José decided that he could be an astronaut, too.

So he kept studying, and graduated high school. He kept studying, earning an engineering degree and a graduate degree. He kept working hard, ending up at a national laboratory, helping to develop a new kind of digital medical imaging system.

And a few years later, he found himself more than 100 miles above the surface of the earth, staring out the window of the Shuttle Discovery, remembering the boy in the California fields with a crazy dream and an unshakable belief that everything was possible in America.

That is what we are fighting for. We are fighting for every boy and girl like José with a dream and potential just waiting to be tapped. We are fighting to unlock that promise, and all that it holds not just for their futures, but for the future of this great country.

Thank you. God bless you. And may God bless the United States of America.

Source: Retrieved from http://www.nationaljournal.com/whitehouse/text-obama-s-speech-on-immigration-from-el-paso-texas-20110510.

INDEX